COMMUNICATION
YEARBOOK 8

COMMUNICATION YEARBOOK 8

edited by

ROBERT N. BOSTROM

Associate Editor
Bruce H. Westley

an Annual Review Published for the
International Communication Association

SAGE PUBLICATIONS
Beverly Hills/London/New Delhi

For information address:

SAGE Publications, Inc.
275 South Beverly Drive
Beverly Hills, California 90212

SAGE Publications India Pvt. Ltd. SAGE Publications Ltd
C-236 Defence Colony   28 Banner Street
New Delhi 110 024, India   London EC1Y 8QE, England

Printed in the United States of America

Library of Congress: 76-45943
ISBN 0-8039-2335-X

FIRST PRINTING

CONTENTS

THE INTERNATIONAL COMMUNICATION ASSOCIATION

Communication Yearbook is an annual review. The series is sponsored by the International Communication Association, one of several major scholarly organizations in the communication field. It is composed of 2,500 communication scholars, teachers, and practitioners.

Throughout its 35-year history, the Association has been particularly important to those in the field of communication who have sought a forum where the behavioral science perspective was predominant. The International Communication Association has also been attractive to a number of individuals from a variety of disciplines who hold communication to be central to work within their primary fields of endeavor. The Association has been an important stimulant to the infusion of behavioral concepts in communication study and teaching, and has played a significant role in defining a broadened set of boundaries of the discipline as a whole.

The International Communication Association is a pluralist organization composed of eight subdivisions: information systems, interpersonal communication, mass communication, organizational communication, intercultural and international communication, political communication, instructional and developmental communication, and health communication.

In addition to *Communication Yearbook*, the Association publishes *Human Communication Research*, the *ICA Newsletter*, and *ICA Directory*, and is affiliated with the *Journal of Communication*. Several divisions also publish newsletters and occasional papers.

INTERNATIONAL COMMUNICATION ASSOCIATION
EXECUTIVE COMMITTEE

President
James A. Anderson, *University of Utah*

Past President
Erwin P. Bettinghaus, *Michigan State University*

President-Elect
Klaus Krippendorff, *University of Pennsylvania*

President-Elect-Select
Brenda Dervin, *University of Washington, Seattle*

Executive Director
Robert L. Cox (ex officio), *ICA Headquarters*

BOARD OF DIRECTORS

Members-at-Large
Joseph N. Cappela, *University of Wisconsin—Madison*
Sue DeWine, *Ohio State University*
Rita Atwood, *University of Texas—Austin*
Ellen Wartella, *University of Illinois*

Division Chairpersons
Information Systems
Rolf T. Wigand, *Arizona State University*

Interpersonal Communication
Mary Anne Fitzpatrick, *University of Wisconsin—Madison*

Mass Communication
Ted Glasser, *University of Minnesota*

Organizational Communication
Raymond Falcione, *University of Maryland*

Intercultural and Development Communication
Felipe Korzenny, *Michigan State University*

Political Communication
Sidney Kraus, *Cleveland State University*

Instructional and Developmental Communication
Gus Friedrich, *University of Oklahoma*

Health Communication
Loyd Pettegrew, *University of South Florida*

Student Members
Charmaine E. Wilson, *University of Washington*
Cynthia Stohl, *Purdue University*

Special Interest Groups
Stanley Deetz, Philosophy of Communication, *Southern Illinois University—Carbondale*
Richard V. Farace, Human Communication Technology, *Michigan State University*

PREFACE

The richness and diversity of the study of communication is nowhere more apparent than in the activities of the International Communication Association. Here the various approaches to communication range from the international to the technical, from the political to the personal, and from considerations of human health to those of the communication classroom. The International Communication Association has developed a range and depth that is at once impressive and stimulating. The dynamic nature of this association is immediately obvious to anyone who examines the *Yearbook* series from its inception to this volume, the eighth in the series. To have been part of this change is exciting.

It is always a pleasure to work with the particular mix of individuals who contribute to the *Yearbook*. The table of contents lists 32 chapters, authored by 62 persons. This, as the old cliché states, is only the tip of the iceberg. Over 70 other persons were involved with the evaluating, selecting, and editing of these chapters. The particular problems with the publication schedule ensure that most of these authors have had little time to edit, rewrite, or otherwise amend their initial offerings to their divisions or to the *Yearbook*. Their good humor and patience are, as always, to be commended. In addition, the patience of the division chairpersons is a marvelous asset, one that the association often needs. Let us hope that, as last year, this patience and good humor persist after all concerned have seen what Westley and I have done to their manuscripts.

Communication Yearbook 8 continues the practice of opening with communication "reviews and commentaries," which allows us to publish many interesting and comprehensive works that would not otherwise be published. Accordingly, this work opens with a number of thoughtful analyses of communication that fall somewhere between book and typical journal manuscript length.

I am particularly thankful to the divisions that provided their authors with helpful criticism and time to revise their chapters before submission. I am also extremely grateful to all of the consulting editors, who gave up substantial periods of time, both at Christmas and after, to read volumes and volumes of material. Since all works in this volume are refereed twice, this means that each chapter that appears in the divisional sections has been evaluated by a minimum of five persons other than the *Yearbook* editors, and, in most cases, judged to be appropriate by all of these. In a field that is especially prone to theoretical and methodological controversy, this kind of testing is especially stringent. The scope of this entire process can be appreciated only if one remembers that over 500,000 words of material were submitted for this volume!

What purpose is served by this stringent and exclusionary process? Would the International Communication Association be better served by a system in which *everything* submitted to a division was made available to the members? Over 300 papers were available for consumption at the San Francisco meeting, and the division chairpersons report that this is substantially less than half of the initial submissions. The *Journal of Communication, Human Communication Research,* and *Communication Yearbook* publish a total of about 150 articles per year. Is the quality of the 600 yearly submissions so poor that no one should read them? We should all have serious doubts about this process.

Perhaps we might begin to think about using the vast information-processing capacity of a typical computing installation for our annual information exchange. For example, each division might well take each study submitted and enter it on a disk filing system. Authors who do not submit on disk, tape, or some other appropriate system could pay to have their work transcribed into appropriate form. Key words and other appropriate identifiers would be entered as part of the file. Divisional referees could then log on the home computer using a remote facility and either have the files dumped (I love that particular interactive command—there is something fun about telling the computer to DUMP when you really mean transfer a file) to their home systems or read them on the long-distance lines. Comments and evaluations could be entered as part of the file in a special subfile. A "top three" (or whatever a division decided to do) could be easily sorted from this group. Following this, the authors could have comments instantly transferred to their original files and the paper could be adapted accordingly. *Yearbook* submissions could be made as simply as logging on a home system and pressing a button that would send the manuscript to the editor's system. Editing could be done electronically, and the results shunted back to the authors for approval. The entire manuscript could then be dumped to Sage, who could then interact with the editors, authors, and division chairpersons to construct the best volume possible.

At the convention, ICA could either lease or borrow an appropriate disk system with a small mainframe to drive it. About forty terminals could be set up in an appropriate setting, and those wishing to read papers could log on (registrants at the convention would be given an account number and a password), scan the offerings, read entire papers, read only abstracts, comment on papers, ask questions, request hard copy of papers, (or abstracts, bibliographies, tables, or whatever). Authors could log on daily and see what kind of reactions their papers were generating and then answer questions, meet particular points of criticism, and set up face-to-face meetings with interested persons.

There may be a good deal of prestige associated with the editorship of one of the association publications or with holding the chair of a division. But it is entirely possible that the days of these prestigious gatekeepers are numbered. The current rationale for having gate-keepers is that space is restricted and judgements must be made to publish only quality pieces. If space is no longer restricted (and the computer age has seen to this), then some other way of presenting information might well be called for. It is entirely possible that some assistant professor with a brand new degree knows more about a particular topic than division chairpersons politically elected and publication editors even more politically chosen. Heresy! Especially heretical coming from one of the graybeards in the association, who has long been the beneficiary of the gatekeeping process.

But enough of this kind of rumination. Our system is probably imperfect, but there are persons who make it tolerable. One is, of course, my associate editor, Bruce Westley, who edits with diligence and sagacity. Another is Murali Nair, who cheerfully accepted the routine and boring task of checking references, cross-checking page numbers, and entering the volumes of material in the index.

Last year, I expressed my gratitude to all in the College of Communication at the University of Kentucky who made these pages possible. This group again worked hard to make my life tolerable during the hectic four months when editing demands were intense. This group includes Mrs. Shirley Seabrook, Mrs. Karen Lindeman, and Dean Herbert Drennon. The support of my friends at Sage Publications is

also greatly appreciated. Finally, my wife Ann once more provided
extended support throughout the whole process.

   Thanks again to the ICA for being a stimulating and interesting
place to work. I am especially pleased that the distinguished
communication scholar, Margaret McLaughlin, has been chosen
to edit *Yearbooks 9* and *10* and already has the process under way.
Good luck to Professor McLaughlin next year, and to all of you in
the ICA who have made this volume possible.

—Robert N. Bostrom
Lexington, Kentucky

OVERVIEW OF THE COMMUNICATION YEARBOOK SERIES

This is the eighth in a series of annual volumes providing yearly reviews and syntheses of developments in the evolution of the science of communication. Each volume in the series provides (1) disciplinary reviews and commentaries on topics of general interest to scholars and researchers no matter what their specialized interest in communication studies, (2) current research in a variety of topics that reflect the scholarly concerns of persons working in designated areas, and (3) subject and author indexes that offer convenient reference for each volume. Reviews and commentaries for this volume were solicited by the series editor and chapters presenting current research were selected through processes of competitive judging. Final acceptance of *all* chapters was based upon refereeing processes established by the editor.

Reviews and Commentaries

Review and Commentary chapters are general discussions and critiques of substantive matters of generic interest and relevance that transcend the more specialized concerns of scholars working in the highly diversified discipline of communication science. This section provides a unique outlet for discussions of issues and ideas not readily adaptable to more restrictive journal formats.

Selected Studies

Communication Yearbook is also a means of publishing edited versions of representative current research that has been selected competitively for presentation at annual conferences of the International Communication Association. *Yearbook 8* presents studies selected for the 34th Annual Conference held in San Francisco in May 1984. These studies represent the papers chosen by competitive evaluation by each of the ICA's divisions and by the *Yearbook* editor and selected reviewers. The papers represent research from the following divisions: information systems, interpersonal communication, mass communication, organizational communication, intercultural and development communication, political communication, instructional and developmental communication, and health communication.

1 • COMMUNICATION REVIEWS AND COMMENTARIES

1 ● Uses and Gratifications: A Theoretical Perspective

PHILIP PALMGREEN

University of Kentucky

S INCE the publication of Blumler and Katz's (1974) landmark volume, *The Uses of Mass Communication,* research into the uses audience members make of the mass media, the gratifications derived from media consumption, and their antecedents and consequences has continued at an accelerating pace. Ten years ago critics argued with some success that such research was basically "atheoretical." Today, such an argument would be more difficult to defend. In fact, an examination of the research agenda reveals that the last decade has been a period of rather vigorous theoretical growth for the uses and gratifications approach. This growth was heralded by Blumler and Katz's (1974, p. 13) observation that "the uses and gratifications approach is well and truly launched on a third major phase of its development: a sort of coming of age." This third phase, they said, is concentrated on attempts to provide explanations of the ways in which audience motives, expectations, and media behaviors are interconnected. In other words, Blumler and Katz felt that after lengthy periods in which researchers concentrated mainly on description and measurement of audience uses and motives, the emphasis had shifted in the 1970s to theory development.

While description and measurement remain important concerns, a growing number of studies have indeed been dedicated to the specification and testing of hypotheses about gratifications and media consumption, the relationship between gratifications sought and obtained, the social and psy-

AUTHOR'S NOTE: The author was on sabbatical leave at the University of Lund, Sweden, when this chapter was written. He is grateful for the insightful suggestions and comments of Professor Karl Erik Rosengren on a preliminary draft of this chapter.

Correspondence and requests for reprints: Philip Palmgreen, College of Communications, University of Kentucky, Lexington, KY 40506.

chological origins of media use, and gratifications and media effects. Many of these studies have begun to bridge certain important gaps observed by Blumler and Katz and others a decade ago, while others represent the first tentative steps down entirely new paths of inquiry. The result has been a significant transformation in an important research tradition as researchers strive for a greater understanding of the roles played in society by media undergoing both rapid change and functional reorganization.

This chapter attempts an assessment of the various strands of uses and gratifications research from a theoretical perspective. It examines in some detail the empirical evidence relating to a number of important theoretical linkages and assumptions, including those stemming from certain relatively new and particularly promising approaches to uses and gratifications phenomena. In turn, the research findings in each of six categories are explored: (1) gratifications and media consumption; (2) social and psychological origins of gratifications; (3) gratifications and media effects; (4) gratifications sought and obtained; (5) expectancy-value approaches to uses and gratifications; and (6) audience activity. The findings in each of these areas are incorporated into an integrative model of gratifications and media consumption representing the rather complex theoretical structure that appears to be emerging from uses and gratifications research and work in related areas. Finally, a few of the many challenges facing uses and gratifications researchers are discussed, including understanding the uses of new communications technologies and the development of a comparative theory of mass media use.

GRATIFICATIONS AND MEDIA CONSUMPTION

In a now classic précis, Katz, Blumler, and Gurevitch (1974, p. 20) describe the uses and gratifications approach as one concerned with "(1) the social and psychological origins of (2) needs, which generate (3) expectations of (4) the mass media or other sources, which lead to (5) differential patterns of media exposure (or engagement in other activities), resulting in (6) need gratifications and (7) other consequences, perhaps mostly unintended ones."

While research concerned with almost any of these diverse elements has been placed rather loosely under the broad uses and gratifications umbrella, researchers have emphasized the broad center of Katz et al.'s list (elements 2-6), while paying less attention to the end points of "social and psychological origins" and "media effects." The actual research agenda, then, contradicts a common interpretation of uses and gratifications research as an approach that evolved out of dissatisfaction with earlier "effects" research, and that sought to utilize gratifications concepts as intervening or interacting variables to improve effects predictions. If the uses and gratifications paradigm were indeed a "modified effects model," it is curious that Katz et al. (1974, p. 28) nearly thirty years after the origins of the approach, would conclude that "hardly any substantial empirical or theoretical effort has been devoted to connecting gratifications and effects." While there has been a welcome upsurge in "uses and effects" studies in recent years, and while the social and psychological origins of needs and gratifications is also an important and legitimate concern, most of the research has been devoted to explaining and explicating processes of individual mass media consumption. Such consumption, which is defined narrowly here as audience members' choices of and exposure to various media and types of media content, is viewed by uses and gratifications adherents as motivated by individuals' needs, wants, and requirements. The perceived fulfillment of these manifold needs and requirements through media consumption constitutes, in the lexicon of uses and gratifications researchers, the perceived "gratifications obtained" from media experience. These gratifications, when sought by audience members, are viewed as one of the major causes of active, purposive media consumption behavior directed at gratification fulfillment.

Empirical Studies

Research on the relationship between gratifications (both sought and obtained) and media consumption falls into two main categories: (1) typological studies of media gratifications and (2) studies that investigate the empirical association between gratifications sought and%or obtained on the one hand and measures of media exposure or medium or content choice on the other. Typological studies are at the core of the uses and gratifications tradition and have as their main purpose the identification of types of motives for media consumption. Typological studies formed the bulk of uses and gratifications research prior to the 1970s, and new typologies, particularly for specific content types (such as television news), continue to appear in the literature. Most of the empirical studies cited in this review, in fact, present one or another typology appropriate to the medium or content type under study.

Becker (1979) and McLeod and Becker (1981) have discussed three techniques that have been employed in such studies to elicit consumption motives and to measure their strength: (1) self-report techniques; (2) observer inference of motivations presumed to intervene between media consumption and antecedent variables (such as age, sex, and social location); and (3) experimental manipulation of motives. Self-report is the most direct method of measurement and is far more commonly used than either observer inference or experimental manipulation, although examples of the latter two methods are treated later in this review. The self-report "technique" actually encompasses a variety of methods, including the writing of essays by respondents about their reasons for media consumption; interviews with audience members, either alone or in "focus groups"; and closed-ended Likert-type gratification scales, usually devised on the basis of the open-ended essays or interviews. The closed-ended measures are usually subjected to factor analysis, multidimensional scaling, or cluster analysis to aid in the identification of various gratification dimensions. Through such methods, typological studies have identified a great variety of motives for media consumption, including information, entertainment, social utility, and personal identity (Katz et al., 1974).

The validity of this type of explanation of media consumption rests in turn on the validity of the different self-report techniques. While self-report measures have a long and respected tradition of use in the social sciences, they also have recognized limitations. In the present context, there is controversy over the extent to which respondents are conscious of their motives for consumption or can be made conscious of such motives through closed- or open-ended techniques. The measures have also been criticized as subject to the influence of social acceptability, respondent educational level, and researcher-imposed conceptualization (Becker, 1979; McLeod & Becker, 1981). The debate about these issues is neither new nor unique to the uses and gratifications tradition. Much doubt about the construct validity of gratification measures would be resolved, however, if it could be shown that such indices relate in theoretically predictable ways to other variables, particularly various measures of media consumption. Such empirical evidence would at the same time support the general postulate that mass media consumption is motivated by the gratifications identified by researchers.

In this regard a survey of the literature reveals more than twenty studies that show empirical associations between various gratification measures (both sought and obtained) and media exposure, medium choice, and content choice (Becker, 1976; Becker & Fruit, 1982; Blood & Galloway, 1983; Blumler & McQuail, 1969; Davis & Woodall, 1982; Greenberg, 1974; Hedinsson, 1981; Hur & Robinson, 1981; Kippax & Murray, 1980; McLeod & Becker, 1974; McLeod, Bybee, & Durall, 1982; McLeod, Durall, Ziemke, & Bybee, 1979; McQuail, 1979; Nordlund, 1978; Palmgreen & Rayburn, 1979, 1982; Palmgreen, Wenner, & Rayburn, 1981; Peled & Katz, 1974; Rosengren & Windahl, 1972; Rubin, 1981, 1983; Rubin & Rubin, 1982; Wenner, 1983). While only one of the above studies provides data of a longitudinal nature (Blood & Galloway, 1983) and the evidence is thus primarily correlational, taken together these studies provide documentation of the ability of a wide variety of gratification indices to predict a still wider variety of media consumption measures in diverse settings ranging from peacetime presidential campaigns to media use in a war zone.

A majority of studies to this point concern television, including total TV exposure, exposure to different program content types—such as television news, debates, and quiz shows—public television viewing, and viewing of specific programs (for example, *Roots*). A number of studies also have shown that gratifications are related to program choice in different ways. For example, Palmgreen et al. (1981) found that respondents consistently perceived that they were obtaining greater gratifications from their favorite network television news program than they obtained (or felt they would obtain) from the two competing programs. Rubin & Rubin (1982) found that specific gratifications sought are related to viewing specific types of programs. Canonical analysis revealed that the seeking of essentially passive-entertainment kinds of gratifications from television (companionship, relaxation, passing time, arousal, and habit) was related to total viewing time and the viewing of daytime serials and game shows. The seeking of informational gratifications, on the other hand, characterized viewers of television news, documentary magazines, and talk shows.

The published research does not relate exclusively to television, however. Kippax and Murray (1980) found that perceived gratifications obtained from each of five different media were generally positively related to exposure. Only newspapers failed to show a consistent relationship. McLeod et al. (1979) report that seeking of surveillance-vote guidance was positively correlated with overall cross-media campaign media exposure for the young, while seeking of content-excitement was a stronger predictor for older voters. Both sets of gratifications predicted exposure to partisan media content among both age groups. Other studies that relate gratifications and needs to exposure to newspapers, radio, and other media include Nordlund (1978), Rosengren and Windahl (1972) Kline, Miller, and Morrison (1974), and Becker and Fruit (1982). The last study also provides evidence that audience members' comparisons of gratifications obtained from different media are related to medium choice. Respondents' evaluations of newspapers and television (relative to one another) concerning the ability of these media to satisfy local and national information needs were related to choice of one or the other medium for either local or national news.

In general, the various media consumption studies show low to moderate correlations (.15 to .40) between the gratifications measures and consumption indices. While not large, the observed correlations are in the range of those generally found in cross-sectional surveys of mass media behavior, including "effects" studies. Also, approximately half of the studies cited employed statistical controls, sometimes multiple ones, for a variety of demographic, exposure, and political variables. In one of the most stringent tests of this type, Wenner (1983), using hierarchical regression analysis, demonstrated that gratification measures (both sought and obtained) accounted for significant additional variance in exposure to network evening news and *60 Minutes* when demographic, exposure, and dependency measures are included. Additional evidence of this type is furnished by Hedinsson (1981), who employed a fifteen-variable structural equation model (LISREL) in a study of television use among Swedish children. Television use associated with identification and interaction with TV content ("capture," according to Rosengren & Windahl, 1972) was positively related to television viewing levels for both fifth graders ($\beta = .16$) and ninth graders ($\beta = .26$). The effect was independent of the numerous social class and socialization variables in the model.

Conclusions

Data, then, from studies in the United States, Britain, Sweden, Israel, and Australia are supportive of the postulate that mass media consumption is motivated by gratifications associated with the consumption experience. Moreover, the research evidence speaks strongly against univariate or bivariate motivational schemes, since several investigations have found consumption predicted by multiple motivations. While much media consumption may be accidental, and though consumption is certainly constrained by such factors as availability and work schedules, as Bogart (1965) and others have contended, there seems to be no denying that motivation also plays a substantial role.

SOCIAL AND PSYCHOLOGICAL ORIGINS OF MEDIA GRATIFICATIONS

In a study of social integration and mass media use among adolescents, Johnstone (1974, p. 35) observes that "members of mass audiences do not experience the media as anonymous and isolated individuals, but rather as members of organized social groups and as participants in a cultural milieu." This is a view shared by the majority of uses and gratifications researchers who "have always been strongly opposed to 'mass audience' terminology as a way of labelling the collectivities that watch TV shows, attend movies, and read magazines and newspapers in their millions" (Blumler, 1979, p. 21). According to this view, then, many of the media-related needs and requirements of individuals spring from their location in and interaction with their social environment.

Blumler has posited three major social origins of media gratifications:

(1) normative influences, which give rise to certain requirements or expectations based on sex, life-cycle position, social roles, and so on; (2) socially distributed life chances, consisting of factors that "facilitate" a richer involvement with media content (for example, organizational affiliations, frequency of social contact) or that are sources of a "need to compensate" for the lack of various social opportunities (for example, lack of friends, telephone, or opportunities for leisure); and (3) the subjective reaction or adjustment of the individual to his or her social situation (for example, job or role satisfaction). Johnstone (1974), in focusing on social integration, has offered a somewhat different conceptualization of the role of social variables. Transcendental uses are those motivated by a desire to escape from the realities of one's social environment. In some ways this concept is subsumed by Blumler's concept of compensatory uses. Experiential uses, on the other hand, spring from a desire to stay in contact with and oriented to the social milieu. Perhaps a more descriptive term for this type of use would be "social orientation."

Psychological factors may also provide the motivational stimulus or point of origin for much media use. This is hinted at by Blumler's "subjective adjustment" to the social situation, but the topic has received its only extensive theoretical treatment in McGuire's (1974) brilliant essay on the psychological motives for media use. His sixteen-cell classification scheme for human motives highlights the relevance of a large number of psychological theories for understanding the cognitive and affective underpinnings of media consumption. Consistency, attribution, complexity, and various personality theories are among those McGuire examines for their utility in generating hypotheses about media gratifications.

McGuire's success in this endeavor stands in stark contrast to the scarcity of empirical investigations of psychological origins within the framework of the uses and gratifications tradition. Only two studies have included explicit consideration of the linkage between psychological variables and gratifications. In a study by Nordlund (1978), neuroticism was shown to be moderately positively related to the perception of obtaining escape gratifications from television quiz programs, magazine serials, entertainment shows, and television serials, in addition to correlating with parasocial interaction with TV characters. Rosengren and Windahl (1977) found that neuroticism and introversion-extraversion were related in complex ways to potential for interaction with the mass media and parasocial interaction with media content. A few other studies have shown correlations between gratifications and attitudes (Greenberg, 1974; Hur & Robinson, 1981). Since generalizations about psychological variables are not possible on the basis of such sparse evidence, the remainder of this section is devoted to the question of social origins.

Empirical Studies of Social Origins

Research has slowly begun to map certain features of the role of social context in generating motivations for media consumption. At least twenty studies may be identified that furnish empirical evidence on the role of demographic and social circumstances. In about half of these studies this examination has been largely exploratory, unguided by specific hypotheses grounded in theory, though in some cases informal "expectations" are voiced (see Becker & Fruit, 1982; Davis & Woodall, 1982; Greenberg, 1974; Hur & Robinson, 1981; Kippax & Murray, 1980; Lometti, Reeves, & Bybee, 1977; Lull, 1980; McQuail, 1979; Peled & Katz, 1974; Rubin, 1981; Rubin & Rubin, 1982). In most of these investigations the social origins of gratifications are not a primary focus of the study, and empirical data on the influence of demographic (in most cases) and social variables on gratifications are presented in subsidiary fashion. Only in a few cases are ex post facto explanations of observed relationships attempted. Still, these studies establish at a minimum that a variety of gratifications sought and obtained do have empirical ties with such variables as age, education, sex, income, family communication patterns, length of residence, discussions with others, and membership in organizations. The theoretical nature of these relationships awaits explanations in most cases.

A number of other studies have taken a more theoretical approach to the question of the social origins of gratifications (see Blumler, 1979; Brown, Cramond, & Wilde, 1974; Hedinsson, 1981; Johnsson-Smaragdi, 1983; Johnstone, 1974; Nordlund, 1978; Palmgreen & Rayburn, 1979; Roe, 1983a, 1983b; Rosengren & Windahl, 1972; Rubin & Rubin, 1981). For example, Rosengren and Windahl (1972), working from a functional and compensatory theoretical framework, hypothesized and found support for a relationship between low potential for social interaction and parasocial interaction with mass media content. A study by Johnstone (1974), while not measuring gratifications directly, illustrates well the use of both compensatory and facilitative theorizing to postulate certain gratifications (escape, social orientation) as variables that intervene between social-structural variables and media consumption. Roe (1983a) proceeded from a similar structural-cultural perspective—but employed a very different sort of methodology—in examining the social uses Swedish adolescents make of videocassettes. Through in-depth group interviews with fifty high school students (age 15), he found that most actively sought more or less clearly perceived social gratifications from videocassette use, including (1) to establish and maintain a shared peer-group activity; (2) to exercise autonomy from parents and adults; and (3) to present an antiestablishment profile. Viewing of highly violent horror films via cassette served the additional function of providing a "test of manhood" for males. The Roe study demonstrates how social demands, interests, and expectations can lead to facilitative uses of a mass medium to promote social integration.

Conclusions

In both the theoretically oriented and more exploratory studies of social origins, generalizations about the strength of observed relationships are more difficult than in the media consumption studies treated in the previous section. In some cases only frequency data are presented, and in others (for example, Roe, 1983a) the methodology employed precludes use of statistical measures of association. Also, only six of the studies cited employed statistical controls. Still, the reported correlations again fall in the low-to-moderate range.

At least two conclusions about the social origins of media-related gratifications seem warranted. First, sufficient empirical evidence has now accumulated for us to state that many uses of the mass media do appear to have their origins in societal structure and social processes. Second, we are only beginning to understand the nature of the theoretical linkages. Certainly Katz et al. (1974) and Levy (1977) are correct in observing that no general theoretical framework exists that links gratifications to their social origins. However, we might ask where else in mass media research such a general theory exists, and, in any case, whether it is fair to apply such a standard at this stage. If theory is treated more as a goal than as an evaluative standard, then some limited progress has been made. Blumler's (1979) concepts of normative influence, social opportunity, and subjective social adjustment, along with Johnstone's (1974) and Roe's (1983a) concept of social orientation, have received some empirical support and deserve further elaboration and testing. Other concepts, such as social integration and life cycle, seem equally promising. Whatever the conceptual framework, many more theoretical studies of social origins are needed if the uses that audience members make of the mass media are to be placed in their proper social and cultural context.

GRATIFICATIONS AND MEDIA EFFECTS

It was noted earlier that Katz et al. (1974) drew the conclusion a decade ago that hardly any empirical or theoretical effort had been expended in attempts to examine the relationship, if any, between motives for media use and subsequent effects. Although it has been argued here that the uses and gratifications approach is concerned principally with media consumption, many researchers have expected that the consideration of audience motives might shed some light on effects processes. More recently Blumler (1979) decried the lack of theoretical advancement brought about by an "exceedingly spare" list of published gratifications-by-effects studies. Windahl (1981) has also called for a merger of the "effects" and uses and gratifications traditions and has proposed a "uses and effects" model that treats the interactive outcome of media content and media use as "conseffects."

A review of the literature reveals that this long looked-for merger, if not actually realized, has at least reached the point of serious negotiations. At least twenty empirical studies of a "uses and effects" variety may now be enumerated, two-thirds of which have appeared in the last five years (Becker, 1976; Blumler & McQuail, 1969; de Bock, 1980; Garramone, 1983; Greenberg, 1974; Hedinsson, 1981; Hur & Robinson, 1981; McLeod & Becker, 1974; McLeod, Becker, & Byrnes, 1974; McLeod, Brown, Becker, & Ziemke, 1977; McLeod, Luetscher, & McDonald, 1980; Nordlund, 1978; Roe, 1983b; Rubin, 1981, 1983; Rubin & Rubin, 1982; Weaver, 1980; Wenner, 1982, 1983; Windahl, Hedinsson, Höjerback, & Nord, 1983).

These studies have shown that a variety of audience gratifications (again, both sought and obtained) are related to a wide spectrum of media effects, including knowledge, dependency, attitudes, perceptions of social reality, agenda setting, discussion, and various political effects variables. Most of the investigations employed statistical controls for media exposure and/or demographic and other variables, with several utilizing multivariate techniques such as hierarchical regression, canonical correlation, multiple classification analysis, and structural equation modeling. The likelihood of spuriousness is therefore greatly reduced. In the studies that used hierarchical regression (McLeod & Becker, 1974; McLeod et al., 1977; Wenner, 1982, 1983), gratifications accounted for additional effects variance after the introduction of exposure and other control variables. In addition, at least three studies using self-report gratification measures have employed panel designs (Blumler & McQuail, 1969; McLeod & Becker, 1974; McLeod et al., 1977), with gratifications sought predicting later media effects. Another study involving inferred gratifications also utilized a panel design (Roe, 1983b). Cross-cultural validation stems from the fact that the investigations were carried out in four countries (United States, Great Britain, Sweden, and the Netherlands). Although the majority of the studies concern television, several studies provide data on newspapers.

Media Dependency

One media "effect" that has been the focus of considerable attention in uses and gratifications investigations is media *dependency*. The variable actually has been given different appellations (dependency, attachment, affinity—even "irritation with missing the newspaper"), but all of these concepts have been operationalized basically by asking respondents to what extent they would miss a particular medium if it were unavailable, how important the medium is, and so on. The prominence of the dependency variable in recent studies probably stems from its connections with the concept of functional alternatives (Rosengren & Windahl, 1972) and with media dependency theory (Ball-Rokeach & DeFleur, 1976; see also Rubin & Windahl, 1982). While treated as an effects variable in most studies, dependency is probably best conceptualized as both an antecedent and a consequence of mass media consumption. In any case, it has been found that dependency is related to a number of motives for attending to the media. In accordance with theoretical expectations, the more motivated persons are in seeking gratifications from a particular medium or the more they perceive they are obtaining gratifications, the more they will come to depend on that medium (Rubin & Windahl, 1982).

The extent to which particular gratifications relate to dependency seems to depend on both medium and content variables. While several motives seem to be related to dependency on television as a medium (for example, companionship, entertainment, passing the time, arousal, relaxation), surveillance or information motives usually exhibit low or nonsignificant relationships (de Bock, 1980; Greenberg, 1974; Rubin, 1981, 1983; Rubin & Rubin, 1982; Windahl et al., 1983). However, in a study of a newspaper strike and a TV blackout in the Netherlands, de Bock (1980) found that an information gratification frustration measure was the strongest predictor of dependency on the newspaper. The information measure was unrelated to television dependency. Data from six studies indicate, then, that people in general do not strongly depend on television as a medium for informational purposes. By comparison, readers of newspapers (at least in the Netherlands) depend on them very much as sources of information. Wenner (1982) presents data indicating that dependency on television news programs and documentaries (60 Minutes) is related to surveillance gratifications, as the nature of these programs might indicate, but even here gratifications such as parasocial interaction and interpersonal utility are stronger predictors of program dependency than are surveillance motives.

Tests of a Theoretical Perspective

Blumler (1979, pp. 15-16) criticizes the few, mostly exploratory, uses and effects studies that had appeared up to that time for the lack of a theoretical perspective, for "feeding a number of audience orientations into the computer at the gratifications end and seeing what emerges at the effects end." Unfortunately, this still constitutes a reasonably accurate description of some uses and effects studies. While gratifications are often shown to enhance or mitigate effects, the theoretical nature of the relationship is sometimes neglected or treated only ex post facto.

In an attempt to stimulate a more theoretical approach, Blumler (1979) offers three hypotheses, based on a tripartite classification of commonly observed gratifications: (1) *Cognitive motivation* will facilitate information gain; (2) *diversion and escape motivations* will favor audience acceptance of perceptions of social situations in line with portrayals frequently found in entertainment materials; and (3) *personal identity motivations* will promote reinforcement effects.

Some empirical evidence relevant to each of these hypotheses has now accumulated. Regarding the hypothesis that cognitive or surveillance motivations should promote learning, McLeod and Becker (1974) found that surveillance was the strongest motivational predictor of knowledge gains during a political campaign. Similarly, McLeod et al. (1980) report that the surveillance motive predicted knowledge of an economic crisis, while communication utility did not. In a related vein, Atkin, Bowen, Nayman, and Sheinkopf (1973) and Atkin and Heald (1976) found that persons who viewed political ads for informational as opposed to "captive-audience" reasons learned more about each candidate.

Two rare (for uses and gratifications research) experimental investigations also lend support to Blumler's hypothesis. Garramone (1983) instructed subjects to attend to a televised political ad "to learn where the candidates stand on issues" (issue motivational set) or "to form an impression of the candidate's personality" (image motivation set). Subjects in the issue set learned more issue information and were more confident in their learning than were those in the image set. Those in the image set paid greater attention to the video portion of the ad (containing much information about personality) and had greater confidence in their recall of video information. They also were more likely than issue attenders to base personality inferences on information contained in the ad, rather than on implicit personality theories.

McLeod and Becker (1981) report the results of a pilot experiment that showed somewhat similar results. Subjects in small groups were seated in a lounge area containing equal numbers of public affairs periodicals. In one condition, subjects were told that they would soon be involved in a test of what they knew about "the current situation in Pakistan." Subjects in a second condition were informed that they would soon be required to write an essay about U.S. policy on military aid to Pakistan. A third group (control) was given no specific instructions. Subjects in the test and essay conditions, who presumably had induced in them different kinds of information-seeking motives, made greater use of the public affairs periodicals than those in the control group. While they displayed no greater knowledge about Pakistan than the control subjects on an objective test, they recalled more pictures about Pakistan from the periodicals. Also, reflecting the fact that there are different kinds of cognitive motivations, subjects in the essay condition used about twice the number of words and distinct pieces of information in postexperiment essays than did subjects in either the test or control conditions. The experimental results, then, support the survey findings in demonstrating that cognitive motivations of different types do facilitate learning from media materials. At the same time, they provide validational evidence for the self-report measures employed in the surveys.

The evidence available on the *diversion* hypothesis is not supportive, however, and suggests that the hypothesis be reformulated. In four studies the strongest motivational correlate of the perceived content realism of television was an *information* (about life) motive (Greenberg, 1974; Rubin, 1979, 1981, 1983). Viewing for escape or to forget, on the other hand, was either unrelated or only weakly related to perceived realism. In retrospect, it makes sense that those who perceive that television is an accurate reflection of life should also be most likely to seek information about life from the medium. Content perceived as true to life, on the other hand, should hold little attraction for those seeking escape from their worldly cares. Notice, though, that this hypothesis treats perceived television reality as a perceptual variable related to motives for media use, rather than as an effect of exposure. It should also be noted that the studies cited deal with the *perceived* reality of media portrayals. Such perception is not necessarily correlated with more objectively determined influence of, or learning from, such portrayals. Further investigation of Blumler's hypothesis employing such objective measures is needed.

Finally, no direct data are available on Blumler's *personal identity* motivation hypothesis. This is due partly to the very broad nature of this audience orientation, encompassing as it seems reinforcement, identification, and parasocial interaction gratifications. Partial and indirect evidence is provided by Blumler and McQuail (1969) and McLeod and Becker (1981), who found that those seeking reinforcement during election campaigns manifested selective exposure to content about their own preferred candidates. Some evidence of selective retention by reinforcement seekers was also found by McLeod and Becker.

Interactive Versus Additive Effects

An important theoretical question concerning the role played by gratifications sought and obtained in media effects is whether the effects of media exposure and motives are additive or interactive. McLeod and Becker and their colleagues generally have found support for an additive model in their research on political communication (Becker, 1976; McLeod & Becker, 1974; McLeod et al., 1977, 1980). Wenner (1982, 1983), in his studies of dependency on television news, also demonstrated that the addition of gratification "main effects" terms to hierarchical regression models containing exposure variables accounted for additional variance in dependency. Wenner, though, did not include interaction terms in his models. By comparison, interactive effects of exposure and gratifications have been found for political campaign variables (Blumler & McQuail, 1969) and agenda setting (McLeod et al., 1974). While the weight of evidence at this time seems to favor additive models, it is possible that *either* additive or interactive models may be appropriate in different research situations involving different settings, variables, and operationalizations. Obviously, more research that directly contrasts the two formulations is needed. Attention should also be paid to the *form* of any observed interaction, since any number of patterns may result in statistically significant interaction terms.

GRATIFICATIONS SOUGHT AND OBTAINED

In the early to mid 1970s a number of media scholars (such as Greenberg, 1974; Katz, Blumler, & Gurevitch, 1973; Lometti et al., 1977) stressed the need to distinguish between the motives for media consumption or gratifications sought (GS) and the gratifications perceived to be obtained (GO) from this experience. Research up to that time had neglected the distinction empirically, and thus an important theoretical link was being ignored. Whether the motivations that lead an individual to media consumption are equivalent to the perceived outcomes of that consumption should have important ramifications for future media behavior, as well as for media evaluation (McLeod et al., 1982).

In the last five years a considerable amount of research has been directed at examining the relationship between GS and GO and the combined and independent impact of these variables on media consumption and effects (Levy & Windahl, 1984; McLeod & Becker, 1981; McLeod et al., 1982; Palmgreen & Rayburn, 1979; Palmgreen, Wenner, & Rayburn, 1980, 1981; Rayburn & Palmgreen, 1984; Rayburn, Palmgreen, & Acker, 1984; Wenner, 1982, 1983).

One major finding is that individual gratifications sought display moderately strong correlations (.40 to .60) with corresponding gratifications obtained (Levy & Windahl, 1984; McLeod et al., 1982, Palmgreen et al., 1980; Rayburn & Palmgreen, 1984; Rayburn et al., 1984; Wenner, 1982, 1983). This, combined with the generally much lower correlations observed between noncorresponding GS and GO, lends support to a feedback model relating gratifications sought and obtained.

On the other hand, gratifications sought are separable empirically as well as conceptually from gratifications obtained. There are several reasons for this conclusion. First, despite the "moderately strong" label that conventional usage would attach to the GS-GO correlations noted above, there is still considerable variance (65-85 percent) that GS and GO measures do not share. Gratifications sought and obtained influence but do not determine one another. Second, the *dimensions* of GS and GO have been found to differ in some studies (McLeod et al., 1982; Palmgreen et al., 1980). Third, mean levels of gratifications sought often differ from mean levels of gratifications obtained. Fourth, at least two studies have found that GS and GO contribute independently to variance in media consumption and effects measures (Wenner, 1982, 1983).

Level of Abstraction

In a cautious attempt to maximize the empirical distinction between GS and GO, researchers have ordinarily measured the two concepts at different levels of media abstraction. For example, Palmgreen et al. (1980, 1981) measured GS from television news in general and GO from network evening news programs. Similarly, McLeod and Becker (1982) measured GS from "presidential campaigns" and GO from the 1976 televised presidential debates. Recently, however, Levy and Windahl (1984) and Rayburn and Palmgreen (1984), in studies involving Swedish and American television news, respectively, measured both GS and GO at the same level of abstraction (that is, "television news"). Both studies found GS-GO correlations near .50, similar to those observed in studies where different levels of abstraction were employed and providing similar evidence of the related but separate nature of GS and GO. These findings are preliminary and should be interpreted cautiously, but, if future research should replicate these results, an important conceptual and methodological step will have been taken. Measurement of GS and GO at the same level of abstraction is crucial to direct comparison of communication outcomes with what is sought. It also eliminates certain contratheoretical results that may occur under certain conditions when GS and GO are measured at different levels of abstraction. For example, as Palmgreen et al. (1981) have discussed at some length, if gratifications obtained from a favorite television program substantially exceed gratifications sought from the program *type*, then GS-GO discrepancies may actually be greater for the favorite program than for less well-liked programs.

There will, of course, be times when measuring GS and GO at different abstraction levels will be preferable. For example, we may wish to predict exposure to various functional alternatives on the basis of gratifications sought and obtained. Measuring GS and GO at the same abstraction level for each functional alternative requires that the audience member make at least some use of each alternative if GS measures are to be obtained for these alternatives. For example, ability to respond meaningfully to the item "I watch CBS news to give me things to talk about" requires at least minimal exposure to CBS news. On the other hand, even in the case of no exposure to CBS news, it should still be possible to obtain meaningful measures of GS from television news in general (assuming some exposure to the program type), while obtaining both actual (in the case of watched news programs) and hypothetical (in the case of unwatched news programs) measures of GO from different programs. While GS and GO discrepancy measures may yield contratheoretical results in this instance, as previously discussed, it would still be possible to employ GS and GO measures separately to examine their role in program choice. This is the approach adopted by Palmgreen et al. (1981) in their study of news program choice.

AN EXPECTANCY-VALUE APPROACH

A concept central to most models of uses and gratifications phenomena is that of "expectancy." Numerous authors have employed the term (see Katz et al., 1974; McLeod & Becker, 1981; Mendelsohn, 1974; Peled & Katz, 1974), and it is a key element in Katz et al.'s (1974) classic précis of the uses and gratifications approach described above. Indeed, the concept of audience expectations concerning the characteristics of the media and potential gratifications to be obtained is essential to the uses and gratifications assumption of an active audience. If audience members are to select from among various media and nonmedia alternatives according to their needs, they must have some perception of the alternatives most likely to meet those needs.

Until recently, however, theory development in the area suffered from the lack of a rigorous conceptualization of expectancy. Expectations have been variously defined as probabilities of satisfaction assigned by audience members to various behaviors (McLeod & Becker, 1981), audience demands upon the media (Peled & Katz, 1974), affective anticipations regarding the prospects of particular events having certain consequences (Mendelsohn, 1974), and gratifications sought (Katz, Gurevitch, & Haas, 1973).

Substantial conceptual clarification results if one adopts an expectancy-value approach to uses and gratifications, as certain authors (Blood & Galloway, 1983; Galloway & Meek, 1981; Palmgreen & Rayburn, 1982; Rayburn & Palmgreen, 1984; Van Leuven, 1981) recently have advocated.[1] Although the various theories under this label differ somewhat in their emphases (Atkinson, 1957; Fishbein, 1963; Fishbein & Ajzen, 1975; Rotter, 1954; Tolman, 1932; Vroom, 1964), all view behavior, behavioral intentions, or attitudes (or all three) as a function of (1) *expectancy* (or belief)— the perceived probability that an object possesses a particular attribute or that a behavior will have a particular consequence; and (2) *evaluation*— the degree of affect, positive or negative, toward an attribute or behavioral outcome.

Palmgreen and Rayburn have been exploring the interrelationships among beliefs, evaluations, gratifications sought, and media exposure. From an expectancy-value perspective (based on Fishbein & Ajzen, 1975), they have expressed gratifications sought as a function of both beliefs and evaluations:

$$GS_i = b_i e_i \qquad [1]$$

where GS_i = the ith gratification sought from some media object, X (some medium, program, content type, or the like); b_i = the belief (subjective probability) that X possesses some attribute or that a behavior related to X will have a particular outcome; and e_i = the affective evaluation of the particular attribute or outcome.

A parallel formulation that predicts a generalized orientation to seek various gratifications from a particular source is as follows:

$$\sum_{i=1}^{n} GS_i = \sum_{i=1}^{n} b_i e_i \qquad [2]$$

Both models successfully predicted gratifications sought from television news, indicating that expectations about the characteristics of television news and evaluations of these characteristics are important antecedents of motives to seek associated gratifications (Palmgreen & Rayburn, 1982).

Further analysis that included gratifications obtained supports the model shown in Figure 1.1 (Rayburn & Palmgreen, 1984). It is a process model that states that the products of beliefs (expectations) and evaluations

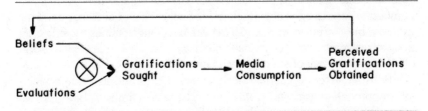

Figure 1.1.   Expectancy-value model of GS and GO.

influence the seeking of gratifications, which in turn influence media consumption. Such consumption results in the perception of certain gratifications obtained, which then feed back to reinforce or alter an individual's perceptions of the gratification-related attributes of a particular newspaper, program, program genre, or whatever. For example, if a person values "information about current issues and events" positively and believes (expects) that television news possesses such information, he or she will be motivated to seek such information from television news. Assuming that television news is available to the audience member, exposure to television news programming should result. If the individual obtains the expected information, this outcome (GO) will feed back to reinforce the initial belief about this program attribute. If he or she obtains the information at a lower or higher level than expected, the associated belief should be altered, with consequent change in motivation to seek information about current issues from television news.

Belief Formation

The expectancy-value approach postulates that beliefs about a source are the primary informational components determining the seeking of gratifications. These beliefs have many origins and derive from the sum of an individual's experiences (direct and indirect) with a particular media object (a medium, program, content type, newspaper, or the like). Fishbein and Ajzen (1975) distinguish among three kinds of belief: (1) descriptive, (2) informational, and (3) inferential.

Descriptive beliefs result from direct observation of an object. Exposure to a particular medium, for example, will lead to the formation and modification of beliefs concerning attributes of the medium.

Informational beliefs are formed by accepting information from an outside source that links certain objects and attributes. We may acquire beliefs about a magazine through a friend who subscribes to that magazine, or we may obtain information through advertising concerning the magazine. Collectively, informational beliefs may constitute a large proportion of our total media belief system, especially concerning media objects with which we have little direct personal experience.

Inferential beliefs are also beliefs about characteristics of objects not yet directly observed, or that are not directly observable. We often infer such beliefs on the basis of formal logic, personal theories of implicit personality (Wiggins, 1973), causal attributions (Kelley, 1973), and stereotyping (Lippmann, 1922). Such inferential processes apply to media attributes and are the basis of many of the beliefs we have about media objects with which we have little direct experience. Here cultural and social stereotypes and norms play a major role in forming both individual and collective expectations about media objects.

From this perspective, it is illuminating to reexamine the criticism that responses to gratifications measures may reflect "only" cultural or social stereotypes or myths, rather than individual "actual" experience with media content. Yet these stereotypes and myths consist of beliefs about the mass media, beliefs that may constitute a very significant proportion of an individual's meaning system for a given medium, program, or channel. From the standpoint of the individual, these beliefs will influence media behavior, regardless of their source. Thus the person who responds principally in terms of stereotypes or other inferential beliefs regarding a source is still yielding valuable information about his or her media perceptions. From the larger social or cultural perspective it is, of course, important to determine the types and sources of beliefs about the mass media. Here studies of belief formation and change could yield valuable insights into the social origins of media expectations.

Gratifications Versus Avoidances

A few uses and gratifications studies (see Becker, 1979; Blumler & McQuail, 1969; McLeod & Becker, 1974) have distinguished between "positive" gratifications (reasons for seeking media consumption) and "negative" gratifications or avoidances (reasons for avoiding media consumption). Becker (1979) found that avoidance motivations are empirically distinct from gratifications, and called for more conceptual attention to avoidance measures.

Taking an expectancy-value approach to uses and gratifications offers a useful way of conceptualizing both gratifications and avoidances, and gives insight into different kinds of motivation for media use. An examination of avoidance items employed in uses and gratifications studies reveals that the majority involve a *negatively* evaluated attribute (presumed to be gratification related) that the media object in question (for example, political content) is believed to possess. An example of such an item tapping avoidance of political content on television is the following: "Because I'm not interested in watching candidates I don't like" (Becker, 1979). Endorsement of such an item would indicate a negative evaluation of information about "candidates I don't like" along with the belief that political content on TV possesses such information. Such a situation would involve a case of *true* and classic avoidance of a disliked entity.

The remainder of avoidance items commonly employed usually involve a positively valued attribute that the media object is believed not to possess. Such an item for political TV is "Because I prefer to relax when

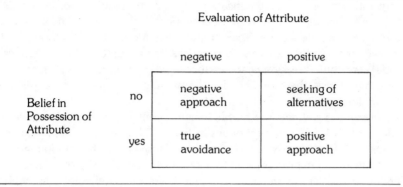

Figure 1.2.   Typology of media motivations.

watching television" (Becker, 1979). Endorsement of this type of item indicates a positive evaluation of "relaxing when watching television" in conjunction with the belief that political TV content is not relaxing. This would reflect not so much true avoidance of political TV as exposure to alternative TV content perceived to be more relaxing. This type of motive will be termed "seeking of alternatives."

Cross-tabulating *evaluation* of media attributes with *belief* in their possession yields, in fact, a fourfold typology of media motivations hypothesized to result from differing perceptions/evaluations of media attributes (see Figure 1.2).

Positive evaluation of a media attribute, combined with belief that the media object has this attribute, will give rise to a motive to seek the associated gratification from that particular source (Palmgreen & Rayburn, 1982). This cell is termed "positive approach" and represents the type of motivation uses and gratifications researchers have studied almost exclusively. Belief in possession of a negatively valued attribute should lead, as discussed above, to "true avoidance," while disbelief in possession of a positively valued characteristic is associated with "seeking of alternatives." Finally, if an individual believes a communication source does not possess a disliked attribute (for example, "At least it's not boring"), he or she may be motivated to use the source, particularly if available alternatives are perceived to have the negative characteristic (are "boring"). Since true seeking of a positive gratification is not involved, we shall call this kind of motivation "negative approach."

It may be argued, of course, that negative approach is merely the mirror image of positive approach; that is, disbelief in the possession of a negative attribute (such as "boring") implies belief in possession of the corresponding positive attribute (such as "exciting"). In some cases this may be true. However, it may be argued that "true avoidance" is also the mirror opposite of positive approach or gratification seeking. A study by Becker (1979), though, indicates that this is not the case. Gratifications and avoidances emerged on separate factors in this study.[2] Also, McLeod and Becker (1974) showed that gratifications and avoidances (mostly of the "true avoidance" type) contributed separately to variance in political effects. Any "mirror image" hypothesis, therefore, needs to be put to empirical test and additional theoretical scrutiny.

Uses and gratifications research might profit from the empirical investigation of all four types of motives in Figure 1.2. Do media consumption patterns differ depending upon the type of motivation that predominates? Does including measures of all four types of motivation lead to increased ability to predict media consumption and associated effects? If so, which type of motivation generally is the strongest predictor? Future investigations might well address these and other research questions raised from an expectancy-value perspective.

AUDIENCE ACTIVITY

Uses and gratifications researchers have long been opposed to the old "hypodermic needle" concept of a passive media audience, absorbing uncritically and unconditionally the symbolic output of all-powerful media. Instead, uses and gratifications researchers have argued that audience members actively confront their media experience, taking from it in accordance with the gratifications they pursue and the perceived abilities of the various media sources to satisfy them. Although this assumption has been severely criticized by some (for example, see Elliot, 1974), it still constitutes one of the essential theoretical underpinnings of the approach. Rosengren has characterized uses and gratifications research as a finalistic or purposive approach based on a voluntaristic perspective, as opposed to media effects research, which is more causal and deterministic in nature (Rosengren, 1983; Rosengren, Roe, & Sonesson, 1983).

As Blumler (1979) has observed, it is unfortunate that uses and gratifications researchers have treated the concept of audience activity more as an "article of faith" than an empirical question deserving of investigation. One of the reasons for this neglect, according to Blumler, is the "extraordinary range of meanings" associated with the activity concept, including utility, intentionality, selectivity, and imperviousness to influence. Swanson (1977, 1979) adds still another connotation in insisting that audience activity be equated with the process of constructing meaning from message elements.

Building upon these and other interpretations, Levy and Windahl,

(1984) have mounted the most serious attempt to date to conceptualize and investigate empirically what is undeniably a complex, multidimensional construct. They conceive of a typology of audience activity constructed from two dimensions. The first dimension, *audience orientation,* is qualitative in nature and consists of three levels: (1) selectivity, (2) involvement, and (3) use. Borrowing from Blumler, they posit a second, temporal dimension that subdivides activity based on its occurrence before, during, or after exposure. The result is a potentially rich ninefold typology that suggests a number of research questions, including the frequency with which different types of activity occur, the relationships among these types of activity, the implications of activity types for media effects, and the distribution of activity levels across media and audience subgroups. Unfortunately, Levy and Windahl present data on only three of the activity types. These lie along the diagonal of the table, thus confounding the orientation and temporal dimensions. These three types they term "Preactivity" (in this study, defined as consciously planning to watch television news), "Duractivity" (defined in a negative sense as engaging in distracting behaviors while viewing), and "Postactivity" (thinking about the news and discussing it with others).

Respondents were found to vary in their activity levels across the three types. Generally, moderately high activity levels were observed for Pre- and Postactivity, with lower levels for Duractivity. Also, while the Preactivity measure was fairly strongly related to Postactivity ($r = .525$), neither Preactivity nor Postactivity was significantly related to Duractivity. All of these findings related to Duractivity, however, may be due to the concept's operationalization, not as "active" involvement in the decoding and interpreting process, but as not engaging in distracting activities (as Levy & Windahl themselves note). The reliability of the Duractivity measure is also rather low (mean interitem correlation of .366). Because of the confounding of the orientation and temporal dimensions, there also was no opportunity to explore whether a particular "orientational" activity (such as selectivity) is correlated across time or, conversely, whether the different orientational measures gathered at the same point in time are related. These are important questions to be addressed in later work.

From a theoretical standpoint, however, Levy and Windahl's most important finding is that measures of gratifications sought and obtained were related consistently and positively to all three measures of activity. That is, the more audience members were motivated in their use of television news and the more they perceived various types of gratification, the more active they were in their television news consumption. This is consistent with theoretical expectations. Replication of this finding is needed in studies that employ the full ninefold typology.

Studies of Medium and Content Choice

While studies that have attempted direct measurement of audience activity are few (see also Levy, 1978, 1983), indirect evidence is available from several studies that speaks to various aspects of the activity question. For example, if activity is guided by motivations for media use and expectations concerning different media channels, audience members should differentiate among these channels on the basis of gratifications sought and/or obtained. There is a good deal of empirical evidence that supports this hypothesis. In a classic study of Israeli media use, Katz, Gurevitch, and Haas (1973) showed through multidimensional scaling that audience members differentiated among five media on the basis of perceived gratifications obtained. Lometti et al. (1977), also using multidimensional scaling, showed that respondents differentiated among six media and two interpersonal channels along three dimensions. Similar empirical data on the ability of audience members to distinguish among different media on the basis of gratifications sought or obtained is provided by Peled and Katz (1974), McLeod and Becker (1981), Becker and Fruit (1982), de Bock (1980), and Mendelsohn and O'Keefe (1976).

Lometti et al. (1977) have noted that such studies confound medium and content characteristics. While an interesting research challenge is thereby posed, nonetheless, such investigations show that gratifications and media choice are related, providing empirical evidence for the "selectivity" and "use" aspects of activity identified by Levy and Windahl (1984). Still other studies, though, have "controlled" for type of medium by investigating the relationship of gratifications to content choice within a single medium. Rubin and Rubin (1982) found through canonical analysis that viewing of daytime serials and game shows was associated with seeking companionship, relaxation, arousal, habit, and passing the time. By comparison, viewing of TV news, documentary magazines, and talk shows was associated most strongly with an information-learning motive. Other studies that relate gratifications to choice of content within a medium are Nordlund (1978), Rubin (1981, 1983), and Palmgreen et al. (1981).

A few studies have failed to find evidence of gratification-related audience activity, but these appear to possess serious methodological difficulties. Bantz (1982) reports no differences between uses of television in general and uses of respondents' favorite programs, an inference based on very similar factor solutions for both medium and program uses. Bantz concludes that respondents do not easily make the differentiations that uses and gratification researchers expect of them. Each respondent in this study, however, nominated his or her favorite program type. Since respondents named a variety of program types, the program type factorial solution represents an across-individual composite of different programs. The medium solution also represents a composite of programs in that each individual's gratification ratings of TV are the result of a complex mental aggregation of programs. In each case the factorial solution is probably weighted toward the most popular or most-viewed programs on television. The similar factor solutions are thus not surprising.

In addition, consideration of dimensional similarities is insufficient evidence of lack of differentiation according to use. Consideration must also be given to differences in mean levels of seeking or obtaining for each item or factor. Finally, possible differences in gratification *domains* for different media channels or content types must be considered. For example, the domain of gratification items for political television content (Blumler & McQuail, 1969; McLeod & Becker, 1974), while similar in many ways to the domain for television as a medium, nevertheless differs in its emphasis on vote guidance and other information relevant to political decisions. The Bantz study does not treat mean gratification levels or possible differences in domain.[3]

Lichtenstein and Rosenfeld (1983) concluded that media usage and media fandom are unrelated to individuals' perceptions of gratifications provided by different media. The researchers elicited measures of ten gratifications sought from each of seven mass media as well as "friends." Concordance W analysis showed almost perfect agreement among the ranking of seven groups (including frequent, moderate, and infrequent users of the medium, and high, moderate, and low "fans") of the gratification items for each of the eight channels. However, the data are rankings and once again no comparison is made of item means across groups for each medium, even though the authors indicate that they fully expected such differences. It may well be that high and low fans or users share the *dimensions* by which they perceive gratification-related attributes of different media, while at the same time perceiving different media quite differently *along* these dimensions. Also, different rank orders of gratifications emerged for different media, indicating intermedia differentiation. there thus seems to be insufficient foundation for the authors' conclusion that media usage and fandom are unrelated to perceptions of gratifications.

Finally, in an oft-cited study, Kippax and Murray (1980) measured perceived importance of each of thirty needs and perceived media helpfulness in fulfilling those needs (that is, perceived GO) for six media. Although perceived gratifications obtained were generally positively related to exposure to the six media (except newspapers), individual measures of need importance generally were not. However, from an expectancy-value perspective the latter finding is not surprising. "Perceived helpfulness" is conceptually similar to "belief" (b_i), as discussed in the previous section of this chapter. "Need importance," on the other hand, is related to "evaluation" (e_i) (see

Galloway & Meek, 1981; Blood & Galloway, 1983). An expectancy-value approach would suggest calculating the $b_i e_i$ product for each need, and summing across the thirty needs (or across items for different factors) in an attempt to predict exposure. We might ask why an individual who feels need A is important should make greater use of medium X without considering the following: (1) perceptions of X's helpfulness in fulfilling need A; (2) other needs; and (3) perceptions of X's helpfulness in fulfilling those other needs. It is the composite of these factors that is likely to predict exposure , not the importance of each need considered in isolation. Again, the heuristic value of taking an expectancy-value perspective is underscored. It may be that a reanalysis of Kippax and Murray's rich data would lead to a different set of conclusions.

Activity and Meaning

As noted earlier, information processing, or the assigning of meaning to message elements, is also an important dimension of audience activity. As reported above, Garramone (1983) experimentally investigated the influence of "motivational set" on the processing of a televised political commercial. Subjects in an "issue set" learned more issue information and were more confident of their learning than those in an "image set." Those in the image set paid greater attention to the video portion of the ad, had greater confidence in recall of video information, and were more likely than issue attenders to base personality inferences on information contained in the ad. McLeod and Becker (1981) have presented similar experimental evidence of the influence of motivations on the processing of media material. While the evidence is preliminary, it indicates that audience members do actively process media content, and that this processing is influenced by motivations. Such processing may be the basis of many of the previously discussed connections between media uses and effects reported in survey studies. Many more such experimental studies are needed of the role of motivation in the processing of media messages. Such studies may draw upon a large and fertile literature on information processing spanning the fields of communication and psychology.

Other Empirical Studies

The selection of media sources, and thus audience activity of this type, is constrained by the number of possible choices available to the audience member. Evidence is beginning to emerge that developments in communication technology that provide audience members with a greatly expanded repertoire of choices are also resulting in increased levels of selectivity. Heeter, D'Alessio, Greenberg, and McVoy (1983) examined channel selection data from 172 subscribers to a Florida interactive cable system. The head-end computer scanned channel-changing behavior once a minute continuously for one week. A great deal of channel changing took place, with a mean of 34 changes per household per day. Analysis of minute-by-minute changes showed change peaks on the hour and half hour, but significant levels of channel changing occurred throughout the hour. Although such data cannot relate such changes to audience motives and expectations, they do indicate that cable viewers are highly active in the process of selecting programs. Similar evidence of activity is found in a study of video recorder use by Levy and Fink (1984), who conclude that in using video recorders for time-shifting and library-building purposes, VCR users are actively altering the broadcast schedule. They also observe that "recording and replay can be interpreted as an attempt by VCR users to maintain and perhaps increase those gratifications associated with certain types of television programs" (Levy & Fink, 1984, p. 59).

Finally, Barwise, Ehrenberg, and Goodhardt (1982) studied 18,000 viewing diaries gathered over a three-year period in New York City, Los Angeles, and San Francisco. Contrary to the earlier work of these authors, which has been cited widely as evidence of nonselectivity in the television audience (Goodhardt & Ehrenberg, 1969; Goodhardt, Ehrenberg, & Collins, 1975), this study indicated a marked degree of "program loyalty." While availability acted as a constraint, repeat-viewing levels averaged 50 percent for most program types. About 60 percent of those viewing one episode of a program are viewing TV at the time the next episode is shown. Of these, 90 percent are engaged in repeat viewing. Repeat viewing was much higher than could be accounted for by *channel* loyalty. While still contending that the first stage of the viewing decision—whether to watch—is passive, Barwise et al. (1982, p. 27) conclude that the second-stage decision—what to watch—"does not seem so passive. Viewers do not just pick a program at random."

AN INTEGRATIVE GRATIFICATIONS MODEL

The preceding review has sought to profile and evaluate the theoretical advances made along several fronts in the last decade by uses and gratifications researchers. While these advances have been uneven and often lacking in coordination, we can now perceive the outlines of a rather complex theoretical structure that has begun to emerge. This structure, while far from parsimonious and in need of strengthening and elaboration in many areas, nevertheless represents a significant increase in our understanding of mass media consumption and related processes. If what is now known about such processes could be reduced to a schematic model, such a model might look like that in Figure 1.3. The model, which is by no means completely original (borrowing in particular from Rosengren, 1974; and McLeod & Becker, 1981), seeks to integrate what is known about media consumption on the basis of uses and gratifications research and research in other social science disciplines.

Space does not allow detailed discussion of each set of relationships depicted. One obvious feature of the model, however, is its complex causal structure, even though such models by definition oversimplify reality. Ten years ago Blumler and Katz (1974, p. 16) expressed the hope that uses and gratifications research could "be detached from its former functionalist moorings." It would appear that his has been achieved successfully, although terminological evidence of the functionalist heritage still remains. Although there are many varieties of functionalism, most have in common the attempt to explain a social pattern of behavior (structure) in terms of the effects or consequences (functions) of the pattern or behavior (Cancian, 1968; Stinchcombe, 1968). It should be clear from an examination of the model that this is no longer the form of uses and gratifications explanations. The integrative model presented here, while taking into account the feedback from gratifications obtained to those sought, also considers (among other things) the social and psychological origins of needs, values, and beliefs, which give rise to motives for behavior, which may be guided by beliefs, values, and social circumstances into seeking various gratifications through media consumption and other nonmedia behaviors.

Mirroring the complex nature of the phenomena under study, the model is both multivariate and nonrecursive. In such a multivariate structure no single element can assume a central explanatory role. Certainly the emphasis is not on gratifications obtained, as it must be in a traditional functional explanation (Cancian, 1968), nor is undue prominence given to needs. If any concept in the theoretical structure can be said to be central it is the gratifications sought from media experience, thus underscoring the motivational nature of uses and gratifications theory. Yet the model makes clear that gratifications sought cannot be viewed in isolation, connected as they are in both antecedent and consequent fashion to a host of media, perceptual, social, and psychological variables.

Given the theoretical structure that has evolved, charges by critics a decade or more ago that uses and gratifications research could only support the status quo now seem curiously outmoded. Carey and Kreiling (1974) and Elliot (1974) argue that (1) the uses and gratifications approach was based on functionalism; (2) functional theories deal with static, equilibrating systems and cannot accommodate change; and (3) policymakers could therefore argue that current media structures were "functional" for audience members and no change in these structures was required. Whatever

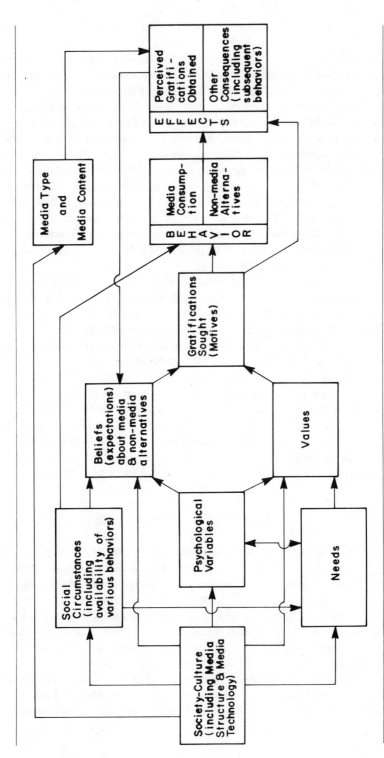

Figure 1.3. Integrative gratifications model of mass media consumption.

the merits of these various contentions, and strong arguments have been advanced against each (see Blumler, 1979; Mendelsohn, 1974; Pryluck, 1975; Rosengren, 1974), this chapter has shown that current uses and gratifications theory is not in the functional tradition unless one is willing to accept a radically altered definition of the term. An examination of the integrative model reveals several potential sources of change in both audience consumption behavior and media structure and content. Of particular relevance is that perceived discrepancies between gratifications sought and obtained, which are frequently observed empirically, may motivate changes in media consumption behaviors to reduce these discrepancies. Such changes in turn will stimulate changes in media structure and content in responsive media systems. Recent empirical evidence does not support the critics' unrealistic assumption of nearly perfect provision by the media of the gratifications that audience members are seeking.

Change may also result from variations in the social and cultural milieu in which media use is embedded. Political and economic trends and upheavals bring with them substantial and sometimes radical alterations in needs, values, beliefs, social circumstances, and the structure and content of the mass media. The rapid evolution of media technology also forces individuals in modern society to confront a constantly varying and expanding array of choices. We would thus expect changes in both media consumption behaviors and media structures to be the norm rather than the exception. Maintenance of the status quo would be indicated only under circumstances in which gratifications obtained match those sought in a steady, unchanging environment, in the absence of reasonable alternatives with unresponsive media systems. Such steady-state conditions, like the "perfect vacuum" of physicists, are approachable only in the laboratory and in the minds of some critics.

CHALLENGES FOR THE FUTURE

From an integrative theoretical perspective, the efforts of uses and gratifications researchers to come to grips with media consumption processes have not been in vain. Yet this progress should not breed complacency in the face of the many serious challenges that remain and that are certain to develop. The integrative gratifications model has heuristic value in identifying these challenges. It is obvious from such an examination that our knowledge of different conceptual areas is very uneven. Although additional research is needed in all of these areas, some have received substantial empirical attention while others have been largely neglected. The broad conceptual block labeled "psychological variables" is included largely on the basis of reputation and McGuire's (1974) persuasive discussion of its relevance. Much research is obviously needed here. Also, while recent research on the social origins of gratifications has done much to negate the charge that gratifications research ignores social context, we are only beginning to understand the ways in which social-structural variables influence the matrix of values, needs, beliefs, and social circumstances that molds media behavior.

The recent trend toward more theoretically oriented studies must also be continued. An emphasis on variance explanation and post hoc theorizing still characterizes too many uses and gratifications investigations. General "expectations" must be replaced by directional hypotheses, and hypotheses must be grounded in well-articulated theoretical rationales. This is not to say that all investigations should follow the hypothetico-deductive model. There is always a need, especially in new substantive areas, for exploratory studies of a descriptive nature. Careful conceptualization within the framework of ethnomethodological studies of media use can also contribute much to theoretical advancement. But whatever the approach, researchers should consider carefully the theoretical relevance and implications of their findings, if the ultimate goal is a deeper understanding of processes of media consumption.

New Communication Technologies

A major challenge that confronts uses and gratifications researchers is the adaptation and molding of the current conceptual framework to deal with new communication technologies. Very little uses and gratifications research has addressed this issue, and yet it is a crucial one if we are to gain a better insight into the uses people have for cable television, teleconferencing, videocassettes, videotext, and other new communication systems. In addressing such issues, researchers should not be wedded to gratification typologies that the very changes under study may have rendered incomplete, if not obsolete. In a study of the gratifications associated with cable television, the two gratifications mentioned most frequently by respondents in focus group interviews were the *variety* provided by the greatly increased number of program choices and the increased *control over viewing* resulting from the highly flexible scheduling of movies, news, weather, sports, and other content on a 24-hour basis (Shaver, 1983). Such gratifications had not been identified in previous studies of television. Roe (1981), however, in a historical study of mass media development concluded that increased choice of content and control over the media consumption decision are major factors in the adoption of any new communication medium. Their emergence as important cable gratifications is not surprising, therefore. The Shaver study illustrates the potential of uses and gratifications research to help in understanding the uses of new communication technologies, while issuing a caution to researchers to be sensitive to new or unforeseen gratifications tied to specific features of the new medium.

Belief Acquisition and Change

An expectancy-value approach emphasizes the importance of understanding processes of belief acquisition and change regarding the mass media. This suggests the need for longitudinal studies of such processes, particularly for media objects such as new television series, magazines, or major technological innovations such as cable television. These studies could also explore life-cycle and age-related developmental changes in media use as a function of changes in the belief system. In both settings longitudinal studies could shed light on the ways in which direct media exposure, inferential processes, and exposure to media and interpersonal sources of information interact to form those beliefs that are the cognitive basis of media consumption. At the same time, the acquisition and change of beliefs could be linked to gratifications sought, media consumption, perceptions of gratifications obtained, and media effects. There is also the opportunity here to forge stronger ties with the belief and value systems characterizing particular societies and cultures.

A Multivariate Comparative Model

The integrative gratifications model presented in Figure 1.3 is based on the collective findings of a large number of uses and gratifications studies and research in related fields. While such first-generation multivariate procedures as factor analysis, multidimensional scaling, multiple regression, and canonical correlation have been employed, the great majority of investigations have been concerned with only limited portions of the integrative model. In many cases only isolated, bivariate relationships are explored, albeit often with statistical controls. Such studies, of course, have the potential to provide an intensive view of the limited topic under investigation, but they do not provide a test of the multiple elements of the model as an integrated theoretical system. The process may be likened to examining an elephant through a magnifying glass. One may learn much about various parts of the anatomy, but it may be difficult to discern the nature of the beast.

What is needed in addition are studies that test large multivariate models incorporating indicators of many of the variable groupings in the integrative model, and that specify the complex relationships among these variables in a priori fashion. Only in this way may a true test of integrative models be accomplished. As Rosengren (1983) has discussed in some detail, recent developments in second-generation multivariate procedures such as linear structural equation modeling now make this possible in uses and gratifications research. Procedures such as LISREL (linear structural relations) and PLS (partial least squares) have the capacity to handle large numbers of manifest and latent variables simultaneously, with either cross-sectional or panel data, and to carry out formal tests of alternative models. LISREL, with its measurement model feature, also has the potential to improve the measurement of gratifications and related variables (for illustrations of LISREL in uses and gratifications studies, see Hedinsson, 1981; Johnsson-Smaragdi, 1983; Roe, 1983b; Rosengren, 1983; Rosengren et al., 1983).

Such techniques may also aid in the development of a comparative model of gratifications, media consumption, and media effects. The selection of a particular medium or interpersonal source does not occur in isolation, but involves a complex cognitive and affective comparison of the available alternatives. While a number of studies reviewed in this chapter have compared gratifications across different channels, none has attempted in a formal multivariate model to relate relative assessments of different media objects to media consumption, its origins, and its effects. Such a model introduces formidable measurement and analytical difficulties, which structural linear equation techniques can help overcome. While the development of such a model may be some years away, it has the potential to provide a deeper understanding of the forces governing media behavior.

NOTES

1. Lundberg and Hultén (1968) provide an early example of a conceptualization similar to expectancy-value theory. Respondents rated the perceived importance to them of certain goals, and the perceived instrumentality of the media in helping them to achieve these goals. A multiplicative index of the two measures successfully predicted reported media use.

2. It is possible that Becker's finding is an artifact of response set sometimes observed in attitude measurement, in which negatively worded and positively worded items appear on separate factors.

3. In addition, of the 37 "use" items employed by Bantz (1982), approximately half appear to tap gratifications sought and the remainder measure gratifications obtained, yet they are factor analyzed together. Since other studies have found different dimensional solutions for GS and GO (McLeod et al., 1982; Palmgreen et al., 1980), the appropriateness of this procedure is questionable.

REFERENCES

Atkin, C. K., Bowen, L., Nayman, O. B., & Sheinkopf, K. G. (1973). Quality versus quantity in televised political ads. *Public Opinion Quarterly, 37,* 209-224.

Atkin, C. K., & Heald, G. (1976). Effects of political advertising. *Public Opinion Quarterly, 40,* 216-228.

Atkinson, J. W. (1957). Motivational determinants of risk-taking behavior. *Psychological Review, 64,* 359-372.

Ball-Rokeach, S. J., & DeFleur, M. L. (1976). A dependency model of mass media effects. *Communication Research, 3,* 3-21.

Bantz, C. R. (1982). Exploring uses and gratifications: A comparison of reported uses of television and reported uses of favorite program type. *Communication Research, 9,* 352-379.

Barwise, T. P., Ehrenberg, A. S. C., & Goodhardt, G. J. (1982). Glued to the box? Patterns of TV repeat-viewing. *Journal of Communication, 32*(4), 22-29.

Becker, L. B. (1976). Two tests of media gratifications: Watergate and the 1974 election. *Journalism Quarterly, 53,* 28-33.

Becker, L. B. (1979). Measurement of gratifications. *Communication Research, 6,* 54-73.

Becker, L. B., & Fruit, J. W. (1982). *Understanding media selection from a uses and motives perspective.* Paper presented at the meeting of the International Communication Association, Boston.

Blood, R. W., & Galloway, J. J. (1983). *Expectancy-value measures of audience uses and gratifications for media content.* Paper presented at the meeting of the International Communication Association, Dallas.

Blumler, J. G. (1979). The role of theory in uses and gratifications studies. *Communication Research, 6,* 9-36.

Blumler, J. G., & Katz, E. (1974). Foreword. In J. G. Blumler & E. Katz (Eds.), *The uses of mass communications: Current perspectives on gratifications research.* Beverly Hills, CA: Sage.

Blumler, J. G., & McQuail, D. (1969). *Television in politics.* Chicago: University of Chicago Press.

Bogart, L. (1965). The mass media and the blue-collar worker. In A. Bennett & W. Gomberg (Eds.)., *The blue-collar world.* Englewood Cliffs, NJ: Prentice-Hall.

Brown, J. R., Cramond, J. K., & Wilde, R. J. (1974). Displacement effects of television and the child's functional orientation to media. In. J. G. Blumler & E. Katz (Eds.), *The uses of mass communications: Current perspectives on gratifications research.* Beverly Hills, CA: Sage.

Cancian, F. M. (1968). Varieties of functional analysis. In D. L. Silla (Ed.), *International encyclopedia of the social sciences.* New York: Macmillan.

Carey, J. W., & Kreiling, A. L. (1974). Popular culture and uses and gratifications: Notes toward an accommodation. In J. G. Blumler & E. Katz (Eds.), *The uses of mass communications: Current perspectives on gratifications research.* Beverly Hills, CA: Sage.

Davis, D. K., & Woodall, W. G. (1982). *Uses of television news: Gratification or edification.* Paper presented at the meeting of the International Communication Association, Boston.

de Bock, H. (1980). Gratification during a newspaper strike and a TV blackout. *Journalism Quarterly, 57,* 61-66, 78.

Elliot, P. (1974). Uses and gratifications research: A critique and a sociological alternative. In J. G. Blumler & E. Katz (Eds.), *The uses of mass communications: Current perspectives on gratifications research.* Beverly Hills, CA: Sage.

Fishbein, M. (1963). An investigation of the relationships between beliefs about an object and the attitude toward that object. *Human Relations, 16,* 233-240.

Fishbein, M., & Ajzen, I. (1975). *Belief, attitude, intention, and behavior.* Reading, MA: Addison-Wesley.

Galloway, J. J., & Meek, F. L. (1981). Audience uses and gratifications: An expectancy model. *Communication Research, 8,* 435-450.

Garramone, G. M. (1983). Issue versus image orientation and effects of political advertising. *Communication Research, 10,* 59-76.

Goodhardt, G. J., & Ehrenberg, A. S. C. (1969). Duplication of television viewing between and within channels. *Journal of Marketing Research, 6,* 169-178.

Goodhardt, G. J., Ehrenberg, A. S. C., & Collins, M. A. (1975). *The television audience: Patterns of viewing.* Lexington, MA: D. C. Heath.

Greenberg, B. S. (1974). Gratifications of television viewing and their correlates for British children. In J. G. Blumler & E. Katz (Eds.), *The uses of mass communications: Current perspectives on gratifications research.* Beverly Hills, CA: Sage.

Hedinsson, E. (1981). *TV, family and society: The social origins and effects of adolescents' TV use.* Stockholm: Almqvist & Wiksell International.

Heeter, C., D'Alessio, D., Greenberg, B. S., & McVoy, D. S. (1983). *Cableviewing.* Paper presented at the meeting of the International Communication Association, Dallas.

Hur, K. K., & Robinson, J. P. (1981). A uses and gratifications analysis of viewing of "Roots" in Britain.*Journalism Quarterly, 58,* 582-588.

Johnsson-Smaragdi, U. (1983). *TV use and social interaction in adolescence.* Stockholm: Almqvist & Wiksell International.

Johnstone, J. W. C. (1974). Social integration and mass media use among adolescents: A case study. In J. G. Blumler & E. Katz (Eds.) *The uses of mass communications: Current perspectives on gratifications research.* Beverly Hills, CA: Sage.

Katz, E., Blumler, J. G., & Gurevitch, M. (1973) *Utilization of mass communication by the individual.* Paper presented at the Conference on Directions in Mass Communication Research, Arden House, New York.

Katz, E., Blumler, J. G., & Gurevitch, M. (1974). Utilization of mass communication by the individual. In J. G. Blumler & E. Katz (Eds.), *The uses of mass communications: Current perspectives on gratifications research.* Beverly Hills, CA: Sage.

Katz, E., Gurevitch, M., & Haas, H. (1973). On the use of the mass media for important things. *American Sociological Review, 38,* 164-181.

Kelley, H. H. (1973). The processes of causal attribution. *American Psychologist, 28,* 107-128.

Kippax, S., & Murray, J. P. (1980). Using the mass media: Need gratification and perceived utility. *Communication Research, 7,* 335-360.

Kline, F. G., Miller, P. V., & Morrison, A. J. (1974). Adolescents and family planning information: An exploration of audience needs and media effects. In J. G. Blumler & E. Katz (Eds.), *The uses of mass communications: Current perspectives on gratifications research.* Beverly Hills, CA: Sage.

Levy, M. R. (1977). *The uses and gratifications of television news.* Unpublished doctoral dissertation, Columbia University.

Levy, M. R. (1978). The audience experience with television news. *Journalism Monographs, 55.*

Levy, M. R. (1983). Conceptualizing and measuring aspects of audience "activity." *Jouranlism Quarterly, 60,* 109-114.

Levy, M. R., & Fink, E. L. (1984). Home video recorders and the transcience of television broadcasts. *Journal of Communication, 34*(2), 56-71.

Levy, M. R., & Windahl, S. (1984). Audience activity and gratifications: A conceptual clarification and exploration. *Communication Research, 11,* 51-78.

Lichtenstein, A. L., & Rosenfeld, L. B. (1983). Uses and misuses of gratifications research: An explication of media functions. *Communication Research, 10,* 97-109.

Lippman, W. (1922). *Public opinion.* New York: Macmillan.

Lometti, G. E., Reeves, B., & Bybee, C. R. (1977). Investigating the assumptions of uses and gratifications research. *Communication Research, 4,* 321-338.

Lull, J. (1980). Family communication patterns and the social uses of television. *Communication Research, 7,* 319-334.

Lundberg, D., & Hultén, O. (1968). *Individen och massmedia.* Stockholm: Norstedt.

McGuire, W. J. (1974). Psychological motives and communication gratification. In J. G. Blumler & E. Katz (Eds.), *The uses of mass communications: Current perspectives on gratifications research.* Beverly Hills, CA: Sage.

McLeod, J. M., & Becker, L. B. (1974). Testing the validity of gratification measures through political effects analysis. In J. G. Blumler & E. Katz (Eds.), *The uses of mass communications: Current perspectives on gratifications research.* Beverly Hills, CA: Sage.

McLeod, J. M., & Becker, L. B. (1981). The uses and gratifications approach. In D. D. Nimmo & K. R. Sanders (Eds.), *Handbook of political communication.* Beverly Hills, CA: Sage.

McLeod, J. M., Becker, L. B., & Byrnes, J. E. (1974). Another look at the agenda-setting function of the press. *Communication Research, 1,* 131-166.

McLeod, J. M., Brown, J.D., Becker, L. B., & Ziemke, D. A. (1977). Decline and fall at the White House: A longitudinal analysis of communication effects. *Communication Research, 4,* 3-22.

McLeod, J. M., Bybee, C. R., & Durall, J. A. (1982). Evaluating media performance by gratifications sought and received. *Journalism Quarterly, 59,* 3-12.

McLeod, J. M., Durall, J. A., Ziemke, D. A., & Bybee, C. R. (1979). Expanding the context of debate effects. In S. Kraus (Ed.), *The great debates 1976: Ford vs. Carter.* Bloomington: Indiana University Press.

McLeod, J. M., Luetscher, W. D., & McDonald, D. G. (1980). *Beyond mere exposure: Media orientations and their impact on political processes.* Paper presented at the meeting of the Association for Education in Journalism, Boston.

McQuail, D. (1979). The uses and gratifications approach: Past, troubles and future. *Massacommunicatie, 2,* 73-89.

Mendelsohn, H. (1974). Some policy implications of the uses and gratifications paradigm. In J. G. Blumler & E. Katz (Eds.), *The uses of mass communications: Current perspectives on gratifications research.* Beverly Hills, CA: Sage.

Mendelsohn, H., & O'Keefe, G. J. (1976). *The people choose a president.* New York: Praeger.

Nordenstreng, K. (1970). Comments on "gratifications research" in broadcasting. *Public Opinion Quarterly, 34,* 130-132.

Nordlund, J. E. (1978). Media interaction. *Communication Research, 5,* 150-175.

Palmgreen, P., & Rayburn, J. D. (1979). Uses and gratifications and exposure to public television: A discrepancy approach. *Communication Research, 6,* 155-180.

Palmgreen, P., & Rayburn, J. D. (1982). Gratifications sought and media exposure: An expectancy value model. *Communication Research, 9,* 561-580.

Palmgreen, P., Wenner, L. A., & Rayburn, J. D. (1980). Relations between gratifications sought and obtained: A study of television news. *Communication Research, 7,* 161-192.

Palmgreen, P., Wenner, L. A., & Rayburn, J. D. (1981). Gratification discrepancies and news program choice. *Communication Research, 8,* 451-478.

Peled. T., & Katz, E. (1974. Media functions in wartime: The Israel homefront in October 1973. In J. G. Blumler & E. Katz (Eds.), *The uses of mass communications: Current perspectives on gratifications research.* Beverly Hills, CA: Sage.

Pryluck, D. (1975). Functions of functional analysis: Comments on Anderson-Meyer. *Journal of Broadcasting, 19,* 413-420.

Rayburn, J. D., & Palmgreen, P. (1984). Merging uses and gratifications and expectancy-value theory. *Communication Research, 11*(4).

Rayburn, J. D., Palmgreen, P., & Acker, T. (1984). Media gratifications and choosing a morning news program. *Journalism Quarterly, 61,* 149-156.

Roe, K. (1981). *Video and youth: New patterns of media use* (Media Panel Report 18). Lund, Sweden: Växjö University College and Lund University.

Roe, K. (1983a). *The influence of video technology in adolescence* (Media Panel Report 27). Lund, Sweden: Växjö University College and Lund University.

Roe, K. (1983b). *Mass media and adolescent schooling: Conflict or co-existence?* Stockholm: Almqvist & Wiksell International.

Rosengren, K. E. (1974). Uses and gratifications: A paradigm outlined. In J. G. Blumler & E. Katz (Eds.), *The uses of mass communications: Current perspectives on gratifications research.* Beverly Hills, CA: Sage.

Rosengren, K. E. (1983). Communication research: One paradigm, or four? In E. M. Rogers & F. Balle (Eds.), *Mass communication research in the United States and Western Europe.* Norwood, NJ: Ablex.

Rosengren, K. E., Roe, K., & Sonesson, I. (1983). *Finality and causality in adolescents' mass media use* (Media Panel Report 24). Lund, Sweden: Växjö University College and Lund University.

Rosengren, K. E., & Windahl, S. (1972). Mass media consumption as a functional alternative. In D. McQuail (Ed.), *Sociology of mass communications.* Harmondsworth: Penguin.

Rosengren, K. E., & Windahl, S. (1977). Mass media use: Causes and effects. *Communications: International Journal of Communication Research, 3,* 336-351.

Rotter, J. B. (1954). *Social learning and clinical psychology.* Englewood Cliffs, NJ: Prentice-Hall.

Rubin, A. M. (1979). Television use by children and adolescents. *Human Communication Research, 5,* 109-120.

Rubin, A. M. (1981). An examination of television viewing motivations. *Communication Research, 8*, 141-165.

Rubin, A. M. (1983). Television uses and gratifications: The interaction of viewing patterns and motivations. *Journal of Broadcasting, 27*, 37-51.

Rubin, A. M., & Rubin, R. B. (1981). Age context, and TV use. *Journal of Broadcasting, 25*, 1-15.

Rubin, A. M., & Rubin, R. B. (1982). Older persons' TV viewing patterns and motivations. *Communication Research, 9*, 287-313.

Rubin, A. M., & Windahl, S. (1982). *Mass media uses and dependency: A social systems approach to uses and gratifications.* Paper presented at the meeting of the International Communication Association, Boston.

Shaver, J. L. (1983). *The uses of cable television.* Unpublished master's thesis, University of Kentucky.

Stinchcombe, A. L. (1968). *Constructing social theories.* New York: Harcourt Brace Jovanovich.

Swanson, D. L. (1977). The uses and misuses of uses and gratifications. *Human Communication Research, 3*, 214-221.

Swanson, D. L. (1979) Political communication research and the uses and gratifications model: A critique. *Communication Research, 6*, 37-53.

Tolman, E. C. (1932). *Purposive behavior in animals and men.* New York: Appleton-Century-Crofts.

Van Leuven, J. (1981). Expectancy theory in media and message selection. *Communication Research, 8*, 425-434.

Vroom, V. H. (1964). *Work and motivation.* New York: John Wiley.

Weaver, D. H.(1980). Audience need for orientation and media effects. *Communication Research, 7*, 361-376.

Wenner, L. A. (1982). Gratifications sought and obtained in program dependency: A study of network evening news programs and "60 Minutes." *Communication Research, 9*, 539-560.

Wenner, L. A. (1983). *Gratifications sought and obtained: Model specification and theoretical development.* Paper presented at the meeting of the International Communication Association, Dallas.

Wiggins, J. S. (1973). *Personality and prediction: Principles of personality assessment.* Reading, MA: Addison-Wesley.

Windahl, S. (1981). Uses and gratifications at the crossroads. In G. C. Wilhoit & H. de Bock (Eds.), *Mass Communication Review Yearbook.* Beverly Hills, CA: Sage.

Windahl, S., Hedinsson, E., Höjerback, I., & Nord, E. (1983). *Perceived deprivation and alternate activities during a television strike.* Paper presented at the meeting of the International Communication Association, Dallas.

2 ● Communicative Competence: An Interactive Approach

MARY E. DIEZ

Alverno College

WHILE "communicative competence" is discussed in a variety of settings, from scholarly conferences to legislative assemblies, the term's widespread use is not indicative of a single meaning, much less a clear one. It has been used to denote a list of observable (and often discrete) skills, to identify abstract knowledge, to stand for global developmental abilities displayed in performance, and to label evaluations of effective interaction. In different disciplines, study of communicative competence has focused to varying degrees on referential, social, and directive functions of communication. In this chapter I will review the three major traditions using the term "communicative competence" (or slight variations on it; i.e., communication skill, oral communication skill, etc.) and argue that a theory of communicative competence needs to integrate aspects of all three if is it to probe effectively the development of human communication.

THE SOCIOLINGUISTIC TRADITION

This set of disciplines using the term communicative competence really represents a multiple tradition involving structural linguistics, sociolinguistics, anthropology, and education. Chomsky's (1965) original use of communicative "competence" was to distinguish *knowledge* of language structure—which he argued was acquired innately—from its *use,* or "performance." The goal of structural linguistic study according to Chomsky was to identify the knowledge of an ideal speaker-listener, elimi-

Correspondence and requests for reprints: Mary E. Diez, Department of Communication, Alverno College, 3401 S. 39th St., Milwaukee, WI 53215.

nating the factors of person and situation that necessarily affect a real speaker-listener's actual performance.

Having ruled out the effects of situation, context, and person, structural linguistics could focus on language in the abstract, seeking a *"purely structural characterization of linguistic knowledge in terms of abstract rules . . . not seen as the direct cause of the subject's performance"* (Ammon, 1981, p. 16). By the late 1960s, however, clear dissatisfaction had developed with what such a limited view of language could contribute. Especially critical was the realization that such a conception of competence could not account for a child's ability to acquire knowledge of sentences not only as grammatical but also as appropriate in particular contexts (Hymes, 1971, 1972).

The break was made most clearly by Hymes (1972, p. 278), recognized as the originator of the view of communicative competence still prevalent in this tradition today:

> We break irrevocably with the model that restricts the design of language to one face toward referential meaning, one toward sound, and that defines the organization of language as solely consisting of rules for linking the two. . . . A model of language must define it with a face toward communicative conduct and human life.

To stimulate development of that model, Hymes (1971, 1972) defined communicative competence as the native speaker's ability, within his or her speech community, to interpret and produce language appropriate to situations.

The focus of concern thus moved from syntax to pragmatics—that is, from concern with abstract structure to examination of the links between speakers and language and its situated use. Moreover, a second refocusing involved a questioning of Chomsky's conceptualization of language development as innate. In the development of this tradition, Vygotsky's (1962) argument that linguistic control and the organization of a child's behavior are at first external was coupled with the phenomenological argument that intersubjectivity (the functional sensitivity to social interaction) develops through interaction with the speech community. Thus studies began to focus more directly on the social and socially developed aspects of communication.

The tradition developed after Hymes's (1971, 1972) redefinition of competence has produced a rich collection of theoretical and empirical work. The organization of a brief review of some of this work below illustrates four essential characteristics that seem to inform the studies in this tradition—namely, that communicative competence is situational, interactional, functional, and developmental. The review will be followed by comments on the methods and conclusions of this tradition and some implications of this research.

Situational

Approaches to communicative competence in the sociolinguistic tradition have tended to view language use as situated (see, for example, Brown & Fraser, 1979; Erickson & Shultz, 1981; Ervin-Tripp, 1968, 1980; Goffman, 1974; Graham, Argyle, Clarke, & Maxwell, 1981; Gregory & Carroll, 1978; Hall & Cole, 1978; Halliday, 1979; Kreckel, 1981; Scherer & Giles, 1979). The elements and their relationships integrated into the notion of "situation" include setting, type of interaction, and the relationships between participants regarding role and status. Perhaps the most important, however, is the so-called built-in sense of goal or purpose typified in situation (Brown & Fraser, 1979; Gregory & Carroll, 1978; Hall & Cole, 1978). The philosophical assumption about a speaker's understanding of "situation" is a phenomenological one: that these elements are somehow learned and become known as part of the stock of common knowledge created in an ongoing way by society—specifically the speech community.

Examples of this research show how the focus on situation has served to clarify the tradition's understanding of communicative competence. Erickson (1981) reports part of a year-long study of kindergarteners and first graders, specifically examining the functions of timing in the social organization of classroom interaction. His study illustrates what Whitehurst and Sonnenschein (1981) call the difference between "knowing how" and "knowing when." Part of the school child's situationally specific communicative competence shown in Erickson's study is the ability to distinguish which communicative acts are appropriate to which segments of the school day (e.g., that one may talk to the teacher freely about any topic during play time but not interrupt her with off-topic comments or questions in a reading lesson).

Hall and Cole (1978) examined the variability of speech of adults and preschool children in two settings, the classroom and a local supermarket. While they expected to find differences in kinds of talk in the two settings, they found contrasts in only one of their two studies. In the other, speech during the supermarket trip was more like speech in the two classrooms than like the other supermarket trip. Their analysis sheds light on how part of communicative competence is the interactants' ability to structure the situation according to its purpose, regardless of the physical setting. While the physical settings of supermarket and classroom were different, the perceived task or purpose (supermarket trip as school field trip) led to the participants' structuring of their discourse as "classroom talk."

School research has naturally received much attention in this tradition, since it is a pervasive setting and one available to researchers (see, for example, Cook-Gumperz, 1977; Gumperz & Herasimchuk, 1981; Shuy & Griffin, 1981; Wilkinson, Clevenger, & Dallaghan, 1981). However, some studies have attempted to explore school and home environments to contrast children's behavior and probe situational differences (Philips, 1972). Other studies have examined bilingual and multilingual societies (for example, see Blom & Gumperz, 1972; Scotton, 1972; Scotton & Ury, 1977).

Interactional

Viewing communicative competence as interactional focuses on speakers' ability to create interaction as an ongoing negotiation of participant identity and task definition (Scotton, in press). Studies in this tradition have tried to uncover evidence of role adaptation (how speakers signal changes in role) and of communication monitoring (whether and how speakers are aware of changes in interaction and/or the effects of their own and others' linguistic choices). In fact, Goffman (1967) asserts that "situations begin when mutual monitoring occurs and lapse when the next to the last person has left."

Much of the work exploring *directives* (a type of speech act calling on another to do something) illustrates the belief that communicative competence is interactional (see Ervin-Tripp, 1976, 1977; Mitchell-Kernan & Kernan, 1977; Olson & Hildyard, 1981). Ervin-Tripp's thesis is that the choice of forms of utterances—specifically directives—is clearly related to the social identity that speakers intend to invoke or simply to recognize as operating in the situation. Her finding in the research on adult use of directives was that "there were relatively consistent differences in the type of directive uses, as a function of the social features of the speech situation" (1977, p. 166). Thus directives provide information (to participants as well as to outside observers) about how to interpret the speaker's view of the ongoing situation, and they also allow participants to evaluate each other's intent. Directives also carry some weight or power to influence the other's action; the idea of *illocutionary force* proposed in Searle's (1969) theory of speech acts is a conceptualization of the interactional power of linguistic choices, clearly dependent upon situationally defined factors.

Recent research with children (Ervin-Tripp, 1977; Mitchell-Kernan & Kernan, 1977) indicates that while there are limits to a child's repertoire, early use of directives and responses to them follow the general adult pattern. The shared knowledge about how to encode situational differences appears to function as interactional communicative competence early, as indicated by Corsaro's (1979) examination of how children gain access to play groups, Edelsky's (1977) account of how sex roles are encoded in speech, and Camaioni's (1979) comparison of child-adult and child-child interactional differences.

Functional

Researchers in this tradition have focused on communicative competence as functional, investigating the ongoing management of interaction and the force of different linguistic options, based on situational and interactional constraints. For example, within mainstream American culture, children learn the organizational functions of turn-taking (Ervin-Tripp, 1979), as well as the politeness routines required by society (Gleason & Weintraub, 1976; Greif & Gleason, 1980). Dore's (1977) study of responses to questions indicates how various forms are "heard" differently, depending on context, showing the functional impact of learning a society's language conventions—another part of shared knowledge. More specifically, Brenneis and Lein (1977) describe children's patterns of settling disputes, a macrofunctional use of language.

Note that in this tradition, function is not seen as able to be examined outside of situational and interactional considerations. Situation or context is ultimately the heart of the study of communicative competence following Hymes; situation consistently directs the understanding of function as well as the design of its study.

Developmental

Throughout these brief reviews of research in the sociolinguistic tradition, it is clear that much of the focus has been on children's acquisition of communicative competence. Some research has involved comparisons to show that children have some aspects basic to adult communicative competence, even at an early age (see Ervin-Tripp, 1977; Gleason & Weintraub, 1976; Greif & Gleason, 1980; Newcombe & Zaslow, 1981). Other research has shown that the communicative competence of young children is different from that of adults—for example, that their patterns for joining groups are adapted to their specific, situated experience (Corsaro, 1970). Finally, there is evidence for continual adaptation to situation; children will adjust their style of language for younger children (Gleason & Weintraub, 1978), for strangers, for grandparents, and so on.

Methods

In the sociolinguistic tradition researchers have examined natural speech, in context, with participants engaged in realistic tasks, in settings where roles and relationships are able to be validated with the participants. Many studies are in-depth examinations of, for example, one or two classrooms over a year-long period, but more and more multiple observation studies have been conducted, probably due to the maturing of this tradition, that is now ready to build on its initial work. In general, studies in this tradition could be described as qualitative or subjective, in that researchers attempt to find out what is happening in natural settings rather than to manipulate independent variables in controlled settings.

Conclusions and Implications

The sociolinguistic tradition has found many ways in which even infants are communicatively competent. Perhaps the methodological bias of looking at what is happening in natural interaction has allowed these researchers to see how even children negotiate their situations to produce and interpret communication appropriate for their age, role, needs, and so on (see especially Cook-Gumperz, 1977; Corsaro, 1979; Ervin-Tripp, 1977; Gleason & Weintraub, 1976).

While some studies have examined children's progress toward attaining an adult repertoire, definitions of communicative competence within this tradition have not been restricted to so-called adult skill and thus have not sparked research designs that test how far children have come toward that standard. Fairly consistently, communicative competence has been conceptualized as an ongoing skill by which persons respond to new demands and incorporate new capabilities (e.g., increased cognitive ability and growing vocabulary).

Two implications for this tradition, then, given the current state of its research art, might be these:

(1) Researchers need to examine further what constitutes the ongoing skill of communicative competence, including situational, interactional, functional, and developmental aspects, in order to draw together a more formulated theory. Qualitative researchers are noted (whether it is truly the case or not) for being willing to probe a corpus of data ad infinitum. As Erickson (1977) has recently suggested, it is time to begin the process of generalization about the findings of the studies in this tradition.

(2) Researchers need to extend their study of communicative competence as developmental to adult competence. The philosophical position that interaction is created in an ongoing manner suggests that communicative competence is constantly open to development—in fact, that it probably *requires* the kind of monitoring that contributes to ongoing learning. Making the processes of monitoring and development explicit would aid in the development of both our understanding of communicative competence and of solutions to problems of adult incompetence needed for therapeutic work.

These implications will be probed further after a consideration of the contributions of the two other traditions and their approaches to the construct of communicative competence.

THE REFERENTIAL COMMUNICATION TRADITION

While the shift from syntax to pragmatics was being made in sociolinguistics, a syntactic and semantic focus on language development had captured the attention of cognitive and educational psychologists and psycholinguists. Interested in language as a carrier of thought and the use of language to communicate ideas so that others might understand them, this tradition focused its study on *referential communication*. Following Piaget (1955), their initial interest was in "seeking to explain levels of performance in terms of underlying cognitive abilities" (Dickson, 1981).

Where sociolinguists were discovering that even infants are communicatively competent in adapting their responses to situational, interactional, and functional factors, referential tradition researchers were concluding that even school-age children were quite incompetent (Dickson, 1981). This apparent contradiction is explained partly by the definition of communicative competence assumed in referential studies and partly by methodological factors.

The conceptualization of communicative competence in the referential tradition moved from an early focus on a single underlying factor—role-taking ability—to a more recent conceptualization of it as consisting of a number of components or subskills (Whitehurst & Sonnenschein, 1981). These skills are generally seen to include role taking as part of a *listener component,* as well as to have a *comparison component,* an *evaluation component,* and "outside" skill factors. Still another conceptualization focuses study in relation to the development of propositional meaning, using the framework of cognitive certainty. Each will be explored briefly, followed by comments on methods, conclusions, and implications.

The Listener Component

The extent to which a speaker takes the characteristics of the listener into account in conversational interaction was first studied within this tradition as "role taking." It was based on the Piagetian notion that a child moves from egocentric ways of organizing thought and speech to the adult, sociocentric standard. While enthusiasm for this framework has waned with the failure of experiments to confirm Piaget's notion (Dickson, 1981; Shantz, 1981; Whitehurst & Sonnenschein, 1981), much of the research in this tradition focused on children's failure to communicate effectively and attributed it to their inability to take the role of listener (Asher & Wigfield, 1981). Criticisms from within the tradition point to the problems of testing role taking and communicating separately within experiments (Asher & Wigfield, 1981) and of not being able to determine if a speaker assumes or infers similarity of the listener—which is crucial to knowing if role taking has occurred (Shantz, 1981).

Flavell (1974) renewed interest in the component of role taking or listener awareness, however, by suggesting subcomponents of this skill: existence—the child's awareness that others have their own perspectives;

need—the child's awareness that examining the other's perspective may affect communication decisions; inference—the child's development of the skill of making accurate assessment of the other's perspective; and application—the child's development of skill in using those inferences to make communication decisions. As will be seen, Flavell's expansion overlaps with the other major components identified in this tradition.

The Comparison Component

Some researchers in this tradition have argued that this skill is logically primary to any of the others—namely, the speaker's ability to analyze "a set of stimuli to determine which attributes of a referent distinguish it from non-referents" (Whitehurst & Sonnenschein, 1981) makes either role taking or evaluation possible. Many of the studies that find improvement in children's referential skills after training have used comparison exercises to build the children's abilities to see differences (Asher & Wigfield, 1981; Dickson, 1981; Whitehurst & Sonnenschein, 1981).

In fact, comparison appears to be the basic analytical component of nearly every approach to referential communication research (Flavell, 1981). Asher and Wigfield (1981), for example, in proposing a "task-analytic" approach to replace the earlier role-taking focus, require comparison at several points in explaining the development of oral communication skills. Communication tasks, they explain, require comparisons of this speaker with other speakers, this task with other tasks; the choice of this referent with other possible referents, and this outcome with other possible outcomes.

The Evaluation Component

Implied by the comparison tasks in communication, speakers are evaluative; that is, while rejecting some messages judged to be uninformative, they formulate alternatives (Whitehurst & Sonnenschein, 1981). Although this aspect of referential communication research appears to be fairly recent, it has been explored in relation to cognitive and comprehension monitoring by Flavell (1981) and Markman (1981), respectively.

To reject a message as uninformative, speakers need first to make a judgment about the message's information value. Being able to make that judgment may be crucial; Markman (1981) points to a number of studies showing that children often report that they have understood material that is ambiguous or inconsistent. Both she and Flavell (1981) argue that conscious attention to task and to accuracy of comprehension is needed for the development and demonstration of referential communication skills. Markman, moreover, argues for the relation of the structure of the information to its comprehensibility and for the need to have children practice evaluative skills in relation to information and explanations.

Thus evaluation as a component is tied to both of the previous abilities: to compare and to take the role of the other. It adds a focus on the ability of the speaker to direct his or her attention consciously to the decisions to be made in communication.

Outside Skill Factors

A number of researchers in this tradition, noting the incomplete or inconsistent results of experimental work, have attempted to account for the development of improved referential communication skills by citing outside or more global developmental factors. For example, some have observed that the acquisition of a wider knowledge base and an increased vocabulary appear to affect performance of referential communication tasks (Asher & Wigfield, 1981). Others have lumped these and other developments into the factor of chronological age. Beaudichon (1981), approaching the stance of the sociolinguistic approach, suggests that interaction with others is a crucial factor in the improvement of referential communication skill, particularly role taking.

Propositional Meaning and Cognitive Certainty

Referential studies are concerned primarily with propositional meaning—the truth value or well-formedness of utterances in their representation of (reference to) objects in the real world. A typical task used in such research is a test reported by Asher (1976) in which children were asked to choose the most effective among a number of messages. They were then given messages that were either moderately associated with the referent but highly unassociated with the nonreferent or highly associated with both the referent and the nonreferent. The question the children had to deal with in choosing the most effective messages was really which were more informative. Greenfield and Zukow (1978) argue that the principle of informativeness functions in the correct choice of referents. They point out that the number of possible alternatives facing a child in a referential task creates uncertainty; the elements that reduce uncertainty most should be chosen as the most informative.

Using the framework of propositional meaning and the principle of cognitive certainty or informativeness, researchers in this tradition combine the components discussed previously. The judgment of informativeness is made both in reference to the possible messages referring to the referent and to what can be presupposed about the information already held by the other—a minimal role-taking involvement. The decision about what message is the most informative implies both a comparison among the alternatives (which created the uncertainty in the first place) and an evaluation of their informativeness. This tradition must also take into account chronological differences, clearly recognized in the differentiation of children at one-word and two-word stages, for example.

Some researchers in developmental pragmatics (actually more a part of the sociolinguistic tradition) have also probed the development of early referential communication skill (Atkinson, 1979; Bates, Camaioni, & Volterra, 1979; Ochs, Schieffelin, & Platt, 1981). In fact, Atkinson (1979) discusses prerequisites for reference in the need of small children first to get the attention of the listener before transmitting propositional content. Ochs et al. (1981) argue that propositions are also constructed over a sequence of utterances, particularly when the speaker is a child at the one-word stage; they also discuss propositions across speakers and utterances. Common to all these studies, however, is the principle of informativeness—used to predict that speakers' choices will be made on the basis of what part of the proposition will reduce uncertainty.

Methods

Typically, research pursued in the referential communication skills tradition takes a random sample of an age group or groups and gives them a (generally complex) referential task, focusing on the evaluation of specific communication skills (Beaudichon, 1981). The task is necessarily artificial in the controlled laboratory setting; care is taken to rule out interference from other factors or to control them. Thus the methodology could be labeled experimental and quantitative. As a variation, some experiments are preceded by "training" the subjects (for example, in comparison skills).

Conclusions and Implications

The referential tradition's approach has been to set up expectations and then to test for failure, concluding that children cannot perform some task because they did not perform the task in the test setting. As Whitehurst and Sonnenschein (1981) point out, that tells us nothing about the situational doing of the task. Thus the limits of the conclusions drawn in the research of this tradition are the limits of experimental design. Specifically, there have been gaps in the age groups studied—mostly under age 11 and above age 17, according to Dickson (1981). He also points to serious limits in the number of items actually tested and to the relative absence of multiple referential communication tasks.

The difficulty in generalizing from these experiments is that they yield few data and few conclusions about how referential meaning is constructed and conveyed in situated interaction. Only the work of the sociolinguists in early propositional meaning has attempted to examine referential communication in natural settings. Thus among the implications for future work, the following two seem particularly clear:

(1) If generalizability is the benefit of the experimental method, then more care should be taken to ensure that what is generalized is truly worth the trouble. More attention should be paid to a wide range of age groups, not merely those that can be easily brought into experimental settings. More items and items that reflect the findings of research in more naturalistic settings ought to be tested to begin to bring the work of the two traditions together.
(2) Related to the latter point, articulation with other traditions asking similar questions and looking through different methodology at similar phenomena is essential. Some movement in this is apparent in developmental pragmatics, but reference to studies outside the referential tradition is typically absent in the field's bibliographies and reference lists.

THE SPEECH COMMUNICATION TRADITION

As persuasion studies began to get "bad press" in the 1960s, with people responding negatively to connotations of "manipulation" (Miller & Burgoon, 1978), scholars trained in the rhetoric and persuasion areas of speech communication picked up the term "communicative competence" as an alternative focus for their study. McCroskey (1982), in fact, recently argued that Aristotle's definition of rhetoric is the earliest definition of communicative competence!

Weinstein's (1969) conception of interpersonal competence as "the ability to control the responses of others" is typical in its persuasion focus. And even Wiemann's (1977) more balanced wording shows the influence of concern with *effect* of communication on the behavior of others. According to Wiemann (1977, p. 198), communicative competence is

the ability of an interactant to choose among available communicative behaviors in order that he (she) may successfully accomplish his (her) own interpersonal goals during an encounter while maintaining the face and line of his (her) fellow interactants within the constraints of the situation.

While not all within the speech communication tradition would agree that social factors are important (see, for example, Monge, Bachman, Dillard, & Eisenberg, 1982), there is a consistent focus in this tradition on the achievement of specific interpersonal goals. Work in the area of communicative competence has proceeded in a number of directions within the tradition, including two that represent the bulk of attention to communicative competence: social perspective taking and effectiveness of communicator style. A third focus, restricted to communication education, has attempted to delimit specific skills appropriate for testing competence in the schools. Each will be discussed briefly, followed by consideration of methods, conclusions, and implications.

Social Perspective Taking

The constructivist school within speech communication (Delia, 1977) built its theoretical position around the concept of role taking, borrowing from the work of Piaget and the research of the referential communication tradition. However, role taking could hardly be considered an alien notion to a tradition that has always focused on audience analysis in both rhetoric and persuasion. What is different in the constructivist view is its attention to how attributional and evaluative aspects of social cognition are developed; the theory is a conscious linking of cognitive-developmental and personal construct theories (Delia & OKeefe, 1979).

Research in this area has examined the developmental path of role taking ability. Clark and Delia (1976, 1977) describe it as moving from the beginning state of the child's having no recognition of the perspective of the other, to a low level of recognition where others' needs and desires are focused on only in terms of the speaker's own needs, to higher levels of including the awareness of others' needs but counterarguing or refuting them in messages, to the highest level, where speakers use messages that highlight the advantages to the persuadee. While the parallel to Flavell's (1974) developmental pattern is evident, the theory reflects the typical assumption of speech communication in its explicit references to persuasion.

Studies reported by constructivists indicate some evidence for the development of interpersonal constructs. Delia and O'Keefe (1979), for example, found marked individual differences in social cognition and communicative performance as a function of the complexity of children's interpersonal cognitive systems. By focusing on individual communicators, these researchers have probed the relationships between cognitive development and communication performance, finding shifts in evaluation and attributional orientation. Delia (1977), Delia and Clark (1977), and Delia and O'Keefe (1979) argue that these shifts explain how language is used to create shared meaning. Understanding adult communicative competence thus requires, for this view, understanding "the processes by which interactants make cognitive assessments of one another's character, emotional state, intentions, and situational understandings" (Delia & O'Keefe, 1979). Hale and Delia (1976) identify role taking as "the capacity to assume and maintain another's point of view [as] the basic social cognitive process in communication."

Effectiveness of Communicator Style

In contrast to this focus on the cognitive development of the speaker, another important strain of work in communicative competence within speech communication focuses on the effectiveness of the communicator *as judged by his or her listener.* Communicative competence as a "socially judged phenomenon" (Wiemann & Backlund, 1980) moves the locus of evaluation from the speaker (where the referential tradition places it) to the receiver of the communication. Thus competence is seen less as a quality or ability of the speaker than as an attribution made by the listener, a judgment of the style of the communicator.

While "appropriateness of behavior" as a criterion is used by these researchers, the means of testing the judgment of what is appropriate is conceived of quite differently by speech communication researchers as opposed to sociolinguists. In much of this research, criterion variables are attitude change, judgments of credibility, or the amount of attraction the listener reports feeling for the speaker. Harris (1977, cited in Wiemann & Backlund, 1980), for example, produced findings of greater listener attraction to competent interaction managers than to incompetent managers, even though background similarity factors were held constant.

The focus is quite clearly on effectiveness, particularly in persuasive communication. In probing the factors that might comprise the broader construct of communicative competence, researchers have found, for example, a two-factor solution of "impression management" and "transaction management" (Rushing, 1976, cited in Wiemann & Backlund, 1980). Even when a three-factor solution like "empathy," "behavioral flexibility," and "interaction management" is generated to explain the construct, the factors are seen as in the service of the speaker's being able to employ "effective tactics" (Weinstein, 1969).

One means of managing effectiveness through control of communicator style, studied in persuasive communication, is the capacity of speakers to be self-monitors (Snyder, 1974, 1979). Generally, high self-monitors are described as people who are conscious of their external environment and able to pick up cues, evaluate information, and adapt their behavior. In contrast, low self-monitors are not attuned to others or to the environment and so are less likely and less able to seek out information or to adapt their behavior. Experiments using this construct generally reveal that high self-monitors make better (more effective) persuaders and are more successful in managing the impressions of others (Elliot, 1979; Miller & Kalbfleisch, 1981).

Communication Education's Skill Identification

While the constructivists are concerned with the development of cognitive interpersonal constructs, and the so-called effectiveness school is interested in abstracting the factors within communicative competence, the communication education subgroup in the discipline has been faced with the demands of producing evidence of skill development in elementary and secondary schools and the challenges of assessing communication skill at the college level.

Various inventories of skills have been produced on the state level and are being used to guide curriculum development (see, for example, the Massachusetts State Board of Education document in Backlund, Brown, Gurry, & Jandt, 1982). Institutions of higher learning have produced exemption tests or collegewide evaluation instruments such as the University of Wisconsin-Parkside's Communication Competency Assessment Instrument (Rubin, 1982) and Alverno College's teaching materials and assessment instruments related to both social interaction and the communication areas of reading, writing, speaking, listening, and media (Alverno College Faculty, 1981).

To varying degrees, the examination of communicative competence as a set or list of skills has also focused on the underlying cognitive or social developmental factors. Unfortunately, in many cases the rush to produce lists of skills under pressure from legislatures or departments of education has short-circuited the process of relating these inventories to the broader conceptualizations of the other traditions, or even to the use of these skills in everyday situations.

Methods

Largely experimental in research design, work in the first two areas has attempted to clarify conceptualizations of communicative competence and proceeded to build theories through operationalization and testing. Delia (1977), Delia and Clark (1977), and Delia and O'Keefe (1979) developed tests of social perspective taking and cognitive complexity. Persuasion research has used experimental designs in which criterion variables (measures of attraction or attitude change) are counted as judgments of competence by listeners. Manipulation of organismic variables like high or low self-monitoring has been used to probe the effects of specific speaker qualities.

Little research has been pursued in the education-focused skill identification area, although Alverno College is systematically validating the assessment instruments in communication areas (Friedman, Mentkowski, Earely, Loacker, & Diez, 1982).

Conclusions and Implications

The two research programs have generated different conclusions. Clark and Delia (1976, 1977) report finding developmental patterns and continue to refine their theoretical integration of cognitive-developmental and social perspective taking. While their work seems to represent a significant breakthrough in connecting theoretical frameworks, they have generally discounted the effects of situation in communicative competence. This may be a serious limitation to their work.

The other, rather abstract approach to probing the dimensions and factors of the construct of communication competence has produced findings that are difficult to link to one another, much less to the experiences of communicators. Moreover, the manipulations conducted in experimental settings have the same drawbacks that some referential studies manifest—they provide little information about actual communication.

To the degree that the identification of communication skills has been grounded in the theoretical frameworks available, these offer a valuable link between the researcher and practical communication situations. Regrettably, few have made use of that link in designing studies to expand the theoretical understandings and to test the validity of the competence lists.

These reflections about the conclusions of speech communication research suggest two implications:

(1) While linking the idea of role-taking with the development of cognitive complexity and the development of communication skill is a good step, at some point it must be linked to the important findings of the sociolinguistic tradition. Perhaps the schemata developed for social perspective taking include a means of including situational information in the assessment of the other's perspective. Indeed "situational understanding" is included by Delia and O'Keefe (1979), but, overall, the idea of situation is given short shrift in this school.

(2) Situation may be the key to breaking the tight link between effectiveness and persuasion as well. Implied in the work of communication researchers who study communicative competence from the standpoint of communicator style is a competitive orientation, the goal of one communicator necessarily being to change the view of the other (or at least to manage it). Higgins, Fondacaro, and McCann (1981) argue that interaction may focus on one or more of variety of goals—including to initiate or maintain a social bond, to achieve a common definition of social reality, to achieve a specific self-presentation, to achieve production of a task or solution of a problem, and even to seek entertainment. Clearly some situations occur more on the collaborative plane, and a theory of communicative competence needs to address what would be effectiveness in those situations. By defining situations as universally persuasive through their choice of operationalizations, these researchers have ruled out an area of communication that needs to be probed.

A further link could be made by combining the study of communication as effective with the evaluation of the lists of skills produced by the communication education school. Students working together in varieties of noncompetitive situations could supply the researcher with a means of probing the broader range of communication goals.

TOWARD AN INTEGRATION OF
THE THREE TRADITIONS

Clearly all three traditions have captured aspects of the communication process and have focused their study using the assumptions and approaches of their disciplines. The argument I will develop in this section is that an integration of the three approaches could offer a more complete understanding of communicative competence—and that the work of each tradition could be enriched through such an integration.

Indeed, an argument for linking at least two parts of the traditions—the social and referential focuses—has been made as a part of speech act theory (Searle, 1969). While Watzlawick, Beavin, and Jackson (1967) were the first to posit the operation of content and relational messages in each utterance, the notion that speech acts do two things at once is increasingly recognized (see, for example, Clark & Clark, 1977; Goody, 1978; Halliday, 1973; Higgins et al., 1981). Speech acts encode propositional content, or referential meaning, which has logical properties independent of context and which is judged on its truth or well-formedness. It is what Goody (1978) calls "report," what Halliday (1973) calls "ideational," and what Clark and Clark (1977) refer to as governed by the "reality principle." But speech acts encode social content as well—"performative" meaning by which the statement itself *is* an action. The social meaning depends on context, has pragmatic properties, and is judged not on truth but on appropriateness. Goody (1978) calls this aspect "command," Halliday (1973) terms it "interpersonal," and Clark and Clark (1977) identify for it a "cooperative principle."

While these two aspects of speech acts can be separated for purposes of analysis, they are not separated in "the state of nature" (Erickson, 1981) and, indeed, may often need to be linked more tightly for analysis than scholars have realized. Olson and Hildyard (1981) pointed out that we often need the social to explain cognition, as in the case of a choice of referent that is mandated by the situation. There may be several accurate or truthful representations in the abstract but only one that will work as a referent in the concrete situation. Moreover, demonstration of referential ability—the ability to *produce* certain propositional meaning—may depend on social or other situational factors, as in Whitehurst and Sonnenschein's (1981) contrasting of knowing how and knowing when.

Perhaps directives give us the clearest sense of how the referential or propositional and the social or interpersonal aspects of a speech act interact.

The propositional meaning of the following three utterances is roughly translatable as the referential meaning as utterance 1:

(1) "Give me a soft drink, please."
(2) "Hey, throw me a Coke."
(3) "I'd appreciate your giving me a cola."

But they may have very different social messages, telling those able to observe the ongoing exchange how the speaker is defining the situation and his or her role in relation to the others present.

The second example implies a casual relationship and an assumption of the other as an equal: native speakers would think nothing of one teenager directing the utterance to another. Consider, however, the same utterance from a gardener to his employer, a society woman proud of her listing in the social register. The utterance would be marked as inappropriate, giving even the casual observer a start and generating speculation about the relationship between the two persons or about the imminent dismissal of the employee. Without belaboring the obvious, one could point out a series of situations in which the third utterance could signal politeness of request, irony (in response to poor service), or even smoldering anger (in response to extremely poor service).

"Social meaning" in this sense covers the whole of the situation—setting, type of interaction, roles of participants relative to each other, relative status, various levels of goals, and so on. It refers not only to the social meaning embedded in the choice of words ("give" versus "throw") that would be "true" in general but also to what is specific to this utterance given what has gone before within the interaction (the quality of service in the time preceding the request, for example). The contribution of the speech communication tradition's persuasion focus may be to reveal a third aspect of communicative competence: the directing or structuring function within ongoing interaction.

To examine this aspect further requires that we move beyond the limits of speech act theory, however, which cannot provide (and was not intended to produce) a theory of interaction. Dore (1979) suggested a helpful conception of a larger unit of analysis, the conversational act; Weick (1979) proposed the double interact, a linking of three utterance units. Whatever is ultimately used to examine natural interaction and to pursue experimental study, the notion of ongoingness of context and goal definition needs to be included, functioning in the structuring work done by a given speech act within that larger whole. For example, in many situations, "Hey, throw me a Coke" could be analyzed as directing the social relationship goal or even an entertainment goal of the speaker in relation to the other. It maintains, rather than attempts to change or establish, the social bond between the speakers. However, if the participants were not already acquainted, the same utterance could serve the purpose of establishing a social bond, signaling through its social aspect that the speaker wants to recognize the other as an equal and pursue small talk.

On the one hand, such an utterance reveals social content and indicates illocutionary force. On the other, it sets up the next move by the other, directing the flow of the interaction while being open to being changed by the other's next move. Goals change in an ongoing way throughout an interaction, sometimes in subtle ways, sometimes more drastically. These changes are communicated through individual utterances interpreted in the ongoing flow of discourse.

Structuring or directing aspects of an utterance are not clearly separable from the referential and social aspects, even as those two occur tightly tied together. But the role of structuring in interaction can be analyzed as a distinct functional aspect, one that regulates the movement of the interaction across utterances. Seen in the broader context of an ongoing interaction, then, the three aspects of communicative competence can be redefined and expanded to show the work they perform together in creating interactional meaning.

Referential

Besides the propositional meaning of the utterance and the referential meaning of individual terms, we could include in this view of referential competence (the skill of making links to previous utterances) the creation of ongoing coherence of discourse. Such a view would focus on the lexical and syntactic skills needed to arrange the structure of sentences and the juxtaposition of words to convey the intended links. Truth and well-formedness would still be appropriate criteria for judgment of referential effectiveness, but they would be truth in relation to the ideational content of previous utterances, well-formedness that takes into account previous references to objects and ideas across the flow of discourse.

Social

The social meaning of the utterance would be defined much the way the sociolinguistic tradition has defined it: tied to language as situated and reflective of the social roles of the participants. However, explicit ties to the impact of the social or referential meaning should be considered part of the social aspect of competence. Such a view would focus on both lexical and pragmatic skills, judged from the standard of culturally determined appropriateness. The idea of fuctionality as part of social meaning would be divided into immediate function and a broader sense of function in relationship to the discourse as an ongoing whole.

Structuring

This aspect shares with the social the pragmatic focus on language as linked to speakers and their intentions in using language. As a functional, social competence, structuring needs to be tied to a recognition of the goal or goals of the interactions. Gleason and Weintraub (1978) offer a different perspective on that relationship between goals and structuring. In asserting that a mature speaker learns "to use language to organize and direct behavior," they argue that this directive function is not a social use, although originating in the interpersonal arena. Rather, they call it an "intrapersonal" behavior-planning function, using language to order thoughts and specify goals. Regardless of how one views the social aspect of structuring, it is clear that monitoring skill would be an important component and a necessary part of this aspect of communicative competence. Such a view would posit a process by which speakers evaluate the success of past structuring in meeting goals and decide on their next choices within the interaction. Effectiveness would be the criterion of structuring competence.

IMPLICATIONS

What are the implications of conceptualizing communicative competence as having referential, social, and structuring aspects? I conclude this chapter with a discussion of three implications linked to the observations made earlier about the separate traditions.

(1) Such a conceptualization could improve articulation between and among the three traditions. While there has been some cross-referencing of studies in the three traditions, or disciplines within them, many articles still fail to cite research outside their own tradition, even when other research is clearly related to the questions under consideration. Without recognition of the work being done in other, related areas, progress in the development of our understanding of human language use and development will be impaired.

By focusing on a conceptualization of communicative competence that attempts to make connections between the past work of all three disciplines, the valuable contributions of each could be brought to bear on the others. Moreover, it could support the burgeoning movement (Erickson, 1977) to find ways to link the work of quantitative and qualitative researches in the area of human language and language development.

(2) Such a conceptualization draws attention to the basic unit of communication as larger than the individual sentence; that is, as interactional. Part of the reason for the disparity in findings of competence or incompetence has been the definition of what will be studied and what will count as

evidence in drawing conclusions. By focusing on interaction rather than on discrete choices from among those provided in an artificial task, referential communication researchers would be challenged to design more realistic experiments yielding more generalizable conclusions. We might then begin to be able to see the extent to which referents are tied to situations and be able to evaluate the mutual influence of speakers' ongoing choiçes of subsequent use of referents in conversation.

Communication research would be encouraged to move beyond the definition of abstract factors and to find links to the work in communication education and other disciplines. The suggestion is not to avoid the abstract or to deny its place in theorizing; rather, the need is to ground that theorizing and make sure it is applicable in real settings.

(3) Such a conceptualization would recognize communicative competence as an ongoing, developmental human ability. Erickson (1981) suggests that socialization is a never-ending process, yet some conceptualizations of communicative competence have provided a rigid, abstract view of a single standard of adult performance. Viewing conversation or interaction as a continually negotiated process leads to the examination of communicative competence as a processing and producing capability best discovered in natural talk. Such a view would call researchers in all traditions to reexamine why they study only small children or undergraduates in basic courses (whatever has been their stock in trade). It might well lead to more programmatic research pursuing questions across age groups and across situations, form simple to complex tasks, in a variety of goal contexts. Getting at the processes involved in the acquisition of beginning competence and in the ongoing refining of the capability is a challenge that sociolinguists need to face, moving beyond current work.

Identification of the three aspects of communicative competence—referential, social, and structuring—is only a beginning in the potential integration of the three separate traditions examined in this chapter. However, because it appears to offer a way to bring a range of important work together in a new way, it offers benefits across all three traditions. Its application depends on the collaborative communicating skills of the practitioners in the three areas—a level of communicative competence needed by effective researchers.

REFERENCES

Alverno College Faculty. (1981). *Liberal learning at Alverno College* (2nd ed.). Milwaukee: Alverno Productions.

Ammon, P. (1981). Communication skills and communicative competence: A neo-Piagetian process-structural view. In W. P. Dickson (Ed.), *Children's oral communication skills*. New York: Academic.

Asher, S. R. (1976). Children's ability to appraise their own and another person's communication performance. *Developmental Psychology, 12,* 24-32.

Asher, S. R., & Wigfield, A. (1981). Training referential communication skills. In W. D. Dickson (Ed.), Children's oral communication skills. New York: Academic.

Atkinson, M. (1979). Prerequisites for reference. In E. Ochs & B. Schieffelin (Eds.), Developmental pragmatics. New York: Academic.

Backlund, P. M., Brown, K. L., Gurry, J., & Jandt, F. (1982). Recommendations for assessing speaking and listening skills. Communication Education, 31, 9-18.

Bates, E., Camaioni, L., & Volterra, V. (1979). The acquisition of performatives prior to speech. In E. Ochs & B. Schieffelin (Eds.), Developmental pragmatics. New York: Academic.

Beaudichon, J. (1981). Problem-solving communication and complex information transmission in groups. In W. D. Dickson (Ed.), Children's oral communication skills. New York: Academic.

Blom, J., & Gumperz, J. (1972). Social meaning in linguistic structures: Code-switching in Norway. In J. Gumperz & D. Hymes (Eds.), Directions in sociolinguistics. New York: Holt, Rinehart & Winston.

Bochner, A. P., & Kelly, C. W. (1974). Interpersonal competence: Rationale, philosophy, and implementation of a conceptual framework. Speech Teacher, 23, 279-301.

Brenneis, D., & Lein, L. (1977). "You fruithead": A sociolinguistic approach to children's dispute settlement. In S. Ervin-Tripp & C. Mitchell-Kernan (Eds.), Child discourse. New York: Academic.

Brown, P., & Fraser, C. (1979). Speech as a marker of situation. In K. Scherer & H. Giles (Eds.), Social markers in speech. Cambridge: Cambridge University Press.

Camaioni, L. (1979). Child-adult and child-child conversations: An interactional approach. In E. Ochs & B. Schieffelin (Eds.), Developmental pragmatics. New York: Academic.

Chomsky, N. (1965). Aspects of the theory of syntax. Cambridge: MIT Press.

Clark, H. H., & Clark, E. V. (1977). Psychology and language. New York: Harcourt Brace Jovanovich.

Clark, R. A., & Delia, J. G. (1976). The development of functional persuasive skills in childhood and early adolescence. Child Development, 47, 1008-1014.

Clark, R. A., & Delia, J. G. (1977). Cognitive complexity, social perspective-taking, and functional persuasive skills in second- to ninth-grade children. Human Communication Research, 3, 128-134.

Cook-Gumperz, J. (1977). Situated instructions: Language socialization of school-age children. In S. Ervin-Tripp & C. Mitchell-Kernan (Eds.), Child discourse. New York: Academic.

Corsaro, W. A. "We're friends, right?": Children's use of access rituals in a nursery school. Language in Society, 8, 315-336.

Delia, J. G. (1977). Constructivism and the study of human communication. Quarterly Journal of Speech, 63, 66-83.

Delia, J. G., & Clark, R. A. (1977). Cognitive complexity, social perception, and development of listener-adapted communication in six-, eight-, ten-, and twelve-year old boys. Communication Monographs, 44, 326-345.

Delia, J. G., & O'Keefe, B. J. (1979). Constructivism: The development of communication in children. In E. Wartella (Ed.), Children communicating: Media and development of thought, speech, understanding. Beverly Hills, CA: Sage.

Dickson, W. P. (1981). Referential communication activities in research and in the curriculum: A meta-analysis. In W. P. Dickson (Ed.), Children's oral communication skills. New York: Academic.

Dickson, W. P. (1981). Children's oral communication skills. New York: Academic.

Dore, J. (1977). "Oh them sheriff": A pragmatic analysis of children's responses to questions. In S. Ervin-Tripp & C. Mitchell-Kernan (Eds.), Child discourse. New York: Academic

Dore, J. (1979). Conversational acts and the acquisition of language. In E. Ochs & B. Schieffelin (Eds.), Developmental pragmatics. New York: Academic.

Edelsky, C. (1977). Acquisition of an aspect of communicative competence: Learning what it means to talk like a lady. In S. Ervin-Tripp & C. Mitchell-Kernan (Eds.), Child discourse. New York: Academic.

Elliot, G. C. (1979). Some effects of deception and level of self-monitoring on planning and reacting to a self-presentation. Journal of Personality and Social Psychology, 1282-1292.

Erickson, F. (1977). Some approaches to inquiry in school-community ethnography. *Anthropology and Education Quarterly, 8*, 58-69.

Erickson, F. (1981). Timing and context in everyday discourse: Implications for the study of referential and social meaning. In W. P. Dickson (Ed.), *Children's oral communication skills*. New York: Academic.

Erickson, F., & Shultz, J. (1981). When is a context? Some issues and methods in the analysis of social competence. In J. L. Green & C. Wallat (Eds.), *Ethnography and language in educational settings*. Norwood, NJ: Ablex.

Ervin-Tripp, S. (1968). An analysis of the interaction of language, topic and listener. In J. A. Fishman (Ed.), *Readings in the sociology of language*. The Hague: Mouton.

Ervin-Tripp, S. (1976). Is Sybil there? The structure of some American English directives. *Language in Society, 5*, 25-66.

Ervin-Tripp, S. (1977). Wait for me, roller skate! In S. Ervin-Tripp & C. Mitchell-Kernan (Eds.), *Child discourse*. New York: Academic.

Ervin-Tripp, S. (1979). Children's verbal turn-taking. In E. Ochs & B. Schieffelin (Eds.), *Developmental pragmatics*. New York: Academic.

Ervin-Tripp, S. (1980). Speech acts, social meaning and social learning. In H. Giles, W. P. Robinson, & P. M. Smith (Eds.), *Language: Social psychological perspectives*. New York: Pergamon.

Ervin-Tripp, S., & Mltchell-Kernan, C. (Eds.). (1977). *Child discourse*. New York: Academic.

Flavell, J. (1974). The development of inferences about others. In T. Mischel (Ed.), *Understanding other persons*. Totowa, NJ: Rowan & Littlefield.

Flavell, J. (1981). Cognitive monitoring. In W. P. Dickson (Ed.), *Children's oral communication skills*. New York: Academic.

Friedman, M., Mentkowski, M., Earley, M., Loacker, G., & Diez, M. (1982). *Validating assessment techniques in an outcome-centered liberal arts curriculum: Valuing and communications generic instruments*. National Institute of Education Grant (NIE-G-77-0058) Final Report. Milwaukee, WI: Alverno Productions.

Garvey, C. (1977). Play with language and speech. In S. Ervin-Tripp & C. Mitchell-Kernan (Eds.), *Child discourse*. New York: Academic.

Garvey, C. (1979). Contingent queries and their relations in discourse. In E. Ochs & B. Schieffelin (Eds.), *Developmental pragmatics*. New York: Academic.

Gleason, J. B., & Weintraub, S. (1976). The acquisition of routines in child language. *Language in Society, 5*, 129-136.

Gleason, J. B., & Weintraub, S. (1978). Input language and acquisition of communicative competence. In K. E. Nelson (Ed.), *Children's language* (Vol. 1). New York: Gardner.

Goffman, E. (1967). *Interaction ritual*. New York: Pantheon.

Goffman, E. (1974). *Frame analysis*. New York: Harper & Row.

Goody, E. N. (1978). Towards a theory of questions. In E. N. Goody (Ed.), *Questions and politeness: Strategies in social interaction*. Cambridge: Cambridge University Press.

Graham, J. A., Argyle, M., Clarke, D., & Maxwell, G. (1981). The salience, equivalence, and sequential structure of behavioral elements in different social situations. *Semiotica, 35*, 1-27.

Gregory, M., & Carroll, S. (1978). *Language and situation*. London: Routledge & Kegan Paul.

Greenfield, P. M. (1979). Informativeness, presupposition, and semantic choice in single-word utterances. In E. Ochs & B. Schieffelin (Eds.), *Developmental pragmatics*. New York: Academic.

Greenfield, P. M., & Zukow, P. G. (1978). Why do children say what they say when they say it?: An experimental approach to the psychogenesis of presupposition. In K. E. Nelson (Ed.), *Children's language* (Vol. 1). New York: Gardner.

Greif, E. B., & Gleason, J. B. (1980). Hi, thanks, and goodbye: More routine information. *Language in Society, 9*, 159-166.

Gumperz, J., & Herasimchuk, E. (1975). The conversational analysis of social meaning: A study of classroom interaction. In M. Sanches & B. G. Blount (Eds.), *Sociocultural dimensions of language use*. New York: Academic.

Hale, C. L., & Delia, J. G. (1976). Cognitive complexity and social perspective-taking. *Communication Monographs, 43*, 195-203.

Hall, W. S., & Cole, M. (1978). On participant's shaping of discourse through their understanding of the task. In K. E. Nelson (Ed.), *Children's language* (Vol. 1). New York: Gardner.

Halliday, M. A. K. (1973). *Explorations in the function of language.* London: Edward Arnold.

Halliday, M. A. K. (1979). *Language as social semiotic.* Baltimore: University Park Press.

Harris, L. M. (1977). *The effect of interaction management and background similarity on perceived communicative competence and attraction during intial interaction.* Unpublished master's thesis, University of Kentucky.

Higgins, E. T., Fondacaro, R., & McCann, C. D. (1981). Rules and roles: "Communication game" and speaker-listener processes. In W. P. Dickson (Ed.), *Children's oral communication skills.* New York: Academic.

Hymes, D. (1971). Competence and performance in linguistic theory. In R. Huxley & E. Ingram (Eds.), *Language acquisition: Models and methods.* New York: Academic.

Hymes, D. (1972). On communicative competence. In J. Pride & J. Holmes (Eds.), *Sociolinguistics.* London: Penguin.

Kreckel, M. (1981). *Communicative acts and shared knowledge in natural discourse.* New York: Academic.

McCroskey, J. C. (1982). Communication competence and performance: A research and pedagogical perspective. *Communication Education, 31,* 1-7.

Markman, E. M. (1981). Comprehension monitoring. In W. P. Dickson (Ed.), *Children's oral communication skills.* New York: Academic.

Miller, G. R., & Burgoon, M. (1978). Persuasion research: Review and commentary. In B. D. Ruben (Ed.), *Communication yearbook 2.* New Brunswick, NJ: Transaction Books.

Miller, G. R., & Kalbfleisch, P. J. (1981). *Effects of self-monitoring and opportunity to rehearse on deceptive success.* Unpublished manuscript, Department of Communication, Michigan State University.

Mitchell-Kernan, C., & Kernan, K. T. (1977). Pragmatics of directive choice among children. In S. Ervin-Tripp & C. Mitchell-Kernan (Eds.), *Child discourse.* New York: Academic.

Monge, P. R., Bachman, S. G., Dillard, J. P., & Eisenberg, E. M. (1982). Communicator competence in the workplace: Model testing and scale development. In M. Burgoon (Ed.), *Communication yearbook 5.* New Brunswick, NJ: Transaction Books.

Newcombe, N., & Zaslow, M. (1981). Do 2½-year-olds hint? A study of directive forms in the speech of 2½-year-old children to adults. *Discourse Processes, 4,* 197-220.

Ochs, E., & Schieffelin, B. (1979). *Developmental pragmatics.* New York: Academic.

Ochs, E., Schieffelin, B., & Platt, M. (1979). Propositions across utterances and speakers. In E. Ochs & B. Schieffelin (Eds.), *Developmental pragmatics.* New York: Academic.

Olson, D. R., & Hildyard, A. (1981). Assent and compliance in children's language. In W. P. Dickson (Ed.), *Children's oral communication skills.* New York: Academic.

Piaget, J. (1955). *The language and thought of the child* (M. Gabain, trans.). New York: World.

Philips, S. U. (1972). Participant structures and communicative competence: Warm Springs children in community and classroom. In C. B. Cazden, V. B. John, & D. Hymes (Eds.), *Functions of language in the classroom.* New York: Teachers College Press.

Rubin, R. B. (1982). Assessing speaking and listening competence at the college level: The communication competency assessment instrument. *Communication Education, 31,* 19-32.

Rushing, J. (1976). *Impression management as communication action: A nonverbal strategy in interpersonal encounters.* Paper presented at the annual meeting of the Western Speech Communication Association, San Francisco.

Scherer, K., & Giles, H. (Eds.). (1979). *Social markers in speech.* Cambridge: Cambridge University Press.

Scotton, C. M. (1972). *Choosing a lingua franca in an African capital.* Edmonton: Linguistic Research.

Scotton, C. M. (in press). The negotiation of identities in conversation: A theory of markedness and code choice. *International Journal of the Sociology of Language.*

Scotton, C. M., & Ury, W. (1977). Bilingual strategies: The social functions of code-switching. *International Journal of the Sociology of Language, 13* 5-20.

Searle, J. (1969). *Speech acts.* Cambridge: Cambridge University Press.

Searle, J. (1976). A classification of illocutionary acts. *Language in Society, 5,* 1-23.

Shantz, C. U. (1981). The role of role-taking in children's referential communication. In W. P. Dickson (Ed.), *Children's oral communication skills.* New York: Academic.

Shuy, R. W., & Griffin, P. (1981). What they do in school *any* day: Studying functional language. In W. P. Dickson (Ed.), *Children's oral communication skills.* New York: Academic.

Snyder, M. (1974). Self-monitoring and expressive behavior. *Journal of Personality and Social Psychology, 30,* 526-537.

Snyder, M. (1979). Self-monitoring processes. In L. Berkowitz (Ed.), *Advances in experimental social psychology* (Vol. 12). New York: Academic.

Van Dijk, T. A. (1977). Context and cognition: Knowledge frames and speech act comprehension. *Journal of Pragmatics, 1,* 211-232.

Vygotsky, C. M. (1962). *Language and thought.* Cambridge: MIT Press.

Wartella, E. (1979). *Children communicating: Media and development of thought, speech, understanding.* Beverly Hills, CA: Sage.

Watzlawick, P., Beavin, J. H., & Jackson, D. D. (1967). *Pragmatics of human communication.* New York: W. W. Norton.

Weick, K. E. (1979). *The social psychology of organizing.* Reading, MA: Addison-Wesley.

Weinstein, E. A. (1969). The development of interpersonal competence. In D. A. Goskin (Ed.), *Handbook of socialization theory and research.* Chicago: Rand McNally.

Whitehurst, G. J., & Sonnenschein, S. (1981). The development of informative messages in referential communication: Knowing when versus knowing how. In W. P. Dickson (Ed.), *Children's oral communication skills.* New York: Academic.

Wiemann, J. M. (1977). Explication and test of a model of communicative competence. *Human Communication Research, 3,* 195-213.

Wiemann, J. M., & Backlund, P. (1980). Current theory and research in communicative competence. *Review of Educational Research, 5,* 185-199.

Wilkinson, L. C., Clevenger, M., & Dollaghan, C. (1981). Communication in small instructional groups: A sociolinguistic approach. In W. P. Dickson (Ed.), *Children's oral communication skills.* New York: Academic.

3 ● Incongruity in Humor: The Cognitive Dynamics

SHIRLEY WILLIS MAASE ● EDWARD L. FINK ● STAN A. KAPLOWITZ

University of Maryland ● Michigan State University

T HE study of humor has spanned more than a dozen centuries[1] and has drawn the interest of researchers from a wide variety of fields: anthropology, communication, philosophy, experimental social psychology, education, and sociology. The use of humor and the humor response has been suggested to be related to a variety of social and communication functions (for example, therapy, education, persuasion, and social influence).[2] However, despite the interest in and the suggested social importance of humor, we are no closer to developing a generalized theory of humor than we were in the first century A.D., when Quintilian complained that no one had yet explained what laughter was, though many had tried (Morreall, 1983).

Some approaches to the study of humor have focused on the *cognitive* activity involved in the response to humor, while others have focused on the *emotional* aspects of that response. Although both cognitive and affective orientations have laid important groundwork for the development of a more generalized theory of humor, often the most basic assumptions of these theories have not been stated precisely or tested empirically.

The purpose of this chapter is to state formally and precisely some of the most basic assumptions shared by a number of humor theories, and to demonstrate the utility of metric multidimensional scaling (MMDS) models for the explication and test of those assumptions from a cognitive perspective. To accomplish these objectives, the remainder of this chapter will be

AUTHORS' NOTE: We wish to thank L. Allen, C. Stein, V. S. Freimuth, J. L. McCaleb, and T. Marron for discussion concerning the ideas in this chapter.

Correspondence and requests for reprints: Edward L. Fink, Department of Communication Arts and Theatre, University of Maryland, College Park, MD 20742.

devoted to the presentation of four topics. First, a review of the relevant humor literature will be presented to establish which assumptions and hypotheses warrant further elaboration and research. Second, existing spatial and temporal models will be reviewed. Third, several general MMDS models will be described and their relevance for the study of humor will be explained. The fourth section uses these models to develop empirically testable hypotheses regarding humor. Finally, a summary of this chapter will be provided.

COGNITIVE AND AFFECTIVE THEORIES OF HUMOR

Although theorists seem to agree that the humor response disturbs the balance of both emotion and thought (e.g., see Clark, 1970; Koestler, 1964; Wicker, Thorelli, Barron, & Ponder, 1981), most research focuses on one or the other aspect rather than on both. Eysenck (1942, pp. 303-305) grouped theories of humor into two major categories: (1) cognitive theories, which stress elements such as incongruity, contrast between ideas, or deceived ideational expectancies; and (2) oretic theories, which equate laughter with the satisfaction of needs or drives, or which stress the emotional correlates of laughter.

Cognitively oriented theories view humor as a result of cognitions that are perceived to be incongruous. The incongruity creates a cognitive imbalance; the presentation of the incongruity is surprising or unexpected, and the imbalance is rapidly resolved. One of the more celebrated of the early incongruity theorists was Kant (1952), who attempted to link the cognitive and physical aspects of laughter. Laughter, according to Kant, is "an affectation arising from a strained expectation being suddenly reduced to nothing" and "in this presentation, the understanding, missing what it expected, suddenly let go its hold, with the result that the effect of this slackening is felt in the body by the oscillation of the organs" (p. 538).

The basic ideas of most incongruity theorists, however, are similar to the two-stage process outlined by Suls (1972). The first stage occurs when the perceiver encounters an incongruity between the anticipated and the actuality. In the second, or problem-solving stage, the receiver reconciles the incongruous elements. The humor is the difference between what is expected and the actual state of affairs. Nerhardt (1970) explored the hypothesis that the presentation of nonhumorous material would also produce a humorous response if there had been a corresponding violation of expectancies. Nerhardt found that subjects lifting weights smiled and laughed when presented with a weight that was divergent from a series of prior weights each subject had also lifted; without this divergence, smiling and laughing occurred significantly less often.

The relationship between incongruity and amusement is not simple, however. While Kenny (1955) found a negative linear relationship between amusement and incongruity, Shurcliff (1968) and Nerhardt (1970) found a positive linear relationship. An additional study by Nerhardt (1975) and evidence provided by Wilson (1979) suggest there is a curvilinear, inverted U-shaped relationship between amusement and incongruity, with moderate levels of incongruity producing the most amusement. Wilson suggests that the earlier studies may have employed a small range of incongruities and thus were reporting only the slope of one side of the inverted U-shaped curve.

Not only is the relation between the amount of incongruity and humor complex, but so is the relation between the type of incongruity and humor. While Kant suggests that the resolution of incongruity is necessary for humor, Clark (1970) suggests that amusement is the enjoyment of perceiving, or indulging in the incongruity. For jokes, moreover, theorists disagree about, or sometimes fail to specify clearly, which parts of a joke are incongruous (Godkewitsch, 1976a). Godkewitsch suggests that incongruity does not lie between joke body and punch line, but rather between occurrences within the joke body; the punch line serves to give the necessary information to resolve the incongruity. In a test of this hypothesis, Godkewitsch found that the relation between incongruity, its placement in a joke (i.e., within the joke body or punch line), and amusement appears to be confounded by the theme of the joke. For example, sex jokes were funnier the more predictable and expected they were and the less surprising their punch lines were. Yet one class of verbal put-ons (nonsense jokes) was rated funnier the more unusual and the more unlikely the occurrences within the joke body were. Funniness of both sexual and nontendentious jokes correlated positively with a measure of punch line *appropriateness*. The results of studies such as this indicate that incongruity is relevant to the cognitive processing of humor, but the wide variety of interpretations and applications of incongruity has yielded inconclusive and sometimes inconsistent results.

Oretic or affective theories assume that the incongruous elements of a joke cause increased tension, drive, or arousal, which is released with the resolution of the joke. Berlyne (1960) distinguishes two ways in which arousal may be linked to humor. The *arousal-boost* hypothesis suggests that the joke creates arousal to a pleasant level, and amusement stems from the short-term maintenance of this rewarding level of arousal. The *arousal-jag* hypothesis proposes that the joke body induces a massive and aversive increase in arousal, which is then rapidly reduced as the punch line is understood. The reduction of arousal is pleasant and is thus the source of humor appreciation. The arousal-jag hypothesis is very similar to the view expressed by Freud (1960):

> We should say that laughter arises if a quota of physical energy which has earlier been used for the cathexis of particular physical paths has become unusable, so that it can find free discharge. (p. 147)

The arousal-boost and arousal-jag hypotheses make different predictions regarding the relation of amusement to degree and timing of arousal. The arousal-boost hypothesis predicts an inverted U-shape relationship, with a modest level of arousal evoking the maximum amount of amusement. Moreover, the amusement should start prior to the punch line. The arousal-jag hypothesis predicts a positive, linear relation between amusement and arousal, and the amusement should start after the punch line reduces the arousal.

Some researchers have attempted to examine empirically the relation between arousal and humor. Goldstein, Harman, McGhee, and Karasik (1975), for example, monitored the heart rate and skin conductance of individuals presented with riddles and with nonhumorous problems. Riddles are jokes that begin with a question that cannot be answered correctly to which, following the respondent's incorrect response, the actual answer is provided. For the nonhumorous problems utilized in this study the answer was also provided after the respondents failed to answer the question. Although heart rate accelerated with the question and decelerated with the answer for both stimuli, there were significant differences for skin conductance in the conditions. This research suggests that autonomic responses may be different for jokes than for ordinary problem-solving situations. Part of the difference may be due to the affective loading that occurs with the presentation of humorous material—that is, people expect to enjoy the riddle. According to Goldstein et al. (1975), an additional possibility for the difference in physiological response to riddles and problems may be that the temporal dimension in the two situations may be fundamentally different. Intuitively, problem solving takes longer, and there is some evidence to suggest that the resolution of a joke must occur rather rapidly in order for the joke to be perceived as humorous.

Goldstein et al., in a test of Berlyne's arousal hypothesis, correlated arousal changes and absolute arousal with funniness ratings of riddles. Humor appreciation was found to be the greatest for subjects who showed a modest amount of arousal. This was consistent with the arousal-boost hypothesis. Wilson (1979) suggests that the best way to distinguish the arousal-boost and arousal-jag hypotheses would be to examine the temporal relation of arousal and amusement. We know of no study, however, that has done this. Hence, while a number of studies (Berlyne, 1960; Godke-witsch, 1976b; Goldstein et al., 1975) suggest that arousal may be neces-sary for humor, they do not tell us how much arousal maximizes humor or whether the increase in arousal or the subsequent reduction in it causes humor.

Thus far we have distinguished theories of humor that emphasize cog-nitive mechanisms from those that emphasize affective mechanisms. Eysenck (1942) warned, however, that the distinction between the two cat-egories must not be carried too far. In practice, cognitive and affective re-sponses are necessarily bound together, and a synthesis of cognitive and affective mechanisms may be necessary to advance our understanding of humor. Clearly, the tension or arousal experienced in humor has a cognitive basis. Hence, an examination of the cognitive correlates of arousal also needs to be made. The magnitude of a physiological response tells us little about the conscious reasoning or unconscious reactions that may have con-tributed to that response.

The cognitive and affective theories depict a process in which there is a disturbance to an existing state, some action to counter or reduce that distur-bance, and some effect that occurs as a result of that action. Some theorists (e.g., Bateson, 1952; Fry, 1963) suggest there may even be a rapid vascilla-tion between alternative meanings as the individual seeks to resolve or re-duce incongruity. Each of the theories suggests, either implicitly or explicitly, that joke resolution is accompanied by a change in the cognitive representa-tion (or meaning) of the concepts involved in the joke. None of the theories, however, has demonstrated empirically the change in the cognitive configu-ration following joke resolution.

HUMOR IN TIME AND SPACE

The consideration of time as a key factor in the cognitive response to humor has been explored minimally. On the interactional or interpersonal level, comedians have long recognized the importance of timing for their success on stage. Eastman (1936, p. 318) suggests that the superior comic takes the audience the "optimal distance down the mental path, where the surprise is the most unexpected," before springing the punch line. Eastman tells how one particular comedian, Bill Robinson, made jokes out of time itself:

> He starts a simple tapping rhythm . . . and gets the audience going with him in that rhythm, and just as they are going "good," with a most dexterous sudden-ness, he stops and leaves them in the air. And they laugh. That is what a joke is . . . getting somebody going and them leaving him in the air. (p. 318)

As stated earlier, in the humor response, time is theoretically very important. Incongruity theories frequently refer to stages; tension release theories discuss a buildup and sudden release of tension; drive theories refer to an imbalance and a motivation to restore equilibrium, followed by a return to balance; arousal theories discuss the buildup of arousal and its consequences. In addition, some theories have described the spatial configuration of the cognitive processing of humor over time. For example, Koestler (1964) describes the comedic situation as a buildup of expectations accompanied by mounting tension. Then there is an explosion as the individual perceives

> a situation or idea, L, on two self-consistent but habitually incompatible frames of reference, M_1 and M_2. The event L, in which the two intersect, is made to vibrate simultaneously, on two different wavelengths, as it were. While this association lasts, L is not merely linked to one associative context, but *bisociated* with two. (p. 35)

Koestler's representation of the cognitive explosion is represented in Figure 3.1.

Koestler suggests that higher forms of sustained humor (such as humorous narratives, comic poems, or satire) rely on "a series of minor explo-

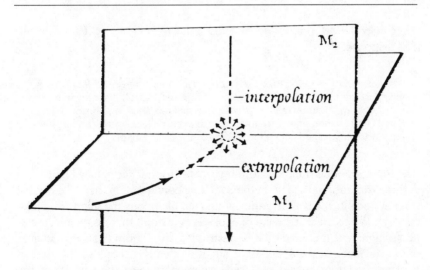

Figure 3.1.   Koestler's bisociation theory of humor represented in a multidimensional space. Reprinted by permission of the Sterling Lord Agency. Copyright© 1964, 1976 by Arthur Koestler.

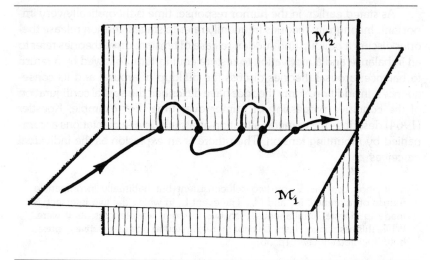

Figure 3.2.   Koestler's representation of sustained humor in a multidimensional space. Reprinted by permission of the Sterling Lord Agency. Copyright © 1964, 1976 by Arthur Koestler.

sions or a continuous state of mild excitement" (p. 37) as the "humorous narrative oscillates between the two frames of reference" (p. 38; see Figure 3.2).

Paulos (1980, pp. 94-95) also discusses a "mental oscillation" in the joke response:

> Thus as a story is being told, the listener oscillates between 1) following it, taking it seriously, and thereby becoming aroused, and 2) responding to the metacues, and thereby realizing the story is make-believe, and becoming deflated. This phenomenon of mental oscillation partially accounts for the pleasant tension associated with good joke-telling, theatre and play.

Paulos models humor according to catastrophe theory (see Figure 3.3) in three-dimensional space. In the cognitive configuration there is a double layer surface in the center, representing simultaneous meanings of a joke concept. When the punch line of a joke is delivered, there is an interpretation switch, accompanied by a "catastrophic drop" from the upper level to the lower layer or surface. Paulos suggests that the shape of the surface explains the importance of timing. The comedian must know where on the surface the meaning might be located; if the second interpretation becomes too obvious too soon, the joke fails. If the comedian is ahead of the audience, the interpretation switch might not occur.

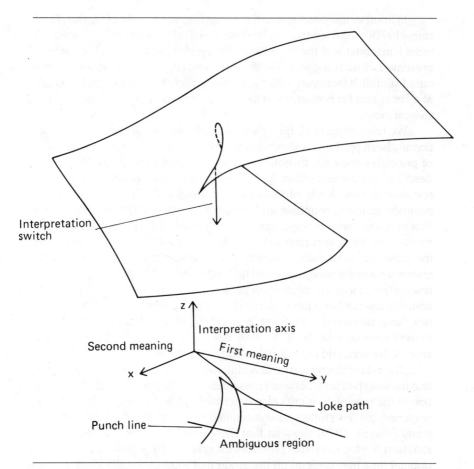

Figure 3.3.   Paulos's representation of the cognitive response to a joke in a three-dimensional space. From *Mathematics and Humor* by J. A. Paulos. Reprinted by permission of the University of Chicago Press. Copyright © 1980 by the University of Chicago.

The representations proposed by Koestler and Paulos have been proposed only theoretically; there has been no empirical evidence to warrant the acceptance of such spatial-temporal representations in the development of a more generalized theory of humor. However, two relevant temporal studies of the cognitive processing of humor have been reported in the literature. Wilson's (1979) findings suggest that the effect of timing on humor depends on the level of incongruity. In particular, for highly incongruous jokes, greater pauses between joke body and punch line led to decreased funniness.

In another temporal study of the cognitive processing of humor, Goldstein (1970) examined the relation between the affective stimuli in joke material (cartoons) and the time it takes subjects to respond to the cartoons presented. Results suggest that response time is shortest for positively evaluated stimuli. It increases with the complexity of the material and increases at a faster rate for nonsense cartoons than for sexually oriented or aggressive cartoons.

We have suggested, first, that although theories of humor have traditionally been predominantly cognitive or affective in orientation, a synthesis of principles common to both approaches may be necessary in order to describe and explain either type of response. Next, several assumptions common to both kinds of theories were discussed. The first assumption common to many cognitive and affective theories is that the response to humor is a dynamic process, occurring in stages and/or over time. Key elements of the process appear to be incongruity, resolution, and time between the presentation of the incongruity and joke resolution. While cognitively oriented theorists have suggested that a change occurs in the cognitive representation of joke concepts from presentation of joke body to joke resolution, this has not been demonstrated empirically. Affectively oriented theories have proposed that there is a change in arousal or tension from presentation of joke body to joke resolution, but the relations among arousal, tension, and the humor response are still unclear.

The role of timing warrants additional research. Many theories suggest that the length of time between presentation of the joke body and presentation of the resolution is critical in determining the magnitude of the humor response, yet few studies have examined this relationship specifically. One study (Wilson, 1979) suggests that there may be an *optimal* time (neither too short nor too long) that produces the greatest magnitude of humor. This optimal time may depend on the amount of incongruity introduced by the joke body. A second study (Goldstein, 1970) suggested that the complexity of a joke affects the time it takes an individual to respond to a joke, with more complex jokes involving longer response times. The next sections will describe several MMDS models and then will discuss their relevance in the development of a theory of humor.

METRIC MULTIDIMENSIONAL MODELS
OF COGNITION

Metric multidimensional models of cognition have been developed by Woelfel and his associates (see Woelfel & Saltiel, 1978; Woelfel, Cody, Gillham, & Holmes, 1980; Woelfel & Fink, 1980) and have been developed further by Kaplowitz and Fink (1982, 1983). These models make assumptions about both the structure and the dynamics of cognition that are relevant to humor.

The Structure of Cognition

Metric multidimensional models of cognition all assume that (1) concepts can be represented as being located in a multidimensional cognitive space; and (2) the greater the perceived dissimilarity between two concepts, the greater their spatial separation.

Such spatial models of cognition have been criticized by Tversky (1977) and Tversky and Gati (1982) on the grounds that empirical data on perceived similarities among concepts sometimes fail to satisfy the axioms of a Euclidean space (axioms that appear to be satisfied by physical space). Of greatest relevance to us is violation of the triangular inequality axiom. This axiom holds that if d(i,j) is the distance between i and j, then for any three points, A, B, and C, d(A,B) + d(B,C) ≥ d(A,C).

While Tversky and his associates regard violation of the triangular inequality as a fatal flaw of spatial models, we do not. First, we argue that violations of the triangular inequality do not destroy possibilities of mathematical representation of the space. Second, we argue that such violations are substantively important for understanding cognition in general and for humor in particular.

Woelfel and his associates (Woelfel & Fink, 1980; Woelfel & Barnett, 1982) acknowledge violations of the triangular inequality but show that such configuration can be represented by means of imaginary dimensions (much as Einsteinian general relativity treats time as an imaginary dimen-

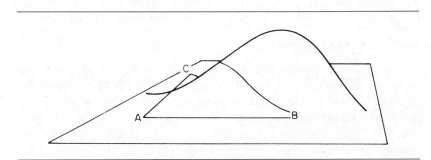

Figure 3.4.   Three points on a curved Riemann surface. From *The Measurement of Communication Processes: Galileo Theory and Method* by J. Woelfel and E. L. Fink. Reprinted by permission of Academic Press. Copyright © 1980 by Academic Press, Inc.

sion in space-time). A space with imaginary dimensions is called a "warped Reimannian manifold." Such a space is drawn in Figure 3.4.

An alternative approach to such representation assumes that the space itself is Euclidean but that the distances reported may be misinterpreted. The spatial structure is typically created from the interconcept distances on the assumption that either the concepts are points or the distances between concepts are distances from the center of one concept to the center of the other. Kaplowitz and Fink (1983), however, suggest that concepts are best represented as regions that encompass all of the meanings and attributes of a concept (hence regions of different size) and that reported distances may not be center to center. In particular, when subjects report d(A,B), they may be reporting distances from a different point within the region defined by concept A than the point within concept A that they use when measuring d(A,C).

Whether the space is genuinely warped or only apparently warped is not, however, crucial to our current concerns. What concerns us is the cause and the consequences of violations of the triangle inequality. It appears that violations of the triangle inequality tend to occur when we examine concepts that contain two or more highly dissimilar attributes or meanings. As an example of the former, Tversky (1977) notes that

> Jamaica is similar to Cuba (because of geographic proximity); Cuba is similar to Russia (because of their political affinity); but Jamaica and Russia are not similar at all (1977, p.329).

Thus Jamaica and Cuba would be located close together, Cuba and Russia would be located close together, and Jamaica and Russia would be located far apart. As an example of the latter, Woelfel and Fink (1980) report that the distance between Red and Tangerine is greater than the distance between Red and Orange plus the distance between Orange and Tangerine.

The Dynamics of Cognition

A number of researchers have used spatial models of cognition as the basis for building dynamic models. Woelfel and his associates regard the message "A is like B" as setting up a cognitive force pushing concepts A and B toward each other in the message recipient's cognitive space. Kaplowitz and Fink (1982) distinguish two different models of this force. Variable mass-impulse models are proposed by Woelfel and his associates and are based on two assumptions: (1) The force created by a message acts like a brief impulse; and (2) messages implicating a concept add inertia to the concept, making it more difficult to accelerate in the future.

Kaplowitz and Fink (1982, 1983) give most of their attention, however, to the development of a spring model. This assumes that a message linking concepts A and B sets up a springlike connection between them. The strength, or restoring coefficient, of this connection is assumed to depend on the recipient's view of the source and the degree to which the message is unexpected. Among the important consequences of this model are that (1) springs created by previous messages serve to anchor a concept to its current location; (2) cognitions may oscillate prior to coming to rest at equilibrium; and (3) stretching or compressing these springlike connections increases the tension within them. This cognitive tension may well be related to the physiological tension we experience.

In sum, a number of potential models might be utilized to represent the cognitive dynamics of humor. We assume that the cognitive response to humor may be explicated by a multidimensional cognitive pattern. Further, it is proposed that joke messages are like other messages that have been modeled with multidimensional cognitive theory; thus joke messages should act like forces to bring together concepts that are not necessarily viewed as similar. By mapping the response to a joke in a multidimensional space as that response occurs over time, we can see the motion of concepts as a result of the cognitive processing of humor.

Relevance of MMDS Models
for the Study of Humor

The first section of this chapter discussed several basic principles common to many humor theories. One of these principles is that the response to humor occurs in stages and/or over time. Although several researchers have proposed spatial representations of such a process (e.g., Koestler, 1964; Paulos, 1980), there has been no empirical test of the dynamic aspects of the response to humor. We propose that the use of MMDS models would enable us to see the change in a cognitive *configuration* in space and over time.

Returning to the MMDS models, recall that concepts are assumed to have location and mass in a cognitive space. Thus the concepts that are presented in a joke body can be mapped with regard to how far apart (or dissimilar) they are. Following the spring model, we could consider a joke as a force that establishes connections between the concepts implicated in the joke body. Many jokes rely on the use of words that have multiple meanings (as, for example, puns), and the joke body usually suggests which meaning of the word is to be understood. As the individual seeks to make sense out of or to solve the joke, there may be accompanying tension in the cognitive springs. Concepts implicated in the joke body may thus be pulled closer together. With the joke resolution, the concepts may change their location with respect to each other, as there is a sudden realization that another meaning of the joke's focal concept is to be understood. The joke resolution may also lead to a released tension in the springlike connections between the concepts.

The location and motion of concepts may occur in a Euclidean space, or it may involve a warping of the cognitive space. The next section of this chapter will discuss models that might represent the cognitive processing of humor. All of these models are testable, given that the location and motion of concepts prior to the presentation of a joke body, following the joke body presentation, and following the joke resolution can all be determined and the violation of the triangle inequality assumption can also be measured.

A second issue we discussed indicated that timing, or the amount of time between the presentation of the joke body and the joke resolution, may be important in determining the magnitude of the response to a humorous message. Theorists and comedians alike have focused on *suddenness* as a prerequisite for humor. This suddenness has been described variously as a "sudden release," a "sudden reversal," a "sudden recognition," or a "sudden realization." Holland (1982), who considers playfulness and suddenness the principal conditions for humor, states: "As early as the 16th century people began to point to the suddenness, unexpected, and surprise as indispensable prerequisites of laughter" (p. 32). Further, Holland suggests that "joking gives us pleasure by converting a conscious process full of energy and tension into an easy unconscious process" (p. 49).

Morreall (1983) suggests that humor involves a conceptual shift and that time can be related to that conceptual shift in the following way:

> Suddenness in a psychological change, then is a function of the amount of change (the difference between the earlier state and the later) and the time over which the change takes place. For a sudden change there must be a relatively large distance between the two states, and the time separating the states must be relatively short. If the time is short, but the change is small, then the change is not sudden, for the person can assimilate what is happening. And if the change is great but the time is also great, here too the rate of change is slow; the person can adjust smoothly to what is happening, and there is no "jolt." Knowing in advance that a certain change is about to take place, as we said, has the same effect in reducing suddenness as spreading the change over more time, for the person who is expecting a certain change has already started to adjust to it. (p. 49)

Recall that both Paulos and Koestler spatially represented the sudden change in the cognitive system due to the humor response. Koestler's (1964) representation is the "explosion" of the joke concepts on two planes simultaneously (see Figure 3.1). Paulos's (1980) representation was a "drop" from one surface to another (see Figure 3.3). However, neither Paulos's nor Koestler's representation provides a mathematical framework in which to examine the existence of the explosion, the drop, or any other sudden change *quantitatively*.

The use of the MMDS model, however, allows us to examine the relationship of timing to the cognitive response to humor. If we describe the change in the cognitive configuration represented by these models as a conceptual shift, we can relate time, or timing, to the models by manipulating the amount of time that lapses between presentation of the joke body and presentation of the joke resolution, and measuring the time between the latter and "getting" the joke. Significant differences in the amount or direction of the shift across the timing conditions would enable us to see the effects of timing. Further, correlations can be computed between various self-report affective measures and differences in timing conditions.

Parallels between Humor and Cognitive Research on Attitude Change

Many studies of humor (e.g., Deckers & Kizer, 1975; Deckers, Jenkins, & Gladfelter, 1977; Deckers & Devine, 1981; Nerhardt, 1970) have associated humor with the difference between the observed and the expected. Nerhardt (1970) found that the greater the divergence of a perceived event (or message) from an expected event (or message), the greater the laughter. A later study by Nerhardt (1975) supported his earlier findings and suggested there is an inverted U-shaped relationship between the ratings of funniness and the divergence from expectancy.

Deckers and Kizer (1975) asked subjects to compare a standard weight with a comparison weight. An incongruity was established between an expected comparison and a critical comparison. Deckers and Kizer found that the greater the number of times the subjects lifted the expected comparison before lifting the critical comparison, the greater the divergence from expectancy and the greater the frequency of laughter.

In attitude change research, some researchers have used a variable that parallels the notion of incongruity used by Nerhardt (1970, 1975) and others. For example, Kaplowitz and Fink (1982, 1983) regard degree of disconfirmation of the message expected from a source[3] as a critical variable for predicting attitude change, and some empirical research (e.g., Wood & Eagly, 1981) supports this claim. Kaplowitz and Fink (1982, 1983) predict that (1) attitude change will be zero both when disconfirmation is zero and when it is infinite, and (2) that there is a nonmonotonic relationship between message disconfirmation and attitude change. This prediction is similar to the humor theorists' claim that there is an inverted U-shaped relationship between humor and expectancy.

Regarding the incongruity as the difference between the actual message and the expected one also helps us to understand why the same message might be funny if stated by one source but not if stated by another. For example, the statement, "Countries will be backward if they are governed by aged leaders whose ideas are firmly fixed in the past," might be funny if stated by Ronald Reagan but not if stated by some other political leader.

Another parallel between attitude change and humor studies is that both consider the effects of prior messages. For example, Kaplowitz and Fink (1982) suggest that information received (and remembered) prior to the reception of a message serves to strengthen the anchoring of the concepts. In humor research, Wilson (1979, p. 66) suggests that a "priming message" may serve to vary the level of the incongruity of a message. To understand the role a priming message plays, consider that some jokes (particularly those involving puns) juxtapose two separate and apparently inconsistent meanings of a focal concept. The joke builds up the expectancy that one of the meanings is to be considered. The punch line then indicates that the other, previously unconsidered meaning is being implicated. Wilson (1979, p. 66) created four levels of initial incongruity through the manipulation of expectancy. Subjects were primed with either synonyms of words in the joke, synonyms of words in the punch line, synonyms of words in both the body and punch line, or with neutral words. Wilson reported that the initial level of incongruity had "an extremely potent" influence on the funniness ratings; a curvilinear relation between the funniness ratings and the initial level of incongruity was found.

The work of the attitude change theorists and the humor researchers suggests that the inclusion of a message, such as a priming message, prior to the presentation of a joke message may strengthen the expectation that one or another meaning is to be understood from the joke body. A priming message will be defined as a message that serves to move or locate an implicated focal concept toward an expected meaning or interpretation and away from the unexpected meaning as revealed by the joke punch line. As an example, consider the following joke:

Q: Why do mice have small balls?
A: Because very few of them can dance.

A priming message is one that would locate or move the concept "balls" (the focal concept) toward the concept "testicles." An example might be "that guy has really got balls." The priming message should significantly affect the cognitive response to humor.

This section has described several multidimensional models of cognition; one of these models, the spring model, might aid in the description and explanation of the cognitive response to humor. This model assumes that concepts have location and mass in a cognitive space, and that messages act like forces to move concepts in that space. We propose that the concepts implicated in a joke (such as a pun) can be located in a multidimensional space, and that the parts of a joke (joke body and joke resolution) will act like forces to change the location of those concepts with respect to each other. Thus the use of an MMDS model will allow us to test the implications of both cognitive and affective approaches to humor; we may evaluate the cognitive dynamics of humor by looking at these changes over time in models that make explicit assumptions as to the cognitive forces involved in these changes.

The next section further develops the use of MMDS by proposing different models that might be used to examine the cognitive dynamics of humor.

THE APPLICATION OF MMDS MODELS
TO HUMOR

The previous section suggested that the concepts within jokes could be mapped in an MMDS space. If we consider the messages presented in the joke body and joke resolution as forces that cause these concepts to change their location, we could examine the cognitive representation of joke concepts prior to the presentation of a joke (t_0), after the presentation of a joke body but before the presentation of the punch line (t_1), and after the presentation of the joke punch line (t_2).

Suppose that with the telling of the joke body, concepts implicated in the joke body move from some initial positions in the cognitive space (P_1) to a new location in the space (P_2). After arriving at the new location, however, the joke resolution is presented and the concepts are pulled to a different location $(P_3,$ which could be the same as $P_1)$. Thus there will be a difference in the location of concepts from time t_0 (prior to joke body), t_1 (following presentation of the joke body but prior to the presentation of the joke resolution), and t_2 (following presentation of the joke resolution).[4] This leads to the presentation of several hypotheses common to all of our models.

First, because the message in the joke body acts like a force to move concepts closer together, if the focal concept is a word with more than one meaning (as in a pun), we hypothesize as follows:

> H_1: The presentation of a joke body (t_1) will cause concepts implicated in the joke body to move closer in the cognitive space than they would be in the absence of the joke body presentation (t_0).

The punch line serves as a force to move other concepts closer together. In particular, the focal concept in a joke is moved from the location implied by the joke body to the unexpected location implied by the punch line. Thus we hypothesize:

H_2: The presentation of a joke body and punch line (t_2) will cause concepts implicated in the joke punch line to move closer in the cognitive space than they would be in the absence of a punch line presentation (t_1).

Third, if we assume that each joke component acts like a force to pull concepts closer together, a priming message will also serve to move concepts (those implicated in the priming message) closer together than they would be located in the absence of a priming message. Stated formally:

H_3: The presentation of a priming message will move the concepts implicated in the priming message closer together in the cognitive space than they would be in the absence of a priming message.

Finally, we need to consider the effect of adding a priming message to a joke body. It is possible that a priming message moves the concept with double meaning implicated in the joke (the focal concept) even closer to the "wrong" meaning implied by the joke body than it would be in the absence of a priming message. This leads to a fourth hypothesis:

H_4: The presentation of a priming message with a joke body will cause concepts implicated in both messages to move closer together in the cognitive space than they would be in the absence of a priming message.

Next, presuming again that the motion of concepts does occur, we need to consider the effect of this motion on humor. Recall that the humor literature suggests that there is a suddenness requirement for humor to occur. The models that will be presented next consider how this suddenness produces a humorous response.

The Feint Model of Humor

All of the versions of the feint model consider that the joke body may serve as a feint, or trick. This moves concepts implicated in a direction that the punch line shows to be the wrong direction.

The distance variant. This variant of the feint model assumes that the joke body causes humor by increasing the *distance* between a focal concept and the meaning implied in the joke resolution. This variant has implications for the relation between the time from the joke body to the joke resolution and the amount of humor. Too short a time would not allow for the concept to reach the wrong place and hence should reduce the humor associated with the joke by reducing the distance between the right and wrong cognitive places. Too much time might also reduce the amount of humor, if during the delay other forces (such as those provided by the cognitive responses due to the individual's attempt to resolve the joke) pull the focal concept toward P_3 (the resolution position). Stated formally as a hypothesis:

H_5: The magnitude of humor associated with a joke will be curvilinearly related to the size of the time interval between t_1 and t_2; the curve will have an inverted U-shape.

The priming message should not reduce the humor, but if hypothesis 4 is supported, then the priming message might increase the humor in that the distance between the wrong and right places should be even greater. This suggests the following:

H_6: There will be more humor associated with a joke when a priming message precedes it than when a priming message does not; this humor should occur more rapidly than in the absence of a priming message.

The acceleration variant. This variant of the feint model suggests that it is the acceleration the moving concepts exhibit that serves to create the condition for the humorous response. First, assume that shortly after the presentation of the joke body, the concepts are moving at some velocity. Second, assume that with a long delay, or with a priming message, the focal concept has come to a rest (or close to rest), as opposed to having *just* arrived at the "wrong" place (the meaning implied by the joke body) and still moving in the "wrong" direction. Since acceleration is defined as the change in velocity over time, a focal concept that is still moving in the wrong direction will require a greater acceleration in order to head in the opposite direction than will a focal concept that has been at rest.[5] A small delay between t_1 and t_2 will also result in a lower magnitude of humor, since the focal concept has not yet had time to accelerate enough in the wrong direction. If the priming message causes the focal concept to arrive at its new location earlier, that concept may be at or near rest at the time of the punch line. Hence, contrary to the distance variant, which predicted (H_6) that the priming message will increase humor, this variant predicts the opposite.

H_7: There will be less humor when the joke body is preceded by a priming message than when there is no priming message.

The jerk variant. A third variant of the feint model is the jerk variant. "Jerk" is the first derivative of acceleration; this version suggests that the rate of change in acceleration causes the humor. Assume that with a long delay, or with a priming message, the focal concept has come to a rest, while with a shorter delay the focal concept is still, as a result of the force from the message, accelerating in the wrong direction. The shorter delay (without a priming message) will result in a greater jerk, and hence a greater level of humor, than if a long delay or a priming message were given.

In both the acceleration and jerk variants, but not the distance variant, the maximum amount of humor arises from a sudden reversal in direction. These variants lead to an additional hypothesis:

H_8: The greater the angle between the $t_1 - t_2$ motion of the focal concept and the $t_2 - t_3$ motion of the focal concept, the greater the magnitude of humor associated with a joke. (The angle will be restricted to be between 0° and 180°).

The three variants of the feint model have very different implications as to the optimal time lag. The distance variant suggests that enough time be alloted for the focal concept to make the entire journey to its new location, P_2. The acceleration variant suggests that the joke resolution should occur when the focal concept has reached its maximum velocity in the wrong direction (i.e., on its way toward P_2). For an undamped oscillatory trajectory, this maximum is reached halfway between the two extreme points of the trajectory, which are P_1 and P_2. (For a damped system, the maximum is reached before the halfway point.) For the jerk variant, humor is maximized if the joke body occurs when acceleration in the wrong direction is at a maximum. This occurs as the joke body is just beginning to move the focal concept toward P_2. (For equations and graphs that suggest why the points that have just been made are true, see Kaplowitz & Fink, 1982.)

In short, of the three variants, the distance variant suggests the greatest time lag for optimal humor and the jerk variant suggests that the optimal time lag is extremely small, a prediction that makes the jerk variant seem rather questionable.

The Resonance Model

Juxtaposing the fact that timing is important to humor with an oscillating spring model of cognition suggests another possible process. Humor may be maximized if the punch line resonates with the oscillatory motion set up by the joke body and/or priming message.

The joke body, we assume, sets up a spring that moves the focal concept toward a new location P_2. The focal concept is assumed to be connected to other springs, which anchor it to its original location, P_1. After moving toward P_2, it will oscillate about its new equilibrium and, hence, there should be a point at which it is moved back in the direction of P_1.

Let us suppose, consistent with the feint model, that the punch line moves the focal concept in a direction that is close to 180° from the direction in which it was moving as a result of the joke body. Resonance occurs if the outside force is in phase with the oscillations that are already in process. Hence, resonance is obtained if the punch line comes just at the point at which the focal concept is instantaneously at rest and is changing direction.[6]

How does the resonance model compare with the variants of the feint model? In this model, humor is maximized if the punch line occurs when the velocity of the focal concept is zero and the focal concept is already accelerating in the direction in which the punch line will pull it. Hence, unlike the acceleration or jerk variant, for maximum humor, the velocity and acceleration are decidedly not at maximum values when the punch line occurs. This model is somewhat similar to the distance variant, in that the point of maximum distance is the point at which the focal concept will begin to oscillate back toward P_1. Unlike the distance variant, however, this model does not predict that the increase in distance, which might result from a priming message, enhances humor.

This model does, however, have certain implications as to the relation between incongruity and timing in humor. The optimal delay between the joke body and the punch line is the time it takes for the focal concept to go from its initial location, P_1, to the point at which it starts to oscillate back. The time it takes is one half of a period of oscillation. The period of oscillation of a spring system is a decreasing function of the restoring coefficient of the spring. Kaplowitz and Fink (1982, 1983) moreover, propose that more unexpected, disconfirmatory messages produce springs with smaller restoring coefficients. Hence, we have hypothesis 9:

H_9: The more the joke body disconfirms prior expectations, the larger is the optimal time delay between the joke body and the punch line.

This hypothesis is consistent with Wilson's (1979) findings about the effect of incongruity and timing on humor.

Warp Models

A third set of models are warp models, which propose that the psychological shift that results in humor is due to the sudden warping or dewarping of the space defined by the concepts. We believe that warping results from the realization that the relevant concepts have double meanings and dewarping occurs from the realization that only one of these meanings is relevant.

Just as arousal theories differ as to whether humor is caused by the increase in arousal or the subsequent decrease, so warp models vary as to whether humor results from the creation of, or the disappearance of, the warp. Below we present several variants of the warp model, which differ as to the shape of the space at different points of time in the joke process.

EEN variant of the warp model. This proposes that the space is Euclidean both before and after the joke body but becomes Non-Euclidean with the resolution of the joke. It is based on the assumption that prior to the resolution, only one meaning of the focal concept is being considered. With the presentation of the resolution, however, the individual suddenly sees two meanings for the focal concept at once. Again, utilizing the mice joke, recall that the cognitive space warps when there has been a violation of the triangle inequality assumption that

$$d\,(A,B) + d\,(B,C) \geqslant d\,(A,C).$$

After the presentation of the resolution, the distance between testicles (T) and dance (D) will be great, but the distance between testicles (T) and balls (B) will be small, and the distance between balls (B) and dance (D) will be small. Thus,

$$d\,(T,D) \geqslant d\,(T,B) + d\,(B,D).$$

and the only way this can be represented on a planar surface is if the space warps. In this model, if this warping is sudden, the message is perceived to be humorous.

Hypotheses associated with the warp model can be stated as follows. First, the existence of the warp can be investigated:

H_{10}: When a joke body and its resolution are presented, there will be a greater violation of the triangle inequality for the joke-relevant concepts than when a joke body is presented without a resolution, or when neither joke body nor joke resolution has been presented.

Since we have stated that the sudden warping results in humor, we may also hypothesize about the magnitude of that humor. As Morreal (1983, p. 79) suggests, suddenness is a function of the relatively large distance between two states and the relatively short time separating them. Thus:

H_{11}: The greater the rate and size of the violation of the triangle inequality for joke-relevant concepts, after the resolution, the greater the humor experienced.

ENE variant of the warp model. The second warp variant is the ENE (Euclidean, non-Euclidean, Euclidean) variant. This model proposes that concepts are normally located in a Euclidean space, but with the presentation of the joke body (without resolution) the force of the message causes the focal concept to be viewed ambiguously, creating a non-Euclidean space (one in which we have violations of the triangle inequality). Next, the joke resolution reduces the ambiguity, forcing or directing thought to one particular meaning of the focal concept, and the cognitive space is once more Euclidean. Thus the space could be described as Euclidean at t_0 (prior to joke body), non-Euclidean at t_1 (following joke body but prior to joke resolution), and Euclidean at t_2 (following joke resolution). This suggests the following hypothesis:

> H_{12}: Joke-relevant concepts will be located in a non-Euclidean space following the presentation of a joke body and prior to the presentation of a joke resolution, but in a Euclidean space at other times.

Further,

> H_{13}: The greater the change in the size of the violation of the trangle inequality for joke-relevant concepts between joke body and joke resolution, the greater the magnitude of humor.

NEN variant of the warp model. This variant suggests that the space begins as non-Euclidean, become Euclidean at t_1 (with joke body presentation), and returns to non-Euclidean at t_2 (with joke resolution). For example, perhaps concepts are ordinarily located in a space that takes in all meanings of a focal concept simultaneously. The joke body then serves to *reduce* the ambiguity. Using the mice joke as an example, we would find that balls, testicles, and dance are represented in a non-Euclidean space prior to the presentation of the joke body. The joke body then directs thought to one meaning of the word "balls" (testicles), and the resulting configuration is represented in a Euclidean space. Presenting this as a hypothesis:

> H_{14}: When a joke body is presented, there will be a smaller violation of the triangle inequality than there will be without the joke body presentation.

The resolution, however, reminds the receiver that there is more than one meaning for the focal concept (here, the word "balls"); thus the joke-relevant concepts return to a non-Euclidean space. If this change is sudden, the receiver will find the joke humorous. In any case, the degree of warp associated with the joke resolution should be greater than that associated with the joke body. The NEN model is consistent with hypothesis 10 presented earlier for the EEN model, and with hypothesis 13; however, the NEN variant posits that the change in the size of the violations of the triangle inequality is

Table 3.1
Comparison of Some Different Warp
Models as to the Geometry of the
Cognitive Space Represented

| | Time | | |
Model	Before Joke Body (t_0)	After Joke Body (t_1)	After Resolution (t_2)
EEN	Euclidean	Euclidean	non-Euclidean
ENE	Euclidean	non-Euclidean	Euclidean
NEN	non-Euclidean	Euclidean	non-Euclidean

in the opposite direction from that proposed by the ENE variant. Table 3.1 lists the warp models that have been proposed and shows how they differ with regard to the geometry of the cognitive space at different times in the joke's unfolding.

SUMMARY AND FUTURE RESEARCH

This chapter has presented some of the assumptions and hypotheses that are shared by both cognitive and affective orientations to humor and that have yet to be tested empirically. One of these assumptions was that the response to humor is dynamic, and that the timing between the presentation of the joke segments (i.e., joke body and joke resolution) is important in determining the magnitude and type of response to humor. We next discussed MMDS models of cognition and suggested ways in which these models might be utilized to specify and test some aspects of humor. Next, we developed three models that might be utilized to represent the cognitive dynamics of humor. These were the feint model, which had distance, acceleration, and jerk variants; the resonance model; and the three variants of a warp model.

We have raised several questions for future research by posing hypotheses derived from our MMDS models. Below are some additional questions that have been posed regarding humor and that await translation into our MMDS models; space precludes our elaboration here.

(1) We have discussed humor of a particular kind—that induced by incongruity. To what extent may all humor (e.g., sexual, aggressive) be so modeled? Can all differences in humorous stimuli be modeled using the tools we have provided?

(2) How may we represent the cognitive processing involved in attempting to get the joke? Is this cognitive Brownian motion, or is something more systematic occurring?

(3) What are the developmental implications of our model? Children's humor appreciation is different from that of adults; how may the models reflect this?

(4) How can these models be used to explain the process of humor creation, as opposed to humor appreciation?

(5) Do the models successfully reflect individual differences in humor appreciation? The spring model implies that all individual differences reflect differences in concepts, their locations relative to other concepts, strength of linkages to these other concepts, and cognitive friction. Can all individual differences be translated into these elements?

Considering the cognitive processing of humor in a multi-dimensional framework allowed us to develop precise and clear models. It is possible that one of the models fully explains humor. It is possible that humor results from some combination of the processes discussed. It is possible that one of the process models best explains the humor response in one kind of joke and another model best explains humor in other kinds. And it is possible that none of the models discussed is ever correct. But in any case, we have now moved beyond verbal theory and have constructed testable alternatives by using a physicalistic analogy. More research is needed, and so is more theory (e.g., full development of a tension release model of humor). We hope we have contributed to the latter.

NOTES

1. Although humor and laughter have been of interest for many centuries, only within the present century have *empirical* studies been reported, and most of these have been within the last twenty years. Prior to this time the study of humor has been basically philosophical supposition.

2. Although purported connections between these communication functions and humor have been made, evidence to support such assumptions is as inconclusive as the basic humor theory research. For example, although politicians and advertisers often suggest that humor enhances persuasion, research suggests that humor does not significantly influence persuasion (Markiewicz, 1974).

3. What we now call disconfirmation was called discrepancy by Kaplowitz and Fink (1982).

4. This assumes that the joke is "gotten."

5. Note also that both the variable mass impulse model and the spring model suggest that priming messages should make the focal concept more resistant to acceleration—the former by changing its mass and the latter by increasing its connections to other concepts.

6. In an empirical test of a spring model of cognition, Kaplowitz, Fink, and Bauer (1983) found the period of oscillation to be 13.5 seconds. Half of this is 6.75 seconds, which is not far from some of the longer time lags used by Wilson (1979).

REFERENCES

Barnett, G. A., & Woelfel, J. (1979). On the dimensionality of psychological processes. *Quality and Quantity, 13*, 215-232.

Bateson, G. (1952). The role of humor in human communication. In C. Von Foerster (Ed.), *Cybernetics*. New York: Josiah Macy, Jr. Foundation.

Berlyne, D. E. (1960). *Conflict, arousal, and curiosity*. New York: McGraw-Hill.

Clark, M. (1970). Humor and incongruity. *Philosophy: Journal of the Royal Institute of Philosophy, 45*, 20-32.

Deckers, L., & Devine, J. (1981). Humor by violating an existing expectancy.*Journal of Psychology, 108*, 107-110.

Deckers, L., Jenkins, S., & Gladfelter, E. (1977). Incongruity versus tension relief. *Motivation and Emotion, 1*, 261-272.

Deckers, L., & Kizer, P. (1975). Humor and the incongruity hypotheseis. *Journal of Psychology, 90*, 215-218.

Eastman, M. (1936). *Enjoyment of laughter*. New York: Simon & Schuster.

Eysenck, H. J. (1942). The appreciation of humor: An experimental and theoretical study. *British Journal of Psychology, 32*, 205-309.

Freud, S. (1960). *Jokes and their relation to the unconscious*. New York: W. W. Norton.

Fry, W. F. (1963). *Sweet madness: A study of humor*. Palo Alto, CA: Pacific Books.

Godkewitsch, M. (1974). Verbal, exploratory and physiological responses to stimulus properties underlying humor. Unpublished Ph.D. thesis, University of Toronto.

Godkewitsch, M. (1976a). Thematic and collative properties of written jokes and their contribution to funniness. *Canadian Journal of Behavioral Science, 8*, 88-97.

Godkewitsch, M. (1976b). Physiological and verbal indices of arousal in rated humor. In A. J. Chapman & H. C. Foot (Eds.), *Humor and laughter: Theory, research, and applications*. London: Wiley.

Goldstein, J. H. (1970). Humor appreciation and time to respond. *Psychological Reports, 27*, 445-446.

Goldstein, J. H., Harman, J., McGhee, P., & Karasik, R. (1975). Test of an information processing model of humor: Physiological response changes during problem and riddle-solving. *Journal of General Psychology, 92*, 59-68.

Holland, N. N. (1982). *Laughing: A psychology of humor*. New York: Cornell University Press.

Kant, I. (1952). *Critique of judgment* (1790). Chicago: University of Chicago Press.

Kaplowitz, S. A., & Fink, E. L. (1982). Attitude change and attitudinal trajectories: A dynamic multidimensional theory. In M. Burgoon (Ed.), *Communication yearbook 6*. Beverly Hills, CA: Sage.

Kaplowitz S. A., & Fink, E. L. (1983). Source-message-receiver relations and attitude change: A dynamic multidimensional theory. Unpublished manuscript, Michigan State University.

Kaplowitz, S. A., Fink, E. L., & Bauer, C. L. (1983). A dynamic model of the effect of discrepant information on unidimensional attitude change. *Behavioral Science, 28*, 233-250.

Kenny, D. J. (1955). The contingency of humor appreciation on the stimulus confirmation of joke ending expectations. *Journal of Abnormal and Social Psychology, 51*, 644-664.

Koestler, A. (1964). *The act of creation*. New York: Dell.

Markiewicz, D. (1974). The effect of humor on persuasion. *Sociometry, 37*, 407-422.

McGhee, P. F. (1979). *Humor: Its origin and development*. San Francisco: W. H. Freeman.

Morreall, J. (1983). *Taking laughter seriously*. Albany: State University of New York Press.

Nerhardt, G. (1970). Humor and inclination to laugh: Emotional reactions to stimuli of different divergence from a range of expectancy. *Scandinavian Journal of Psychology, 11*, 185-195.

Nerhardt, G. (1975). Rated funniness and dissimilarity of figures: Divergence from expectancy. *Scandinavian Journal of Psychology, 16*, 156-166.

Paulos, J. A. (1980). *Mathematics and humor*. Chicago: University of Chicago Press.

Saltiel, J., & Woelfel, J. (1975). Inertia in cognitive processes: The role of accumulated information in attitude change. *Human Communication Research, 1*, 333-344.

Schmidt, N. E., & Williams, D. J. (1971). The evolution of theories of humor. *Journal of Behavioral Science, 1,* 95-106.

Shurcliff, A. (1968). Judged humor, arousal, and the relief theory. *Journal of Personality and Social Psychology, 8,* 1-14.

Suls, J. M. (1972). A two-stage model for the appreciation of jokes and cartoons: An information processing analysis. In J. H. Goldstein & P. E. McGhee (Eds.), *The psychology of humor.* New York: Academic Press.

Tversky, A. (1977). Features of similarity. *Psychological Review, 84,* 327-352.

Tversky, A., & Gati, I. (1982). Similarity, separability, and the triangle inequality. *Psychological Review, 89,* 123-154.

Wicker, F. W., Thorelli, J. M., Barron, W. L., & Ponder, M. R. (1981). Relationships among affective and cognitive factors in humor. *Journal of Research in Personality, 15,* 359-370.

Wilson, C. P. (1979). *Jokes: Form, content, use and function.* New York: Academic Press.

Woelfel, J., & Barnett, G. A. (1982). Multidimensional scaling in Riemann space. *Quality and Quantity, 16,* 469-491.

Woelfel, J., Cody, M., Gillham, J., & Holmes, R. (1980). Basic premises of multidimensional attitude change theory. *Human Communication Research, 6,* 153-167.

Woelfel, J., & Fink, E. L. (1980). *The measurement of communication processes: Galileo theory and method.* New York: Academic Press.

Woelfel, J., & Saltiel, J. (1978). Cognitive processes as motions in a multidimensional space. In F. Casimer (Ed.), *International and intercultural communication.* New York: University Press.

Wood, W., & Eagly, A. (1981). Stages in the analysis of persuasive messages: The role of causal inferences and message confirmation. *Journal of Personality and Social Psychology, 40,* 246-259.

4 ● The Second Electronic Revolution: The Computer and Children

WILLIAM PAISLEY ● MILTON CHEN

Stanford University

INTERACTIVE MEDIA TODAY

The "New Literacy"

The "first electronic revolution" of radio and television undermined literacy as the foundation of learning by providing (or, often, seeming to provide) preliterate children and nonliterate adults with knowledge that had been sealed from them in books. Paradoxically, the "second electronic revolution" of interactive media (microcomputers, videotex, interactive cable, and so on) depends *more* on literacy than even traditional print media. Unlike radio and television, the interactive media do not promise learning without literacy. They will not be expected to close the "knowledge gap" between literate and nonliterate populations. They will probably widen the "knowledge gap," and the advantages they provide to users will certainly raise questions of equity.

It is also possible, however, that early exposure to interactive media, which are gamelike in many of their applications, may motivate children to acquire cognitive skills and knowledge, including both reading literacy and computer literacy, at an earlier age. This chapter focuses on the personal, social, and technological factors that may affect children's learning from interactive media.

Although interactive media will be common in schools by the end of this decade, many of the installed systems on which we now base our observations are found in homes. Typical teletext, videotext, and interactive cable

Correspondence and requests for reprints: Milton Chen, Institute for Communication Research, Stanford University, Stanford, CA 94305.

systems serve middle-class homes in cities such as Los Angeles, Columbus, Philadelphia, Dallas, and Salt Lake City. The most widely publicized systems, such as QUBE in Columbus, find the majority of their subscribers in well-educated, information-rich homes where the additional benefits of interactive media are hard to distinguish from the many educational advantages that the children already enjoy. Microcomputer homes are also skewed toward higher education and socioeconomic status (SES).

There are exceptions to this pattern of diffusion. For example, the USDA-sponsored Green Thumb Box videotext system operated in 200 representative farm homes in Kentucky during 1980 and 1981. Stanford researchers who were charged with evaluating Green Thumb had an opportunity to observe use of the videotext system in low-SES as well as high-SES homes (Paisley, 1983).

Children in low-SES homes have had access to interactive media in several other sites. These include, for example, Channel 2000 (Viewtel) in Columbus, Ohio; WETA Teletext and the Capital Children's Museum in Washington, D.C.; KCET Teletext in Los Angeles, California; and, more anonymously, microcomputer learning centers in an increasing number of schools.

Children's use of interactive media is a new phenomenon. Except by analogy to the previous era of research on television, we lack a theoretical framework for designing research on the effects of the new media on children. A new theoretical framework must take account of the *diversity of systems and settings* that constitute children's exposure to the new media. It must take account of *user-directed interaction* rather than "viewing behavior." And it must take account of the high *ratio of information to entertainment content* that characterizes the new media.

Microcomputers

In the aggregate, it is safe to say that children spend far more time with microcomputers than with other interactive media. Microcomputers are making their way into homes and classrooms at an impressive pace. By early 1983, more than 5 million microcomputers had been sold nationally, at least half of them to homes ("The Computer Moves in," 1983). School purchases totaled more than 100,000 (compared with 52,000 by mid-1980), for a national average of 1 computer for every 400 students. Minnesota leads the nation in school adoption of microcomputers, with 1 for every 50 students.

Accompanying the increasing rate of diffusion of computers is a dramatic decrease in cost. Full-featured 64K microcomputers are being sold in 1983 at less than $200. A complete microcomputer system, capable of performing the work of a $25,000 minicomputer of ten years ago, now costs less than $1,000.

Microcomputers are the most amorphous of the interactive media described in this chapter. Except in limiting cases, their possible applications are not dictated by their design. They are the chameleons of the new media; they take on the coloration of the software that is used with them. To describe microcomputers beyond minimal engineering specifications, one must describe their software.

Most microcomputer software used by children falls into the categories of games and instruction. It is widely agreed that "first-generation" software for children was poor. The games were violent and unimaginative; the instructional programs did not teach, but merely drilled existing knowledge.

A new genre of software has begun to emerge, sometimes called "discovery" software, which takes advantage of the motivating features of games to teach or to facilitate self-expression with words, pictures, or music. The second generation of software for children can be dated from the introduction of the best known of the discovery programs, LOGO.

Good software and inviting settings are combined in the Computer Gallery at each of the Sesame Place theme parks now opening in Pennsylvania, Texas, and other states. The Children's Television Workshop (CTW), creator of Sesame Place, has designed more than 70 educational games to run on specially adapted microcomputers in each park's Computer Gallery. CTW's oversize, alphabetically organized keyboard simplifies use by younger children. Several of CTW's games feature the *Sesame Street* Muppets. For example, in a recognition game the child guesses the Muppet's identity as the screen slowly resolves the features of a Muppet face. Some of the CTW-Sesame Place programs have now been released for public sale.

The Capital Children's Museum in Washington, D.C., is another example of an inviting setting in which children can become familiar with microcomputers. The museum has established a Future Center, in which use of the computers is free. A staff of teenagers offers classes in computer literacy and programming for students ranging from 3-year-olds to adults. During free hours, children can come to the center, play learning games, and even write games of their own. During many sessions, parents accompany their children for a rare educational experience in which both parents and children acquire new skills together.

The Bank Street College of Education in New York City combines a research and teacher-training facility with the real-world testing ground of a private elementary school. In 1980, the college established a Center for Children and Technology with the purpose of studying the role of various educational media in the lives of children. Three of their projects are especially relevant to an understanding of the educational potential of microcomputers. One is a study of how children acquire programming skills in LOGO and how such skills are related to other cognitive and social abilities.

A second area of research involves the effects of the use of word processors on children's writing. A third Bank Street project joins an established educational technology with the more recent technology of the microcomputer. The Project in Science and Mathematics Education combines a television series for elementary schoolchildren with microcomputer exercises and simulations.

Bank Street researchers have observed that computer activities elicit more collaboration and peer interaction than other types of classroom tasks. Their research is also directed toward understanding the social context of computer use in classrooms and how computer interactions differ from other classroom work.

Teletext Systems

During the brief history of electronic text transmission (see, for example, Bloom, Hanson, Linfield, & Wortendyke, 1980), the terms "videotex," "videotext," and "teletext" have been used inconsistently. Conventionally, "videotex" encompasses both broadcast and "wired" transmission. Videotex is distinguished from broadcast or cable transmission of camera images, which are not textual, and from microcomputer displays, which are not transmitted.

"Teletext," or broadcast videotex, refers to text transmitted during the vertical blanking interval of a television signal, although teletext is also transmitted in dedicated channels such as FM subcarriers. Teletext "frames" are broadcast in a constantly repeated sequence; the number of frames is limited by the length of time the sequence takes to repeat, since the user must wait for a given frame to be broadcast before it can be "captured" by the teletext decoder and displayed on the screen. At a transmission rate of about five frames per second (high-resolution frames take longer), one thousand frames constitute a maximum sequence. In order to minimize waiting time for popular frames, these are broadcast two or more times in each sequence.

The typical content of a teletext system reflects the content resources that are available to broadcasters as teletext operators. News (including sports, weather, and financial information), timetables and event calendars, directories, advertisements, and shopping catalogs are the preferred content of a teletext system because they are concise, widely used, and in some cases profitable.

Despite teletext's limitations, there are compensating features, particularly for children's use. The teletext user does not need to establish a telephone or cable connection before accessing frames of text; the teletext signal is already available at the television receiver, ready to be decoded and displayed. Furthermore, since teletext is a child of the mass media, it is acquiring much of the slickness and accessibility of its parents. At their best, teletext frames are well written and colorfully illustrated. Their brevity makes them attractive to children.

KCET, the Los Angeles PBS station, has introduced the NOW! teletext service using Antiope technology from France. KCET transmits from 60 to 80 pages of text each day, including news, sports, weather, book and movie reviews, an entertainment guide, financial trends, and two children's features. During the trial period, decoders were placed in 100 homes, 6 schools, and about 15 public sites throughout Los Angeles. The 100 homes participated in an ongoing study of teletext usage. Meters attached to the television sets recorded the time, channel, and teletext pages accessed.

KCET's feature for in-home viewing by children is called Popsicle. Broadcast during after-school hours, Popsicle provides information, quizzes, and children's activities. The feature for in-school viewing, Think Shop, is often keyed to two instructional programs broadcast by KCET. Formative research conducted in the six schools participating in the Think Shop trial indicates that the series has positive effects on students' motivation and learning. Think Shop primarily is used in three ways:

(1) *Teaching current events:* Students read news stories appearing in NOW! and answer questions posed by Think Shop. Quizzes take advantage of the system's "reveal button." When the button is pressed, answers appear on the screen next to the questions.

(2) *Reinforcing instructional programs:* After viewing a KCET television program, students work on exercises broadcast over Think Shop.

(3) *Enriching the curriculum:* Stand-alone units have been developed, often at teachers' request, to address topics such as handicapped awareness, space exploration, and computer literacy.

WETA, the PBS station in Washington, conducted a teletext trial utilizing the Canadian Telidon system. The Alternate Media Center of New York University provided implementation, software, and research support. Beginning in 1981, WETA teletext was made available to 40 selected households and 10 public sites, including the public library, the Capital Children's Museum, the Smithsonian Institution, and the Jewish Community Center.

About 120 pages were sent daily with the WETA broadcast signal, using 4 lines of the vertical blanking interval. Of the 120, about 80-90 were new each day; the rest were weekly features. The service was organized in 9 categories: news, weather, money, sports, library, entertainment, consumer comparison shopping, a special feature, and consumer news. Providers of pages included the *Washington Post,* the National Weather Service, a consumer advocacy group called Consumer Checkbook, the District of Columbia Public Library, and the Capital Children's Museum. The last two contributed pages for the Saturday children's feature, which has included information on collecting postcards, making puppets, dinosaurs, book reviews, and local events for children.

The Alternate Media Center's research design included in-home interviews with the 40 randomly selected user households, diaries kept by each family on their usage, and a transaction tape of each keystroke and page accessed. Of the 35 households that provided age data on their families, 13 had children under the age of 18; 11 had children 12 and under. Anecdotal data indicated that the entertainment pages, including horoscopes, movie listings, and movie reviews, were most popular with adolescents. Sports and the weather maps also were frequently accessed.

Videotext Systems

"Videotext," or wired videotex, refers to text transmitted via cable, telephone, or other nonbroadcast channels. Typically, videotext is also received on ordinary television sets fitted with decoders. Unlike teletext, which merely captures a signal that is being broadcast anyway, videotext requires a request channel from the user to the distribution center. Requested frames are sent to the individual user alone. Because it is not necessary to broadcast videotext frames in a constantly repeated sequence, the content of a videotext system can be orders of magnitude larger than the content of a teletext system.

However, content differences between teletext and videotext are overshadowed by differences in *interactivity,* which can be defined as the ratio of user activity to system activity. At one extreme, known to users of conventional cable systems, bulletins scroll on the screen without any user control. Since the bulletin display doesn't "need" the user to complete its programmed sequence, interactivity is zero. At the other extreme, exemplified by the "CB" service of videotext systems, there is near parity between user activity and system activity. The interactivity ratio is about 1:1.

Videotext's request channel provides opportunities for interaction that are missing from teletext use. Videotext users can take an additional step beyond requesting information; they can make decisions, answer questions, place orders, vote, and in other ways express themselves to the videotext system's host computer, which will then respond accordingly. Teletext's frame-capturing codes and "reveal button" represent a lower level of interactivity.

Kentucky's Green Thumb Box videotext system was a typical early (1980) installation with simple keypads connected to home telephones and television sets. About 250 frames of information were available from the system; these included weather maps and forecasts, market prices, information and advice on farming, home management information, and 4-H news and activities.

Of 194 Green Thumb households surveyed in 1981, more than two-thirds had children living at home. Children were regular users of the system; in several families, they were delegated the responsibility of accessing weather or market information for their parents to view. Of greatest interest to the children, however, were the frames of 4-H information, in particular a sequence on career exploration that included game activities.

The Channel 2000 videotext experiment in Columbus was undertaken as a joint venture between the Online Computer Library Center (OCLC), which developed and operated the system, and Bank One, which offered on-line financial services and provided incremental funding for the field test. Channel 2000 videotext was used by 200 Columbus-area households from October through December 1980.

Seven principal types of services were offered by Channel 2000. These can be grouped in four categories:

(1) *Academic or reference information:* The Video Encyclopedia, otherwise known as the Academic American Encyclopedia, contained 32,000 articles ranging in length from 1 frame to more than 300 frames. The Video Catalog contained 300,000 records of the Columbus and Franklin County Public Library catalog.

(2) *Community information:* A Public Information Service and a Community Calendar were searchable on-line.

(3) *Learning tools:* Early Reader and Math that Counts, both developed by Ohio State University, were intended for preschool and elementary school children, respectively. Early Reader frames taught word relationships through rhymes. The problem sets of Math that Counts were grouped by grade level from kindergarten through sixth grade.

(4) *Home banking:* Channel 2000 users who were also customers of Bank One could monitor their accounts and pay bills through the system.

Services most frequently used by children in the 200 households included the Video Encyclopedia, the Video Catalog, Early Reader, and Math that Counts. However, they also used the community information services, in particular the Community Calendar. Availability of the on-line Video Encyclopedias and Video Catalog made it possible for children to access encyclopedia articles related to school assignments and arrange for home delivery of books of interest from the local library's holdings.

Interactive Cable

In 1977 the Warner Cable Company launched the first American interactive cable system in Columbus. QUBE has approximately 30,000 users, for the most part middle- to upper-class families in Columbus and adjoining suburbs. A home console presents the viewer with 10 selections from each of 3 services, for a total of 30 channels. The premium service offers first-run movies, sports, a children's channel, and other features on a pay-per-view basis. The regular service offers the network affiliates and independent stations. The community service includes local community programming and special programs that may be narrowcast to specific households among the QUBE subscribers. Five response buttons on the console are used for viewer response in interactive mode.

The interactive capability of QUBE typically is used three or four times daily, for example, in posing community issues to the audience during local talk/variety shows. Test households indicated a "novelty effect" for the interactive capability. They responded interactively to programs during the early months of QUBE operations, but their viewing of such programs gradually decreased.

A further innovation on QUBE was to make CompuServe, a national videotext system based in Columbus, available to ten selected households via a microcomputer. For the first time, data bases usually accessed via terminals and telephone lines became available to cable subscribers: full text of eight major newspapers (including the *New York Times* and the *Washington Post*), sports, weather, home management, an encyclopedia, electronic mail, national bulletin board, and stock market quotations. The potential also existed to have CompuServe's MicroNET software downloaded into users' microcomputers for home/business computing.

The ten households participating in QUBE's CompuServe trial were selected to represent a range of experience with microcomputers and videotext. Questionnaires and interviews collected data on use of and attitudes toward QUBE/CompuServe. From early anecdotal findings, games, newspapers, and electronic mail appeared to be the most popular CompuServe features.

Features Analysis of Interactive Media

Research on the uses and effects of any communication medium requires a conceptual framework for specifying the mode(s) of content presentation that the medium utilizes. In an earlier era of communication research, when presentation differences among media appeared to be qualitative rather than quantitative (for example, newspapers versus television), the conceptual framework for specifying differences was largely informal. However, as technological advances produce new media with composite features (such as teletext—newspaper content on the television screen), it becomes necessary to formalize the conceptual framework and to define new dimensions of presentation differences.

In research on interactive media (see Martin, 1974; Paisley & Butler,

1977), the conceptual framework is called a "features analysis." Without describing it as such, Bretz (1971) conducted a features analysis of audiovisual and electronic media in use at that time. Subsequent features analyses have been modeled to a considerable degree on Bretz's work, and Bretz (1983) has recently extended his analysis to several forms of interactive media.

Interactive media are remarkably varied in their operating characteristics or, within the narrower context of this chapter, the "features" that they present to users at the "interface." The dividing line between structure and function, quite distinct in older print and electronic media, is blurred in the interactive media by the equivalence of features implemented in hardware or software. Because hardware-implemented features are more expensive to change when systems are being modified to perform different functions, there is a design preference for software-implemented features. Software rather than hardware thus determines much of what a user sees and uses in the interactive media.

For this reason, we cannot say that a system has microcomputer features, teletext features, videotext features, or interactive cable features per se. Feature differences within one of these categories can be as great as differences between the categories. A features analysis of an interactive medium used by children can be specific only when both hardware and software (and, in some cases, setting) are specified.

A few features common to all interactive media make up their *species* definition, while individual features make up their *differentia*. The primary common feature, of course, is *interactivity,* which has already been defined as the ratio of user activity to system activity. Among the interactive media, teletext has less interactivity than videotext, interactive cable, or microcomputers, but the teletext user's control over what will be displayed still distinguishes teletext from its parent media, conventional television and newspapers.

All interactive media also share the feature of *digital storage* of information, which has four important advantages over modes of analog storage such as printed pages and video frames. Digitally stored information can be (1) updated integrally by deleting unwanted sections and inserting others; (2) accessed using relational logic, since all digitally stored information can "identify itself" when the user-directed computer is searching for key terms; (3) transferred from one storage location to another, using low-bandwidth lines if necessary; and (4) brought out for display in any of the textual, numeric, and graphic modes into which the digital codes can be transformed.

A third common feature of interactive media that is easy to overlook is *processing speed.* Several videotext systems now provide access to millions of pages of information in seconds. Microcomputers compress the manual labor of weeks into minutes. The behavioral implications of the new momentum of knowledge work wait to be studied.

The differentiating features of interactive media can be grouped in three categories: (1) features associated with the presentation of information; (2) features associated with inputting and commanding; and (3) features associated with content. Selected features from each category are described below.

Features Associated with the
Presentation of Information

With the exception of *synthesized speech*, the presentation features of interactive media pertain to the *display*. The following display features are hypothesized to affect user behavior, learning, and satisfaction:

(1) *Display rate* was as slow as 15 characters per second (CPS) 10 years ago. While a rate of 2 or 3 words per second may be suitable for young children, it causes older readers to "read at the edge" —that is, to read each word as soon as it appears on the screen. This is a fatiguing procedure. On the other hand, current fast displays (960 CPS is now common) must be interruptable so that text does not scroll off the screen before it is read.

(2) *Character resolution* is a second major feature of displays. It is also a major source of dissatisfaction with the current generation of interactive media. On many displays, characters are generated within 5 × 7 dot matrices. Typographically, the quality of text that children read from displays is much inferior to the quality of text in children's books.

(3) *Uppercase-only* displays are another source of dissatisfaction with some microcomputers and videotex systems. Among children and others who read with difficulty, uppercase letters are involved in more recognition errors than lowercase letters. Furthermore, rules of capitalization and distinctions between common nouns and proper nouns are not reinforced in uppercase-only displays.

(4) *Line length* ranges from as few as 22 characters on one of the popular microcomputers to as many as 80 characters. Most videotex displays have 40-character lines. The average number of words per line thus ranges from as few as 3 to as many as 10. In contrast, lines in children's books range from an average of 8 words in double-column format to 12 words in single-column format.

(5) *Lines per screen* range from 16 to 25. This variable, combined with line length, causes full-screen displays to range from 75 words to 300 words. At the lower limit, little more than a paragraph can be displayed at a time, providing children with a minimum of context for "decoding."

(6) *Graphics resolution* has both cognitive and motivational implications for children's use of interactive media. Low-resolution graphics use less memory and are transmitted faster by videotex systems; however,

"low-res" creates cartoonlike representations and may impede children's understanding of form. Second-generation microcomputer software for children contains excellent examples of "high-res" graphics.

(7) *Motion* is another feature of graphic displays. Convincing simulation of real-world processes (such as growth, flow, collision, and rebound) require rapid motion, but not all interactive media are capable of depicting rapid motion.

(8) *Color* is a feature of most videotex and interactive cable systems, but many microcomputers have monochrome displays. Earlier research on the benefits of color in instructional film, television, and so on indicates that color has little effect on cognitive learning but may be an important motivator.

(9) *Music* and *sound effects* are common features of microcomputers but are not yet practical on videotex systems. Music may be an appropriate reinforcer or attention-focuser in interactive media use, but the "untempered" scales of most microcomputers are not considered acceptable for music instruction itself.

(10) *Synthesized speech* is now available for most microcomputers. Since 1980 the vocabulary and vocal quality of synthesized speech have improved markedly. New synthesizers that follow complex phonetic instructions to pronounce words, phrases, and even entire texts can show children the relationship of written to spoken language.

(11) *Keyboard symbols, labels, and layouts* are not usually regarded as presentation features, but in fact children may learn much about language and the control of computer/communication devices from them. Optimal arrangement of keyboard letters for children's use is an unresolved issue. Advocates of an "ABCDEF" arrangement believe that children's keyboard use should reinforce language learning, while advocates of the "QWERTY" arrangement argue that children should learn from the first where to find keys on conventional keyboards.

Other features of the keyboard, such as punctuation, mathematical symbols, and function keys, probably help children to understand the range of symbols used in human communication. The keyboard shows all symbols simultaneously and in an orderly pattern that children can study.

Features Associated with Inputting and Commanding

Ideally, an interactive medium would respond to the user's spoken commands. The amount of machine intelligence and memory required to accomplish this feat routinely place it in the future. Even now, however, children experimenting with first-generation voice recognition devices can learn valuable lessons about pronunciation and articulation.

Apart from voice recognition, there are four categories of features associated with inputting and commanding:

(1) *Keyboards and keypads* are indeed the "key" to most control over an interactive medium. All microcomputers in general use are controlled by full alphanumeric keyboards averaging 70 or so keys, while most videotex, interactive cable, and interactive videodisc systems are controlled by numeric keypads averaging 16 keys.

Full keyboards allow users to interact with interactive media in two ways: (a) responding to "menu" choices and (b) initiating interaction through a command language (see below). Keypads generally allow response to menu choices only. In most applications other than microcomputers, full keyboards have more interaction capacity than is needed, while keypads have too little interaction capacity for microcomputers.

(2) *Analog input devices* such as joysticks, paddles, and mouses can provide responses to instructional programs as well. Children like the vigorous action of these devices and may prefer moving a pointer to the correct response with a joystick rather than typing the response.

Inexpensive graphics tablets for microcomputers, introduced in 1983, have fostered the development of more powerful and versatile graphics software. Children's eye-hand coordination will be affected—we hope for the better—by practice in drawing invisibly on the graphics tablet while watching the result on the microcomputer screen.

(3) *Menus and other structured choices* are often a user's first exposure to the way interactive media "think." Menus are implicit or explicit decision trees. Choices are made between substantive alternatives, such as addition problems versus multiplication problems, and between procedural alternatives, such as "review" versus "continue."

Users become impatient with menus after a number of practice sessions, especially if the menus are verbose. Given the choice, users often prefer a command language that allows them to proceed directly to an activity that may be located several branches down a decision tree.

(4) *Command languages* are sometimes programming languages. That is, a user can command microcomputer functions directly in BASIC or other high-level languages. More often, command languages are embedded in programs whose statements the user doesn't see. However, a well-written command language makes the user feel that he or she has a large measure of control over the system. Most important, command languages allow the user to *initiate* interaction and not merely *respond* to the system's menus.

Features Associated with Content

Important as the foregoing features are in creating contexts for interaction, the major effects of interactive media on children's learning are probably determined by systems' content features—their substantive programs and data bases. The features of four categories of content are discussed below.

(1) *Recreational software* includes three categories of programs to which children are devoted: (a) motor skill games, (b) thinking games, and (c) creativity experiences. These categories are exemplified by Space Invaders, Adventure, and various music and graphics programs.

(2) *Instructional software* is also divided into three categories of programs: (a) drill and practice, (b) tutorial, and (c) simulation. Drill and practice programs emerged first because they are relatively easy to program and require the least memory. With the advent of high-resolution graphics, it has become possible to add detailed graphs, diagrams, and pictures to tutorial programs that are lacking in drill and practice programs. Simulation requires not only large memory capacity and high-resolution graphics, but also an algorithm of the physical, biological, or social process being simulated.

(3) *Utilities* are designed to facilitate users' own tasks. Utilities create task environments in which users can process words, organize and tabulate numbers, store and retrieve files, design and schedule projects, communicate with other users, and so on. The success of a utility lies in an accurate analysis of the requirements of users who are performing a common task for individual reasons. That is, the reasons for using a word processor are highly individual, but most users of word processors need a work space for composition, an editing procedure, a file-handling procedure, a printing and/or file-transmission procedure, and so on. Well-written utilities free the user to be productive or creative by supplying the common requirements of his or her task.

(4) *Data bases* may be called "knowledge utilities." They have grown in the past decade from a handful of experimental files to library-size collections that include bibliographic tools, catalogs and directories, numerical records, and an increasing number of full-text resources such as encyclopedias. Because of their memory requirements, data bases have been mounted primarily on mainframe computers. However, conversions to mini- and microcomputers are keeping pace with the increasing memory of small computers. Although data bases frequently duplicate the contents of books and journals, they are more powerful resources because of the computer's ability to locate any reference, key word, phrase, or statistic in a data base.

A more complete account of content features would include programming languages, which have both substantive and procedural content. A lively but inconclusive debate focuses on the use of the BASIC language to introduce children to computer programming. Adherents of other languages criticize the front-runner on several grounds, although research has not yet shown whether BASIC, PASCAL, LOGO, and other popular microcomputer languages have differing cognitive advantages or disadvantages.

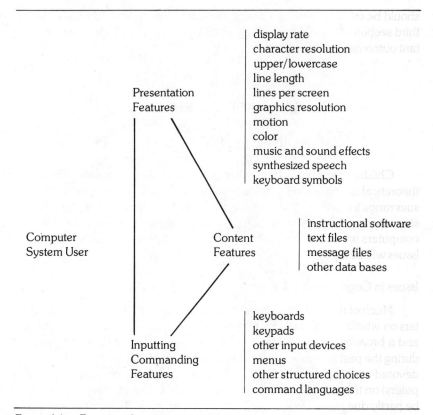

Figure 4.1.   Features of computer systems.

Figure 4.1 summarizes the three categories of interface features that differentiate interactive media.

An extended, social definition of the "interface" now appears in research on group processes in interactive media use (Butler & Paisley, 1983). We have consistently observed that a child using (for example) a microcomputer alone will soon be joined by other children if the situation permits. Some of the children seek advice, others give advice. They do not form an audience in the sense of a "television audience"; they participate in the interaction. Each of them is a resource for the others and, in a sense, an extension of the "interface."

Of course, this social definition of the interface goes beyond the features for which designers can take credit or responsibility. However, group use, especially among children, follows so predictably from the "intrinsically motivating characteristics" of interactive media (Malone, 1980) that it should be encompassed in a description of the interface. As discussed in the third section of this chapter, group processes may affect some of the important outcomes of interactive media use.

BEHAVIORAL ISSUES IN
CHILDREN'S USE OF
INTERACTIVE MEDIA

Children's use of, and learning from, interactive media raises important theoretical issues related to their cognitive and social development. The issues range in diversity from the surgeon general's concern about the aggressive nature of video games to teachers' observations of the benefits of microcomputers with learning-disabled children. In this section, several of these issues will be addressed.

Issues in Cognitive Development

Much of the current discussion of the benefits of interactive media centers on whether they can aid children to acquire more mature thinking skills and a broader base of knowledge. Within the past decade, and especially during the past four years, a growing number of behavioral researchers have devoted attention to the effects of interactive media (most often, microcomputers) on the cognitive development of children. The learning benefits may be partly due to the observed motivational aspects of these media (Levin & Kareev, 1980; Lepper, 1982). For children, the media have a dual identity—as games and as intelligent machines. Their gamelike qualities attract and hold the interest of children, much like the entertainment qualities of television. At the same time, the skills and knowledge learned in order to use and in the process of using interactive media may lead children to assimilate and analyze information, discover processes of thinking, and acquire strategies for problem solving.

The Piagetian Perspective

In discussions of the effects of interactive media on children's thinking abilities, frequent mention is made of the work of Jean Piaget, the Swiss psychologist and epistemologist. While there is a growing trend in developmental psychology questioning the broad and general nature of stage theories such as Piaget's (Flavell, 1982), many of Piaget's specific insights continue to be widely acknowledged. Seymour Papert, one of the earliest and best-known researchers in the field of computers and children, worked with Piaget. In his book *Mindstorms* (1980) Papert discusses the impact of computers upon children's progress through Piaget's concrete- and formal-operational stages of cognitive development.

The stage of concrete operations, typically seen in children between the ages of 7 and 11, is characterized by the development of the child's ability to create and manipulate mental representations of the physical world. For instance, one aspect of the concrete-operational child's thinking is conservation of mass, length, and weight. The child is able to perceive the constancy of an object despite outward changes in shape. The child is also able to classify (organize objects into hierarchies of classes) and seriate (organize objects in order along one dimension, such as height). He or she is able to take the perspective of others, in a visual sense. In general, the concrete-operational child is engaging in logical thinking involving the perception, representation, and manipulation of concrete physical objects in the immediate world.

The stage of formal operations, which typically begins around age 12 and continues into adulthood, signifies the child's transition into more abstract and, in that sense, "formal" thinking. The formal thinker moves away from dependence on the physical world for representations of logical operations into a symbolic world of hypotheses, inferences, and multiple alternatives. Formal operations involve more systematic thought and an ability to arrive at more general and abstract statements to explain classes of phenomena.

The differences between concrete and formal operations can be exemplified by the task of forming all possible paired combinations of a group of colored beads (Papert, 1980). Concrete-operational children can generate only a random assortment of the combinations. Formal-operational children recognize the rule or "system" for generating all possible alternatives by fixing the color of a first bead and pairing it with all possible colors of a second, then repeating until all possible first colors have been exhausted.

Papert believes that these systematic thinking skills can be discovered and modeled by children working with computers. The above problem of "combinatorial thinking" becomes as easy as instructing the computer to execute a nested loop. Papert's hypothesis is that the computer, by providing a rich environment of models, maps, and systematic procedures, can encourage children to become better thinkers, often earlier than traditional studies have shown. Other studies have shown an earlier development of formal operations when children are confronted with problems that exercise such skills (see Kuhn & Angelev, 1976). In a specific test of these notions, Sheingold and Pea (1981) are studying the effects of learning LOGO on children's planning and problem-solving abilities.

A frequent observation on the ease with which children learn to use computers may be cast in such Piagetian stage terms. It has been said that the reason adults have more difficulty in becoming accustomed to computers is that they, as formal thinkers, need explanations of how the computer works, not only heuristically but even electronically. Such detailed explanations are difficult to present and are unconvincing or confusing to the electronics novice.

On the other hand, concrete-thinking children do not desire such explanations. Using the cognitive tools at their disposal, they employ trial and error, induction, and persistence to arrive at conclusions concerning operations the computer can perform and how it can be made to perform them. Computers are relatively unambiguous about correct versus incorrect procedure. This quality may make them more accessible to the minds of children. That is, at some level of use, the concrete-operational thinking of young children may find a congenial match in the cognitive skills required for using interactive media.

Implied above is the computer's power to mirror children's own thought processes. That is, the computer can lead children to engage in meta-cognition, or thinking about one's own thinking. For instance, the process of writing and debugging a computer program is an exercise in partitioning a problem into smaller and more manageable subproblems. Often called "procedural thinking," this cognitive skill is one that can be constantly aided by the computer as it detects errors and informs the user about them. The concepts of a "bug" as a problem and "debugging" as problem solving are significant preparation for acquisition of more advanced cognitive skills. As another example, interactive media using decision trees as structures for locating desired information may model useful hierarchical organizations for a child's own knowledge.

Visual Thinking

One interesting hypothesis is that interactive media, by displaying graphs, maps, and other visualizations, can encourage visual thinking skills (Arnheim, 1969; McKim, 1980). Salomon (1979) presents evidence that televised presentation of certain visualizations (such as rotation of simple objects) can help children to internalize such representations. The stimuli involved are well within the graphics capability of microcomputers used by children. Visual thinking is often discussed as a basis for creative thinking (Adams, 1974). Many popular video games, such as Adventure, require players to hold in their minds mental representations of complex scenes (such as a floor plan or a room filled with objects). Research based on Salomon's concepts and utilizing the graphics capabilities of interactive media may lead to a better understanding of the processes involved in visual thinking.

Domain-Specific Knowledge

Recent research has suggested that much of human cognitive growth can be attributed to the gradual acquisition of knowledge and expertise in specific domains (Flavell, in press). Insofar as interactive media enable children to explore multiple domains of interest and information, they may promote the acquisition of more mature thinking skills and strategies.

As indicated above, knowledge of computer programming may be one specific yet powerful type of expertise that can be transferred to other cognitive tasks. Because of their convenience and attractiveness, other interactive media, such as videotext and teletext, can offer children new access to knowledge in many subject areas. We have observed children using these systems to learn more about science, mathematics, health, current events, history, art, and writing.

The proficient use of interactive media has the common requirement of developed reading skills. Reading research has documented the importance of a supportive environment and motivating activities that encourage the child to extract meaning from print (Strickland, 1982). Because interactive media can be designed to be nonpunitive and entertaining, they may provide an impetus to children's development of reading and language skills crucial to their continued cognitive growth.

Cognitive Style

Exposure to interactive media may also affect "cognitive style," or those differences in perception, disposition, or temperament that can be distinguished from the exercise of cognitive skills alone (Kagan, 1965, 1966). While further research is needed to distinguish these stylistic aspects of thinking from measures of intelligence and motivation (Gardner, 1978; Haertel, 1978), use of interactive media can be related to at least one dimension of cognitive style: "reflective" versus "impulsive" thought. Programming, word processing, and other applications permit successive approximations that may allow the impulsive thinker to try out alternative solutions. Reflective children, who are often blocked by anxiety over being wrong, can benefit from the nonpunitive and diagnostic support offered by well-designed systems.

Sex Differences in Cognition

Maccoby and Jacklin (1974) present a thorough review of the literature on sex differences. Some differences between boys and girls on various cognitive abilities emerge during the elementary school years. For instance, after age 10, girls exhibit greater mastery over some verbal skills, while boys begin to excel in spatial and analytic abilities at around age 6 (Haertel, 1978). Such differences may be compounded in the early adolescent years by social and attitudinal factors. Girls often develop negative attitudes toward math and science by age 12, with the result that, through their avoidance of essential high school courses, their career opportunities are thereafter limited (Fox, 1977). Since interactive media can exercise a wide range of verbal and spatial skills, boys and girls using these media in informal as well as formal settings may be able to acquire compensatory training in abilities needing further development.

Issues in Social Development

Our observations, as well as those of other researchers, suggest that interactive media may have effects not only on children's cognitive development but on their social development as well. Continued exposure to and facility with interactive media may affect a child's self-confidence, interest patterns, and relations with peers, teachers, and parents—in short, the child's sense of self in the social world. Research points to the crucial nature of successful early experiences, beginning in the preschool years, on the development of a positive self-image (Maccoby, 1980).

Development of Self-Esteem

During their first ten years, children engage in a process of self-definition and gradually build a self-concept. They begin to acquire perceptions of their appearance, their skills, and their limitations. They become concerned about how others perceive them—their friends, their teachers, their parents. They set standards for their own performance in school, hobbies, and friendships.

Children's use of interactive media raises interesting theoretical issues related to the development of self-esteem. "Competence" is one important component of self-esteem (Coopersmith, 1967), and experiences with interactive media provide one area for the development of competence. The insecurity of many adults regarding interactive media may provide a source of even greater reinforcement for children who are able to use the media. The microcomputer may be the most sophisticated tool that children frequently show adults how to use. Until computer literacy becomes widespread among both children and adults, children who can command computers may be finding their skills valued and reinforced among peers and adults.

There is another sense in which interactive media can help build self-esteem. The psychological literature on "locus of control" identifies a feeling of control over one's environment as one important component of self-esteem (Epstein, 1973; Brim, 1976). When children program computers, they are exerting power over a powerful machine.

The patience and versatility of microcomputers may especially benefit children whose self-confidence suffers in other learning or performance situations. Children with physical, mental, or emotional disabilities may see themselves as unable to compete with other students at school or with siblings at home. Microcomputers can be "equalizers" for such children (see Weir, 1981). For example, through the use of templates fitted over the keyboard, cerebral-palsied children exhibit impressive writing skills, unhampered by the motor-coordination requirements of handwriting. Interactive media can thus enable children with learning or other disabilities to reveal and master skills that have remained hidden in the past.

Relations with Peers and Adults

Observations of children's use of interactive media in classrooms have often shown a high degree of peer sharing, teaching, and interaction. The exchanges occur in the beginning stages of learning to use interactive media and continue through more advanced tasks. This collaboration in using interactive media seems to occur with greater frequency than in other classroom activities.

Over the longer term, children's use of interactive media may help to break down traditional perceptions of children based on age, sex, ethnicity, or academic achievement. For instance, girls who are "local experts" with computers can help overcome the stereotype (held by parents, teachers, and other children) that only boys are skilled with machines. Through the sharing of computer experiences, children with varying personality or learning styles may enter into new social relations with their peers. Already, children and teenagers are often knowledgeable members of adult computer users' groups. There are indications that the interactive media may lead us to a redefinition of the behaviors and competencies associated with the period known as "childhood." (See Ariès, 1962 for changing conceptions of childhood through the centuries.)

FUTURE RESEARCH ON
CHILDREN AND INTERACTIVE MEDIA

Analogy with Television Research

Beginning with landmark studies such as *Television and the Child* (Himmelweit, Oppenheim, & Vince, 1958) and *Television in the Lives of Our Children* (Schramm, Lyle, & Parker, 1961), research on children and television has occupied scores of researchers over the past quarter century. Thanks to the development of close relationships between researchers and producers, the growing knowledge of television's effects on children has led to more effective programming (Lesser, 1974; Palmer, 1974).

The issues that merit research on children and interactive media, and the potential benefits of such research, parallel those of television. However, it is unlikely that research on interactive media will parallel television research in two important aspects. First, it is often suggested that the new media will have *transformative* rather than *supplemental* effects on children's learning. Thus researchers studying children's use of interactive media may need to derive new paradigms of effects. Second, whereas television technology changed little in a quarter century, interactive media are changing at a rate that outstrips studies before they can be completed.

Basic and Applied Research

Basic research on children and interactive media should be committed to long-term programs organized, initially, around the psychological and sociological effect paradigms of previous research on learning media. Lest we imply that such research will shift entirely to new paradigms, we will predict that many basic problems investigated by researchers in the past will continue to be investigated in a similar manner. One of the most significant of these, in our opinion, is *aptitude-treatment interaction,* ably studied by Cronbach and Snow (1977). Their research design can encompass interactions between the features of interactive media and individual differences among learners. Other continuities of research will be discovered when new topics receive their first careful examination. For example, the principles of learning from discovery software may be found to be rooted in Gestalt psychology.

At the same time, *applied* research on interactive media should be adapted to the changing media and the new users and uses. Issues of quality and equity in the next decade should not be ignored or deferred because of the prospect that interactive media will be easy to use or ubiquitously available by the century's end.

Lasswellian Paradigm

Research on interactive media may follow a variation of Lasswell's (1948) paradigm for communication research: *Who says what to whom through which channel and with what effects?* The variation, which will necessarily be receiver oriented rather than sender oriented, may be: *Who learns what from which interactive system and with what effects on other learning and behavior?*

This paradigm raises research questions at three levels of inquiry—demographic, sociological, and psychological. We will discuss several such questions below.

Who . . .

Which groups in the society have access to interactive media? Present access to interactive media is strongly influenced by socioeconomic status and place of residence. Socioeconomic status affects not only the purchase of equipment (for example, microcomputer, teletext, and videotext terminal/decoder) but also the perception of utility in such technology. For example, up-to-the-minute financial reports are valued more by investors than by noninvestors.

Place of residence affects teletext, videotext, and interactive cable service. These services will spread in metropolitan areas during this decade, but small towns and rural areas not served by metropolitan broadcasting will be slow to receive teletext service. Small towns will have access to interactive cable and videotext service, albeit more slowly than metropolitan areas. Rural areas will be poorly served until rooftop reception from satellites becomes cheaper. Cable operators avoid the front-end costs of running lines to widely separated rural homes. Videotext service is not available to the many rural families who have party-line telephones.

What are the barriers to access and how can they be overcome? Cost will soon be the least significant barrier to access. Market forces have already reduced the cost of microcomputers to a level that households have long been paying for color television sets and related equipment. The $100 microcomputers on sale in 1983 may fill household niches much as radios now do—that is, two or more such microcomputers will be located around the house where adults or children wish to use them. Teletext and videotext terminals and decoders will become trivially cheap (by the standards of other household expenses) in mass production. Interactive cable service may always be somewhat more expensive than the other interactive media because of the rising costs of the dedicated lines and the required personnel (based on the QUBE model).

Where place of residence limits access to some interactive media, as in rural areas, alternate solutions may be explored. The first solution, which rural dwellers have traditionally chosen, is self-sufficiency. Microcomputers and their extensive software libraries do not depend on telephone or cable lines or on broadcast signals from metropolitan areas. Videodiscs are a complementary storage medium for random access to high-resolution graphic or pictorial images.

A second solution is more rapid development of low-cost satellite transmission to homes. Direct satellite transmission is becoming, by necessity, a major communication link in the Third World. Equipment tested in these applications is now reaching the domestic market, but it is still too expensive for widespread adoption. A small number of satellite channels can meet the needs of a rural area for television signals and digital transmissions to microprocessor equipment.

Which groups make greater or lesser use of public-access systems (that is, those in public facilities such as libraries and museums)? This question cannot be discussed without a hard look at the concept of "equal access." If public libraries begin to offer access to interactive media (as they will) to all persons in a community, is that equal access? In the "formalist" sense of equity (Harvey, 1980), the answer is yes. In the "actualist" sense, the answer is no. Formal equity is concerned with barriers to access that lie outside a person—laws, sanctions, customs, and the like. If there are no such barriers to access, then formal equity is said to be present. However, barriers to access also lie within people—in lack of education, experience, self-confidence, or sense of personal efficacy, or in inability to formulate strategies. These internal barriers largely account for the gap between formal equity and actual equity.

Other media, rich with relevant information and simple to use, are widely available in communities, but they are not used equally by everyone. Contrary to equity goals, these media are used more by the groups that already have the most information—the "information haves."

We believe that interactive media *do* differ from traditional information media and services in the balance of perceived benefit relative to accessibility. Whether these media can overcome internal use barriers is a question for research, however.

Within social groups, what are the group roles of those who make greater or lesser use of interactive media? Social groups can be analyzed in terms of many permanent and temporary roles that members play. In addition to the roles of leader and facilitator (and, of course, follower and obstructor), the role of innovator is significant in groups that are undergoing change. If the decision to adopt new practices is "top down" rather than "bottom up," then the leader's role may be more important than the innovator's. If the decision is "bottom up," then the innovator comes into his or her own.

In groups of children, up to the present time, those who have interest and ability in working with interactive media have often been characterized as "outsiders" and "loners." The machines that they used were mysterious; so, by association, were they. They had little influence with their peers, and they could not induce their peers to use interactive media, since the media were not widely available. However, we believe that both the facts and the stereotypes concerning "computer kids" are changing. As suggested in the previous section, children with interest and expertise in computers may be acquiring new social roles as well. Study of group roles in settings where interactive systems are extensively used by children is one promising area for research.

What are the individual characteristics of those who make greater or lesser use of interactive media? Demographic analyses of the child audience for television have continued from the 1950s to the present day. Such analyses confirm some hypotheses about children as television viewers and disconfirm others. Demographic analyses, by sex, age, race, school achievement, and other variables, should now be conducted for children using interactive media. In other words, the field needs a study entitled *Interactive Media in the Lives of Our Children* to complement the pioneering study of television by Schramm et al. (1961).

Learns What . . .

Which content resources are used? By which groups of users? Steiner (1963) noted the differing "diets" that television audience subgroups chose from the "menu" of television fare. Newspaper and magazine readership studies are a similar genre of research. By further analogy to audience analysis in television research, research on interactive media should study differential use of recreational software, instructional software, utilities, data bases, and so on.

It may be difficult to determine which content resources are used in the case of proprietary interactive media, since they lack the economic incentive of older media to reveal the popularity of their offerings. However, an independent survey could begin with randomly sampled homes and schools in order to determine, from the statements of users themselves, which content resources are being used, and by whom.

What levels of learning are attained? Levels of learning can be categorized as association, discrimination, rule learning, and principle learning (Gagne, 1970) or as knowledge of specifics, comprehension, application, analysis, synthesis, and evaluation (Bloom, Englehart, Hill, Furst, & Krathwohl, 1956). What levels of learning are attained by users of instructional software? When instructional software can be "played" with casually, how do learning benefits compare with its use in directed (that is, study) mode? What are the learning benefits of casual versus directed use of utilities and data bases?

What are the secondary and/or unintended learning outcomes? Each learning medium and setting, including school itself, teaches students many lessons beyond those provided for in the curriculum. To paraphrase McLuhan (1964), the medium is a message in each case. Sometimes it is surprising to find out what the message is. Interactive media have a variety of implicit messages—in this case, facts about the world that children learn while using the systems for other purposes. At the very least, children may note the ways in which knowledge is organized and information conveyed. They may learn lessons about themselves; they may be surprised that they can understand information intended for adults and kept largely insulated from them by school experience.

Secondary learning of *skills* is almost certain. Computer usage provides opportunities for children to practice reading, to translate written instructions and choices into action, to compose statements and commands, to coordinate eyes and hand, and more.

From Which Interactive Medium . . .

For "interactive medium" the reader may wish to substitute "combination of interactive features." As discussed in the first section of this chapter, these features are remarkably varied. Many features, furthermore, are under software control, which allows them to be changed instantly. For example, information in memory can be presented to the user in various formats. As the information is retrieved from memory, it can be edited in length or terminology. It can be transformed from text to other forms of representation. Instead of being displayed on the screen, it can be directed to a speech synthesizer. Combining the capabilities of several existing systems, it is within the state of the art to display (or speak) the following to the user:

> I have located the information you requested. Would you prefer to review it in the form of . . .
>
> 1. spoken synopsis
> 2. spoken full text
> 3. displayed synopsis
> 4. displayed full text
> 5. statistical tables
> 6. graphs and pictures

The user can choose one or any combination of these formats. And, in addition to *alternative* formats, there are *supplementary* formats, as when contrasting colors, blinking words, or "voice-overs" provide emphasis, or when background music cues a transition in the text. Given the range of user-selectable formats now possible and soon to be common, can we say that children are sharing the same information when they use the same interactive medium to complete the same assignment?

Is there differential use of particular interactive media by group or individual characteristics? There is much functional overlap among interactive media, but, to choose extreme examples, children who used only teletext systems and other children who used only microcomputers would probably develop different knowledge, skills, and attitudes. The "teletext children" would be observers of a world crowded with bulletins, reports, and updates on events of all kinds—a world where facts beggar the imagination. The "microcomputer children" would be actors in a smaller world where they control events, where relationships between causes and events are presented, where problems are solvable. Although neither of these extreme cases is likely to occur, it will be important to know the extent to which differential use of the systems is occurring and which groups or individuals account for the differential use.

Over time, which interactive media seem to have an increasing potential for learning, while other systems reach limits inherent in their technology or use environments? Do all the interactive media have equally bright futures? Or will the simplest system, teletext, soon be passed over for the power of videotext or interactive cable? In the not-distant future, will schools and homes both opt for the combination of microcomputers and interactive cable systems over which entire libraries of programs can be "downloaded"? Should researchers try to foresee the outcomes of technological progress and market competition in order to study the effects, and the more effective use, of the eventual winners rather than the eventual losers?

With What Effects on Other Learning...

Does learning from interactive media reinforce, or conflict with, other forms of learning? Ten years ago the advocates of individualized instruction had to admit that children could not be started in individualized programs in grade school, then funneled into conventional whole-class programs in middle or high school. The one experience "maladjusted" them for the other, not only in level of preparation (some children had progressed individually far beyond the whole-class curriculum, while other children were not ready for it) but also in attitude. Will interactive media "maladjust" children for other classroom learning, including instruction from the teacher? Will they be less able to learn without buttons for "back up" and "go forward faster"? Or, on the contrary, will learning from interactive media be a catalyst for classroom instruction and discussion?

Do children who use interactive media extensively have a richer or poorer home and school experience otherwise? With interactive media in both environments, will school days and home evenings flow together in a continuous learning experience? Will children come to school with unfulfilled curiosity and enthusiasm from interactive media use at home, and will they take home the stimulation of interactive media use at school? Or will there be "information burnout" —too much information, too many questions, too many possibilities, all of it too fast?

With What Effects on Behavior...

What are the effects of interactive media use on children's personal adjustments? On their social development? On their interaction with other children and with adults? These questions all ask, in different ways, whether interactive media will help children grow personally and socially. On the one hand, the answer may be, "It depends," which is as close to a final verdict as 25 years of research on children and television has reached. On the other hand, interactive media are different from television, and these questions are pregnant with possibilities for research.

On one point, we believe that fears concerning interactive media are wrong. Interactive media do not separate people, but bring them together. A roomful of microcomputers produces not only conversation but conviviality among children. The most popular features of videotext systems include their "CB" conversations, their electronic mail, and their bulletin boards. In homes where computers are used by both children and adults, "what's on the system" is a livelier topic of conversation than "what's on TV." The general finding may be that instructive, funny, difficult, disastrous and/or rewarding experiences with intelligent machines are irresistible topics of conversation. This is not a trivial finding *when,* as we have observed, the conversations cross age lines and their content becomes quite technical.

The larger questions of the effects of interactive media on children's personal and social growth must be left for research. The potential for some adverse effects is inherent in the often-compelling nature of the interaction that the systems provide. Malone's (1980) analysis of "what makes things fun to learn" identifies the elements of *challenge, fantasy, curiosity, variable difficulty level, multiple-level goals, hidden information,* and *randomness* in learning as well as play. How these variables interact with individual traits and learning styles remains to be studied. For instance, some children may find frustration in levels of pacing and difficulty that others find enjoyable.

Temporal Frames of Reference

More than one temporal frame of reference is implicit in these questions. Interactive media are still a relatively new phenomenon. Outside of computer-related professions, few adults and even fewer children were knowledgeable users of interactive media prior to this decade. Most children we have observed are still learning to use the systems. We have observed a high proportion of *procedural* learning relative to *content* learning.

Social researchers sometimes use the "loaf of bread" analogy to describe differences between periods when new behaviors are initiated and later periods when the behaviors have reached equilibrium with respect to other behaviors. The majority of slices in a loaf of bread are uniform, and one or more of them can be sampled to represent the others. However, the end of the loaf has some slices that differ from the majority and from each other in size and texture. Similarly, the early adoption period of a social or technological innovation almost certainly differs in "size and texture" from later periods (Rogers, 1983).

To complicate matters further, "early" and "late" can refer both to *the life cycle of a technological innovation itself* and to *an individual's contact with it.* By the turn of the century, which we assume will be fairly late in the life cycle of interactive media as we now know them, there will still be individuals who have no contact with the systems. Others at that time will just be initiating contact. Even apart from technological progress per se, initial contact with interactive media in 2000 will be qualitatively different than in 1983.

Thus research on children's use of interactive media should focus on both the period of initial contact, when use procedures are being learned and attitudes toward the systems are being formed, and the later period of proficient regular use integrated with other activities. These periods of *individual* contact with interactive media should be studied continuously throughout a substantial part of the life cycle of the *systems* as well.

RESEARCH ON INTERACTIVE MEDIA LITERACY: "RITHMS" OF THE FUTURE

The introduction of interactive media will almost certainly widen the gap between the "information haves" and "have nots." However, the particular *information-processing deficit* of the "have nots" may not be widely recognized. They will be criticized for not availing themselves of interactive media resources that are increasingly affordable, comprehensive, and easy to use.

Interactive media literacy, a concept that takes us back to the beginning of this chapter, will separate the "information haves" from the "have nots" in the future. Millions of children and adults will have such literacy; other millions may not.

Computer literacy is the closest concept under investigation today, but some studies of computer literacy confuse *skills* with *understanding* and focus on programming courses. Such courses, and even less so the particular languages that are taught, are not at the heart of computer literacy.

Computers and other interactive media become "friendlier" over time. Users need to know fewer protocols and virtually no programming commands. However, the benefit differential between "information haves" and "have nots" who actually use the systems *increases* as the systems become friendlier. For example, a system that reports back to users on the results of a data base search, or the "bottom line" of a spread sheet, or the optimal decision in business or home management is providing a valuable service for users who understand its *algorithms* and can structure their *own* tasks algorithmically.

The future environment of interactive media use will be, above all, an algorithmic one. As requirements for technical knowledge of interactive media use procedures decrease, requirements for algorithmic thinking will increase. Interactive media offer extraordinary access to information, but only to those who understand the algorithms of information seeking. Interactive media offer extraordinary analytic power, file management, communication, and so on, but only to those who understand the corresponding algorithms.

It is important to emphasize that algorithms of tasks such as information seeking, analysis, file management, and communication have no *intrinsic* connection with interactive media, but the "computerization" of tasks often brings the algorithms into clear focus for the first time. With or without the computer, the tasks can thereafter be performed at a higher level, because they are better understood.

The "rithms" of the future are already well-entrenched in business, science, and the professions. While it is expected that business, research, and professional work will be algorithmic, it is surprising to note how rapidly the "rithms" of the future have come home, with interactive media, to the tasks of everyday life.

However, interactive media are scarcely five years old in most of the applications discussed in this chapter. On the strength of their present capabilities alone, we believe they may be able to provide children with the literacies and modes of thought that the future requires.

REFERENCES

Adams, J. L. (1974) *Conceptual blockbusting: A pleasurable guide to better problem solving.* New York: W. W. Norton.

Ariès, P. (1962). *Centuries of childhood: A social history of family life.* New York: Vintage.

Arnheim, R. (1969) *Visual thinking.* Berkeley: University of California Press.

Becker, H. J. (1982). *Microcomputers in the classroom: Dreams and realities.* Baltimore: Johns Hopkins University, Center for Social Organization of Schools.

Becker, H. J. (1983, April). *How schools use microcomputers: First report from a national survey.* Paper presented at the annual meeting of the American Educational Research Association, Montreal.

Bloom, B. S., Englehart, M. D., Hill, W. H., Furst, E. J., & Krathwohl, D. R. (Eds.). (1956). *Taxonomy of educational objectives, handbook 1: Cognitive domain.* New York: David McKay.

Bloom, L. R., Hanson, A. G., Linfield, R. F., & Wortendyke, D. R. (1980). *Videotex systems and services.* Boulder, CO: U.S. Department of Commerce, National Telecommunications and Information Administration.

Bretz, R. (1971). *A taxonomy of communication media.* Englewood Cliffs, NJ: Educational Technology Publications.

Bretz, R. (1983). *Media for interactive communication.* Beverly Hills, CA: Sage.

Brim, O. G. (1976). Life span development of the theory of oneself: Implications for child development. In H. W. Reese (Ed.), *Advances in child development and behavior* (Vol. 11). New York: Academic.

Butler, M. L., & Paisley, W. J. (1983, March). *Convivial computing.* Paper presented at the Eleventh Annual Math/Science Conference, Arizona State University, Tempe.

The computer moves in. (1983, January 3). *Time,* pp. 14-24.

Coopersmith, S. (1967). *The antecedents of self-esteem.* San Francisco: W. H. Freeman.

Cronbach, L. G., & Snow, R. E. (1977). *Aptitudes and instructional methods: A handbook for research on interactions.* New York: Irvington.

Epstein, S. (1973). The self-concept revisited. *American Psychologist, 28,* 404-416.

Flavell, J. H. (1982). On cognitive development. *Child Development, 53,* 1-10.

Flavell, J. H. (in press). *Cognitive development* (2nd ed.). Englewood Cliffs, NJ: Prentice-Hall.

Fox, L. H. (1977). The effects of sex-role socialization on mathematics participation and achievement. In L. H. Fox et al., *Women and mathematics: Research perspectives for change.* NIE Papers in Education and Work No. 8. Washington, DC: National Institute of Education.

Gagne, R. M. (1970). *The conditions of learning.* New York: Holt, Rinehart & Winston.

Gardner, H. (1978). *Developmental psychology: An introduction.* Boston: Little, Brown.

Haertel, G. D. (1978). Literature review of early adolescence and implications for programming. In *Early adolescence: Perspectives and recommendations.* Washington, DC: Government Printing Office.

Hald, A. (1981, March). *The making of a genius generation.* Paper presented at the Ninth Annual Math/Science Conference, Arizona State University, Tempe.

Harvey, G. (1980). *Information equity in the field of education: A concept paper.* San Francisco: Far West Laboratory for Educational Research and Development.

Hawkins, J. (1983). Learning LOGO together: The social context. In *Chameleon in the classroom: Developing roles for computers.* Symposium presented at the annual meeting of the American Educational Research Association, Montreal.

Hess, R., & Miura, I. T. (1983). *Gender and socioeconomic differences in enrollment in computer camps and classes.* Stanford, CA: Stanford University, School of Education.

Himmelweit, H. T., Oppenheim, A. N., & Vince, P. (1958). *Television and the child.* London: Oxford University Press.

Kagan, J. (1965). Impulsive and reflective children: Significance of conceptual tempo. In J. Krumboltz (Ed.), *Learning and the educational process.* Chicago: Rand McNally.

Kagan, J. (1966). Reflection-impulsivity: The generality and dynamics of conceptual tempo. *Journal of Abnormal Psychology, 71,* 17-24.

Kane, J. H. (1983). Computers for composing. In *Chameleon in the classroom: Developing roles for computers.* Symposium presented at the annual meeting of the American Educational Research Association, Montreal.

Kuhn, D., & Angelev, J. (1976) An experimental study of the development of formal operational thought. *Child Development, 47,* 697-706.

Lasswell, H. D. (1948). The structure and function of communications. In L. Bryson (Ed.), *The communication of ideas.* New York: Harper & Row.

Lepper, M. R. (1982). *Microcomputers in education: Motivational and social issues.* Stanford, CA: Stanford University, Department of Psychology.

Lesser, G. (1974). *Television and children: Lessons from Sesame Street.* New York: Random House.

Levin, J. A., & Kareev, Y. (1980). *Personal computers and education: The challenge to schools.* La Jolla: University of California at San Diego, Center for Human Information Processing.

Liebert, R. M., Sprafkin, J. N., & Davidson, E. S. (1982). *The early window: Effects of television on children and youth* (2nd ed.). New York: Pergamon.

Maccoby, E. (1980). *Social development.* New York: Harcourt Brace Jovanovich.

Maccoby, E., & Jacklin, C. (1974). *The psychology of sex differences.* Stanford, CA: Stanford University Press.

Malone, T. W. (1980). *What makes things fun to learn? A study of intrinsically motivating computer games.* Palo Alto, CA: Xerox Palo Alto Research Center.

Many schools buying computers find problems using them. (1983, April 7). *Wall Street Journal.*

Martin, T. H. (1974). *A features analysis of interactive retrieval systems.* Standord, CA: Stanford University, Institute for Communication Research.

McKim, R. (1980). *Experiences in visual thinking.* Monterey, CA: Brooks/Cole.

McLuhan, M. (1964). *Understanding media.* New York: McGraw-Hill.

Paisley, W. J. (1980). Information and work. In B. Dervin & M. Voight (Eds.), *Progress in the communication sciences* (Vol. 2). Norwood, NJ: Ablex.

Paisley, W. J. (1983). Computerizing information: Lessons of a videotext trial. *Journal of Communication, 33*(1), 153-161.

Paisley, W. J., & Butler, M. L. (1977). *Computer assistance in information work.* Report to the National Science Foundation. Palo Alto, CA: Applied Communication Research, Inc.

Paisley, W. J., & Chen, M. (1982). *Children and electronic text: Challenges and opportunities of the "new literacy."* Stanford, CA: Stanford University, Institute for Communication Research.

Palmer, E. (1974). Formative research in the production of television for children. In D. R. Olson (Ed.), *Media and symbols: The forms of expression, communication, and education.* Chicago: University of Chicago Press.

Papert, S. (1980). *Mindstorms: Children, computers, and powerful ideas.* New York: Basic Books.

Pea, R. D. (1983). LOGO programming and problem-solving. In *Chameleon in the classroom: Developing roles for computers.* Symposium presented at the annual meeting of the American Educational Research Association, Montreal.

Phi Delta Kappa. (1983, May). *Sex differences in computer training: Why do boys outnumber girls?* Center for Evaluation, Development, and Research.

Rogers, E. M. (1983). *Diffusion of innovations* (3rd ed.). New York: Free Press.

Rogers, E. M., Daley, H. & Wu, T. (1982). *The diffusion of home computers.* Stanford, CA: Stanford University, Institute for Communication Research.

Salomon, G. (1979). *Interaction of media, cognition, and learning.* San Francisco: Jossey-Bass.

Schramm, W., Lyle, J., & Parker, E. B. (1961). *Television in the lives of our children.* Stanford, CA: Stanford University Press.

Sheingold, K. (1981). *Issues related to the implementation of computer technology in schools: A cross-sectional study.* Paper presented at the National Institute of Education Conference on Issues Related to the Implementation of Computer Technology in Schools, Washington, D.C.

Sheingold, K., & Pea, R. D. (1981). *The impact of a classroom computer experience on children's problem solving, planning, and peer collaboration.* New York: Bank Street College of Education.

Steiner, G. (1963). *The people look at television.* New York: Knopf.

Strickland, D. (1982). *Reading and the young child.* New York: Teachers College, Columbia University.

Weir, S. (1981, September). LOGO and the exceptional child. *Microcomputing,* pp. 76-84.

Weizenbaum, J. (1976). *Computer power and human reason.* San Francisco: W. H. Freeman.

Williams, F. & Williams, V. (1984). *Microcomputers in elementary education.* Belmont, CA: Wadsworth.

5 ● The Employment Screening Interview: An Organizational Assimilation and Communication Perspective

FREDRIC M. JABLIN ● KAREN B. McCOMB

University of Texas–Austin

IT seems that every few years a paper is presented at an International Communication Association convention, or an article is published in a journal, reviewing the employment interviewing literature and calling for more *communication*-oriented research on the interview. For example, Daly (1978, p. 1) suggests in his review of the literature that one of his goals is "to propose that scholars claiming interest in applied or organizational communication pay more attention to the interview as a topic of research." More recently, Goodall and Goodall (1982, p. 21), in a "selective" review of the literature, conclude by observing that "while there is a virtual abundance of research and opinion about employment interviewing to be found in a variety of professional technical journals, trade magazines, and popular books and magazines, very little research has been done by speech communication scholars."

Even taking into consideration the proclivity of researchers to close their articles and papers with calls for more research, one wonders why scholars seem to be persistently calling for more communication-oriented employment interviewing research. The obvious response to this query is that researchers are recalcitrant in conducting communication-oriented interviewing research, and thus need to be admonished to correct this lacuna

Correspondence and requests for reprints: Fredric M. Jablin, Department of Speech Communication, University of Texas, Austin, TX 78712.

in our knowledge of human behavior. The less than obvious reply is that these recurrent literature reviews that call for more communication-oriented interviewing research are not themselves providing sufficient theoretical and empirical guidance to stimulate research.

In fact, it is our position that one of the major weaknesses of extant employment interviewing literature reviews prepared by communication scholars (such as Daly, 1978; Goodall & Goodall, 1982) is their failure to focus on *communication* behaviors and attitudes inherently involved in the interviewing process. Even a cursory examination of these reviews indicates that they are almost indistinguishable from the reviews conducted by personnel psychologists and management experts (for example, see Arvey & Campion, 1982; Schmitt, 1976). From our perspective, if a literature review in this area is to stimulate communication-oriented research, it must focus attention on examining studies that either describe interview communication processes or utilize communication-related attitudes and behaviors as independent or dependent variables in research designs. Thus we do not find it surprising that literature reviews that, for example, summarize studies of the effects of an applicant's age on interviewers' employment decisions do not stimulate communication-oriented interviewing research.

In addition to the above weaknesses in existing employment interviewing literature reviews prepared by communication scholars, we feel that these research analyses have not provided adequate theoretical models to serve as the bases for future study. For example, the reviews often suggest the need for more "process"-oriented research, more attention to the communication behavior of the interviewee, and so forth, but fail to incorporate these recommendations into integrative and heuristic models of communication in the employment interview.

Given the limitations of previous "communication-oriented" reviews of employment interviewing research, this chapter proposes to follow a different approach in analyzing the characteristics of the interviewing literature. Specifically, the first part of this report presents a review and analysis of *empirical* research exploring the employment *screening* (vs. determinant) interview from a communication perspective for the period of 1976-1982. The period of 1976-1982 was chosen for review since at the time we initiated our literature search the last major review of the employment interviewing literature had been published in 1976 by Neal Schmitt. Given typical publication lag time, we assumed Schmitt had reviewed the literature through about 1975. After our literature review we briefly discuss recent theoretical papers written concerning communication in the employment interview, and then conclude by presenting a model of the interview that we feel may be useful in stimulating future communication-oriented employment interviewing research.

COMMUNICATION-RELATED EMPIRICAL RESEARCH ON THE EMPLOYMENT SCREENING INTERVIEW: 1976-1982

The following literature review is based on an examination of major communication, psychology, personnel, management, and guidance journals, as well as *Dissertation Abstracts International* for the period of 1976 through 1982. Readers interested in literature reviews and analyses prior to this period are directed to a number of previously published general compilations of research (Wagner, 1949; Mayfield, 1964; Ulrich & Trumbo, 1965; Wright, 1969; Schmitt, 1976). In addition, it should be noted that during the preparation of this chapter, Arvey and Campion (1982) published a literature review that, in part, surveyed several of the years encompassed by the present analysis. However, their review does not focus on communication-oriented research, nor does it attempt to organize and thoroughly analyze this literature (though they do have a category of studies related to "nonverbal behavior"). Still, rather than be overly redundant with Arvey and Campion's review, we have truncated our analysis for the early years the two reviews overlap, while devoting greater attention to examining studies conducted during the 1980s (a period that received considerably less scrutiny in the Arvey and Campion review). In addition, it should be noted that we have included in our review only studies that directly or indirectly involve the interview as a selection device. Hence research exploring the effects of variations in information presented about applicants in resumes, application forms, and the like have been excluded from analysis, unless the interview is also utilized in the research design.

The following review is organized into four major sections. The first two sections review studies solely of either interviewee or recruiter interview communication behaviors and attitudes. In turn, the third section summarizes research that simultaneously explores interviewer and interviewee communication behaviors and attitudes, and compares the two. The final section provides a brief summary and critique of the literature reviewed in the preceding sections. In addition, it should be noted that each of the major sections is subdivided into a number of more specific areas of research. Some of the studies examined share more than one category, but were classified into distinct clusters for purposes of review and, ultimately, model building.

The Interviewee

Research exploring interviewee perceptions and behaviors in employment interviews during the period reviewed can be classified into three major groupings: (1) studies investigating factors affecting applicants' perceptions of interview outcomes, (2) research examining interview variables predictive of applicants' interview satisfaction, and (3) inquiries exploring interviewee perceptions of the credibility and trustworthiness of their interviewers.

Interview Outcomes

Several recent studies have examined factors affecting applicants' perceptions/expectations of interview outcomes and the likelihood of their accepting job offers from their recruiters' organizations. In addition, one investigation has explored relationships between applicants' perceptions of interview variables and whether or not they *actually* receive second interview offers from the organizations with which they interviewed.

Building upon Alderfer and McCord's (1970) seminal research examining relationships between the interpersonal need structures of job applicants and their expectations of a variety of interview outcomes, Schmitt and Coyle (1976) explored the effects of interviewees' evaluations of their interviewers on the likelihood of their receiving and accepting job offers from their interviewers' organizations. Based upon the results of a mail questionnaire requiring respondents (undergraduates interviewing at a university placement center) to recollect the last interview in which they had participated, Schmitt and Coyle's findings suggest that the "interpersonal capability" of interviewers is significantly related to applicants' interview outcome perceptions/expectations. Specifically, their data analyses indicate that an interviewee's perception of the likelihood of a job offer is related to his or her perceptions of an interviewer as interpersonally warm and thoughtful, well organized in presentation of ideas, and providing the applicant with job information. In turn, an applicant's likelihood of accepting a job offer was found to be related to perceptions of an interviewer as interpersonally warm and business-like, and well organized in his or her thoughts and speech patterns.

In related research, Fisher, Ilgen, and Hoyer (1979), in an interview experiment created by paper-and-pencil measures, report that business seniors are less likely to accept a job offer from an interviewer if he or she is the only source of information about a company than if the source of information were a friend, a job incumbent, or a professor. In addition, their results showed that a job applicant was more likely to accept a job offer with an organization if he or she was given positive *and* negative information about the company.

Finally, and in contrast to the above research, Jablin, Tengler, and Teigen (1982) conducted a study in which both applicants' perceptions/expectations of interview outcomes *and* actual outcomes were used as dependent measures. Obtaining data from applicants immediately subsequent to their interviews at a college placement center, Jablin et al. found that those interviewees who perceived a strong likelihood of receiving second (on-site) interview offers from their recruiters' organizations were more satisfied with their interviews as communication events than applicants who were uncertain that they would receive offers or who perceived offers as an unlikely interview outcome. Moreover, Jablin et al. found that the more interviewees perceived their interviewers as trustworthy, competent, and composed, the greater their expectations of receiving second interview offers. However, it is of interest that these researchers did *not* discover any differences between applicants who *actually* did and did not receive second (on-site) interview offers with respect to the above variables. Further, their analyses revealed that "while 81% of those persons who actually received a second interview offer accurately predicted it (the others were uncertain), only 24% of those persons not receiving an offer accurately predicted that outcome" (Jablin et al., 1982, p. 12).

In summary, findings from the above studies suggest that applicants' interview outcome expectations and the likelihood of their accepting job offers are related to their perceptions of their interviewers as competent, trustworthy, well-organized, and composed communicators. Moreover, it appears that the greater an applicant's interview communication satisfaction, the more likely it is that he or she will expect positive interview outcomes. On the other hand, interviewees appear to be hesitant to accept job offers with organizations when their only sources of information are interviewers. In conclusion, it should be noted that findings from at least one study have shown that communication variables associated with interviewees' *expectations* of receiving second (on-site) interview offers do not appear to be related to whether or not they *actually* receive offers.

Interview Satisfaction

During the period of 1976-1982, two studies explored variables contributing to applicants' interview satisfaction. Collecting questionnaire data from seniors and graduate students interviewing on a university campus, Karol (1977) discovered that the factors contributing most to applicant satisfaction involved the recruiter's "interpersonal conduct" during the interview (smiling, recalling information about the interviewee, summarizing) and the degree to which the recruiter provided information to the interviewee (about the job, prospects with the company).

Focusing specifically on applicants' perceptions of interview communication satisfaction, Tengler (1982) recently completed a study exploring relationships between the types (open/closed) and orientations (primary/secondary) of interviewers' questions and applicants' levels of interview communication satisfaction. Measuring interview communication satisfaction by an adapted version of Hecht's Interpersonal Communication Satisfaction

Inventory, and using data from actual employment interviews, Tengler's (1982, p. 77) results suggest that "the more open-ended questions an employment interviewer asks, the more satisfied the applicant with the interview as a communication event." In addition, he reports significant correlations between the amount of time interviewees spend answering questions and talking in their interviews and their interview communication satisfaction.

In summary, applicant interview satisfaction appears in part to be a function of (1) the degree to which an interviewer asks an applicant open-ended questions and allows him or her to talk during the interview, (2) the amount and quality of job and organizational information the interviewer provides, and (3) the extent to which an interviewer shows interest in an interviewee.

Interviewer Credibility

Factors contributing to applicants' perceptions of interviewer credibility have also been a focus of investigation in recent research. Manipulating interviewer behavior via a simulated audio-recorded employment interview, Rogers and Sincoff (1978) present evidence suggesting that an interviewer's job title and age, as well as speech fluency, may affect applicants' perceptions of interviewer credibility. On the other hand, Fisher et al. (1979) report that of four possible sources of information (job incumbent, friend, professor, interviewer), interviewers are least trusted and liked by applicants. Interestingly, they also found that the perceived expertise and trustworthiness of all the sources increased when they presented negative/realistic job information to applicants.

Finally, in related research Jablin et al. (1982) discovered that interviewees who perceived their interviews as high in quality (in comparison to other interviews in which they had participated) perceived their interviewers as more credible and trustworthy than applicants who rated their interviews as low in quality. Further, they found most dimensions of interviewer credibility to be significantly associated with applicants' feelings of interview communication satisfaction. However, their analyses also revealed little association between an applicant's interviewing experience (number of previous interviews, interview training) and their perceptions of interviewer credibility.

In summary, investigations exploring interviewees' perceptions of interviewer credibility indicate that in comparison to other sources of employment information, interviewers are not particularly trusted or liked. Yet, when examining applicants' perceptions when interviewers are the primary source of information, it appears that the more interviewers present negative/realistic job information and the more fluently they speak, the greater the likelihood they will be perceived as credible and trustworthy sources of information by applicants. Moreover, while several interviewer characteristics (job title and age) appear related to applicants' perceptions of interviewer credibility, interviewee characteristics (interviewing experience, interview training) do not seem to be related to credibility perceptions. In addition, research evidence suggests that interviewees' perceptions of interviewer credibility are closely associated with their feelings of interview communication satisfaction.

The Interviewer

Studies examining interviewer perceptions and behaviors in screening interviews can be grouped into three major categories: (1) investigations exploring the effects of applicant characteristics on recruiters' decisions, (2) research aimed at determining the effects of variations in an applicant's interview communication behavior on interviewers' decisions, and (3) studies directed at understanding how and what information interviewers process in making decisions about applicants.

Applicant Characteristics

Research exploring the effects of applicants' physical attributes and psychological characteristics on employers' interview decisions can be classified into three major categories: (1) studies manipulating the gender, race, or physical attractiveness of applicants, (2) research exploring the effects of interviewees' self-presentation styles, and (3) investigations evaluating the effects of applicants' handicaps/disabilities on recruiters' interview decisions.

Utilizing simulated videotaped selection interviews, Nolan (1979), in his dissertation research, attempted to determine the influence of an applicant's race, gender, and physical attractiveness on "interviewers' " (college students) evaluations of a job applicant's communication ability, work motivation, and sociability. Results of the study indicated that black interviewees were perceived to be significantly more sociable than white applicants. In addition, a significant race/gender/physical attractiveness interaction for communication ability was found, but it accounted for little variance.

Diboye and Wiley (1977,1978) also explored the effects of applicants gender on interviewers' decisions, but in addition varied applicants' levels of self-presentation style. In the first of their studies, college recruiters were shown experimentally manipulated videotapes of male and female interviewees presenting themselves in either passive or moderately aggressive interaction styles. Findings revealed that interviewers favored the moderately aggressive applicant over the passive one, and believed that the passive interviewee answered questions poorly (usually responding with yes or no answers). Moreover, recruiters liked the female interviewee more than they liked the male applicant. However, raters judged the moderately aggressive male and female applicants approximately equal in favorability, and similarly perceived the passive male and female interviewees to be equally unfavorable. In their second study, Diboye and Wiley essentially replicated the results of the first investigation, but in addition found that interviewers may possess stereotypes of the self-presentation styles appropriate for different types of positions. In addition, it should be noted that Sands (1979) has recently reported findings supportive of Diboye and Wiley's research.

During the period reviewed, two investigations examined the effects of applicants' handicaps/disabilities on recruiters' interview decisions. In one study (Stone & Sawatzki, 1980), MBA students received experimentally manipulated (physically disabled, psychiatrically disabled, no disability) packets of information on an interviewee, and then heard the same simulated audiotaped employment interview. Subsequently, these judges rated the applicant on twelve Likert-type items, essentially evaluating the interviewee's communication competency (communication skills, ability to stay focused on interview topics, explanation skills, expressions of enthusiasm, appropriate closure). Data analyses revealed that evaluations of the interviewee were *not* significantly different across the three disability conditions.

In contrast, Sigelman, Elias, and Danker-Brown (1980) investigated the effects of the nonverbal and verbal behaviors of mentally retarded adults on "interviewer" ratings of their employability. Specifically, videotaped segments of simulated employment interviews were shown to students in a personnel management course, who rated the interviewees on a number of scales. Results of analyses indicated that the verbal behaviors of the interviewees were better predictors of interviewers' hiring decisions than were their nonverbal behaviors: "Interviewees whose speech was intelligible, who spoke at length, and who responded appropriately to questions were likely to make favorable impressions" (Sigelman et al., 1980, p. 67). The authors speculate that verbal factors may be more important predictors of the employability of mentally retarded job applicants than they are for "normal" job applicants (for whom research often shows nonverbal behaviors to be powerful predictors of interviewers' employment decisions).

In summary, the studies reviewed in this section concerned with the effects of applicants' characteristics on interviewers' evaluations of their communicative behavior suggest few significant findings. However, of those studies examined the research of Sigelman et al. (1980) may hold the most promise for future investigation. If it can be substantiated that psychologically disabled job applicants are evaluated more on their verbal than on their nonverbal communication during interviews, an important form of interviewer bias (and possibly discrimination) will have been uncovered.

Interviewee Communication

A number of studies have attempted to determine the effects of variations in applicant communicative behavior on interviewers' employment decisions. Most of these investigations have manipulated either interviewees' (1) nonverbal communication or (2) language/dialect styles.

Inquiries exploring the impact of interviewee nonverbal communication on interviewers' decisions have generally controlled applicant verbal behaviors while employing a "high/low" nonverbal behavior experimental paradigm. For example, McGovern and associates (McGovern & Ideus, 1978, McGovern & Tinsley, 1978) and Trent (1979) created "low" and "high" nonverbal interviewees by manipulating their levels of eye contact, energy (as expressed by smiles, gestures, and body movement), voice modulation and vocal expression of affect, and speech disturbances (hesitations, "ah," "um"). In each of these studies simulated interviews were videotaped and shown to actual employment interviewers. Findings from these studies suggest that interviewers (1) overwhelmingly prefer "high nonverbal" job candidates, (2) probably perceive applicant nonverbal communication as a cluster of behaviors versus distinct ones, and (3) evaluate interviewee nonverbal behavior throughout the entirety of an interview. However, it should be noted that, in contrast to the findings of the above studies, Sterrett (1978), in research utilizing a similar type of methodology and manipulating interviewees' intensities of body language (length of eye contact, number of hand gestures, level of dress, and length of pause before answering a question), found no differences in interviewers' ratings of applicants.

Focusing on somewhat different dimensions of nonverbal communication, Imada and Hakel (1977) report a study of the influence of interviewer-interviewee proximity and interviewee nonverbal "immediacy" on decisions in employment interviews. In this simulated interview experiment, proximity was operationalized by assigning raters (students) to one of three roles: interviewer, "live" observer (seated in the interview room next to the interviewer), or TV observer (seated in a different room). In other words, proximity was manipulated in both physical and psychological senses. The two levels of applicant nonverbal immediacy (immediate, nonimmediate) were created by manipulating the applicants' (confederates) levels of eye contact, smiling, posture, interpersonal distance, and body orientation. Results of the experiment indicated that applicants evidencing immediate nonverbal behaviors were rated more favorably than applicants in the nonimmediate condition. No significant proximity main effects were found in the data analyses.

In addition to examining the effects of applicants' nonverbal behavior on interviewers' employment decisions, researchers have also manipulated the verbal behavior (in particular the language styles) of interviewees to determine its impact on their employability. Hopper (1977), exploring the effects of "standard" and "nonstandard" speech dialects and applicants' race (black, white), obtained recruiters' impressions of experimentally manipulated simulated screening interviews. Results of his study revealed that black applicants who spoke "standard" dialect were favored by interviewers over the other job candidates. In general, findings suggested that the interviewees' ethnicity was not an important component of their interviewers' attitudes toward them. In related research, de la Zerda and Hopper (1979) had recruiters listen to simulated audiotaped interviews of Mexican Americans speaking English with varying degrees of accent. Findings showed that the applicant's accent did affect hiring decisions. Specifically, interviewees whose accents were standard sounding were favored by recruiters for supervisory positions, but were less likely to be hired for semiskilled positions. The researchers suggest that recruiters may be matching jobs to their stereotypes of interviewees based on their accents.

Interested in the effects of the vocal activity and race of applicants on interview selection decisions, Byrd (1980) showed interviewers (students in management courses) a slide of either a black or white male interviewee while they listen to audiotaped interviews in which the interviewee's vocal activity level was manipulated. Results of the experiment indicated that (1) vocal activity was a more powerful predictor of interviewer's selection decisions than applicant race, (2) black applicants were favored over white applicants, and (3) high vocal activity was perceived by interviewers as a more desirable trait in applicants than low vocal activity.

In contrast to the above studies, Watson and Ragsdale (1981) conducted an investigation of the linguistic characteristics of truthful and deceptive responses of applicants to questions in simulated employment interviews. Interviewees (undergraduate students in basic communication courses) were asked either to lie or to be truthful in response to four questions asked by an interviewer. Deceptive responses were found to contain more total word usage, negated second-person pronouns, positive first-person pronouns, negated existential references, and positive generalized other references, and fewer group references and past-tense verbs. Overall, deceptive responses were less specific and more abstract than truthful responses.

In one of the few studies found analyzing data from actual employment interviews, Einhorn (1981) examined the rhetorical communication of "successful" and "unsuccessful" interviewees (success defined as pre/post-interview improvement in interviewers' attitudes toward interviewees). Her nonstatistical analyses of fourteen interview videotapes led her to conclude that successful (compared to unsuccessful) interviewees "displayed more

behaviors that identified them with employers, supported arguments, organized thoughts, clarified ideas, contributed to effective delivery, and conveyed positive images" (Einhorn, 1981, p. 220).

In related research, Greenwald (1978) reported a study designed to
explore the effects of an applicant's physical attractiveness, experience, and
social performance upon interviewer decision making. Social performance
was operationalized as either "high" or "low" based on the manipulated
audiotaped responses of an applicant to three commonly asked interview
questions. Of the three independent variables studied, social performance
was the best predictor of recruiters' ratings. Yet findings revealed that "interviewers as a group consistently underestimated the influence of verbal interview performance on their evaluations" (Greenwald, 1978, p. 1956-B).

Finally, the only research we discovered that simultaneously explored
the verbal and nonverbal dimensions of communication in employment interviews warrants discussion. In this study, Hollandsworth, Kazelskis,
Stevens, and Dressel (1979) obtained recruiters' ratings of applicants immediately after their interviews at a college placement office. Results of a discriminant analysis indicated that "appropriateness of content, fluency of
speech, and composure were of greatest importance in contributing to a
favorable employment decision" (Hollandsworth et al., 1979, p. 359). The
researchers add that their findings bring into question some of the recent
research that emphasizes the impact of nonverbal versus verbal behaviors
on interview decisions.

In summary, several conclusions can be drawn from studies examining
the effects of variations in applicants' communicative behaviors upon interviewers' decisions. First, it appears that interviewees who demonstrate high
versus low levels of nonverbal immediacy are favored by recruiters. However, this conclusion should be tempered by the knowledge that in most of
this research, interviewees were portrayed at the extremes of the immediacy
continuum. As McGovern and Tinsley (1978, p. 163) observe, "In real life,
however, such differences may be less absolute." With respect to studies
manipulating the speech behavior of interviewees, findings seem to suggest
that vocally active interviewees who speak a standard English dialect are
preferred by recruiters. However, this conclusion may also be limited, since
most of the speech samples employed in these investigations have been of
very brief durations (60-90 seconds), and consequently of questionable
generalizability to actual employment interviews (which are typically 30
minutes long). In closing, it should also be noted that of the research reviewed here only one investigation explored simultaneously the effects of
verbal and nonverbal applicant communication upon interviewers' selection decisions. Though the results of that study and several others suggest

that the verbal, compared to the nonverbal, communication of applicants may have more influence on interviewers' decisions, future research will be required before we can accept that conclusion even tentatively.

Information Processing

The manner in which interviewers process information about applicants prior to and during interviews traditionally has been a popular area of research. However, though a considerable number of studies were conducted in this area during the period reviewed, only a handful directly explored communication variables and the processing of information in interviews (versus information from resumes, application forms, and so on). Of those communication-related investigations reviewed, most tended to explore either (1) the effects of information characteristics presented during interviews, or (2) the effects of interviewer attributional processes on selection decisions.

In an investigation of information favorability in the employment interview, Constantin (1976) had interviewers (management students) rate audiotaped simulated interviews that were manipulated with respect to information normativity (socially normative-deviant), relevancy (relevant-irrelevant), and favorability (favorable-unfavorable) about the applicant. Results of the experiment indicated that raters evaluated "information that deviated from the social norms more extremely than information that was normative; judges responded to unfavorable information that was relevant by rating the applicant lower than when same information was irrelevant; and judges responded to favorable information by rating the applicant high regardless of the relevancy of the information" (Constantin, 1976, p. 748). On the other hand, Downs and Tanner (1982), in a more general study of decision making in interviews, report that recruiters' decisions about applicants tend to be based more on their assessment of the "total" person than on individual qualities.

The question of *how* information, versus what information, is processed by interviewers in their decision making has also been a focus of recent research. Applying principles of attribution theory, Tucker and Rowe (1979) present the results of an experiment in which they had students read a series of interview transcripts in which the applicant discussed either a successful or an unsuccessful situation from his or her past. However, before the judges read the transcripts, expectations of the interviewees were established by providing the judges with either a favorable or unfavorable letter of reference for the applicant. Findings from the study revealed that a recruiter with an unfavorable expectancy is likely to attribute less credit to an applicant for his or her past successes, while attributing more responsibility to the applicant for past failures, and is less likely to find the interviewee an acceptable job candidate.

In related research, Sackett (1981) examined the effects of preinterview expectancies of applicants on interviewers' question-asking behaviors. Extrapolating upon Snyder and Swann's (1978) expectancy-confirmation research, Sackett hypothesized that during interviews recruiters would adopt questioning strategies that would be directed at confirming experimentally manipulated preinterview expectations of applicants. In general, the results of his research did not support this hypothesis, and they suggest limited generalizability of Snyder and Swann's "hypothesis testing" research to the selection interview.

In summary, the studies reviewed here confirm the rather intuitive proposition that interviewers find applicants more acceptable if they receive favorable information about them either prior to or during their interviews. In addition, it appears that if recruiters do possess preinterview applicant expectancies, these expectations do not necessarily result in interviewers adopting confirmatory question strategies; rather, they seem to base their questions on the types of answers they receive from applicants in their interviews.

Interviewee-Interviewer Meta-Perceptions

In addition to research that has focused solely on either interviewers' or applicants' behaviors and perceptions of themselves, recent studies have also attempted to determine the degree to which interviewers' and interviewees' perceptions of interview processes and behaviors are similar. Most of these studies have explored the degree to which interviewers' and interviewees' value structures, perceptions of intrinsic and extrinsic job characteristics, and the like parallel one another. However, a few investigations have examined interviewer-interviewee perceptual congruence with respect to communication-related variables.

Cheatham and McLaughlin (1976) asked interviewers and interviewees at a college placement center to respond to questionnaires immediately after their interviews, evaluating their own and the "other" parties' interview communication behaviors. Results of their study showed that interviewees tended to rate themselves and their interviewers higher on verbal communication behaviors (vocal communication, percentage of talk time, questioning behavior, and the like) than did their recruiters. In particular, "compared to applicant self-perceptions, interviewers saw applicants as more talkative and less effective in listening and question-answering behaviors" (Cheatham & McLaughlin, 1976, p. 13).

In a study peripherally related to communication in interviews, Harlan, Kerr, and Kerr (1977) had recruiters, managers, supervisors, clerical workers, and high school students respond to a questionnaire in which they were asked to indicate work-related topics they would and would not discuss in employment interviews. Of interest is the rather consistent finding that each of the sampled groups felt that they would not discuss with interviewers information about "interpersonal relationships" with supervisors and peers on past jobs or what they expected those relationships would be like in the jobs for which they were applying. One might infer from these results that during interviews, recruiters and applicants do not feel it is appropriate to discuss or ask about communication relationships with supervisors and peers on previous jobs or expectations of these relationships on jobs being applied for.

Focusing on the effects of applicant-interviewer similarity on employment decisions, Daly, Richmond, and Leth (1979) explored whether or not similarities in interviewee-interviewer levels of social communicative anxiety are related to personnel selection decisions. Results of the research clearly showed that regardless of an interviewer's (students judging paper-and-pencil interview situations) own level of anxiety, the interviewer would rate the highly anxious applicant lower than he or she would rate the applicant low in communicative anxiety.

Finally, an investigation that does not compare interviewer-interviewee communication perceptions/attitudes, but rather their actual interview "talk," requires discussion. In this study Ragan and Hopper (1981) qualitatively described "aligning talk" in six simulated interviews with one recruiter. According to these researchers, aligning actions/talk are "conversational tactics used to repair enigmatic meanings and to aid actors in understanding each other's intentions" (Ragan & Hopper, 1981, p. 85). Four characteristics of aligning actions were examined (accounts, formulations, meta-talk, and qualifiers), and the results of their investigation revealed that interviewees used almost twice as many alignment actions as interviewers. These findings led the authors to conclude that in the interview context, alignment talk is used to create and preserve the differential roles/status of an interviewee and interviewer.

In summary, based upon the few studies discussed here it appears that interviewers and interviewees possess differential perceptions of communication in employment interviews, and may evidence distinct types of actual communicative behaviors.

Summary and Critique

Several descriptive statistics computed from the preceding literature review may be of interest to the reader. First, in our search of the general employment interviewing literature for the period reviewed, we identified 53 empirical studies. Of those studies, 30, or 57 percent, explored communication-related variables. Moreover, within the category of interviewee studies,

100 percent investigated communication-related variables, while in the other two categories approximately 50 percent of the studies explored communication-related factors (51 percent of the interviewer studies and 57 percent of the interviewer-interviewee articles). In turn, of the communication-oriented investigations, 17 percent (n = 5) focused solely on the interviewee, 70 percent (n = 21) examined interviewer communication exclusively, and 13 percent (n = 4) were concerned with comparing interviewer-interviewee perceptions and behaviors.

The above statistics are revealing in that they suggest that over half of the employment interviewing studies published between 1976 and 1982 examined communication-related variables. However, it should be noted that to the best of our knowledge only about one-third of these communication-oriented investigations were reported by scholars associated with the speech and communication disciplines. Thus, if one is not provincial in one's attitudes about *who* (with respect to academic disciplines) does communication research, it is apparent that a considerable amount of communication-related employment interviewing research was conducted between 1976 and 1982. This would seem to indicate that if debilities exist in communication-related employment interviewing research, they may be associated less with the *amount* of research being conducted and more with the *types* of inquiries being executed.

The above conclusion seems to be supported by the statistics reported earlier showing that the great majority (70 percent) of the communication-related interviewing research is concerned exclusively with interviewer perceptions and behaviors. This research bias is evident in the general employment interviewing literature as well, and reflects the traditional partiality of applied researchers to the organization's (in this case the interviewer representing the organization) perspective or definition of "reality." In other words, we have a tendency to view the interview as a selection tool for the organization and often lose sight of the fact that it is also a communication event in which the interviewee is *recruited* by the organization and evaluates the organization and its representative with respect to potential employment. In fact, given recent research indicating that the average applicant spends only about ten minutes of the typical thirty-minute screening interview talking (see Tengler, 1982), it is obvious that a considerable amount of interview time is spent recruiting the applicant (or at least creating a favorable public relations image).

It is also evident from our review that most communication-oriented interviewing studies have focused on exploring isolated interview factors, typically from static research perspectives. Little of the research explores the interview process, and in particular message-exchange patterns between interviewer and interviewee. Of equal significance is the fact that none of the research effectively examines the role of communication in the interview as an integral part of the overall process of assimilating new members into organizations. Specifically, almost all the research utilizes the interviewer's offering/not offering of a job to an applicant as the major outcome of an employment interview, and consequently fails to realize that the interview is also setting initial job expectations for applicants, and is therefore a significant factor in subsequent organizational assimilation processes.

In addition, the selection of a "job offer" as the major criterion for measuring the "success" of an interview is not an accurate representation of the typical outcome of an employment screening interview. The purpose of the screening interview is not to make a decision whether or not to hire an applicant, but merely to determine if the organization and applicant wish to continue the selection/recruitment process (see Stewart & Cash, 1982). Thus the more appropriate variable to measure the "success" of an interview is an organization's offer to an applicant of a second or on-site interview, and the applicant's acceptance of that offer. It is only after the on-site interview that job offers are typically made. Consequently, an applicant's decision to accept a job offer is the result of more factors than merely his or her interaction with a screening interviewer.[1]

On a more positive note, it is our impression from examining the recent literature that paper-and-pencil interview studies are diminishing in number, while investigations utilizing audio- and videotaped simulated interview stimuli are increasing in popularity. This trend is obviously desirable and it is only hoped that in the future more studies will investigate communication processes in actual versus simulated interviews.

In summary, it appears that (1) over 50 percent of the employment interviewing studies conducted between 1976 and 1982 examined communication-related variables; (2) over two-thirds of the communication-related studies focused exclusively on exploring the communication behaviors and perceptions of interviewers; (3) most of the research has failed to consider both the selection and recruitment functions of the interview; (4) few studies have examined message-exchange processes in interviewing or the communicative role of the interview in the organizational assimilation process; (5) investigators have tended to use the offer/not offer of a *job* as their major screening interview outcome variable when the offer/not offer of a second or *on-site interview* seems more appropriate; and (6) paper-and-pencil interviewing studies are decreasing in number while more investigations are being conducted utilizing audio- and videotape simulated interviews.

Given the deficiencies in the interviewing literature discussed above, the following section examines recent interviewing reviews and theoretical reports to determine the degree to which their research recommendations present viable solutions to the aforementioned issues.

RESEARCH RECOMMENDATIONS OF
RECENT THEORETICAL EMPLOYMENT
INTERVIEWING PAPERS: AN ANALYSIS

In the last few years two articles have been published in communication journals that are somewhat theoretical in nature and set forth directions for future communication-related employment interviewing research. The first of these articles is a rhetorical analysis of the employment interview published by Einhorn (1981) and is based on her dissertation research, while the second was written by Goodall and Goodall (1982) and is a selected review of the literature with "implications" for communication research. In addition to the "typical" recommendations for research in this area (such as more case studies of interviews in specific job categories, greater methodological care in conducting studies, more process studies), these authors advocate that future research should be oriented more toward exploring the employment interview as a *persuasive* communication event. Goodall and Goodall (1982, p. 122) clearly state this position:

> While it is fashionable to look at employment interviews, or any interview, as a form of interpersonal communication (Downs, Smeyak, & Martin, 1980; Stewart & Cash, 1978), it is perhaps more profitable to look at the persuasiveness of the situation and the individual rhetorics used to further individual causes (Einhorn, 1981).

While we have no objection to exploring employment interviews from a rhetorical perspective, we do take issue with the above suggestion that researchers should base their analyses of interviews on the premise that interviews are primarily persuasive events in which rhetors attempt "to further their individual causes." In fact, we believe that the adoption of such a position will just reinforce some of the major weaknesses already existing in the employment interviewing literature.

There are a number of reasons we believe embracing a persuasion model of the employment interview would hinder rather than foster the quality of research in this area. First, given the already existing tendency of researchers to examine the interview as a linear versus reciprocal interaction process, utilization of the persuasion paradigm would likely result in an even greater emphasis on how the interview parties "act" versus "interact" with one another. Second, we fear that a by-product of the persuasion approach will be a focus on the interview as a form of "manipulative" versus "open" persuasion (Porter, Allen, & Angle, 1981). Research findings that may be generalized to teaching applicants and recruiters how better to enact interpersonal facades are certainly not likely to enhance the already-limited validity of the interview as a selection and recruitment device.

Related to the above issues is a concern that arises based on the results of research on the job expectations of new organizational recruits. Specifically, results of these studies (for reviews, see Wanous, 1980; Jablin, 1981) indicate that recruits who have "realistic" (accurate) expectations of their jobs and organizations prior to their employment evidence lower turnover rates and higher levels of job satisfaction once on the job than recruits who have "unrealistic" expectations. From our perspective, these findings seem to suggest that it is in both the organization's and the applicant's best interests to view the interview as an *information-sharing,* expectation-matching communication event, rather than one in which both parties are trying to persuade each other that they are something they are not.

Obviously, the above criticisms of the persuasion model of the employment interview are in part based on the assumption (and fear) that the approach encourages one to view the interview as a context in which interviewer and interviewee are adversaries, each attempting in some manner to manipulate the other. Certainly one can argue that this is a very biased perspective of persuasion, but as it applies to the employment interview we feel it is a very realistic one. For anyone who has ever taught college students employment interviewing, it is apparent that most students (applicants) are primarily interested in learning what they *need to say* to recruiters to receive on-site interviews. In other words, they do in fact usually perceive the interviewer as an adversary whom they must somehow control. Not only is that perspective shortsighted, but, as indicated above, it is likely to result in the creation of unrealistic expectations for both the interviewee and the interviewer.

In summary, our analysis suggests that acceptance of a persuasion model of the employment interview poses several dangers. We feel it may (1) encourage viewing the interview as a linear rather than a reciprocal interaction process; (2) foster research promoting the perspective that interviewers and interviewees are adversaries versus allies; (3) result in the creation of unrealistic expectations on the parts of both interviewers and interviewees (which in the long run may have undesirable individual and organizational consequences); and therefore (4) probably not provide information that will increase the validity of the interview as a selection and recruitment device. An alternative approach, which we believe may be more productive in guiding future communication-oriented employment interviewing research, is discussed in the next section.

THE EMPLOYMENT SCREENING INTERVIEW: A MODEL FROM A COMMUNICATION AND ORGANIZATIONAL ASSIMILATION PERSPECTIVE

Rather than suggest that future research focus on analyzing the screening interview as a persuasive communication event, we recommend that it be investigated as an *information-sharing* interaction. Viewing the interview as an information-sharing interaction eliminates most of the deficiencies noted above with respect to the persuasive approach, while still allowing for those who wish to examine the rhetorical properties of the process. In addition, we advise that the interview be studied as an essential element in the organizational assimilation process. Adoption of this perspective will mean that the interview will not only be explored as a process, but its communicative role in the assimilation of new members into organizations will be considered.

According to Jablin (1982, p. 256), organizational assimilation "refers to the process by which organizational members become a part of, or are absorbed into, the culture of an organization." The process essentially combines the organization's attempt at socializing new employees with the new recruits' efforts to "individualize" or negotiate their organizational roles. This socialization-individualization process is typically reported to contain three basic phases: anticipatory socialization, encounter, and metamorphosis. Our concern here is with the first two stages of the process.

Anticipatory socialization occurs prior to an individual's entry into an organization. Feldman (1976, p. 434) has suggested that the "main activities the individual engages in at this stage are forming expectations about jobs—transmitting, receiving and evaluating information with prospective employers—and making decisions about employment." In turn, it has recently been proposed that the anticipatory socialization phase can be divided into two separate but related stages—anticipatory *vocational* (or occupational socialization) and anticipatory *organizational* socialization (Jablin, 1982). The first of these phases is concerned with the process by which a person chooses a career direction and develops expectations about what that profession or career will be like. The latter stage describes the process by which an individual forms expectations of a particular job and organization prior to actually becoming a member of the organization. This phase is directly concerned with the employment interview, as Jablin (1982, p. 263) observes:

> The information sharing that takes place between the recruit and organization during the selection-recruitment process is considered to be a key part of this stage, particularly in terms of how it affects employment decisions. One of the

primary vehicles for information exchange between applicant and organization is the selection interview.

Subsequent to the anticipatory socialization phase, and assuming an applicant is offered and accepts a position in an organization, he or she begins the "encounter" stage of assimilation. This is a "breaking-in" period and, while it may be a "reality shock" for the new employee, it typically "involves a pattern of day-to-day experiences in which the individual is subjected to the reinforcement policies and practices of the organization and its members" (Porter, Lawler, & Hackman, 1975, p. 164). As a result of this "encounter" the new employee may need to reformulate his or her existing attitudinal and behavioral work patterns so that they are aligned with the "reality" of the organization of which he or she is now a member. However, as was noted earlier, the more an employee's initial expectations are not congruent with organizational "reality," the greater the probability that he or she will not successfully adapt to the "encounter" phase, and consequently will experience job dissatisfaction and possibly job turnover.

With these issues in mind, Figure 5.1 presents a model of the relationships among the employment screening interview, communication, and organizational assimilation. An assumption of this model is that the screening interview is both a selection and a recruitment device, through which the interview parties share information, consequently permitting them to determine if an adequate "match" or fit exists between their respective needs and goals (see Jablin, 1975). Though not included in the model, the assumption is made that organizations will likely use other devices (such as testing or assessment centers) along with the interview as part of their selection procedures.

As is evident in Figure 5.1, the first stage of the model is concerned with the expectations the interviewee develops as a result of vocational anticipatory socialization. In particular, the model suggests that these expectations will be affected by the various sources from which vocational information has been derived, as well as the degree to which these sources have provided realistic/accurate portrayals of the desired career/occupation. In turn, it is anticipated that job expectations originating from an applicant's vocational anticipatory socialization will affect his or her organizational anticipatory socialization. During the organizational socialization phase it is possible that a job candidate might obtain information either from literature available from the organization or via interpersonal contacts. Thus prior to a screening interview an applicant might inspect the organization's most recent annual report, talk to professors familiar with the organization, or converse with other applicants who may have already interviewed with the organization. Regardless of the particular sources from which the recruit has obtained information, it is expected that with respect to accuracy/realism these data will exist along a continuum (from very accurate to very inaccurate).

The interaction of information and corresponding attitudes derived from vocational and organizational anticipatory socialization is hypothesized to affect the dynamics of the screening interview directly. In addition, it is assumed that a variety of individual difference/attribute factors particular to the interviewee and interviewer will affect communication in the interview. Several of these factors are included in the model and are extrapolated from the preceding review. Obviously, the degree to which interviewer and interviewee personal attributes complement one another will influence the character of the interview message exchange process.

With respect to the character of the interview message exchange process, it is important to note that each party's actual *and* perceived behaviors will affect the dynamics of the communication process. Based primarily upon our literature review, several dimensions of the message exchange process are posited to be of importance. Obviously, the topics that are discussed, as well as the quality of information obtained on each topic (for example, quantity, relevancy, specificity, accuracy of information), are basic properties of the message exchange process. In addition, it is expected that the interaction pattern—question/response or a more conversational response/response—that evolves in the interview will influence interview outcomes. The analysis of such patterns seems particularly important since recent research suggests that applicants who receive on-site interview offers (compared to those who do not) tend to spend less total time answering questions in their interviews, but more total time talking with their interviewers (Tengler & Jablin, 1983). Finally, the nonverbal behaviors (particularly the degree of nonverbal immediacy) of the interview parties, as well as the attributions each party makes of the other's messages, are considered integral elements of the interview communication process.

The model posits that there will be immediate and long-term outcomes generated directly and indirectly from the employment screening interview. In terms of immediate outcomes, each interview party will experience some degree of interview communication satisfaction. Additionally, the applicant will probably possess a set of expectations with respect to a possible on-site interview, a job offer, and the character of the organization and position applied for. The actual offer of a second interview (usually occurring within a week or two of the interview) is also considered an immediate outcome. Long-term outcomes include the further development of both the recruiter's and the applicant's interview skills, possible alterations and refinements in the interviewee's vocational expectations, and some form of impression (which may be accurate or inaccurate) formed by the applicant of the organization and job for which he or she had applied.

Obviously, if the applicant does not receive a second (on-site) interview offer, the selection-recruitment process with the particular organization terminates. On the other hand, assuming that the applicant participates in the

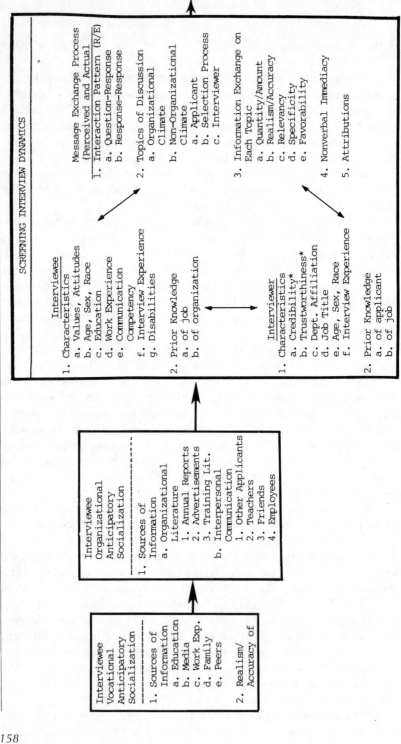

SCREENING INTERVIEW DYNAMICS

Interviewee
1. Characteristics
   a. Values, Attitudes
   b. Age, Sex, Race
   c. Education
   d. Work Experience
   e. Communication
      Competency
   f. Interview Experience
   g. Disabilities
2. Prior Knowledge
   a. of job
   b. of organization

Interviewer
1. Characteristics
   a. Credibility*
   b. Trustworthiness*
   c. Dept. Affiliation
   d. Job Title
   e. Age, Sex, Race
   f. Interview Experience
2. Prior Knowledge
   a. of applicant
   b. of job

Message Exchange Process
(Perceived and Actual
1. Interaction Pattern (R/E)
   a. Question-Response
   b. Response-Response
2. Topics of Discussion
   a. Organizational
      Climate
   b. Non-Organizational
      Climate
      a. Applicant
      b. Selection Process
      c. Interviewer
3. Information Exchange on
   Each Topic
   a. Quantity/Amount
   b. Realism/Accuracy
   c. Relevancy
   d. Specificity
   e. Favorability
4. Nonverbal Immediacy
5. Attributions

Interviewee
Organizational
Anticipatory
Socialization
1. Sources of
   Information
   a. Organizational
      Literature
      1. Annual Reports
      2. Advertisements
      3. Training Lit.
   b. Interpersonal
      Communication
      1. Other Applicants
      2. Teachers
      3. Friends
      4. Employees

Interviewee
Vocational
Anticipatory
Socialization
1. Sources of
   Information
   a. Education
   b. Media
   c. Work Exp.
   d. Family
   e. Peers
2. Realism/
   Accuracy of

158

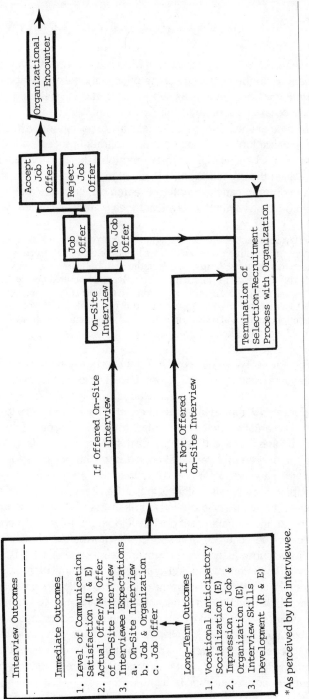

Interview Outcomes

Immediate Outcomes

1. Level of Communication Satisfaction (R & E)
2. Actual Offer/No Offer of On-Site Interview
3. Interviewee Expectations
   a. On-Site Interview
   b. Job & Organization
   c. Job Offer

Long-Term Outcomes

1. Vocational Anticipatory Socialization (E)
2. Impression of Job & Organization (E)
3. Interview Skills Development (R & E)

If Offered On-Site Interview

If Not Offered On-Site Interview

On-Site Interview

Job Offer

No Job Offer

Accept Job Offer

Reject Job Offer

Organizational Encounter

Termination of Selection-Recruitment Process with Organization

*As perceived by the interviewee.

Figure 5.1.   The employment screening interview, communication, and organizational assimilation.

on-site interview and receives and accepts a job offer, he or she will subsequently embark upon the next stage of the organizational assimilation process, organizational "encounter." As suggested earlier, it is likely that the new recruit's success in adapting to this "encounter" will be related to the degree to which he or she has developed realistic expectations as a result of anticipatory socialization and the selection-recruitment process.

In summary, we believe that the above model of the employment interview and its role in the organizational assimilation process can be useful in guiding future communication-oriented research on the interview. The assimilation approach has a number of advantages, as recently noted:

> An assimilation approach allows one simultaneously to explore individual cognitive and communicative processes, as well as organizational processes, in dynamic rather than static terms; that is, individual behavior and organizational processes are viewed as interactive, reciprocal (although not necessarily always of equal magnitude), and occurring over time. Furthermore, this framework assumes that cognition and communication behaviors in organizations are developmental and historic in nature and, as a result, may have some degree of predictability. (Jablin, 1982, p. 261)

Even a cursory consideration of the model and the earlier literature review suggests some exciting research possibilities. For example, several studies discussed in the review (for example, Diboye & Wiley, 1977, 1978; de la Zerda & Hopper, 1979) indicate that recruiters may have a tendency to stereotype the oral presentation styles appropriate for different types of positions and job levels. If this is the case, then it may be that those applicants who fail to demonstrate the desired oral presentation styles for the positions for which they are applying have not experienced the breadth, depth, or realism of vocational anticipatory socialization that is indicative of more successful applicants. Moreover, the issues of the relative influences of different sources of information on an individual's vocational development, how one reconciles inconsistencies in the accuracy and realism of information obtained from these sources, and subsequent effects on an applicant's interviewing behavior are all aspects of the interviewing and organizational assimilation processes we know little about. In fact, at present we still do not have an adequate understanding of the effects of an applicant's interview preparation (anticipatory organizational socialization) on his or her interview communication behavior. On the other hand, our knowledge of the effects of an interviewer's organizational department affiliation—particularly if the interviewer is an incumbent from the hiring department or a personnel representative—on the quality of interview communication is minimal.

Essentially, it is our position that future research needs to take into consideration that applicants and interviewers enter screening interviews with job and organizational expectations they derive from numerous sources of communication. Until we start to consider the effects of those factors, as well as the communicative dynamics of the interview itself, it is unlikely that our understanding of the employment interview will advance. Moreover, discernment of the types of expectations that are communicated to the recruit via the screening (and on-site) interview appears necessary if we are to comprehend difficulties new organizational members often experience later, during organizational "encounter" and "metamorphosis."

In summary, our goals in this chapter have been (1) to provide a review of communication-oriented research on the employment screening interview for the period of 1976-1982; (2) to critique that literature; (3) to consider the viablity of recent suggestions to study the interview primarily as a persuasive interaction; and (4) to propose an alternative approach for guiding future communication-related research on the screening interview. Toward this end, a model of the employment screening interview, communication, and organizational assimilation was presented and explicated in the final section of the chapter. We hope this model will be valuable in stimulating future communication-oriented research on the screening interview and its role in the organizational assimilation process.

NOTE

1. It is assumed that organizations that conduct screening interviews do have available positions in which to place qualified applicants. If an organization were merely conducting "courtesy" interviews, which does occur to some degree during depressed economic periods, the offer/no offer of an on-site interview would probably not be a suitable interview outcome criterion.

REFERENCES

Alderfer, C. P., & McCord, C. G. (1970). Personal and situational factors in the recruitment interview. *Journal of Applied Psychology, 54,* 377-385.
Arvey, R. D., & Campion, J. E. (1982). The employment interview: A summary and review of recent research. *Personnel Psychology, 35,* 281-322.
Byrd, M. L. V. (1980). The effects of vocal activity and race of applicant on the job selection interview decision (Doctoral dissertation, University of Missouri—Columbia, 1979). *Dissertation Abstracts International, 41,* 1834A.
Cheatham, T. R., & McLaughlin, M. (1976). A comparison of co-participant perceptions of self and others in placement center interviews. *Communication Quarterly, 24,* 9-13.
Constantin, S. W. (1976). An investigation of information favorably in the employment interview. *Journal of Applied Psychology, 61,* 743-749.
Daly, J A. (1978). *The personnel selection interview: A state of the art review.* Paper presented at the annual convention of the International Communication Association, Chicago.
Daly, J. A., Richmond, V. P., & Leth, S. (1979). Social communicative anxiety and the personnel selection process: Testing the similarity effect in selection decisions. *Human Communication Research, 6,* 18-32.
de la Zerda, N., & Hopper, R. (1979). Employment interviewers' reactions to Mexican American speech. *Communication Monographs, 46,* 126-134.
Diboye, R. L., & Wiley, J. W. (1977). Reactions of college recruiters to interviewee sex and self-presentation style. *Journal of Vocational Behavior, 10,* 1-12.

Diboye, R. L., & Wiley, J. W. (1978). Reactions of male raters to interviewee self-presentation style and sex: Extensions of previous research. *Journal of Vocational Behavior, 13,* 192-203.

Downs, C. W., Smeyak, G. P., & Martin, E. (1980). *Professional interviewing.* New York: Harper & Row.

Downs, C. W., & Tanner, J. E. (1982). Decision-making in the selection interview. *Journal of College Placement, 42,* 59-61.

Einhorn, L. J. (1981). An inner view of the job interview: An investigation of successful communicative behaviors. *Communication Education, 30,* 217-228.

Feldman, D. C. (1976). A contingency theory of socialization. *Administrative Science Quarterly, 21,* 433-452.

Fisher, C. D., Ilgen, D. R., & Hoyer, W. D. (1979). Source credibility, information favorability, and job offer acceptance. *Academy of Management Journal, 22,* 94-103.

Goodall, D. B., & Goodall, H. L. (1982). The employment interview: A selective review of the literature with implications for communication research. *Communication Quarterly, 30,* 116-123.

Greenwald, M. A. (1978). The effects of physical attractiveness, experience, and social performance on employer decision-making in job interviews (Doctoral dissertation, University of Wisconsin—Madison, 1978). *Dissertation Abstracts International, 39,* 1956B.

Harlan, A., Kerr, J., & Kerr, S. (1977). Preference for motivator and hygiene factors in a hypothetical interview situation: Further findings and some implications for the employment interview. *Personnel Psychology, 30,* 557-566.

Hollandsworth, J. G., Kazelskis, R., Stevens, J., & Dressel, M. E. (1979). Relative contributions of verbal, articulative and nonverbal communication to employment decisions in the job interview setting. *Personnel Psychology, 32,* 359-367.

Hopper, R. (1977). Language attitudes in the employment interview. *Communication Monographs, 44,* 346-351.

Imada, A. S., & Hakel, M. D. (1977). Influence of nonverbal communication and rater proximity on impressions and decisions in simulated employment interviews. *Journal of Applied Psychology, 62,* 295-300.

Jablin, F. M. (1975). The selection interview: Contingency theory and beyond. *Human Resource Management, 14,* 2-9.

Jablin, F. M. (1981). *Organizational entry and organizational communication: Job retrospections, expectations, and turnover.* Paper presented at the annual convention of the Academy of Management, San Diego.

Jablin, F. M. (1982). Organizational communication: An assimilation approach. In M. E. Roloff & C. R. Berger (Eds.), *Social cognition and communication* (pp. 255-286). Beverly Hills, CA: Sage.

Jablin, F. M., Tengler, C. D., & Teigen, C. W., (1982). *Interviewee perceptions of employment screening interviews: Relationships among perceptions of communication satisfaction, interviewer credibility and trust, interviewing experience, and interview outcomes.* Paper presented at the annual convention of the International Communication Association, Boston.

Karol, B. L. (1977). Relationship of recruiter behavior, perceived similarity, and prior information to applicants' assessments of the campus recruitment interview (Doctoral dissertation, Ohio State University, 1977). *Dissertation Abstracts International, 38,* 2411B.

Mayfield, E. C. (1964). The selection interview: A reevaluation of published research. *Personnel Psychology, 17,* 234-260.

McGovern, T. V., & Ideus, H. (1978). The impact of nonverbal behavior on the employment interview. *Journal of College Placement, 37,* 51-53.

McGovern, T. V., & Tinsley, H. E. A. (1978). Interviewer evaluations of interviewee nonverbal behavior. *Journal of Vocational Behavior, 13,* 163-171.

Nolan, J. L. (1979). The influence of race, sex, and physical attractiveness on observers' evaluations of job applicants' communication ability, work motivation, and sociability in a simulated selection interview (Doctoral dissertation, Ohio University, 1978). *Dissertation Abstracts International, 34,* 6396A.

Porter, L. W., Allen, R. W., & Angle, H. L. (1981). The politics of upward influence in organizations. In L. L. Cummings & B. M. Staw (Eds.), *Research in organizational behavior* (Vol. 3). Greenwich, CT: JAI.

Porter, L. W., Lawler, E. E., & Hackman, J. R. (1975). *Behavior in organizations*. New York: McGraw-Hill.

Ragan, S. L., & Hopper, R. (1981). Alignment talk in the job interview. *Journal of Applied Communication Research, 9,* 85-103.

Rogers, D. P., & Sincoff, M. Z. (1978). Favorable impression characteristics of the recruitment interviewer. *Personnel Psychology, 31,* 495-504.

Sackett, P. R. (1981). The interviewer as hypothesis tester: The effects of impressions of an applicant on subsequent interviewer behavior (Doctoral dissertation, Ohio State University, 1979). *Dissertation Abstracts International, 40,* 4009B.

Sands, L. (1979). The influence of sex, competency and style of self-presentation on interviewee decisions (Doctoral dissertation, University of South Florida, 1978). *Dissertation Abstracts International, 39,* 3568B.

Schmitt, N. (1976). Social and situational determinants of interview decisions: Implications for the employment interview. *Personnel Psychology, 29,* 79-101.

Schmitt, N., & Coyle, B. W. (1976). Applicant decisions in the employment interview. *Journal of Applied Psychology, 61,* 184-192.

Sigelman, C. K., Elias, S. F., & Danker-Brown, P. (1980). Interview behaviors of mentally retarded adults as predictors of employability. *Journal of Applied Psychology, 65,* 67-73.

Snyder, M., & Swann, W. B. (1978). Hypothesis-testing processes in social interaction. *Journal of Personality and Social Psychology, 36,* 1202-1212.

Sterrett, J. H. (1978). The job interview: Body language and perceptions of potential effectiveness. *Journal of Applied Psychology, 63,* 388-390.

Stewart, C. J., & Cash, W. B. (1982). *Interviewing: Principles and practices*. Dubuque, IA: Wm. C. Brown.

Stone, C. I., & Sawatzki, B. (1980). Hiring bias and the disabled interviewee: Effects of manipulating work history and disability information of the disabled job applicant. *Journal of Vocational Behavior, 16,* 96-104.

Tengler, C. D. (1982). *Effects of question-type and question orientation on interview outcomes in naturally occurring employment interviews*. Unpublished master's thesis, University of Texas—Austin.

Tengler, C. D., & Jablin, F. M. (1983). Effects of question type, orientation, and sequencing in the employment screening interview. *Communication Monographs, 50,* 245-263.

Trent, L. W. (1979). The effect of varying levels of interviewee nonverbal behavior in the employment interview (Doctoral dissertation, Southern Illinois University, 1978). *Dissertation Abstracts International, 39,* 5116B.

Tucker, D. H., & Rowe, P. M. (1979). Relationship between expectancy, causal attributions, and final hiring decisions in the employment interview. *Journal of Applied Psychology, 64,* 27-34.

Ulrich, L., & Trumbo, D. (1965). The selection interview since 1949. *Psychological Bulletin, 63,* 100-116.

Wagner, R. (1949). The employment interview: A critical summary. *Personnel Psychology, 2,* 17-46.

Wanous, J. P. (1980). *Organizational entry: Recruitment, selection and socialization of newcomers*. Reading, MA: Addison-Wesley.

Watson, K. W., & Ragsdale, J. D. (1981). Linguistic indices of truthful and deceptive responses to employment interview questions. *Journal of Applied Communication Research, 9,* 59-71.

Wright, O. R. (1969). Summary of research on the selection interview since 1964. *Personnel Psychology, 22,* 391-413.

6 ● Black Children's Esteem: Parents, Peers, and Television

STEVEN T. McDERMOTT ●
BRADLEY S. GREENBERG

University of Georgia ● Michigan State University

T HIS chapter presents a study of the effects of race-related inter-personal communication from parents and peers and television experiences on preadolescent black children's esteem. The past developmental research in esteem, while focusing on independent influences such as schools, parents, and peers, has not adhered to a multi-influence model of the esteem process (Liebert & Poulos, 1976), nor has it focused on the effects of communication, especially the identification of specific types of communication and their effects on beliefs and attitudes (Maccoby, 1964: Atkin, Greenberg, & McDermott, 1983).

Also, an examination of black children's esteem from a communication perspective requires a distinction, rarely made, between self- and racial esteem (Gray-Little & Appelbaum, 1979; McDermott, 1983). One part of a person's esteem is a result of his or her communication with others and how his or her role in society is viewed. Some of the information a person receives about role is based upon such limited characteristics as gender, age, and race. For instance, a black child forms a sense of self by communication received about black people in comparison with other role groups such as white people.

Another part of a person's overall esteem may not necessarily be based on such society role-group conceptions, such as race, but may be thought of as a result of the individual's unique reinforcement scheduling. In other words, a person's overall esteem may be thought to contain two major parts, a conception of his or her own racial group (hereafter referred to as *racial*

Correspondence and requests for reprints: Steven T. McDermott, Department of Speech Communication, University of Georgia, Athens, GA 30602.

esteem) and his or her *self-esteem,* which may not be directly tied to racial conceptions (McDermott, 1983).

Thus, with these conceptions in mind, the research examines both racial and self-esteem while accounting for the multiple communication influences of interpersonal communication and television. Attention is also given to the interpersonal communication influences on children's attitudes toward television characters, an important mediator of television effects.

ESTEEM

Research on esteem has followed two major lines. The first, epitomized by the pioneering research of Clark and Clark (1947), conceived and operationalized esteem as racial esteem. In these studies, children were asked to make play choices or to choose the "nice" doll between a black doll and a white doll. If a child chose a doll whose color matched the child's own racial group, it was construed as evidence for high self-esteem. Note that although the doll choices were made on presumed racial characteristics (racial esteem), the researchers inferred that the choice indicated self-esteem.

In the first two decades of this research line, black children consistently demonstrated a preference for the white doll over the black doll (Clark & Clark, 1947; Goodman, 1952; Morland, 1962; Radke, Sutherland, & Rosenberg, 1950; Stevenson & Stewart, 1958; Armstrong & Gregor, 1964; Greenwald & Oppenheim, 1968; Asher & Allen, 1969). In the past decade or so, the results from similar studies have been mixed (Greenwald & Oppenheim, 1968; Katz & Zalk, 1974; Katz, 1976). These results have been explained as measurement problems and unstable racial awareness (Katz, 1976).

The second line of research is that exemplified by Rosenberg (1965) and Coopersmith (1967), in which black and white children were given validated indices of self-esteem. Questions dealt with self-feelings, such as "I feel I'm a person of worth." These questions do not ask the children to make explicit comparisons between black and white, thus assuming racial esteem may be inferred from reports of self-esteem by comparing white children's responses to those of black children. Results are similar to those mentioned earlier; black children tended to have lower self-esteem than white children until the late 1960s (Duncan, 1968; Rosenberg, 1965; Porter, 1971), but higher self-esteem levels have been found for some black children in more recent years (E. Greenberg, 1972; Caplan, 1970; Katz, 1976).

In positing an impact of communication, these research lines do not account for self-versus racial esteem. For instance, it is quite possible that communication from a parent or peer about one's racial group (racial esteem) might be more readily acceptable than communication about oneself

(self-esteem); the latter may be perceived as more directly related to the child's behavior. Or, television may have more impact upon racial esteem, rather than being understood in terms of self-esteem.

Communication Influences on Esteem

Communication to a child about his or her racial group (or others) should be directly related to that child's racial conceptions, but it may also indirectly influence the child's self-esteem, especially in light of recent evidence that indicates that racial identity is fairly strong among black children (Katz, 1976).

Although Katz (1976) argues that attitudes toward race crystallize in late grade school years, a black child's self-esteem seems to be adversely affected by contact with white children (Amir, 1976). Social comparison processes may be one reason for this, but it may be that parental attitudes are reflected in children (Proshansky & Newton, 1968). Thus interpersonal communication from parents about one's racial group may affect esteem development, as may communication from peers. Given the lack of research demonstrating interpersonal communication influences on esteem development, it in not entirely clear whether parents or peers are likely to be more important sources of influence. There is parallel research pointing out the importance of peer versus parental communication regarding informational and judgement matters. As children enter adolescence they appear to increase their commitment to good socioemotional relationships and to begin to conform more to peers than to parents in matters of judgment (see Saltzstein, 1976). Inasmuch as preadolescent children are still making this transition, the following hypothesis was formulated:

> H_1: Frequency of *parental* (1a) and *peer* (1b) communication emphasizing positive characteristics of black children will be positively related to *self-esteem* ($1a_1$; $1b_1$) and *racial esteem* ($1a_2$; $1b_2$).

Along with interpersonal communication, television is a large source of influence in the lives of black children (Poindexter & Stroman, 1981), but the socializing impacts of television are not simple. Television and interpersonal communication affect each other as well as the child (Comstock, Chaffee, Katzman, McCombs, & Roberts, 1978). For this reason the interactive and unique effects of each are examined here.

Furthermore, attitudes toward television characters are probably mediators of the effect of exposure to television on esteem. For instance, Atkin, et al. (1979) found little relationship between mere exposure to black television programs and general attitudes toward real-life black people. Identification studies also support a mediation effect (Maccoby & Wilson, 1957; Rosekrans, 1967; Reeves & Greenberg, 1977). More to the point, Dimas (1975) found that exposure to high-status film models led to high self-concept. With these studies in mind, the following hypothesis was proposed:

H_2: Frequent viewers of black family television programs who have highly positive attitudes toward black *child* (1) and *adult* (2) television characters will have higher *self* (Ha) and *racial* (Hb) esteem than those who are infrequent viewers.

What is appropriate to view and how television portrays characters are topics of conversation between a child and others (Wand, 1968; Barcus, 1969; McLeod, Atkin, & Chaffee, 1972; Atkin & Greenberg, 1977). One of the most significant social influences may be the family (Atkin & Greenberg, 1977). Not only do parents direct children away from certain types of programs, they also may interpret or evaluate program content for children (Hicks, 1968; Atkin & Greenberg, 1977; Bogatz & Ball, 1971; Atkin & Gantz, 1975). Yet communication from peers may also have an effect especially during these preadolescent years of transition.

H_3: Frequency of *parental* (3a) and *peer* (3b) communication emphazizing positive characteristics of black *child* ($3a_1$; $H3b_1$) and *adult* ($3a_2$; $3b_2$) television characters will be related to more positive attitudes toward black television characters than communication that does not emphasize positive characteristics.

Exposure to television is also a likely part of the process. First, there is sufficient research demonstrating that, despite the small number of black family shows on television, black children watch them frequently. In addition, they tend to judge black characters favorably (Atkin et al., 1979; B. Greenberg, 1972) and identify with them (Dates, 1979), especially the more black shows the child watches. Thus exposure should be related to attitudes toward television characters:

H_4: Children who are more frequent viewers of black family television programs will have more positive attitudes toward black *child* (4a) and *adult* (4b) television characters than children who are less frequent viewers.

In testing these simple hypotheses, the conjoint and relative influence of television, peer, and parental communication on esteem and the influence of peer and parental communication and television exposure to black family programs on children's attitudes toward black television characters were also studied.

METHODS

The respondents were 82 fourth- and fifth-grade black children in naturally integrated schools in a middle- to lower-middle-class section of a large metropolitan city in the western United States. Questionnaires were administered by a black male, a black female, and three white female graduate students.[1]

Dependent Variables

A five-item index of self-esteem was constructed using concepts similar to those used by Rosenberg (1965) and Coopersmith (1967). It was a shortened version of a measure adapted to fourth- and fifth-grade children from an index designed and validated by Schwartz and Tangri (1965), transformed to a form more suitable for a fourth- and fifth-grade sample (see Coopersmith, 1967). The measure of self-esteem stated, "Please tell us what you are like: I think I am . . ." followed by response categories of "very [concept]," "pretty [concept]," "not very [concept]," and "not [concept]." The concepts forming the index were "good," "important," "friendly," "kind," and "superior." The measure of absolute racial esteem was "I think black kids in real life are . . ." followed by the five concept categories indicated above. Items were summed to form the indices.

Each of the esteem indices had a possible range of 5 (low esteem) to 20. The overall response to both the self-esteem and the absolute racial esteem index resulted in a mean higher than the theoretical midpoint of 12.5 (absolute racial esteem, $\bar{X} = 15.7$, SD = 2.7, skew = 0.22; self-esteem, $\bar{X} = 15.9$, SD = 1.75, skew = +0.41).

Independent and Mediating Variables

Interpersonal Communication. Parental and peer communications about black children were measured by asking about the amount and content of communication the children engage in with parents and peers about black children: "How often do your parents [friends] tell you that black kids are good, important, friendly, kind, superior." Responses included "a lot," "sometimes," "not often," and "never." Items were summed to form an index.

Each of the indices of parental and peer communication about black children had a theoretical mean of 12 and a range of 4 to 20. Inspection of the means (parental communication, $\bar{X} = 13.27$, SD = 4.07, skew = -0.47; peer communication, $\bar{X} = 13.51$, SD = 4.075, skew = -0.33) indicates that the responses were well distributed around the theoretical mean. A t-test of the differance between parent and peer communication was non-significant.

Television Exposure. The measure of television exposure tapped the children's exposure to programs in which black people were cast as central characters. The programs included *What's Happening, Good Times, Dif-f'rent Strokes, The Jeffersons,* and *Fat Albert.* Programs that featured black characters in major roles but in which the main characters were white were not included. Thus the measure of overall exposure to black programming consisted of the sum of the rating given to the five black shows with central black characters. Children were asked, "How often do you watch [name of program]," with "every week," "most weeks," "some weeks," and "once in a while or never" as response options. Scores ranged from 5 to 20 $\overline{X} = 10.68$, SD = 4.42, skew = +0.58).

Attitudes Toward Black Television Characters. An index of favorableness was formed by summing the children's response to "Here is a list of people on TV; please tell us which ones you like or don't like." A list of black and white characters, both children and adults, followed the item. Two indices were formed. The adult index measured preference for Mrs. Walker (on *What's Happening*), Bill Cosby (on *Fat Albert*), Florida Evans (on *Good Times*), and Louise and George Jefferson (on *The Jeffersons*). The child index measured preference for Dee, Roger, and Rerun (on *What's Happening*), Thelma and JJ (on *Good Times*), and Arnold (on *Diff'rent Strokes*). Possible answers were "like a lot," "like a little," and "don't like."

The child index had a possible range of 6 to 18 and the adult index had a range of 5 to 15; for child characters, $\overline{X} = 14.94$, SD = 2.24, skew = $-.373$; for adult characters, $\overline{X} = 11.63$, SD = 2.31, skew = -0.23. A constant of 1 was added to the adult index to make the indices comparable and a t-test of the difference between attitudes toward the black adult characters and black child characters was significant ($t = 7.91$, $p < .001$).

Interpersonal Communication About Television Characters. A set of measures assessed the content and amount of communication the child received about black television characters from both parents and friends. Children were told, "Here is a list of people on TV, please tell us which ones your [parents, friends] like or don't like." Respondents were asked to indicate if they thought their parents [friends] "like a lot," "like a little," or "don't like" each of the same characters. As with the measure of the child's own attitude toward the characters, two indices were formed by summation, one for child actors and the other for adult actors.

Ranges of 5 to 15 for adult characters and 6 to 18 for child characters were possible; for child television characters, $\overline{X} = 13.71$, SD = 2.77, skew = -0.27; for adult television characters, $\overline{X} = 10.40$, SD = 2.58, skew = -0.27. After a suitable transformation a t-test revealed significant differences ($t = 4.02$, $p < .001$).

Similar differences were found between communications from parents about adult and child characters ($t = 3.70$, $p < .001$). The parental communications about children on television ($\overline{X}$ = 14.06, SD = 3.10, skew = 0.43) and about adults on television ($\overline{X}$ = 11.04, SD = 2.93, skew = 0.33) were both positive, and parent and peer communications were both significantly more positive about child characters.

Analysis

Each hypothesis was considered supported if the appropriate Pearson product-moment correlation coefficient was significant at alpha <.05. The mediation hypothesis was considered supported if the correlation coefficients reached the p <.05 level. Given 82 respondents, the correlation coefficient would have to exceed .19 to be significant at p < .05. In addition, regression analyses were done to assess the relative influence of the exogenous variables on esteem as well as on attitudes toward black television characters. In addition, the variance accounted for by the three sources of communication are presented for assessment of the conjoint influences of communication on esteem.

RESULTS

The first hypothesis stated that frequency of peer and parental communication emphasizing positive characteristics of black people would be positively related to self-esteem and racial esteem. The relationship between peer communication and racial esteem (H1a$_2$) was significant (r = .376, p < .002), as were the relationship between parental communication and self-esteem (H1b$_1$; r = .290, p < .006), and the relationship between parental communication and racial esteem (H1b$_2$; r = .418, p < .002). The relationship between peer communication and self-esteem (H1b$_1$) was the only nonsignificant relationship (r = .112, p .171). Thus three of the four tests of H1 were supported.

The second hypothesis predicted that exposure to black family programs would be related to more positive esteem primarily among those who have positive attitudes toward child and adult television characters. The relationship between exposure and self-esteem was significant (r = .200, p < .05) but the relationship between exposure and racial esteem was not (r = .184, p < .07). To elaborate the mediation hypothesis, the relationship between exposure and self-esteem was calculated separately for those who had attitudes above the mean toward adult TV characters (r = .263) and those whose attitudes were below the mean (r = .027). A z transform test (Blalock, 1972) indicated that the two correlations were significantly different (z= 4.724, p < .001). The correlation between exposure and racial esteem also differed (z = 3.432, p < .002) for those who had more positive

attitudes toward adult characters (r = .206) and those who had more negative attitudes (r = .030). There were no differences in attitudes toward child
characters; for self-esteem the r = .152 for positive attitudes and r = .170
for those lower, and for racial esteem the r = .151 for positive and r = .115
for lower attitude levels. Two of four tests of the hypothesis were supported.

The third hypothesis predicted that interpersonal communication that
emphasizes positive characteristics of black television characters will be related to more positive attitudes toward television characters than communication that does not emphasize positive characteristics. This hypothesis was
broken out to look at parental (3a) and peer (3b) communication about both
child ($3a_1$; $3b_1$) and adult ($3a_2$; $3b_2$) television characters. All tests of this
hypothesis were supported. Positive communication from parents about
television characters was strongly related to children's positive attitudes toward black adult TV characters (r = .747, p < .001) and to the attitudes
toward black child characters (r = .572, p < .001). Similarly, hypothesis $3a_2$
relating positive interpersonal communication about TV characters from
peers, was strongly related to the children's attitudes about adult TV characters (r = .744, p < .001) and the children's attitudes about child TV characters (r = .777, p < .001) were supported.

Regressions

In order to determine the conjoint and relative influences of the three
major determinants of esteem—that is, interpersonal communication from
peers and attitudes toward adult characters—multiple regressions were performed for each of the esteem variables. One regression set was done with
communication about children and attitudes toward child TV characters,
while the other was done with communication about adults and attitudes
toward adult TV characters. The three determinants in the first set account
for nearly 16 percent of the variance in self-esteem, with parental communication about black children the major contributor. For the second set, 21
percent of the variance was accounted for with attitudes toward black adult
TV characters being the lone significant predictor (see Table 6.1). Although
amount of variance accounted for by the predictors of racial esteem was
similar to self-esteem (20 percent for child communication and 20 percent
for communication about adults), there was no single variable determinants
in the sets.

A test of the relative influence of communication experiences—(1) frequency of viewing of black family television programs, (2) communication
from parents about black television characters, and (3) communication from
peers about black television characters—on attitudes toward black television characters was also completed. Parental communication was a significant predictor of attitudes toward black child characters and the three deter-

Table 6.1
Regression of Parental and Peer Communication
and Attitudes Toward Black Television
Characters on Self-Esteem

Predictor	Unstandardized Beta	Standardized Beta	F	Multiple R^2
Parental communication about black children	.181	.422	7.455*	.158
Peer communication about black children	−.142	−.331	3.752	
Attitudes toward child TV characters	.022	.284	4.733	
Parental communication about black adults	.102	.238	2.005	.214
Peer communication about black adults	−.123	−.287	3.121	
Attitudes toward black adult TV characters	.324	.428	8.836*	

*$p < 0.5$.

minants accounted for 63 percent of the variance in attitudes toward characters. For the adult characters, 71 percent of the variance in attitude was accounted for by the communication variables, with both parental communication about the characters and exposure to black family TV shows as significant predictors (see Table 6.2).

DISCUSSION

Descriptive Summary

Both racial and self-esteem levels were moderately positive, thus supporting the shift to more positive esteem reported in the past decade or so from earlier rather low self-esteem levels for black children.

The amount of television exposure to black family programs by black children confirmed earlier research showing that black television program viewing is fairly high for black children (B. Greenberg, 1972; Atkin et al., 1979).

The children had a fairly positive evaluation of black adult and child television characters, suggesting the possibility of favorable modeling influences. Interpersonal communication from both parents and peers about child television characters was, on the average, very positive. However, re-

Table 6.2
Regression of Exposure and Parental and Peer Communication About Television Characters on Attitudes Toward Black Television Characters

Predictor	Unstandardized Beta	Standardized Beta	F	Multiple R^2
Exposure to black child TV characters	−.021	−.042	<1.0	.630
Parental communication about black child TV characters	.544	.673	43.375*	
Peer communication about black child TV characters	.149	.205	3.845	
Exposure to black adult TV characters	.164	.313	14.409*	.710
Parental communication about black adult TV characters	.364	.407	13.571*	
Peer communication about black adult TV characters	.230	.291	6.275	

*$p < .05$.

ported communication from parents and peers about adult television characters was significantly less positive.

These findings suggest several possibilities. Perhaps television programs display child behaviors that are acceptable to children and display adult behaviors that are less acceptable. Previous demographic research has not identified such differences. Another, perhaps more likely, reason for the difference might be related to what the child viewer regards as acceptable behaviors: Similar behaviors from an adult or child—for the example, being funny—are less acceptable from an adult actor than from a child. Or it could be that children are less severe critics of child actor's behavior than of adult behavior. Whatever the reasons, this difference has implications for modeling hypotheses, discussed below.

Hypotheses

Of the fourteen hypotheses proposed in this chapter, eleven were supported. Communication is a factor in the development of the black child's esteem. Both interpersonal communication and television experiences are related to black children's esteem. Interpersonal communication works two ways: It is related to esteem, and it is related to children's attitudes toward television characters. Specifically, children's racial esteem—that is, their general attitudes toward black children and adults—was related to communication from the child's parents and peers. Self-esteem was related to communication from parents. Such communication also relates to how the children view television characters: Racial attitudes toward black television characters were related to communication received from both parents and peers.

Television viewing was also related to attitudes toward television characters as well as to esteem as mediated by children's attitudes toward the characters.

Regression analyses examining the relative influence of communication on esteem and on the hypothesized mediation variable (attitudes toward TV characters) found that (1) parental communication is an important covariate and (2) attitude toward adult television characters is an important mediator of viewing and esteem.

The present data underline the Liebert and Poulos (1976) recommendation that socialization research be approached from a multi-influence perspective. Thus it was found that parental communication is a most important factor in esteem development for preadolescent children. Parental communication was related to both attitudes toward television characters and self-esteem.

The research also shows that attitudes and esteem are in fact related to communication behaviors, a finding that casts doubt on the efficacy of Katz's (1976) observation that racial attitudes tend to crystallize at the fourth- and fifth- grade levels. However, it should be noted that there are variations in the relationships between communication variables and the different esteem types as conceptualized and operationalized here. Although the simple relationships between both parental and peer communication and racial esteem were all significant, only those for parental communication were significant for self-esteem. Thus the utility of the esteem distinctions argued for in the rationale section is apparent; theoretically, communication may differ in influence depending on whether it is (a) directed to how the child functions in a rather direct way, that is, self-esteem, or (b) directed at the child in rather indirect ways by referring to the child's cultural or racial group, and thus influences the child's racial esteem.

The differences in communication may be due to the willingness of children to accept communication from different sources or the sources' willingness to give certain types of communication depending on whether it is direct or indirect. Perhaps, for instance, it may be more difficult for children to communicate to other children directly about their characteristics (self-esteem), while children are still able to accept and get communication from their parents about themselves directly. On the other hand, communication that is not so direct—for instance, references to the child's race in the form of racial esteem—may be more easily communicated and more acceptable for children when coming from either parents or peers.

Past research on mediation effects shows that exposure to black family programs should influence esteem only when children have positive attitudes toward black television character models. This was a hypothesis that extended the past research and found modeling effects when children identified strongly with the model. The present research results show that attitudes toward the television characters may be a significant mediator for television learning of racial and self-esteem.

That adult television models were the most import mediators suggests several possible explanations. First, preadolescent children may rely mostly on adults for information, as the developmental research indicates (see, for example, Saltzstein, 1976), and adult television models may be more potent sources of influence. Second, adult television models may actually have more favorable images than child models. A third explanation may be that children are more critical of the appropriateness of child TV characters' behavior than they are of the behavior of adult characters.

Although this research has shown that fourth- and fifth-grade children's esteem is related to communication inputs, future research efforts should look at the influence process over time, to broaden our knowledge of esteem formation by helping to identify critical stages of racial esteem formation and when communication sources gain or lose impact on these processes. Longitudinal investigations are needed to verify causal order, such as the causal relationship between exposure to television and attitudes toward television characters. Does level of exposure to black family programs change attitudes toward the television characters, or do attitudes change the level of exposure? Exposure and attitudes might also be functions of self-esteem.

NOTE

1. Precautions were taken in the administration to avoid instrumentality effects. Variation in item ordering was just one precaution. The questionnaire items were intermixed so that those items that appeared repetitive (that is, those that asked for responses of "good," "important," and so on) were never next to one another or followed one another. Instead, questions about the characters, TV use, program exposure, and the like were mixed in among similar item sets. Also, all items were paced as they were read aloud by the administrators and there was no possibility for interaction among the children. To avoid respondent fatigue, a brief stretch break was called halfway through the questionnaire administration.

REFERENCES

Amir, Y. (1976). The role of intergroup contact in change of prejudice and ethnic relations. In P. Katz (Ed.), *Towards the elimination of racism* (pp. 245-308). New York: Pergamon.

Armstrong, C. P., & Gregor, A. J. (1964). Integrated schools and Negro character development. *Psychiatry, 27,* 69-72.

Asher, S. R., & Allen, V. L. (1969). Racial preference and social comparison processes. *Journal of Social Issues, 25,* 157-165.

Atkin, C. K., & Gantz, W. (1975). *The role of television news in the political socialization of children.* Paper presented at the meeting of the International Communication Association, Chicago.

Atkin, C. K., & Greenberg, B. S. (1977). *Parental mediation of children's social behavior learning from television* (CASTLE Report 4 to the U.S. Office of Child Development). East Lansing: Michigan State University, Department of Communication.

Atkin, C. K., Greenberg, B., & McDermott, S. (1979). Race and social role learning from television. In H. S. Dordick (Ed.), *Proceedings of the Sixth Annual Telecommunications Policy Research Conference.* Lexington, MA: D. C. Heath.

Barcus, F. E. (1969). Effects of parental learning on children's television viewing. *Television Quarterly, 8,* 63-73.

Blalock, H. M. (1972). *Social statistics.* New York: McGraw-Hill.

Bogatz, G. A., & Ball, S. J. (1971). *The second year of Sesame Street: A continuing evaluation.* Princeton, NJ: Educational Testing Service.

Caplan, N. (1970). The new ghetto man: A review of recent empirical studies. *Journal of Social Issues, 26.*

Clark, K. B., & Clark, M. P. (1947). Racial identification and preference in Negro children. In T. M. Newcomb & E. L. Hartley (Eds.), *Readings in social psychology* (pp. 169-178). New York: Holt, Rinehart & Winston.

Comstock, G., Chaffee, S., Katzman, N., McCombs, M., & Roberts, D. (1978). *Television and human behavior.* New York: Columbia University Press.

Coopersmith, S. (1967). *The antecedents of self-esteem.* San Francisco: W. H. Freeman.

Dates, J. L. (1979). *The relationship of demographic variables and racial attitudes to adolescent perceptions of black television characters.* Unpublished doctoral dissertation, University of Maryland.

Dimas, C. (1975). The effect of motion pictures portraying black models on the self-concept of black elementary school children. In G. Comstock (Ed.), *Television and human behavior: The key studies.* Santa Monica, CA: Rand Corporation.

Duncan, O. D. (1968). Inheritance of poverty or inheritance of race? In D. P. Moynihan (Ed.), *Understanding poverty: Perspectives from the social sciences* (pp. 85-110). New York: Basic Books.

Goodman, M. E. (1952). *Race awareness in young children.* Reading, MA: Addison-Wesley.

Gray-Little, B., & Appelbaum, M. I. (1979). Instrumentality effects in the assessment of racial differences in self-esteem. *Journal of Personality and Social Psychology, 7,* 1221-1229.

Greenberg, B. S. (1972). Children's reaction to TV blacks. *Journalism Quarterly, 49,* 5-14.

Greenberg, E. S. (1972). Black children, self-esteem and the liberation movement. *Politics and Society, 2,* 293-307.

Greenwald, H. D., & Oppenheim, D. B. (1968). Reported magnitude of self-misidentification among Negro children: Artifact? *Journal of Personality and Social Psychology, 8,* 49-52.

Hicks, D. J. (1968). Effects of co-observer's sanctions and adult presence on imitative aggression. *Child Development, 38,* 303-309.

Katz, P. S. (Ed.). (1976). *Towards the elimination of racism.* New York: Pergamon.

Katz, P. S., & Zalk, S. R. (1974). Doll preferences: An index of racial attitudes. *Journal of Educational Psychology, 66,* 663-668.

Liebert, R. M., & Poulos, R. W. (1976). Television as a moral teacher. In T. Kikona (Ed.), *Moral development and behavior.* New York: Holt, Rinehart & Winston.

Maccoby, E. E. (1964). Effects of the mass media. In M. L. Hoffman & L. W. Hoffman (Eds.), *Review of child development research.* New York: Russell Sage.

Maccoby, E. E., & Wilson, W. C. (1957). Identification and observational learning from films. *Journal of Abnormal and Social Psychology, 55*, 67-87.

McDermott, S. T. (1983). A reconstitution of racial esteem with regard to communication. *Communication, 11*(2), 69-75.

McLeod, J., Atkin, C., & Chaffee, S. (1972). Adolescents, parents, and television use: Adolescent self-report measures from Maryland and Wisconsin sample. In J. Rubenstein, G. Comstock, & M. Murray (Eds.), *Television and social behavior* (Vol. 3). Washington, DC: U.S. Department of Health, Education and Welfare.

Morland, J. K. (1962). Racial acceptance and preference of nursery school children in a southern city. *Merrill-Palmer Quarterly, 8*, 271-280.

Poindexter, P. M., & Stroman, C. A. (1981). Blacks and television: A review of the research literature. *Journal of Broadcasting, 25*(2), 103-121.

Porter, J. D. R. (1971). *Black child, white child.* Cambridge, MA: Harvard University Press.

Proshansky, H., & Newton, P. (1968). The nature and meaning of Negro self-identity. In M. Deutsch, I. Katz, & A. R. Jensen (EDs.), *Social class, race and psychological development.* New York: Holt, Rinehart & Winston.

Radke, M. J., Sutherland, J., & Rosenberg, P. (1950). Racial attitudes in children. *Sociometry, 13*, 154-171.

Radke, M. J., Trager, H., & Davis, H. (1950). Children's perceptions of the roles of Negroes and Whites. *Journal of Psychology, 29*, 3-33.

Reeves, B., & Greenberg, B. S. (1977). Children's perceptions of television characters. *Human Communication Research, 3*, 113-127.

Rosekrans, M. A. (1967). Imitation in children as a function of perceived similarities to a social model of vicarious reinforcement. *Journal of Personality and Social Psychology, 7*, 307-315.

Rosenberg, M. (1965). *Society and the adolescent self-image.* Princeton, NJ: Princeton University Press.

Saltzstein, H. D. (1976). Social influence and moral development. In T. Lickona (Ed.), *Moral development and behavior: Theory, research and social issues* (pp. 253-265). New York: Holt, Rinehart & Winston.

Schwartz, M., & Tangri, S. S. (1965). A note on self-concept as an insulator against delinquency. *American Sociological Review, 30*, 922-926.

Stevenson, H. W., & Stewart, E. C. (1958). A developmental study of race awareness in young children. *Child Development, 29*, 399-410.

Wand, B. (1968). Television viewing and family choice differences. *Public Opinion Quarterly, 32*, 84-94.

7 ● Listening Behavior: Definition and Measurement

KITTIE W. WATSON ● LARRY L. BARKER

Tulane University ● Auburn University

INFORMAL measures of listening ability have been in existence for several centuries in the classroom setting. After listening to various types of information, students have been expected to perform well on both oral and written examinations. Yet not until the mid-1950s did theorists begin to differentiate among intelligence, reading, and listening ability.

The first formal listening studies were concerned with listening comprehension in elementary classroom settings. Thus most of the early listening tests were designed to discover the relation between listening and verbal ability. In 1937, Durrell and Sullivan developed a test to measure how well children understood spoken language or "auditory comprehension." Unfortunately, few people realized it was a listening test because it was named the Durrell-Sullivan Reading Capacity Test. Later, in 1941, Miller examined the relationship between reading and listening comprehension.

In 1948, Ralph Nichols, referred to as the modern-day Father of Listening, attempted to identify specific factors that influence classroom listening comprehension. His initial listening study, one of the earliest to use factor analysis, identified 14 factors that affected listening comprehension and 12 factors that were likely to affect listening comprehension. His preliminary research suggested that it would be possible to measure listening comprehension quantitatively when and if valid and reliable tests were designed.

Not long after Nichols's research was reported, Blewett (1949) developed his two-part Test of Listening Comprehension, which consisted of a test of content retention and a test of drawing conclusions. The test of content retention measured immediate recall of factual information, and the test

Correspondence and requests for reprints: Kittie W. Watson, Department of Communication, Tulane University, New Orleans, LA 70118.

of drawing conclusions measured the ability of students to draw conclusions, make inferences, and identify speaker attitudes. The relatively low correlation between the tests suggested that they were measuring different types of listening.

Based on the scores from his test and their correlation with the scores on various standardized tests and school grades, Blewett presented 14 conclusions with educational implications. The most important findings regarded the relation between listening and reading comprehension. The results suggested that despite some overlap, reading and listening are dissimilar skills. In addition, Blewett found that listening contributes approximately as much to scholastic achievement as does reading achievement. With the contributions from Blewett and Nichols, listening theorists began to study listening factors rather than pure verbal factors.

At about the same time, two theorists, D. P. Brown and J. G. Caffrey (cited in Russell, 1964) introduced "auding" as a more precise term to describe the ability to comprehend spoken language. Along this line, Caffrey developed the California Auding Test to measure vocabulary, the ability to follow directions, and comprehension of spoken language (talk/lecture). The preliminary work by Brown and Caffrey supported the existence of a separate auding factor for which reading tests could not account, similar to Blewett's findings.

The Brown-Carlsen Listening Comprehension Test, the first standardized listening (auding) test, was developed by J. I. Brown and G. R. Carlsen in 1955. Their test was designed for grades 9 through 12 and included 76 items divided over five subtasks involved in the comprehension of the spoken word. The subtasks included immediate recall (17 items), following directions (20 items), recognizing transitions (8 items), recognizing word meanings (10 items), and lecture comprehension (21 items).

In addition to the Brown-Carlsen Test, two other important listening tests were developed in 1955. Clyde Dow (1955) attempted to find an objective measure of listening comprehension. His test, later known as the Michigan State College Listening Test, was first used with high school seniors and college freshmen.

During the same year, Mary Hollow (1955) expressed concern about whether or not listening could be taught to elementary school students. She developed the Hollow Listening Test as a pre- and posttest instrument to follow 30 twenty-minute lessons in listening comprehension. Hollow found that the ability of students to summarize, draw inferences, recall facts in sequence, and remember facts accurately could be improved with direct instruction.

Pratt (1956) was one of the first theorists to advocate the inclusion of interpersonal variables in listening tests. He divided listening into receptive and reflective listening skills. Receptive skills revolved around accuracy and included (1) keeping related details in mind, (2) observing a single detail, (3) remembering a series of details, and (4) following oral directions. Reflective skills required (1) using contextual cues, (2) recognizing organizational elements, (3) selecting main ideas as opposed to subordinate ideas or details, (4) recognizing relations between main and subordinate ideas, and (5) drawing justifiable inferences.

Like Pratt, Larter and Scott (1956) included listening factors other than the traditional lecture listening factors in their test. Their listening factors included (1) listening to music, (2) listening to phonics, (3) listening for main ideas, (4) listening for sequences and details, and (5) listening to follow directions.

The second commercially produced standardized listening test was introduced in 1957 by the Educational Testing Service. The Sequential Tests of Educational Progress: Listening Test (STEP) was included as part of a battery of achievement tests available in different forms for different grade levels. The test was composed of 12 to 13 passages for each grade level. The passages ranged from twenty-five seconds to three minutes in length. The first half of the passages included informational articles, poems, or stories and the second half included argumentative talks, oral directions, instructions, and explanations. Currently on the market, STEP uses 80 items to measure at least 28 subskills, grouped in the areas of plain sense comprehension, interpretation, and evaluation/appreciation.

About the same time, the Listening Skill Builders (LSB), prepared by the Science Research Associates, introduced another training program with some overlap in subskills with STEP (Katz, 1959). LSB was designed to provide students with training in auditory discrimination, instant recall of facts, following directions, listening for cause and effect, visualizing and listening for mood, making inferences, and distinguishing fact from opinion.

An important listening test contribution was made by E.E. Ongman in 1960. Although this test was not widely marketed, his was the first listening test to contain background noises as part of the testing instrument.

In 1962, using factor analysis Spearritt examined the results of 34 tests. The tests he analyzed included measures of reading comprehension, reasoning, memory, auditory ability, attention, and the STEP listening test. His work supported the earlier work of Brown and Caffrey by revealing a separate factor: listening comprehension of verbal material. The next year, Sarah Lundsteen (1963) developed a test that required fifth- and sixth-grade students to (1) detect the speaker's purpose, (2) analyze and judge propaganda, and (3) analyze and judge arguments. She found evidence of two separate listening abilities (critical and general) that were distinct from verbal ability (Russell, 1964).

The next several years were marked by the introduction of a number of commercially produced tests. Warren Graham and David Orr (1968) constructed the Orr-Graham Listening Test as an auditory alternative to the conventional reading comprehension test. Their commercially available test was designed primarily to be used with disadvantaged junior high school boys. The content of the test (stories concerning sports, adventure, and natural lore) was designed to coincide with the interests of the group being tested. Test results suggested that it was uniquely capable of identifying educational potential in disadvantaged junior high school boys.

Another commercially designed listening test, the Assessment of Children's Language Comprehension (ACLC), introduced in 1969, was developed as "an assessment tool which would reveal levels of receptive difficulty in children with language problems" (Till, 1978, p. 608).

During the same year, research from the Educational Development Laboratories provided educators with a number of subskills identified as necessary for effective listening comprehension. A partial list of factors considered important to the "Listen and Think" (Mallis & Anderson, 1969) module were (1) recognizing sounds in the environment; (2) finding the stated main ideas in a story; (3) noticing the correct order of happenings; (4) listening for details; (5) noting likenesses and differences between people and countries; (6) making mental pictures of something that is being described; (7) understanding how attitudes and customs are affected by the setting; (8) identifying the elements of exaggeration that make a tall tale amusing; (9) learning to recognize such propaganda techniques as name-calling, testimony, and bandwagon; and (10) learning to recognize the climax of a story. The subskills that were identified were not in agreement with the Science Research Associates' or Educational Testing Service's findings discussed earlier.

In 1971-1972, the New Zealand Council for Educational Research constructed the Progressive Achievement Tests of Listening Comprehension (PAT). PAT was developed based on the factors found in earlier measuring instruments. In 1973, Elizabeth Carrow of Learning Concepts developed the Tests for Auditory Comprehension of Language (TACL). TACL was designed to be used with the mentally retarded and hearing impaired and has been discussed as the "best single measure of language comprehension currently available" (Hatten, 1978, p. 611). Although one instrument cannot provide a complete language profile, TACL was designed to measure auditory comprehension, to determine developmental level, and to provide diagnostic information concerning language problem areas.

As listening scholars and theorists began to identify factors that affected listening comprehension, researchers began to modify existing instruments and to create additional instruments to answer criticisms about test construction and administration procedures. Until this time, most of the listening tests focused on a lecture retention model of listening (Bostrom &

Waldhart, 1980a) rather than an interpersonal or varied context model of listening.

During the mid-1970s, listening tests began to examine interpersonal listening in addition to lecture comprehension listening factors. The Jones-Mohr Listening Test (1976), for example, examined the effects of nonverbal cues during listening comprehension. Their test required participants to listen to voices on a test tape and then to select the appropriate meaning based on paraverbal cues such as vocal intonation, rate, and volume. A more traditional instrument, the Critical Listening Test, was also developed in 1976 by Richards. His test required listeners to (1) identify assumptions and inferences, (2) recognize main ideas and arguments, (3) identify fallacies in the use of data, (4) judge relevance of data, (5) recogniz bias in persuasive discourse, (6) distinguish between statements of fact and statements of opinion, and (7) recognize errors in deductive reasoning.

After investigating the relation between memory and listening research, Robert Bostrom and Enid Waldhart constructed the Kentucky Comprehensive Listening Test (KCLT) in 1979 (Bostrom & Waldhart, 1980b). The KCLT, used with college students, is designed to measure listening skills systematically and to control for the effects of memory during listening comprehension. Revised in 1980, the KCLT is presented on audiotape and uses 48 items to measure a complex of four skills: (1) short-term listening, (2) short-term listening with rehearsal (20-50 seconds), (3) lecture listening, and (4) interpretive listening.

The Watson-Barker Listening Test (WBLT) was developed in 1983 to examine interpersonal listening comprehension. Instructions, listening content material, and test questions are contained on audiotape. In addition, the test focuses on topics used in a business context and uses speakers with different regional dialects. Fifty items measure a complex of five interpersonal skills: (1) interpretive short-term listening; (2) interpretive dialogue short-term listening; (3) short-term lecture listening; (4) interpretive-emotional-connotative meaning short-term listening; and (5) short- and long-term instruction-following listening.

Listening theorists have borrowed measurement techniques used in other disciplines. One technique that has received special attention in recent years is the Cloze Procedure (Alderson, 1980; Neville & Pugh, 1976; Templeton, 1977; Theobald & Alexander, 1977; Weaver, 1972). Auditory cloze procedures are patterned after reading cloze procedures. Using deletions of every eighth word, research focuses on students' comprehension of instructional talk (Theobald & Alexander, 1977).

Along with the tests mentioned above, a number of listening tests have been developed during the last few years that were designed and categorized for specific educational levels. A description and listing of these tests is provided in the October 1982 issue of *Communication Education* (Rubin,

Daly, McCroskey, & Mead, 1982). In addition to the listening tests discussed in this chapter and in *Communication Education*, numerous tests have been used in individual studies (Cochran, 1960; Dorval, 1959; Edgar, 1961; Farrow, 1964; Goldhaber & Weaver, 1968; Graham, 1966; Hill, 1963; Larter & Scott, 1956; Lewis, 1955; Richards, 1976; Ward, 1980).

One common complaint about listening tests has been the variability in factors they attempt to measure. The inconsistency has led many theorists to speculate about whether or not listening can be measured as a unitary skill. With this in mind, Tipton and Weaver (1973) examined programs developed by the Educational Development Laboratories, Science Research Associates, and Educational Testing Service. After consulting with teachers and subject matter experts, they identified 11 subskills necessary for fourth, fifth, and sixth graders: following directions; recognizing transitions; inference-making; differentiating among contextual clues; getting the main idea; sequential listening; getting details; listening for meaning in imagery; perceiving causal relations; perceiving relations; and getting the critical elements.

In 1977, Binford investigated tests of listening comprehension and found 22 different but highly related listening skills. The results of the previously mentioned studies listed above provide valuable information for the listening theorist. The following section addresses the topic of comprehension-related variables in the listening process.

VARIABLES THOUGHT TO AFFECT LISTENER COMPREHENSION

Pioneering work designed to identify variables affecting listening behavior was conducted by Ralph Nichols. Nichols (1948) identified 14 factors that influenced listener comprehension, including the following: intelligence, reading comprehension, recognition of correct English usage, size of listener's vocabulary, ability to make inferences, ability to structuralize a speech (organization/main ideas), listening for main ideas, use of special techniques to improve concentration, real interest in subject, emotional adjustment to speaker's thesis, ability to see significance in subject discussed, curiosity about subject, physical fatigue of listener, and audibility of the speaker. In addition to these 14 factors, Nichols found evidence to suggest that the following 12 factors also affected listening comprehension: speaker effectiveness, admiration of the speaker, respect for listening as a method of learning, susceptibility to distraction, parental occupation, gender of the listener, room ventilation and temperature, use of only the English language in the home, rearing in an only-child home environment, high school scholastic achievement, high school speech training, and experience in listening to difficult expository material. These factors have been grouped into the categories of listener characteristics; speaker characteristics; message characteristics; and environmental characteristics (Barker, 1971).

Listener Characteristics

Variables related to a listener's physical attributes, demographic characteristics, experiences, and mental abilities have been found to affect listening ability. A listener's organizational ability (Thompson, 1960), intelligence (Bonner, 1960; Crook, 1957; Palmer, 1966; Vineyard, 1960), reading skill (Palmer, 1966; Reeves, 1965; Ross, 1964), linguistic aptitude (Blewett, 1949), and academic achievement (Palmer, 1966) correlate positively with listening comprehension. Extrinsic motivation such as grades or perceived rewards or punishments tend to improve listening efficiency (Beatty, Behnke, & Froelich, 1980; Blubaugh, 1963; Bohn, 1964; Goodyear, 1969; Petrie & Carrel, 1976; Plax & Rosenfeld, 1979; Smeltzer & Watson, 1983).

Early studies indicated little correlation between notetaking and listening comprehension (Crawford, 1925; Eisner & Rohde, 1959; Nichols, 1948; Petrie, 1961). However, more recent research findings suggest that notetaking does influence listening comprehension (Bostrom, Waldhart, & Brown, 1979; Divesta & Gray, 1973; Lashbrook, 1976; Waldhart & Bostrom, 1981). For example, Aiken and others (1975) found that students who interchange listening and notetaking score higher than students who take notes concurrently or do not take notes.

In addition, until recently most listening research indicated minimal gender differences in listening comprehension (Ferris, 1964; Hedrick, 1976; Hopkins, 1966; Laurent, 1967; Rossiter, 1972). More recently, however, results of some research suggest that there were differences between what males and females paid attention to during a lecture (Weaver, 1972), that men and women differed in the amount of notes they took during a lecture (Waldhart & Bostrom, 1981), that women were more accurate at reading or interpreting nonverbal cues (Lafrance & Mayo, 1979), and that women scored higher than men on an objective test after a lecture.

Factors such as ego involvement, personal anxieties (Haberland, 1959; Prince, 1948; Stromer, 1955; Sullivan, 1946; Wheeless, 1975), and fatigue (Sorenson, 1948; Widener, 1950; Wiskell, 1946) appear to decrease listening efficiency. Recently, increased attention has been paid to the negative effects of one type of communication anxiety: listener apprehension (Beatty, 1981; Scott & Wheeless, 1977; Wheeless, 1975). Variables shown to have little or no influence on listening behavior include birth order (Nichols, 1948) and expressed interest in the topic (Karraker, 1952; Nelson, 1948; Petrie & Carrel, 1976).

Speaker Characteristics

The rate of speaking, fluency of the speaker, visibility of the speaker, credibility of the speaker, and delivery variables are said to influence listening comprehension. Speaker rates from 120 to 250 words per minute produce reasonable listening comprehension scores (Asher, 1955; Ernest, 1968; Goldstein, 1940; Goodman-Malamuth, 1956; Harwood, 1955; Nelson, 1948). In addition, rapidly delivered phrases were more difficult for subjects to remember than were phrases delivered more slowly (Bostrom & Bryant, 1980).

Research findings indicate that when a speaker is liked, listeners comprehend more of the message (Haiman, 1949). However, there is no clear evidence to suggest that gestures (Haiman, 1949) or visibility of the speaker (Anderson, 1951; Heron, 1946; Loder, 1937; Tabor, 1967; Utigard, 1962) influence listener comprehension.

Message Characteristics

Several message-related variables appear to influence listening comprehension. Clear, unambiguous statements (Zimbardo, 1960), active voice (Devito, 1969), message organization (Johnson, 1970; Spicer & Bassett, 1976), similar values or viewpoints (Carlton, 1954; Edwards, 1941; Gilkinson, Paulson, & Sikkik, 1953), and disconfirmation of audience expectations (Buchli & Pearce, 1974) have been associated with increased listening comprehension.

Environmental Characteristics

Variables in the environment such as temperature, seating arrangement, and noise have been associated with listener comprehension. Adequate room ventilation and comfortable temperature are positively related to listening comprehension (Nichols, 1948). A seating arrangement that is compact has a more positive relation to listening comprehension than have scattered seating arrangements (Furbay, 1965). Theorists have speculated that background noise or music would hinder listening comprehension, yet Tanner (1961) reports that listening comprehension was not significantly affected by musical or other background sounds.

MODES OF LISTENING TEST ADMINISTRATION

A number of theorists have investigated the effects of test administration on listening tests scores. Since the Brown-Carlsen and STEP Listening

Tests have been widely distributed for classroom use, they have been used in a number of investigations.

Studies have examined the effects of the differing channels, speakers, and rates on listening test scores. Johnson and Frandsen (1963) administered the Brown-Carlsen test to three groups of freshman students via taped, filmed, and live presentations. The best results were obtained through the taped presentation; least satisfactory results were obtained when the test was presented by film. Hopkins (1966) administered the Brown-Carlsen Test three ways (videotape, audio portion only, and video portion with placards).to 235 students. No significant differences were found with gender, mode of presentation, class size, or time of day. Jones (1961) found no significant differences between presenting live and taped presentations of the Brown-Carlsen Test.

Other studies have investigated differences in speaker presentations. Homan (1958) found that performance increased on the Brown-Carlsen Test when it was presented by a person with a normal speech pattern as compared to a person who stuttered. The increased performance, however, was not statistically significant. Nonsignificant results were found by Haberland (1958) when he compared results of the Brown-Carlsen Test when it was presented by a person with speech training and a person without speech training.

Klinger (1959) found no statistically significant differences in results on the STEP Test when it was presented by a person speaking normally, mildly stuttering, or severely stuttering. In another study, the STEP Test was administered to 252 students by a reader in the same room, a reader viewed on a closed-circuit television, and sound from the television (Coffman & Stodola, 1961). No significant differences were found in the mean test scores across the different modes of presentation. Significant differences, however, were found among the classes that had different readers. Likewise, no significant differences were found between four modes of presentation (teachers trained in test administration, teachers trained in the STEP Test, film with trained speaker, and audio of film) when the STEP Test was administered to fourth through twelfth graders (Stodola, Schwartz, & Kolster, 1962).

Even so, Richards (1976) suggests that using different voices to administer listening tests serves as a distraction to students and thus lowers critical listening scores. Carver (1969) found that young black males preferred and were more motivated to do their best on a listening test recorded by a black announcer than on a test recorded by a white announcer. In another study, the Brown-Carlsen and STEP tests were administered by effective and ineffective speakers (Barker, Watson, & Kibler, 1984). Subjects hearing the effective speakers scored significantly higher on both tests. In addition to the presenter variations, Brown (1959) found that performance of the STEP Listening Test improved when a brief introductory statement was made about the test.

Another area of test administration that has received considerable attention is the rate of presentation. For example, Nelson (1948) presented recorded newscasts to subjects at 125, 150, 175, 200, 225, and 250 words per minute and found no significant differences in comprehension. Fergen (1955) administered listening test at 80, 130, 180, and 230 words per minute. He found the best results at 130 words per minute but satisfactory results at all four speeds. Fairbanks, Guttman, and Miron (1957) found small but insignificant differences when information was presented at 141, 201, and 282 words per minute. Later, Foulke (1968) found a significant decline in comprehension when the speaking rate exceeded 250 words per minute. More recently, Behnke and Beatty (1977) reported a significant difference in comprehension scores between groups hearing presentations at 140 and 275 words per minute. Continued research has found that increased presentation rates accompany a significant decrease in comprehension scores (Beatty et al., 1977). Finally, it appears that lowered comprehension scores caused by increases in the rate of a presentation can be reduced through the use of extrinsic motivation or achievement incentives (Petrie & Carrel, 1976; Beatty, Behnke, & Froelich, 1980).

In addition to examining the mode of presentation, presentor effects, and the rate of presentation, other studies have examined the relation between administering tests in oral and written formats (Briggs & Armacost, 1933; Brown, 1948; 1952); with or without background noise (Ongman, 1960; Tanner, 1961); at different difficulty levels (Dolcini, 1965); and with true-false (Briggs & Armacost, 1933; Lehman, 1929; Odom & Miles, 1951; Stump, 1928), multiple choice (Sims & Knox, 1932), or Braille responses (Davis & Nolan, 1961; Hartlage, 1963). Considerable research has examined the effects of administration on listening test scores. Yet these results are of limited value unless the instruments are reliable and valid measures of listening comprehension.

QUESTIONS OF LISTENING TEST RELIABILITY AND VALIDITY

Most listening tests currently on the market have been criticized by communication scholars and educators. Critics have questioned the tests' validity, the relations among types of listening required, generalizability to the real world, norming procedures, passage length, and methods of administration (Barker et al., 1984).

The most widely used tests on the market are the Brown-Carlsen (out of print but available through Lyman K. Steil) and STEP Listening tests. For years the Brown-Carlsen and STEP tests were the primary measuring instruments used to study listening comprehension. However, as early as 1959 Lindquist questioned the Brown-Carlsen and STEP Test norming procedures, validity, and methods of administration. In fact, when researchers found high reliability for the Brown-Carlsen and STEP tests independently, they also found low correlations between the two tests for men (.58) and for women (.53; see Higgins, 1964). More important, theorists such as Petrie (1961) reported that the Brown-Carlsen and STEP tests measured factors other than listening.

Even so, educators were disappointed and surprised when Kelly (1965, 1967) analyzed both the Brown-Carlsen and STEP tests and found that they were related more closely to general mental ability than to listening. He reasoned that if these listening tests were indeed measuring a distinct skill, they should have correlated more closely with each other than with achievement or intelligence tests. As they did not, he attributed the differences in listening test scores to general mental ability rather than to listening comprehension differences. Kelly (1967) summarized the problem with listening tests as one of obtaining normalcy in test results. He listed five possible sources of error: (1) test versus nontest conditions (some subjects test better than others), (2) experimental set (purpose of the test), (3) motivational potential of the testing setting, (4) interestingness of the test, and (5) receptiveness of subject population.

In addition to problems with validity, these tests appear to have other measurement difficulties. For example, alternate forms of the same test do not have significant equivalents (Anderson & Baldauf, 1965); the test items are too easy for the designated grade levels (Spearitt, 1962); tests are a source of intelligence or cultural bias (Smith, 1956); and black children score lower on tests than do white children (Nolan, 1967). Other complaints have concerned testing procedures. For example, theorists question whether or not STEP uses too few items to test so many factors (Ross, 1964).

A number of additional criticisms of both published and unpublished listening tests include the mode of presentation (Lindquist, 1959), testing time (Johnson & Frandsen, 1963), test item difficulty (Langholz, 1966), test norming procedures (Ross, 1964), shortness of test passages, written rather than oral style (Thomas, 1956), gender-interestingness bias (Tipton & Weaver, 1973), communication purpose or activity (Halliday, 1973; Stohl, 1983), and test reading-writing requirements (Caffrey, 1950). Until measuring instruments address these criticisms, listening test score results will provide little meaningful information.

The inconsistency in listening test results has led theorists to surmise that because of the nature of listening, validity is difficult to judge (Lorge, 1959). However, validation difficulties are no reason to accept and use instrumentation that provides little useful information. Fortunately, rather than abandoning listening research, some theorists have attempted to examine the listening process more carefully. Results of their analyses suggest that listening test development is difficult without a clear definition of listening.

Listening has been defined as a process or series of steps used in various listening situations (Barker, 1971; Weaver, 1972; Steil, Barker, & Watson, 1983). Listening research has focused primarily on lecture comprehension listening. For this reason, many listening tests have failed to measure critical situational elements of the listening process (Kelly, 1967). More recently, however, Bostrom and Waldhart (1980a) suggested that theorists need to differentiate listening into three separate abilities: short-term listening, short-term listening with rehearsal, and lecture listening. In fact, short-term listening was found to be distinct from lecture listening and related more closely to oral skills than previous operational definitions of listening comprehension indicated (Bostrom & Waldhart, 1980a). By measuring the three separate listening abilities, listening—particularly short-term listening—was found to be separate from general mental ability for the first time (Bostrom & Waldhart, 1980a). In addition, short-term listening was found to be significantly different from short-term memory (Bostrom & Bryant, 1980).

Current research suggests that listening is a complex process rather than a singular skill. Therefore, listening tests must be identified and/or constructed to meet the complexities and challenges of such a construct.

CRITERIA FOR
LISTENING TEST CONSTRUCTION

Developing a reliable and valid measure of listening comprehension is difficult, and thus far no single listening test has gained universal acceptance. Several theorists have made suggestions about what to avoid or be aware of during listening test construction. Caffrey (1950) identified three basic problems in evaluating listening: elimination of irrelevant factors as items to be measured by the test (such as attention), isolation of test items from reading factors, and standardization of methods of presentation to nullify variations. McCarthy (1958) warned that since listening is closely related to general information, it is important to control for content familiarity. If familiarity is not controlled, those individuals who are more familiar with the information will have higher listener comprehension scores. Langholz (1966) stressed that listening tests need more discriminating items in order to ensure that tests are reliable across grade levels.

Although many theorists have presented suggestions for listening test construction, recent mandates that hold the educational system accountable for a student's communication skill development have led to an increased interest in listening test development and validation. Concern about communication skill deficiencies in high school and college graduates has led to the inclusion of speaking and listening as basic skills requirements in the Public Education Title II Program. With these requirements, educators found that their most pressing need was to develop a valid, reliable, and cost-efficient measurement instrument. With this in mind, a task force was appointed to recommend speaking and listening skills necessary as a minimal requirement for high school graduation. They identified functional, educational, and general skills (Bassett, Whittington, & Staton-Spicer, 1978). The skills they identified as peculiar to listening included listening effectively to spoken English, identifying main ideas, distinguishing fact from opinion, distinguishing persuasive from informative messages, recognizing when another does not understand your message, answering questions effectively, summarizing messages, describing another point of view, and describing differences of opinion.

Backlund, Brown, Gurry, and Jandt (1982) worked with the state of Massachusetts to conceive, implement, and evaluate basic skills. They identified 11 key listening skills and then established criteria by which to judge published listening tests. The criteria are as follows: (1) Stimulus requires responder to perform as a listener, (2) Instrument distinguishes listening performance from reading and writing, (3) Instrument is free of gender, cultural, racial, ethnic content, and/or stereotyping, (4) Instrument assesses presence or absence of skills. Of the seven listening instruments they evaluated, no instrument met their predetermined cutoff point (50% of the identified skills and criteria).

In addition to establishing criteria by which to judge listening tests, Backlund et al. (1982) provided the following recommendations for developing future listening tests:

(1) Stimulus materials should be taped (audio-video).
(2) Passages should use spoken, not written, passages that are read aloud.
(3) Stimulus materials should call for simple, minimal responses.
(4) Both the stimulus messages and questions should be produced on tape.
(5) Test booklets should contain test items in writing (should not be difficult or require excessive reading).
(6) Stimulus materials (messages and test questions) should be short (thirty seconds to three minutes).
(7) Stimulus materials should be interesting (meaningful/real-life).
(8) Vocalizations used in the stimulus materials should be controlled.

In addition to these suggestions, theorists should remember to construct tests that differentiate among short-term listening, short-term listening with rehearsal, and lecture listening (Bostrom & Bryant, 1980). Based on principles of memory, short-term listening lasts up to fifteen seconds; short-term listening with rehearsal lasts up to forty seconds; and long-term listening (affected by rehearsal techniques and organizational schemes) is not activated until at least one minute after the presentation (Norman & Rumelhart, 1975; Siegel & Allik, 1973; Smith, 1978). It is also important for listening tests to include a test-retest component in order to measure the critical effects instructional strategies.

CONCLUSIONS AND IMPLICATIONS

On the basis of the studies reviewed in this chapter, several conclusions seem warranted:

(1) Listening measurement is important in a variety of educational levels from elementary grades through adult audiences,
(2) Interest in listening has preceded scholarship in many areas of the discipline, leading to inconclusive and, at times, contradictory findings,
(3) Listening scholars, like social scientists in other disciplines, often neglect to build on previous research when formulating models or formats of listening tests,
(4) Problems in identifying and defining important listener characteristics, variables, and constructs have hindered general acceptance of most listening tests to date,
(5) Before valid and reliable listening tests can be developed, listening theorists (perhaps through the influence and leadership of the International Listening Association) need to agree on standardized operational definitions of the listening process,
(6) Both new and old listening tests need to be retested for reliability and validity,
(7) Finally, additional normative data need to be provided for past and future listening tests.

Future listening scholars, it is hoped, will avoid many of the pitfalls of earlier researchers by developing measures that provide more accurate reflections of the subtle differences in the type and quality of listening abilities. In addition, with refined statistical procedures, contemporary researchers should be able to provide more objective reliability and validity data than was possible in previous generations of listening research.

REFERENCES

Aiken, E. G., Thomas, G. S., & Shennum, W. A. (1975). Memory for a lecture: Effects of notes, lecture rate, and informational density. *Journal of Educational Psychology, 67,* 439-444.

Alderson, J. C. (1980). Native and non-native speaker performance on cloze tests. *Language Learning, 30,* 59-76.

Anderson, H. M., & Baldauf, R. J. (1965). A study of listening. *Journal of Educational Research,* 57, 128-198.

Anderson, J. C. (1951). The relative effectiveness of personal and recorded presentation of persuasive speeches. *Speech Monographs, 18,* 200.

Asher, J. J. (1955). *An experimental study of listener comprehension of news commentary when rate of delivery is varied.* Unpublished master's thesis, University of Houston.

Backlund, P. M., Brown, K. L., Gurry, J., & Jandt, F. (1982). Recommendations for assessing speaking and listening skills. *Communication Education, 31,* 9-17.

Baldauf, R. J. (1963). A study of a measure of listening comprehension and its relation to the school achievement of fifth grade pupils. *Journal of Educational Research, 57,* 197-200.

Barker, L. L. (1971). *Listening behavior.* Englewood Cliffs, NJ: Prentice-Hall.

Barker, L. L., Watson, K. W., & Kibler, R. J. (1984). An investigation of the effect of presentation by effective and ineffective speakers on listening test scores. *Southern Speech Communication Journal, 48,* 309-318.

Bassett, R. E., Whittington, N., & Staton-Spicer, A. (1978). The basics in speaking and listening for high school graduates. *Communication Education, 27,* 293-303.

Beatty, M. J. (1981). Receiver apprehension as a function of cognitive backlog. *Western Journal of Speech Communication, 45,* 275-279.

Beatty, M. J., Behnke, R. R., & Froelich, D. L. (1980). Effects of achievement incentive and presentation rate on listening comprehension. *Quarterly Journal of Speech, 66,* 193-200.

Beatty, M. J., Behnke, R. R., & Goodyear, F. H. (1977). True knowledge: A new measure of comprehension. *Center for Controlled Rate Newsletter, 11,* 3-4.

Beatty, M. J., & Payne, S. (1981). Receiver apprehension and cognitive complexity. *Western Journal of Speech Communication, 45,* 363-369.

Behnke, R. R., & Beatty, M. J. (1977). Effects of time-compressed speech on confidence weighted comprehension scores. *Southern Speech Communication Journal, 42,* 309-317.

Binford, F. E. (1977). *A study of interrelationships among different approaches to measuring listening comprehension.* Unpublished doctoral dissertation, University of Iowa.

Blewett, T. T. (1949). *An experiment in the measurement of listening at the college level.* Unpublished doctoral dissertation, University of Missouri.

Blubaugh, J. A. (1963). *An experimental study of the effects of information, instruction, and motivation on listening behavior.* Unpublished master's thesis, Lawrence, Kansas.

Bohn, T. W. (1964). *A study of immediate and delayed recall as a function of mode of presentation and anticipation of reward.* Unpublished master's thesis, Southern Illinois University.

Bonner, M. S. (1960). A critical analysis of the relationship of reading ability to listening ability. *Dissertation Abstracts, 21,* 2167-2168.

Bostrom, R. (1980). *Communication attitudes and communication abilities.* Paper presented at the International Communication Association Convention, Minneapolis.

Bostrom, R. N., & Bryant, C. (1980). Factors in the retention of information presented orally: The role of short-term listening. *Western Journal of Speech Communication, 44,* 137-145.

Bostrom, R. N., & Waldhart, E. S. (1980a). Components in listening behavior: The role of short-term memory. *Human Communication Research, 6,* 222-227.

Bostrom, R. N., & Waldhart, E. (1980b). *The Kentucky Comprehensive Listening Test.* Lexington: University of Kentucky.

Bostrom, R. N., Waldhart, E., & Brown, M. H. (1979). *Effects of motivational instructions on listening behavior.* Paper presented at the International Communication Association Convention, Philadelphia.

Briggs, T. H., & Armacost, G. H. (1933). Results of an oral true-false test. *Journal of Research, 26,* 595-596.

Brown, C. T. (1959). Studies in listening comprehension. *Speech Monographs, 26,* 288-294.

Brown, J. I. (1948). A comparison of listening and reading ability. *College English, 10,* 105-107.

Brown, J. I. (1951). The objective measurement of listening ability. *Journal of Communication, 1,* 44-48.

Brown, J. I. (1952). Teaching listening through listening type tests. *College English, 13,* 224-225.

Brown, J. I. (1954). Can listening be taught? *College English, 15,* 290-291.

Brown, J. I., & Carlsen, G. R. (1955). *Brown-Carlsen Listening Comprehension Test.* New York: Harcourt Brace Jovanovich.

Brown, K. L., Backlund, P., Gurry, J., & Jandt, F. (1980). Evaluating speaking and listening skill assessment instruments: Which one is best for you? *Language Arts, 57,* 621-627.

Buchli, V., & Pearce, W. (1974). Listening behavior in coorientational states. *Journal of Communication, 24*(3), 62-70.

Caffrey, J. (1950). The establishment of auding-age norms. *Education Digest, 15,* 18-20.

Canfield, G. R. (1961). A study of the effect of two types of instruction on the listening comprehension of fifth grade children. *Elementary School Journal, 62,* 146-151.

Carlton, R. (1954). An experimental investigation of the relationships between personal value and word intelligibility. *Speech Monographs, 21,* 142-143.

Carroll, B. J. (1980). *Testing communication performance: An interim study.* Oxford, England: Pergamon.

Carver, R. (1969). Use of recently developed listener comprehension test to investigate the effect upon verbal proficiency. *American Education Research Journal, 6,* 263-270.

Cochran, J. R. (1960). Validated batteries of speaking and listening predictors.*Dissertation Abstracts, 20,* 3427.

Coffman, W. E., & Stodola, Q. (1961). *The effect of conditions of administration on listening comprehension test scores.* College Entrance Examination Board Research and Development Reports, Research Bulletin RB. Princeton, NJ: Educational Testing Service.

Crawford, C. C. (1925). The correlation between college lecture notes and quiz papers.*Journal of Educational Research, 12,* 282-291.

Crook, F. E. (1957). Interrelationships among a group of language arts test. *Journal of Educational Research, 51,* 305-311.

Davis, C. J., & Nolan, C. Y. (1961). A comparison of the oral and written methods of administering achievement tests. *International Journal for the Education of the Blind, 10,* 80-82.

Devine, T. G. (1978). Listening: What do we know fifty years of research and theorizing? *Journal of Reading, 21,* 296-304.

Devito, J. A. (1969). Some psychological aspects of active and passive sentences. *Quarterly Journal of Speech, 55,* 401-406.

Dickson, W. P., & Patterson, J. H. (1981). Evaluating referential communication games for teaching speaking and listening skills. *Communication Education, 30,* 11-21.

Divesta, F. J., & Gray, G. S. (1973). Listening and note taking II: Immediate and delayed recall as functions of variations in thematic continuity, note taking, and length of listening review intervals. *Journal of Educational Psychology, 64,*278-287.

Dolcini, M. E. (1965). Children's listening comprehension of fictional and factual materials at two levels of difficulty. *Dissertation Abstracts, 25,* 6428.

Dorval, B. M. (1959). *A descriptive study of a series of units on listening in a fifth grade.* Unpublished master's thesis, Boston.

Dow, C. W. (1955). The development of a listening comprehension test for Michigan State College freshmen. *Speech Teacher, 4,* 239-246.

Durrell-Sullivan Reading Capacity Test. (1937). Yonkers, World Book.

Edgar, K. F. (1961). The validation of four methods of improving listening ability. *Dissertation Abstracts, 22,* 1084.

Edwards, A. (1941). Political frames of reference as a factor in influencing recognition. *Journal of Abnormal Social Psychology, 36,* 34-50.

Eisner, S., & Rohde, K. (1959). Note taking during or after a lecture. *Journal of Educational Psychology, 50,* 301-304.

Ernest, C. H. (1968). Listening comprehension as a function of type of material and rate of presentation. *Communication Monographs, 35,* 154-158.

Fairbanks, G., Guttman, N., & Miron, M. S. (1957). Auditory comprehension in relation to listening rate and selective verbal redundancy. *Journal of Speech and Hearing Disorders, 22,* 23-32.

Farrow, V. L. (1964). An experimental study of listening attention at the fourth, fifth, and six grade. *Dissertation Abstracts, 24,* 3146.

Fergen, G. K. (1955). Listening comprehension at controlled rates for children in grades IV, V, and VI. *Dissertation Abstracts, 15,* 89.

Ferris, M. E. (1964). *A study of the relationship between reading comprehension and listening comprehension.* Unpublished master's thesis, University of Tennessee.

Foulke, E. (1968). Listening comprehension as a function of word rate. *Journal of Communication, 18,* 198-206.

Furbay, A. L. (1965). The influence of scattered versus compact seating on audience response. *Communication Monographs, 32,* 144-148.

Gilkinson, H., Paulson, S. F., & Sikkik, D. E. (1953). Conditions affecting the communication of controversial statements in connected discourse: Forms of presentation and the political frame of reference of the listener. *Speech Monographs, 20,* 253-260.

Goldhaber, G. R., & Weaver, C. H. (1968). Listening comprehension of compressed speech when the difficulty, rate of presentation, and sex of the listener are varied. *Speech Monographs, 35,* 20-25.

Goldstein, H. (1940). *Reading and listening comprehension at various controlled rates.* New York: Bureau of Publications-Teachers College, Columbia University.

Goodman-Malamuth, L. (1956). *An experimental study of the effects of rate of speaking upon listenability.* Unpublished doctoral dissertation, the University of Southern California.

Goodyear, H. (1969). *An experimental study of the motivational effect of punishment and reward anticipation on the listening comprehension of college students.* Unpublished doctoral dissertation, the University of Texas at Austin.

Graham, J. L. (1966). The teaching of listening skills through music lessons in fourth and fifth grade classrooms. *Dissertation Abstracts, 26,* 7114-7115.

Haberland, J. A. (1958). Speaker effectiveness and the Brown-Carlsen Listening Test. *School and Society, 86,* 198-199.

Haberland, J. A. (1959). A comparison of listening tests with standardized tests. *Journal of Educational Research, 102,* 301-302.

Haiman, F. (1949). An experimental study of the effect of ethos on public speaking. *Speech Monographs, 16,* 190-202.

Halliday, M. (1973). *Explorations in the functions of language.* London: Edward Arnold.

Hartlage, L. C. (1963). Differences in listening comprehension of the blind and sighted. *International Journal for the Education of the Blind, 13,* 1-6.

Harwood, K. A. (1955). Listenability and rate of presentation. *Speech Monographs, 22,* 57-59.

Hatten, J. T. (1978). Tests of auditory comprehension. In O. K. Buros (Ed.), *The eighth mental measurements yearbook.* Highland Park, NJ: Griphon Press.

Hedrick, D. L. (1976). *A developmental investigation of children's abilities to respond to competing messages varied in intensity and content.* Unpublished doctoral dissertation, University of Washington.

Heron, W. T., & Ziebarth, E. W. (1946). A preliminary experimental comparison of radio and classroom lectures. *Speech Monographs, 13,* 54-57.

Higgins, I. D. (1964). *An empirical study of listening related to anxiety and to certain other measures of ability and achievement.* Unpublished doctoral dissertation. University of Southern California.

Hill, P. (1963). *An informal survey of listening skills.* Unpublished master's thesis.

Holleran, B. P. (1966). *A comparison of oral and written listening tests.* Unpublished master's thesis, Columbus, Ohio.

Hollow, K. S. M. (1955). *An experimental study of listening comprehension at the intermediate grade level.* Unpublished doctoral dissertation, New York.

Homan, H. W. (1958). *The effect of recorded stuttering on listening comprehension.* Unpublished master's thesis, Kalamazoo, Michigan.

Hopkins, J. E. (1966). *The Brown-Carlsen Test: An investigation of the influence of modes of presentation, class size, sex, and time of presentation on listening comprehension.* Unpublished master's thesis, Athens, Ohio.

Jackson, A. E. (1966). An investigation of the relationship between listening and selected variables in grades four, five and six. *Dissertation Abstracts, 27,* 53A.

Jenson, M. B. (1930). An evaluation of three methods of presenting true-false examinations. *School and Society, 32,* 675-677.

Johnson, F. C., & Frandsen, K. (1963). Administering the Brown-Carlsen Listening Comprehension Test. *Journal of Communication, 13,* 38-45.

Johnson, M. (1970). *The construction and analysis of a listening test for the immediate grades.* Unpublished doctoral dissertation, Ohio University.

Jones, J. A. (1961). *An investigation of scores on the Brown-Carlsen listening test as correlated with subjective instructor ratings and as influenced by media of presentation.* Unpublished master's thesis. Seattle, Washington.

Jones-Mohr Listening Test. (1976). La Jolla, CA: University Associates.

Karraker, M. E. (1952). An evaluation of the influence of interest and 'set' on listening effectiveness in the basic communication class. *Speech Monographs, 19,* 117-118.

Katz, M. (Eds). (1959). *Listening skills builders.* Princeton, NJ: Educational Testing Service.

Kelly, C. M. (1965). An investigation of the construct validity of two commercially published listening tests. *Speech Monographs, 32,* 139-143.

Kelly, C. M. (1967). Listening: Complex of activities—and a unitary skill? *Speech Monographs, 34,* 455-466.

Klinger, H. N. (1959). *The effects of stuttering on audience listening comprehension.* Unpublished doctoral dissertation, New York University.

Kramer, E. J. (1952). A study of listening test scores on orally presented expository material with the speaker seen and with the speaker not seen. *Speech Monographs, 19,* 160.

Lafrance, M., & Mayo, C. (1979). A review of nonverbal behaviors of women and men. *Western Journal of Speech Communication, 43,* 96-107.

Langholz, A. P. (1966). A study of the relationship of listening test scores to test item difficulty. *Dissertation Abstracts, 26,* 6912.

Larter, M. J., & Scott, C. T. (1956). *Construction and validation of a listening test for grades I and II with evaluation of listening exercises.* Unpublished master's thesis. Boston.

Lashbrook, V. J. (1976). *The effects of cueing and storage strategies on the processing of oral messages.* Unpublished doctoral dissertation, West Virginia University.

Laurent, M. J. (1967). The construction and evaluation of a listening curriculum for grades 5 and 6. *Dissertation Abstracts, 27,* 4167A-4168A.

Lehman, H. (1929). The oral versus the mimeographed true-false test. *School and Society, 30,* 470-472.

Lewis, M. S. (1955). The construction of a diagnostic test of listening comprehension for grades 4, 5, and 6. *Abstracts of Field Studies for the Degree of Doctor of Education, 16,* 18-52.

Lieb-Brilhart, B. (1965). The relationship between some aspect of communicative speaking and communicative listening. *Journal of Communication, 15,* 35-46.

Lindquist, E. F. (1959). Review of Brown-Carlsen listening comprehension test. In O. K. Buros (Ed.), *Fifth mental measurements yearbook* (650-651, 652-654). Highland Park, NJ: Griphon Press.

Loder, J. E. (1937). A study of aural learning with or without the speaker present. *Journal of Experimental Education, 6,* 46-60.

Lorge, I. A. (1959). Review of sequential test of educational progress. In O. K. Buros (Ed.), *Fifth mental measurements yearbook* (654-655). Highland Park, NJ: Griphon Press.

Lundsteen, S. W. (1963). *Teaching ability in critical listening in the fifth and sixth grades.* Unpublished doctoral dissertation, University of California.

Mallis, J., & Anderson, L. A. (Eds.). (1969). *Listen and think.* New York: McGraw-Hill.

McCarthy, E. L. (1958). Auding ability related to achievement in two telecourses. *Dissertation Abstracts, 18,* 531-532.

Nelson, H. D. (1948). The effect of rate on the recall by radio listeners of "straight" newscasts. *Speech Monographs, 15,* 179.

Neville, M. H., & Pugh, A. K. (1976). Context in reading and listening: Variations in approach to cloze tasks. *Reading Research Quarterly, 12,* 13-31.

Nichols, R. G. (1948). Factors in listening comprehension. *Speech Monographs, 15,* 154-163.

Nolan, C. Y. (1967). Listening and reading in learning. In E. Foulke (Ed.), *Proceedings of the Louisville conference on time compressed speech.* Louisville, KY: Center for the Rate Controlled Recordings.

Norman, D. A., & Rumelhart, D. E. (1975). Explorations in cognition. San Francisco: W. H. Freeman.

Odom, C. L., & Miles, R. W. (1951). Oral versus visual presentation of true-false achievement tests in the first course in psychology. Educational and Psychological Measurements, 11, 470-477.

Ongman, E. E. (1960). Construction of a listening comprehension test for the sixth, seventh, and eight grades. Unpublished master's thesis, Chicago.

Orr, D. B., & Graham, W. R. (1968). Development of a listening comprehension test to identify educational potential among disadvantaged junior high school students. American Educational Research Journal, 5, 167-180.

Palamatier, R. A., & McNinch, G. (1972). Source of gains in listening skills. Experimental or pre-test experience? Journal of Communication, 22, 70-76.

Palmer, B. M. (1966). A study of the relationship between reading comprehension and listening comprehension of selected high school freshmen. Unpublished master's thesis. DePaul University.

Petrie, C. R. (1961). An experimental evaluation of two methods for improving listening comprehension abilities. Unpublished doctoral dissertation, Purdue University.

Petrie, C. R., & Carrel, S. D. (1976). The relationship of motivation, listening capability, initial information, and verbal organizational ability to lecture comprehension and retention. Communication Monographs, 43, 187-194.

Plax, T. G., & Rosenfeld, L. B. (1979). Receiver differences and the comprehension of spoken messages. Journal of Experimental Education, 48, 23-28.

Pratt, L. E. (1956). Experimental evaluation of a program for the improvement of listening. Elementary School Journal, 56, 318.

Prince, B. L. (1948). A study of classroom listening effectiveness in basic communication and its relation to certain other factors. Unpublished master's thesis, University of Denver.

Reeves, H. R. (1965). The effect of training in listening upon reading achievement. Unpublished doctoral dissertation, Florida State University.

Richards, R. A. (1976). The development and evaluation of a test of critical listening for use with college freshmen and sophomores. Unpublished doctoral dissertation, New York University.

Roach, D.A. (1981). State of the art in listening comprehension: A compendium of measures. Paper presented at the International Listening Association Convention, Denver.

Rogers, G.W. (1960). Lecture listening skills: Their nature and relationship to achievement. Dissertation Abstracts, 20, 4165.

Ross, R. (1964). A look at listeners. Elementary School Journal, 64, 369-372.

Rossiter, C. M. (1972). Sex of the speaker, sex of the listener, and listening comprehension. Journal of Communication, 22, 64-69.

Rubin, D. L., Daly, J., McCroskey, J. C., & Mead, N. A. (1982). A review and critique of procedures for assessing speaking and listening skills among preschool through grade twelve students. Communication Education, 31, 285-303.

Russell, D. H. (1964). A conspectus of recent research on listening abilities. Elementary English, 41, 262-267.

Scott, M., & Wheeless, L. R. (1977). The relationship of three types of communication apprehension to classroom achievement. Southern Speech Communication Journal, 42, 246-255.

Sequential Tests of Educational Progress (STEP). (1959). Princeton, NJ: Educational Testing Service.

Siegel, A. W., & Allik, J. P. (1973). A developmental study of visual and auditory short-term memory. Journal of Verbal Learning and Verbal Behavior, 12, 409-418.

Sims, V. M., & Knox, L. B. (1932). The reliability and validity of multiple response tests when presented orally. Journal of Educational Psychology, 23, 656-662.

Smeltzer, L., & Watson, K. W. (1983). Improving listening skills used in business: An empirical investigation of discussion length, modeling and level of incentive. Paper presented at the Speech Communication Association Convention, Washington, D.C.

Smith, E. E. (1978). Theories of semantic memory. In W. K. Estes (Ed.), Handbook of learning and cognitive processes. Hillsdale, NJ: Lawrence Erlbaum.

Smith, T. W. (1956). Auding and reading skill as sources of cultural bias in the Davis-Ellis Games and *California Test of Mental Maturity.* Unpublished doctoral dissertation, University of Southern California.

Sorenson, H. (1948). *Psychology in education* (2nd ed.). New York: McGraw-Hill.

Spearritt, D. (1962). *Listening comprehension—A factorial analysis.* Melbourne, Australia: Australian Counsel for Educational Research, Series Number 76.

Spicer, C., & Bassett, R. E. (1976). The effect of organization on learning from an informative message. *Southern Speech Communication Journal, 41,* 290-299.

Steil, L. K., Barker, L. L., & Watson, K. W. (1983). *Effective listening.* Reading, MA: Addison-Wesley.

Sticht, T. G., & Glasnapp, D. R. (1972). Effects of speech rate, selection difficulty, association strength, and mental aptitude on learning by listening. *Journal of Communication. 22,* 174-188.

Stodola, Q., Schwartz, D. F., & Kolstoe, R. H. (1962). Administering a listening comprehension test through the use of teacher-readers, sound film, and tape recorders. *North Dakota Teacher, 41,* 13-17.

Stohl, C. (1983). The development of a communicative competence scale. In R. N. Bostrom (Ed.), *Communication yearbook 7.* Beverly Hills, CA: Sage.

Stromer, W. F. (1955). Listening and personality. *Education, 75,* 322-326.

Stump, N. F. (1928). Oral versus printed method in the presentation of true-false examinations. *Journal of Educational Research, 18,* 423-424.

Sullivan, G. (1946). Listening behavior in the secondary schools. *American Teacher, 31,* 12-13.

Tabor, D. D. H. (1967). *Differential effectiveness of various instructional methods involved in a listening comprehension program.* Unpublished doctoral dissertation, University of Nebraska.

Tanner, D. B. (1961). *A comparison of the influence of three environments upon critical listening in the fifth grade.* Unpublished master's thesis.

Templeton, H. (1977). A new technique for measuring listening comprehension. *English Language Teaching Journal, 31,* 292-299.

Theobald, J. T., & Alexander, J. E. (1977). An auditory cloze procedure for assessing the difficulty level of teacher instructional talk in the intermediate grades. *Elementary School Journal, 77,* 389-394.

Thomas, G. L. (1956). Effect of oral style on intelligibility of speech. *Speech Monographs, 23,* 46-54.

Thompson, E. C. (1960). *An experimental investigation of the relative effectiveness of organizational structure in oral communication.* Unpublished doctoral dissertation, University of Minnesota.

Till, J. A. (1978). Tests and reviews: Miscellaneous listening. In O. K. Buros (Ed.), *Eighth mental measurements yearbook.* Highland Park, NJ: Griphon.

Tipton, M. J., & Weaver, C. H. (1973). A listening test for the intermediate grades. *Central States Speech Journal, 24,* 5-12.

Utigard, C. N. (1962). *A comparison of the effectiveness of magnetic tape and the regular classroom teacher upon growth in listening ability.* Unpublished master's thesis, University of Washington.

Vineyard, E. E., & Bailey, R. B. (1960) Interrelationships of reading ability, listening skill, intelligence, and scholastic achievement. *Journal of Developmental Reading, 3,* 174-178.

Waldhart, E. S., & Bostrom, R. N. (1981). *Notetaking, listening, and modes of retention.* Paper presented at the International Listening Association Convention, Washington, D.C.

Ward, K. K. (1980). *Listening skills test.* Canton, Ohio: Kent State University-Stark Campus.

Watson, K. W., & Barker, L. L. (1983). *Watson-Barker Listening Test.* Auburn, AL: SPECTRA, Inc.

Weaver, C. H. (1972). *Human listening: Process and behavior.* Indianapolis: Bobbs-Merrill.

Wheeless, L. R. (1975). An investigation of receiver apprehension and social context dimensions of communication apprehension. *Speech Teacher, 24,* 261-268.

Widener, R. W. (1950). *A preliminary study of the effects of training on listening.* Unpublished master's thesis, University of Oklahoma.

Wiskell, W. (1946). Problems of listening. *Quarterly Journal of Speech, 32,* 505-508.

Zimbardo, P. G. (1960). Involvement and communication discrepancy as determinants of opinion conformity. *Journal of Abnormal and Social Psychology, 60,* 86-94.

8 ● Communication Development in Children

BETH HASLETT

University of Delaware

RESEARCHERS have advocated different theories and methods for studying human communication from a pragmatic perspective, especially in research on developmental pragmatics. This area of study offers a rich and bewildering array of studies; many scholars are recognizing, however, that these studies need integration and synthesis so that more adequate theory building and research can be done. In this overview I have attempted to integrate research in developmental pragmatics and to discuss critical research issues that have emerged.

THE DEVELOPMENT OF PRAGMATIC COMMUNICATION

Given the diversity of theory and method in developmental pragmatics, I shall begin by discussing children's developing communicative skills. However, the view being presented here does *not* imply that prior stages of development are causally related to subsequent stages. Although some researchers are making such claims, it is not at all clear that such claims are theoretically sound or empirically verifiable.[1] This analysis of the child's developing communicative skills will concentrate on the first five years of life.

Early pragmatic communicative skills appear to develop in four broad stages. The first stage, *recognizing the interpersonal basis of communication,* is the stage during which infants recognize that communication is the means by which we establish and maintain relationships with others. The second stage, *creating communicative effects,* develops from approximately four months to three years of age. Development during this stage occurs in

Correspondence and requests for reprints: Beth Haslett, Department of Communications, University of Delaware, Newark, DE 19711.

three substages: (1) preverbal routines—in which the child acquires an understanding of the requirements of dialogue, such as role reciprocity and turn taking; (2) communicative intentionality—in which the child begins to signal his or her needs intentionally; and (3) linguistic communication—in which the child demonstrates a functional mastery of language in accomplishing social goals. The discussion of the substage of linguistic communication shall include two approaches to language use—speech act analysis and functional analysis of language. The third stage of pragmatic development, *using communicative strategies*, begins at approximately three years of age. During this period, the child develops an increasingly diverse set of linguistic forms to accomplish a variety of communicative goals. Thus communication becomes increasingly adapted to different participants in different communicative settings. The final stage of pragmatic development, *monitoring communication*, emerges at around five years of age. Children now develop the ability to evaluate the adequacy of messages and to make repairs, when needed, in conversing with others.

Research on pragmatics has not only been concerned with the communicative skills children demonstrate, but with characterizing the relevant social knowledge about communication that permits one to adjust one's communication appropriately in varying social situations. Children appear to acquire this knowledge gradually. First, infants develop an *awareness of self as distinct from others*, which emerges during the first year of life; then, *knowledge of others* becomes increasingly differentiated during the second and third years, and, finally, *knowledge of communicative contexts* begins to emerge at the third year. A more thorough discussion of each of these developmental stages follows.

Stage I:
Recognizing the Interpersonal Basis
of Communication

The first stage of development is the appearance of the motivation to communicate. The work of Trevarthen (1977, 1979a, 1979b, 1980a, 1980b, 1982) has been most prominent in this area of study. Trevarthen suggests that humans possess an innate ability for intersubjectivity. Further studies of human brain growth suggest that the "human brain has systems which integrate interpersonal and practical aims together from the first few months after birth" (Trevarthen, 1982, p. 77). He advocates a balanced holistic perspective in studying infants' mental life; in particular, he stresses the internal processes by which infants regulate their mental activities.

Intention, as defined by Trevarthen (1982, p. 80), involves *regulating* one's behavior by anticipating alternatives for action. Intentional behaviors are guided by motives: "The choice of a particular . . . intentional action satisfying that motive" is largely a matter of free individual choice.

Trevarthen claims that motives and intentions develop in two stages: primary intersubjectivity and secondary intersubjectivity. Each stage reflects the infant's growing ability to act cooperatively in accomplishing goals.

The first stage takes place in three substages. The first substage, primary interpersonal life, is from birth to approximately 10 weeks. The infant moves from an initial negative period (in which the infant appears to be controlling the amount of stimulation he or she receives) to a period in which complex, expressive exchanges occur between the adult caretaker and the child (Bates, 1979; Murray, 1980; Sylvester-Bradley, 1980). The following substages, object prehension and games, occurs from approximately 11 to 30 weeks. Social development of motives appears to occur in cycles of avoidance and approach: Motives for affectionate and cooperative interaction with others alternate with motives for withdrawal and avoidance. The final substage, development of cooperative understanding and expression of meaning, occurs from 31 to 60 weeks. The infant now shows strong interest in others' actions, movements, and statements; cooperative activity now emerges. After 9 months, according to Trevarthen (1982, p. 100), communicative signals "clearly conceive of others [as] having interests, purposes and helpful powers."

The second stage in the development of motives and intentions, secondary intersubjectivity, emerges during the second year and occurs in periods of little growth followed by periods of enriched growth. By 15 months, symbolic representation seems to be clearly established. Infants also appear to recognize that humans possess the capability for shared intention and awareness; thus this stage is marked by inventiveness and creativity in interactions with familiar others (Hubley & Trevarthen, 1979, p. 216).

In summary, by the end of the second year of life, infants understand the basic intersubjective function of language—its communicative use. The development of primary intersubjectivity is the essence of the first stage of communicative awareness; the infant now possesses a functional social sensitivity that is necessary for human communication.

Stage II:
Creating Communicative Effects

The child's growing awareness of communication during this stage reflects increasing elaboration and differentiation in the child's understanding of the communication process and of the effects of particular communicative acts. This elaboration occurs in three substages: (1) preverbal routines, (2) communicative intentionality, and (3) linguistic communication. During this stage, the transition from prelinguistic to linguistic communication occurs. This discussion, while focusing on the use of language for communication, will not be concerned with the acquisition of language itself.

Preverbal Routines

During this period, from approximately two to six months of age, infants establish interactive routines with adults. Among these early routines are patterned social exchanges during bathing, bedtime, feeding, and so forth. Subsequently these routines incorporate games, such as peekaboo. Through participating in such routines, infants develop an understanding of the fundamental nature of communication such as role reciprocity, role reversibility, turn taking, and strategies for gaining and maintaining joint attention (Bates, 1979; Bruner, 1975; Snow, 1977; Stern, 1977). Nelson (1981) has termed this learning "anticipatory imitation," in which the infants' performance completes the social routine. Bruner (1982) prefers to call these routines "formats," stressing their "formal" nature.

Such routines emphasize the interactive aspects of social encounters. Infants begin to develop expectations about how one goes about the communication game; they appreciate role reciprocity, role reversibility, a sense of sequence in communication, and so forth. One communicative skill emerging during this period is the concept of turn taking; dialogue clearly implies that there will be an exchange of speaking and listening roles and many scholars suggest that this appreciation first develops during preverbal routines.

Infants appear to have an early appreciation of turn taking. According to Bruner (1975b), role reciprocity (taking turns and assuming the other's role, as, for example, in conversational exchanges) emerges from action in give-and-take games with objects and games such as peekaboo. These social exchanges become communicative (that is, intentional) around 9-10 months (Bates, 1976). Exchanges become more complex and organized around tasks. As Bruner (1975b, p. 277) points out, the task "is gradually being structured into reciprocating roles, the roles defined into rounds, each composed of turns, often with turns interchangeable. . . . the striking thing about such task formats is that they are rule bound and constraining."

Keenan (1974), in her analysis of dialogues between twin boys, found that they took turns, handled interruptions, and made audible and appropriate responses to one another. A study by Schaffer, Collis, and Parsons (1977) found that 12- and 24-month-old children exchanged talking turns smoothly with their mothers; any overlaps were brief and were caused equally by mothers and children. Bloom, Rocissano, and Hood (1976) also found children at the two-word stage (18 months) able to respond to adults and take turns. Schaffer (1979) points out, however, that in normal mother-infant dyadic exchanges it is difficult to assess the extent of the infant's interactive skill or the degree to which the mother maintains the exchange. Through object manipulation, games, and interactive routines, the child at 12 months appears to "comprehend, in a practical sense, the notion of reciprocity with its attendant ideas of complementarity, synchrony and role reversal" (Schaffer, 1979, p.

294). The child's understanding of speaker-listener roles develops through vocal exchanges with his or her mother. Turn taking thus appears to develop from biological patterns of temporal sequencing and interactional synchrony; in the context of communication, sequencing and synchrony develop into role reciprocity and role complementarity.

As we have seen, many of the rudimentary skills necessary for interpersonal communication begin during preverbal routines. The degree to which these skills come under the control of the infant, however, has been a subject of much controversy. In discussing the next stage of development, that of *communicative intentionality*, the ways in which the infant's emerging ability to control his or her communicative skills have been characterized will be assessed.

Communicative Intentionality

Bates, Benigni, Bretherton, Camaioni, and Volterra (1979, p. 36) view intentionality as behavior in which "the sender is aware *a priori* of the effect a signal will have on his listener, and he persists in that behavior until the effect is obtained or failure clearly indicated." Researchers have examined the infant's efforts to engage an adult in achieving a goal. These efforts develop as follows: (1) the infant visually checking the adult for feedback; (2) the infant altering his or her signal upon changes in adult behavior toward achieving a goal; and (3) signaling becomes shorter and ritualized (that is, signals are becoming conventionalized). Thus infants recognize the conventional purpose of speech acts as being the effect intended by the speaker; this conventional purpose is recognized by both speaker and listener. Conventional signals thus enable regular and predictable communication between adult and child to occur.

For conventional signals to be symbolic, the child must be aware of the relationship between the conventional sign and its referent, and this recognition must exist in varied situations. Bates, Benigni, Bretherton, Camaioni, and Volterra (1979) found that at 13 months, infants used conventional signals symbolically in their utterances. They conclude that symbolic capacity emerges at the same time in both play and language, and that parallels exist in their levels and sequences of development. Studies by Nicolich (1975) also uncovered structural parallels between children's language and symbolic play. Such evidence indicates that the underlying cognitive basis for language and symbolic play may be the same.

A broader perspective on the emergence of intentionality is offered by the work of John Dore (1983). Dore suggests that intentionality emerges in three stages. First, there is the intent to act, in which "the infant is aware of a practical end and can institute various means to achieve it, largely by sensorimotor actions on objects" (Dore, 1983, p. 174). There is a transitional stage, that of expressing, and the final stage is the intent to convey, in which the child uses recognizable words intentionally. Dore is most concerned with the transitional stage of expressing and the role of mother-infant interaction in transforming expressing to intending.

The transitional stage of expressing has two substages (this expressing stage coincides with the period of indexical expressions). In intending *in* expressing, the first substage, infants use vocalizations that are immediate and spontaneous—behaviorally, it is manifested by vocalization plus gesture or gaze at an object, but not both. The second substage, intending *to* express, has vocalizations that are premeditated, designed to express "something to be done or said about an object" (Dore, 1983, p. 175). Infants are able to synchronize their activities across persons, movements, and objects—that is, they coordinate their behavior along those three dimensions.

What changes this expressing into intending? Dore argues that mother-child interaction is crucial for language onset (the use of first words). Mothers, when responding to their children's vocalizations, may analogue, complement, or imitate the baby's affect state (that is, the baby's expressing). Through the mother's responses, she transforms the baby's affect expressions into "intents to express those affect-states" (Dore, 1983, p. 169). According to Dore (1983, p. 169), this marks the origin of intention—"when the motivation for an expression finds an observable form that can be focussed upon and then reproduced." The baby's motivation to change from expressing to intending is the necessity for adapting to the mother's "ways of doing and expressing in order to achieve, maintain, repair, and later renegotiate their relationship" (Dore, 1983, p. 169).

While varying approaches have been taken to try to account for intentionality, all approaches view intentionality in terms of altering behavior. This emphasis on the infant's ability to alter his or her communicative behavior also highlights the interactive nature of communicative intentionality. Infants need the responses of others in order to have feedback about their own behavior. Not only is feedback needed, but infants also rely on others' interpretations of their behavior. The infant cannot progress from intentional communication to use of conventional communicative signals *without* the adult's interpretation of those signals. Thus intentionality must be expressed via some conventional communicative signals.

Finally, we need to note that the child gradually increases his or her control over expressing intentions. This matter of control is, in part, a function of the child's growing awareness of his or her effect on others. While researchers place the earliest behavioral evidence of intentionality at approximately nine months, it is clear that infants continue to develop increasing mastery over the communicative means by which they express their intentions.

Both preceding substages, preverbal routines and communicative intentionality, are prelinguistic stages. The final substage, *linguistic communication,* develops between the ages of twelve and eighteen months. During this period, the child begins to communicate using language. Two theoretical approaches have been used to account for the emergence of verbal communication: speech act theory and functional approaches. Before presenting the research from both perspectives, I shall briefly highlight some differences between these two approaches.

Linguistic Communication

Language has often been discussed in terms of linguistic form (nouns, verbs, questions and so forth) and linguistic function (the purpose for which language is being used—to persuade, to warn, to threaten, and the like). Speech act analyses emphasize linguistic form, whereas functional approaches emphasize linguistic function. A speech act analysis deals not only with linguistic form itself, but also with the intentions, presuppositions, and implications of a particular linguistic form. For example, in making a request, what are the different ways in which one can make a request, and what are the presuppositions inherent in making a request? In contrast, functional analyses deal with analyzing the purposes for which children use language. While functional analyses may seem similar to analyzing the illocutionary force of a speech act, there are several points of contrast. First, functional analyses can incorporate the perlocutionary effect as well as illocutionary force; that is, the function of an utterance can be viewed as effect, intention, or both. Speech act theory has generally ignored perlocutionary effect altogether. This, in my opinion, has weakened speech act theory because it obviates the important linkage between intent and effect: People intend to do things in order to create a desired effect—concentrating only on the intent deals with only part of the communicative process. Second, speech act analyses typically focus on a single proposition, whereas a functional analysis may incorporate more than a single utterance. Finally, functional approaches allow for the multi-functionality of utterances, whereas speech act analysis focuses on only one function an utterance could perform. Keeping these differences in mind, let us now look at developmental research from both these perspectives.

Speech Acts

From approximately twelve to eighteen months, children develop single words that signal intentions more explicitly. Although there is some debate as to whether single words can be viewed as propositional utterances, the view is beginning to dominate research perspectives at this substage, and that is the view that will be taken here.

Bates (1976) suggests that infants substitute words for those preverbal gestures used to signal their intentions. Children encode whatever they consider most important in a given context (that is, whatever is most interesting to them). Thus an infant's utterance "presupposes that situation, treating the uncoded elements [presuppositions] as the topic for the one-word comment" (Bates, 1976, p. 159).

Indirect Speech Acts. With respect to understanding indirect speech acts, Bates (1976) found that children aged 2 to 4 responded equally to both direct and indirect forms used by their mothers. Shatz (1974a, 1974b) found that 2-year-olds obeyed indirect and direct requests equally frequently. Ervin-Tripp (1976) found that children produced requests that ranged from imperatives (that is, direct speech acts) to requests (indirect speech acts). Grimm (1975) found that older children used more indirect forms than did younger children. All these researchers, in their discussion of results, highlight the reliance of young children on contextual and nonverbal features in the interaction. Mitchell-Kernan and Kernan (1977) found that older children (ages 7-12) correctly produced a variety of indirect forms and inferred information about social roles in their understanding of indirect forms. Generally, there is no evidence to support the view that direct speech acts are learned prior to indirect speech acts. There is, however, some controversy over how indirect forms are understood; Gordon and Lakoff's (1971) proposal appears to be too complex cognitively for young children (Bates, 1979) and it appears that some indirect forms may be learned idiomatically (Sadock, 1974).

Directives. Directives are speech acts that function as requests for action. Directives may be direct (imperatives) or indirect (interrogatives). Garvey (1975) found that children aged 3 to 5 years produced both direct and indirect requests for action, and older children produced more indirect requests than did the younger children. Ervin-Tripp (1977) found that the earliest directives used by children were accompanied by gestures, the name of the desired object, or linguistic markers, such as "want." Eventually children produce a variety of indirect forms, although it appears that the desired goal or action must be specified for preschoolers. Read and Cherry (1978) found that older children (4½ years old) produced more verbal directives and fewer gestures than younger children (2½ to 3½ years). They conclude that preschoolers possess a flexible array of directive forms that may be alternated and combined in making requests. Haslett (1983a) found that directives among 2-year-olds were frequently accompanied by gestures.

Interrogatives. Interrogatives have been widely studied in a variety of contexts, including their use for clarification and information seeking (Garvey, 1975, 1977; Cosaro, 1977), their use in turn-taking allocation (Snow, 1977a), and their use as an indirect request for action (Bates, 1976; Shatz, 1974b). Ervin-Tripp and Miller (1977) suggest that answering questions is a discourse obligation to which children are very sensitive. Ervin-Tripp (1970) found that children first understand yes-no, what, and where questions. "Wh" questions were understood in the following order: why, who (subject), where from, when, and who (object). This acquisition order was also found in a study by Tyack and Ingram (1977), who also found that "what" and "where" questions were closely tied to the immediate environment.

As we have seen, the preoperational child has developed some ordering of topic-comment (that is, the proposition-presupposition relationship). The preoperational child also develops a higher level of pragmatic skill in which he or she manipulates his or her symbolic structures, reflects on communicative procedures, and controls the listener's interpretation of his or her messages. Part of this increasing communicative skill is due to the child's emerging ability to talk about communication.

Metapragmatic Skills

Bates has also examined the development of the ability to talk about speech acts (that is, metapragmatics). Metapragmatic skills develop in three stages during the preoperational period. First, children refer explicitly to hearers and speakers, and use locatives of space and time to identify the participants and location under discussion specifically. Second, children use conjunctions that link utterances together (for example, connectives such as "and" and "if not"). According to Bates (1976, p. 152) the third metapragmatic stage depends upon the cognitive capacity to coordinate three or more information units such that the third unit is "coordinated with a relationship established between the other two."

According to Bates (1976), the child controls not only his or her own pragmatic structures, but also begins to control the listener's interpretation. With the cognitive operations of reversibility and conservation, an increased information base, and increased cognitive processing capabilities, the child can create indirect speech acts. In addition, Bates cites the development of counterfactuals and politeness conventions as important pragmatic developments during this period.

Counterfactuals. According to Bates, the prerequisites of counterfactuals are built up gradually. First, the child begins to appreciate the distinction between real and possible worlds. Then the child becomes capable of expressing entailment (for instance, two objects may be linked causally). Finally, the child begins to appreciate when it is necessary to comment on the "unreality" of the situation so that listeners can make appropriate inferences (Bates, 1976, pp. 248-249). In sum, counterfactuals require the child to "consider divergent views, perform complex coordinations on truth conditions, and carry out reversible operations up and down an objective time continuum" (Bates, 1976, p. 254).

Politeness Conventions. Three linguistic forms—imperatives, declaratives, and interrogatives—can be substituted for one another and can serve to "soften" utterances (make utterances polite or more polite). For example, the imperative "close the door" can be softened by using the interrogative—"Could you close the door?" By the age of 2½, children used polite forms (such as "please") to soften requests. At age 3, children seem to have a general concept of politeness. They can correctly judge gradients of politeness of various linguistic forms, and their judgments match those of adult judges.

Putting forth a version of Sadock's model (1974), Bates suggests a three-stage model for the acquisition of politeness terms. First, up to about 3½ to 4 years of age, children apparently do not use indirect speech acts. They decide what aspect of their desire to express, and they state this directly in their utterances. Children may also acquire direct, idiomatic rules of use for various performatives, without analyzing the internal syntactic structure of the idiom. Next, children are able to vary linguistic form and function, to separate means and ends, and to take another's perspective. However, they must still express the object of the act (that is, the goal) in their utterances. Finally, children are able to manipulate both linguistic form and content to achieve goals.

During the sensorimotor and preoperational stages, children's implicit pragmatic procedures change into explicit pragmatic signals. Also, Bates suggests that at 2½ years of age, speech act usage shifts from an emphasis on efficiency to an emphasis on politeness. Some evidence suggests that children may be polite as a way to get what they want. Bates suggests that more research is needed to identify when and how children reason about the pragmatic value of various request forms.

During the linguistic communication stage, the child moves from "primitive" speech acts to fully formed speech acts (that is, multiword utterances that have a clear propositional value and illocutionary force). The child also develops distinct types of speech acts such as directives and interrogatives, and the use of communicative strategies such as politeness conventions and indirect speech acts. Next, development during the linguistic communication substage will be assessed from the functional perspective. As mentioned previously, functional approaches focus on the purposes for which children use language. Two of the most prominent functionalist researchers are M.A.K. Halliday and Joan Tough.

Communicative Functions

Halliday (1975) provides a developmental account of communicative functions and argues that language plays a key role in socialization and that the structure of language reflects the functions for which language is used.

The functional use of language develops in three phases. Phase I develops from the age of 10½ to 18 months. Each utterance, whether a sound or actual utterance, has only one function. According to Halliday, four language functions appear from 10½ months to 17½ months: *instrumental* (stating desires and demands), *regulatory* (controlling the actions of others), *interactional* (expressing social or affective bonds), and *personal* (informing others about one's own actions). At 18 months, two further functions develop: the *heuristic* (explaining actions and events) and the *imaginative* (imagining events, actions, and objects).

During the transitional Phase II period, from 18 to 24 months of age, language functions become more complex and abstract. The six functions in Phase I merge into three broad functions: the *pragmatic* function (a blend of the earlier instrumental and regulatory functions), the *mathetic* function (a blend of the earlier personal and heuristic functions), and the *interactional* function. Another function, the *informative* function (which expresses information that is not apparent to listeners from the immediate context), also appears at this time. Grammatical structure begins to develop during this time as well; according to Halliday, grammatical structures allows an utterance to perform more than one function and thus is necessary for the adult language system to emerge. Dialogue (that is, the linguistic exchanges in ordinary conversations) also develops and is a prerequisite of mastery of communicative roles. Much of the development during this phase occurs through the opposition of the pragmatic (action) and mathetic (reflective) functions; Halliday points out that things are both acted upon and thought about.

The final phase, Phase III, marks the onset of the adult functional system. Two basic functions, the *ideational* function (derived from the mathetic function and used to "talk about the world") and the *interpersonal* function (derived from the interactional function and used to establish and maintain social relations), emerge during Phase III. A third function, the *textual,* reflects how language can be organized to serve other functions. The textual function is built up from (1) focusing on information by using tonic (tonal) prominence; (2) interrelating sentences by using cohesive devices such as "but" or "that"; and (3) establishing patterns of texture that relate to particular communicative events (that is, establishing specific structures for narrative, dialogue, and so on; Halliday, 1979). These three basic functions allow the speaker to accomplish an infinite variety of purposes. Rees (1978) suggests that the ideational and interpersonal functions parallel the noncommunicative and communicative functions of language (or, to use Halliday's [1978] terms, the reflective and action-oriented functions of language).

Tough's (1973, 1977) research provides an extension and validation of Halliday's functional analysis. Tough's approach centers on how language functions in the child's development of meaning, in both its social and cognitive aspects. Her theoretical perspective integrates the work of Halliday and

Piaget. In addition, Tough's approach also provides an interactive approach emphasizing the relationships interlocutors develop with one another.

Tough's theoretical perspective distinguishes four language functions, each of which expresses a different mode of thinking. Each function of language can be accomplished in different ways; these alternative means are designated *uses* of language. Tough (1973, p. 47) points out that "within particular uses of language there is need for further differentiation to take account of the different devices that may be used. . . . we refer to these as *strategies* and distinguish a number that may also serve the several different uses that are distinguished within the functions." Thus *strategies* are devices that accomplish particular uses of language; these language *uses,* in turn, fulfill particular language functions.

The four major language functions, each reflecting different modes of thinking, are as follows:

(1) *Directive function:* concerned with directing actions and operations. At its simplest level a directive may be a child's egocentric monologue while performing some activity; at its most complex level, directives may serve to coordinate the actions of others in accomplishing a task. There are two uses of the directive function: self-directing and other directing.

(2) *Interpretive function:* concerned with communicating the meaning of events and situations the child witnessed. There are two uses of the interpretive function: reporting and reasoning.

(3) *Projective function:* concerned with projecting and exploring situations, which the child is not actually experiencing, through imagination and past experiences. There are three uses of the projective function: predicting, empathizing, and imagining.

(4) *Relational function:* concerned with language functioning to establish and maintain relationships between people. There are two uses of the relational function: interactional and self-maintaining.

Tough found that disadvantaged 3-year-olds used language focusing on their present experiences and monitoring their own activities. Advantaged 3-year-olds used language for reasoning, anticipating future events, and creating imaginary contexts more than did disadvantaged peers. Disadvantaged 5- and 7-year-olds had shorter utterances, and their statements demonstrated a less complex level of thinking than did those of their advantaged counterparts.

Using Tough's hierarchical analysis of language functions, uses, and strategies, Haslett (1983a) found developmental differences in the communicative functions and strategies used by preschoolers in their conversations with peers. At age 3, the most important communicative functions were to master information about the environment (*interpretive* function) and to express needs and ideas (*relational* function). Interpretative strategies included labeling and elaboration of detail; this enabled children to explore their environment through verbal means. Relational strategies reflected predominantly (75 percent) self-emphasizing strategies. At age 4, a major developmental shift occurred, with the *projective* function becoming most important, followed by the *relational* function. Within the *projective* function, imagining strategies enabled children to create new roles and contexts for their play. Both imagining and relational strategies incorporated increasingly adaptive communication directed toward others. Generally it was found that females appeared to develop language strategies (utilized by both sexes) earlier than males. Females also achieved a more advanced level of cognitive complexity and communicative adaptability in their relational and projective strategies.

One language function, that of referential communication, has received considerable attention in the literature. The referential or informative function, which will be examined next, appears to be among the earliest functions mastered by the child, and is viewed as a prerequisite of later acquisition of knowledge, especially in educational settings. The studies reported here cover ages 2 to 8.

Referential Communication

The referential, or informative, function of language serves to convey information about particular referents. The speaker's task is to enable the listener to identify correctly the referent from other alternative referents in the environment. Asher (1979) suggests that the referential function of language has received great attention due to its simplicity, pervasiveness, and importance in educational settings and because it serves as a component in other complex types of communication.

Recent research has explored the component skills needed for referential communication tasks. Three research perspectives, each focusing on one of the component skills outlined by Glucksberg, Krauss, and Higgins (1975), can be identified. The *task-analytic* perspective assesses the child's ability to fulfill the information-processing demands of the referential task. The *role-taking* perspective focuses upon the child's ability to analyze the listener's perspective and to produce messages with this perspective in mind. Finally, the *message-evaluation* perspective explores young children's ability to recognize inadequate messages, and to attribute blame for communicative inadequacy correctly.

Task-Analytic Perspective. This perspective stresses the child's ability to fulfill the requirements of communication tasks. Asher and Wigfield (1981) suggest that the child's improved performance on referential communicative tasks over age could be due to (1) improved vocabulary or knowledge, or (2) the child's increased awareness of the need for comparison. Young children fail to compare in a variety of such tasks (Alvy, 1976; Asher, 1976; Asher & Oden, 1976; Asher & Parke, 1975; Whitehurst, 1976). Whitehurst and Sonnenschein (1981) questioned whether children fail at comparison activity because they do not have comparison skills (that is, comparison is a *novel* skill) or because they do not understand the relevance of using comparison in the referential task (that is, comparison is an accustomed skill that children fail to use in referential communication). They conclude that for 5-year-olds comparison is an accustomed skill; however, young children do not know that comparison is necessary for effective communication. In a follow-up series of experiments designed to train children to make comparisons, they found that children increased their comparison activities after specific instructions to describe perceptual differences and feedback as to whether or not they did so correctly. The training improvement, however, did not transfer from a speaking task to a listening task.

Role Taking. Research on role taking stresses the speaker's ability to assess the listener's perspective and formulate a message with this perspective in mind. According to Piaget (1926, 1952), children's egocentrism prevents them from analyzing and accommodating the perspective of another, and this leads to communication failure.

Flavell (1973) proposed the following model of the component skills in role taking. First, the child becomes alert to others' perspectives, thoughts, and feelings. Second, the child realizes that analyzing another's perspective is important in some situations (such as conflict or persuasion). Third, the child develops inferences about others' perspectives. Finally, the child translates these inferences into effective social behaviors. Flavell has termed these steps "existence," "need," "inference," and "application," respectively. Studies among preschoolers have demonstrated their ability to modify messages for different listeners: They communicate differently to a blindfolded listener than to a sighted one (Maratsos, 1973); to naive listeners than to listeners knowledgeable about a game (Menig-Peterson, 1975); and to adults and older children than to younger children (Shatz & Gelman, 1973). Studies among older children (Flavell, Botkin, Fry, Wright, & Jarvis, 1968; Higgins, 1977) found that communication accuracy increased over age and, as speakers, children continued to be sensitive to the need to vary content according to listener characteristics. Although accuracy of communication improves, role-taking ability is only modestly correlated with this improvement (Asher, 1979; Dickson, 1981).

Shantz (1981) argues that role taking facilitates message effectiveness; one is more likely to send an adequate message if there is recognition of potential differences between the self and the other. Shantz also notes that the speaker must not only recognize the need for role taking, but must also make accurate inferences, appropriately alter the message, and continually monitor the message and listener feedback. Although children have demonstrated the ability to change messages for different age addressees, these situations have been relatively straightforward and simple (for example, picking out a present for an adult or a child). The degree to which children can take roles, then, still remains problematic. Chandler (1977) has pointed out that some message adjustments may be due to children's social category knowledge (what teachers would expect, what police officers would expect, and the like) rather than role-taking ability. However, studies of children's disputes reveal that children are capable of adapting messages in order to gain their goals, and often these messages are altered to accommodate others' views (Haslett, 1983c; O'Keefe & Delia, 1982). What does seem clear, however, is that children do adapt their messages in socially appropriate ways. What is not so clear is how children are able to accomplish this. I suspect that social category knowledge, role-taking ability, understanding situational constraints, and the like may all play a role in adjusting one's messages; each of these skills may be called into play in different situations.

Message Evaluation. This perspective focuses on only one dimension of listening skill—the ability to use message information appropriately. Typically this is measured by having subjects choose the correct referent from among a group of referents. Recently, other dimensions of listening skills have been studied and our understanding of listener competence has been broadened.

Glucksberg et al. (1975, p. 331) point out that listeners can pursue at least three strategies to improve message effectiveness: (1) They can identify noninformative messages; (2) if they recognize a message as inadequate, they can convey this to the speaker; and (3) they can give the specific information needed to clarify the message. In a review of listener's skills, Patterson and Kister (1981) point out that listeners' skills can be assessed along four dimensions: their ability to assess message quality; their understanding that message quality is related to communicative success; their responses to adequate message; and their responses to inadequate messages.

The studies reviewed thus far reveal a wide range of developing skills in referential communication tasks. One additional concern has been whether or not it is possible to train children to use or develop these skills. Training in this area has generally been successful. It has been found that both modeling and emphasizing the importance of asking questions facilitate elementary schoolchildren's responses to inadequate messages (Asher, 1979). Asher and Wigfield (1981) conclude that comparison training procedures are effective in teaching children to attend to referents and nonreferents in constructing messages. Whitehurst and Sonnenschein (1981) found that perceptual feedback is critical in teaching children to describe significant differences among referents. However, training programs have experienced problems in generalizing these skills to other tasks or from the speaker's role to the listener's role (Shantz, 1981; Whitehurst & Sonnenschein, 1981).

Beaudichon (1981) reports a series of studies investigating referential communication that attempts to avoid prior methodological weaknesses in the referential communication paradigm. These weaknesses include (1) confronting children with a very atypical communication situation, and their creating novel responses; and (2) conducting naturalistic studies that allow little control or manipulation of variables. Beaudichon's findings were that (1) young children showed little ability to say only the necessary information; (2) interaction with other listeners sometimes led to confusion about the message and its referent; and (3) listeners' performances improved when they were able to ask questions of the speaker.

Beaudichon argues that interaction is vital for improving decoding and encoding skills. Adults have already acquired a general mental representation of a listener's needs, whereas children are in the position of acquiring this representation little by little. Thus children need to interact with others to understand what information speakers need to convey for accurate comprehension; this knowledge comes from interaction with and feedback from others. Beaudichon also emphasizes the importance of testing communicative behavior in situations in which the subjects are motivated and can "make sense" out of the situation (Donaldson, 1978).

The trend in analyzing children's referential communication skill is to explore the component cognitive and social skills that make referential communication possible and effective. Thus global causal concepts, such as egocentrism, have been rejected, and specific component skills, such as role-taking or comparison skills, have been scrutinized. Generally, there is growing acknowledgment that any communicative behavior is interactive (that is, there are dependencies and interrelationships between speakers and listeners). Erickson (1981) found that timing "mismatches" between speaker and listener resulted in communication failure. Olson and Hilyard (1981) also point out that young children appear to scan statements for their social implications; such implications are dependent upon the social situation and the other interactants.

The functional uses of language that begin to emerge at around 12 to 18 months have become well established by age 3. The three basic functions of language appear to be ideational (informational), interpersonal (relational), and textual (organization of language itself). Although other functional systems can become more elaborated depending upon the needs of the researcher (see, for example, Tough, 1977, or Dore, 1977, for more detailed functional schemes), all of these schemes can collapse into those three fundamental functions outlined by Halliday. Referential communication has been examined closely because of its general communicative and educational significance; the ability to communicate clearly about objects and events in the surrounding environment is certainly a necessary prerequisite of effective communication. Each of the approaches—the task analytic, role taking, or message appraisal—highlights a different aspect of referential communication. Taken together, these approaches reflect the gradual increase in children's referential communication skills; this gradual development of referential communication appears to culminate around middle childhood (Chandler, 1977). Although most scholars regard these three approaches to referential communication as competing paradigms, I believe that children may utilize each of these strategies in different situations. For example, when asked to describe an object, a child may use a task-analytic strategy—focusing on the task of describing rather than role taking. Message-appraisal skills may be used when a child is asked to evaluate the accuracy of a description. And role taking may be needed when informing someone who is younger than the speaker, or who comes from a different culture.

In retrospect, as we summarize the communicative accomplishments of the linguistic communication substage, we can see the tremendous growth achieved during this period. At the beginning of this substage, children had just begun with language acquisition; by age 3, children have acquired the ability to produce multiword utterances designed to achieve particular social ends. Children can produce both direct and indirect speech acts, and have begun to use politeness conventions in their interactions with others.

The second stage of pragmatic development, *creating communicative effects,* includes the transition from prelinguistic to linguistic communication. Many scholars have regarded this transition as the most important communicative development in early childhood (see Golinkoff, 1983). I have characterized this transition as occurring during three substages: preverbal routines, communicative intentionality, and linguistic communication. Through participation in preverbal routines, infants acquire an understanding of the fundamental nature of dialogue through turn taking, role reversibility, and role reciprocity. The emergence of communicative intentionality marks the child's awareness of communication as a vehicle for accomplishing social goals. Communicative signals also become conventionalized during this period and the child is able to establish interpersonal relationships with others. As a result of these prelinguistic experiences, the child possesses a considerable fund of knowledge and skill about the process of interpersonal communication.

With the addition of language, communication becomes much more explicit and less dependent upon the immediate context. Two approaches have been used to characterize communicative development during this period: speech act analyses and functional approaches. Speech act analyses emphasize linguistic form, while functional analyses emphasize linguistic functions. By age 3, children have mastery of a variety of linguistic forms (for instance, children can produce both direct and indirect speech acts, ask questions, make requests, and the like) and use language to achieve a variety of purposes. While both these approaches detail the complexity of communicative skills children acquire during this time, each approach reflects only partial understanding of communicative development. If an adequate theory of human communication is to evolve, I believe the unfortunate split between linguistic form and linguistic function must come to an end. When we communicate, form and function interact; therefore, our communication models ought to devote considerable attention to their interaction. This interplay between form and function undoubtedly emerges during early childhood, and developmental research and theory should reflect this as well. Thus, while we have an understanding of how linguistic forms and functions emerge, we have yet to develop models explaining their complex interrelationships with one another during communication. These interrelationships also need to be assessed in light of a particular social relationship and given social contest.

During the next stage of developmental pragmatics, *using communicative strategies,* children experience a substantive increase in interactions with others. By age 3, children experience interaction with other peers and unfamiliar adults (preschool teachers and others), as a result, children must adapt their messages to a variety of interactants in a diverse range of settings. The increased complexity of these communicative demands requires children to establish communicative strategies. These strategies enable children to communicate clearly, to establish and maintain conversational topics, and to interpret the remarks of others accurately. In sum, the skills that emerged during the previous 18 months are refined and expanded.

Stage III:
Using Communicative Strategies

Communicative strategies, enabling children to sustain conversations with others, emerge and expand from approximately 3 to 5 years of age. Children can now initiate and maintain conversational topics (Ochs & Schieffelin, 1979), adapt messages to others (Shatz & Gelman, 1973), link statements together to pursue a particular line of reasoning or arguments (Eisenberg & Garvey, 1981; Haslett, 1983c), creatively role play in free play with peers (Garvey, 1974; Haslett, 1983a), and so forth. In sum, children begin to show considerable skill in interacting with others in a variety of communicative settings. We shall look particularly at three communicative strategies—deixis, topicalization, and conversational postulates—that support children's conversational dialogues.

Deixis

"Deixis" refers to linguistic devices that clearly identify person, place, and time when communicating. Thus deixis serves to "anchor the utterance to the communicative setting in which it occurs" (Rees, 1978, p. 210). The most basic deictic element, of course, is the "I-you" (that is, speaker-listener) distinction in communication. Other linguistic devices, such as demonstratives and adverbs, locate discourse referents in place ("here," "this," and the like) and in time ("now," "later," and so on). Rees (1978) suggests that deictic features convey a significant amount of conversation meaning. According to Bruner (1975a), an understanding of reciprocal roles in discourse is necessary for deixis, and this develops in early mother-child interaction. The infant's learning to follow his or her mother's gaze becomes combined with reaching and pointing to ensure a joint focus of attention for mother and child. These accomplishments mark the primitive bases for spatial and person deixis, according to Bruner, and lay the foundation for later naming.

Keenan and Schieffelin (1976) found that children at the two-word stage use pronouns to refer to objects in the present environment, but not to refer to nonpresent objects. Bloom et al. (1976) found that when children recoded adult utterances in conversations, children at around 18 months recoded person deixis (that is, changed from the parental "you" to the personal "I") and at 36 months recoded place deixis. Charney (1979) found that by age 3½ children understand "here" and "there" from the speaker's perspective and that they do not show an egocentric stage in the acquisition of "here" and "there." DeVilliers and deVilliers (1979) conclude that appropriate use of pronouns and demonstratives are not mastered until 4 or 5 years of age. Appropriate use of deixis reflects the emerging understanding of relationships among objects, events, and entities. Finally, deictic elements have been analyzed in light of their role in cohesion and topic maintenance (deVilliers & deVilliers, 1979; Halliday & Hasan, 1976; Haslett, 1983b).

Topicalization

"Topicalization" refers to the abilities speakers need to establish and maintain a topic of discourse. In order for a dialogue to be coherent, both speaker and listener must know the discourse topic. According to Keenan and Schieffelin (1976), four conditions must be met: (1) the speaker must have the listener's attention; (2) the listener must be able to decipher the speaker's utterance; (3) the listener must be able to identify the referents being talked about; and (4) the listener must be able to identify the intended semantic relations between referents. Some speech acts, such as questions and answers, are directly linked by a common discourse topic. At other times, discourse topics may be marked explicitly (for instance, by statements such as "that reminds me of . . ." through which a specific topic is introduced) or developed through the use of presuppositions. Keenan and Schieffelin note that at the one- and two-word stages, children are capable of completing the first three conditions for topicalization: Children have a variety of well-developed attention-getting devices, speak clearly and intelligibly, and specify objects being talked about. Many of these strategies for getting attention and identifying referents are nonverbal (pointing, touching, and so on).

Conversational Postulates

Conversational postulates are a set of pragmatic presuppositions or assumptions about the nature of human interaction (Bates, 1976, p. 27). Grice (1975) has analyzed these conversational postulates into four general rules: (1) Be cooperative (that is, truthful); (2) be relevant; (3) be clear; and (4) be efficient (that is, tell only what is required—avoid redundancy). Of course, not all of these postulates are followed by interactants; Grice suggests that these postulates are used so that when speakers violate them, this additional information facilitates the listener's interpretation of the message. According to Bates (1979, p. 447), conversational postulates need to be viewed "as intentions, or rules for using utterances the speaker uses a sentence to comment upon or intentionally violate an assumed rule of conversation." Bates (1979, p. 447) further comments that "the ability to predict whether or not the listener shares a given assumption and to plan one's utterances accordingly is one of the highest achievements in pragmatic development." Bates's research on conversational postulates has centered upon politeness judgements. Bates suggest that, by age 3, children have a general concept of politeness and that, by 2½ years of age, children appear to shift from a focus on the efficiency dimension of utterances (that is, economy and informativeness) to a focus on the politeness dimension.

During the communicative strategies stage, the complexity of communication increases substantially; language itself has become more complex, and children are interacting with peers as well as adults in diverse settings. In order to meet these demands, children further develop and refine basic skills learned previously. Joint attention and reference, developed earlier between mother and infant in their preverbal routines, now is precisely detailed through the child's use of deictic elements. Children use pronouns, demonstratives, and locatives to specify the relationships among objects, events, and individuals, and to focus attention on those relationships.

At first, children are primarily reactive (that is, they primarily *respond* to stimuli, rather than actively initiate their own messages; see Haslett, 1983c). However, as children develop skills for initiating and maintaining dialogues with others (that is, maintaining topic), they actively initiate new topics and use presuppositions in maintaining conversations. Also aiding in their ability to sustain interaction with others is children's growing understanding of conversational postulates; children have a general understanding of the communicative requirements of relevancy, informedness, clarity, and the like.

Up to this point in the child's developing pragmatic communicative skills, the child's abilities focus on expanding his or her competency as a speaker. In the final stage, *monitoring communication*, the child begins to shift attention to the communicative message—its accuracy, clarity, and effectiveness. This message orientation rests on the child's ability to metacommunicate—that is, the act of communication itself must be treated as an object of evaluation and discussion. This metacommunicative ability begins to emerge at around 5 years of age. In middle childhood, children have a well-established set of metacommunicative strategies that they apply to messages and listeners (see, for example, Flavell, Speer, Green, & August, 1981; O'Keefe & Delia, 1982). A more thorough discussion of communicative monitoring follows.

Stage IV:
Monitoring Communication

The process by which humans assess their progress toward accomplishing any cognitive goal is referred to as "metacognition." "Metacommunication" is the application of metacognitive monitoring to communication tasks; it enables communicators to reflect on messages, detaching and diagnosing their deficiencies and assessing the import and implications of those deficiences (Flavell et al., 1981).

While metacognition applies to any cognitive endeavor, we are particularly concerned about its application to communication. Flavell (1981) observes that much of communication seems metacognitive in nature; for example, the listener's ideas about the speaker's intent, the speaker's ideas about the listener's comprehension, and so forth. He argues that since communication, as a cognitive process, cannot be analyzed apart from other cognitive processes, the nature and development of communicative monitoring may not be "adequately understood if examined in isolation from cognitive monitoring" in other areas (Flavell, 1981, p. 37). Flavell's research suggests that young children may fail at communication tasks because they do not treat "messages as analyzable cognitive objects" (Flavell, 1981, p. 37).

Studies of referential communication skills among young children have explored their judgments of message adequacies. One of the most consistent findings in referential communication studies is that children do not understand that speakers are obligated to send messages that uniquely identify a referent (Asher, 1979; Asher & Wigfield, 1981; Whitehurst & Sonnenschein, 1981). Furthermore, young children do not appear to recognize inadequate instructions and are less likely to ask questions for further information than are older children (Flavell, 1981; Robinson & Robinson, 1978b, 1978c). Generally, young children appear to be ignorant concerning message failure (Lloyd & Beveridge, 1981). Children also appear to go through stages in which they initially blame listeners for communicative failure; then they move toward blaming speakers (this occurs irrespective of whether or not the speaker or listener *really* was blameworthy in a given situation). It is not until approximately 8 years of age that children seem to acknowledge that communication is interactive—that both listener and speaker contribute to effective communication.

The referential communication literature has focused primarily on message evaluation and attribution of blame. What is needed, however, is research focusing on message evaluation and message repair in nonreferential contexts. The research of Jesse Delia and his associates (Applegate & Delia, 1980; Delia & Clark, 1977; Delia, Kline, & Burleson, 1979; Delia & O'Keefe, 1979; O'Keefe & Delia, 1979) offers some promising lines of research in this area. O'Keefe and Delia (1981, p. 2) argue that the "speaker's knowledge of the listener constitutes a basis for selecting among alternative messages or message elements so as to produce a message tailored to the listener's perspective or needs." Their research has established a "clear correlational relationship between communicative strategy quality and the development of differentiated and abstract sets of interpersonal constructs employed in person perception" (O'Keefe & Delia, 1981, p. 4). However, O'Keefe and Delia (1981) believe that this research is problematic with respect to supporting a model of listener-adapted message strategies and have offered a reconceptualization of their message hierarchy. Rather than analyzing messages in terms of the degree to which these messages reflect adaptation to the listener's perspective, O'Keefe and Delia (1981, p. 42) argue that the hierarchic ordering of messages reflects the degree to which "multiple dimensions (obstacles and aims) of complex communication situations are recognized and reconciled in messages." They suggest that when individuals face complex message tasks they have three basic techniques for resolving conflicts between aims and obstacles to those aims: (1) *selection,* in which one aim is given priority over a conflicting aim; (2) *temporal* or *behavioral separation,* in which the conflicting aims and/or obstacles are resolved through addressing them in either temporally or behaviorally separated components of a message; and (3) *integration,* in which messages can advance multiple aims at the same time or simultaneously advance aims and remove obstacles.

O'Keefe and Delia's reconceptualization can also be viewed from the perspective of metacognition. Flavell's conceptualization of metacognition explicitly discusses monitoring of strategies for pursuing goals. The degree to which speakers and listeners recognize conflicting goals and adjust their messages accordingly is evidence of metacommunicative monitoring. It appears that metacommunicative monitoring skills are a prerequisite of *effective* communication. The research of both Delia and his associates and scholars studying referential communication indicates that these monitoring skills begin to develop in middle childhood; prior to that time, children seem unaware of message inadequacy. Flavell (1981) suggests that it would be of interest to discover the precursors of metacognitive monitoring.

The research on preschoolers' early language may reveal some of these precursors. For example, Bates (1979) reports "metapragmatic" comments ("He said no"; "She said it was red") occurring in the talk of children between 30 and 36 months of age. These comments, however, appear to perform a report or verification function rather than a monitoring function. Yet they reflect an important awareness among young children— namely, that talk can be treated as an object (that is, talk can be talked about) and as part of the context. Studies showing that children as young as 4 years old adjust their speech to different aged listeners (Shatz & Gelman, 1973) also are demonstrating that children have an awareness of "what it takes" to be understood by another.

The use of polite forms also indicates monitoring activity; Bates (1976) found that by 30 months children were using polite or indirect forms to "soften" their utterances, and that by 36 months children had a general concept of politeness. As Bates points out, children may be polite to get what they want efficiently; this presupposes that children have previously "monitored" the relationship between politeness and goal achievement and learned the pragmatic value of various request/politeness forms. When Bates asked children to judge the degree of politeness of various utterances, she found that (1) children's judgments were similar to adult judgments of politeness; (2) children's subsequent requests became more polite when they were told their initial request had failed; and (3) children who made correct passive judgments concerning the politeness of various statements could not give reasons to support their judgments. This latter point is not surprising since politeness conventions tap deeply rooted cultural values and such metacognitive knowledge, as Flavell points out, may not be readily available for conscious processing.

In a series of studies, Applegate and Delia (1980) found that abstractness of cognitive constructs was correlated with person-centered adaptive communication in both regulative and interpersonal contexts. They conclude that "individual differences in the development of an abstract system of constructs forms the basis for the development of person-centered communicative ability" (Applegate & Delia, 1980, p. 273). Abstract constructs are necessary, but not sufficient, for adapted communication—children must also possess behavioral routines and strategies needed to express those understandings. These conclusions seem to parallel similar findings in referential communication studies—listener-adapted communication is only one component of those needed for effective communication.

Another promising line of research is that of assessing young children's strategies in settling disputes. Disputes provide an ideal opportunity for the observation of monitoring since children usually want very much to win (that is, the dispute is very salient) and usually the conflict between competing goals is very clear (for example, both children may want to play with the same toy). Piaget theorizes that conflict with peers begins to trigger sociocentric communication among preschoolers. Thus disputes in which goals are divergent and highly salient appear to be communicative situations in which monitoring would be particularly relevant (that is, necessary for constructing strategies and gaining one's ends). Researchers have analyzed the communicative rules and strategies children use in arguments (Benoit, 1981; O'Keefe & Benoit, in press). With increasing age, children rely more on messages that contain more information (Eisenberg & Garvey, 1981); that reflect more adaptation to listeners (Delia et al., 1979); and that become cognitively and communicatively more complex and more coordinated with the messages of others (Haslett, 1983c). All this suggests that children become more aware of the communicative demands of disputes and more adept at trying to accomplish their goals. Such ability, again, presupposes growing elaboration and differentiation in the child's metacognitive knowledge about him- or herself, about others and relationships with others, and about task demands.

In summary, monitoring communication focuses the speaker's attention on the message and addressees. Children begin to evaluate message adequacy, to alter messages when needed, to adapt their messages when conflict with others' goals are recognized, to discuss the communication process explicitly, and to utilize knowledge of others in constructing their communicative strategies. These skills are just beginning to emerge at age 5, and they become well established in middle childhood. Through monitoring communication, children become increasingly adept at sending socially appropriate messages in a variety of contexts.

Thus far, the development of communicative skills as they emerge in early childhood have been examined. First, infants develop a basic sensitivity to, and understanding of, the nature of human communication; the necessary role of communication in establishing contact and cooperation with others is recognized. Second, infants become cognizant of their ability to signal their own desires, to initiate and to alter their own communicative activity—they begin to communicate *intentionally*. Third, as language emerges at around 12 to 18 months, children begin using language to communicate. Linguistic communication gradually increases in complexity as the child's interactions broaden to include varied participants, topics, goals and social settings. Children thus, over time, develop communicative strategies that enable them to begin to adjust their communication appropriately. Finally, children begin to develop the capacity to metacommunicate—to monitor and repair their messages.

Each developmental stage represents added communicative and cognitive complexity. The process of communication itself becomes more difficult over time, as language is added as a communicative tool, as tasks become more varied and complex, and as interactants and settings become more varied. As children mature, adults also expect more (Bruner, 1983; Dore, 1983); adults thus "up the ante" and communicative demands are correspondingly increased. The increase in peer-peer interaction, at around 3 years, also adds considerable complexity to interpersonal interaction. While adults typically accommodate their communication to the child's cognitive level, no such accommodation is possible with peers. Given such complexity, children develop communicative strategies that enable them to send socially appropriate, adapted messages. Such ability, however, is not just a matter of pragmatic skills and strategies that we have discussed: *Children also need to acquire social knowledge about communication that enables them to exercise these skills and strategies in appropriate settings and at appropriate times.* The ability to communicate effectively involves a complex assessment of the communicative task, the interactants, and the social setting.

Before turning to a more thorough discussion of the acquisition of social knowledge about communication, a brief caution is in order. The unfortunate dichotomy between linguistic form and linguistic function is also present between communicative skills and communicative knowledge. In order to communicate effectively, one needs to possess the necessary communicative skills; however, those skills are relatively useless without the communicative knowledge that enables one to exercise them in an appropriate manner. The interaction between communicative knowledge and communicative skill is the central concern of pragmatic approaches to human communication. However, virtually all researchers focus on either pragmatic skills or pragmatic knowledge: Only two research teams—Lubin and Forbes, and Delia and his associates—relate pragmatic knowledge to pragmatic skills. It is not hard to understand why this is the case: Tracing the development of either the pragmatic skills or the pragmatic knowledge base for communication is in itself tremendously complex.[2] However, for pragmatic theories of communication to develop such integration is necessary. It is hoped that the synthesis and views expressed here will be a first step in these efforts.

As previously discussed, when we examine the pragmatic communicative skills children develop in early childhood, we see only one aspect of the child's pragmatic competence. Communication scholars utilizing pragmatic approaches are also interested in representing the child's social knowledge that enables him or her to communicate appropriately. It is this underlying social knowledge that will be explored next.

DEVELOPING SOCIAL KNOWLEDGE
ABOUT COMMUNICATION

Social knowledge relevant to communication appears to develop in three broad stages. The most fundamental social distinction needed for communication is the I-thou, speaker-listener distinction. This distinction between self and others appears to develop during the first year of life. As more interactions occur with a wider variety of interactants, a more finely differentiated knowledge of others is necessary for effective communication (Chandler, 1977; Flavell et al., 1981; Shantz, 1981). This increasingly differentiated knowledge of others gradually emerges during early childhood; at age 5, children have internalized interpersonal constructs of others (O'Keefe & Delia, 1982).

As knowledge of others increases, so too does the child's knowledge of social situations and their communicative requirements. Knowledge of others and of social situations appears to develop concomitantly; knowledge of others is undoubtedly facilitated by interacting with others in a variety of contexts that emphasize different dimensions of other individuals. Also, knowledge of the communicative demands in particular settings may be facilitated by observing how different individuals handle that situation. In sum, assessing children's developing social knowledge—knowledge relevant to their interpersonal interactions with others—gives us insight as to how individuals begin to establish and maintain interpersonal relations with one another and insight into the essential role communication plays in this process. Each of these aspects of social knowledge—knowledge of self as distinct from others, knowledge of others, and knowledge of social situations—will be discussed in turn. Although knowledge of self as distinct from others appears to be prior to, and necessary for, knowledge of others and of social situations, no other interrelationships are being advocated here.[3]

Knowledge of Self as
Independent from Others

An infant's interactions with responsive others are believed to be radically different from other interchanges (Brazelton, Koslowski, & Main, 1974; Stern, 1977). By 8 or 9 months, infants appear to have a sense of personal agency since they use objects to obtain goals (Wolf, 1981). Wolf argues that from 9 to 15 months infants recognize and react to the separateness of self and others; attachment and fear of separation from familiar others also become evident during this time. This sense of separate identity is fundamental to the I-thou, speaker-listener distinction in dialogue. Gelman and Spelke (1981) point out that the distinction between animate and inanimate objects develops in the first month of life, and that this understanding is necessary for communication and action. By 24 months, these distinctions have become more complex and differentiated (Harding & Golinkoff, 1979).

While there appears to be substantial controversy over whether cognitive and social cognitive processes are similar (Chandler, 1977; Damon, 1977; Higgins, 1981), Wolf (1981) believes that substantial differences exist between them. Hoffman (1981) emphasizes that the complexity of social cognition is due to the fact that it operates in interactional settings. Individuals act and react in diverse ways; their reactions are mediated by internal states and the nature of the interpersonal relationship between interactants. Meanings of actions vary as a function of interactants' social relationships, and emotional factors operating in interaction may be intense. Glick (1978) contrasts the domains of cognition and social cognition and suggests that the social cognitive domain is characterized by less predictability. Damon (1981, p. 157) emphasizes the "potential of social objects for social interaction," as does Bruner (1982). The point here is not to resolve the controversy about the relationships between cognitive and social cognitive processes, for, as Wolf (1981) points out, there are undoubtedly similarities and dissimilarities between them. The task here has been to highlight some distinctive qualities about social cognition and to emphasize its interactional base.

Wolf (1981) claims that any child who has the concept of independent agency recognizes that individuals can produce distinct goals. This involves the understanding of the following: (1) simple agency—that something or someone produces an effect; (2) separateness—that self and others are physically separate; (3) humanness—that people are animate beings who function in human ways (for example, move in cars) and possess human psychological traits; and (4) independence—that individuals have different roles and goals. These realizations develop during the first three years of life.

Knowledge of Others

Gelman and Spelke (1981, p. 51) suggest that by age 4 children are beginning to develop "a systematic set of beliefs about the thoughts, feelings, intentions, motives, knowledge, and capacities of other people." Researchers have approached the study of social knowledge of others from two general perspectives: the *person-perception* perspective, which focuses upon various cues others give off that children must accommodate;

and the *role-taking* perspective, which emphasizes children's tendency to oversubjectivize their experience (Chandler, 1977). Chandler argues that the person-perception perspective focuses on children's accommodation, while the role-taking perspective emphasizes the process of assimilation.

Person-perception studies are based upon a sequential information processing model; one registers cues given off by another, encodes these cues, and draws inferences from them. Chandler (1977) points out that these studies have found that children, with increasing age, move from statements about concrete characteristics of others to describing others' feelings and thoughts. With increasing age, children rely more on abstract dispositional constructs, and the number and abstractness of these constructs also increase. Preschool children seldom use these constructs, but they become a regular part of children's vocabulary by 9 or 10 years of age.

Scholars in the Wernerian tradition argue that these attributions (dispositional constructs) become increasingly ordered, differentiated, and hierarchically ordered with increasing age. In studying impression formation, Scarlett, Press, and Crockett (1971) found that age was correlated with the number, variety, and differentiation of interpersonal constructs. With increasing age, children's judgments of personal characteristics were moderated by situational or temporal factors or by the internal states of the person being judged. Bigner (1974), in a study of kindergartners through eighth graders, found that with increasing age children's characterizations of others become more abstract and hierarchically organized. Gollin (1958) found that with increasing age children used qualitatively different inference models in forming impressions of others; older children were more able to recognize and resolve incongruent cues. Chandler (1977) points out that children's increasing sensitivity to potential social stimuli must depend, in part, on how they integrate these stimuli with their own perspective; that is, it must depend on the child's capacity to differentiate his or her own view from that of another.

Role Taking

Role taking is assumed to rest on the degree to which an individual can differentiate himself or herself from others; thus role taking is seen as a "special case of a more fundamental capacity to decenter or departicularize the focus of one's conceptual activities and simultaneously to consider and coordinate two or more points of view" (Chandler, 1977, p. 10). Role taking has thus been viewed along a continuum of egocentrism (that is, a person's view is limited to an individual, personalized perspective) to perspectivism (that is, a person is increasingly able to distinguish between his or her view and others' views). Because of various methodological difficulties (such as stimulus objects being selected to give maximum contrasts for alternative perspectives and difficulty of distinguishing between role taking and stereo-typic responses to situations), Shantz (1981) and Chandler (1977) conclude that studies of role-taking abilities have generally produced inconsistent and contradictory results.

However, some clear findings have emerged (Chandler, 1977). Ego-centrism has been found to decline and role-taking skills to increase with age. Children fail to distinguish between public and private information and generally assume that others understand more than they do (that is, chil-dren mistakenly assume that private information, known only by them, is also known by others). Although Flavell (1973) has found rudimentary role taking among 2- and 3-year-old children, generally recognition and coordi-nation of multiple items of information seem to develop in middle child-hood. Greenspan, Barenboim, and Chandler (1974), in a study of first and third graders, found that older children who were sensitive to incongruent cues given by a central character were reluctant to make inferences about the character and were uncertain about their judgments. Younger children appeared to ignore the incongruent cues and expressed confidence in their judgments.

Chandler (1977) claims that this prolonged horizontal decalage has presented some critical theoretical problems—why, if some initial compe-tence in role taking is evident in early childhood, does it take so long for social role taking to develop fully? One explanation has been that various nonsocial and social dimensions on which attention may be centered or de-centered become salient at different ages (Chandler, 1977, p. 19). Another explanation offered is that different decentering tasks require qualitatively different cognitive structures.

Shantz (1981), like Chandler, argues that studies relating role-taking skills to communicative effectiveness need to be conducted more rigor-ously. She points out that individuals may be able to take the role of another, yet fail to make necessary discriminations or encode them appropriately; studies of role taking in referential communication seem to suggest this, as the earlier discussion pointed out. Furthermore, some communication tasks may require very little role taking, especially if there is great similarity be-tween speaker and listener. In one study, Cowan (1967) paired children according to their performance on a spatial egocentrism task into low-low role takers, high-high role takers, and mixed (high-low) role takers. When these children, aged 8 to 10, performed a referential communication task, Cowan found that there was a high relationship among role-taking ability, metacommunication (that is, talking about the task), and nonegocentric messages. Shantz (1981) concludes that role-taking ability facilitates effec-tive communication, but it is not sufficient for effective communication; very able listeners and contextual information can compensate for role-tak-ing omissions.

Higgins (1981) suggests a developmental order in role taking: First, there is situational role taking (that is, what would I do/think in that situation); second, there is an acknowledgment that people in the same situation may react differently; and, finally, there is a comparison and contrast of one's own views with those of another. Higgins points out that controlling the intrusion of one's own view is critical in the last stage, when comparisons of viewpoints are needed. Depending upon the situation, the individuals involved, and so forth, controlling the intrusion of one's view may vary in difficulty (Ross, 1981).

Our ability to interact effectively with others is dependent upon our acknowledgment of them as independent actors and our knowledge of them as individuals. The final component of social knowledge needed for effective communication is knowledge of context. Contextual knowledge may be subdivided into two areas: knowledge of social relationships and knowledge of social situations. While relational knowledge will be separated from situational knowledge here for heuristic reasons, it is important to remember that these knowledge bases do not develop in isolation, but are closely interrelated. I suspect, in fact, that what has been termed "world knowledge" (Clark & Clark, 1977) or "tacit knowledge" (Bransford & McCarrell, 1974) is a complex network of relevant social knowledge (of self, of others, and of context) that is activated in given social encounters and that guides our interpretation of "what is going on" in a given encounter.

Knowledge of Social Context

Knowledge of Social Relationships

Damon (1981) points out that children, to become interactionally competent, have to distinguish among various types of intended social actions and reactions; they need to classify themselves and others with respect to varying affiliations and social significances. Damon argues that interactions characterized by similar intentions can be grouped together, each group having a specific social purpose. For example, social relations between peers in childhood are often characteristic of the friendship relationship, while adult-child interaction is characteristic of the authority relationship.

Olson and Hilyard (1981) suggest that an understanding of social relations is necessary to interpret utterances; utterances not only establish a propositional content but express a social order as well (Bateson, 1972; Watzlawick, Beavin, & Jackson, 1967). In a study that asked children to recall final key statements made in a story, Olson and Hilyard (1981) found children interpreted the statement "You have more than me" not just as a true statement, but as an indirect request as well—and younger children tended to give the "request" when asked to recall what was said. Older children, aged 7 and 8, recalled the statement verbatim and its intent (that is, to get more).

A number of studies have demonstrated that the form of speech acts that serve to regulate the actions of others (directives, questions, requests, and so on) is determined by factors such as status and politeness. Mitchell-Kernan and Kernan (1977) found that some children give commands to other children just to establish a dominant status relationship. Ervin-Tripp (1977) found that children varied their directives according to the age, familiarity, or dominance of the listener. Ackerman (1978) found that young children can recognize the intentionality in unconventional directive forms. A number of studies (Bates, 1976; Ervin-Tripp, 1977; Erickson, 1981; Gelman & Shatz, 1977; Shatz, 1978) suggest that young children focus on the social meaning of the utterance rather than on its propositional content.

Erickson (1981, p. 243) claims that social and referential meanings are expressed simultaneously in messages: Humans "talk together in order to accomplish social purposes, making use of the human capacity to transmit social and referential meaning simultaneously, implicitly and explicitly, verbally and nonverbally, and to read off these meanings inferentially against (or better, within) the context of action itself." Just as there is a comparison process in referential communication between the referent and the message describing it, Erickson suggests that interpreting a message's social form involves (1) a "reading off" of the message form against the social context and (2) a judgment concerning the "fit" or "lack of fit" between the message form and message context. Asking individuals to attend only to the text (as in referential communication tasks) is contradictory to everyday experience in interactions; speakers usually choose, from among equivalent alternative referential utterances, the message form that signals the social meaning the speaker intended. Ethnomethodologists have termed this the "principle of recipient design," in which the speaker encodes both the social and propositional meanings that are intended.

A number of scholars (Cicourel, 1972; Erickson, 1981; Cook-Gumperz & Gumperz, 1976) have pointed out that role and status are continually being negotiated in conversation. In face-to-face interaction, "what looks on the surface to be a series of discrete, successive 'turns' is actually a process of continuous, simultaneously reflexive behaving and monitoring by the two players" (Erikson, 1981, p. 246).

As we have seen, social relationships between interactants tend to guide their interpretations of the ongoing interaction. The interpersonal dimension thus plays a substantial role in communication since both the decoding and encoding of messages are governed by social relationships. However, these relationships need to be considered in light of particular social contexts. The context, for example, may govern the set of social relationships possible in that context. In like manner, social relationships may also influence the social context; they may, for example, render a business meeting less formal. While it is heuristically useful to separate relational from contextual knowledge, as we have seen, they influence one another in a complex variety of ways. Let us now turn to consider the influence of context, defined as the surrounding social situation, on communication.

Knowledge of Social Situations

A speaker's belief about the type of communication engaged in (such as a lecture as opposed to a casual discussion) may be mentioned explicitly in interactions, especially if speakers need to make some conversational repairs. In this way, interactants make the context a shared cognitive construct and thus interactants are creating context as well as communicating in a given social situation. Cook-Gumperz and Gumperz (1976) view context as a creative interpretation of ongoing interaction—an interpretation that is created by both participants.

Research by Cook-Gumperz and Cosaro (1976) and Gumperz and Herasimchuck (1973) found that children and adults differ in their use of contextualization cues and thus misunderstandings may arise. While adults focus their attention on the semantic-syntactic information against a background of constantly monitored nonverbal information, children appear to "regard all the available information as similarly weighted for the purpose of what is being said" (Cook-Gumperz & Gumperz, 1976, p. 19). Children also do not signal their intentions through multiple channels; this produces sudden topic or attention shifts that often are confusing to adults.

Cook-Gumperz and Cosaro (1976) investigated how different settings in nurseries provide different socially defined possibilities for interaction; these possibilities are governed by conventionalized expectations and by past behavior produced in those settings (Cook-Gumperz & Casaro, 1976, p. 412). They found that a child's interactions are guided by his or her expectations about "what goes on" in various areas in the nursery (conventionalized role playing in the playhouse, fantasy play in the sandbox, and so on) and that different communicative strategies are used to sustain these interactions. Cook-Gumperz and Cosaro (1976, p. 431) conclude that "specific properties of social context are part of the information children make note of and utilize in combination with conventionalized expectations to create cultural and normative sense throughout ... interactive episodes." Conventionalized role playing appeared less complex than children's interaction in fantasy play. Fantasy play relied on repetition, description of action, and expansion of previous utterances as important communicative strategies for maintaining the interaction.

Cook-Gumperz (1981, p. 48), in her study of children's persuasive talk, suggests that children rely on their "accumulated situational knowledge" as much as they rely on their linguistic knowledge in interpreting others' utterances. Mishler's (1979) analysis of children's trading talk found that speech acts needed to be interpreted in context—a subsequent remark could alter a prior interpretation of an utterance. Schieffelin's (1981) analysis of sibling relationships in Kaluli society found that mothers carefully "school" their children in this relationship through formulaic messages that co-occur with a specific set of contextualization cues.

As previously discussed, contextual knowledge—in terms of both relational and situational knowledge—provides an important basis for interpreting ongoing interactions. With the increase in pragmatic research on human communication, attention has also been directed to how humans acquire this contextual knowledge. Let us take a brief look at the research of Katherine Nelson (1981), in which she suggests that social knowledge, especially that knowledge relevant to interpersonal communication, is acquired via scripts.

Acquiring Social Knowledge

The work of Argyle (1975, 1981) and Cook-Gumperz (1981) suggests that adults interpret messages by analyzing information across various communication modalities (eye gaze, intonation, stress, posture, and so on). Cook-Gumperz and Gumperz (1976, p. 18) suggest that information available in a context is interpreted against "a developed notion of what constitutes a 'normal array' of information in the background and the foreground features." It seems unlikely that this "normal array" of knowledge is learned piecemeal; children appear to learn the "whole" first and only later begin to differentiate particular dimensions or routines. According to Nelson (1981), social cognition is defined as knowledge about people and their relationships; this knowledge is acquired via social interaction. These social interactions may be represented by scripts. Scripts, as defined by Nelson, reflect a concrete, well-specified sequence of actions, located in a spatial and temporal context, that are designed to accomplish a particular goal. Scripts also specify roles for participants and distinguish obligatory from optional actions. Young children possess general script knowledge (for example, of everyday events such as going to a restaurant) that is consistent over time and socially accurate. A study by Nelson (1978) found that preschoolers can verbalize and act out scripts, that experienced preschoolers had more script knowledge than newcomers, and that scripts became more skeletal in form as activities became more varied. Young children are very skilled at extracting the main idea or purpose of an event, and use sequencing to connect central events in a script.

Nelson (1981) argues that children acquire scripts through experience. Adults usually arrange exchanges with infants (for example, Bruner's formats) and infants acquire their roles through participation in the interaction. Children's roles become progressively more different (Bruner, 1977) and eventually children begin acting out scripts (playing house, playing school, and the like). This social knowledge guides routine encounters, and when these encounters become well established, individuals "run through" the sequence of actions automatically. When an individual is freed from attending to the ongoing action, Nelson suggests that "cognitive space" is gained and thus attention can be focused upon on problematic aspects of an encounter.

Thus far, the child's developing communicative skills as well as the child's developing social knowledge about communication have been examined. These two areas of pragmatic development have been discussed separately; this, unfortunately, reflects the fact that researchers have studied one or the other, and only rarely the interrelationships between the two pragmatic components of communication. In the section that follows, I shall briefly discuss the research of Lubin and Forbes, and Delia and his associates, which links aspects of social knowledge with communicative strategies. In my view, such research is needed if our theories are to capture the dynamic complexity of human communication accurately.

Social Cognition and Communication

With increasing age, children develop more complex cognitive systems for regulating social behavior. This general development is complicated by many factors, including motivation and the influence of the peer culture. Lubin and Forbes (1981) view social behavior as goal-oriented activity and social reasoning as the planful regulation of social behavior. As such, social reasoning relies on specific social and cognitive skills, such as making inferences and applying script knowledge to everyday encounters.

In a study of children's interactions, Lubin and Forbes (1981) postulated three levels of social reasoning (that is, levels of making inferences). Level 1, Mechanistic Stereotypy, reflects a one-to-one correspondence between environmental effects and individual psychological reactions; in similar situations, an individual believes that others would react in the same way as he or she would. In Level 2, Reactive Subjectivism, everyone *interprets* the situation in the same way (for example, situation X is an unhappy occasion), but individuals may *evaluate* and *react* to the situation differently (situation X may make person A sad, while person B is not bothered by it). On Level 3, Constructive Subjectivism, individuals acknowledge that both evaluation and interpretation of events may vary.

In attempting to link levels of social reasoning with social behavior, Forbes and Lubin (1981a, 1981b) first interviewed children about their inferences about children's behavior after watching three different videotaped interactions. Subjects were asked to make inferences about the videotaped children's psychological states, and to explain why they thought their inferences were correct. Subsequently, the subjects themselves were videotaped in a play group. Only persuasive episodes in the first four play sessions were analyzed, since Forbes and Lubin believed that generalized social reasoning would be most influential with unfamiliar others. They found that with increasing age, children moved from Level 1 to Level 3 social reasoning; the movement from Level 1 to Level 2 reasoning appears to be a move toward increasing decentration, and the shift from Level 2 to Level 3 moves from a passive view of humans to viewing others as active, intentional actors. Level 3 also appears similar to reciprocal role taking (Selman, 1971) and to metacognition (Flavell, 1981); thus these skills may develop earlier than previously thought.

Persuasive strategies were found to be significantly related to level of social reasoning. Ritualistic strategies, like appeals to rules or norms, reflected Level 1 reasoning; affect-oriented strategies reflected Level 2 social reasoning, and construal strategies, focusing upon clarification of the referent and/or intent, reflected Level 3 reasoning. Furthermore, these strategies were hierarchically stratified, with ritualistic strategies being the least complex and construal strategies the most complex. Forbes and Lubin conclude that children regulate their behavior, in part, by reasoning processes that are verbal-explanatory in nature.

According to Applegate and Delia (1980), research linking social-cognitive and communicative development has produced mixed results because no clear conceptual ties have been developed between aspects of social-cognitive development and aspects of communicative behavior. The work of Jesse Delia and his colleagues (Applegate & Delia, 1980; Clark & Delia, 1976, 1977; Delia & Clark, 1977; Delia et al., 1979; Delia & O'Keefe, 1979) links cognitive complexity (number of cognitive constructs) and construct abstractness with level of persuasive strategy. Persuasive strategies were classified according to the degree of sensitivity to the target's perspective. Such strategies have been found to be correlated with cognitive complexity and construct abstractness. Significant correlations were found between level of persuasive strategies, and independent assessments of perspective-taking skills and cognitive complexity in elementary school-aged children.

Another promising line of research linking social reasoning to social behavior is that concerning children's arguments, for in arguments, as in persuasion, there is conflict between the participant's goals. It is in this conflict of ideas, goals, or intentions that cognitive growth occurs (Chandler, 1977; Damon, 1981; Piaget, 1970). A number of studies have shown that with increasing age children's argumentative strategies become less rigid, more complex and adaptive (Haslett, 1983c), more informative (Eisenberg & Garvey, 1981), and more numerous, complex, and rule governed (Benoit, 1981; O'Keefe & Benoit, in press). All of these studies document children's increasing social knowledge of others and their skill in utilizing this knowledge.

Thus far, this review of developmental pragmatics has explored the child's emerging communicative skills and growing social knowledge about interpersonal communication. Early in infancy, children appear to have an innate motivation to interact with others; children have a sensitivity to and understanding of communication as a means of establishing relationships and cooperating with others. This first stage of development was termed *recognizing the interpersonal nature of communication.* The next stage, *creating communicative effects,* spans from approximately four months to three years; during this stage, the child moves from preverbal routines to well-established linguistic communication. The child intentionally communicates her or his views utilizing a variety of speech acts to accomplish differing goals; language is used to express a range of functions (expressive, directive, informative, and so on). In the next stage, *utilizing communicative strategies,* children refine and extend communicative strategies such as turn taking, maintaining topic, using deixis, and coordinating their messages with others to accomplish differing purposes. This stage, from approximately 3 to 5 years of age, is also marked by increased interaction with peers. Communicative strategies may expand because children are not just communicating with adults, who often anticipate and "fill in the gaps" in children's messages; rather, they must effectively interact with peers whose knowledge and capacities are roughly equivalent to their own. The final stage of children's pragmatic communicative skills, *monitoring communication,* develops at around 5 years. Here the child begins to metacommunicate, at times commenting on his or her own talk, making conversational repairs, and so forth.

As we survey these developing communicative skills, the direction of growth has always been in terms of increasing cognitive and communicative complexity. As children mature, they develop new skills, put old skills to work at accomplishing new goals, and combine previously separate skills to achieve a given purpose. These functional skills, however, in order to be utilized effectively in interpersonal communication, need to be activated at appropriate times during our interactions with others. For example, one needs to know how to "soften" one's demands (that is, follow politeness conventions), but one also needs to know *when* to be polite. The child's developing social knowledge about communication provides him or her with the necessary knowledge that permits socially adapted communication to occur. Both pragmatic dimensions—the skills themselves and the social knowledge needed to activate those skills—must be accounted for in any adequate theory of developmental pragmatics.

When we review the development of social knowledge relevant to children's communication, this development also reflects increasing cognitive and communicative complexity. In the first stage of this social knowledge, the infant separates the self from others; this separation depends upon the recognition of people as independent agents and as animate beings. Bruner (1983) and Damon (1981) suggest that this understanding enables the infant to recognize other people as having a unique potential for social interaction. In the next stage of developing social knowledge, knowledge of others becomes more finely differentiated and knowledge of context also develops. Contextual knowledge incorporates knowledge of social relationships as well as knowledge of social situations. At this point, in my view, it is not possible to separate clearly the growth of knowledge of others from the growth of knowledge about context. Both sources of knowledge are embedded within scripts that children acquire in early childhood; it appears that children begin to separate personal dispositions (knowledge of others) from situational constraints (knowledge of context) in middle childhood (Higgins, 1981; Ross, 1981). Thus, from a developmental point of view, it does not seem useful—or at this point possible—to separate them. Indeed, knowledge of social relationships may well turn out to be a reflection of both knowledge of others and knowledge of social situations.

At this point, then, we have reviewed *what* pragmatic communicative skills and knowledge have been acquired. But since we are concerned with the development of pragmatic communication, it is not sufficient to discuss only what has been acquired. While this overview is of value in itself— because there has been no previous attempt to integrate the diversity of pragmatic accomplishments outlined here—nevertheless, a developmental perspective implies a concern for *how* these communicative accomplishments are achieved, not merely a concern for what those accomplishments happen to be. Now that the development of pragmatic communicative skills and knowledge has been charted, the remainder of this chapter will explore issues in the acquisition of the pragmatic dimension of human communication.

CRITICAL ISSUES IN THE
ACQUISITION OF COMMUNICATION

This section is titled as it is rather than as "acquiring communication" because there is no single theoretical account that attempts to explain how we acquire our communicative abilities. Given that pragmatics is a newly emerging paradigm, this is not surprising (Kuhn, 1970). As Kuhn points out, new paradigms are characterized by controversy over how the area of study ought to be defined, what appropriate methods of analysis are, and conflict over competing explanations. All of these characteristics are evident in research on the acquisition of pragmatics. This review, in fact, can be viewed as an attempt to define pragmatics as an area of study.

At the present time, there appear to be two competing paradigms for explaining the acquisition of pragmatics: those using cognitive bases as explanatory principles, and those using principles of social interaction as explanatory principles (Atkinson, 1981; Bates, Bretherton, Beeghly-Smith, & McNew, 1981). A third paradigm, nativism, has been used to explain how language itself is acquired, but does not concern itself with the appropriate and socially adapted use of language[4] and thus is not relevant to this discussion.

Cognitively oriented researchers can be divided into two groups. The first group uses Piagetian concepts—such as tool use, object permanence, conservation, and reversibility—to explain communicative development. Examples of this type of research would be studies relating communicative intentionality to Stage 5 of the sensorimotor intelligence, or relating the infant's developing sense of self to the concept of object permanence. In contrast, the second group uses information-processing theories and artificial intelligence research—employing constructs such as scripts, frames, and plans— as explanatory principles. Nelson's use of scripts to explain communicative behavior and acquisition would exemplify this approach. Both cognitive approaches, whether from a Piagetian or information-processing perspective, argue that communicative behavior can be explained by reference to, or can be reduced to, a set of underlying cognitive abilities (Atkinson, 1981; Bates, 1979).

On the other hand, researchers taking a social interaction perspective argue that communicative behavior is acquired within, and explained by, social interaction. Bruner (1983), has divided these researchers into two groups, one supporting a "functional substitution hypothesis" and one supporting a "fine-tuning hypothesis." Those advocating the functional substitution hypothesis argue that prelinguistic infants, through gestures, vocalizations, and the like, already have a communication system that expresses their desires; language, when it is developed, just substitutes for these already-existing functions. The fine-tuning hypothesis, however, argues that the adult caretaker provides communicative input that is adapted to the child's level so that the child's own acquisition of communication is greatly facilitated.

The difference between the cognitive and social interaction perspectives is one of degree and of emphasis, rather than one of diametric opposition. Both positions acknowledge that language and communication are acquired in an interactive context (Rees, 1978). However, the cognitive theorist tends to emphasize the mental abilities of the individual and their role in communication, whereas the social interaction perspective emphasizes the dialogue and interaction that occurs among interlocutors. Each researcher, of course, selects a perspective that highlights variables of most interest to him or her.

My own sympathies lie with the social interaction perspective, although I am not advocating any particular approach that has been discussed. I believe the social interaction perspective offers a richer, more inclusive perspective from which a unified theory of pragmatics may develop. Most important, such a perspective focuses on the fundamental nature of human communication—its interpersonal nature; communication is a *shared* social activity, an interpersonal dialogue. Any model of pragmatics, in my view, must accommodate this fundamental fact of communication.

The preceding discussion provides a frame of reference for our discussion of critical issues in acquiring pragmatic communicative skills. These issues have emerged as major, current controversies among developmental researchers attempting to explain how these pragmatic abilities are acquired. Four general issues seem critical. First, the early relationship between the adult caretaker and infant seems critical for communicative development. What is the nature of this relationship, and what relationships can be said to facilitate communicative development and why? Second, the question of intentionality: To what extent do communicators seem aware of their communicative behavior? Third, are communicative skills continuous or discontinuous (that is, is there continuity from preverbal behavior to verbal behavior?)? And, finally, what is the relationship between communication and other cognitive skills? This last question may be dealt with in two distinct ways: (1) Can communicative skills be accounted for or subsumed under other cognitive skills? (2) Can communication facilitate the learning of other cognitive skills? It is to these issues we now turn.

Adult Caretaker-Child Interaction

Although both the cognitive and social interaction approaches acknowledge that language is acquired in the context of dialogue (Rees, 1978), the social interaction approach emphasizes environmental factors more (Bates et al., 1981). One such environmental factor has been the dialogue between the adult caretaker and infant. Early studies argued that the nature of the adult language (as input) determined the subsequent quality of the child's language (for example, see Snow, 1977). More recently, the child has been recognized as playing an active role as a communicative partner in dialogue with the adult caretaker (Nelson, 1977). We now turn to a careful examination of the nature of the dialogue between the adult caretaker (usually the mother) and infant, and its influence upon the child's communicative development.

Within the general area of adult caretaker and infant interaction, several questions have emerged; these questions concern the nature of linguistic input from the adult caretaker, the general pattern of interaction between caretaker and child, and individual differences in language acquisition. Other issues of concern include the directionality of effects (that is, who is influencing whom) and the affective bond between caretaker and child.

Linguistic Input

Mothers' speech to their children has been found to be simpler, more repetitious, and more focused on immediate events; to contain more questions and imperatives; and to be higher pitched and more exaggerated in emphasis than adult-to-adult speech (Sachs, 1977; Snow, 1972, 1977). Mothers' speech to children varies as a function of the communicative demands of the situation (Snow, 1977a, 1977b). Other researchers have correlated aspects of mothers' speech (such as "motherese" or baby talk) with various measures of language production and comprehension. However, "the interpretation of correlations between relatively gross measures of language is problematic" and many researchers have turned to more specific measures of linguistic form and production (deVilliers & deVilliers, 1979, p. 141). For example, researchers have looked at the frequency of specific grammatical forms in parental speech and related that to the child's age or have looked at changes in parental speech forms as paralleled in the child's speech (Sellinger, 1979; van der Geest, 1977). Nelson, Carskaddon, and Bonvillian (1973) conclude that for normal language acquisition to occur, the linguistic input needs to match the child's cognitive abilities.

Bates et al. (1981) conclude that—while more language input is related to more and better language in children—specific claims linking specific types of input to specified outcomes need to be tested. Studies reporting efforts to use specific types of input (expansions, recasting sentences, and so on) to enhance language development have reported some success (Brown, 1976; Nelson, 1977). This linkage is particularly difficult to assess in spontaneous speech (deVilliers & deVilliers, 1979). DeVilliers and deVilliers (1979, p. 148) conclude that "while such studies may establish the effectiveness of particular training procedures in enhancing acquisition, sometimes with important implications for therapy programs with language-delayed children, it is an extra step to establish that these processes actually play any substantial role in the natural language acquisition of the normal child." Snow (1977b, p. 39) notes that expansions, for example, may facilitate language development because they are ways to provide "relevant, responsive and interesting input at all stages of language development." Thus quality of conversation may be the crucial variable. It is this possibility, that the quality of interaction between adult and child significantly influences language and communication development, that we shall explore next.

Patterns of Interaction
Between Adult and Child

Rees (1978), following Steiner (1969), claims that the child must participate in interactions with others in order to develop a concept of self and of
his or her social role. Sugarman (1973) points out that by the time the child
uses language, at around 9 to 12 months of age, he or she already has well-
developed communicative schemes that have emerged through interactions with others.

Researchers have noted the role that adults play in keeping the interaction with children "going," often relying on the use of questions or turn-
passing devices such as "well" or "but" (Bloom et al., 1976; Ervin-Tripp,
1977; Kaye & Charney, 1981; Mishler, 1975, 1976; Shugar, 1978). Moerk
(1974) found that mothers were very sensitive to their children's language
abilities and adapted their messages to these abilities; with children's increasing age, mothers move from explicit modeling in their interactions to
using questions to cue the child's response, and, finally, the child spontaneously encodes through actions and explanations. Wells, Montgomery, and
Maclure (1979) are engaged in a program of research designed to target
adult-child interaction patterns. They are particularly concerned about investigating how adult utterances are "appropriately responsive to the child's
contributions in particular sequences of interaction" (Wells et al., 1979,
p. 341).

In an analysis of two excerpts from a longitudinal study, Wells et al.
(1979, p. 368) found differences in their two subjects with respect to the
children's "ability to contribute new and contextually relevant matter to the
conversation." They attribute these differences, in part, to varying ways in
which mothers interpreted their children's conversational abilities and thus
constrained their interaction in varying ways. A study by Wells (1981, p. 47)
found that "insofar as there is variation in children's experience of linguistic
interaction which can be interpreted as differentially facilitative of development, this emerges from the actual topics proposed and from the way they
are collaboratively negotiated and to this both child and adult contribute in
varying proportions." Howe (1980, p. 40), in an analysis of videotaped
mother-child conversations, found that mother-initiated exchanges with the
child appeared to influence the motivation for semantic development:
"Given high motivation, the children will learn from maternal replies and
will be influenced by percentages of minimal and extended replies." According to Howe, previous attempts to look at mother-child interaction have
stressed the informational value of the exchange, whereas her findings suggest there is a motivational value as well that could help explain individual
differences in language development.

Social class differences in maternal language styles and their implications for children's development have also been assessed. Bernstein (1970, 1972, 1973) emphasizes the role of language in his theories of socialization. Elaborated communication codes are more complex, more flexible, and permit more explicit, individualized meanings to be expressed, whereas restricted communication codes are more stereotyped, condensed, and reliant on nonverbal means and primarily reflect commonly shared social meanings. Bernstein (1972) suggests that the middle class uses both codes, whereas the lower class uses mainly the restricted code.

Cook-Gumperz (1973) analyzed social class differences in mothers' language and modes of social control with their children. She found that middle-class mothers used predominantly an elaborated code and *personal* modes of control (that is, their modes of control focused on individual motivations and needs), whereas lower-class mothers used predominantly a restricted code and *positional* modes of control (their modes of control focused on the status and role the individual possessed). Turner (1973) found that middle-class children tended to use positional modes of control (based on status obligations and the like), while lower-class children tended to use imperative modes (commands, directives, and so on).

A series of studies by Hess and his colleagues (Hess & Shipman, 1965, 1967, 1968; Hess, Shipman, Bear, & Brophy, 1968) further tested Bernstein's theory. Their studies found that three modes of maternal control could be linked to complementary styles of their children: (1) the children whose mothers use an imperative mode tend to acknowledge and obey authority, (2) the children whose mothers use a subjective mode tend to acknowledge personal considerations, and (3) the children whose mothers use a cognitive-rational mode focus on task and rational principles.

Robinson and Rackstraw (1978) analyzed maternal strategies in answering questions. Middle-class mothers were more likely to answer questions, give more factual and accurate information, and use more analogies and cause-effect relationships in their responses than were lower-class mothers. Lower-class mothers tended to restate a question as a statement, or to respond that things were "always done" in a particular way; thus their responses appealed to authority. When middle-class children asked questions, they gave more information and the information was more accurate and relevant than information given by lower-class children. Lower-class children tended to reply by appealing to authority or to general behavioral rules (for example, "You can't do that because it's naughty").

Hartmann and Haavind (1981) criticize the studies of Cook-Gumperz and Hess et al. because they analyze how mothers say they will behave rather than actual social interaction between mother and child. Furthermore, the global measures used to assess social class are "too gross for the necessary detailed description of the mediating process. . . . it is necessary to separate the problem of how social mediation influence cognitive development from the problem of how differences in social structure produce different forms of social mediation" (Hartmann & Haavind, 1981, p. 132). Hartmann and Haavind explored this mediation in a study that assessed social and cognitive processes in a game-learning situation, with the mother as teacher and the child as learner, across dyads of differing social status. Mothers were found to use three strategies in teaching their children how to play a new game: (1) the informing teaching strategy, which focuses on explaining rules and different action options; (2) the imperative teaching strategy, which focuses on telling the child what to do, but with little or no explanation; and (3) the competitive-expressive teaching strategy, which focuses on competitive and interpersonal skills. These three teaching strategies correlated with three educational strategies found among the children. Respectively, these strategies are (1) the active mastering strategy, which reflects an active, questioning learning approach; (2) the passive strategy, which is characterized by superficial imitation and guessing; and (3) the expressive strategy, which is characterized by emotional and/or competitive responses. Hartmann and Haavind are particularly interested in exploring the influence of parent-child communication on language functions and on cognitive development generally. They suggest that although others serve as socializing agents, since the mother's task (usually) as the main caretaker results in her having considerable social interaction with the child, her strategy may have considerable influence on the child.

Robinson (1981a) suggests that researchers need to consider the psychological significance, if any, of the social differences that are found in interactive patterns. Robinson observed mother-child interactions, across a range of social classes, in which children were asked to tell what they knew about familiar objects to an experimenter and then they could question their mothers if they wanted to know more about the objects. In mother-child dialogues, Robinson found that middle-class mothers asked more questions of their children, regardless of the objects being discussed; their answers were given with reference to the child's experience and used more referential comparisons. Middle-class children tended to give more appropriate responses to their mothers' questions. Both lower-class mothers and children used language predominantly to inform. Robinson (1981a, p. 179) concludes that social class differences appear to stem from differences in the frequency of certain responses; both groups clearly used speech "mainly to seek or relay information of a propositional nature."

Generally, differing patterns of maternal interaction are viewed as individual differences; their linkage to social class differences needs to be explored further. Many researchers (Harding, 1983; Hartmann & Haavind, 1981; Robinson, 1981; Schieffelin & Ochs, 1983; Snow & Gilbreath, 1983) have commented on the need to explore parental attitudes toward child rearing and relate these expectations and attitudes to parental behavior.

From the limited research done on cultural differences in language and communication behavior, striking differences appear to exist in maternal interaction styles (Schieffelin & Ochs, 1983); these styles appear to reflect the cultural socializing patterns of different societies. Isbell and McKee (1980, p. 340) suggest that differences in the structure of caretaker relations influences communication patterns; these communicative patterns, in turn, contribute to differences in cognitive orientation. Isbell and McKee (1980, p. 350) argue for an interactive view of cognition in which "perceptual schemata result from the selective attention of the child to the available and salient information in her/his environment." These differences in maternal interaction style across cultures have also focused attention on the question of individual differences in communicative development.

Individual Differences in
Communicative Development

With the former emphasis on humans' innate predisposition for language, little attention was paid to individual differences in communicative development. As researchers analyzed the nature of the input for language acquisition, interaction patterns between adult caretakers and infants were systematically studied. This, in turn, raised questions about individual differences and directionality of effects.

Nelson et al.'s (1973) monograph found that individual differences in language learning were related to differences in early experiences with language. Differences were found between object-oriented (referential) children, who acquired vocabulary more rapidly, and personal-social-oriented (expressive) children, who developed syntax more rapidly. Nelson et al. suggest that these differences might be a function of maternal interaction styles that emphasize either naming objects or social action in the environment. A subsequent study by Nelson (1976) argues that differences in children's language experiences predispose them to focus on different uses of language. Dore (1974), in a study of two children, found that one child was oriented to word form (vocabulary) while the other child was oriented to intonation (prosodic features that reflect different language functions). Greenfield and Smith (1976) claim that the social situation may provide structure as well as content in early language learning; thus different contexts provide different learning opportunities for children.

As with the issue of individual differences, the issue of directionality of effects was similarly ignored in earlier work on language acquisition. It was assumed that the adult caretaker was the teacher or role model, and the infant/child was a passive learner. However, recent research emphasizes the active role of the child as a participant in a two-way dialogue with the adult caretaker.

Directionality of Communicative Effects

As Bates et al. (1981) have pointed out, with correlational studies, the direction of influence could flow from child to adult caretaker, or the reverse. As a result, they have raised questions about previous research. First, they observe that "motherese" reflects a communicative style that is used frequently when a listener fails to understand a speaker (e.g., simplification and repetition frequently occur). Thus, motherese may be a response to the child's failure to understand. Bohannon and Marquis (1977) found that when children indicated lack of understanding, adults reduced utterance length. However, Bates et al. (1981, p. 54) point out that motherese could also aid comprehension: "Any positive influence that motherese may have on the child is canceled out by the original negative relationship between motherese and child failure." A study by Carlson-Luden (1979) found a large number of negative correlations between maternal interventions and measures of children's success in completing tasks; rather than arguing that these interventions inhibit learning, Bates et al. (1981, p. 55) suggest that "the most sensible interpretation is that mothers intervene to the degree their children fail to understand the task."

Studies by McNew (1981), Belsky, Goode, and Most (1981), Nelson, Carskaddon, and Bonvillian (1973), and Nelson (1977) all support the positive effects of motherese on child language development. In the Nelson studies, the maternal interventions were linked with specific aspects of language development. Bates et al. (1981, p. 59) conclude that these studies support effects from parent to child although the "learning process in recast experiments is essentially child driven." Snyder-McLean and McLean (1978) point out that infant strategies for language learning are distinct from adult facilitation strategies; infants use interactive strategies (information-gathering strategies) as well as cognitive strategies (information-processing strategies).

The issue of directionality of effects suggests that earlier research results might need to be reinterpreted since the infant is now viewed as being an active, directive participant in his or her dialogues with adult caretakers. Studies of interaction have revealed the synchrony in interaction between mother and child, and have suggested that the infant may have substantial control over this process (Stern, 1977).

Analysis of caretaker-child interactions has also been confounded by the emotional attachment between the caretaker and the child. For example, closer attachment probably means that the caretaker and child interact more; more interaction provides more communicative opportunities and thus language and communicative development is undoubtedly facilitated. I shall now examine recent research efforts that have attempted to analyze the relationship between attachment and communicative development.

The Influence of Attachment
Between Adult Caretaker and Child

Bretherton, Bates, Benigni, Camaioni, and Volterra (1979) look at how the quality of the caretaker/infant relationship influences cognitive and communicative development. They suggest two hypothesized relationships between quality of attachment and cognitive/communicative development:

(1) *Attachment-exploration:* The infant uses the mother as a secure base from which to explore the environment.
(2) *Attachment-teaching:* The infant and mother establish an interactive synchrony that permits increased opportunities for the child to develop cognitive/communicative skills.

The first hypothesized relationship rests on motivational factors, while the second rests upon motivational and learning factors. In a review of studies on attachment and its relationship to cognitive and communicative development, Bretherton et al. (1979, p. 236) report that "a substantial number of investigators have discovered positive relationships between quality of attachment as measured by the strange situation and cognitive functioning. . . . relationships between quality of attachment and language competence so far reported have been weaker, with a higher proportion of studies finding no differences." A study by Bretherton et al. (1979, p. 257) of 11- and 12-month-old children found a "fairly strong correlation of strange situation variables with gestural communication level . . . but none whatsoever with language competence." They suggest that infant-mother attachment needs to incorporate not only their social interaction and the mother's function as a secure base, but other aspects of their relationship as well, such as the mother's role as teacher. Bretherton et al. conclude that much further exploration needs to be done in this general area, especially in seeking new measures of relational quality, separating maternal stimulation from social interaction and looking at relational quality at differing times and in differing knowledge domains.

Recent work by John Dore (1983) extends Stern's analysis of the affective nature of the mother/child dyad. During the transitional period from babbling to words, Dore hypothesizes that when the baby expresses a marked affect, the mother responds by matching it (that is, "analoguing" the same affect), by complementing it (responding with a different state), or by imitating it. These matches, according to Dore, transform the child's affect state into "intents to express those affect-states."

Dore's work places the development of communicative intentionality and of conventional communication signals in the context of the mother-child affective relationship. More important, Dore's work may begin to explain how the dual nature of human communication—that utterances express both propositional and relational content—is established. Finally, and in my view quite accurately, Dore emphasizes the importance of the relational element in human communication. As both Dore and Trevarthen point out, communication is, at heart, the way in which we establish relationships with others. Pragmatic models of communication, while concerned about how language is used to communicate, are centered upon how language operates in the context of interpersonal relationships. Trevarthen claims that the human need to establish relationships with others is a fundamental motivation for acquiring communicative skills. And Dore's research argues that testing and expressing relational states is a fundamental aspect of the communicative process.

While Dore's view needs to be worked out more fully, his model clearly shifts emphasis from cognitive to social and motivational factors, focusing particularly on the interactional, situated nature of early communicative development. This view also offers yet another perspective on the nature of adult caretaker-infant interaction; a view that is centered upon the affective quality of the caretaker-infant relationship.

As we have seen, caretaker-child interaction is a multifaceted issue; critical aspects seem to be the nature of the linguistic imput, patterns of interaction, directionality of effects, individual differences, and the influence of affective bonds between caretaker and child. Emerging themes concerning caretaker-child interaction and its influence on the acquisition of pragmatic skills, while still in need of further research, seem to (1) focus on the child as an *active* participant in his or her acquisition of communication; (2) acknowledge that children may utilize a variety of acquisition strategies; (3) acknowledge that different interactive contexts provide different learning experiences for the child, and thus different levels and types of communicative skills may be learned; (4) focus on the quality of interaction, especially the relational, affective quality of the caretaker-child bond; and (5) suggest that there may be complex interactive effects that operate in the acquisition of communication.

Communicative Intentionality

The degree to which communication is an intentional activity has been a subject of increasing debate. Langer (1978), for example, argues that much of communicative behavior is relatively "mindless." Indeed, some suggest that the routinized nature of communication, which frees interactants from the need to concentrate fully on the communicative process, enables participants to focus on problematic aspects of encounters (Nelson, 1981) or on learning other complex skills (Shatz, 1978, 1982). On the other hand, often we devote particular attention to trying to ascertain others' intentions and use this information as a basis for our interpretation of what is going on in those encounters. Thus intentionality appears to be a central concern for pragmatics—and, of course, for any model of communication. While most researchers acknowledge the centrality of communicative intentionality and the necessity to deal with intentionality in modeling communicative processes, there is little agreement on how intentionality is to be conceptualized, and even less agreement about "what counts" as evidence of intentionality. For developmental pragmatics, the issue becomes even more complex since we are dealing here with the development of intentionality. In the following section, some of the ways in which developmental researchers have tried to resolve this issue will be explored.

Researchers in developmental pragmatics have focused on intentionality as reflected in the infant's communicative behavior. Dore's work emphasizes the mother's use of accountability procedures in helping the child achieve a desired goal. Bruner, however, focuses on the routinized nature of formats in helping the child accomplish an expected or desired goal. Ryan (1974) has identified cues adults use in trying to understand and interpret the child's communicative behavior. Finally, Bates's discussion of intentionality has focused on the child's ability to alter his or her communicative behavior in response to adult feedback.

Two important points about intentional communicative behavior are reflected in these varying approaches. First, communicative intentionality is accomplished in an *interpersonal* context. Whether through formats, accountability procedures, interpreting cues, or giving feedback, the *response* of another to the message is critical to achieving that message's intended effect. And these responses by adult caretakers, in early infancy, appear to aid the infant in recognizing the conventional and intentional qualities of his or her early communicative signals, and to alter those signals correctly when needed.

Second, intentionality is related to the concept of *control* over one's message-sending abilities. In its earliest stage, the infant's control over communication may consist only of his or her recognition of the value of communication as a means of establishing relationships with others (Trevarthen's concept of intersubjectivity). As the infant matures, he or she participates in routines and develops an appreciation of what is required in order to complete these routines; particular activities take on specified meanings and the infant becomes "held accountable" for completing these routines. Finally, infants become able to alter their messages as a result of feedback from adults (Bates's use of intentionality). Over time, children become increasingly adept at altering messages in response to feedback and at encoding messages in light of *anticipated* consequences and effects from a given message. The earliest developments of intentionality, then, are experienced in interpersonal contexts and reflect increasing control over communication, in terms of both understanding and performing communicative acts.

As the child's mastery of verbal communication grows, children recognize that any utterance can convey more than one intended meaning. In addition, children realize that there are many messages that can express the same intent (for instances, indirect versus direct requests). This recognition of the complexity of messages is accompanied by growing complexity in the interpersonal contexts in which children communicate. Increasing interaction with both peers and adults involves the child in a wide range of social relationships and social contexts. The child learns that he or she must deal with the intentions of others as well as with his or her own.

Given this communicative complexity, speech act theory seems very limited in its view of intentionality (illocutionary force) and, in my opinion, is fundamentally inaccurate since this view does not acknowledge the interactive nature of intentionality. Damon (1981, p. 109) has expressed the fundamental links between intentionality and interaction most cogently:

> What, then, are the principles unique to social interaction that call for a special kind of knowing? Most significantly, there is the ability of persons *intentionally* to coordinate their actions, thoughts, and perspectives with one another. Persons do not simply react to one another, but do so consciously, purposefully, with mutual intent, reciprocal exchanges unimaginable in the inanimate world. . . . Of course the character of the reciprocity changes as the social relation (as well as the participants in it) develop. Mother-infant reciprocity originates with primitive turn taking between mother and child in act and sound (Brazelton, Koslowski, & Main, 1974). . . .
>
> But regardless of its form or its relative level of sophistication, the communication and reciprocity at the heart of all social interaction is brought about by persons intentionally coordinating their actions and thoughts with one another.

Whatever the particular viewpoint being advocated, researchers acknowledge the fundamental importance of intentionality in any theory of pragmatics.

Much greater conceptual clarity is needed to delineate the assumptions concerning intentionality implied in a particular perspective. Careful methods for ascertaining "what counts" as evidence of intentionality also need to be delimited clearly. Shatz (1978) points out that we need to be very cautious about the skills we impute to children. Intentionality, like egocentrism, has been used as a global construct; just as research has broken down the global construct of egocentrism into a number of more specific constructs (such as role-taking skills) and specific underlying processes (decentration), so too future research must more explicitly identify, both conceptually and methodologically, what we mean by intentionality. Special attention should be given to avoiding confusion between goals and means, or between motives and the realization of those motives.

Another issue that appears to be as vexing as that of intentionality is the issue of the relationship between prelinguistic and linguistic communication. In what ways, if any, does prelinguistic communication influence later linguistic development? As we shall see, there are a variety of positions taken on this issue. While some theorists argue that there may be a sharp break between the two (that is, prelinguistic and linguistic communication are *discontinuous*), others suggest a gradual transition between the two (*continuity*), and still others argue that the question needs to be reformulated in a more meaningful way.

Continuity and Discontinuity in Human Communication

In her discussion of this issue, Sugarman (1983) distinguishes three types of relationships between earlier and later behavior: (1) Antecedents denote behaviors that reliably precede other behaviors; (2) precursors denote behaviors that both precede and share some feature with other behaviors; and (3) prerequisites denote behaviors that are antecedent and causally necessary for other behaviors. She claims that only antecedents may be empirically justified; precursors and prerequisites are matters of theoretical interpretation. Given these considerations, let us turn now to a closer examination of the support for continuity between preverbal and verbal communication.

Bruner (1975b) presents one of the strongest claims for linking preverbal communication to language. He discusses four major preverbal precursors to language: (1) the mother's interpretation of the child's communicative intent; (2) the shift of prespeech topic-comment organization to linguistic predication; (3) joint reference as a precursor to deixis; and (4) children's strategies in accomplishing a task with another. Two lines of research have pursued these linkages: The first perspective links "functionally equivalent forms" prior to and after the onset of speech (for example, gesturally making a request in prespeech is linked to asking a question in verbal communication); the second perspective looks for the constituent skills necessary for linguistic mastery (for example, it is suggested that action schemas derived earlier aid the child in making linguistic distinctions such as agent or object).

Bruner (1975b, p. 250) argues that support for continuity rests on demonstrating that a specific precursor is "an instrumental prerequisite to a more involved utterance" and recognition of the social, meaningful nature of speech. It is this latter sense of continuity with which Bruner is most concerned; if the child knows many communicative conventions, such as reciprocity of roles, then he or she is better equipped to learn language.

Bruner argues that formats frame an interaction so that children discover how to use language to accomplish certain goals. Formats limit the range of interpretation and action so that the child can signal his or her steps in accomplishing a specific goal. Such reciprocal fine-tuning, suggests Bruner (1983, p. 40), requires an interplay between pragmatic and linguistic factors; he believes it "impossible to learn a *language in use* without knowing in advance or learning concurrently the perspectival complexities involved in using a set of symbols both to represent and to communicate." These "perspectival complexities" seem to reflect the social cognitive knowledge of self, others, and relations with others that was discussed earlier (Damon, 1981).

Cognitive precursors to communicative skills have also been researched widely. For example, the development of communicative intentionality has been linked to the achievement of Stage 5 in sensorimotor development (Bates, 1976; Frye, 1981; Sugarman, 1977). Bates et al. (1981) categorize cognitive researchers into two groups: those advocating structural approaches and those advocating process approaches. Structural approaches attempt to establish a semantic basis for grammatical rules while process approaches relate language development to changes in general information-processing procedures (Bates et al., 1981, p. 13).

Bates (1979, pp. 15-36) claims that homologous relationships exist between language and proto-dialogues (postural synchrony, patterns of turn taking, and so on) because of their shared cognitive base. She argues that "language can be viewed as a new machine created out of various cognitive and social components that evolved initially in the service of completely different functions"; this developed through changes in cognitive-social growth patterns (that is, heterochrony). These capacities, in turn, reached new quantitative levels that allowed for "qualitatively new interactions" (Bates, 1979, p. 31). In a correlational study by Bates, Benigni, Bretherton, Camaioni, and Volterra (1979) of 25 American and Italian children, they found that symbolic play, imitation, tool use, and combinatorial play appeared to have a homologous relationship with language. Also, the same cognitive capacities that related to language development were also related to some preverbal communicative behaviors that correlate with language:

> In short, we have located a package of related structures, capacities that are implicated in the development of linguistic and nonlinguistic symbols. There is also supporting evidence from abnormal language developement, and from comparisons across species, suggesting that the same capacities that are *present* when language emerges are *absent* when language fails to emerge. (Bates, Benigni, Bretherton, Camaioni, & Volterra, 1979, p. 316)

In a follow-up study of the same infants, Bates, Bretherton, Carlson, Carpen, and Rossen (1979, p. 317) found that cognitive developments at 9 months do not appear to "correlate with symbol use and communication beyond 13 months." However, communicative development still correlates with symbol use at 18 months.

Thus far the arguments showing continuity (or alleged continuity) between preverbal communication and language development have been analyzed. A serious methodological issue can be raised because, as Bates (1979) points out, homologies may be difficult to distinguish from analogies (that is, structural similarities may be difficult to distinguish from surface similarities). Correlations, of course, suggest that two items covary but do not reveal the specific relationships between those items. The question of continuity versus discontinuity, for many reasons, is thus a difficult one to address.

Sugarman (1983) states that communication, as it moves from preverbal to linguistic, is both continuous and discontinuous; the communication is the continuity, but the means are different (discontinuous). She argues that we must look for the points of continuity and discontinuity in communication and specify the units of analysis (dimensions) being assessed. If one focuses on language as a communicative system, one sees more continuity than if one focuses on language as a formal, symbolic rule system.

Although preverbal communicative experiences may be helpful, Sugarman (1983, p. 137) concludes that even evidence across different contexts "does not conclusively demonstrate that children *must* engage in preverbal communication before they talk."

Snow and Gilbreath (1983, p.284) group the social interaction researchers into two camps: One group argues that the social interactive process "minimizes the demands on the child at each point, such that no major transition is ever necessary"; the other camp argues that the social environment provides the structure that makes the transition possible. Snow and Gilbreath cite research on naming and on the transition from one-word to two-word utterances showing that these developmental changes now appear to occur in more gradual increments. However, Snow and Gilbreath (1983, p. 243) point out that both cognitive and social interaction play roles in communicative development: "Any claim about the desirable social environment is equally a claim about cognitive mechanisms."

Cognitive hypotheses are relevant because the transition is a cognitive transition. Also, if certain types of social information are most beneficial, then so are the cognitive mechanisms needed to process that information. They go on to discuss several claims about the role of social interaction in communicative development and analyze the underlying cognitive assumptions of these claims. For example, the claim that language acquisition is aided when adults provide semantically meaningful responses to the child's utterances presumes cognitive processes that search for sound-meaning pairs and for more information about a topic, and that focus only slowly on a new topic.

The analysis of social interaction has also documented the divergent interactive processes found across cultures. Different social variables appear to be relevant in some cultures, but not in others (Brazelton, 1977;

LeVine, 1977; Schieffelin & Ochs, 1983). Bates (1979) reaches a somewhat similar conclusion when she argues that social interaction may affect language development by providing some minimal "threshold level" that can be achieved in a number of different ways.

Shatz (1983) suggests that the continuity-discontinuity issue has outlived its usefulness; when the transition from preverbal to linguistic communication is viewed from a broad model of communicative development, it loses its special significance:

> Communicative skill is situated at the interface between linguistic, cognitive, and social abilities. As such, its development depends on growth in each of those areas, although growth in any one may be relatively independent of factors in the other. Even within these large domains there are systems of knowledge which affect communicative growth and that may develop at different rates. One thing we have learned from recent research is that communicative and grammatical developments do not proceed in lock step. . . . The evidence seems to point to sets of simultaneously developing subsystems (or variables), each with its own sets of constraints, precedence conditions, and mechanisms of change. Some of these conditions and mechanisms are undoubtedly shared, but each subsystem is by definition at least partially different. (Shatz, 1983, p.52)

Thus far, the discussion of continuity and discontinuity has pointed to the following tentative conclusions. First, some achievements that were viewed in the past as representing new developments (that is transitions) now appear to be the result of more gradual shifts in development. Second, while there generally appears to be a sharp distinction between cognitive and social interactive explanations of development, theorists are now beginning to acknowledge their interactive effects (Bates, 1979; Bruner, 1983; Nelson, 1977; Snow & Gilbreath, 1983). Third, variables must be more carefully specified and linked to specific outcomes. In particular, it appears that there are multiple pathways to achieving communicative competence, and that cultural and individual differences play a role in communicative development. One final consideration of the continuity/discontinuity issue needs to be noted; if language is innate to some degree, how does this influence the continuity-discontinuity issue and, more broadly, does this rule out the possibility of important social interaction influences on language development?

Most theorists have argued that the innateness hypothesis is a separate issue (Bates, 1979; Bruner, 1975b; Snow, 1979; Sugarman, 1983); Chomsky (1965) himself did not rule out the possibility of considerable environmental "fine-tuning" for communicative development. As Sugarman (1983, p. 135) states, "that we are somehow constrained to develop the language that we do does not say how we do it." Bruner (1975, p. 256) makes a similar point:

Even if it were literally true (as claimed by Chomsky), *that the child mastering a particular language initially possesses a tacit knowledge of an alleged universal deep structure of language, we would still have to know how he managed to recognize these universal deep rules as they manifest themselves in the surface structure of a particular language.* Even an innate "language acquisition device" would require a programme to guide such recognition and it would fall to the *psychologist* to discover the nature of the programme by investigating the alleged recognition process (Chomsky, 1965, p. 27). . . . At the most general level, we may say that to master a language a child must acquire a complex set of broadly transferable or generative skills—perceptual, motor, conceptual, social, and linguistic—which when appropriately coordinated yield linguistic performances.

Finally, Brown (1973) points out that the innateness position depends, to a large extent, on how one views language—that is, on what one considers the nature of language to be. Depending on the features one selects to characterize language, one may find aspects of continuity (that is, similarities) or discontinuity (unique differences) between human communication, including language, and animal communication. As our knowledge of human and animal communication grows, our thinking about the discontinuities and continuities between preverbal communication and language will change with respect to the research questions we ask, and with respect to the evidence required to support different perspectives. It seems to me to be most helpful not to set aside the innateness hypothesis, but to reframe the issue in terms of continuities and discontinuities across a range of human communicative behaviors, including that of handicapped individuals such as the deaf and blind, and in terms of how human communicative behaviors compare with communicative behaviors of primates.

Communication and Other Cognitive Abilities

This last section discusses the cognitive abilities needed for communication. In addition, the role of communication in acquiring cognitive skills is discussed.

Cognitive Abilities Underlying Communication

In *Language and Context,* Bates (1976) states that children's earliest signals of communicative intentionality have been correlated with Stage 5 of sensorimotor intelligence. An underlying symbolic capacity, necessary for both language and symbolic play, is correlated with Stage 6 of sensorimotor intelligence. Bates (1979, p. 13) suggests that structural relations between nonlinguistic and linguistic capacities exist at an underlying cognitive level that enables certain behaviors to emerge. Nicolich (1975) suggests that structural parallels between the domains of gestural and vocal communication exist through the age of two. We have also seen that aspects of social cognitive knowledge, such as the distinction between self and others, both contribute to and derive from social interaction with others (Chandler, 1977; Rees, 1978; Wolf, 1981). Clearly, in early communicative development, communication skills require certain cognitive prerequisites.

At later stages, communicative skills seem dependent upon cognitive complexity, including increasingly complex information-processing procedures and increasingly differentiated cognitive constructs (Bates, 1976; O'Keefe & Sypher, 1981). For example, research on referential communication, argument strategies, and metacommunicative monitoring documents the complex relationships between cognitive capacities and communication.

Communication's Impact upon Cognition

On the other hand, as we have seen, cognition seems equally dependent upon communication. Piaget (1926) and Nelson (1977) have pointed out the role communication plays in cognitive development, especially in exposing the child to new viewpoints and thus giving the child opportunities for cognitive growth. Luria (1959), Steiner (1969), and Mead (1934) acknowledge the role of social interaction in forming concepts of the self and others, and its impact on further cognitive developments. Bernstein's (1970, 1973) theory argues that communication codes differentially influence a child's learning, and thus his or her cognitive growth.

Recent research has begun to explore the impact of communication on different cognitive tasks. Perret-Clermont and Schubauer-Leoni (1981) suggest that learners learn more when they are participants in an interactive communicative process. A series of studies by Doise and his coworkers found that some children acquired the concept of conservation in interaction with other peers, especially when there was a cognitive conflict between partners (that is, one partner was a conserver and the other a nonconserver, and thus their answers to the problem being posed differed; as cited in Perret-Clermont & Schubauer-Leoni, 1981, p. 220). Two studies by Perret-Clermont and Schubauer-Leoni (1981) found that sociocognitive conflicts between children in a cooperative task enabled cognitive restructuring to occur. In general, communication serves to gain new information and knowledge, which the child uses to restructure his or her cognitive world. In Piagetian terms, communication may be viewed as assimilation and cognition as accommodation. With respect to language acquisition, Shatz (1982) has suggested that social interaction patterns, when learned, "free up" cognitive processing for the acquisition of syntax. So in general, cognition, in terms of both knowledge of and processing of information, is the fundamental frame in which communication occurs. Communication, in turn, is the process by which humans acquire new knowledge, and thus are able to restructure cognition. As the complexity of both communication and cognition increases, so does the complexity of their interaction. Examining the ways in which they interact will continue to provide a fascinating research challenge.

CONCLUDING REMARKS

Communicative development, as Shatz (1983, p. 52) points out, is "situated at the interface between linguistic, cognitive and social abilities." In the discussion of communicative development presented here, I have focused primarily on social and cognitive abilities: to a lesser degree, the relationship of social and cognitive abilities to language acquisition has been discussed. Thus the emphasis has been on communication—not language—and I believe that the study of pragmatics should be viewed as the study of communication. It has also been assumed here that cognition is the context in which communication occurs, and that communication is the context in which language is acquired. These contextual frames, of course, influence the communicative process, regardless of whether or not any innate predisposition for language exists. This review has explored the acquisition of communication and has examined the interrelationships among cognition, social cognition, and language in this acquisition.

Given the interdisciplinary and complex nature of research on communicative development, the task of synthesizing this research is difficult, but some general trends seem to be emerging. Although researchers will emphasize those theoretical aspects most closely aligned with their own disciplines, nevertheless the following trends seem to be developing across varying disciplines.

(1) The child is viewed as an active partner in conversational dialogues with an adult caretaker. Children actively initiate and modify dialogue patterns; increasing attention is now focused on those influences that flow from child to caretaker as well as on those influences that flow from caretaker to child.

(2) The use of global constructs such as egocentrism and role taking is becoming less frequent. Researchers are attempting to specify variables with greater precision, to analyze skills across different domains of knowledge, to link specific variables to particular outcomes, and to integrate variables across different domains. In order to accomplish these goals, Bates et al., (1981), Robinson (1981a), and others suggest more sophisticated data reduction techniques, use of nonnormal populations (such as the blind and deaf) for comparative analysis, and use of a variety of data-gathering strategies, from experimental to observational settings.

(3) There is increasing concern for describing the types and strengths of interrelationships between variables. What are the implications of a variable being a precursor or prerequisite for a later skill? Sugarman (1983) and Shatz (1983) have particularly useful discussions of this issue.

(4) There is growing attention directed to the *why* of communication— that is, there is concern for motivation and for affect, and their influence upon communication development. The research of Trevarthen and Dore is especially directed at possible motivational forces and crises that govern the infant's acquisition of communication. Researchers studying the caretaker-child relationship are investigating the quality of that relationship, especially affect, and its impact on emerging communicative skills. Sugarman (1983) and Snow and Gilbreath (1983) suggest that maternal responsiveness may be a critical variable in developing communication skills.

(5) Information-processing models are now being applied to explain cognitive mechanisms operative in language and communication. Shatz (1978, 1982) explores connections among cognitive processing, communication, and language from an information-processing model. She suggests that social interaction processes may "free up" cognitive processing so that other skills, like syntax, may be acquired. Nelson (1981) uses script analysis as a way of explaining how interactive processes may be acquired, and one could also argue that scripts "free up" cognitive processes for other tasks as well.

(6) There is growing acknowledgment that communication is a multi-faceted process. As such, varied aspects of communication may be acquired by different mechanisms, at different times, and in different domains. Not only does the process of acquisition vary, but also the interrelationships among communicative components may vary as a function of age, task, and social relationships.

(7) The relationship between communication and a variety of other cognitive skills, such as sociocognitive knowledge of others, will be of continuing research interest. Here researchers will be exploring the linkages among communication, cognition, and language. Of special interest will be the study of these relationships as they are manifest in different cultures.

(8) Finally, more attention will be focused on the problem of salience or relevance. The importance of a task to an individual may determine what degree of effort or attention is given to the task; saliency may thus determine, in part, the cognitive, communicative, or linguistic strategies selected in accomplishing a particular goal.

Implicit in the perspective developed throughout this review is the idea that verbal communication is a complex system dependent upon interactions among cognitive, social, and linguistic factors. To understand fully the dynamics of human communication, we need to look at how individuals interact with one another in a variety of situations. Different relationships among cognitive social and linguistic factors may occur as a function of the different participants, topics, and contexts. The role of verbal communication in social action must be explored, as well as the structures and processes of verbal communication itself. While considerable progress has been made in understanding the emergence of verbal communication, much remains to be done; unresolved problems and new insights will continue to present challenging research puzzles.

NOTES

1. The relationship between antecedent stages or variables and later stages is discussed more fully in the section on continuity and discontinuity in communication. For an excellent discussion of the problems with making causal claims, see Bates et al. (1981).

2. One of most glaring lacks in pragmatically oriented research has been the lack of research on the interaction between communicative skills and social knowledge underlying or supporting those skills. Our research and theory needs to deal with their complex interactions in everyday communicative encounters. Not only has the relationship between skill and knowledge been relatively ignored, but researchers also have largely ignored the interrelationships among communicative skills themselves (for example, possible relationships between referential communication skills and metacommunicative monitoring) or among aspects of social knowledge about communication (for example, the relationship between social setting and social relationships with others).

3. Research on social knowledge about communication, at this point, does not warrant statements concerning the interdependencies among various aspects of social knowledge. I suspect that one difficulty has been the controversy concerning distinctions between cognition and social cognition. Researchers in social cognition have devoted considerable time and effort to pointing out that people have unique capabilities for interaction, whereas objects do not, and thus social cognitive processes (that is, processes involving people's understanding of themselves, others, and their relationships) should be viewed as distinct from cognition (that is, knowledge and understanding of objects and events in the world). Until this debate is resolved, or set aside, the "status" of knowledge about communication is problematic (see, for example, Damon, 1981; Chandler, 1977).

4. Although Chomsky and the transformational grammarians exclude language use (that is, performance) from their considerations, the distinction between use and form has been blurred in the work of generative semanticists. The inclusion of increasingly broad-based perspectives on semantics—presuppositions, real-world knowledge, and the like—in grammars has caused many to claim that the old dichotomy between form and function is no longer viable (Atkinson, 1981; Bates et al., 1981; Pinker, 1979).

REFERENCES

Ackerman, B. P. (1978). Children's understanding of speech acts in unconventional directive frames. *Child Development, 49,* 311-318.

Alvy, K. (1976). Relation of age to children's egocentric and cooperative communication. *Journal of Genetic Psychology, 12,* 24-32.

Applegate, J., & Delia, J. (1980). Person-centered speech, psychological development, and the contexts of language usage. In R. St. Clair & H. Giles (Eds.), *The social and psychological contexts of language.* Hillsdale, NJ: Lawrence Erlbaum.

Argyle, M. (1975). *Bodily communication.* London: Methuen.

Argyle, M., Furnham, A., & Graham, J. (1981). *Social situations.* Cambridge: Cambridge University Press.

Asher, S. (1976). Children's ability to appraise their own and another person's communication performance. *Developmental Psychology, 12,* 24-32.

Asher, S. (1979). Referential communication. In G. Whitehurst & B. Zimmerman (Eds.), *The functions of language and cognition.* New York: Academic.

Asher, S., & Oden, S. (1976). Children's failure to communicate: An assessment of comparison and egocentrism explanations. *Developmental Psychology, 12,* 132-139.

Asher, S., & Parke, R. (1975). Influence of sampling and comparison processes on the development of communication effectiveness. *Journal of Educational Psychology, 67,* 69-75.

Asher, S., & Wigfield, A. (1981). Training referential communication skills. In W. Dickson (Ed.), *Children's oral communication skills.* New York: Academic.

Atkinson, M. (1981). *Explanations in the study of child language development.* Cambridge: Cambridge University Press.

Bates, E. (1976). *Language and context: The acquisition of pragmatics.* New York: Academic.

Bates, E. (1979). *The emergence of symbols: Cognition and communication in infancy.* New York: Academic.

Bates, E., Benigni, L., Bretherton, I., Camaioni, L., & Volterra, V. (1979). Cognition and communication from nine to thirteen months: Correlational findings. In E. Bates, *The emergence of symbols: Cognition and communication in infancy.* New York: Academic.

Bates, E., Bretherton, I., Beeghly-Smith, M., & McNew, S. (1981). Social bases of language development: A reassessment. In H. Reese & L. Lipsett (Eds.), *Advances in child development and behavior* (Vol. 16). New York: Academic.

Bates, E., Bretherton, I., Carlson, V., Carpen, K., & Rosser, M. (1979). Next steps: A follow-up study and some pilot research. In E. Bates, *The emergence of symbols: Cognition and communication in infancy.* New York: Academic.

Bateson, G. (1972). *Steps to an ecology of mind.* New York: Ballantine.

Bateson, G. (1976). A theory of play and fantasy. In J. Bruner, A. Jolly, & K. Sylva (Eds.), *Play: Its role in evolution and development.* London: Penguin.

Bateson, M. C. (1975). Mother-infant exchanges: The epigenesis of conversation interaction. *Annals of the New York Academy of Science, 263,* 101-113.

Bearison, D., & Levey, L. (1977). Children's comprehension of referential communication: Decoding ambiguous messages. *Child Development, 48,* 716-721.

Beaudichon, J. (1981). Problem solving communication and complex information transmission in groups. In W. Dickson (Ed.), *Children's oral communication skills.* New York: Academic.

Bellinger, D. (1979). Changes in the explicitness of mothers' directives as children age. *Journal of Child Language, 6,* 443-458.

Belsky, J., Goode, M., & Most, R. (1981). Maternal stimulation and infant exploratory competence: Cross-sectional, correlational and experimental analyses. *Child Development, 52.*

Benoit, P. (1981). *The use of argument by preschool children: The emergent production of rules for winning arguments.* Unpublished manuscript.

Berko-Gleason, J., & Weintraub, S. (1976). The acquisition of routines in child language. *Language in Society, 5,* 129-136.

Berko-Gleason, J., & Weintraub, S. (1978). Input language and the acquisition of communicative competence. In K. Nelson (Ed.), *Children's language* (Vol. 1). New York: Gardner.

Bernstein, B. (1970). Language and socialization with some reference to educability. In F. Williams (Ed.), *Language and poverty.* Chicago: Markham.

Bernstein, B. (1972). *Class, codes and control* (Vol. 2). London: Routledge & Kegan Paul.

Bernstein, B. (1973). A brief account of the theory of codes. In The Open University, *Educational studies: Language and learning* (Block 3). London: The Open University.

Bigner, J. (1974). A Wernerian developmental analysis of children's descriptions of siblings. *Child Development, 45,* 317-323.

Bloom, L., Rocissano, L., & Hood, L. (1976). Adult-child discourse: Developmental interaction between information processing and linguistic interaction. *Cognitive Psychology, 8,* 521-552.

Blount, B. (1977). Prosodic, paralinguistic and interactional features in parent-child speech, English and Spanish. *Journal of Child Language, 4,* 67-87.

Bohannon, N., & Marquis, A. (1977). Children's control of adult speech. *Child Development, 48,* 1002.

Bransford, J., & McCarrell, N. (1974). A sketch of a cognitive approach to comprehension: Some thoughts about understanding what it means to comprehend. In W. Weimer & D. Palermo (Eds.), Cognition and the symbolic process. New York: John Wiley.

Brazelton, T. (1977). Implications of infant development among the Maya Indians of Mexico. In P. Leiderman, S. Tulkin, & A. Rosenfeld (Eds.), Culture and infancy: Variations in the human experience. New York: Academic.

Brazelton, T., Koslowski, B., & Main, M. (1974). The origins of reciprocity: The early mother-child interaction. In M. Lewis & L. Rosenblum (Eds.), The infant's effects on the caregiver. New York: John Wiley.

Bretherton, I., & Bates, E. (1979). The emergence of intentional communication. New Directions for Child Development, 4, 81-100.

Bretherton, I., Bates, E., Benigni, L., Camaioni, L., & Volterra, V. (1979). Relationships between cognition, communication and quality of attachment. In E. Bates, The emergence of symbols: Cognition and communication in infancy. New York: Academic.

Bronfenbrenner, U. (1979). The ecology of human development: Experiments by nature and design. Cambridge, MA: Harvard University Press.

Brown, R. (1973). A first language: The early stages. Cambridge, MA: Harvard University Press.

Brown, R. (1976). New paradigm of reference. Cognition, 4, 125-153.

Bruner, J. (1975a). The ontogenesis of speech-acts. Journal of Child Language, 2, 1-19.

Bruner, J. (1975b). From communication to language: A psychological perspective. Cognition, 3, 255-287.

Bruner, J. (1977). Early social interaction and language acquisition. In H. Schaffer (Ed.), Studies in mother-infant interaction. London: Academic.

Bruner, J. (1983). The acquisition of pragmatic commitments. In R. M. Golinkoff (Ed.), The transition from prelinguistic to linguistic communication. Hillsdale, NJ: Lawrence Erlbaum.

Carlson-Luden, V. (1979). Causal understanding in the 10-month-old. Unpublished doctoral dissertation, University of Colorado.

Carter, A. (1975). The transformation of sensori-motor morphemes into words: A case study of the development of more and mine. Journal of Child Language, 2, 233-250.

Carter, A. (1978a). The development of systematic vocalizations prior to words: A case study. In N. Waterson & C. Snow (Eds.), The development of children. Chichester, England: John Wiley.

Carter, A. (1978b). From sensori-motor vocalizations to words: A case study of the evolution of attention-directing communication in the second year. In A. Lock (Ed.), Action, gesture and symbol. New York: Academic.

Chandler, M. (1977). Social cognition: A selective review of current research. In W. Overton (Ed.), Knowledge and development. New York: Plenum.

Charney, R. (1979). The comprehension of "here" and "there." Journal of Child Language, 6, 69-80.

Chomsky, N. (1965). Aspects of a theory of syntax. Cambridge: MIT Press.

Cicourel, A. (1972). Basic and normative rules in the negotiation of status and role. In D. Sudnow (Ed.), Studies in social interaction. New York: Free Press.

Clark, H., & Clark, E. (1977). Psychology and language. New York: Harcourt Brace Jovanovich.

Clark, R., & Delia, J. (1976). The development of functional persuasive skills in childhood and early adolescence. Child Development, 47, 1008-1014.

Clark, R., & Delia, J. (1977). Cognitive complexity, social perspective-taking, and functional persuasive skills in second- to ninth-grade children. Human Communication Research, 3, 128-134.

Cole, M., Hood, L., & McDermott, R. (1978). Ecological niche picking: Ecological invalidity as an axiom of experimental cognitive psychology. Unpublished manuscript, Rockefeller University, Institute for Comparative Human Development.

Cook-Gumperz, J. (1973). Social control and socialization. London: Routledge & Kegan Paul.

Cook-Gumperz, J. (1975). The child as a practical reasoner. In M. Sanches & B. Blount (Eds.), Sociocultural dimensions of language. New York: Academic.

Cook-Gumperz, J. (1977). Sociocultural knowing in conversational inference. In M. Saville-Troike (Ed.), *GURT*. Georgetown University Press.

Cook-Gumperz, J. (1981). Persuasive talk: The social organization of children's talk. In J. Green & C. Wallat (Eds.), *Ethnography and language in educational settings*. Norwood, NJ: Ablex.

Cook-Gumperz, J., & Cosaro, W. (1976). Social-ecological constraints on children's communicative strategies. In J. Cook-Gumperz & J. Gumperz (Eds.), *Papers on language and context*. Berkeley: University of California, Language Behavior Research Laboratory.

Cook-Gumperz, J., & Gumperz, J. (1976). Context in children's speech. In J. Cook-Gumperz & J. Gumperz (Eds.), *Papers on language and context*. Berkeley: University of California, Language Behavior Research Laboratory.

Cosaro, W. (1977). The clarification request as a feature of adult interactive styles with young children. *Language in Society, 6*, 183-208.

Cosgrove, J., & Patterson, C. (1977). Plans and development of listener skills. *Developmental Psychology, 13*, 557-564.

Cowan, P. (1967). *The link between cognitive structure and social structure in two-child verbal interaction*. Paper presented at the meeting of the Society for Research in Child Development, Santa Monica.

Cromer, R. (1974). The development of language and cognition: The cognition hypothesis. In B. Foss (Ed.), *New perspectives in child development*. Harmondsworth: Penguin.

Cross, T. (1978). Motherese: Its association with rate of syntactic acquisition in young children. In N. Waterson & C. Snow (Eds.), *The development of communication*. New York: John Wiley.

Damon, W. (1977). *The social world of the child*. San Francisco: Jossey-Bass.

Damon, W. (1981). Exploring children's social cognition on two fronts. In J. Flavell & L. Ross (Eds.), *Social cognitive development*. Cambridge: Cambridge University Press.

Delia, J., & Clark, R. (1977). Cognitive complexity, social perception, and the development of listener-adapted communication in six-, eight-, ten-, and twelve-year-old boys. *Communication Monographs, 44*, 326-345.

Delia, J., Kline, S., & Burleson, B. (1979). The development of persuasive communication strategies in kindergartners through twelfth-graders. *Communication Monographs, 46*, 241-256.

Delia, J., & O'Keefe, B. (1979). Constructivism: The development of communication in children. In E. Wartella (Ed.), *Children communicating*. Beverly Hills, CA: Sage.

deVilliers, P., & deVilliers, J. (1979). *Early language*. Cambridge, MA: Harvard University Press.

Dickson, W. P. (1981). Referential communication activities in research and in the curriculum: A metaanalysis. In W. Dickson (Ed.), *Children's oral communication skills*. New York: Academic.

Doise, W., Mugny, G., & Perret-Clermont, A. N. (1975). Social interaction and the development of cognitive operations. *European Journal of Social Psychology, 5*, 365-383.

Donaldson, M. (1978). *Children's minds*. Glasgow: Fontana.

Dore, J. (1974). A pragmatic description of early language development. *Journal of Psycholinguistic Research, 3*, 343-350.

Dore, J. (1975). Holophrases, speech acts and language universals. *Journal of Child Language, 2*, 21-39.

Dore, J. (1977). Children's illocutionary acts. In R. Freedle (Ed.), *Discourse production and comprehension*. Hillsdale, NJ: Lawrence Erlbaum.

Dore, J. (1978). Variation in preschool children's conversational performances. In K. Nelson (Ed.), *Children's language* (Vol. 1). New York: Gardner.

Dore, J. (1983). Feeling, form and intention in the baby's transition to language. In R. Golinkoff (Ed.), *The transition from prelinguistic to linguistic communication*. Hillsdale, NJ: Lawrence Erlbaum.

Dore, J., Gearhart, M., & Newman, D. (1978). The structure of nursery school conversation. In K. Nelson (Ed.), *Children's language* (Vol. 1). New York: Gardner.

Eisenberg, A., & Garvey, C. (1981). Children's use of verbal strategies in resolving conflicts. *Discourse Processes*.

Ellis, R., & Wells, C. G. (in preparation). *Enabling factors in adult-child discourse.*

Erickson, F. (1981). Timing and context in everyday discourse: Implications for the study of referential and social meaning. In W. Dickson (Ed.), *Children's oral communication skills.* New York: Academic.

Ervin-Tripp, S. (1970). Discourse agreement: How children answer questions. In J. Hayes (Ed.), *Cognition and the development of language.* New York: John Wiley.

Ervin-Tripp, S. (1976). Is Sybil there? The structure of some American English directives. *Language in Society, 5,* 25-66.

Ervin-Tripp, S. (1977). Wait for me, roller-skate. In S. Ervin-Tripp & C. Mitchell-Kernan (Eds.), *Child discourse.* New York: Academic.

Ervin-Tripp, S., & Miller, W. (1977). Early discourse: Some questions about questions. In M. Lewis & L. Rosenblum (Eds.), *Interaction, conversation and the development of language.* New York: John Wiley.

Flavell, J. (1973). The development of inferences about others. In T. Mischel (Ed.), *Understanding other persons.* Oxford: Blackwell.

Flavell, J. (1979). Metacognition and cognitive monitoring: A new area of psychological inquiry. *American Psychologist, 34,* 906-911.

Flavell, J. (1981a). Cognitive monitoring. In W. Dickson (Ed.), *Children's oral communication skills.* New York: Academic.

Flavell, J. (1981b). Monitoring social cognitive enterprises: Something else that may develop in the area of social cognition. In J. Flavell & L. Ross (Eds.), *Social cognitive development.* Cambridge: Cambridge University Press.

Flavell, J., Botkin, P., Fry, C., Wright, J., & Jarvis, P. (1968). *The development of role taking and communication skills in children.* New York: John Wiley.

Flavell, J., Speer, J., Green, F., & August, D. (1981). *The development of comprehension monitoring and knowledge about communication.* Monograph, Society for Research on Child Development.

Forbes, D., & Lubin, D. (1981a, April). *The development of applied strategies in children's social behavior.* Paper presented at the biennial meeting of the Society for Research in Child Development, Boston.

Forbes, D., & Lubin, D. (with Schmidt, M., & Van der Laan, P.). (1981b). *Verbal social reasoning and observed persuasion strategies in children's peer interactions.* Report from NSF (BNS-78-09119) and NIMH (1-ROI-MH34723).

Foucault, M. (1971). *L'ordre du discouis.* Paris: Gallimard.

Frye, D. (1981). Developmental changes in strategies of social interaction. In M. Lamb & L. Sherrod (Eds.), *Infant social cognition: Empirical and theoretical considerations.* Hillsdale, NJ: Lawrence Erlbaum.

Garvey, C. (1974). Some properties of social play. *Merrill-Palmer Quarterly, 20.*

Garvey, C. (1975). Requests and responses in children's speech. *Journal of Child Language, 2,* 41-60.

Garvey, C. (1977). Play with language and speech. In S. Ervin-Tripp & E. Mitchell-Kernan (Eds.), *Child discourse.* New York: Academic.

Garvey, C., & Hogan, R. (1973). Social speech and social interaction: Egocentrism revisited. *Child Development, 44,* 562-568.

Gelman, R., & Shatz, M. (1977). Appropriate speech adjustments: The operation of conversational constraints on talk to two-year-olds. In M. Lewis & L. Rosenblum (Eds.), *Interaction, conversation and the development of language.* New York: John Wiley.

Gelman, R., & Spelke, E. (1981). The development of thoughts about animate and inanimate objects: Implications for research on social cognition. In J. Flavell & L. Ross (Eds.), *Social cognitive development.* Cambridge: Cambridge University Press.

Gleitman, L., Gleitman, H., & Shipley, E. (1972). The emergence of the child as grammarian. *Cognition, 1,* 137-164.

Glick, J. (1978). Cognition and social cognition: An introduction. In J. Glick & K. A. Clarke-Stewart (Eds.), *The development of social understanding.* New York: Gardner.

Glucksberg, S., Krauss, R., & Higgins, E. T. (1975). The development of referential communication skills. In F. Horowitz, E. Hetherington, S. Scarr-Salapatek, & G. Siegel (Eds.), *Review of child development research* (Vol. 4). Chicago: University of Chicago Press.

Glucksberg, S., Krauss, R., & Weisberg, R. (1966). Referential communication in nursery school children: Method and some preliminary findings. *Journal of Experimental Child Psychology, 3,* 333-342.

Goffman, E. (1974). *Frame analysis.* New York: Harper & Row.

Golinkoff, R. (Ed.). (1983). *The transition from prelinguistic to linguistic communication.* Hillsdale, NJ: Lawrence Erlbaum.

Gollin, E. (1958). Organizational characteristics of social judgement: A developmental investigation. *Journal of Personality, 26,* 139-154.

Goody, E. (1978). *Questions and politeness.* Cambridge: Cambridge University Press.

Gordon, D., & Lakoff, G. (1971, April). Conversational postulates. In *Proceedings of the 7th Annual Meeting of the Chicago Linguistic Society.* Chicago: Univesity of Chicago Press.

Green, J., & Harker, J. (1982). Reading to children: A sociolinguistic-perspective. In J. Langer & M. T. Smith-Burke (Eds.), *Reader meets author: Bridging the gap.* Newark, DE: International Reading Association.

Greenfield, P., & Smith, J. (1976). *Communication and the beginnings of language: The development of semantic structures in one-word speech and beyond.* New York: Academic.

Greenspan, S., Barenboim, C., & Chandler, M. (1974). *Children's affective judgements in response to videotaped stories.* Paper presented at the southeastern regional meeting of the Society for Research in Child Development, Chapel Hill.

Grice, H. (1975). Logic and conversation. In P. Cole & J. Morgan (Eds.), *Syntax and semantics: Vol. 3. Speech acts.* New York: Academic.

Grimm, H. (1975). *Analysis of short-term dialogues in 5-7-year-olds: Encoding of intentions and modifications of speech acts as a function of negative feedback loops.* Paper presented at the Third International Child Language Symposium, London.

Gumperz, J., & Herasimchuk, E. (1973). Conversational analysis of social meaning. In R. Shuy (Ed.), *Sociolinguistics: Current trends and prospects.* Georgetown: Georgetown University Press.

Halliday, M.A.K. (1975). *Learning how to mean: Explorations in the functions of language.* London: Edward Arnold.

Halliday, M.A.K. (1978). Meaning and the construction of reality in early childhood. In H. Pick & E. Saltzman (Eds.), *Modes of perceiving and processing information.* Hillsdale, NJ: Lawrence Erlbaum.

Halliday, M.A.K. (1979). Development of texture in child language. In T. Myers (Ed.), *The development of conversation and discourse.* Edinburgh University Press.

Halliday, M.A.K., & Hasan, R. (1976). *Cohesion in English.* London: Longman.

Harding, C. (1983). Setting the stage for language acquisition: Communication development in the first year. In R. Golinkoff (Ed.), *The transition from prelinguistic to linguistic communication.* Hillsdale, NJ: Lawrence Erlbaum.

Harding, G., & Golinkoff, R. (1979). The origins of intentional vocalizations in prelinguistic infants. *Child Development, 50,* 33-40.

Harkness, S. (1977). Aspects of social environment and first language acquisition in rural Africa. In C. Snow & C. Ferguson (Eds.), *Talking to children.* Cambridge: Cambridge University Press.

Hartmann, E., & Haavind, H. (1981). Mothers as teachers. In W. Robinson (Ed.), *Communication in development.* New York: Academic.

Haslett, B. (1983a). Communicative functions and strategies in children's conversations. *Human Communication Research, 9,* 114-129.

Haslett, B. (1983b). Children's strategies for maintaining cohesion in their written and oral stories. *Communication Education, 31,* 91-106.

Haslett, B. (1983c). Preschoolers' strategies for resolving conflict: A developmental study. *Quarterly Journal of Speech, 68,* 84-100.

Heber, M. (1981). Instruction versus conversation as opportunities for learning. In W. Robinson (Ed.), *Communication in development.* New York: Academic.

Hess, R., & Shipman, V. (1965). Early experience and the socialization of cognitive modes in children. *Child Development, 36,* 869-886.

Hess, R., & Shipman, V. (1967). Cognitive elements in maternal behavior. In J. Hill (Ed.),

Minnesota Symposium on Child Development (Vol. 1). Minneapolis: University of Minnesota Press.

Hess, R., & Shipman, V. (1968). Maternal influences upon early learning. In R. Hess & R. Bear (Eds.), *Early education*. Chicago: Aldine.

Hess, R., Shipman, V., Bear, R., & Brophy, J. (1968). *The cognitive environments of urban preschool children*. Chicago: University of Chicago Press.

Higgins, E. T. (1977). Communication development as related to channel, incentive and social class. *Genetic Psychology Monographs, 96,* 75-141.

Higgins, E. T. (1981). Role taking and social judgement: Alternative developmental perspectives and processes. In J. Flavell & L. Ross (Eds.), *Social cognitive development*. Cambridge: Cambridge University Press.

Higgins, E. T., Feldman, N. S., & Ruble, D. N. (in press). Accuracy and differentiation in social prediction: A developmental perspective. *Journal of Personality*.

Hoffman, M. L. (1981). Perspectives on the difference between understanding people and understanding things: The role of affect. In J. Flavell & L. Ross (Eds.), *Social cognitive development*. Cambridge: Cambridge University Press.

Hubley, P., & Trevarthen, C. (1979). Sharing a task in infancy. *New Directions for Child Development, 4,* 57-80.

Hymes, D. (1974). *Foundations in sociolinguistics: An ethnographic approach*. Philadelphia: University of Pennsylvania Press.

Ironsmith, M., & Whitehurst, G. (1978). The development of listener abilities in communication: How children deal with ambiguous information. *Child Development, 49,* 348-352.

Isbell, B., & McKee, L. (1980). Society's cradle: An anthropological perspective on the socialization of cognition. In J. Sant (Ed.), *Developmental psychology and society*. London: Macmillan.

Kaye, K., & Charney, R. (1981). Conversational asymmetry between mothers and children. *Journal of Child Language, 8,* 35-49.

Keenan, E. (1974). Conversational competence in children. *Journal of Child Language, 1,* 163-183.

Keenan, E., & Klein, E. (1975). Coherency in children's discourse. *Journal of Psycholinguistic Research, 4,* 365-380.

Keenan, E., & Schieffelin, B. (1976). Topic as a discourse notion: A study of topic in the conversations of children and adults. In C. Li (Ed.), *Subject and topic* (pp. 335-385). New York: Academic.

Kuhn, T. (1970). *The structure of scientific revolutions* (rev. ed.). Chicago: University of Chicago Press.

Langer, E. J. (1978). Rethinking the role of thought in social interaction. In J. H. Harvey, W. J. Ickes, & R. F. Kidd (Eds.), *New directions in attribution research* (Vol. 2). Hillsdale, NJ: Lawrence Erlbaum.

Leonard, L., Wilcox, J., Fulmer, K., & Davis, G. (1978). Understanding indirect requests: An investigation of children's comprehension of pragmatic meanings. *Journal of Speech and Hearing Disorders, 21,* 528-537.

LeVine, R. (1977). Child rearing as cultural adaptation. In P. Leiderman, S. Tulkin, & A. Rosenfeld (Eds.), *Culture and infancy: Variations in the human experience*. New York: Academic.

Lloyd, P., & Beveridge, M. (1981). *Information and meaning in child communication*. London: Academic.

Lloyd, P., & Pavlidis, G. (1978). Child language and eye movements: The relative effects of sentence and situation on comprehension. *Bulletin of the British Psychological Society, 31,* 70-71 (abstract).

Lubin, D., & Forbes, D. (1981, April). *Understanding sequential aspects of children's social behavior: Conceptual issues in the development of coding schemes*. Paper presented at the biennial meeting of the Society for Research in Child Development, Boston.

Luria, A. (1959). The directive function of speech in development and dissolution. *Word, 15,* 341-352.

MacMurray, J. (1961). *Persons in relation*. London: Faber.

MacWhinney, B., & Bates, E. (1978). Sentential devices for conveying givenness and newness: A cross-cultural development study. *Journal of Verbal Learning and Verbal Behavior, 17,* 539-558.

Maratsos, M. (1973). Nonegocentric communication abilities in preschool children. *Child Development, 44,* 697-701.

McNew, S. (in preparation). *Maternal gestures: An exploration of contingency.*

McShane, J. (1980). *Learning to talk.* Cambridge: Cambridge University Press.

Mead, G. (1934). *Mind, self and society.* Chicago: University of Chicago Press.

Menig-Peterson, C. (1975). The modification of communicative behavior in preschool-aged children as a function of the listener's perspective. *Child Development, 46,* 1015-1018.

Messer, D. (1983). The redundancy between adult speech and nonverbal interaction: A contribution to acquisition. In R. Golinkoff (Ed.), *The transition from prelinguistic to linguistic communication.* Hillsdale, NJ: Lawrence Erlbaum.

Miller, G., Galanter, E., & Pribram, K. (1960). *Plans and the structure of behavior.* New York: Holt, Rinehart & Winston.

Mishler, E. (1975). Studies in dialogue and discourse: II. Types of discourse initiated by and sustained through questioning. *Journal of Psycholinguistic Research, 4,* 99-121.

Mishler, E. (1976). Studies in dialogue and discourse: III. Utterance structure and utterance function in interrogative sequences. *Journal of Psycholinguistic Research, 5,* 279-305.

Mishler, E. (1979). Would you trade cookies for popcorn: Talk of trade among six-year-old children. In O. Garnica & M. L. King (Eds.), *Language, children and society.* New York: Pergamon.

Mitchell-Kernan, C., & Kernan, K. (1977). Pragmatics of directive choice among children. In S. Ervin-Tripp & C. Mitchell-Kernan (Eds.), *Child discourse.* New York: Academic.

Moerk, E. (1974). Changes in verbal child-mother interactions with increasing language skills of the child. *Journal of Psycholinguistic Research, 3,* 101-115.

Mueller, E. (1972). The maintenance of verbal exchanges between young children. *Child Development, 43,* 930-938.

Mueller, E., & Lucas, T. (1975). A developmental analysis of peer interaction among toddlers. In M. Lewis & L. A. Rosenblum (Eds.), *Friendship and peer relations.* New York: John Wiley.

Murray, L. (1980). *The sensitivities and expressive capacities of young infants in communication with their mothers.* Unpublished doctoral dissertation, Edinburgh University.

Nelson, K. (1976). Some attributes of adjectives used by young children. *Cognition, 4,* 13-30.

Nelson, K. (1977). Facilitating syntax acquisition. *Developmental Psychology, 13,* 101-107.

Nelson, K. (1978). Early speech in its communicative context. In F. Minific & L. Lloyd (Eds.), *Communicative and cognitive abilities: Early behavioral assessment.* Baltimore: University Park Press.

Nelson, K. (1981). Social cognition in a script framework. In J. Flavell & L. Ross (Eds.), *Social cognitive development.* Cambridge: Cambridge University Press.

Nelson, K., Carskaddon, G., & Bonvillian, J. (1973). Syntax acquisition: Impact of experimental variation in adult verbal interaction with the child. *Child Development, 44,* 497-504.

Nicolich, L. (1975). *A longitudinal study of representational play in relation to spontaneous imitation and development of multiword utterances: Final report.* (ERIC Document Reproduction Service No. PS007 854).

Ochs, E., & Schieffelin, B. (1979). *Developmental pragmatics.* New York: Academic.

O'Keefe, B., & Benoit, P. (in press). Children's argument. In R. Cox & C. Willard (Eds.), *Advances in argumentation theory.* Carbondale: Southern Illinois University Press.

O'Keefe, B., & Delia, J. (1979). Construct comprehensiveness and cognitive complexity as predictors of the number and strategic adaptation of arguments and appeals in a persuasive message. *Communication Monographs, 46,* 221-240.

O'Keefe, B., & Delia, J. (1981). *Impression formation processes and message production.* Paper presented at the convention of the International Communication Association.

O'Keefe, B., & Sypher, H. (1981). Cognitive complexity measures and the relationship of cognitive complexity to communication. *Human Communication Research, 8,* 72-92.

Olson, D., & Hilyard, A. (1981). Assent and compliance in children's language. In W. Dickson (Ed.), *Children's oral communication skills.* New York: Academic.

Patterson, C., Cosgrove, J., & O'Brien, R. (1980). Nonverbal indicants of comprehension and noncomprehension in children. *Developmental Psychology, 16,* 38-48.

Patterson, C., & Kister, M. (1981). Listener skills for referential communication. In W. Dickson (Ed.), *Children's oral communication skills.* New York: Academic.

Pentz, T. (1975). *Facilitation of language acquisition: The role of the mother.* Unpublished doctoral dissertation, Johns Hopkins University.

Perret-Clermont, A., & Schubauer-Leoni, M. (1981). Conflict and cooperation as opportunities for learning. In W. Robinson (Ed.), *Communication in development.* New York: Academic.

Piaget, J. (1926). *The language and thought of the child.* London: Routledge & Kegan Paul.

Piaget, J. (1952). *The origins of intelligence in children.* New York: Norton.

Piaget, J. (1970). Piaget's theory. In P. H. Mussen (Ed.), *Carmichael's manual of child psychology.* New York: John Wiley.

Pinker, S. (1979). Formal models of language learning. *Cognition, 1, 217-283.*

Read, B., & Cherry, L. (1978). Preschool children's production of directive forms. *Discourse Processes, 1,* 233-245.

Rees, N. (1978). Pragmatics of language. In R. Schieffelbusch et al. (Eds.), *The bases of language.* Baltimore: University Park Press.

Robinson, E. J. (1981). Conversational tactics and the advancement of the child's understanding about referential communication. In W. P. Robinson (Ed.), *Communication in development.* New York: Academic.

Robinson, E. J., & Robinson, W. P. (1976a). Development changes in the child's explanation of communication failure. *Australian Journal of Psychology, 28,* 155-165.

Robinson, E. J., & Robinson, W. P. (1976b). The young child's understanding of communication. *Development Psychology, 12,* 328-333.

Robinson, E. J., & Robinson, W. P. (1977a). The child's understanding of life-like communication failures. *Australian Journal of Psychology, 729,* 137-142.

Robinson, E. J., & Robinson, W. P. (1977b). Development in the understanding of causes of success and failures in verbal communication. *Cognition, 5,* 363-378.

Robinson, E. J., & Robinson, W. P. (1978a). Explanations of communication failure and ability to give bad messages. *British Journal of Social and Clinical Psychology, 17,* 219-225.

Robinson, E. J., & Robinson, W. P. (1978b). Development of understanding about communication: Message inadequacy and its role in causing communication failure. *Genetic Psychological Monographs, 98,* 233-279.

Robinson, E. J., & Robinson, W. P. (1978c). The roles of egocentrism and weakness in comparing in children's explanations of communication failures. *Journal of Experimental Child Psychology, 26,* 147-160.

Robinson, W. P. (1981a). Mothers' answers to children's questions. In W. P. Robinson (Ed.), *Communication in development.* New York: Academic.

Robinson, W. P. (1981b). Some problems for theory, methodology, and methods for the 1980s. In W. P. Robinson (Ed.), *Communication in development.* New York: Academic.

Robinson, W. P., & Arnold, J. (1977). The question-answer exchange between mothers and young children. *European Journal of Social Psychology, 7,* 151-164.

Robinson, W. P., & Rackstraw, S. J. (1978). Social class differences in posing questions for answers. *Sociology, 12,* 265-280.

Rosenberg, S., & Cohen, B. (1966). Referential processes of speakers and listeners. *Psychological Review, 73,* 208-331.

Ross, L. (1981). The "intuitive scientist" formulation and its developmental implications. In J. Flavell & L. Ross (Eds.), *Social cognitive development.* Cambridge: Cambridge University Press.

Ryan, J. (1974). Early language development. In M. P. M. Richards (ed.), *The integration of the child into a social world.* Cambridge: Cambridge University Press.

Sachs, J. (1977). The adaptive significance of linguistic input to prelinguistic infants. In C. Snow & C. Ferguson (Eds.), *Talking to children.* Cambridge: Cambridge University Press.

Sacks, H., Schegloff, E. A., & Jefferson, G. (1974). A simplest systematics for the organization of turn taking for conversation. *Language, 50,* 696-735.

Sadock, J. (1974). *Toward a linguistic theory of speech acts.* New York: Academic.

Scarlett, H., Press, A., & Crockett, W. (1971). Children's descriptions of peers: A Wernerian developmental analysis. *Child Development, 42,* 439-453.

Schaffer, H. R. (1979). Acquiring the concept of dialogue. In M. Bornstein & W. Kessen (Eds.), *Psychological development from infancy: Image to intention.* Hillsdale, NJ: Lawrence Erlbaum.

Schaffer, H. R., Collis, G. M., & Parsons, G. (1977). Vocal exchange and visual regard in verbal and preverbal children. In H. Schaffer (Ed.), *Studies in mother-infant interaction.* London: Academic.

Schank, R., & Abelson, R. (1977). *Scripts, plans, goals and understanding.* Hillsdale, NJ: Lawrence Erlbaum.

Schieffelin, B. (1981). A sociolinguistic analysis of a relationship. *Discourse Processes, 4,* 189-196.

Schieffelin, B., & Ochs, E. (1983). A cultural perspective on the transition from prelinguistic to linguistic communication. In R. Golinkoff (Ed.), *The transition from prelinguistic to linguistic communication.* Hillsdale, NJ: Lawrence Erlbaum.

Schultz, J. (1977). *It's not whether you win or lose, it's how you play the game.* Unpublished manuscript, American Educational Research Association.

Searle, J. R. (1969). *Speech acts.* Cambridge: Cambridge University Press.

Searle, J. R. (1975a). Indirect speech acts. In P. Cole & J. Morgan (Eds.), *Syntax and semantics: Vol. 3. Speech acts.* New York: Seminar.

Searle, J. R. (1975b). Speech acts and recent linguistics. In D. Aaronson & R. Rieber (Eds.), *Developmental psycholinguistics and communication disorders.* New York: New York Academy of Sciences.

Selman, R. (1971). Taking another's perspective: Role taking development in early childhood. *Child Development, 42,* 1721-1734.

Shantz, C. (1981). The role of role taking in children's referential communication. In W. Dickson (Ed.), *Children's oral communication skills.* New York: Academic.

Shatz, M. (1974a). *The influence of conversational rules on speech modifications.* Paper presented at the Conference on Language Input and Acquisition, Social Science Research Council, Boston.

Shatz, M. (1974b). *The comprehension of indirect directives: Can two-year-olds shut the door?* Paper presented at the Linguistic Society of America, Amherst.

Shatz, M. (1978). The relationship between cognitive processes and the development of communication skills. In B. Keasey (Ed.), *Nebraska Symposium on Motivation, 1977.* Lincoln: University of Nebraska Press.

Shatz, M. (1982). On mechanisms of language acquisition: Can features of the communicative environment account for development? In L. Gleitman & E. Warren (Eds.), *Language acquisition: The state of the art.* New York: Cambridge University Press.

Shatz, M. (1983). On transition, continuity, and coupling: An alternative approach to communicative development. In R. Golinkoff (Ed.), *The transition from prelinguistic to linguistic communication.* Hillsdale, NJ: Lawrence Erlbaum.

Shatz, M., & Gelman, R. (1973). The development of communication skills: Modifications in the speech of young children as a function of listener. *Monographs of the Society for Research in Child Development, 38* (5).

Shugar, G. (1978). Text analysis as an approach to the study of early linguistic operations. In N. Waterson & C. Snow (Eds.), *The development of communication.* New York: John Wiley.

Snow, C. (1972). Mothers' speech to children learning language. *Child Development, 43,* 549-565.

Snow, C. (1977a). The development of conversation between mothers and babies. *Journal of Child Language, 4,* 1-22.

Snow, C. (1977b). Mother's speech research: From input to interaction. In C. Snow & C. Ferguson (Eds.), *Talking to children.* Cambridge: Cambridge University Press.

Snow, C. (1979). The role of social interaction in language acquisition. In M. A. Collins (Ed.), *Children's language and communication: Vol. 12. The Minnesota Symposium on Child Psychology.* Hillsdale, NJ: Lawrence Erlbaum.

Snow, C., Arlman-Rupp, A., Hassing, Y., Jobse, J., Joosten, J., & Vorster, J. (1976). Mother's speech in three social classes. *Journal of Psycholinguistic Research, 5,* 1-20.

Snow, C., & Gilbreath, B. (1983). Explaining transitions. In R. Golinkoff (Ed.), *The transition from prelinguistic to linguistic communication.* Hillsdale, NJ: Lawrence Erlbaum.

Snyder-McLean, L., & McLean, J. (1978). Verbal information gathering strategies: The child's use of language to acquire language. *Journal of Speech and Hearing Disorders, 43,* 305-326.

Steiner, G. (1969). The language animal. *Encounter, 33,* 7-24.

Stern, D. (1974). Mother and infant at play: Dyadic interaction involving facial, vocal and gaze behavior. In M. Lewis & L. Rosenblum (Eds.), *The effect of the infant on its caretaker.* New York: John Wiley.

Stern, D. (1977). *The first relationship.* Cambridge, MA: Harvard University Press.

Sugarman, S. (1973). *Description of communicative development in the prelanguage child.* Unpublished manuscript, Hampshire College.

Sugarman, S. (1977). A description of communicative development in the prelanguage child. In I. Martova (Ed.), *The social context of language.* London: John Wiley.

Sugarman, S. (1983). Empirical versus logical issues in the transition from prelinguistic to linguistic communication. In R. Golinkoff (Ed.), *The transition from prelinguistic to linguistic communication.* Hillsdale, NJ: Lawrence Erlbaum.

Sylvester-Bradley, B. (1980). *A study of young infants as social beings.* Unpublished doctoral dissertation, Edinburgh University.

Tough, J. (1973). *Focus on meaning.* London: Allen & Unwin.

Tough, J. (1977). *The development of meaning.* New York: John Wiley.

Trevarthen, C. (1977). Descriptive analyses of infant communication behavior. In H. R. Schaffer (Ed.), *Studies in mother-infant interaction.* London: Academic.

Trevarthen, C. (1978). Modes of perceiving and modes of acting. In H. Pick & E. Saltzmann (Eds.), *Modes of perceiving and processing information* (pp. 99-136). Hillsdale, NJ: Lawrence Erlbaum.

Trevarthen, C. (1979a). Communication and co-operation in early infancy: A description of primary intersubjectivity. In M. Bullowa (Ed.), *Before speech: The beginnings of human communication.* London: Cambridge University Press.

Trevarthen, C. (1979b). Instincts for human understanding and for cultural co-operation: Their development in infancy. In M. von Cranach, K. Foppa, W. Lepenies, & D. Ploog (Eds.), *Human ethology.* Cambridge: Cambridge University Press.

Trevarthen, C. (1980a). Brain development and the growth of psychological functions. In J. Sants (Ed.), *Developmental psychology and society.* London: Macmillan.

Trevarthen, C. (1980b). The foundations of intersubjectivity: Development of interpersonal and co-operative understanding in infants. In D. Olsen (Ed.), *The social foundations of language and thought: Essays in honor of J. S. Bruner.* New York: Norton.

Trevarthen, C. (1981). Basic patterns in psychogenetic change in infancy. In T. Bever (Ed.), *Dips in learning.* Hillsdale, NJ: Lawrence Erlbaum.

Trevarthen, C. (1982). The primary motives for cooperative understanding. In G. Butterworth & P. Light (Eds.), *Social cognition.* Chicago: University of Chicago Press.

Trevarthen, C., & Hubley, P. (1978). Secondary intersubjectivity: Confidence, confiding and acts of meaning in the first year. In A. Lock (Ed.), *Action, gesture and symbol: The emergence of language.* London: Academic.

Turner, G. (1973). Social class and children's language of control at ages five and seven. In B. Bernstein (Ed.), *Class, codes, and control* (Vol. 2). London: Routledge & Kegan Paul.

Tyack, D., & Ingram, D. (1977). Children's production and comprehension of questions. *Journal of Child Language, 4,* 211-225.

van der Geest, T. (1977). Some interactional aspects of language acquisition. In C. Snow & C. Ferguson (Eds.), *Talking to children.* Cambridge: Cambridge University Press.

Van Lancker, D. (n.d.). *Heterogeneity in language and speech: Neurolinguistic studies.* UCLA Working Papers in Phonetics, No. 29.

Watzlawick, P., Beavin, J., & Jackson, D. (1967). *Pragmatics of human communication.* New York: Norton.

Wellman, H., & Lempers, J. (1977). The naturalistic communicative abilities of two-year-olds. *Child Development, 48,* 1052-1057.

Wells, G., Montgomery, M., & Maclure, M. (1979). Adult-child discourse: Outline of a model of analysis. *Journal of Pragmatics, 3,* 337-380.

Whitehurst, G. (1976). The development of communication: Changes with age and modeling. *Child Development, 47,* 473-482.

Whitehurst, G., & Sonnenschein, S. (1978). The development of communication: Attribute variation leads to contrast failure. *Journal of Experimental Child Psychology, 25,* 454-490.

Whitehurst, G., & Sonnenschein, S. (1981). The development of informative messages in referential communication: Knowing when versus knowing how. In W. Dickson (Ed.), *Children's oral communication skills.* New York: Academic.

Winnicott, D. (1974). *Playing and reality.* Harmondsworth: Penguin.

Wolf, D. (1981). Understanding others: A longitudinal case study of the concept of independent agency. In G. Forman (Ed.), *Action and thought.* New York: Academic.

9 ● Automaticity, Arousal, and Information Exposure

R. LEWIS DONOHEW ● MURALI NAIR ●
SETH FINN

University of Kentucky ● University of North Carolina

ALTHOUGH many contemporary theories involving human communication behavior hold that individuals are proactive seekers of information and conscious decision makers, there is growing research evidence that much of the time this is not true. Instead, individuals often are only dimly aware—if at all—of the choices they are making.

In research supporting this view, Berger (1979, 1980) referred to this condition as one in which the individual is on "automatic pilot," Laberge and Samuels (1974) and Finn (1982) called it "automaticity," and Langer (1980) and Roloff (1980) described it as "mindlessness." All of these refer to an individual's capacity to process automatically what is critical for comprehension in multicomponent, complex skills such as are involved in exposure to visual material for reading or viewing.

Implications of these findings for the study of human communication behavior are promising. First, it is apparent that most major contemporary theories, those that embrace assumptions that individuals are proactive and aware of choices they are making, are inadequate as general models. Some theories still assume that information is sought primarily to reduce uncertainty rather than, for example, to achieve pleasure. In fact, individuals often are reactive and unaware of choices they are making, and information sometimes is sought for no nobler reason than the pleasurable responses it produces.

The level of human attention and self-awareness appears to range along a broad continuum. At the low self-awareness end of the continuum, it is possible that cognition plays a very small role, with guidance provided largely

Correspondence and requests for reprints: R. Lewis Donohew, College of Communications, University of Kentucky, Lexington, KY 40506.

267

by affect. As awareness progresses upward, cognition exerts a greater force, although clearly affect continues to play a part even at the highest levels of self-awareness. There is a need for rethinking old theories and developing new ones that account for these more complex human behaviors.

These behaviors might include daydreaming or thinking through a complex problem while driving an automobile through a complicated series of maneuvers—obeying traffic signals, making turns, and changing gears— while driving home from work. Or they might include turning away from or attending to a television or newspaper message not on the basis of informational needs but because of more subtle clues such as style, movement, color, or intensity, of which readers or viewers are at most slightly aware even after their focus of attention has shifted.

Only a few researchers have examined the functioning of this phenomenon in mass communication situations. In this chapter we review some of the research literature that appears to support automaticity or information processing under a condition of low self-awareness and examine some of its psychological and physiological bases as they apply to exposure to mass media.

INTERPERSONAL AND MASS COMMUNICATION: AN EXAMPLE

To offer a quick orientation to this topic, let us begin with an illustration from personal experience.

We have a friend who in our judgment is quite intelligent and who appears to have a high need for stimulation, a need to be involved in something exciting all the time. Our conversations with him invariably are one way. He talks and one or the other of us listens or responds to what he says.

There are lots of times we want to do something more than listen to him, however. We also want to express ideas and have him react to them. If one of us hands him something to read, this works all right. He zips through it almost as if he were skimming, then works on it awhile and provides valuable suggestions.

But when someone tries to *talk* with him, it doesn't work very well. After a few sentences have been uttered, our friend's eyes start glazing over and it becomes apparent that he is off thinking about something else. As an alert communicator, the one who has been trying to talk with him will try to change course somewhat, to move, to do something else to reattract him, but none of this is very effective. We can receive messages from him, but we can't get them through very well orally.

Previously, we had attributed this problem to his high need for activation. We weren't providing enough variety. Perhaps we misinterpreted the implications of the glazed eyeballs. An alternative is an automatic pilot interpretation of his behaviors. Instead of tuning us out, his system may merely have noted that it could process our input and have room left over for other things. It may then have gone on to other problem-solving, for example, but still have been with us.

AUTOMATICITY

LaBerge and Samuels (1974), who conducted one of the pioneer studies of automaticity, are of the opinion that the processing of visual material by individuals is learned and the degree of this learning is evaluated with respect to two criteria: accuracy and automaticity. At the first stage, attention is assumed to be necessary for processing; at the automatic level it is not.

> During the execution of a complex skill, it is necessary to coordinate many component processes within a very short period of time. If each component process requires attention, performance of the complex skill will be impossible, because the capacity of attention will be exceeded. But if enough of the components and their coordinations can be processed automatically, then the load on attention will be within tolerable limits and the skill can be successfully performed. (LaBerge & Samuels, 1974, p. 293)

Individuals process visual information through a series of processing stages before arriving at total comprehension. According to Finn (1982), "The better practiced a reader is, the greater opportunity there is to focus attention on the semantic meaning and the implications of what is being read." In a study that compared information processing of an issue by experts and novices, Fiske, Kinder, and Larter (1983) found that novices focused on information consistent with a provided expectation, whereas experts focused to a larger extent on inconsistencies. The authors concluded that increasing automaticity that comes with skill acquisition frees up processing capacity.

Describing automaticity, Finn (1983, pp. 6-7) adds:

> This concept asserts that the mind's capacity to process information is infinitely expandable, because any well-known stimuli will be processed unconsciously (automatically), thereby allowing the scarce resource of attention to be focused exclusively on less familiar stimuli.

Shiffrin and Schneider (1977) have formulated a theory based on two basic processing modes: controlled and automatic. Controlled search, as defined by the authors, requires a great deal of attentional capacity, whereas automatic detection is based on long-term memory and demands attention only under certain conditions. Describing benefits of this system, Shiffrin and Schneider (1977, p. 93) state:

A system based on the two basic processing modes . . . has many advantages. In novel situations or in situations requiring moment-to-moment decisions, controlled processing may be adopted and used to perform accurately, though slowly. Then as the situations become familiar, always requiring the same sequence of processing operations, automatic processing will develop, attention demands will be eased, other controlled operations can be carried out in parallel with the automatic processing, and performance will improve.

SELF-AWARENESS AND INFORMATION SEEKING

Individuals vary in their degree of self-awareness and subsequently are not always reflective of their attitudes, beliefs, or previous behaviors prior to and during a specific action. Thus the theory of objective self-awareness suggests that some situations promote an examination of beliefs, attitudes, and behaviors more than do others.

Langer (1980), who conducted a number of studies on self-awareness, asserts that human behavior is often mindless. She claims that people operate at the low end of awareness and engage in scripted behavior. This notion of a script also underlies top-down theories of information processing in which it is assumed that a reader, for instance, makes sense of a narrative text by automatically accessing from long-term memory an appropriate schema that details a stereotypical sequence of events (Schank & Abelson, 1977).

Langer believes that a person who engages in a particular behavior over time develops a pattern or script for that situation and, as a result, does not devote a great deal of consciousness to carrying out that behavior when encountering a similar situation in the future. It is suggested that in many situations people have scripts that tell them what response they must give to a particular situation and that these scripts do not require cognitive processing.

In previous research, Donohew and Tipton (1973) described this as a stored repertoire of coping strategies that were part of the individual's overall image of reality or cognitive map. We didn't know at the time, however, that this set of responses was quite possibly automatic.

Langer (1980) notes that actions guided by cues that result from scripts or overlearning often may take a different form from that following conscious processing of information. Langer suggests that most behavior, even complex social interaction, may be enacted without paying attention to it. She suggests that persons may believe they have been thinking, but in fact tend to behave according to well learned and general scripts rather than on the basis of new, incoming information. "Minds" are virtually at rest much of the time, or free to focus attention on other matters.

A FIELD EXPERIMENT

Langer (1980) observes that persons tend to respond differently to stimuli when they appear to be operating at a low level of self-awareness than when at a higher level. She cites a field experiment at a library in which subjects were persons standing in a line waiting to use a photocopier. Her expectation was that persons would draw on scripted behavior when responding to familiar sequences of events and would respond differently when the cue for calling up the script was not present or when novelty was introduced into the situation, presumably increasing the level of self-awareness. Persons in the line were asked by an experimenter one of three questions: (1) May I make five copies ahead of you (no reason given)? (2) May I make five copies ahead of you because I need to copy them (meaningless reason given, but one expected to call up a prior script)? and (3) May I make five copies ahead of you because I'm in a hurry?

Langer expected subjects in so-called mindless states to respond according to the script: "favor + reason → comply." In response to the requests in which no reason was given, 60 percent of the subjects agreed to let a person move ahead of them, 93 percent agreed to the request with a meaningless reason given, and almost exactly the same proportion—94 percent—agreed when a simple reason was given.

When a much larger number of copies (25) was requested in each of the conditions, introducing more effort into the situation, it was expected that self-awareness would be heightened and the number of refusals would increase. This was supported. The favorable response proportions changed to 24 percent with no information, 24 percent with meaningless information, and 42 percent with real information. In other words, the larger request appears to have caused subjects to respond in nonscripted ways.

A number of other studies in differing situations produced similar results.

A Comment on "Mindlessness"

In view of what the human system appears to do, the term "mindless" may be misleading here. Instead of being lazily at rest much of the time as Langer suggests, evidence from other sources supports the idea that the system seems to be ready to do whatever is appropriate for the situation, as Shiffrin and Schneider (1977) proposed. If what is happening falls in the overlearned category, the system may use the leftover attention to daydream or to solve problems. On the other hand, if events require full attention—as indicated by the perception of something novel or important in the situation, for example—the system is alerted to a self-aware state in which it may use its full processing capacities.

INFORMATION THEORY

Information theory plays a central role in discussions concerning the communication process when the impact of novel messages on mental capacity is at issue (Miller, 1956). Finn (1982) approaches the subject by relating how information can be a significant component in determining reader enjoyment of journalistic prose. Hypothesizing that an individual attending to a news story possesses a positive association between the unpredictability of its verbal content and his or her level of enjoyment, Finn proposes a model that includes entertainment-seeking and information-seeking as two distinct forms of behavior.

Finn's study employs cloze procedure (systematically eliminating words in news stories and asking listeners or readers to supply them) as a basis for computing content unpredictability scores—what Cherry (1957) called "surprise value"—which he then relates to assessments of enjoyability for the same articles. Finn's study is in sharp contrast to the traditional approach in which it is assumed that a reader or listener would be attracted to a specific item based on his or her interests and information needs. While not totally rejecting this notion, Finn does reject a corresponding idea, incorporated in simple information-seeking models, that the news reader is fundamentally motivated by a need to reduce uncertainty.

Watt and Krull (1974), who developed a procedure for measuring six elemental forms of entropy in television messages, have shown how children's attention is linked to higher amounts of program entropy (Krull, Watt, & Lichty, 1977). In an unpublished study, Donohew and Baseheart (1982) also examined the relationship of an individual's need for arousal (Pearson, 1970, 1971) and cognitive complexity (Bryson & Driver, 1972) to average entropy scores of television programs they watched. The design generated a strong main effect of need for arousal on entropy in a negative (or information) direction. In other words, persons with a high need for arousal watched programs with significantly higher information (or "surprise value") scores than did those with a low need for arousal. Individual differences in need for arousal also have been found to affect responses to television dramas (Bryant, 1979) and to film selection and liking (Johnson, 1981).

IMPLICATIONS FOR MASS COMMUNICATION

What implication does all this have for mass communication, for those who send messages through the media and for those who expose themselves, actively or passively, to those messages?

Our society has made a number of assumptions about the role of mass media and has offered them special protections because of this role. A principal role assigned to the press in our society, for example, is that it survey the environment and provide the public with information that will assist it in functioning effectively. We assume that people search out information on vital topics—in documentaries or in newspaper articles exposing wrongdoing in society—and that they will act on this information in ways that protect us all. Some do watch and read thus, of course, and wrongdoers sometimes do get their comeuppance. It is quite possible that for others, exposure to public information comes about because it also entertains, and so long as the message contains these devices providing entertainment, we will stay tuned in or continue to read, but with little or no long-term effect. When those pleasurable cues run out, the audience will turn to something else.

All of this is not to challenge the effectiveness of the surveillance role assigned the media. Rather, it is to question assumptions about how consumers of the media react to those messages they select or have selected for them. Glasser (1980, p. 243) quotes Stephenson as characterizing newsreading as "communication-pleasure" and proposing that experientially "news consumption is an interlude, a departure from the day's responsibilities and obligations." Holmlöv (1982) demonstrated that reader interest in municipal affairs and amount of newspaper reading in general are uncorrelated with knowledge of muncipal affairs. Holmlöv's results indicate that there must be an orientation toward learning, or else the information is processed for fun rather than knowledge.

In picking up their morning newspapers, are readers "thinking" anything much different from what they think when bringing in the milk? In tuning in *Good Morning America,* is the television watcher doing much more than when he or she pops the bread into the toaster or turns on the coffeemaker? Both are behavior routines overlearned through long practice and could be carried out without much thought. Quick scanning of the headlines to find something to read or hearing something on TV to which one attends while scrambling the eggs might well reflect a kind of mindless behavior. But as our discussion of the need for arousal later illustrates, such mindless behavior may not be useless but rather may fulfill definite physiological needs for stimulation of the brain and energy for the body. It is more than conjecture to suggest that when a person finds it impossible to get going in the morning without a cup of coffee and a few minutes perusing the newspaper, or plops down in front of a television set after a frantic day at the office, these behaviors may be motivated by a need to achieve a more satisfactory level of arousal.

This point was addressed many years ago from a different vantage point in Berelson's (1949) classic study of what it means to be without a newspaper during a strike. He observed what he called the "ritualistic and near compulsive character of news reading" in reporting what most bothered his respondents as they sought activities to fill the void (p. 125). Some read old newspapers from the attic, others old magazines. Many admitted feeling lost, losing sleep, being tense and irritable. Some went to the newsstands every day, even though they did not expect to find newspapers there.

Alternatively, missing the newspaper may not make much difference to others. Some years ago, one of the authors was doing some lifestyle research for a mass media chain in which we were looking at female users and nonusers of the research sponsor's medium. Although there was a hard core of persons who actively sought information and in whose lives this information clearly played a significant role, the largest group of users responded to it as one more product in their environment, something they were accustomed to using but that could disappear from their lives, probably without leaving a measurable gap. We are among those who grew up believing in the considerable importance of the media in providing information and were disturbed by our inference that their actual uses were peripheral to the lives of many of their "consumers."

We have long known, of course, that uses of the mass media are highly varied, and the spate of research in recent years on uses and gratifications has borne this out (Katz, Blumler, & Gurevitch, 1974; Greenberg, 1974; McLeod & Becker, 1974; Palmgreen & Rayburn, 1979; Palmgreen, Wenner, & Rayburn, 1980). Gratifications sought or obtained—or both—range far beyond the mythical ideal of readers or watchers out there seeking the truth that will keep them free.

If, in fact, individuals do much of their newspaper scanning or television watching while operating at a low level of self-awareness (that is, that they often tune themselves out when tuning in the media), what implications does this have for persons who prepare messages for use on those media? After all, the message itself is about the only part of the process over which the reporters, editors, and producers have much control. As Finn noted elsewhere:

> Clearly . . . we cannot assume that the public is comprised of inveterate information-seekers. We have to look to other motivating factors when attempting to attract the attention of an apathetic audience. (1983, p. 3)

In previous research, some of us (Donohew, Palmgreen, & Duncan, 1980; Donohew, 1981; Finn 1982, 1983) have operated under the assumption that even while individuals are seeking information, much of the attention focused on mass media is motivated by a search for stimulation rather than a need for information about a specific topic. The "primary criteria for evaluation of media content often stem not from the individual's degree of uncertainty (information-seeking), but from his or her need for unpredictable stimuli" (Finn, 1982, p. 15).

In his play theory of communication mentioned earlier, Stephenson (1967) stated that mass communication is utilized more for pleasure than for information or improvement. Beyond this, of course, is that portion of media content that is intentionally entertainment oriented. Here, one might speculate that automatic processing is even more likely to prevail.

We should note here that in this section we have referred to mass media, news media, newspapers, and television almost as if they were interchangeable. Clearly, these are different packages of stimuli, each with their own unique properties. Our intention here is to indicate that readers or viewers seek them out at least in part because each contains some elements that generate a pleasurable arousal response for the consumer.

Before describing some of the underlying assumptions of the Donohew et al. and Finn paradigms, let us take a brief look at some early models of exposure to information through the mass media.

NATURE OF NEWS

Schramm's "The Nature of News" (1949) is among the earliest to focus on the attributes of news at the receiver's end. Schramm (1949, p. 260) suggests that an individual's response to a news item is in anticipation of a reward that could be either immediate or delayed:

> In general, immediate rewards are news of crime and corruption, accidents and disasters, sports and recreation, social events and human interest. Delayed reward comes from news of public affairs, economic matters, social problems, science, education and health. News of the first kind pays its rewards at once, the second kind has a sort of "threat value" and is read so that the reader may be informed and prepared.

Under the immediate reward category, a stimulus is presented for which a response is made, and this response may be rewarded. If it is not rewarded, the tendency to respond in a given way progressively loses ground. Based on the Freudian concept of mental functioning, the reward process includes what Freud called the pleasure principle and the reality principle.

Some researchers did not accept the universality of these two categories, however (Stephenson, 1967; Pietila, 1969). Stephenson maintained that any content would be pleasurable or painful depending on the needs and experience of the individual reader.

PLAY THEORY OF NEWSREADING

Stephenson, in proposing his theory of newsreading, emphasizes the inherent "play" involved in the communication process between a source and receiver. On that point, Glasser (1982, p. 104) observes:

One of Stephenson's most telling observations is that newsreading is a complex skill, "the importance of which is little understood." Reading the day's news for enjoyment, playing in and with communication, requires a certain aptitude, an ability to see the story through the facts, so to speak, a capacity for appreciating images, not just assimilating information. Analogously, anyone can read Chaucer and Shakespeare but not everyone will truly enjoy the experience; reading as an intrinsic delight, consumption as an immediately pleasurable activity, is an acquired taste developed over time and only with experience. (p. 104)

Glasser notes that Stephenson's treatment of play and its relation to newsreading has not been widely and favorably received. Nevertheless, we believe it clearly presages current models of information processing that predicate comprehension of a message on the automatization of subskills that comprise the complex skill of reading (LaBerge & Samuels, 1974) and prior familiarity with underlying scripts appropriate to understanding the text at hand (Schank & Abelson, 1977).

USES AND GRATIFICATIONS MODELS

Uses and gratifications research has come in for increased criticism of late, although it remains a crucial and formative influence on thinking about the mass media. One of the arguments against the approach is that audience members are asked why they consumed particular items in the media when they may not know why. Howitt (1982), a critic of the approach, says:

> The uses and gratifications approach has certain intuitive appeal. It seems to give the audience a new dignity: they are seen as active and self-determining rather than passive absorbers of mass communication. Instead of being manipulated, the audience is the manipulator. The approach is not a fully unified body of theory and research. It is a loose conglomerate of particular types of research questions and methodology. Clear formulations of the aims, purposes and objectives of the functionalist approach are difficult to find. There are plenty of reviews, but they leave the limits and intents of the approach loosely stated. (p. 14)

Criticisms of the audience's ability to describe *why* it watched what it watched or read what it read become even more acute when we take into account that much of the time the audience may be operating on automatic pilot, unaware of the mechanisms that attracted their attention and unable to explain why decisions about viewing or reading were made.

Goodhart, Ehrenberg, and Collins (1975) argued that there is little evidence to suggest the viewing selectivity propounded by the uses and gratifications model. Finding lack of evidence that certain program types attract a special audience, the authors propose the duplication of viewing law, which states that "the size of the audience common to two different programs on different days depends on the ratings of the programs and the channels on which they are shown, rather than the content of the program" (p. 19).

SEARCHING FOR MODELS

Underlying the activities for which we invent behavior theories are biological processes. It is useful to examine these biological underpinnings both for checking the validity of new theories to determine if what they describe is within the realm of possibility and as a source of information for inventing new explanations to cover unaccounted-for phenomena. By this we do not mean that all our theories should be quasi-biological. That would be far too constraining. Rather, we might employ this knowledge more for its heuristic value to us in our search for new explanations.

Haskins (1982) contributed a substantial review of psychobiological connections to communication behavior, with special attention to human attraction to negative messages.

Bostrom (1983) argued that in the study of communication we have put too much emphasis on cognitive theories, whereas affect is often determined by factors other than cognitive ones. He states: "Few connections are stronger or better formed than the biological-affect link."

Perhaps the most obvious place to turn in search of a general model is the attention process itself and some of the arousal or activation theories that spring from it. Arousal or activation models provide an explanation of that part of the process that is going on under conditions of automaticity and, to some extent, when the reader or viewer is aware that decisions are being made. Although they do not explain the more complex information processing that takes place in many instances, they appear to explain more about this phenomenon than do cognitive theories.

GENERAL MECHANISMS OF ATTENTION

At any given time, individuals are exposed to numerous stimuli. The sifting of stimuli and identifying the one needing attention is an ongoing process making it possible for individuals to attend to important messages and ignore those that are not important (Donohew & Palmgreen, 1971). "Once a stimulus has been selected," says Weaver (1972), "it is said to have your attention."

Physiologists have been working on this process of selective attention for a long time and have proposed that the brain stem reticular formation serves as the center for the attention-involving process. This portion of the brain intercepts stimuli, sending the low-value stimuli off into other circuits of the brain and sending high-value ones up to the cortex for attention. Thus a process of cognitive handling or structuring takes place at the cortex.

Arousal

At the heart of the attention process is arousal, which provides the organism with energy to act (Kroeber-Riel, 1979). Since the findings of earlier research that excitatory phenomena on television contribute to an individual's arousal in a positive or negative direction, several researchers have tried to probe the cause and effect of arousal and its relationship to mass media, as noted by Chaffee and Tims (see Comstock, Chaffee, Katzman, McCombs, & Roberts, 1978).

Considering the impact of television on the American public, many arousal studies have been conducted with the idea of showing arousal responses during or after viewing television fare. Research has indicated that individuals experiencing stress maintain a high level of arousal, and that watching television is likely to involve and absorb the ruminating person more effectively than many alternative activities.

Zillmann (1982) developed a model of excitation transfer, which in part suggests that "contents that relate to the individual's acute emotional state potentially reiterate arousal maintaining cognitions" (p. 55).

Information Exposure

Now let us look at some implications of an attention or arousal model of information exposure, a principal research area of the senior author and his colleagues for more than a decade. Early in this research (Donohew & Palmgreen, 1977), when we were still enamored of cognitive consistency theories, we observed:

> The mediator of two important elements in this process—arousal and stimulus selection—appears to be the reticular formation, a type of nerve tissue in the subcortical region of the brain. Functions of the reticular formation bear a remarkable resemblance to the homeostatic function inferred in cognitive consistency theories. The reticular formation seems to have the power to actually inhibit the neuronal transmission of certain stimuli to the higher brain centers while facilitating the transmission of others. This inhibition or facilitation appears to be based upon the general pleasantness or unpleasantness of stimuli determined by the desires, interests, norms, values, etc. of the receiver. . . . Certain items which might cause anxiety or unpleasantness are apparently excluded from consciousness through the activity of the reticular formation. (p. 628)

The arousal—or activation—model of information exposure has developed in the intervening years, and we have come to believe that noncontent characteristics of messages play a larger role in their being attended to than generally is recognized. The notion of automaticity is consistent with this approach. If we are engaging in a familiar activity, such as reading the newspaper, it is plausible that we make our selections on the basis of these more subtle cues that help to make a story more pleasant or unpleasant for us to attend to rather than on the basis of loftier goals that have been attributed to such behaviors.

Finn, in fact, while drawing on the arousal-based approach, offers support for a three-stage model of newsreading that has ease of decoding as the first stage, entertainment-seeking as the second stage, and information-seeking as the uppermost level. His model is based on the assumptions given in Figure 9.1. At the decoding stage, ink dots on paper are transformed into symbolic codes for processing at higher levels. Ordinarily such behavior would be automated, except that uncommon or complex syntactical forms or unfamiliar vocabulary could require increased attention. At the entertainment-seeking level, it is assumed that a physiological need for novel stimuli causes individuals to attend to messages that may conform to

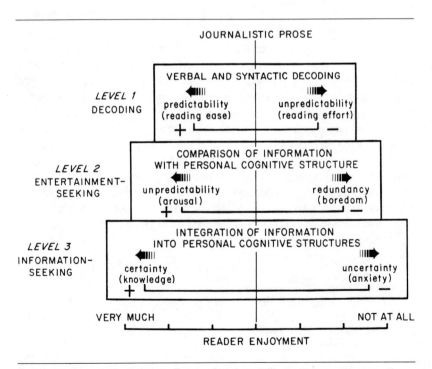

Figure 9.1.   An information-theoretic model of reader enjoyment. Adapted from Finn (1982).

schematized or scripted structures but nonetheless are characterized by a large quantity of unexpected detail. Here novelty promotes attention to the text, a notion first developed by the Russian formalists who argued that the function of literary style was to "deautomatize" reading of a text (Ejxenbaum, 1978).

At the information-seeking level, however, novel stimuli may be threatening to the reader's belief structure. As Berlo (1978) pointed out, the assumption that information always reduces uncertainty is valid at best in the short term. In the long term, information may either reduce or increase uncertainty depending on how the message complements the receiver's previous knowledge, attitudes, and beliefs. Uncertainty and anxiety resulting from cognitive conflicts may motivate two types of behavior: simple avoidance or a search for more consistent information.

In summary, Finn's model assumes at the entertainment-seeking level that the reader's reaction to an unexpected message is arousal, which often is desirable for its own sake. However, at the information-seeking level, some messages may contribute to a pleasurable feeling of control over the environment, but some highly salient messages may increase uncertainty and cause greater anxiety.

Previously the senior author and associates (Donohew et al., 1980) offered a two-stage activation theory of information exposure in conjunction with a research design that emphasized the importance of individual characteristics as well as message properties. The basic assumption of this theory, which grew in part out of studies of sensory deprivation and more general activation and attention studies, is that individuals have an optimal level of activation (or arousal) at which they feel most comfortable. Individuals enter information exposure situations with the expectation of achieving or maintaining this optimal state of activation and will experience a positive or negative affect—a feeling of pleasantness or unpleasantness—depending on whether or not this optimal state is achieved. If activation falls below or exceeds the desired level, individuals will tend to experience a negative affective state and will turn away from the source of information that led to the state. If activation level reaches or remains within some range perceived to

Figure 9.2.   An activation model of information exposure. Based on material in
                Donohew et al. (1980).

be acceptable, the affective state will be more positive and individuals will continue to expose themselves to the information. Research findings by the author and associates involving printed messages (Donohew et al., 1980), film selection (Johnson, 1981), and television viewing (Donohew & Baseheart, 1982) have offered support for this model (Figure 9.2).

This model as well as Finn's draws on Hebb's (1955) classic inverted U-curve of performance responses to arousal. Hebb's curve suggests that messages that become too boring (generate too little arousal) or too threatening (generate too much arousal) will not be well attended. Those at the middle of the curve (optimal level of arousal) will be best attended. Results of studies conducted by both authors are consistent with this curve.

In a subsequent study undertaken by Donohew (1981), arousal responses were measured more directly. Skin conductance response and a mood scale were used to measure physiological and affective responses to style of writing. Stimulus materials were news stories about the Guyana suicides (November 1978), with style factors manipulated. Although it was considered possible that readers would turn away from materials because arousal level became too high, as the inverted-U hypothesis holds, the more likely alternative would be that readers would not be aroused enough. As we noted:

> The human sensory system is attracted not only to the content of messages, but also by such characteristics as color, contrast, intensity, and movement. . . . Thus, messages lacking most of these properties—such as those presented in the form of black marks on paper by the print media—must offer particularly appealing content if they are to compete with other mass media or with other elements of an individual's environment. (Donohew, 1981, p. 109)

We should note here that although the Donohew et al. model, unlike Finn's, was designed without taking automaticity into account, the verbal responses it requires (to questions on "how do you feel right now?") are capable of being answered whether or not the individual was on automatic pilot at the time the information was being processed.

It is plausible that in a story of tragedy such as the Guyana suicides, greater arousal might have generated greater negative affects and lower arousal might have generated lower negative affects. In this study we found that when arousal was higher, mood change tended only slightly in a negative direction, if at all. When arousal was lower, however, mood level tended in a strongly negative direction. In other words, excitement appears to be treasured more than drabness, even when bad news is conveyed. All this seems to argue for affect over cognition, at least in situations where "safe" thrills (that is, from situations not directly involving the reader) are concerned. Although it would be stretching our findings considerably to indicate that the individual was operating on automatic pilot here, clearly the involuntary arousal response is predominant over the cognitive response.

In recent years, as attention has shifted to cognitive processes that assume self-awareness, the amount of attention paid to effects of message characteristics has been rather scant. Now that it appears that a substantial number of decisions about attending to messages are made by individuals under conditions of low self-awareness, some rethinking is in order. If an individual is unaware of the course he or she steers through audio, video, and print channels, what are the overlearned procedures he or she employs? What leads to turning away or staying with messages? Are there guideposts that stand out? From the researcher's point of view, how do we determine when the message consumer is at different levels of self-awareness? We can track subjects through some sequence of events, measuring their physiological and exposure responses to sources of information, but that does not tell us their level of conscious awareness.

In this chapter we have concentrated primarily on the notion of automaticity, its relationship to arousal, and its implications for information exposure. The questions we have raised cover only a small fraction of those which can be raised, not only about message exposure but also about comprehension, learning, attitude change, or many other possible message effects. We are hopeful that some of these questions will be addressed by other investigators in the near future.

REFERENCES

Berelson, B. (1949). What missing the newspaper means. In P. Lazarsfeld & F. N. Stanton (Eds.), Communications research, 1948-1949. New York: Harper & Row.

Berger, C. R. (1979). Interpersonal interaction and self-awareness. Paper presented at the International Conference on Social Psychology and Language, Bristol, England.

Berger, C. R. (1980). Self-consciousness and the adequacy of theory in relationship development. Western Journal of Speech Communication, 44, 93-96.

Berlo, D. K. (1978). Communication as process: Review and commentary. In B. D. Ruben (Ed.), Communication yearbook 1. New Brunswick, NJ: Transaction.

Bostrom, R. N. (1983). Biological factors in communication. Paper presented at the meetings of the Speech Communication Association, Washington, D.C.

Bryant, J. (1979). The effect of sensation-seeking on the enjoyment of the climax and the resolution of suspenseful drama. Paper presented at the meetings of the International Communication Association, Philadelphia.

Bryson, J., & Driver, M. (1972). Cognitive complexity, introversion and preference for complexity. Journal of Personality and Social Psychology, 23, 3206-3207.

Cantor, J. R., & Zillman, D. (1973). The effect of affective state and emotional arousal on music appreciation. Journal of General Psychology, 89, 97-108.

Cherry, C. (1957). On human communication. Cambridge: MIT Press.

Comstock, G. S., Chaffee, S., Katzman, N., McCombs, M., & Roberts, D. F. (Eds.). (1978). Television and human behavior. New York: Columbia University Press.

Donohew, L. (1981). Arousal and affective response to writing styles. Journal of Applied Communication Research, 9, 109-119.

Donohew, L., & Baseheart, J. (1982). Need for activation and television viewing. Unpublished paper, University of Kentucky, Lexington.

Donohew, L., & Palmgreen, P. (1971). A reappraisal of dissonance and the selective exposure hypothesis. *Journalism Quarterly, 48,* 412-420, 437.

Donohew, L., & Palmgreen, P. (1977). An investigation of "mechanisms" of information selection. *Journalism Quarterly, 48,* 627-639, 666.

Donohew, L., Palmgreen, P., & Duncan, J. (1980). An activation model of information exposure. *Communication Monographs, 47,* 295-303.

Donohew, L., & Tipton, L. (1973). A conceptual model of information-seeking, avoiding, and processing. In P. Clarke (Ed.), *New models for mass communication.* Beverly Hills, CA: Sage.

Exjenbaum, B. M. (1978). The theory of the formal method. In L. Matejka & K. Pomorska (Eds.), *Readings in Russian poetics.* Ann Arbor: University of Michigan Press.

Finn, H. S. (1982). *An information theory approach to reader enjoyment of print journalism.* Unpublished doctoral dissertation, Stanford University.

Finn, S. (1983). *Beyond readability formulae: Predicting reader enjoyment of popular science writing.* Paper presented at the meetings of the International Communication Association, Dallas.

Fiske, S. T., Kinder, D. R., & Larter, M. The novice and the expert: Knowledge-based strategies in political cognition. *Journal of Experimental Social Psychology, 19,* 381-400.

Glasser, T. L. (1980). The aesthetics of news. *ETC.: A Review of General Semantics, 37,* 238-247.

Glasser, T. L. (1982). Play, pleasure, and the value of news reading. *Communication Quarterly, 30,* 101-107.

Goodhardt, G. J., Ehrenberg, A. S., & Collins, M. A. (1975). *The television audience: Patterns of viewing.* Farnborough, England: Saxon House.

Greenberg, B. S. (1974). Gratifications of television viewing and their correlates for British children. In J. G. Blumler & E. Katz (Eds.), *The uses of mass communication: Current perspectives on gratifications research.* Beverly Hills, CA: Sage.

Haskins, J. (1982). *Toward a psychobiological theory of motives for human communication behavior.* Paper presented at the meetings of the International Communication Association, Boston.

Hebb, D. O. (1955). Drives and the CNS (conceptual nervous system). *Psychological Review, 62,* 243-254.

Holmlöv, P. G. (1982). Motivation for reading different content domains. *Communication Research, 9,* 314-320.

Howitt, D. (1982). *The mass media and social problems.* Oxford, England: Pergamon.

Johnson, A. (1981). *Need for activation, film preferences and film-going behavior.* Unpublished master's thesis, University of Kentucky.

Katz, E., Blumler, J. G., & Gurevitch, M. (1974). Utilization of mass communication by the individual. In J. G. Blumler & E. Katz (Eds.), *The uses of mass communication: Current perspectives on gratifications research.* Beverly Hills, CA: Sage.

Kroeber-Riel, W. (1979). Activation research: Psychobiological approaches to consumer research. *Consumer Research, 5,* 240-250.

Krull, R., Watt, J., & Lichty, L. (1977). Entropy and structure: Two measures of complexity in television programs. *Communication Research, 4,* 61-86.

LaBerge, D., & Samuels, S. J. (1974). Toward a theory of automatic information processing in reading. *Cognitive Psychology, 6,* 293-323.

Langer, E. (1980). Rethinking the role of thought in social interaction. In H. Harvey, W. Ickes, & R. Kidd (Eds.), *New directions in attribution research* (Vol. 2). Hillsdale, NJ: Lawrence Erlbaum.

McLeod, J. M., & Becker, L. B. (1974). Testing the validity of gratification measures through political effects analysis. In J. G. Blumler & E. Katz (Eds.), *The uses of mass communications: Current perspectives on gratifications research.* Beverly Hills, CA: Sage.

Miller, G. A. (1956). The magical number seven, plus or minus two: Some limits on our capacity for processing information. *Psychological Review, 63,* 81-97.

Palmgreen, P., & Rayburn, J. D. (1979). Uses and gratifications and exposure to public television: A discrepancy approach. *Communication Research, 6,* 155-180.

Palmgreen, P., Wenner, L. A., & Rayburn, J. D. (1980). Relations between gratifications sought and obtained: A study of television news. *Communication Research, 7*, 161-192.

Pearson, P. H. (1970). Relationship between global and specified measures of novelty-seeking. *Journal of Consulting and Clinical Psychology, 34*, 199-204.

Pearson, P. H. (1971). Differential relationships of four forms of novelty experiencing. *Journal of Consulting and Clinical Psychology, 37*, 23-30.

Pietila, V. (1969). Immediate versus delayed reward in newspaper reading. *Acta Sociologica, 12*, 199-208.

Roloff, M. E. (1980). Self-awareness and the persuasion process: Do we really know what we are doing? In M. E. Roloff & G. R. Miller (Eds.), *Persuasion: New directions in theory and research.* Beverly Hills, CA: Sage.

Schank, R. C., & Abelson, R. P. (1977). *Scripts, plans, goals, and understanding: An inquiry into human knowledge structures.* Hillsdale, NJ: Lawrence Erlbaum.

Schramm, W. (1949). The nature of news. *Journalism Quarterly, 26*, 259-269.

Shiffrin, R. M., & Schneider, W. (1977). Controlled and automatic human information processing, II: Perceptual learning, automatic attending, and a general theory. *Psychological Review, 84*, 127-190.

Stephenson, W. (1967). *Play theory of mass communication.* Chicago: University of Chicago Press.

Watt, J. H., & Krull, R. (1974). An information theory measure for television programming. *Communication Research, 1*, 44-68.

Weaver, H. C. (1972). *Human listening: Processes and behavior.* Indianapolis, IN: Bobbs-Merrill.

Zillmann, D. (1982). Television viewing and arousal. In D. Pearl, L. Bouthilet, & J. Lazar (Eds.), *Television and behavior: Ten years of scientific progress and implications for the eighties* (Vol. 2). Rockville, MD: National Institute of Mental Health.

10 ● Organizational Climate, Communication, and Culture

RAYMOND L. FALCIONE ● ELYSE A. KAPLAN

University of Maryland ● Marriott Corporation

PREVIOUS reviews of organizational communication theory and research have provided the reader with excellent analyses of the issues and problems facing researchers (Daly & Korinek, 1982; Dennis, Goldhaber, & Yates, 1978; Downs & Hain, 1982; Jablin, 1980; Redding, 1979; Richetto, 1977). They also point out the difficulties in attempting to develop appropriate boundaries for the field of organizational communication, primarily because of the field's eclectic nature. This eclecticism can be exemplified by Greenbaum and Falcione's (1982) 9 major classifications and 72 subclassifications of organizational communication literature. As Jablin (1980, p. 327) observes,

> Given the complexities of human communication and man-made communication systems, an eclectic orientation to the study of organizational communication appears appropriate and equivalent to the nature of the phenomenon being investigated. However, when the field adopts concepts and approaches from other disciplines, it also needs to be cognizant of the theoretical and methodological issues associated with the appropriate *application* of these tools.

The purpose of this chapter is to examine this research and discuss the issues and problems facing researchers in organizational climate, communication climate, and organizational culture.

ORGANIZATIONAL CLIMATE

Investigations of a set of organizational phenomena have proliferated in the research literature under the rubric "organizational climate." Much

Correspondence and requests for reprints: Raymond L. Falcione, Department of Communication, University of Maryland, College Park, MD 20742.

effort has been expended in an attempt to isolate, define, and explain the effects of this construct on the way the member, and the organization as a whole, functions. Unfortunately, these efforts have not been conducted under a consensual definition of the construct, or even with agreement as to whether the term represents an underlying theoretical construct that is distinct from other well-investigated organizational variables (such as job satisfaction). The purposes of this section are as follows: (1) to review briefly the prevailing perspectives from which organizational climate is defined; (2) to identify the areas of consensus and dissensus in these perspectives; (3) to suggest ways in which the differing perspectives affect the development of research hypotheses; and (4) to relate these perspectives and the research questions they generate to communication research.

Extensive reviews of the literature (Hellriegel & Slocum, 1974; James & Jones, 1974) reveal three major perspectives from which organizational climate has been approached. The first perspective treats climate as an attribute, or set of attributes, belonging to an organization. These attributes are considered to be possessed by the organization itself, independent of the perceptions or attributions made by individual members. James and Jones (1974, p. 1097) deem this approach the "multiple measurement-organizational attribute approach," which corresponds roughly to the assumption of an organizational "personality." The research that proceeds from this perspective (Forehand & Gilmer, 1964; Litwin & Stringer, 1968) assumes that an organization possesses a set of traits that distinguish it from other organizations and that are relatively stable (that is, they persist over time), thus influencing individual behavior. While these "traits" (size, structure, systems complexity, leadership style, and so on) bear remarkable similarity to components of "situational variance," as James and Jones note, the assumption inherent in treating these traits as an enduring *set* is that organizational climate may be more than a simple additive function of the values of the variables constituting it. This is, just as an individual's personality may be said to be more than his or her degree of dogmatism plus degree of self-esteem plus intelligence, so the construct "climate" may be more than the sum of the organization's size, predominant leadership style, and so on. The implication is that climate is "greater than the sum of its parts"; the phenomenon of the interest results from the interrelationships of the traits that make it up. Thus studies that take one or two so-called climate variables and attempt to relate them to outcome variables may not be tapping the construct that is of interest (for example, see Litwin & Stringer, 1968).

Of concern to investigations undertaken from this perspective would be the identification of those traits that determine organizational climate, and the interrelationships among these traits. Having found these, the researcher could then go on to investigate climate's impact on outcome variables. The underlying assumptions of this perspective include the following:

(1) Organizations exist and persist despite fluctuations in membership.
(2) Organizations develop a set of characteristics that may be specified.
(3) These specified characteristics are relatively enduring.
(4) The specification of these organizational characteristics may be accomplished objectively; that is, once the set of characteristics is specified, the levels or values of these characteristics may be found independent of individual members' idiosyncratic perceptions of the organization.
(5) Consensus across observers as to the levels of the characteristics, and thus the climate, would be expected to obtain.

The second perspective treats "climate" as an interaction of an organization's traits or characteristics and the individuals' perceptions of these traits. James and Jones (1974) call this perspective the "perceptual measurements-organizational attribute" approach. As with the first approach, researchers adopting this perspective assume that organizations have distinguishable attributes that are relatively enduring over time. However, climate is seen as a "perceptual measure that describe[s] the organization and [is] different from attitudinal, evaluative, and need satisfaction variables" (James & Jones, 1974, p. 1100). The key distinctions of this perspective are as follows: (1) Climate is considered a perceptual variable, dependent on the reports of individual members; (2) the perceptions of climate are descriptive, rather than evaluative; and (3) reports of the individual members are expected to exhibit considerable congruence. Thus climate from this perspective is essentially a consensual perception of an organization's attributes.

Given this perspective, the issue of consensus among perceivers is crucial to an understanding of the climate construct. Research has shown that within a given organization, subgroups may differ as to perceptions of climate. For example, Payne and Mansfield (1973) and Gorman and Malloy (1972) found that perceptions of organizational climate differed by hierarchical level of organizational participants, while Pritchard and Karasick (1973) reported that organizational climate in dispersed organizations varied from location to location as a function of both overall climate and local environmental demands. Johnston (1976 p. 101) suggests that his field study data imply "that the small organization studied had two climates," and that the "concept of climate as a joint function of situational and personality variables provides a direct and unequivocal answer to the otherwise difficult question . . . of whether climate is an attribute of the organization or of its members" (p. 102). Although Johnston fails to show the link between personality traits (for example, locus of control) that were unmeasured in his study and situational characteristics of an individual (such as tenure in the organization) that were measured, the suggested approach argues for a definition of climate based on consensual perceptions of the organization by subgroups. Under this perspective the climate becomes defined according to the networks of consensus found within the organization. Hence researchers would look not for the simple perceptual summation of all members of an organization to define the organizational climate, as Hellriegel and Slocum (1974) suggest, but rather for patterns of consensus among individuals and their characteristics that might account for the occurrence of such consensus.

Whether a molar or subsystems approach is taken, the assumptions characterizing the perceptual measurements-organizational attribute approach include those made by the first perspective, with the exception of the fourth assumption, that is, that specification of organizational climate may be accomplished objectively. Instead, climate is assumed to be a joint function of organizational properties and the individual's perception of these properties.

The third approach to organizational climate is termed "perceptual measurement-individual attribute approach" by James and Jones (1974) and is an individual, psychological approach to organizational climate. Research undertaken from this perspective has been accomplished, according to Schneider (1975a, p. 447), under two "infrequently specified assumptions . . . 1) humans attempt to apprehend order in their environment and to create order through thought; 2) humans apprehend and/or attempt to create order in their environment so they can effectively adapt their behavior to the work environment." Consequently, this approach assumes that "what is psychologically important to the individual must be how he perceives his work environment, not how others might choose to describe it" (Schneider & Bartlett, 1970, p. 510). Climate, from this perspective, is an individual's summary perceptions of his or her encounters with the organization.

Attempts have been made to distinguish this approach from the other two by differentiating between "organizational" climate and "psychological" climate (James & Jones, 1974). Ultimately this distinction is based upon the unit of analysis to be utilized in an investigation, as well as the assumptions under which the investigation is to be pursued. The distinction is both a theoretical and an operational issue. Powell and Butterfield (1978) point out that approximately half the studies they surveyed performed their analyses at the individual level, while purporting to measure an organizational construct.

Moreover, several researchers have agreed that organizations have multiple climates (for example, see Johnston, 1976; Schneider, 1975b). Research findings cited by Powell and Butterfield (1978) support the multiple subsystems approach to climate by numerous studies that showed differences in perceived climate within the same organization. Differences have been found according to (1) hierarchical level, (2) line or staff positions, (3) department/subunit, (4) biographical influences, (5) personality characteristics interacting with structural perceptions, (6) personality characteristics such as activity or passivity, or task orientation, and (7) length of service, for instance, first or second generation.

Explanation of these phenomena are offered by those who suggest that, because perceptions are influenced by the experiences one has with ones immediate environment, it would be difficult to assess the global perceptions of an entire organization from employees who interact within a limited subsystem environment. Job tenure, the degree to which jobs are boundary spanning, and organizational level can be very important variables when the research calls for global perceptions.

Powell and Butterfield (1978, p. 155) conclude:

(1) Climate is a property of subsystems in organizations. Subsystems may consist of organizational members taken individually, in groups formed on any basis, or as a whole.

(2) As a conceptual construct, climate exists independently for separate subsystems. In fact, the relationships may, but do not necessarily, exist between climates for separate subsystems (for example, the climate for new employees who are also managers).

The many organizational-level studies actually conducted at the individual level exemplify a significant dilemma in climate research. Payne, Fineman, and Wall (1976) attempt to clarify the unit of analysis dilemma by suggesting three criteria to be used in climate research to distinguish various concepts:

(1) the unit of analysis—individual or organization;
(2) the element of analysis—job or group/organization; and
(3) the nature of the measurement—descriptive or affective.

Using the above criteria, the following distinctions obtain: The construct of *organizational climate* emerges when the focus of analysis is in the organization and the nature of the measurement is descriptive; *perceived organizational characteristics* emerge when the individual is used as the unit of analysis. These compare roughly to the second and third perspectives suggested by James and Jones (1974).

Regardless of the perspective employed, the research investigations share a common concern with the impact of the entity of the organization on the individual within it. This point of convergence may be more critical than the points of divergence that have constituted many of the scholarly discussions concerning organizational climate. The often-discussed differences among the conceptualizations of the construct lie in the locus of appropriate observation. The first conceptualization assumes the "objective" observer as the appropriate "definer" of the organization's climate; the second assumes the interrelationship of the objective and subjective (organization member) observer as the appropriate definer of the construct; and the third perspective assumes the subjective observer as the appropriate locus of observation of the construct. Pivotal to these distinctions is whether the observer of the climate construct can and/or should be external or internal to the system. Likewise, the differing conceptualizations dictate that different units of analysis be employed in research investigations.

The importance of making these differences explicit is to facilitate the comparison of the differing lines of inquiry that each of the perspectives generates. The first perspective tends to generate research in which climate is used as a predictor variable posited to affect outcome variables such as satisfaction or performance (for example, see Litwin & Stringer, 1968). By stipulating the elements of climate, these elements can be varied systematically in a laboratory setting to assess their impact on selected criterion variables. In contrast, the second perspective yields research that is concerned with the impact of climate on criterion variables as well as with determinants of and the accuracy of the perception of organizational attributes (see Campbell, Dunnette, Lawler, & Weick, 1970). The third perspective yields research that treats climate as predictor, a criterion and a moderating variable. The emphasis in this school of research is the prediction of the individual member's behavior. Thus, given that making attributions concerning the characteristics of the organization is considered "behavior" on the part of the individual, this body of research is concerned with the causal mechanisms responsible for the development of such attributions, as well as their impact on satisfaction and performance with the organization (for example, see Friedlander & Margulies, 1969; Schneider & Bartlett, 1970).

More recently, Schneider and Reicher (1983) developed an integrative conceptual approach to the etiology of organizational climates. The perspective is based heavily on Mead's (1934) symbolic interactionism as the process through which individuals attach meaning to events. The perspective is labeled the "selection-attraction-attrition" (SAA) approach. Schneider and Reicher maintain that the organizational processes of selection by the organization, attraction to the organization and its members, and the attrition from the organization combine to create memberships that are relatively homogeneous.

Specifically, Schneider and Reicher theorize that individuals are attracted to and select organizations that fit their personalities and needs. As members, individuals will naturally be attracted to and interact with those individuals who share similar values, needs, attitudes, and expectations. While the selection and attraction processes appear as logical influences toward homogeneity, the attrition process works to increase homogeneity further by "weeding out" individuals who have inconsistent values, needs, attitudes, and expectations. The SAA approach suggests that organizational members tend to attach similar meanings to events primarily because the members themselves are homogeneous in their values, needs, attitudes, and expectations. This approach is particularly interesting because it views the climates of organizations as a function of communication transactions.

Despite calls for investigation of the relationship of organizational communication practices to organization climate (see Lawler, Hall, & Oldham, 1974), the relationship between organizational communication and organizational climate from all three perspectives remains virtually unexplored. Muchinsky (1977, p. 593) asserts that "there are no previous empirical studies in the literature relating climate to communication upon which to draw specific hypotheses." However, as Muchinsky suggests, the previous climate research suggests areas in which relationships between the two constructs may be found. For example, from the first climate perspective, correlates between elements of organizational climate and communication structure within the organization could be sought. Of interest would be the directionality of the relationship, as well as the impact of these constructs on the outcome variables previously investigated. From the second perspective, investigations of the relationships between the structures and functions of communication within the organization as they are perceived by members and the accuracy of the perceptions of organizational climate would be of interest. From the third perspective, the impact of the perceptions of organizational climate and organizational communication on each other, as well as on outcome variables, would be useful. The list is far from exhaustive and will be elaborated upon further in the following sections. What is crucial, however, is to maintain the distinction among the three research traditions in organizational climate, as the relationships between climate and communication are explored.

ORGANIZATIONAL CLIMATE RESEARCH

Organizational Climates as a Moderating Variable

Forehand and Guetzkow (Forehand, 1968) developed a 25-item organization description questionnaire that measured the degree to which an organization is "rules" or "autonomy" oriented. Data collected on 120 individuals, 60 in the autonomy-oriented and 60 in the rules-oriented organizations, were correlated with measures of innovativeness. Significant correlations for 8 out of 9 ability measures were found in the autonomy-oriented conditions, while no significant correlations were found in the rules-oriented conditions.

Andrews (1967) used the Thematic Apperception Test to measure nAch and nPow. These two personality characteristics were viewed as predictors of performance. It was hypothesized the nAch would be the better predictor of performance in an entrepreneurial environment. Two Mexican firms were chosen in the research—one for its aggressive, achievement orientation, the other for its conservative, stagnant orientation. Data collected from management trainees showed significant positive correlations between progress in the organization and high nAch, and significant negative correlations for nPow in the achievement-oriented firm, with the reverse being true for the conservative firm.

Hand, Richards, and Slocum (1973) found that employees who participated in a human relations training program and perceived their organization as supportive and consultative developed higher job performance than employees who perceived their organization as autocratic. Litwin and Stringer (1966) found that different styles of leadership can have an intervening effect on organizational climate. Using leadership styles as the independent variable, "authoritarian," "friendly," and "achieving" climates were created, all producing different effects on motivation and performance. Pritchard and Karasick (1973) and Cawsey (1973) found that individual need orientations and perceptions of organizational climate interact to influence performance and satisfaction. Finally, research by Frederickson, Jensen, and Beaton (1972), Dunnette (1973), and Schneider (1974) found differences in the prediction of performance when climate was viewed as a mediating variable.

In summary, although the findings are still tentative, research suggests that performance and satisfaction are more predictable as the climates are modified. Climates allowing for individual differences such as supportive leadership, autonomy, innovation, equitable rewards, and task variety appear to be conducive to higher performance and satisfaction.

Organizational Climate as
a Criterion Variable

Numerous researchers have viewed climate as a function of organizational structure. It is suggested that the structural characteristics of organizations influence the communication patterns and consequently affect perceptions of climate. Research by Pheysey, Payne, and Pugh (1971), Payne and Mansfield (1973), and Lawler et al. (1974) views climate as the criterion variable with somewhat limited results. Research by George and Bishop (1971) and Stimson and LaBelle (1971) found that extremely bureaucratic educational systems were perceived by teachers to have more "closed" climates.

Structural variables such as organizational size, structuring of activities, and centralization of authority were used by Inkson, Hickson, and Pugh (1968) and Inkson, Schwitter, Pheysey, and Hickson (1971) as predictors of perceived innovative role expectations, actual innovative behavior, and perceived interpersonal conflict. The studies were conducted in British manufacturing companies and in U.S. manufacturing companies. Data were collected from 3 groups: top managers from 25 large, highly structured British firms; top managers from 17 large, highly structured Ohio organizations; and managers from all levels in 17 more decentralized Ohio organizations.

Wide differences appeared between the two countries. While the British sample showed larger correlations between larger size and higher structuring of activities with higher expectations of innovative roles, perceived actual innovative behavior, and less interpersonal conflict, only interpersonal conflict was similar for the Ohio top managers sample. The top managers in the large, highly structured Ohio organizations perceived less interpersonal conflict as a consequence of size and structured activities, but also expected and perceived less innovative behavior in their organizations. While centralization of authority was unrelated to all the climate variables for the British firms, the more decentralized Ohio firms' top managers tended to report less innovative behavior, and managers from all levels of the more decentralized Ohio firms reported less interpersonal conflict. Child and Ellis (1973) replicated the Inkson et al. (1968, 1971) studies. When viewing all three studies, we find that relationships among structured activities, centralization, and expected and perceived innovative behavior vary greatly.

The one structural variable that appears to affect climate pervasively is organizational size (Payne & Pheysey, 1971; Indik, 1965). Size is more often related to different climate variables than any other structural variable (Payne & Pugh, 1975). In their investigation of 14 manufacturing organizations, Payne and Mansfield (1973) found that size showed correlations of at least .34 with each of 16 (out of 20) organizational climate scales.

Another structural property that appears to influence climate perceptions is hierarchical level (Hall & Lawler, 1969; Schneider & Bartlett, 1970; Schneider & Hall, 1972; Stimson & LaBelle, 1971). It appears from the above-mentioned studies that climate perceptions vary as a function of different levels in the organization hierarchy. Employees at different levels tend to report significant differences in their descriptions of their organizations' climate as well as their satisfaction with their jobs. In the same vein, Dieterly and Schneider (1974) found that climate perceptions varied as a function of the employee's level of participation, orientation to the environment, and position level.

In summary, we can see that organizational climate has been viewed extensively as a function of organizational structure. The multidimensionality of structure, however, has created some significant problems for generalization across organizational contexts. The one structural variable of size appears to be pervasive in the research, and should be considered in organizational climate research.

Organizational Climate as
a Predictor Variable

Performance is often viewed as a function of organizational climate perceptions. For example, Friedlander and Greenberg (1971) found higher performance from the hard-core unemployed who perceived a "supportive" climate than from those who perceived a less "supportive" climate. The findings on performance as a function of climate perceptions is far from conclusive, however. Research by Kacyka and Kirk (1968) found that an employee-centered climate did not lead to higher performance. Pritchard and Karasick (1973) found that only two of their eleven climate items correlated significantly with performance, and Cawsey (1973) found conflicting performance findings as a function of need orientations and organizational technology. Hellriegel and Slocum (1974) suggest that because of the multiple levels of technology varying within organizations, the subsystems studied also vary. Consequently, there is a lack of consistency in the research on performance and climate.

Job satisfaction has often been shown to vary as a function of climate perceptions. Hackman and Lawler (1971) found job satisfaction to be a function of their four core dimensions: (1) variety, (2) autonomy, (3) task identity, and (4) feedback. Hackman and Lawler (1971) found that when jobs are high on the above core dimensions, employees experience higher motivation and job satisfaction.

Research by Friedlander and Margulies (1969), Schneider (1972, 1973), and Litwin and Stringer (1966) has found job satisfaction to be a function of organizational climate, particularly in relation to interpersonal relations, group cohesiveness, task involvement, and the like. Hellriegel and Slocum (1974) provide an overview of the instruments, samples, variables, and results of numerous climate research studies.

Schneider (1975b, p. 464) provides us, however, with a profound word of caution concerning job satisfaction and organizational climate:

> For climate, perceptions of practices and procedures may be organized into a theme characterizing the organization: the organization's order is apprehended. For satisfaction, the same perceptions may be organized into a theme representing the affective state of the *individual.* By referencing structural conditions to some internal system of values, the result is a summary of the person rather than a way of characterizing the organization.

In summary, the relationship between performance and climate is apparent, but research is often confounded by changes in the level of technology between subsystems. This environmental diversity has caused a good deal of inconsistency in performance/climate findings. Additionally, the relationship between job satisfaction and organizational climate is also apparent. However, as Schneider points out, the unit of analysis is a significant issue to be addressed.

RESEARCH TOOLS

Perceptual Measures of
Organizational Climate

Perceptual measures of climate are often used in research. The following descriptions of these measures are not intended to be exhaustive, but are designed to give limited perspective of the dimensions the instruments purport to measure. There are, however, some measures that we feel are representative of climate research and are worth describing.

Organizational climate dimensions have been quite varied across the literature. Campbell et al. (1970) have suggested a useful description of four major climate dimensions: (1) individual autonomy; (2) degree of structure imposed on the position; (3) reward orientation; and (4) consideration, warmth, and support. Although the above dimensions are extremely helpful in understanding the nature of the construct, Hellriegel and Slocum (1974) found a fair amount of diversity among instruments. They found some much more narrow in scope (Dewhirst, 1971; Halpin, 1967; Halpin & Croft, 1962) than others; they also found some instruments that were more encompassing (Burns & Stalker, 1961; House & Rizzo, 1972; Payne & Pheysey, 1971; Pritchard & Karasick, 1973).

Using Leavitt's (1965) typology that organizations consist of task, structure, people, and technology dimensions, Hellriegel and Slocum (1974) suggest that there appears to be an overemphasis on "people"-oriented scales. They further suggest that this overemphasis is partially a consequence of abstracting climate items from satisfaction scales (see Johannesson, 1971, 1973).

The purposes of the next section are to identify some recently developed communication climate instruments and to examine their possible relationship to the organizational climate construct.

Perceptual Measures of
Communication Climate

The construct of "ideal communication climate" was postulated by Redding (1972). These climate dimensions consist of (1) supportiveness; (2) participative decision making; (3) trust, confidence, and credibility; (4) openness and candor; and (5) high performance goals.

More recently, Dennis (1975) envisioned communication climate to consist of at least seven components: the five hypothesized by Redding (1972), plus "information adequacy/satisfaction" and "semantic-information distance." Factor analysis produced five dimensions accounting for 52 percent of the total variance. The identified factors related to (1) superior-subordinate communication, particularly supportiveness; (2) perceived quality and accuracy of downward communication; (3) perceived openness of the superior-subordinate relationship; (4) opportunities and degree of influence of upward communication; and (5) perceived reliability of information from subordinates and coworkers.

Using a canonical correlation procedure, Dennis compared his communication climate measure with Taylor and Bowers's (1972) Survey of Organizations measure. Dennis found that his five communication climate factors shared considerable variance with the leadership and climate factors of Likert (1967). A multiple regression analysis revealed that 62 percent of the variance in Likert's variable of "supervisory leadership," and 72 percent of the variance in Likert's "organizational climate" variables of communication flow, human relations, and participation in decision making. The above findings suggest that the communication climate factors identified by Dennis are significantly related to important *causal* factors (as identified by Likert) in the climate of the organization, suggesting a considerable degree of overlap in the two constructs.

Based on the research conducted by Read (1962), Roberts and O'Reilly (1974) developed a climate-type measure of organizational communication. The instrument consists of 36 items that measure 16 dimensions of organizational communication. Of the 16 dimensions, 8 consist of trust (3 items); influence (3 items); mobility (2 items); desire for interaction (3 items); accuracy (3 items); summarization (3 items); gatekeeping (3 items); and overload (2 items). Another 3 dimensions deal with the percentage and direction of communication time: directionality-upward (3 items); directionality-downward (3 items); and directionality-lateral (3 items). There are also 4 single-item scales dealing with the percentage of time written, face-to-face, telephone, and "other" communication modes are used. The last dimension consists of a single-item scale measuring overall communication satisfaction in the organization.

After correlating the above dimensions with job satisfaction, leadership, and organizational competence and commitment, Roberts and O'Reilly found that job satisfaction was positively related to all of the communication items except for upward communication and overload, which were negatively related. Leadership "consideration" was positively related to trust, influence, mobility, desire for interaction, and amount of information received. Perceived organizational competence was positively related to trust, influence, mobility, desire for interaction, and the accuracy of information received. Organizational commitment was positively related to trust, influence, mobility, desire for interaction, accuracy of information received, and the amount of downward communication.

The research by Dennis (1975) and Roberts and O'Reilly (1974) appears to support the notion that perceptions of the quality of superior-subordinate relationships and communication are significant variables to consider when analyzing the climate of an organization. This appears particularly evident concerning trust, supportiveness, openness, and influence as they relate to leadership, decision making, perceptions of the organization's competence, and the degree of commitment to the organization.

Another measure considered here was developed by Downs, Hazen, Quiggens, and Medley (1973). The instrument purports to measure "communication satisfaction," which may be defined loosely as the totality or sum of an individual's satisfaction with the informational and relational variables in the organization's environment. Communication climate is considered to be only one of the eight dimensions affecting one's satisfaction with the organizational environment. Specifically, the instrument measures employee satisfaction with (1) communication climate, (2) supervisors, (3) organizational integration, (4) media quality, (5) horizontal and informal communication, (6) organizational perspective, (7) subordinates, and (8) personal feedback. Downs (1979) found that the communication satisfaction dimensions, when correlated with job satisfaction, varied dramatically across six different organizations. However, the communication climate, personal feedback, and relationship with supervisor dimensions displayed consistently high correlations across the six organizations.

An interesting study was conducted by Muchinsky (1977). His purpose was to explore the relationships among measures of organizational communication (Roberts & O'Reilly, 1974), organizational climate (modified Litwin & Stringer instrument; Muchinsky, 1976) and job satisfaction (Smith, Kendall, & Hulin, 1969). Muchinsky's findings are particularly relevant to communication researchers. He found the organizational communication dimensions of trust, influence, accuracy, directionality-downward, directionality-lateral, and communication satisfaction to be significantly related to all or most of the climate dimensions, while gatekeeping, overload, written modality, and other modality were unrelated to any climate dimensions. Somewhat similar findings were reported for the relationship between the communication dimensions and the job satisfaction dimensions. It should be noted that the five dimensions of job satisfaction and the six dimensions of organizational climate were highly correlated.

It is important to note that the trust and influence scales were the more consistent correlates of perceived climate. Both scales had their highest correlations with the climate factor affective tone toward management/organization. Muchinsky (1977) suggests that perceptions of trust and influence in supervision may be related to perceptions of management generally. The above two factors were consistently found to be related to climate and satisfaction. These findings partially support previous findings concerning the perception of immediate supervision and its relationship with satisfaction (Falcione, 1973, 1974a, 1975; Daly, McCroskey, & Falcione, 1976; Falcione, McCroskey, & Daly, 1977).

Falcione (1978) developed a 26-item, 5-dimension communication climate instrument. The dimensions were (1) communication receptivity, (2) decision making, (3) organizational commitment, (4) coordination, and (5) communication satisfaction/expectations. The above 5 climate dimensions and 4 perceived supervisor credibility dimensions (safety [character/sociability], competence, extroversion, and emotional stability; Falcione, 1974b) were viewed as predictors of satisfaction with immediate supervision. A total of 20 percent of the variance in supervisor satisfaction was accounted for by the credibility dimension of safety (18 percent) and the climate dimension of communication receptivity (2 percent). Since the climate dimension described supervisor behaviors to a large extent, another regression analysis was conducted with safety as the dependent variable and the 5 climate dimensions as predictors. A total of 33 percent of the variance in safety was accounted for by communication receptivity. Tentatively, at least, it appears that perception of one dimension of a supervisor's credibility is partially a function of how receptive he or she is to the communication needs of the subordinate.

The unit of analysis issue that burdens organizational climate research appears to be as troublesome for communication climate. The measures discussed previously may not view the organization as the unit of analysis, but the individual. Items dealing with subsystem and systemwide variables that go beyond the individual level departments, units, branches, work groups, and so on—are often disregarded. Schneider (1975a, p. 470) makes the following suggestion:

When the decision has been made to use climate as an index of each person's "psychology of the organization" then it is appropriate to develop measures in which individuals are the unit of analysis. For example, a common strategy is to write a set of somewhat molar descriptors, administer them to people in an organization and factor analyze the resultant item-item correlation matrix. It is clear that the resultant factors will reflect the individual differences in the way people report the system's practices and procedures. These factors, because they represent *individual* differences should not be used in research when the chosen unit of analysis is other than the individual.

Beyond the problems concerned with unit of analysis, the research does not currently show the multidimensional nature of climate, whether it be "psychological," "organizational," or "communication" climate. Using different measures that purport to measure a construct, but at a different level of analysis, can be hazardous business. What we find may be more artifactual than real. Muchinsky (1977) suggests the use of convergent and discriminant validity techniques. He recommends the use of multitrait-multimethod approaches to climate research, whether it be "organizational" climate or "communication" climate. Unless the variables that constitute the climate construct can be determined, the research will remain somewhat confused.

The ICA Communication Audit project developed by members of the International Communication Association has made a commendable effort to clarify some of the confusion in communication climate research. The project uses a multimethod procedure for the measurement of communication at the system, subsystem, and individual level by employing five measurement instruments that can be administered independently or in conjunction with one another. The five instruments consist of (1) questionnaire survey, (2) interviews, (3) network analysis, (4) communication experiences instrument, and (5) communication diary. All of the instruments can be said to measure the communication climate from micro and macro perspectives.

Using the ICA Audit survey instrument, Daly, Falcione, and Damhorst (1979) identified some of the dimensions of an organization's communication climate and examined their relationships with the employee's satisfaction with the job, the organization, and the relationships within the organizational environment. The communication climate dimensions assessed were the amount of communication sent and received by an individual to others in the organization (in terms of discrepancy scores between what respondents perceived as needed and what was reported as sent and received), the discrepancy between the amount of follow-up perceived necessary and completed by organizational sources, the timeliness of responses, and the degree of discrepancy between the information sent and perceived as needed by different levels of personnel. Each was hypothisized to have a significant relationship with organizational satisfaction (overall organization functioning, organizational concerns, and job satisfaction) and with relationships (satisfaction with top management, middle management, immediate supervisors, coworkers, and self-influence). The results generally supported the hypotheses. The ICA Communication Audit is one of the more sophisticated and carefully designed efforts to measure the communication systems of organizations.

In summary, much of the research on communication climate shares considerable variance with the organizational climate construct. Moreover, just as the unit of analysis is a significant issue in the measurement of organizational climate, the same can be said for communication climate.

ORGANIZATIONAL CULTURES

As indicated earlier, the variety of approaches to organizational climate has resulted in theoretical and empirical muddy waters. Contributing to the confusion is the construct of organizational *culture*. The purpose of this section is to explore the theoretical and empirical approaches used in the study of organizational culture, and to relate these approaches to those of the climate construct.

Unlike organizational climate, the organizational culture construct has not been investigated extensively. However, two conceptual approaches to organizational culture have already emerged. The first treats culture solely as a context in which the organization members function and that shapes their behavior (for example, see Schwartz & Davis, 1980). Culture, from this perspective, is "usually long-term and strategic . . . difficult to change . . . [and] rooted in deeply-held beliefs and values in which individuals hold a substantial investment as the result of some processing or analysis of data about organizational life" (Schwartz & Davis, 1980,p. 5). This perspective focuses on culture as a force, influencing or constraining the behavior of the organization as a whole, as well as of individuals within it. Culture, as defined, would be consistent across organizational subsets and relatively stable over time.

The second perspective views culture as both process and context (see Pacanowsky & O'Donnell-Trujillo, 1982). Endeavoring to "see" the organizing process, this perspective focuses on the interaction of events within an organization. Of interest is "understanding how . . . organizational life is accomplished communicatively" (Pacanowsky & O'Donnell-Trujillo, 1982, p. 122).

These perspectives have several similarities. Both perspectives have their theoretical bases in anthropology. Both assume that patterns of behavior can be found within organizational boundaries, unique to that organization, and determined as a function of membership in the organization. Moreover, culture is an attribute of the organization, not of the individuals within it.

However, the differences in these perspectives may yield highly different research programs. The first perspective would view culture as a predictor variable, influencing outcomes of organizational decisions, determining organizational processes, and affecting individual perceptions and attributions. The second perspective yields investigations of the processes leading to the establishment and maintenance of organized behavior. Simply stated, the first perspective asks, "What is the culture and how does it influence the organization?" while the second perspective asks, "How are the processes of interaction behaving in this organization?"

RELATION OF ORGANIZATIONAL CULTURE AND ORGANIZATIONAL CLIMATE

The culture construct, as viewed from the first perspective, bears remarkable resemblance to the climate construct defined from the "multiple measurement-organizational attribute" approach defined by James and Jones (1974). According to Jablin (1980, p. 329), "This orientation characterizes organizational climate as a global construct, potentially inclusive of almost all organizational characteristics; e.g., organizational structure, system and subsystem values, contexts, norms, and processes." It is important to note that this definition also implies that climate is relatively stable over time, as changes cannot be effected quickly in values, norms, and structures. Comparing this definition to the definition of culture offered by Schwartz and Davis (1980), it might be argued that organizational climate and organizational culture are isomorphic. However, empirical support for this argument is limited. As a practical matter, such an assertion assumes that climate would be measured from multiple perspectives designed to identify organizational behavior apart from the perceptions of individual members. Few organizational studies (see Litwin & Stringer, 1966) have utilized techniques not solely relying on members' self-reported perceptions. More important, if the definition holds, homogeneous perceptions of an organization's climate/culture would be expected to obtain. However, findings by several researchers (for example, Hall & Lawler, 1969; Johnston, 1976; Schneider, 1975a, 1975b; Stimson & Belle, 1971) support the notion that climate differs by subgroup, whether functional or hierarchical.

What, then, is the relationship of climate and culture? We suggest that *culture* may be usefully viewed as the organization's system of values, norms, beliefs, and structures that persist *over time*, while climate is the assessment of these elements *at a given moment*.

This definition reflects a historical perspective of organizations. Conceptually, at the inception of an organization, climate and culture would be isomorphic. However, over time, as the organization becomes an entity aside from the persons who belong to it, *climate* would become an indicator of the goodness of fit between an organization's *culture* and its people.

This definition has several implications. First, the definition suggests that the culture of an organization, measured over time, will show little change. Studies of organizational resistance to change (see Coch & French,

1948; compare Beer, 1971; Greiner, Leitch, & Barnes, 1968) indicate that organizations do tend to retain existing perceptions and patterns of behavior, even in the presence of change agents. Second, the definition suggests that in studies of climate, regardless of subgroup variation, some common variance would be shared, across subgroups and over time. Schwartz and Davis (1980, p. 3) posit that while subgroups may differ among themselves, "an overall umbrella culture, however, exists as a common denominator for the organization as a whole." Of interest in previous studies would be the amount of variance *shared* across groups, as well as the unique variance explained by subgroups.

The utility of this definition of culture is yet to be evaluated empirically. Little formal study has been conducted on the subject, and a search of the literature reveals that no formal longitudinal investigations have been reported. Anecdotal case studies, however (for example, Deal & Kennedy, 1982), suggest the viability of systematic investigations of the construct.

The second perspective of organizational culture, which treats culture as both process and context, also has implications for climate studies. By studying the content, structure, and context of communicative events, this line of research seeks to discover the "sense-making" devices used by organizational members. Investigations from this perspective may be said to operationalize the assumptions of climate research, identified by Schneider (1975a, p. 451) that "people (a) apprehend order in their work world based on perceived and inferred cues; and (b) behave in ways that fit the order they apprehend." This perspective would also lend behavioral insight to study of the socialization process of organizational members, which has previously relied primarily on cognitive theoretical models (see, for example, Feldman, 1981; Wiener, 1982).

As with the first perspective, investigations from the "culture as context and process" perspective would expect to find consistency over time, especially in organizations that have extensive histories. Moreover, it might be argued that the findings of a single study may be indications of *communication* climate, which would be expected to reflect organizational culture over time.

From both perspectives on culture, a close relationship between culture and communication climate would exist. From the first perspective, communication practices are considered indicators of the culture. From the second perspective, culture consists of the communication regularities in the organization.

Implications

The usefulness of the organizational culture construct may be twofold. Theoretically, it may provide richer understanding of the findings of climate research. The culture construct may serve to clarify seemingly disparate findings by adding a contextual dimension to field research. Empirically, it may refocus research efforts from perceptual self-reports to a greater variety of data collection methods. The construct requires both longitudinal research and a variety of data collection methods. The use of method "triangulation" (Jick, 1979) is crucial in the study of organizational culture.

CONCLUSIONS AND RECOMMENDATIONS

This chapter has reviewed the equivocal conceptualization of the organizational climate and organizational culture constructs. Research was reviewed that treats climate as a moderating, criterion, and predictor variable. It was also suggested that climate may be usefully viewed as a subsystem variable, while culture may be viewed as the shared variance among subsystems.

The relationships between *communication* climate and organizational climate were also reviewed. Difficulties in interpreting research findings due to varying units of analysis are shared by both communication and organizational climate studies. The need for future research concerning the relationships among climate and culture was also suggested.

The conclusions and recommendations may be summarized as follows:

(1) Many unresolved methodological and conceptual issues continue to exist in organizational climate and communication climate research.
(2) Individual and organizational attributes are often confounded, particularly when the individual is used as the unit of analysis and the research conclusions are drawn at the organizational level of analysis.
(3) When using multiple instruments to measure more than one concept (organizational climate, communication climate, satisfaction, productivity, and so on) the unit of analysis should be the same across concepts.
(4) Organizations probably have many subsystem climates, and care must be taken in sample selection and statistical analyses to deal with them.
(5) Researchers who treat organizational climate as a criterion variable might also consider investigating communication behavioral correlates as predictors. At various subsystem levels, the corresponding climates should show differing degrees of variance in communication behavior. Schneider (1975a, pp. 474-475) presents this case very well in his following definition of climate:

> Climate perceptions are psychologically meaningful molare descriptions that people can agree characterize a system's practices and procedures. By its practices and procedures a system may create many climates. People perceive climates because the molare perceptions function as frames of references for the attainment of some congruity between behavior and the system's practices and procedures. However, if the climate is one which regards and supports the display of individual differences, people in the same system will not behave similarly.

(6) In order for us to understand better both the cultures and the climate constructs, multiple methods must be employed. Both objective and perceptual measures of climate, as well as experimental manipulation, can be utilized to determine congruency across approaches. Moreover, research on the culture construct needs to employ several methodologies (that is, triangulation) and should be longitudinal in nature.

(7) More rigorous conceptualizations of the culture construct are needed to yield more formalized operationalizations.

(8) In general, greater care in defining what constitutes an organization is needed. Research has tended to *assume,* a priori, that a given business concern is an organization, on the basis of a label. That is, that which shows the same name, or incorporating documents, qualifies as an organization. Consequently, unit of analysis arguments abound, as "subsystems" (that is, recognizable entities) within the assumed degree of entitivity exhibited by an "assumed" organization.

The studies of organizational climate, communication climate, and organizational culture have sparked fascinating research questions. Communication scholars can make significant contributions by determining the relationship of communication practices and the development of organizational climate and culture.

REFERENCES

Andrews, J. D. W. (1967). The achievement motive and advancement in two types of organizations. *Journal of Personality and Social Psychology, 6,* 163-169.

Beer, M. (1971, September). Organizational climate: A viewpoint from the change agent. In *Organizational climate.* Symposium presented at the American Psychological Association, Washington, D.C.

Bohrnstedt, G. (1969). A quick method for determining the reliability and validity of multiple item scales. *American Sociological Review, 34,* 542-548.

Burns, T., & Stalker, G. (1961). *The management of innovation.* London: Tavistock.

Campbell, J. P., Dunnette, M. D., Lawler, E. E., & Weick, K. E. (1970). *Managerial behavior, performance and effectiveness.* New York: McGraw-Hill.

Cawsey, T. (1973, April). *The interaction of motivation and environment in the prediction of performance potential and satisfaction in the life insurance industry in Canada.* Paper presented at the Sixteenth Annual Meeting of the Midwest Academy of Management, Chicago.

Child, J., & Ellis, T. (1973). Predictors of variation in managerial roles. *Human Relations, 26,* 250-277.

Coch, L., & French, J. R. P. (1948). Overcoming resistance to change. *Human Relations, 1,* 512-532.

Costley, D., Downey, K., & Blumberg, M. (1973). *Organizational climate: The effects of human relations training.* Unpublished manuscript, Pennsylvania State University.

Csoka, L. S. (1975). Relationship between organizational climate and the situational favorableness of dimension of Fiedler's contingency model. *Journal of Applied Psychology, 60,* 273-277.

Daly, J. A., Falcione, R. L., & Damhorst, M. L. (1979). *Communication correlates of relational and organizational satisfaction: An audit based investigation.* Paper presented at the annual convention of the International Communication Association, Philadelphia.

Daly, J. A., & Korinek, J. T. (1982). Organizational communication: A review via operationalizations. In H. H. Greenbaum & R. L. Falcione, *Organizational communication: Abstracts, analysis, and overview* (Vol. 7, pp. 11-46). Beverly Hills, CA: Sage.

Daly, J. A., McCroskey, J. D., & Falcione, R. L. (1976). *Communication apprehension, supervisor communication receptivity and satisfaction with supervisors*. Paper presented at the annual convention of the Eastern Communication Association, Philadelphia.

Davis, J. (1968). Rules, hierarchy, and organizational climate. *Personnel Administration, 31*, 50-55.

Deal, T., & Kennedy, A. (1982). *Corporate cultures*. Reading, MA: Addison-Wesley.

Dennis, H. S. (1975). *The construction of a managerial communication climate inventory for use in complex organizations*. Paper presented at the annual convention of the International Communication Association, Chicago.

Dennis, H. S., Goldhaber, G. M., & Yates, M. P. (1978). Organizational communication theory and research: An overview of research method. In B. Ruben (Ed.), *Communication yearbook 2* (pp. 243-269). New Brunswick, NJ: Transaction.

Dewhirst, D. (1971). Impact of organizational climate on the desire to manage among engineers and scientists. *Personnel Journal, 50*, 160-203.

Dieterley, D., & Schneider, B. (1974). The effect of organizational environment on perceived power and climate: A laboratory study. *Organizational Behavior and Human Performance, 11*, 316-337.

Downey, H. K., Hellriegel, D., Phelps, M., & Slocum, J. (1974). Organizational climate and job satisfaction. *Journal of Business Research, 2*, 233-248.

Downey, H. K., Hellriegel, D., & Slocum, J. (1975). Congruence between individual needs, organizational climate, job satisfaction, and performance. *Academy of Management Journal, 18*, 149-155.

Downs, C. (1979). The relationship between communication and job satisfaction. In R. Huseman, C. Logue, & D. Freshley (Eds.), *Readings in interpersonal and organizational communication* (3rd ed.). Boston: Allyn & Bacon.

Downs, C., & Hains, T. (1982). Productivity and communication. In M. Burgoon (Ed.), *Communication yearbook 5* (pp. 435-453). New Brunswick, NJ: Transaction.

Downs, C., Hazen, M., Quiggens, J., & Medley, J. (1973). *An empirical and theoretical investigation of communication satisfaction*. Paper presented at the annual meeting of the Speech Communication Association, New York.

Dunnette, M. D. (1973). *Performance equals ability and what?* Technical Report No. 4009. Unpublished manuscript, University of Minnesota, Department of Psychology.

Falcione, R. L. (1973). The relationship of supervisor credibility to subordinate satisfaction. *Personnel Journal, 52*, 800-803.

Falcione, R. L. (1974a). Communication climate and satisfaction with immediate supervision. *Journal of Applied Communication Research, 2*, 13-20.

Falcione, R. L. (1974b). The factor structure of source credibility scales for immediate supervisors in the organizational context. *Central States Speech Journal, 25*, 63-66.

Falcione, R. L. (1974c). Credibility: Qualifier of subordinate participation. *Journal of Business Communication, 11*, 43-54.

Falcione, R. L. (1975). *Subordinate satisfaction as a function of perceived supervisor credibility*. Paper presented at the annual convention of the International Communication Association, Chicago.

Falcione, R. L. (1978). *Subordinate satisfaction as a function of communication climate and perceptions of immediate supervision*. Paper presented at the annual convention of the Eastern Communication Association, Boston.

Falcione, R. L., McCroskey, J. C., & Daly, J. A. (1977). Job satisfaction as a function of employees' communication apprehension, self-esteem, and perceptions of their immediate supervisors. In B. Ruben (Ed.), *Communication yearbook 1* (pp. 363-375). New Brunswick, NJ: Transaction.

Feldman, D. (1981). Multiple socialization of organizational members. *Academy of Management Review, 6*, 309-318.

Forehand, J. A. (1968). On the interaction of persons and organizations. In R. Tagiuri & G. Litwin (Eds.), *Organizational climate: explorations of a concept*. Boston: Harvard Business School, Division of Research.

Forehand, J. A., & Gilmer, B. V. (1964). Environmental variation in studies of organizational behavior. *Psychological Bulletin, 62*, 361-382.

Frederickson, N. (1966). *Some effects of organizational climates on administrative perform-ance.* Research memorandum RM-66-21, Educational Testing Service.

Frederickson, N., Jensen, O., & Beaton, A. E. (1972). *Prediction of organizational behavior.* Elmsford, NY: Pergamon.

Friedlander, F., & Greenberg, S. (1971). Effect of job attitudes, training and organizational climates on performance of the hard-core unemployed. *Journal of Applied Psychology, 55,* 287-295.

Friedlander, F., & Margulies, N. (1969). Multiple impacts of organizational climate and individ-ual value systems upon job satisfaction. *Personnel Psychology, 22,* 171-183.

Gavin, J. F. (1975). Organizational climate as a function of personal and organizational varia-bles. *Journal of Applied Psychology, 60,* 135-139.

George, J., & Bishop, L. (1971). Relationship of organizational structure and teacher personal-ity characteristics to organizational climate. *Administrative Science Quarterly, 16,* 467-476.

Goldhaber, G., Porter, D. T., & Yates, M. (1977). *ICA communication audit survey instrument: 1977 organizational norms.* Paper presented at the annual convention of the International Communication Association, Berlin.

Golembiewski, R. (1970). Organizational properties and managerial training: Testing alterna-tive models of attitude change. *Academy of Management Journal, 13,* 13-34.

Golembiewski, R., & Carrigan, S. (1970). The persistence of laboratory-induced changes in organizational styles. *Administrative Science Quarterly, 15,* 330-340.

Golembiewski, R., Unzenrider, R. M., Blumberg, A., Carrigan, S. B., & Meade, W. R. (1971). Changing climate in a complex organization: Interactions between a learning design and an environment. *Academy of Management Journal, 14,* 465-483.

Gorman, L., & Malloy, E. (1972). *People, jobs and organizations.* Dublin: Irish Productivity Center.

Greenbaum, H. H., & Falcione, R. L. (1982). *Organizational communication: Abstracts, analy-sis, and overview* (Vol. 7). Beverly Hills, CA: Sage.

Greiner, L. E., Leitch, D. P., & Barnes, L. B. (1968). The simple complexity of organizational climate in a governmental agency. In R. Tagiuri & G. H. Litwin (Eds.), *Organizational cli-mate.* Cambridge: Harvard University, Graduate School of Business Administration, Divi-sion of Research.

Hackman, J. R., & Lawler, E. E., III. (1971). Employee reactions to job characteristics. *Journal of Applied Psychology, 55,* 259-286.

Hackman, J. R., & Oldham, G. R. (1975). Development of the job diagnostic survey. *Journal of Applied Psychology, 60,* 159-170.

Hall, D., & Lawler, E. E., III. (1969). Unused potential in research development organizations. *Research Management, 12,* 339-354.

Halpin, A. (1967). Change and organizational climate. *Journal of Educational Administration, 5,* 5-25.

Halpin, A., & Croft, D. (1962). *The organizational climate of schools.* U.S. Office of Education, Department of Health, Education and Welfare, Contract No. SAE 543 (8639). Washing-ton, DC: Government Printing Office.

Hand, H., Richards, M., & Slocum, J. (1973). Organizational climate and the effectiveness of a human relations training program. *Academy of Management Journal, 16,* 185-195.

Hellriegel, D., & Slocum, J. W. (1974). Organizational climate: Measures, research and contin-gencies. *Academy of Management Journal, 17,* 255-280.

Holloman, R. (1973, May). *A problem-solving approach to changing organizational climate.* Paper presented at Tenth Annual Meeting of the Eastern Academy of Management, Phila-delphia.

House, R. J., & Rizzo, J. R. (1972). Toward the measurement of organizational practices: Scale development and validation. *Journal of Applied Psychology, 56,* 388-396.

Indik, B. P. (1965). Organizational size and member participation: Some empirical tests of alter-native explanations. *Human Relations, 18,* 339-350.

Inkson, J. H., Hickson, D. J., & Pugh, D. S. (1968). *Administrative reduction of variances in orga-nization and behavior.* London: British Psychological Society.

Inkson, J. H., Schwitter, J. P., Pheysey, D. C., & Hickson, D. J. (1971). *Comparisons of Birmingham, England and Ohio, U.S.A. organizations.* Unpublished manuscript, University of Aston, Birmingham, England.

Jablin, F. M. (1980). Organizational communication theory and research: An overview of communication climate and network research. In D. Nimmo (Ed.), *Communication yearbook 4* (pp. 327-347). New Brunswick, NJ: Transaction.

James, L. R., & Jones, A. P. (1974). Organizational climate: A review of theory and research. *Psychological Bulletin, 81,* 1096-1112.

Jick, T. (1979). Mixing qualitative and quantitive methods: Triangulation in action. *Administrative Science Quarterly, 24,* 602-611.

Johannesson, R. E. (1971). Job satisfaction and perceptually measured organization climate: Redundancy and confusion. In M. W. Frey (Ed.), *New developments in management and organization theory: Proceedings of the eighth annual conference, Eastern Academy of Management,* (1976) 27-37.

Johannesson, R. E. (1973). Some problems in the measurement of organizational climate. *Organizational Behavior and Human Performance, 10,* 118-114.

Johnston, H. R., Jr. (1976). A new conceptualization of source of organizational climate. *Administrative Science Quarterly, 21,* 95-103.

Kacyka, E., & Kirk, R. (1968). Managerial climate, work groups and organizational performance. *Administrative Science Quarterly, 12,* 252-271.

LaFollette, W. R., & Sims, H. P., Jr. (1975). Is satisfaction redundant with organizational climate? *Organizational Behavior and Human Performance, 13,* 257-278.

Lawler, E. E., Hall, D. F., & Oldham, G. R. (1974). Organizational climate: Relationship to organizational structure, process, and performance. *Organizational Behavior and Human Performance, 11,* 139-155.

Leavitt, H. (1965). Applied organizational change in industry: Structural, technological and humanistic approaches. In J. March (Ed.), *Handbook of organizations* (pp. 1144-1170). Chicago: Rand McNally.

Lesniak, R., Yates, M., Goldhaber, G., & Richards, E. (1977). *NETPLOT: An original computer program for interpreting NEGOPY.* Paper presented at the annual convention of the International Communication Association, Berlin.

Likert, R. (1967). *The human organization.* New York: McGraw-Hill.

Litwin, G., & Stringer, R. (1966). *The influence of organizational climate on human motivation.* Paper presented at a conference on organizational climate, Foundation for Research on Human Behavior, Ann Arbor, Michigan.

Litwin, G., & Stringer, R. (1968). *Motivation and organizational climate.* Cambridge, MA: Harvard University Press.

Lyon, H. L., & Ivancevich, J. M. (1976). An exploratory investigation of organizational climate and job satisfaction in a hospital. *Academy of Management Journal, 17,* 635-648.

Marrow, A., Bowers, D., & Seashore, S. (1967). *Management by participation.* New York: Harper & Row.

Mead, G. H. (1934). *The social psychology of George Herbert Mead (A. Strauss, Ed.).* Chicago: University of Chicago Press.

Muchinsky, P. M. (1976). An assessment of the Litwin and Stringer organization climate questionnaire: An empirical and theoretical extension of the Sims and LaFollette study. *Personnel Psychology, 29,* 371-392.

Muchinsky, P. M. (1977). Organizational communication: Relationships to organizational climate and job satisfaction. *Academy of Management Journal, 20,* 592-607.

Pacanowsky, M., & O'Donnell-Trujillo, N. (1982). Communication and organizational cultures. *Western Journal of Speech, 46,* 115-130.

Payne, R. L., Fineman, S., & Wall, T. D. (1976). Organizational climate and job satisfaction: A conceptual synthesis. *Organizational Behavior and Human Performance, 16,* 45-62.

Payne, R., & Mansfield, R. (1973). Relationships of perceptions of organizational climate to organizational structure, context, and hierarchical position. *Administrative Science Quarterly, 18,* 515-526.

Payne, R., & Pheysey, D. (1971). G. G. Stern's organizational climate index: A reconceptualization and application to business organizations. *Organizational Behavior and Human Performance, 6,* 77-98.

Payne, R. L., Pheysey, D. C., & Pugh, D. S. (1971). Organizational structure, organizational climate, and group structure: An exploratory study of their relationship in two British manufacturing companies. *Occupational Psychology, 45,* 45-46.

Payne, R. L., & Pugh, D. S. (1975). Organizational structure and organization climate. In M. D. Dunnette (Ed.), *Handbook of industrial and organizational psychology.* Chicago: Rand McNally.

Peterson, R. B. (1975). The interaction of technological process and perceived organizational climate in Norwegian firms. *Academy of Management Journal, 18,* 288-299.

Pheysey, D. C., Payne, R. L., & Pugh, D. S. (1971). Influence of structure at organizational and group levels. *Administrative Science Quarterly, 16,* 61-73.

Porter, D. T. (1976). *CAAS—communication audit analysis system.* Unpublished computer program, Buffalo, NY.

Powell, G. N., & Butterfield, D. A. (1978). The case for subsystem climates in organizations. *Academy of Management Review, 3,* 151-157.

Pritchard, R., & Karasick, B. (1973). The effects of organizational climate on managerial job performance and job satisfaction. *Organizational Behavior and Human Performance, 9,* 110-119.

Read, W. (1962). Upward communication in industrial hierarchies. *Human Relations, 15,* 3-16.

Redding, W. C. (1972). *Communication within the organization: An interpretive review of theory and research.* New York: Industrial Communication Council.

Redding, W. C. (1979). Organizational communication theory and ideology: An overview. In D. Nimmo (Ed.), *Communication yearbook 3*(pp. 309-341). New Brunswick, NJ: Transaction.

Richards, W. (1975). *A manual for network analysis: Using the NEGOPY network analysis program.* Stanford, CA: Stanford University, Institute for Communication Research.

Richards, W. (1978). *Network analysis: A state of the art.* Paper presented at the annual convention of the International Communication Association, Chicago.

Richetto, G. (1977). Organization communication theory and research: An overview. In B. Ruben (Ed.), *Communication yearbook 1* (pp. 331-346). New Brunswick, NJ: Transaction.

Roberts, K., & O'Reilly, C. (1974). Measuring organizational communication. *Journal of Applied Psychology, 59,* 321-326.

Schneider, B. (1972). Organizational climate: Individual preferences and organizational realities. *Journal of Applied Psychology, 56,* 211-218.

Schneider, B. (1973). The perception of organizational climate: The customer's view. *Journal of Applied Psychology, 57,* 248-256.

Schneider, B. (1974). *Organizational type, organizational success, and the prediction of individual performance.* Unpublished manuscript, University of Maryland.

Schneider, B. (1975a). Organizational climate: An essay. *Personnel Psychology, 28,* 447-479.

Schneider, B. (1975b). Organizational climate: Individual preferences and organizational realities revisited. *Journal of Applied Psychology, 60,* 459-465.

Schneider, B., & Bartlett, C. (1968). Individual differences and organizational climate I: The research plan and questionnaire development. *Personnel Psychology, 21,* 323-334.

Schneider, B., & Bartlett, C. (1970). Individual differences and organizational climate II: Measurement of organizational climate by multitrait multirater matrix. *Personnel Psychology, 23,* 493-512.

Schneider, B., & Hall, D. (1972). Toward specifying the concept of work climate: A study of Roman Catholic diocesan priests. *Journal of Applied Psychology, 56,* 447-456.

Schneider, B., & Reicher, A. E. (1983). On the etiology of climates. *Personnel Psychology, 36,* 19-39.

Schneider, B., & Snyder, R. A. (1975). Some relationships between job satisfaction and organizational climate. *Journal of Applied Psychology, 60,* 318-328.

Schwartz, H., & Davis, S. (1980, Spring). *Matching corporate culture and business strategy.* Unpublished manuscript, Management Analysis Center.

Sims, H. P., & LaFollette, W. R. (1975). An assessment of the Litwin and Stringer organizational climate questionnaire. *Personnel Psychology, 28,* 19-38.

Smith, P. C., Kendall, L. M., & Hulin, C. L. (1969). *The measurement of satisfaction in work and retirement.* Chicago: Rand McNally.

Sorcher, M., & Danzig, A. (1969). Charting and changing the organizational climate. *Personnel, 46,* 16-28.

Stimson, J., & LaBelle, T. (1971). The organizational climate of Paraguayan elementary school: Rural-urban differentiation. *Education and Urban Society, 3,* 333-349.

Taylor, J., & Bowers, D. (1972). *Survey of organizations.* Ann Arbor: University of Michigan, Institute for Social Research.

Walters, L. K., Roach, D., & Batlis, N. (1974). Organizational climate dimensions and job-related attitudes. *Personnel Psychology, 27,* 465-476.

Watson, J. R. (1973). *Communication effectiveness in university executive management programs: A field experiment.* Unpublished doctoral dissertation, University of Illinois.

Weiner, Y. (1982). Commitment in organizations: A normative view. *Academy of Management Review, 7,* 418-428.

Yates, M., Porter, D., Goldhaber, G., Dennis, H., & Richetto, G. (1976). *The ICA communication audit system: Results of six studies.* Paper presented at the annual convention of the International Communication Association, Portland, Oregon.

11 ● Organizing Communication Behavior: The Role of Schemas and Constructs

HOWARD E. SYPHER ● JAMES L. APPLEGATE

University of Kentucky

O VER the last decade in the fields of communication and psychology groups of researchers have been moving in similar directions in their conceptualizations of the processes through which individuals define and act on their definitions of reality. These moves most generally have led to a view of persons as active and purposeful agents. As a result, we have seen less focus on the causes of human cognition and behavior in the traditional sense and increased concern for describing and explaining the mechanisms employed by individuals to make sense of their world. In psychology there has been a pervasive shift from behavioristic approaches to perception and learning to a more active view of information processing. Social and cognitive psychologists have developed a number of common concerns within this type of information-processing framework regarding such issues as the nature of cognitive structure, verbal memory, the processing of stories and visual information, impression formation, and stereotyping.

In communication research we have seen similar (though not as pervasive) shifts resulting in greater attention to the cognitive mechanisms undergirding and influenced by social interaction. Most illustrative of this shift has been work done within constructivist communication theory (see Delia, O'Keefe, & O'Keefe, 1982, for a comprehensive review) and various cognitive approaches to communication (e.g., Planalp & Hewes, 1982; Roloff &

Correspondence and requests for reprints: Howard E. Sypher, College of Communications, University of Kentucky, Lexington, KY 40506.

Berger, 1982). For obvious reasons these research efforts have focused on those aspects of cognition and social cognition seeming to have the most direct implications for the quality of face-to-face communication behavior, although some others (Woodall, Davis, & Sahin, 1983) have recently explored the role of cognition in understanding and remembering mass communication messages.

In this chapter we first briefly review selected research on models of cognitive structure and critique a part of this recent work in psychology done under the general rubric of "schema" research. Then we offer an analysis of the implications of schema research (particularly work on memory processes) for our thinking about the nature of interpersonal construct system development (particularly interpersonal cognitive differentiation) and its relation to communication behavior.

COGNITION, COGNITIVE STRUCTURE, AND COMMUNICATION

Much of our everyday interactions are unplanned, spontaneous, and appear to involve memory and deeper cognitive processes only marginally. The impact of cognition is probably felt most in its influence on perception, understanding, and motor production processes. Yet a great deal of what constitutes communicative effectiveness in interpersonal contexts and spontaneous communicative activities requires memory (Sypher, in press). Listening, for example, requires that we utilize short-term memory (Bostrom & Waldhart, 1980) and that we be able to integrate knowledge that we gain with related already stored information. Conversation requires that we recall relevant information for input into our conversational bouts and that we participate in a reasonably standard format (we recall the rules). Some conversations are reenacted so many times that they become relatively scripted (Berger & Douglas, 1982). When someone breaks from a script we notice, but often even here routinized repair procedures are performed without the need to focus many cognitive resources on the task. Many researchers would argue that such conversational routines or procedures are stored in memory, recalled, and then replayed in appropriate situations.

Hence memory processes are probably more central to communication and communication research than has been acknowledged. For example, for little apparent reason sometimes we are asked to recall conversations we have had with friends or teachers. Obviously, our reports rely on our memories and reflect whatever biases are inherent in memory. Similarly, in much of our research on communication we ask respondents to recall conversations, behaviors, their style of communication, or the television programs they watch. In asking these kinds of questions we are really asking respondents to recall information stored in memory, often without concern for how this information is stored. Unfortunately, there is no single widely accepted view or dominant model of event or memory storage on which researchers can rely. Memory researchers have suggested a number of plausible cognitive structures for event or person memory. In a recent review, Hastie and Carlston (1980) suggested four ways that information about a communication event or data about a particular person might be stored: (1) undifferentiated associative networks, (2) storage bins or stacks, (3) hierarchical networks, and (4) schema models including frames or scripts.

The first type of cognitive structure, the associative network, can be conceived as an undirected graph where communication episodes or events are nodes or points and the associative links connect similar nodes. In an undirected graph model the relation between two nodes or points is symmetrical and corresponds to a very simple association theory. Alternatively, one might imagine a graph structure in which persons are nodes who are linked to similar persons in an associative network.[1] Unfortunately, this model has limited utility because some of the earliest work on social learning (Ebbinhaus, 1885) showed such paths to be directional.

Recently, Wyer and Srull (1980) provided a second alternative structuring of memory for communication events or person information. These authors contend that information about episodes or individuals is located in "storage bins" that are connected by associative pathways. Within bins, information is sorted according to recency, making new information the most accessible. However, other processes (e.g., rehearsal) can move information to the top of the bin for easy and rapid access. Wyer and Srull's alternative has been applied successfully in computer science.

Hastie and Carlston (1980) suggest another model where hierarchical network structures store person or event data. The assumption is that data entry to the network is limited to higher-level points and that the search for information moves downward. In this model, higher-level nodes represent abstract information (e.g., the construct of extravert or extraversion). Lower-level nodes represent concrete behavioral events or inferences. The base of this hierarchical model is made up of a host of interconnected concrete episodes. These events may be interconnected because they co-occurred in perception or because they were linked by some inference mechanism.

Finally, Hastie and Carlston (1980) point out that a number of researchers have suggested or used frame or script models of episode memory. These schematic structures tend to be very complex and cannot be represented as associative graph structures primarily because they represent geometric, causal, and categorical information as well as simple proximity. The next section analyzes these script and schema frameworks.

THE GROWTH OF SCHEMA RESEARCH

While numerous positions have been advanced, there is general agreement that recent verbal memory research reflects a move away from the Ebbinghaus tradition of detailed analyses of memory components and toward the more holistic orientation forwarded by Bartlett (1932). Research has turned to examination of increasingly complex phenomena (sentences, paragraphs, stories, and persons) and away from the study of nonsense syllables and word lists. Recent work has been characterized by incorporation of association network models of memory. A major goal has been to understand sequential processes in human cognition. A number of memory models (outlined above) are currently employed and, while not entirely isomorphic, they tend to employ similar terminology.

The basic elements of cognitive systems are *nodes*. Nodes are most typically defined as simple ideas or components of a semantic network. However, researchers interested in social cognition have expanded the concept and suggested that nodes exist for persons as well as for events and abstract concepts. Person nodes are not defined by any specific feature but rather are said to embody an amalgamation of relevant cognitions about a person. Furthermore, these person nodes are thought to be connected in associative networks by pathways that can activate and be activated by other nearby nodes. Nodes grouped within thematic clusters are generally thought of as *schemas*.

It is, in fact, the concept of schema that has come to occupy center stage as an explanatory device, not just in memory research but in cognitive and social psychology generally. Although the notion of schema is still defined rather ambiguously (we will have more to say about this problem later), schemas are pictured as organizing frameworks, built up through experience, that are necessary for interpretation, comprehension, and enhanced recall of information. Most researchers believe they are utilized in both the encoding and reconstructive retrieval stages of information processing.

Despite its vagueness (or perhaps because of it), the schema notion has heavily influenced research on a large variety of phenomena in psychology. Rosch and Lloyd (1978) reviewed much of this work, so we point to only a few examples here. There is Schank and Abelson's (1977) scripts model, specifically directed at explaining the processing of stories, as well as Cantor and Mischel's (1977) work using the prototype notion (borrowed from "fuzzy set" theory) in analysis of the development of personality impressions. Hastie, Ostrom, Ebbesen, Wyer, Hamilton, and Carlston (1980), Nisbett and Ross (1980), and Taylor and Crocker (1981) also have been influenced heavily by schema logic in their recent work on impression formation and social judgment. Recent work on attitude change and polarization shows the influence of the schema concept (Smith, 1982; Tesser, 1978).

Work on stereotyping and social cognition has been reconceptualized with schema notions in mind (Hamilton, 1981; Sypher & Waltman, 1983; Taylor, Fiske, Etcoff, & Ruderman, 1978). Other researchers have argued for the utility of employing schemas in understanding visual information processing (Spoehr & Lehmkuhle, 1982). The list of applications of the concept is extensive.

Conceptual Problems with Schema
as a Theoretic Construct

The broad application of schema notions across a variety of research areas in cognitive and social psychology, while producing a number of important and intriguing pieces of research, also has revealed serious conceptual problems, which, unresolved, threaten the possibility of generating an integrated theoretical understanding of cognitive processing from current research. These problems are related to and stem primarily from the fact that so-called schema research has few, if any, coherent philosophical or theoretic underpinnings.

Although a number of researchers have attempted to offer general schema (or frame) models (Bobrow & Winograd, 1977; Minsky, 1975; Rumelhart & Norman, 1978; Rumelhart & Ortony, 1977), it is widely agreed that the term "schema" has no fixed definition (Alba & Hasher, 1983; Taylor & Crocker, 1981). Schemas are variously referred to as organizing frameworks, scripts, plans, abstract hypotheses, organizing principles, implicational molecules, prototypes, or thematic clusters.

Hastie (1981) posits at least three types of schemas, which he labels "central tendency, template, and procedural." Central tendency schemas are prototypic categorical members located at the statistical center of a set of objects or as a categorical member with the most attributes common to other members of the set. Template schemas are said to be frameworks for categorizing, storing, and coordinating stimulus information. Procedural schemas are abstract general frameworks that establish links between events or objects and further determine whether incoming information is congruent with an existing framework.

Although Hastie's analysis begins to add needed specificity to our definitions, and although it is true that more articulated conceptualizations for frames and scripts are available in the literature, the bulk of research (particularly memory research) does not utilize these more articulated definitions of schema. The vagueness and variety of operationalizations of the general schema notion have hindered systematic explication of the concept. Moreover, in reviewing much schema research we find it difficult to imagine what kind of research finding could be inconsistent with a schema explanation. For example, the schema literature predicts that schema-congruent information will be recalled more readily, and a number of studies have shown this to be the case. Unfortunately, the schema literature also predicts that schema-incongruent information will also be better recalled, and a variety of studies have found this to be the case as well (Taylor & Crocker, 1981).

In addition to the lack of specification of the concept of schema, in the literature we find disagreement about how schemas function in encoding and storing information. Schema researchers argue that memory is selective and abstract; that we select from incoming information and retrieve most readily from memory what is schema-consistent. Information is thus available as it has been abstracted and integrated into networks of schemas. However, everyday experience as well as a number of memory studies make clear that not all information is selected and abstracted in such a way. For example, Keenan, MacWhinney, and Mayhew (1977) found that in memory for utterances from a lecture, subjects were able to remember the actual form of the lecture and did not rely on abstracted impressions with few details. This and other studies lead us to conclude that memory contains far more syntactic and lexical detail than is consistent with most schema theory positions (Alba & Hasher, 1983).

Finally, in addition to the vagueness in current conceptualizations of the nature of a schema and its functional role in cognitive processing, as yet we find no satisfactory explanation for the development of schemas. Anderson (1976) and others have argued that schema, as a unit of knowledge, is too large and unwieldy a structure to provide an adequate account of the ways in which units of knowledge are acquired, combined, and recombined. Numerous investigations of learning and cognitive development make it apparent that learning does not proceed in a series of schema-sized scaddic jerks. Problems in developing an explanation of schema development recently led Rumelhart and Norman (1982) to suggest that we never learn new schemas but only modify existing ones. This appears to be an indefensibly restrictive view of learning. It flies in the face of countless investigations documenting the nature of social cognitive development and the role of communication in that process. (For example, see the various constructivist analyses of development reviewed in Delia et al., 1982.)

In summary, even a sympathetic review of the broad range of schema research in various research traditions must conclude that its progress in explaining social cognitive and communicative processes is hampered by (a) a wide variety of generally global definitions of the basic unit of analysis (with some exceptions—e.g., work with scripts and frame analyses), (b) as yet little consensus on how schemas function in organizing cognition and behavior, and (c) no adequate account of the developmental principles that guide the differentiation and organization of schemas within the cognitive system.

The point of these criticisms is not that research should reflect one master conception of schema to be applied across domain. In fact, we would argue that just the reverse is needed. Research should continue to differentiate clearly particular types of schemas (e.g., scripts, frames, personal constructs) and examine directly their differing roles in the organization of information and behavior. But more research of the type done to date is not sufficient. We would argue that future schema research should proceed in some specific directions if it is to respond to the problems we have outlined. Two seem particularly important.

First, attempts to specify schema types and functions must be wed to interaction goals and behavioral production. Research to date has given limited attention to the richest and most available source of clues for uncovering schema types and functions: communication behavior. If we ask, "Why do people structure and access information as they do?" a reasonable response would be, "To accomplish the tasks they face in everyday life: to engage effectively in conversations, persuade, form personal relationships, complete work projects, etc." If that answer is correct, then the cognitive structures they employ should be evidenced in the way persons organize interactional goals and structure behavior to accomplish those goals.

O'Keefe (1984) has argued that the tendency of researchers to underemphasize the status of social goals and interaction behavior as determinants and instantiations of cognitive structures and functioning is due to their embracing of the metaphor of "man as scientist": seeker of information and certainty for its own sake; theory builder. This metaphor has encouraged the search for an overarching structure and logic organizing first-order theories of the everyday world: logics grounded in statistical models, associationist frameworks, or some other system consistent with the epistemology of scientific thought.

O'Keefe argues and presents evidence suggesting that an equally fruitful metaphor is "man as worker": seeking to develop a variety of social tools and the skill to use each in different ways to accomplish practical tasks. O'Keefe's analysis suggests just the type of specific research we feel is needed—research indexing varieties of schema structures employed in particular ways to understand persons, structure conversations, simplify complex information to solve problems, and so on. We believe research programs with this orientation are more likely to provide specific conceptualizations of the types of schemas that operate in accomplishment of particular tasks in given domains.

Some of the most unambiguous work in the schema area reflects such a specific and behavior-linked focus (e.g., the work on plans, goals, and scripts). We also believe that work examining the particular role of personal constructs in interpersonal behavior can be seen in this way. That is, personal constructs have been studied as a central yet particular type of schema used to structure specific types of information used, most typically, for particular social tasks.

In addition to differentiating types and functions of schemas in relation to the goals and structure of behavior, we believe schema research must be integrated more fully with some general theory of cognitive and communication development, one that allows not only assessment of the development of various aspects of cognitive structure across childhood but allows comparative analysis of differential development among adults. Moreover, whatever developmental position(s) is (are) adopted, they should tie development to the idea of persons as workers developing (to varying degrees of efficacy) the skills to manage the central perceptual and behavioral challenges of everyday life. A variety of developmental positions are available (e.g., Piagetian or Wernerian frameworks) that, in fact, may be seen as schema-based in their formulation and operationalizations. Such a developmental base would greatly aid in the creation of coherent accounts of schema development and change tied to parallel assessments of changes in the organization of behavior.

As researchers interested in social cognition and communication, we have focused our work on explaining how people come to understand other people and situations and the ways those understandings affect their communication with others. Not surprisingly, given our own research, we believe the elaboration of George Kelly's (1955) theory of personal constructs, provided by Walter Crockett and his colleagues in psychology and Jesse Delia and other constructivist researchers in communication, offers an example of a specific and theoretically based conception of the nature, development, and use of a particular type of interpersonal schema (constructs) for which we have been arguing.

Detailed descriptions of this work are available elsewhere and need not be elaborated here. Suffice to say that this line of research has worked successfully to tie particular aspects of interpersonal construct system development and use to various features of strategic organization and production (see the review of Delia et al., 1982). This success is due in large part to a clear conceptualization of constructs as a type of interpersonal schema central to the organization of particular social cognitive and communicative processes—a definition firmly grounded in a general developmental theory constructed primarily from the work of Kelly (1955) and the comparative view of development forwarded by Heinz Werner (1957).

In the remaining part of this essay, we wish to examine critically current work on the nature of construct system development, the measures of construct system development (particularly the Role Category Questionnaire measure of interpersonal complexity or differentiation), and the relation of constructs and communication as an example of research taking the directions for which we are calling. This thinking has been stimulated by the recent work of Crockett (1982, 1983; Crockett & Thom, 1983) and O'Keefe and Delia (1982) integrating certain schema notions within constructivist logic. The analysis is supported by our own intuitions from doing research on construct development and communication as well as recent schema research (particularly in the areas of memory and impression formation).

INTERPERSONAL DIFFERENTIATION AND THE ORGANIZATION OF PERSON KNOWLEDGE

Our research and that of our colleagues has been concerned mainly with the relation of individual differences in interpersonal construct system development (e.g., in degree of differentiation, abstractness, integration, comprehensiveness) on the strategic organization of communicative interactions. Such developments, through their influence on processes of impression formation, social evaluation, goal formation, and so on, are seen as necessary (though not sufficient) causes for parallel shifts in the quality of communication behavior in varieties of contexts. (For a more detailed analysis of the nature of this necessary relationship, see Clark & Delia, 1977; Applegate, Burke, Burleson, Delia, & Kline, in press.) The greatest attention has been given to the effects of increases in interpersonal differentiation or complexity on communication.

We are not unique in this interest. Complexity, particularly, has been conceptualized within several frameworks. In a semantic network structure (Anderson, 1983), greater complexity would mean a greater number of nodes or more links between nodes. In multidimensional scaling representations (e.g., Rosenberg & Sedlak, 1972), greater complexity can be represented in terms of a greater number of dimensions. And in a hierarchical feature tree model (e.g., Sattath & Tversky, 1977), greater complexity may be conceptualized in terms of a greater number of levels in a hierarchy. For the most part, we have operationalized complexity or differentiation as the number of constructs one uses in judging others and have measured differentiation with Crockett's (1965) Role Category Questionnaire (RCQ).[2]

As many readers are aware, the RCQ is a free response measure, and while it lacks many of the problems associated with provided construct and grid measures of interpersonal cognitive differentiation it is not without its critics. Recently, for example, a number of individuals have suggested that the RCQ is really a better measure of verbal ability (Leitner, Landfield, & Barr, 1975) or locquacity (Powers, Jordan, & Street, 1979) than it is a measure of cognitive differentiation or complexity. While examination of the

RCQ lends superficial credence to their positions, we have consistently failed to find any evidence for a verbal ability (Sypher & Applegate, 1982) or locquacity interpretation (Burleson, Applegate, & Neuwirth, 1981).

Recently, however, we have come to believe that the impressions that compose the RCQ might be fruitfully conceptualized in another manner. Early work by Crockett and his colleagues illustrates that free response impressions of known and unknown others are often composed of thematic elements. In the process of forming developmentally advanced impressions, cognitively differentiated persons are capable of linking together positive, negative, and neutral qualities into thematic wholes (Nidorf & Crockett, 1965). A number of investigations also have shown that their less differentiated peers tend to form scattered and, at best, univalent impressions of stimulus targets (Meltzer, Crockett, & Rosenkrantz, 1966). This thematic clustering of constructs suggests that some individuals are better able to access person information and creatively develop plausible construals of others—even others manifesting inconsistent or contradictory traits and behaviors.

These and related findings recently led O'Keefe and Delia (1982) to suggest that the Role Category Questionnaire may not be measuring the number of constructs available for making discriminations, but rather it may be tapping the extent to which a perceiver puts information from working memory and retrieved information together. O'Keefe and Delia suggest that the RCQ may more be a measure of the organization among a person's constructs than an index of the actual number of interpersonal constructs available in the construct system.

We tend to agree with this analysis. Analysis of free response impressions generated by the RCQ suggests that while each impression is somewhat unique, there emerges within, and to some extent shared across individuals, common groupings of concrete and dispositional person qualities. The degree to which the impression is influenced by the particular person described (defined in a kind of episodic memory) as opposed to the general organization of the subject's person knowledge (maintained across persons and situations in semantic memory) is an open question.

When respondents are asked to recall impressions of liked and disliked others, essentially a memory experiment has been created. Anderson (1981) says that schemas "refer to what is deposited in memory as a function of making the correspondence between presented material and a schema" (p. 134). In memory studies the experimental material has been organized by the respondent to reflect the structure of the schema. When subjects are asked to form an impression of another, are they not being asked to organize qualities in terms of the schematic organization of person knowledge in memory?

Although we are in the early stages of pursuing the implications of this sort of conceptualization of the RCQ, in a recent paper Crockett (1983) sketched out a picture of the type of organization of person knowledge the RCQ may be tapping that we find extremely promising. We briefly cast up his analysis in terms of the argument we are making here. Crockett suggests our knowledge of people is made up of "concrete representations" of their appearance and behavior and "interpersonal constructs" defining dispositional qualities. Concrete representations "are more than just sensory patterns; instead, they are organizations of and selections from sensory patterns" (p. 2). They are more closely tied to the particular person and situations they characterize and are stored in episodic memory. Interpersonal constructs are organized within semantic memory, are more stable, and tend to be applied across persons. In more or less complex ways interpersonal constructs are tied to certain prototypical patterns of concrete representations (this idea is consistent with Kelly's [1955] contention that each construct has a particular range and focus of convenience). Construal of certain prototypical patterns of concrete representations leads to application of some part of the individual's system of interpersonal constructs, and application of constructs leads to the expectation that certain patterns of concrete representations will emerge. Construals change when appropriate patterns do not emerge.

This analysis suggests that impressions (such as those generated in the RCQ) reflect the application of the individual's system of concrete representational prototypes and the interpersonal constructs tied to those prototypes. As such, they are a measure of the organization of the individual's person knowledge as a product of his or her culture and individuality.

If the RCQ is a measure of the organization of person knowledge, why do some people recall more about the dispositional character of others in a more organized way? One answer points to differential *development*. For reasons of socialization, varying exposure to personal relationships, relational conflicts, and a variety of other antecedents, some people expend more cognitive effort developing prototypical patterns of concrete person features and go further in the construction of a system of constructs implied by these prototypes.

A second additional reason for the differences in impression quality found in previous research (and this especially for differences among adults) may have to do with *accessibility*. Development aside for the moment, if we accept the idea that some people are more person-oriented than others (are more "person experts," so to speak) they should spend a great deal more time thinking about others (see Little, 1972; Applegate et al., 1984). If we conceptualize dispositional person qualities (Crockett's interpersonal constructs) as nodes in a hierarchical associationist network, it seems likely that people give these nodes differential attention and as a result they are more or less accessible in memory. O'Keefe and Delia (1982) addressed this issue in their speculations about the differential activation or "mobilization" of constructs. Memory research has consistently shown that more recently activated concepts or constructs are more quickly recalled (Anderson, 1983). What we are arguing is that the differences in impression quality indexed by the RCQ may reflect (in addition to the relative development of person knowledge) differences in the accessibility of certain types of interpersonal constructs.

These differences may be due to the frequency with which the concrete representations to which the constructs are tied emerge in everyday life, the number of concrete prototypes to which they are tied, and/or general differences in the degree to which individuals are person-oriented in their thinking. We have a pretty good idea that accessibility rather than the simple availability of verbal descriptions is the issue here, given that differential availability of verbal descriptions should be evidenced on general verbal knowledge tests and they are not (Sypher & Applegate, 1982).

Some research evidence supports the notion that differentiated perceivers not only have more interpersonal constructs with which to construe but that these constructs are more accessible to them in the formation and recall of impressions than are those constructs held by their less differentiated counterparts (Higgins, King, & Mavin, 1982; O'Keefe et al., 1977; also see McCann & Higgins's [1984] review of research on construct accessibility and its effects on communication).

It seems clear that the differences in impression quality tapped by the RCQ are not simply differences in the complexity of concepts held in working *or* episodic memory but reflect in part differences in individuals' ability to access a more stable system of interpersonal constructs. When we ask people to recall another, that person scheme, composed of concrete representations and interpersonal constructs, becomes available in working memory. Anderson (1981) calls this an expansion of the cognitive unit. The degree of expansion is affected in part by the accessibility of constructs stored in semantic memory. We would expect that fewer of the constructs available to the less differentiated perceiver would be activated or expanded, perhaps because the links (with concrete representations and between constructs) are so underutilized that they fail to "fire." Indeed, Anderson (1983) suggests just such a possibility when he argues that each node in declarative memory (which we see as a type of semantic or long-term memory) has an associative strength that is a function of the frequency of use of that cognitive element.

Further examination of the internal features of the RCQ provides even more support for the role of accessibility in influencing impression quality. As we mentioned earlier, much of the work utilizing the RCQ has used a two-peer version of the Role Category Questionnaire. This version requires respondents to describe a liked peer and a disliked peer. Researchers using this measure consistently find that the impressions respondents form of liked peers are more complex than the impressions the same respondents form of disliked peers. Traditionally, this difference has been explained with reference to an "avoidance" or "frequency of interaction" hypothesis (Crockett, 1965). However, it can be argued that the effects of more frequent interactions on impressions are the result of differential accessibility. We have more interactions with our friends, and consequently the person nodes we utilize for thinking about them receive more attention and are in a higher state of activation.

This viewpoint receives additional support from the results of recent work by Ferguson, Rule, and Carlson (in press). These authors report that not all representations of people are equally well differentiated. More specifically, they find that the representations of disliked others are not as well organized as representations of the self or well-liked others. While their methodology is somewhat different, their findings are entirely consistent with previous research using the RCQ.

Thus far we have identified what we see as serious problems in current schema theory and research that limit its promise as an approach for understanding the nature, development, and use of systems for understanding other people. However, we have argued that recent research with schemas as well as some constructivist research does have implications for our conceptualization of the organization of interpersonal constructs as a part of individual's person knowledge and of the RCQ as a measure of the quality of person knowledge. The RCQ has been presented as a measure of the organization of person knowledge influenced by both the development and the accessibility of a system of prototypical concrete representational patterns tied to a hierarchically organized network of interpersonal constructs housed in episodic and semantic memory.

Ultimately, of course, as communication researchers we are not interested in the RCQ, impressions, or even the organization of person knowledge generally as ends in themselves. We are interested in how the organization of person knowledge guides our communicative behavior.

Our analysis of that relationship begins with an outline of the organization of communication closely tied to the practical tasks to which everyday talk is addressed. We then analyze when and how constructs and person knowledge most typically should be used to accomplish communicative goals, recognizing at the outset that the relative importance of person knowledge for differing goals and related strategic formulations in an empirical question (see also Applegate, 1983; O'Keefe & Delia, 1982).

CONSTRUCTS, INTERACTION GOALS, AND THE ORGANIZATION OF COMMUNICATION

At the heart of the conception of communication forwarded in our previous work is the contention that messages *do* things. People do not communicate in order to evidence the behavioral correlates of personality traits, consistency drives, or schema structures. Rather, talk is tied most directly to interactions goals such as comforting, persuading, or negotiating personal relationships. The functions of communication messages may be explicit (i.e., closely tied to actors' intentions) or implicit (i.e., embedded in tacit knowledge). Researchers investigating the effects of constructs on communication have integrated aspects of symbolic interactionist theory in sociology, including W. I. Thomas's conception of the "definition of the situation" (see Ball, 1972; Blumer, 1969) and a variety of sociolinguistic analyses (e.g., Bernstein, 1974; Halliday, 1973; Hymes, 1974) to construct a beginning taxonomy of communicative functions. Clark and Delia (1979) argue that every communicative transaction involves the overt and/or tacit negotiation of identities and relationship definitions between interactants. Moreover, the transaction may (and typically does) involve pursuit of instrumental goals (e.g., persuasion, comforting, transmitting information).

Communication behavior is most directly influenced by *communication-relevant beliefs* organized within the actor's definition of the situation. Interactants have some expected definition as they enter the situation that is modified as they accommodate to the behavior of others. Included in this changing definition are impressions of self and other, a definition of the relationship that exists with the other, and beliefs about type of context, expectations for behavior in that context, and so on. Also included—either as explicit intentions or tacitly embedded in beliefs about self, other, and/or the situation—are identity, relational, and instrumental interaction goals (Clark & Delia, 1979). Moreover, the interactant typically has some beliefs about his or her partner's definition of the situation (e.g., the other's impression of him or her, self-concept, goals).[3]

Now, not all beliefs embodied in the actor's definition of the situation are communication-relevant. Only those beliefs that embody communicative goals, means of achieving, and/or obstacles to those goals and hence have implications for the content and form of strategic behavior are communication-relevant. Previous research and common sense suggest that situated person knowledge generated from application of interpersonal constructs typically will contain communication-relevant beliefs. Moreover, the quality and organization of person knowledge in memory (as indexed by the RCQ and other construct system measures) will affect what individual's take to be communication-relevant in the situation.

For example, for one individual the fact that Tom's socks do not match may seem irrelevant for strategic behavior designed to persuade him to loan his BMW. Another person with a more extensive, integrated, accessible system of person knowledge might recognize that Tom's sock behavior is related to other behaviors reflecting a sloppiness that is itself tied to a desire to be seen as nonmaterialistic. That information, unavailable to a less advanced perceiver, could be seen as relevant to the form of the strategic persuasive effort (i.e., by suggesting the effectiveness of casting the loan as yet another example of how Tom values people and their needs over material concerns).

More advanced systems of person knowledge can affect not only *how* interaction goals are pursued but *what* goal(s) are perceived (tacitly or explicitly). The quality and accessibility of the system of person knowledge could affect the degree to which our persuader recognizes and addresses identify or relationship related issues present in the situation. Does he or she recognize that since everyone asks to borrow Tom's BMW, Tom might take the request as an indication that his friendship with the persuader is materially based? If so, how can the goal of preserving the friendship with Tom be addressed in the strategic effort?

In short, access to an organized system of person knowledge should provide individuals with a more complex understanding of the goal structure in social situations as well as the features of the situation that suggest means of achieving or obstacles to those goals—this by providing a more extensive, organized understanding of the perspective of other actors and their definition of the situation. To date there has been little effort to relate personal construct development directly to the number and quality of communication-relevant beliefs embodied in actors' situational definitions (see O'Keefe, et al., 1983). Some research has addressed the issue indirectly by asking subjects to provide rationales for the strategies they employ (Applegate, 1980a, 1980b, 1982). Such rationales display the goals that inform behavior and beliefs about self, others, the situation, and so on perceived as relevant to reasons for the strategies employed. These studies show that subjects with more advanced systems of personal constructs (1) offer greater numbers of beliefs about the subjective perspective of others (e.g., their self-image, perception of the subject, needs, feelings) as communication-relevant; and (2) perceive a more complex goal structure in the situation (e.g., spontaneously indicate that identity and/or relationship goals were also influential in the formulation of persuasive strategies).

Obviously, situations vary in the types and number of goals and obstacles they present. Similarly, individuals will vary in the typical types and number of goals, means, and obstacles they perceive as present and in their ability to construct integrated strategic responses to communication-relevant features of contexts. It is just those individual differences that should be central to our study of communication and the effects of the quality of accessible person knowledge on communication.

In closing, we should reemphasize that we would expect interpersonal constructs and the system of person knowledge they provide to be but one source for communication-relevant beliefs (albeit an important one). Obviously, perceptions of the physical features of setting, temporal and spatial constraints, and shared social scripts for situations affect communication-relevant beliefs. At times these so-called nonpersonal sources may simply add to the number of beliefs informing communication. At other times they will interact with our person knowledge affecting what features of the latter system we access as we communicate with persons in situations. In many contexts, and for some goals, the type of dispositional knowledge of others provided by personal constructs may be irrelevant to communication behavior. Research has shown certain contexts to be heavily scripted, requiring little or no reference to person knowledge (e.g., the now famous restaurant script). O'Keefe (1984) suggests a limited function for personal constructs in impression formation in highly task-oriented groups, suggesting that other task-related schemes are more central to forming impressions of others. Nevertheless, past research does suggest that in a variety of important communicative contexts the quality of constructs, of person knowledge, does strongly affect the nature of our efforts to persuade, comfort, inform, and instruct our friends, work partners, and children. Future research should further delineate the role of constructs and other types of cognitive schemas in the way people pursue particular communicative goals in particular types of contexts.

In this chapter we have briefly presented some of our current thinking on the status of the RCQ (and, by inference, other measures of construct quality) as measures of the organization and accessibility of person knowledge stored in semantic memory. We believe current schema research, while flawed in a number of ways, is suggestive for conceptualizing what construct measures tap. It suggests as well a direction for integrating what we have found about the effects of individual differences in the quality of person knowledge on communication within a more comprehensive account of the combined influence of person and situation knowledge on communication-relevant beliefs and the organization of strategic communication behavior. While our observations are admittedly speculative, we hope they are suggestive for future research integrating current schema notions within research on the relation between personal constructs and communication.

NOTES

1. This raises a question that has emerged repeatedly and to date has eluded an answer: Is social information organized by episode or by individual persons? Part of the reason this question remains unanswered is that it is really two questions. The first concerns the *content* of social

information; the second, its *structure*. By content, researchers mean the representation of social information in memory; by structure, the way the representation is linked. The content of knowledge is determined by the processes that create it before it is retained in memory. The structure of social knowledge is determined by what happens as the knowledge is stored in memory. We believe that it is entirely possible to have situation-based information stored in a person-based structure or vice versa.

2. A host of instruments have been proposed for measuring cognitive differentiation, but this is not the place to chronicle them. For reviews of these measures see Crockett (1965), Goldstein and Blackman (1978), and O'Keefe and Sypher (1981).

3. Metacognition research has shown perception to operate at even more abstract levels involving assessments of "what I think you think I think; what I think you think I think you think, etc."

REFERENCES

Alba, J. W., & Hasher, L. (1983). Is memory schematic? *Psychological Bulletin, 93,* 203-231.

Anderson, J. R. (1976). *Language, memory, and thought.* Hillsdale, NJ: Lawrence Erlbaum.

Anderson, J. R. (1981). Effects of prior knowledge on memory for new information. *Memory and Cognition, 9,* 237-246.

Anderson, J. R. (1983). *The architecture of cognition.* Cambridge, MA: Harvard University Press.

Applegate, J. L. (1980a). Person- and position-centered teacher communication in a day-care center: A case study triangulating interview and naturalistic methods. In N. K. Denzin (Ed.), *Studies in symbolic interaction* (Vol. 3). Greenwich, CT: JAI Press.

Applegate, J. L. (1980b). Adaptive communication in educational contexts: A study of teacher's communicative strategies. *Communication Monographs, 29,* 158-170.

Applegate, J. L. (1982). *Construct system development and identity-management skills in persuasive contexts.* Paper presented at the meeting of the Western Speech Communication Association, Denver.

Applegate, J. L. (1983). *Constructs, interaction goals, and communication in relationship development.* Paper presented at the Fifth International Congress on Personal Construct Psychology, Boston.

Applegate, J. L., Burke, J. A., Burleson, B. R., Delia, J. G., & Kline, S. L. (1984). Reflection-enhancing parental communication. In I. E. Sigel (Ed.), *Parental belief systems: The psychological consequences for children.* Hillsdale, NJ: Lawrence Erlbaum.

Ball, D. W. (1972). The definition of the situation: Some theoretical and methodological consequences of taking W. I. Thomas seriously. *Journal for the Theory of Social Behavior, 2,* 61-68.

Bartlett, F. C. (1932). *Remembering: A study in experimental and social psychology.* London: Cambridge University Press.

Berger, C. R., & Douglas, W. (1982). Thought and talk: "Excuse me, but have I been talking to myself?" In F. E. X. Dance (Ed.), *Human communication theory.* New York: Harper & Row.

Bernstein, B. (1974). *Class, codes, and control (Vol. 1): Theoretical studies towards a sociology of language.* New York: Schocken.

Blumer, H. (1969). *Symbolic interactionism: Perspectives and method.* Englewood Cliffs, NJ: Prentice-Hall.

Bobrow, D. G., & Winograd, T. (1977). An overview of KRL, a knowledge representation language. *Cognitive Science, 1,* 3-46.

Bostrom, R., & Waldhart, E. S. (1980). Components in listening behavior: The role of short-term memory. *Human Communication Research, 6,* 221-227.

Burleson, B. R., Applegate, J. L., & Neuwirth, C. M. (1981). Is cognitive complexity loquacity? A reply to Powers, Jordan, and Street. *Human Communication Research, 7,* 212-225.

Cantor, N., & Mischel, W. (1977). Traits as prototypes: Effects on recognition memory. *Journal of Personality and Social Psychology, 35,* 38-48.

Clark, R. A., & Delia, J. G. (1977). Cognitive complexity, social perspective-taking, and functional persuasive skills in second-to-ninth grade children. *Human Communication Research, 3,* 128-134.

Clark, R. A., & Delia, J. G. (1979). Topoi and rhetorical competence. *Quarterly Journal of Speech, 65,* 187-206.

Crockett, W. H. (1965). Cognitive complexity and impression formation. In B. H. Maher (Ed.), *Progress in experimental personality research* (Vol. 2) New York: Academic.

Crockett, W. H. (1982). The organization of construct systems: The organization corollary. In J. C. Mancuso & J. R. Adams-Webber (Eds.), *The construing person.* New York: Praeger.

Crockett, W. H. (1983). *Constructs, impressions, actions, responses, and construct change: A model of processes in impression formation.* Paper presented at the Fifth International Congress on Personal Construct Psychology, Boston.

Crockett, W. H., & Thom, M. (1983). *Prototypic behaviors and the inference of interpersonal constructs.* Paper presented at the Conference on Social Cognition and Interpersonal Behavior, University of Kansas.

Delia, J. G., O'Keefe, B. J., & O'Keefe, D. J. (1982). The constructivist approach to communication. In F. E. X. Dance (Ed.), *Human communication theory.* New York: Harper & Row.

Ebbinghaus, H. E. (1885). *Memory: A contribution to experimental psychology.* New York: Dover.

Ferguson, T. J., Rule, B. G., & Carlson, D. (in press). Memory for personally relevant information. *Journal of Personality and Social Psychology.*

Goldstein, K. M., & Blackman, S. (1978). *Cognitive style: Five approaches and relevant research.* New York: Wiley.

Halliday, M. A. K. (1973). *Explorations in the functions of language.* London: Edward Arnold.

Hamilton, D. L. (Ed.). (1981). *Cognitive processes in stereotyping and intergroup behavior.* Hillsdale, NJ: Lawrence Erlbaum.

Hastie, R. (1981). Schematic principles in human memory. In E. T. Higgins, C. P. Herman, & M. P. Zanna (Eds.), *Social cognition: The Ontario symposium* (Vol. 1). Hillsdale, NJ: Lawrence Erlbaum.

Hastie, R., & Carlston, D. (1980). Theoretical issues in person memory. In R. Hastie, T. M. Ostrom, E. B. Ebbesen, R. S. Wyer, D. L. Hamilton, & D. E. Carlston (Eds.), *Person memory.* Hillsdale, NJ: Lawrence Erlbaum.

Hastie, R., Ostrom, T. M., Ebbesen, E. B., Wyer, R. S., Hamilton, D. L., & Carlston, D. E. (Eds.). (1980). *Person memory.* Hillsdale, NJ: Lawrence Erlbaum.

Higgins, E. T., King, G. A., & Mavin, G. H. (1982). Individual construct accessibility and subjective impressions and recall. *Journal of Personality and Social Psychology, 43,* 35-47.

Hymes, D. (1974). *Foundations of sociolinguistics: An ethnographic approach.* Philadelphia: University of Pennsylvania Press.

Kelly, G. A. (1955). *The psychology of personal constructs* (2 vols). New York: Norton.

Keenan, J. M., MacWhinney, B., & Mayhew, D. (1977). Pragmatics in memory: A study of natural conversation. *Journal of Verbal Learning and Verbal Behavior, 16,* 549-560.

Leitner, L. M., Landfield, A. W., & Barr, M. A. (1975). *Cognitive complexity: A review and elaboration within personal construct theory.* Unpublished manuscript, University of Nebraska-Lincoln.

Little, B. (1972). Psychological man as scientist, humanist, and specialist. *Journal of Experimental Research in Personality, 6,* 95-118.

McCann, C. D., & Higgins, E. T. (1984). Individual differences in communication: Social cognitive determinants and consequences. In H. E. Sypher & J. L. Applegate (Eds.), *Communication by children and adults: Social cognitive and strategic processes.* Beverly Hills, CA: Sage.

Meltzer, B., Crockett, W. H., & Rosenkrantz, P. S. (1966). Cognitive complexity, value congruity, and the integration of potentially incompatible information in impressions of others. *Journal of Personality and Social Psychology, 4,* 338-343.

Minsky, M. (1975). A framework for representing knowledge. In P. H. Winston (Ed.), *The psychology of computer vision.* New York: McGraw-Hill.

Nidorf, L. J., & Crockett, W. H. (1965). Cognitive complexity and the organization of impressions of others. *Journal of Social Psychology, 66,* 165-169.

Nisbett, R., & Ross, L. (1980). *Human inference: Strategies and shortcomings of social judg-ment.* Englewood Cliffs, NJ: Prentice-Hall.

O'Keefe, B. J. (1984). The evolution of impressions in small working groups: Effects of construct differentiation. In H. E. Sypher & J. L. Applegate (Eds.), *Communication by children and adults: Social cognitive and strategic processes.* Beverly Hills, CA: Sage.

O'Keefe, B. J., & Delia, J. G. (1982). Impression formation and message production. In M. E. Ro-loff & C. R. Berger (Eds.), *Social cognition and communication.* Beverly Hills, CA: Sage.

O'Keefe, B. J., Delia, J. G., & O'Keefe, D. J. (1977). Construct individuality, cognitive complex-ity, and the formation and remembering of interpersonal impressions. *Social Behavior and Personality, 5,* 229-240.

O'Keefe, B. J., Murphy, M., Meyers, R., & Bobrow, A. (1983). *The development of persuasive communication skills: The influence of developments in interpersonal constructs on the ability to generate communication-relevant beliefs and on level of persuasive strategy.* Paper presented at the meeting of the International Communication Association, Dallas.

O'Keefe, D. J., & Sypher, H. E. (1981). Cognitive complexity measures and the relationship of cognitive complexity to communication. *Human Communication Research, 8,* 72-92.

Planalp, S., & Hewes, D. E. (1982). A cognitive approach to communication theory: Cogito ergo dico? In M. Burgoon (Ed.), *Communication yearbook 5.* New Brunswick, NJ: Transaction.

Powers, W. G., Jordan, W. J., & Street, R. L. (1979). Language indices in the measurement of cognitive complexity: Is complexity loquacity? *Human Communication Research, 6,* 69-73.

Roloff, M. E., & Berger, C. R. (Eds.). (1982) *Social cognition and communication.* Beverly Hills, CA: Sage.

Rosch, E., & Lloyd, B. (Eds.). (1978). *Cognition and categorization.* Hillsdale, NJ: Lawrence Erlbaum.

Rosenberg, S., & Sedlak, A. (1972). Structural representations of implicit personality theory. In L. Berkowitz (Ed.), *Advances in experimental social psychology* (Vol. 6). New York: Academic.

Rumelhart, D. E., & Norman, D. A. (1978). Accretion, tuning, and restructuring: Three modes of learning. In J. W. Cotton & R. L. Klatzky (Eds.), *Semantic factors in cognition.* Hillsdale, NJ: Lawrence Erlbaum.

Rumelhart, D. E., & Norman, D. A. (1982). Simulating a skilled typist: A study of skilled cogni-tive-motor performance. *Cognitive Science, 6,* 1-36.

Rumelhart, D. E., & Ortony, A. (1977). The representation of knowledge in memory. In R. C. Anderson, R. J. Spiro, & W. T. Montague (Eds.), *Schooling and the acquisition of knowl-edge.* Hillsdale, NJ: Lawrence Erlbaum.

Sattath, S., & Tversky, A. (1977). Additive similarity trees. *Psychometrica, 42,* 319-345.

Schank, R., & Abelson, R. (1977). *Scripts, plans, goals, and understanding: An inquiry into human knowledge structures.* Hillsdale, NJ: Lawrence Erlbaum.

Smith, M. J. (1982). Cognitive schemata and persuasive communication: Toward a contingency rules theory. In M. Burgoon (Ed.), *Communication yearbook 6.* Beverly Hills, CA: Sage.

Spoehr, K. T., & Lehmkuhle, S. W. (1982). *Visual information processing.* San Francisco: W. H. Freeman.

Sypher, H. E. (in press). Memory: The forgotten canon. In B. Dervin & M. Voight (Eds.), *Ad-vances in communication science* (Vol. 7). Norwood, NJ: Ablex.

Sypher, H. E., & Applegate, J. L. (1982). Cognitive differentiation and verbal influence: Clarify-ing relationships. *Educational and Psychological Measurement, 42,* 537-543.

Sypher, H. E., & Waltman, M. S. (1983). *Dialect-cued social stereotypes: Differential utilization of base-rate information.* Paper presented at the annual meeting of the Speech Commu-nication Association, Washington, D.C.

Taylor, S. E., & Crocker, J. (1981). Schematic bases of social information processing. In E. T. Higgins, C. P. Herman, & M. P. Zanna (Eds.), *Social cognition: The Ontario symposium* (Vol. 1). Hillsdale, NJ: Lawrence Erlbaum.

Taylor, S. E., Fiske, S. T., Etcoff, N., & Ruderman, A. (1978). Categorical and contextual bases of person memory and stereotyping. *Journal of Personality and Social Psychology, 36,* 778-793.

Tesser, A. (1978). Self-generated attitude change. In L. Berkowitz (Ed.), *Advances in experimental social psychology* (Vol. 2). New York: Academic.

Werner, H. (1957). The concept of development from a comparative and organismic point of view. In D. B. Harris (Ed.), *The concept of development*. Minneapolis: University of Minnesota Press.

Woodall, W. G., Davis, D. K., & Sahin, H. (1983). From the boob tube to the black box: Television news comprehension from an information processing perspective. *Journal of Broadcasting, 27,* 1-23.

Wyer, R. S., & Srull, T. K. (1980). The processing of social stimulus information: A conceptual integration. In R. Hastie, T. M. Ostrom, E. B. Ebbesen, R. S. Wyer, D. L. Hamilton, & D. E. Carlston (Eds.), *Person memory*. Hillsdale, NJ: Lawrence Erlbaum.

12 ● Fear-Arousing Persuasive Messages

FRANKLIN J. BOSTER ● PAUL MONGEAU

Arizona State University ● Michigan State University

THE effects of including fear-arousing material in a persuasive message have been debated frequently (Sussman, 1973).[1] The antecedents of modern debate on this question reside in paradoxical experimental results. Some experiments show that there is more conformity to message recommendations when the amount of fear in the persuasive message is high than when it is low (for example, see Beck & Davis, 1978). Other experiments report data in which there is more conformity to message recommendations when the amount of fear in the persuasive message is low than when it is high (see Janis & Feshbach, 1953). Still other experiments present data that demonstrate that the amount of fear in the persuasive message has no impact on the extent to which a listener conforms to the recommendations of the persuasive message (see Wheatley & Oshikawa, 1970).

Moreover, there is no consensus among persuasion scholars as to how these conflicting data are to be reconciled. Some explanations suggest that messages high in fear-arousing content are more effective in obtaining conformity to message recommendations than are messages low in fear-arousing content (for example, see Leventhal, 1970). Other explanations suggest that the opposite relationship holds (see Miller, 1963). A third class of explanations posits that appeals low in fear and high in fear are relatively ineffective, while appeals with a moderate amount of fear-arousing content are relatively effective (see Janis, 1967). Yet another class of explanations argues that fear inter-

AUTHORS' NOTE: We wish to acknowledge Drs. John Crawford, Norman K. Perrill, William D. Stinnett, and Karen Beyard-Tyler for their valuable comments on an earlier draft of this chapter. We would like to thank Dr. Kenneth Frandsen for providing additional information concerning one of his fear appeal articles, and Dr. John E. Hunter for his "meta-analytical" assistance. Finally, we would like to thank Jeanne Conrad, Suzanne Kroll, and Carra Sleight for their help in preparing the manuscript.

Correspondence and requests for reprints: Franklin J. Boster, Department of Communication, Arizona State University, Tempe, AZ 85287.

acts with other variables, so that in some cases high fear messages are more effective than low fear messages, but in other cases low fear messages are more effective than high fear messages (see Leventhal, 1971).

This monograph addresses two issues. First, the available data are reviewed, and conclusions are drawn concerning the effect of incorporating fear-arousing material into a persuasive message. Second, implications of these conclusions for a theory of fear appeals are drawn. As a necessary preliminary step, the major explanations of fear appeal effects are sketched.

The Drive Explanation

The drive explanation, outlined, but not advocated, by Leventhal (1970) and Sutton (1982), suggests that the effect of persuasive messages, which vary in fear-arousing content, is the production of varying amounts of fear in the audience. While the relationship between the fear-arousing content of the persuasive message and the amount of fear generated in the audience is unlikely to be without error, the two variables are expected to be positively correlated. Put another way, high fear messages produce more perceived fear on the average than do moderate fear messages, and moderate fear messages produce more fear on the average than do low fear messages. Fear, in turn, is predicted to be positively correlated with the audience's attitude toward the topic in question. Thus, as perceived fear increases, the audience's attitude more closely approaches the attitude recommended in the persuasive message. Again, this correlation is not expected to be without error, but is expected to be substantial.

According to the drive explanation, the process that produces this set of relationships is a drive-reduction process. The perceived fear that is aroused by the persuasive message creates a state of drive, which audience members find unpleasant. Thus the audience members must perform some action in order to reduce the drive. Although there are many potential drive-reducing actions that persons might perform, the drive explanation posits that persons change their attitudes and/or behaviors as a means of drive reduction.

This relationship may be construed as a causal model. According to the mathematics of path analysis, this model predicts that the correlation between the fear-arousing content of the persuasive message and the attitude of the audience toward the topic in question is the product of the correlation between the fear-arousing content of the persuasive message and the amount of perceived fear generated in the audience and the correlation between the amount of perceived fear generated in the audience and the attitude of the audience toward the topic in question. If x represents a fear-arousing message, y perceived fear, and z the resultant attitudes, then $r_{xz} = r_{xy} r_{yz}$. This model predicts that if both r_{xy} and r_{yz} are positive, then r_{xz} is positive.

Put substantively, according to the drive explanation, the greater the amount of fear-arousing material in a persuasive message, the more closely the attitudes of audience members become to the attitude recommended in the persuasive message.

The Resistance Explanation

In an early review of the literature, Miller (1963, p. 119) concludes,

A strong fear appeal is not effective in producing the desired audience response, but this conclusion is tempered by personality differences among audience members, the relevance and interest value of the communication for the audience, and other relevant factors that affect the relationship.

According to Miller a process of defensive avoidance produces this result. When a process of defensive avoidance is activated, "the audience becomes motivated to ignore, minimize, or deny the importance of the threat" (Janis, 1967, p. 293). Conversely, listeners attend to persuasive messages low in threatening content. Since the recommendations contained in low fear messages are heard, and the recommendations contained in high fear messages are ignored, the former are likely to be more persuasive.

The resistance explanation is similar to the drive explanation in two ways. First, the explanations posit a similar causal model. Put differently, both explanations predict that the effect of persuasive messages that vary in the amount of fear-arousing content is to produce differing amounts of fear in listeners, and that perceived fear, in turn, affects attitudinal and/or behavioral conformity to the recommendations of a persuasive message. Second, both explanations posit that the relationship between the amount of fear-arousing content in persuasive messages and the amount of perceived fear in listeners is positive.

The resistance explanation differs from the drive explanation concerning the relationship between perceived fear and attitude. The drive explanation hypothesizes that as perceived fear increases, listeners' attitudes and/or behaviors more closely resemble those recommended in the persuasive message. The resistance explanation hypothesizes that as perceived fear decreases, listeners' attitudes and/or behaviors more closely resemble those recommended in the persuasive message. Utilizing the mathematics of path analysis, it follows that the resistance explanation predicts a negative correlation between the amount of fear-arousing material in a persuasive message and listeners' conformity to the recommendations in that persuasive message, while the drive explanation predicts a positive correlation between these variables. Thus, according to the resistance explanation, r_{xz} is negative.

Curvilinear Hypotheses

As with the previous two explanations, advocates of curvilinear hypotheses suggest that as the fear-arousing content of a persuasive message increases, the amount of perceived fear in listeners increases. The curvilinear hypotheses differ from both the drive explanation and the resistance explanation in the specification of the link between perceived fear and the listeners' acceptance of message recommendations. According to the curvilinear hypotheses, the regression of attitude onto perceived fear is an inverted U. Thus when a listener is either extremely fearful or has very little fear, little attitudinal and/or behavioral conformity results. When, however, a listener is moderately fearful, an optimal amount of attitudinal and/or behavior conformity is produced. Similarly, persuasive messages that are either low in fear-arousing content or high in fear-arousing content are relatively ineffective. Alternatively, those persuasive messages that contain a moderate amount of fear-arousing content are most effective in yielding conformity to message recommendations. There are three different versions of the curvilinearity hypothesis. Following is a discussion of each variation.

Janis (1967) and Janis and Leventhal (1968) were the first to articulate a curvilinear hypothesis. Janis and Leventhal (1968, p. 1056) assert that at low levels of perceived fear,

> the average person remains unaffected by warning communications because he dismisses all information about the threats as inconsequential by means of blanket reassurances.

Thus no change in attitude is predicted when there is a low level of fear in the persuasive message, since the audience is not convinced that a need for change exists.

When the level of fear in the persuasive message is high, Janis and Leventhal (1968, p. 1056) argue that

> the average person's state of intense emotional excitement will be characterized by preoccupation with hypervigilant speculations and ruminations which generate defensive maneuvers—such as denial, detachment, and minimizing rationalizations that interfere with acceptance of the safety measures recommended by the communicator.

Therefore, at high levels of perceived fear Janis and Leventhal argue that audience members defensively avoid the threat, instead of accepting message recommendations.

On the other hand, at moderate levels of fear, the

average person's vigilance and reassurance tendencies are stimulated, which is the optimal condition for developing compromise attitudes of the type required for sustained acceptance of whatever plausible safety measures are recommended by the communicator. (Janis & Leventhal, 1968, p. 1056)

Hence at moderate levels of fear listeners conform most closely to the recommendations in the persuasive message.

Janis and Leventhal (1968, p. 1056) maintain that the optimal fear content for producing attitudinal and/or behavioral conformity depends upon any number of "content, situational, and dispositional factors." Therefore, the specific point on the fear continuum at which attitude toward the topic in question is closest to that advocated by the persuasive communication depends upon a number of other factors. These factors create a family of inverted-U curves that incorporate the effects of other factors upon the relationship between the fear-arousing content of a persuasive message and the listeners' conformity to message recommendations.

The second derivation of the curvilinear hypothesis is McGuire's (1968, 1969) two-factor explanation. McGuire hypothesizes that fear acts both as a drive and as a cue. As a drive, perceived fear increases the probability of an individual's yielding to the recommendations made in the persuasive message. As a cue, perceived fear increases the probability of an individual's resisting the message recommendations. These yielding and resisting functions are exponential, according to McGuire (1968, p. 1164), and their combination results in "an overall nonmonotonic relation between anxiety and influenceability . . . with maximum susceptibility coming at intermediate levels of anxiety."

In a third statement of the curvilinear hypothesis, Higbee (1970) suggests the importance of two variables: severity of the threat and the probability that the threat will occur given that no preventive action is taken. Higbee predicts that these two variables are negatively correlated. He posits that as the level of perceived fear increases, perceived severity increases exponentially, while probability of occurrence decreases exponentially. These two effects combine to produce the inverted-U function in much the same manner as McGuire's two factors.

The Parallel Response Explanation

Several scholars suggest that fear interacts with other variables to affect attitudes and behaviors. Leventhal's (1970, 1971) parallel response explanation is one such hypothesis. The parallel response explanation asserts that fear-arousing persuasive messages activate two primary processes within the audience: fear control and danger control. The function of these

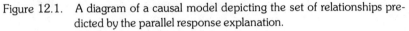

Figure 12.1.   A diagram of a causal model depicting the set of relationships predicted by the parallel response explanation.

processes is to assist the listener in coping with the threat. The listener's
attitude toward the topic in question is predicted to be a function of the
amount of fear control and danger control aroused by the persuasive message. This set of relationships is depicted in Figure 12.1 From this figure one
may observe that fear control and danger control mediate the relationship
between the amount of fear-arousing material in the persuasive message
and the listener's attitude toward the topic in question.

Danger control is conceived as a problem-solving process in which the
listener scans the external environment for information pertinent to dealing
with the threat presented in the persuasive message. When a danger control
process is operative, the focus of attention is the danger that the threat
poses. The danger control process produces responses that are instrumental in averting the threat.

Fear control is an emotional coping process in which listener strives to
reduce the fear generated by the persuasive message. When a process of
fear control is operative, listeners focus on their internal emotional responses, not on the threat. Thus the process of fear control may produce
action that interferes with the acceptance of the recommendations of the
persuasive message.

Leventhal (1970, 1971) asserts that these two processes interact to affect the extent to which listeners conform to message recommendations.
The specific nature of this interaction, however, is unspecified. When a fear-
arousing persuasive message generates solely a danger control process a
positive relationship between the amount of fear-arousing material in the
message and the listener's attitude toward the topic in question is predicted.
When the fear-arousing persuasive message generates solely a fear control
process an inverse relationship between the amount of fear in the message
and listener's attitude toward the topic is predicted.

Overall, Leventhal (1970, p. 127) predicts that

> with respect to main effects, the parallel response model clearly leads us to
> expect that for the most part there will be positive associations between fear
> and persuasion.

The parallel response explanation has also been extended to predict a curvilinear relation between the level of fear-arousing material in a persuasive message and the listener's attitude toward the topic in question. Sternthal and Craig (1974, p. 26) argue that

> from parallel response analysis, it is predicted that incremental increases in emotional material ultimately lead to disruption of danger control resulting in a nonmonotonic relationship between fear and persuasion.

Put another way, Sternthal and Craig contend that as fear increases both the danger control process and the fear control process increase. At moderate levels of fear the danger control process is relatively strong and the fear control process is relatively weak. Consequently, listeners concentrate on reducing the threat by accepting the message recommendations. At low levels of fear both processes are weak. There is no reason for the listener to accept the message recommendations, since the threat does not appear to be serious. At high levels of fear both processes are strong. The tendency to control fear interferes with the process of danger control, and listeners fail to exhibit substantial attitudinal or behavioral shifts.

Rogers (1975) points out two inadequacies in the parallel response explanation. First, Rogers contends that the parallel response explanation fails to specify the stimulus variables that predict the extent to which the fear and danger control processes operate. Since, according to Leventhal, the amount of fear control and danger control generated by the persuasive message predict the listener's attitude toward the topic in question, this ambiguity makes it difficult to construct an adequate test of the explanation.

Second, Rogers argues that the constructs and linking statements in the parallel response explanation are too ambiguous to derive precise predictions regarding the relationship between fear and persuasion. Beck and Frankel (1981) concur, referring to the parallel response explanation as untestable.

In summary, the parallel response explanation contributes to this body of knowledge by introducing the fear control and danger control constructs. The major flaw in the explanation is the ambiguous nature of the concepts and linking statements. This ambiguity results in the parallel response explanation predicting all possible outcomes of a fear appeal experiment without specifying the conditions under which the different outcomes are expected to occur. This characteristic results in the explanation being untestable. Put differently, it is unfalsifiable in principle, and hence is of little scientific value.

The Protection Motivation Explanation

The premise central to Rogers's (1975) protection motivation explanation is that fear-arousing persuasive messages are composed of three factors:

(a) the magnitude of noxiousness of a depicted event; (b) the conditional probability that the event will occur provided that no adaptive behavior is performed or there is no modification of an existing behavioral disposition; and (c) the availability and effectiveness of a coping response that might reduce or eliminate the noxious stimulus. (Rogers, 1975, p. 97)

Rogers claims that the greater the extent to which these three factors are present in a persuasive message, the greater the extent to which they are perceived by the audience. Listeners' perceptions of these three variables then combine multiplicatively to produce a state of protection motivation in the listeners. For Rogers, protection motivation refers to a listener's drive to take steps to avoid a potential threat. Thus the greater the noxiousness (fear), efficacy, and probability in a persuasive message, the greater the aroused protection motivation. Moreover, if any of these elements is missing from a persuasive message—that is, has a value of zero—then the message does not induce any protection motivation. Put another way, each of the three message components is necessary to produce protection motivation. A listener's attitude toward the topic in question is hypothesized to be a function of the amount of protection motivation produced in the listener by the persuasive message. Specifically, as the amount of protection motivation increases, the amount of conformity to the recommendations in the persuasive message increases proportionally. The correlation between protection motivation and attitude toward the topic is expected to be positive, but not without error.

This set of relationships is depicted in Figure 12.2. From this figure one may observe that the listener's perceptions of the message components mediate the relationship between the message components and protection motivation. Protection motivation, in turn, mediates the relationship between the perceived message components and the audience's attitude toward the topic in question. Since all causal links are predicted to be positive, the correlation between the three message characteristics and attitude is expected to be positive. Since there are several mediating links, however, this correla-

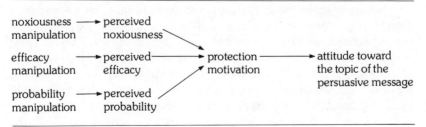

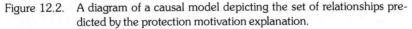

Figure 12.2.   A diagram of a causal model depicting the set of relationships predicted by the protection motivation explanation.

tion may be low. Moreover, if any of the links between the perceived message characteristics is absent, then no protection motivation is aroused, and no conformity to message recommendations is expected to occur. In such a case the correlation between the message characteristics and attitude is predicted to be zero.

The Threat Control Explanation

The common thread running through all of the previous explanations is that listener's perceived fear, and in some cases other factors, mediates the relationship between the fear-arousing material in the persuasive message and the listener's attitude toward the topic in question. The threat control explanation, on the other hand, posits that the response to fear appeals depends entirely upon cognitive, rather than emotional, factors.

In the most recent attempt at theoretical integration, Beck and Frankel (1981, p. 211) state that "the important factor mediating the effects of health threat communications is not fear but the degree to which the communication depicts a real, but controllable threat." From this point of view negative correlations between the fear-arousing content in a persuasive message and the listener's attitude toward the topic in question (for example, see Janis & Feshbach, 1953) are said to be a result of the depiction of an uncontrollable threat and not the result of a defensive avoidance process.

The threat control explanation asserts that fear-arousing persuasive messages arouse two fundamental processes in the listener—response, efficacy and personal efficacy. Response efficacy is "the perceived contingency between the performance of the recommended response and the reduction of the depicted event" (Beck & Frankel, 1981, p. 212). In order for response efficacy to be high the listener must perceive that the performance of the recommended response is effective in eliminating or reducing the probability of the threat's occurrence. Personal efficacy is "the person's perceived ability to perform the recommended action successfully" (Beck & Frankel, 1981, p. 212). If personal efficacy is to be high, the recommended action must be perceived as something the listener is capable of doing.

Response efficacy and personal efficacy combine to create perceived threat control. Perceived threat control is "the extent to which recipients possess expectations of success in controlling the threat" (Beck & Frankel, 1981, p. 212). While Beck and Frankel fail to specify the way in which response efficacy and personal efficacy combine to produce threat control, they do claim that attitude toward the topic in question is a function of the amount of perceived threat control generated by the message. Specifically, as threat control increases, attitudes more closely approximate those recommended in the persuasive message. This relationship is assumed to be linear. Furthermore,

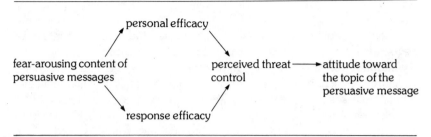

Figure 12.3.   A diagram of a causal model depicting the set of relationships predicted by the threat control explanation.

although the correlation between threat control and attitude is not without error, it is expected to be both positive and substantial.

This set of relationships is depicted in Figure 12.3. This figure illustrates that personal efficacy and response efficacy mediate the relationship between the fear-arousing persuasive message and perceived threat control. Perceived threat control, in turn, mediates the relationship between personal efficacy and response efficacy and the listener's attitude toward the topic in question. When all causal links are assumed to be positive, the threat control explanation yields the prediction that as the amount of fear-arousing material in a persuasive message increases, the amount of attitude change produced in the listener increases. This relationship may be weak, however, since there are several mediating variables. On the other hand, it is possible that a fear appeal might have an inverse impact on either response efficacy or personal efficacy. In such cases the correlation between the amount of fear-arousing content in the persuasive message and conformity with message recommendations is expected to be negative.

Conclusion

The characteristic that distinguishes these classes of explanations is that they make different predictions about the relationship between the amount of fear in a persuasive message and the amount of attitudinal and/or behavioral conformity with the recommendations of the persuasive message. Thus it is possible to eliminate a number of these competing explanations, if not all of them, by gaining an understanding of how the amount of fear in a persuasive message affects attitudes and conforming behavior. The method of gaining this understanding that was employed in this study is meta-analysis. A brief discussion of meta-analysis follows.

METHOD

As the number of studies on a topic increases, the difficulty in integrating the results of the studies increases. Providing an accurate summary of any literature requires a method for combining the results of independent studies on a topic. Several methods of accomplishing this goal are available (for example, see Rosenthal, 1978). Meta-analysis is one such method.

Meta-analysis is "the quantitative cumulation and analysis of descriptive statistics across studies" (Hunter, Schmidt, & Jackson, 1982, p. 137). In performing a meta-analysis, the investigator computes the relevant statistic, or statistics, for each pertinent study. Subsequently, the investigator cumulates these data across studies. These computations yield an estimate of the population parameter of interest. Since the sample size of the cumulative estimate is the sum of the sample sizes of all of the pertinent studies, this estimate probably provides a more accurate estimate of the population parameter than does the estimate from any one study.

Furthermore, when the focus of the meta-analysis is the relationship between variables, it is possible to search for variables that moderate the relationship. There are two ways in which to conduct this search. The direct method requires that one estimate the size of interaction effects in those studies in which there are multiple independent variables. The indirect method requires that one examine the variance in the computed relational statistic(s) (for example, r or d) and ascertain if that variance is attributable to sampling error. If not, then there must be moderator variables that cause the effect size to vary across studies. For a comprehensive discussion of meta-analysis, see Glass, McGaw, and Smith (1981) and Hunter et al. (1982).

The Data

The data for this project consist of statistics and various characteristics of the experiments from which these statistics derive. The statistics include the correlations between fear appeal manipulations and perceived fear (manipulation checks), attitude, and behavior; the quadratic effect of the fear appeal manipulations on the same set of criterion measures; and sample size. The experimental characteristic measures include topic of the fear appeal message, the year of publication of the study, the nature of the participant population, whether the participants volunteered or did not volunteer to participate in the study, the type of fear appeal manipulation employed, the nature of the experimental design, and the number of items constituting each dependent measure.

These data were obtained from articles in which the effect of fear appeals on various criterion measures was assessed. The articles were obtained by inspecting reference lists from major fear appeal review articles (Higbee, 1970; Janis, 1967; Leventhal, 1970; McGuire, 1969; Sutton, 1982). Any article relevant to the topic was reviewed, and the reference list searched for additional citations. Moreover, recent volumes (the last five years) of major social psychology, communication, and marketing journals were examined for relevant citations.

The literature search was restricted to studies published in journals; that is, dissertations, theses, convention papers, and other unpublished reports were eliminated from consideration. Since the majority of such reports located in the literature search were eventually published, this restriction is not likely to affect the results of this analysis.

Abstracts and computer search procedures were not used to locate articles. Since this analysis was restricted to published studies, the search procedure employed was sufficient to find applicable articles. Since more than 100 reference lists were inspected, the probability of omitting a substantial number of relevant studies is minimal. Furthermore, given the larger data base generated by the literature search, the results of an omitted study would have to be extreme in order to alter the substantive conclusions drawn here.

Criteria for Inclusion

Four criteria were used to determine if a study was pertinent for this meta-analysis. First, the study had to include data that had not been published previously. Thus review articles, reanalyses, and "think pieces" were eliminated.

Second, the persuasive message(s) had to include a fear manipulation, and the fear manipulation had to be relevant to the topic of the message. Thus studies investigating the effects of threats to attitudinal freedom (for example, Smith, 1977), the effects of irrelevant fear (for example, Simonson & Lundy, 1966), and emotional role playing (for example, Janis & Mann, 1965) were excluded.

Third, one or more of three dependent variables had to be measured in the study. These dependent variables were (1) perceived fear, (2) attitudes, and (3) behavior. These variables require explication.

Perceived fear measures are those items designed to tap how anxious or fearful participants felt during exposure to the persuasive message. For example, Rogers and Thistlethwaite (1970) asked their participants to indicate how they felt while they watched a film on smoking and lung cancer. Participants indicated their fright, tension, nervousness, anxiety, discomfort, and nausea on 9-point rating scales.

Attitude measures are those items designed to assess the participants' affect toward the persuasive message's recommendations. For example,

Horowitz and Gumenik (1970) asked their participants to indicate their agreement with the three basic recommendations included in a persuasive message concerning the dangers of drug abuse. These ratings were made on 10-point scales.

Behavior measures are assessments of whether or not, or the extent to which, participants' actions conform to the persuasive message's recommendations. For example, Leventhal and Niles (1965) measured whether or not participants had a chest X-ray after exposure to a persuasive message concerning smoking and lung cancer.

Several additional criterion measures were taken in the studies examined. These measures were not included in this analysis, since there were relatively few studies that examined these measures and since they are not as relevant as the obtained measures to the theoretical controversy outlined previously.

Fourth, the study had to provide sufficient information to allow the computation of the correlation, and quadratic effect when possible, between the fear manipulation and at least one of the pertinent dependent variables. For example, Kirscht and Haefner (1969) report the effects of a fear appeal manipulation on several dependent measures. They do not, however, report the results in sufficient detail to compute the correlations between the fear manipulation and these dependent variables.

Measuring Effects

Pearson's r was chosen as a measure of the strength of the linear effect of a fear appeal manipulation on perceived fear, attitude, and behavior. While there are other measures, such as d, which are useful for this purpose, Pearson's r has a number of advantages. First, it is simple to compute. Second, since a discussion of Pearson's r appears in almost all introductory textbooks, the majority of social scientists are familiar with the measure. Third, it has a metric that is easily interpreted. Fourth, the sampling distribution of Pearson's r is known, and an examination of this sampling distribution shows that Pearson's r has properties that make it a desirable measure of linear association. Fifth, it is a flexible measure. It can be used in further multivariate analyses, such as multiple regression and multiple correlation, the analysis of covariance, and path analysis. And, in any case, if one prefers other measures, then r can be transformed to yield values of d, t, and F (Hunter et al., 1982, p. 98).

None of the studies examined presented the correlation between the fear manipulation and the dependent variables of interest. The presentation of these data took the form of either the analysis of variance or the t-test. Thus Pearson's r had to be computed from this information. The computation was performed in two ways. First, if sufficient information was given in the report, the analysis of variance table was reconstructed. The unweighted means algorithm was employed. Since Pearson's r equals η (that is, the square root of the correlation ratio, η^2) for the linear trend, the correlation coefficient was easily obtained from this table. Since η was calculated from an unweighted means analysis of variance, the obtained correlation is corrected for unequal cell size (see Hunter et al., 1982, p. 99). Second, since values of F or t can be transformed to yield values of r, these transformations were used to obtain a value of the correlation coefficient. When sufficient information was available in a report, both methods were used as a means of minimizing computational errors. In some instances, only the latter information was available. In these cases there were no available means of checking computations.

The quadratic effect was computed in the same manner. The value of η for the quadratic effect was taken as the effect size measure.

Special Problems

Some articles presented special computational problems. These problems were treated in a consistent manner. In this section the most crucial and frequent problems and the methods employed in dealing with them are discussed.

In several instances authors failed to report statistical information for variables that did not produce statistically significant findings. For example, Shelton and Rogers (1981) manipulated fear, empathy, and efficacy, and measured their effects on several dependent variables. While they report statistical information concerning the main effects of fear and empathy, they report only that efficacy main effect and all interactions did not exert statistically significant effects on the dependent variables. Since the size of the effect of all variables must be known in order to compute Pearson's r accurately, such omissions proved problematic.

In such cases Pearson's r was computed in two ways. First, r was calculated assuming that all statistically nonsignificant effects were zero. The resulting value provided an estimate of the maximum fear correlation. Second, r was computed assuming that all statistically nonsignificant effects were as large as possible without being statistically significant at the .05 level. The resulting value provided an estimate of the minimum fear correlation. These two correlations were averaged, and the mean correlation was entered as the estimate of Pearson's r. In each case in which this problem was encountered, the two estimates were within .02 of each other. Thus the amount of error introduced into these data is probably not substantial.

A second problem concerned the analysis of dependent variables for which there were multiple measures. For example, Leventhal, Singer, and

Jones (1965) discuss the effect of a fear manipulation on perceived fear. In their study, perceived fear was measured by seven items. In reporting these data Leventhal et al. present separate analyses for each of the seven items. That is, they did *not* sum participants' responses to all seven items and assess the effect of fear on this index. In this case, and in related cases, the effect of the fear appeal manipulation on each measure was calculated and the correlations were averaged. The mean correlation was entered, and it was treated as being computed from a one-item measure.

Control group analyses produced two problems. In some experiments the control group and the experimental groups were not comparable. For example, Janis and Feshbach (1953) exposed three experimental groups to a persuasive message concerning dental hygiene. The control group, in contrast, was exposed to a persuasive message on the structure and operation of the human eye. Since the persuasive message to which the control group was exposed differed from that of the experimental groups on a factor in addition to fear, the control group was not included in the computations.

The second control group problem concerned those designs in which the control group did not fit into a factorial design. For example, Powell (1965) manipulated both the amount of fear in a persuasive message (low, high) and the target of the appeal (self, family, nation). In addition, Powell included a control group that received no persuasive message. In such cases the analysis of variance was performed first excluding the control group, and the effects were computed for each variance component. Subsequently, the control group data were used to recompute the effect of the fear appeal manipulation. The sums of squares for the other variance components were adjusted for the increase in sample size produced by the addition of the control group participants. The initial analysis was used to estimate the strength of interaction effects. The latter analysis was used to estimate the strength of the effect of the fear appeal manipulation. This technique is similar to a procedure recommended by Himmelfarb (1975).

A final problem involved collapsing quantitative dependent variables. For example, although Janis and Feshbach (1953) measured attitude change on quantitative scales, they presented the results as the percentage of participants who exhibited change toward the recommendations in the persuasive message, change away from the recommendations in the persuasive message, and those exhibiting no change. Since the report precluded determining the extent of change, a value of $+1$ was assigned to those participants who changed toward the recommendations in the persuasive message, a value of -1 was assigned to those participants changing away from the recommendations in the persuasive message, and a value of 0 was assigned to those participants exhibiting no change. This procedure was followed in all such cases.

RESULTS

The presentation of the results of the meta-analysis is organized by dependent variable. The effects of the fear-arousing content of persuasive messages on perceived fear, attitude, and behavior are discussed in sequence.

Perceived Fear

Pertinent data are available from 40 studies. These 40 studies have a combined sample size of 7016 participants. The correlation between the fear manipulation and perceived fear ranges from .17 to .81, with a weighted mean of .36. The weighted (by sample size) variance in this distribution of correlations is .018. A weighted variance of .004 is expected by sampling error alone. Thus the obtained variance is larger than that expected by chance. The χ^2 test indicates that the variance in the distribution of correlations is significantly greater than that expected by sampling error alone ($\chi^2 = 168.14$, df $= 39$, $p < .001$; for a discussion of these computations, see Hunter et al., 1982, pp. 40—74).

The regression of perceived fear onto the fear manipulation is linear. There are 12 studies in which a quadratic effect can be estimated. These studies have a combined sample size of 3437 participants. The quadratic effect ranges from .03 to .19, with a mean of .07. Thus the degree of nonlinearity in these data is trivial.[2] The quadratic effect is substantially smaller than the linear effect. Moreover, with a mean sample size in these 12 studies of approximately 286, the mean quadratic effect is within sampling error of zero.

There is little evidence suggesting nonadditivity in these data. Several studies report that other variables interact with the fear manipulation to affect perceived fear, but these effects are small (see Chu, 1966; Leventhal, Jones, & Trembly, 1966; Leventhal & Singer, 1966; Rogers & Deckner, 1975). Specifically, none of these effects exceeds a correlation of .19. They reach accepted levels of statistical significance because of large sample sizes.

While there is little evidence of nonadditivity in these data, it is clear from a number of studies that the manipulation of other independent variables (that is, independent variables other than fear) is confounded with fear. Several investigators report that other independent variables have main effects on perceived fear (for example, see Hendrick, Giesen, & Borden, 1975; Powell, 1965; Powell & Miller, 1967; Ramirez & Lasater, 1977; Shelton & Rogers, 1981).

The variance in the distribution of perceived fear correlations, is, in part, attributable to methodological artifacts. For example, it is known that, ceteris paribus, the more items employed to measure a construct, the higher the reliability of the measure. Since unreliability has the systematic effect of attenuating correlations, the number of items measuring perceived fear is expected to be positively correlated with the size of the fear manipulation-perceived fear correlation ($r = .11$, $df = 36$, $p = .27$). In addition, it is known that, ceteris paribus, change scores are less reliable than static scores. Thus the fear manipulation-perceived fear correlation is expected to be larger in posttest-only designs than in pretest-posttest designs. Type of design is correlated in the expected direction with the size of the fear manipulation-perceived fear correlation ($r = -.28$, $df = 40$, $p = .04$). While these correlations are not exceptionally large, the data suggest that these variables suppress the effect of each other. Hence, if the size of the fear manipulation-perceived fear correlation is regressed onto both number of items measuring perceived fear and type of design, then the standardized regression coefficients are found to be larger than the zero-order correlations ($B = .24$ and $-.36$, respectively; $R = .36$).

In general, authors do not report the reliability of the perceived fear measure. The exceptions are Beck and Davis (1978), who report that $\alpha = .86$; Mewborn and Rogers (1979), who report that $\alpha = .88$; and Shelton and Rogers, who report that $\alpha = .80$. The former two measures are composed of six items. The latter measure is composed of five items. Moreover, Janis and Terwilliger (1962) report an interrater correlation of .85 for their content analysis measure of perceived fear. Finally, Leventhal and Watts (1966) report that their six-item measure of perceived fear has an average item-total correlation of .60.

While no formal analyses, such as correcting all correlations for attenuation and performing the meta-analysis on the corrected correlations, can be performed on these data, some speculation concerning the effect of unreliability is warranted. If one assumes that the reliability of a six-item measure is .87, the mean of the Beck and Davis (1978) and Mewborn and Rogers (1979) data, then using the Spearman-Brown formula to calculate the estimated reliability of a one-item measure yields an estimated reliability of $\alpha = .52$. If this figure is used to correct the mean fear manipulation-perceived fear correlation for attenuation due to error of measurement, then a corrected correlation of .50 is obtained. Since approximately one-third of the studies in this sample employ a one-item measure of perceived fear, it is likely that many of these studies provide a substantial underestimate of the fear manipulation-perceived fear correlation. Had all studies been able to be corrected for attenuation due to error of measurement, it is not unlikely that there would have been substantially less variance in the distribution of fear manipulation-perceived fear correlations.

There is also evidence that another methodological artifact affects these results. For example, as a result of an extremely strong set of fear messages, Chu (1966) reports little difference in perceived fear among three experimental groups. Thus the fear manipulation-perceived fear correlation is attenuated due to restriction of range in these data. If the variance among treatment conditions could be assessed, then these data could be corrected. Such a correction could reduce the variance in the fear manipulation-perceived fear correlations further.

Attitude[3]

Pertinent data are available from 25 studies. These studies have a total sample size of 3892 participants. The correlation between the fear manipulation and attitude ranges from $-.25$ to $.63$, with a weighted mean of $.21$. The weighted variance in this distribution of correlations is $.03$. A weighted variance of $.01$ is expected by sampling error alone. Thus the obtained variance is larger than the variance expected by chance. The χ^2 test indicates that the variance in this distribution of correlations is significantly greater than that expected by sampling error alone ($\chi^2 = 137.91$, df $= 24$, p$< .001$).

The regression of attitude onto the fear manipulation is linear. There are 14 studies in which a quadratic effect can be estimated. These studies have a total sample size of 2056 participants. The quadratic effect ranges from $.00$ to $.26$, with a weighted mean of $.09$. Thus the quadratic effect is substantially smaller than the linear effect, and with a mean sample size of approximately 147 the quadratic effect is within sampling error of zero.

Since the variance in this distribution of correlations is greater than that expected by chance, it is possible that there are variables that moderate the fear manipulation-attitude relationship. Prior to entertaining such a hypothesis, however, a search for possible artifacts is necessary.

The strength of the fear manipulation-perceived fear correlation differs across studies. Moreover, the size of the fear manipulation-perceived fear correlation is correlated with the size of the fear-attitude correlation (r $= .41$). Thus, as the size of the former increases, the size of the latter increases. It is possible that differences in the strength of the fear appeal manipulation produce differences in the fear manipulation-attitude correlations. For example, strong manipulations may produce high correlations with attitude, while weak manipulations may produce low correlations with attitude. In order to test this possibility the fear manipulation-attitude correlation is divided by the fear manipulation-perceived fear correlation. This quotient is interpretable in at least two ways. First, it is a measure of the strength of the fear manipulation-attitude correlation when corrected for the strength of the fear manipulation. Second, if perceived fear mediates the relationship between the fear manipulation and attitude, it is an estimate of the correlation between perceived fear and attitude.

There are 17 studies from which both a fear manipulation-perceived fear correlation and a fear manipulation-attitude correlation can be obtained. These studies have combined sample size of 2572 participants. The ratio of the fear manipulation-perceived fear correlation to the fear manipulation-attitude correlation ranges from $-.61$ to 1.57, with a weighted mean of $.57$. The weighted variance of this distribution is $.24$. A weighted variance of $.004$ is expected by sampling error alone. Thus the obtained variance is substantially larger than the variance expected by chance. The χ^2 test indicates that the variance of this distribution is significantly greater than that expected by sampling error ($\chi^2 = 1354$, df $= 16$, p $< .001$).

The variance of the distribution of corrected correlations is larger than the variance of the distribution of uncorrected correlations. Therefore, the strength of the fear manipulation masks some of the variance in the fear manipulation-attitude correlations. One possible explanation for this result is that the stronger fear manipulations occur in those studies in which the perceived fear-attitude relationship is relatively weak, and the weaker fear manipulations occur in those studies in which the perceived fear-attitude relationship is relatively strong. Alternatively, the increased variance may be due to methodological artifacts. For example, assuming that the ratio of the fear manipulation correlation to the fear manipulation-attitude correlation is constant, differences in the reliability of the perceived fear measure and/or the attitude measure serve to attenuate correlations differentially and thus produce an increase in the variance of the distribution of the correlation ratio.

There are two pieces of indirect evidence that indicate that differential reliability increases the variance in the distribution of the fear manipulation-attitude correlations. First, the type of experimental design is correlated with the size of the fear manipulation-attitude correlation ($r = -.20$, df $= 23$, p $= .17$).[4] Although this correlation is not statistically significant at the .05 level, it does indicate a tendency for larger correlations in posttest-only designs than in pretest-posttest designs. Second, there is a statistically significant correlation between the number of items used to measure attitude and the size of the fear manipulation-attitude correlation ($r = .36$, df $= 21$, p $= .05$). This correlation indicates that the more items used to measure attitude, the higher the fear manipulation-attitude correlation. Again, suppressor effects are in evidence. Regressing the fear manipulation-attitude correlation onto both type of design and number of items, the standardized regression coefficients are found to be larger than the zero-order correlations ($B = -.24$ and $.39$, respectively; $R = .43$).

There is also evidence that fear manipulation-attitude correlations are attenuated due to restriction in range. There is a substantial correlation between the number of levels of the fear manipulation and the size of the fear manipulation-attitude correlation ($r = .31$, df $= 23$, p $= .07$). The greater the number of levels of the fear manipulation, the larger the variance of the independent variable. The larger the variance of the independent variable, the less the fear manipulation-attitude correlation is attenuated due to restriction in range. Therefore, in general, fear manipulations that employ several levels of fear tend to produce larger fear manipulation-attitude correlations than those fear manipulations that employ only few levels of fear.

The extent to which the variance in the fear manipulation-attitude correlations is due to methodological artifacts may be estimated by the multiple correlation of the fear manipulation-attitude correlation with type of design, number of items employed to measure the criterion variable, and number of levels of the independent variable. This correlation is $R = .50$. Hence methodological artifacts are responsible for a considerable amount of the difference in the fear manipulation-attitude correlation distribution.

While methodological artifacts provide a partial explanation of why fear manipulation-attitude correlations differ across studies, moderator variables are responsible for a portion of the difference as well. Several studies include manipulations of independent variables in addition to fear. Some of these studies report that these other independent variables interact with fear to affect attitude. These results are discussed below.

Three experiments report the effect of both fear and source credibility on attitude (Hewgill & Miller, 1965; McCroskey & Wright, 1971; Powell & Miller, 1967). Two of these studies report a statistically significant fear × source credibility interaction (McCroskey & Wright, 1971; Powell & Miller, 1967). The third experiment reports a statistically nonsignificant interaction (Hewgill & Miller, 1965). Moreover, the effect size for the interaction in that study is small, $r = .04$.

The effect sizes for the two studies that report a statistically significant interaction are not trivial. There is reason to believe, however, that these interactions result from unusual features of the experimental designs, rather than a substantive fear × source credibility interaction. These studies are detailed below.

The effect size of the fear × source credibility interaction in the Powell and Miller (1967) experiment is large, $\eta = .36$ (4 df). The source credibility manipulation is primarily a trustworthiness manipulation in this experiment. The manipulation has a strong effect on trustworthiness ratings, but not on competence ratings. No dynamism ratings are reported. There are three source credibility treatments in this study: (1) low source credibility, (2) high source credibility, and (3) an unattributed source. The fear × source credibility interaction effect is due primarily to the unattributed source condition. If the unattributed source condition is removed, the size of the fear × source credibility interaction decreases dramatically, $\eta = .10$ (2 df). This effect is not statistically significant at the .05 level.

This interaction effect is difficult to derive from theory. While Powell and Miller present a hypothesis suggesting such an effect, there is no ration-ale for the hypothesis. An important omission in their analysis is that, while there are credibility manipulation check data for the low credibility and high credibility sources, there are no credibility manipulation check data for the unattributed source. While the authors appear to assume that the unattribu-ted source has higher source credibility than the low credibility source but lower credibility than the high credibility source, there is no evidence to support the claim. Moreover, it is undoubtably the case that the subjects in this experiment made some attribution of the source's credibility in the unat-tributed source condition. From an observation of the fear manipulation check data and the attitude data, a reasonable hypothesis is that partici-pants assume that the unattributed source is highly credible. The rationale for this hypothesis is that the pattern of fear manipulation check data and attitude data is the same for both the high credibility source and the unattri-buted source. An alternative hypothesis is that there are vast individual dif-ferences in the credibility attributions made in the unattributed source con-dition. The interaction of these individual differences with fear, or with both fear and source credibility, might produce an apparent fear × source credi-bility interaction. While this hypothesis is extremely speculative, without a replication of this effect and data probing the process that produces the ef-fect, it is reasonable to be skeptical of its validity.

In the McCroskey and Wright (1971) experiment two levels of source credibility are manipulated. The source credibility manipulation has no ef-fect on dynamism ratings, but does affect both authoritativeness (compe-tence) and character (trustworthiness), especially the former. The effect size of the interaction is smaller than in the Powell and Miller data, $\eta = .12$ (2 df).

The interaction is due to a strange control group difference. In both the low fear and high fear conditions more favorable attitudes are produced by the high credibility source than by the low credibility source. But in the control group the opposite effect occurs. This difference is not too large— witness the effect size—but it is sufficient to be statistically significant at the .05 level. If the control group data are removed, there is no interaction, r = .00. There is no satisfying rationale for the control group difference that produces the interaction. Unless this effect replicates, it is reasonable to be skeptical of its validity.

All three source credibility experiments have the common feature of including manipulations of two levels of source credibility and two levels of fear. When the data from the 2 × 2 design are analyzed, there is no evi-dence of substantial fear × source credibility interactions (Hewgill & Miller, 1965, r = .04; McCroskey & Wright, 1971, r = .00; Powell & Miller, 1967, η = .10, 2 df). Thus, despite some claims to the contrary, there is no strong evidence that source credibility is a powerful moderator of the fear manipu-lation-attitude relationship.

In a series of studies Leventhal and his associates have examined the effect of both fear and the specificity of instructions on attitude (Leventhal et al., 1965, 1966; Leventhal, Watts, & Pagano, 1967). Two of these reports claim statistically significant interactions involving fear and the specificity of recommendations. The third experiment reports no such effect. These experiments are reviewed chronologically.

Leventhal et al. (1965) report that fear, specificity of instructions, and whether or not one has had a prior tetanus shot interact to affect attitudes toward obtaining a tetanus shot. The nature of the interaction is that for those participants who have a prior shot there is no effect of fear when the message is accompanied by specific recommendations, but as fear increases participants conform more closely to message recommendations when the message does not include specific recommendations. For those participants not having a prior shot there is a small effect for fear when the message does not include specific recommendations, and a stronger fear effect when the message includes specific recommendations. Again, the nature of the fear effect in both instances is that as fear increases, conformity with message recommendations increases. The effect size for this three-way interaction is $r = .16$. The fear $\times$ specificity interaction is neither statistically significant at the .05 level nor substantial, $r = .02$.

Leventhal et al. (1966) report that fear and specificity of instructions interact to affect attitudes toward tetanus. Specifically, they produce data showing that as fear increases, conformity with message recommendations increases when the recommendations are specific. The size of this interaction effect is $r = .14$. There is no evidence of the three-way interaction that Leventhal et al. (1965) report. It is neither statistically significant at the .05 level nor substantial, $r = .03$.

Leventhal et al. (1967) include both a fear manipulation and an instructions manipulation in a study that assesses the effects of these and other independent variables on attitudes toward smoking and lung cancer. They do not report sufficient data to allow the estimation of interaction effects. Since they report statistically significant interaction effects in their analyses of other dependent variables, it is reasonable to conclude that there is no statistically significant fear $\times$ specificity interaction. With 118 participants providing data in this experiment, the effect size for the fear $\times$ specificity interaction cannot have exceeded $r = .16$ without being statistically significant at the .05 level. Therefore, it is probably reasonable to assume that fear and specificity do not interact to produce a substantial effect on attitude.

Thus the overall picture regarding how fear and specificity of instructions interact to affect attitudes is unclear. Leventhal et al. (1965) report a fear $\times$ specificity $\times$ prior shots interaction, but no fear $\times$ specificity interaction. Leventhal et al. (1966) report no fear $\times$ specificity $\times$ prior shots interaction, but do report a fear $\times$ specificity interaction. Leventhal et al. (1967)

report no fear × specificity interaction. Parenthetically, it is notable that these data are, in the main, inconsistent with Leventhal's hypothesis that a fear effect occurs only in the specific recommendations condition.

Hence, as with source credibility, it is reasonable to be skeptical of the validity of claims that fear and specificity of recommendations interact to affect attitudes. Since these three studies include only approximately 700 participants, a larger data base is needed in order to perform a meta-analysis of the fear × specificity interaction. Only such an analysis allows one to judge whether the paradoxical results from these three studies are due to sampling error, if there are additional moderator variables, or if some other explanation accounts for these data.

In a study of attitudes toward building community fallout shelters, Powell (1965) provides data that yield a statistically significant fear × target interaction. Powell reports that when the target of the persuasive message is the listener, there is a slight, but statistically nonsignificant, tendency for an increase in fear to produce a decrease in conformity to message recommendations. When the target of the persuasive message is the listener's family, however, an increase in fear produces an increase in conformity to the recommendations of the persuasive message. When the target of the persuasive message is the listener's nation, there is no effect of fear on attitude. The size of this effect is $\eta = .19$ (2 df).

There are several factors that prohibit accepting the conclusion that fear and target interact to affect attitudes. First, this study is the only one in which the effect of fear and target on attitude can be assessed. Second, it is a relatively small sample study—N = 80 for this analysis. Third, the effect size is relatively small; while the effect is statistically significant at the .05 level, it is not statistically significant at the .025 level. Fourth, the internal validity of the target manipulation is questionable. The target manipulation has a large effect on perceived fear, $\eta = .46$ (2df). One plausible hypothesis is that the target manipulation and the fear manipulation combine additively to produce perceived fear, which, in turn, directly affects attitude. There is some evidence consistent with this hypothesis. The correlation between the mean perceived fear scores and the mean attitude scores for the six experimental conditions is substantial, r = .67. While it is premature to embrace such a hypothesis, there are sufficient questions concerning the Powell experiment to make embracing the veracity of the fear × target interaction premature.

Burnett and Oliver (1979) report data that describe the effect of both fear and various demographic, sociopsychological, and health attitude variables on attitudes toward health maintenance organizations. A cluster analysis of the demographic, sociopsychological, and health attitude variables is presented, and the relationship between fear and attitude toward health maintenance organizations is broken down by cluster. Two clusters, labeled "older liberals" and "older blue-collar blacks," prove to be the most receptive to fear appeals. In other words, for these clusters as fear increases attitudes toward health maintenance organizations conform more closely to those recommended in the persuasive message.

The recondite character of the results of the cluster analysis makes it difficult to assess which demographic, sociopsychological, and/or health attitude variable(s) interacts with fear to affect attitude. Nevertheless, Burnett and Oliver's results suggest that age is such a variable.

In order to probe the fear × age interaction, the estimated age of the participants in each of the studies is correlated with the fear manipulation-attitude correlation.[5] From this analysis a correlation of r = .52 is obtained (df = 23, p = .004). Thus, as in the Burnett and Oliver (1979) study, the effect of fear manipulations on attitude is stronger as the age of the participants increases. Specifically, as fear increases attitudes conform more closely to message recommendations for older participants. An increase in fear produces either no effect or a decrease in conformity to message recommendations for younger participants.

Four studies report data pertinent to assessing the effect of both fear and anxiety on attitude (Goldstein, 1959; Janis & Feshbach, 1954; Millman, 1968; Wheatley & Oshikawa, 1970). Two of these experiments meet the criteria for this meta-analysis (Goldstein, 1959; Wheatley & Oshikawa, 1970). In neither of these experiments is the fear × anxiety interaction statistically significant at the .05 level. Moreover, in neither of these experiments is the effect size for the fear × anxiety interaction substantial. On the other hand, the effect size is consistent. In both experiments r = .12. Furthermore, the nature of the interaction effect is similar in all four experiments. Specifically, for low-anxiety participants there is either no correlation between manipulated fear and attitude or a small positive correlation between manipulated fear and attitude. For high-anxiety participants there is either no correlation between manipulated fear and attitude or a small negative correlation between manipulated fear and attitude. Given the consistency of this effect, and given that there is reason to believe that methodological artifacts attenuate the effect size in these experiments, they are detailed below.

A low fear message and a high fear message compose the fear manipulation in the Goldstein (1959) experiment. Mainord's (1956) adaptation of the Sentence Completion Test is employed as a measure of coping/avoiding tendencies.[6] The extreme quartiles are used to define copers and avoiders. The sample is composed of high school students. A pretest-posttest design is utilized to examine changes in attitudes toward dental hygiene. Five items, each with a five-point response scale, are included as attitude measures. The results are presented, however, as a trichotomy. Specifically, the participant changes in a negative direction, does not change, or changes in a positive direction.

For copers, or low-anxiety participants, the fear manipulation has no effect, r = −.01 (df = 65, p > .05). For avoiders, or high-anxiety partici-pants, an increase in fear produces a decrease in attitude change, r = −.25 (df = 70, p < .05). The anxiety-attitude change correlation reflects that the low fear message is more successful with avoiders than with copers, al-though the correlation is not statistically significant at the .05 level (r = .12, df = 61, p > .05). The high fear message is more successful with copers than with avoiders, although the correlation is not statistically significant at the .05 level (r = −.13, df = 74, p > .05).

While the effect size for the fear × anxiety interaction is not large in this experiment, it may be seriously attenuated because of several features of the experimental design. First, the design of the experiment is pretest-post-test and, as previously discussed, the unreliability of change scores tends to attenuate correlations to a greater extent than the more reliable posttest-only measures. Second, the experimental design includes only two levels of manipulated fear and only two levels of anxiety. As shown previously, range restriction tends to attenuate correlations in such studies. Third, while the dependent measure contains five items, a considerable amount of the vari-ance in this scale is lost when the data are trichotomized. Again, the ex-pected result is attenuation of the effect size. Fourth, high school students constitute the sample in the Goldstein experiment. As shown previously, the manipulated fear-attitude correlation is weaker for such relatively young participants. It is likely that the same is true for interaction effects. In sum, there is reason to suspect that a larger fear × anxiety interaction may be obtained if a replication of the Goldstein study is conducted with some de-sign modifications. Or, given Goldstein's design, the application of statistical corrections for unreliability and restriction in range may be sufficient to pro-duce a substantial fear × anxiety interaction.

A low fear message and a high fear message compose the fear manipula-tion in the Wheatley and Oshikawa (1970) experiment. Wheatley and Oshi-kawa employ the Sarason Lack of Protection Test to measure anxiety. The bottom one-third and the top one-third of the anxiety distribution divide par-ticipants into the low-anxiety and the high-anxiety groups. College students provide the data for this experiment. A pretest-posttest design is employed to examine changes in attitudes toward life insurance. Six items, each with a seven-point response scale, are utilized to measure attitude change.

For low-anxiety participants, as the amount of fear in the persuasive message increases, the amount of attitude change increases proportionally (r = .15, df = 75, p > .05), although the effect is not statistically significant at the .05 level. For high-anxiety participants, as the amount of fear in the persuasive message increases, the amount of attitude change decreases proportionally (r = −.07, df = 75, p > .05), although the effect is not statis-tically significant at the .05 level. The anxiety-attitude change correlation indicates that the low fear message is more successful with high-anxiety participants than with low-anxiety participants (r = .12, df = 75, p > .05). Again, this effect is not statistically significant at the .05 level. The high fear message, however, is more successful with low-anxiety participants than with high-anxiety participants (r = −.11, df = 75, p > .05). This effect is not statistically significantly at the .05 level.

Some of the same factors that may serve to attenuate the effect size of the fear × anxiety interaction in the Goldstein (1959) experiment may serve to attenuate the Wheatley and Oshikawa (1970) effects as well. Particularly, the design is a pretest-posttest design, and both the fear manipulation and the anxiety measure are dichotomized. So again there is reason to believe that a larger effect size for the fear × anxiety interaction may be obtained in a modified replication of the Wheatley and Oshikawa experiment. Alternatively, statistical corrections applied to data collected from a direct replication of the Wheatley and Oshikawa experiment are likely to produce the same result.

Neither the Janis and Feshbach (1954) experiment nor the Millman (1968) experiment report data in a way that allows the estimation of effect sizes. But their data appear consistent with those of the Goldstein experiment and the Wheatley and Oshikawa experiment. Janis and Feshbach (1954) report similar fear × anxiety interactions for two dependent measures: (1) change in dental practice and (2) resistance to counterpropaganda. Millman (1968) reports that chronic anxiety and acute anxiety interact to affect opinion change. While she interprets these data as consistent with the curvilinearity hypothesis, an alternative interpretation is that they are evidence of a fear × anxiety interaction. Put differently, acute anxiety is similar to the effect that a fear manipulation produces. Assuming that these variables indicate a common factor, Millman's interaction is of exactly the same form as Goldstein's, Wheatley and Oshikawa's, and Janis and Feshbach's fear × anxiety interaction.

In sum, the available evidence indicates that fear and anxiety interact consistently to affect attitude change. While that effect is weak, there are methodological artifacts that serve to suppress it. Therefore it is possible that future carefully designed experiments may produce data that indicate that fear and anxiety interact substantially to affect attitude. Or application of statistical corrections for unreliability and restriction in range may produce the same result.

Three studies present data examining the effects of both fear and whether the participant is a volunteer or a nonvolunteer on attitude (Horowitz, 1969, 1972; Horowitz & Gumenik, 1970). In each of these experiments the fear × volunteer interaction is substantial: r = .25 (Horowitz, 1969); r = .15 (Horowitz & Gumenik, 1970); and η = .23 with 4 df (Horowitz, 1972). These studies are detailed below.

Horowitz (1969) provides data that examine the effect of fear, whether the participant volunteered or did not volunteer for the experiment, and number of exposures to the persuasive message on attitude toward drug abuse. He reports a main effect for the volunteering manipulation, volunteers conform more closely to message recommendations than nonvolunteers, and a fear × volunteer interaction. Specifically, for volunteers, as fear increases, conformity to the message recommendations increases ($r = .46$, $df = 58$, $p < .05$). For nonvolunteers, as fear increases, conformity to the message recommendations decreases ($r = -.21$, $df = 58$, $p > .05$), although this effect is not quite statistically significant at the .05 level. Both the low fear message and the high fear message produce more conformity to message recommendations. For the low fear message this effect is not statistically significant at the .05 level ($r = -.15$, $df = 58$, $p > .05$). For the high fear message this effect is statistically significant at the .05 level ($r = -.42$, $df = 58$, $p < .05$).

Horowitz and Gumenik (1970) manipulate fear, whether the participant is a volunteer or nonvolunteer, and whether or not the participant has a choice of experiments in which to participate, and assess their impact on attitude toward drug abuse. In addition to their decision to manipulate choice instead of number of exposures, the Horowitz and Gumenik design differs from the Horowitz (1969) design in one important way: The volunteering manipulation is different. Horowitz's (1969, p. 35) nonvolunteer participant sample was recruited from a "subject file-card index." The volunteer participant sample was composed of persons responding to a request to participate. Horowitz and Gumenik (1970), on the other hand, posted a request for participants to take part in a psychological experiment. Those persons volunteering to participate in that experiment are considered volunteers, whereas those persons not volunteering to participate in that experiment are considered nonvolunteers. Horowitz and Gumenik then canceled the experiment. Subsequently, they required persons to participate in another experiment, choosing both those volunteering for the previous experiment (volunteers) and those refusing to participate in the previous experiment (nonvolunteers).

Horowitz and Gumenik (1970) report substantial volunteer and choice main effects. Volunteers conform more closely to message recommendations than do nonvolunteers. Participants given a choice of experiments conform more closely to message recommendations than do participants not given a choice. They also report a statistically significant fear × volunteer interaction, and a statistically significant fear × volunteer × choice interaction, the latter being an especially large effect ($r = .34$).

For volunteers, as fear increases, attitudes more closely resemble those advocated in the persuasive message ($r = .33$, $df = 58$, $p < .05$). For nonvolunteers, as fear increases, attitudes are unaffected ($r = -.02$, $df = 58$, $p >$

.05). For both the low fear message and the high fear message volunteers conform more closely to message recommendations than do nonvolunteers, the difference being more pronounced in the high fear condition. For the low fear message, $r = -.22$ (df = 58, p > .05). For the high fear message, $r = -.52$ (df = 58, p < .05).

The triple interaction occurs because of a difference among the nonvolunteers. Put another way, for volunteers whether or not the participant has a choice of experiments makes little difference ($r = .35$ and $r = .33$, respectively). For nonvolunteers, however, choice makes a substantial difference in the size of the fear manipulation-attitude correlation. When nonvolunteers are given a choice, an increase in fear produces an increase in conformity to message recommendations ($r = .20$, df = 28, p > .05), although this effect is not statistically significant at the .05 level. When nonvolunteers are not given a choice an increase in fear produces a decrease in conformity to message recommendations ($r = -.24$, df = 28, p > .05), although this effect is not statistically significant at the .05 level. While neither of these correlations significantly differs from zero, they are very close to being significantly different from each other ($z = 1.62$, p = .0526).

Horowitz (1972) provides data that examine the effects of fear and whether or not the participant volunteered for the experiment on attitude toward drug abuse. The volunteering manipulation is the same as that used by Horowitz and Gumenik (1970). The fear manipulation, however, differs from both of the previous experiments. Both Horowitz (1969) and Horwitz and Gumenik (1970) varied fear by providing participants with pamphlets and films that differed in the amount of fear-arousing content. Horowitz (1972), on the other hand, manipulated fear by the use of false heart rate feedback.

Horowitz (1972) reports two significant main effects, and a substantial, but not statistically significant, interaction effect. Volunteers conform more closely to message recommendations than do nonvolunteers. The high fear message produces more conformity to message recommendations than does the low fear message. For both volunteers and nonvolunteers, as fear increases, conformity to the message recommendations increases ($r = .48$, df = 58, p < .05 for volunteers; $r = .20$, df = 58, p > .05 for nonvolunteers). There were five levels of the fear manipulation. In all but the second lowest fear condition volunteers conformed more closely than nonvolunteers to message recommendations. The volunteer/nonvolunteer-attitude correlations were $-.33$ (lowest fear), .10, $-.20$, $-.41$, and $-.57$ (highest fear), respectively. Only the last two correlations are statistically significant at the .05 level (df = 22 for each correlation).

In sum, the Horowitz research program illustrates that whether the participant volunteers or does not volunteer for the experiment is a strong moderator of the fear manipulation-attitude correlation. Specifically, for volunteers an increase in the fear-arousing content of a persuasive message produces an increase in conformity to the recommendations contained in that message. This effect is a strong one. The mean correlation in these three studies is r= .42. For nonvolunteers there is considerable variance in the fear-attitude correlation across the three studies. The mean correlation is r = −.01. Given the small mean correlation, and since none of the fear manipulation-attitude correlations differ significantly from zero at the .05 level, the most reasonable conclusion is that for nonvolunteers fear has no impact on conformity to message recommendations.

Since whether or not participants volunteered for the experiment is one of the study characteristics coded in the meta-analysis, additional data are available to replicate the Horowitz results. In twelve studies, including the Horowitz studies, it is clear that the participants are volunteers. In eight studies, including the Horowitz studies, it is clear that the participants are nonvolunteers. An observation of these twenty studies shows that the fear manipulation-attitude correlation is much higher for volunteers than for nonvolunteers. There are two ways of illustrating this point. First, the weighted mean fear manipulation-attitude correlation is larger for volunteers than for nonvolunteers ($\bar{r}$ = .32 for volunteers; .07 for nonvolunteers). Second, the volunteer/nonvolunteer variable correlates substantially with the fear manipulation-attitude correlation (r = −.55, df = 18, p < .05). Thus these data are consistent with the Horowitz data and with the hypothesis that whether or not one volunteers to participate in the experiment moderates the relationship between fear manipulations and attitude.

While it is important to note the variables that moderate the relationship between fear manipulations and attitude, it is equally important to note those variables that do not moderate this relationship.[7] In the fear appeal literature there are several variables that have not interacted with fear to exert a statistically significant and/or a substantial effect on attitudes. For example, Beck and Davis (1978) report that importance is not a moderator of the fear manipulation-attitude relationship. Berkowitz and Cottingham (1960) show that relevance does not interact with fear to exert a substantial effect on attitude. Frandsen (1963) reports a small fear × medium of presentation interaction effect. An experiment by Hendrick, Giesen, and Borden (1975) presents data that show a small fear × fear reduction interaction effect. Insko, Arkoff, and Insko (1965) demonstrate that time is not a strong moderator of the fear manipulation-attitude relationship. Leventhal et al. (1966) report no interaction effects among several independent variables, including sex, eligibility for a tetanus shot, and delay of attitude measurement. Finally, Leventhal et al. (1967) produce no evidence that fear interacts with smoking, smoking habit, and/or time to affect attitudes concerning smoking and lung cancer. The potential moderating effect of several of these independent variables has been tested in only one experiment. Therefore it is premature to dismiss them as potential moderators until replications are conducted. Nevertheless, at this time there is no evidence to suggest that these variables are important moderators of the fear manipulation-attitude relationship.

Moreover, several study characteristics show no evidence of moderating the fear manipulation-attitude relationship. While there are not many studies per topic, the available evidence suggests that the fear manipulation-attitude correlation does not vary substantially across topic. Moreover, there is little evidence that either the method of manipulation or year of publication are strong moderators of the fear manipulation-attitude relationship.[8]

Behavior

Pertinent data are available from 15 studies, which have a combined sample size of 3080 participants. The correlation between the fear manipulation and behavior ranges from −.36 to .69, with a weighted mean of .10. The weighted variance in this distribution of correlations is .04. A weighted variance of .005 is expected by chance alone. Thus the obtained variance is larger than the variance expected by chance. The χ^2 test indicates that the variance in this distribution of correlations is significantly greater than that expected by sampling error alone ($\chi^2 = 125.70$, df = 14, p < .001).

The regression of behavior onto the fear manipulation is linear. There are eight studies in which a quadratic effect can be estimated. The quadratic effect ranges from −.22 to .43, with a weighted mean of .03. Thus, despite one study with an abnormally high quadratic effect, the mean quadratic effect is smaller than the linear effect. With a mean sample size of approximately 250 cases it is within sampling error of zero, while the linear effect is not ($\alpha = .05$).

Since the variance in this distribution of correlations is greater than that expected by chance, it is possible that there are variables that moderate the fear manipulation-behavior relationship. Prior to entertaining such a hypothesis, however, a search for artifacts is required.

First, the fear manipulation-behavior correlations are corrected for the strength of the manipulation. Of the 15 studies allowing the calculation of the fear manipulation-behavior correlation, 13 also allow the calculation of the fear manipulation-perceived fear correlation. These 13 studies include a total of 2951 participants. The ratio of the fear manipulation-behavior correlation to the fear manipulation-perceived fear correlation in these studies ranges from −.91 to .85, with a weighted mean of .45. The weighted variance of this distribution is .19. A weighted variance of .004 is expected by chance alone. Thus the obtained variance is larger than the variance expected by chance alone. The χ^2 test indicates that the variance of this distribution is significantly greater than that expected by sampling error alone (χ^2 = 881.58, df = 12, p < .001).

As with attitudes, the variance of this distribution of corrected correlations is larger than the variance of the distribution of obtained correlations. One possible explanation of this result is differential reliability of the behavior measures. There is evidence consistent with this explanation. The correlation of the number of items measuring behavior with the fear manipulation-behavior correlation is r = .76 (df = 13, p = .001).

In addition to methodological artifacts, such as reliability, it is possible that other variables moderate the fear manipulation-behavior relationship. An observation of the 15 relevant studies shows that several of them include the manipulation of other independent variables. Few of them, however, yield either statistically significant interaction effects and/or substantial effect sizes for the interaction effect(s). These data are discussed below.

Chu (1966) reports that fear, imminency, and efficacy interact to affect whether or not children take a drug to inoculate them against roundworm. The effect size is small (η = .11, 4 df), but since Chu's experiment includes the measurement of 1071 participants, the three-way interaction is statistically significant at the .05 level. Chu's interpretation of this interaction is that imminency makes a difference in drug-taking behavior only when the perceived efficacy of the solution is high and the amount of fear arousal in the message is low.

Griffeth and Rogers (1976) report that fear, probability, and efficacy interact to affect high school students' error rates on a driving simulator task. This three-way interaction effect is statistically significant at the .05 level. The effect size is r = .15. The nature of the interaction is that the low probability-high efficacy and high probability-low efficacy cells contain more errors than the low probability-low efficacy and high probability-high efficacy conditions, and that this effect is stronger under conditions of low fear (low noxiousness).

As with the Chu (1966) experiment, there are no other experiments that manipulate these three independent variables and assess their effect on behavior. Rogers and Mewborn (1976), however, examine the effect of these three manipulations on behavioral intention. In this experiment the three-way interaction is not statistically significant at the .05 level. Moreover, the effect size is not substantial.

Ramirez and Lasater (1977) report that fear and self-esteem interact to affect participants' tooth-brushing behavior. This interaction is statistically significant at the .05 level. The effect size is r = .16. The nature of this interaction is that for high self-esteem participants there is no effect of fear on tooth-brushing behavior (r = −.01, df = 100, p > .05). For low self-esteem participants, as fear increases, behavioral conformity to message recommendations increases ($r = .20$, $df = 100$, $p < .05$). For low fear messages, as self-esteem increases, behavior conformity to message recommendations decreases ($r = -.15$, $df = 100$, $p > .05$), although this effect is not statistically significant at the .05 level. For high fear messages, as self-esteem increases, there is no effect on behavioral conformity to message recommendations ($r = .04$, $df = 100$, $p > .05$).

Again, there are no other studies that manipulate both fear and self-esteem, assess their effect on behavior, and report sufficient information to allow further analysis. Leventhal and Trembly (1968), however, mention that self-esteem and fear interact to affect their criterion variable. But the interaction that they report is different from that reported by Ramirez and Lasater (1977). Specifically, they claim that as fear increases, conformity increases for the high self-esteem participants but not for the low self-esteem participants.

There are several variables that did not interact with fear to produce statistically significant effects on behavior. For example, Chu (1966) reports neither statistically significant nor substantial fear × immediacy and fear × efficacy two-way interactions. Dabbs and Leventhal (1966) indicate neither statistically significant nor substantial fear × effectiveness, fear × pain of shots, and fear × effectiveness × pain of shots interactions. Griffeth and Rogers (1976) offer no evidence of either a fear × probability or a fear × efficacy interaction. Leventhal et al.'s (1965) paper shows no evidence of a fear × recommendations interaction. Leventhal and Watts (1966) report no fear × smoking, fear × susceptibility, or fear × smoking × susceptibility interactions. Ramirez and Lasater (1977) indicate no fear × ethnicity of communicator and no fear × ethnicity of communicator × self-esteem interactions. Finally, Skilbeck, Tulips, and Ley (1972) report no evidence of a fear × sidedness, fear × exposure, or fear × sidedness × exposure interaction.

Interestingly, Hill and Gardner (1980) found a statistically nonsignificant fear × sensitizer/repressor interaction, $r = .18$. The nature of the interaction is that there is a slight positive effect for sensitizers, $r = .27$, and a slight negative effect for repressors, $r = -.08$. Since sensitizers are similar to low-anxiety participants, and since repressors are similar to high-anxiety participants, these data resemble the effect of the fear × anxiety interaction on attitude. They may indicate a mediated moderator effect. That is, had Hill and Gardner measured attitude, they would likely have found a substantial fear × sensitizer/repressor interaction effect. If attitude mediates the effect of this interaction on behavior, then the impact of the interaction on behavior is expected to be less substantial.

Given the small number of experiments that include behavior as a dependent measure, the correlations of study characteristics with the fear manipulation-behavior correlation are highly unstable. Nevertheless, several of these results deserve comment. The age of the participants is highly correlated with the fear manipulation-behavior correlation ($r = -.43$, $df = 13$, p $= .06$). Interestingly, this correlation is in the direction opposite that of the correlation of age with the fear manipulation-attitude correlation. Other coefficients exhibit the same pattern. For example, the fear manipulation-behavior correlation is stronger for nonvolunteers than for volunteers ($r = .37$, $df = 10$, $p = .12$). Given the small number of studies, it is necessary to remain cautious when interpreting these data. The safest course of action is to suspend judgment pending more evidence.

In sum, the behavior data are difficult to interpret. The large variance in the distribution of the fear manipulation-behavior correlation distribution indicates the possibility of moderator variables. Moreover, some authors report statistically significant, although not extremely large, interaction effects. There are, however insufficient data to allow firm conclusions to be drawn concerning these effects. Moreover, the large correlation between number of behavioral measures and the fear manipulation-behavior correlation suggests that error of measurement is an important contributor to the variance in the distribution of fear manipulation-behavior correlations.

DISCUSSION

In this section the results of the meta-analysis are summarized. The theoretical, methodological, and pragmatic implications of these results are discussed.

Meta-Analytic Findings

The mean fear manipulation-perceived fear correlation, $r = .36$, indicates that, in the main, researchers do not create strong fear appeal manipulations. Nevertheless, the data do indicate that strong fear appeal manipulations are possible. For example, persuasive messages that generate high amounts of fear do exist (Chu, 1966). Moreover, persuasive messages that generate low amounts of fear do exist (Leventhal et al., 1966). Finally, there are studies in which researchers construct strong fear appeal manipulations (Griffeth & Rogers, 1976; Rogers & Thistlethwaite, 1970).

It is important to note that, according to most theories, perceived fear moderates the relationship between manipulated fear and attitude. If these theories are accurate, then it follows that if the fear appeal manipulation is not strong (if the fear manipulation-perceived fear correlation is small), then it is not possible for the fear manipulation to have a strong impact on attitude.

For example, given the mean fear manipulation-perceived fear correlation $r = .36$, if the perceived fear-attitude correlation is perfect, $r = 1.00$, then the fear manipulation-attitude correlation is not able to exceed $r = .36$ to within sampling error. In a study in which $N < 25$ this correlation is not statistically significant at the .05 level.

This example is a conservative one. Since there are determinants of attitude in addition to fear, the assumption that the perceived fear-attitude correlation is $r = 1.00$ is untenable. If one assumes that the correlation is still substantial, but more reasonable, then the case is made more dramatically. For example, if the perceived fear-attitude correlation is $r = .50$, then the fear manipulation-attitude correlation is not able to exceed $r = .17$ to within sampling error. This figure is approximately the mean fear manipulation-attitude correlation obtained in this meta-analysis. Such a correlation is statistically significant at the .05 level when $N > 92$. Of the studies reviewed in this chapter, 15 report measurements on fewer than 92 participants.

Thus future researchers must be sensitive to the problems of manipulating fear. Materials must be prepared and pretested carefully. Manipulation checks require several items in order to achieve levels of reliability sufficient to guard against attenuating the manipulated fear-perceived fear correlation. Moreover, it is wise to consider adding manipulation check items in order to see if fear manipulations bring about sources of variance in addition to or other than fear. For example, high fear messages may be more attitude discrepant than low fear messages. Such a potential confound is detectable if an experiment includes a discrepancy manipulation check.

There is no evidence of either nonlinearity or nonadditivity in the perceived fear data. The variance in the distribution of the fear manipulation-perceived fear correlations is larger than expected by chance, but this result may be due to methodological artifacts.

The weighted mean fear manipulation-attitude correlation of $r = .21$ appears to indicate that fear appeal manipulations do not exert a strong impact on attitudes. There are both substantive and methodological reasons that mitigate this conclusion.

Substantively, the data suggest that age of the participants, trait anxiety of the participants, and whether the participant volunteers or does not volunteer are potentially strong moderators of the fear manipulation-attitude relationship. Thus the mean fear manipulation-attitude correlation does not adequately represent the impact of fear on attitudes. For example, if the fear manipulation-attitude correlation is strong and positive for volunteers, but zero for nonvolunteers, then the fear manipulation-attitude correlation for all participants is positive, but weak.

These data are insufficient, however, to illuminate one important theoretical point. It is conceivable that these moderator variables interact with the fear manipulation to affect perceived fear, which then has a direct impact on attitudes. Alternatively, the fear manipulation may exert a direct impact on perceived fear, which then interacts with moderator variables to affect attitudes. While these two suggestions do not exhaust the pool of potential hypotheses, clarification of this point is an important question for future investigators.

Methodologically, the data illustrate the importance of artifacts. Both unreliability of measurement and restriction of range in the independent variable seriously attenuate fear manipulation-attitude correlations. The same recommendations made for the perceived fear data apply to attitudes as well.

While there is evidence of nonadditivity in these data, there is no strong evidence of nonlinearity. This finding is particularly relevant, given theories that predict that the regression of attitude onto fear is curvilinear.

The weighted mean fear manipulation-behavior correlation of $r = .10$ is the expected size, given previous data. Expanding upon this point, if perceived fear mediates the fear manipulation-attitude relationship, and if attitude mediates the perceived fear-behavior relationship, then the fear manipulation-behavior correlation must be smaller than the correlation of the fear manipulation with attitude, which in turn must be less than the correlation of the fear manipulation with fear. This pattern of data is observed in the obtained results.

The behavior data are sparse. With only 15 experiments reporting relevant data, it is difficult to draw any firm conclusions concerning moderator variables and/or methodological artifacts. The warranted conclusion is that future researchers need to consider incorporating behavioral measures into their designs, in addition to manipulation check measures and attitude measures. Some fear appeal topics either preclude behavioral measures or make obtaining them very difficult (for example, such topics as seat belts, population control, or drug abuse). On the other hand, there are several topics that make obtaining such measures relatively easy (blood donation, tetanus shots, or taking a roundworm drug). In addition, there are ingenious methods of obtaining behavioral measures for topics that appear to preclude such measures (dental hygiene and safe driving). Therefore, there does exist a pool of topics for which such measures are easily obtained.

As with the attitude data, there is little evidence that the regression of behavior onto fear is nonlinear. One experiment reports such results (Krisher, Darley, & Darley, 1973). This study, however, employs a small sample. Moreover, the results of other experiments for which a quadratic effect could be computed are inconsistent with this finding.

Implications for Existing Theory

These results have implications for judging the veracity of fear appeal explanations. For example, the presence of a number of negative correlations between fear manipulations and attitude (Goldstein, 1959; Janis & Feshbach, 1953; Janis & Terwilliger, 1962), negative correlations between fear manipulations and behavior (Janis & Feshbach, 1953; Leventhal, et al., 1965; Leventhal & Watts, 1966), no correlation between fear manipulations and attitude (Kohn, Goodstadt, Cook, Sheppard, & Chan, 1982; Wheatley & Oshikawa, 1970), and the evidence that variables moderate the fear manipulation-attitude relationship show that the drive explanation is an inadequate explanation of the effect of fear-arousing messages. Similarly, the presence of numerous studies reporting a positive correlation between fear manipulations and attitudes (Beck & Davis, 1978; Berkowitz & Cottingham, 1960; Burnett & Oliver, 1979; Frandsen, 1963; Hendrick et al., 1975; Hewgill & Miller, 1965; Horowitz, 1969, 1972; Horowitz & Gumenik, 1970; Insko et al., 1965; Leventhal et al., 1965; McCroskey & Wright, 1971; Powell, 1965; Powell & Miller, 1967) is sufficient to show that the resistance explanation is inadequate to explain the effect of fear-arousing messages.

The various forms of curvilinearity hypotheses are inconsistent with the obtained data. For both attitude measures and behavior measures the mean quadratic effect is small. Moreover, there are few studies that report substantial effects and, of those studies that do report curvilinear effects that are not trivial, they are not of the functional form predicted by the curvilinear hypotheses (Powell, 1965). The one exception is the Krisher et al. (1973) experiment. Given the small sample size in this study ($N = 60$), this result may be due to sampling error.

To anticipate an argument from curvilinearity hypothesis advocates, the lack of strong quadratic effects cannot be attributed to the fear appeal manipulations. It is not the case that studies that manipulate low to moderate fear produce positive effects on attitudes and behavior, and that studies that manipulate moderate fear to high fear produce negative effects on attitudes and behavior. For example, Chu's (1966) manipulation is clearly moderate fear to high fear. Nevertheless, Chu reports that an increase in fear produces an increase in behavioral conformity to message recommendations. Furthermore, both Janis and Feshbach (1953) and Janis and Terwilliger (1962) report fear manipulations that clearly range from low to moderate, and in both experiments the fear manipulation-attitude correlation is negative. Thus there is little evidence consistent with the curvilinearity hypotheses, and there is considerable evidence inconsistent with these hypotheses.

There are few data consistent with the hypotheses that suggest that fear interacts with other variables to affect both attitudes and behavior. The parallel response explanation cannot be falsified, since it is not stated with sufficient precision to allow an empirical test. The protection motivation explanation is tested in at least one experiment (Griffeth & Rogers, 1976). While this explanation predicts that fear, efficacy, and probability interact to affect attitudes and behavior, and while such an interaction is reported, it is not the type of interaction predicted by the protection motivation explanation. Specifically, Rogers (1975) argues that the high fear, high efficacy, high probability cell produces the most conformity to message recommendations. That prediction is not consistent with the result reported by Griffeth and Rogers (1976). Moreover, Rogers and Mewborn (1976) report further falsifying evidence in an experiment in which behavioral intention is the dependent variable.

Finally, the threat control explanation has not received a rigorous test. Nevertheless, a notion central to this explanation is that fear manipulations and efficacy interact to affect attitudes and/or behavior. Both Chu (1966) and Griffeth and Rogers (1976) report statistically nonsignificant or small interaction effects of fear and efficacy on behavior. While these data are not a strong test of this explanation, the conclusion that there is no evidence consistent with the threat control explanation is warranted.

In sum, none of the fear appeal explanations are consistent with the available evidence. While no theory is offered here, a sketch of what an adequate theory must explain is presented in the next section.

Implications for Future Theory

While the variance in the distribution of fear manipulation-perceived fear correlations is larger than that expected by chance, there is no evidence of nonadditivity in these data. The results of the meta-analysis suggest that the variance may be due to methodological artifacts, such as error of measurement or restriction in range. Thus it is plausible that fear manipulations are generally successful in bringing about a state of perceived fear in the participants. In the main, however, these manipulations are weak. Moreover, two possible problems require consideration. First, there is evidence that other independent variables bring about varying degrees of perceived fear. Second, it is possible that fear manipulations bring about other affective/cognitive states in addition to fear. Put differently, both the manipulation of fear and the manipulations of other relevant independent variables are often confounded.

Since there is little nonadditivity in the perceived fear data, it is likely that the interactions of fear manipulations with age, trait anxiety, and volunteering actually reflect interactions of these variables with perceived fear. In other words, a plausible hypothesis is that fear manipulations directly affect perceived fear, which interacts with age, trait anxiety, and volunteering to affect attitudes.

Furthermore, it is possible that these moderator variables are not unique. It may be the case that they are alternate indicators of the same underlying factor. For example, both the fear × anxiety and the fear × volunteering interactions may reflect a common factor. If volunteers have low anxiety and nonvolunteers have high anxiety, then a single factor could account for both interactions. The available evidence concerning the anxiety of volunteer and nonvolunteer participants is mixed, however (Rosenthal, 1965).

There is no strong evidence of nonadditivity in the fear manipulation-behavior data. One explanation of this result is that moderator variables, such as age, trait anxiety and volunteering, interact with perceived fear to affect attitudes, which then mediate the relationship between these interaction effects and behavior. One implication of such a model is that the interactions of fear with other variables have stronger effects on attitudes than on behavior, since the latter effects are mediated by attitudes.

A causal model depicting these effects is presented in Figure 12.4. This model is a reasonable representation of the results of the meta-analysis. Moreover, it is a null hypothesis against which future researchers may test experimental data. The model is not, however, a theory. If future data are shown to be consistent with this model, then a satisfactory theory must delineate the mechanisms that produce the model. In particular, such a theory must include an explanation of individual differences. Why, for example, are low-anxiety, older volunteers more susceptible to fear appeals than high-anxiety, younger nonvolunteers?

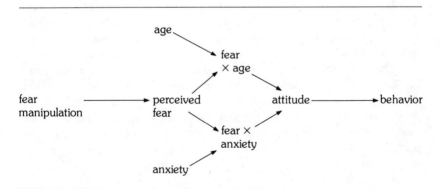

Figure 12.4.   A model of a fear appeal experiment.

Methodological Implications

It is clear from the results of the meta-analysis that reliability of measurement has a substantial impact on the results of experimental studies. Both the type of experimental design—pretest-posttest or posttest only—and the number of items employed to measure the dependent variable are indicators of the reliability of the measurement of the dependent variable. Both measures correlate substantially with the size of the fear manipulation-attitude correlation. The multiple correlation of the fear manipulation-attitude correlation with these two study characteristics, R = .50, indicates the impact of error of measurement on experimental results. Experiments in which the dependent variable is measured reliably are more likely to find large effects of fear manipulations, and hence statistically significant findings. Those experiments in which the dependent variable is not measured with high reliability are likely to find that the effect of the fear manipulation is attenuated by error of measurement. Therefore, such studies are less likely to find statistically significant effects of the fear manipulation.

Clearly, it is possible to obtain reliable measures of the criterion variables discussed in this study. Generally, obtaining satisfactory levels of reliability is a function of pretesting and employing a sufficient number of items to measure the variables in question. While it may be difficult to obtain multiple behavioral measures, both Griffeth and Rogers (1976; safe driving) and Ramirez and Lasater (1977; dental hygiene) report multiple measures of behavior.

Finally, there are few studies that report the reliability of criterion measures. Thus it is impossible to apply corrections to obtained statistics. At least two advantages accrue if reliability coefficients are presented. First, the mean corrected correlation can be calculated, and thus a better estimate of the effect of fear on the criterion variable(s) may be obtained. Second, the distribution of corrected correlations may be examined. In this way a more accurate estimate of the relative contributions of methodological artifacts and moderator variables to the variance in the fear manipulation-criterion variable correlation distribution may be obtained.

There is also evidence consistent with the hypothesis that restricting the range of experimental manipulations attenuates the correlations of fear manipulations with the criterion variables. For example, the correlation between the number of levels of the fear manipulation and the size of the fear manipulation-attitude correlation is substantial. There are reasons to include more than two levels when manipulating fear, in addition to the restriction in range artifact. For example, only if more than two levels of fear are manipulated can quadratic effect estimates be obtained.

There is a paradoxical implication of including more than two levels in fear manipulations. While higher correlations of fear with the criterion variable(s) are likely to result, the main effect for fear is less likely to be statistically significant. Such a phenomenon is produced by the increased degrees of freedom associated with the main effect. For example, consider a design in which fear is the only independent variable, it is an independent groups factor, and there are two levels of the manipulation. Further, suppose that the sum of squares for the fear effect is 25 and the sum of squares for subjects nested within fear is 500. In this example the correlation of fear and the criterion variable is approximately $r = .22$. With $N = 85$ the analysis of variance yields an $F = 4.15$, which is statistically significant at the .05 level with 1 and 83 degrees of freedom. Assume that an exact replication of this study is performed, except that three levels of fear are included in the manipulation. Suppose that the sum of squares for fear increases by a factor of 1.48, so that it equals 37. And assume that the sum of squares is due to the linear effect. In this case the correlation of fear with the criterion variable is larger, $r = .26$. On the other hand, the results of the analysis of variance show that $F = MS_B/MS_W = 18.5/6.02 = 3.07$, which is not statistically significant at the .05 level with 2 and 83 degrees of freedom. In order to obtain consistent results from the F test in such a case one must decompose the sum of squares for the fear effect into linear and quadratic components and conduct the test on these components separately (Keppel, 1982, pp. 135-140).

The results of the meta-analysis suggest that demographic variables and/or personality traits may moderate the fear manipulation-criterion variable relationship. In order to test for interaction effects these variables are often dichotomized or trichotomized. For example, in the experiments that examine the effects of both fear and anxiety on attitudes, participants are divided into low-anxiety and high-anxiety groups for purposes of analysis. Restricting the variance of such a variable in this way is likely to attenuate the interaction effect. More important, it makes comparison across experiments difficult, especially when different measures of the demographic characteristic/personality trait are employed or descriptive statistics on the demographic characteristic/personality trait are not reported. An alternative method is to use regression techniques to estimate the strength of interaction effects (Cohen, 1968), although one may wish to dichotomize or trichotomize the presentation of results in order to illustrate the nature of the interaction effect. Moreover, a description of the distribution of the demographic characteristic/personality trait is an important piece of information to include in the report.

The discussions of fear appeal explanations and of the meta-analysis results rely heavily on path-analytic techniques. Although Costner (1971) illustrates how this technique may be used to illuminate experimental data, there are few experiments that utilize the technique. Path analysis is necessary to provide an adequate test of some of the fear appeal explanations. For example, if the drive explanation is accurate, then the correlation between the fear manipulation and attitude must be equal to the product of the fear manipulation-perceived fear correlation and the perceived fear-attitude correlation. Finding that the fear manipulation exerts a statistically significant effect on both perceived fear and attitude is not sufficient to conclude that the data are consistent with the drive explanation. For example, a fear manipulation-attitude correlation of .5 is not consistent with the drive explanation if the fear manipulation-perceived fear correlation is .3 and the perceived fear-attitude correlation is .7. Such data suggest, for example, that the fear manipulation may bring about another variable in addition to fear, and that that variable also has an impact on attitude.

While path-analytic techniques can suggest the existence of an experimental confound, being theoretically blind algorithms, they are unable to specify what variables are confounded in the fear manipulation. Thus, when designing the experiment, and considering the possibility of confounding variables, one may construct measures of these variables and include them in the experiment. During analysis the hypothesis that these variables mediate the fear manipulation-attitude relationship may be tested directly by path-analytic techniques.

Pragmatic Implications

There are several important implications of these data for those desiring to use fear-arousing persuasive messages in applied contexts. First, judging from the perceived fear results, experimenters generally do not create strong manipulations. Thus one might well come to the conclusion that manipulating fear is not an easy task. What appears to be a highly fear-arousing persuasive message to the experimenter may not induce much fear into the recipient of the persuasive message. Thus, at minimum, a practitioner must pretest persuasive messages before using them in an applied context, such as a public service campaign. Moreover, both the practitioner and the theorist need to reconsider the question of message design. It is not clear exactly what features of a persuasive message are fear arousing.

Second, the finding that demographic characteristics and personality traits moderate the relationship between fear manipulations and attitudes suggests the importance of audience analysis. The focus of the Burnett and Oliver (1979) paper illustrates that marketing researchers are aware of, and concerned with, this problem. More accurate techniques of analyzing properties of audiences are necessary, however, before the results presented here can be of use to the practitioner.

These two pragmatic implications suggest the possibility of a union of both scientific and rhetorical approaches to the development of communication theory (Miller, 1975). Rhetorical scholars have long examined the properties of persuasive messages and persuasion situations. This knowledge base is of utility for the purposes of message design and audience analysis (see, for example, Sussman, 1973).

Third, in order to specify precisely the relationship between fear and attitude (and/or behavior), data must be collected from the entire range of fear stimuli. Many of the manipulations of fear fall within a relatively restricted range, however. There is an important question involved in employing stronger fear manipulations. Is it justifiable ethically to elicit high levels of fear with experimental materials? Is the potential harm that participants may incur as a result of being exposed to a highly fear-arousing message outweighed by the benefit of the data produced by the reactions to such messages? We can provide no concrete answer to this question. Nevertheless, it is perhaps the most important question researchers must confront when studying the effects of fear-arousing persuasive messages. It is also one of the least-discussed issues in the fear appeal literature.

Summary and Conclusion

This chapter reexamined the question of the effects of fear-arousing persuasive messages. Meta-analytic techniques were employed in order to assess quantitatively the effect of fear manipulations on three criterion variables: perceived fear, attitude, and behavior. The results of this analysis illustrate that existing explanations of the effects of fear-arousing persuasive messages are inadequate to account for the data. The theoretical, methodological, and pragmatic implications of the results are discussed.

NOTES

1. A fear appeal is an argument of the following form:

(1) You (the listener) are vulnerable to a threat.
(2) If you are vulnerable, then you should take action to reduce your vulnerability.
(3) If you are to reduce your vulnerability, then you must accept the recommendations contained in this message.
(4) Therefore, you should accept the recommendations contained in this message.

For example:

(1) If the USSR launches a nuclear attack you would be killed.
(2) Since you do not want to die, you should do something to protect yourself in the event of such an emergency.
(3) The only effective action that can be taken is to build a fallout shelter.
(4) Therefore, you should build a fallout shelter.

In order to prove the validity of the structure of such an argument, let V = one is vulnerable; A = take action to eliminate vulnerability; and R = accept the message recommendations. Then, the premises of the argument may be symbolized as follows:

(1) V
(2) V ⊃ A
(3) A ⊃ R
(4) ∴ R

where   ⊃   is the symbol for a conditional statement and   ∴.   symbolizes "therefore." The proof is as follows:

(5) V ⊃ R   2, 3 hypothetical syllogism
(6) R   5, 1 by modus ponens

For a discussion of the hypothetical syllogism and modus ponens inference rules, as well as a discussion of propositional logic in general, see Copi (1967). While the validity of the form of argument is easily demonstrated, the soundness of any fear appeal depends upon the quality of the evidence that supports the premises of the argument.

2. There was no evidence of strong higher-order nonlinearities, such as cubic effects or quartic effects, in any of the data examined in this monograph. Since there was no evidence of such effects, and since no theory predicts such effects, they are not presented in detail.

3. Only those studies that assessed attitude immediately after the message were considered. Since few studies included delayed attitude measures, there was not sufficient information to draw conclusions about the relationship between fear manipulations and delayed attitudes, or attitude change.

4. This correlation is computed using the absolute value of the fear manipulation-attitude correlation as the dependent variable. The absolute value is employed, since it is the strength of r, and not its sign, which is of theoretical interest in this case. Unless indicated otherwise, absolute values are used for both the fear manipulation-attitude correlations and the fear manipulation-behavior correlations when these variables are correlated with study characteristics.

5. The signed, rather than absolute value, of the fear manipulation-attitude correlation was used for this analysis.

6. Goldstein reports that the Mainord measure is not correlated substantially with the Janis and Feshbach (1954) anxiety measure, and concludes that the Mainord measure is not a measure of anxiety. Since there are no data to suggest that the Janis and Feshback measure is valid, the possibility exists that the Mainord scale is a measure of anxiety, but the Janis and Feshback measure is a weak indicator of anxiety. Moreover, since the Mainord scale looks like a measure of trait anxiety, and since it interacts with fear in the same manner as other known anxiety scales, it is reasonable to treat it as an anxiety measure.

7. Brown (1979) manipulated fear, and classified participants as either high conformers or low conformers, based upon their responses to a Crutchfield simulated group pressure situation. Brown found a strong fear × conformity interaction, r = .30. Specifically, for conformers the fear manipulation-attitude correlation was r = .79, while it was only .41 for nonconformers. The correlation between conformity and attitude was r = −.36 in the control condition and .42 in the experimental condition. The Brown study is the only known experiment that crossed these two independent variables. Thus, while it holds promise of being a moderator, this conclusion must await replication.

8. The latter correlates substantially with the fear manipulation-attitude correlation, r = .25. While this correlation is not statistically significant at the .05 level, the number of studies upon which is it based is small. When this correlation is controlled for other study characteristics, such as the type of design, however, the correlation decreases (r = .17 when controlling for type of design). Thus it does not appear to be an important moderator.

REFERENCES

Beach, R. I. (1966). The effects of a "fear-arousing" safety film on physiological, attitudinal and behavioral measures: A pilot study. *Traffic Safety Research Review, 10,* 53-57.
Beck, K. H., & Davis, C. M. (1978). Effects of fear-arousing communications and topic importance on attitude change. *Journal of Social Psychology, 104,* 81-95.

Beck, K. H., & Frankel, A. (1981). A conceptualization of threat communications and protective health behavior. *Social Psychology Quarterly, 3*, 204-217.

Beck, K. H., & Lund, A. K. (1981). The effects of health threat seriousness and personal efficacy upon intentions and behavior. *Journal of Applied Social Psychology, 1*, 401-415.

Berkowitz, L., & Cottingham, D. R. (1960). The interest value and relevance of fear-arousing communications. *Journal of Abnormal and Social Psychology, 60*, 37-43.

Brown, R. A. (1979). Fear-induced attitude change as a function of conformity and drinking pattern in alcoholics. *Journal of Clinical Psychology, 35*, 454-456.

Burnett, J. J. (1981). Internal-external locus of control as a moderator of fear appeals. *Journal of Applied Psychology, 66*, 390-393.

Burnett, J., & Oliver, R. (1979). Fear appeal effects in the field: A segmentation approach. *Journal of Marketing Research, 16*, 181-190.

Chu, G. C. (1966). Fear arousal, efficacy and imminency. *Journal of Personality and Social Psychology, 5*, 517-524.

Cohen, J. (1968). Multiple regression as a general data-analytic system. *Psychological Bulletin, 70*, 426-443.

Copi, I. M. (1967). *Symbolic logic* (3rd ed.). New York: Macmillan.

Costner, J. L. (1971). Utilizing causal models to discover flaws in experiments. *Sociometry, 34*, 398-410.

Dabbs, J. M., & Leventhal, H. (1966). Effects of varying the recommendations in a fear-arousing communication. *Journal of Personality and Social Psychology, 4*, 525-531.

Evans, R. I., Rozelle, R. M., Lasater, U. M., Dembroski, T. M., & Allen, B. P. (1968). New measure of effects of persuasive communications: A chemical indicator of toothbrushing behavior. *Psychological Reports, 23*, 731-736.

Evans, R. I., Rozelle, R. M., Lasater, T. M., Dembroski, T. M., & Allen, B. P. (1970). Fear arousal, persuasion, and actual versus implied behavioral change: New perspective utilizing a real-life dental hygiene program. *Journal of Personality and Social Psychology, 16*, 220-227.

Frandsen, K. D. (1963). Effects of threat appeals and media of transmission. *Speech Monographs, 30*, 101-104.

Glass, G. V, McGaw, B., & Smith, M. L. (1981). *Meta-analysis in social research*. Beverly Hills, CA: Sage.

Goldstein, M. J. (1959). The relationship between coping and avoiding behavior and response to fear arousing propaganda. *Journal of Abnormal and Social Psychology, 58*, 247-252.

Griffeth, R. W., & Rogers, R. W. (1976). Effects of fear-arousing components of driver education on students' safety attitudes and simulator performance. *Journal of Educational Psychology, 68*, 501-506.

Haas, J. W., Bagley, G. S., & Rogers, R. W. (1975). Coping with the energy crisis: Effects of fear appeals upon attitudes toward energy consumption. *Journal of Applied Psychology, 60*, 754-756.

Hendrick, C., Giesen, M., & Borden, R. (1975). False physiological feedback and persuasion: Effect of fear arousal vs. fear reduction on attitude change. *Journal of Personality, 43*, 196-214.

Hewgill, M. A., & Miller, G. R. (1965). Source credibility and response to fear-arousing communications. *Speech Monographs, 32*, 95-101.

Higbee, K. L. (1970). Fifteen years of fear arousal: Research on threat appeals: 1953-1968. *Psychological Bulletin, 72*, 426-444.

Hill, D., & Gardner, G. (1980). Repression-sensitization and yielding to threatening health communications. *Australian Journal of Psychology, 32*, 183-193.

Himmelfarb, S. (1975). What do you do when the control group doesn't fit into the factorial design? *Psychological Bulletin, 82*, 363-368.

Horowitz, I. A. (1969). Effects of volunteering, fear arousal, and number of communications on attitude change. *Journal of Personality and Social Psychology, 11*, 34-37.

Horowitz, I. A. (1972). Attitude change as a function of perceived arousal. *Journal of Social Psychology, 87*, 117-126.

Horowitz, I. A., & Gumenik, W. E. (1970). Effects of the volunteer subject, choice, and fear arousal on attitude change. *Journal of Experimental Social Psychology, 6*, 293-303.

Hunter, J. W., Schmidt, F. L., & Jackson, G. B. (1982). *Meta-analysis: Cumulating research find-ings across studies.* Beverly Hills, CA: Sage.

Insko, C. A., Arkoff, A., & Insko, V. M. (1965). Effects of high and low fear-arousing communica-tions upon opinion toward smoking. *Journal of Experimental Social Psychology, 1,* 255-266.

Janis, I. L. (1967). Effects of fear arousal on attitude change: Recent developments in theory and research. In L. Berkowitz (Ed.), *Advances in experimental social psychology,* (Vol. 3). New York: Academic.

Janis, I. L., & Feshback, S. (1953). Effects of fear-arousing communications. *Journal of Abnor-mal and Social Psychology, 48,* 78-92.

Janis, I. L., & Feshback, S. (1954). Personality differences associated with responsiveness to fear-arousing communications. *Journal of Personality, 23,* 154-166.

Janis, I. L., & Leventhal, H. (1968). Human reactions to stress. In E. Borgatta & W. Lambert (Eds.), *Handbook of personality theory and research.* Chicago: Rand McNally.

Janis, I. L., & Mann, L. (1965). Effectiveness of emotional role playing in modifying smoking habits and attitudes. *Journal of Experimental Research in Personality, 1,* 84-90.

Janis, I. L., & Terwilliger, R. (1962). An experimental study of psychological resistance to fear arousing communications. *Journal of Abnormal and Social Psychology, 65,* 403-410.

Keppel, G. (1982). *Design and analysis: A researcher's handbook* (2nd ed.). Englewood Cliffs, NJ: Prentice-Hall.

Kirscht, J. P., & Haefner, D. P. (1969). Reactions to a sequence of fear-arousing messages. *Pro-ceedings, 77th Annual Convention of the American Psychological Association,* 373-376.

Kohn, P. M., Goodstadt, M. S., Cook, G. M., Sheppard, M., & Chan, G. (1982). Ineffectiveness of threat appeals about drinking and driving. *Accident Analysis and Prevention, 14,* 457-464.

Krisher, H. P., Darley, S. A., & Darley, J. M. (1973). Fear-provoking recommendations, inten-tions to take preventative actions, and actual preventative actions. *Journal of Personality and Social Psychology, 26,* 301-308.

Leventhal, H. (1970). Findings and theory in the study of fear communications. In L. Berkowitz (Ed.), *Advances in experimental social psychology* (Vol. 5). New York: Academic.

Leventhal, H. (1971). Fear appeals and persuasion: The differentiation of a motivational con-struct. *American Journal of Public Health, 61,* 1205-1224.

Leventhal, H., Jones, S., & Trembly, G. (1966). Sex differences in attitude and behavior change under conditions of fear and specific instructions. *Journal of Experimental Social Psy-chology, 2,* 387-399.

Leventhal, H., & Niles, P. (1964). A field experiment on fear arousal with data on the validity of questionnaire measures. *Journal of Personality, 32,* 459-479.

Leventhal, H., & Niles, P. (1965). Persistence of influence for varying durations of exposure to threat stimuli. *Psychological Reports, 16,* 223-233.

Leventhal, H., & Singer, R. P. (1966). Affect arousal and positioning of recommendations in persuasive communications. *Journal of Personality and Social Psychology, 4,* 137-146.

Leventhal, H., Singer, R. P., & Jones, S. (1965). The effects of fear and specificity of recommen-dation. *Journal of Personality and Social Psychology, 2,* 20-29.

Leventhal, H., & Trembly, G. (1968). Negative emotions and persuasion. *Journal of Personal-ity, 36,* 154-168.

Leventhal, H., & Watts, J. C. (1966). Sources of resistance to fear-arousing communications on smoking and lung cancer. *Journal of Personality, 34,* 155-175.

Leventhal, H., Watts, J. C., & Pagnao, F. (1967). Effects of fear and instructions on how to cope with danger. *Journal of Personality and Social Psychology, 6,* 313-321.

Mainord, W. A. (1956). *Experimental repression related to coping and avoidance behavior in the recall and relearning of nonsense syllables.* Unpublished doctoral dissertation, Uni-versity of Washington.

McCroskey, J. C., & Wright, D. W. (1971). A comparison of the effects of punishment-oriented and reward-oriented messages in persuasive communication. *Journal of Communica-tion, 21,* 83-93.

McGuire, W. J. (1968). Personality and susceptibility to social influence. In E. Borgatta & W. Lambert (Eds.), *Handbook of personality theory and research.* Chicago: Rand McNally.

McGuire, W. J. (1969). The nature of attitudes and attitude change. In G. Lindzey & E. Aronson (Eds.), *The handbook of social psychology* (Vol. 3., 2nd ed.). Reading, MA: Addison-Wesley.

Mewborn, C. R., & Rogers, R. W. (1979). Effects of threatening and reassuring components of fear appeals on physiological and verbal measures of emotion and attitudes. *Journal of Experimental Social Psychology, 15,* 242-253.

Miller, G. R. (1963). Studies on the use of fear appeals: A summary and analysis. *Central States Speech Journal, 14,* 117-125.

Miller, G. R. (1975). Humanistic and scientific approaches to speech communication inquiry: Rivalry, redundancy, or rapprochement. *Western Speech Communication, 39,* 230-239.

Millman, S. (1968). Anxiety, comprehension and susceptibility to social influence. *Journal of Personality and Social Psychology, 9,* 251-256.

Powell, F. A. (1965). The effects of anxiety-arousing messages when related to personal, familial and impersonal referents. *Speech Monographs, 32,* 102-106.

Powell, F. A., & Miller, G. R. (1967). Social approval and disapproval cues in anxiety-arousing communications. *Speech Monographs, 34,* 152-159.

Radelfinger, D. (1965). Some effects of fear-arousing communications on preventive health behavior. *Health Education Monographs, 19,* 2-15.

Ramirez, A., & Lasater, T. M. (1977). Ethnicity of communicator, self-esteem, and reactions to fear-arousing communications. *Journal of Social Psychology, 102,* 79-91.

Rogers, R. W. (1975). A protection motivation theory of fear appeals and attitude change. *Journal of Psychology, 91,* 93-114.

Rogers, R. W., & Deckner, C. W. (1975). Effects of fear appeals and physiological arousal upon emotions, attitudes, and cigarette smoking. *Journal of Personality and Social Psychology, 32,* 222-230.

Rogers, R. W., & Mewborn, C. R. (1976). Fear appeals and attitude change: Effects of a threat's noxiousness, probability of occurrence, and the efficacy of coping responses. *Journal of Personality and Social Psychology, 34,* 54-61.

Rogers, R. W., & Thistlethwaite, D. L. (1970). Effects of fear arousal and reassurances on attitude change. *Journal of Personality and Social Psychology, 15,* 227-233.

Rosen, T. J., Terry, N. S., & Leventhal, H. (1982). The role of esteem and coping in response to a threat communication. *Journal of Research in Personality, 16,* 90-107

Rosenthal, R. (1965). The volunteer subject. *Human Relations, 18,* 389-406.

Rosenthal, R. (1978). Combining results of independent studies. *Psychological Bulletin, 85,* 185-193.

Shelton, M. L., & Rogers, R. W. (1981). Fear-arousing and empathy arousing appeals to help: The pathos of persuasion. *Journal of Applied Social Psychology, 11,* 366-378.

Simonson, N. R., & Lundy, R. M. (1966). The effectiveness of persuasive communication presented under conditions of irrelevant fear. *Journal of Communciation, 16,* 32-37.

Skilbeck, C., Tulips, J., & Ley, P. (1972) The effects of fear arousal, fear position, fear exposure and sidedness on compliance with dietary instructions. *European Journal of Social Psychology, 7,* 221-239.

Smith, M. J. (1977). The effects of threats to attitudinal freedom as a function of message quality and initial receiver attitudes. *Communication Monographs, 44,* 196-206.

Sternthal, F., & Craig, C. (1974). Fear appeals: Revisited and revised. *Journal of Consumer Research, 7,* 22-34.

Sussman, L. (1973). Ancients and moderns of fear and fear appeals: A comparative analysis. *Central States Speech Journal, 24,* 206-211.

Sutton, S. R. (1982). Fear-arousing communications: A critical examination of theory and research. In J. R. Eisner (Ed.), *Social psychology and behavioral medicine.* New York: John Wiley.

Wheatley, J. J., & Oshikawa, S. (1970). The relationship between anxiety and positive and negative advertising appeals. *Journal of Marketing Research, 7,* 85-89.

II ● INFORMATION SYSTEMS

13 ● Message Structure, Inference Making, and Recall

MARGARET FITCH HAUSER

University of Oklahoma

F OR years communication scholars have conducted research on communication-related factors that seem to affect message output. Those factors include source variables, receiver variables, and message variables. Even our communication textbooks teach that a message can be adapted so that receivers properly understand the meaning. Despite everything that we have learned about the way human beings communicate with each other, we are still unable to exchange messages without some kind of distortion taking place.

Several attempts have been made to explain information distortion. These explanations have focused primarily on distortion caused by selective perception and distortion caused by information storage and recall processes in either long-term or short-term memory. All of these are valid attempts to explain information distortion, but some types of information distortion still have not been adequately addressed. One of these is the distortion caused by inference making.

Much of the existing literature that focuses on inference making has been reported in the literature of cognitive psychology. This research is based on the notion of cognitive schemata or cognitive structures that are used in such processes as perception (Bartlett, 1932), comprehension (Ortony, 1978; Folger & Woodall, 1982), and memory (Bobrow & Norman, 1975). According to these researchers, schemata provide plans or maps for perceiving incoming information. In that capacity, schemata are large units of knowledge that organize much of what we know about the world around

Correspondence and requests for reprints: Margaret Fitch Hauser, College of Business Administration, University of Oklahoma, OK 73019.

us. As large units of knowledge, schemata establish sets of expectations for incoming information. As we learn about the surrounding world, we learn that certain events occur in certain ways. This knowledge, in turn, forms a set of expectations designated as schema which we use to predict or perceive incoming information. One schema that will be discussed in this chapter causes us to expect information to be presented in a particular sequence. This expectation is especially applicable to information in story form.

As we perceive incoming information, we categorize it according to the appropriate schemata or schema. However, our memory systems can process the message only as it is presented. The fact that differences exist between an original message and a recalled message suggests that an interaction may occur between the original message and our schema. As our memory systems perceive and integrate a message into memory, the schema probably determines what is stored and recalled by making the information fit existing expectations. Evidence indicates that this type of process does indeed occur. Although there is some agreement on the overall necessity of a concept of knowledge integration, there is less agreement on the details of such information processes, particularly on the nature and process of inference making.

Some researchers, for example, believe that during schematic processing, inferences are created as messages are first comprehended (Graesser, Robertson, & Anderson, 1981). Other researchers (Schank, 1973, 1975; Schank & Abelson, 1977) believe a foundation exists for constructing conceptual representations that include both information that was truly in the message as well as inferences about the information during schematic processing. The evidence strongly suggests that the message and the receiver's schema do interact and the interaction determines what is remembered.

This study examines the interaction of a particular type of message— stories—and schemata in an attempt to see if the interaction between the two may explain part of the information distortion, in the form of inferences, that occurs in the recall of some messages. Before moving to a discussion of the means by which I address this specific issue, two applicable areas of literature will be presented: (1) attempts that have been made to delineate when and where inferences occur in the memory process, and (2) attempts to explicate the notion of an interaction between story structure and schematic processing.

INFERENCES

Inferences can be defined as the process by which an individual tries to represent incoming information in a well-defined structure (Schank, 1975).

During this process, inferences fill gaps in the structure of incoming information (slot-filling) and connect events in the structure with other events in order to provide a higher level of organization (text connection).

Warren, Nicholas, and Trabasso (1979) postulate that inferences are based primarily on three identifiable sources of information. The first involves logical relations between events in the text. Those relations include causes, motivations, and conditions surrounding the events, and focus on answering the questions "why?" and "how?" An example of an inference based on logical relations would occur if a receiver inferred why a particular act was done. The second source of inferences focuses on the informational relations between events in the text. Examples are specific people, instruments, objects, times, places, and contexts of events. These inferences address the questions "who?" "what?" "when?" and "where?" If a receiver infers that an act in a story was performed by using a particular tool, then the inference is based on informational relations. The third source of inference making involves one's knowledge of the world. This source includes knowledge about vocabulary, items referred to, and the functional relations among them. This category is based on prior knowledge and perceptions and affects the other two categories.

Using these sources of information, an individual (listener or reader) focuses on the present (focal point) and uses this focal point to connect events from the past to predict future events. Warren et al. (1979) also believed that these same sources of information are used to fill empty slots in a story. They felt that individuals use their world knowledge (past experience and knowledge) to infer information that is missing in a story.

A quick review of research shows that inferences do occur in predictable locations in recalled messages. The first area seems to be where information is missing or implied in the original story. Individuals infer implied information when they integrate pieces of information. This notion was tested by Bransford and Franks (1972) in a classic study in which they presented related sentences (a story) to four groups of subjects. During the recall phase of their study, many subjects stated with a high degree of confidence that they had "heard" sentences that combined the original four sentences. In actuality, however, no combination sentences were presented in the experiment. Bransford and Franks perceived that their results strongly supported the notion that information gathered from the semantic interpretation of related sentences is stored together and integrated in memory.

In addition, Bransford and Franks postulate that information is integrated as inferences are made. As the subjects in the previously cited experiment remembered the information, they also inferred relations among the parts of the whole. These inferences seemed to be a spontaneous part of the reconstruction of information in memory. These conclusions have been supported by other researchers, such as Paris (1965; Paris & Carter, 1973). Other research indicates that inferences are made by adding information to the original messages. Several studies have found that when certain types of information are not explicitly stated, the subjects will infer the information when they are asked to recall the message. Paris and Lindauer (1976) presented subjects with statements that implied, but did not state, an instrument or tool of action in a story. During the recall phase, subjects "remembered" the implied tool as well as if it had actually been named in the study. The findings of these authors were further supported by Paris and Upton (1976); Stein and Glenn (1979); Kintsch (1974); Kintsch and Monk (1972); and Johnson, Bransford, and Soloman (1973).

Finally, inferences may be caused by the presence of an inconsistency or contradiction in a message. Research indicates that when incoming stimuli are consistent with the expectations of the receiver, the information is assimilated and recalled with relative ease. When information is highly inconsistent with one's expectations, the information is rejected as not valid. However, when information is only mildly inconsistent with expectations, it is easily recalled in short-term memory but tends to be converted to fit the expectations in long-term recall (Taylor & Crocker, 1980; Kintsch & Van Dijk, 1978). In other words, the presence of a mild inconsistency in a message will cause a receiver to make an inference in order to attain consistency. This information also implies that any message that is contradictory to a receiver's expectations is subject to distortion by inference.

The inference research discussed so far suggests that some relations exist between original messages and the inferences people tend to produce. In all of the studies discussed, subjects remembered the information presented as well as the inferences. These results strongly point to the possibility that there is some interaction between the way a message is presented and the way it is remembered. To explore this notion further, the following section will focus on the way a message is presented and the interaction of that message with the semantic processing system.

STORY STRUCTURE AND SCHEMATIC PROCESSING

Research of story structure, an underlying organization holding sentences together, indicates that the more highly a story is structured, the more accurately the story is recalled. However, the story structure does not remain static from input to recall. Mandler and Johnson (1977) defined story structure as the idealized internal representation of story parts and the relations among those parts. They believed that the structure of a story provides a framework for the comprehension of the ideas expressed in the story. In turn, this framework is believed to provide several functions:

(1) It directs attention to certain aspects of incoming material.
(2) It helps the listener keep track of what has gone before. In this capacity the story structure provides a summary that increases the predictability of what information will immediately follow.
(3) It tells the listener when some part of the story is complete and can be stored or is incomplete and must be held until more material is encoded.

The pioneer in the study of story structure was Bartlett (1932). As he studied memory he tried to find some explanation for the memory of prose information. He postulated that "perceiving, recognizing, and recalling [were] all functions which [belonged] to the same general series" of information processing (p. 187). Bartlett's notion indicates that the original form of a message, as the receiver perceives it, influences how the story will be stored and recalled. Current research and literature seems to support this notion.

For example, Bartlett and others found that subjects have a much easier time recalling stories that are presented in an organized format than stories with little organization (Rumelhart, 1975; Mandler, 1978; Mandler & Johnson, 1977). In order to test these assertions, these researchers developed grammars that delineate the parts of a story in an attempt to discover more about the effect of story structure on recall. Research using these grammars has shown that stories that fit the grammars closely are recalled in more detail and with more accuracy than stories that are not as structured. However, the structure of the original story and the one evident in the recalled version does not seem to be the same (Tulving & Thomson, 1973); Rumelhart, 1975; Mandler & Johnson, 1977). The discrepancy between the two structures led Mandler and Johnson to conclude that recall approximates an idealized story structure more than the actual form of the story.

Mandler and Johnson (1977) also found that information distortion or inferences occur in certain types of situations. The first occurs when an important part of the story structure is weak or missing. Another distortion occurs when a subject reverses the order of events in a story. Finally, distortion occurs when information is added to the original story. These findings are further verified by Mandler (1978) and Stein and Glenn (1979).

In order to determine why story structure changes in recall, we need to examine the concept of schematic processing. Some memory theories postulate that information is stored in an orderly, structured fashion somewhat similar to the story structure discussed in the previous section. One such group of theories addresses the use of schema in memory.

After surveying various memory models that utilize the notion of schema, Thorndyke and Hayes-Roth (1979) reached the general conclusion that "schema" represents an abstraction of a set of concepts and relations that explicitly occur in a number of unique contexts. These representations provide a pattern for the individual to use in encoding and decoding information. Based on this notion, "schema" is defined as data structures for representing generic concepts that are stored in memory as well as those structures used to put the story together for transmission (Rumelhart & Ortony, 1977).

Keeping this definition in mind, Rumelhart and Ortony (1977) found four characteristics of schema that qualify it as a means of representing knowledge in memory. The first characteristic is that schema has variables. Second, schemata can embed one within the other. Third, schemata represent generic concepts that vary in their levels of abstraction. The fourth characteristic is that schemata represent knowledge areas and definitions. These four aspects seem to rationalize a schema's ability to cope with encoding and decoding information. This is especially relevant in light of postulations about how information is processed in memory.

One example of such a notion about memory was postulated by Bobrow and Norman (1975). They theorized that the human memory system is guided by a central, limited processor that utilizes schemata. The use of schemata allows the system to process information in an efficient manner. The researchers believed their central processor utilized schemata in at least two situations. First, schemata are used when the system attempts to reduce any ambiguity or fill gaps in an existing information category. In other words schemata provide the guidelines for the system's search for the information needed to complete a category so it can achieve closure. The system also utilizes schemata when it tries to associate new information with existing information categories. In this capacity, the schemata help the reader to be sensitive to novel information or help confirm or dispute hypotheses (Rumelhart, 1975).

The notion of a schematic processing system (a memory system using schemata) can easily be applied to the processing of linguistic information. Aaronson and Scarborough (1977) found evidence that an underlying structure exists into which incoming information is integrated. Since the evidence indicated that chunking occurs in the recall of sentences, individuals must be identifying, organizing, and integrating linguistic information. Their model suggests "that there is a level of linguistic processing at which words must be integrated into a larger context across phrase units (p. 301)." Schemata can provide the larger context.

Interaction of Story Structure and the Schematic Processing System

The schematic processing system is not static; rather, it changes so that new and old information can be integrated during information processing. Because the system does change to accommodate new information, or to fit the new and old information together, inferences often become part of the information that is recalled.

When a story is presented to the schematic processing system, it has its own structure. If the structure is strong enough, the system integrates the story structure into the mind's system. If, however, the story structure is weak or has missing or incongruent parts, the mind probably changes the story to fit an existing set of ideas or the schema. Distortion of the story results not only from changes in the schema but also because of weaknesses in the original story structure. The difference between information at input and at recall has led some researchers to conclude that the original story structure cannot predict the structure of the recalled version of the story (Craik & Lockhart, 1972; Mandler & Johnson, 1977).

The fundamental assumption of the schema theory approach to language comprehension is that neither spoken nor written text carries the meaning itself—the text only provides directions to the receivers as to how they should retrieve or construct the intended meaning from each individual's own previous knowledge (Adams & Collins, 1979). The words in a message and their organization help an individual remember past associations and interrelationships. From this information, the individual infers the meaning of the text. The derivation of meaning from the text comes from two component processes: the application of prior knowledge and the making of inferences (Bartlett, 1932; Warren et al., 1979). All of this occurs during schematic processing.

The research cited in this study shows that information distortion in the form of inferences occurs in several ways. First, a receiver can combine a relocated idea and infer the underlying relationships. The individual also seems to infer information that is missing from or is incongruent in the story.

Research also supports the idea that the structure of the message itself partially influences inference production. Experimenters have manipulated the presence or absence of and the strength or weakness of story structure. In so doing, they found that certain components are essential to strong story structure and are thus easy to recall. These elements include a setting, a goal, a beginning, a reaction, an attempt, an outcome, and an ending (Freedle & Hale, 1979; Stein & Glenn, 1979; Mandler & Johnson, 1977). Paris and Upton (1971) and Mandler and Johnson (1977) each combined these elements into broader units:

cause: goals and attempts

consequence: reactions, outcomes, and endings

setting: actual action in the story

event: background information

Research has not, however, addressed the possibility that manipulating story structure internally may influence the production of inferences in recall. For example, research has not tested whether or not manipulating one part of story structure influences the recall of the rest of the story. Research also has not addressed the possibility that one story node is more critical to recall than another. Another issue that has not been adequately tested is the effect of incongruency in a story. Therefore, the following questions about the effect of manipulating story structure on inference production arise:

(a) Will the deletion of a story node cause inferences about the rest of the story as well as the missing node?
(b) Will the manipulation of one node create more inferences than the manipulation of other nodes in the same story?
(c) Will an incongruency in the story cause inferences?

In order to address these three questions, the following hypotheses are put forth:

H_1: More inferences will be produced in the recall of a story missing the cause node than in the recall of an unaltered story.

H_{1a}: More cause nodes will be inferred when the cause node is deleted than when it is presented.

H_{1b}: The deletion of the cause node will produce more inferences in the recall of all story nodes than the recall of an unaltered story.

H_2: More inferences will be produced in the recall of a story missing the consequence node than in the recall of an unaltered story.

H_{2a}: More consequence nodes will be inferred when the node is deleted than when it is present.

H_{2b}: The deletion of the consequence node will produce more inferences in the recall of all story nodes than the recall of an unaltered story.

H_3: More inferences will be produced when the cause node is deleted than when the consequence node is deleted.

H_4: More inferences will be produced in the recall of a story when one node is incongruent than when all story nodes are congruent.

METHODOLOGY

Subjects

The subjects were 152 students enrolled in the basic communication course at a Midwestern university.

Design

The research design of this study contains one independent variable and three dependent variables cast into a one-way, four-group comparison. The independent variable, story structure, was manipulated to create four conditions: unaltered story structure (UA), cause deleted story structure (CA), consequence deleted story structure (CQ), and incongruent story structure (IC). The dependent variables were the recall of the cause, the consequence, and the incongruency.

Stimulus Material

Three communication case studies were parsed into four nodes: background, cause, event, and consequence. *Background* is defined as information providing the setting of the story. The *cause* is defined as the reason the action occurred. The *event* is the main action that occurs. The final node, *consequence,* was defined as the result of the event. All parsing was validated by a panel of judges who were not familiar with the research. The criterion for acceptance of the parsing was set at four of five judges agreeing.

In order to test the fourth hypothesis, an incongruency, or an illogical ideal, was written into a node of each story. The incongruency was judged by a separate group of raters. The criterion for acceptance was set at two of three judges.

Instrument

The instrument used in this study was a multiple-choice questionnaire composed of questions addressing the cause node, the consequence node, and either the background or event nodes. One question also addressed any incongruity that might be in the story. The questions covered each story.

Each question had four possible responses: three content related and a fourth choice, "(d) the story doesn't say." Each question had only one correct response. The correct answer, of course, depended on which group the respondent was in. (The correctness of the responses had been previously validated in a pretest.)

Procedure

The subjects were divided into four groups. Each group heard three stories presented via a video monitor in the classroom. The same source presented all of the stimulus material. Each group was placed in a different experimental condition. Group 1 heard condition 1 (CA) in which stories were missing the cause node. The consequence node was deleted in condition 2 (CQ) for Group 2. The third group heard condition 3 (IC) which contained an incongruent conclusion. The final group heard condition 4 (UA) in which the stories were unaltered.

Two days after the students heard the stimulus material, a questionnaire covering the stories was administered.

Statistical Analysis

The data gathered in this study were coded into inference scores and recall scores. Inference scores were the number of inferential responses, or incorrect answers, summed across all three stories for each subject. These scores were computed for the cause, the consequence, and the congruency questions. Each subject could have an inference score ranging from 0 to 3 for each of the dependent variables.

After the data were coded, they were submitted to a series of Hotelling's T-squares (Winer, 1979). The UA group's inference and recall scores served as a baseline against which the other groups' scores were compared. If the Hotelling statistic produced a significance F value (an alpha level of .05 or better), Student's t-tests were performed to determine where the differences existed.

RESULTS

The data analysis used only the responses to the cause, the consequence, and the congruent questions collapsed across all three stories. The filler questions were not submitted to analysis because they addressed neither any manipulated portion of the stories nor any specific node as did the other three questions.

The mean inference scores were computed for all four groups.[1] The means of the UA group served as a baseline against which all other groups were compared during the data analysis. The tests for each hypothesis are presented briefly below and in Table 13.1.

Hypothesis 1 speculated that more inferences would occur when the cause node was deleted than when it was present. The hypothesis specifically predicted that inferences would occur in the recall of the cause node (H_{1a}) as well as all other nodes (H_{1b}). A Hotelling's T-square produced a significant F value (F = 38.69; p < .0004), thus supporting the hypothesis. Because of the significant finding, Student's T-tests were performed on each dependent variable. The analysis showed that the CA group made significantly more cause (t = 10.29, p < .04) and congruency (t = 2.02; p < .047) inferences than did the UA group. They did not, however, make more inferences in response to the consequence question.

Table 13.1
Results of Hypothesis Testing

Groups	Hyp. No.	Variables	Test	Test Value	d.f.	P Value
Cause deleted vs.	1	All	Hotelling's T	F = 38.69	3,61	.0004
unaltered	1a	Cause	t	t = 10.29	64	.04
	1b	Consequ.	t	t = −.53	64	NS
		Congruent	t	t = 2.02	64	.047
Consequence	2	All	Hotelling's T	F = 8.21	3,70	.0004
deleted vs.	2a	Consequ.	t	t = 4.62	73	.0004
unaltered	2b	Cause	t	t = −.32	73	NS
		Congruent	t	t = 2.89	72	.005
Cause deleted vs.	3	All	Hotelling's T	F = 52.45	3,71	.0004
consequence		Consequ.	t	t = −5.32	73	.0004
deleted		Cause	t	t = 9.48	73	.0004
		Congruent	t	t = 1.02	73	NS
Incongruent vs.	4	All	Hotelling's T	F = 6.29	3,71	.001
unaltered		Consequ.	t	t = 3.37	74	.001
		Cause	t	t = −.73	74	NS
		Congruent	t	t = 1.99	73	.05

Note: NS = not significant.

Hypothesis 2 and its components stated that the deletion of the consequence node would produce inferences in recall. Once again Hotelling's T-square produced a significant F (F = 8.21; p < .0004). The individual t-tests on the dependent variables showed that the CQ group made significantly more inferences to the consequence question (H_{2a}: t = 2.89; p < .005). They did not, however, make more cause inferences. Therefore, the hypothesis was only partially supported.

Hypothesis 3 speculated that the CA group would make more inferences than the CQ group in recall. Hotelling's T again produced a significant F value (F = 52.45; p < .0004). Individual comparisons revealed that the difference was caused by the greater number of cause inferences made by the CA group (t = 9.48; p < .0004). The results, then, support the hypothesized idea that the effect of cause deletion produces more inferences than consequence deletion.

Hypothesis 4 postulated that more inferences would be produced when an incongruency was present in a story. A Hotelling's T comparing the IC and UA groups produced an F value of 6.29 (p < .001). Therefore, the results support the hypothesized idea that the presence of an incongruity produces inferences. Individual comparisons revealed that the difference occurred in the responses to the consequence (t = 3.37; p < .001) and the congruency (t = 1.99; p < .05) questions.

DISCUSSION

A summary of the results shows that, overall, the hypotheses were confirmed.

(1) The deletion of a cause node produced an inferred cause in recall.
(2) The deletion of a consequence node produced an inferred consequence in recall.
(3) The deletion of the cause node produced more inferences than the deletion of the consequence node.
(4) A node that is incongruent causes subjects to infer congruent nodes in an attempt to keep the message congruent.

Several observations can be made about these results. First, they support the notion that the manipulation of story structure causes inferences to occur. This conclusion suggests that the sender of a message can have some control over the type of inferences the receiver makes. Obviously, if the sender leaves out an important factor in a message or introduces incongruity into a message, the receiver will very probably infer the missing information or infer congruent information.

Second, the evidence supports the notion that an interaction occurs between the message and the receiver's schema or expectations of that message. When a message does not meet those expectations, the recalled version of that message is restructured to fit those expectations. For example, the schema for a story says that all stories must have a cause and a consequence, and that all story parts must be congruent with each other. As the data analysis showed, when these expectations are violated, the subjects inferred the appropriate information and thus made the recalled version of the story congruent with their story schemata.

The finding that the deletion of the cause node produced significantly more inferences than the deletion of the consequence node suggests a third observation. The evidence supports that all nodes are not equally important to the story schema. However, only the cause and consequence nodes were tested in this study, so the interpretation cannot be extended to all story nodes. Further research might examine other story nodes as well as other types of message schemata.

The final observation is that the existence of an incongruity in a message causes information distortion to occur during recall. The data analysis clearly supported this point. However, the only node that was manipulated in this condition was the consequence node. This limitation suggests that further research is needed to test the generalizability of the observation.

As previously indicated, the results of this study also suggest directions for future research. First, researchers need to explore the effect of incongruous story nodes, other than the consequence nodes, in order to explore more fully the influence of incongruity on the recall of a message. Second, the research presented in this story needs to be expanded to include more complex messages. Only then can the notion that one particular node is the focal point of story structure be confirmed or disconfirmed.

A final suggestion involves the need to develop more reliable and less structured methods of coping with free recall. Current methods tend to either shape recall responses via the particular grammars that are used or to test for recognition, which restricts the range of subjects' possible responses (for example, a subject might make an inference that was not included in the possible responses). As an illustration, a pilot study conducted by the author and others attempted to test inference making in free recall (Fitch, Gorcyca, & Goss, 1979). Methodological problems precluded any significant findings. Perhaps if the methodology of that study and this one were combined, the type of inferences made in free recall could be explored and stimulus material could include messages other than stories.

NOTE

1. Mean recall scores were also computed for all variables. The analysis of these scores further supported the findings of this study, but they are not reported because of time and space limitations. The reader may refer to Fitch (1982) for full details.

REFERENCES

Aaronson, D., & Scarborough, H. S. (1977). Performance theories for sentence coding: Some quantitative models. *Journal of Verbal Learning and Verbal Behavior, 16,* 227-303.

Adams, M. J., & Collins, A. (1979). A schema-theoretic view of reading. In R. Freedle (Ed.), *New directions in discourse comprehension,* Norwood, NJ: Ablex.

Barclay, J. R. (1973). Comprehension and sentence memory. *Cognitive Psychology, 4,* 229-254.

Bartlett, F. C. (1932). *Remembering.* Cambridge, England: Cambridge University Press.

Binder, A. (1963). Further considerations on testing the null hypothesis and the strategy and tactics of investigating theoretical models. *Psychological Review, 70,* 107-115.

Bobrow, D. G., & Norman, D. A. (1975). Some principles of memory schemata. In D. G. Bobrow & A. Collins (Eds.), *Representation and understanding.* New York: Academic.

Bransford, J. D., Barclay, J. R., & Franks, J. J. (1972). Sentence memory: A constructive versus interpretive approach. *Cognitive Psychology, 3,* 193-209.

Bransford, J. D., & Franks, J. J. (1972). The abstraction of linguistic ideas: A review. *Cognition, 1,* 211-249.

Cairns, H. S., & Cairns, C. E. (1976). *Psycholinguistics: A cognitive view of language.* New York: Holt, Rinehart & Winston.

Collins, A. (1977). Processes in acquiring knowledge. In R. C. Anderson, R. J. Spiro, & W. E. Montague (Eds.), *Schooling and the acquisition of knowledge*. Hillsdale, NJ: Lawrence Erlbaum.

Craik, F. I. M., & Lockhart, E. S. (1972). Levels of processing : A framework for memory research. *Journal of Verbal Learning and Verbal Behavior, 11*, 123-136.

Craik, F. I. M., & Tulving, E. (1975). Depth of processing and the retention of words in episodic memory. *Journal of Experimental Psychology: General, 104*, 268-294.

Epstein, W. (1969). Recall of word lists following learning of sentences and anomalous and random strings. *Journal of Verbal Learning and Verbal Behavior, 8*, 20-25.

Fisher, R. A. (1949). *The design of experiments*. Edinburgh: Oliver & Boyd.

Fitch, M. (1982). *The effect of message structure on inference making in recall*. Unpublished doctoral dissertation, University of Oklahoma.

Fitch, M. E., Gorcyca, D. A., & Goss, L. B. (1979). *A developmental approach to sentence reconstruction*. Paper presented to the International Communication Association, May.

Folger, J. P., & Woodall, W. G. (1982). Nonverbal cues as linguistic context: An information processing view. In M. Burgoon (Ed.), *Communication yearbook 6*. Beverly Hills, CA: Sage.

Freedle, R., & Hale, G. (1979). Acquisition of new comprehension: Schemata for expository prose by transfer of a narrative schema. In R. O. Freedle (Ed.), *New directions in discourse processing*, Norwood, NJ: Ablex.

Graesser, A. C., Robertson, S. F., & Anderson, P. A. (1981). Incorporating inferences in narrative representations: A study of how and why. *Cognitive Psychology, 13*, 1-26.

Gough, P. B. (1965). Grammatical transformations and speed of understanding. *Journal of Verbal Learning and Verbal Behavior, 5*, 492-496.

Gough, P. B. (1966). The verification of sentences: The effects of delay of evidence and sentence length. *Journal of Verbal Learning and Verbal Behavior, 5*, 492-496.

Hayes-Roth, B., & Hayes-Roth, F. (1977). The prominence of lexical information in memory representations of meaning. *Journal of Verbal Learning and Verbal Behavior, 16*, 119-136.

Johnson, M. K., Bransford, J. D., & Solomon, S. K. (1973). Memory for tacit implications of sentences. *Journal of Experimental psychology, 98*, 203-205.

Kintsch, W. (1974). *The representation of meaning in memory*. Hillsdale, NJ: Lawrence Erlbaum.

Kintsch, W., & Monk, D. (1972). Storage of complex information in memory: Some implications of the speed with which inferences can be made. *Journal of Experimental Psychology, 94*, 25-32.

Kintsch, W., & Van Dijk, R. A. (1978, Sept. 5). Toward a model of text comprehension and production. *Psychological Review, 85*, 363-394.

Mandler, J. (1978). A code in the node: The use of a story schema in retrieval. *Discourse Process, 1*, 14-35.

Mandler, J. M, & Johnson, N. S. (1977). Remembrance of things passed: Story structure and recall. *Cognitive Psychology, 9*, 111-151.

Marks, L. E., & Miller, G. A. (1964). The role of semantic and syntactic constraints in the memorization of English sentences. *Journal of Verbal Learning and Verbal Behavior, 3*, 1-5.

Mehler, J. (1963). Some effective grammatical transformations on the recall of English sentences. *Journal of Verbal Learning and Verbal Behavior, 2*, 346-351.

Meyer, B. J. F. (1977). The structure of prose: Effects on learning and memory and implications for educational practice. In R. C. Anderson, R. J. Spiro, & W. E. Montague (Eds.), *Schooling and the acquisition of knowledge*. Hillsdale, NJ: Lawrence Erlbaum.

Miller, G. A., Galanter, E., & Pribram, K. H. (1960). *Plans and the structure of behavior*. New York: Holt, Rinehart & Winston.

Neyman, J., & Pearson, E. N. (1928). On the use and interpretation of certain test criteria for purposes of statistical inference. *Biometrika, 20A*, 175-240.

Ortony, A. (1978). Remembering, understanding, and representation. *Cognitive Science, 2*, 53-69.

Paris, S. G. (1965). Integration and inference in children's comprehension and memory. In F. Restle, R. Shiffrin, J. Castellan, J. Lindman, & D. Pisoni (Eds.), *Cognitive theory* (Vol. 1). Hillsdale, NJ: Lawrence Erlbaum.

Paris, S. G., & Carter, A. Y. (1973). Semantic and constructive aspects of sentence memory in children. *Developmental Psychology, 9,* 109-113.

Paris, S. G., & Upton, L. R. (1976). Children's memory for inferential relationships in prose. *Child Development, 47,* 660-668.

Perfetti, C. A. (1973). Retrieval of sentence relations: Semantic versus syntactic deep structure. *Cognition, 2,* 95-102.

Rubin, D. C. (1978). A unit analysis of prose memory. *Journal of Verbal Learning and Verbal Behavior, 17,* 599-620.

Rumelhart, D. E. (1975). Notes on a schema for stories. In D. G. Bobrow & A. Collins (Eds.), *Representation and understanding: Studies in cognitive science.* New York: Academic.

Rumelhart, D. E., & Ortony, A. (1977). The representation of knowledge in memory. In R. C. Anderson, R. J. Spiro, & W. E. Montague (Eds.), *Schooling and the acquisition of knowledge.* Hillsdale, NJ: Lawrence Erlbaum.

Sachs, J. S. (1967). Recognition memory for syntactic and semantic concepts of connected discourse. *Perception and Psychophysics, 2,* 437-442.

Savin, H. B., & Perchonock, E. (1965). Grammatical structure and the immediate recall of English sentences. *Journal of Verbal Learning and Verbal Behavior, 4,* 348-353.

Schank, R. C. (1973). Indentification of conceptualizations underlying natural language. In R. C. Schank & K. M. Colby (Eds.), *Computer models of thought and language.* San Francisco: W. H. Freeman.

Schank, R. C. (1975). The structure of episodes in memory. In D. G. Bobrow & A. Collins (Eds.), *Representation and understanding; Studies in cognitive science.* New York: Academic Press.

Schank, R. C., & Abelson, R. (1977). *Scripts, plans, goals, and understanding.* Hillsdale, NJ: Lawrence Erlbaum.

Slobin, D. I. (1966). Grammatical transformations and sentence comprehension in childhood and adulthood. *Journal of Verbal Learning and Verbal Behavior, 5,* 219-227.

Spiro, R. J. (1977). Remembering information from text: The "state of schema" approach. In R. C. Anderson, R. J. Spiro, & W. E. Montague (Eds.), *Schooling and the acquisition of knowledge.* Hillsdale, NJ: Lawrence Erlbaum.

Stein, N. L., & Glenn, C. G. (1979). An analysis of story comprehension in elementary school children. In R. Freedle (Ed.), *New directions in discourse comprehension.* Norwood, NJ: Ablex.

Taylor, S. E., & Croker, J. (1980). Schematic bases of social information processing. In E. T. Higgins, P. Hermann, & M. P. Zanna (Eds.), *The Ontario symposium on personality and social psychology* (Vol. 1). Hillsdale, NJ: Lawrence Erlbaum.

Thorndyke, P. A, & Hayes-Roth, B. (1979). The use of schemata in the acquisition and transfer of knowledge. *Cognitive Psychology, 2,* 82-106.

Tulving, E., & Thomson, D. M. (1973). Encoding specificity and retrieval processes in episodic memory. *Psychological Review, 80,* 352-373.

Waller, T. G. (1976). Children's recognition memory for written sentences: A comparison of good and poor readers. *Child Development, 47,* 90-95.

Warren, W. H., Nicholas, D. W, & Trabasso, T. (1979). Event chains and inferences in understanding narratives. In R. Freedle (Ed.), *New directions in discourse comprehension.* Norwood, NJ: Ablex.

Winer, B. J. (1979). *Statistical principles in experimental designs.* New York: McGraw-Hill.

14 ● Choice Shifts:
Argument Qualities or
Social Comparisons

FRANKLIN J. BOSTER ● MICHAEL MAYER

Arizona State University

FOR the past 25 years, a substantial research effort has been directed toward the study of the group polarization effect, or the choice shift. Two explanations, the social comparison hypothesis and the persuasive arguments hypothesis, have been most successful in predicting the outcomes of choice shift experiments. In this chapter the results of a test of these explanations are reported. Initially, however, a sketch of each explanation is provided below.

The Social Comparison Hypothesis

Originating from Festinger's (1950, 1954) theory of social comparison, the idea most central to the social comparison hypothesis is that merely exposing group members to the choices of other group members is both necessary and sufficient to produce a choice shift (Pruitt, 1971). Laughlin and Earley (1982) argue that three postulates summarize the position of current social comparison theorists. First, group members desire to equal or exceed other group members on certain positively valued, task-relevant characteristics, such as risk and caution. Second, prior to group discussion group members believe that they do equal or exceed others on such characteristics. Third, by comparing themselves to others in the course of group discussion some group members realize that they were incorrect. Then, according to Laughlin and Earley (1982, p. 274):

> A choice shift results to the extent that these members change in the positively valued direction in order to present themselves as at least the equal of the average group member on the positively valued dimension.

Correspondence and requests for reprints: Franklin J. Boster, Department of Communication, Arizona State University, Tempe, AZ 85287.

There are considerable data consistent with this set of postulates. For example, group members tend to estimate the average group member's position as less extreme than their own, but they estimate their own positions as being less extreme than their ideal positions (Carlson & Davis, 1971; Castore, Goodrich, & Peterson, 1970; Castore & Roberts, 1972; Ferguson & Vidmar, 1971; Fraser, Gouge, & Billig, 1971; Horne & Long, 1972; Lamm, Schaude, & Trommsdorff, 1971; Lamm, Trommsdorff, & Rost-Schaude, 1972; Levinger & Schneider, 1969; McCauley, Kogan, & Teger, 1971; Myers & Bishop, 1971; Myers, Wong, & Murdoch, 1971; Schroeder, 1973; Stoner, 1968; Vidmar & Burdeny, 1971; Wallach & Wing, 1968). Moreover, when asked to rate persons varying in extremity, group members rate extreme others as more socially desirable (Jellison & Riskind, 1970, 1971; Main & Walker, 1973).

The evidence is mixed concerning whether or not mere exposure to the choices of others is sufficient to produce the choice shift. Several studies present data consistent with this hypothesis (Clark & Willems, 1969; Goethals & Zanna, 1979; Myers, Bach, & Schreiber, 1974; Myers et al., 1971; Stokes, 1971; Teger & Pruitt, 1967; Willems & Clark, 1969, 1971), but several others report contradictory results (Bell & Jamieson, 1970; Burnstein, Vinokur, & Trope, 1973; Clark, Crockett, & Archer, 1971; Myers & Bishop, 1971; Wallach & Kogan, 1965). A thorough review of this literature is provided by Lamm and Myers (1978).

The Persuasive Arguments Hypothesis

Central to the persuasive arguments hypothesis is the notion that the choice shift is produced by the arguments advanced during group discussion. Laughlin and Earley (1982) argue that three postulates summarize the position of current persuasive arguments theorists. First, there is a pool of arguments for and against a given alternative. These arguments vary in persuasiveness, and they are skewed. Specifically, for items that consistently produce a risky shift, the pool of arguments is predominantly risky. For items that consistently produce a cautious shift, the pool of arguments is predominantly cautious. Second, not all group members are aware of all arguments in the pool. Third, during group discussion persuasive arguments from the pool of arguments are advanced. Then, according to Laughlin and Earley (1982, p. 274) "a choice shift results to the extent that group members who had not previously considered these partially shared arguments are convinced of their merits."

Considerable data are consistent with this hypothesis. For example, the direction of the arguments advanced during group discussion predicts the direction of the choice shift (Silverthorne, 1971; Vinokur & Burnstein, 1974). Moreover, discussion elicits choice shifts, even when there is no exposure to others' positions (Boster, Mayer, Hunter, & Hale, 1980; Boster, Fryrear, Mongeau, & Hunter, 1982; Burnstein & Vinokur, 1973, 1975; Clark et al. 1971; Ebbeson & Bowers, 1974; Morgan & Aram, 1975; Roberts & Castore, 1972; Silverthorne, 1971; Vinokur & Burnstein, 1974, 1978a, 1978b). To our knowledge there is no evidence of data that are clearly inconsistent with the persuasive arguments hypothesis.

Critical Experiments

Experiments have attempted to pit the social comparison hypothesis against the persuasive arguments hypothesis (Boster et al., 1982; Burnstein & Vinokur, 1973; Morgan & Aram, 1975). None of these experiments has eliminated either of the hypotheses. There are two primary difficulties in designing a critical experiment that would eliminate one of the hypotheses.

First, both hypotheses predict that there will be choice shifts, and both hypotheses predict that group member opinion change produces the shifts. The difference in the explanations is in specifying the process that produces the opinion change. A typical choice shift experiment involves an individual pretest opinion measurement, a group discussion, a group decision, and an individual posttest opinion measurement. These outcomes cannot be used to separate the two hypotheses. For example, if one observes a group member advancing an argument and then observes other group members gradually coming to agree with the position advocated in that argument, either of the two processes or both might be operating. It might have been the quality of the persuasive argument that produced the group consensus, or it might have been the mere fact that the group member let her or his position be known to the others. Alternatively, suppose that one observes a group member simply stating an opinion on an issue, without any supporting argument. Further, suppose that one observes that the other group members come to agree with that opinion. Again, either or both of the two processes might be operating to produce the group consensus. It might have been the mere fact that the group member let her or his position be known to the others that produced the consensus, but it may just as well have been that the other group members inferred an argument, or set of arguments, from the stated opinion.

Second, ingenious manipulations have been employed in an attempt to block one of the other of the processes. This strategy is also insufficient to eliminate either of the explanations. The problem with this strategy is that the existence of data consistent with one of the explanations does not warrant the conclusion that the other explanation is false. The possibility remains that both social comparison processes and persuasive arguments processes contribute to the direction and the magnitude of the polarity shift.

In this experiment both group discussion and process blocking manipulations were rejected. Instead, subjects were exposed to a transcript of a (fictitious) group discussion. This transcript incorporated manipulations designed to induce both social comparison processes and persuasive arguments processes. The former involved manipulating the position taken by the majority of participants in the transcript. The latter involved manipulating the quality of both the risky arguments and the cautious arguments. In this way several possible experimental outcomes could be assessed. For example, it is possible that one process operates to the exclusion of the other, that both processes operate additively, that the two processes interact to produce the choice shift, or that one process mediates the effect of the other.

METHOD

Subjects

Subjects were 636 undergraduates enrolled in an introductory communication course at a large southwestern university. Subjects were assigned randomly to treatments.

Design

A 2 × 2 × 2 factorial design was employed in which the strength of arguments favoring the cautious position (weak, strong), the strength of arguments favoring the risky position (weak, strong), and the composition of the majority (risky, cautious) were varied. The quality of both the risky arguments and the cautious arguments was ascertained from a pilot study in which the participants rated the quality of a pool of both pro-risky and pro-cautious arguments. The most highly rated three risky/cautious arguments and the three risky/cautious arguments with the lowest ratings were chosen for this study. The majority manipulation was accomplished by having three persons favor the risky/cautious alternative and one person favor the cautious/risky alternative.

Materials

The stimulus item utilized in this experiment was the employment item (Stoner, 1968). This item describes the life dilemma of a recent college graduate who is faced with choosing between a job offer from a new firm with an uncertain future but high potential for growth and a job offer from an old firm with a certain future but low potential for growth. This item was selected because of its ability to elicit both weak and strong arguments for both the risky and cautious options.

Procedure

Upon entering their introductory communication class, subjects received a booklet. Each booklet contained a set of personality scales, a copy of the employment item, a pretest measure of the subject's opinion as to the option that the recent college graduate should select, a 1¼-page script labeled "Excerpt from a Group Discussion of the Employment Item," a series of manipulation check items, and a posttest assessment of the subject's opinion as to the option that the recent college graduate should select.

After filling out the personality scales, reading the employment item, and responding to the employment item, subjects were instructed to read the script. Ostensibly, the purpose of reading the script was so that subjects could give their judgments of the "quality of communication patterns in a group discussion, and how they affect the quality of group decisions." After reading the scripts subjects completed the manipulation check measures. Finally, they completed the posttest opinion measure.

The script contained the experimental manipulations. In the script an experimenter interrupts a group discussion in order to poll the members. Participant 1 always took the majority position, and offered three arguments in support of that position. Participant 2 always took the minority position, and offered three arguments in support of that position. Participants 3 and 4 simply indicated agreement with the first participant. The experimenter then indicated that the group members should continue discussing the issue until they reached agreement.

Majority was manipulated by varying the position that Participants 1, 3, and 4 advocated. Quality of arguments was manipulated by varying whether Participant 1's arguments were weak or strong, and by varying whether Participant 2's arguments were weak or strong. Thus there were eight forms of the booklet distributed to the subjects.

The procedure confounds the majority manipulation with a possible order effect. Pilot study data indicate that order had no main effect on opinion change, and that order did not interact with the other independent variables to affect opinion change. Hence it was not considered important in this study, and order was held constant across conditions.

Instrumentation

The personality scales included Spielberger, Gorsuch, and Lushene's (1970) Trait Anxiety Scale, Rosenberg's (1965) Self-Esteem Scale, and Snyder's (1974) other-directedness subscale of the Self-Monitoring Scale. Pretest and posttest measures of opinion on the employment item utilized the Fraser et al. (1971) 5-point Likert response scale. Quality of arguments judgments were made on four 5-point Likert scales (strong-weak, convincing-unconvincing, persuasive-lacking in persuasiveness and reasonable-unreasonable). The majority manipulation check consisted of one item that asked whether the majority had favored the Company A job option (risky option) or the Company B job option (cautious option).

RESULTS

The data indicate that the majority manipulation was successful. Of the 628 subjects who responded to the majority manipulation check item, 567 (90 percent) responded correctly. If the 8 who did not respond to the item are assumed not to have known the correct answer, then the proportion of correct responses drops to 89 percent. Moreover, the errors in perception of the majority were unaffected by the independent variables. The success of the majority manipulation may be illustrated in another way. The correlation of the majority manipulation with the subjects' perception of the majority was $r = .79$ (df = 626, p. < .05).

Table 14.1
Confirmatory Factor Analysis Performed on the
Quality of Risky Arguments Measure

	Strong	Convincing	Persuasive	Reasonable
Obtained Correlations				
strong	1.00			
convincing	.49	1.00		
persuasive	.51	.60	1.00	
reasonable	.47	.40	.43	1.00
Predicted correlations				
strong				
convincing	.51			
persuasive	.54	.55		
reasonable	.43	.43	.46	
Residuals				
strong				
convincing	−.02			
persuasive	−.03	.05		
reasonable	.04	−.03	−.03	

Item	F
Strong-weak	.71
Convincing-unconvincing	.72
Persuasive-lacking in persuasiveness	.76
Reasonable-unreasonable	.60

The data are consistent with the hypothesis that the 4-item quality of risky arguments measure is unidimensional. A confirmatory factor analysis performed on these data is presented in Table 14.1 (Hunter & Cohen, 1970). Each predicted correlation is within the 95 percent confidence interval of its respective obtained correlation. Moreover, the matrix of residuals is within sampling error of zero ($\chi^2 = 4.58$, df $= 6$, p $> .05$). The reliability of this scale is estimated by Cronbach (1951) α and is substantial, $\alpha = .79$.

Descriptive statistics for these data were broken down by condition and subjected to an analysis of variance. This analysis demonstrated that the risky arguments manipulation was unsuccessful. The only substantial effect was the main effect for majority. Subjects perceived the quality of risky arguments to be higher when the majority was risky than when the majority was cautious.

The data are consistent with the hypothesis that the four-item quality of cautious arguments measure is unidimensional. A confirmatory factor analysis performed on these data is presented in Table 14.2. Each predicted correlation is within the 95 percent confidence interval of its respective ob-

Table 14.2
Confirmatory Factor Analysis Performed on the
Quality of Cautious Arguments Measure

	Strong	*Convincing*	*Persuasive*	*Reasonable*
Obtained Correlations				
strong	1.00			
convincing	.70	1.00		
persuasive	.64	.69	1.00	
reasonable	.55	.57	.50	1.00
Predicted correlations				
strong				
convincing	.71			
persuasive	.64	.67		
reasonable	.54	.57	.51	
Residuals				
strong				
convincing	−.01			
persuasive	.00	.02		
reasonable	.01	.00	−.01	

Item	*F*
Strong-weak	.82
Convincing-unconvincing	.86
Persuasive-lacking in persuasiveness	.78
Reasonable-unreasonable	.66

Table 14.3
Descriptive Statistics for the Differential Argument
Quality Measure, Broken Down by Condition

	Risky Majority		Cautious Majority	
	Weak Risky Arguments	Strong Risky Arguments	Weak Risky Arguments	Strong Risky Arguments
Strong cautious arguments	$\overline{X}$ = 1.09 s = 4.14 N^x = 78	$\overline{X}$ = .81 s = 3.30 N^x = 74	$\overline{X}$ = −1.58 s = 4.32 N^x = 81	$\overline{X}$ = −1.17 s = 4.02 N^x = 84
Weak cautious arguments	$\overline{X}$ = 2.47 s = 3.63 N^x = 73	$\overline{X}$ = 1.68 s = 4.09 N^x = 80	$\overline{X}$ = −1.53 s = 4.45 N^x = 74	$\overline{X}$ = − .74 s = 4.29 N^x = 82

Table 14.4
Unweighted Means Analysis of Variance Performed on
the Differential Argument Quality Measure

Source	Var	SS	df	MS	F	p	n^2	r
Majority (M)	1.92	1200.81	1	1200.81	72.51	<.05	.10	−.32
Risky arguments (R)	.00	.25	1	.25	<1.00	>.05	.00	.00
Cautious arguments (C)	.12	72.37	1	72.37	4.37	<.05	.01	−.08
M × R	.09	54.24	1	54.24	3.28	>.05	.00	.07
M × C	.06	36.40	1	36.40	2.20	>.05	.00	.06
R × C	.00	1.20	1	1.20	<1.00	>.05	.00	.01
M × R × C	.00	.00	1	.00	<1.00	>.05	.00	.00
S/M, R, C	16.35	10236.67	618	16.56	—	—	.88	—
Total	—	11601.94	625	—	—	—	.99	—

Note: F_{MAX} = 1.81, df = 8, 78, p > .05.

tained correlation. Moreover, the matrix of residuals is within sampling error of zero (χ^2 = .45, df = 6, p > .05). The reliability of this scale is substantial, α = .86.

Descriptive statistics for these data were broken down by condition, and subjected to an analysis of variance. The analysis demonstrated that the cautious arguments manipulation was unsuccessful. Although the main effect for the cautious arguments manipulation was statistically significant at the .05 level, the effect size was extremely small. The only substantial effect found in this analysis was the main effect for majority. Subjects perceived that the cautious arguments were of higher quality when the majority was cautious than when the majority was risky.

Thus, while the majority manipulation was successful, both of the argument manipulations were unsuccessful. Another way to demonstrate this result is to form an index that incorporates both of the argument variables. Such an index, differential argument quality, was formed by subtracting subjects' perceptions of the quality of the cautious arguments from their perceptions of the quality of the risky arguments. Descriptive statistics for this index are broken down by condition and are presented in Table 14.3. The corresponding analysis of variance is presented in Table 14.4. From these tables it may be observed that the majority manipulation exerted a strong impact on differential argument quality. When the majority was risky, subjects perceived the risky arguments to be superior to the cautious arguments. When the majority was cautious, subjects perceived the cautious arguments to be superior to the risky arguments. Neither of the argument manipulations had a strong effect on perceptions of differential argument quality, although the main effect of the cautious arguments manipulation is statistically significant at the .05 level. Moreover, these effects were not seriously attenuated due to error of measurement, since $\alpha = .86$ for the differential argument quality measure.

Given the status of the experimental manipulations, it is not surprising that neither of the argument manipulations affected change in opinion on the employment item. Descriptive statistics for opinion change are broken down by condition and are presented in Table 14.5. The corresponding analysis of variance is presented in Table 14.6. From these tables it is clear that none of the independent variables exerted a strong effect on opinion change. The majority main effect is statistically significant at the .05 level; a risky majority produced a risky shift and a cautious majority produced a cautious shift. On the other hand, the effect size for this variance component

Table 14.5

Descriptive Statistics for the Opinion Change Measure,
Broken Down by Condition

| | Risky Majority | | Cautious Majority | |
	Weak Risky Arguments	Strong Risky Arguments	Weak Risky Arguments	Strong Risky Arguments
Strong cautious arguments	$\overline{X} = .14$ $s = .81$ $N^x = 79$	$\overline{X} = .08$ $s = .67$ $N^x = 76$	$\overline{X} = -.01$ $s = .78$ $N^x = 81$	$\overline{X} = .05$ $s = .78$ $N^x = 84$
Weak cautious arguments	$\overline{X} = .25$ $s = .77$ $N^x = 76$	$\overline{X} = .13$ $s = .66$ $N^x = 82$	$\overline{X} = -.05$ $s = .91$ $N^x = 75$	$\overline{X} = -.07$ $s = .78$ $N^x = 83$

Table 14.6
Unweighted Means Analysis of Variance Performed on
the Opinion Change Measure

Source	Var	SS	df	MS	F	p	n^2	r
Majority (M)	.01	4.60	1	4.60	7.54	<.05	.01	−.11
Risky arguments (R)	.00	.14	1	.14	<1.00	>.05	.00	−.02
Cautious arguments (C)	.00	.00	1	.00	<1.00	>.05	.00	.00
M × R	.00	.81	1	.81	1.32	>.05	.00	.05
M × C	.00	1.02	1	1.02	1.67	>.05	.00	.05
R × C	.00	.25	1	.25	<1.00	>.05	.00	.03
M × R × C	.00	.00	1	.00	<1.00	>.05	.00	.00
S/M, R, C	.60	380.81	628	.61	—	—	.98	—
Total	—	387.63	635	—	—	—	.99	—

Note: $F_{MAX} = 1.91$, df = 8, 80, p > .05.

is small, reaching an acceptable level of statistical significance only because of the large sample size.

While one might be tempted to conclude that these data are consistent with a social comparison explanation, and that they are not an adequate test of the persuasive arguments explanation, there are two pieces of mitigating evidence. First, if subjects' perceptions of the quality of arguments are considered, then it is clear that arguments are not irrelevant to opinion change. Specifically, the correlation between perceived differential argument quality and opinion change is $r = .31$, and $r' = .33$ when corrected for attenuation due to error of measurement (df = 634, p < .05). Second, the majority manipulation exerted a stronger effect on perceptions of differential argument quality than on opinion change. These two pieces of evidence suggest the possibility of perceived differential quality of arguments mediating the relationship between the majority effect and opinion change.

Figure 14.1 presents a causal model consistent with this hypothesis. In this model a causal string is posited. The majority manipulation induces the subjects to perceive that a majority favors either the risky or the cautious alternative. The subjects' perception of the majority then affects the way in which they perceive the quality of arguments. If they perceive that the majority is risky, then they rate the risky arguments as superior to the cautious arguments. On the other hand, if they perceive that the majority is cautious, then they rate the cautious arguments as superior to the risky arguments. Finally, the differential quality of arguments has a direct effect on opinion change. If subjects rate the risky arguments as superior to the cautious arguments, then they tend to shift their opinions in a risky direction. If they rate

.79	.39	.31
majority manipulation ———→	majority perception ———→	differential ———→ opinion argument change quality

Figure 14.1. Causal model of the experiment.

Table 14.7
Test of the Causal Model

	Majority Manipulation	Majority Perception	Differential Argument Quality	Opinion Change
Obtained correlations				
majority manipulation	1.00			
majority perception	.79	1.00		
differential				
argument quality	.32	.39	1.00	
opinion change	.13	.12	.31	1.00
Predicted correlations				
majority manipulation				
majority perception	*			
differential				
argument quality	.31	*		
opinion change	.10	.12	*	
Residuals				
majority manipulation				
majority perception				
differential				
argument quality	.01			
opinion change	.03	.00		

*Constrained by estimation.

the cautious arguments as superior to the risky arguments, then they tend to shift their opinions in a cautious direction.

The path coefficients are estimated by the method of ordinary least squares and are presented in Figure 14.1. A test of the model is presented in Table 14.7. All of the path coefficients are statistically significant at the .05 level. Moreover, they are of reasonable magnitude. An analysis of the residual matrix in Table 14.7 illustrates that the model provides a close fit to the data. All predicted correlations fall within the 95 percent confidence interval of their respective obtained correlations. Moreover, the matrix of residuals does not differ significantly from zero ($\chi^2 = .64$, df = 3, p > .05).

The personality variables did not exert a direct effect, or mediated effect, on any of the dependent variables. Moreover, they did not moderate the effect of any of the independent variables on the dependent variables.

DISCUSSION

These data are consistent with the hypothesis that both a social comparison process and a persuasive arguments process contribute to produce the choice shift. Specifically, the majority manipulation induces a social comparison process. The social comparison process, in turn, affects perceptions of the quality of persuasive arguments. Perception of the quality of persuasive arguments has a direct impact on the direction and magnitude of the choice shift. Put differently, the "correct" judgment of the quality of a persuasive argument is unclear, or, to use Festinger's (1950) phrase, is dependent upon social reality rather than physical reality. Under such conditions people use the opinions of others to guide their judgments of the "correctness" of persuasive arguments. When a majority of similar others voice the opinion that a particular set of arguments is "correct," then there is a tendency to concur with their judgment. Having made the judgment that a set of arguments is "correct," or more "correct," than another set of arguments, there is a tendency to shift one's opinion in the direction advocated by those "correct" arguments. The outcome is a choice shift.

This experiment is pertinent to recent experiments that examine the multiple source effect. In several experiments Harkins and Petty (1981a, 1981b) report that multiple sources presenting multiple arguments are more persuasive than multiple sources presenting a single argument, a single source presenting multiple arguments, or a single source presenting a single argument. The primary difference between these experiments and the experiment reported in this chapter is that the latter includes arguments from both sides of an issue. Nevertheless, the same processes may operate in both types of experiments.

Harkins and Petty (1981a, 1981b) rule out a pool of arguments interpretation of their results, and demonstrate that the multiple source effect is mediated by favorable thoughts about the persuasive messages. If arguments are of high quality, then the multiple source/multiple arguments condition produces more favorable thoughts than the other conditions, and hence is more persuasive. On the other hand, if arguments are of poor quality, then the multiple source/multiple arguments condition produces counterarguing, and hence less persuasion.

This result provides a possible explanation of the link between the majority perception and differential argument quality found in this experiment.

Specifically, arguments advanced by the majority generate more favorable thoughts than do the minority arguments, and are perceived as of higher quality. Little counterarguing is likely to have occurred, since both sets of arguments are judged to be of relatively high quality.

The generation of favorable thoughts from the persuasive messages may be a matter of processing time. In this experiment one of the majority participants presents arguments first. Counterarguments are then presented by a minority participant. These two presentations take approximately equal amounts of time, and hence are expected to generate a similar number of favorable thoughts. When the remaining two participants express their agreement with Participant 1, however, the subject is likely to review Participant 1's arguments. This review makes it possible for the subject to generate more favorable thoughts, such as additional reasons for the soundness of these arguments. The minority participant does not have a similar opportunity. Hence subjects feel more favorable about the majority arguments and rate them as superior to the minority arguments.

This explanation does not contradict the Festinger (1950) explanation. Rather, it expands upon this hypothesis by specifying how people use the judgments of others to guide their perceptions of the quality of persuasive arguments. If others' judgments are reasoned, then they cause persons to reflect on them and to generate additional reasons for their soundness. If others' judgments are of poor quality, then they cause persons to reflect on them and to generate additional reasons for their incorrectness. In other words, they produce counterarguing.

While processing time may explain the differential generation of favorable thoughts, and while this process may explain the perceived majority-differential argument quality link in the data reported in this chapter, this explanation is unsatisfactory for the Harkins and Petty (1981a, 1981b) data. There is no reason the multiple source/multiple argument condition should result in more processing time than the single source/multiple argument condition. Hence there is no reason for more favorable thoughts in one condition than in the other. Nevertheless, Harkins and Petty's (1981b) data clearly show that the former condition produces more favorable thoughts than the latter condition.

The explanation of this result may reside in the nature of the topic. The issues involved were senior comprehensive examinations (Harkins & Petty, 1981a, 1981b) and raising the driving age to 21 (Harkins & Petty, 1981a). The subjects may well have reasoned that the examination proposal would not pass before they graduated, and thus would not apply to them. Moreover, many were probably close to 21 years of age, so that a change in the driving laws would be inapplicable to them as well. While it is impossible to be certain about this matter without more information about the Harkins and Petty materials and about their subjects, it is likely that these topics were uninvolving for the subject.

Furthermore, Petty, Cacioppo, and Goldman (1981) show that when the topic is not highly involving for the subject, the expertise of the source is a better predictor of attitude change than is the quality of the persuasive arguments. When the issue is highly involving, the quality of the persuasive arguments is a better predictor of attitude change than is the expertise of the source. It is reasonable to assume that subjects attributed high expertise to the stimulus persons appearing on the Harkins and Petty tapes. They were likely to reason that the experimenters selected stimulus persons precisely because they were extremely knowledgeable and/or articulate concerning the issue in question.

It is possible then that in the Harkins and Petty experiments the number of sources enhanced the subjects' perception of source expertise in the multiple-source conditions relative to the single-source conditions. The combined contributions of arguments and expertise may have produced the difference in favorable thoughts across conditions. While the employment issue used in this study is also not highly personally involving, the presence of a source arguing against the majority may have attenuated any expertise effect in these data. Moreover, the stimulus materials were presented in such a manner that the supposed discussion participants were seen as four undergraduate students who were drafted to participate in a study. Thus there was no particular reason to attribute high expertise to them.

While the model presented in this report has intuitively appealing causal links, and while it is consistent with the limited pertinent data base (see Vinokur & Burnstein, 1974), there may be conditions under which the model would either fail to fit relevant data or fit the data only with extremely different path coefficients. Such conditions may be predicted from data presented in an experiment by Laughlin and Earley (1982). Laughlin and Earley suggest that choice dilemma items may be arrayed on a continuum ranging from those items that are highly intellective to those that are highly judgmental. The former are those items for which there is a demonstrably correct solution. They are identified by extremely skewed pretest scores. The latter are those items that require group consensus on some subjective judgment. They are identified by relatively normally distributed pretest scores. Laughlin and Earley go on to suggest, and provide data to show, that a persuasive arguments process is more important in the former case, while a social comparison process is more important in the latter instance.

From pretest data it is clear that the choice dilemma item employed in this study falls toward the judgmental end of the intellective-judgmental continuum. Therefore, a social comparison process is expected to be an important component of the obtained choice shift. Items that fall toward the intellective end of the continuum may produce very different results. For example, for such items perceived majority may have no effect on differential argument quality. In fact, it may not be possible to find arguments that are strong and also support the "incorrect" solution for such an item. Putting the matter another way, in an experiment in which the type of item (intellective/judgmental), majority, and quality of arguments are manipulated, one would anticipate finding that majority and type of item interact to affect differential argument quality.

In summary, in this chapter data are presented that synthesize previous research. It is shown that both a persuasive arguments process and a social comparison process are important in predicting the nature of the choice shift. Moreover, the way in which these processes combine to produce the choice shift is detailed.

The lack of a strong majority effect in other studies (for example, see Boster et al., 1982; Boster & Hale, 1983) is easily explained by the model presented in this chapter. Since the majority effect is mediated by differential quality of arguments, the correlation of majority with opinion change is a product of three correlations (manipulated majority-perceived majority, perceived majority-differential argument quality, differential argument quality-opinion change). This triple product is necessarily lower than the correlation of those variables that have a direct impact on opinion change. This result does not imply that majority is less important than arguments in understanding the choice shift. Rather, both variables must be assessed before a coherent picture of the dynamics of the choice shift can be developed, at least for choice dilemma items that are judgmental in nature.

Speculation concerning the precesses underlying the links in the causal model suggests several important avenues for future research. First, there is an experimental design paradox. Can one manipulate the quality of arguments and majority independently? If the item is relatively judgmental, then majority is likely to affect persons' perceptions of the arguments. Thus independent manipulations would prove impossible. If, on the other hand, the item were intellective, then it would be difficult to find arguments that are strong risky/weak cautious if the "solution" to the item were cautious, or strong cautious/weak risky if the "solution" to the item were risky.

Second, there are several variables that, if controlled, might add important details to the causal model presented in Figure 14.1. For example, it is unclear what role personal involvement with the topic and expertise of the stimulus persons play in determining the direction and the magnitude of the choice shift.

Finally, this study suggests the importance of measuring additional variables that may mediate the variables in the causal model developed here. It is particularly important to assess individuals' favorable thoughts and counterarguments in order to test whether or not they mediate the relationship between perceived majority and differential argument quality.

REFERENCES

Bell, P. R., & Jamieson, B. D. (1970). Publicity of initial decisions and the risky shift phenomenon. *Journal of Experimental and Social Psychology, 6,* 329-345.

Boster, F. J., Fryrear, J. E., Mongeau, P. A., & Hunter, J. E. (1982). An unequal speaking linear discrepancy model: Implications for the polarity shift. In M. Burgoon (Ed.), *Communication yearbook 6* (pp. 395-418). Beverly Hills, CA: Sage.

Boster, F. J., & Hale, J. L. (1983, May). *Social comparison and the polarity shift.* Paper presented at the meeting of the International Communication Association, Dallas.

Boster, F. J., Mayer, M. E., Hunter, J. E., & Hale, J. L. (1980). Expanding the persuasive arguments explanation of the polarity shift: A linear discrepancy model. In D. Nimmo (Ed.), *Communication yearbook 4* (pp. 165-176). New Brunswick, NJ: Transaction.

Burnstein, E., & Vinokur, A. (1973). Testing two classes of theories about group induced shifts in individual choice. *Journal of Experimental Social Psychology, 9,* 123-137.

Burnstein, E., & Vinokur, A. (1975). What a person thinks upon learning he has chosen differently from others: Nice evidence for the persuasive arguments explanation of choice shifts. *Journal of Experimental Social Psychology, 11,* 412-426.

Burnstein, E. Vinokur, A., & Trope, Y. (1973). Interpersonal comparison versus persuasive argumentation: A more direct test of alternative explanations for group induced shifts in individual choice. *Journal of Experimental Social Psychology, 9,* 236-245.

Carlson, J. A., & Davis, C. M. (1971). Cultural values and the risky shift: A cross-cultural test in Uganda and the United States. *Journal of Personality and Social Psychology, 20,* 392-399.

Castore, C. H., Goodrich, T. S., & Peterson, K. (1970). The veridicality of subjective estimates of relative risks. *Psychonomic Science, 21,* 321-322.

Castore, C. H., & Roberts, J. C. (1972). Subjective estimates of own relative riskiness and risk taking following a group discussion. *Organizational Behavior and Human Performance, 7,* 107-120.

Clark, R. D., III, Crockett, W. H., & Archer, R. L. (1971). Risk-as-value hypothesis: The relation between perception of self, others, and the risky shift. *Journal of Personality and Social Psychology, 20,* 425-429.

Clark, R. D., III, & Willems, E. P. (1969). Risk preferences as related to judged consequences of failure. *Psychology Reports, 25,* 827-830.

Cronbach, L. J. (1951). Coefficient alpha and the internal structure of tests. *Psycholmetrika, 16,* 297-334.

Ebbeson, E. B., & Bowers, R. J. (1974). Proportion of risky to conservative arguments in a group discussion and the choice shift. *Journal of Personality and Social Psychology, 29,* 316-327.

Ferguson, D. A., & Vidmar, N. (1971). Effects of group discussion on estimates of culturally appropriate risk levels. *Journal of Personality and Social Psychology, 20,* 436-445.

Festinger, L. (1950). Informal social communication. *Psychological Review, 57,* 271-282.

Festinger, L. (1954). A theory of social comparison process. *Human Relations, 7,* 117-140.

Fraser, C., Gouge, C., & Billig, M. (1971). Risky shifts, cautious shifts, and group polarization. *European Journal of Social Psychology, 1,* 7-30.

Goethals, G. R., & Zanna, M. P. (1979). The role of social comparison in choice shifts. *Journal of Personality and Social Psychology, 37,* 1469-1476.

Harkins, S. G., & Petty, R. E. (1981a). Effects of source magnification of cognitive effort on attitudes: An information-processing view. *Journal of Personality and Social Psychology, 40,* 401-413.

Harkins, S. G., & Petty, R. E. (1981b). The multiple source effect in persuasion: The effects of distraction. *Personality and Social Psychology Bulletin, 1,* 627-635.

Horne, W. C., & Long, G. (1972). Effect of group discussion on universalistic-particularistic orientation. *Journal of Experimental and Social Psychology, 8,* 236-246.

Hunter, J. E., & Cohen, S. H. (1970). *PACKAGE: User's Manual.* East Lansing: Michigan State University, Computer Institute for Social Science Research.

Jellison, J. M., & Riskind, J. (1970). A social comparison of abilities interpretation of risk taking behavior. *Journal of Personality and Social Psychology, 15*, 375-390.

Jellison, J. M., Riskind, J. (1971). Attribution of risk to others as a function of their ability. *Journal of Personality and Social Psychology, 20*, 413-415.

Lamm, H., & Myers, D. G. (1978). Group induced polarization of attitudes and behavior. In L. Berkowitz (Ed.), *Advances in experimental social psychology* (Vol. 11). New York: Academic.

Lamm, H., Schaude, E., & Trommsdorff, G. (1971). Risky shift as a function of group members' value of risk and need for approval. *Journal of Personality and Social Psychology, 20*, 430-435.

Lamm, H., Trommsdorff, G., & Rost-Schaude, E. (1972). Self-image, perception of peers' risk acceptance and risky shift. *European Journal of Social Psychology, 2*, 255-272.

Laughlin, P. R., & Early, P. C. (1982). Social combination model, persuasive arguments theory, social comparison theory, and choice shift. *Journal of Personality and Social Psychology, 42*, 273-280.

Levinger, G., & Schneider, D. J. (1969). A test of the "risk as value" hypothesis. *Journal of Personality and Social Psychology, 11*, 165-169.

Main, E. G., & Walker, T. G. (1973). Choice shifts and extreme behavior: Judicial review in the federal courts. *Journal of Social Psychology, 91*, 215-222.

McCauley, C., Kogan, N., & Teger, A. I. (1971). Order effects in answering risk dilemma for self and others. *Journal of Personality and Social Psychology, 20*, 423-424.

Morgan, C. P., & Aram, J. D. (1975). The performance of arguments in the risky shift phenomenon. *Journal of Experimental Social Psychology, 11*, 25-34.

Myers, D. G., Bach, P. J., & Schreiber, F. B. (1974). Normative and informational effects of group interaction. *Sociometry, 37*, 275-286.

Myers, D. G., & Bishop, G. D. (1971). Enhancement of dominant attitudes in group discussion. *Journal of Personality and Social Psychology, 20*, 386-391.

Myers, D. G., Wong, D. W., & Murdoch, P. H. (1971). Discussion arguments, information about others' responses and the risky shift. *Psychonomic Science, 24*, 81-83.

Petty, R. E., Cacioppo, J. T., & Goldman, R. (1981). Personal involvement as a determinant of argument based persuasion. *Journal of Personality and Social Psychology, 41*, 847-855.

Pruitt, D. G. (1971). Choice shifts in group discussion: An introductory review. *Journal of Personality and Social Psychology, 20*, 339-360.

Roberts, J. C., & Castore, C. H. (1972). The effects of conformity, information, and confidence upon subject's willingness to take risk following a group discussion. *Organizational Behavior and Human Performance, 8*, 384-394.

Rosenberg, M. (1965). *Society and the adolescent self-image*. Princeton, NJ: Princeton University Press.

Schroeder, H. E. (1973). The risky choice shift as a general choice shift. *Journal of Personality and Social Psychology, 27*, 297-300.

Silverthorne, C. P. (1971). Information input and the group shift phenomenon in risk taking. *Journal of Personality and Social Psychology, 20*, 456-461.

Snyder, M. (1974). The self-monitoring of expressive behavior. *Journal of Personality and Social Psychology, 30*, 526-537.

Spielberger, C. D., Gorsuch, R. L., & Lushene, R. E. (1970). *Manual for the state-trait anxiety inventory*. Palo Alto, CA: Consulting Psychologists Press.

Stokes, J. P. (1971). Effets of familiarization and knowledge of others' odd choices on shifts to risk and caution. *Journal of Personality and Social Psychology, 20*, 407-412.

Stoner, J. A. F. (1968). Risky and cautious shifts in group decisions: The influence of widely held values. *Journal of Experimental Social Psychology, 4*, 442-459.

Teger, A. I., & Pruitt, D. G. (1967). Components of group risk taking. *Journal of Experimental Social Psychology, 3*, 189-205.

Vidmar, N., & Burdeny, T. C. (1971). Effects of group size and item type on the "risky shift" effect. *Canadian Journal of Behavioral Science, 3*, 393-407.

Vinokur, A., & Burnstein, E. (1974). Effects of partially shared persuasive arguments on group induced shifts. *Journal of Personality and Social Psychology, 29*, 305-315.

Vinokur, A., & Burnstein, E. (1978a). Depolarization of attitudes in groups. *Journal of Personality and Social Psychology, 36,* 872-885.
Vinokur, A., & Burnstein, E. (1978b). Novel argumentation and attitude change: The case for polarization following discussion. *European Journal of Social Psychology, 8,* 335-348.
Wallach, M. A., & Kogan, N. (1965). The roles of information, discussion, and consensus in group risk taking. *Journal of Experimental Social Psychology, 1,* 1-19.
Wallach, M. A., & Wing, C. W., Jr. (1968). Is risk a value? *Journal of Personality and Social Psychology, 9,* 101-106.
Willems, E. P., & Clark, R. D., III. (1969). Dependence of the risky shift on instructions: A replication. *Psychological Reports, 25,* 811-814.
Willems, E. P., & Clark, R. D., III. (1971). Shift towards risk and heterogeneity of groups. *Journal of Experimental Social Psychology, 7,* 304-312.

III ● INTERPERSONAL COMMUNICATION

15 ● Affect and Social Information Acquisition: Sit Back, Relax, and Tell Me About Yourself

KATHY KELLERMANN ●
CHARLES R. BERGER

University of Wisconsin–Madison ● Northwestern University

A LTHOUGH considerable research attention has been directed to understanding the various baises and shortcomings that plague social decision makers (Kahneman, Slovic, & Tversky, 1982; Nisbett & Ross, 1980), relatively little work has been done to explain how persons acquire the social information they process. Snyder's work on hypothesis testing (see Snyder, 1981, for review) has revealed that when persons have a hypothesis they wish to test about another, they tend to ask questions that will confirm the existence of the hypothesized trait rather than ask questions that disconfirm its existence. However, Troupe and Bassok (1982) found that under certain conditions persons seek diagnostic information rather than confirmatory information about others. In addition to this line of research is a study by Major (1980) that revealed that persons utilize relatively little information made available to them when they are asked to make attributions about others.

In general, the hypothesis-testing research has placed persons in the position of asking questions in order to obtain information about target others. However, Berger (1979) suggested that social information seekers can employ three broad classes of strategies to seek information relevant to their goals: (1) passive, (2) active, and (3) interactive. Passive strategies involve

AUTHORS' NOTE: We would like to thank Angela Bognano, Hyo-Seong Lee, Tom Nowinski, Pip Powell, Lynn Turner, and Lynda Willer for their coding efforts and Dan Berger for drawing the figures.

Correspondence and requests for reprints: Kathy Kellermann, Department of Communication Arts, Vilas Communication Hall, University of Wisconsin, Madison, WI 53706.

the unobtrusive observation of target persons with no direct interaction between the observer and the target. Research directed toward understanding these strategies was reported by Berger and Perkins (1978, 1979) and by Berger and Douglas (1981). When using active strategies, observers structure a set of conditions to which the target person reacts, similar to the way in which a social scientist might set up a laboratory experiment. Active strategies do not involve direct interaction between observers and targets, however. Interactive strategies require direct interaction between observers and targets. Among the information acquisition modes that are possible here are interrogation, self-disclosure, and deception detection. Persons can ask questions to obtain information and/or disclose information about themselves with the hope that their partners will reciprocate their disclosures (Gouldner, 1960; Sermat & Smyth, 1973; Worthy, Gary, & Kahn, 1969).

In the domain of interactive strategies, Berger and Kellermann (1983) reported findings concerning patterns of question-asking in initial encounters. Their findings suggested that interactive information acquisition strategies might be placed in a two-dimensional space defined by *efficiency* and *social appropriateness*. Thus interrogation might be a relatively efficient way by which to acquire information from another, but it might be perceived to be socially inappropriate because of its intrusiveness. Self-disclosure, by contrast, is a more subtle way to acquire social information, but it might be somewhat less efficient because of its indirectness. A third strategy, not considered by Berger (1979) but mentioned by research participants in the Berger and Kellermann (1983) study, is that of *relaxing the target person* as a means of inducing him or her to reveal information. Obviously, this interactive strategy is extremely indirect and unobtrusive, but it may also be the least efficient of the three strategies discussed here. A relaxed target may reveal considerable amounts of information about himself or herself but not the particular information that the observer desires. Thus *control* of the interactive sequence underlies the efficiency dimension and is in tension with the social appropriateness of behaviors employed for seeking information. The focus of the present study is on the kinds of verbal and nonverbal behaviors displayed by persons who are attempting to extract information from their conversational partners using the relaxation strategy.

Psychotherapeutic literature dealing with therapist-client communication generally argues that in order to encourage clients to verbalize about their problems, therapists must establish a permissive (Ruesch, 1961) or a warm (Rogers, 1951) relationship with their clients. Both of these authors emphasize the necessity of establishing a nonevaluative atmosphere in which clients feel free to talk about their feelings and perceptions without fear of negative sanctions.

From the point of view of the information seeker, we argue that under most conditions seekers will attempt to ingratiate themselves to target persons in order to encourage them to reveal information about themselves. Employing relaxation as an information-gaining strategy involves two distinct steps: (1) inducing the target to like and feel at ease with the seeker; (2) as a consequence, the target becomes willing to talk about himself or herself. Extant theory and research have investigated both of these links. First, Jones (1964) and Jones and Wortman (1973) discussed and documented a number of strategies persons may use to ingratiate themselves to each other. In addition, Rosenfeld (1966) found that when persons were asked either to seek or to avoid gaining approval from others, there were a considerable number of differences in individuals' verbal and nonverbal behaviors. Approval seekers spoke more frequently and for longer durations than did avoiders. Moreover, seekers showed more smiles, positive head nods, and gesticulations than did their approval-avoiding counterparts. In a subsequent study, Rosenfeld (1967) reported that approving responses from an interviewer encouraged interviewees to reciprocate both smiles and positive head nods more frequently. In a similar study, Mehrabian and Williams (1969) found that persons who were asked to attempt to persuade another were more likely to display greater eye contact, increased rates of positive head nodding, gesticulation, facial activity, speech rate, speech volume, and intonation. Obviously, there is some degree of convergence between the findings of this study and Rosenfeld's (1966), even though participants in these studies were asked to achieve what are ostensibly different interaction objectives. One explanation for this convergence is that those persons in the persuasion study were employing the implicit hypothesis that to be persuasive with their targets they must first win their approval. In support of such reasoning, Clore and McGuire (1974) found that the primary determinants of attraction to conversational partners were the extent to which they displayed positive responses, negative responses, and dissimilarity statements during their interactions. Other studies (Bond, 1972; Coutts, Schneider, & Montgomery, 1980; Ickes, Patterson, Rajecki, & Tanford, 1982) examined the impact of preinteraction expectations on subsequent interaction behavior.

Research investigating the second link in our proposed chain has examined the relationship between liking and self-disclosure. Our concern here is with the proposition that liking induces self-disclosure rather than the opposite relationship, although attempts have been made to study both causal directions (for reviews, see Cozby, 1973; Taylor, 1979). Colson (1968) found that persons who received social approval from an interviewer were more likely to disclose information about themselves. Similarly, Taylor, Altman, and Sorrentino (1969) reported that persons receiving positive reinforcement both talked more and disclosed more about themselves than did persons receiving negative reinforcement. However, Taylor et al. failed to find support for Aronson and Linder's (1965) gain-loss of esteem hypothesis, which asserts that persons who give constant approval to others will be less attractive to them than will persons who first give disapproval and then give approval.

While the research reviewed above supports the notions that persons who are given the goal of ingratiating themselves to others will display verbal and nonverbal behaviors that are different from those of persons not instructed to do so and that persons who are more attractive are more likely to receive both more talk and more intimate disclosures from others, there is no direct evidence to support the proposition that persons who are interested in gaining information from others will adjust their verbal and nonverbal behavior in ways that will make themselves potentially more likable to the targets of their information-seeking attempts.

Thus conversational participants in the present study were given one of the following three conversational goals: (1) find out as *much* as possible about their partner (High Seekers), (2) find out as *little* as possible about their partner (Low Seekers) or (3) carry out a "normal" interaction (Normals). Examination of verbal and nonverbal behaviors, observers' ratings, and participants' self-reports were performed to determine the ways in which persons given these conversational goals would differ from each other. Based upon the research reviewed earlier, we expected that persons placed in the High Seeker role would be most likely to display behaviors that would enhance their attractiveness and put their conversational partners at ease, while Low Seekers would be least likely to manifest such behaviors. We felt that normals would fall somewhere between the High and Low Seekers.

METHOD

Since the data analyzed in the present study are part of a larger project, another segment of which has been reported previously (Berger & Kellermann, 1983), only a summary of methods and procedures will be presented here. The interested reader can consult Berger and Kellermann (1983) for a more detailed discussion.

Participants

Participants in this study were 96 Northwestern University undergraduates enrolled in various communication courses. These individuals were paired in 48 dyads.

Procedure

Participants were randomly assigned to one of four conditions. The conditions were created by varying instructional sets given the participants before they entered the interaction situation. Participants were asked not to talk about their instructions during the interaction, and participants were strangers to each other. After reading their instructions, participants interacted for a period of five minutes, during which their interactions were videotaped with their knowledge. Participants were then ushered into separate rooms, where they indicated on audiotape what their goals were in the interaction and how they achieved those goals.

Manipulations

Three different sets of instructions were used to create four conditions. The first part of the instructions was identical for all participants. Those receiving High Seeker instructions were told to find out as much as possible about their partners during their conversations. Low Seekers were instructed to find out as little as possible about their conversational partners. The wording of these instructions was virtually identical, with the exception of the critical wording differences. Normal instructions said nothing about how much or how little information a participant was to acquire from his or her partner. The instructions contained no directions concerning how much or how little information participants should reveal about themselves, nor did the instructions indicate how long the conversations would last. No suggestions were made concerning how conversational goals might be reached. Four types of dyads were created randomly by pairing persons with similar or different instructions: High-High, Low-Low, High-Low, and Normal-Normal. The Normal-Normal dyads served as a baseline from which to assess between-condition differences.

Interaction Indices

Three sources of data were employed to investigate relaxation as an information-gaining strategy. First, coders who were blind to the experimental conditions of participants independently recorded judgments about the frequency and duration of various verbal and nonverbal behaviors. Second, judges made several global judgments (impressions) about the interaction participants on a number of rating scales. Finally, the postinteraction protocols were analyzed to determine the extent to which the participants could verbalize about their use of the relaxation strategy. For analytic purposes, the five-minute interactions were divided into ten 30-second intervals. The frequency and duration judgments were made on the basis of these intervals; however, the global judgments were made only once at the

Table 15.1
Relaxation Indices

	r	n
Frequency/Duration Indices		
questions (frequency)	.88	40
verbal backchannels (frequency)	.96	40
positive head nods (frequency)	.93	40
smiles (frequency)	.62	480
forward body lean (duration)	.99	50
vocalizations		
average duration	.79	10
total duration	.96	10
frequency	.86	10
pauses		
average duration	.83	10
total duration	.89	10
frequency	.77	10
switching pauses		
average duration	.82	10
total duration	.86	10
frequency	.82	10
floor possessions		
average duration	.89	10
total duration	.99	10
frequency	.85	10
simultaneous speech		
average duration	.68	10
total duration	.77	10
frequency	.80	10
Global Judgments		
evaluative-nonevaluative	.77	10
pleasant-unpleasant	1.00	10
directive-nondirective	.94	10
relaxation of self	.86	48
make partner comfortable	.95	48
encourage partner to talk	.68	48
fluency	.77	48
social appropriateness	.58	48
efficiency	.67	36

Note: For frequency/duration indices, n represents judgments across 10 time intervals for n/10 number of conversations. For global judgments, n represents ratings of n different individuals in n different conversations. Reliabilities are expressed as correlations between coders.

conclusion of the five-minute interaction. Both the frequency/duration measures and the global judgments were selected as empirical indicators of the relaxation strategy. These indices are displayed in Table 15.1, along with coder reliabilities for each index.

Consistent with previous research on approval seeking and positive reinforcement, the frequency of questions (Mehrabian, 1971), verbal back-channels (Yngve, 1970), positive head nods (Mehrabian & Ksionzky, 1971), and smiles (Mehrabian, 1971) was coded by one of three pairs of observers. Frequency counts were also made for speech parameters of vocalizations, pauses, switching pauses, floor possessions, and simultaneous speech, employing Jaffe and Feldstein's (1970) definitions.[1] These speech parameters have been isolated as important expressive behaviors (for review, see Cappella, 1981; Harper, Wiens, & Matarazzo, 1978; Siegman & Feldstein, 1979). In addition, the average and total durations of these speech parameters were obtained. Duration information was also collected on forward body lean (Mehrabian & Ksionzky, 1971). These behaviors have been identified by Mehrabian (1971) as affiliative, relaxing, or ingratiation-based behaviors. Intercoder reliabilities were calculated over 30-second intervals for a varying number of conversations, with four as a minimum. As can be seen from Table 15.1, the coders were able to count and time reliably these behavioral indices of relaxation.

The global judgments employed to index the relaxation strategy were obtained by having observers rate each participant on the extent to which the participant was pleasant (Mehrabian & Ksionzky, 1971), evaluative, and directive, measures suggested by the psychotherapeutic literature (Rogers, 1951). Furthermore, observers made global judgments about the extent to which participants were relaxed or comfortable (self-relaxation), the extent to which participants tried to make their partner relaxed or comfortable (other-comfortableness), and the extent to which participants encouraged their partners to talk (encouragement). A dyadic rating was made of the fluency of the conversation and assigned to each participant in the conversation. For theoretic purposes, participants were judged on the social appropriateness of their behavior and the efficiency with which they pursued their interaction goal. Given the nature of the efficiency judgment, raters were informed of each participant's goal; Normals, who were not given an explicit interaction goal, were not rated. Seven-point scales were used for all ratings of global judgments (1 = low; 7 = high).

Postinteraction Protocols

The postinteraction protocols were analyzed in two different ways. First, two judges, blind to the condition of the participants, read each protocol and estimated which instruction set the participant had received and

Table 15.2
Distribution of Relaxation-Related Techniques
as Reported by Participants

Technique	Frequency of Mention			
	High Seekers	Low Seekers	Normals	Totals
Encouragement	4	1	0	5
Discouragement	1	3	0	4
Comfort (total)	7	0	7	14
make self comfortable	(0)	(0)	(4)	(4)
make other comfortable	(6)	(0)	(1)	(7)
make conversation comfortable	(1)	(1)	(1)	(3)
Discomfort (total)	0	5	0	5
make self uncomfortable	(0)	(2)	(0)	(2)
make other uncomfortable	(0)	(1)	(0)	(1)
make conversation uncomfortable	(0)	(2)	(0)	(2)
Positive feedback (total)	7	2	2	11
behavior	(5)	(2)	(0)	(7)
appearance	(2)	(0)	(2)	(4)
Negative feedback (total)	0	16	0	16
behavior	(0)	(6)	(0)	(6)
appearance	(0)	(10)	(0)	(10)
Positive self-presentation	2	0 ·	3	5
Negative self-presentation	0	3	0	3
Noncontrolling	6	1	2	9
Controlling	0	3	0	3
Total strategies mentioned				75

whether the instructions had been understood. The two judges agreed 100 percent of the time on these estimates. The postinteraction protocols were also coded by two judges with reference to the strategies that participants indicated they used to achieve their goals. Persons who indicated that they utilized relaxation or discomfort strategies in some way were coded into one of the categories shown in Table 15.2.

Strategy coding was done in two steps. First, judges independently read each protocol and decided whether or not the participant indicated that he or she had used relaxation or discomfort to achieve the objective. Across all participants' protocols, the two judges agreed 94.7 percent of the time on this judgment. Disagreements were discussed until a decision could be made. For those participants identified as using relaxation or discomfort, the specific techniques mentioned were then coded into the categories shown in Table 15.2. Since a participant could mention more than one technique, some individuals contributed multiple responses to the categories shown in Table 15.2. Of the 75 strategies mentioned, two judges agreed on the placement of these strategies into categories 93.4 percent of the time. As before, disagreements were discussed until they could be placed into a category.

The encouragement and discouragement categories in Table 15.2 refer to the extent to which the participant aided or hindered talking by the conversational partner; whether the partner was "drawn out" or "interrupted" and "cut off." The comfort and discomfort categories refer to the ease (informality) or awkwardness (formality) of the interaction. Positive feedback behavior includes head nods, backchannels ("uh-huh," saying "yes") and other positive cues, whereas negative feedback behavior references gaze avoidance, crossed arms, crossed legs, distant body position, and negative cues. Positive feedback appearance refers to such behaviors identified as "appearing interested," while negative feedback appearance includes "reacting strangely," "being nonresponsive," and "being silent." A positive self-presentation includes being "friendly," "interesting," "expressive," and "pleasant," whereas "rudeness" and "insensitivity" define the negative self-presentation category. Noncontrolling and controlling refer to directing the action in the conversation, noncontrolling including such ideas as "don't push," "don't direct conversation," "just talk," and "listen." Controlling is referenced by such statements as "direct conversation" and "dominate conversation."

RESULTS

For all results to be reported, one participant from each dyad was randomly deleted from the analysis to assure independence of observations in the various conditions. This procedure was deemed necessary because between-dyad correlations within conditions revealed significant correlations on many of the measures. This deletion procedure presents spurious interactions stemming from mutual influence effects from being reported (Kraemer & Jacklin, 1979). Thus the data from 48 individuals (one individual per dyad) were used in all analyses.

Manipulation Checks

All of the participants included in this analysis accurately identified their interaction goal related to information seeking. Furthermore, judges reliably ($r = .92$) made ratings on five-point scales of the extent to which each participant sought information from his or her partner. A one-way ANOVA by the participant's condition (High Seeker, Low Seeker, Normal) on these information-seeking ratings revealed a significant main effect ($F = 31.24$, df $= 2/93$, $p < .001$), with the mean for Normals at 3.15, High Seekers at 3.88, and Low Seekers at 2.11. Newman-Keuls tests indicated that each group was significantly different from every other group ($p < .05$). Thus not only were the participants aware of their information-seeking instructions, but judges were able to detect differences in information-seeking behavior that were consistent with the instruction sets.

That the use of the relaxation strategy varied significantly by the participant's information-seeking condition was demonstrated in two ways. First, inspection of the postinteraction protocol data presented in Table 15.2 reveals that High Seekers reportedly encouraged their partners to talk; made themselves, their partners, and the conversations comfortable; used positive feedback; employed positive self-presentations; and were noncontrolling in the conversation. Low Seekers, by contrast, discouraged their partners from talking; made themselves, their partners, and the conversation uncomfortable; employed negative feedback; offered negative self-images; and controlled the conversation. Second, the extent to which participants tried to make their conversational partners comfortable was analyzed. Ratings of information seeking correlated .41 with ratings of other-comfortableness. A one-way ANOVA by participant's information-seeking condition revealed that other-comfortableness varied significantly as a function of the participant's condition ($F = 4.87$, df $= 2/45$, $p < .01$). Newman-Keuls tests indicated that High Seekers ($M = 5.03$, $SD = 1.44$) and Normals ($M = 5.33$, $SD = 1.33$) tried significantly more than did Low Seekers ($M = 3.77$, $SD = 1.69$) to make their conversational partners comfortable. Thus not only was the experimental induction of information seeking successful, but the underlying assumption of variations in relaxation strategy use was verified as well.

Intermeasure Relationships

Given the potential for the various measures employed as indices of relaxation to be correlated, a factor analysis was conducted to determine if combined measures could be constructed. In order to include the behavioral measures (frequency/duration ratings), a total for each behavior was computed for the conversation. A principal components factor analysis with orthogonal rotation was conducted on all totaled behavioral measures and on all global judgments excluding social appropriateness and efficiency; information seeking was included. Caution in interpreting the results is necessary, as the matrix to be decomposed was nearly singular, one negative eigenvalue occurred, and the iterative procedure was stopped after only two iterations because the communalities exceeded one.

Table 15.3
Factor Analysis of Overall Measures

	Factors						
Measure	Talk Time	Atmosphere	Monologue Rhythm	Control	Turn Taking	Interaction Rhythm	Nonverbal Backchannels
	1	2	3	4	5	6	7
Average vocalization duration	.68						
Total vocalization duration	.93						
Average floor possession length	.75						
Total floor possession length	.89				−.41		
Fluency		.59					
Self-comfort		.66					
Other-comfort		.76					
Pleasantness		.67					
Vocalization frequency			.70		.59		
Pause number			.91				
Total pause length			.89				
Information seeking				.79			
Question frequency				.75	.42		
Directiveness				.69			
Encouragement		.42		.67			
Switching pause frequency					.64		
Floor possession frequency					.92		
Average switching pause duration						.88	
Total switching pause duration						.92	
Head nods							.80
Smiles							.69
Eigenvalue	6.70	4.29	3.41	1.80	1.52	1.35	1.20
% variance explained	23.90	15.30	12.20	6.40	5.40	4.80	4.30

For the 28 variables entered into the factor analysis, 7 factors emerged (with eigenvalues greater than one) explaining 72 percent of the variance. Of the 28 variables, 7 failed to load on any of the seven factors—average pause duration, average simultaneous speech duration, total simultaneous speech duration, simultaneous speech frequency, evaluation, body lean duration, and verbal backchannels. Table 15.3 summarizes the results of the factor analysis for the seven factors that did emerge. The first factor, labeled "talk time," essentially refers to utterance duration. The second factor, "atmosphere," is based on perceptions of relaxation, comfort, and pleasantness. The third factor, "monologue rhythm," is defined by speech parameters governing verbal production *within* a floor possession. The "control" dimension (Factor 4) appears to define the extent to which a participant directs the conversation—that is, controls it. "Turn-taking" (Factor 5) is self-explanatory: the number of switching pauses must necessarily (by definition) be correlated with the number of floor possessions. Factor 6, "interaction rhythm," defines the patterning *between* speaker changes of the floor. Factor 7, "nonverbal backchannels," indicates that head nods and smiles are highly related.

It is clear the factor solution is not optimal. The potentially unreliable results stemming from problems in the rotation process, and the fact that 28 measures are reduced to only 7 factors and 7 leftover measures, seriously undermine the ability to analyze the data in reduced form. Furthermore, similar loadings of totaled behavioral measures does *not* imply that similar trends in these measures will occur over time. Consequently, the factor analysis was used only as a guideline for generating expectations about which measures might perform similarly across conditions and over time. No reduced or composite measures were constructed.

Information Seeking and Relaxation

It was hypothesized that the participant's information-seeking set would influence the use of the relaxation strategy. One-way ANOVAs were employed to analyze the global judgments; repeated measures ANOVAs were used to analyze the behavioral indicators that were repeated over the ten 30-second intervals. Since no interaction effects were located for information-seeking conditions over time, the main effects for all measures will be reported as a group in order to assess the hypothesized differences in relaxation strategy use. The results will be grouped according to the factors emerging in the factor analysis.

Nonverbal backchannels (head nods, smiles) operated similarly across information-seeking conditions; that is, neither varied significantly. However, the number of verbal backchannels was found to be different across information-seeking conditions ($F = 3.15$, df $= 2/45$, $p < .05$). Newman-

Keuls tests indicated that High Seekers (M = 22.26, SD = 11.99) and Normals (M = 20.00, SD = 7.68) engaged in more verbal backchanneling than did Low Seekers (M = 14.53, SD = 6.73). These data indicate that the *form* of backchanneling, verbal or nonverbal, matters in discriminating the use of a relaxation strategy. Like nonverbal backchannels, forward body lean duration did not differ significantly across information-seeking conditions.

Talk time speech parameters (total and average vocalization length, total and average floor possession duration) also failed to vary significantly by the condition of the participant. Similarly, monologue rhythm speech parameters did not vary in response to differences in participants' information-seeking levels. However, a significant condition of participant (High Seeker, Low Seeker) × condition of partner (High Seeker, Low Seeker) interaction did occur for vocalization frequency (F = 4.45, df = 1/32, p < .04). Analysis of the simple effects revealed that when High Seekers were paired with Low Seekers (M = 77.57, SD = 27.07), the frequency of vocalization was higher (F = 7.77, df = 1/32, p < .05) than when Highs were paired with other Highs (M = 56.33, SD = 13.87) or when Lows were paired with other Lows (F = 5.45, df = 1/32, p < .05; M = 55.17, SD = 17.53). Lows paired with High Seekers (M = 62.60, SD = 20.68) produced equivalent frequencies of vocalizations as Lows paired with other Lows or Highs paired with Highs. Thus vocalization frequency is higher for High-Low dyads than for any other pairing. In general, however, talk time and monologue rhythm parameters tend not to be affected by differing levels of information seeking.

The turn-taking parameters did not differ significantly by information-seeking conditions; however, the interaction parameters (average and total switching pause duration) did vary as a function of information-seeking conditions (average switching pause duration: F = 3.32, df = 2/45, p < .04; total switching pause duration: F = 4.43, df = 2/45, p < .02). While Newman-Keuls tests were unable to locate the between-groups differences for average switching pause duration (Highs: M = 1.33, SD = .65; Normals: M = 1.32, SD = .50; Lows: M=2.46, SD = 2.31), the means are dispersed in a manner similar to the means of total switching pause duration. In the case of total switching pause duration, Newman-Keuls tests revealed that Lows (M = 52.77, SD = 47.27) spent significantly more total time engaging in switching pauses than did Normals (M = 27.50, SD = 14.10) or Highs (M = 24.79, SD = 16.17). The frequencies underlying rhythms of floor exchange, therefore, appear less important than the time/duration parameters in discriminating use of a relaxation strategy. Closely related to these results is the finding that Low Seekers paused significantly longer, on the average, than did High Seekers or Normals (F = 5.47, df = 2/45, p < .007; Highs: M = 1.43, SD = .62; Normals: M = 1.63, SD = .83; Lows: M = 2.58, SD = 1.56). Thus duration of various pausing behaviors appears to be a strong indicator of strategies of relaxation or discomfort. Simultaneous speech in terms of average length, number of interruptions, or total length did not differ significantly by information-seeking conditions.

The behavioral measures indicate that that High Seekers, compared to Lows and Normals, used more verbal backchannels, paused for less time within their own vocalizations, and paused for less time when gaining possession of the floor. These behavioral measures correlate with the extent to which participants made their partners comfortable (verbal backchannels: $r = .36$; average pause duration: $r = .45$; average switching pause duration: $r = -.45$; total switching pause duration: $r = -.44$), suggesting that these differences in behavior are related to varying use of relaxation and/or discomfort strategies.

The perceptual correlates of relaxation were analyzed as well. The effects of global judgments loading on the atmosphere dimension (fluency, self-relaxation, other-comfortableness, pleasantness) did not perform similarly when analyzed as a function of information-seeking conditions. Fluency did not vary significantly across instructional sets. It was reported earlier that High Seekers and Normals attempted to make their partners more comfortable than did Low Seekers. In a similar manner, pleasantness was found to differ across information-seeking conditions ($F = 3.87$, $df = 2/45$, $p < .03$). High Seekers ($M = 4.58$, $SD = 1.12$) and Normals ($M = 4.42$, $SD = .90$) were judged to be significantly more pleasant than were Lows ($M = 3.71$, $SD = .85$). These findings indicate that other-directed behavior (other-comfortableness, pleasantness) more likely discriminates use of relaxation or discomfort strategies than do self-directed (fluency, self-relaxation) behaviors in creating an atmosphere for the interaction.

Such attempts as are made to create a more positive atmosphere might be the result of high levels of control behavior; that is, individuals exhibiting control in the interaction might try to decrease any negative effects of such control by creating a more positive atmosphere with reference to the conversational partner. Measures of control differed significantly across information-seeking conditions (directiveness: $F = 6.42$, $df \neq 2\%45$, $p < .004$; encouragement: $F = 4.84$, $df = 2/45$, $p < .01$; information seeking: $F = 13.88$ $df = 2/45$, $p < .001$; question asking; $F = 7.45$, $df = 2/45$, $p < .002$). In contrast to the information-seeking analyses reported earlier, Newman-Keuls tests indicate that while Low Seekers are less directive ($M = 3.24$, $SD = 1.82$), less encouraging of talk ($M = 4.24$, $SD = 1.48$), and less inclined to ask questions ($M = 5.65$, $SD = 4.77$) than are High Seekers (directiveness: $M = 5.21$, $SD = 1.55$; encouragement: $M = 5.50$, $SD = .99$; question asking: $M = 13.78$, $SD = 8.26$), Normals cannot be differentiated from Highs on the basis of directiveness ($M = 4.33$, $SD = 1.56$), encouragement ($M = 5.38$, $SD = 1.46$), or question asking ($M = 12.92$, $SD = 6.79$). Thus, contrary to their self-reports, High Seekers employed control techniques more than did Lows.

The evaluative aspects of verbal interaction did not differ significantly by the participant's information-seeking condition. These findings indicate that High Seekers did attempt to make their conversational partners more comfortable than did Lows while seeking social information, indicated by the differences in the use of verbal backchanneling, switching pause duration, and pause duration. Furthermore, Highs were perceived as being more pleasant, directive, and encouraging than were Lows.

Determinants of Relaxation

Given that relaxation is not the sole interactive strategy individuals might employ to seek social information from others, exploratory data analyses were conducted to assist in the isolation of behaviors and judgments that typically accompany relaxation strategy use. Participants were divided into three approximately equal groups based on the extent to which they were judged to have made their partners comfortable, as this measure indi-

Table 15.4
Discriminant Analysis of Other Comfort

Standardized Discriminant Coefficients	
Variable	Coefficient
fluency	.91
pause frequency	.90
total switching pause duration	.84
question frequency	.66
self-relaxation	.60
positive head nod frequency	.50
average floor possession length	−.44
body lean duration	.37
verbal backchannels	.28
efficiency	−.22

Group Centroids	
low other-comfort	−1.56
medium other-comfort	1.08
high other-comfort	1.26

Classification Analysis (percentages)			
	lows	mediums	highs
lows	85.0	15.0	0.0
mediums	8.7	73.9	17.4
highs	0.0	20.0	80.0
			79.17 correct

cates use of relaxation most directly. A stepwise discriminant analysis was conducted to isolate the most important indices of the relaxation strategy. Although two discriminant functions are possible, sufficient discriminating information did not remain after the first discriminant function to justify use and/or examination of a second (Wilks's lambda = .70, chi-square = 14.54, df = 9, p < .10). The canonical correlation for the first discriminant function was .83. Table 15.4 summarizes the results of the discriminant analysis, including information on the standardized discriminant coefficients, group centroids, and the classification analysis summary table.

Of the 29 measures in Table 15.1, 10 are contained in the first discriminant function, although the frequency of interruptions (simultaneous speech), average vocalization duration, and encouragement to talk were entered and then removed. The most important discriminators of the relaxation strategy are fluency, pause frequency, and switching pause duration; as these measures increase, more extensive use of the relaxation strategy occurs. Relaxation is also positively related to the number of questions asked and the relaxation of the target. As head nods, duration of forward body lean, and verbal backchannel frequency increase, the social information seeker is perceived as increasing the attempt to make his or her conversational partner comfortable. Shorter floor possessions are also indicative of relaxation strategy use. In partial confirmation of the two-dimensional space posited to underlie interactive information-seeking strategies, efficiency was perceived to decrease as employment of a relaxation strategy increased. The classification analysis indicates that the discriminant function has a great deal of power, in that almost 80 percent of the participants could be correctly classified into their actual group.

Relating Behaviors to Judgments

The results of the factor analysis suggested that behavioral indicators of relaxation do not overlap to any significant degree with judgments of relaxation. To explore further the behavioral basis of the various global judgments, a series of stepwise regression analyses were conducted. Each global judgment was regressed on behavioral measures totaled for the conversation as a whole. The control factor (question-asking, information seeking, directiveness, encouragement) can be viewed as a relatively stable factor given the ANOVA results across information-seeking conditions. Similarly, the regression analyses isolate consistent predictor measures that are behaviorally based. Given that question-asking is a *behavioral* measure, it was expected that interrogation frequency should serve as a significant predictor of other control factors. As can be seen in Table 15.5, question-asking frequency is an important behavioral cue in all three remaining control measures—directiveness, information seeking, and encouragement. The total switching

Table 15.5
Regression Analyses on Control Factor Measures

Dependent Variable	R^2	Adj R^2	Predictors	Beta	F	p
Information seeking	.60	.57	question frequency	.61	37.16	.001
			total switching pause duration	−.39	13.57	.001
			total simultaneous speech duration	−.27	6.94	.012
Directiveness	.46	.41	question frequency	.54	16.46	.001
			floor possession frequency	−.44	9.74	.003
			total switching pause duration	−.28	5.72	.021
			vocalization frequency	.27	4.30	.044
Encouragement	.48	.46	question frequency	.53	22.63	.001
			total switching pause duration	−.31	7.88	.007

pause duration is another consistent cue in all three judgment control factors; the more time allotted to switching pauses, the less controlling the participant is perceived to be—the less directive, the less encouraging, the less seeking of information.

While the judgment measures of control have similar behavioral bases, these judgments can be differentiated in terms of behavioral cues only serving as predictors of one of the judgments. For example, the more time a dyad is engaged in simultaneous speech, the less a participant is perceived to be seeking information. Directiveness also has behavioral correlates of floor possession and vocalization frequency; as the number of floor possessions increases, directiveness decreases, whereas vocalization frequency is related positively to directiveness. More exchanges of the floor apparently permit less dominate or directive behavior by one participant in the dyad. Similarly, attempts to gain the floor rapidly (simultaneous speech, short switching pause duration) are used as cues for judgments of control.

The atmosphere factor (fluency, self-relaxation, other-comfortableness, pleasantness) tends not to be as cohesive in terms of the behavioral correlates of the individual measures. Table 15.6 summarizes the regression results for the atmosphere factor measures. While the ANOVA results indicated pleasantness and other-comfortableness performed similarly across information-seeking conditions, the regression analyses suggest that the behavioral cues for fluency and other-comfortableness are most similar. For

Table 15.6
Regression Analyses of Atmosphere Measures

Dependent Variable	R^2	Adj R^2	Predictors	Beta	F	p
Fluency	.41	.40	average pause duration	−.64	31.70	.001
Self-relaxation	.13	.11	switching pause frequency	−.36	7.02	.011
Other-comfortableness	.37	.34	average pause duration	−.62	24.53	.001
			pause frequency	.33	7.07	.011
Pleasantness	.25	.23	verbal backchannel frequency	.50	15.13	.001

these latter two judgments, average pause duration is inversely correlated. While pausing behavior of some kind tends to be the cue for most of the atmosphere measures, verbal backchannels serve as a behavioral predictor of pleasantness. As verbal backchannels and average pause duration are negatively correlated ($r = -.27$), the filling of pauses appears to be the cue for pleasantness judgments.

Relaxation Behaviors Over Time

The factor analysis of relaxation measures was computed on totals for the behavioral indices across the conversation. While totals for behavioral indices may load similarly on dimensions, trends over time may differ. However, the factor analysis results will serve as guidelines for expectations about the form of trends over time. Repeated measures ANOVAs over the ten 30-second intervals were conducted to examine the consistency of the use of behavioral relaxation techniques over the course of the conversation.

Nonverbal backchannels (head nods, smiles) behave differently over time. The frequency of head nods did not vary significantly over time, whereas the frequency of smiles did ($F = 5.35$, df = $9/405$, $p < .001$). A trend analysis revealed significant linear ($F = 21.10$, df = $1/45$, $p < .001$), quadratic ($F = 7.01$, df = $1/45$, $p < .01$), and octal ($F = 5.65$, df = $1/45$, $p < .02$) components. Figure 15.1, which displays the relationship of smiles to

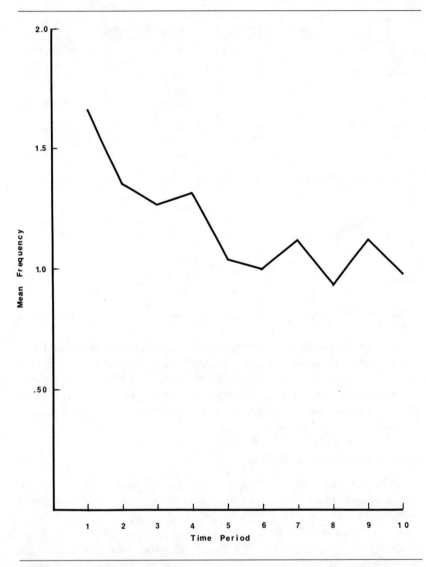

Figure 15.1.   Smile frequency over time.

time, indicates the cyclical and downward trend in smile frequency during
the conversation.

Verbal backchannel frequency also varied significantly as a function of
time ($F = 2.71$, df = $9/405$, $p < .055$). A trend analysis reveals significant
quartic ($F = 6.61$, df = $1/45$, $p < .01$) and quintic ($F = 4.81$, df = $1/45$, $p <$

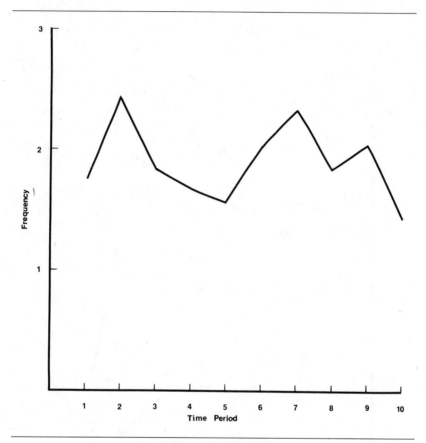

Figure 15.2.   Verbal backchannel frequency over time.

.03) components to changes in verbal backchannel frequency over time. In Figure 15.2 it can be seen that verbal backchannels *cycle* upward and downward around an equilibrium of the sample mean (M = 1.90, SD = .98). Backchanneling, whether verbal or nonverbal, clearly depends on the exact type of backchanneling behavior when considering time effects. Positive head nods remain relatively stable, smiles cyclically decrease, and verbal backchannels cycle around an equilibrium.

Forward body lean duration evidenced a significant time × partner's information-seeking condition interaction (F = 2.55, df = 9/288, p < .008). As can be seen in Figure 15.3, except at intervals 1 and 4, participants conversing with High Seeking partners exhibited significantly different forward body lean duration than did participants conversing with Low Seeking part-

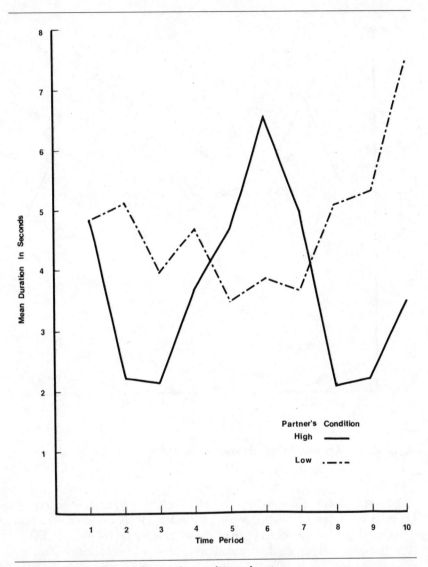

Figure 15.3.   Body lean duration by condition of partner.

ners. Where one type of dyad peaks, the other reaches a trough. Participants with High Seeking partners appear to have sped up the overall cycle of forward body lean duration by four or five intervals; a phase shift appears to be occurring.

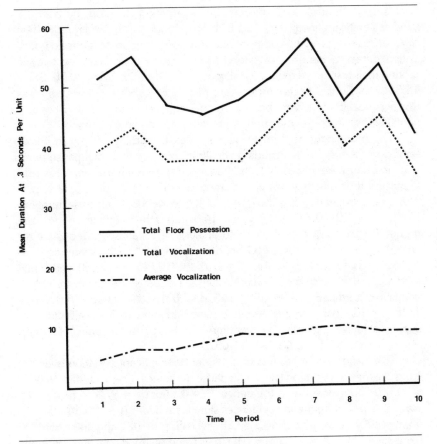

Figure 15.4. Talk time parameters over time.

All but one of the talk time measures varied significantly over the course of the conversation. Only average floor possession length fails to change significantly over time. Average vocalization duration ($F = 2.47$, df = $9/405$, p $< .01$), total vocalization duration ($F = 3.19$, df = $9/405$, p $< .001$), and total floor possession duration ($F = 3.15$, df = $9/405$, p $< .001$) are not stable over time, though the trend analyses do not yield completely similar results. As Figure 15.4 illustrates, total vocalization duration and total floor possession duration have almost identical trajectories over time; both evidence a significant cubic component to the trend (total vocalization duration: $F = 11.38$, df = $1/45$, p $< .002$; total floor possession duration: $F = 12.37$, df = $1/45$, p $< .001$) and a significant quartic component (total vocalization duration: $F = 4.31$, df = $1/45$, p $< .04$; total floor possession duration: $F = 4.32$, df = $1/45$, p < .04). A trend analysis of average vocalization duration, by contrast, yielded significant linear (F = 15.51, df = 1/45, p < .001) and quartic (F = 5.92, df = 1/45, p < .02) components. Thus total floor possession and vocalization duration, parameters ignoring the *frequency* of each event, cycle around their respective means (total vocalization duration: M = 40.50, SD = 14.34; total floor possession duration: M = 49.64; SD = 14.31), whereas average vocalization duration (including frequency and duration components) tends to increase over time even with some downward motion.

The monologue rhythm measures index the timing of speech within floor possessions. While including vocalization frequency, total pause duration, and pause frequency, only the frequency speech parameters evidenced significant time effects (vocalization frequency: F = 9.71, df = 9/405, p < .001; pause frequency: F = 2.67, df = 9/405, p < .005; total pause duration: F = 1.81, df = 9/405, p < .06). Figure 14.5 graphs the frequency monologue rhythm measures over time. A trend analysis of vocalization frequency revealed significant linear (F = 54.38, df = 1/45, p < .001), quadratic (F = 4.59, df = 1/45, p < .04), cubic (F = 6.75, df = 1/45, p < .003), and septic (F = 6.75, df = 1/45, p < .01) components. The pause frequency trend had significant quartic (F = 4.95, df = 1/45, p < .03) and septic (F = 5.07, df = 1/45, p < .03) components. As can be seen in Figure 15.5, vocalization frequency is decreasing cyclically over time, whereas pause frequency is cycling around its mean (M = 2.43, SD = 1.65).

The turn-taking measures both evidence significant variation over the course of the conversation (switching pause frequency: F = 5.11, df = 9/405, p < .001; floor possession frequency: F = 14.46, df = 9/405, p < .001). Switching pause frequency evidences significant linear (F = 20.54, df = 1/45, p < .001), quadratic (F = 5.89, df = 1/45, p < .02), and cubic components (F = 7.11, df = 1/45, p < .01) to its trend over the conversation; floor possession frequency follows a similar trajectory (linear: F = 101.21, df = 1/45, p < .001; quadratic: F = 12.78, df = 1/45, p < .001; cubic: F = 6.12, df = 1/45, p < .02). Examination of Figure 15.6 reveals, however, that switching pause frequency cycles through its trend about two intervals before floor possession frequency; the valleys and troughs of switching pause frequency occur just prior to the valleys and troughs of floor possession frequency. However, both turn-taking parameters, even though cyclically varying, decrease over time.

The interaction parameters (average and total switching pause duration) do not follow the same trajectory over the course of the conversation; average switching pause duration remains stable, whereas total switching pause duration varies significantly (F = 2.35, df = 9/405, p < .02). A trend analysis for switching pause duration revealed significant linear (F = 4.71, df

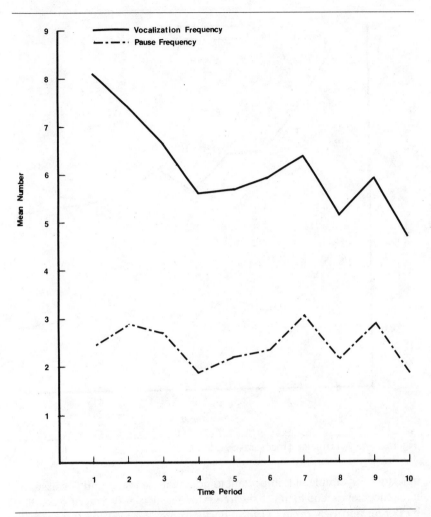

Figure 15.5.   Monologue rhythm measures over time.

$= 1/45$, $p < .04$) and quadratic components ($F = 4.26$, $df = 1/45$, $p < .05$). As can be seen in Figure 15.7, switching pauses are longer in the initial stages of a conversation than in later stages. Average pause duration, average simultaneous speech duration, total simultaneous speech duration, and simultaneous speech frequency failed to show any significant changes over time.

In sum, many of the behavioral indices of relaxation exhibited cyclical

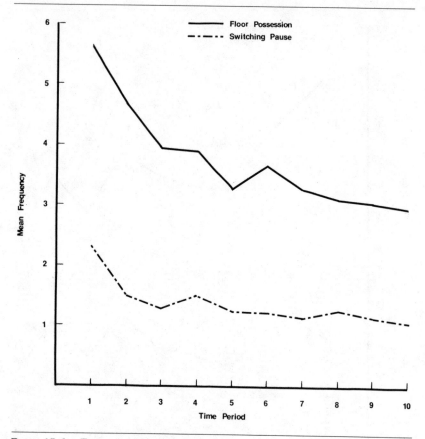

Figure 15.6.   Turn-taking measures over time.

trajectories over time. It is important to note that the pause and vocalization frequency trends tend to match the trends for question-asking reported earlier by Berger and Kellermann (1983). Furthermore, the total switching pause duration trajectory tends to peak when question-asking troughs, and vice versa. The verbal backchannels frequency trend is quite similar to those of total floor possession duration and total vocalization duration. The behavioral measures of relaxation thus appear to vary over time in related trajectories.

DISCUSSION

The findings of the present study suggest a number of different tactical variations individuals employ when seeking social information in interaction

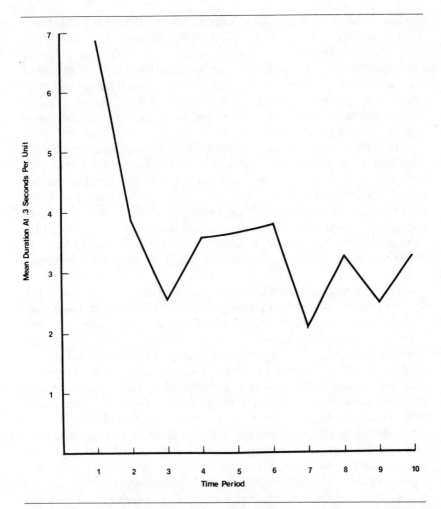

Figure 15.7.   Total switching pause duration over time.

contexts through a strategy of relaxing their conversational partners. High Seekers employed a number of behavioral techniques in pursuit of this relaxation goal. In contrast to Lows, Highs behaviorally engaged in more verbal backchannels and questions, and less lengthy pauses and switching pauses. Furthermore, High Seekers were perceived as more pleasant, more directive, and more encouraging than were Lows. While Highs attempted to control the conversation more so than Lows, they simultaneously engaged in behaviors that made the interaction more pleasant for their conversational partners. The results of the discriminant analysis on other-comfortableness indicate that a relaxation strategy is employed *in conjunction* with behaviors typically associated with an interrogation strategy (Berger & Kellermann, 1983). Use of relaxation techniques might therefore be a means of offsetting potentially intrusive interrogation sequences while still allowing information-seeking goals to be accomplished efficiently. In other words, continuous and relentless interrogation might be considered socially inappropriate; to maximize efficiency without violating social norms, a relaxation strategy may be implemented to balance optimally the tension between appropriateness and efficiency.

The rather consistent results indicating that Normals are comparable to High Seekers on almost all relaxation techniques suggests that a ceiling effect on this optimization process may occur, at least with respect to employment of relaxation behaviors. Earlier research (Berger & Kellermann, 1983) reported that Highs and Normals were relatively similar with respect to interrogation strategy use. It may well be that our initial interaction scripts (Abelson, 1976, 1981; Berger & Roloff, 1980, 1982; Schank & Abelson, 1977) cognitively direct information seeking to be optimally appropriate and efficient.

This optimality hypothesis is consistent with the assumptions and predictions of uncertainty reduction theory (Berger, 1979; Berger & Calabrese, 1975). In this theory, information seeking is posited to be a primary means of reducing uncertainty about, or coming to know, other individuals. Furthermore, this optimization hypothesis implies that the differences between High and Low Seekers are due to Low Seekers engaging in *discomfort* strategies rather than High Seekers employing relaxation strategies to any greater extent than individuals typically do in routine social encounters. Initial social interaction might therefore be characterized as balancing the competing desires of seeking information efficiently and acting appropriately. Engaging in a discomfort strategy would thus be indicative of a minimal desire to reduce uncertainty through the suppression of information-seeking behaviors and the engagement of discomfort behaviors.

It is clear that the tension between efficiency and appropriateness is not directly perceived by social actors. High Seekers indicated in their post-interaction protocols that they did *not* engage in controlling behaviors, whereas Low Seekers reported they attempted to control the conversation. All behavioral and observer-perceived measures of control, however, were highest for the High Seekers and correlated with efficiency. These results verify the hypothesis that control is the distinguishing feature of efficiency. A potential explanation for the disjunction between High Seekers' behavior and cognition about control can be found in work on inconsistent messages in the psychotherapeutic literature. While therapists *verbally* report the desire for, and actuality of, use of nondirective interaction strategies with clients, Truax (1966) found that nonetheless *nonverbal* cues were used to shape the behaviors of clients. Haley (1963) argues that the therapist may be sending inconsistent messages—nondirective verbally but directive nonverbally. Mehrabian (1970) argues that such inconsistent messages are beneficial for camouflaging intentions, an outcome social information seekers as well as therapists may desire. The effectiveness of a Rogerian therapist can thus "be attributed in some measure to his use of implicit reinforcers in a context which, explicitly at least, [he] claims to wish not to openly influence the patient" (Mehrabian, 1970, p. 81).

The efficient but socially appropriate social information seeker may be analogous to a Rogerian therapist—masking intentions by giving inconsistent cues but nonetheless reinforcing information provision by conversational partners through nonverbal relaxation techniques. The regression analyses revealed that switching pause duration, floor possession number, vocalization frequency, and question-asking frequency—all nonverbal cues—are the behaviors underlying judgements of directiveness and control of a conversation. While no judgments were made solely on the directiveness of verbal content, it is likely that observers were basing their directiveness judgments on nonverbal cues while High Seekers were reporting directiveness of verbal content. Earlier research reported a bias in the postinteraction protocols for content-related information rather than structure or strategy information (Berger & Kellermann, 1983). Thus it is likely that efficient and appropriate information seeking utilizes inconsistent messages of control to balance optimally the tension between efficiency and appropriateness.

The inconsistent message hypothesis also may be used to explain Low Seekers' disjunction between cognition and behavior. While Lows may have verbally attempted to control the conversation, their nonverbal behaviors may have granted directing power to High Seekers. Such an explanation is reasonable given the longer pause and switching pause durations exhibited by Low Seekers, indicating *abdication* of control rather than assumption of control.

If the constraint of efficiency in seeking information were removed, fewer control behaviors might be exhibited. The discriminant analysis of the three other-comfortableness groups (High, Medium, Low) are supportive of this expectation. Behaviors Mehrabian (1971) identified as affiliative, ingratiating, or relaxing are variables in the discriminant function. Furthermore, many of these measures—fluency, pause frequency, self-relaxation, positive head nods, floor possession duration, forward body lean duration—do not discriminate across information-seeking conditions where efficiency constraints may be present. However, switching pause duration, verbal backchannels, and question-asking frequency are not only variables in the discriminant function but also serve to differentiate High Seekers from Low Seekers. Such findings imply that constraints related to participants' achieving their information-seeking goals interfered with performance of behaviors that would maximize the conversational partner's comfortableness at the expense of efficiency. Examining conversations where so-called pure forms of interrogation and relaxation strategies occur would be useful for verifying these optimization hypotheses.

The results of this study also lend support to the two-step chain model of goal achievement described earlier. Behaviors other researchers have identified as promoting attitude change, attraction, approval-seeking, or approval-inducing goals were employed here by individuals to facilitate social information seeking. That identical behaviors are employed to achieve different and seemingly unrelated goals suggests that some common process is mediating the movement from goal acceptance to goal fulfillment. It is our belief that when goal fulfillment depends on the actions or reactions of another person, an individual will first attempt to induce the target to like or feel at ease with the individual, under the assumption that positive regard will promote more favorable target response. For this mediation hypothesis to become operative, the goal seeker must perceive himself or herself to be *dependent* on others for goal fulfillment: ingratiation and positive regard would seemingly be unnecessary when an individual could achieve a goal independently. Increasing dependence upon another for achievement of some goal has been shown to elevate information-seeking behaviors (Berscheid, Graziano, Monson, & Dermer, 1976; Swann, Stephenson, & Pittman, 1981; Tjosvold & Fabrey, 1980).

This interdependence hypothesis suggests the operation of a generic schema in which the superordinate goal—in this case the acquisition or non-acquisition of social information—is achieved by reaching the subordinate goal of gaining or failing to gain social approval. While we have suggested that gaining social approval might also be employed to reach the superordinate goal of persuading a target person, social approval might not always be employed as a means to achieve various social goals. Obviously, both persuasion and information acquisition can be accomplished through a number of less positive means, such as threat and intimidation. Here again note that while such means for achieving persuasion or information may be potentially efficient, assuming that one has the requisite power to make threats credible, they are toward the low end of the social appropriateness dimension.

Regardless of the information-seeking goal of the social actor, relaxation behaviors tend to exhibit cyclical trajectories over time. While some cyclically decrease, others cycle around an equilibrium point. Such cyclicity was also revealed for interrogation behaviors (Berger & Kellermann, 1983). Perhaps most interesting is the patterning of the cycles across behavioral measures. Trajectories for pause and vocalization frequencies tend to match trends for question-asking frequency, whereas switching pause duration follows a trajectory cyclically opposite that of question-asking. In other words, when switching pause durations start on the downward part of a cycle, question-asking frequency tends to increase. Such findings provide even stronger support for the "power up-glide" hypothesis suggested by Berger and Kellermann (1983). Immediately following longer pausing between floor possessions, it appears that questions are asked to "power up" the conversation, letting it "glide" until the next time "powering up" is required. McLaughlin and Cody (1982) recently reported that a question-answer sequence is a "verified behavior sequence" following conversational lapses. What the present study adds is the cyclical nature of such conversational lapses and the interaction between lapses and question-asking behavior over time.

The patterns of cyclicity evidenced by the behavioral measures clearly differ over the course of initial interactions. Both total and average duration measures for pausing, simultaneous speech, average duration for floor possessions and switching pauses, and frequency measures for positive head nods and simultaneous speech are insensitive to conversational length, remaining stable throughout initial conversations. Cyclically decreasing patterns occur for total switching pause duration and the frequency measures for vocalizations, switching pauses, floor possessions, and smiles. Cyclicity around an equilibrium occurs for the frequency of verbal backchannels and pauses, as well as for the total durational measures for forward body lean, floor possession, and vocalizations. Only average vocalization duration evidences an increasing cyclical pattern.

Except for vocalization duration, all *average* measures of speech parameters remain stable over the course of initial conversational encounters. Although such stability might be indicative of actual conversational regularities, the stability is more likely an artifact of measurement. Average measures are confounded, having total duration as well as frequency components. In all cases but simultaneous speech, the frequency and total duration components are not stable across the conversational encounter. Frequency components decrease cyclically while total duration components cycle around an equilibrium, except for total switching pause duration and pause frequency, wherein the cyclical patterns are inverted. Smile frequency and forward body lean duration also maintain the speech parameter cyclical differences in frequency and duration.

Why do frequency measures tend to decrease cyclically and total durational measures cycle around an equilibrium? It would be tempting to argue that decreases in frequency with simultaneous equilibria in duration would lead to increases in average duration. However, only average vocalization duration demonstrates such a cyclical increase. Shifts in behavior must therefore be occurring across behaviors; that is, the expected increases in average duration of floor possessions, switching pauses, and the like are translated into an increase in average vocalization duration over time. In the framework of uncertainty reduction theory, the need to prevent information power decreases as uncertainty decreases, thus allowing for more and longer distortions from the point of "equal" power. An indicator that uncertainty has probably decreased can be seen in the shift away from switching pauses as a regulator of turn-taking behavior over the course of initial interactions; both total switching pause duration and frequency decrease over time. As switching pauses are often perceived as indicators of stress or anxiety (see, for example, Harper et al., 1978), a reduction in stress may allow for more synchronized behavior between interactants (Cappella, 1981) that provides a larger confidence band around deviations from the power equilibrium. Thus relaxation may be an implicit goal of most initial interactions regardless of the strategy employed to achieve it.

If this reasoning is valid, behaviors cycling around an equilibrium should promote relaxation of the partner more so than behaviors decreasing cyclically. Our results indicate that most of the behavioral measures with an equilibrium cycle discriminate use of a relaxation strategy, whereas only one of the measures with a decreasing cycle serves a similar function. Particularly interesting is the phase shift occurring in forward body lean behavior dependent on the goal of the partner. Participants with High Seeking partners went through the cycle of forward body lean duration prior to participants with Low Seeking partners. As increases in forward body lean are related to increases in relaxation (Mehrabian & Williams, 1969), High Seeking partners were more successful in creating the state of relaxation in participants and maintaining that state than were Low Seeking partners. However, forward body lean duration is the only behavior evidencing differences across information-seeking sets and over time. The lack of set differences over time serves as strong evidence for a relaxation goal, implicit or explicit, for social actors in initial encounters. The issue then becomes the strategy of achieving such a goal—its appropriateness and efficiency. Our data indicate that initial social interaction can be modeled as a cyclical phenomenon, with a goal of information seeking through optimally efficient and socially appropriate behaviors. Although not all initial interactions would necessarily adhere to this model, typical interactions (as indexed by our Normal participants) closely align themselves to such a perspective.

NOTE

1. A button box was constructed and attached to a two-track tape recorder. Two chronographers were trained to depress their button when the participant they were viewing on the videotape was speaking. Each participant in a dyad was "button-pressed" onto a separate track of the tape. When the buttons were depressed, a tone was placed on the appropriate tracks of the tape. The tape served as the input for analog to digital conversion on a PDP-12 computer. Computer programs were written to sample the tape at 200/minute, "reading" the

tape for sound or silence. These readings then served as input to a computer program designed to calculate the frequency and duration of speech parameters according to Jaffe and Feldstein's (1970) six-state model.

REFERENCES

Ableson, R. P. (1976). Script processing in attitude formation and decision-making. In J. S. Carroll & J. W. Payne (Eds.), *Cognition and social behavior.* Hillsdale, NJ: Lawrence Erlbaum.

Abelson, R. P. (1981). Psychological status of the script concept. *American Psychologist, 36,* 715-729.

Aronson, E., & Linder, D. (1965). Gain and loss of esteem as determinants of interpersonal attractiveness. *Journal of Experimental Social Psychology, 1,* 156-171.

Berger, C. R. (1979). Beyond initial interaction: Uncertainty, understanding, and the development of interpersonal relationships. In H. Giles & R. St. Clair (Eds.), *Language and social psychology.* Oxford, England: Basil Blackwell.

Berger, C. R., & Calabrese, R. J. (1975). Some explanations in initial interaction and beyond: Toward a developmental theory of interpersonal communication. *Human Communication Research, 1,* 99-112.

Berger, C. R., & Douglas, W. (1981). Studies in interpersonal epistemology: III. Anticipated interaction, self-monitoring, and observational context selection. *Communication Monographs, 48,* 183-196.

Berger, C. R., & Kellermann, K. A. (1983). To ask or not to ask: Is that a question? In R. N. Bostrom (Ed.), *Communication yearbook 7.* Beverly Hills, CA: Sage.

Berger, C R., & Perkins, J. W. (1978). Studies in interpersonal epistemology: I. Situational attributes in observational context selection. In B. D. Ruben (Ed.), *Communication yearbook 2.* New Brunswick, NJ: Transaction.

Berger, C. R., & Perkins, J. W. (1979). *Studies in interpersonal epistemology. II. Self-monitoring, involvement, facial affect, similarity, and observational context selection.* Paper presented at the Speech Communication Association convention, San Antonio, Texas.

Berger, C. R., & Roloff, M. E. (1980). Social cognition, self-awareness and interpersonal communication. In B. Dervin & M. Voigt (Eds.), *Progress in communication sciences* (Vol. 2). Norwood: ABLEX.

Berger, C. R., & Roloff, M. E. (1982). Thinking about friends and lovers: Social cognition and relational trajectories. In M. E. Roloff & C. R. Berger (Eds.), *Social cognition and communication.* Beverly Hills; CA: Sage.

Berscheid, E., Graziano, W., Monson, T., & Dermer M. (1976). Outcome dependency: Attention, attribution, and attraction. *Journal of Personality and Social Psychology, 34,* 978-989.

Bond, M. H. (1972). Effect of an impression set on subsequent behavior. *Journal of Personality and Social Psychology, 24,* 301-305.

Cappella, J. N. (1981). Mutual influence in expressive behavior: Adult-adult and infant-adult dyadic interaction. *Psychological Bulletin, 89,* 101-132.

Clore, G., & McGuire, H. (1974). *Attraction and conversational style.* Paper presented at the Society of Experimental Social Psychology Meetings, Urbana, Illinois.

Colson, W. N. (1968). *Self-disclosure as a function of social approval.* Unpublished master's thesis, Howard University.

Coutts, L. M., Schneider, F. W., & Montgomery, S. (1980). An investigation of the arousal model of interpersonal intimacy. *Journal of Experimental Social Psychology, 16,* 545-561.

Cozby, P. C. (1973). Self-disclosure: A literature review. *Psychological Bulletin, 79,* 73-91.

Gouldner, A. W. (1960). The norm of reciprocity: A preliminary statement. *American Sociological Review, 25,* 161-178.

Haley, J. (1963). *Strategies of psychotherapy.* New York: Grune & Stratton.

Harper, R. G., Wiens, H. N., & Matarazzo, J. D. (1978). *Nonverbal communication: The state of the art.* New York: John Wiley.

Ickes, W., Patterson, M. L., Rajecki, D. W., & Tanford, S. (1982). Behavioral and cognitive consequences of reciprocal versus compensatory responses to preinteraction expectancies. *Social Cognition, 1,* 160-190.

Jaffe, J., & Feldstein, S. (1970). *Rhythms of dialogue.* New York: Academic.

Jones, E. E. (1964). *Ingratiation.* New York: Appelton-Century.

Jones, E. E., & Wortman, C. (1973). *Ingratiation: An attributional approach.* Morristown, NJ: General Learning Press.

Kahneman, D., Slovic, P., & Tversky, A. (Eds.). (1982). *Judgment under uncertainty: Heurisitics and biases.* Cambridge: Cambridge University Press.

Kraemer, H. C., & Jacklin, C. N. (1979). Statistical analysis of dyadic social behavior. *Psychological Bulletin, 86,* 217-224.

Major, B. (1980). Information acquisition and attribution processes. *Journal of Personality and Social Psychology, 39,* 1010-1023.

McLaughlin, M. L., & Cody, M. J. (1982). Awkward silences: Behavioral antecedents and consequences of the conversational lapse. *Human Communication Research, 8,* 299-316.

Mehrabian, A. (1970). *Tactics of social influence.* Englewood Cliffs, NJ: Prentice-Hall.

Mehrabian, A. (1971). Nonverbal communication. In J. K. Cole (Ed.), *Nebraska Symposium on Motivation* (pp. 107-162). Lincoln: University of Nebraska Press.

Mehrabian, A., & Ksionzky, S. (1971). Factors of interpersonal behavior and judgment in social groups. *Psychological Reports, 28,* 483-492.

Mehrabian, A., & Williams, M. (1969). Nonverbal concomitants of perceived and intended persuasiveness. *Journal of Personality and Social Psychology, 13,* 37-58.

Nisbett, R., & Ross, L. (1980). *Human inference: Strategies and shortcomings of social judgment.* Englewood Cliffs, NJ: Prentice-Hall.

Rogers, C. R. (1951). *Client-centered therapy: Its current practice, implications, and theory.* Boston: Houghton-Mifflin.

Rosenfeld, H. M. (1966). Approval-seeking and approval-inducing functions of verbal and nonverbal responses in the dyad. *Journal of Personality and Social Psychology, 4,* 597-605.

Rosenfeld, H. M. (1967). Nonverbal reciprocation of approval: An experimental analysis. *Journal of Experimental Social Psychology, 3,* 102-111.

Ruesch, J. (1961). *Therapeutic communication.* New York: W. W. Norton.

Schank, R., & Abelson, R. (1977). *Scripts, plans goals and understanding: An inquiry into human knowledge structures.* Hillsdale, NJ.: Lawrence Erlbaum.

Sermat, V., & Smyth, M. (1973). Content analysis of verbal communication on the development of a relationship: Conditions influencing self-disclosure. *Journal of Personality and Social Psychology, 26,* 332-346.

Siegman, A. W., & Feldstein, S. (Eds.). (1979). *Of speech and time: Temporal speech patterns in interpersonal contexts.* Hillsdale, NJ: Lawrence Erlbaum.

Snyder, M. (1981). Seek and ye shall find: Testing hypotheses about other people. In E. T. Higgins, C. P. Herman, & M. P. Zanna (Eds.), *Social cognition: The Ontario symposium on personality and social psychology.* Hillsdale, NJ: Lawrence Erlbaum.

Swann, W. B., Stephenson, B., & Pittman, T. S. (1981). Curiosity and control: On the determinants of the search for social knowledge. *Journal of Personality and Social Psychology, 40,* 635-642.

Taylor, D. A. (1979). Motivational bases. In G. J. Chelune & Associates (Eds.), *Self-disclosure: Origins, patterns, and implications of openness in interpersonal relationships.* San Francisco: Jossey-Bass.

Taylor, D. A., Altman, I., & Sorrentino, R. (1969). Interpersonal exchange as a function of rewards and costs and situational factors: Expectancy confirmation-disconfirmation. *Journal of Experimental Social Psychology, 5,* 324-339.

Tjosvold, D., & Fabrey, L. (1980). Motivation for perspective taking: Effects of interdependency and dependence on interest in learning others' intentions. *Psychological Reports, 46,* 755-765.

Troupe, Y., & Bassok, M. (1982). Confirmatory and diagnosing strategies in social information gathering. *Journal of Pesonality and Social Psychology, 43,* 22-34.

Truax, C. B. (1966). Reinforcement and nonreinforcement in Rogerian psychotherapy. *Journal of Abnormal Psychology, 71,* 1-9.

Worthy, M., Gary, A. L., & Kahn, G. M. (1969). Self-disclosure as an exchange process. *Journal of Personality and Social Psychology, 13,* 59-64.

Yngve, V. H. (1970, April). *On getting a word in edgewise.* Paper presented at the sixth regional meeting of the Chicago Linguistic Society.

16 Global Impressions of Social Skills: Behavioral Predictors

JAMES P. DILLARD ● BRIAN H. SPITZBERG

University of Wisconsin–Madison ● North Texas State University

SOCIAL skill has become an almost ubiquitous concept. The importance of social skill is evidenced by the numerous constructs in which it has been implicated as a causal factor. Social skill is hypothesized to be involved in the etiology of delinquency (Freedman, Rosenthal, Donahoe, Schlundt, & McFall, 1978), depression (Fisher-Beckerfield, 1979), loneliness (Spitzberg & Canary, 1983), social anxiety (Curran, 1977; Curran et al., 1980; Farrell, Mariotto, Conger, Curran, & Wallander, 1979), mental illness (Trower, Bryant, & Argyle, 1978), and numerous other psychosocial disorders (Barrios, 1980; Finch & Wallace, 1977; Monti, Corriveau, & Curran, 1982; Numbers & Chapman, 1982). Conversely, mastery of social skills commonly is assumed to facilitate psychological and social adjustment (Breen, Donlon, & Whitaker, 1977; Foote & Cottrell, 1955). It is no surprise, therefore, that behavioral social skills training has become a major mode of intervention for individuals experiencing interpersonal and psychological problems (Curran, 1977; Ladd & Mize, 1983).

Despite the ubiquity of the social skills concept, the very nature of social skills is a mystery (Eisler, 1978; Trower, 1982). Definitions of social skill range from cognitively oriented views (for example, see Hargie, Saunders, & Dickson, 1981) to purely behavioral approaches (see Gambrill, 1977; Hersen & Bellack, 1977). McFall (1982) clarifies this continuum by identifying two models of social skills: the trait model and the molecular model. Trait

Correspondence and requests for reprints: James P. Dillard, Department of Communication Arts, Vilas Communication Hall, University of Wisconsin, Madison, WI 53706.

models assume that certain cross-situational psychological dispositions enable or impair one's social performances. In contrast, the molecular model makes no explicit assumptions regarding interpersonal phenomena or cross-situational tendencies. The molecular model focuses on discrete, observable behaviors that are associated with ratings of social skill. While trait models have proven useful in explaining social behavior and the maintenance of skill deficits over time, they are limited by their general inability to specify behavioral targets or processes for therapeutic intervention and change. On the other hand, molecular models are consistent with behaviorally based social skills training programs. The molecular models offer the advantage of precision in identifying the specific behaviors that should be taught or extinguished (Curran, 1979). However, this precision may be illusory if the behaviors most frequently investigated are unrelated to global perception of social skill. While it might seem a simple task to examine available research on social skills to address this issue, there are several problems associated with taking the findings of individual studies at face value.

To begin with, there is little theoretical guidance regarding which molecular behaviors are likely to be important predictors of social skills. Social skills studies are generally atheoretic in their rationale. "Because of the lack of well formulated theoretical models within the heterosocial skill domain, investigators have typically synthetically derived component behaviors from the anxiety literature in general or simply 'intuited' the relevant skills" (Conger, Wallander, Mariotto, & Ward, 1980, p. 244). Such a haphazard approach to designing social skills studies hardly contributes to the systematic accumulation of findings.

Furthermore, in the absence of strong theoretical rationale, the empirical evidence for various molecular social skills appears inconsistent. There is simply little collective empirical support for the behaviors most commonly studied (Bellack, 1983; Curran, 1979). Behaviors (head movements, minimal encourages, and the like) that are significantly related to social skills in one study may not be so in another study. For example, Conger and Farrell (1981) found talk time, gaze, and smiles to be significantly and positively related to social skill ratings in both role-play situations and *in vivo* waiting periods. Spence (1981) also found talk time, eye contact, and response latencies to be related significantly to rated social skills in interview situations. However, Romano and Bellack (1980) failed to find a significant relationship between the behaviors of talk time, smiles, and response latencies and ratings of social skills. Greenwald (1977) found a null relation between social skills ratings and response latencies and eye contact. Other behaviors (questions, adaptors, and so on) appear to be related to social skill impressions, but the effect sizes vary too much among studies for sound conclusions about their relative importance to be drawn. "It is entirely unclear how much variance in the impact or effectiveness of behavior is accounted for by each of the components typically assessed" (Bellack, 1979, p. 169). Thus there seems to be neither strong theoretical nor empirical justification for choosing certain molecular behaviors as representative of social skills.

Among the obvious reasons that different studies produce different results are low statistical power, sampling error, and methodological inconsistencies. Most molecular social skills studies suffer from low statistical power and sampling error. Given the investment of time and resources required for the recording and rating of molecular behaviors, most social skills studies rely on very small samples. Small samples restrict the power of a statistical test, thereby increasing the likelihood of type II error. Consequently, conclusions based on the findings of any given study must be highly tentative.

Another problem with drawing inferences from molecular social skills studies is that they differ in their methodological procedures.

> There is tremendous variability in the selection and definition of target behaviors, specific measurement procedures and the level of observation (e.g., molar vs molecular). The major problem with this variability *per se* is that it makes interstudy comparisons difficult. (Bellack, 1983, p. 30)

Research indicates that slight differences in demand characteristics (Martinez-Diaz & Edelstein, 1980; Nietzel & Bernstein, 1976), confederate prompt delivery style (Steinberg, Curran, Bell, Paxson, & Munroe, 1982), pretesting procedures (Mungas & Walters, 1979), types of rater involvement (Gormally, 1982) and training (Corriveau et al., 1981), use of selection instruments (Wallander, Conger, Mariotto, Curran, & Farrell, 1980), and role-playing instructions (Galassi & Galassi, 1976) can affect the results of the study. If these characteristics systematically influence findings, and if they vary across studies, then relationships between behaviors and social skill ratings may be study specific.

The dangers of "eyeballing" the literature to make behavioral inferences from social skills studies are apparent. The hazard is magnified when the effects of inappropriate inferences are considered. If the behaviors selected for study or training are incorrect or weakly related to social skill ratings, then valuable research resources my be wasted and client outcomes may be jeopardized. Clearly, if molecular behaviors are an object of social skills training and research, there needs to be greater certainty regarding which behaviors are related reliably to social skill ratings, and to what extent. While establishing a theory of social skills is beyond the scope and intent of the current study, it is clear that we cannot hope to develop theories until we possess accurate empirical information about the relationship of given behaviors to global impressions of social skill. There is, therefore, an undeniable need to synthesize this research quantitatively, both systematically and empirically. The study reported here addresses this need. Specifically, this study provides a meta-analysis of a selected sample of molecular social skills studies.

METHOD

Meta-analysis is a technique for quantitatively cumulating the findings of multiple studies (Glass, McGaw, & Smith, 1981; Hunter, Schmidt, & Jackson, 1982). In contrast to primary analysis, which utilizes the responses of individuals as data, meta-analysis takes as the unit of analysis the value of the statistic that summarizes a relationship among two variables in the primary-level data. For example, in the present study we were interested in the relationship between the amount of time an individual spoke and others' perceptions of his or her social skill. In most studies that information was expressed as a correlation coefficient. Thus each correlation coefficient was treated as an individual datum.

Once these data were collected by compiling a group of studies that empirically assessed the relationship between talk time and social skill, the distribution of correlation coefficients was described in terms of its mean and variance. The sample-size-weighted mean and variance of this distribution may be taken as estimates of the population parameters. However, as Hunter et al. (1982) note, these estimates are subject to distortion as a function of sampling error, measurement error, and restriction or enhancement of range. The effects of these artifacts may be estimated and the mean and variance of the population estimates adjusted accordingly. The present study corrects for the impact of sampling and measurement error.

The procedures followed in the present study were composed of three steps. First, the literature was searched and a pool of studies selected for analysis. Next, the findings were converted to a common statistic and the mean and variance of each distribution was computed. Third, the data were examined for statistical artifacts and the observed variance was tested against the variance expected by chance. A chi-square test of significance was used for the last step. If this test showed that the variability across studies was artifactual—that is, attributable to sampling error—then the meta-analysis stopped. If the test showed that the variability was greater than could be expected by chance alone, then the pool of studies was examined for moderator variables. When hypotheses were formed regarding moderator variables, feature correlations were computed to assess the validity of those hypotheses. A feature correlation is the simple correlation between some feature of the study—for example, patient sample versus student sample—and the value for the dependent variable produced by that study. Where the feature correlations indicated support for the hypothesis, subgroups were formed and the meta-analytic procedures repeated. The analysis stopped when the chi-square test showed that the remaining between-study variability could be attributed to sampling error.

Selection of the Studies

The criteria for selection of studies consisted of the following: Each study must (a) be published; (b) use an English-speaking sample; (c) be of an adult or adolescent sample; and (d) relate molecular behavioral predictors to molar ratings of social skill. The requirement that studies be published was adopted because of evidence indicating that effect sizes and methodological quality differ significantly between published and unpublished studies (Rosenthal & Rubin, 1978; Smith & Glass, 1977). The last criterion was required for both conceptual and methodological reasons. Conceptually, our interest is in the molecular or component skills model, in which behaviors related to impressions of social skill are isolated for purposes of training. Methodologically, molecular behaviors are readily identified and defined. If interstudy comparisons are to be made, it is vital that the variables compared be similar in their operationalizations. Molecular behaviors usually are defined precisely enough so as to permit straightforward comparisons across studies.

Given these criteria, computer-assisted search of *Psychological Abstracts* was performed. Since our interest was in molecular behavioral predictors, we first accessed articles referencing "behavioral adjustment assessment," "behavior adjustment analysis," "coding," "rating,," and "videotape." This procedure indicated 9616 abstracts. The next parameter terms entered were "social adjustment," "social skills," "social competence," "interpersonal adjustment," and "competence." This resulted in a pool of 2233 articles. By cross-referencing these two samples, 132 articles remained. This pool was further focused by excluding references to dissertations ($n = 27$), foreign languages ($n = 4$), and children subject samples ($n = 23$), producing a final abstract list of 78 studies between 1967 and 1982. However, only 4 of these turned out to be studies relating molecular behavioral predictors to molar social skill ratings. In an attempt to expand the sample, current issues (1981-1982) of *Behavior Modification, Journal of Applied Behavior Analysis, Journal of Behavioral Assessment,* and *Journal of Consulting and Clinical Psychology* were examined. In addition, all issues of *Behavior Therapy* were searched. These journals were chosen because of their obvious emphasis on behavioral and social skills concerns. These procedures resulted in a total of 18 studies presented in 14 different articles in which data were presented relating at least one molecular behavior to an overall rating of social skill.

Characteristics of the Studies

When a report included multiple independent samples, each study was treated as a single data point. Sample sizes for individual studies ranged from 10 to 93, with a mean of 46. A total of 824 subjects participated in the investigations. Half of the 18 studies that formed the meta-analytic sample relied on constructed distributions of subjects, that is, equal numbers of subjects in high, medium, and low groups on some variable of interest. Although it is known that range enhancement inflates the magnitude of the correlation coefficient, it was not possible to estimate quantitatively the extent of bias due to the relatively small number of studies in the analysis.

Behavioral Predictors

The 14 reports were examined for common behavioral predictors. The reporting of operational definitions was rarely complete, although several predictors clearly appeared to be common to many studies. A total of 12 molecular behaviors were isolated that were used in a minimum of 3 studies and were operationalized in similar ways across studies. Of these behaviors, 9 are nonverbal and 3 are verbal. *Latency* is the amount of the time between the end of the partner's speaking turn and the subject's initiation of a verbal utterance, sometimes scored as a number of 10-second silences. *Gaze* is the amount of time a subject appears to be looking at the partner's facial area. *Eye contact* is the amount of time a subject and partner look directly into each other's eyes. *Smiles* is the number of times a subject retracts the corners of his or her lips upward, usually revealing the teeth. *Gestures* is the number (per minute) of hand or arm movements used to illustrate or emphasize speech. *Head movements* is the number of times (per minute) the subject moves the head in an up-and-down or side-to-side motion indicating agreement or disagreement, and is not associated with postural shifts. *Adaptors,* also referred to as "self-manipulations" and "fidgeting," is the number of times (per minute) the subject displays small movements of hands unrelated to speech, including facial stroking and picking, scratching, playing with hair, or tapping with an object such as a pencil. *Volume* is the loudness of the subject's voice, usually rated on a 5-point scale (for example, very loud to very soft). *Talk time,* or speech duration, is the amount of time the subject is speaking. *Questions* refers to verbal utterances that request information from the partner. *Compliments* represents statements that possess positively valenced references to the partner. *Minimal encourages,* or attention feedback responses, is the number of verbal responses made while in a listening role that indicate acknowledgement (for example, "mm"; "yes"; "I see") or question feedback responses (for example, "Oh?" "Did you?" "Really?").

While minor variations occurred among the studies in the ways in which these variables were defined (for instance, sometimes they were frequency counts rather than duration counts), the same behavioral content apparently was being observed across studies.

Analysis

The first computational step in preparing the data is that of converting the various studies to a common statistic. The estimate of effect strength used in the present analysis was the Pearson correlation coefficient. Although most investigations relied on the correlation coefficient, some analyses reported t or F statistics. When this occurred the difference statistics were converted to r using formulas provided in Hunter et al. (1982). Since the desired outcome of this investigation was to make general statements about the relationships between verbal and nonverbal behaviors and global perceptions of social skill, data within studies were aggregated at the highest level possible. Thus, for example, when subjects engaged in multiple role plays the statistic describing the behavior-skill relationship was averaged across role plays to yield one estimate per study.

Once the data were aggregated within individual investigations, distributions of coefficients were formed for each of the twelve independent variables. Next, these distributions were summarized in terms of their means and variances. After correction for sampling error the variances were subjected to formal chi-square tests. A null finding for this statistic was taken as an indication that the variability in the distribution was the result of sampling error. Hunter et al. (1982) note that this test has very high statistical power and consequently may reject the null even when the variation across studies is substantively trivial. Thus if the null is not rejected this is strong evidence that the variation across studies is inconsequential.

When a statistically significant chi-square was obtained it was necessary to evaluate this finding in conjunction with other aspects of the data; for example, the ratio of error variance to observed variance. For one variable in the present study, it was concluded that the variation across studies was both statistically and substantively significant. In this case, predictions were developed regarding the source of that additional variation. To afford a preliminary test of these predictions features of studies were correlated with the value of the dependent variable produced by individual studies. Where these feature correlations supported the existence of a moderator variable, the studies were broken into smaller groups and new means, variances, and chi-square tests were computed for each subgroup. As with the earlier analyses, if these tests indicated that the variance was attributable to sampling error then no additional analyses were conducted.

Finally, it was considered important to correct the obtained values for the effects of measurement error. Since a large number of studies reported only some of the necessary reliability information, it was not possible to correct the correlations at the level of individual studies. Instead, it was necessary to form distributions of reliability coefficients based on the available information. Frequently, this required conversion from a simple correlation coefficient and an adjustment for the number of raters. The Spearman-Brown formula was used to correct the reliability estimates where an average interrater correlation coefficient was given by considering each rater as a unit increment in test length. The artifact distributions of reliability estimates are available from the authors upon request. After estimating the reliability of each of the independent variables and social skill, the obtained correlations were corrected for attenuation due to measurement error using the formula provided by Nunnally (1967, p. 204).

Results

Twelve meta-analyses were conducted to examine the relationships between global social skill and each of the twelve microscopic behaviors. The results, which are reported individually below, are summarized in Table 16.1. In the following paragraphs N is used to designate the total number of subjects included in a meta-analysis, and K is used to represent the number of studies.

Social Skill. Reliability information was gathered from 13 studies. Computation of the mean reliability yielded a value of .87. This coefficient was used in the subsequent analyses in the correction for measurement error.

Response Latency. A total of 9 studies reported usable data on response latency. Included in these studies were 526 subjects. Calculation of the summary statistics yielded a mean r of −.30. Formation of the ratio of expected variance to observed variance indicated that 100 percent of the variability across studies could reasonably be attributed to sampling error. A nonsignificant chi-square test confirmed this. Based on data from four studies the reliability of the response latency measures was estimated to be .99. Using this value in combination with the reliability estimate for social skill produced a corrected estimate of correlation of −.33.

Gaze. Data from 218 subjects in 4 studies were analyzed to assess the impact of gaze upon ratings of social skill. The meta-analytic procedures revealed a mean r of .31. The ratio of error variance to observed variance yielded a value of 100 percent. The chi-square test was nonsignificant, indicating that the between-study variation was artifactual. Use of the average

Table 16.1
Results of the Meta-Analysis Relating Verbal
and Nonverbal Behaviors to Global
Ratings of Social Skill

Behavior	Correlation of Behavior with Social Skill (ρ)	Standard Deviation of Rho($\sigma\rho$)	Number of Subjects (N)	Number of Studies (K)	% of Variance Attributable to Sampling Error	χ^{2a}
Nonverbal						
latency	−.33	.00	526	9	100	4.31
gaze	.35	.00	218	4	100	2.46
eye contact	.24	.00	268	5	100	4.63
smiles	.25	.00	189	9	100	2.79
gestures	.45	.00	170	4	100	1.45
head movements	.24	.00	110	3	100	1.38
adaptors	−.18	.00	104	3	100	2.81
volume	.31	.00	184	5	100	5.58
talk time						
nonpatients/ in vivo	.68	.00	137	7	100	5.27
nonpatients/ role play	.42	.04	289	6	91	6.59
Verbal						
questions	.41	.00	338	8	100	7.05
compliments	.41	.11	168	3	52	5.78
minimal encourages	.22	.11	100	4	75	5.37

a. df = k− 1. None of these chi-square values attained significance at the .05 level.

reliability coefficient of .98 to correct for measurement error produced an estimate of correlation of .34.

Eye Contact. For this variable K = 5 and N = 268. Meta-analysis of this sample showed a mean r of .21. The variances ratio was again 100 percent. This was consistent with the outcome of the chi-square test, which was nonsignificant. The reliability estimate for eye contact was .92. The final estimate of the population parameter was .24.

Smiles. The association between the number of smiles and perceptions of social skill was examined in 9 studies, with a combined sample of 189 subjects. For this sample, the mean correlation was .23. The variances ratio was 100 percent and the accompanying chi-square test was nonsignificant.

The reliability of this measure was .94. The final outcome of the smiles analysis was a mean r of .25.

Gestures. Analysis of the gestures data yielded a combined sample of 170 subjects in 4 studies, with a mean correlation of .41. The variances ratio was 100 percent, and the corresponding chi-square test was nonsignificant. The reliability of the gestures variable was estimated at .96. Correction for the attenuation caused the estimate of correlation to rise to .45.

Head Movements. There were 3 studies (N = 100) containing data on the relationship between head movements and social skill. The average correlation was .22, and the variances ratio was 100 percent, with a nonsignificant chi-square test. The reliability for head movements was .94, and the estimate of mean correlation was .24.

Adaptors. Treatment of the adaptors data from 3 studies (N = 104) showed a mean r of −.17. The variances ratio was 100 percent. The chi-square test was nonsignificant. Reliability for this variable was quite high at .99. The estimate of the population parameter was −.18, indicating that adaptors are only slightly correlated with global judgments of social skill.

Volume. Consideration of 5 investigations (N = 184) of the association between volume and social skill revealed a correlation of .28. The variances ratio was 100 percent and the chi-square test was nonsignificant. Using the reliability value of .94 to adjust the estimate of the population parameter yielded a mean correlation of .31.

Talk Time. Initially 14 studies (N = 635) were relied upon to estimate the correlation between talk time and social skill. The meta-analysis produced a mean r of .35 and a standard deviation of .25. This very large standard deviation was the first indication of a high degree of variability in the data. The error to observed variances ratio was 21 percent, indicating that some 79 percent of the between-study variation was attributable to some source other than chance. The chi-square test offered formal confirmation of this, χ^2 (13) = 66.34, p < .001.

Examination of the studies for moderator variables suggested that differences in populations sampled and the type of induction employed might explain the between-study variability. For the sample variable, studies were coded 1 if a patient population was drawn upon and 0 if a student or nonpatient sample was used. For the type of induction variable studies were coded 1 if the data were gathered unobtrusively and 0 for role-play situations.

The feature correlations were −.69 for sample (n of studies = 13) and .49 for induction (n of studies = 17). These findings indicated support for both of the predicted moderator variables. However, since type of sample and type of induction were themselves correlated −.42 it was reasoned that controlling for one variable might eliminate the effects of the other. Thus, because the correlation for sample was the largest, the studies were initially

Table 16.2
Effects of Talk Time on Global Ratings of
Social Skill, as Moderated by Type of
Sample and Type of Induction

	Sample	
Induction	Patient	Nonpatient
Role play	(K = 0)	$\bar{r}$ = .39
		sdρ = .04
In vivo	$\bar{r}$ = .08	$\bar{r}$ = .63
	sdρ = .34	sdρ = .00

split on that variable. When both subgroups showed highly significant chi-square values, it was concluded that type of sample alone could not account for the unexplained variation between studies. Next, subgroups were formed on the basis of type of induction. Those analyses yielded similar results: Both subgroups showed greater than chance variation.

Finally, a bivariate split was performed that placed studies into one of four cells: patient/role play, patient/in vivo, nonpatient/role play, and nonpatient/in vivo. This analysis indicated the existence of a two-way interaction in which both sample and induction moderate the effects of talk time on ratings of social skill. The results are summarized in Table 16.2

The strongest findings were for the two nonpatient cells. In the nonpatient/role play cell, the mean correlation was moderate at .39, and the standard deviation was small at .04. The variances ratio was 91 percent and the chi-square was nonsignificant, χ^2 (5) = 6.59, ns. Thus the data are homogeneous within this cell. This analysis was based on K = 6 and N = 289.

The effect was substantially larger in the nonpatient/in vivo cell, with a mean correlation of .63 and a standard deviation of .00. This analysis, which was based on 137 subjects in 7 studies, produced a variances ratio of 100 percent and a nonsignificant chi-square test, χ^2 (6) = 5.27, ns. The latter two statistics show that the within-cell variation is artifactual.

As shown in Table 16.2, there were no studies that placed patients in role-play situations. Thus this cell was empty. The remaining patient/in vivo subgroup consisted of three studies (drawn from two articles) that used a total of 144 subjects. Analysis of these three data points suggested that the studies were not homogeneous. The mean correlation was .08, and the standard deviation was .34. The variances ratio was 15 percent, resulting in a significant chi-square, χ^2 (2) = 20.31, p < .001. Clearly, these findings suggest the existence of some systematic source of variance. However, due to the small number of studies it is impossible to determine empirically the cause of that variance.

Questions. A total of 8 studies, using 338 subjects, assessed the relationship between question asking and perceptions of social skill. The analyses revealed a mean r of .37, a variances ratio of 100 percent, and a nonsignificant chi-square statistic. Reliability for question asking was .92 and the final estimate of correlation was .41.

Compliments. Analysis for this variable was based on 168 subjects in 3 studies. The mean correlation coefficient was .37 and its corresponding standard deviation was .11. Although the variances ratio was 52 percent, suggesting substantial nonartifactual variation, the nonsignificant chi-square test indicated that for this sample size this amount of variation could easily be the result of chance. Given the high power of the chi-square test, it was reasonable to conclude that the studies were relatively homogeneous. A likely explanation for the discrepancy between the variances ratio and the chi-square test is that the variances ratio is relatively inaccurate with very small numbers of studies. The reliability of compliments was .94. The overall estimate of the population parameter was .41.

Minimal Encourages. A group of 4 studies yielded 100 subjects for this analysis. The mean correlation was .19, with a variances ratio of 75 percent and a nonsignificant chi-square. The reliability of this variable was .90. The final estimate of the population parameter was .22.

Summary of the Results

All of the verbal and nonverbal variables included in this investigation exhibited meaningful relationships with global ratings of social skill. However, the magnitude of these relationships varied considerably. The only strong correlation (.68) in these data was between talk time and social skill for nonpatients in non-role-play inductions. Correlations above .40 were observed for questions, compliments, and gestures, and for talk time for nonpatients in role-play situations. Latency, gaze, and volume all showed relationships with social skill ratings in excess of .30. The remaining correlations were comparatively small but nontrivial. Eye contact, smiles, head movements, and minimal encourages showed coefficients in the mid .20s. The correlation between adaptors and social skill was .18.

DISCUSSION

The results of the meta-analysis are reassuring. It appears that the behaviors most commonly chosen as predictors of social skill ratings are, in fact, related consistently to overall judgments of social skill. While the effect sizes are not overwhelming, neither are they inconsequential. Only one behavior (adaptors) explained less than an average of 5 percent of the social skill ratings variance. The empirical relationships provide a basis for future efforts at theory construction.

Limitations

Before considering the theoretical and practical importance of these findings, it is important to note certain limitations of the study. First, despite all attempts at locating relevant social skills studies, the sample was surprisingly small. However, the results were still relatively robust due to the apparently homogeneous samples. Second, it is clear that the domain of behaviors studied is incomplete. In surveying over 30 studies relevant to social skills, there were more than 11 verbal and 22 nonverbal behaviors identified. However, there were only enough data across studies to examine 12 behaviors in this meta-analysis. Even 33 behaviors seem insufficient to describe the judgments relevant to social interaction and skill. The effects of these other behaviors need to be observed and measured empirically. Third, half of the studies in this meta-analysis relied on constructed samples, which suggests the possibility of inflated effect sizes. Relationships are often enhanced when the entire range is modified to include only high, medium, and low subgroups, thus allowing the construct under study to manifest its effect more "purely." Again, it was impossible to assess the precise extent of this inflation due to the small number of investigations.

Implications

With these reservations in mind, the results appear to support the importance of the behaviors used to operationalize social skills. Knowing how, and to what extent, these behaviors are related to judgments of social skill still leaves unanswered the question of why. While the study was not designed to answer this question, several interpretations can be inferred from the results. Two nonverbal behaviors (gestures, talk time in nonclinical samples) and two verbal behaviors (questions, compliments) obtained average correlations over .40. The nonverbal behaviors appear to reflect an activity or expressiveness component of social interaction. Talk time has also been found to be an important predictor of perceptions of interpersonal influence (Brandt, 1980; van de Sande, 1980). The verbal behaviors seem to represent other-oriented or positively reinforcing components of social intercourse. It seems intuitively appealing to interpret socially skilled behavior as expressive, effective, and positively reinforcing. Unfortunately, this is too simplistic. Smiles and head movements would seem to be expressive behaviors, yet they did not produce similar correlations to talk time and gestures. Minimal encouragements to speak would seem to be positively reinforcing, despite their low correlation relative to questions and compliments.

Closer examination of the zero-order correlations reveals a less ambiguous conclusion. Of the behaviors studied, only adaptors and response latencies consistently obtained negative relationships to social skill ratings. Adaptors resulted in the smallest average effect size of all the behaviors studied. Response latencies, by definition, indicate a *lack* of activity or expressiveness. All the remaining behaviors can then be viewed as forms of activity. Taken as a whole, the results suggest that social activity, arousal, and intensity, in virtually all their forms, tend to lead to impressions of social skill. Obviously, however, too much of a good thing can be expected to detract from perceptions of social skill. But in "normal" social interaction, a person's social skill appears to depend significantly on his or her ability to be active and expressive in the interaction.

Another interesting finding concerns the results for talk time. Talk time was a significant predictor of social skill ratings only among nonclinical samples and, within these samples, it was a stronger predictor in unobtrusive contexts than in role-play situations. Concerning the first finding, clinical or patient samples may reflect a relatively more homogeneous population. As such, talk-time patterns may demonstrate less variability overall, thereby restricting potential systematic relationships to perceptions of social skill. Variability also provides a possible explanation for the nonpatient sample. Role-play situations are more structured than in vivo contexts. With more structure comes less variation in response patterns. Typical in vivo situations (such as waiting-room interaction) place few restrictions on the potential speech duration of the subjects. The greater behavioral freedom allows a wider range of talk-time behavior. Therefore, if systematic variations exist, they are more likely to be found in this condition. These speculations suggest the importance of selecting social skills that are relevant to the sample and context being studied. It is not a foregone conclusion that a behavior relevant to one sample and context will be relevant to another sample and context.

Application

Among the implications of this study are those concerning the clinical application of social skills training. It is apparent that molecular behaviors do make a difference. The often implicit assumption underlying molecular behavior research is that all observed behaviors are skills. That is, a subject who is capable of *producing* a behavior is also capable of *reproducing* that behavior. The task for the clinician is not always to instill the skill, but to increase or decrease its production in certain contexts. There is now reliable empirical support for the training of these behaviors in therapeutic contexts. However, caution should be taken in overextending the results of this meta-analysis. Some behaviors are likely to be much easier to train than others. For example, eye contact is a discrete, observable type of interactive behavior; talk time, on the other hand, is made up of sequences and continuous streams of behaviors. How things such as talk time and response latencies can be modified needs further study.

Another concern is that molecular behaviors will be overemphasized relative to cognitive skills. Two centuries ago the elocutionists believed that certain behaviors (gestures) should be taught as representing specific *natural* meanings. The elocutionists failed partly because people vary in the degree to which they naturally represent meanings through behavior and in the ways they interpret behavior. It is important to avoid the elocutionist trap that by simply learning how to increase or decrease certain social skills (such as eye contact or questions) people will be viewed automatically as more socially skilled. People must also possess the cognitive and judgmental competence to determine when and where to perform such skills for the behavior to be effective. While this meta-analysis has emphasized molecular skills, it is important to note that any successful clinical approach must necessarily include both behavioral and cognitive, as well as expressive and interpretive, components.

The State of the Literature

A final set of concerns arises indirectly from this meta-analysis. Most of the social skills studies that could be located for this analysis suffered from a common set of shortcomings. For example, the interrelationships of the behavioral predictors is a relatively unexplored question. Some behaviors that are individually related to social skill ratings may be unrelated (or more related) when combined with other behaviors. Other domains of behavior need to be examined more extensively (body lean, intonation, nonfluencies, facial expression, distance, speech rate, personal attention, interruptions, negative verbal content, turn-taking rhythms, and so on). As research accumulates for these behaviors, a more comprehensive picture can emerge regarding the relative importance of specific social behaviors.

A second problem of social skills research concerns the general lack of attention to verbal behavior. Researchers seem more content to emphasize nonverbal behaviors presumably because of the nature of many nonverbal behaviors. For example, while not every context calls for assertive responses, virtually all contexts call for eye contact. The assumption seems to be that nonverbal behaviors are more stable across contexts than verbal behavior. However, it is the verbal content and form that constitutes much of the substance of interaction. Without verbal interaction conversation is nothing more than a mysterious choreography of movements with little or no apparent meaning. The verbal content provides the basis for topic maintenance, personal involvement, and much of what is involved in defining the situation. Consequently, future research might pay closer attention to verbal content and structure.

Third, most social skills studies examine only initial interactions. Despite distinctions among interview, assertion, and heterosocial situations, the vast majority of subjects studied are meeting their conversational partners for the first time when observed. While initial interactions clearly are important in their own right, they constitute only one of many types of context. Social skills research runs the risk of finding out a great deal about how social skills operate only within a relatively narrow range of social interaction. It is even reasonable to ask how often people engage in extended face-to-face interactions with total strangers. Instead, interactions with peers, intimate relations, and colleagues seem just as important as initial interactions—if not more so—to a person's psychological well-being. Future research in social skills may even find that established relationships have developed idiosyncratic standards in which such things as eye contact and response latencies are far less important than in initial interactions. Certainly, this is a question deserving empirical study.

Finally, the studies located for this analysis almost uniformly demonstrated poor reporting procedures. We had to contact several authors personally to obtain such basic information as zero-order correlations and instrument reliabilities (all authors contacted graciously provided the information). In other studies, reliability analysis was not even performed. Many times it was difficult to determine how a behavior was defined conceptually or operationally. The minimal condition of responsible editorial and scientific practice should be to report reliabilities and a total zero-order correlation matrix of the social skills involved in these studies and to offer the coding instruments or manuals upon request. Only by such consistent practices can researchers hope to cumulate social scientific information in a systematic and useful manner.

REFERENCES

Arkowitz, H. (1977). Measurement and modification of minimal dating behavior. *Progress in Behavior Modification, 5,* 1-61.

Arkowitz, H., Lichtenstein, E., McGovern, K., & Hines, P. (1975). The behavioral assessment of social competence in males. *Behavior Therapy, 6,* 3-13.

Barrios, F. X. (1980). Social skills training and psychosomatic disorders. In D. P. Rathjen & J. P. Foreyt (Eds.), *Social competence: Interventions for children and adults* (pp. 271-303). New York: Pergamon.

Bellack, A. S. (1979). A critical appraisal of strategies for assessing social skill. *Behavioral Assessment, 1,* 157-176.

Bellack, A. S. (1983). Recurrent problems in the behavioral assessment of social skill. *Behaviour Research and Therapy, 21,* 29-41.

Brandt, D. R. (1980). A systematic approach to the measurement of dominance in human face-to-face interaction. *Communication Quarterly, 28,* 31-43.

Breen, P., Donlon, T. F., & Whitaker, U. (1977). *Teaching and assessing interpersonal competence: A CAEL handbook.* Columbia, NJ: CAEL, 1977.

Conger, A. J., Wallander, J. L., Mariotto, M. J., & Ward, D. (1980). Peer judgments of heterosexual-social anxiety and skill: What do they pay attention to anyhow? *Behavioral Assessment, 2,* 243-259.

Conger, J. C., & Farrell, A. D. (1981). Behavioral components of heterosocial skills. *Behavior Therapy, 12,* 41-55.

Corriveau, D. P., Vespucci, R., Curran, J. P., Monti, P. M., Wessberg, H. W., & Coyne, N. A. (1981). The effects of various rater training procedures on the perception of social skills and social anxiety. *Journal of Behavioral Assessment, 3,* 93-97.

Curran, J. P. (1977). Skills training as an approach to the treatment of heterosexual-social anxiety: A review. *Psychological Bulletin, 84,* 14-157.

Curran, J. P. (1979). Pandora's box reopened? The assessment of social skills. *Journal of Behavioral Assessment, 1,* 55-71.

Curran, J. P., Monti, P. M., Corriveau, D. P., Hay, L. R., Hagerman, S., Zwick, W. R., & Farrell, A. D. (1980). The generalizability of a procedure for assessing social skills and social anxiety in a psychiatric population. *Behavioral Assessment, 2,* 389-401.

Dow, M. G., Glaser, S. R., & Biglan, A. (1981). The relevance of specific conversational behaviors to ratings of social skill: An experimental analysis. *Journal of Behavioral Assessment, 3,* 233-242.

Eisler, R. M. (1978). Behavioral assessment of social skills. In M. Hersen & A. S. Bellack (Eds.), *Behavioral assessment: A practical handbook.* Oxford: Pergamon.

Farrell, A. D., Mariotto, M. J., Conger, A. J., Curran, J. P., & Wallander, J. L. (1979). Self-ratings and judges' ratings of heterosexual social anxiety and skill: A generalizability study. *Journal of Consulting and Clinical Psychology, 47,* 164-175.

Finch, B. E., & Wallace, C. J. (1977). Successful interpersonal skills training with schizophrenic inpatients. *Journal of Consulting and Clinical Psychology, 45,* 885-890.

Fisher-Beckfield, D. E. (1979). *The relationship of competence to both depression and depression-proneness in male college students.* Unpublished master's thesis, University of Wisconsin, Madison.

Freedman, B. J., Rosenthal, L., Donahoe, C. P., Jr., Schlundt, D. G., & McFall, R. M. (1978). A social-behavioral analysis of skill deficits in delinquent and nondelinquent adolescent boys. *Journal of Consulting and Clinical Psychology, 48,* 1448-1462.

Foote, N. N., & Cottrell, L. S., Jr. (1955). *Identity and interpersonal competence.* Chicago: University of Chicago Press.

Galassi, M. D., & Galassi, J. P. (1976). The effects of role playing variations of the assessment of assertive behavior. *Behavior Therapy, 7,* 343-347.

Galassi, J. P., Hollandsworth, J. G., Jr., Radeki, J. C., Gay, M. L., Howe, M. R., & Evans, C. L. (1976). Behavioral performance in the validation of an assertiveness scale. *Behavior Therapy, 7,* 447-452.

Gambrill, E. D. (1977). *Behavior modification: Handbook of assessment, intervention, and evaluation.* San Francisco: Jossey-Bass.

Glasgow, R. E., & Arkowitz, H. (1975). The behavioral assessment of male and female social competence in dyadic heterosexual interactions. *Behavior Therapy, 6,* 488-498.

Glass, G. V., McGaw, B., & Smith, M. L. (1981). *Meta-analysis in social research.* Beverly Hills, CA: Sage.

Gormally, J. (1982). Evaluation of assertiveness: Effects of gender, rater involvement, and level of assertiveness. *Behavior Therapy, 13,* 219-225.

Greenwald, D. P. (1977). The behavioral assessment of differences in social skill and social anxiety in female college students. *Behavior Therapy, 8,* 925-937.

Hargie, O., Saunders, C., & Dickson, D. (1981). *Social skills in interpersonal communication.* London: Croom Helm.

Hersen, M., & Bellack, A. S. (1977). Assessment of social skills. In A. R. Ciminero, K. S. Calhoun, & H. S. Adams (Eds.), *Handbook of behavioral assessment* (pp. 509-544). New York: John Wiley.

Hunter, J. E., Schmidt, F. L., & Jackson, G. B. (1982). *Meta-analysis: Cumulating research findings across studies.* Beverly Hills, CA: Sage.

Kern, J. M. (1982). The comparative external and concurrent validity of three role-plays for assessing heterosocial performance. *Behavior Therapy, 13,* 666-680.

Ladd, G. W., & Mize, J. (1983). A cognitive-social learning model of social skill training. *Psychological Review, 90,* 127-157.

Martinez-Diaz, J. A., & Edelstein, B. A. (1980). Heterosocial competence: Predictive and construct validity. *Behavior Modification, 4,* 115-129.

McFall, R. M. (1982). A review and reformulation of the concept of social skills. *Behavioral Assessment, 4,* 1-33.

Minkin, N., Braukman, C. J., Minkin, B. L., Timbers, G. D., Timbers, B. J., Fixen, D. L., Phillips, E. L., & Wolf, M. M. (1976). The social validation and training of conversational skills. *Journal of Applied Behavior Analysis, 9,* 127-139.

Monti, P. M., Corriveau, D. P., & Curran, J. P. (1982). Social skills training for psychiatric patients: Treatment and outcome. In J. P. Curran & P. M. Monti (Eds.), *Social skills training* (pp. 185-223). New York: Guilford.

Mungas, D. M., & Walters, H. A. (1979). Pretesting effects in the evaluation of social skills training. *Journal of Consulting and Clinical Psychology, 47,* 216-218.

Nietzel, M. T., & Bernstein, D. A. (1976). Effects of instructionally mediated demand on the behavioral assessment of assertiveness. *Journal of Consulting and Clinical Psychology, 44,* 500.

Numbers, J. S., & Chapman, L. J. (1982). Social deficits in hypothetically psychosis-prone college women. *Journal of Abnormal Psychology, 91,* 255-260.

Nunnally, J. C. (1967). *Psychometric theory.* New York: McGraw-Hill.

Romano, J. M., & Bellack, A. S. (1980). Social validation of a component model of assertive behavior. *Journal of Consulting and Clinical Psychology, 48,* 478-490.

Rosenthal, R., & Rubin, D. B. (1978). Interpersonal expectancy effects: The first 345 studies. *Behavioral and Brain Sciences, 3,* 377-415.

Royce, W. S. (1982). Behavioral referents for molar ratings of heterosocial skill. *Psychological Reports, 50,* 139-146.

Smith, M. L., & Glass, G. V (1977). Meta-analysis of psychotherapy outcome studies. *American Psychologist, 32,* 752-760.

Spence, S. H. (1981). Validation of social skills of adolescent males in an interview conversation with a previously unknown adult. *Journal of Applied Behavior Analysis, 14,* 159-168.

Spitzberg, B. H., & Canary, D. J. (1983). *Attributions of loneliness and relational competence.* Paper presented at the meeting of the International Communication Association, Dallas.

Steinberg, S. L., Curran, J. P. Bell, S., Paxson, M. A., & Munroe, S. M. (1982). The effects of confederate prompt delivery style in a standardized social stimulation test. *Journal of Behavioral Assessment, 4,* 263-272.

St. Lawrence, J. S. (1982). Validation of a component model of social skill with outpatient adults. *Journal of Behavioral Assessment, 4,* 15-26.

Trower, P. (1980). Situational analysis of the components and processes of behavior of socially skilled and unskilled patients. *Journal of Consulting and Clinical Psychology, 48,* 327-339.

Trower, P. (1982). Toward a generative model of social skills: A critique and synthesis. In J. P. Curran & P. M. Monti (Eds.), *Social skills training* (pp. 399-427). New York: Guilford.

Trower, P., Bryant, B., & Argyle, M. *Social skills and mental health.* Pittsburgh: University of Pittsburgh Press, 1978.

van de Sande, J. P. (1980). Cue utilization in the perception of dominance. *British Journal of Social and Clinical Psychology, 19,* 311-316.

Wallander, J. L., Conger, A. J., Mariotto, M. J., Curran, J. P., & Farrell, A. D. (1980). Comparability of selection instruments in studies of heterosexual-social problem behaviors. *Behavior Therapy, 11,* 548-560.

17● Deception: Paralinguistic and Verbal Leakage

MICHAEL J. CODY ● PETER J. MARSTON ● MYRNA FOSTER

University of Southern California ● Pennsylvania State University

S INCE the publication of work by Ekman and Friesen (1969, 1972 1974) and Knapp, Hart, and Dennis (1974), communication scholars have demonstrated considerable concern and effort in determining reliable, valid, and generalizable nonverbal, paralinguistic, and linguistic differences between deceptive and truthful communications (Bauchner, Brandt, & Miller, 1977; Brandt, Miller, & Hocking, 1981; Cody & O'Hair, 1983; Comadena, 1982; DePaulo, Davis, & Lanier, 1980; Dulaney, 1982; Feldman, Devin-Sheehan, & Allen, 1978; Fugita, Hogrebe, & Wexley, 1980; Geis & Moon, 1981; Geizer, Rarick, & Soldow, 1977; Hocking, Miller, & Fontes, 1978; Hocking, Bauchner, Kaminski, & Miller, 1979; Hocking & Leathers, 1980; Knapp & Comadena, 1979; Miller & Burgoon, 1982; Miller, deTurck, & Kalbfleisch, 1983; O'Hair, Cody, & McLaughlin, 1981; Zuckerman, DePaulo, & Rosenthal, 1981). In these endeavors, two methodologies have prevailed: the deception detection accuracy study (asking how accurate observers are in identifying deception and how accurate observers are in using different channels) and the cue leakage study (asking whether or not deceptive and truthful messages can be differentiated from one another on the basis of measurable variables). Most of these studies have addressed the issue of controllability, with Ekman and Friesen's sending capacity hypothesis as the typical focus. Ekman and Friesen argue that when liars do not want to be detected, they will control

Correspondence and requests for reprints: Michael J. Cody, Department of Communication Arts, University of Southern California, Los Angeles, CA 90089.

channels high in sending capacity (the face) and that the low sending channels (feet, legs) will result in greater cue leakage. Considerable evidence indicates that observers who have access to the body channel are often more accurate in detecting deception than other observers and that more body-related cues are leaked than facial cues (Ekman & Friesen, 1969, 1972, 1974; Ekman, Friesen, & Scherer, 1976; Hocking et al., 1979; Fugita et al., 1980; Littlepage & Pineault, 1978, 1979; Zuckerman et al., 1981).

Recently, however, interest has focused on the potential usefulness of message characteristics in providing accurate cues to detection. Indeed, a number of studies suggest that the auditory channel is "leakier" than all other channels. For example, Hocking et al. (1979) found some support for the Ekman and Friesen sending capacity hypothesis for lies of emotional concealment when they found that body-only observers were more accurate than other groups of observers. However, transcript-only observers were just as accurate as body-only observers. Furthermore, for lies about facts, the transcript-only and audio-only groups were more accurate than other groups (Hocking et al., 1979). Zuckerman et al. (1981) reviewed additional studies that compared all channels and likewise concluded that the message itself served as a leaky channel. In fact, Zuckerman et al. argue that exposure to tone of voice or transcripts only provides cues to accurate detection, with the transcript-only group often having higher accuracy scores. Evidence also indicates that the audio-only channel elicits higher accuracy scores than visual-only channels regardless of level of arousal experienced by liars (DePaulo, Lanier, & Davis, 1981; Zuckerman et al., 1981). Further, when all deception studies were compared, Zuckerman et al. found only three out of ten commonly studies visual behaviors to be consistently related to deception (adaptors, pupil dilation, and shrugs), while five out of nine auditory variables reviewed were consistently related to deception (speech hesitations, speech errors, irrelevant information, pitch, and negative statements). This comparison of consistency is important, since a common limitation of deception studies related to the visual channel (illustrators, leg/foot movements, and so on) is that of inconsistency of results and failures to replicate (Knapp & Comadena, 1979; Hocking et al., 1978; O'Hair et al., 1981). The possibility that some vocal and message-related cues may be more generalizable than nonverbal performance behaviors across experimental conditions should be investigated, since the advantages of such increased generalizability to hypothesis testing, theory construction, and practical prescriptions are clear.

Our purpose is threefold. First, since greater leakage and more consistent leakage is to be found in the auditory channel, we focus attention on the auditory channel and review how processes underlying deception might affect message leakage. Second, we argue that increased leakage is evidenced when lies are unplanned and narrative in nature, and we comment on how the timing of questions eliciting spontaneous narratives may influence the amount of effort required to construct fabrications. Third, we present the results of a study that tests our hypotheses.

REVIEW OF THE LITERATURE

Zuckerman et al. (1981) note that little is known of either the "semantics of deception" or how words reveal deception. In part, this lack of insight is due to the fact that many studies have explored laboratory-induced lies that are relatively brief in nature (for example, see Hocking & Leathers, 1980; O'Hair et al., 1981; but see also Knapp et al., 1974; Kraut, 1978). In such studies emphasis has been placed on variables such as response latency, response length, speech rate, and speech errors. Only a few studies have explored variables such as self-reference statements (Zuckerman et al., 1981; Knapp et al., 1974), irrelevant information (Zuckerman et al., 1981), dependence statements (Knapp et al., 1974), concreteness or vagueness (Knapp et al., 1974; Kraut, 1978), and nonimmediacy (Wagner & Pease, 1976). This is unfortunate since the few studies that have explored variables such as concreteness and irrelevant information have consistently related them to deception.

However, it is also clear that any attempt to construct a typology of auditory variables must be grounded in the theoretical processes underlying deception. Otherwise, were one simply to compile variables offered in the literature, one would find 25 auditory-related variables in Knapp et al. (1974), additional variables offered by Kraut (1978) and by Hocking and Leathers (1980), and several more alluded to in Zuckerman et al. (1981). Below, we review how processes operating during deception are associated with specific behaviors. It follows that by manipulating the processes affecting the behaviors it is possible to increase message leakage.

Deception is not itself an affect and therefore no specific verbal or non-verbal expression is directly associated with it (Zuckerman et al. 1981). Indeed, a number of processes underlying deception influence behavior (Zuckerman et al., 1981; Knapp et al., 1974; Kraut, 1980). Three processes are discussed here: arousal, attempted control, and cognitive processes.[1]

Deception induces a state of arousal, which influences respiration, heartbeat, and galvanic skin response (see Waid & Orne, 1981), presumably because of fear of punishment, felt conflict over lying, and the like (see Zuckerman et al., 1981). Zuckerman et al., conclude that three behaviors consistently related to deception can be attributed to arousal: pupil dilation, pitch, and speech errors. The first two variables are related to arousal because they represent autonomic responses associated with fear and/or stress. Speech errors are linked to manipulations of arousal during interviews (Kasl & Mahl, 1965; Zuckerman et al., 1981) and are related to deception presumably because fear of punishment disrupts normal encoding processes. Are there other cues leaked by liars that are associated with arousal? Generally, methods of increasing motivation to succeed heighten arousal (as well as attempted control) and research indicates that highly motivated liars blink less, exhibit fewer head movements, use fewer adaptors, and engage in fewer postural shifts than liars with less motivation: In short, liars become more behaviorally rigid as their motivation increases (Zuckerman et al., 1981). It is also interesting to note that motivated liars are likely to talk for a shorter duration and provide more negative statements than less motivated liars, while less motivated liars are somewhat more likely to make irrelevant statements (Zuckerman et al., 1981). However, most (if not all) of these effects seem to be interpreted more properly as a result of the liar's increased attempts at control rather than his or her state of arousal. Increased behavioral rigidity may be expected to occur when liars concentrate on encoding their messages (Ekman & Friesen, 1972), and shorter messages encoded without an increase in irrelevant information are more likely to occur when control over the message is affected. Thus it is safest to conclude that arousal effects are limited to pitch and speech errors in the auditory channel.

Controlled deceptive responses leave listeners with the impression that the speaker lacks personal involvement and that the message is prepared, rehearsed, and lacking in spontaneity (Zuckerman, DeFrank, Hall, Larrance, & Rosenthal, 1979; DePaulo, Davis, & Lanier, 1980; DePaulo et al., 1981). The lack of personal involvement is likewise reflected in the fact that liars are often vague (Knapp et al., 1974) or produce messages low in concreteness (Kraut, 1978). It also appears that there exists a difference in the level of specificity with which messages are encoded by liars and truthers. Liars are less likely to provide specific details than truthers [fewer factual statements, fewer statements of self-experience, fewer statements of past reference, and fewer self-interest statements (Knapp et al., 1974)], and liars are more likely to produce statements that are general and nonspecific or even irrelevant (Zuckerman et al., 1981). In Knapp et al. (1974), these variables include "other references," "disparaging statements," and possibly "other experiences." Since liars presumably find it difficult to encode specific facts and details, they substitute more general statements (Zuckerman et al., 1981). It is possible that more pronounced differences occur when lies are spontaneously induced (Kraut, 1978).

Since prepared liars anticipate what they will say, prepared lies differ little from truthful responses in terms of speech errors, speech rate, pauses, and word/phrase repetitions (Knapp et al., 1974; Hocking & Leathers,

1980; Zuckerman et al., 1981). In fact, spontaneously induced lies contain more speech errors and pauses (at least when liars are low self-monitors), and manifest higher rates of pausing (Miller et al., 1983). However, prepared liars often have shorter response latencies and speak more briefly than "truthers" (O'Hair et al., 1981; Knapp et al., 1974). Spontaneous lies may be preceded by a longer latency when the lie requires elaboration (Kraut, 1978) than when it requires only a brief answer (O'Hair et al., 1981), presumably because the construction of complex messages requires more processing time (see below). There is some evidence that prepared liars may speak more slowly, but this is apparently true only when the prepared response is for a relatively long duration (Knapp et al., 1974; Motley, 1974).

One obviously understudied factor underlying deception is the cognitive difficulty of encoding the message. Liars must devise a message that contains no inconsistencies, that does not contradict the listener's knowledge, and that provides sufficient detail so as to seem plausible and truthful (Zuckerman et al., 1981; Knapp et al., 1974). Although Zuckerman et al. provide no constitutive or operational definition of cognitive effort, it is generally understood that effort increases as the number of decisions the speaker must make increases (Siegman, 1979). Increased speech hesitation (pauses, response latency) is evidenced when individuals are required to interpret (as opposed to describe) stimuli, or when answers must be composed for ambiguous or abstract questions (as opposed to specific or concrete ones) (Siegman & Feldstein, 1978; Goldman-Eisler, 1968; Siegman, 1979). Lying is generally more difficult than telling the truth, as indicated by the length of time required to prepare deceptive and truthful messages (De-Paulo, Finkelstein, Rosenthal, & Eisenstat, 1980; Zuckerman et al., 1981). Yet it is also clear that some lies require greater effort to construct than others. For example, lies that require only a yes or no response require fewer decisions and less effort (see O'Hair et al., 1981) than narrative responses (Knapp et al., 1974) or answers to open-ended questions about such matters as personnel problems (Kraut, 1978).

Obviously, the more a question requires a narrative response ("What did you do in San Francisco?"), the more likely liars will have difficulty in encoding as much detail as truthers. Liars may provide briefer answers with only the minimally sufficient information to answer a particular question, and they may offer less additional elaboration of related facts (Horvath, 1973). Questions requiring narrative responses are also more likely than closed-ended questions to find liars using fewer words and producing briefer messages than their truthful counterparts (Knapp et al., 1974; Kraut, 1978). Lengthier lies requiring more decisions are also more likely to result in more leveling (or generalizing) terms and speech hesitations (Knapp et al., 1974; Zuckerman et al., 1981). Finally, it appears that liars may speak more slowly when forced to encode a longer deception (Knapp et al., 1974) and that the likelihood of eliciting longer latencies from liars is enchanced when the lie is both spontaneously induced and requires elabortion (Kraut, 1978; see review above).[2]

Our brief review of the literature suggests four general conclusions:

(1) Increases in speech errors are evidenced when liars are aroused and unprepared, and when lies are narrative. Further, arousal generally experienced by liars during all types of lies may result in more speech errors (in comparison to truthing), but our review of the literature indicates that unplanned and narrative lies should increase the likelihood of obtaining more speech errors than planned and brief lies.

(2) Increases in speech disturbances (pausing), lack of specific detail, increases in references to general detail, and longer response latencies are evidenced when lies are unplanned and narrative.

(3) Slower speech rates and increases in the use of leveling or generalizing terms are evidenced when lies are narrative.

(4) Shorter message durations, fewer total words, and fewer different words are evidenced when lies are either planned or narrative.

TIMING OF QUESTIONS AND THE RETRIEVAL OF INFORMATION

Predictable and pronounced leakage should be evidenced when lies are unplanned and narrative in nature. However, it is obvious that not all unplanned/narrative responses are equivalent in the amount of effort required for their construction. Two critical questions requiring fabrication from liars may both prompt respondents to make a number of decisions when constructing the narrative responses, but may vary in the amount of time required to retrieve information from long-term memory. Cognitive psychologists inform us of a number of factors relevant to speed of recall (see Anderson, 1976, 1980; Norman, 1976). First, speed of recall is related positively to the degree of learning (Anderson, 1976, 1980). Truthers obviously should be able to retrieve information from long-term memory more quickly than liars during spontaneous responses. Second, learned or rehearsed material requires more time to recall if the respondent is distracted from the rehearsal (Anderson, 1980). Third, retrieval of information is facilitated when the category from which the information is recalled is still active in short-term memory (Loftus, 1974; Anderson, 1980). Fourth, when information concerning a construct is activated in short-term memory, there exists a propositional network linking the retrieved information to related concepts and constructs. This "spread of activation" or priming facilitates retrieval of associated information (Anderson, 1980; Collins & Loftus, 1975).

These observations have obvious implications for the amount of effort required to construct unplanned deceptions. For example, O'Hair et al. (1981) induced liars to tell a prepared lie by having them report fabricated grade point averages to a conversational partner. After the grade point averages were communicated, the confederate/partner asked a series of questions designed to trap individuals in "spontaneous" lies. However, since the questions occurred immediately after the prepared critical question, the concept of grades and grade point averages is active in short-term memory and retrieval of information relevant to the construction of the spontaneous response is readily available. In fact, liars and truthers did not differ significantly from each other in response latency during the spontaneous response. On the other hand, high cognitive effort associated with lying when retrieval of information is not facilitated by short-term memory activation (for example, when instructed to lie when prompted by a randomly flashing light) resulted in strong influences on speech disturbances and concreteness (Kraut, 1978).

We argue that difficulty in constructing messages is influenced both by the number of decisions a speaker must make and by the length of time required to retrieve information from long-term memory. To test this hypothesis we devised a procedure that required subjects assigned to the deception condition to construct three deceptive messages. Briefly, liars were induced to report false locations as their favorite vacation spots (prepared critical question) during a "get-acquainted" self-disclosure task (see the section on methods for details). The topic, vacation areas, was selected because it lends itself readily to a number of possible spontaneous and narrative questions. After participants answered the prepared critical question, the conversational partner/confederate asked, "Oh, really? What did you do there?" (immediate spontaneous/narrative critical question). After securing an answer to this question, the confederate asked five additional questions from a prearranged list of interview questions and then ended the interview by asking, "Listen, you said you went to [name of place given]. What were the people like there?" (delayed spontaneous/narrative question).

This framework included the construction of two spontaneous/narrative responses, which should elicit greater effort from liars than truthers. However, since the delay or distraction is included (in this case, the completion of an interview protocol), and since liars are expected to have no memory traced for events that never took place (and, therefore, responses must be constructed on the basis of stereotypes or whatever related constructs the liars can retrieve), we anticipate that liars would evidence longer latencies during the delayed spontaneous/narrative response than during the immediate spontaneous/narrative response. Further, if we are correct that question difficulty is generally increased by the necessity of retrieving information from long-term memory, it follows that the impact on response latency should generalize to additional variables indicative of effort. Specifically, if liars must retrieve information from long-term memory concerning stereotypes and so on in order to construct fabrications, then the increased effort involved in the delayed response (versus the immediate one) should have an impact on pausing (Siegman, 1979; Siegman & Feldstein, 1978) and speech disturbances (errors)(Kraut, 1978). The latter is included because speech errors might be expected when liars must retrieve, encode, and transmit a fabricated message simultaneously and yet not appear to lie. Concreteness (Kraut, 1978) is not included because liars are generally expected to be less concrete than truthers across all critical responses (Knapp et al., 1974; hypothesis 5). In sum, liars should evidence greater effort than truthers during both spontaneous responses by exhibiting longer latencies, shorter messages, more pauses, more speech errors, slower speech rates, and more generalizing/leveling terms; liars should use fewer words, fewer different words, and fewer statements of fact than truthers; and liars should evidence longer latencies, more pausing, and more speech errors during the delayed response than during the immediate response.

HYPOTHESES

Certain variables are predicted to differentiate liars and truthers across all deceptive messages (although, as noted above, the size of the effect is expected to vary across the type of lie being constructed):

H_1: Liars will construct messages of shorter duration than truthers during critical responses (when liars are deceiving).

H_2: Liars will employ fewer words and fewer different words than truthers during the critical responses.

For prepared lies, liars and truthers are not expected to differ significantly in terms of speech rate, speech errors, pauses, or generalizing/leveling terms.
However,

H_3: When prepared to lie, liars will evidence shorter latencies than truthers.

For spontaneous/narrative responses, liars should differ from truthers on a number of criteria related to effort and so on. Again, the size of the effect is expected to vary as a function of lie-type, but as a general hypothesis we predict:

H_4: Liars will exhibit greater difficulty in encoding spontaneous/narrative responses than truthers. Liars will exhibit longer response latencies, slower speech rates, more speech errors, more generalizing/leveling terms, and more pauses than truthers.

(We concede that including a number of variables in one hypothesis makes it difficult to reject or accept the hypothesis clearly. However, we decided to present hypotheses in a fairly parsimonious manner. It should be understood that if a number of the above variables discriminate between liars and truthers in our multivariate tests, then some support exists for the role of cognitive effort in encoding processes; we will then attempt to explain why all the variables were not included in the discriminant function.)

In the present analysis, we have made the concept of verbal concreteness (Kraut, 1978) less vague by coding verbal statements on the basis of specific types of information individuals present in their messages (see below). Generally, we anticipate that liars will provide information minimally sufficient to answer a particular question, but that truthers will provide more details of related facts that make the message more concrete. For example, when asked about what people are like (delayed spontaneous/narrative response), liars may provide statements describing people more than truthers (or, perhaps, at the same rate as truthers), while truthers will provide more statements of specific places (where the interactions took place), specific activities (that occurred during the interaction), and so on (see below concerning categories of verbal statements). Since liars are more vague than truthers even when prepared and rehearsed to lie (Knapp et al., 1974), concreteness is hypothesized as consistently differentiating between liars and truthers across fabrications, although it is understood that the size of the effect will be greater for spontaneous responses:

H_5: Liars will be less concrete than truthers during the critical responses.

Finally, given the above discussion of effort, we hypothesize the following:

H_6: Liars will exhibit longer latencies, more pauses, and more speech errors during the delayed response then during the immediate response.

METHODS

Participants

Participants were students enrolled in freshman, sophomore, and junior courses at Texas Tech University (TTU) who received course credit for volunteering. All participants were recruited to be in a study on "conversational analysis" and were told they would be videotaped. The students were presented with a variety of time slots for which to volunteer, spanning mid-morning to early evening each weekday for three weeks. Each volunteer was assigned a number; all even-numbered volunteers were assigned to the deception condition and all odd-numbered volunteers were assigned to the truthful condition. Nine male truthers, nine male liars, twelve female truthers, and twelve female liars provided data for this analysis.[3]

Procedures

Procedures similar to those used by O'Hair et al. (1981) were employed. When a participant arrived at the test site, he or she was told that the purpose of the study was to find out what topics students talk about during interactions with strangers. The female experimenter told each subject that she would introduce the participant to a person in the next room, that the person was another student, and that the two would ask each other twelve questions to get acquainted. The experimenter then told the participants that they and their partners were to talk about anything that came to mind for the remaining time allowed to them (half an hour). Each participant was then told the name of the confederate, to check whether the two were indeed strangers. The experimenter then gave each participant a checklist of twelve questions (ordered as follows): What is your major? Do you have any brothers and sisters, and if so, what do they do? What are your career goals? What do you do in your leisure time? What part of the country do you plan to live in after you graduate? What is your favorite vacation spot? What organizations or clubs do you belong to? What sports do you prefer? What type of music do you prefer? Who are your favorite authors? What do you enjoy most about TTU?

The experimenter then said:

> One of you will start the get-acquainted interview by asking the partner the twelve questions. Ask the questions in the order they appear on this sheet. Then, after the first partner asks all the questions, the two of you should reverse roles, with the other person asking the questions. Then you can talk about anything that comes to mind for the remainder of the half hour. Look over the twelve questions while I go and talk to your partner. You will be videotaped, as we told you earlier, but you will not see the equipment and you should not worry about being videotaped.

In fact, two cameras videotaped the interaction, both outside the participants' fields of vision. One camera was attached to the ceiling and videotaped the body, while the second camera videotaped the face from behind a two-way mirror. A cassette recorder was placed under a table in the experimental room to secure quality audio recordings.

Similar procedures were employed for participants in the deception condition. However, after the participants were provided the list of questions, the experimenter told them that actually they had been assigned the role of confederate in the study and that the experimenter would appreciate their assistance. The experimenter told the participants that they had been randomly assigned to a condition in which they were to report a false favorite vacation spot to their partners. The experimenter told the participants that the purpose of the study was to determine the effects of this communication on the subsequent conversation. All participants agreed to be confederates in the study.

At this point, the experimenter presented a list of ten vacation spots from which one was selected as the falsely reported vacation spot. This list of vacation areas was constructed by calling seven local travel agencies in order to identify the most common vacation areas about which people seek information. The ten most frequently mentioned areas included the Colorado mountains (several skiing and summer resorts), Hawaii, Los Angeles, Orlando (Florida), New Orleans, New York City, San Diego, San Francisco, Puerto Rico, and the Virgin Islands. On the basis of several tosses of a coin, a fabricated vacation area was assigned. If a liar had visited the area, the location that followed the originally assigned area was selected (the areas were listed alphabetically). This method of assigning the prepared lie offered several advantages. First, the vacation areas were all familiar, so it is reasonable to assume that liars could construct at least some details of an alleged vacation. There would be no fair test of the hypotheses if extremely unusual locations were employed. Second, by rotating liars through a list of locations, the potential problems due to some locations being either easier or more difficult to lie about are reduced. Third, since fairly common locations were selected, some liars and truthers described the same places thereby reducing the ability of blind confederates and coders to guess who were liars and who were truthers. After the vacation area was selected, the experimenter reminded the participants, "Of course, it is important that you be honest while responding to the other eleven questions."

Each participant was left in a waiting room for approximately ten minutes with the list of questions. Presumably, during this time, the participant believed that the experimenter was giving instructions to the partner. The participant was then led down a corridor and taken to the experimental room, where the true confederate was waiting. After the participant and confederate were introduced, the experimenter gave the list of questions to the true confederate and told her to start the questioning. The experimenter thanked the participants for volunteering, and then told them she would return in half an hour and left. The true confederate asked the questions on the list, and immediately after the participant provided an answer to the prepared critical question, the true confederate looked up at the participant and said, "Oh really? What did you do there? "After receiving an answer the confederate returned to the list of questions. After the last question on the list was asked, the confederate looked up again and asked, "Listen, you said you went to [name of place mentioned]. What were the people like there?" After this last question was answered, the confederate announced, "That's all the questions I have, " and handed the list of questions over to the participant. As the participant started to ask the questions, the experimenter entered the room and announced the the experiment was over. Each participant was led to another waiting room for debriefing, where the true purpose of the study was revealed and where the experimenter confirmed that the truthers told the truth on all the questions, and that the liars told the truth on the eleven non-critical questions. Two female confederates were employed in the study as conversational partners; both were blind to the lie/truth condition.

Coding

Responses to five questions were coded: the three critical responses and two truthing responses. The two truthing responses included answers to one question prior to the prepared critical question (referred to hereafter as the "precritical" truthing) and one question occurring after the prepared critical question (referred to hereafter as the "second" truthing). The two questions were selected because they required some elaboration in their responses (What are your career goals? What do you enjoy most about TTU?), so that there was a basis for comparison of the two spontaneous/narrative responses. The inclusion of the two truthing responses is important because if liars and truthers differed in regard to truthing, then any difference obtained between liars and truthers may not be attributed solely to deception (see the section on results, below).

Definitions and examples of the variables coded in this study are provided in Figure 17.1. Definitions for many variables are common to nonverbal research, and need no further explanation here (message duration, response latency, number of words, number of different words). *Speech errors* included grammatical errors (errors of noun-verb agreement), stuttering (any repetition of a monosyllabic sound), and sentence changes or false starts (in which a speaker begins a sentence a second time after having once initiated it, but with a different noun or verb; see example in Figure 17.1) *Generalizing terms* included leveling terms (the use of universals such as "all" or "everyone"), generalizing terms that indicated reluctance or inability to mention specific detail ("stuff like that," "they were crazy, *you know*"), and frequency of using the word "just" (as in *"just* hung out," *"just* drank a

Paralinguistic variables

message duration . . . . Length of time from the first syl-
(.999; .999)   lable of an answer to the last syl-
                                                           lable of the answer, excluding
                                                           any filled pause that may have
                                                           occurred prior to the occur-
                                                           rence of the first syllable.

response latency . . . . Length of time from the end of
(.995; .993)   the interviewer's question to the
                                                           start of the interviewee's an-
                                                           swer.

number of words. . . . . A count of the number of words
(.999; .993)   used in the message; included
                                                           in the count were word/phrase
                                                           repetitions.

number of different words . . . . The number of words used mi-
(.995; .993)   nus the number of words used
                                                           twice or more.

speech errors. . . . . Included grammatical errors
(.900; . 919)   (switching   plural/singular,
                                                           omissions of verbs, omissions of
                                                           contractions), stuttering (any
                                                           repetition of a sound), and sen-
                                                           tence fragments/false starts
                                                           (e.g., "You have a lot/I mean
                                                           there's a lot of things you can do
                                                           there. They're ah/they don't
                                                           even/they're not even from the
                                                           state themselves"—these two
                                                           sentences contained three false
                                                           starts).

Figure 17.1.   List of variables associated with the auditory channel, with defini-
               tions, estimates of coder reliabilities, and examples.

speech rate..........................The number of words used divided by the message duration.

generalizing term rate ....Included generalizing terms denoting lack of specific detail ("stuff like that," "you know" at the end of a sentence, as in "you know what I mean"), repetition of the word "just," and leveling terms (the use of any universal).
(.846; .758)

pauses (frequency)....................The number of times during a message the respondent exhibited either a silent pause or a filled pause. A pause had to be at least .2 of a second in duration to be recorded.
(.943; .715)

pauses (duration) ....The total length of time of either filled pauses or silent pauses during an answer.
(.876; .778)

Concreteness variables

factual statements about area ....Included the number of statements concerning facts about the area ("a lot of land up there is owned by oil people"; "in the winter there's nothing to do there but snowmobile or something like that"; "they have their own zoo and everything"; "there was a huge waterfall"; "20 miles north of Winter Park").
(.968; .883)

specific activities......................Included the number of activities referred to that inform the listener of an exact experience, one that is not likely to be open to interpretation: swam; skiied; laid out in sun; got blisters; went hang gliding; went to Mardi Gras, etc.
(.985; .688)

Figure 17.1 (Continued)   (continued)

specific persons . . . . Included references to self ("I"
(.990; .921)   or "me") and included all refer-
                                                     ences to persons who were
                                                     uniquely identified and who are
                                                     not interchangeable: my grand-
                                                     mother; dad; my husband; my
                                                     wife; my girlfriend; my cousins;
                                                     John Denver, etc.

descriptions of people. . . . . Included statements concerning
(.963; 1.00)   meeting people, interacting
                                                     with people, and reactions to
                                                     people ("they're just really laid
                                                     back up there"; "high on some-
                                                     thing"; "they called us Texas
                                                     Turkeys").

temporal references/justifications . . . . Included any temporal refer-
(.967; 1.00)   ence that fixed and located the
                                                     trip in time (end of the fall se-
                                                     mester; just before the tourist
                                                     season, etc.) and any reference
                                                     concerning why the trip was
                                                     taken: Mardi Gras; to go skiing;
                                                     graduation party, etc.

specific places . . . . Included all references to lo-
(.947; 1.00)   cales that were uniquely defined
                                                     within a geographic area or
                                                     within a state or city: the Davis
                                                     Mountains; the Hyatt Regency;
                                                     Winter Park; San Diego Zoo;
                                                     Bourbon Street; Hollywood and
                                                     Vine; the Biltmore, etc.

Concreteness (nonspecific)

nonspecific activities . . . . Included the number of activi-
(.968; 1.00)   ties referred to that fail to inform
                                                     the listener of an exact experi-
                                                     ence ("stayed out all night";
                                                     "taste the high country"; "lazy
                                                     stuff"; "hung out"; "had fun").

Figure 17.1 (Continued)

nonspecific persons . . . . (.971; 1.00)	Included all references to "we" and included all group references (Texans, New Yorkers, etc.).
Nonspecific places . . . . (.999; 1.00)	Included names for general areas which did not differentiate specific subareas such as streets, hotel names, and the like: Colorado, West Coast, New Orleans, Los Angeles, etc.

Figure 17.1 (Continued)

lot"). *Frequency of pausing* was measured by counting the number of silent pauses or filled pauses ("er," "ah," "hmmm") that were longer than .2 second in duration and that occurred during the delivery of the message. *Duration of pausing* was the total amount of time in which the speaker engaged in either silent or filled pausing during the delivery of the message.

Several categories were included to measure both specific and nonspecific details because it was felt that the number of details that differentiate liars and truthers may differ slightly from one narrative response to another, and that liars may use one or two categories of details while truthers may provide reference to more different types of specific details across responses. A message was considered to be highly elaborated and rich in detail if it contained *factual statements about an area;* statements mentioning *specific activities, specific places, specific persons,* and *descriptions of people;* statements of *temporal reference* and of *justification* (that is, providing reasons for taking the vacation). A message was considered less concrete if it mentioned *nonspecific activities, nonspecific places,* and *nonspecific persons.* Of course, a message was not concrete at all if no details of any kind were mentioned.

Factual statements about an area included any reference to the activities offered by the area, the ownership of the land, the expense of staying in the area, features of the area, geographic relations to other areas, and opinions about the area (such as "It's a good place to get away from the city and relax"; see examples in Figure 17.1). *Specific activities* included any reference to an activity the speaker engaged in that was described in sufficient detail to inform the listener of exactly what was experienced—a description that was not open to misinterpretation ("laid out in the sun, got blisters," "went to Mardi Gras"). In contrast, *nonspecific activities* failed to inform the listener of an exact activity ("stayed out all night," "lazy stuff," "hung out").

Specific persons included references to self (" I," "me") and any reference to a person who was precisely identifiable by the reference ("dad," "my boy-friend," "grandmother," "my cousins," "John Denver"), while *nonspecific persons* included references to groups ("Texans," "New Yorkers," "Califor-nians") and any reference to "we." *Specific places* included references to locales that are unique within a general geographic area or within a state or city, including names of specific streets or hotels ("San Diego Zoo," "Bour-bon Street," "the Biltmore," "the Davis Mountains"); *nonspecific places* in-cluded only references to general areas without differentiating subareas ("Miami," "West Coast," "Denver"). *Descriptions of people* included any statement concerning meeting people, interacting with people, and reac-tions to people. *Temporal references/justifications* included any statement as to when or why the vacation was taken. Originally separate categories, the two were collapsed together because there were few temporal refer-ences, and justification for a trip often concurred with when a trip was taken ("snow skiing in winter," "a Mardi Gras trip in the spring," "we went to my brother's graduation in Hawaii in June").

RESULTS

Coder Reliability

There were 2 coders, blind to the lie/truth condition, and each coded half of the 42 tapes; 2 estimates of intercoder reliability were computed. The experimenter who assigned subjects to conditions did not code tapes. After the responses for one participant were used as a training tape, each coder began transcribing and coding responses. After each coder coded 7 to 10 tapes, 1 tape coder B had completed was randomly selected for coder A to code and 2 tapes coder A had completed were given to coder B to transcribe (and these 2 tapes were embedded in the second tapes coder B was to transcribe and code). Each coder measured the 17 variables (excluding speech rate) for 5 responses for the 3 participants. Reliability was assessed by computing Pearson product-moment correlations between coders. The correlations are presented as the first number in parentheses under each variable heading in Figure 17.1; these ranged from .846 to .999. Later, when the last several tapes assigned to coder B were given to the coder, 3 tapes were included that were randomly selected from the tapes coder A had already completed. The resulting correlations are presented as the sec-ond number in parentheses in Figure 17.1. Of the correlations, 13 were well above a desired level of .80, reliabilities for 2 variables approached the de-sired level (generalizing/leveling, .758; duration of pauses, .778) and reli-abilities were somewhat lower for frequency of pauses (.715) and for references to specific activities (.688). Disagreements between coders were resolved by having the coders jointly listen to the tapes and mutually agree about how the behaviors were to be coded. The time required to transcribe and code a tape ranged from 1.5 to 7 hours.

Hypotheses

Since the duration of responses varied considerably across deceiving/ truthing conditions and across types of questions, all behaviors except response latency, message duration, number of words, and number of different words were computed as rates by dividing frequency of occurrence (or duration, as in the case of duration of pauses) by message duration. Hypotheses were explored in two ways. First, since a fairly large number of variables are included in the analysis, a stepwise multiple discriminant analysis was conducted for each of the three critical responses in order to obtain one linear combination of variables that differentiated between liars and truthers. Second, a series of 5 (trials) × (truth/deception) ANOVAs (Dixon & Brown, 1977) were computed, with supplementary contrasts. The second procedure confirmed the expectation that liars and truthers did not differ from each other on any variable during the two truthing responses. However, since it is clear that the variables under study undoubtedly correlate with each other, we shall present and emphasize the mutivariate tests and add information concerning the second analysis when relevant to the questions of question difficulty and consistency of leakage.

Table 17.1 presents the summary of the multiple discriminant analysis for the prepared critical response. The significant function (eigenvalue = .7833; R = .6628; Wilks's lambda =.5607; chi-square = 21.11; df = 7; p = .0036) included seven variables and accounted for 43.9 % of the between-groups variance. Liars had shorter response latencies ($\bar{X}$ = .624) than truthers ($\bar{X}$ = 2.057), were less likely to employ generalizing/leveling terms ($\bar{X}$ = .000) than truthers ($\bar{X}$ = .028), and were slightly more likely to engage in speech errors ($\bar{X}$ = .040) than truthers ($\bar{X}$ = .032). In regard to concreteness, liars ($\bar{X}$ = 2.555) made more references to nonspecific places than truthers ($\bar{X}$ = .997), as expected, but truthers made more temporal references ($\bar{X}$ = .032) than liars ($\bar{X}$ = .000), made more references to specific places ($\bar{X}$ = .193) than liars ($\bar{X}$ = .000), and made more references to specific persons ($\bar{X}$ = .100) than liars ($\bar{X}$ = .081). Liars did not construct shorter messages with fewer words and fewer different words. Hypotheses 1 and 2 were not supported for the prepared critical response. Liars did engage in shorter latencies, supporting hypothesis 3. Further, the fact that liars only reported nonspecific places in their messages and made fewer references to time and so on is supportive of our expectation of concreteness (hypothesis 5). However, we did not anticipate that liars would use fewer generalizing/

Table 17.1
Summary of Multiple Discriminant Analysis Results:
Prepared Critical Response

Canonical Discriminant Function:

Eigenvalue	Percent of Variance	Canonical Correlation	After Function	Wilks's Lambda	Chi-Square	d.f.	p
.7833	100.00	.6628	0	.5607	21.11	7	.004

Standardized Canonical Discriminant Function Coefficients:

	Function 1
Latency	.3325
Generalizing/leveling	.5838
Temporal references	.4088
Nonspecific places	−.4693
Specific persons	.5023
Specific places	.4968
Speech error rate	−.8209

Canonical Discriminant Function Evaluated at Group Means:

	Function 1
Group 1 (liars)	−.8637
Group 2 (truth tellers)	.8637

Means for Variables Included in Function:

	Liars' $\overline{X}$	Truthers' $\overline{X}$
Latency	.624	2.057
Generalizing/leveling	.000	.029
Temporal references	.000	.032
Nonspecific places	2.255	.997
Specific persons	.081	.100
Specific places	.000	.193
Speech error rate	.040	.032

leveling terms than truthers, although such an outcome is compatible with the notion that prepared lies appear rehearsed and lacking in spontaneity (DePaulo, Davis, & Lanier, 1980; DePaulo et al., 1981). Further, the slight increase in speech error rate among liars is compatible with the effects of arousal, as noted above, although we had not predicted the effect for prepared, brief lies.

Table 17.2 presents the summary of the results for the immediate response. The function (eigenvalue = .8624; R = .6805; Wilks's lambda = .5369; chi-square = 23.32; df = 5; p = .003) included five variables and accounted for 46.3 percent of the between-groups variance. Liars exhibited

Table 17.2
Summary of Multiple Discriminant Analysis Results:
Immediate Spontaneous Response

Canonical Discriminant Function:

Eigenvalue	Percent of Variance	Canonical Correlation	After Function	Wilks's Lambda	Chi-Square	d.f.	p
.8624	100.00	.6805	0	.5369	23.32	5	.003

Standardized Canonical Discriminant Function Coefficients:

	Function 1
Latency	.3088
Number of words	−.6500
Generalizing/leveling	.5132
Pause duration rate	.2901
Specific persons	−.3968

Canonical Discriminant Function Evaluated at Group Means:

	Function 1
Group 1 (liars)	.9063
Group 2 (truth tellers)	−.9063

Means for Variables Included in Function:

Variables	Liars' $\bar{X}$	Truthers' $\bar{X}$
Latency	1.124	.752
Number of words	14.238	39.524
Generalizing/leveling	.318	.071
Pause duration rate	.235	.180
Specific persons	.042	.175

longer latencies ($\bar{X} = 1.124$) than truthers ($\bar{X} = .752$), used fewer words ($\bar{X} = 1.238$) than truthers ($\bar{X} = 39.524$), used more generalizing/leveling terms ($\bar{X} = .318$) than truthers ($\bar{X} = .071$), and paused for longer durations ($\bar{X} = .235$) than truthers ($\bar{X} = .180$). Only the concreteness variable references to *specific persons* differentiated liars from truthers: truthers made more such references than liars ($\bar{X}$s = .175 and .042, respectively). Partial support was thus obtained for hypothesis 2: Liars employed fewer words than truthers. Partial support was also obtained for hypothesis 4: Liars exhibited longer latencies, used more generalizing/leveling terms and paused longer than did truthers. Some support was also obtained for hypothesis 5: Truthers made more specific statements concerning people than did liars.

Table 17.3 presents the summary of the results for the delayed response. The significant function (eigenvalue = 1.6921; R = .7928; Wilks's lambda = .3714; chi-square = 35.65; df = 8; p = .001) included eight

Table 17.3
Summary of Multiple Discriminant Analysis Results:
Delayed Spontaneous Response

Canonical Discriminant Function:

Eigenvalue	Percent of Variance	Canonical Correlation	After Function	Wilks's Lambda	Chi-Square	d. f.	p
1.6921	100.00	.7928	0	.3714	35.65	8	.0001

Standardized Canonical Discriminant Function Coefficients:

	Function 1
Message duration	−.3999
Pause duration rate	.8171
Temporal references	−.3953
Nonspecific places	−.4375
Specific places	−.5905
Nonspecific activities	.3476
Descriptions of people	.5324
Speech error rate	.5233

Canonical Discriminant Function Evaluated at Group Means:

	Function 1
Group 1 (liars)	1.2695
Group 2 (truth tellers)	−1.2695

Means for Variables Included in Function:

Variables	Liars' $\bar{X}$	Truthers' $\bar{X}$
Message duration	12.962	23.919
Pause duration	.271	.168
Temporal references	.003	.018
Nonspecific places	.010	.038
Specific places	.002	.037
Nonspecific activities	.013	.003
Descriptions of people	.351	.165
Speech error rate	.157	.127

variables and accounted for 62.9 percent of the between-groups variance. Liars talked more briefly $\bar{X}$ = 12.962) than truthers ($\bar{X}$ = 23.919) and paused for longer durations ($\bar{X}$ = .271) than truthers ($\bar{X}$ = .168). Liars also engaged in slightly more speech errors ($\bar{X}$ = .157) than truthers ($\bar{X}$ = .127). The results provide strong evidence that liars found it difficult to improvise specific detail when they constructed the delayed response. Truthers mentioned more specific places ($\bar{X}$ = .0367) than liars ($\bar{X}$ = .0018), mentioned more nonspecific places ($\bar{X}$ = .0380) than liars ($\bar{X}$ = .0101), and made slightly more temporal references ($\bar{X}$ = .0177) than liars ($\bar{X}$ = .0032). Liars, however, only made more statements describing people ($\bar{X} = .3515$) than truthers ($\bar{X} = .1648$). Some support for hypothesis 1 was obtained (liars spoke more briefly). However, in hypothesis 4 we predicted that a number of variables associated with the difficulty of encoding spontaneous responses would differentiate liars and truthers. Yet only two variables (duration of pauses and speech errors) did so. Thus less support for hypothesis 4 was obtained than anticipated. However, strong support was obtained for hypothesis 5 (liars were less concrete than truthers).

In hypothesis 6 we predicted that liars would exhibit longer latencies, more pauses, and more speech errors during the delayed response than during the immediate response. However, little evidence was obtained that indicated that liars found the delayed response more difficult (than the immediate) than did truthers. Liars did exhibit longer latencies during the delayed response 2.314) than during the immediate ($\bar{X} = 1.238$; $t = 3.42$; df = 20; $p = .002$; one-tailed distribution). However, truthers also exhibited longer latencies during the delayed response ($\bar{X} = 1.814$) than during the immediate one ($\bar{X} = .752$; $t = 3.27$; $p = .002$). Both liars and truthers required more processing time during the delayed response. It should be noted, however, that the interpretation of the significant trials × deception interaction ($F = 5.41$, 4/160; $p = .001$) revealed evidence highly supportive of the impact of retrieval time on length of response latency. Specifically, liars exhibited the shortest average latency when prepared to lie ($\bar{X} = .624$), while truthers required longer retrieval times ($\bar{X} = 2.057$; $t = 2.89$; df = 40; $p = .003$), and truthers exhibited the shortest average latency during the immediate spontaneous response, when the topic was active in short-term memory ($\bar{X} = .752$; $\bar{X} = 1.124$ for liars; $t = 2.21$; $p = .002$). Thus retrieval time influenced response latency, and both liars and truthers required a longer retrieval time during the delayed response. The only support for hypothesis 6 occurred for speech errors. Liars exhibited more speech errors during the delayed response ($\bar{X} = .157$) than during the immediate response ($\bar{X} = .083$; $t = 1.86$; $p = .039$); no such difference occurred for truthers ($p = .165$). Liars did not differ in the two responses for either frequency of pauses ($p = .783$) or duration of pauses ($p = .538$), and neither did truthers ($p = .169$ and .639, respectively). While liars exhibited longer durations of pauses than truthers during both spontaneous responses (see above), there was no evidence that liars increased pausing behavior during the delayed response.

DISCUSSION

Based on the previous work that suggested that the auditory channel is a "leaky" channel, we sought to identify what cues are leaked by liars in the auditory channel and to assess how attempted control and amount of effort influence cue leakage. Our results provide strong support for the importance of these two processes. First, when control is high (prepared response), liars require little processing time and simply answer the question; subsequently, response latencies are short and liars do not fill in details that would locate the described event in time and so on, which would make the message concrete. However, hypotheses 1 and 2 (message duration, number of words) were not supported for the prepared lie. This was due to the fact that the answer to this question was relatively short for both liars and truthers.

The more important results have to do with effort. Clearly, liars found both the spontaneous responses more difficult than did truthers (although, as noted above, liars did not find a particular one of the spontaneous responses any more difficult than the other). First, liars were more likely than truthers to be reticent (fewer words in the immediate response, shorter message duration in the delayed response) and paused for longer durations than truthers during both spontaneous responses. Further, when no associative linkages existed to facilitate answering a question (even when the topic was active in short-term memory), liars had longer latencies and generalized more than did truthers. However, the clearest support of difficulty in encoding occurred when the liars had to construct a narrative lie when they felt their role as liar had been completed. Liars talked more briefly, paused more, had more speech errors, and made references only to descriptions of people (and slightly more references to nonspecific activities) without filling in specific details concerning time, specific places where the event occurred, and so on.

There are several inconsistencies with these data that need to be addressed. Specifically, while liars had longer durations of pauses than truthers during both spontaneous responses, liars generalized more than truthers during the immediate response (but not during the delayed response) and exhibited more speech errors than truthers during the delayed response (but not during the immediate one). If both responses required effort (and if the delayed response required more effort), then one would expect either consistency in leakage or perhaps more leakage during the delayed response. However, our results seem to reflect some external influence we had not previously considered. One possible explanation for these results is the issue of question ambiguity (Siegman, 1979; Siegman & Feldstein, 1978). Specifically, it is possible that subjects felt that being asked to describe activities was a more ambiguous task than being asked to describe people. While we have no evidence for this explanation, it should be noted that both liars ($p = .010$) and truthers ($p = .036$) talked for a longer duration during the delayed response than during the immediate one (in fact, both talked twice as long during the descriptions of people as they did during the descriptions of events). Since interactions with people are more general and more pervasive than activities that occur only in one locale, and since sub-jects talked longer when discussing people, it would seem to follow that perhaps the immediate question was a more ambiguous task. Consequently, liars generalized more during the immediate response, while during the de-layed response they thought of more to say but engaged in more speech errors when processing and transmitting the information.

Our results suggest a number of implications for work in hypothesis testing and theory construction in deception research. Clearly, the underly-ing processes of attempted control and cognitive effort influence the type of cue leaked and the amount of leakage obtained. Our results indicate that deception theorists need to examine mechanisms underlying effort more closely (number of decisions, retrieval time, question ambiguity), since these variables have a clear impact on latency, speech errors, pausing, and gener-alizing terms. Further, we recommend that deception theorists employ ma-nipulation checks on the types of lies subjects are induced into constructing. Admittedly, if we had our subjects listen to their taped interviews and pro-vide evidence concerning difficulty, ambiguity, and so on, not only would the interpretation of our results be more straightforward, but more direct evidence concerning the impact of underlying processes would be available. To date, only Matarazzo, Wiens, Jackson, and Manaugh (1970) have at-tempted a postexperimental interview, and it is long overdue for deception theorists to provide more direct evidence of the impacts of anxiety and other factors. Subsequently, in our latest project, we had subjects rate their re-sponses in terms of confidence, difficulty, controllability, and the like, and we feel that this is a useful extension of the present analysis. Second, our results have implications concerning research on deception detection accu-racy. Obviously, we feel that observers should be more accurate in detecting deception when effort is high, as in the delayed spontaneous/narrative re-sponse. This should be especially true if observers use concreteness when making judgments of veracity (Kraut, 1978).

Some limitations must be stipulated concerning generalizability. The lies explored in this project were sanctioned by an experimenter, we inten-tionally dealt only with lies of fact, and the liars' motivation to lie successfully was not manipulated (as, for example, in Miller et al., 1983). Obviously, we recommend that future research extend our analysis to other types of lies and types of liars.

NOTES

1. Zuckerman et al. (1981) also included felt emotions (negative affect, anxiety, and so on) as a fourth process. However, there was somewhat less support for this particular process in comparison to other processes. Many people feel uncomfortable during lying, and thus theo-rists (and even naive observers, as survey data indicate—see Hocking & Leathers, 1980; Zuck-erman et al., 1981) believe that gestures such as adaptors, facial unpleasantness, and eye con-

tact should differentiate liars and truthers. However, literature concerning most of these variables contains contradictory findings. Zuckerman et al. (1981) conclude that only adaptors and negative statements represent behaviors related to negative affects that are consistently leakage by liars. In part, the lack of consistency for many guilt- or anxiety-related cues may stem from the facts that there are gender differences and personality differences in how liars exhibit negative affects (see Cody & O'Hair, 1983; Miller et al., 1983) and personality differences exist in liars' abilities under stressful conditions (Exline et al, 1970; Geis & Moon, 1981). Also, as Zuckerman et al. (1981) and Ekman (1980) have noted, some liars may experience negative feelings while others may enjoy the experience of duping others. Since different people may experience or manifest anxiety/negative affects differently, and since less consistency is evidenced, we decided to focus more attention on processes underlying deception that would be more fruitful than the affective approach.

2. We do not, of course, argue that the variables summarized here represent an exhaustive set of variables relevant to the processes underlying deception. Consistency and plausibility (Kraut, 1978), powerless style speech, and nonimmediacy are some additional variables worthy of future study.

3. A total of 59 participants were recruited. One volunteer knew the confederate, and so was given credit and allowed to leave. One female assigned to the deception condition had actually visited all ten vacation areas and was simply given credit and allowed to leave. On three of the interviews the confederates asked either the prepared-critical or immediate-critical question in a manner inconsistent with the way it was asked of other subjects. Poor audio recordings were obtained for six participants. Further, since we did not want to sample a higher portion of one sex over the other (see Cody & O'Hair, 1983), we decided to equalize the number of males and females assigned to the two conditions.

REFERENCES

Anderson, J. R. (1976). *Language, memory and thought.* Hillsdale, NJ: Lawrence Erlbaum.

Anderson, J. R. (1980). *Cognitive psychology and its implications.* San Francisco: W. H. Freeman.

Bauchner, J., Brandt, D. R., & Miller, G. R. (1977). The truth/deception attribution: Effects of varying levels of information availability. In B. R. Ruben (Ed.), *Communication yearbook 1.* New Brunswick, NJ: Transaction.

Brandt, D. R., Miller, G. R., & Hocking, J. E. (1981). *Familiarity and lie detection: A replication and extension.* Paper presented at the meeting of the Speech Communication Association, Anaheim, CA.

Cody, M. J., & O'Hair, H. D. (1983). Nonverbal communication and deception: Differences in deception cues due to gender and communicator dominance. *Communication Monographs, 50,* 175-192.

Collins, A. M., & Loftus, E. F. (1975). A spreading-activation theory of semantic processing. *Psychological Review, 82,* 407-428.

Comadena, M. E. (1982). *Observer accuracy in detecting deception in intimate and friendship relationships.* Paper presented at the meeting of the International Communication Association, Boston.

DePaulo, B. M., Davis, T., & Lanier, K. (1980). *Planning lies: The effects of spontaneity and arousal on success at deception.* Paper presented at the meeting of the Eastern Psychological Association, Hartford, CT.

DePaulo, B. M., Finkelstein, S., Rosenthal, R., & Eisenstat, R. A. (1980). *Thinking about deceit.* Unpublished manuscript, University of Virginia.

DePaulo, B. M., Lanier, K., & Davis, T. (1981). *The effects of planning and arousal on telling and detecting lies.* Unpublished manuscript, University of Virginia.

Dixon, W. J., & Brown, M. B. (Eds.). (1977). *BMD-77 biomedical computer programs, p-series.* Berkeley: University of California Press.

Dulaney, E. F. (1982). Changes in language behavior as a function of veracity. *Human Communication Research, 9,* 75-82.

Ekman, P. (1980). *Mistakes when deceiving.* Paper presented at the Conference on the Clever Hans Phenomenon, New York Academy of Sciences, New York.

Eckman, P., & Friesen, W. V. (1969). Nonverbal leakage and clues to deception. *Psychiatry, 32,* 88-106.

Ekman, P., & Friesen, W. V. (1972). Hand movements. *Journal of Communication, 22,* 353-374.

Ekman, P., & Friesen, W. V. (1974). Detecting deception from the body or face. *Journal of Personality and Social Psychology, 29,* 288-298.

Ekman, P., Friesen, W. V., & Scherer, K. E. (1976). Body movement and voice pitch in deceptive interaction. *Semiotica, 16,* 23-27.

Exline, R. V., Thibaut, H., Hickey, C. B., & Gumpert, P. (1970). Visual interaction in relation to Machivellianism and an unethical act. In R. Christie & F. L. Geis (Eds.), *Studies in Machiavellianism.* New York: Academic.

Feldman, R. S., Devin-Sheehan, L., & Allen, V. L. (1978). Nonverbal cues as indicators of nonverbal dissembling. *American Education Research Journal, 15,* 217-231.

Fugita, S. S., Hogrebe, M. C., & Wexley, K. N. (1980). Perceptions of deception: Perceived expertise in detecting deception, successfulness of deception and nonverbal cues. *Personality and Social Psychology Bulletin, 6,* 637-643.

Geis, F. L., & Moon, T. H. (1981). Machiavellianism and deception. *Journal of Personality and Social Psychology, 41,* 766-775.

Geizer, R. A., Rarick, D. L., & Soldow, G. F. (1977). Deception and judgment accuracy: A study in person perception. *Personality and Social Psychology Bulletin, 3,* 446-449.

Goldman-Eisler, F. (1968). *Psycholinguistics: Experiments in spontaneous speech.* New York: Academic.

Hemsley, G. D. (1977). *Experimental studies in the behavioral indicants of deception.* Unpublished doctoral dissertation, University of Toronto.

Hocking, J. E., Bauchner, J., Kaminski, E., & Miller, G. R. (1979). Detecting deceptive communication from verbal, visual and paralinguistic cues. *Human Communication Research, 6,* 33-46.

Hocking, J. E., & Leathers, D. G. (1980). Nonverbal indicators of deception: A new theoretical perspective. *Communication Monographs, 47,* 119-131.

Hocking, J. E., Miller, G. R., & Fontes, N. E. (1978). Videotape in the courtroom. *Trial, 14,* 52-55.

Horvath, F. S. (1973). Verbal and nonverbal clues to truth and deception during polygraph examinations. *Journal of Police Science and Administration, 1,* 138-152.

Horvath, F. S. (1978). An experimental comparison of the psychological stress during polygraph examinations. *Journal of Applied Psychology, 63,* 338-344.

Kasl, S. V., & Mahl, G. F. (1965). The relationship of disturbances and hesitations in spontaneous speech to anxiety. *Journal of Personality and Social Psychology, 1,* 425-433.

Knapp, M. L., & Comadena, M. E. (1979). Telling it like it isn't: A review of theory and research on deceptive communication. *Human Communication Research, 5,* 270-285.

Knapp, M. L., Hart, R. P., & Dennis, H. S. (1974). An exploration of deception as a communication construct. *Human Communication Research, 1,* 15-29.

Kraut, R. E. (1978). Verbal and nonverbal cues in the perception of lying. *Journal of Personality and Social Psychology, 36,* 380-391.

Kraut, R. E. (1980). Humans as lie detectors: Some second thoughts. *Journal of Communication, 30*(4), 209-216.

Littlepage, G. E., & Pineault, M. A. (1978). Verbal, facial and paralinguistic cues to the deception of truth and lying. *Personality and Social Psychology Bulletin, 4,* 461-464.

Littlepage, G. E., & Pineault, M. A. (1979). Detection of deceptive factual statements from the body and the face. *Personality and Social Psychology Bulletin, 5,* 325-328.

Littlepage, G. E., & Pineault, M. A. (1981). Detection of truthful and deceptive interpersonal communication across information transmission modes. *Journal of Social Psychology, 114,* 57-68.

Loftus, E. F. (1974). Activation of semantic memory. *American Journal of Psychology, 86,* 331-337.

Matarazzo, J. D., Wiens, A. N., Jackson, R. H., & Manaugh, T. S. (1970). Interviewee speech behavior under conditions of endogenously-present and exogenously-induced motivational states. *Journal of Clinical Psychology, 26,* 141-148.

Miller, G. R., & Burgoon, J. K. (1982). Factors affecting assessments of witness credibility. In N. L. Kerr & R. M. Bray (Eds.), *The psychology of the courtroom.* New York: Academic.

Miller, G. R., DeTurck, M. A., & Kalbfleisch, P. J. (1983). Self monitoring, rehearsal and deceptive communication. *Human Communication Research, 10,* 97-118.

Motley, M. T. (1974). Acoustic correlates of lies. *Western Speech, 38,* 81-87.

Norman, D. A. (1976). *Memory and attention: An introduction to human information processing.* New York: John Wiley.

O'Hair, H. D., Cody, M. J., & McLaughlin, M. L. (1981). Prepared lies, spontaneous lies, Machiavellianism and nonverbal communication. *Human Communication Research, 7,* 325-339.

Siegman, A. W. (1979). Cognition and hesitation in speech. In A. W. Siegman & S. Felstein (Eds.), *Of speech and time: Temporal patterns in interpersonal contexts.* Hillsdale, NJ: Lawrence Erlbaum.

Siegman, A. W., & Feldstein, S. (Eds.). (1978). *Nonverbal behavior and communication.* Hillsdale, NJ: Lawrence Erlbaum.

Wagner, H., & Pease, K. 1976). The verbal communication of inconsistency between attitudes held and attitudes expressed. *Journal of Personality, 44,* 1-16.

Waid, W. M., & Orne, M. T. (1981). Cognitive, social and personality processes in the physiological detection of deception. In L. Berkowitz (Ed.), *Advances in experimental social psychology* (Vol. 14). New York: Academic.

Zuckerman, M., DeFrank, R. S., Hall, J. A., Larrance, D. T., & Rosenthal, R. (1979). Facial and vocal cues of deception and honesty. *Journal of Experimental Social Psychology, 15,* 378-396.

Zuckerman, M., DePaulo, B. M., & Rosenthal, R. (1981). Verbal and nonverbal communication of deception. In L. Berkowitz (Ed.), *Advances in experimental social psychology* (Vol. 14). New York: Academic.

IV ● MASS COMMUNICATION

18● Fear and Victimization: Exposure to Television and Perceptions of Crime and Fear

RON TAMBORINI ● DOLF ZILLMANN ● JENNINGS BRYANT

Michigan State University ● Indiana University ● University of Evansville

I
N forming perceptions about the social world, individuals can draw on different types of experience for information to be used in making judgments. This information may come directly from personal experience or indirectly through communication with friends and contact with the mass media. Recently, social scientists have been interested in determining the extent to which media experiences alone can contribute to these social perceptions (see Hawkins & Pingree, 1982). Investigations have attempted to link media exposure to family values (Pingree, Starrett, & Hawkins, 1979), racial concerns (Vogly & Schwarz, 1980), attitudes about the elderly (Gerbner & Signorielli, 1979), and perceptions about home health care programs (Tyler, Cook, & Gordon, 1981). Most research in this area, however, has concentrated on the impact of television exposure on judgments about crime and safety (e.g., Doob & Macdonald, 1979; Gerbner & Gross, 1976a, 1976b). The purpose of this inquiry is to look more closely at this relation, building, in part, on an experimental investigation of this issue conducted by Bryant, Carveth, and Brown (1981). In particular, this study is concerned with two issues: (1) At what level (personal versus societal) does television exposure affect perceptions? (2) What is the duration of any such effect?

The first issue, the impact of television exposure on personal- versus societal-level perceptions of crime and safety, has not been investigated in any great detail. Although the separation between personal- and societal-

Correspondence and reprint requests: Ron Tamborini, Department of Communication, Michigan State University, East Lansing, MI 48824.

level judgments can be made on a conceptual basis, little research on mass media effects has dealt with this distinction. Most studies in this area have looked at what might be considered societal-level perceptions, those that deal more with population estimates and the general state of the environment rather than the personal implications of the environment for the individual. Research of this type has attempted to determine the effect of media exposure on beliefs about the prevalence of violence in society (Pingree et al., 1979) and on interpersonal mistrust (Neville, 1980; Gerbner, Gross, Eleey, Jackson-Beeck, Jeffries-Fox, & Signorielli, 1977a, 1977b). At the same time, several studies have employed measures that deal with more personal-level perceptions, those having greater implications for the individual; however, these studies fail to distinguish perceptual-level differences in exposure effects (Doob & Macdonald, 1979; Gerbner, Gross, Jackson-Beeck, Jeffries-Fox, & Signorielli, 1978a, 1978b; Gerbner, Gross, Signorelli, Morgan, & Jackson-Beeck, 1979a, 1979b).

Although little research on media exposure and perceptions of crime has dealt specifically with differences between personal- and societal-level judgments, work in the field of cognitive social psychology more directly addresses this issue. Of particular interest here is the research on base rates. This literature indicates that although base rates may have a marginal impact on judgments about others, this type of statistical information does not appear to influence judgments about the self (Borgida & Brekke, 1981; Borgida & Nisbett, 1977; Hansen & Stoner, 1978; Kahneman & Tversky, 1973). Information associated with personal and societal judgments is thought to be segregated in processing so that information related to judgments about the general population do not translate into changes in personal perceptions concerning fear of victimization (Tyler, 1980). In addition, some evidence indicates that similar judgmental-level differences can result from this type of base rate information when it is received through the mass media (Tyler, Cook, & Gordon, 1981), and suggests that the media can affect general perceptions while having little impact on personal-level perceptions.

Within the literature on media exposure and perceptions of crime, however, the separation between personal- and societal-level judgments is less clear. Although they do not deal with this distinction in particular, several authors have suggested that exposure to television violence can have an important effect on perceptions about crime and safety that might be considered both personal and societal in nature. In their "cultivation hypothesis," Gerbner and Gross (1976a, 1976b) assert that the overemphasis of violence on television drama gives viewers an exaggerated impression of the extent of threat and danger in society (a societal-level effect), and that these impressions cultivate fear and distrust of fellow citizens in real life (a personal-level effect). They propose that heavy exposure to media violence causes viewers to perceive the world as television portrays it, and to consider it increasingly likely that they might become victims of violent crime. As a consequence, they become acutely fearful for their personal safety. In support of their "scary world" proposition, Gerbner and Gross provide correlational data that indicate a relatively weak but statistically reliable positive association between amount of television viewing and a tendency to give the "television answer" to questions concerning estimates of law enforcement, social distrust, and anticipated victimization. More recent research conducted by Gerbner et al. (1977a, 1977b, 1979a, 1979b) produced similar results with child populations.

The finding of Gerbner and his colleagues have been challenged strenuously, however. In research similar to that conducted by Gerbner and Gross (1976a, 1976b), Doob and MacDonald (1979) report that after controlling for the density of crime in a viewer's neighborhood, no relation was found between media use and fear of crime except in high-crime neighborhoods. Hughes (1980) and Hirsch (1980), in a reanalysis of the same data reported in Gerbner et al. (1977a), used simultaneous rather than individual controls for demographic factors such as age, sex, and education and failed to obtain most of the correlations originally reported. Gerbner and his colleagues (Gerbner, Gross, Morgan, & Signorielli, 1980a, 1980b) account for these inconsistencies in a refinement to the cultivation hypothesis known as "resonance." They assert that television's effect is strongest among viewers whose real-life situations most closely parallel those portrayed on television. When an issue is relevant to a viewer's everyday life, television's images will "resonate" and amplify the cultivation effect. Thus Doob and MacDonald's (1979) finding that only city dwellers who live in high-crime neighborhoods demonstrate the cultivation of fear is consistent with this notion because the portrayal of crime on television should be particularly salient to their lives. In addition, Gerbner et al. (1980a, 1980b) point to more recent research that exhibits a relation between television viewing and perceptions of danger even after simultaneous controls are applied.

Although the research by Gerbner and his colleagues may suggest that exposure to television can influence both personal- and societal-level perceptions about violence, research designed to look at this distinction more directly indicates that exposure to the mass media does not affect perceptions at both levels. The reports of several recent surveys comparing first-hand experience and indirect experience through the mass media have demonstrated that exposure to media is related positively to judgments about crime and violence on the societal level but is unrelated to fear of personal crime victimization (Skogan & Maxfield, 1981; Tyler, 1980). This research shows that personal judgments about vulnerability are best predicted by direct experience with crime and by conversations about crime with others. In addition, it suggests that societal-level judgments about crime are related most strongly to media exposure due to the informativeness of the media event, not because of the affectivity of its images.

Despite the claims made by Gerbner or other researchers, the correlational nature of the data presented in all of these studies precludes an assessment of causality. While exposure to television crime drama may, in fact, cultivate fear and apprehension at either personal or societal levels, any observed association between television exposure and perceptions of fear is amenable to several alternative explanations. The relation may be spurious and noncausal; it may be causal but in the opposite direction of that proposed by cultivation rationales; or it may be a reciprocal relation in which forces are operating in different directions. Along these lines, the cultivation interpretation has recently been challenged as being in conflict with several psychological principles suggesting that anxiety-creating programs should be avoided if they produce aversive states (Zillmann, 1980). This interpretation asserts that the general theme of most television crime drama is the restoration of a safe and just world. Criminals are caught and removed from society, an image that should be particularly comforting and attractive to fearful viewers. If this reasoning is accepted, the observed correlations between television exposure and perceptions of fear are consistent with the proposition that exposure to television crime drama does not cause viewers to be more fearful, but that fearful viewers selectively expose themselves to crime drama in order to reduce their anxieties. Regardless of which rationale one accepts, alternative interpretations like this make it clear that the exploration of a causal direction in this situation cannot be accomplished through correlational research.

To date, the only experimental evidence of television exposure's impact on judgments about crime and safety is a study by Bryant, Carveth, and Brown (1981). Because the results of this research apply directly to the two issues addressed by the present investigation (duration and judgmental level of effect), the study will be discussed here in greater detail. In this experiment designed to test the cultivation hypothesis, subjects' exposure to television was manipulated (heavy versus light) over a period of six weeks. The heavy exposure condition was subdivided into exposure to crime fare that featured either just or unjust resolutions. This variation was introduced to test for the possibility that if crime drama breeds fear (Gerbner & Gross, 1976a), it should breed the most fear in drama that fails to present a just, pacifying resolution (Zillmann, 1980). Measures of perceptions of crime and violence were obtained through subjects' responses to three items said to be similar to those employed by Gerbner and Gross (1976a). The first question was, "How likely is it that you personally will someday be a victim of some type of violent behavior?" The second question asked, "How fearful are you that some harm will befall you someday because of someone's act of violence?" The third question was, "If you were to be a victim of an act of violence, how likely would it be that your assailant would be caught and punished?" Questions one and three appear to measure the type of base rate estimates of probability discussed earlier, whereas question two appears to measure a general perception associated with fear of some harm at some indefinite time in the future. Although it can be argued that these questions deal with the individual, as a whole they appear to be more along the line of societal-level judgments—those that are associated with broad estimates of general states or the environment.

The results of this study, while not showing effects on all measures, did yield several reliable differences. Exposure to drama that features just resolutions appeared to increase manifest anxiety, expectations of being a victim of violence, fear of victimization, and perceptions about the likelihood of an assailant being punished. In addition, exposure to drama with just endings led to significant increases in expectations of being a victim of violence, and fear of victimization. To the extent that this investigation simulates the presumably cumulative effects of exposure to violence-laden drama, it gives some support to the cultivation hypothesis. However, in view of the fact that (a) crime drama on television almost always features a just resolution, (b) the expected breeding of fear was observed on only two measures in this condition, (c) only four items were used to measure perceptions, and (d) these items do not clearly differentiate levels of perception, support for the proposition that television exposure cultivates personal- and societal-level perceptions is tenuous.

Although the research by Bryant et al. (1981) appears to provide at least some support for the cultivation hypothesis, limitations of the methods employed cast doubt on even this support and focus attention on the second issue of the present investigation, the duration of media effects on social perceptions. As acknowledged by Bryant et al., there is some doubt that (a) the effects observed are long term and (b) attributable to the cumulative effect of long-term exposure rather than one (the last) exposure to crime drama. In their investigation, measures of fear and anxiety were taken immediately after exposure to a crime drama (during the last experimental session). Thus the data can be taken to support the contention that any observed effects were due to watching this last program rather than a series of programs over the six-week period. Likewise, assertions concerning the duration of any lasting effects are questionable.

A considerable amount of evidence suggests that there may be some short-term effect on social perceptions following exposure to even a single crime drama. In their discussion of heuristic principles, Tversky and Kahneman (1973) assert that judgments about the frequency and probability of an event occurring is affected by the ease with which instances of the event come to mind. This view implies that individuals often rely on an availability heuristic that reduces the complex task of making such judgments to simpler operations (Tversky & Kahneman, 1974); it also implies that because of this, judgments are based on only a fraction of the relevant information that is stored in memory (Wyer & Srull, 1980). The rationale has been applied to social perceptions in general to propose that any judgment derived from memory should be biased in the direction of salient cues (Reyes, Thompson, & Bower, 1979), and it has been suggested that media exposure can play a part in this by making instances of a construct highly accessible when judgments are being made (Higgins & King, 1980).

Research on the processing of social stimuli has repeatedly reported that salient events, those more recently activated or accessible in memory, can have a strong influence on social perceptions (e.g., Kahneman & Tversky, 1973; Nisbett & Ross, 1980; Ross, 1977; Taylor & Fiske, 1979). It has been demonstrated, for example, that priming different trait characteristics can bias evaluations of another individual (Higgins, Rholes, & Jones, 1977), that more vivid arguments and evidence are better recalled and have a disproportional impact on judgments of guilt in mock jury situations (Reyes et al., 1980), and that students' evaluations of college courses vary depending on whether procourse or anticourse behaviors have been activated recently (Salancik & Conway, 1975). Most recently, Reeves and Garramone (1984) demonstrated that television exposure can serve as a stimulus to momentarily activate certain concepts and bias perceptions of others. In this study, television exposure designed to prime the trait "funny" was found to influence children's ratings of another child on several dimensions.

The results of these studies are consistent with both the "storage bin model" (Wyer & Srull, 1980) and the "spreading activation model" (Collins & Quillian, 1968; Collins & Loftus, 1975) of memory, both of which suggest that perceptions may often be affected substantially by unrelated events that lead one or another concept to be more accessible to an individual at the time judgments are made. Both models imply that exposure to different descriptions can activate a trait schema and temporarily increase its availability for use in the interpretation of social stimuli. These rationales have been used to explain how impression formation works (Higgins et al., 1977), as well as how judgments are made about the likelihood of events occurring (Tversky & Kahneman, 1973).

In addition to suggesting how exposure and availability can affect judgments, the social perception literature also tells us something about the duration of these influences. The impact of priming has been found to disappear after a matter of seconds in research on semantic decision tasks (Collins & Quillian, 1968; Meyer & Schvanevelt, 1971), or to remain after several hours in research on social stimulus judgments (Srull & Wyer, 1979). In fact, in the research on vividness (Reyes et al., 1979), more vivid arguments were found to influence judgments of guilt up to two days after presentation. It is generally accepted, however, that the accessibility and use of primed schemata for processing social stimuli decrease over time, and it has been demonstrated in several studies that the overall effect of priming on judgments dissipates as the interval between activation and stimulus presentation increases (Wyer & Srull, 1980).

The rationales presented in the social perception literature dealing with level of judgment and impact of available concepts encourages alternative interpretations of the research by Bryant et al. (1981). First, with regard to differences in the type of perception that might be influenced by media, it could be argued that the research by Bryant et al. measured only very general perceptions of crime and anxiety. According to Tyler (1980), perceptions at this level should be most susceptible to influence by media exposure, whereas personal-level judgments go relatively unchanged. Thus it would be predicted that more personal-level judgments should remain unaffected by comparison in research similar to that of Bryant et al. Second, concerning the duration of media exposure's impact on judgments, it can be pointed out that the Bryant et al. study failed to account for the possible short-term effect of priming cognitions relevant to perceptions of fear and violence during the last experimental session. Consistent with the research on cognitive availability, it would be expected that a single exposure to a similar crime drama should activate relevant schemata and temporarily bias subjects' judgments to produce perceptions that a greater likelihood of crime and victimization exists in society. Therefore, if measures were taken a few days later, initially observed effects should disappear. As it is, the results of the Bryant et al. study cannot be interpreted as indicating anything beyond a temporary effect of the last exposure.

The present study was conducted to investigate these issues. Specifically, it was designed to (1) examine the effect of a single exposure to several types of television programming on judgments about crime and safety; (2) distinguish this effect, if there is any, at different judgmental levels (societal versus personal) and dimensions (situation-specific perceptions); and (3) discover whether or not this effect dissipates quickly. To anwer these questions, procedures similar to those used in earlier research were employed with several additions. First, questions designed to measure perceptions of crime and fear on several dimensions were created to help distinguish societal- from personal-level judgments and to measure situation-specific perceptions within these levels. Second, in addition to taking measures of perception immediately after viewing a television program, measures were obtained three days after exposure in order to determine the effect due to priming. Third, in the study by Bryant et al. (1981), a no crime drama, a justice-depicting crime drama, and an injustice-depicting crime drama exposure condition were used to test Gerbner's scary world hypothesis. Crime drama was used because it has been the main target in earlier claims that television presents an exaggerated view of danger in our society (e.g., Gerbner & Gross, 1976a, 1976b; Gerbner et al., 1980a, 1980b). In the present investigation a crime documentary exposure condition was added to compare the impact of more realistic portrayals of crime in our society with typical television crime drama. If, as asserted by Tyler (1980), it is the informativeness and not the affectivity of media exposure that influences general perceptions of crime, we would expect that crime documentary to have a greater effect on these perceptions than the crime dramas.

The basic design resulting from these procedural considerations was a 4 × 2 factorial arrangement with exposure condition and measurement-delay time as the two factors. Subjects were exposed to one of four programs: a control film, a just-resolution crime drama, an unjust-resolution crime drama, or a news-documentary program dealing with crime. After exposure, measures of (a) general anxiety, (b) general perceptions about crime, and (c) fear for safety in specific situations were obtained. For half of the subjects, measures were taken immediately after exposure; for the other half, measures were taken three days later.

If, as expected, the results reveal that on the same measures used by Bryant et al. (1981) increased anxiety occurs immediately after exposure and disappears three days later, then Bryant's claim to have demonstrated a cumulative effect that supports the cultivation hypothesis becomes seriously questionable. Such an outcome would indicate instead that television can prime certain constructs for use in making judgments and temporarily influence these decisions. If, however, no differences due to exposure are found on immediate measures, or if no reduction in immediate effects is found on delayed measures, then the support for cultivation claimed by Bryant et al. remains unchallenged. In addition, if the impact of exposure to the crime documentary equals or surpasses the effect of exposure to crime drama, it would suggest that real-world images have an equal or stronger influence on perceptions than the so-called exaggerated picture presented by television crime drama. Finally, if effects due to exposure are found to differ on measures designed to distinguish between societal- and personal-level judgments, the generalizability of television's influence on perceptions of crime would be limited severely.

METHOD

Subjects

Undergraduates (56 male and 59 female) enrolled in an introductory mass communication course receiving class credit for participation served as subjects. Subjects were contacted in class and, if willing to participate, signed an informed consent statement. All subjects were informed that they were free to leave during the course of the experiment and would not be penalized if they chose to do so.

Experimental Materials

Four videotaped television programs, each approximately 60 minutes in length, were edited specifically for use in this experiment. The programs served as stimuli in the four experimental exposure conditions: (1) a control condition, (2) a justice-depicting condition; (3) an injustice-depicting condition; and (4) a crime documentary condition. The first program was an episode of *The Love Boat,* which served as the control stimulus. The second and third programs were two different edited versions of a movie made for television, *High Midnight.* The first was a justice-depicting version in which the transgressive behavior of the criminals in the program was punished. The second was an injustice-depicting version in which transgressive acts by the criminals went unpunished. The same program was used to create both versions in order to keep all program content the same except the conclusion. The conclusion shows a criminal about to shoot the film's hero. In the first version, a police officer arrives and kills the criminal. In the second version, a criminal shoots and kills the hero. The different versions were created by editing materials in an undetectable manner. The fourth program consisted of a 30-minute broadcast of the *CBS Evening News* with Walter Cronkite taped on November 28, 1979, and a 30-minute documentary on crime in Harlem, New York, called *They Get What They Pay For.*

The *Love Boat* episode was selected as the control film because it contained no scenes of crime or violence that might make these issues salient for the viewer. The film made for television, *High Midnight,* was selected because it was a fictional drama focusing on crime and violence: the type of "violence-laden dramatic fare" referred to by Bryant et al. (1981) and Gerbner and Gross (1976a, 1976b) that deals with social norms and the "risks of life and price for transgressions of society's rules." It was set in an urban environment and featured the violent death of the wife and child of the protaganist. In addition, the structure of the film made it possible to edit it in such a way that both the justice-depicting and injustice-depicting conditions could be created from the same film. The *CBS Evening News* program included several stories dealing with real-life violence, as did the documentary. Among others, the news program included several stories about the Iranian hostage situation, a story about a plane crash killing 257 people, and a story about the unmotivated murder of a 106-year-old man and two other individuals. The crime documentary included scenes of street life in Harlem, along with reports of the prevalence of gambling, prostitution, drug use, and violent crime. The two programs were selected for the crime documentary condition because they provided factual information about real-life social conditions dealing with crime and violence.

Procedure

Subjects randomly assigned to conditions were tested in groups of three and four. A male experimenter greeted subjects and told them they would be taking part in two studies: one on that day and a second study two days later at another location with a different experimenter. The experimenter then played taped instructions informing subjects that they were taking part in an experiment designed to determine empathetic reactions to characters seen in different types of documentary and entertainment programs. Subjects were told that this would be done by taking measures of heart rate and blood pressure, and that to do so a probe would be attached to their fingers. After attaching a bogus finger probe to each subject, the experimenter played one of the four experimental videotapes on a 17-inch color television monitor.

After exposure, all subjects were thanked and told that the first study was completed. Subjects in the delayed-measures condition were reminded to go to another location two days later for the second study and then dismissed. Two days later subjects were greeted at the new location by a second male experimenter. Subjects in the immediate-measures condition were told that the experimenter for the second study wanted them to fill out an initial questionnaire before they left. The first experimenter left and returned with the second male experimenter. The second experimenter introduced the second study and asked subjects in both conditions, immediate and delayed measures, to fill out a questionnaire. Taped instructions informed subjects that they were taking part in a study of the relation between radio use and personality characteristics. Subjects were told that apprehensiveness was a trait of particular interest in the study and were given a questionnaire dealing with this.

After filling out the apprehension questionnaire, subjects were debriefed, thanked, and dismissed. During the debriefing, the experimenter attempted to determine if any subjects had seen the experimental stimuli before or understood the true purpose of the experiment. One male suggested that the two sessions were part of the same study (he could not say how the sessions were related, however). Two males and four females had been exposed to experimental stimuli before. The exclusion of these six participants left 53 males and 55 females as subjects.

Dependent Measures

Four measures of anxiety used by Bryant et al. (1981) were employed here. The first measure was the subject's response to Taylor's Manifest Anxiety Inventory (Taylor, 1953). The other three measures were subjects' response to the three perception of safety items employed by Bryant et al. (1981). The first question—"How likely is it that you personally will someday be a victim of some type of violent behavior?"—had a 10-point response scale ranging from "absolutely certain of no violence" (0), "50/50 chance of violence" (5), and "absolutely certain of violence" (10). Question two—"How fearful are you that some harm will befall you someday because of someone's act of violence?"—was followed by a 10-point scale labeled "not at all fearful" (0), and "extremely fearful" (10). Question three—"If you were to be a victim of an act of violence, how likely would it be that your assailant would be caught and punished?"—had a response scale ranging from 0 ("not at all likely") to 10 ("extremely likely").

In addition to the items employed by Bryant et al. (1981), 21 hypothetical situation questions were created for use in this research. All items were designed to measure concern for safety in different hypothetical situations (for example: "You are visiting Chicago and have made plans to visit a friend who lives in the city. Your friend gives you directions to a bar where you are going to meet for a drink. When you arrive, you find yourself in a dark unfamiliar bar, and your friend is nowhere to be found. How concerned would you be that you might be assaulted?"). A 10-point response scale was provided, ranging from "not very concerned" (0), to "very concerned" (10). All 21 items dealt with a specific hypothetical situation and provided details about location of the setting, people involved in the situation, and reasons for the people being there at the time. Some items were designed to measure concern for the safety of the subjects themselves; some dealt with concern for familiar and unfamiliar others. In addition, both rural and urban settings were used as locations for the hypothetical situations. These dimensions of concern (personal safety versus the safety of others; safety in urban versus rural settings) were included to help determine differences in apprehension across these dimensions.

RESULTS

A principal-components factor analysis with varimax rotation was performed on the three perceptions of safety items and the 21 hypothetical situation items. The results of this solution, reported in Table 18.1, yielded five factors (eigenvalues > 1) that accounted for more than 60% of the variance. The first factor appeared to reflect concern for safety in local, nonurban settings and was labeled "rural fear." The second factor appeared to reflect concern for safety in urban areas and was labeled "urban fear of assault." The third factor appeared to reflect concern for safety of one's mate and was labeled "fear for mate." The fourth factor appeared to reflect concern for one's personal safety and was labeled "personal fear of assault." The fifth factor appeared to reflect perceptions of the likelihood of one's being assaulted and the assailant being caught and punished, labeled "perceptions of crime." The items that loaded cleanly on this last factor were questions one and three of Bryant's perception of safety items.

Factor scores were generated for all five factors by summing, for all items that loaded cleanly on each factor, the product of the factor score coefficient and the standardized value of the item. Factor scores on all five factors and scores on Taylor's Manifest Anxiety Inventory (TMAI) were subjected to $2 \times 4 \times 2$ analyses of variance, with delay time, exposure condition, and gender being the independent variables.

The analysis of manifest anxiety data yielded significant main effects of time $[F(1,92) = 3.76, p = .05]$, and film condition $[F(3,92) = 3.22, p = .03]$, whereas differences failed to yield significance for gender and for all interactions $[F \approx 1]$. For the main effect of time, manifest anxiety was higher immediately after exposure $(M = 9.12)$ than three days later $(M = 7.55)$. Subsequent tests on means associated with the film condition, shown in Table 18.2, indicate that subjects viewing the injustice-depicting crime drama were more anxious than subjects in all other conditions.

The analysis on the perceptions of crime factor yielded a significant main effect of exposure condition $[F(3,92) = 6.27, p < .01]$, and a significant interaction between delay time and exposure conditions $[F(3,92) = 3.19, p < .03]$, with differences for gender $[F(1,92) = 2.55, p = .11]$ and the interaction of delay time, film and gender $[F(3,92) = 1.94, p = .12]$ only approaching significance. All other differences were trivial $[F < 1]$. Subsequent tests comparing cell means for the interaction of delay time and exposure revealed that in the immediate-measure condition, exposure to the injustice-depicting drama and the crime documentary increased subject's estimates of the probability that they would be assaulted and the criminal would go unpunished compared to subjects in the control condition. In the delayed-measure condition, however, the difference remained only for subjects who had earlier watched the crime documentary. In this condition, subject's scores on perceptions of crime were higher than were their scores in all other conditions (Table 18.3).

The analysis of variance on the "urban fear" factor produced a significant interaction between delay time and exposure $[F(3,92) = 6.19, p < .01]$, while all other differences were minimal $[F \approx 1]$. Subsequent tests on means associated with the interaction of delay time and exposure, displayed in Table 18.4 show that immediately after exposure, subjects in the injustice condition were more concerned about assault in urban areas than were subjects in the control condition, and that subjects in the crime documentary group were more con-

Table 18.1

Factor Loadings[a] for Principal Components Analysis with Varimax Rotation of the Apprehension Questionnaire

Abbreviated Items	Factor 1	Factor 2	Factor 3	Factor 4	Factor 5
Concerned you will be assaulted in small town home you have lived in for years.	.55*	.29	-.22	.15	.29
Concerned that mother will be assaulted in parking lot of local Bloomington shopping mall.	.70*	.13	.22	.14	.02
Concerned that woman will be assaulted on campus in Bloomington.	.72*	.21	.10	-.06	-.16
Concerned that woman will be assaulted at library in Bloomington.	.56*	.22	.30	-.05	-.08
Concerned that child will be assaulted at nearby park in Bloomington.	.67*	.00	.43*	.09	.01
Concerned that man will be assaulted on highway near Bloomington.	.52*	.09	.40*	.09	.01
Concerned that you will be assaulted in small rural town in Massachusetts.	.58*	.10	.02	.47*	.21
Concerned that friend will be assaulted while walking home in Bloomington.	.65*	.08	-.05	.40	-.06
Concerned that child will be assaulted in downtown Los Angeles.	.38	.43*	.13	-.01	.28
Concerned that you will be assaulted in New York's Central Park.	.22	.72*	-.03	.24	-.20
Concerned that friend will be assaulted in Watts district of Los Angeles.	.31	.55*	.15	.24	-.03

Concerned that man will be assaulted walking across town in New York.	.20	.72*	.14	.09	−.15
Concerned that man will be assaulted working in South Chicago.	−.00	.75*	.18	.10	.03
Concerned that father will be assaulted at bus station in South Chicago.	.17	.72*	.32	.06	.13
Concerned that boyfriend will be assaulted on Sunset Strip in Los Angeles.	.02	.52*	.62*	.12	.23
Concerned that mate will be assaulted waiting on campus.	.16	.08	.85*	.06	.01
Concerned that woman will be assaulted in New York subway.	.31	.21	.51*	−.05	−.04
Concerned that mate will be assaulted at local Bloomington drugstore.	.25	.09	.69*	.09	−.12
Concerned that mate will be assaulted in San Francisco's Chinatown district.	.00	.24	.63*	.55*	.03
Concerned that you and mate will be assaulted in New York's Times Square.	.08	.20	.41*	.56*	−.28
Likelihood that you will be assaulted in unfamiliar Chicago bar.	.26	.43*	−.22	.59*	.04
Fear that some harm will befall you someday because of someone's act of violence.	.10	.10	.16	.76*	.03
Likelihood that you will be a victim of violence.	−.02	.31	.38	.02	−.44*
Likelihood that your assailant would be caught and punished.	−.03	.01	.04	−.00	.82*

*Selected for inclusion in generating factor scores.

Table 18.2

Mean Scores of Manifest Anxiety as a
Function of Exposure Condition

	Exposure Condition		
Control	Justice	Injustice	Documentary
7.21	8.00	10.71a	7.92

a. Injustice condition means differs from other means significantly at p < .05 by Newman-Keuls test.

Table 18.3

Means Scores of Perceptions of Crime as a
Function of Delay Time and
Exposure Condition

	Exposure Condition			
Delay Time	Control	Justice	Injustice	Documentary
Immediate	−.46	−.10	.58a	.25a
Three days later	−.28	−.06	−.21	.47a

Note: Comparisons are within delay time only (horizontal).
a. Means differ significantly at p < .05 by Newman-Keuls test.

cerned than subjects in both the control and justice-depicting conditions. Three days later, however, no differences among groups remained.

The analysis of the fear for mate factor produced a significant main effect for gender [$F(1,92) = 7.08$, p < .01], and a significant interaction between delay time and exposure condition [$F(3,92) = 4.64$, p < .01]; whereas differences only approached significance for delay time [$F(1,92) = 2.29$] and all other effects were trivial [$F \approx 1$]. For the main effect of gender, fear for the safety of one's mate was greater among males (M = .25) than among females (M = −.25). Subsequent tests of means associated with the delay time × exposure condition interaction revealed that immediately after viewing, concern for mate was greater for subjects viewing the crime documentary than for subjects viewing the control film. Once again, however, three days later no differences remained among exposure conditions Table 18.5.

Analysis of the rural fear factor yielded a significant main effect of gender [$F(1,92) = 4.38$, p < .04], whereas all other differences were trivial [$F \approx 1$]. As might be expected, for the main effect of gender, females expressed greater concern for safety in rural areas (M = .22) than did males (M = −.21).

Table 18.4

Mean Scores of Urban Fear as a Function of

Delay Time and Exposure Condition

Delay Time	Exposure Condition			
	Control	Justice	Injustice	Documentary
Immediate	−.86[a]	−.05[b]	.35[bc]	.97[c]
Three days later	.24	−.22	.04	−.40

Note: Comparisons are within delay time only (horizontal). Means having no superscript letter in common differ significantly at p < .05 by Newman-Keuls' test.

Table 18.5

Mean Scores of Fear for Mate as a

Function of Delay Time and

Exposure Condition

Delay Time	Exposure Condition			
	Control	Justice	Injustice	Documentary
Immediate	−.51[a]	.04[ab]	.28[ab]	.87[b]
Three days later	.07	−.17	.10	−.51

Note: Comparisons are within delay time only (horizontal). Means having no superscript letters in common differ significantly at p < .05 by Newman-Keuls test.

Analysis of the personal fear factor revealed no significant differences, with all Fs ≈ 1.

DISCUSSION

The results of the present investigation indicate that (a) perceptions about crime and safety vary along several dimensions, (b) exposure to a television program dealing with crime has a different effect on these perceptions in different dimensions, and (c) the immediate effect of such exposure disappears over time.

The factor analysis on items designed to differentiate perceptions that are situation-specific and vary at judgmental level demonstrates that fear of crime is not a unidimensional construct, and suggests that earlier research failing to make this distinction should be reinterpreted. The solution provided factors that distinguished fear in urban areas from fear in rural settings, fear for personal safety from fear for someone else, and a separate factor that reflected estimates of risk rather than fear of victimization. This indicates that situation-specific perceptions may differ (e.g., urban versus rural) and

that personal-level perceptions are separate from more general perceptions, such as estimates of society risk and perceptions associated with danger to people other than oneself (e.g., personal fear versus perceptions of
crime and fear for mate). The distinctions indicate that theoretical rationales
predicting media effects only on certain dimensions of perception should be
given greater consideration.

Perhaps the most interesting result of this research is its demonstration
that exposure to a television program dealing with crime can influence certain perceptions while leaving other associated judgments unaffected. Exposure to the crime documentary and to the injustice-depicting crime
drama led to more exaggerated perceptions of crime and fear of assault in
urban environments. In addition, watching the injustice-depicting crime
drama increased manifest anxiety, whereas viewing the crime documentary
elevated fear for one's mate. However, although differences were found on
these perceptions, no effects were found on personal fear or fear of assault in
rural environments. These results are consistent with recent survey research
suggesting that media effects on perception differ at personal and societal
levels (Skogan & Maxfield, 1981; Tyler, 1980), as well as with theories of
social cognition suggesting that the priming of different concepts will affect
only perceptions relevant to those activated categories (Reyes et al., 1979;
Srull & Wyer, 1979; Wyer & Srull, 1980). With regard to the societal- versus
personal-level distinction, the demonstration of an effect on general perceptions of crime and on fear for one's mate (without influencing personal fear)
supports the notion that information associated with societal-level judgments is segregated in processing and does not influence personal perceptions (Kahneman & Tversky, 1973). One explanation for this is that individuals overestimate their own ability to deal with situations relative to the
abilities of others (Einhorn & Hogarth, 1978). Hence, an exaggeration of
one's own ability to deal with the danger of crime may reduce the impact of
information about threat to others on fear for one's own safety. In a similar
manner, the present data indicating that fear in urban environments increased while rural fear remained unchanged support rationales that limit
effects to cognitions more relevant to media content. All experimental exposure conditions dealt with crime and violence in urban settings. This indicates that although exposure effects may generalize to some extent (e.g., to
nonpersonal perceptions of crime and fear in several urban settings), it has a
much more limited influence than previously asserted.

The data strenuously challenge the assertions by Bryant et al. (1981)
that their data support the cultivation hypothesis (Gerbner & Gross, 1976a,
1976b). The present study demonstrated that a single exposure to crime
drama can create the kind of result found by Bryant et al., but this effect is
transitory. Since a single exposure increased subjects' apprehension about

crime on items used by Bryant as well as on other measures, the Bryant study can be interpreted as showing an effect due only to the last exposure and not a cumulative effect resulting from the six-week exposure period. Further, the fact that all differences resulting from exposure to crime drama in the present study dissipated quickly suggests that any relation illustrated in the Bryant study may also have been short term.

In addition to the issues dealing with exposure duration, the observed variation in the effect of exposure to different types of crime-related programming has implications for the cultivation hypothesis. Although predictions based on cultivation rationales do not clearly distinguish between just-ending and unjust-ending crime drama, Bryant et al. (1981) suggest that injustice presents a "scarier world" image and creates greater apprehension than does the depiction of justice. The results of the present study are consistent with this reasoning, in that increased apprehension was found on only urban fear after exposure to justice-depicting drama, whereas exposure to injustice-depicting drama led to greater increases and perceptions of crime. However, the demonstrated effect of exposure to the crime documentary conflicts with the cultivation interpretation. Exposure to this real-world information equaled the impact of viewing injustice on measures of urban fear and general perceptions of crime and led to an increase in fear for one's mate, which was not matched by viewing injustice. In addition, the only effect remaining three days after exposure was an increase on measures of general "perceptions of crime" in the crime documentary condition. This is inconsistent with the view that an exaggerated sense of danger presented by television drama increased apprehension. Rather, it indicates that presenting information about the real dangers in society has a somewhat greater impact on perceptions.

It could be maintained that crime documentary is a component of television's portrayal of society that should be included as part of television content said to cultivate perceptions. The evidence here, however, suggests an interpretation distinct from cultivation. The differences found on measures taken immediately after exposure are in accord with previously discussed rationales predicting a short-term impact of construct accessibility on social perceptions (Tverskey & Kahneman, 1973; Wyer & Srull, 1980). Rather than suggesting that exposure cultivated greater apprehension, these data indicate that exposure primed schemata relevant to crime and victimization that temporarily biased perceptions in the direction of increased apprehension. The lasting effect of the crime documentary on general perceptions of crime cannot be explained by this interpretation, however, and indicates that another process was involved as well. The more enduring influence on general perceptions is consistent with Tyler's (1980) reasoning that it is the informativeness of media exposure that influences more stable perceptions. This rationale is based on an image of the individual as a so-called naive scientist who uses information conveyed in experience to form perceptions about the social world (Heider, 1958; Kelly, 1967, 1973). Such an explanation of the present data would project that whereas a crime documentary contains information pertinent to perceptions of the real world, a crime drama does not. According to this understanding, in the short term perceptions are influenced by the salience of events, whereas lasting images are based on the relevant information provided by television experiences. Given that crime drama's vivid images can remain salient momentarily, they have a momentary impact on perception.

Although the category accessibility interpretation conflicts with the cultivation hypothesis, its application here could result in similar predictions. Wyer and Srull (1980) show that the frequency of activating a construct can elevate the initial impact of priming and result in its sustained influence. This implies that Gerbner and Gross (1976a, 1976b) are correct in suggesting that repeated exposure to television images can have a cumulative effect, although here it is only an effect that should take longer to dissipate. In addition, it could be argued that heavy exposure to television primes relevant concepts repeatedly, so that when the impact of an earlier exposure has dissipated, the recent exposure will keep these schemata activated. In this case, the most recent image primed by television should influence perceptions. If this is true, the issue becomes one of determining exactly what impact these primed images have and how long it lasts. This is not an easy task, however. For example, it has been suggested that the last image activated by a typical television crime drama is that justice prevails and the world is safer (Zillmann, 1980), but there is some disagreement about the salience of such endings compared to the victimization portrayed in this type of program (Bryant et al., 1981). In addition, it is not clear whether or not watching some other type of program devoid of threat to safety following exposure to a crime drama will remove the impact of this initial exposure.

The outcome of this study has theoretical implications beyond those associated with television viewing and crime. As discussed previously, the data support theories proposing that societal- and personal-level judgments operate independently. In addition, the results are compatible with both the storage bin and spreading activation models of information processing. The short-term effects are consistent with spreading activation logic (see Collins & Loftus, 1975; Collins & Quillian, 1968), suggesting that exposure stimulated concept nodes beyond the threshold value required to influence immediate behaviors. Three days later, however, the excitation at these nodes should no longer remain activated enough to affect perceptions. This, of course, does not explain the persisting impact found in the documentary condition. To account for this, Wyer and Srull (1980) suggest that a different process occurs. The storage bin model could project that in the three days following exposure, little use is made of the concept category containing the crime documentary; therefore, the information contained in the documentary would still be near the top of this cognitive bin and would continue to influence perceptions.

In addition to the theoretical implications, the outcome of this research has practical implications. First, it indicates that attempts by media producers to change personal-level perceptions are likely to meet with little success, and that unintentional effects at this level may be more limited than is generally believed. Further, it suggests that attempts to influence societal-level perceptions should use realism and not sacrifice the informativeness of a message for an affectively powerful dramatic appeal. Of course, this does not mean that crime drama has no influence; nor does it mean that affect is unimportant. Crime drama as well as crime documentary have been demonstrated here to have short-term effects on apprehension and on perceptions of crime. In addition, it is reasonable to posit that these observed effects at the cognitive level are matched by similar influences on behaviors. Previous research has shown, for example, that programming of this kind can temporarily influence selective exposure to different types of television content (Wakshlag, Vial, & Tamborini, 1984). From this it is easy to project that temporary changes in cognitive availability can affect any other form of behavior that is influenced by salient cognitions. This suggests that an experience such as media exposure can have a temporary impact on a wide range of behaviors with important implications.

REFERENCES

Borgida, E., & Brekke, N. (1981). The base rate fallacy in attribution and prediction. In J. H. Harvey, W. J. Ickes, & R. F. Kidd (Eds.), *New directions in attribution research* (Vol. 3). Hillsdale, NJ: Lawrence Erlbaum.

Borgida, E. & Nisbett, R. E. (1977). The differential impact of abstract vs. concrete information on decisions. *Journal of Applied Social Psychology, 7*, 258-271.

Bryant, J., Carveth, R., & Brown, D. (1981). Television viewing and anxiety: An experimental examination. *Journal of Communication, 31(1)*, 106-119.

Collins, A. M., & Loftus, E. F. (1975). A spreading-activation theory of semantic processing. *Psychological Review, 82*, 407-428.

Collins, A. M., & Quillian, M. R. (1968). Retrieval time from semantic memory. *Journal of Verbal Learning and Verbal Behavior, 8*, 240-247.

Doob, A. W., & MacDonald, G. E. (1979). Television viewing and fear of victimization: Is the relationship causal? *Journal of Personality and Social Psychology, 37*, 170-179.

Einhorn, H. J., & Hogarth, R. M. (1978) Confidence in judgment: Persistence of the illusion of validity. *Psychological Review, 85*, 395-416.

Gerbner, G., & Gross, L. (1976a). Living with television: The violence profile. *Journal of Communication, 26(2)*, 173-199.

Gerbner, G., & Gross, L. (1976b). The scary world of TV's heavy viewer. *Psychology Today, 89*, 41-45.

Gerbner, G., Gross, L., Eleey, M., Jackson-Beeck, M., Jeffries-Fox, S., & Signorielli, N. (1977a). TV violence profile No. 8. *Journal of Communication, 27*(2), 171-180.

Gerbner, G., Gross, L., Eleey, M., Jackson-Beeck, M., Jeffries-Fox, S., & Signorielli, N. (1976b). *Violence Profile No. 8: Trends in network television drama and viewer conceptions of social reality 1967-1976.* Philadelphia: Annenberg School of Communications, University of Pennsylvania.

Gerbner, G., Gross, L., Jackson-Beeck, M., Jeffries-Fox, S., & Signorielli, N. (1978a). Cultural indicators: Violence Profile No. 9., *Journal of Communication, 28*(3), 176-207.

Gerbner, G., Gross, L., Jackson-Beeck, M., Jeffries-Fox, S., & Signorielli, N. (1978b). *Violence Profile No. 9: Trends in network television drama and viewer conceptions of social reality 1967-1977.* Philadelphia: Annenberg School of Communications, University of Pennsylvania.

Gerbner, G., Gross, L., Morgan, M., & Signorielli, N. (1980a). Some additional comments on cultivation analysis. *Public Opinion Quarterly, 44,* 408-410.

Gerbner, G., Gross, L., Morgan, M., & Signorielli, N. (1980b). The "mainstreaming" of America: Violence Profile No. 11. *Journal of Communication, 30* (3), 19-29.

Gerbner, G., Gross, L., Signorielli, N., Morgan, M., & Jackson-Beeck, M. (1979a). The demonstration of power: Violence Profile No. 10. *Journal of Communication, 29,* 177-196.

Gerbner, G., Gross, L., Signorielli, N., Morgan, M., & Jackson-Beeck, M. (1979b). *Violence Profile No. 10: Trends in network television drama and viewer conceptions of social reality 1967-1978.* Philadelphia: Annenberg School of Communications, University of Pennsylvania.

Gerbner, G., & Signorielli, N. (1979). *Women and minorities in television drama 1969-1978.* Philadelphia: Annenberg School of Communications, University of Pennsylvania.

Hansen, R. D., & Stonner, D. M. (1978). Attributes and attributions: Inferring stimulus properties, actors' dispositions, and causes. *Journal of Personality and Social Psychology, 36,* 657-667.

Hawkins, R. P., & Pingree, S. (1982). Television's influence on social reality. In D. Pearl, L. Bouthilet, & J. Lazar (Eds.), *Television and behavior: Ten years of scientific progress and implications for the eighties* (Vol. 2). Rockville, MD: National Institute of Mental Health.

Heider, F. (1958). *The psychology of interpersonal relations.* New York: Wiley.

Higgins, E. T., & King, G. (1981). Accessibility of social constructs: Information-processing consequences of individual and contextual variability. In N. Cantor & J. Kihlstrom (Eds.), *Cognition, social interaction, and personality.* Hillsdale, NJ: Lawrence Erlbaum.

Higgins, E. T., Rholes, C. R. & Jones, C. R. (1977). Category accessibility and impressions formation. *Journal of Experimental Social Psychology, 13,* 141-154.

Hirsch, P. M. (1980). The "scary world" of the nonviewer and other anomalies: A reanalysis of Gerbner et al.'s findings on cultivation analysis. Part 1. *Communication Research, 7,* 403-456.

Hughes, M. (1980). The fruits of cultivation analysis: A reexamination of some effects of television watching. *Public Opinion Quarterly, 44,* 287-302.

Kahneman, D., & Tversky, A. (1973). On the psychology of prediction. *Psychological Review, 80,* 237-251.

Kelley, H. H. (1967). Attribution theory in social psychology. In D. Levine (Ed.), *Nebraska symposium on motivation* (Vol. 15). Lincoln: University of Nebraska Press.

Kelley, H. H. (1973). The processes of causal attribution. *American Psychologist, 28,* 107-128.

Meyer, D. E., & Schvaneveldt, R. W. (1971). Facilitation in recognition between pairs of words: Evidence of a dependence between retrieval operations. *Journal of Experimental Psychology, 90,* 227-234.

Neville, T. (1980). *Television viewing and the expression of interpersonal mistrust.* Unpublished doctoral dissertation, Princeton University.

Nisbett, R. E., & Ross, L. D. (1980). *Human inference: Strategies and shortcomings of social judgment.* Englewood Cliffs, NJ: Prentice-Hall.

Pingree, S., Starrett, S., & Hawkins, R. (1979). *Soap opera viewers and social reality.* Unpublished manuscript, Women's Studies Program, University of Wisconsin-Madison.

Reeves, B., & Garramone, G. (1984) Television's influence on children's encoding of person information. *Human Communication Research, 10,* 257-268.

Reyes, R. M., Thompson, W. C., & Bower, G. H. (1979). Judgmental biases resulting from dif-fering availabilities of arguments. *Journal of Personality and Social Psychology, 37,* 357-368.

Ross, L. (1977) The intuitive psychologist and his shortcomings: Distortions in the attribution process. In L. Berkowitz (Ed.), *Advances in experimental social psychology* (Vol. 10). New York: Academic.

Salancik, G. R., & Conway, M. (1975). Attitude inferences from salient and relevant cognitive content about behavior. *Journal of Personality and Social Psychology, 32,* 829-840.

Skogan, W. G., & Maxfield, M. G. (1981). *Coping with crime.* Beverly Hills, CA: SAGE.

Srull, T. K., & Wyer, R. S. (1979). The role of category accessibility in the interpretation of information about persons: Some determinants and implications. *Journal of Personality and Social Psychology, 37,* 1660-1672.

Taylor, J. A. (1953). A personality scale of manifest anxiety. *Journal of Abnormal and Social Psychology, 48,* 285-290.

Taylor, S. E., & Fiske, S. T. (1979). Salience, attention, and attribution: Top of the head phe-nomena. In L. Berkowitz (Ed.), *Advances in experimental social psychology* (Vol. 11). New York: Academic.

Tversky, A., & Kahneman, D. (1973). Availability: A heuristic for judging frequency and proba-bility. *Cognitive Psychology, 5,* 207-232.

Tversky, A., & Kahneman, D. (1974). Judgment under uncertainty: Heuristics and biases. *Sci-ence, 185,* 1124-1131.

Tyler, T. R. (1980) The impact of directly and indirectly experienced events: The origin of crime related judgments and behavior. *Journal of Personality and Social Psychology, 39,* 13-28.

Tyler, T. R., Cook, F. L., & Gordon, M. T. (1981) *The nature of mass media effects: Personal versus societal level impact.* Paper presented at the meeting of the Midwest Association for Public Opinion Research, Chicago.

Volgy, T., & Schwartz, J. (1980). Television entertainment programming and sociopolitical atti-tudes. *Journalism Quarterly, 57,* 150-155.

Wakshlag, J., Vial, V., & Tamborini, R. (1984). Selecting crime drama and apprehension about crime. *Human Communication Research, 10,* 227-242.

Wyer, R. S., & Srull, T. K. (1980). Category accessibility: Some theoretical and empirical issues concerning the processing of social stimulus information. In E. T. Higgins, C. P. Herman, & M. P. Zanna (Eds.), *Social cognition: The Ontario Symposium on personality and social psychology.* Hillsdale, NJ: Lawrence Erlbaum.

Zillmann, D. (1980). Anatomy of suspense. In P. H. Tannenbaum (Ed.), *The entertainment functions of television.* Hillsdale, NJ: Lawrence Erlbaum.

19 ● Public Views on Crime: Television Exposure and Media Credibility

GARRETT J. O'KEEFE

University of Denver

T HE contention that television plays a major role in shaping public perceptions and attitudes regarding crime has received a great deal of attention of late, but empirical evidence on the issue has often been piecemeal and contradictory. This study examines the issue in the context of its theoretical and policy-related implications, and provides a broader array of evidence in terms of the type and scope of the concepts considered.

REVIEW OF PREVIOUS RESEARCH

Media Crime Content

The news media provide extensive coverage of certain kinds of crime-related events. Several recent content analyses of newspaper and television news indicate that crime stories are a staple of both (Graber, 1980; Skogan & Maxfield, 1981; Gordon & Heath, 1981), probably in large part because they appeal to news audiences and are relatively cost-effective to handle journalistically. The frequency of appearance of stories about crime tends to be disproportionate to actual incidence of crime, at least in urban areas

AUTHOR'S NOTE: The research reported was supported in part by funding from the National Institute of Justice, U.S. Department of Justice. I wish to thank Kathaleen Reid-Nash, Harold Mendelsohn, Elise Henry, and Beth Rosenzweig for their assistance on various phases of the project.

Correspondence and requests for reprints: Garrett J. O'Keefe, Department of Mass Communications, University of Denver, Denver, CO 80208-0187.

(Graber, 1980). And news media tend to report violent crimes, such as murder and rape, far out of proportion to their occurrence as compared to such other types of crime as burglary and white-collar crime (Graber, 1980; Skogan & Maxfield, 1981). Depictions of crime are prevalent on the most popular entertainment medium—television—as well. A content analysis of prime-time network programs during the 1980-1981 television season indicated that crime content pervaded the viewing schedule, with murder the most common offense (Lichter & Lichter, 1983). Violent crimes dominated the screen in far greater proportion to their real-life incidence. Criminals were predominantly either professional mobsters or "respectable" businessmen motivated by greed; they were older than their real-life counterparts and likelier to be apprehended. Police were generally depicted as positive and somewhat effective but nowhere near as competent as private investigators in solving crimes. These finding support a similar reality gap between televised and actual crime reported in previous content analyses of entertainment television (Dominick, 1978; Gerbner, Gross, Signorielli, & Jackson-Beeck, 1979).

Pubic Response to Media Crime Content

Popular journalistic and entertainment media tend to emphasize giving their audiences "what they want to hear about," and the case of crime appears to be no exception. In a limited 21-person panel survey, Graber (1980) found that respondents paid substantial attention to crime-related stories and that they were likely to name the media as their main source of information about crime. However, recall of specifics of particular crime stories appeared quite low, and respondents were likely to name more personalized sources of information about crime as a neighborhood issue. Insofar as television entertainment programming is concerned, the prevalence of crime on consistently highly rated shows suggests that audiences attend to and are interested in crime.

Skogan and Maxfield (1981) suggest that newspaper crime stories reach the more affluent audiences characteristic of print media, while televised crime stories are likelier to be blue-collar and lower-class audiences. More data on both attention to media crime content and the demographic and sociographic makeup of such audiences are needed.

Public Impact of Media Crime Content

Few studies have dealt directly with the key issue of the effects of media crime content on audience perceptions, beliefs, attitudes, and behaviors regarding crime, and their results tend to be inconclusive. Perhaps the most extensive data sets pertinent to the role of media in shaping citizen perceptions of crime have been reported under the cultivation or "scary world" hypothesis (Gerbner & Gross, 1976; Gerbner, Gross, Eleey, Jackson-Beeck, Jeffries-Fox, & Signorielli, 1977; Gerbner, Gross, Jackson-Beeck, Jeffries-Fox, & Signorielli, 1978).

Briefly, the proposition asserts that commercial television on the whole presents an "organically composed total world" of patterned and interrelated themes and symbols. Content analysis supports such interrelatedness and indicates a relatively high proportion of imagery depicting crime and violence. It is argued that such imagery "cultivates" among television viewers a cognitive structure that is used to interpret the world around them. The more frequent the viewing, the hypothesis goes, the greater the cultivation effect.

More specifically, the hypothesis predicts that heavier viewers of television will perceive crime more closely in tune with televised depictions of it than with its reality. Furthermore, the crime-related values of heavy viewers are predicted to be more reflective of the television view of reality, particularly in terms of greater personal mistrust, alienation, and fear. Thus the "scary world" of television cultivates a similar perspective of the world among the viewing public. The hypothesis presents the amount of time spent with television as the independent variable; it is not particularly concerned with individual patterns of viewing based on content choices. That is, greater exposure to the world of television in its totality is what cultivates inaccurate citizen perceptions and values, regardless of specific exposure to crime-relevant or violent programming.

Data addressing the hypothesis do not invariably support it. Initial correlational findings of Gerbner et al. (1977, 1978) based on the NORC General Social Survey appeared to be supportive in that heavier viewers were more likely than lighter viewers to score high on indices of interpersonal mistrust, anomie, and fear of walking alone at night, and these relationships held when age, gender, and education were controlled separately. Corroborative evidence was found for children in smaller (and far less generalizable) samples. In one of the few content-specific analyses, frequency of viewing of crime and police shows on television was found to be related to fear of walking alone at night and to reported ownership of dogs for protection, special locks, and guns (Gerbner et al., 1978).

Since the publication of those findings, several other studies have shown no support for them, including reanalyses of the same data. Hughes (1980) reanalyzed the NORC data used by Gerbner et al. but included several measures they excluded and controlled for a wider set of potentially confounding variables (income, hours employed, organizational membership, etc.) Hughes used these controls simultaneously rather than one at a time, and found virtually none of the relations reported previously and no evidence of a cultivation effect on any of the additional dependent variables considered. Similarly, Hirsch (1980a, 1980b, 1981a, 1981b), in an extensive theoretical and methodological critique of the cultivation approach, found virtually no relations supporting cultivation in the NORC data when he applied a series of controls using a multiple classification analysis technique.

Two studies dealing with exposure to more specific content areas offer evidence somewhat contrary to cultivation as well. Skogan and Maxfield (1981) found no relation between fear of victimization and viewership of television news (or readership of newspaper crime news) in their large-scale survey of residents of three urban areas when age, education, race, and gender were simultaneously controlled. In a survey of Toronto residents, Doob and McDonald (1979) found no overall relation between television use and fear of crime when controls for demographics and actual reported neighborhood crime levels were inserted. However, their results did suggest a positive association between viewership and fear within the highest crime neighborhoods.

Moreover, in the aforementioned limited panel case study, Graber found indications that respondents were more likely to perceive criminals as nonwhite and lower class, contrary to what media portrayals would suggest. However, respondent evaluations of the criminal justice system, largely negative, appeared to be based in part on the relatively unorganized milieu of crime-related information presented in the news media. That is, the respondents may have developed from the media the idea that crime is rampant and thus inferred that the justice system was lacking. Graber concludes that public perceptions of crime may be based partly on news coverage, but that individuals take an active role in assimilating that information along with other inputs to form their own unique cognitive maps vis-à-vis crime as a public issue.

Gordon and Heath (1981) offer correlational evidence that readers of newspapers with greater crime coverage are more likely to call crime their most important neighborhood problem. It remains unclear whether the newspapers were helping to set the public issues agenda for those readers, or whether individuals simply chose the paper that spoke more to their already existng concerns.

A review of studies dealing with cultivation and related hypotheses by Hawkins and Pingree (1981b) finds some limited support for cultivation. It argues, however, that research taking into account media content differences and individual dispositions of audience members, including their social and environmental circumstances, is likely to be more productive in sorting out the impact of television and other media on public perceptions of social reality, including crime-related ones.

RATIONALE FOR THE PRESENT RESEARCH

This study is concerned specifically with the relation between viewership of television and orientations toward crime, from the viewpoints of both public policy considerations and media effects theory.

From a policy perspective, it has been observed that fear of crime out of proportion to its actual occurrence and severity may be an emerging social problem, and the impact of both news and entertainment television on such fear could yield dysfunctional influences, particularly given the biases in the content of both (Lavrakas, 1980; Skogan & Maxfield, 1981). Such influences may affect not only citizen perceptions of the severity of crime and vulnerability to it, but also views of how crime can best be dealt with and the social and political ramifications of such views. Such citizen orientations obviously may affect not only individual behaviors but system-level legislative and judicial action as well.

From a theoretical perspective, the concerns here are with, first, bringing new evidence to bear on the cultivation hypothesis itself, utilizing data derived from a more recent national sample survey of the U.S. public, and including both a broader and more specific array of independent and dependent variables.

A second major concern is examining the potential impact of total television viewing and of specific exposure to crime-oriented entertainment programming and crime news content. Previous work has suggested that exposure to such particular programming content as crime adventure shows is more likely than other types of programming to be related to perceptions of criminal violence (Hawkins & Pingree, 1981). It is hypothesized here that persons exposed more often to crime-oriented news and entertainment programming would hold perceptions and attitudes more congruent with the content of such programming (e.g., in the direction of seeing crime as more serious; having greater fear of victimization, particularly in terms of violent crime; etc.).

The final concern of this chapter is investigating the role of the psychological predispositions of audience members as either reducing or enhancing the relationship between viewing and orientations toward crime. The cultivation hypothesis has been criticized for not sufficiently taking into account analyses of individual dispositions of audience members, as well as their social and environmental settings. Studies using such paradigms as uses and gratifications and examining such variables as the extent of reliance on media have been helpful in explaining the influences of media content on, for example, political orientations and behaviors (see O'Keefe & Atwood, 1981). Although a number of potentially intervening variables may be considered, one that has proven productive in social reality studies is that of the perceived reality, or credibility, of television content to the viewer (Hawkins & Pingree, 1981; Slater & Elliott, 1982; Elliott, Mudd, & Good, 1983). These studies suggest that the more "real" or credible the content, the more likely that content will influence perceptions of social reality. It is hypothesized that the greater the credibility attached to crime news and to crime entertainment content, the more that content will influence viewers' crime orientations.

If television content is capable of affecting citizens' cognitions, attitudes, and behaviors regarding crime, those effects are likely to be found across a far broader spectrum of crime-related dispositions than has previously been examined. Given the content characteristics described above, television is likely to affect not only citizens' perceptions of the extent of crime within their own neighborhoods, but their own perceptions of their personal vulnerability to crime (that is, their felt risk of and extent of worry about victimization). Furthermore, we would expect perceptions of police performance in abetting crime to be influenced, perhaps as well as assessments of the performance of the courts. Citizen values concerning the most appropriate means for dealing with crime could well be affected, as well as individuals' sense of fatalism regarding crime in society.

METHODOLOGY

The methodology involved a secondary analysis of national sample data gathered for a study of the public impact of crime prevention information campaigns (O'Keefe, 1983; O'Keefe & Mendelsohn, 1983).[1] As in any secondary analysis, the measures used do not always form a perfect fit; yet they are arguably adequate.

Sample

The survey, with fieldwork subcontracted to The Roper Organization, was conducted with a standard multistage probability sample of 1188 adults interviewed in their homes for approximately 45 minutes each in November 1981.

The population included national civilian noninstitutionalized U.S. residents over the age of 17. A one-call quasi-probability design was employed based on Roper's master national probability sample of interviewing areas. At the first selection stage, 100 counties were drawn randomly after all counties in the nation had been stratified by population size within geographic regions. At the second stage, cities and towns within the sample counties were drawn at random, proportionate to population. Four blocks or segments were then drawn within each location. Where block statistics were available, blocks or rural route segments were drawn at random. A specific method of proceeding from the starting household was prescribed at the block or route level. Quotas for gender and age levels, as well as for employed women, were imposed to ensure proper representation. Interviewing was conducted by Roper's staff of regularly employed personnel. Their work was consistently monitored, with work samples systematically validated. The resulting sample was highly comparable to 1980 Census Bureau statistics on key demographics.

Measurement

The key independent variables included the following:

(1) *Overall exposure to television.* "On the average weekday, how much time do you usually spend watching television from the time you get up until you go to sleep?" (3 levels)

(2) *TV crime entertainment exposure.* "How often do you watch police, crime, or detective programs on television? Do you watch them often, sometimes, or hardly ever at all?" (3 levels)

(3) *TV crime news exposure.* "How much attention do you ordinarily give to news about crime on television—a lot, some, or hardly any?" (3 levels)

(4) *TV crime entertainment credibility.* "Do you think that police, crime, and detective programs on television give a very accurate picture of crime in America, a somewhat accurate picture, or not a very accurate picture at all of crime in America?" (3 levels)

(5) *TV crime news credibility.* "Which statement do you agree most with?: Crime is more serious than the newspapers and TV say; crime is about as serious as the newspapers and TV say; crime is less serious than the newspapers and TV say."

The TV crime news credibility item has the weakness of incorporating newspapers and television, but there is neither evidence nor reason to suspect that one medium has greater credibility than any other in crime coverage. Responses to the item were coded on two levels: (1) Crime is about as serious; (2) crime is more/less serious. (Only 4 percent regarded it as less serious, while 59 percent called it more serious.)

Citizen crime orientations studied previously have centered almost exclusively on sense of personal security and have typically used slight variants of only one questionnaire item basically asking about one's sense of personal safety or fearfulness in being out alone at night. In the present study, several categories of measures were used:

(1) *Neighborhood crime perceptions,* including perception of increase in neighborhood crime rate; sense of safety in being out alone at night in the neighborhood; and how dangerous the neighborhood was viewed compared to others.[2]

(2) *Perceived likelihood of victimization,* or how likely respondents thought it was that (a) their residences would be burglarized and (b) they personally would be attacked or robbed.[3]

(3) *Worry about victimization,* or the extent of worry about being either burglarized or attacked or robbed.[4]

(4) *Assessment of performance of the criminal justice system,* including how good a job both the local police and the local courts were seen as doing in preventing or reducing crime.[5]

(5) *Perceived effectiveness of various social and political policies for reducing crime,* including improving societal conditions; having citizens act responsibly with others to protect themselves and their property; punishing criminals to the fullest extent possible; and putting more police on the streets.[6]

(6) *Fatalistic values about crime,* included feelings that crime can't be prevented regardless of measures taken, and that "there will always be crime and criminals."[7]

(7) *General psychological characteristics,* including measures of trust in people, anomie, and altruism.[8]

Control variables consisted of a number of demographic characteristics that have been shown to be related to both television viewing habits and crime orientations, including gender, age, race, income, education, social class or neighborhood, dwelling type (single detached versus multiple), and community size. In addition, respondents' direct experience with crime was used as a control variable, using a weighted measure taking into account whether the respondent had personally been victimized or had known relatives, neighbors, or other people who had been victimized.

The general plan for analysis called for zero-order correlations between the independent and dependent variables to be examined as indicators of basic descriptive relations, and then for the use of hierarchical regression equations to determine the significance of those relations with appropriate controls inserted. The general model included demographics to be used as block one of the equation, direct crime or victimization experience as block two, overall television exposure as block three, crime news and entertainment exposure as block four, and crime news and entertainment credibility as block five.

As in the previous studies on this issue, the single time point data used here do not allow for causal inference building. However, they do allow baselines to be set in terms of whether the potential exists for causal relations and what the parameters of those relations are likely to be.

FINDINGS

A descriptive overview of audience orientations toward crime on television by demographic characteristics and victimization experience appears in Table 19.1. Education and, to a lesser extent, income and neighborhood

Table 19.1
Correlations Among Television Orientations
and Demographics
(n = 1188)

	Total TV Exposure	TV Crime Entertainment Exposure	TV Crime News Exposure	TV Crime Entertainment Credibility	TV Crime News Credibility
Gender					
(fem. = 0)	−.05	.08**	−.09**	.04	−.01
Age	.02	−.09**	.02	−.07*	−.03
Race					
(white = 0)	.05	.20**	.13**	.13**	.04
Income	−.17**	−.11**	−.15**	−.02	−.08**
Education	−.21**	−.18**	−.15**	−.11**	−.12**
Neighborhood					
class	−.14**	−.10**	−.09**	−.08*	.04
Dwelling type					
(sing. = 0)	−.05	−.08**	.02	.03	−.01
Community					
size	.02	.00	−.05	.01	−.01
Victimization					
experiences	.00	.01	−.08**	.10**	.00

*p < .05; **p < .01.

class occur as the primary predictors. Generally, lower socioeconomic groups watch more television overall, watch more crime-related entertainment and news programming, and find such programming more credible. Younger persons watch more crime entertainment programs and also find them more believable. Men watch more crime entertainment shows; women are more exposed to crime news. Previous direct contact with crime appears to make little difference in viewing habits, except for persons with more victimization experience watching less news about crime who find crime entertainment programs more credible.

Neighborhood Crime Perceptions

Perceptions of danger due to crime in one's own neighborhood were generally well predicted by demographic characteristics and in directions to be expected. The environmental characteristics of community size and social class of neighborhood were key indicators, with urban dwellers and residents of lower-class neighborhoods likelier to perceive their neighborhoods as less safe. Similarly, residents of multiple dwelling units saw greater danger in their neighborhoods. Apart from environmental considerations, the lesser educated perceived greater danger, as did nonwhites and women; older

Table 19.2
Regression Analysis of Neighborhood Crime Perceptions
by TV Orientations and Controls
(n = 1188)

	Crime Rate		Danger at Night		Comparative Danger	
	zero	B	zero	B	zero	B
Block 1						
gender (fem. = 0)	−.01	−.03	−.31	.30**	−.07	−.06**
age	.13	.16	.10	.12**	−.01	.02
race (white = 0)	.06	.05	.15	.07**	.20	.12**
income	−.02	.01	−.16	−.04	−.14	−.04
education	−.05	−.05	−.15	−.07**	−.12	−.06**
neighborhood class	.00	.02	−.14	−.07**	−.20	−.11**
dwelling type (sing. = 0)	−.03	−.01	.09	.06*	.15	.10**
community size	.04	.03	.13	.13**	.11	.11**
Block 2						
victimization experiences	.17	.21**	.07	.13**	.11	.13**
Block 3						
total TV exposure	.01	−.02	.12	.03	.06	−.01
Block 4						
TV crime entertainment exposure	.04	.02	.08	.02	.07	−.02
TV crime news exposure	.06	.04	.18	.06**	.13	.05
Block 5						
TV crime entertainment credibility	.05	.05	.11	.12**	.10	.11**
TV crime news credibility	.07	.06*	.10	.08**	.03	.02
	(R^2 = .06)		(R^2 = .21)		(R^2 = .11)	

persons were more concerned for their personal safety when out at night. Having had direct experience with victimization also enhanced perception of danger (see Table 19.2).

Relations between perceptions of danger and television viewing characteristics proved to be somewhat mixed. Clearly, however, the greater the credibility attached to entertainment crime programs, the greater the perception of danger. Higher crime news credibility was associated with feeling more unsafe when out at night. Frequency of exposure to television crime content appeared less important, although greater attendance to crime news was positively associated with perceived danger at night. Total television exposure was unrelated to perceived danger when other variables were accounted for. However, total exposure was significantly associated with

Table 19.3
Regression Analysis of Perceived Likelihood of Victimization
by TV Orientations and Controls
(n = 1188)

	Burglary Probability		Violent Crime Probability	
	zero	B	zero	B
Block 1				
gender (fem. = 0)	−.09	−.10**	−.02	−.02
age	−.01	.04	−.07	−.05
race (white = 0)	.14	.09**	.08	.03
income	−.09	−.05	−.10	−.15**
education	−.05	−.02	−.01	.01
neighborhood class	−.11	−.06*	−.04	−.03
dwelling type (sing. = 0)	.04	.02	−.05	.01
community size	.05	.04	.04	.05*
Block 2				
victimization experiences	.23	.26**	.18	.19**
Block 3				
total TV exposure	.04	−.01	.01	−.03
Block 4				
TV crime entertainment exposure	.06	.01	.09	.05
TV crime news exposure	.08	.04	.04	.06*
Block 5				
TV crime entertainment credibility	.09	.07**	.09	.02
TV crime news credibility	.07	.06**	.05	.04
	(R^2 = .10)		(R^2 = .06)	

perceived danger at night before controls were inserted. Although this find-ing corroborates that of Gerbner et al., a plausible alternative explanation is that those afraid of going out at night simply watch more television because they spend more time at home.

Perceived Likelihood of Victimization

There was also mixed support for the possible influence of television on respondents' beliefs about the likelihood that they would be victimized. The findings varied according to whether the concern was with burglary or more violent assault.

Women, nonwhites, and lower social class neighborhood residents—in addition to those with direct victimization experience—saw a greater chance of being burglarized. In addition, the more credibility attached to both crime entertainment and crime news programming, the greater the

Table 19.4
Regression Analysis of Worry About Victimization
by TV Orientations and Controls
(n = 1188)

	Worry About Burglary		Worry About Violent Crime	
	zero	B	zero	B
Block 1				
gender (fem. = 0)	−.09	−.09**	−.23	−.22**
age	−.08	−.03	−.06	−.03
race (white = 0)	.08	.04	.11	.06*
income	.02	.01	−.07	−.06*
education	−.00	−.01	−.04	−.01
neighborhood class	−.04	−.01	−.07	−.02
dwelling type (sing. = 0)	.03	−.01	−.05	−.02
community size	.10	.08**	.10	.10**
Block 2				
victimization experiences	.22	.21**	.14	.15**
Block 3				
total TV exposure	.08	.03	.07	.01
Block 4				
TV crime entertainment exposure	.07	−.02	.04	−.03
TV crime news exposure	.11	.17**	.11	.13**
Block 5				
TV crime entertainment credibility	.21	.10**	.16	.08**
TV crime news credibility	.03	.02	.08	.07**
		$(R^2 = .10)$		$(R^2 = .12)$

perceived burglary risk. Television exposure patterns were unrelated to perceived likelihood of burglary. However, greater crime news attendance was positively associated with perceived likelihood of being attacked or robbed, with income, victimization experience, and community size the only other significant correlates (see Table 19.3).

Apparently each kind of crime lends itself to different risk perceptions among different kinds of people. Not easily explained at this point is why people who believe more of what they watch see higher risk from burglary, whereas those who simply watch more crime news, regardless of how much they believe it, see violent crime as more likely.

Worry About Victimization

The extent to which respondents reported worrying about being victimized presented a somewhat different pattern of correlates. Women and urban residents clearly were more likely to worry about being burglarized or attacked, with nonwhites and lower-income persons more likely to worry about attack but not burglary. Among the television orientations, exposure to crime news was a dominant factor: The more crime news watched, the greater the extent of worrying about both burglary and attack. Crime entertainment exposure was unrelated to either type of worry, but those seeing such entertainment as more credible were likelier to worry more. Crime news credibility was associated positively with greater worry as well (see Table 19.4).

Thus the reality of news programming is reasonably tied to greater felt concern about crime as a consequence of increased exposure, whereas entertainment programming appears to be accepted more for what it is and remains unrelated to degree of worry about crime—except among those who see such programming as more believable.

Directly supportive of the "scary world" hypothesis are significant zero-order correlations between total television exposure and each type of worry. However, the beta values drop to minimal levels, indicating the greater importance of intervening variables.

Assessments of Criminal Justice System Performance

Younger persons, nonwhites, and residents of lower-class neighborhoods tended to be more critical of the performance of police in helping prevent or reduce crime, whereas older individuals and residents of larger communities were more critical of the courts. Persons with direct victimization experience were more likely to be more critical of both elements of the justice system. In neither case was exposure to television a significant factor, but credibility was, and in a curiously inverse way. The more accurate respondents thought entertainment crime programming was, the more positively they rated both the police and the courts. However, the more credibility attached to crime news, the more negatively the police and the courts were viewed (see Table 19.5).

Although the limited content analyses of crime-related entertainment and news programming cannot reliably bear this out, one could argue that crime entertainment programs generally show the police in a more effectual light (noted by Lichter & Lichter, 1983), and the action-based nature of the shows may reveal little that is detrimental to court proceedings. However, televised crime news may reflect the journalistic tendency to emphasize the wrongs of the justice system and to highlight instances in which the police and courts are either ineffective or in error. The extent to which citizens' views about the justice system are influenced by television is open to debate here, but the findings suggest a strong corroboration between varying views of citizens regarding the justice system and how believable are two differing media depictions of it.

Table 19.5

Regression Analysis of Perceptions of Police and Courts Performance by TV
Orientations and Controls (n = 1188)

	Police Performance		Courts Performance	
	zero	*B*	*zero*	*B*
Block 1				
gender (fem. = 0)	−.04	−.03	−.07	−.05
age	.15	.14**	−.03	−.06*
race (white = 0)	−.13	−.10**	.04	.05
income	.06	.03	−.06	−.01
education	.04	.05	−.08	−.06
neighborhood class	.15	.10**	−.01	.04
dwelling type (sing. = 0)	.08	.01	−.00	.00
community size	−.05	−.05	−.12	−.11**
Block 2				
victimization experiences	−.11	−.09**	−.11	−.09**
Block 3				
total TV exposure	.01	.02	.03	.02
Block 4				
TV crime entertainment exposure	−.00	.03	.03	.01
TV crime news exposure	.07	.04	.11	−.03
Block 5				
TV crime entertainment credibility	.01	.07**	−.02	.08**
TV crime news credibility	.09	−.08**	−.11	−.11**
		(R² = .06)		(R² = .04)

Perceived Effectiveness of Crime Prevention Policies

Somewhat similarly, the more credibility attached to both entertainment and news crime content, the more likely were respondents to regard punitive crime prevention measures as effective. While previous content analyses have not addressed this area, the suggestion is that media crime content appears congruent with views that greater punishment of criminals and enhanced police powers would be effective means of reducing crime. The extent of television exposure, however, was unrelated to the perceived efficacy of either policy. Demographically, less educated persons and whites were likelier to espouse both policies, while women and residents of upper-

Table 19.6

Regression Analysis of Crime Prevention Effectiveness Values by TV Orientations
and Controls (n = 1188)

	"Full Punishment"		"More Police"	
	zero	B	zero	B
Block 1				
gender (fem. = 0)	−.01	−.00	−.07	−.05*
age	.11	.07**	.08	.04
race (white = 0)	−.12	−.12**	−.02	−.06*
income	−.02	.03	−.07	−.03
education	−.13	−.13**	−.11	−.08**
neighborhood class	.04	.04	.02	.06*
dwelling type (sing. = 0)	.07	.04	−.03	−.03
community size	−.06	−.02	.06	.08**
Block 2				
victimization experiences	−.05	−.02	−.10	−.07**
Block 3				
total TV exposure	.03	.01	.07	.04
Block 4				
TV crime entertainment exposure	.01	−.00	.03	−.00
TV crime news exposure	.07	.05	.03	.03
Block 5				
TV crime entertainment credibility	.05	.06*	.09	.07**
TV crime news credibility	.10	.08**	.08	.07**
	(R^2 = .05)		(R^2 = .03)	

class neighborhoods and urban areas particularly favored greater police authority (see Table 19.6).

More socially conscious crime reduction policies were predicted less well by the media variables or by any of the others, for that matter. Taking responsible preventive actions was positively associated with crime news exposure, for which there is no ready explanation. Women and residents of smaller communities also supported such actions, whereas minority group members regarded the general improvement of social conditions as a positive factor in reducing crime (see Table 19.7).

Table 19.7
Regression Analysis of Crime Prevention Effectiveness Values by TV Orientations
and Controls (n = 1188)

	"Improving Conditions"		"Responsible Citizens"	
	zero	B	zero	B
Block 1				
gender (fem. = 0)	−.06	−.05	−.05	−.06*
age	−.04	−.05	−.03	−.01
race (white = 0)	.10	.09**	−.01	−.01
income	−.05	−.02	.01	.01
education	−.03	−.02	.03	.04
neighborhood class	−.04	−.01	−.03	−.04
dwelling type (sing. = 0)	−.02	.00	−.01	−.02
community size	−.02	−.02	−.06	−.07**
Block 2				
victimization experiences	−.01	−.01	−.02	−.03
Block 3				
total TV exposure	−.01	−.03	−.04	−.05
Block 4				
TV crime entertainment exposure	.01	−.02	−.02	−.03
TV crime news exposure	.04	.03	.06	.09**
Block 5				
TV crime entertainment credibility	.04	.04	−.01	−.02
TV crime news credibility	−.04	.04	−.03	−.03
	(R^2 = .01)		(R^2 = .01)	

Fatalistic Value Toward Crime

The more believable respondents found both entertainment and news crime content, the more likely they were to express feelings that self-protection was useless "if criminals really wanted to get you," perhaps a reflection on the seeming inevitability of crime as portrayed on television. Simple exposure was unrelated to such feeling, however; men, members of lower SES groups, and urban residents were more likely to express such sentiments (see Table 19.8).

Table 19.8
Regression Analysis of Crime Fatalism Values by TV Orientations and Controls
(n = 1188)

	"No Use Protecting Self"		"Always Be Crime"	
	zero	B	zero	B
Block 1				
gender (fem. = 0)	.04	.07*	.01	.00
age	.07	.01	.10	.09**
race (white = 0)	.12	.05	.01	−.00
income	−.20	−.13**	−.03	−.02
education	−.21	−.15**	−.06	−.06*
neighborhood class	−.12	−.01	.03	.04
dwelling type (sing. = 0)	−.06	.00	.01	.01
community size	.06	.10**	.03	.04
Block 2				
victimization experiences	−.03	−.02	−.03	−.00
Block 3				
total TV exposure	.07	.02	−.07	−.10**
Block 4				
TV crime entertainment exposure	.03	−.03	.03	.07*
TV crime news exposure	−.02	−.05	−.00	−.03
Block 5				
TV crime entertainment credibility	.10	.08**	−.03	.01
TV crime news credibility	.10	.07*	.01	−.00
	(R^2 = .08)		(R^2 = .01)	

A somewhat different pattern was found in response to the item suggesting "there will always be crime." Persons viewing more television in general were significantly more in disagreement with the statement, whereas those more exposed to crime entertainment shows were more likely to agree with it. The reasons for differential responses remain unclear, but the findings are a good indication that total television viewership does not necessarily yield the same type of attitudes regarding crime as does specific viewership of crime content per se. Older persons and the lesser educated were also more likely to agree with the statement.

Table 19.9
Regression Analysis of Psychological Characteristics by TV Orientations and Controls (n = 1188)

	Trust in People		Altruism		Anomie	
	zero	B	zero	B	zero	B
Block 1						
gender (fem. = 0)	.03	.01	−.07	−.09**	.04	.06**
age	.07	.10**	−.04	.00	−.02	−.09**
race (white = 0)	−.19	−.14**	−.12	−.07**	.18	.09**
income	.20	.12**	.13	.02	−.31	−.17**
education	.20	.13**	.15	.10**	−.34	−.23**
neighborhood class	.14	−.00	.14	.08	−.22	−.04
dwelling type (sing. = 0)	−.09	−.03	.09	.04	−.11	−.02
community size	.05	.03	−.07	.09**	.04	.00
Block 2						
victimization experiences	−.03	−.06*	.13	.12**	−.02	−.03
Block 3						
total TV exposure	−.07	.00	−.04	−.01	.15	.06*
Block 4						
TV crime entertainment exposure	−.07	.04	−.04	.01	.13	−.02
TV crime news exposure	−.11	−.09**	−.02	.02	.06	.02
Block 5						
TV crime entertainment credibility	−.14	−.07**	−.00	.01	.06	−.01
TV crime news credibility	−.13	−.11**	−.06	−.04	.14	.10**
	(R^2 = .10)		(R^2 = .06)		(R^2 = .17)	

General Psychological Characteristics

Lack of trust in other people apparently carries over to trust in media as well, with both news and entertainment credibility negatively related to trust in people. Greater attendance to crime news also was associated with such distrust, as was victimization experience. Older persons, whites, and members of upper SES groups tended to be more trustful. Sense of altruism was unrelated to any of the media variables (see Table 19.9).

Anomie proved to be significantly predicted by greater overall exposure to television, a finding supportive of Gerbner et al.; anomie was also related positively to greater crime news credibility. Those scoring higher on anomie also tended to be male, younger, lower SES group members, and minorities.

CONCLUSIONS AND DISCUSSION

The findings indicate no support for the proposition that total time spent viewing television has an impact on public perceptions and attitudes regarding crime, or that television viewing per se increases feelings of fearfulness among citizens. Moreover, the amount of time spent viewing televised crime entertainment programs was similarly unrelated to nearly all of the crime perceptions and attitudes examined here. However, the extent of attendance to crime-related television news content was significantly associated with certain kinds of citizen orientations toward crime, notably including perceptions of neighborhood danger, perceived likelihood of being a victim of violent crime, and the extent of worry over being victimized. Persons regarding either televised crime entertainment or news content as being more credible differed significantly from other individuals in terms of their perceptions and attitudes regarding crime.

Insofar as the cultivation hypothesis is concerned, significant zero-order correlations were found between total viewing time and perceptions of danger when out alone at night and worry about being victimized. However, these relations dropped to well below significance when demographic and other variables were controlled. While the "scary world" hypothesis per se receives no support here, it is quite possible (as well as plausible) that such variables as education, income, race, and living environs influence both crime orientations and general television viewing habits, and the interactions among these variables deserve further study. It should also be noted that total viewing time was significantly associated with the anomie index, even with controls. This finding generally corroborates earlier data of Gerbner et al. in which anomie-related items were used. Whether higher anomie respondents are more frequent viewers of television as a function of greater isolation or other reasons, or whether television viewing stimulates such a psychological disposition, remains an unanswerable question at this point, however.

Despite frequent criticisms of the nature of crime-related entertainment programming on television, there is no evidence here that the people viewing them differ from others in their basic perceptions and attitudes regarding crime, the only exception being a tendency among those audiences to regard crime as being an inevitable social ill.

The potential impact of televised crime news on audiences appears somewhat more problematic. The basic quandary is whether citizens who are already more concerned about crime selectively attend more to such news or whether attendance to crime news stimulates greater concerns and fears. The chances are that the answer is not "either-or," but that some form of reciprocal or mutually reinforcing interaction is taking place. Persons already more concerned about crime may be more attentive to crime news for such purposes as getting more information about the issue, or having their own biases reinforced. In such cases such exposure could well stimulate even greater concern.

Two more recently posed components of the cultivation hypothesis—"mainstreaming" and "resonance" (Gerbner et al., 1980b)—may also assist in clarifying some of the more subtle processes at work here, but adequate investigation of their role remains beyond the scope of these data. (Briefly, mainstreaming is proposed to occur as the "television world" cognitions and attitudes of distinctively heavy television viewers become more congruent over time, despite differences in the general background and predispositions of those viewers. Resonance refers to a heightened effect of television on heavy viewers as the "television world" scenario more closely matches the real environment of heavy viewers.)

It is very clear that psychological dispositions among audiences need to be taken into account in examining television's potential for influencing orientations toward crime. The strongest predictor across the board among media variables was the extent of believability or credibility of crime entertainment shows and news as perceived by individuals. Either crime entertainment or crime news credibility, or in some cases both, was significantly related to virtually every crime orientation indicator measured here—including perceptions of neighborhood danger, likelihood of victimization, worry about crime, and justice system evaluations and values. Once again, the directions of causality are unclear, but it could well be that a mutually reinforcing phenomenon is also at work here.

NOTES

1. Funded under a grant to the author by the National Institute of Justice, U.S. Department of Justice.

2. The items used were as follows: (a) "Within the past year, do you think that crime in your neighborhood has increased, decreased, or remained the same?" (b) "How safe do you feel or would you feel being out alone in your neighborhood at night—very safe, reasonably safe, somewhat unsafe, or very unsafe?" (c) "How dangerous do you think this neighborhood

is compared to other neighborhoods in terms of crime? Do you believe it is much more dangerous, more dangerous, about average, less dangerous, or much less dangerous?"

3. Questionnaire items follow: (a) "How likely do you think it is that your residence will be
broken into or burglarized during the next year—do you think it is very likely, somewhat likely,
or not very likely?" (b) "How likely do you think it is that you personally will be attacked or
robbed within the next year—do you think it is very likely, somewhat likely, or not very likely?"

4. The first item read: "Is having your residence burglarized or broken into something that
you worry about a great deal, or something that you worry about somewhat, or something that
you hardly worry about at all?" The second item read: "Is being attacked or robbed something
that you worry about a great deal, or something that you worry about somewhat, or something
that you hardly worry about at all?"

5. "How good a job of prevention would you say (a) the local police are doing? (b) the
local courts are doing? (responses: very good, good, fair, poor).

6. "On this card are four statements telling about different ways of possibly reducing
crime. For each statement, please tell me whether you think it is a very effective way of reducing
crime, a somewhat effective way, or not a very effective way at all of reducing crime:

    (a) by improving conditions as much as possible for all people in our society;
    (b) by punishing criminals to the fullest extent of the law possible;
    (c) by having individual citizens acting responsibly by themselves or with others to pro-
        tect themselves and their property;
    (d) by putting more policemen on the streets and giving them more ability to control
        criminals."

7. "Please tell me whether you agree or disagree with each statement on this card:

    (a) There is not much use trying to protect yourself from crime these days—if criminals
        want to get you, they'll get you.
    (b) Human nature being what it is, there will always be crime and criminals."

8. Composites of standard scales reported in O'Keefe and Mendelsohn (1983).

REFERENCES

Campbell, D. T., & Stanley, J. (1966). *Experimental and quasi-experimental designs for re-
search.* Chicago: Rand McNally.
Cohen, J., & Cohen, P. (1975). *Aplied multiple regression and correlational analysis for the
behavioral sciences.* Hillsdale, NJ: Lawrence Erlbaum.
Cook, T. D., & Campbell, D. T. (1979). *Quasi-experimentation.* Chicago: Rand McNally.
Dominick, J. (1978). Crime and law enforcement in the mass media. In C. Winick (Ed.), *Devi-
ance and the mass media.* Beverly Hills, CA: Sage.
Doob, A., & MacDonald, G. (1979). Television viewing and fear of victimization: Is the relationship causal? *Journal of Personality and Social Psychology, 37,* 170-179.
Elliott, W. R., Mudd, R., & Good, L. (1983). *Measuring the perceived reality of television: Per-
ceived plausibility, perceived superficiality, and the degree of personal utility.* Paper presented at annual meeting of the Association for Education in Journalism and Mass Communication, Corvallis, Oregon.
Gerbner, G., & Gross, L. (1976). Living with television: The Violence Profile. *Journal of Communication, 26*(2), 173-199.
Gerbner, G., Gross, L., Eleey, M., Jackson-Beeck, M., Jeffries-Fox, S., & Signorielli, N. (1977).
TV Violence Profile No. 8. *Journal of Communication, 27*(2), 171-180.
Gerbner, G., Gross, L., Jackson-Beeck, M., Jeffries-Fox, S., & Signorielli, N. (1978). Cultural
indicators: Violence Profile No. 9. *Journal of Communication, 28*(3), 176-207.
Gerbner, G., Gross, L., Morgan, M., & Signorielli (1980a). Some additional comments on culti-
vation analysis. *Public Opinion Quarterly, 44,* 408-410.
Gerbner, G., Gross, L., Morgan, M., & Signorielli, N. (1980b). The "mainstreaming" of Amer-
ica: Violence Profile No. 11. *Journal of Communication, 30*(3), 10-29.

Gerbner, G., Gross, L., Morgan, M., & Signorielli, N. (1981). A curious journey into the scary world of Paul Hirsch. *Communication Research, 8,* 39-72.

Gerbner, G., Signorielli, N., & Jackson-Beeck, M. (1979). The demonstration of power: Violence Profile No. 10. *Journal of Communication, 29*(3), 177-196.

Gordon, M., & Heath, L. (1981). The news business, crime, and fear. In D. Lewis (Ed.), *Reactions to crime.* Beverly Hills, CA: Sage.

Graber, D. B. (1980). *Crime news and the public.* New York: Praeger.

Hawkins, R. P., & Pingree, S. (1981a). Uniform messages and habitual viewing: Unnecessary assumptions in social reality effects. *Human Communication Research, 7,* 291-301.

Hawkins, R. P., & Pingree, S. (1981b). Using television to construct social reality. *Journal of Broadcasting, 25,* 347-364.

Heise, D. (1979). Separating reliability and stability in test-retest correlation. *American Sociological Review, 44,* 93-101.

Hirsch, P. M. (1980a). On Hughes's contribution: The limits of advocacy research. *Public Opinion Quarterly, 44,* 411-413.

Hirsch, P. M. (1980b). The "scary world" of the nonviewer and other anomalies: A reanalysis of Gerbner et al.'s finding on cultivation analysis. Part I. *Communication Research, 7,* 403-456.

Hirsch, P. M. (1981a). Distinguishing good speculation from bad theory: Rejoinder to Gerbner et al. *Communication Research, 8,* 73-95.

Hirsch, P. M. (1981b). On not learning from one's own mistakes: A reanalysis of Gerbner et al.'s findings on cultivation analysis. Part II. *Communication Research, 8,* 3-37.

Hughes, M. (1980). The fruits of cultivation analysis: A reexamination of some effects of television watching. *Public Opinion Quarterly, 44,* 287-302.

Lavrakas, P. (1980). *Factors related to citizen involvement in personal, household, and neighborhood anti-crime measures.* Report submitted to the U.S. Department of Justice.

Lewis, D. A. (1981). *Reactions to crime.* Beverly Hills, CA: Sage.

Lichter, S., & Lichter, R. (1983). *Prime time crime.* Washington, DC: The Media Institute.

O'Keefe, G. J. (1983). *Taking a bite out of crime: The impact of a public information campaign.* Paper presented at the annual meeting of the Association for Education in Journalism and Mass Communication, Corvallis, Oregon.

O'Keefe, G. J., & Atwood, L. E. (1981). Communication and election campaigns. In D. Nimmo & K. Sanders (Eds.), *Handbook of political communication.* Beverly Hills, CA: Sage.

O'Keefe, G. J., & Mendelsohn, H. (1983). *Taking a bite out of crime: The public impact of a crime prevention information campaign and implications for communication strategies.* Report submitted to the National Institute of Justice, U.S. Department of Justice.

O'Keefe, G. J., & Reid-Nash, K. (1982). *Fear arousal in a media information campaign.* Paper presented at the annual meeting of the Midwest Association for Public Opinion Research, Chicago.

Podolefsky, A., & Dubow, F. (1981). *Strategies for community crime prevention: Collective responses to crime in urban America.* Springfield, IL: Charles C. Thomas.

Skogan, W. G., & Maxfield, M. E. (1981). *Coping with crime.* Beverly Hills, CA: Sage.

Slater, D., & Elliott, W. R. (1982). Television's influence on social reality. *Quarterly Journal of Speech, 68,* 69-79.

Solomon, D. (1981). Social marketing and health promotion. In R. Rice & W. Paisley (Eds.), *Public communication campaigns.* Beverly Hills, CA: Sage.

Stinchcombe, A. L., Adams, R., Hiemer, C. A., Scheppele, K. L., Smith, T. W., & Taylor, D. G. (1980). *Crime and punishment: Changing attitudes in America.* San Francisco: Jossey-Bass.

U.S. Department of Health and Human Services. (1982). *Television and behavior: Ten years of scientific progress and implications for the eighties.* Washington, DC: Author.

V ● ORGANIZATIONAL COMMUNICATION

20 ● Managerial Communication and Work Perception

TERRANCE L. ALBRECHT

University of Washington

I T is an accepted notion that an individual's cognitive orientation is a function of the extent to which societal structure regulates exposure to varied kinds of experiences (Holzner, 1972; Parks, 1977). Managers in the organization world are no different; the ways they view their jobs and see themselves are shaped in large part by their positions in the social system. Their social participation roles facilitate or impede what they can do, whom they can contact, and what they can learn.

As in other social aggregates, a position in the social structure of the workplace emerges from the pattern of one's communication transactions with others. A social order is established based on the configuration of strong and weak links among members. The emergent networks of information flow have consequences not only for the cognitive processes of the individuals involved but also for power and influence, politics, members' perceptions of the social climate, and the overall functioning effectiveness of the organization (Albrecht, 1979; Danowski, 1980; Farace, Taylor, & Stewart, 1978; Goldhaber, Dennis, Richetto, & Wiio, 1979; Jablin, 1980; Thurman, 1979).

Although the notion of structure and the impact on individual perceptions is important for understanding motivation and behavior, it has been examined only a few times in research on organizational communication (Jablin, 1982). Recent work has generally concerned the relation between network integration and attitude formation. Albrecht (1979) found that cognitive maps representing work climate attitudes were a function of members' communication network roles in a unionized manufacturing plant. Taylor (1977) studied the relation between degree of attitude change and

Correspondence and requests for reprints: Terrance L. Albrecht, Department of Speech Communication DL-15, University of Washington, Seattle, WA 98195.

network roles of administrators in a statewide educational setting. His results supported hypotheses predicting rate of acceptance of an OD effort based on message impact and network centrality.

The present study was based on a theoretical framework integrating assumptions from uncertainty reduction theory (Berger & Calabrese, 1975), force aggregation theory (Gillham & Woelfel, 1977), and communication structure (Farace, Monge, & Russell, 1977; Rogers & Kincaid, 1981). The purpose was to investigate how managers viewed themselves and their jobs in terms of relational and motivational factors in the organization. Following the mounting empirical evidence for cognitive and behavioral differences among communication role incumbents (e.g., Albrecht, 1979; MacDonald, 1976; Schwartz & Jacobson, 1977; Taylor, 1977), we hypothesized specific ways in which perceptions would differ for those in linking or central roles versus others. This research extended previous studies in two ways: (1) The focus was specifically on the relation between communication behavior and the very personal views managers had about their self-concepts and their jobs; and (2) unlike most previous network and perception studies that have been based on data only from a single time point (e.g., Albrecht, 1979; MacDonald, 1976; Moch, 1980; Roberts & O'Reilly, 1979), this research design was conducted over three points in time. The intent was to examine whether differences in personal perceptions held across time, and how reports of those perceptions fluctuated given highly sensitive measurement techniques.

THEORETICAL FRAMEWORK AND HYPOTHESES

Managers in organizations communicate so as to reduce uncertainty and ambiguity (Farace et al., 1978; Weick, 1979), thereby enabling them to gain some control over their environments. Whether a manager achieves control is determined by several things, including his or her access to information, and the quality of relations with subordinates and superiors. Hence the outcomes of moves to reduce uncertainty and ambiguity are colored by the manager's location and level of interaction with others. Meaning for significant aspects of the organization, as well as one's sense of self and work role, are negotiated products of the range and quantity of interaction with others.

The central notion of force aggregation theory is that attitudes about objects develop at a level commensurate with the rate of acquisition of information about those "objects," such as an issue, a product, the organization, or the self (Albrecht, 1979; Barnett, Serota, & Taylor, 1976; Taylor, Farace, & Monge, 1976). Information is acquired through interactions with others; through this process objects come to develop definition and meaning, which is then shared among members (Taylor et al., 1976).

Specifically, force aggregation theory, an outgrowth of symbolic inter-action notions (Woelfel & Haller, 1971) and learning theory (Burgoon, Burgoon, Miller, & Sunnafrank, 1981), incorporates hypotheses where attitudes are a product of the amount of weighted information organization members receive about objects they perceive as salient in the organization. Information is weighted by the number of messages received, whether the messages are positive or negative, and the level of significance of the source (Gillham & Woelfel, 1977; Taylor, 1977).

For managers at work, perceptions about themselves and their jobs have been developed and reinforced by many messages over a long period. Managers at all levels accumulate information about themselves by working and interacting with others in the organization; the effect is an impact, a shaping of one's self-concept, and perceptions about success on the job. These are developed through positive or negative communication over time with significant others and acquaintances.

Further, the assumption of most force aggregation studies (e.g., Albrecht, 1979) has been that perceptions about objects (such as a product, a candidate, or an innovation) will be positive to the extent that individuals perceive them to be associated with themselves or "close" to their self-concepts in their psychological distance judgments. "Positive" in this sense means they will be disposed to "buy" the product, "vote" for the candidate, or "adopt" the innovation (Albrecht, 1979; see Barnett et al., 1976; Taylor et al., 1976; Taylor, 1977). For managers in the organization, minimal psychological distance between themselves and their views of their jobs (and their coworkers, bosses, salaries, and so on) reflect strong self-definitions and imprinted involvement with work. For a manager to lack that identification with the job and the organization reflects what Westley (1979) has argued: a psychological detachment—in short, alienation.

Given that messages frame attitudes and perceptions, it is important to understand the nature of a manager's access to them. Communication structure refers to the pathways of information flow that link organization members (Farace et al., 1977). One's position or communication role in the network represents the frequency of interaction, integration in the system, and degree of diversity among contacts.

As noted previously in this chapter, different levels of network integration have been related to differences in attitudes and motivation (e.g., Albrecht, 1979; Albrecht, Irey, & Mundy, 1982; Moch, 1980; Roberts & O'Reilly, 1979; Taylor, 1977). Reynolds and Johnson (1982) reviewed selected findings on differences between liaisons and nonliaisons and found that liaisons were unique in terms of motivational and relational factors. Following the line of work advanced in these previous studies, the present research was designed to further explore such motivation and relationship factors as related to fluctuations in managers' perceptions of themselves and their jobs. The hypotheses were based on predictions of differences in cognitive orientation between managers identified as *linkers* (those in bridge or liaison communication roles) and *nonlinkers* (group members and other, more isolated roles).

Hypotheses

At the motivational level, it was expected that linkers would identify more with their jobs because they had more positive orientations to their roles in the system. This was consistent with previous findings. Albrecht (1979) found that liaisons and bridges identified more with their jobs and that their concepts of their jobs were at the center of their cognitive MDS spaces. She reasoned that key linkers would see themselves as more central, given that they had access and influence in the communication system. In contrast, nonlinkers would have less involvement in the communication flow and would encounter fewer messages to shape their perceptions. They viewed little about the organization in ways they could relate to themselves and their jobs. Roberts and O'Reilly (1979) found that participants in a communication network of navy personnel had more job satisfaction than did nonparticipants. Finally, MacDonald (1976) found that liaisons were more satisfied with their jobs and the communication system (Reynolds & Johnson, 1982).

The hypotheses are as follows:

H_1: The magnitude of the psychological distance between the concepts of "self" and "my job" will be less for linkers than for nonlinkers.

H_2: The association between the concepts of "self" and "my job" reported by linkers will become closer over time than will the association reported by nonlinkers.

Given that linkers were expected to identify more with their jobs and generally be more satisfied with their work, it was also hypothesized that they would attribute more positive concepts in connection to themselves and their jobs than would nonlinkers. It was expected that these would be perceived as an increasingly closer set of associations over time:

H_3: Linkers will associate their jobs and their concepts of themselves more with positive concepts than will nonlinkers.

H_4: Linkers will report closer associations over time between the concepts in Hypothesis 3 than will nonlinkers.

At the relational level, it was expected that linkers would perceive less distance between themselves and their coworkers and superiors because of the range and frequency of their communication behavior. Amend (1971) found that liaisons had greater peer communication contact and network centrality. Hence liaisons likely perceive closer relationships between themselves and others because of greater contact. And Albrecht (1979) found that those in linking positions perceived less psychological distance between themselves and the plant foremen and general management. What this means is that the volume of interactions functions to reduce linkers' levels of uncertainty toward others, which in turn facilitates continued interaction. As Parks and Adelman (1983) noted, the reduction of uncertainty motivates further interaction by increasing levels of affiliation between persons.

H_5: The magnitude of the psychological distance between the concepts of "my job" and "my boss" and between "my job" and "my coworkers" will be less for linkers than for nonlinkers.

H_6: The magnitude of the psychological distance between the concepts of "me" and "my boss" and between "me" and "my coworkers" will be less for linkers than for nonlinkers.

H_7: The distances reported by linkers between the concepts noted in Hypotheses 5 and 6 will decrease more over time than will the distances reported by nonlinkers.

In understanding the perceptions linkers have about their relationships in organizations, it was necessary to consider the nature of their reported communication contacts—the strength and/or frequency and range of contact with others. This helps construe the level of certainty linkers have over their personal communication environments. Investigating the organization system from a communication network perspective means that the phenomena under study are the retrospective accounts of people about their communication behavior (Albrecht & Ropp, 1982), a reflection of the assumptions they hold about their relationships and relative positions in the organization. These assumptions vary across organization members systemwide, to the extent that there can be much disagreement among respondents as to the nature of their links to others. That is, people may disagree not only on the number of times they communicated during a given period (strength of the link) but also on whether the link even existed at all.

Hence we explored how linkers and nonlinkers differed in their perceptions of their communication patterns, as well as how others in the system reported interacting with them. High agreement with others over the nature of one's interactions indicates a level of perceived personal control and certainty over actions. Schwartz and Jacobson (1977) found that liaisons had higher levels of reciprocity (agreement over the existence of a link) than did nonliaisons. Given that Amend (1971) found that liaisons had more control over the general flow of information in the organization, it was expected that linkers would have greater awareness of the scope and volume of their interactions; that they had greater certainty about the environments in which they communicated. They would be less likely to err in the estimates they reported for the range and frequency of their contacts.

H_8: Linkers will have a higher level of reciprocated contact and less discrepancy in the volume of their perceived interactions with others than will nonlinkers.

H_9: The reciprocity and discrepancy levels in Hypothesis 8 will remain stable over time more for linkers than for nonlinkers.

METHOD

The organization used for the research site was an electronics manufacturing plant in the Southwest. Respondents were all salaried personnel (n = 65). The number of respondents at each time point were (1) 89 percent, (2) 80 percent, and (3) 75 percent. Of the respondents at time 1, 65 percent were male. The age range was 19-58 (mean = 38, s = 8.9). The average length of time employed in the facility was 3.02 years (s = 1.75). There were 17 percent considered upper-level managers, 20 percent middle-level, and 63 percent lower-level. Nearly all were white. A total of 48 percent had completed one year of college; 51 percent had finished college.

Measurements. Job and self-perceptions were measured using a paired comparison technique developed in attitude measurement (Gillham & Woelfel, 1977; Woelfel & Fink, 1980). The form of measurement is a set of paired comparisons among concepts and attributes salient to organization members and native to their shared code system. These words were identified through content analysis of personal interview data collected just prior to the main study with a random sample of 20 percent of the salaried individuals. Respondents were asked open-ended questions concerning their descriptions of the work environment, their jobs, superiors, coworkers, and so on. Concepts and attributes mentioned most frequently across respondents were chosen for the final study instrument and included "teamwork," "knowledgeable," "effectiveness," "pressures," "problems," "frustration," "my salary," and "my boss." Concepts added as part of the research purpose were "me," "my job," and "coworkers" (see also Albrecht, 1979; Taylor, 1977).

Each word was paired with the concepts "me" and "my job." The items for the final instrument were the paired comparisons; respondents were asked to indicate the degree of perceived similarity between the concepts of each pair by making distance judgments. The judgments were made using open-ended ratio scales (Gillham & Woelfel, 1977).

Communication structure properties and communication role were assessed using network-analytic techniques developed by Richards (1975). The work network among salaried persons was measured by asking respondents how often they had talked with other personnel during the previous week about their jobs, work in the plant, or the general day-to-day business of the company. The roster method (Rogers & Kincaid, 1981) was used to facilitate memory recall for respondents. Names of all respondents were listed on the instrument in alphabetical order.

The data were analyzed using program NEGOPY (Richards, 1975) to determine each member's communication role. Those managers classified by the program as bridges or liaisons were coded as communication linkers. Group members, dyad members, and isolates were coded as nonlinkers.

Values for additional communication properties used for the reciprocity and discrepancy analyses were obtained from the NEGOPY results.

Reciprocity. This variable referred to the extent to which two people independently agreed they had a communication link (Farace et al., 1977; Richards, 1975). If a respondent reported that communication with an individual took place but the individual did not report the occurrence, the link was considered unreciprocated. Level of reciprocity was calculated for each respondent based on the ratio of reported reciprocated links to total links (reciprocated and unreciprocated).

Link strength. Following Richards (1975) and Farace et al. (1977), link strength was measured by reports of communication frequency. Although two managers may have agreed they had a communication link, they may or may not have agreed on the number of times they communicated during the specified period. Hence, "outgoing reciprocated link strength" referred to the respondent's total report of frequency of communication with all of his or her reciprocated contacts. "Incoming reciprocated link strength" was the total frequency of interaction that all the respondent's contacts reported they had with him or her. A similar analysis was made of the respondent's unreciprocated links. "Outgoing unreciprocated link strength" referred to the total number of interactions reported by the respondent with others who did not report any connection to him or her. "Incoming unreciprocated link strength" was a measure of all reports of communication frequency with the respondent (who did not acknowledge that such transactions occurred). Finally, discrepancy totals were calculated to reflect the sum of differences between the repondent's record of reciprocated and unreciprocated interactions and the number of interactions reported by those others with the individual.

Data collection. Data were collected in two stages: (1) telephone interviews and (2) distribution of final study questionnaires at three points in time. The study was a three-wave panel design with one-week intervals between data collection time points. The first collection was held formally on plant premises. Verbal instructions were given to small groups of mixed-level managers participating in the study. Assurances were made regarding confidentiality of the data for each individual. For the second and third waves of data collection, respondents were asked to complete the forms on their own time during each of the two designated 24-hour periods. The company was given a final report of summary trends in the data.

RESULTS

Communication Role Analysis

Of the 58 respondents at time 1, 22 were identified as linkers. Of those, 32 percent were upper-level managers, 23 percent were middle-level, and 45 percent were lower-level personnel. Thirty-six persons were identified as nonlinkers in the organization. About 11 percent were upper-level managers, 19 percent middle-level, and approximately 69 percent were lower-level personnel. The two groups did not differ markedly in terms of representation of management level. Results of a chi-square test showed that the two distributions of management levels were not significantly different ($\chi^2 = 4.42$, p > .05, df = 2).

Differences in Motivational Factors

Hypotheses 1 and 2. In general, linkers tended to identify more closely with their jobs than did nonlinkers. They consistently reported lower mean interpoint distances (Tables 20.1 and 20.2) and were less variable in their perceptions (see the lower standard deviations). The difference in perceptions was significant across time (Table 20.3).

Hypothesis 2 was also supported, in that linkers tended to perceive that the concepts of self and job moved closer over time. In contrast, the pattern for nonlinkers remained relatively steady; managers who were nonlinkers at time 3 perceived their jobs more than three times as distant from themselves as did linkers.

Hypotheses 3 and 4. The results show some support for Hypothesis 3. In contrast to those in nonlinking positions, linkers tended to associate their jobs with the notions of teamwork and effectiveness; they also saw more of a parallel between their jobs and their salaries. They clearly characterized themselves as knowledgeable. Linkers consistently reported the least association with feelings of frustration, a notion that moved further away in space over time. Interestingly, although linkers saw closer associations with positive factors, they also saw their jobs more in terms of problems and pressures than did nonlinkers. They also reported a closer tie to problems at

Table 20.1
Descriptive Statistics for Job Concept Pairs

Concept Pairs	Time 1 $\overline{x}$	(s)	Time 2 $\overline{x}$	(s)	Time 3 $\overline{x}$	(s)
My job and my boss						
linkers	32.73	(27.93)	25.25	(17.05)	21.05	(16.72)
nonlinkers	33.49	(32.05)	22.74	(23.55)	26.20	(27.60)
My job and pressures						
linkers	31.82	(25.89)	34.05	(29.01)	32.11	(27.55)
nonlinkers	35.24	(30.57)	38.39	(26.03)	29.50	(26.17)
My job and my salary						
linkers	26.59	(29.70)	35.71	(29.64)	36.39	(36.70)
nonlinkers	33.68	(29.80)	45.65	(34.25)	42.67	(34.56)
My job and problems						
linkers	25.62	(29.09)	27.14	(26.25)	22.63	(25.46)
nonlinkers	33.76	(31.80)	35.32	(23.24)	29.67	(27.67)
My job and coworkers						
linkers	25.91	(24.53)	28.25	(23.91)	28.42	(24.84)
nonlinkers	28.65	(29.56)	26.94	(25.19)	31.50	(29.42)
My job and teamwork						
linkers	17.05	(18.62)	18.57	(16.97)	20.26	(20.85)
nonlinkers	23.28	(30.74)	28.91	(27.23)	25.00	(21.81)
My job and effectiveness						
linkers	15.91	(14.93)	19.52	(17.24)	15.79	(15.21)
nonlinkers	22.36	(26.39)	22.58	(24.66)	25.50	(29.46)
My job and me						
linkers	15.00	(20.18)	8.81	(11.50)	6.32	(12.00)
nonlinkers	22.32	(30.57)	19.36	(24.79)	20.50	(28.20)

a personal level than did the nonlinkers at time 1 (though this did not hold stable across time points 2 and 3).

The results generally did not support Hypothesis 4. Contrary to expectation, linkers did not tend to perceive a steadily closer association between themselves and their jobs with the more positive concepts. The only relationship where this occurred was with an increased self-characterization of being knowledgeable.

Differences in Relational Factors

Hypotheses 5, 6, and 7. There was little consistent support for Hypotheses 5 and 6. Linkers and nonlinkers did not differ consistently in their perceptions of their relationships with bosses and coworkers. Although the

Table 20.2
Descriptive Statistics for Self-Concept Pairs

Concept Pairs	Time 1 $\bar{x}$	(s)	Time 2 $\bar{x}$	(s)	Time 3 $\bar{x}$	(s)
Frustration and me						
linkers	50.23	(31.45)	74.29	(114.87)	102.63	(160.90)
nonlinkers	45.78	(31.92)	44.65	(31.92)	51.50	(32.59)
Problems and me						
linkers	37.50	(32.98)	42.86	(35.73)	39.17	(33.97)
nonlinkers	41.54	(36.96)	35.32	(27.02)	36.70	(31.97)
My boss and me						
linkers	29.32	(26.43)	26.75	(21.42)	19.21	(15.12)
nonlinkers	30.54	(33.90)	28.55	(27.73)	33.00	(33.67)
Knowledgeable and me						
linkers	21.36	(23.96)	15.43	(19.76)	12.50	(13.20)
nonlinkers	26.08	(28.41)	26.94	(26.10)	27.33	(30.65)
Coworkers and me						
linkers	16.14	(14.22)	26.43	(28.07)	18.16	(16.18)
nonlinkers	28.54	(31.71)	26.94	(28.97)	31.00	(32.28)
My job and me						
linkers	15.00	(20.18)	8.81	(11.50)	6.32	(12.00)
nonlinkers	22.32	(30.57)	19.36	(24.79)	20.50	(28.20)

Table 20.3
t-Test Results for Differences Between Communication Roles
for All Concept Pairs Over Time (one-tailed tests)

Concept Pairs	Time 1 df	t	Time 2 df	t	Time 3 df	t
My job and my boss	57	0.51	49	2.15**	47	3.80***
My job and pressures	57	2.45**	50	2.84***	47	1.64
My job and my salary	57	4.83***	50	5.59***	46	2.90***
My job and problems	57	5.41***	50	5.96***	47	4.47***
My job and coworkers	57	1.40	50	0.97	48	1.94*
My job and teamwork	57	4.87***	50	8.21***	47	3.75***
My job and effectiveness	57	6.09***	50	2.59**	47	6.99***
My job and me	57	5.72***	50	9.82***	47	11.02***
Frustration and me	57	2.84***	50	1.33	47	1.58
Problems and me	57	2.34**	50	4.29***	46	1.23
My boss and me	57	0.82	49	1.28	47	8.90***
Knowledgeable and me	57	3.63***	50	8.96***	46	10.30***
Coworkers and me	57	10.20***	50	0.32	48	8.61***

*p < .05; **p < .025; ***p < .005.

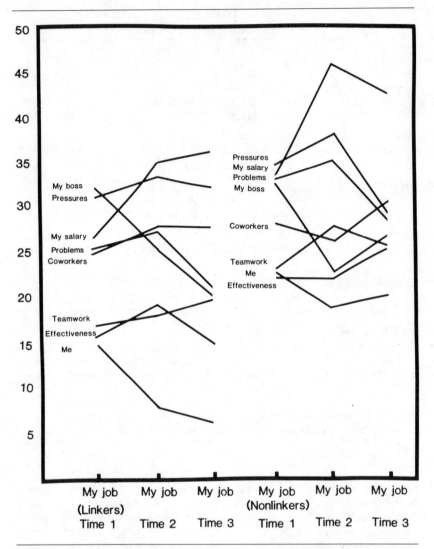

Figure 20.1.   Differences in job perceptions between linkers and nonlinkers across
                three points in time.

association between themselves and their coworkers was closer for linkers
than for nonlinkers, it was not significant at time 2.

The findings did provide some evidence for the prediction in Hypothesis 7 that linkers would report increased identification with others over time.
This was not true for their perceptions of their coworkers, but the interpoint
distances between self and job with the boss moved increasingly closer
across the time points.

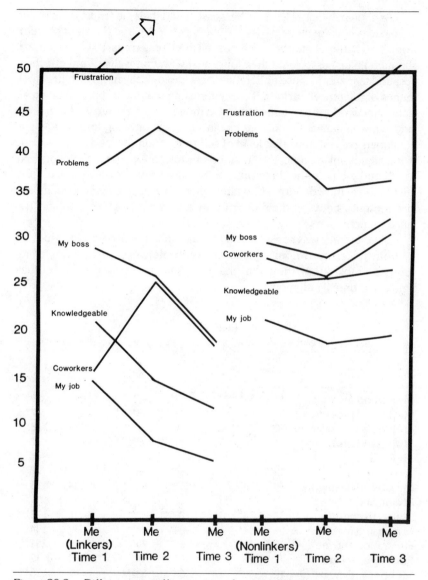

Figure 20.2.   Differences in self-perceptions between linkers and nonlinkers across three points in time.

Summary of paired comparisons. The ways in which linkers differed from nonlinkers are better depicted by a visual representation of the average distances reported. Figures 20.1 and 20.2 are comparisons of the approximate mean interpoint distances between the concept pairs tested in Hypotheses 1-7.

As shown in Figure 20.1, linkers associated their jobs most closely with themselves and the characteristics of being effective and the spirit of teamwork. This pattern held strongly across all three times measured. In contrast, although linkers associated their jobs most with themselves, and effectiveness and teamwork, these notions were psychologically more distant in their frames of reference. Further, it was interesting that the notions of being effective and working as a team tended to move further away over time. Similarly, while linkers felt a notably increased sense of being knowledgeable, nonlinkers did not have that level of self-perception. It was also interesting that whereas linkers perceived their bosses to come closer to their concepts of self and job over the three time points, nonlinkers showed much more fluctuation in their patterns. And although both groups perceived increased incongruency between their jobs and their salaries, this was a greater distance for nonlinkers.

Finally, there was considerable fluctuation in the perceptions reported by both linkers and nonlinkers over time. Interwave correlations of responses (Table 20.4) show that the groups were steadiest between their time 2 and time 3 judgments.

Table 20.4
Stability Analysis of Association Judgments for All Concept Pairs[a]

Concept Pairs	r_{12} L[b]	NL[c]	r_{23} L	NL	r_{13} L	NL
My job and my boss	.24	.66***	.64**	.87***	.18	.39*
My job and pressures	.51	.33	.71***	.53**	.38	.37*
My job and my salary	.50*	.71***	.79***	.81***	.72***	.58***
My job and problems	.12	.26	.81***	.68***	.26	.22
My job and coworkers	.59**	.46**	.64**	.90***	.68***	.28
My job and teamwork	.39	.30	.57**	.66***	.34	.33
My job and effectiveness	.07	.35*	.79***	.72***	.18	.73***
My job and me	−.01	.44*	.64**	.71***	.17	.44*
Frustration and me	.28	.42*	.66**	.70***	.17	.51**
Problems and me	.42	.26	.93***	.14	.30	.12
My boss and me	.10	.58***	.63**	.63***	.02	.55**
Knowledgeable and me	.54*	.49**	.48*	.35*	.14	.09
Coworkers and me	.14	.28	.82***	.83***	.19	.45**

a. Correlations are based on data obtained over time for waves 1, 2, and 3.
b. L = linkers.
c. NL = nonlinkers.
*p < .05; **p < .01; ***p < .001.

Table 20.5
Descriptive Statistics for Network Variables

Variable	Time 1 $\bar{x}$	(s)	Time 2 $\bar{x}$	(s)	Time 3 $\bar{x}$	(s)
Reciprocity level						
linkers	0.47	(0.11)	0.45	(0.11)	0.45	(0.11)
nonlinkers	0.38	(0.13)	0.39	(0.10)	0.41	(0.19)
Outgoing recipro- cated link strength						
linkers	224.59	(179.11)	165.86	(123.15)	128.44	(99.02)
nonlinkers	66.32	(88.20)	91.04	(103.79)	78.69	(80.57)
Incoming recipro- cated link strength						
linkers	181.23	(96.39)	147.10	(80.22)	120.17	(70.62)
nonlinkers	93.88	(58.66)	97.00	(48.12)	82.31	(49.38)
Outgoing unrecipro- cated link strength						
linkers	86.05	(62.17)	64.38	(37.31)	52.00	(40.58)
nonlinkers	30.09	(34.67)	33.71	(33.84)	22.42	(22.85)
Incoming unrecipro- cated link strength						
linkers	18.32	(19.32)	20.55	(20.81)	21.14	(34.25)
nonlinkers	48.06	(56.43)	29.00	(25.11)	24.36	(23.99)
Discrepancy of reported link strengths						
linkers	131.10	(104.20)	113.90	(90.27)	85.83	(64.68)
nonlinkers	79.06	(77.38)	93.61	(75.74)	65.27	(58.18)

Hypotheses 8 and 9. The results showed that linkers had a higher level of reciprocity in their relationships, although this was not significantly higher than the levels for nonlinkers at times 2 and 3 (see Tables 20.5 and 20.6). The level was, however, more stable over time for linkers than for non-linkers (i.e., time 1 and time 2 correlations: $z = 7.31$, $p < .05$; time 1 and time 3 correlations: $z = 5.13$, $p < .05$). See Table 20.7.

However, there was no support for the hypothesis that linkers would have a generally lower level of discrepancy in their perceptions of the volume of contacts they had with others. They did have a mean discrepancy rate consistently higher than the one for nonlinkers, but the difference was significant only at time 1. It is noteworthy that the discrepancy levels for nonlinkers reflected more unstable perceptions about their communication over the duration.

An additional breakdown and analysis of the data provided several in-

Table 20.6
t-Test Results for Differences Between Communication Roles for
Network Variables Over Time (one-tailed tests)

Variables	Time 1		Time 2		Time 3	
	df	t	df	t	df	t
Reciprocity level	54	3.00**	47	0.67	42	0.80
Outgoing reciprocated link strength	54	4.46**	47	2.30*	42	2.11*
Incoming reciprocated link strength	54	4.28**	47	2.72**	42	2.09*
Outgoing unreciprocated link strength	54	4.38**	47	3.00**	42	3.07**
Incoming unreciprocated link strength	54	2.42**	47	1.25	42	0.37
Discrepancy of reported link strengths	54	2.14*	47	0.85	42	1.10

*p < .025; **p < .005.

Table 20.7
Stability Analysis of Communication Linkage Patterns
(work network)[a]

Variable	r_{12}		r_{23}		r_{13}	
	L[b]	NL[c]	L	NL	L	NL
Reciprocity level	.78**	.30	.62**	.55**	.72**	.42*
Outgoing recipro-cated link strength	.74**	.32	.86**	.70**	.68**	.63**
Incoming recipro-cated link strength	.72**	.28	.94**	.66**	.74**	−.10
Outgoing unrecipro-cated link strength	.66**	.52**	.56**	.51**	.44*	.37*
Incoming unrecipro-cated link strength	.31	.61**	.06	.30	−.02	.02
Discrepancy of reported link strengths	.79**	.10	.88**	.38*	.43*	.25

a. Correlations are based on network data obtained over time from waves 1, 2, and 3.
b. L = linkers.
c. NL = nonlinkers.
*p < .025; **p < .005.

teresting trends. Linkers tended to report significantly greater link strength for their reciprocated and unreciprocated contacts than did nonlinkers. They also had contacts who reported stronger relationships with them than did the nonlinkers' contacts, and they were fairly stable levels. The most unstable findings were the reports of incoming unreciprocated link strengths, which could be interpreted as the most random data given.

Finally, we found that in comparing the reports on the strengths of contact, linkers continually perceived more interactions with their reciprocated and unreciprocated contacts than those people reported having with them. In a sense, they overreported rather than underreported their communication frequency. This finding was not significant in every case, but it was a consistent trend. Conversely, nonlinkers did not report the levels of contact with others that those people reported with them. The difference was not significant, but nonlinkers did tend to underreport rather than overreport their interactions.

DISCUSSION AND IMPLICATIONS

Glazer and Moynihan suggested in their book *Beyond the Melting Pot* (1963) that in America, you are what you do for a living. This is particularly true for those in a culture where values center on success and "getting ahead" as important to the purpose of one's life. So much of what we do for work is tied up with our self-concepts; self-definition is often a consequence of the nature of our jobs. It is in work and the workplace that we receive many messages about who we are as contributors, what we are capable of doing, and how well.

Managers are certainly individuals whose concepts of self are especially a function of their work. An important reason is that good management is often related to many personal (as well as task or expertise) factors such as skills in persuasion, impression management, information processing, and political tact. We found in this study that identification with work was particularly a function of one's position in the network of communication patterns that exist in the organization.

Our findings extended earlier research on these issues by demonstrating that over repeated measurements, the reports of those in potentially powerful linking roles in the social order saw increased congruency between who they were as people and who they were as managers. That the concepts of self and job moved closer together over time dramatized the strong identification with work held by linkers, unlike others with more restricted interaction patterns.

This was certainly not a surprising result. Linkers in the organization have tremendous potential access to diverse communication channels; they are generally more active and involved in the workplace than are others. They often emerge as people who are influential and have control over the direction of the decisions that are made. From a force aggregation standpoint, their intense activity easily brings them many messages of a self-defining nature, messages that help them see themselves in terms of their jobs. Of course, if these messages enable these same people to see themselves as knowledgeable, part of a team effort, and effective, that is an important bonus.

Contrary to expectation, this study did not find that linkers had any greater cognitive orientation toward their coworkers and bosses than did others in the organization. This was probably because the linkers selected in this study were from the job network, where the sense of affiliation is likely tempered by strong task orientation and competition. Perhaps the linkers identified in a more social-personal network might reveal a closer association pattern.

But is was useful to find also that linkers did not have to have a close cognitive association with others to perceive a stronger sense of teamwork. This may demonstrate that it is the work of the company that is the salient objective first, and sheer relational activity comes second. And it was interesting that over time, the concept of "my boss" moved closer and closer to the idea of self and job for linkers but showed a highly fluctuating movement for nonlinkers. This may be due to the need linkers have to reduce their ambivalence or uncertainty toward their bosses in such a way that enables them to accomplish tasks. Communication with superiors likely has a direct effect on linkers' perceptions, one that is picked up readily with this form of measurement. In contrast, nonlinkers may have more distance because of less interaction with higher-ups and more uncertainty toward those roles.

The data showed that linkers were not without problems and pressures, however. Clearly, involvement and personal investment in the uncertain business world is stress producing, as are linkers' diverse patterns of interactions (Albrecht et al., 1982). Linkers are no more immune to problems at a personal level than are others; they are probably more vulnerable given their high internalization of the job. This points out a double bind of the linking role. Strong cognitive orientation to one's work means that success, as well as difficulties, is going to have its effects. However, linkers are also able to see themselves with more positive attributes that may serve as a buffer to the stress. Nonlinkers, on the other hand, identify less with the job and are thus able to achieve more distance from pressures and problems at a personal level. However, they perceive less in terms of rewards associated with professional life. Based on these data, it is clear that there are costs and benefits to be borne in either set of roles.

A final distinguishing feature of linkers and nonlinkers is the way they perceive their communication environments. Linkers had a slightly higher level of agreement with others over contact, which reflected more of an awareness and monitoring in their relationships with others. However, in both reciprocated and unreciprocated contacts, they perceived that substantially more interactions took place with others than with those individuals acknowledged having with them. This is not a case of who was right in their reports of whether the interactions occurred; rather, it is an issue of perception about one's communication in the organization: the salience, concern and sensitivity one has to those behaviors, perhaps even to the point of exaggeration. It is likely that linkers attach more of a premium to the act of communication than do nonlinkers, as a critical function of production processes. Nonlinkers had the converse pattern in their data: They generally did not report having had as many interactions as others reported having with them. This type of discrepancy reflects less communication awareness among managers who occupy nonlinking roles. Their vision of the organization and their behavior in it may be colored by their more restricted interactions. They are more likely to discount the worth of many of their interactions, or not understand their potential effects on others. In short, they could be missing a sense of their own importance, possibly not thinking of communication as a strategic means the way linkers might. Their scope of certainty is more limited; in reporting their relationships, nonlinkers tend to identify close ties to work cliques and hence reflect a more limited image of themselves.

In short, the powerful tie of communication structure to cognitive process has key implications for quality of work life issues. This has been a central notion since Durkheim articulated this relationship (Nisbet, 1974). The force aggregation framework gives us a better way to explain how messages affect managers and their views of themselves and the quality of what they do and the environments in which they work. The data are, of course, limited to a case study of one organization, but the analysis over time provides some insights into how strongly managers' perceptions of themselves and their behavior are held, and further evidence for an increasing pool of knowledge in this area.

REFERENCES

Albrecht, T. (1979). The role of communication in perceptions of organizational climate. In D. Nimmo (Ed.), *Communication yearbook 3*. New Brunswick, NJ: Transaction.

Albrecht, T., Irey, K., & Mundy, A. (1982). Integration in communication networks as a mediator of stress: The case of a protective services agency. *Social Work, 27*, 229-235.

Albrecht, T., & Ropp, V. (1982). The study of network structuring in organizations through the use of method triangulation. *Western Journal of Speech Communication, 46*, 162-178.

Amend, E. (1971). *Liaison communication roles of professionals in a research dissemination organization*. Unpublished doctoral dissertation, Michigan State University.

Barnett, G. A., Serota, K. B., & Taylor, J. (1976). Campaign communication and attitude change: A multidimensional analysis. *Human Communication Research, 2,* 227-244.

Berger, C., & Calabrese, R. (1975). Some explorations in initial interaction and beyond: Toward a developmental theory of interpersonal communication *Human Communication Research, 1,* 99-112.

Burgoon, J., Burgoon, M., Miller, G. R., & Sunnafrank, M. (1981). Learning theory approaches to persuasion. *Human Communication Research, 7,* 161-179.

Danowski, J. A. (1980). Group attitude uniformity and connectivity of organizational communication networks for production, innovation, and maintenance content. *Human Communication Research, 6,* 299-308.

Farace, R. V., Monge, P., & Russell, H. (1977). *Communicating and organizing.* Reading, MA: Addison-Wesley.

Farace, R. V., Taylor, J. A., & Stewart, J. (1978). Criteria for evaluation of organizational communication effectiveness: Review and synthesis. In B. Ruben (Ed.), *Communication yearbook 2.* New Brunswick, NJ: Transaction.

Gillham, J., & Woelfel, J. (1977). The Galileo system of measurement: Preliminary evidence for precision, stability, and equivalence to traditional measures. *Human Communication Research, 3,* 222-234.

Glazer, N., & Moynihan, D. (1963). *Beyond the melting pot.* Cambridge: MIT Press/Harvard University Press.

Goldhaber, G. M., Dennis, H. S., Richetto, G., & Wiio, O. (1979). *Information strategies: New pathways to corporate power.* Englewood Cliffs, NJ: Prentice-Hall.

Holzner, B. (1972). *Reality construction in society.* Cambridge, MA: Schenkman.

Jablin, F. (1979). Superior-subordinate communication: The state of the art. *Psychological Bulletin, 86,* 1201-1222.

Jablin, F. (1980). Organizational communication theory and research: An overview of communication climate and network research. In D. Nimmo (Ed.), *Communication yearbook 4.* New Brunswick, NJ: Transaction.

Jablin, F. (1982). Formal structural characteristics of organizations and superior-subordinate communication. *Human Communication Research, 8,* 338-347.

MacDonald, D. (1976). Communication roles and networks. *Human Communication Research, 2,* 365-375.

Moch, M. (1980). Job involvement, internal motivation, and employees' integration into networks of work relationships. *Organizational Behavior and Human Performance, 25,* 15-31.

Nisbet, R. (1974). *The sociology of Emile Durkheim.* New York: Oxford University Press.

Parks, M. R. (1977). Anomia and close friendship communication networks. *Human Communication Research, 4,* 48-57.

Parks, M., & Adelman, M. (1983). Communication networks and the development of romantic relationships: An expansion of uncertainty reduction theory. *Human Communication Research, 10,* 55-79.

Reynolds, E. V., & Johnson, J. D. (1982). Liaison emergence: Relating theoretical perspectives. *Academy of Management Review, 7,* 551-559.

Richards, W. (1975). *A manual for network analysis.* Stanford, CA: Institute for Communication Research, Stanford University.

Roberts, K., & O'Reilly, C. (1979). Some correlates of communication roles in organizations. *Academy of Management Journal, 22,* 42-57.

Rogers, E. M., & Kincaid, D. (1981). *Communication networks: Toward a new paradigm for research.* New York: Free Press.

Schwartz, D., & Jacobson, E. (1977). Organizational communication network analysis: The liaison communication role. *Organizational Behavior and Human Performance, 18,* 158-174.

Taylor, J. (1977). *Communication and organizational change: A case study.* Unpublished doctoral dissertation, Michigan State University.

Taylor, J., Farace, R., & Monge, P. (1976). *Communication and the development of change among educational practitioners.* Paper presented at the World Education Conference, Honolulu, Hawaii.

Thurman, B. (1979). In the office: Networks and coalitions. *Social Networks, 2,* 47-63.

Weick, K. (1979). *The social psychology of organizing.* Reading, MA: Addison-Wesley.

Westley, W. (1979). Problems and solutions in the quality of working life. *Human Relations, 32,* 113-123.

Woelfel, J., & Fink, E. (1980). *The measurement of communication processes: Galileo theory and method.* New York: Academic.

Woelfel, J., & Haller, A. (1971). Significant others, the self-reflexive act, and the attitude formation processes. *American Sociological Review, 36,* 37-74.

21 ● Managerial Control and Discipline: Whips and Chains

GAIL T. FAIRHURST ● STEPHEN G. GREEN ● B. KAY SNAVELY

University of Cincinnati ● Miami University

L IKE the party whip whose job it is "to enforce party discipline and to secure the attendance of party members at important sessions" (Kellerman, 1975), it is also part of the manager's role to ensure the performance and attendance of his or her staff. While political whips coax and even cajole, they rarely use punishment to "whip" members into line (Cooper, 1978). In contrast, managers must sometimes use both punishment (that is, discipline) and persuasion-based strategies, especially when poor performance manifests itself in a mounting chain of incidents that become increasingly difficult to deal with. Consider the following example:

> The third time we talked I called Cheri into the office to talk about her tardiness. On numerous occasions, Cheri would walk in anywhere from 5 to 10 to 15 minutes late. Not one word was offered as explanation—I'm sorry, I had car trouble; I'm sorry, my kids were sick. So I told her that I expected her to be prepared to work at 9:30. To do that she should be here by 9:25 or 9:26. She became very belligerent. That's the only word I can use. She actually sat there and yelled at me. The tellers across the lobby could hear her yelling at me. I have never had anyone act that way to me before. . . . She did not think that she should be here one minute before 9:30 when her time card said 9:30 to 5:30. I again told her of the many times she had started work past 9:30 which I actually kept a record of and never said a word to her. I actually showed her the card and she actually denied ever being late.

Over six months, this manager held three consecutive discussions with this employee before issuing a warning to correct the problem. The employee quit

Correspondence and requests for reprints: Gail T. Fairhurst, Department of Communication, Mail Location #184, University of Cincinnati, Cincinnati, OH 45221.

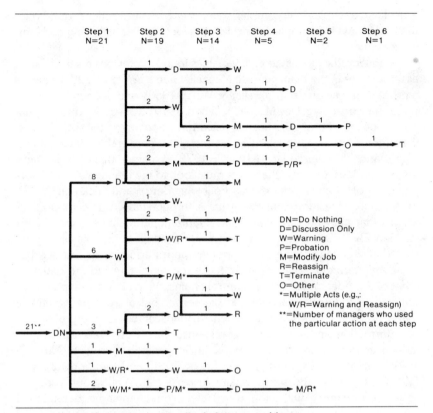

Figure 21.1. Control chains for teller balancing problems.

the job soon after the warning was issued. Over a twenty-month period, another bank branch manager took a series of six consecutive control actions to correct a recurring teller balancing problem: (1) discussion only, (2) discussion with a written warning, (3) discussion only, (4) discussion only, (5) discussion with probation, and, finally, (6) termination. Such sequences of performance problems and resultant control actions are perhaps more common than single incidents of poor performance (Bureau of National Affairs, 1978; Green, Fairhurst, & Liden, 1981; Liden, 1981; O'Reilly & Weitz, 1980). Thus we have recently argued that the appropriate unit of analysis in research on the control of ineffective performance should be the entire chain of control episodes, not a single episode. This focus should more closely approximate managerial experience (Green & Fairhurst, 1981; Green, Fairhust, & Snavely, 1983; Fairhurst, Green, & Snavely, in press).

In attempting to explain these control chains, we first looked to organizational policy. In no case did we find policy statements to be highly enough articulated to explain the complex sequences of control actions found (Figure 21.1 shows the complex control chains for the teller balancing problem, for example).

Similarly, the examination of variables found in previous research, such as attributions of the manager (see Mitchell, Green, & Wood, 1981), characteristics of the actors (see O'Reilly & Weitz, 1980), and seriousness of the performance problem (see Mitchell & Wood, 1979), was equally dissatisfying.

Since the control of ineffective performance seems on the surface to be the antithesis of the rational, rule-governed, and predictable process it was organizationally intended to be (Weick, 1976), it seemed that to understand the psycho-logic of these chains we must look to the managers' own interpretations of the chains themselves. Following Berger and Luckman (1967), it is through these interpretations—that is, through the words, symbols, and actions that managers invoke—that organizational reality is socially constructed. By focusing upon how and why meanings come to exist and be shared in situations defined as controlling poor performance, our task became an interpretive one. As such, these meanings directed our development of a model-in-use for the control chains, which in turn helped us to understand the ways managers "make sense" out of poor performance, that is, how managers detect a problem, diagnose its cause, interpret available information, and select a control response. Our efforts were significantly influenced by the interpretive paradigm in general (Burrell & Morgan, 1979; Putnam, 1983; Deetz, 1982; Louis, 1981) and the work of Louis (1980) on surprise and sense making in particular. While Louis's specific sense-making model will be discussed later in this chapter, her definition of sense making is a central focus now.

According to Louis (1980), sense making is a special kind of thinking process that occurs when what is expected differs from what is observed, a process of providing reasons for outcomes and for observed discrepancies. Consequently, sense making is often both retrospective and revealed in language. Following Weick (1977) and Garfinkel (1967), sense making is a posteriori because actors reflect upon previous actions to see what actions they have taken and to see what the meaning of those action is. Consider the following example:

> So again I tried to reassure her. . . . I guess I probably tried to reassure her the first time too, although the first time having been so angry myself, I got much more into "You can't do this!" because of the way it reflects on the other people in the office. This time I just simply went into that this is your imagination. Finally, she became more calm. It might have taken her longer to calm down that time because I wasn't reacting. But I was just simply letting her get it all out, and just listening, and sympathizing—being aware that she does have such deep problems.

Note the retrospective nature of sense making in this example when the manager now sees his early behavior as "reacting" when contrasted with his later "good listening" behaviors.

Sense making is also accomplished and displayed through language because, as Tompkins and Cheney (1982, p. 8) state, "in the language of social actors, we find many accounts, rich with vocabularies of motive, attitude, reason, and action." Thus it is the language of social actors that reveals the logic that makes their actions meaningful or sensible (Mills, 1940; Harré, 1977; Scott & Lyman, 1968; Pondy, 1978; Pettigrew, 1979; Tompkins & Cheney, 1982; Harré & Secord, 1973). Given our view of sense making and given the iterative nature of control problems, contextually sensitive, qualitative methods (Van Maanen, 1979; Van Maanen, Dabs, & Faulkner, 1982; Glaser & Strauss, 1967; Morgan & Smircich, 1980; Evered & Louis, 1981) were required that would provide managers the opportunity to inspect their own control actions retrospectively, reflectively, sequentially, and linguistically. Two types of data were consistent with these criteria.

In-depth, taped interviews (one to two hours in length) were conducted with 84 bank branch managers and 5 branch administrators in 3 midwestern banks. The purpose of the interviews was to gather managers' reflections of specific performance problems they had recently faced. These could be anything the managers considered ineffective performance; however, 76 percent of the problems fell into one of the following categories: (1) absenteeism/tardiness; (2) balancing; (3) staff conflict; and (4) customer relations. The interview protocol started at the point the manager first recognized a performance problem and then required the manager to retrace his or her actions as they occurred. At each step, the manager explained what had occurred, his or her action, and recounted as closely as possible to verbatim (often in a role-playing mode) any discussion with the employee at that time. From the taped managers' descriptions and explanations of their behavior and the behavior of their subordinates, transcripts were prepared.

Archival records, in the form of memos prepared by managers written at the time each action was taken served as the second type of data. While these records are retrospective, sequential, and amenable to language analysis, they are not as reflective as the interviews, or as rich. Frequently, the contents of the memos simply describe the nature of the infraction, the manager's actions, and the subordinate's response. They do, however, allow us to attempt to assess the convergence between "real-time" descriptions of the control chains and the interview data descriptions, the former being unobtrusive measures taken much closer in time to the infraction (Jick, 1979; Faulkner, 1982). Two of the three banks (83% of the sample) made written records available for inspection (210 separate documents).

The remainder of this chapter presents the results of our analyses of the interview transcripts and the written documents. The information obtained about a manager's sense making seemed meaningful only when the relative location of the manager in the control chain was explicitly considered. Therefore, the first analysis presents a construction of a model of the control process as we believe managers have consciously or unconsciously done. This model-in-use serves as our context for describing managers' sense making in the control process, the second part of our analysis.

A MODEL-IN-USE
FOR THE CONTROL OF
INEFFECTIVE PERFORMANCE

We began this investigation with a very rudimentary model in mind. Previous research suggests that the process of controlling poor performance is iterative, and performance problems typically surface at irregular intervals (Green et al., 1981). Because poor performance is obviously distinguished from acceptable performance, the subordinate's role behavior in this process can be conceptualized as an ongoing stream of acceptable performance that is punctuated by episodes of poor performance. Borrowing Kiesler and Sproull's (1982) term "breakpoint," a salient event that segments an ongoing stream of behavior, the ongoing stream of a marginal performer's behavior can be seen as punctuated by poor performance breakpoints.

In turn, the presence of poor performance breakpoints prompts responses from managers that are both perceptual and behavioral: perceptual in the sense that the manager's definition of his or her work relationship with the subordinate changes because the subordinate now poses a problem requiring action; behavioral in the sense that managers often take some concrete control action. Moreover, there is reflexivity between the control actions and the definition of the work relationship because a control action is initiated when the relationship changes, and the relationship in turn changes in light of the control action. Add to this reflexivity the iterative nature of control problems, and an evolutionary dynamic develops between the control actions and the definition of the work relationship. The logic of this evolutionary dynamic seems to hinge on the nature of the manager's redefinition of the work relationship in response to poor performance breakpoints. Two major redefinitions of the work relationship appear to occur. Following our previous logic, these redefinitions can be seen as breakpoints in the ongoing stream of the relationship. We have termed one the "problem-solving breakpoint" and the other the "elimination breakpoint" (see Figure 21.2).

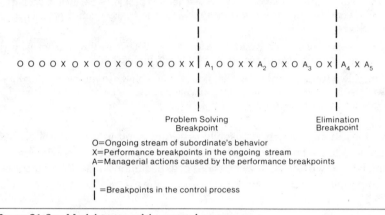

O O O O X O X O O X O O X O O X X | A₁ O O X X A₂ O X O A₃ O X | A₄ X A₅

Problem Solving   Elimination
Breakpoint   Breakpoint

O=Ongoing stream of subordinate's behavior
X=Performance breakpoints in the ongoing stream
A=Managerial actions caused by the performance breakpoints

| =Breakpoints in the control process

Figure 21.2.   Model-in-use of the control process.

Problem-Solving Breakpoint

The problem-solving breakpoint occurs in managerial perceptions when a manager first perceives a problem requiring corrective action and the problem is assumed (or hoped) to be correctable. This breakpoint may occur after a single incident of poor performance or after a series of incidents, depending upon such elements as the severity of the problem, the employee's work history, or causal attributions. In the present sample, it typically appeared to occur after numerous poor performance breakpoints ($\bar{x} = 5$) in almost all cases. The key issue is the manager's "recognition" (a retrospective judgment) that the poor performance incident(s) will probably repeat unless he or she acts. The manager redefines his or her relationship with the employee from one of day-to-day supervision to one of intervention.

A number of factors within the data support the notion of the problem-solving breakpoints. First, and most obvious, is the onset of control actions by the manager. It is obvious that some redefinition of the relationship has occurred when the manager first employs a specific control action. Second, the initial actions the managers reported using were frequently problem solving in nature. For example, managers reported things such as going back over the task to discover errors, monitoring in various forms to discover the source of the problem, questioning subordinates to discover how they can be helped, retraining, and offering help and support. Moreover, the managers themselves defined the activities as "helping," "problem solving," "counseling," or "teaching."

We are a branch and we all have to pull together and we will be talking to each of the tellers individually and we are going to try and *solve* the situation.

> It's not an unusual situation that a new teller has problems balancing, seeing that's what we're here for, to *teach* them and to make them a productive employee.
>
> On three or four occasions each time we tried to determine the problem, why she was having problems and what we could do to *help* her.
>
> OK, now I want to show you what you're doing on these transactions and I want to time it and I want to show you what *you should* be doing on the same transaction and time that.

Also, these types of actions usually occurred early in the control chains, contiguous to the first action, our best indicant of the problem-solving breakpoint. Finally, we find clear expressions of expectations of positive outcomes accompanying the descriptions of these activities:

> I felt sure she was going to make it, and it was just the matter of what to do to overcome the possibility of individual differences.
>
> We had some feelings that perhaps her attitude was less than it should have been, and we were hoping that after the conversation that her attitude would really change.

All of these factors argue for the existence of the problem-solving breakpoint. Furthermore, the existence of this breakpoint is consistent with certain characteristics of the control chains. This view would help explain the great variance we find in the length of control chains—longer chains should be associated with the manager maintaining a problem-solving posture for extended periods of time. Moreover, by conceptualizing the control process in this manner we now can account for apparent anomalies where, for example, the manager appears to regress in control actions (for instance, he or she goes from probation back to discussion only). Essentially, the manager is problem solving and casting about for solutions and feels no need to proceed in a linear fashion. This casting about during problem solving is also consistent with the great variety of control actions one finds in the early steps of a control chain (see Figure 21.1). Finally, this view also clarifies that the interpretation of a single control action depends upon understanding the context of that action. At one point in the process probation is an attempt to get the employer back on track; at another point, it is a legally required prelude to termination.

Elimination Breakpoint

When the problem is no longer judged to be soluable, the elimination breakpoint is reached. Again, this may occur after one violation-control action iteration or, more typically, after a series of iterations all aimed at correcting the problem. The elimination breakpoint is usually reached be-

```
Problem:   Balancing, Absenteeism

Documentation:            Date              Action Taken

                          4/80:             First Noticed Problem;
                          |                 < 10 times
                          |
                          |
                          5/80:             First Action;
                          |                 Discussion/Warning
                          |
                          |
                          6/80:             Second Action;
                          |                 Discussion/Warning
                          |
                          |
                          7/80:             Third Action;
                          |                 Discussion/Warning/Modify Job
                          |
                          |
Letter from Doctor        :10/2/80
                          |
                          |
Employee Requests         :10/8/80
Medical Leave             |
                          |
                          |
Official Leave Request    :10/8/80
                          |
                          |
Letter from Doctor        :10/14/80
                          |
                          |
Discussion of             :10/27/80:        Fourth Action;
Employee's Cancelling                       Employee Quit Before Being Terminated
of Leave & Subsequent
Absence Problem
```

Figure 21.3.   Documentation flurry.

cause the manager's actions have failed to correct the problem, the problem begins to dominate the total work relationship, and the employee is not seen as salvageable or not worth salvaging given the costs.

A number of factors within the data support the existence of the elimination breakpoint: documentation flurry, verbal case building, and expressions of pessimism. All three of these activities typically occur toward the end of the control chain, where the elimination breakpoint logically would appear.

Documentary Flurry

Because of the increasing likelihood of legal action taken against organizations, documentation of employee infractions and subsequent actions is a

Problem: Balancing, Absenteeism

Documentation:	Date	Action Taken:
	12/15/80:	First Noticed Problem; 8 Absences
Teller Shortage Noted	:2/23/81:	First Action; Discussion
Memo Documenting Conversation; Not Probation	:4/1/81:	Second Action; Discussion/Probation
Memo Documenting Conversation and Probation & Possible Termination	:7/30/81:	Third Action; Discussion/Probation
Teller Using Money for Personal Use	:9/14	
Teller Balancing Problem Noted; Put Through Retraining	:9/15:	Fourth Action; Retraining
Retraining Discussed	:9/16	
Teller Cashed Own Check and Possible Termination	:9/17:	Fifth Action; Reprimand/Warning
Memo Documenting Conversation and Probation and Possible Termination	:10/16:	Sixth Action; Discussion/Probation

Figure 21.4.   Documentation flurry.

Problem: Balancing, Absenteeism

Documentation:	Date	Action Taken:
	6/81:	First Noticed Problem; > 10 times
	6/81:	First Action; Discussion
	8/81:	Second Action; Probation
Memo Documenting Probation	:10/2/81:	Third Action; Indefinite Probation
Memo Documenting Discussion of Balancing Problem	:12/1/81:	Fourth Action; Discussion
Memo Documenting Continuing Balancing Problems	:12/29	
Memo Documenting Probation and Possible Termination	:1/27/82:	Fifth Action; Discussion and Probation with New Guidelines
Memo Documenting Termination	:2/12/82:	Sixth Action; Termination

Figure 21.5.   Documentation flurry.

protection mechanism vital to an organization's ability to terminate a person legally (Asherman & Vance, 1981). Therefore, we thought it possible that strict attention to documentation might be an indication of the elimination breakpoint and examined the pattern of documentation to see if we could find a flurry of activity near the end of the control chain, indicating that the manager was anticipating possible termination. Figures 21.3 through 21.5 present the documentation patterns of three representative case histories.

Figure 21.3 reflects the flurry of documentation near the end of the control sequence most dramatically. In Figure 21.4, there is less evidence of a flurry of documenting activity near the end. However, (1) eight absences occurred without documentation or action, (2) the employee was put on probation for his second action but this was not documented, and (3) once possible termination is raised during the third action, the manager begins documenting at an accelerating rate. In Figure 21.5, the manager did not document until his third action, but once this was initiated, the pattern of documentation was steady.

In all three cases documentation was either nonexistent or incomplete until the third action. We do not suggest that the elimination breakpoint always occurs around the third action, but it may be a possibility. The elimination breakpoint most likely occurs either when the flurry of activity is striking, as in Figure 21.3 or when the manager raises the possibility of termination by specifying a time period under which no more rule violations may occur. We shall return to this point later.

Verbal Case Building

An attempt on the part of the manager to recount the employee's problems verbally, the steps taken by the manager to solve the problems, and the failure of those steps was termed "verbal case building." Verbal case building is seen as an indication of the elimination breakpoint because it appears to lay the groundwork for elimination by making the eventual termination of the employee *appear* justifiable and reasonable, a desirable position both in legal and moral terms. Consider this manager's efforts at verbal case building:

> We have reviewed everything we had done with Kathy . . . all the steps, the different memos, the probation, and the whole thing. We first informed her that we had gone through all these steps and she had sort of failed all of them.

In the following example, the employee questions this process, forcing the manager to explain the necessity of verbal case building.

> We brought her complete personnel file out and went through it—the good, the bad, and definitely the ugly. We went over from memo one to memo twenty. She sat there and shook her head, and I guess it took us the better part of two hours. As we were doing this we asked her for input, negative or positive. We got basically none. She agreed that this did take place. At the end we looked at her and said, "Because of these things we are dismissing you for procedural irregularities." Her first comment was, "Why did you make me sit here for over an hour to listen to that?" And then I got upset. [I said] "Would you rather that I would have called you in, sat you down, and said you're fired? And not give you any explanation why?" And she said that would have been easier. And I said, "For who? You would have left not knowing why in the hell you were fired." And then she started to cry. She never did apologize or offer any excuses. She just cried pretty heavy at that point. And I told her to quit crying.

The manager in this example took nearly two hours to build a case for termination of this employee. The extremes this manager went to suggest that the verbal case building was not necessarily done to explain to the employee why she was being fired (after all, that could have been accomplished in much less time) as much as it was done to make his actions *appear* justifiable and reasonable to all parties, including himself.

Expressions of Pessimism

A final indication of the elimination breakpoint was that of expressions by the manager of low expectations of correcting the problem. Consider the following example of a manager's account of a third meeting with an employee:

> It was an emotional type of meeting, but it was one everyone knew was eventually coming, we just never knew when it was coming. She had been a good worker, but we all knew it was coming, because of the policies, plus all the little considerations we had given her. [We] couldn't let it go any farther. In fairness to other employees, we wanted to be consistent, although we weren't consistent. I think we bent over backwards for her. We thought that she could *never* regain her proper attitude, or gain her skills.

The statement "We thought that she could never regain her proper attitude or gain her skills" significantly departs from the "hope" this manager expressed when describing the second action he took: "We were hoping that after the conversation that her attitude would really change." This indicates to us that for this particular case the elimination breakpoint was reached between the second and third actions.

This example also reveals an element of "must" or inevitability that surrounds the impending termination, which the manager acknowledges: "but it was one everyone knew was eventually coming, we just never knew when." Thus actions once seen as "helpful" or "problem solving" are now seen as failed attempts, which are the antecedent conditions that trigger an inescapable and inevitable conclusion.

Conclusion

Based on the different types of activities, their timing, and the evaluative statements that accompany them, we find evidence for two major redefinitions of the control process as a result of their impact: a problem-solving breakpoint, occurring when a manager initiates action to correct a problem; and an elimination breakpoint, occurring when the problem is deemed insoluble.

There are several points to note. First, we stated earlier that an evolutionary dynamic emerges between the control actions and the work relationship. Unless a problem is serious immediately (such as embezzlement), the performance problem initially will not occupy a large share of the work relationship between a manager and a subordinate. Nevertheless, just as a cancer spreads, as the problem continues it begins to occupy a greater and greater share of the relationship. As the control problem continues without resolution, the relationship becomes coterminous with the control process such that when the control process is judged a failure at the elimination breakpoint, termination of the relationship is sought.

Second, the suggestion that the manager defines the control process as problem solving should not be taken to imply that all of the actions are equally accompanied by expectations of success. In the language of decision theory (Edwards, 1954; Lee, 1971), the subjective expected utility of each successive action would likely decline until the manager finally reached the decision to eliminate.

Third, we recognize that the sequence of breakpoints suggested is not inviolate. Under certain rare circumstances, a problem-solving breakpoint may never be extant. A number of factors (such as severity of problem or legal issues) could cause the manager initially to redefine the relationship in elimination terms. The sequence suggested, however, is considered to be most common.

Finally, the model we propose is itself situationally specific. Any number of factors, such as the number of poor performance breakpoints preceding the problem-solving breakpoints or the number of actions preceding the elimination breakpoint, are expected to vary from organization to organization and from manager to manager. Part of this will be due to the great variability in performance contexts. Part of it, however, is thought to be due to the sense-making processes that underlie our model-in-use. The next section addresses those sense-making processes and attempts to show how they are related to the model proposed here.

SENSE MAKING IN
THE CONTROL PROCESS

In addressing entry experiences of new employees, Louis (1980) proposes a sense-making model as an explanation of how they cope with the change and new experiences associated with entry. Fundamentally, it is seen as "a process through which interpretations of discrepancies are developed" (Louis, 1980). She suggests a recurring cycle of three key activities: detection, diagnosis, and interpretation. Thus the *meaning* of discrepancies and the concomitant behavioral responses are seen as an *outcome* of the sense-making process. Our data and interactions with managers suggest that a similar sense-making process is operating when managers attempt to cope with the changes and discrepancies in performance inherent in control chains.

For each of the three activities, we will discuss the following: (1) the specific mechanisms used to accomplish the activity; (2) the activity as it is likely to surface in the control process from acceptable performance to the problem-solving breakpoint (Stage 1), from the problem-solving breakpoint to the elimination breakpoint (Stage 2), and from the elimination breakpoint to termination (Stage 3); and (3) the reflexivity of detection and diagnosis with interpretive processes. We will then have some final comments about selection of control responses. Obviously, our attempt to pull this process apart is somewhat artificial in that these activities may occur simultaneously or in close succession, consciously or unconsciously, rapidly and automatically or slowly and deliberately. Nevertheless, we feel that attempting to map the cycle of detection, diagnosis, and interpretation within the control process, however artificial, will be useful to our understanding of the construction of the control chains.

Problem Detection

As suggested earlier, in problem detection the manager acknowledges an unmet expectation, that is, a change or break in the ongoing stream of the subordinate's role behavior. Initially this break in the performance is not yet labeled "poor performance," but rather is simply perceived as something different or contrary to expectations. A deceptively simple, epistemological question that must be posed is, how do managers know that there has been a break in the subordinate's role behavior? Managers seem to recognize breaks because they "know" what poor performance is and knowing poor performance tells them what to look for, what counts as "a break." Then, we must ask, how do managers know poor performance?

Managers, and subordinates for that matter, know poor performance because through the creation of a culture (Pacanowsky & O'Donnell-Trujillo, 1982, 1983; Louis, 1981; Pettigrew, 1979) organizations invest their settings with meaning about acceptable performance, and through socialization individuals come to learn and appreciate those meanings (Brim, 1966; Louis, 1980; Van Maanen, 1976; Van Maanen & Schein, 1979). As Louis (1981, p. 250) has stated, "Culture provides a background through which particular types of events and behaviors are noticed." This is accomplished in several ways. First, there are written policies and procedures that specify behaviors that are obligatory, permissible, or preferred. Consider the following example of policy from Bank B's employee handbook:

You may be discharged without prior notice for several reasons including but not limited to the following: falsification of bank records, misuse of bank property, drinking on the job, usage of drugs on the premises, and various arrests with subsequent convictions occurring outside banking hours.

Further, there are agreed-upon procedure norms shared within the work group. For example, one branch administrator, addressing the dollar limit set for teller outages, said, "$300 has been the magical figure. At $300 we mandate retraining. At $600 they must leave the job." Note that the arbitrariness of these standards is acknowledged by this branch administrator when he uses the word "magical" to refer to this limit.

A second way organizations invest their settings with meaning is through the inculcation of a set of values in its members. Values form the core of an organization's culture by articulating what is important in the organization, and what meanings and role behaviors reflect those values (Weick, 1969; Geertz, 1983; Deal & Kennedy, 1982). In customer service organizations such as banks, the value placed on the customer is primary and was heard with striking consensus throughout:

The customer is always right.

When you're in the service industry, you can't stress customer service enough.

We must bite our tongues in dealing with the public at times and realize the customer comes first.

Thus "knowing" poor performance depends upon interpretive processes (that is, a set of meanings for what constitutes poor performance derived through socialization into an organization's culture), and detection in our context is dependent upon knowing poor performance. Also, by recognizing that what is interpreted as poor performance is constrained by what is noticed (that is, behavior that is not noticed cannot be labeled), the reflexivity between problem detection and interpretive processes is quite apparent.

It is important to recognize that a break in the subordinate's role behavior will always be interpreted as poor performance if it falls into one of the prohibitive categories of behavior imposed by the organization and the body of knowledge its members share. But it is not necessarily seen as a "real problem" warranting a corrective response. This is because many poor performance incidents faced by bank managers become serious cumulatively. Absenteeism and teller outages are two examples. How, then, does a manager know a "real problem"? Consider the remarks of a branch administrator:

I would hope that if there is some consistency in their dollar amount or the percentages that we would be counseling the individual. A manager is going to have to wait 2-3 weeks until there is a trend there. We are all capable of going crazy for a week or so.

A "trend," in this branch administrator's terms, would be constituted by two types of detection. First, "basic detection" involves recognizing performance breaks. Second, "pattern detection" involves looking across the breaks, which, while individually interpreted as poor performance, are collectively defined as a real problem. As a real problem, the pattern of breaks is taken as evidence that individual performance breaks are not illusory or chance occurrences that are likely to go away by themselves.

That pattern detection was a widely shared organizational practice by managers is quite apparent. By administrators' own admission, however, what constitutes a pattern appears to be more a case of individual judgment than a shared norm. Thus, returning to our model in Figure 21.2, our hypothetical manager perceived a pattern and decided to take action after the sixth performance breakpoint. However, another manager may just have easily perceived a "real problem" after the second, fifth, or eighth performance breakpoint. Just what accounts for these differences in pattern detection is a fruitful area for future research.

Problem Detection in the Control Process

At this point, detection processes are seen as contributing to the manager moving through Stage 1 by allowing him or her to recognize poor performance breakpoints as such and patterns in those breakpoints that are the prelude to the problem-solving breakpoint (see Figure 21.6). The basic discussion of detection through Stage 1 of the control process generalizes to all three stages with some minor changes. In Stage 2, however, problem detection also involves tracking the covariance of control actions and subordinate's performance. This is because expectations about future subordinate role behavior come not only from knowledge of what is acceptable performance, but also from having intervened with the purpose of turning a performance problem around. From the problem-solving breakpoint to the elimination breakpoint, every time the manager acts, he or she expects corrected performance and thus tracks the covariance between the action taken and subsequent performance by the subordinate. With the lack of covariance, problem detection as in Stage 1 repeats itself. We would hypothesize that one other difference between Stages 1 and 2 is that fewer performance breakpoints will prompt a manager to act in the latter phase as the pattern or trend will have been well established.

In Stage 3, as a result of continued poor performance, the adjudged failure of the control process, and the desire to rid the organization of the employee legally, a manager may direct a heightened awareness toward the performance of the employee. In other words, the manager is ready to

Sense Making

		Stages of Control Chain		
		Stage 1	Stage 2	Stage 3
Process	Mechanisms	Accept Problem Solving Perform. Breakpoint	Problem Solving Eliminate Breakpoint Breakpoint	Eliminate Term-Breakpoint ination
Problem Detection	-Basic Detection -Pattern Detection -Heightened Detection	-Acknowledge disjunction in stream of performance as a pattern	-Track covariance of control actions and performance.	-Heightened awareness
Problem Diagnosis	-Monitoring -Questioning -Role Taking	-Seeks information to: -assign problem realness -speculate on causes (Monitoring)	-Seeks information to: -reassign causes -consider solutions -decide if problems correctable (Monitoring, Questioning, Role Taking)	-Seeks information to: -execute a speedy termination (Monitoring)
Interpreta-tion	-Interpretive schemas -Action schemas	-Stimulates and Channels Detection and Diagnosis -Helps Fill In Information -Assimilates Information	-Stimulates and Channels Detection and Diagnosis -Helps Fill In Information -Assimilates and accommodates to information	-Stimulates and Channels Detection and Diagnosis -Helps Fill In Information -Assimilates to Information

Figure 21.6.   Mechanisms and foci of sense making, by stages of control chain.

pounce on any false move by the employee because it may speed the "inevitable" elimination process.

Thus problem detection involves both the recognition of poor performance and the recognition of a real problem. Further, culturally based interpretive processes obviously are involved and are crucial in directing the manager in what to look for throughout the control process and how to "see" it.

Problem Diagnosis

Once the manager detects poor performance and makes the most fundamental diagnosis that there is a problem, there are a number of other diagnostic issues throughout the control process that a manager faces, such as the cause of the problem, potential solutions, when action should be taken, and whether the problem is amenable to correction. The uncertainty surrounding these issues prompts managers to employ a variety of information-yielding devices, all designed to increase their understanding of the situation. Based on our data, monitoring, questioning, and role taking appear to be three of the most common.

Monitoring

One way managers can gain information as to the cause of a performance problem is to scan the ongoing stream of the subordinate's role behavior more closely. Thus past, present, and future performance breakpoints become magnified during this process. Kiesler and Sproull (1982, p. 562) state:

> In other words, under uncertainty, increased information is automatically available to the perceiver by his adjusting the level of his analysis of the environment so that segmented units or categories are divided at more (and less obtrusive) breakpoints. Up to a point, finer units provide more detailed information for encoding and organizing in memory.

Managers' use of monitoring, however, goes somewhat beyond additional observation, as the following two examples show:

> I had moved her between two experienced tellers, but so far, there has been no difference. . . . And they took extra steps, I believe, in the days that she was there to try to help her. They would make her make totals every half hour, which is different for anyone to take more than 2 or 3 totals a day, and then review her work.

> The only way we ever found out [the problem] would be to go back and go through all her work. And then sometimes it was tough. She was not consistent. I think consistent was a word I must have used a thousand times in the first

conversation. Above all you have to be consistent. Now I may do things wrong, but I consistently do them the same way. She didn't consistently do anything the same way.

Here monitoring took the form of appointing official "watchers," who would test or institute additional duties for the subordinate, retrace the subordinate's steps through previous tasks while he or she is being observed, and make additional observations during the normal performance of the subordinate's tasks.

Questioning

Weick (1977) suggests that equivocality removal is essentially an interpersonal process whereby communication reduces uncertainty, frequently through questions posed by the manager to the poor performers. In our previous research, sense-making questions frequently were used by managers to elicit the cause of the problem and suggestions as to how to solve it (Fairhurst et al., in press). Consider the following:

> I think with your first meeting . . . you would have to offer help. What did she feel that we could do to help her improve in these areas? Why did she feel she had those problems? Was there anything within the system that we could do to help her with that?

Yet the distinguishing features of these questioning routines are that they were quickly abandoned by managers and they frequently failed to yield satisfactory answers (Fairhurst et al., in press). One reason for their failure to reduce uncertainty may be due to the inability of subordinates to separate the report and command functions of a question (that is, to recognize that each question carries content and information about how the content should be taken; Watzlawick, Beavin, & Jackson, 1967). Goody explains (1978, p. 39):

> But if roles are very clearly defined . . . then the role expectations will bias the interpretation of any questions asked. Thus, it is very difficult for a person in a clearly defined authority role to ask a pure information question—that is, to ask a question which is perceived as being just about facts and not also about fixing responsibility or threatening control.

What Goody is suggesting is that subordinates are incapable of seeing or are unwilling to see managers' questions as "strictly fact-finding" without also feeling blamed. If the managers' questions caused subordinates to feel defensive, then a common defensive reaction is to withhold or to distort information (Gibb, 1961). By withholding or distorting information, the subordinate does not reinforce the manager for this posture and the manager quickly abandons questioning routines for a more punitive stance. Unfortunately, this stance minimizes the flow of information the manager needs in order to understand the problem better.

Role Taking

Another way managers can get information is through role taking. According to Stryker (1957), role taking refers to "anticipating the responses of others implicated with one in some social act." A manager does not have to agree with the subordinate's acts, but can understand them better by putting him- or herself in the subordinate's place. Consider the following example:

> I noted that at that time in talking to her, that 18 months after being hired she still did not know how to look for her own outages. And her work continued to be sloppy and recovery time continued to be time-consuming. At this point I made a note that she continued to perceive that she was doing a good job. And at that point I had to admit that she was probably working to her own potential as she perceived it, not as I perceived it. I didn't say that to her because if I admitted that to her I felt like we wouldn't make any progress at all. And the interesting thing about this particular case is that she is a smart young lady. We tested her. This is a young lady who had the ability to assert herself with her family but not with anyone else. If she could have used the level of confidence that she used in talking to her parents on the phone with the customers, she would have been fine.

This quote suggest several things about role taking as a diagnostic aid. First, role taking depends on already having enough information to create a "sense of the situation" as perceived by the subordinate. In this case, the manager had three previous sessions at which "nervousness" was given as an excuse as well as an opportunity to observe the subordinate at work and talking with family. Second, role taking is useful when the subordinate's behavior is perplexing and because the excuses lack explanatory power from the manager's perspective. Because this teller is "a smart young lady" and she appears confident in talking with family, from the manager's perspective nervousness is not a believable reason for her performance problem. But by taking the role of the subordinate, that is, by allowing that she may have a different perspective, her behavior is explainable.

Third, role taking may prompt managers to take actions that they would not otherwise take—actions that are specifically suited to the employee's needs. Consider the following example:

> So it was very important to take care of the customers and not argue with them. If you are at a point where you just feel like you had to argue with somebody, I told her to send them to a supervisor. I knew it was going to be

difficult for her to learn how to back away all the time because of her personality. I suppose in the situation she just felt she had to say something.

In this example, the manager shows he understands that people with argumentative personalities "feel they just have to say something." The manager
then gives this teller a situation-specific suggestion for what to do the next
time she feels she has to argue (that is, send the customer to a supervisor).

Use of Diagnostic Devices
in the Control Process

As might be expected, the diagnostic devices would be used differently
depending upon which stage of the control process a manager was currently
in. As shown in Figure 21.6, during Stage 1 the manager is attempting to
assess the problem's realness, speculate on causes, and consider his or her
first action. Since there was little or no communication about the problem
prior to the first action, monitoring of the employee in the form of additional
observation is the predominant device to yield information. With the manager's first action Stage 2 begins, and monitoring in all forms, questioning,
and role taking are all used because information gathering is so critical to the
problem-solving process. The manager is still seeking to assign causes, consider solutions, and, perhaps most important, decide if the problem is solu-
ble. The information requirements of these decisions are substantial, thus
leading managers to rely on as many information-yielding devices as possible. In Stage 3, the manager's primary task is elimination of the employee
and his or her readiness to detect any poor performance that could speed
elimination suggests that monitoring once again becomes the primary way
to gather information. Thus it is only during Stage 2, where the information
requirements are the greatest, that all three information sources were used,
with monitoring characterizing the other two stages.

In summary, problem diagnosis involves information-yielding devices,
such as monitoring in various forms, questioning, and role taking. Further,
their use is shaped by the information requirements of each particular stage of
the control chain as well as by what the organization values and chooses to
sanction. Finally, if interpretive processes guide managers in detecting poor
performance, they also guide managers in diagnosing it. Knowing how to
diagnose a problem is dependent upon knowing (that is, having interpretive
frameworks for) what are likely causes of poor performance, what factors are
related to improving performance, and how managers should proceed in diagnosing performance problems. It follows that if what one interprets as appropriate diagnostic behavior constrains how one collects information, the
information obtained constrains what is available for interpretation. One can-

not interpret what one does not have. Thus there is a reflexivity between diagnosis and interpretation, our next sense-making process.

Interpretation

We have already suggested that detection and diagnosis are interpretively driven activities. We have not, however, discussed the specific mechanisms that both drive them and embellish their output. Bartlett (1932, p. 21) suggested years ago that perception and memory are not merely reproductive but reconstructive in character, guided by "an active organization of past reactions or past experiences." This "an active organization" translates to a set of anticipatory assumptions or "cognitive schemata" that give meaning to and specify appropriate forms of goal-oriented behavior (Taylor & Crocker, 1981).

Two types of schemas commonly identified are interpretive schemas and action schemas. *Interpretive schemas* (Louis, 1980) impart meaning to objects and have been variously described as "schemas" (Tesser, 1978), "frames" (Minsky, 1975), "prototype schemata" (Tversky, 1977), "template schemata" (Norman & Bobrow, 1975), "constitutive rules" (Searle, 1969), and "constructs" (Kelly, 1955). Tesser (1978, p. 291) argues that interpretive "schemas vary in levels of abstraction and can embed themselves one within the other." *Action schemas* (Taylor & Crocker, 1981) regulate preexisting forms of behavior (Searle, 1969) by specifying that which is appropriate to the achievement of one or more goals. Action schemas also have been variously described as "scripts" (Schank & Abelson, 1977; Abelson, 1976), "plans" (Schank & Abelson, 1977), "procedural schemata" (Neisser, 1976), and "regulative rules" (Searle, 1969).

Managers' schemas arise from many sources—the organization's culture, other managers, society, their own experience, and so on. Evidence of these schemas and hints of their origins can be seen in those that guide both detection and diagnosis. For example, one organization states in its employee handbook that falsification of bank records, drug and alcohol usage on the job, misuse of bank property, and arrest and conviction are "cause" for immediate dismissal. This organization is simultaneously providing to its managers interpretive schemas for what shall constitute poor performance (thus directing problem detection), and action schemas as to how the manager should respond to certain performance problems. Similarly, there is evidence that organizations provide schemas that guide problem diagnosis. For example, managers appear to learn, through cultural training, when and how to question problem employees to avoid unnecessary risk (primarily legal) to the organization:

> I was programmed not to accuse her. I can understand why because I had no
> proof but I strongly felt that there were problems. In fact, I asked her about a
> specific transaction, and she could not explain it.

In this quote, the phrase "I was programmed not to accuse her" very clearly
reflects the organization's role in shaping how managers go about collecting
information. Coupling this phrase with "I had no proof" also suggests that
the manager's behavior was influenced by societal action schemas that negatively sanction accusations without proof.

The preceding example is particularly notable because it depicts what
we feel is a common managerial experience in control processes. The organization frequently seems to make clear what a manager cannot do, but then
does not provide cultural schemas to direct what he or she should do. Under
these circumstances the manager's "interpretation" of what is going on and
what to do must derive from societal and personal schemas. In the previous
case, the manager switched to such schemas when he went "off record,"
that is, the intention of his remarks was left ambiguous so that he could not
be held to have committed himself (Brown & Levinson, 1978):

> I asked her, "If you were in my position, and you saw this [cash shortage],
> what would you ask the employee?" She looked at me and said, "You think I
> stole it, don't you?" and I said that I didn't say that.

The manager's off-record schema allows him to let his true feelings be
known and to extend his diagnosis, yet to remain equivocal publicly.

It is also clear from this example that the manager anticipated an attempt by the subordinate to get him to "own" the theft interpretation he
implied when the manager readily makes reference to the ambiguity of his
remarks ("I didn't say that"). The anticipatory nature of schemas reveals just
how they are used in sense making. As Louis (1980) suggests, schemas
provide the individual with predictions of event sequences and outcomes.
When individuals take in information from the environment, events are
matched with schema-based expectations. Discrepancies between events
and schema-based expectations, then, are the root of the motivation for
sense making to occur, as the following example shows:

> Unfortunately, it is necessary to oversee the simple tasks she performs to see
> that they are done in a timely fashion. She is certainly gracious to our help and
> willing to accept suggestions, but she appears to have a lack of logic or under-
> standing as to why I do not feel she is performing adequately.

In this example, the manager recognizes that his action schema for acceptable teller performance (that is, simple tasks should be performed in a timely
fashion without supervision) is not shared by this employee. This then

prompts him to engage in sense making, that is, to speculate about plausible reasons for her having the problem, when he says, "She appears to have a lack of logic or understanding."

The interpretation or meaning assigned to the performance discrepancy in control problems will be fueled by a number of inputs, among them the development of the manager's own schematic structures (more experienced managers should have better-developed schemas than less experienced managers), the detection and diagnosis capability of the manager, and the willingness and ability of the subordinate to volunteer information about the problem. Consider the following example of a manager dealing with a subordinate's customer relations problem:

> We reviewed the fact that he cannot have a customer reduce him to their level when he is dealing with a difficult customer. I alluded to one time when he was rude in refusing to cash an unemployment check. He admitted that he was. And I said why and he said because that's the way they were to me. I treated them the way they treated me. I said you can't do that.

When the manager asked why the subordinate was rude in refusing to cash a check, the manager reported that the subordinate was immediately forthcoming with the latter's action schema for dealing with customers, namely, "I treat them the way they treat me." Thus the subordinate's willingness to volunteer that information makes it easier for the manager to make sense of the situation. But subordinates may not always be aware of why they act as they do, or they may be aware but unwilling to volunteer information, or the manager simply may not be skilled at "drawing out" the necessary facts. All of these factors limit the "reality testing" of the manager and force him or her to fill in the uncertain or incomplete information obtained. To do this, managers will rely on past experience, general predispositions (such as to attribute the locus of control to events external or internal to the individual; Rotter, 1966), and their preexisting schemas, such as implicit theories (see, for example, Markus, 1977; Bem & Allen, 1979; Lord, Binning, Rush, & Thomas, 1978; Schneider, 1973). These theories would allow the managers to fill in information to provide whole meaning to their observations. Thus we can see that schemas play an important role in interpretation. That role may change character, however, depending upon the stage of the control chain.

Interpretation in the Control Chain

The "filling-in" function of schemas reflects their assimilative character, that is, the tendency to make one's cognitions about an object more like the schema. Nevertheless, according to Tesser (1978, p. 294), schemas also exhibit accommodation, which "often results in making the schema a more complete and veridical 'theory' of the stimulus domain." Whether schemas assimilate or accommodate depends upon a variety of factors. Chief among them is certainly the information that is available.

Although our data do not allow us to address questions of assimilation and accommodation directly, what we know of the control chains does suggests a plausible relationship between stage of the chain and these processes. In the interest of hypothesis generation, we suggest that since Stages 1 and 3 of the control process are not characterized as high information-yielding stages, the opportunity to reality test is minimized, which suggests that the assimilative character of schemas would be quite strong (see Figure 21.6). In Stage 1, the manager is beginning to define the problem and develop a frame of reference from available schemas. In Stage 3, the manager is no longer concerned with correcting the situation and seeks only to rid the organization of the employee. Information exchange with the employee in both of the stages is minimal. Since information yielding is potentially the highest in Stage 2 during problem solving, the accommodative character of schemas may predominate. If the information a subordinate is willing to volunteer attenuates accommodation, however, so must the receptivity of the manager to that information. Moreover, it seems likely that experienced managers with already well-developed schemas may exhibit less accommodation than other less experienced managers even under high information-yielding conditions. Careful, longitudinal tests of these possibilities are needed.

In summary, we made the following points about interpretation in sense making. First, managers use interpretive and action schemas to understand subordinates' behavior and to guide their own actions. Second, schemas are supplied by the organization's culture, but also by the society, specific groups, and the individuals themselves in varying degrees. Third, the lack of fit between the schematic structures of the manager and events in the work environment is what prompts sense making. Fourth, several factors influence the character of sense making, including the opportunity to reality test and the development of the managers' own schematic structures. Finally, the assimilative versus the accommodative character of schemas was hypothesized to vary depending upon the relative location of the manager in the control chain.

SENSE MAKING AND THE
SELECTION OF A CONTROL RESPONSE

In order to understand the relationship between sense making and resulting control behavior, we must reconsider the nature of the exchange between a manager and a subordinate in the control chain. To begin with, because of the temporal flow of communication, each person's behavior is both the antecedent and the consequent of the other. According to Cronen, Pearce, and Harris (1982), this alternation produces a behavioral logic in which an act by one person is assigned meaning by the interpretive schemas of the other and serves also as the antecedent condition of the other's action schemas. For example, each manager has an interpretive schema for how many absent days constitute a trend and thus a "real problem." Thus a pattern of absences is seen as a "real problem" and simultaneously serves as the antecedent condition for the manager's action schemas (remind the employee of policy, discover the cause of the problem, and so on). The dynamics of the exchange, then, between a manager and a subordinate can be characterized by the "fit" between their respective schematic structures.

It is the lack of fit between events and the manager's schemas that a manager must address him- or herself to when confronted with a performance problem. This lack of fit provides the exigence for sense making and the exercise of control. The nature of sense making and control depends upon a manager's inclination and ability to apprehend the interpretive and action schemas guiding the employee, that is, the operative schema. If the manager is able to apprehend the subordinate's operative schema through sense making, then he or she can formulate a response that can potentially incorporate that information and so adapt itself. In the following example, the manager's opportunity to adapt a control response was thwarted until his third discussion, when sense making occurred:

> She was disgusted at me and she didn't tell me that until we hit the parking lot, and I said, OK, I'm so glad you said that. I felt, hooray, breakthrough! Now I felt I knew what was bugging her; I was loading this work on her and the tellers weren't doing this and the other tellers weren't doing that and I said, "You know what I'm going to do; I'm going to put blinders on you. You're going to be so much happier. Just do your work and if they don't perform, I will take care of that."

In this example, the manager's sense making permitted her to formulate a response specifically adapted to this subordinate's gripes about the performance of the other tellers. Previous suggestions by this manager contained somewhat vague statements of support during the first discussion and the need to get along with people one works with during the second discussion, neither of which directly addressed the real problem or corrected it.

We now see a key link between sense making and the selection of control responses. Until the elimination breakpoint is reached, regardless of the specific control action employed by a manager, the basic aim of the control process is to influence the employee to accept the manager's schematic structures about what work is (interpretive schemas) and how it should be accomplished (action schemas). After the elimination breakpoint, it is immaterial whether the employee accepts the manager's schemas or not because he or she will be leaving the work environment. In the following classic example we see a manager negotiating both interpretive (what do we mean by "sick") and action (the relationship between attendance and sickness) schemas during the first discussion of the problem:

> I said the following to Kim . . . I've called you in this morning to talk about your absence record and your tardiness. It is just something that is just going to have to stop. I certainly would be the last one to want someone to come in here and work if they *truly* are *sick*. And if you are *really sick*, I don't want you to come in because I don't want other people getting sick. I don't want you to get worse, as a result of coming in. But if you have that kind of sickness, I am in a position where I need someone who can be relatively reliable. And if you *really* are that *sick*, I don't know if you will be able to fill the part of what I need here at the office. I just think that it is something that we are going to have to make an effort to work on. Also, if you *really* are that *sick*, you need to see a doctor or something. At that point, I advised her that if she is *really* that *sick*, that maybe she should have some sort of doctor's note for the absences.

Schema replacement, then, is the essence of the problem-solving stage in the control chains. But it is important to bear in mind that "replacement" can be accomplished either through persuasion with the goal of internalization or with the explicit use of threat with the goal of compliance. If the manager's sense making allows him or her to apprehend the subordinate's operative schema and it is not yet perceived as resistant to change, then we would expect more influence attempts, at least initially, to be based on persuasion. This is because the manager can use the additional information gleaned through sense making to formulate a more credible, subordinate-adapted argument.

One caveat is in order, however. Even though sense making should make it easier to be persuasive and avoid the exclusive use of threat, it does not presuppose success. According to Pondy (1978), leadership is a language game and it is the *dual capacity* to make sense of the situation and to put it into language that is meaningful to the recipient that characterizes the effective leader. The customer relations problem in the following example never surfaced again, and this may be because sense making was easily accomplished when the subordinate freely volunteered his operative schema, namely, "I treat them the way they treat me," and the *manner* in which this manager chose to articulate his action schema for dealing with customers.

> You have a job and you can't let the customer drag you down and let them get under your skin. You have got to treat them with respect. You have to be

reasonably friendly. And you smile at them while they are yelling at you. You have to act like you are listening. And I say the one thing you always tell a customer to cut the edge is 'I want to help you but . . .' List the things that they need to accomplish before you can complete their transaction.

The manager used two metaphors, "You can't let the customer drag you down," and "let them get under your skin." Then, no less than six specific behaviors were delineated that reflect appropriate role behavior (for example, "treat them with respect"). This type of response is much different than merely saying, "The customer is always right." A less articulate or well-reasoned manager might not have been so successful.

On the other hand, a manager may be thwarted by lack of information in his or her attempt to apprehend the operative schema. Or, sense making may occur but the operative schema may be resistant to change or replacement. In either case, the discrepant behavior still must be rectified. The manager still faces the basic dilemma of getting the employer to accept his or her schematic structure. Here, the manager may try a variety of control actions, including persuasion, hoping one will trigger the correct responses. However, persuasion attempts would likely be more quickly abandoned in lieu of threat-based compliance-gaining attempts. Thus the manager offers to the employee a basic action schema that says "failure to do a behavior will result in increasing punishment." We can now see progressive discipline in a new light. It represents a series of increasingly harsh action schemas that are designed to replace or override whatever other schemas are operating with a poor performer. The following example depicts these processes in all their complexity:

The first time . . . We got nothing more than a blank stare. For some unknown reason she just simply didn't do it right [balancing]. When confronting with it, she always just shrugged it off and said I don't know.
[Action: Discussion]

The second time . . . She gave us the impression that . . . she didn't care. Everything you would say to her she would nod yes and say, "I understand, I understand." Then she would go back and do the same thing again.
[Action: Warning]

The third time . . . I brought the teller into my office to question her to find out why she didn't wait on this particular customer. She informed me that this particular customer had never been at her window. She didn't know that the customer had been standing in front of her. It was at that particular point I realized that there was some kind of a problem with either not remembering, knowing, or something; and this in part was causing some of her problems. My tellers had mentioned on a couple of occasions, it never even hit me, that she would act strange. That could mean a lot of things, OK? Generally speaking,

the acting strange would be just kind of staring out in space, like she wasn't there, not knowing what was going on around her.
[Action: Discussion]

The fourth time . . . It was in the window, it was in late afternoon. We called the city life squad and they came and took her to the hospital and she was released that night and she was back to work the next day happy, joking with the tellers, just as though nothing had happened. I called her into my office and she did not volunteer the information that she was epileptic. I had to ask her and at that point she confirmed it. At that particular point I sent her on over to the teller window and she ran her window fine; there were no problems. At that point, I think I realized that some of these blank stars, these lost feelings were because she was on the verge of going and she could control it. She didn't know where she was for a minute or two and then she came back, and it was during some of these periods when she created mistakes in her work, and had no idea why there was a mistake. It was because she wasn't even there, didn't even know what happened.
[Action: Discussion]

The fifth time . . . She had a medical problem, OK; we found out about it. But her performance was still suspect. She cashed some stolen Series E bonds and it was substantial—$1,500.00, on top of her other teller outages. She cashed some bad checks. We told her her performance was to improve over the next three months. If it did not, she would be fired.
[Action: Probation]

The sixth time . . . Her performance did not improve and when the time period was up, the decision was made to terminate her.
[Action: Termination]

As this example demonstrates, at first the manager tried to apprehend the operative schema but failed (Action 1). Making no progress in understanding, he tried discipline to force compliance (Action 2). With more information (Actions 3 and 4) the manager made sense of the events and abandoned discipline, trying to negotiate (discussions) the action schemas. Unfortunately, the operative schema here (a medical problem) was resistant to change and the manager switched back to discipline to try to force compliance and/or set up the eventual elimination (Actions 5 and 6).

When one studies poor performance from a control chain perspective (versus single episodes), it is apparent that information about the problem can surface at different times, in different amounts, and in differing degrees of clarity for employees ostensibly with the "same" problem (for example, absenteeism). Thus, because the character of sense making is different, each problem is quite unique. When information does become available (that is, sense making occurs), it then interacts with the prevailing conditions, such as problem severity to that point. Had the teller's epilepsy in the previous example been discovered earlier, the control chain might be quite different because other control actions, such as transfer to a noncustomer contact position, might have been more viable.

Predicting a Control Response

We believe the answer to the question of a priori versus post hoc analysis depends upon which breakpoint managers are closer to in the control process. When managers are near the problem-solving breakpoint, they are arriving at a definition of the situation; they seek to determine the problem's realness, assess its impact, determine cause, attribute blame, project future instances, determine fixability, and so on. The judgments that they make are continually revised as information becomes available and experience is accumulated. Because of their need to interact with the environment to acquire and adapt to any information that will help them make sense of the situation and solve the problem, managers appear to operate much like open systems (von Bertalanffy, 1968; Hall & Fagan, 1956).

Open systems are characterized by greater interaction with the environment, adaptability, and one other characteristic that managers also appear to share—lower predictability. Based on our current knowledge of the control process, which in its early stages appears unfolding and adaptive in character, there appears to be no "formula" of necessary ingredients for determining whether a manager will issue a warning, choose only to "counsel" the employee, request retraining, or whatever. Certainly, we can say that the control process will probably begin with some sort of lower-level control action such as counseling, unless precluded by a formal, organizational action schema. We also can say that the control process will probably escalate as the problem continues and grows more serious. But, returning to the schematic in Figure 21.1, we cannot yet say how long counseling will continue or if it will suddenly reappear later in the control chain.

We also cannot say whether or not managers will continue with the same level of control action or "regress" with a lower-level action before again escalating. Rather, it appears that at this stage there is only the general goal of problem solving (schema replacement), and, following Garfinkel (1967), a set of ad hoc tactics for adapting to the present circumstances that vary considerably with each subordinate, the problem that is posed, and the character of the sense making. These tactics are shaped by policy and the organization's culture, individual management styles, the history of the relationship between the parties, and the subordinate's response, among other things. But these tactics appear so circumstantially prescribed that they are generally unelaborated and in principle unpredictable to both theorist and participant, hence the retrospective character of sense making. This notion is quite consistent with the open system's property of equifinality, where "results" are not determined so much by the set of initial conditions as by the nature of the process or system parameters (von Bertalanffy, 1962). In other words, the same problem-solving action may arise from a quite different set of circumstances and, correspondingly, similar circumstances may yield quite different problem-solving actions even by the same manager. And the rather imprecise and ambiguous nature of bank policy and the unwillingness of bank administrators to enforce it to the letter appear to be tacit acknowledgments of this state of affairs.

As the manager reaches the elimination breakpoint, however, he or she has arrived at a definition of the situation that is likely to endure, the contents of which suggest that the employee is not worth salvaging, the problem is not fixable (the operative schemas are beyond negotiation), and a decision to terminate is made. The manager now takes on the characteristics of a closed system, which is characterized by a lack of interaction with the environment, no adaptiveness, and higher predictability because the initial conditions determine the final state of the system (von Bertalanffy, 1968; Hall & Fagan, 1956). Because a termination decision is difficult to make and even more difficult to carry out, there is a strong need on the part of managers to make such a decision appear justifiable and reasonable to themselves as well as to others. We discussed the use of verbal case building by managers when the model was first introduced. There is, however, a stronger mechanism at work here. As an open system during problem solving, the manager sees him- or herself as the force behind the rules, that is, as the originator or chief interpreter of the rules governing the system. As one manager put it, "I want to feel like we were controlling this ourselves." As a closed system during the elimination phase, the manager sees him- or herself as subject to the force of the rules. That is, both the manager and the subordinate are components of a determined system such that when certain initial conditions are met, there are irreversible consequences totally outside of the manager's control. Either the system or the subordinate who triggered the initial conditions is responsible for the termination, not the manager. Consider the following examples:

> Her attitude would have to change before a training program could be set up for her and be considered for any type of advancement. If not, it could lead to termination and there would be no other alternative. It was her choice to make, either change and work to advancement to increase her potential, or keep her attitude and face termination.

> Sandy, I'm sorry to have to meet with you this morning, but you realize that you have been on probation and I warned you that continuance of your past history could result in your termination, and you've been absent since our last meeting; I have no other alternative than to terminate your employment as of today.

In these examples, the manager states that the employee will trigger or has triggered the initial condition (that is, not changing an attitude or one more absence) and the inescapable conclusion. Phrases in the above passages, such as "her choice," and other phrases such as "It was his problem, not mine," and "The employee has got to realize that they are responsible for their termination, not the manager" all reflect the conscious shift of ownership of the problem to the subordinate. Indeed, the following statement by a manager is rather explicit in this regard: "I guess what I was doing was shifting the blame. If I had to fire her, it wasn't going to be my fault."

Thus, in Weick's (1976) terms, the logic of the control chains can best be understood as a sequence of first loosely and then tightly coupled events. At or near the problem-solving breakpoint, when uncertainty is the highest, the manager's actions are highly adaptive and thus may only be weakly linked or loosely coupled with previous or immediately ensuing actions. At or near the elimination breakpoint, however, the manager's actions are tightly coupled by his or her public portrayal as components of a determined system. When the manager announces to the subordinate the initial conditions that, when met, will lead to termination, he or she feels no choice but to carry out those actions, hence the tight coupling of the session that spells out the initial conditions and the session that carries out the consequences of their being met. The issue of predictability of a manger's control behavior, then, is relegated to the location of the manager in the control process.

CONCLUSION

At the beginning of this chapter we argued that the state of current control research led us to reconceptualize the process by which managers control poor performers in terms of control chains rather than single control episodes. Our reconceptualization prompted a shift toward understanding sense making in poor performance through contextually sensitive, qualitative methods. What have we learned and what have we yet to learn?

First, we have a model of the control process the complexity of which stems from tracking it in its entirety as well as examining it in the context of an ongoing relationship. As such, the model captures the control process in a way no other research model of controlling poor performance has. There are several reasons for this. The unit of analysis in previous research has been single incidents. An examination of the schematic in Figure 21.1 clearly calls this practice into question. Further, "single incidents" are contextualized not only by previous actions taken but by the definition of the work relationship itself. Unless future research incorporates these factors by locating a dyad at a particular stage in the control process, external validity is seriously compromised. Second, our ability to define the control process was the result of a focus on sense making during poor performance incidents and the use of contextually sensitive qualitative methods. During sense making managers not only explained observed vs. expected performance discrepancies, but they explained the control process as they enacted it.

Two areas remain for future investigation, however. First, the model-in-use was derived from a managerial perspective. What is needed at this point is the subordinate's sense making of the control process to see to what extent it coincides with the manager's view, to see if and at what point the subordinate perceives an elimination breakpoint, or just how the subordinate perceives the work relationship changing as poor performance continues. Second, a more precise specification of the problem-solving and elimination breakpoints might be obtained by a shift from retrospective case histories to a longitudinal method.

The second contribution of this research is a better understanding of how managers make sense out of poor performance. For example, problem detection, which is a pre-sense-making activity, was shown to involve basic detection of poor performance and pattern detection or the recognition of a "real problem." We need to know more about "real problem" recognition, however, and its impact on the effectiveness of a manager's control. Problem diagnosis was shown to involve three basic mechanisms for this sample: monitoring, questioning, and role taking. Again, the issue of effectiveness is a relevant one here. To what extent is a manager's diagnostic skill linked to his or her ability to manage performance problems effectively? During interpretation, managers were shown to employ interpretive and action schemas. The dynamics of the exchange between a manager and a subordinate was defined in terms of the "fit" between their respective schematic structures. Future research should continue to explore the schematic structures of both managers and subordinates from both perspectives, especially to assess the impact of misunderstandings. Further, the role the organization plays in supplying schemas to its managers should be explored.

In our final section, on selection of a control action, we imposed a systems metaphor to explain the basic functioning of managers' treatment of subordinates during the control process. During problem solving, managers are seen as adapting to the circumstances, "casting about" for solutions, and less predictable in their actions. During elimination, however, managers have committed themselves to a decision to terminate and thus set up conditions that can trigger the outcome and simultaneously relieve them of any direct responsibility. Future research should be directed at a better understanding of the problem-solving phase. The situation changes substantially during elimination, and future research would do well to explore the "tipping points" of managers who reach the elimination breakpoint early as opposed to late in the control process. What causes managers to fall within these groups? What is their effect on the rest of the staff? These questions have implications not only for the performance of subordinates, but for the costs associated with retaining a poor performer.

One final word should be said about the generalizability of our findings in terms of our sample. While our own research has been limited to banks thus far, we have every reason to expect our findings and model to generalize to other organizational settings. This is because such performance problems as absenteeism, staff conflict, customer relations, and the handling of financial transactions occur with some frequency in other organizational settings and they are also iterative.

In light of this conclusion, we believe we have contributed a better understanding of the whips and chains of controlling poor performance, and we would encourage future research to pursue the directions initiated here.

REFERENCES

Abelson, R. P. (1976). Script processing in attitude formation and decision making. In J. S. Carroll & J. W. Payne (Eds.), *Cognition and social behavior* (pp. 33-46). Hillsdale, NJ: Lawrence Erlbaum.

Asherman, I. G., & Vance, S. (1981, August). Documentation: A tool for effective management. *Personnel Journal,* pp. 641-643.

Bartlett, F. C. (1932). *Remembering.* Cambridge: Cambridge University Press.

Bem, D. L., & Allen, A. (1979). On predicting some of the people some of the time: The search for cross-situational consistencies in behavior. *Psychological Review, 81,* 506-620.

Berger, P., & Luckman, G. (1967). *The social construction of reality.* Garden City, NY: Doubleday.

Bertalanffy, L. von (1962). General systems theory: A critical review. *General Systems Yearbook, 7,* 1-20.

Bertalanffy, L. von (1968). *General systems theory, foundations developments, applications.* New York: Braziller.

Brim, O. G., Jr. (1966). Socialization through the life cycle. In O. Brim, Jr., & S. Wheeler (Eds.), *Socialization after childhood: Two essays* (pp. 1-49). New York: John Wiley.

Brown, P., & Levinson, S. (1978). Universals in language usage: Politeness phenomena. In. E. N. Goody (Ed.), *Questions and politeness.* Cambridge: Cambridge University Press.

Bureau of National Affairs Editorial Staff. (1978). *Grievance guide.* Washington, DC: Bureau of National Affairs, Inc.

Burrell, G., & Morgan, C. (1979). *Social paradigms and organizational analysis.* London: Heinemann.

Cooper, A. (1978, May 27). House Democratic whips: Counting, coaxing, cajoling. *Congressional Quarterly Weekly Report,* pp. 1301-1306.

Cronen, V. E., Pearce, W. B., & Harris, L. M. (1982). The coordinated management of meaning. In F.E.X. Dance (Ed.), *Human communication theory* (pp. 61-89). New York: Harper & Row.

Deal, T. E., & Kennedy, A. A. (1982). *Corporate cultures.* Reading, MA: Addison-Wesley.

Deetz, S. (1982). Critical interpretive research in organizational communication. *Western Journal of Speech Communication, 46,* 131-149.

Edwards, W. (1954). The theory of decision making. *Psychological Bulletin, 51,* 380-417.

Evered, R., & Louis, M. R. (1981). Alternative perspectives in the organizational sciences: "Inquiry from the inside" and "inquiry from the outside." *Academy of Management Review, 6,* 385-396.

Fairhurst, G. T., Green, S. G., & Snavely, B. K. (in press). Face support in controlling poor performance. *Human Communication Research.*

Faulkner, R. R. (1982). Improvising on a triad. In J. Van Maanen, J. M. Dabbs, Jr., & R. R. Faulkner (Eds.), *Varieties of qualitative research.* Beverly Hills, CA: Sage.

Garfinkel, H. (1967). *Studies in ethnomethodology.* Englewood Cliffs, NJ: Prentice-Hall.

Geertz, C. (1983). *The interpretation of cultures.* New York: Basic Books.

Gibb, J. R. (1961). Defensive communication. *Journal of Communication, 11,* 141-168.

Glaser, B. G., & Strauss, A. L. (1967). *The discovery of grounded theory.* Chicago: Aldine.

Goody, E. N. (1978). Towards a theory of questions. In E. N. Goody (Ed.), *Questions and politeness: Strategies in social interaction* (pp. 17-43). Cambridge: Cambridge University Press.

Green, S. G. & Fairhurst, G. T. (1981, August). Episodes and rules: The context of managerial control. In *Doing power.* Symposium conducted at the National Academy of Management, San Diego.

Green, S. G., Fairhurst, G. T., & Liden, R. C. (1981). *Control of ineffective performance: History and sequences.* Unpublished manuscript, University of Cincinnati.

Green, S. G., Fairhurst, G. T., & Snavely, B. K. (1983). *Context, history, and outcomes in the control of poor performance.* Paper presented at the annual conference of the Academy of Management, Dallas.

Hall, A. D., & Fagan, R. W. (1956). Definitions of a system. *General Systems, 1.*

Harré, R. (1977). The ethnogenic approach: Theory and practice. In L. Berkowitz (Ed.), *Advances in experimental social psychology* (Vol. 10). New York: Academic.

Harré, R., & Secord, P. E. (1973). *The explanation of social behavior.* Totowa, NJ: Littlefield, Adams.

Jick, T. D. (1979). Mixing qualitative and quantitative methods: Triangulation in action. *Administrative Science Quarterly, 24,* 602-612.

Kellerman, D. F. (Ed.). (1975). *New Webster's dictionary of the English language.* New York: Consolidated.

Kelly, G. A. (1955). *A theory of personality.* New York: Norton.

Kiesler, S., & Sproull, L. (1982). Managerial response to changing environments: Perspectives on problem sensing from social cognition. *Administrative Science Quarterly, 27,* 548-570.

Lee, W. (1971) *Decision theory and human behavior.* New York: John Wiley.

Liden, R. C. (1981). *Contextual and behavioral factors influencing perceptions of ineffective performance and managerial responses.* Unpublished doctoral dissertation, University of Cincinnati.

Lord, R. G., Binning, J. F., Rush, M., & Thomas, J. C. (1978). The effect of performance cues and leader behavior on questionnaire ratings of leadership behavior. *Organizational Behavior and Human Performance, 21,* 27-39.

Louis, M. R. (1980). Surprise and sense making: What newcomers experience in entering unfamiliar organizational settings. *Administrative Science Quarterly, 25,* 226-251.

Louis, M. R. (1981). A cultural perspective on organizations: The need for and consequences of viewing organizations as culture-bearing milieux. *Human Systems Management, 2,* 246-258.

Markus, H. (1977). Self-schemata and processing information about the self. *Journal of Personality and Social Psychology, 35,* 63-78.

Mills, C. W. (1940). Situated actions and vocabularies of motives. *American Sociological Review, 5,* 904-913.

Minsky, M. A. (1975). A framework for representing knowledge. In P. Winston (Ed.), *The psychology of computer vision.* New York: McGraw-Hill.

Mitchell, T. R., Green, S. G., & Wood, R. E. (1981). An attributional model of leadership and the poor performing subordinate: Development and validation. In B. Staw & L. Cummings (Eds.), *Research in organizational behavior.* Greenwich, CT: JAI.

Mitchell, T. R., & Wood, R. E. (1979). An empirical test of an attributional model of leaders' responses to poor performance. *Proceedings of the National Meetings of the Academy of Management.*

Morgan, G., & Smircich, L. (1980). The case for qualitative research. *Academy of Management Review, 5,* 491-500.

Neisser, V. (1976). *Cognition and reality: Principles and implications of cognitive psychology.* San Francisco: W. H. Freeman.

Norman, D. A., & Bobrow, D. G. (1975). On the role of active memory processes in perception and cognition. In C. Cofer (Ed.), *The structure of human memory.* San Francisco: W. H. Freeman.

O'Reilly, C. A., III, & Weitz, B. A. (1980). Managing marginal employees: The use of warnings and dismissals. *Administrative Science Quarterly, 25,* 467-483.

Pacanowsky, M. E., & O'Donnell-Trujillo, N. (1982). Communication and organizational cultures. *Western Journal of Communication, 46,* 115-130.

Pacanowsky, M. E., & O'Donnell-Trujillo, N. (1983). Organizational communication as cultural performance. *Communication Monographs, 50,* 126-147.

Pettigrew, A. M. (1979). On studying organizational cultures. *Administrative Science Quarterly, 24,* 570-581.

Pondy, L. R. (1978). Leadership is a language game. In M. W. McCall, Jr., & M. M. Lombardo (Eds.), *Leadership: Where else can we go?* Durham, NC: Duke University Press.

Putnam, L. L. (1983). The interpretive perspective: An alternative to functionalism. In L. L. Putnam & M. E. Pacanowsky (Eds.), *Communication and organizations: An interpretive approach* (pp. 31-54). Beverly Hills, CA: Sage.

Rotter, J. B. (1966). Generalized expectancies for internal versus external control of reinforcement. *Psychological Monographs, 80.*

Schank, R. C., & Abelson, R. P. (1977). *Scripts, plans, goals, and understanding.* Hillsdale, NJ: Lawrence Erlbaum.

Schneider, D. J. (1973). Implicit personality theory: A review. *Psychological Bulletin, 79,* 294-309.

Scott, M. B., & Lyman, S. M. (1968). Accounts. *American Sociological Review, 33,* 46-62.

Searle, J. R. (1969). *Speech acts: An essay in the philosophy of language.* Cambridge: Cambridge University Press.

Stryker, S. (1957). Role-taking accuracy and adjustment. *Sociometry, 20,* 286-296.

Taylor, S. E., & Crocker, J. (1981). Schematic bases of social information processing. In E. T. Higgens, C. P. Herman, & M. P. Zanna (Eds.), *Social cognition: The Ontario Symposium* (Vol. 1). Hillsdale, NJ: Lawrence Erlbaum.

Tesser, A. (1978). Self-generated attitude change. In L. Berkowitz (Ed.), *Advances in experimental social psychology* (Vol. 2). New York: Academic.

Tompkins, P. R., & Cheney, G. (1982). *The uses of account analysis: A study of organizational decision making and identification.* Paper presented at the annual meetings of the International Communication Association, Boston.

Tversky, A. (1977). Features of similarity. *Psychological Review, 84,* 327-352.

Van Maanen, J. (1976). Breaking in: Socialization to work. In R. Dubin (Ed.), *Handbook of work, organization, and society* (pp. 67-130). Chicago: Rand McNally.

Van Maanen, J. (Ed.). (1979). Qualitative methods. *Administrative Science Quarterly, 24,* 519-711.

Van Maanen, J., Dabbs, J. M., Jr., & Faulkner, R. R. (1982). *Varieties of qualitative research.* Beverly Hills, CA: Sage.

Van Maanen, J., & Schein, E. H. (1979). Toward a theory of organizational socialization. In B. M. Staw (Ed.), *Research in organizational behavior* (Vol. 1, pp. 209-264). Greenwich, CT: JAI.

Watzlawick, P., Beavin, J. H., & Jackson, D. D. (1967). *Pragmatics of human communication.* New York: Norton.

Weick, K. (1969). *The social psychology of organizing* (2nd ed.). Reading, MA: Addison-Wesley.

Weick, K. (1976). Educational organizations as loosely coupled systems. *Administrative Science Quarterly, 21,* 1-19.

Weick, K. (1977). Enactment processes in organizations. In B. M. Staw & G. Salancik (Eds.), *New directions in organizational behavior.* Chicago: St. Clair.

22 ● Assimilating New Members into Organizations

FREDRIC M. JABLIN

University of Texas— Austin

P ROBABLY without question, communication scholars would agree at the theoretical level that communication is a dynamic, ongoing process (for example, see Berlo, 1960). Yet few of us, in researching human communication, regardless of the setting, study it as a process. Rather, most investigations are typified by one-shot, static research designs. This is particularly true of organizational communication research, despite the fact that we frequently admonish one another for failing to consider *time* as a major independent variable (Dennis, Goldhaber, & Yates, 1978; Richetto, 1977). As Dennis et al. (1978, p. 264) observe, there is an obvious and immediate need to "replace the historical emphasis on the one-shot case study and/ or the single measurement of variables undifferentiated in terms of their time-bound or time-free properties" and replace them with longitudinal and time-series research.

The investigation reported here is of a longitudinal and developmental study of the process by which new employees are assimilated into their organizations' communication systems. An inherent assumption of this research is that time may be a major independent variable affecting the development of organizational communication attitudes and behaviors. Further, an underlying supposition of this research is that recruits typically enter an organization with work-related communication histories as well as expectations of the communication environments of their new jobs and organizations. These factors, as well as actual communication-related experiences on their new jobs, are posited to interact in a developmental fashion to create within new employees an understanding of what their organizations consider to be "appropriate" communication behavior and perceptions of their organizations' communication climates/cultures. In summary, this study is exploratory in nature and part of an ongoing programs of research attempting to answer the following question: How do organizational members, and in particular new recruits, become assimilated into (and remain assimilated in) organizational communication systems?

REVIEW OF THE LITERATURE

Organizational Assimilation

"Organizational assimilation refers to the process by which organizational members become a part of, or are absorbed into, the culture of an organization" (Jablin, 1982, p. 256). This process, in turn, can be divided into two reciprocal components: (1) the organization's efforts to "socialize" the new employee, and (2) the new employee's attempts to "individualize" his or her role in the organization. Elsewhere I have recently described these processes in detail (Jablin, 1982); consequently, the following review is merely an abstracted version of this earlier presentation.

Organizational Socialization

Van Maanen (1975a, p. 67) suggests the following general definition of organizational socialization: "the process by which a person learns the values, norms and required behaviors which permit him to participate as a member of the organization." Schein (1968, p. 2) adds that is is also the "process of 'learning the ropes,' the process of being indoctrinated and trained, the process of being taught what is important in an organization." Further, in exploring organizational socialization it is imperative to keep in mind that the process is a continuous one that will "change and evolve as the individual remains longer with the organization" (Porter, Lawler, & Hackman, 1975, p. 161). Moreover, most researchers and theorists are in agreement that organizational socialization is "best viewed as a special division of the more general adult socialization model" (Van Maanen, 1975a, p. 69).

The organizational socialization process is generally depicted as involving a number of sequential phases or stages. The initial stage in the process has been labeled the "prearrival" (Porter et al., 1975) or "anticipatory socialization" stage (Van Maanen, 1975a). Feldman (1976, p. 434) notes that "the main activities the individual engages in at this stage are forming expectations about jobs—transmitting, receiving, and evaluating information with prospective employers—and making decisions about employment." Thus as a result of an individual's education, previous work experience, cultural background, and the like, and the organization's recruitment procedures (see Wanous, 1980), the prospective employee acquires a set of expectations about what life will be like in the organization. Consequently, if the prospective recruit does become a member of the organization, the "organization's socialization process does not construct a brand-new individual, so to speak, but rather attempts to reconstruct him" (Porter et al., 1975, p. 164).

Upon entry into the organization the recruit begins the "encounter" phase of socialization. Sometimes this encounter can be a "reality shock"

(Hughes, 1958), but more often it "involves a pattern of day-to-day experiences in which the individual is subjected to the reinforcement policies and practices of the organization and its members" (Porter et al., 1975, p. 164). Basically, if the recruit's expectations resulting from anticipatory socialization are accurate with the reality of organizational life, the encounter stage is one of reaffirmation and reinforcement of existing beliefs and behaviors. On the other hand, if the new employee's expectations are not congruent with organizational reality, the stage involves a "destructive phase (analytically similar to the Lewinian concept of unfreezing) which serves to detach the individual from his former expectations" (Van Maanen, 1975a, p. 84).

The final major stage in the organizational socialization process has been termed the "metamorphosis" (Van Maanen, 1975a) or "change and acquisition" phase (Porter et al., 1975). As a result of his or her "encounters," the recruit during this stage attempts to become an accepted, participating member of the organization by learning new attitudes and behaviors or modifying existing ones to be consistent with the organization's expectations. Caplow (1964) suggests four acquisition requirements: (1) developing a new self-image, (2) establishing new interpersonal relationships, (3) acquiring new values, and (4) learning a new set of behaviors (Schein, 1968, notes that these behaviors can be subdivided into those that are "pivotal," "relevant," and "peripheral").

In summary, organizational socialization can be characterized as the process by which new (and continuing) organizational members learn and adapt to the norms, expectations, and perspectives of their organizations and its members. As Schein (1968) observes, this adaption is often "defined as the price of membership" in the organization.

Individualization

While most organizational assimilation research has focused on the process from the organization's perspective (that is, socialization), there is an equally important reciprocal process occurring from the employee's perspective—"individualization." As Porter et al. (1975, p. 170) suggest, "At the same time that an organization is attempting to put its distinctive stamp on the individual, he in turn is striving to influence the organization so that it can better satisfy his ideas about how it can best be operated."

Numerous classification schemes have been developed to describe employee individualization behaviors (for example, see Schein, 1968; Van Maanen, 1975a). However, regardless of the classification method, it is probably most important to note that "(1) the intensity of an employee's individualization efforts is often determined by the magnitude of the organization's socialization attempts, and (2) individualization initiatives occur along a continuum from high to low in intensity" (Jablin, 1982, p. 258), though they are often presented in the literature as discrete "types."

In addition, it is essential to observe that most existing research indicates that a recruit's superior is of central importance to the employee's individualization efforts (see Graen & Ginzburgh, 1977; Katz & Tushman, 1983; Weiss, 1977). As Graen (1976, p. 1206) argues:

> One of the crucial mechanisms that is assumed to modify the role during the process of assimilating a new member into the organization . . . is the interpersonal exchange relationship between the new role incumbent (member) and his immediate superior (leader). Although other members of the new person's role set can enter the negotiation of the definition of the new person's role, their bargaining tools are limited to informal sanctions. Only the leader is granted the authority to impose formal sanctions to back up his negotiations.

In summary, most existing research suggests that new organizational members can take an active part in defining their organizational roles and that the primary individuals who negotiate this set of expectations with recruits are their immediate supervisors. As Porter et al. (1975, p. 184) observe, "To the new hire, the supervisor *is* the organization. If he is good, the organization is usually viewed favorably. If he is ineffective in working with the newcomer, the organization itself is seen negatively."

Job Expectations and the Initial Employment Period

Most job turnover studies indicate that the first few months of a recruit's employment are critical to his or her development of "healthy" attitudes and behavior patterns within the organization (see, for example, Berlew & Hall, 1966; Dunnette, Avery, & Banas, 1973; Gomersall & Myers, 1966; Herzberg, Mausner, Peterson, & Capwell, 1957; Schein, 1968). As Porter et al. (1975, p. 178) note, "It is in this initial period of contact that the two sets of expectations—those of the individual and those of the organization—come into direct confrontation." Thus it is not surprising to discover that there is evidence suggesting that job turnover is higher among employees during this "break-in" period than at any other time (see Brodman & Hellman, 1947, cited in Herzberg et al., 1957).

Research has also revealed that when an employee first begins work in an organization he or she experiences a considerable amount of ambiguity, stress, and anxiety (Gomersall & Myers, 1966). However, at the same time, new employees do have certain specific expectations about their job duties and work environments, including the type of supervision they will receive (Jones, 1983; Porter et al., 1975; Porter & Steers, 1973). In fact, Porter and

Steers (1973), in an extensive review of research on employee turnover and absenteeism, suggest that employees who experience "met expectations" have a lower turnover rate than employees whose expectations are not met. In addition, there is considerable evidence indicating that employees who have realistic expectations (usually obtained via job previews) of their job duties and environments are more satisfied with their jobs and have a lower turnover rate than employees who do not have realistic expectations (see, for example, Ilgen & Seely, 1974; Macedonia, 1969; Wanous, 1980; Weitz, 1956; Youngberg, 1963). Further, research by Schneider (1972, 1973; Schneider & Hall, 1972) suggests that if new employees have accurate perceptions of the "climates" of their organizations when they initially begin work, they will be more satisfied with their jobs and organizations and have a higher probability of job survival. Additionally, at least one study has demonstrated that those individuals who have realistic expectations tend to have better on-the-job performance than those persons who do not have realistic expectations (Gomersall & Myers, 1966).

In summary, organizational assimilation has been viewed as a process containing two basic reciprocal dimensions: organizational socialization and employee individualization. Moreover, the organizational socialization process has been described as involving at least three major phases—anticipatory socialization, encounter, and metamorphosis. Furthermore, it has been noted that the recruit's individualization efforts are closely related to his or her relationship with his or her immediate superior, as well as the intensity of the organization's socialization process. Finally, as indicated above, it appears that a recruit's initial employment tenure in an organization is crucial to his or her development of "healthy" work-related attitudes and behaviors. Specifically, there seems to be a strong correlation between a recruit's initial expectations about job duties and the work environment and his or her later job satisfaction and job survival.

THE PRESENT STUDY

While in recent years organizational psychologists and sociologists have increasingly focused attention on describing and analyzing organizational assimilation processes, little research has been pursued in this area by communication scholars (with some notable exceptions). This is quite ironic given that communication plays perhaps the key role in the organizational assimilation process (Elsea, 1979). The effect of this paucity of communication research on our knowledge of organizational assimilation is particularly obvious when one examines extant studies in the area. For example, while several assimilation studies have examined relationships between job expectations and organizational outcome variables (such as turnover), they have in only a peripheral manner focused attention on the role that expectations about the communication environment play upon job satisfaction and job survival. Yet some of these investigations conclude that changes in organizational communication approaches and procedures during the break-in period can reduce later job turnover and increase job performance and job satisfaction (for example, see Gomersall & Myers, 1966). While such conclusions *may* be valid, research *explicitly* exploring the role of communication in the organizational assimilation process is needed before we can accept the validity of such assertions.

Consequently, the purpose of the present study is to explore the relationships among "anticipatory organizational communication socialization," "organizational communication encounter," and "organizational communication metamorphosis." Moreover, data pertinent to both the organization's *and* the recruit's perceptions and behaviors during these stages of the assimilation process are presented (when available). Specific research questions related to each of the assimilation phases are elucidated below.

Anticipatory Organizational
Communication Socialization

As noted earlier, the anticipatory socialization phase of organizational assimilation occurs prior to a recruit's entry into an organization. Two very basic components of a recruit's anticipatory organizational socialization are his or her previous work experiences and his or her expectations about the communication system and environment of the new organization. The importance of previous job/organizational experiences in the organizational assimilation process has recently been stressed by Jones (1983, p. 466), who suggests that "the extent and variety of past experiences in, for example, other organizational contexts and in dealing with a wide variety of role holders will affect the way newcomers respond to new situations." However, as Jones (1983, p. 465) also observes, to date "little attention has been paid to the events in the newcomer's life that occur before entry."

On the other hand, a considerable amount of research attention has focused on recruits' initial expectations of their new organizations' climates and their propensities for later job turnover (see earlier discussion). However, no existing research has explicitly explored recruits' expectations of the communication environments of their new jobs/organizations and the relationships of these variables to job survival. Moreover, the effects of recruits' retrospections about the communication environments of their past jobs on their expectations of the communication environments of their new jobs remains unexplored. Thus this study will attempt to answer the following research questions:

Q_1: Do new recruits who later voluntarily withdraw from their organizations and those who stay differ in their perceptions of the communication environments of their last jobs?

Q_2: Do new recruits who later voluntarily withdraw from their organizations and those who stay differ in their initial expectations of their organizations' climates?

Q_3: Do new recruits' perceptions of the communication climates of their last jobs and their expectations of the communication climates of their new jobs interact to affect their job survival?

Organizational Communication Encounter

Upon entry into a new organization and during the initial weeks of employment, the recruit experiences the "encounter" phase of assimilation. It is during this period that the new employee will probably feel the most "role shock" and will realize the degree to which his or her job and organizational expectations are congruent with the "reality" of organizational life. Consequently, during the encounter stage the effects of the "met expectations hypothesis" (see earlier discussion) will probably have its greatest impact.

As suggested earlier, the basic position advanced by the met expectations hypothesis is that "when an individual's expectations—whatever they are—are not substantially met, his propensity to withdraw [will] increase" (Porter & Steers, 1973, p. 152). While previous research has focused on exploring the met expectations hypothesis as it relates to recruits' initial job expectations and their later attitudes and turnover propensities (see Gomersall & Myers, 1966; Schneider, 1972; Wanous, 1977), none of these inquiries have focused specifically on the potential associations between recruits' attributions of their new organizations' communication systems and their subsequent attitudes and job survival. However, given the encouraging results of Schneider's (1972) research, which peripherally tapped a number of communication climate dimensions (such as managerial support and structure), it does not seem unreasonable to conjecture that such relationships may exist. Specifically, it might be argued that recruits who possess more inflated expectations of their organizations' communication climates will have greater difficulty meeting those "unrealistic" expectations once on the job than recruits with less inflated expectations. In turn, as a result of the large discrepancies between expectations and reality, recruits with inflated communication climate expectations may have a higher probability of job turnover. Consequently, this research will attempt to answer the following research question:

Q_4: Do new recruits' expectations of the communication climates of their new jobs and their perceptions of these factors after six weeks of employment interact to affect their job survival?

In addition, since at present little is known about the nature of the "actual" communication interactions recruits experience during the encounter phase of assimilation, or their attitudes toward these interactions, this study will also attempt to answer the following question:

Q_5: What kinds of interaction episodes characterize the new employee's communication during his or her entry period of employment (third week of work), and how does the new employee feel about these interactions?

Organizational Communication Metamorphosis

During the metamorphosis stage of assimilation the new recruit attempts to become an "accepted" member of the organization by learning "accepted" attitudes and behaviors and/or modifying existing ones. Communication-related research on the metamorphosis stage is scarce, but Feldman and Brett (1983), in a study of exempt employees in a consumer products firm, report that new hires during their initial six months of employment actively seek out information from others concerning job duties, performance appraisal procedures, coworkers, and specific task responsibilities. In addition, Feldman and Brett report that recruits generally attempt to develop a social support network during this period. Thus, in an attempt to replicate Feldman and Brett's research and explore further communication-related attitudes and behaviors during the metamorphosis stage, this study will attempt to answer the following research questions:

Q_6: Do new recruits' perceptions of the communication climates of their jobs/ organizations differ among their sixth, twelfth, eighteenth, and twenty-fourth weeks of employment?

Q_7: Do potential differences between recruits' perceptions of the communication climates of their jobs/organizations during the metamorphosis stage (operationalized as sixth through twenty-fourth weeks of employment) interact to affect their job survival?

Q_8: What kinds of interaction episodes characterize the new employee's communication during the metamorphosis period of employment (here operationalized by one point in time—ninth week of work), and how does she or he feel about these interactions?

Q_9: What differences exist between the interaction episodes that characterize the new employee's communication during the encounter (third week) and metamorphosis (ninth week) stages of assimilation?

Q_{10}: What differences exist between the new employee's attitudes toward his or her communication interaction episodes during the encounter (third week) and metamorphosis (ninth week) stages of assimilation?

In addition, as noted earlier, research has shown that the new employee's supervisor plays a key role in the recruit's assimilation into the organization. Given that the metamorphosis stage is a period in which the recruit strives to learn appropriate attitudes and behaviors, it would seem to follow that to the extent that the recruit's immediate supervisor understands the recruit's "sense-making" (Louis, 1980), the greater the probability of effective assimilation. In other words, it is likely that if a recruit's supervisor understands how the recruit is experiencing the job and organization, the supervisor will be in a better position to assist the recruit in learning necessary work-related behaviors and attitudes. As Jones (1983, p. 467) observes, "A distance or gap between the perceptions of newcomers and the perception of significant others . . . makes the learning process ambiguous." Moreover, given that existing research on established superior-subordinate communication relationships indicates substantial amounts of "semantic/information distance" between members of the dyad (see Jablin, 1979), the question naturally follows whether or not this phenomena characterizes this relationship even during its early stages of development.

Further, it should be noted that it is likely that if a large gap in understanding exists between superior and subordinate during the metamorphosis stage of assimilation, it will be very difficult for the recruit to negotiate (individualize) his or her role with the superior (see Graen, 1976). Failure of superiors and subordinates to achieve mutually satisfying role negotiations may thus result in increased employee turnover. In summary, based on the preceding discussion, this study will attempt to answer the following research questions:

Q_{11}: What differences exist between a new employee's perceptions of his or her organization's communication climate during the metamorphosis stage (sixth, twelfth, and eighteenth weeks of employment) of assimilation and his or her supervisor's perceptions of the recruit's perceptions of communication climate?

Q_{12}: Do potential differences in a new employee's perceptions of his or her organization's communication climate during the metamorphosis period and his or her supervisor's perceptions of the recruit's perceptions of communication climate interact to affect the new employee's job survival?

Finally, in an attempt to determine the extent to which recruits' perceptions of their organizations' communication systems are related to recruits' job performance, the following research question is posed:

Q_{13}: To what degree are a recruit's perceptions of his or her organization's communication system related to the recruit's job performance during the metamorphosis period (sixth, twelfth, and eighteenth weeks of employment) of organizational assimilation?

METHODOLOGY

Research Setting

The Organizations

Data for the study were collected from three different nursing homes located in the same large midwestern city. The nursing homes were approximately equal in size (containing roughly 200 beds), and provided health care primarily to elderly patients. The nursing homes were quite similar in organizational structure, and provided new employees with their own two-week in-house orientation/training programs.

The Subjects

All subjects participating in the study were newly hired nursing assistants. In total, usable data were collected from 44 subjects: 13 from one nursing home, 15 from the second, and 16 from the third. Participants in the research can be characterized as follows: Approximately 95 percent of the subjects were female and 5 percent male; the great majority of both groups (73 percent) were under 25 years of age. Approximately 70 percent of the participants had no more than a high school education. Approximately 95 percent of the subjects had held at least one job in the last ten years, though 91 percent of the aides had no previous working experience in a health care institution. On their last jobs, approximately 70 percent of the subjects perceived themselves to be in the lower levels of their organizations' hierarchies.[1]

Procedure

During a period of approximately six weeks, any nursing assistants who were hired at the nursing homes were asked to participate in the study; all recruits participated willingly in the research. Since each of the nursing homes provided newly hired nursing assistants with in-service orientation/ training, data were initially collected from subjects early in the morning during their first day of instruction (which in all cases was also the first day of employment). The researcher initiated these sessions by explaining the nature of the investigation, responding to questions, and assuring participants of the anonymity of all information collected from them. In addition, all subjects were requested to sign a release of information allowing the researcher to obtain information from their personnel records; all subjects complied with this request. Participants were then asked to complete two "organizational communication questionnaires." Recruits were instructed to respond to one of these questionnaires in terms of what they *expected* communication would be like in their new jobs and organizations, and to the second questionnaire in terms of what communication was like in their *last* jobs and organizations. The questionnaires themselves were identical. Upon completing the questionnaires, participants were thanked for their assistance and were informed that some of them would be contacted in a few weeks to provide some additional information.

During the third week of work (which in all cases was also the first week that employees were working alone on the job) a sample (33 percent) of nursing assistants were requested to keep a communication log for one day during the middle of their work weeks. These logs were designed to provide self-reports of all communication interactions the subjects were involved in during that day, and the aides' attitudes toward these interactions.

After six weeks of employment all subjects were again contacted and requested to complete the organizational communication questionnaire, but this time in terms of what communication was actually like on their new jobs. In addition, at this point each nursing assistant's supervisor was asked to complete the same questionnaire, but to respond to the items as he or she believed the subordinate would if the subordinate were completing the questionnaire. Each supervisor was also asked at this time to provide an appraisal (via an appraisal rating form) of his or her subordinate's job performance.

During their ninth weeks of employment those aides who had completed the communication logs earlier were contacted again and asked to complete another log for a day. However, because of attrition, only seven of the fourteen aides who had completed the first log completed the second (this resulted in a 23 percent sample, given the attrition to that point in time).

After 12, 18, and 24 weeks of employment, all subjects (who still worked at the homes) were again contacted and asked to complete the organizational communication questionnaire. Similarly, each subordinate's superior was contacted at these points and asked to complete the questionnaire with respect to how she or he felt the subordinate would respond. Further, job performance appraisals were collected from the superiors for their subordinates at each of these three points.

The Questionnaires

The organizational communication questionnaire utilized in this research is an eclectic instrument exploring a number of facets of organizational communication climate. Since previous research has indicated that the superior-subordinate relationship is especially important in the organizational assimilation process (for example, see Porter et al., 1975; Weiss, 1977), greater emphasis was placed on exploring perceptions of the climate of superior-subordinate communication than on other areas. The major component scales of the questionnaire are described below.

A number of scales were abstracted from the ICA Communication Audit (Goldhaber & Rogers, 1978):

(1) *Receiving information from others* (15 items): Asks respondents to indicate the amount of information they receive on a variety of topics, for example, job duties, organizational policies, pay and benefits, problems faced by management.

(2) *Sending information to others* (7 items): Asks respondents to indicate the amount of information they send on a variety of topics, for example, reporting what they are doing on the job, reporting job-related problems, asking for work instructions.

(3) *Sources of information* (8 items): Asks respondents to indicate the amount of information they are receiving from a variety of sources, such as coworkers, immediate supervisor, department meetings, grapevine.

(4) *Timeliness of information received* (5 items): Asks respondents to indicate the extent to which the information they receive from their sources is timely, for example, from coworkers, immediate supervisor, management, grapevine.

(5) *Channels of information* (7 items): Asks respondents to indicate the amount of information they receive through a variety of channels, such as face-to-face contact, group interactions, telephone, writing, bulletin boards.

(6) *Organizational outcomes*/satisfaction (13 items): Asks respondents to indicate the degree to which they are satisfied with a number of "outcomes," such as job, pay, progress in organization, work, rewards, organization's communication.

(7) *Satisfaction with coworkers* (3 items): Abstracted from the Organizational Communication Relationships scale of the ICA Communication Audit.

(8) *Satisfaction with management* (4 items): Abstracted from the Organizational Communication Relationships scale of the ICA Communication Audit.

For each of the above scales, subjects responded to items on five-point, Likert-type scales with responses ranging from "a very great extent" (scored 5) to "a very little extent" (scored 1).

The remaining scales contained in the questionnaire focused upon aspects of the superior-subordinate communication relationship:

(1) *Superior-subordinate communicative openness* (15 items): Assesses the climate of openness in message sending and message receiving in superior-subordinate interaction (Jablin, 1978).

(2) *Superior's upward influence* (13 items, 2 subscales): Assesses subordinates' perceptions of their superior's upward hierarchical influence. Includes items indicative of two major areas of upward influence: influence on *strategic* (personnel and administrative) decisions, and influence on *work-related* decisions (Jablin, 1980).

(3) *Subordinate's work dependency* (5 items): Assesses a subordinate's work-related dependency on superior.; For example, the extent to which the supervisor personally assigns the subordinate's work, sets work procedures, and establishes standards of quality. A factor analysis (principal-components varimax rotation) of this scale revealed it to be unidimensional in structure.

(4) *Supervisory leadership* (13 items, 4 subscales): Developed by Taylor and Bowers (1972) to assess four basic dimensions of supervisory leadership: supervisory *supportiveness* (3 items), supervisory *work facilitation* (4 items), supervisory *interaction facilitation* (3 items), and supervisory *goal emphasis* (3 items).

(5) *JDI-supervision* (18 items): Assesses satisfaction with supervision (Smith, Kendall, & Hulin, 1969).

With the exception of JDI-supervision, all of the above scales were responded to on five-point, Likert-type scales with responses ranging from "a very great extent" (scored 5) to "a very little extent" (scored 1). JDI-supervision was responded to on three-point scales (yes, ?, no) and was scored by a weighting method described by Smith et al. (1969).[2]

The Communication Log

As noted earlier, a sample of subjects completed the communication log for one day during their third and ninth weeks of employment. The third week of work was chosen for the initial administration of the logs since it was the first week in which new employees worked alone on the job. During the first two weeks of employment recruits were receiving classroom instruction, working with other (typically more experienced) nursing assistants, or both. Thus it was felt that logs completed during the third week of work, rather than earlier, would be a more accurate indicant of the types of interactions the new employee could be expected to experience initially in his or her work environment. The ninth week of work was selected for the second log administration because of the high rate of turnover in the nursing homes (a later administration would have reduced the sample size beyond the point of practicality).

The communication log was adapted from those used in earlier research by Burns (1954) and Lawler, Porter, and Tennenbaum (1968). The log asked the employee to report factual information about each interaction episode she or he was involved in during the day, as well as her or his attitude toward each of the episodes. In a method similar to that used by Lawler, et al., five semantic differential scales were utilized to tap the employee's "global evaluation" of each episode (valuable-worthless, satisfying-dissatisfying, interesting-boring, precise-vague, challenging-not challenging).

Each employee who completed the communication log was given a pocket-size booklet containing the self-recording forms. The instructions for using the forms followed those used by Lawler et al. (1968), and asked the employee to complete a form "at the conclusion of each behavioral episode that occurs during the working day." A behavioral episode was defined as "any situation that has an integrity of its own." The researcher carefully explained each question on the form to each of the subjects, and, to ensure that each individual understood the procedure, provided several hypothetical interactions and asked the subject to indicate how she or he would complete the form. The subject was then provided with an envelope in which to place the completed communication log booklet and was assigned a location in which to deposit the booklet upon completing the log.

The Performance Appraisal

Prior to initiating the investigation, the researcher obtained from each of the nursing homes copies of the appraisal forms that supervisors used to evaluate the performance of nursing assistants. Since these forms were quite similar in evaluation criteria, a new eclectic standardized form was constructed that included criteria from each of the original forms. Five major levels of performance were included in the evaluation criteria: job skills, dependability, personal relationships, emotional stability, and personal appearance. In total, the appraisal form contained thirty items on which supervisors rated their subordinates' performance on five-point scales (excellent, good, satisfactory, poor, failure). A reliability analysis on data collected from the scale indicated that it was internally consistent (Cronbach's alpha = .98), though somewhat negatively skewed (mean = 113,87, s.d. = 19.01, median = 113.00).

Job Turnover

Information concerning turnover among the aides was obtained via an examination of organizational records. During the six months in which data for this study were collected, employee turnover across the three nursing homes was approximately 67 percent. Though this may seem like a very high turnover rate, it was typical of the turnover rate previously experienced by these facilities (and for this service industry in general).

Data Analysis

Since an examination of the median zero-order correlation coefficients among the scales contained within the organizational communication questionnaire indicated considerable collinearity between the variables, multivariate statistical techniques were used to test the research questions (when applicable). For the majority of the research questions, orthogonal, generalized multivariate analyses of variance (MANOVA) were used to explore the data. Repeated measures analyses were not feasible because of the attrition that was experienced among the subjects across the time periods during which data were collected. The use of the orthogonal analyses represents a more conservative series of tests of the research questions than would result from a set of repeated measures analyses. Consequently, results reported here represent conservative rather than liberal estimates of statistical significance. Significant effects within the MANOVAs were explored by examination of univariate F-ratios and related univariate statistical probing procedures. A series of stepwise multiple regression analyses were utilized to explore the last research question. The alpha level for all statistical tests was set a the .05 level of significance.

RESULTS

Research Questions 1, 2, and 3

Taken together, the first three research questions addressed whether or not recruits' job retrospections and expectations differed and/or interacted to affect their job survival. These questions were explored through a 2 × 2 MANOVA in which the job expectations and job retrospections of those recruits who voluntarily withdrew and remained in their organizations through the sixth week of work were compared.

Results of the MANOVA revealed a nonsignificant interaction effect (mult. $F = .73$, df = 17,64, $p < .76$, $R^2 = .16$), but a significant main effect for job expectations/retrospections ($F = 2.52$, df = 17,64, $p < .004$, $R^2 = .40$). In addition, the main effect for job turnover approached statistical significance ($F = 1.53$, df = 17,64, $p < .10$, $R^2 = .29$). An examination of the univariate effects for the significant retrospections/expectations effect revealed statistically significant differences for information received from others ($F = 4.25$, df = 1,80, $p < .04$), information sent to others $F = 4.07$, df = 1,80, $p < .05$), sources of information ($F = 3.88$, df = 1,80, $p < .05$), the timeliness of information ($F = 5,14$, df = 1,80, $p < .03$), the channels through which information would be received ($F = 4.02$, df = 1,80, $p < .05$), and organizational outcomes/overall job satisfaction ($F = 20.15$, df = 1,80, $p < .0005$). An examination of the univariate effects for job turnover ($p < .10$) indicated two statistically significant differences: sending information to others ($F = 4.44$, df = 1,80, $p < .04$) and organizational outcomes/overall job satisfaction ($F = 4.22$, df = 1,80, $p < .04$). Table 22.1 displays the means and standard deviations for the variables involved in the analysis of questions 1, 2, and 3.

Table 22.1

Means and Standard Deviations for Job/Organizational Retrospectives and Expectations, by Turnover Before the Sixth Week of Work (Anticipatory Socialization)

| Dependent Variables | Job/Organization Retrospectives | | | | Job/Organization Expectations | | | |
| | Job Withdrawers (n = 14) | | Job Survivors (n = 26)[a] | | Job Withdrawers (n = 14) | | Job Survivors (n = 30) | |
	Mean	S.D.	Mean	S.D.	Mean	S.D.	Mean	S.D.
Receive info	53.21	8.46	46.50	11.43	54.57	9.80	52.73	9.99
Send info	24.36	4.55	20.65	6.23	25.36	4.34	23.67	5.14
Sources info	25.50	7.31	23.69	6.63	28.86	4.49	26.17	6.57
Timely info	15.57	3.61	14.46	4.82	17.86	2.77	16.20	3.49
Channels info	22.14	6.05	21.27	5.11	23.79	3.79	23.73	4.84
Sup support	10.86	2.47	10.11	3.22	11.29	2.02	10.63	2.22
Sup work facil	13.57	3.25	12.58	3.93	13.71	3.22	13.70	2.63
Sup inter facil	10.21	1.93	9.85	2.96	11.50	1.79	10.63	1.96
Sup goal emp	11.21	2.42	10.73	2.97	11.64	2.41	11.60	1.83
Sup work influ	15.00	2.66	15.46	3.61	14.93	1.94	15.10	2.83
Sup strat influ	27.93	5.98	28.92	8.17	28.93	4.67	28.13	4.44
Sup-sub openness	52.43	15.61	48.00	17.70	52.21	11.12	51.30	10.65
Sub work depend	18.79	3.09	18.81	3.42	18.07	3.58	19.47	2.53
JDI-supervision	36.43	10.99	38.50	13.90	38.36	10.54	42.33	7.41
Sat coworkers	12.00	2.00	11.77	2.32	11.21	1.53	10.87	2.11
Sat management	13.29	2.64	12.46	3.43	14.36	2.71	13.00	3.37
Overall satisf	45.86	5.20	38.31	12.35	51.86	8.91	49.47	8.70

a. Four subjects had never before been employed.

An examination of Table 22.1 reveals that recruits expected to *receive* more information (53.32 versus 48.85), *send* more information (24.42 versus 21.95), receive more information from *key sources* (27.02 versus 24.33), receive more *timely* information (16.73 versus 14.85), receive information from more *channels* (23.75 versus 21.57), and be more *satisfied* on their new jobs (50.73 versus 40.95) than they were on their last jobs. In addition, to some degree results suggest that the withdrawers and survivors differed in their attitudes (retrospections and expectations taken together) of their organizations' communication climates. Specifically, withdrawers did/expected to *send* more information (24.23 versus 21.98) and be more *satisfied* with their jobs (49.21 versus 42.24) than did the job survivors.

Research Questions 4 and 5

Research question 4 concerned whether or not recruits' expectations of the communication climates of their new jobs and their perceptions of these factors after six weeks of employment interact to affect their job survival. On the other hand, research question 5 concerned the kinds of interactions that characterize recruits' communication interactions during their third week of employment, and their corresponding attitudes toward these interactions.

Question 4 was explored by a 2 × 2 MANOVA in which the job expectations of recruits on their first day of work were compared to their job perceptions after six weeks of work. Moreover, these expectations/perceptions were further examined with respect to whether or not the recruits withdrew or remained as members of their organizations after each period—that is, for expectations, was the recruit still employed at the six-week point of job tenure; for perceptions, was the recruit still employed at twelve weeks of job tenure.

Results of the MANOVA revealed a nonsignificant multivariate interaction effect ($F = .92$, df $= 17,54$, $p < .56$, $R^2 = .22$), as well as a nonsignificant main effect for job turnover ($F = .90$, df $= 17,54$, $p < .58$, $r^2 = .22$). However, the main effect for job expectations/perceptions was significant ($F = 3.31$, df $= 17,54$, $p < .001$, $R^2 = .51$). Examination of the univariate effects for job expectations/perceptions indicated significant differences for receiving information ($F = 28.61$, df $= 1,70$, $p < .0006$), sending information ($F = 10.92$, df $= 1.70$, $p < .001$), sources of information ($F = 8.71$, df $= 1,70$, $p < .004$), timeliness of information ($F = 9.00$, df $= 1,70$, $p < .002$), channels of information ($F = 10.55$, df $= 1,70$, $p < .002$), supervisor work facilitation ($F = 8.23$, df $= 1,70$, $p < .005$), supervisor interaction facilitation ($F = 9.70$, df $= 1,70$, $p < .003$), supervisor strategic upward influence ($F = 26.15$, df $= 1,70$, $p < .0006$), satisfaction with management ($F = 10.79$, df $= 1,70$, $p < .002$), and organizational outcomes/overall job satisfaction ($F = 16.28$, df $= 1,70$, $p < .0004$). Table 22.2 displays the means and standard deviations for the variables explored in the above analyses.

Table 22.2

Means and Standard Deviations for Job/Organizational Expectations at Sixth Week of Work, by Turnover After Each Period (Organizational Encounter)

| Dependent Variables | Job/Organization Expectations | | | | Job/Organization Perceptions – Sixth Week | | | |
| | Job Withdrawers (n = 14) | | Job Survivors (n = 30) | | Job Withdrawers (n = 8) | | Job Survivors (n = 22) | |
	Mean	S.D.	Mean	S.D.	Mean	S.D.	Mean	S.D.
Receive info	54.57	9.80	52.73	9.99	39.37	10.04	40.14	11.63
Send info	25.36	4.34	23.67	5.14	19.63	3.86	20.59	5.17
Sources info	28.86	4.49	26.17	6.57	21.25	7.23	23.14	6.22
Timely info	17.86	2.77	16.20	3.49	12.75	5.85	14.64	3.29
Channels info	23.79	3.79	23.73	4.84	18.63	4.84	20.64	5.23
Sup support	11.29	2.02	10.63	2.22	9.63	3.42	11.14	1.88
Sup work facil	13.71	3.22	13.70	2.63	10.38	4.10	12.14	3.06
Sup inter facil	11.50	1.79	10.63	1.96	8.50	2.51	9.77	1.97
Sup goal emp	11.64	2.41	11.60	1.83	8.88	3.68	11.27	2.05
Sup work influ	14.93	1.94	15.10	2.83	14.13	3.31	14.23	2.89
Sup strat influ	28.93	4.67	28.13	4.44	22.25	5.23	21.77	6.68
Sup-sub openness	52.21	11.12	51.30	10.65	44.13	15.80	49.64	10.48
Sub work depend	18.07	3.58	19.47	2.53	16.38	4.44	18.18	3.45
JDI-supervision	38.36	10.54	42.33	7.41	40.88	9.11	42.36	8.42
Sat coworkers	11.21	1.53	10.87	2.11	9.25	2.71	11.05	2.52
Sat management	14.36	2.71	13.00	3.37	10.25	3.73	10.95	3.64
Overall satisf	51.86	8.91	49.47	8.70	39.75	10.79	42.14	9.10

In summary, as the above results indicate, recruits' perceptions after six weeks of work differed on a number of factors from their initial expectations of what their jobs and organizations' communication environments would be like. In all cases the recruits' expectations were significantly more inflated than the "reality" of their organizations as perceived after six weeks of work. However, it should be noted that both recruits who withdrew and recruits who remained in their organizations demonstrated similar patterns of expectations/perceptions of their organizations' communication climates.

Research question 5 was answered by compiling the self-recording forms from the communication logs. In total, 314 interaction episodes were recorded by the 14 subjects who completed logs. The average number of entries within a log booklet was 22.4. These episodes were first categorized by the position of the other interactant. Since only four major "others" were discovered in the logs, five categories of other interactants were formed—superior, peer, patient, patient's family, and miscellaneous other. In turn, each of these interactions with others was classified into four additional categories: percentage total communication, type of contact (group, dyadic, other), initiator of the episode (self, other), and the purpose of the interaction (give information or instructions, receive information or instructions). Table 22.3 reports the results of the breakdown of the interaction episodes into these categories.

Inspections of the data in Table 22.3 and corresponding chi-square tests of statistical significance suggest a number of conclusions: (1) Most of the recruits' interactions were with patients (40.8 percent) and peers (37.6 percent), while less than 18 percent of the communication episodes involved their superiors; (2) the overwhelming majority of the new employees' communication contacts were dyadic encounters ($\chi^2 = 129.69$, df $= 8$, p $< .001$); (3) with the exception of interactions with patients, most communications were initiated by the other interactant ($\chi^2 = 20.40$, df $= 4$, p $< .0004$); (4) the purpose of most interactions with superiors was to *receive instructions*, while the purpose of most interactions with peers was to *receive information*. On the other hand, the purpose of most interactions with patients was to *give information or instructions* ($\chi^2 = 129.84$, df $= 12$, p $< .0001$).

In order to determine the recruits' attitudes toward their interaction episodes, data from the five semantic differential-type attitude scales contained in the communication log forms were grouped according to the position of the other interactant—that is, superior, peer, or patient (patient's family and miscellaneous others were not included in these analyses since

Table 22.3
Recruits' Communication Interactions: Third Week of Work

Position of Other Interactant	% Total Communication	Type of Contact			Initiated by		Purpose of Interaction			
		Group	Dyadic	Other	Self	Other	Give Information	Give Instructions	Receive Information	Receive Instructions
Superior	17.8	21.4	75.0	3.6	37.5	62.5	16.1	8.9	23.2	51.8
Peers	37.6	18.6	81.4	0.0	46.6	53.4	31.4	5.1	49.2	14.4
Patient	40.8	0.8	97.7	1.6	64.8	35.2	25.0	45.3	24.2	5.5
Patient's family	2.5	0.0	100.0	0.0	12.5	87.5	12.5	0.0	87.5	0.0
Other	1.3	25.0	0.0	75.0	75.0	25.5	50.0	0.0	25.0	25.0

Note: Entries are percentages based upon a total of 314 interactions.

Table 22.4

Recruits' Attitudes Toward Interaction Episodes with Superiors,
Peers, and Patients: Third Week of Work

Attitude Scale	Position of Other Interactant					
	Superior (n = 56)		Peer (n = 118)		Patient (n = 128)	
	Mean	S.D.	Mean	S.D.	Mean	S.D.
Valuable*	6.13	1.13	5.82	1.36	5.09	1.73
Satisfying*	5.63	1.47	5.75	1.18	4.78	1.62
Interesting*	5.02	1.45	5.17	1.52	4.41	1.61
Precise*	5.54	1.69	5.42	1.37	5.02	1.54
Challenging	4.54	1.84	4.29	1.81	4.53	1.90

*Significant (p. < 05) difference between the means. Missing data = 12 interactions.

they accounted for few of the recruits' self-reported interactions—3.8 percent). The recruits' attitudes toward interactions with superiors, peers, and patients were then analyzed by a three-groups, one-way MANOVA.

The F-ratio for the multivariate test was significant (F = 5.03, df = 10,590, p < .005, R^2 = .15). Examination of the univariate F-ratios for each of the attitude scales indicated significant effects for "valuable" (F = 12.10, df = 2,299, p < .005), "satisfying" (F = 15.71, df = 2,299, p < .007), "interesting" (F = 8.06, df = 2,299, p < .004), and "precise" (F = 3.12, df = 2,299, p < .05). Cell means and standard deviations for each of the scales are reported in Table 22.4.

Post hoc Newman-Keuls multiple comparison tests on the significant univariate effects indicated that for each scale recruits' attitudes toward their interactions with patients were significantly less positive than their attitudes toward interactions with peers and superiors. Attitudes toward interactions with peers and superiors did not differ significantly from one another.

Research Questions 6 and 7

Taken together, research questions 6 and 7 were concerned with whether the perceptions of recruits who withdrew or remained employed in their organizations differed between their sixth, twelfth, and eighteenth weeks of employment. This question was answered by computing a 2 × 3 MANOVA in which the perceptions of recruits during their sixth, twelfth, and eighteenth weeks of employment, partitioned by whether or not they were still employed in their organizations after each of these periods, were compared.

Results of the MANOVA revealed a nonsignificant interaction effect (F = 1.04, df = 34,90, p < .42, R^2 = .49) and nonsignificant main effects for perceptions over time (F = .83, df = 34,90 p < .72, R^2 = .42) and job turnover (F = .70, df = 17,45, p < .79, R^2 = .21).

In summary, the results of the above tests suggest that during the encounter-metamorphosis stage of assimilation recruits' perceptions of their organizations' communication climates did not change significantly. Moreover, these findings suggest that both those recruits who left their jobs and those that remained evidenced the same patterns of perceptions across the three time periods.

Research Questions 8, 9, and 10

Research question 8 addressed the interaction episodes that characterized the recruits' communication during their ninth week of work, as well as their corresponding attitudes toward those interactions. In turn, questions 9 and 10 concerned whether or not the character of the recruits' interactions differed between their third week and their ninth week of work; changes in corresponding attitudes toward these interactions were also a focus of inquiry.

Procedures similar to those used to explore research question 5 were employed to answer question 8. In other words, the data from the seven communication log booklets collected during the ninth week of employment were categorized by the position of the "other" interactant, percentage of total communication, type of contact, initiator of the episode, and purpose of the interaction. Table 22.5 reports the results of the breakdown of the interaction episodes into these categories.

Inspection of the data in Table 22.5 and corresponding chi-square tests of statistical significance suggest a number of conclusions: (1) Most of the recruits' interactions were with patients (37.5 percent) and peers (47.5 percent), while approximately 14 percent of their interactions were with superiors; (2) most contacts were dyadic in nature ($\chi^2 = 60.32$, df $= 8$, p $< .0001$); (3) with the exception of contact with superiors (in which recruits and superiors each initiated interactions 50 percent of the time), most communication contacts were initiated by recruits ($\chi^2 = 12.84$, df $= 4$, p $< .01$); and (4) the purpose of most interactions with superiors was to *receive instructions*, while the purpose of most interactions with peers was either to *give or to receive information*. The purpose of most interactions with patients was either to *give information* or to *give instructions* ($\chi^2 = 95.33$, df $= 12$, p $< .0001$).

In order to determine the recruits' attitudes toward their interaction episodes, data from the semantic differential scales were grouped according to the position of the other interactant. The recruits' attitudes toward their interactions with superiors, peers, and patients were then analyzed by a three-groups, one-way MANOVA. The F-ratio for the multivariate test of mean vectors was significant (F $= 3.00$, df $= 10,382$, p < 001, $R^2 = .14$). Examination of the univariate F-ratios for each of the attitude scales indicated significant effects for "valuable" (F $= 4.29$, df $= 2,195$, p $< .02$), "satisfying" (F $= 10.32$,

Table 22.5
Recruits' Communication Interactions: Ninth Week of Work

Position of Other Interactant	% Total Communication	Type of Contact			Initiated by		Purpose of Interaction			
		Group	Dyadic	Other	Self	Other	Give Information	Give Instructions	Receive Information	Receive Instructions
Superior	14.0	14.3	71.4	14.3	50.0	50.0	14.3	0.0	17.9	67.9
Peers	37.5	14.7	84.0	1.3	59.5	40.5	36.0	10.7	42.7	10.6
Patient	47.5	6.3	93.7	0.0	77.7	22.3	26.3	46.3	18.9	8.4
Patient's family	.5	100.0	0.0	0.0	0.0	100.0	0.0	0.0	0.0	100.0
Other	.5	0.0	0.0	100.0	100.0	0.0	100.0	0.0	0.0	0.0

Note: Entries are percentages based upon a total of 200 interactions.

Table 22.6
Recruits' Attitudes Toward Interaction Episodes with Superiors,
Peers, and Patients: Ninth Week of Work

| Attitude Scale | Position of Other Interactant | | | | | |
| | Superior (n = 28) | | Peer (n = 75) | | Patient (n = 95) | |
	Mean	S.D.	Mean	S.D.	Mean	S.D.
Valuable*	5.61	1.23	5.27	1.43	4.80	1.51
Satisfying*	5.68	1.22	5.03	1.20	4.48	1.38
Interesting*	5.11	1.23	4.19	1.12	4.14	1.50
Precise*	5.93	1.36	5.35	1.30	4.71	1.68
Challenging	4.68	1.69	4.57	1.23	4.33	1.82

*Significant (p. < 05) difference between the means. Missing data = 2 interactions.

df = 2,195, p < .0001), "interesting" (F = 6.13, df = 2,195, p < .003), and "precise" (F = 8.56, df = 2,195, p < .0001). Cell means and standard deviations for each of the scales are reported in Table 22.6.

Post hoc Newman-Keuls multiple comparison tests on the significant univariate effects indicated that (1) recruits perceived their interactions with patients to be significantly less "valuable" and "precise" than their interactions with peers and superiors; (2) recruits perceived their interactions with their superiors to be significantly more satisfying than their interactions with peers or patients, though they perceived their interactions with peers to be more satisfying than their interactions with patients; and (3) recruits perceived their interactions with their superiors to be significantly more interesting than their interactions with peers or patients.

Research questions 9 and 10 were answered by comparing the log data collected during the third week of the recruits' employment with the log data collected during the ninth week of work. Chi-square tests were then conducted between the interaction data collected during the two time periods. Attitudes toward the interactions across the two time periods were compared by a 2 × 3 MANOVA (third/ninth week by superior/peer/patient). Results of the breakdown of interaction episodes across the two time periods are reported in Table 22.7, while the cell means and standard deviations for the attitude scales across the third and ninth weeks of employment are displayed in Table 22.8.

Results of the chi-square tests on the interaction episodes revealed only one major change in the nature of the recruits' communication over the two time periods. Specifically, test results indicate that recruits initiated more of their interactions during the ninth week of work than they did during their third week of work ($\chi^2 = 10.23$, df = 1, p < .001).

Findings from the MANOVA performed to ascertain differences in the recruits' attitudes toward the interaction episodes across the two time periods revealed a significant multivariate interaction effect (F = 2.60, df =

Table 22.7

Comparison of Recruits' Communication Interactions:
Third Week Versus Ninth Week of Work

Week at Work	Position of Other Interactant				Type of Contact			Initiated by		Purpose of Interaction			
	Superior	Peer	Patient	Patient's Family	Group	Dyadic	Other	Self	Other	Give Information	Receive Information	Give Instructions	Receive Instruction
Third	17.8	37.6	40.8	2.5	11.5	86.3	2.2	51.9	48.1	25.8	35.0	22.0	17.2
Ninth	14.0	37.5	47.5	.5	11.0	86.0	3.0	66.7	33.3	28.5	27.5	26.0	28.0

Note: Entries are percentages based upon a total of 514 interactions.

Table 22.8

Comparison of Recruits' Attitudes Toward Interaction Episodes
with Superiors, Peers, and Patients:
Third Week Versus Ninth Week of Work

	Position of Other Interactant											
	Superior				Peer				Patient			
	Week at Work				Week at Work				Week at Work			
	Third (n = 56)		Ninth (n = 28)		Third (n = 118)		Ninth (n = 75)		Third (n = 128)		Ninth (n = 95)	
Attitude Scale	Mean	S.D.	Mean	S.D.	Mean	S.D.	Mean	S.D.	Mean	S.D.	Mean	S.D.
Valuable	6.13	1.30	5.61	1.23	5.83	1.37	5.27	1.43	5.09	1.72	4.80	1.51
Satisfying	5.63	1.47	5.67	1.22	5.75	1.18	5.03	1.20	4.78	1.62	4.48	1.38
Interesting	5.02	1.45	5.11	1.23	5.17	1.52	4.19	1.12	4.40	1.61	4.14	1.50
Precise	5.54	1.69	5.93	1.36	5.42	1.37	5.35	1.29	5.02	1.54	4.71	1.68
Challenging	4.54	1.84	4.86	1.84	4.29	1.81	4.57	1.23	4.53	1.90	4.33	1.82

Note: Total number of interactions = 500. Missing data = 14 interactions.

10,980, p < .004, R^2 = .05), as well as significant main effects for the logs (F = 6.00, df = 5,490, p < .0001, R^2 = .06) and the position of the other interactant (F = 6.12, df = 10,980, p < .001, R^2 = .11). Examination of the univariate interaction effects showed only one significant effect, "interesting" (F = 4.67, df = 2,494, p < .01). Subsequent post hoc tests further revealed that during the third week of work recruits perceived their interaction with superiors and peers to be significantly more interesting than their interactions with patients, while during their ninth week of work recruits perceived their interactions with superiors to be significantly more interesting than their interactions with peers and patients. Moreover, tests showed that, overall, recruits perceived their interactions to be less interesting during their ninth week of work than during their third week of work.

On the other hand, an examination of the univariate main effects for the other dependent variables indicated that (1) recruits perceived their interactions during the ninth week of work to be significantly less valuable and less satisfying than during their third week of work (valuable, F = 12.66, df = 1,494, p < .001; satisfying, F =13.28, df = 1,494, p < .001); and (2) across the two time periods recruits perceived their interactions with superiors and peers to be significantly more valuable, satisfying, and precise than their interactions with patients (valuable, F = 16.11, df = 2,494, p < .001; satisfying, F = 23.56, df = 2,494, p < .001; precise, F =10.05, df = 2,494, p < .001).

Research Questions 11 and 12

Research questions 11 and 12 were directed at determining whether or not differences exist between a new employee's perception of his or her organization's communication climate during the metamorphosis stage (sixth, twelfth, eighteenth weeks of employment) of assimilation and his or her supervisor's perceptions of the recruit's perceptions of communication climate. In addition, the potential interaction of such differences on the recruit's job survival was a focus of inquiry. These questions were explored by a 2 × 2 × 3 MANOVA (subordinate/superior perceptions, job withdrawer/survivor, sixth/twelfth/eighteenth week of employment).

Results of the MANOVA failed to show a significant three-way interaction effect (F = .87, df = 34, 212, p < .63, R^2 = .23) or any meaningful two-way interactions (the interaction for week at work by job survival was significant, but its meaning is dubious since it collapses across superior and subordinate perceptions). However, a main effect was evident for superior/ subordinate perceptions (F = 5.45, df = 17,106, p < .0001, R^2 = .05). An examination of the univariate tests showed significant main effects for sending information to others (F = 3.78, df = 1,122, p < .05), satisfaction with coworkers (F = 6.76, sd = 1,122, p < .01), supervisor's upward work influence (F = 4.71, df = 1,122, p < .03), and supervisor's upward strategic influence (F = 18.93, df = 1,122, p < .0001). In addition, the main effect for organizational outcomes/ overall satisfaction approached statistical significance (F = 3.26, df = 1,122, p < .07).

In summary, the results of the above analyses suggest that superiors (across time periods and for both job withdrawers and survivors) tended to *overestimate* the amount of information recruits perceived they were sending to others on their jobs and the amount of upward work influence the superiors possessed. On the other hand, superiors tended to *underestimate* recruits' satisfaction with their coworkers, the amount of upward strategic influence possessed by the superiors, and recruits' overall levels of job satisfaction (organizational outcomes).

Research Question 13

The final research question sought to ascertain the degree to which recruits' perceptions of their organizations' communication systems are related to the recruits' job performance during their sixth, twelfth, and eighteenth weeks of employment. Three separate stepwise multiple regression analyses were conducted in order to answer this research question (one analysis for each time period).

Results of the regression analysis for job performance at the sixth week of employment indicated that thirteen of the independent variables significantly entered the regression equation. However, once all of the variables were in the equation only two variables remained significant predictors: subordinate's work dependency (F = 9.05, p < .006, r = .49, beta = .77) and satisfaction with management (F = 8.75, p < .006, r −.09, beta = −.51). Together the two variables accounted for 43 percent of the variance in job appraisal ratings.

In contrast, the regression analysis for job performance at the twelfth week of work indicated that seven of the independent variables significantly entered the regression equation. However, once all of the variables were in the equation only one variable remained a significant predictor, JDI-supervision (F = 5.05, p < .04, r = .45, beta = .45). This one variable accounted for 20 percent of the variance in job appraisal ratings.

Finally, the regression analysis for job performance at the eighteenth week of employment indicated that after all the variables had entered the regression equation only two remained significant predictors: supervisory supportiveness (F = 5.72, p < .03, r = .57, beta = .63) and supervisory upward work influence (F = 8.77, p < .01, r = −.48, beta = −.55). Together the two variables accounted for 62 percent of the variance in job performance ratings.

In summary, the results of the above analyses suggest that different sets of variables were predictive of job performance ratings for each of the time periods for which job appraisal data were collected.

DISCUSSION

The purpose of this investigation was to explore the processes by which new employees become assimilated into their organizations' communication systems. Findings from the investigation are interpreted and discussed below with respect to the three basic phases of the assimilation process: (1) anticipatory socialization, (2) encounter, and (3) metamorphosis.

Anticipatory Organizational
Communication

Three research questions were posed exploring issues related to anticipatory socialization, and were essentially concerned with whether or not individuals who voluntarily withdraw from their organizations and those who stay differ in their initial expectations of their organizations' communication climates, and their perceptions of the communication climates of the last organizations in which they were employed. Results provide some tentative answers to the issues raised by the research questions, but in addition suggest several new areas of study.

The absence of a significant multivariate interaction effect in the MANOVA conducted to explore the research questions makes it very difficult to draw any firm conclusions from the findings. One's initial conclusion might be that since the interaction effect did not obtain, the recruits' perceptions of the communication climates of their last jobs and their expectations of the communication climates of their new jobs did not interact to affect their job survival. However, an inspection of the means in Table 22.1 suggests that the communication climate expectations of job survivors were consistently lower than those of recruits who terminated their employment. Moreover, the pattern of means suggests that recruits who terminated their new jobs had more positive perceptions of the communication climates of their last jobs/organizations than did individuals who remained in their new organizations. Hence, while results were not statistically significant (possibly because of the small sample size), there is some evidence to indicate that job withdraws' exaggerated perceptions of their last jobs may have served to inflate their expectations of the communication climates of their new organizations. Clearly, future research should explore this possibility.

It is also interesting to note that for both the job withdrawers and the job survivors there is a general tendency for job expectations to exceed job retrospections. Obviously, this is not a surprising finding, since one would expect that the recruits left their last positions (in part) because they were not completely satisfied with their organizations' communication climates. However, it is intriguing to discover that the means in Table 22.1 also show that the job withdrawers' perceptions of their last jobs exceeded or generally were equivalent to the job *expectations* of the job survivors. This trend in results certainly suggests that there may be some very basic differences in the ways that job withdrawers and job survivors perceive their communication environments. The nature and causes of these differences would appear to be a fruitful area for future research.

Organizational Encounter

Results related to the organizational encounter phase of the assimilation process suggest some interesting conclusions. First, it appears that recruits' perceptions after six weeks of work were significantly deflated from their initial job expectations. This finding is consistent with previous research (for example, see Lawler, Kuleck, Rhode, & Sorenson, 1975; Vroom & Deci, 1971), which has shown a substantial drop in employees' job and organizational satisfaction from their first day of employment to several months of employment. As Wanous (1977, p. 615) has observed, "Increasing experience in a new organization is associated with a less favorable view of it."

The fact that significant effects were evident for *all* of the communication climate scales from the ICA Communication Audit, however, is of particular importance. These results may suggest that the new employees are experiencing a form of "communication deprivation." In fact, if one compares the means from the recruits' preceptions at six weeks of employment with their job retrospections, it becomes evident that in many ways the communication environments of their new jobs are much more limited than the communication environments of their old jobs. Moreover, given that the communication log data from the third week of employment indicate that recruits are not initiating the majority of their interactions with others, it would appear that the new employees do not compensate for their organization- and job-related communication/information deprivation by seeking out information from others, but rather wait for others to supply them with relevant information. Future research should be directed at determining whether or not communication deprivation is a common characteristic of the encounter phase of assimilation.

Other findings from the interaction log data collected during the third week of employment are also of interest. These data indicate that the primary communication activity in which recruits engage during the encounter period is that of *receiving* information and instructions. Moreover, the recruits' attitudes toward these types of interactions are more positive than their attitudes toward the interactions in which they give information or instructions (though those also usually involve patients). Consequently, it appears that during the encounter stage of assimilation recruits are most interested in obtaining as much information from others as possible so that they can successfully learn the behavioral and attitudinal norms of their organizations (though they wait for others to initiate these interactions).

Organizational Metamorphosis

The absence of any changes in recruits' perceptions of the communication climates of their organizations after the sixth week of work is also intriguing. These results may suggest that the metamorphosis stage of assimilation is very rapid for the employees of the organizations examined in this research or that the recruits are not very successful in individualizing their roles and thus affecting their communication environments. The generalizability of these findings to other types of organizations and occupations should be a focus of future research.

While recruits' perceptions of their communication environments did not vary significantly between their sixth and eighteenth weeks of work, the nature of their communication interactions and their corresponding attitudes toward those interactions did shift somewhat. Specifically, results suggest that by their ninth week of work recruits were initiating most of their interactions with others rather than waiting for others to initiate interactions with them. Moreover, by their ninth week of employment recruits perceived their interaction episodes with their superiors to be significantly more satisfying and interesting than their interactions with peers and patients. Further, findings indicate a general trend for the recruits to perceive all of their interactions with others in a less positive manner during their ninth week of work than during their third week of work. These findings seem to suggest that changes in recruits' communication behaviors and attitudes are occurring during the metamorphosis stage of assimilation, but that these changes are directed more toward those persons with whom they have contact than toward the organization as a whole.

Results related to superior-subordinate semantic/information distance occurring during the metamorphosis phase suggest only a minimal amount of perceptual incongruency between members of the dyad. However, gaps in understanding do appear to exist in some areas, though they do not differentiate job withdrawers from job survivors. Perhaps of most interest is the fact that superiors believe that their subordinates are less satisfied with their coworkers and their jobs/organizations than they actually are. For this expectation set to occur so early in the superior-subordinate relationship may set a dangerous precedent for the future growth of the relationship. Specifically, a type of "Pygmalion Effect" (Rosenthal, 1969) may result, since supervisors may be communicating somehow to their subordinates that they expect them to be dissatisfied with their jobs and employers. Of course the converse can also be true, as Porter et al. (1975, p. 186) observe: "If the person in the supervisory or teaching position has positive expectations concerning how well the subordinate can perform, and these expectations are communicated or made known to the subordinate, his performance may actually be facilitated."

Finally, findings related to the relationship between recruits' levels of job performance and communication climate perceptions during the metamorphosis period suggest some interesting conclusions. First, it should be noted that the key variables that are related to performance ratings are either satisfaction factors or dimensions of the superior-subordinate relationship. Second, it is important to observe that at the point of six weeks of employment the best predictor of an employee's job performance rating is the degree to which he or she is dependent on his or her superior for information. This finding seems to add support to the notion that a recruit's supervisor is a key person in the organizational assimilation process, since "effectiveness" during the entry period of employment seems closely tied to acknowledging the subordinate's dependent position in the superior-subordinate relationship. Moreover, it is interesting to note that by the eighteenth week of employment dependency is no longer the best predictor of a recruit's job performance, but rather the degree to which the recruit perceives his or her superior as "supportive" and possessing upward work influence in the organization. In short, it appears that at any one point a recruit's job performance rating is closely associated with his or her relationship with his or her superior, but that the qualities of the relationship that lead the superior to perceive the recruit as an effective performer vary over time. This notion warrants additional research.

In summary, this study is part of a longitudinal investigation into the organizational communication assimilation process. The research focused upon the relationships between recruits' (newly hired nursing assistants) perceptions of the communication climates of their last jobs, their expectations of the communication climates of their new jobs, and their corresponding attitudes after six, twelve, and eighteen weeks of employment. In addition, the investigation sought to determine the nature of the communication interactions recruits experienced during the encounter and metamorphosis stages of organizational assimilation. Given the exploratory nature of this research, conclusions should be drawn from it cautiously. In particular, it should be noted that since over 90 percent of the subjects who participated in the study were female, generalizability of research findings may be limited to that group. Further, it is important to keep in mind that the turnover patterns and communication perceptions and behaviors of only one type of occupational group (nursing assistants) were examined in this study, thus limiting the generalizability of the findings.

NOTES

1. An analysis of the demographic characteristics of those nursing assistants who were to later voluntarily withdraw from their jobs and those who remained indicated that they did not differ significantly with respect to (1) gender, (2) age, (3) education, (4) number of previous jobs, (5) previous experiences in health care facilities, (6) length of employment on last job, (7) position in hierarchy on previous job, or (8) if they were also employed at another job while working at the nursing home.

2. Median scale reliabilities (Cronbach's alpha) across administrations of the questionnaires were as follows: receiving information, $\alpha = .91$; sending information, $\alpha = .83$; sources of information, $\alpha = .76$; timeliness of information, $\alpha = .65$; channels of information, $\alpha = .70$; superior-subordinate openness, $\alpha = .96$; superior's work influence, $\alpha = .80$; superior's strategic influence, $\alpha = .88$; supervisory supportiveness, $\alpha = .86$; supervisory work facilitation, $\alpha = .73$; supervisory interaction facilitation, $\alpha = .59$; supervisory goal emphasis, $\alpha = .76$; subordinate work dependency, $\alpha = .69$; JDI-supervision, $\alpha = .70$; satisfaction coworkers, $\alpha = .78$; satisfaction management, $\alpha = .84$; and overall satisfaction, $\alpha = .92$.

REFERENCES

Berlew, D. E., & Hall, D. T. (1966). The socialization of managers: Effects of expectations on performance. *Administrative Science Quarterly, 11*, 207-223.

Berlo, D. K. (1960). *The process of communication.* New York: Holt, Rinehart & Winston.

Burns, T. (1954). The direction of activity and communication in a departmental executive group: A quantitative study in a British engineering factory with a self-recording technique. *Human Relations, 7*, 73-97.

Caplow, T. (1964). *Principles of organization.* New York: Harcourt Brace Jovanovich.

Dennis, H. S., Goldhaber, G. M., & Yates, M. P. (1978). Organizational communication theory and research: An overview of research methods. In B. D. Ruben (Ed.), *Communication yearbook 2.* New Brunswick, NJ: Transaction.

Dunnette, M. D., Avery, R., & Banas, P. (1973). Why do they leave? *Personnel, 50*(3), 25-39.

Elsea, K. (1979). *The role of communication in organizational socialization: A review of relevant literature.* Paper presented at the annual convention of the International Communication Association, Philadelphia.

Feldman, D. C. (1976). A contingency theory of socialization. *Administrative Science Quarterly, 21*, 433-452.

Feldman, D. C., & Brett, J. M. (1983). Coping with new jobs: A comparative study of new hires and job changers. *Academy of Management Journal, 26*, 258-272.

Goldhaber, G. M., & Rogers, D. P. (1978). *Auditing organizational communication systems: The ICA Communication Audit.* Buffalo: SUNY at Buffalo.

Gomersall, E. R., & Myers, M. S. (1966). Breakthrough in on-the-job training. *Harvard Business Review, 44*, 62-72.

Graen, G. (1976). Role making processes within complex organizations. In M. D. Dunnette (Ed.), *Handbook of industrial and organizational psychology.* Chicago: Rand McNally.

Graen, G., & Ginzburgh, S. (1977). Job resignation as a function of role orientation and leader acceptance: A longitudinal investigation of organizational assimilation. *Organizational Behavior and Human Performance, 19*, 1-17.

Herzberg, F., Mausner, B., Peterson, P. D., & Capwell, D. F. (1957). *Job attitudes: Review of research and opinion.* Pittsburgh: Psychological Services of Pittsburgh.

Hughes, E. C. (1958). The study of occupations. In R. K. Merton, L. Broomand, & L. Cotrell (Eds.), *Sociology today.* New York: Basic Books.

Ilgen, D. W., & Seely, W. (1974). Realistic expectations as an aid in reducing voluntary resignations. *Journal of Applied Psychology, 59*, 452-455.

Jablin, F. M. (1978). Message-response and "openness" in superior-subordinate communication. In B. D. Ruben (Ed.) *Communication yearbook 2.* New Brunswick, NJ: Transaction.

Jablin, F. M. (1979). Superior-subordinate communication: The state of the art. *Psychological Bulletin, 86*, 1201-1222.

Jablin, F. M. (1980). Superior's upward influence, satisfaction, and openness in superior-subordinate communication: A reexamination of the "Pelz Effect." *Human Communication Research, 6*, 210-220.

Jablin, F. M. (1982). Organizational communication: An assimilation approach. In M. E. Roloff & C. R. Berger (Eds.), Social cognition and communication (pp. 255-286). Beverly Hills, CA: Sage.

Jones, G. R. (1983). Psychological orientation and the process of organizational socialization: An interactionist perspective. Academy of Management Review, 8, 464-474.

Katz, R., & Tushman, M. L. (1983). A longitudinal study of the effects of boundary spanning supervision on turnover and promotion in research and development. Academy of Management Journal, 26, 437-456.

Katzell, M. E. (1968). Expectations and dropouts in schools of nursing. Journal of Applied Psychology, 52, 154-157.

Lawler, E. E., Kuleck, W. J., Rhode, J. E., & Sorenson, J. E. (1975). Job choice and post decision dissonance. Organizational Behavior and Human Performance, 13, 133-145.

Lawler, E. E., Porter, L. W., & Tennenbaum, A. (1968). Managers' attitudes toward interaction episodes. Journal of Applied Psychology, 52, 432-439.

Louis, M. (1980). Surprise and sense-making: What newcomers experience in entering unfamiliar organizational settings. Administrative Science Quarterly, 25, 226-251.

Macedonia, R. M. (1969). Expectations—Press and survival. Unpublished doctoral dissertation, New York University.

Porter, L. W., Lawler, E. E., & Hackman, J. R. (1975). Behavior in organizations. New York: McGraw-Hill.

Porter, L. W., & Steers, R. M. (1973). Organizational, work, and personal factors in employee turnover and absenteeism. Psychological Bulletin, 80, 151-176.

Richetto, G. M. (1977). Organizational communication theory and research: An overview. In B. D. Ruben (Ed.), Communication yearbook 1. New Brunswick, NJ: Transaction.

Rosenthal, R. (1969). Interpersonal expectations: Effects of experimenter's hypothesis. In R. Rosenthal & R. L. Rosnow (Eds.), Artifact in behavioral research. New York: Academic.

Ross, I. C., & Zander, A. (1957). Need satisfaction and employee turnover. Personnel Psychology, 10, 327-338.

Schein, E. H. (1968). Organizational socialization and the profession of management. Industrial Management Review, 9, 1-16.

Schneider, B. (1972). Organizational climate: Individual preference and organizational realities. Journal of Applied Psychology, 56, 211-217.

Schneider, B. (1973). The perception of organizational climate: The customer's view. Journal of Applied Psychology, 57, 248-256.

Schneider, B., & Hall, D. T. (1972). Toward specifying the concept of work climate: A study of Roman Catholic diocesan priests. Journal of Applied Psychology, 56, 447-455.

Smith, P., Kendall, L., & Hulin, C. (1969). The measurement of satisfaction in work and retirement. Chicago: Rand McNally.

Taylor, J., & Bowers, D. G. (1972). The survey of organizations: A machine-scored standardized questionnaire instrument. Ann Arbor: University of Michigan, Institute for Social Research.

Van Maanen, J. (1975a). Breaking in: Socialization to work. In R. Dubin (Ed.), Handbook of work, organization and society. Chicago: Rand McNally.

Van Maanen, J. (1975b). Police socialization: A longitudinal investigation of job attitudes in an urban police department. Administrative Science Quarterly, 20, 207-228.

Vroom, V. H., & Deci, E. L. (1971). The stability of post-decision dissonance: A follow-up study of the job attitudes of business school graduates. Organizational Behavior and Human Performance, 6, 36-49.

Wanous, J. P. (1977). Organizational entry: Newcomers moving from outside to inside. Psychological Bulletin, 84, 601-618.

Wanous, J. P. (1980). Organizational entry: Recruitment, selection, and socialization of newcomers. Reading, MA: Addison-Wesley.

Weiss, H. M. (1977). Subordinate imitation of supervisor behavior: The role of modeling in organizational socialization. Organizational Behavior and Human Performance, 19, 89-105.

Weitz, J. (1956). Job expectancy and survival. Journal of Applied Psychology, 40, 245-247.

Youngberg, C. F. (1963). An experimental study of job satisfaction and turnover in relation to job expectations and self-expectations. Unpublished doctoral dissertation, New York University.

VI • INTERCULTURAL AND INTERNATIONAL COMMUNICATION

23 ● "A Little Good News": Development News in Third World Newspapers

CHRISTINE L. OGAN ● JO ELLEN FAIR ●
HEMANT SHAH

Indiana University

T HE call for a "little good news" has come from many quarters in recent years—from President Reagan as well as from leaders of many Third World governments. In fact, "good news" has sparked an international controversy over the value of development news or development communication in the world press. In the now well-worn debate over the establishment of a New International Information Order (NIIO), the old order proponents argue that the inclusion of more development news will only mean the acceptance of government handouts from national leaders full of self-serving praise for their economic and social accomplishments. And this news will replace the hard-hitting investigative reporting characteristics of the large international wire services and other press correspondents of the West. Calling the "good news" in government public relations releases "development news" will not change the situation, say the critics (Ogan, 1982).

But not everyone looks upon development news as government-controlled information and not everyone is convinced that development news will be uncritical in its approach to reporting the process of development. The

AUTHORS' NOTE: We would like to thank representatives of Interlink, Gemini, and Pacific News Service for the news copy they provided for this study. Thanks also go to the members of the graduate class in communication and national development for the coding of material and for their overall contribution to the research project. This chapter is reprinted, with permission, from *Gazette*.

Correspondence and requests for reprints: Christine L. Ogan, School of Journalism, Indiana University, Bloomington, IN 47405.

most often quoted advocate of development journalism is Narinder Aggarwala, regional information officer for Asia and the Pacific at the United Nations Development Program. He claims that most Western correspondents are interested in spot news about the sensational, strange, and exotic and neglect information about "movements on the development front in the problem-ridden Third World" (Aggarwala, 1981, p. 8). He would have such news take on the form of investigative reporting (Aggarwala, 1978, p. 200). The journalist's job on a development newsbeat is to "critically examine and evaluate the relevance of a development project to national and local needs, the difference between a planned scheme and its actual implementation, and the difference between its impact on people as claimed by government officials and as it actually is" (Aggarwala, 1979, p. 181).

Other people writing about the importance of covering news of development have been dismayed about the lack of such news in the Western press and that of developing countries where AP, UPI, Reuters, and AFP are the main sources of foreign news. Schramm and Atwood (1981, p. 88), in their study of the circulation of news in Asia, claim that the reason more development news is not covered in the world (and they define development news as positive news about development accomplishments) lies in the nature of news and news flow itself:

Neither the pace of news itself nor the training of the typical newsman have been especially well suited to development news. News moves in a series of bulletins and retakes and revised leads and new bulletins, events piling on events so that an editor always has the sense of covering the world inadequately, always having to leave out items of importance, sometimes not able even to follow up events that he has already published to let his readers learn how the story "came out." The flow of news typically does not encourage the intellectual leisure an editor needs to sit back and analyze a pattern of events that must be interpreted in depth before it becomes truly meaningful. A newsman is typically trained to report events rather than to analyze situations. News is timely. It is a change in something; it can be dated and specified.

In spite of the difficulties in reporting on the process-oriented development news, recent attempts have been made by major news organizations to alter their approach to such reporting. The new owners of UPI promised qualitative changes in reporting the Third World when they purchased the agency in 1982:

This half of UPI's new ownership team (Douglas Ruhe and William Geissler) also expresses some sympathy for the elements of the UNESCO attack on coverage of the Third World by Western reporters. "If you come from the richest country in the world, it's very easy to take a cynical attitude toward those countries," Ruhe observes. To improve coverage of minorities and the Third World, Ruhe says some efforts will be made to "broaden the pool of talent and the diversity of the people" at UPI. (Stephens, 1982, p. 58)

David Anable, foreign news editor of the *Christian Science Monitor,* a newspaper already dedicated to the coverage of news in and features on Third World countries, recently announced the hiring of a correspondent who would specialize only in Third World and development news:

> His main task is to synthesize the growing volume of information on develop-
> ment, on food and hunger, population and literacy, and so on. He will travel
> extensively and can, incidentally, draw on an increasing number of specialist
> and regional news services and magazines which focus on development—a
> publication hand we tend to forget. (Anable, 1983, p. 14)

Some newly established organizations have been developed to fill in the gaps in coverage of development news in both the U.S. press and that of Third World countries. These organizations are discussed in the conclusion of this chapter in light of findings concerning the current use of their services.

No matter how many alternatives are offered to the news media of a developing country from the outside, however, it will remain the responsi- bility of the press within the developing country to cover its own progress in development endeavors. Aggarwala (1980, p. 26) has found Third World journalists remiss in this effort:

> Third World papers have evinced very little desire to change their acute politi-
> cal orientation (in most developing countries, a clear residue of the struggle for
> independence). They show even less interest in news of national economic
> and social development. Most editors in the Third World have a strong prefer-
> ence for news about the West over news about other developing countries,
> even their neighbors; a seemingly incurable hangover from the colonial era.

Only a few studies have been conducted to determine the validity of Ag- garwala's observation. Vilanilam (1979, p. 40), in his content analysis of the development news in four major Indian newspapers, found that little atten- tion was paid to developmental categories of "family planning, housing, eco- nomic activity, education and literacy, employment and labour welfare, health hygiene and medicine, rural and urban development and social change." Po- litical activity constituted the majority of news in the four papers, while some attention was paid to agriculture technology and scientific and industrial de- velopment. Vilanilam's research was limited to a study of the amount of such news in the four papers of one country for a constructed week.

Other content analyses of development news have concerned print media in Asia and Africa. Vilanilam (1979) studied whether any significant difference existed between independent and conglomerate-controlled newspapers in the amount of development, political, and government news carried. The results of his investigation showed that although there was no statistically significant difference between newspapers, development news received considerably less coverage than did government and political news.

In a similar study, Mustafa (1979) examined the coverage of development news in three Malaysian newspapers: one English-language and two Malay-language dailies. He hypothesized and later found that Malay-language newspapers devoted half of their newsholes to development news, while the English-language daily carried 32 percent development news.

Six Indonesian national newspapers were analyzed to find how often and in which ways the newspapers supported development programs outlined in the government's Guidelines for State Policy and Development. Sutopo (1983) concluded that Indonesian newspapers used more development than non-development news and that each newspaper had a different view about which development issue was most deserving of attention.

From Africa, Osae-Asare (1979) studied the amount of development news covered in two daily newspapers and the Ghanian wire service. In a comparison of the newspapers and wire service, it was found that the proportion of total development news content, as measured in standardized column inches, was significantly greater in the Ghanian news agency than in the two newspapers.

Since little systematic study of development news had been conducted previously, and since content analyses of such news had indicated only amount and topics considered in development news, the precursor to the present study examined both the amount and the nature of development news in important daily newspapers of Third World countries (Ogan & Swift, 1982).[1] The 1982 study, based on the development content of news in papers of Botswana, Israel, Cuba, China, Romania, South Africa, Kenya, Nigeria, Zimbabwe, Mexico, and Saudi Arabia, found that about half of the development news items were positive in tone and only about one-fourth contained information from critical sources. Little evaluation or analysis of development issues was found in the stories.

When the newspapers were broken down by ownership—privately owned (little government control), socialist, and nonsocialist government owned (or largely controlled)—the privately owned newspapers were generally found to take a more balanced or neutral tone and were more likely to contain critical sources than either the socialist or the government-owned newspapers.

METHODOLOGY

This study was undertaken to determine the amount and nature of development news since 1981. Since the earlier study there has been increasing discussion of the need for such news and alternative news services have become increasingly more responsive to that need. Specifically, the purposes of the study were to discover if there were differences in the way development news was treated in the 1982 study and in 1982-1983; to determine if there has been an increase in the use of alternative news services as providers of development news since 1981; and to see if patterns of development news usage by government-controlled and privately owned newspapers have changed since 1981. We also sought to expand the focus of the original study by examining more newspapers as cases. With these purposes in mind, we addressed the following research questions:

(1) What priority was given to development news in the newspapers of the selected countries?
(2) What development topics receive the greatest attention?
(3) What types of sources are consulted in the reporting of development news?
(4) To what extent do sources make critical statements about development issues?
(5) Does the reporting of development news differ in privately owned newspapers and government-owned newspapers?
(6) What use is made of alternative news services?

To answer these questions a content analysis was undertaken. Development news was operationalized as news that deals with topics such as culture, education, medicine, nutrition, shelter, health, transportation, telecommunications, employment, political participation, and a more equitable distribution of resources. "Development news" was considered to be information with the potential to satisfy the needs of a population. In that effort, the news item may provide context or background material, describe a process rather than an event, answer "how" and "why" questions, and explain the consequences of an event or process.[2]

Based on availability of newspapers and language skills of the coders, nine newspapers were selected for examination. The following is a description of the newspapers examined:[3]

- *Al-Nahar* (Beirut, Lebanon) is a family-owned newspaper known for its fair and objective reporting of a variety of politically divergent views. However, concessions are made to foreign companies that subsidize the newspaper (Fisher, 1982a, p. 565).

- *Daily Times* (Lagos, Nigeria) is Nigeria's largest and most influential newspaper. Although the government owns 60 percent of the newspaper, the *Times* attempts to maintain its editorial distance from the government and is at times critical of government policies (Nwankwo & Kurian, 1982, p. 687).

- *Al-Jazirah* (Riyadh, Saudi Arabia) is published by the Corporation for Press Printing and Publishing. Although under private ownership, printing and publishing institutions are licensed by the Saudi government and administered by a board of directors with autonomous power. Saudi press law declares that the press is private and free from state interference except where the general welfare is concerned (*Europa Yearbook,* 1983, p. 1357).

- *Excelsior* (Mexico) is cooperatively owned. The Mexican government, however, controls the release of information and can purchase advertising and news space. The government is also responsible for allocating newsprint. Censorship is often imposed by the newspaper itself (Sewell, 1982, p. 627).

- *Fraternite Matin* (Abidjan, Ivory Coast) is the Ivory Coast's only daily. The newspaper is owned and operated by the government and financed through advertising. As a government-operated institution, *Fraternite Matin* follows national integration and development policies set by the government (Nwankwo & Kurian, 1982, pp. 1075-1077).

- The *Herald* (Harare, Zimbabwe) is a government owned newspaper (the government has a 45 percent controlling interest). Officially, the government has promised not to interfere with the paper's news operations. The *Herald* supports the NIIO (Fisher, 1982b, p. 1059).

- *Jerusalem Post* (Jerusalem, Israel) is an independently owned newspaper financed through advertising. Censorship of information related to military and national security is strict. A board of military and national security censors must examine such information before it can be published (Moore, 1982, p. 517).

- *New Nigerian* (Lagos, Nigeria) is the second largest newspaper in Nigeria and is government-owned. Like the *Daily Times,* the *New Nigerian* has been relatively free to criticize the government, although the government in recent years has retaliated by firing journalists critical of the government. The *New Nigerian* supports the NIIO (Nwankwo & Kurian, 1982, p. 687).

- The *Rand Daily Mail* (Johannesburg, South Africa) is part of the South African Associated Newspapers chain and the most widely read paper in South Africa. Although it has been threatened with government controls, it has supported many minority- and black-rights movements (Merrill, 1982, p. 793).

Development news items appearing in these papers were analyzed only if they appeared as spot or feature articles, photographs, illustrations, or combinations thereof. Editorials, comics, sports news, crime news, letters to the editor, classified ads, announcements, and obituaries were excluded from the analysis. Coders analyzed a total of 953 items.

Originally, the analysis was to include all newspapers issued during October 1982. However, because of difficulties in obtaining a complete set of October issues for some newspapers, the sample period was supplemented with issues from months as close to October as possible. In the final analysis, each newspaper was examined for one month between September 1982 and January 1983. About 80 percent of the development news items came from October issues of the newspapers. Although use of the same month for all newspapers would have been better methodologically, it can be argued that no matter what the time frame, a newspaper dedicated to covering development news would cover such news at all times of the year. The amount and nature of the news should not vary substantially from month to month.

For all development news items in the selected newspapers, coders answered 36 questions relating to news sources, geographic origin, priority, tone, size, and content of the item. After several training sessions, reliability checks were conducted on a sample of content across several English-language development news items. The first check, toward the beginning of the study, resulted in an intercoder reliability coefficient of about .80. The second check resulted in a coefficient of .93 (see Holsti, 1969, p. 137).

Newspaper content was analyzed according to the relationship of the press with its government. Countries that exercised little control over press content were South Africa, Israel, Lebanon, and Mexico. Countries where the government exerted a relatively strong influence on the press were Nigeria, Ivory Coast, Saudi Arabia, and Zimbabwe. Countries were grouped accordingly for one part of the analysis.

For another stage of the analysis, answers to questions requiring multiple responses—topics in item, sources used in item, provider of item—were combined to create a single variable. For example, the main and two subsidiary topics were collapsed into a single variable.

RESULTS

A total of 953 stories, or an average of 6.4 per day per newspaper, were coded as development news in the 9 papers for the 1-month period. Development news items were relatively evenly distributed over the days of the month. Of the newspapers selected, 6 were broadsheet and 3 were tabloid format. Only 27.7 percent of the stories were accompanied by a picture.

Development news has been described as news written in news-feature style, carrying analysis, and as process oriented rather than even oriented. In this sample, spot news[5] constituted nearly two-thirds of the news stories and the length and position of all stories were relatively low; for example, 44 percent of the stories took up one-eighth of a page or less (see Table 23.1).

Advocates of development news content also argue that the large agencies carry little regional news. In this study, more than four out of five (83 percent) of the stories were of national origin, while very few (2.6 percent) came from an adjacent country and less than one in ten from other developing countries (see Table 23.1).

It is also said that little news about the rural countryside is included in coverage by international news agencies. In this study, only 11.3 percent of the stories were predominantly about rural development.

Development news topics were related to home news 80.7 percent of the time, and only 13.1 percent dealt with foreign news. Most development news in the study was written by home providers—the newspaper's own reporter, the national news agency, a reader of the newspaper, or one of the paper's foreign correspondents.

Consistent with the charge that the "Big Four" international wire services provide little news about development, this study found only 4.8 percent of

Table 23.1
Comparison of Story Characteristics and Sources
for 1982 and 1983 (in percentages)

	1982	1983
Type of story		
spot	58.9	65.2
feature	40.4	34.8
Priority of story		
high priority	28.5	11.9
medium priority	49.0	32.6
low priority	22.5	55.5
Size of story		
⅛ page or less	58.0	44.0
⅛ to ¼ page	25.0	22.7
¼ to ½ page		15.1
½ page or more	17.0	13.2
Writer's sources		
predominantly human	51.4	72.3
predominantly document	23.7	6.9
both human and document	7.5	6.0
other (no attribution)	17.4	14.8
Providers		
international news services	4.9	4.8
alternative news services	.5	1.1
home sources	84.3	83.5
other foreign sources	—	4.1
no sources cited/unidentifiable	10.3[a]	6.5

a. The stories coded in this category were mostly from socialist newspapers that often do not cite providers of the stories.

Table 23.2
Article Topics

	Frequency of Mention[a]	Percentage of Total
Social service (consumerism, family planning, housing, health, transportation, welfare)	321	16.9
Food and agriculture	264	13.9
Economics	223	11.7
Education (kindergarten through high school, university education)	222	11.7
National integration and human relations	222	11.7
Commerce (tourism, trade, foreign aid)	206	10.9
Science and industry (industry, science, energy, resources)	187	9.9
Mass media and culture (mass media, telecommunications, culture)	161	8.5
Labor and migration to urban areas	92	4.8
Total	1898[b]	100

a. Includes coding of a main and two subsidiary topics, which were aggregated by the multiple response routine of SPSS.
b. Missing one case.

the development news attributed to any of those agencies. Tass, the Soviet Union's international news agency, was listed as the source of only one news story in the study. (It is not known, of course, how many development items were made available by the wire services, only how many were used.)

Topics and Sources

The coding allowed up to three topics per story. When the total number of topics addressed was collapsed into a single category, social services (health, family planning, housing, welfare, consumerism, and transportation) was the most frequently mentioned topic (16.9 percent), with food and agriculture second (13.9 percent). Three topics tied for third: economics, national integration, and education (see Table 23.2).

Government sources were consulted more often (54.9 percent of the time) than nongovernment sources (45.2 percent of the time) and were cited as a first source in 63.1 percent of the stories. When second and third sources were consulted, they were predominantly nongovernment sources (64.2 percent of the second sources and 69.1 percent of the third sources used). However, second sources were used in only about one-fourth of the stories and a third source in only 6.0 percent of the stories. The largest portion of the 111 high-priority items consulted only government sources (30.6 percent) and the largest portion of the 512 low-priority items consulted no government sources (39.3 percent).

Although critics charge that government handouts are the usual source of development news, live (or human) sources were consulted more frequently than were documents in most of the stories (78.3 percent of the stories relied on human sources or a combination of live sources and documents). When predominantly human or predominantly document sources were used, or when no sources were attributed, the story was more often spot than feature news. But when a mixture of human and document sources was used, the story was more likely to be a feature. However, regardless of the location of the item, humans were most often used as sources; when documents were used, it was predominantly in stories about foreign events.

While foreign experts are often considered to be overly relied on in the drafting and administration of development projects, only 12.1 percent of the development news stories used only foreign sources and an additional 8.4 percent used both foreign and native sources. When only foreign sources were consulted, it was most often regarding the development topics of commerce, economics, and social services. When only native sources were consulted, it was more frequently on topics related to social services, food and agriculture, or education. When both foreign and native sources were included in a story, it was more likely on the topics of commerce, economics, and food and agriculture.

Story Tone and
Use of Criticism and Analysis

Not all development news is necessarily good news. Negative or critical commentary, while not predominant, was found in 16.1 percent of the stories. A distinctly positive tone was found in 34.0 percent of the stories, and a neutral or balanced tone in the rest. Since most stories were short, it is likely

Table 23.3
Responses to Questions Concerning Comparative
and Evaluative Content of Development News
Items, 1982 and 1983 (in percentages)

	1982	1983
Item contains critical sources	23.2	20.4
Item compares outcome of development with original goals	31.3	22.1
Item compares success of the subject with government claims for success	34.4	12.2
Item speculates on the future of the development	65.5	53.0
Item compares subject to same subject in other developing countries	21.3	12.6

that more news in the neutral or balanced category was neutral rather than balanced, but since it was difficult for coders to agree upon what constituted a balanced story, the two categories were merged.

Of the 147 stories judged to be negative in tone, the majority were found in government-owned or -controlled newspapers (57 percent), while the rest were found in privately owned, less controlled papers.

All providers of news supplied neutral or balanced stories except the alternative news services. Of the 11 alternative news service stories used by the newspapers in this study, 6 were positive in tone. Critical sources were consulted in 58.3 percent of the stories provided by alternative news sources. The stories of all other providers—home reporter, national news agency, Big Four international agencies, and so on—contained predominantly noncritical sources. In fact, overall, only one in five of the stories contained information from sources critical of the development topic being addressed (see Table 23.3).

There was limited analysis of the development topic by comparison of the present situation with the original goals, accomplishments in other countries, or comparison of the outcome with the government claims for success (Table 23.3). More than half of the stories (53 percent) did speculate on the future of the development issue, however, and most stories (69.4 percent) did relate the issue to local needs. When comparison of the outcome with the original goals was made, it was done more often in the government-controlled papers than in the privately owned papers (by more than a three to one margin).

Ownership and
Control of the Press

Government-controlled presses of Zimbabwe, Ivory Coast, Saudi Arabia, and Nigeria relied less on foreign sources and foreign wire services (7.1 percent) than did privately owned newspapers (15.6 percent) of South Africa, Lebanon, Israel, and Mexico.

Domestic providers for both spot and feature news were used most often (91.2 percent). Of all sources used in development news items—domestic, foreign, Big Four wire services, or alternative news services—the alternative news services most frequently used critical sources (54.5 percent), while the Big Four (38.7 percent), home providers (20.3 percent) and foreign providers (10.8 percent) carried fewer critical sources.

According to Aggarwala (1979), a journalist's task in a developing country is to examine and evaluate development critically, but in both privately owned (26 percent) and government-controlled (17.8 percent) newspapers few critical sources appeared. When critical sources were carried, the surprising finding is that they most frequently appeared in government-controlled newspapers (62.0 percent).

Although it was expected that government-controlled newspapers would carry fewer critical sources than privately owned newspapers, other comparisons of government-controlled and privately owned newspapers reveal mixed findings. Government-controlled newspapers contained only slightly more stories that relied on only government sources (36.2 percent) than stories that cited no government sources (34.4 percent). Although privately owned newspapers more frequently used no government sources, government-controlled newspapers used only 5 percent more "only government sources" than did their privately owned counterparts. Generally, privately owned and government-controlled newspapers used more government sources (52.2 percent and 67.0 percent, respectively) than non-government sources (40.3 percent and 31.6 percent, respectively).

Both government-controlled and privately owned newspapers did little comparing of development subjects with similar problems in other countries. When the subjects were compared, the government-controlled presses did most of the comparing (59.2 percent). Similarly, when newspapers examined the relevance of development problems and projects to national or local levels, the government-controlled newspapers (78.1 percent) did so more often than privately owned newspapers (21.9 percent).

Comparison with Previous Study

In the 1982 study (based on 1981 data), five of the same newspapers were examined (the *New Nigerian, Excelsior,* the *Herald,* the *Rand Daily*

Mail and the *Jerusalem Post*). Three socialist papers were also studied (*Granma,* Havana, Cuba; *Neuer Weg,* Bucharest, Romania; and the *People's Daily,* Beijing, China), along with the *Daily Nation,* Nairobi, Kenya; *Botswana Daily News,* Gabarone, Botswana; and *al-Madinah,* Jeddah, Saudi Arabia.

Not much change or progress can be seen in the overall coverage in the two time periods for the entire sample or for the same newspapers over time. And in fact, some development news coverage was better in the previous study. A few of the changes were interesting (but might be explained by the absence of socialist newspapers in the present study). The level of priority placed on development news appears to have declined over the period, while the amount of space devoted to the stories increased (Table 23.1). There was also less reliance on documents than on live sources in the current study. No major shift in the use of news agencies or alternative news services was observed. There was a slight increase in the use of alternative news services, but no change in the use of international wire services was seen (Table 23.1). Even less critical analysis of a comparative nature was made about the development issues in this study than in the previous study (see Table 23.3).

DISCUSSION

If development news is ever to reach its potential as a genuine service to the cause of development, the findings of this research have shown that certain changes will have to be made: There must be greater use of critical sources, news analysis of development topics, and less dependence on government as the sole sources of information.

The findings also reveal very little use of available alternative news services. Such services have been offered as a partial or complete solution to problems of gaps in development coverage. In this study only three of the nine papers made any use of alternative news services and that use was extremely minimal. Inter Press Service, DEPTHnews, the Non-Aligned News Pool, and the Pan African News Agency were the agencies mentioned. We found the lack of use surprising in light of the increased number of these services and the emphasis placed on their use.

Robert Savio, director general of Inter Press Service (IPS), in a speech to the annual general meeting of the Netherlands Organization for International Development Co-operation in 1982, said that the present system of information distribution needs to be complemented with other "alternative flows of information, based on values, needs and actors which are currently absent." IPS, which Savio claims is the world's sixth largest news network, is an attempt to provide an alternative to the established news agencies. In 1981 IPS had 36 bureaus and by 1983 that number had increased to 42 (Giffard, 1983, pp. 16-17). IPS serves more than 400 clients—newspapers, governments, and universities—in 4 or 5 languages (Hamelink, 1983, p. 77).

Giffard (1983, p. 14), in an analysis of the IPS's English and Spanish output in October 1983 (the primary month of this study), concludes that IPS is precisely the kind of news source called for by developing countries: "More than three-quarters of the news carried on the two networks was sourced in the developing nations and deals with topics and actors of relevance to them."

Only seven stories attributed to IPS could be found in this analysis, even though IPS has bureaus in Beirut, Mexico City, and Lagos, the homes of four of the newspapers in this study.

Many other alternative news services exist for use by newspapers in the Third World. Although the Non-Aligned News Pool has been considered by some to consist largely of information emanating from heads of state, the service has been touted as a useful source of development news. Information transmitted by the pool is carried by IPS under a special agreement with that agency. This study produced only two Non-Aligned News Pool stories. DEPTHnews, based on Manila, one of the more firmly established feature services, was the source of one story. Other feature services currently available but that were unused here include Gemini, a London-based commercial feature service that focuses on development issues; WorldPaper, a Boston-based organization that produces a monthly newspaper supplement focusing on in-depth analysis of international issues and claiming a readership in excess of a million; and CANA, the most successful of several regional news agencies based in and serving the Caribbean (Cuthbert, 1981).

When all these alternative sources exist, it is difficult to understand why so little use was made of them by the newspapers included in this and the previous study. Savio (1982) comments that editors of international pages working for Third World newspapers may be blocking the use of alternative services:

> None of them—whether in the North or the South—has taken part in the debate on the new information order. They are professionals basically tied to the concept of "spot news," that is information which is to succeed in the market must have impact, and must be exceptional, it must attract attention. As we say in the jargon, it must be "sexy."

Giffard's (1983) analysis of the content of the IPS wires indicates that much of the information is "critical of the shortcomings of Third World nations." As the results of this study show, little development news is critical in nature, lending some support to the charge that development news is only "good news."

Although a detailed examination of the output of the alternative news service was beyond the scope of this study, samples of output from the Non-Aligned News Pool, IPS (through its U.S. base, Interlink), and Gemini were examined to determine the general nature of their services and possible reasons the papers in this study did not use them. The Non-Aligned News Pool copy consists of a fairly large number of very short (one- or two-paragraph) stories, which originate in and concern the Third World. However, the stories generally make no attempt at analysis and could be considered spot news, with heavy reliance on government sources and political or economic content.

Gemini, a service of London-based Interpress (a different organization than the Rome-based Inter Press Service), sends out a twice-weekly package of about six features to about thirty countries (J. Blyth, personal communication, September 8, 1983). The file emphasizes analysis of political situations in a variety of Third World countries, and includes maps, photographs, and other usable graphics.

Inter Press Service produces the most complete news services of the three examined. All stories originate in or relate directly to problems of development in Third World countries. Considerable analysis and background is included with each story. However, the stories tend to be event-oriented hard news and discuss problems of development without offering solutions for other countries with similar problems. The IPS copy is characterized by a style and format like that of any Western international news agency; the difference is that IPS transmits in-depth accounts of news usually neglected by other agencies. While it emphasizes economic and political problems, a full range of health, agriculture, and other social services topics is covered, stories that should be of interest to newspapers in Third World countries. Whether this service is not used because of its cost or because it includes material critical of Third World governments is a matter for speculation.

Good development-oriented information is available, therefore, and it is time that the editors and publishers of Third World newspapers began to avail themselves of those services and to expect their own reporters to write more critically and analytically about development. If adequate development coverage is a goal of the Third World press, then government leaders need to stop criticizing the Western press for its failings and begin to examine the situation at home and coordinate efforts to improve coverage in their own countries.

NOTES

1. The previous study was done in 1982 and based on 1981 data.
2. Development was defined by the graduate class in communication and national devel-

opment as follows: a process by which a country works toward relative economic self-reliance. Self-reliance is characterized by heterogeneous, but cooperative, sectors of the economy operating efficiently to meet the demands of a majority of a nation's population. (A nation's needs include culture, education, medicine, nutrition, shelter, health, transportation, telecommunication, employment, political participation, and a more equitable distribution of resources.)

3. Newspapers were selected from those available at the main university library. Although three class members who spoke French, Spanish, and Arabic were able to code in those languages, the remaining papers had to be selected from the English-language papers available in the library. The class selected a time period for study of the papers based on common availability of the newspapers.

4. The SPSS multiple-response facility was used to collapse this variable, but statistics are not computed in the multiple-response subprogram.

5. Spot news was distinguished from feature news as follows: Spot news was defined as news about an event, where timeliness of publication affects reader interest; feature news was defined as news about a process or a series of events, where timeliness does not affect reader interest.

REFERENCES

Aggarwala, N. (1978). News with Third World perspectives: A practical suggestion. In P. C. Horton (Ed.), *The Third World and press freedom* (pp. 197-208). New York: Praeger.

Aggarwala, N. (1979). What is development news? *Journal of Communication, 29* (2), 181-182.

Aggarwla, N. (1980). A new journalism. *Intermedia, 8* (1), 26-27.

Aggarwala, N. (1981). The issues at stake and a new information model. *Media Development, 28* (1), 7-12.

Anable, D. (1983,September). Helping a Third World advance. *IPI Report*, p. 14.

Cuthbert, M. (1981). The Carribbean News Agency: A Third World Model. *Journalism Monographs, 71.*

Europa Yearbook. (1983). London: Europa Publishers.

Fisher, H. A. (1982a). Lebanon. In G. Kurian (Ed.), *World press encyclopedia* (Vol. 1, pp. 595-603). New York: Facts on File.

Fisher, H. A. (1982b). Zimbabwe, In G. Kurian (Ed.), *World press encyclopedia* (Vol. 2, pp. 1059-1060). New York: Facts on File.

Giffard, C. A. (1983, August). *Inter Press Service: News from the Third World.* Paper presented at the annual convention of the Association for Education in Journalism and Mass Communication, Corvalis, Oregon.

Hall, P. (1983, January/February). What's all the fuss about Inter Press? *Columbia Journalism Review*, pp. 53-57.

Hamelink, C. (1983). *Cultural autonomy in global communication: Planning national information policy.* New York: Longman.

Holsti, O. (1969). *Content analysis for the social sciences and humanities.* Reading, MA: Addison-Wesley.

IPS—An information alternative for a new information order. *Development Dialogue, 2,* 98-102.

Merrill, J. C. (1982). South Africa. In G. Kurian (Ed.), *World press encyclopedia* (Vol. 2, pp. 793-806). New York: Facts on File.

Moore, S. R. (1982). Israel. In G. Kurian (Ed.), *World press encyclopedia* (Vol. 1, pp. 517-525). New York: Fact on File.

Mustafa, J. D. (1979). A comparative analysis of the use of development news in three Malaysian dailies during 1974. In J. A. Lent & J. V. Vilanilam (Eds.), *The use of development news* (pp. 56-70). Singapore: AMIC.

Nwankwo, R. L. (1982). Nigeria. In G. Kurian (Ed.), *World press encyclopedia* (Vol. 2, pp. 687-697). New York: Facts on File.

Nwankwo, R. L., & Kurian, G. (1982). Ivory Coast. In G. Kurian (ed.), *World press encyclopedia* (Vol. 2, pp. 1075-1077). New York: Facts on File.

Ogan, C. L. (1982). Development journalism/communication: The status of the concept. *Gazette, 29,* 3-13.

Ogan, C. L., & Swift, C. (1982, August). *Is the news about development all good?* Paper presented at the annual convention of the Association for Education in Journalism and Mass Communication, Athens, Ohio.

Osae-Asare, E. (1979). The Ghana press and national development: A comparative content analysis of development news in the national daily newspapers and the wire services, April-September 1976. In J. A. Lent & J. V. Vilanilam (Eds.), *The use of development news* (pp. 72-90). Singapore: AMIC.

Savio, R. (1982). *Communications and development in the '80s.* Speech to the annual general meeting of the Netherlands Organization for International Development Cooperation.

Schramm, W., & Atwood, E. (1981). *Circulation of news in the Third World: A study of Asia.* Hong Kong: Chinese University Press.

Sewell, M. (1982). Mexico. In G. Kurian (Ed.), *World Press Encyclopedia* (Vol. 1, pp. 627-639). New York: Facts on File.

Stephens, M. (1982, September/October). Can UPI be turned around? *Columbia Journalism Review,* pp. 54-58.

Sutopo, I. K. (1983). *Development news in Indonesian dailies.* Occasional Paper 15. Singapore: AMIC.

Vilanilam, J. V. (1979). Ownership versus development news content: An analysis of independent and conglomerate newspapers of India. In J. A. Lent & J. V. Vilanilam (Eds.), *The use of development news* (pp. 31-54). Singapore: AMIC.

24 ● International Communication Media Appraisal: Tests in Germany

J. DAVID JOHNSON

Arizona State University

E VER since George Gallup (1930) first examined reader interests, the study of media exposure and appraisal has been a topic of continuing interest within the field of communication. Studies to date have concentrated primarily on who reads and what is read. The question of why people expose themselves to media and have particular appraisals of them has not been explored adequately, however. This study examines this question exhaustively by testing a causal model of international communication media appraisal with readership surveys of three magazines—*Dialogue, Economic Impact,* and *Problems of Communism*—distributed in Germany.

This is the third in a series of tests of this model in differing countries. Previous tests of this theoretical framework were supportive of the general model examined here (Johnson, 1983a, 1983b). The model used in this programmatic research seeks to link respondent evaluations of the media directly with overall appraisal of them. Thus it stands in contrast to prior research approaches that investigated the relationships of loosely interrelated variables that have no direct explanatory linkage to the dependent variable focused on here, such as demographic research (for example, see Stamm, Jackson, & Bowen, 1978) and psychographic research (for example, see Urban, 1980).

The model, in general, posits determinative relationships between the three exogenous variables and appraisal. The first two variables, editorial tone and communication potential, primarily relate to message content attributes and the utility dimension represents a judgment of how these attri-

Correspondence and requests for reprints: J. David Johnson, Department of Communication, Arizona State University, Tempe, AZ 85282.

butes serve individual needs (Atkin, 1973). Thus this research relates attributes of the medium to the functions they serve for the reader, a focus shared by other recent programmatic research in this area (Burgoon & Burgoon, 1979, 1980).

Editorial tone reflects a reader's perception of the overall credibility and intentions of a medium. If an individual perceives that a medium has motives other than the mere provision of information, this will weigh heavily in his or her evaluation and exposure decisions. In a comprehensive examination of newspapers in the United States, Burgoon and Burgoon (1979) have found this dimension, particularly as it relates to fair-mindedness, to be the critical factor in determining overall satisfaction with a medium.

Another component of editorial tone is the perceived accuracy of information, regardless of motives. Burgoon and Burgoon (1979) have found that an editorial production index that included accuracy was positively related to satisfaction. For magazines of the type examined here, which are extensions of the U.S. government, designed to impart its views to elites in foreign countries, this dimension is critical. It can be expected that higher ratings on this dimension will be associated with higher summary appraisals.

Communication potential refers to an individual's perception of the manner in which information is presented. This dimension relates to issues of style and comprehension. For example, is a magazine clear, stimulating, and attractive? Burgoon and Burgoon (1980) have found for newspapers that indicants such as quality of visuals and of organization contained in an editorial production index related to satisfaction with a newspaper (Burgoon & Burgoon, 1979). Visual attractiveness of magazines has also been related to exposure cross-nationally (Johnson & Tims, 1981). Thus the model developed here predicts generally that the higher the evaluation of the communication potential of a magazine, the higher will be an individual's exposure to and appraisal of it.

The preceding dimensions involve a direct evaluation by an individual of a particular medium. The final dimension, utility, relates the characteristics of a medium directly to the needs of an individual. For example, is the information contained in the medium important for the individual's purposes, relevant, and topical? Atkin (1973) has argued that mass media exposure will result from a combination of such needs of the receiver and the attributes of a message reflected in the first two dimensions. Indeed, perceived utility of information has been found to relate to newspaper readership (Wang, 1977) and a satisfaction index that included a current information measure was found to have the strongest relationship with newspaper readership in a variety of communities (Burgoon & Burgoon, 1980). For the print media it has been argued that indicants of this dimension, such as interest, usefulness, and importance for achieving one's goals, are interrelated, and they have been found to be associated with readership (Carlson, 1960).

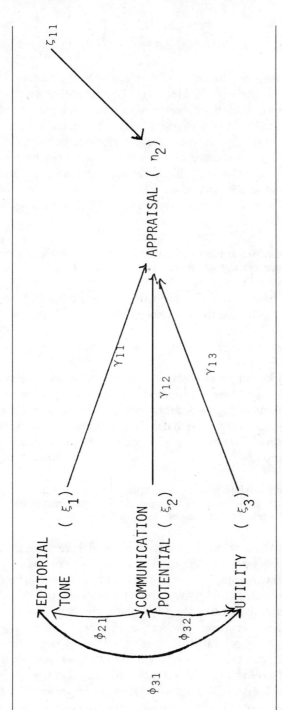

Figure 24.1. Theoretical model of factors affecting media appraisal.

Previous tests were conducted in India on *Economic Impact* and *Problems of Communism* (Johnson, 1983a) and in Nigeria on *Topic* and *Interlink* (Johnson, 1983b). Thus this research represents a unique attempt to validate cross-nationally a model of communication processes. While the previous tests, which rested on the literature just referenced, were quite supportive of the model, they indicated that some specific changes were necessary. These changes are reflected in the following hypotheses and in other changes in the model detailed in Figure 24.1.

First, previous findings in four tests in India and Nigeria suggest the following hypothesis:

H_1: The model specified in Figure 24.1 will provide a good overall fit to the observed system of intercorrelations.

In all four of the previous tests the path between editorial tone and appraisal has been positive, as the literature would predict. Thus:

H_2: There will be a positive relationship between editorial tone and appraisal.

In three out of four of the previous tests there has been a positive and significant relationship between communication potential and appraisal. The only exception was the highly pedantic magazine *Problems of Communism*. For this, and similar magazines, the more boring and "academic" their presentation of material, the more highly valued they may be by highly educated readers. Accordingly,

H_3: Generally there will be a positive relationship between communication potential and appraisal, except in the case of highly pedantic publications, where negative relationships may be expected.

In three of four of the tests in Phase I and Phase II there was a positive, significant relationship between utility and appraisal. The only exception to this in previous tests was *Topic* in Nigeria. The inverse relationship found in this instance was probably attributable to both the high utility of its content for readers in Nigeria, since it deals largely with African issues, and its high number of competitors—a greater number than that for any other magazine examined. Thus a greater relevance when combined with a competing medium of high quality can result in a situation where higher levels of utility result in lower appraisal ratings, since a more exacting standard might be applied to the magazine, which, as a result, suffers in comparison to its competitors.[1] Conversely, low utility ratings may cause readers to be more generous in their evaluations of a particular magazine.

H_4: Generally, there will be a positive relationship between utility and appraisal.

The results in Phases I and II also found positive associations among the exogenous variables. For example, the model specifies a positive relationship between the incomprehensibility of a medium, reflected in communication potential, and accuracy. If an article is subject to multiple interpretations, then its accuracy may be unverifiable.

H_5: There will be positive interrelationships among the variables of editorial tone, communication potential, and utility.

The previous tests of the model also incorporated an endogenous latent variable of exposure that is not included in the current tests for several reasons: the measurement of this variable proved problematic, partly as a result of the disparate characters of its indicators (see Johnson, 1982); the low relationship between exposure and appraisal indicated that the path between them should be trimmed from the model (Johnson, 1983a, 1983b); and, finally, this variable appeared to be affected substantially by situational factors not explicitly incorporated in the current theoretical framework.

In sum, the completely specified theoretical model attempts to move beyond the demographic and psychographic approaches that have characterized research in this area. This phase of the current research is designed to advance our understanding of this research problem in the following ways: (1) to see if the model can be extended to developed countries; (2) to focus on the effects of the exogenous variables on appraisal; and (3) to make some specific suggestions on the nature of contingent effects on the paths contained in the model.

METHOD

Background and Sample

The data for this analysis are drawn from personal interview readership surveys of elites conducted by a commercial contracting firm in West Germany. The samples were drawn randomly from individuals on the mailing lists of *Dialogue* (N = 294), *Problems of Communism* (N = 109), and *Economic Impact* (N = 124). These magazines primarily feature reprinted articles from leading U.S. publications and commissioned articles by major writers. Both *Problems of Communism* and *Economic Impact* are magazines of opinion somewhat similar in presentation of material to *Harper's*.

Problems of Communism is concerned primarily with critical, balanced essays on communism and East-West relations. *Economic Impact* reports on a broad range of economic development issues. *Dialogue,* on the other hand, is intended to be more of a general interest magazine, with wide-ranging articles on a variety of topics.

Readers of these magazines are primarily older, educated male elites drawn from the following occupational groups: media related, academic, government, businessmen, professionals, artists, writers, and students. The elite nature of the audience reflects the demographics generally found for magazines in the United States (see Anast, 1966).

Statistical Tests

LISREL (linear structural relationships), a general computer program for estimating structural equation systems involving multiple indicators of latent variables, was used to test the model developed in the previous section.[2] It has the following advantages over conventional multiple regression techniques when used to examine models of the sort tested here: (1) It simultaneously estimates all of the parameters in a model (Jöreskog, 1970); (2) it is specifically designed for the analysis of causal relationships (Goldberger, 1973); and (3) it permits the simultaneous specification and estimation of theoretical and measurement relationships (Fink, 1980).

Perhaps the most useful feature of LISREL for the analysis proposed here is its test of the goodness of fit of a model. The probability associated with this χ^2 test "is defined as the probability of getting a χ^2 value larger than that actually obtained given that the hypothesized model is true" (Jöreskog & van Thillo, 1972, p. 32). For this test probability levels approaching 1.0 are indicants of increasingly better fits of the model to the data. However, Jöreskog (1974) has indicated that this test should be interpreted cautiously, since for increasingly large sample sizes almost any hypothesized model becomes untenable. A less problematic test is the χ^2 to degrees of freedom ratio (Maruyamu & McGarvey, 1980; Wheaton, Muthen, Alwin, & Summer, 1977). In this test values less than 5.00 are indicants of increasingly better fits of the model to the data (Wheaton et al., 1977).

Observed Indicants

Although administered separately, all questionnaires used identical question wordings. To correct for some measurement error problems found in Phase I, different observed indicants were used for the latent, unobserved variables in this test (see Johnson, 1983a).[3] The indicants were contained in a battery of 7-point, bipolar adjective rating scales. As a convention, only the positive pole of the scale is used in this text. The battery of questions had the following introduction:

These next questions deal with your opinions of the magazines you read. Please look at these cards. Note that they show a number of scales indicated at each end with descriptive words or phrases. Please rate each magazine I mention on these scales.

For example, if you feel the magazine is always accurate rate it "7". If you feel it is neither always accurate nor always inaccurate choose one of the middle numbers, i.e., 1 through 7, that best describes your opinion. We will do this for each set of words or phrases.

This battery of questions was asked only of respondents who reported they read the magazines at least on occasion, which ensures that respondent evaluations are based on prior exposure.

The following bipolar scale items served as indicants for the editorial tone latent variable (ξ_1): accurate (x_1) and impartial (x_2). The lively (x_3), clear (x_4), and stimulating (x_5) observed indicants were used for communication potential (ξ_2). The indicants for utility (ξ_3) were: current (x_6) and important to me (x_7). The indicants for appraisal (η_1) was best magazine of its kind (y_1).

RESULTS

Tables 24.1, 24.2, and 24.3 contain the Pearson correlations of the observed indicants for *Dialogue, Economic Impact,* and *Problems of Communism,* respectively. *Dialogue* had more moderate correlations than the

Table 24.1
Pearson Correlations for *Dialogue*

Observed Indicant	y_1	x_1	x_2	x_3	x_4	x_5	x_6	x_7
y_1 best magazine of its kind — worst magazine of its kind								
x_1 accurate — inaccurate	.24							
x_2 impartial — prejudiced	.20	.30						
x_3 lively — dull	.27	.33	.25					
x_4 clear — confusing	.21	.27	.18	.26				
x_5 stimulating — bland	.30	.31	.28	.54	.38			
x_6 current — dated, old	.24	.27	.21	.34	.25	.39		
x_7 important to me — unimportant to me	.22	.23	.21	.41	.16	.36	.33	

Table 24.2
Pearson Correlations for *Economic Impact*

Observed Indicant	y_1	x_1	x_2	x_3	x_4	x_5	x_6	x_7
y_1 best magazine of its kind — worst magazine of its kind								
x_1 accurate — inaccurate	.41							
x_2 impartial — prejudiced	.20	.37						
x_3 lively — dull	.39	.34	.24					
x_4 clear — confusing	.20	.49	.27	.13				
x_5 stimulating — bland	.29	.42	.26	.17	.54			
x_6 current — dated, old	.25	.46	.29	.34	.51	.33		
x_7 important to me — unimportant to me	.47	.31	.28	.51	.18	.24	.29	

other tests. The results for *Problems of Communism* were more variable and generally higher than the other tests. The most dramatic differences between the correlation matrices were in the intercorrelations between the x_3, x_4, and x_5 indicants of communication potential.

Results for *Dialogue*

The results for the maximum likelihood tests of the theoretical model for each magazine are contained in Table 24.4. The model provides a quite acceptable fit to the data for *Dialogue* ($\chi^2 = 13.49$, 15 d.f.). The probability level was .565 and the chi-square to degrees of freedom ratio was .899 — quite exceptional for this sort of test. The paths (γ) between exogenous true variables and endogenous true variables ranged from $\gamma 12$, .150 to $\gamma 11$, .341. There was a moderate degree of association between the exogenous variables with values ranging from $\phi 31$, .256 to $\phi 32$, .358. The zeta variance was quite high, indicating that the model does not systematically account for a substantial proportion of the variance in appraisal.[4]

The results for the measurement model for *Dialogue* as well as the other two magazines are shown in Table 24.5. All of the observed indicants (except x_4, which has only a moderate value; .647) load heavily on their respective latent variables. The measurement errors range from moderate ($\theta_\delta 5 = .417$) to high ($\theta_\delta 4 = .794$). However, the coefficient of determination of .867 suggests that all together the x indicators are excellent measures of the latent variables.

Table 24.3
Pearson Correlations for *Problems of Communism*

	Observed Indicant	y_1	x_1	x_2	x_3	x_4	x_5	x_6	x_7
y_1	best magazine of its kind — worst magazine of its kind								
x_1	accurate — inaccurate	.34							
x_2	impartial — prejudiced	.33	.50						
x_3	lively — dull	.54	.25	.30					
x_4	clear — confusing	.25	.34	.23	.40				
x_5	stimulating — bland	.19	.46	.40	.27	.50			
x_6	current — dated, old	.03	.38	.23	.21	.40	.50		
x_7	important to me — unimportant to me	.58	.30	.23	.58	.29	.21	.10	

Table 24.4
Maximum Likelihood Results for Theoretical
Model for the Three Magazines

Parameter	Dialogue	Economic Impact	Problems of Communism
$\gamma 11$	.341	1.015	.135
$\gamma 12$	.150	.253	.869
$\gamma 13$	.272	−.562	−.210
$\zeta 11$	.812	.720	.676
$\phi 21$	.314	.411	.374
$\phi 31$	.256	.437	.228
$\phi 32$	.358	.371	.303
χ^2	13.49	60.32	73.16
Degrees of freedom	15	15	15
Ratio	.899	4.021	4.877
Probability level	.565	.001	.001

Results for *Economic Impact*

The model again provides an acceptable fit to the data for *Economic Impact* with a chi-square to degrees of freedom ratio of 4.021. The relationships between exogenous and endogenous variables ranged from −.562 for $\gamma 13$ to 1.015 for $\gamma 11$. The zeta variance for appraisal is lower than for

Table 24.5
Maximum Likelihood Results for Measurement
Models for the Three Magazines

Param- eter	Dia- logue	Eco- nomic Impact	Problems of Com- munism	Param- eter	Dia- logue	Eco- nomic Impact	Problems of Com- munism
λ_{y1}	1.000[a]	1.000	1.000	$\theta_{\epsilon1}$[b]	.000	.000	.000
λ_{x1}	1.000	1.000	1.000	$\theta_{\delta1}$	.636	.462	.424
λ_{x2}	.824	.636	.868	$\theta_{\delta2}$	.753	.782	.566
λ_{x3}	1.000	1.000	1.000	$\theta_{\delta3}$	.508	.727	.541
λ_{x4}	.647	1.088	.872	$\theta_{\delta4}$	.794	.676	.651
λ_{x5}	1.088	.959	.843	$\theta_{\delta5}$	.417	.749	.673
λ_{x6}	1.000	1.000	1.000	$\theta_{\delta6}$	.660	.680	.935
λ_{x7}	.971	.874	1.547	$\theta_{\delta7}$	.680	.756	.845
$\phi11$	.364	.538	.576	$\phi33$	.340	.320	.065
$\phi22$	.492	.273	.459				

a. For identification purposes the λ_{y1}, λ_{x1}, λ_{x3}, and λ_{x6} parameters were fixed at 1.000 (see Jöreskog & van Thillo, 1972).
b. The measurement error variance for y_1 was fixed at .000 since it was the sole indicator of η_1. This results in the measurement error being incorporated in the zeta variance (ζ_1) estimate of this latent variable.

Dialogue, indicating a higher proportion of variance explained by the latent exogenous variables.

The results for the measurement model for the Economic Impact tests are shown in Table 24.5. Except for $\lambda \times 2$, which has only a moderate value (.636), all of the observed indicants load heavily on their respective latent variables. Again the measurement errors range from moderate ($\theta_\delta1 = .462$) to high ($\theta_\delta 2 = .782$). The coefficient of determination of .586 indicates that these indicators provide acceptable measures for the latent variables.

Results for Problems of Communism

The model provides an acceptable fit to the data for Problems of Communism with a ratio of 4.877. The values for the gammas range from −.210 for $\gamma13$ to .869 for $\gamma12$. The results for this magazine also reveal the highest proportion of variance explained for these particular tests ($\zeta11 = .676$).

All of the observed indicators load heavily on their respective latent variables, while the measurement errors for the individual indicants are also higher than the previous tests. However, the coefficient of determination of .687 indicates that the observed indicants provide good measures of the latent exogenous variables.

DISCUSSION

In general, the results indicate that the model provides an acceptable fit to the data in three separate tests, with *Dialogue* in particular exhibiting exceptional results.[5] Thus Hypothesis 1 is confirmed. Since none of the values for estimated parameters fall below .05, none of them should be "trimmed" from the model (see Land, 1969). In general, the measurement errors are acceptable and there are high loadings of the observed indicants on the latent variables. This, coupled with the coefficient of determination results, suggests that the measurement model is quite acceptable.[6] The amount of variance explained in appraisal was similar to that reported in other tests (see Burgoon & Burgoon, 1979) and actually the results reported here were generally superior. All of these factors taken together are quite supportive of the general theoretical framework advanced earlier.

Hypothesis 2 was confirmed; there was a positive relationship between editorial tone and appraisal in all of the tests. In the three phases involving seven tests this result has been consistent, adding further weight to the findings reported here. In addition, this finding reaffirms the importance of editorial tone for magazines of this kind distributed by a foreign government (Johnson & Tims, 1981).

Consistent with the overall framework adopted here, and in support of the general prediction made in Hypothesis 3, all of the paths for communication potential indicated a positive relationship between it and appraisal. However, this does conflict with the previous results for *Problems of Communism* in India, where a negative relationship was found. There are several possible explanations for this discrepancy. First, it could be attributable to cultural differences between the two countries. Second, it could reflect a more general predisposition on the part of the Germans toward a positive appraisal of a magazine with this type of content. Thus these conflicting results may reveal the differing basic orientations of elites in these countries to the United States. In India and Nigeria, elites typically view themselves as being in the nonaligned bloc of nations. German elites, for the last 30 years allies of the United States, may desire a more one-sided treatment of issues related to communism. Thus they view the magazine more favorably in general, a factor that may spill over into favorable evaluations on the dimension of communication potential.

The most discrepant findings in the current research are associated with Hypothesis 4. Except for a magazine such as *Topic,* for which the content was highly valued and which was in a highly competitive situation, this path has been positive in previous tests. It can be argued that *Economic Impact* and *Problems of Communism,* both of which exhibited negative relationships, fall into this category.[7] On the other hand, *Dialogue,* with content that is of the same high utility, is not faced with the same competitive situation.

Another explanation for this discrepant finding may lie in the editorial slant given to issues in a magazine such as *Economic Impact*. Economic issues are probably the biggest source of strain in U.S.-German relations; however, the two nations need to maintain close ties for political and security reasons. Thus appraisals of this magazine's content, which deals largely with U.S.-foreign economic relations, may be clouded by conflicting reactions on the part of the readers. On the one hand, heightened economic performance results in greater perceptions of U.S. strength; on the other, it may come at the cost of direct economic impacts on the German economy and trade.

As predicted in Hypothesis 5, all of the covariances between exogenous latent variables in all three tests were positive. Thus all three phases bear out the important interrelationships among these variables.

One of the advantages of this sort of programmatic research is the evidence it provides concerning the nature of contingent factors that should be incorporated in future modeling. First, the nature of competing sources appears to have a direct effect on the results, particularly when tied to utility, as it has in other studies (Burgoon & Burgoon, 1980; Buss, 1967; Urban, 1980). Second, the predispositions of individuals to a particular source also appear to have important impacts. In this instance, the closer allegiance of German elites, when compared to Nigerian and Indian elites, probably produced some instability in the model.

In summary, this is the third phase of a programmatic research effort that seeks to develop a general model of media exposure and appraisal. The current tests focused on appraisal with data drawn from three separate research surveys conducted among German elites. While there were some differences in the results of the tests of the model in this and the other phases, they are probably attributable to the contingent factors already discussed. What is remarkable is the generally high degree of similarity of the tests of the model, especially in the overall goodness of fit to the data, in three different countries with seven magazines. These results suggest that the model provides a basic framework in which to pursue continued research aimed at specifying more directly various contingent factors.

NOTES

1. This points to a general problem with the test of the model in Germany. The USICA has traditionally been criticized for distributing its media products in Western Europe, given the wide availability of quality media products that are concerned with the United States (U.S. General Accounting Office, 1974). In this context the magazines examined here might be evaluated in a considerably different light than in previous tests. Nevertheless, based on prior literature and previous tests, the model still bases its predictions on the prior results.

2. For a complete description of LISREL, the program and its associated terminology, consult Jöreskog and Sörbom (1981).

3. While all of the previous tests involved the same latent exogenous variables, there are slight differences in the indicants from test to test. In the Indian tests an interest in public affairs indicant was used for utility. This indicant proved to be very troublesome and it was not used in the current test. The remaining indicants are the same except that in the current test well intentioned is not used as an indicant for editorial tone and relevant was not used as an indicator for utility, since it correlated so closely with the importance indicant.

The Nigerian tests used a slightly different scaling procedure for the questions. They also included the additional indicant of authoritative for editorial tone, visually attractive and thought provoking as the sole indicants of communication potential, and also relevant as an additional indicant of utility. Of course, differences in results between these tests might be attributable to the differences between the indicators used.

4. Since there was only one indicator for appraisal, its measurement error was fixed at .000; as a result, measurement error is incorporated in its zeta variance. This probably accounts in part for their slightly higher values.

5. LISRELV provides several new measures of goodness of fit; the pattern of these additional indicators provides further support for the model. The values of the goodness of fit index ranged from .828 for *Problems of Communism* to .988 for *Dialogue*. For this statistic, higher values indicate better fits of the model to the data. The residuals plot for the three tests ranged from acceptable to good for this sort of test. The highest number of residuals greater than two, which indicate problems in the model's ability to specify observed correlations, was two for *Problems of Communism*. In general, the modification indices were quite low, indicating that there was no unestimated parameter that could contribute substantially to a better model.

6. The measurement model results were similar to those in previous tests. The measurement model used in the Nigerian tests was somewhat better than that used here and the model used in India exhibited more instability than the present one.

7. The path for *Problems of Communism* may be attributable in part to a low intercorrelation between the indicators of utility (.10). This result may stem from the characteristics of these respondents. Since their opposition to communism is probably deep-seated, the indicator of utility probably does not weigh as heavily for them as it does for other magazines the agency disseminates.

REFERENCES

Anast, P. (1966). Personality determinants of mass media preferences. *Journalism Quarterly, 43,* 729-732.

Atkin, C. (1973). Instrumental utilities and information seeking. In P. Clarke (Ed.), *New models for mass communication research.* Beverly Hills, CA: Sage.

Burgoon, J. K., & Burgoon, M. (1980). Predictors of newspaper readership. *Journalism Quarterly, 57,* 589-596.

Burgoon, M., & Burgoon, J. K. (1979). Predictive models of satisfaction with a newspaper. In D. Nimmo (Ed.), *Communication yearbook 3.* New Brunswick, NJ: Transaction.

Buss, L. J. (1967). Motivational variables and information seeking in the mass media. *Journalism Quarterly, 44,* 130-133.

Carlson, E. R. (1960). Psychological satisfaction and interest in news. *Journalism Quarterly, 37,* 547-551.

Fink, E. L. (1980). Structural equation modeling: Unobserved variables. In P. R. Monge & J. N. Cappella (Eds.), *Multivariate techniques in communication research.* New York: Academic.

Gallup, G. (1930). A scientific method for determining reader interest. *Journalism Quarterly, 7,* 1-13.

Goldberger, A. S. (1973). Structural equation models: An overview. In A. S. Goldberger & O. D. Duncan (Eds.), *Structural equation models in the social sciences.* New York: Seminar.

Johnson, J. D. (1982). The dimensionality of readership measures. *Communication Research, 9,* 607-616.

Johnson, J. D. (1983). A test of a model of magazine exposure and appraisal in India. *Communication Monographs, 50,* 148-157.

Johnson, J. D. (1983b). *A test of a model of media exposure and appraisal of two magazines in Nigeria.* ERIC Clearinghouse on Reading and Communication Skills, ED 219-758.

Johnson, J. D., & Tims, A. R. (1981). Magazine evaluations and levels of readership: A cross-national comparison. *Journalism Quarterly, 58,* 96-98.

Jöreskog, K. G. (1970). A general method for the analysis of covariance structures. *Biometrika, 57,* 239-251.

Jöreskog, K. G. (1974). Analyzing psychological data by structural analysis of covariance matrices. In D. H. Krantz, R. C. Atkinson, R. D. Luce, & P. Suppes (Eds.), *Contemporary developments in mathematical psychology: Measurement, psychophysics, and neural information processing* (Vol. 2). San Francisco: W. H. Freeman.

Jöreskog, K. G., & Sörbom, D. (1981). *LISRELV: Analysis of linear structural relationships by maximum likelihood and least square methods.* Chicago: International Educational Services.

Jöreskog, K. G., & van Thillo, M. (1972). *LISREL: A general computer program for estimating a linear structural equation system involving multiple indicators of unmeasured variables.* Princeton, NJ: Educational Testing Service.

Katz, E., Blumler, J., & Gurevitch, M. (1974). Utilization of mass communication by the individual. In J. Blumler & E. Katz (Eds.), *The uses of mass communication: Current perspectives on gratifications research.* Beverly Hills, CA: Sage.

King, C. W., & Summers, J. O. (1971). Attitudes and media exposure. *Journal of Advertising Research, 11,* 26-32.

Land, K. C. (1969). Principles of path analysis. In E. F. Borgatta (Ed.), *Sociological methodology: 1969.* San Francisco: Jossey-Bass.

Lehmann, D. R. (1971). Television show preference: Applications of a choice model. *Journal of Marketing Research, 8,* 47-55.

Maruyama, G., & McGarvey, G. (1980). Evaluating causal models: An application of maximum likelihood analysis of structural equations. *Psychological Bulletin, 87,* 502-512.

McCombs, M. (1977). Newspaper readership and circulation. *ANPA: News Research Report, 3,* 1-6.

Stamm, K. R., Jackson, K. M., & Bowen, L. (1978). *Antecedents to newspaper subscribing and using.* Unpublished manuscript, University of Washington, Communication Research Center.

U.S. General Accounting Office. (1974). *Telling America's story to the world: Problems and issues.* U.S. Information Agency Report B-118654. Washington, DC: Government Printing Office.

Urban. C. D. (1980). Correlates of magazine readership. *Journal of Advertising Research, 20,* 73-84.

Wang, G. (1977). Information utility as a predictor of newspaper readership. *Journalism Quarterly, 54,* 791-794.

Wheaton, B., Muthen, B., Alwin, D. P., & Summer, G. F. (1977). Assessing reliability and stability in panel models. In D. R. Heise (Ed.), *Sociological methodology: 1977.* San Francisco: Jossey-Bass.

25 ● Translation Accuracy: Using Multidimensional Scaling

GEORGE A. BARNETT ● MARK T. PALMER ● HANA NOOR AL-DEEN

State University of New York — Buffalo ● University of Wisconsin — Madison ● State University of New York — Buffalo

ACCURATE language translation is a vital issue in bilingual and multilingual societies. National development and social progress rely to a great extent on the mutual understanding and cooperation of linguistic groups. The problems resulting from the lack or distortion of information transfer across cultural boundaries affect the vital areas of science, industry, government, and education. The level of technology and production achieved is directly dependent on the quality of available information. Ethnic minorities and other culture-bound groups, when deprived of the opportunity to develop or adopt to technological innovations, are handicapped in modern competitive economies. Policy decisions in business and government can also be severely distorted by poor communication through inaccurate translation, which can limit political participation and thus the process of national integration.

Finally, intercultural understanding as a whole suffers from poor-quality translation because it places groups and individuals into positions of high uncertainty. If information is inaccurate or uninterpretable, the potential for mutual understanding and trust diminishes and the potential for conflict in-

AUTHORS' NOTE: We would like to thank Charles Petrie, Kenneth Day, Nicholas Illich, and Mark Feldman, without whom this research would not have been possible.

Correspondence and requests for reprints: George A. Barnett, Department of Communication, State University of New York, Buffalo, NY 14260.

659

creases. This chapter tests a method to ensure quality translation that has the potential to facilitate intercultural communication and mutual understanding.

BACKGROUND[1]

Communication can be thought of as a continuous process in which information is shared between individuals or groups. The convergence theory of communication describes this process as being directed toward the goal of mutual understanding (Kincaid, 1975; Rogers & Kincaid, 1981; Barnett & Kincaid, 1983; Palmer, 1981; Palmer & Barnett, 1982; Kincaid, Yum, Woelfel, & Barnett, 1983). Participants continue to exchange information as long as there are perceived differences in their understanding of each other or of the content of their communication.

In a single-culture context, this can be represented as a unique, functional system of concepts or meanings (a system of symbols) that facilitates the social interaction of the members. When communication is limited to a particular topic, the reference frames are also limited for the participants.

> When we communicate with others we are endeavoring to present our concepts in the domain of our conversation and to learn from them about the separate relations among concepts in the same domain. (Woelfel & Fink, 1980, p. 37)

In an intercultural or bilingual context, mutual understanding is the result of the same convergence process, the increased similarity between the semantic/conceptual frameworks of the participants from different cultures or linguistic groups (Barnett, 1974; Palmer & Barnett, 1984).

Translation is a vital means of communication between language-bound cultures. From the convergence perspective, mutual understanding may be represented in translation as the equivalence of two texts (one being the translation of the other). If the texts are substituted for the individuals participating in the convergence process, equivalence is the goal of the translation process. This results when the semantic/conceptual domains relevant to the content of the texts are the same. Accuracy or clarity in translation is then a function of bringing the domains into equivalence.

Therefore, the fundamental issue lies in how we judge equivalence. What are the indicators of the degree of similarity or difference in the conceptual/semantic frameworks of the participants and how can an observer know when the cyclical process has reached its goal of equivalence or mutual understanding?

Ideally, the bilingual translator stands at the meeting of the two languages and their cultures (MacNamara, 1970; Nida, 1975; Barnett, 1977a,

1977b). However, it is not always the case that a bilingual is trained in the particular subject matter dealt with in the material to be translated. Also, there is no guarantee that one translator is equally competent in both languages. As a result, equivalence of technical documents should not be determined by the judgments of bilinguals. Some empirical measure of the cognitive/semantic frameworks involved in translated texts must be used. This measure must take a behavioral approach using responses of a sample of the intended users of the text to the actual text itself. These individuals should be viewed as judges or observers of the text rather than as subjects involved in an experiment. Their responses should be taken to be an evaluation of the translation.

Back-translation has thus far shown the best results in bilingual/expert judged situations (Ervin & Bowers, 1952; Ervin & Osgood, 1954; Brislin, 1972; Brislin & Sinaiko, 1973). Typically, in this method a document is translated back into its original language and both original-language versions are compared by bilinguals acting in the place of single-language users. Using the same cyclical process, but modifying it to include objective measures, would eliminate the variance accounted for by bilingual judges.

The most effective methods of representing the relationship between concepts (meaning) in semantic domains as they are embedded in language have been developed through spatial modeling using either the semantic differential scale or multidimensional scaling (Osgood, Suci, & Tannenbaum, 1957; Osgood, May, & Miron, 1975; Barnett, 1976). These techniques present the relationship, through the mathematical manipulation of data, along comparative dimensions and across linguistic boundaries. The result is a mathematically defined space describing the semantic/conceptual frameworks of the language groups in relation to the text. This is simply a way of comparing concepts that users of the texts consider important. Because there are several problems that make the semantic differential scale less than ideal as a measure of meaning and therefore as a measure of equivalence, metric multidimensional scaling is preferred to determine the degree of semantic/conceptual equivalence (Barnett, 1976; Woelfel & Fink, 1980).

Proposed Methods

The most versatile measurement method available for determining the quality of translation is the Galileo system of metric multidimensional scaling (MMDS). It meets the qualifications specified above and has been shown reliable and theoretically valid in several linguistic and cross-cultural studies (Barnett, 1974, 1977a, 1977b, 1979, 1980; Barnett & McPhail, 1980; Wigand & Barnett, 1976; Barnett, Wigand, Harrison, Woelfel, & Cohen, 1981; Kincaid et al., 1983).

The process of measuring semantic/conceptual frameworks begins with determination of the key concepts in the document to be translated. This is done through in-depth interviews with representative samples from the population of intended users in the original language after they have read the document. For the translation of a technical document, these individuals would be professionally equivalent to the intended users in the target language.

The second step is to measure precisely the relationship among the key concepts to generate the semantic/conceptual space of the users. This is done using the original text, a tentative translation, and back-translation as stimuli. Measurement is done using the method of pair-comparisons (Thurstone, 1927). Subjects estimate the dissimilarity between the relevant concepts against a criterion standard. Typically, the questions are worded in the following way: If X and Y are U units apart, how far apart are concepts A and B?

This format allows respondents to report any positive number, rather than limiting their responses by forcing them to choose a point on a fixed scale, as with Likert and Osgood's semantic differential scales (Barnett et al., 1981). This increases the variability of responses, their precision, and the scale's ability to describe change over time. Further, it allows for direct comparison among the symbols, requiring none of the assumptions of the semantic differential.

The completion of the data collection operations results in a concepts × concepts × subjects matrix (S) that is square and symmetrical. Each cell in the matrix (s_{ij}) represents the distance between concepts i and j. To determine the linguistic characteristics of a group, S is averaged. Any entry s_{ij} is the mean distance between concepts i and j, as seen by the average member of the group (Barnett, 1977a, 1977b).

Matrix S may be converted to a multidimensional space. Mathematically, the process is analogous to converting a matrix of intercity distances to a Cartesian coordinate system where latitude and longitude are the reference axes and the cities' locations on these dimensions are given. From the coordinates a graphic representation such as a map may be drawn. In that special case, an n × n matrix of cities may be reduced to a two-dimensional configuration with little loss of information. However, in semantics, this may not be the case. Semantic space is often multidimensional, and when comparing the semantic/cognitive frameworks across languages for equivalence, all the dimensions used to differentiate the symbols should be taken into account (Barnett & Woelfel, 1979).

Change or difference in language may be examined by repeating the pair-comparison phase and transforming the data for each language. Translated equivalents of the key concepts are used for the language into which the text is being translated. Comparisons of measurements in both languages make it possible to examine the differences between the texts and how individual concepts differ across languages. In this way one can determine where the translation is in error and how to manipulate the concepts to modify the translated document to achieve equivalence.

This assumes that the semantic/cognitive space generated from readers of the original document represents a fixed criterion against which the translation is evaluated. If this assumption is made, then the translator may engage in a cybernetic process of reducing the differences between the spaces (error in translation) through an iterative process of testing and adjusting the translated document (Palmer & Barnett, 1982, 1984). Alternatively, the original document may be adjusted to make it more amenable to the translation process. This is known as "pretranslation" (Nida, 1966). This dynamic interplay between the original document and its translation, which would result in their congruence, is more consistent with the tenets of convergence theory. It is appropriate for many nonscientific materials, especially, governmental documents in multilingual societies.

AN EMPIRICAL EXAMPLE

The goal of this research is to evaluate the utility of metric multidimensional scaling as a procedure to determine the accuracy of translation of written materials in natural language. Once the translation's accuracy and the locations of discrepancies from equivalence are known, the researcher may intervene to ensure that both documents have a common meaning. This section will demonstrate these procedures through a translation of a document from English to Arabic. No specific hypotheses will be presented or tested because this research is evaluative and therefore descriptive in nature.

Methods

Step 1:
Selection of the Document for Translation

The first step in the process is the selection of a document for translation. The following selection criteria were employed:

(1) The document must be precise and technical to control for variance in interpretation. That is, the relations among the concepts in the text must be clear.
(2) There should be a limited number of key concepts. They should be clear, standing out from the surrounding text, which should describe the relationships among these symbols. There should be a high level of agreement among the subjects as to which are the key concepts in the text.
(3) While the document should be technical, it must at the same time be translatable. Symbols for the concepts in the text must have counterparts in the lan-

guage into which it is to be translated. Since English has become the *lingua franca* of science and commerce, many documents cannot be used because the English symbols for many technical concepts have been borrowed directly.

(4) The document should not be mathematical or contain graphics. The text should avoid universal symbols; it should not present information in a manner that need not be translated.

(5) The document should not be too difficult for the subjects to comprehend. It should present a complete, unambiguous set of relations in a relatively short space—two or three pages. This will prevent subject mortality and ensure subject motivation to complete the testing procedures.

(6) The document should not be in the subjects' area of academic experience. In this way, subject equivalence across language can be assumed. Simply, the subjects can be matched using knowledge of the subject matter as the criterion.

The selected document was a portion of Ball-Rokeach and De Fleur's "A Dependency Model of Mass Media Effects" (1982, pp. 157-158). It met all the criteria mentioned above. The only limitation on the subject selection was that subjects be unfamiliar with mass communication.

Step 2:
Selection of the Samples

The samples for this study included a group of subjects for which Arabic was the first language and a group of English speakers. The 50 Arabic speakers were enrolled at the State University of New York at Buffalo. The majority were Palestinian. Others came from throughout the Middle East and North Africa. The majority were engineering majors, but some were studying physics, linguistics, education, management, sociology, pharmacy, computer science, geography, and chemistry. There were no communication majors among the Arabic sample.

The English speakers were drawn from introductory communication classes and were excused from the research if they had taken a mass communication course or were not native English speakers. The total English-speaking sample was 208. These subjects performed three tasks: (1) They identified the key concepts in the text; (2) they estimated the relations among the selected key concepts in the original text; (3) they estimated the relations among the key concepts after reading the back-translation.

Step 3:
Pretesting to Determine the Key Concepts

After the text and samples were chosen, a portion of the English sample (N = 31) read the text and identified the "key words" or "key concepts," as well as the topic sentence or the theme of the text. The key concepts and topic sentence were elicited because it cannot be expected that single words alone in any language will convey the meaning of a text or translate directly into single words in another language. Since equivalence is measured through the relationships among concepts, word-for-word equivalence need not be expected.

A content analysis of the responses revealed that the most frequently mentioned words or phrases were as follows:

word or phrase	frequency
(1) audience	18
(2) mass media	24
(3) society	19
(4) dependency	29
(5) information	20
(6) social conflict and change	10
(7) needs	9
(8) fantasy and escape	7
(9) cognition	5
(10) feelings	6
(11) behavior	8

These concepts formed the basis of a Galileo questionnaire. There was variation in consensus regarding how "key" each symbol was. While "dependency" was selected by 29 of 31 respondents (94 percent), "cognition" was chosen by only 5 (16 percent). This lack of agreement on the document's central concepts may prove problematic.

Step 4:
Translation of the Text

Portions of the essay were translated from English to Arabic through standard back-translation procedures. One of the authors translated the document into Arabic. She is an Iraqi studying for a doctorate in communication. Her course work has focused upon the mass media. She has one master's degree in behavioral science and another in English. Her Arabic translation was translated back into English by an Egyptian doctoral student majoring in educational administration, with course work in communication.

There were substantial differences between the original English text and the back-translation due to variations in dialect between Egypt and Iraq and differences in expertise on the topic. Among the discrepancies were semantic variations involving the words "public," "people," and "society." These differences were resolved in discussions until there was agreement on the sample translation. The back-translation was edited to make it grammatical.

The translation process resulted in three versions of the text: the original English version, an Arabic translation, and a back-translation in English. This allowed for the comparison between the original text and both the translation and the back-translation. Comparisons between the original and the back-translation have certain advantages. First, often translations are performed in one society and then sent to another. In that case, sufficiently large samples in the second language may be unavailable. Comparisons using the back-translation allows the researcher to evaluate the translations for discrepancies without leaving the society where the original was produced.

The second advantage of comparing the back-translation to the original is that cultural differences between the two language groups do not enter into the evaluation of the translation. All subjects come from the same culture. Thus the only source of variation across the two conditions is the text, either the original or its back-translation.

However, the goal of the translation process, following convergence theory, is for the two different language groups to reach a common understanding of the meaning of the text, despite cultural differences. For this reason it is essential to focus on the responses of the actual users of the translation in their own language. Thus it is necessary to compare the original text and the translation directly.

Step 5:
Perform Galileo Analysis in Original Language

A Galileo instrument was created by randomly ordering the concepts from the pretest and then forming all possible pairs of words or phrases. The criterion pair was "needs and dependency are 10 units apart." This instrument was given to two groups of English speakers after they had read either the original text or its back-translation. They were instructed to base their estimates upon the essay they had just read. Subjects were systematically assigned to either condition. A total of 86 subjects read the original text and completed the Galileo instrument; 91 read the back-translation and completed the pair comparisons. Data collection took place in the classroom.

Step 6:
Perform Galileo Analysis in the Translated Language

The Galileo instrument was then translated into Arabic and checked through standard back-translation procedures. It was administered to the 50 Arabic speakers after they read the translated text. They were also instructed to base their estimates upon the essay they had just read. Data were collected while students were socializing in the cafeteria.

Results

Step 7:
Analysis of the Differences Among the Versions

In all, 23 (.2 percent) estimates were removed from 9664. No values were removed from the translated data set. The mean reported value for the original group was 15.81; it was 16.72 for the back-translation and only 6.99 for the Arabic group. Clearly, the Arabic subjects perceived the differences among the scaled concepts to be smaller than did the two English-language groups. This may be due either to the text, which did not differentiate the terms to the same degree, or to the use of smaller numbers by the Arabic speakers. Evidence in support of the latter interpretation may be found by examining the mean reported value for the criterion standard. The Arabic subjects reported that "needs" and "dependency" were only 6.40 units apart, significantly less than the standard of 10.0 ($t = 5.11$, $p < .001$). The original text group reported a value of 10.07, and the back-translation group, 10.53. There was no difference between these two groups ($t = .03$, $p > .05$). To control for the smaller metric, all values were multiplied by 1.55 to adjust them to the same metric as the one used by the original group. All further analyses were based upon these adjusted values.

One difference between the original group and the group that read the back-translation was that there was more variance in the estimates of differences among the pairs for the back-translation. The mean standard deviation for the original was 18.49; this figure was 23.46 for the back translation. The ratio of the variance produced an F of 1.49. If the degrees of freedom are equal to the number of observations (the number of pair comparisons times the sample size), they are 4715, 4923. F is significant, indicating greater overall variance in the back-translation.

This result indicates that there is greater uncertainty about the relations among the key concepts in the back-translation. That is, the translation and back-translation resulted in the loss of information. This result would be expected from information theory (Shannon & Weaver, 1949), which suggests that there is never perfect fidelity in communication. Each time a message is communicated it is distorted to a certain degree. In this case, the code system of the message was intentionally altered twice, once into Arabic and once back into English, causing the loss of information. Since the goal of the translation process is the production of an equivalent document, one without the loss of information, it may prove useful to examine the respective variances of each group to ensure that they are equivalent. This analysis could not be performed with the Arabic group because the use of a smaller standard of comparison is reflected in the variance.

The means of each group were next converted into spatial coordinates. Due to a clerical error only the first ten concepts were scaled. "Feelings" was excluded from the measurement process. The first two dimensions of each data set are graphically represented in Figure 25.1.[2] These two dimensions accounted for 59 percent of the variance for the original group, 54 percent for the back-translation, and 52 percent for the Arabic group. The correlations of the concepts' locations on these axes with the locations of the origi-

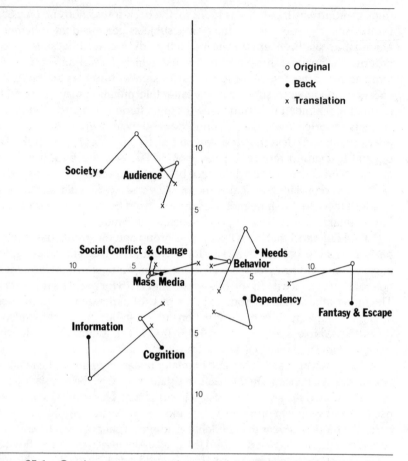

Figure 25.1   Graphic representation for original, translation, and back-translation groups.

nal group were .98 and .93 for dimensions 1 and 2 for the back-translation group, and .92 and .99, respectively, for the Arabic group.

All three groups used the same dimensions to evaluate the concepts in the essay. Dimension 1 differentiates reality from fantasy. The concepts "information" and "fantasy and escape" are bipolar. Dimension 2 differentiates "society" and "audience" from "information" and "cognition," suggesting a social to mental or psychological dimension. These dimensions were labeled without statistical verification. Since they are only orthonormal reference vectors, meaning should not be attributed to them unless regression analysis confirms the attribution (Barnett & Woelfel, 1979).

Figure 25.1 reveals that the Arabic group's concepts (the x's) are closer to the origin than the other two groups. This indicates that they did not differentiate the concepts to the same degree as the other groups. Since these dimensions account for the greatest proportion of the variance, this interpretation is justified.

Figure 25.1 also reveals the sources of the discrepancies among the translations. The length of the lines connecting the equivalent concepts indicates the degree of discrepancy, such that the longer the line, the greater the problem in that concept's translation. These lines are relatively long for "society," "information," "social conflict and change," and "fantasy and escape." Special attention should be given to these concepts when changing the document to improve the translation. The discrepancies are considerably less for "mass media," "behavior," and "audience," suggesting that these concepts were translated with little error. However, since these two dimensions account for only about 55 percent of the total variance, the graphic representation should be viewed somewhat skeptically. Greater emphasis should be placed upon the mathematical description that is presented later.

While there is a high degree of similarity among the spaces, there are systematic differences among the three groups. The traces or sum of the eigenroots of the spatial coordinates matrices indicates that the groups differentiated the key concepts to a greater or lesser degree (Danowski, Stoyanoff, & Barnett, 1977; Stoyanoff & Fink, 1981). The original group's trace was 1052.34; the back-translation, 1097.65; and the Arabic group only, 554.62. This was after the values in the distance matrix were adjusted to account for their use of a smaller criterion standard. The individuals evaluating the text in Arabic failed to differentiate the concepts to the same degree as the readers of the English versions, suggesting that the translated text did not differentiate the key concepts to the same degree as the English versions.

The spatial coordinates of the two translated groups were next rotated to a least-squares best fit, which minimized the departure from congruence with the coordinates of the group that evaluated the original English text (Woelfel, Holmes, & Kincaid, 1979). This made it possible to examine the overall differences between the texts and which key concepts, when translated, were responsible for these discrepancies. The differences between the spaces for each concept and the correlations of the concepts on all the dimensions with the original space are presented in Table 25.1.

Unlike the plot, which describes only about one-half of the variance (that which is attributable to dimensions 1 and 2), the values in Table 25.1 account for the differences on all the dimensions upon which there is variation.[3] As a result, when evaluating the differences between the texts, one should not place too much emphasis on the plot; rather, one should examine the differences across all dimensions (Table 25.1). The correlations allow

Table 25.1

Differences and Correlations Between the Original
Text and the Arabic and Back-Translations

| | Arabic | | Back-Translation | |
	Difference	Correlation	Difference	Correlation
Society	5.25	.95	5.11	.91
Audience	4.94	.90	3.21	.95
Fantasy and escape	4.95	.90	3.21	.98
Social conflict and change	5.32	.69	4.97	.89
Needs	.66	.94	2.43	.96
Cognition	3.65	.97	3.52	.94
Mass media	3.54	.84	1.54	.97
Information	5.15	.89	3.58	.93
Behavior	1.66	.91	2.62	.98
Dependency	3.28	.96	2.34	.98
Mean	3.71	.895	3.25	.949

one to determine if the discrepancies are due simply to the use of larger or smaller values when differentiating the concepts or to a discrepancy in the relations among the concepts. A high correlation and a high difference between groups suggest that the difference is due to scale size, while discrepancies in relations among concepts are indicated by a low correlation and a high difference.

Table 25.1 reveals that the overall discrepancies among the spaces are small, only 32.5 percent to 37.1 percent of the distance between "needs" and "dependency." Overall, the correlations among the spaces are quite high (r = .895 and .949, respectively), indicating that most of the differences between the texts were due to the differentiation of the key concepts. This high level of agreement was expected because the "same" text served as the stimulus for all three groups.

An examination of the individual differences and the correlations reveals that six concepts warrant particular attention in the Arabic translation. They are "society," "audience," "fantasy and escape," "social conflict and change," "mass media," and "information." The correlations suggest that the discrepancies involving "society," "audience," and "fantasy and escape" are largely due to the subjects' inability to differentiate these terms to the same degree as the readers of the English texts. The mean of the pair comparisons involving "society" was 16.53 for the original group and 11.37 for the Arabic group. This difference, 5.20, represents nearly all the discrepancy involving that concept. For "audience," the mean values for the two groups were 15.08 and

12.14, and for "fantasy and escape," 17.31 and 14.57. The differences, 2.94 and 2.74, represent smaller proportions of the total discrepancies that are reflected in their lower correlations, indicating that much of the discrepancy is due to relational differences with other concepts.

"Social conflict and change" was the most discrepant concept between the two conditions. There was 5.32 units difference and its correlation was only .69. Clearly, this concept's meaning was altered during the translation process. In particular, its relations with "audience" and "fantasy and escape" changed 5.19 and 9.17 units, respectively. This accounts for the other portion of the change in these concepts' locations.

According to the translators, the Arabic speakers do not differentiate between "information" and "mass media" to the same degree as Americans. The data bear this out. The mean difference between these two concepts was 8.07 in English and only 6.91 in Arabic. This difference altered the concepts' pattern of relations with the other concepts and produced the somewhat lower correlations across the conditions.

The comparison between the evaluation of the original text and the back-translation revealed slightly greater correspondence than between the original and Arabic treatments. The mean difference was 3.25 compared to 3.71, and the mean correlation was .949 compared to .895. The reason for the greater correspondence is that cultural differences do not affect the results. The process of translation is the only source of differences between the groups.

The primary areas of difference between these two treatments are the concepts "society" and "social conflict and change." The former was 5.11 units different and it correlated .91. The later was 4.97 units different and it correlated .89. The greatest difference between "society" and the two groups was its relation with "information." The difference was 5.46 units and accounted for the discrepancy in the position held by "information" (3.58, r = .93). "Social conflict and change" differences were spread fairly evenly among the other nine concepts, although "fantasy and escape" was 5.63 units different. This suggests that the translation of "social conflict and change" warrants special attention in subsequent translations.

Step 8:
Intervention by the Research to Reduce Discrepancies

The analysis of the differences reveals several points of discrepancy. These areas should be given special attention when the document is re-translated to reduce the discrepancy between the texts. The first problem in the translation is that the Arabic version does not differentiate the concepts to the same degree as the English versions. One way to adjust the Arabic text is through the use of adjectives and adverbs. Cliff (1959) and Woelfel and Fink (1980) have shown that adjectives and adverbs act as multipliers when attached to concepts. For example, the sentence "The one we focus upon first is the high level of dependence of audience on mass media" could be translated as "The one one we focus upon first is the very high level of dependence of audience on mass media." This should expand the differences within the Arabic space to produce the same differences among the concepts.

In this data set, the concepts of concern are "society" and "social conflict and change." Particular attention should be paid to these concepts when translating the document a second time. What are the relations of these terms to the others in the document? How are they different in the back-translation from the original text? The relations between "society" and "information" and between "social conflict and change" and "fantasy and escape" should be clarified in the translation by using modifiers, or additional words or phrases, to specify the relations as precisely as possible. The discrepancy between the latter pair of concepts involved multiple-word concepts. These have the greatest potential for ambiguity, suggesting that special care may be necessary when translating phrases.

The Galileo analysis may not give sufficient information regarding the domain of concepts evoked by a particular concept. For example, "social conflict and change" may require greater specification than allowed from a single measurement. In that case, it may be necessary to perform additional research by first eliciting those key concepts within the domain of a concept that is particularly difficult to translate. This may be done using interviews by asking subjects in the original language to describe the concept; for example, "Please describe 'social conflict and change' " or "What does 'social conflict and change' mean to you?" As with the pretest, a content analysis of these interviews should reveal those concepts used to define "social conflict and change." At this point, a second Galileo could be conducted to describe the term's relations with the other concepts used to define it. This increase in resolution or power should help guide the translator when making adjustments in the translated text.

Step 9:
Retranslate and Retest

At this point the text should be retranslated with the guidance of the Galileo analysis. The researcher may wish to retest to ensure that the distortion is reduced. The process may be repeated until the discrepancy between all versions of the text is zero. At this point, the translation process has converged and the texts have reached equivalence.

DISCUSSION

This chapter has demonstrated how the Galileo system may be applied to evaluate the accuracy of translation of technical documents. The analysis showed that the translation did not differentiate among the concepts and produced greater uncertainty in the relations among the key concepts. Further, it indicated the sources of difference or error in the translation. In this example, those discrepancies concerned the concepts "society" and "social conflict and change." Procedures to modify the translated text to ensure equivalence with the original text have been suggested, including the use of adjectives and adverbs and simply devoting special attention to the most discrepant terms. This example involved only a single iteration of the translation-evaluation process. The next iteration should use the knowledge of the differences among the original, the translation, and the back-translation to guide adjustments in the translation. Future research should be conducted to see if the use of these methods results in convergence, or equivalent texts.

There are methodological problems with this research that should be pointed out. They concern internal and external validity. Regarding the former, it was assumed throughout this chapter that the only source of error or discrepancy between the texts was the translation process. Other sources of error could have been differences in the environments in which the data were collected and measurement error. The mean percentage of relative error was 13.7 percent for the original group, 15.4 percent for the back-translation group, and 9.8 percent for the Arabic group. This error may have been responsible for the perception of the discrepancies among the conditions. This error is in part a function of the number of observers of the text (the sample size). It could be reduced as a function of the square root of the increase in sample size (Woelfel, Cody, Gillham, & Holmes, 1980).

Another possible source of error was the variance in the identification of the key concepts. "Society" and "social conflict and change," the two most discrepant concepts, were selected by only 19 and 10 observers, respectively, from the group of 31. Problems concerning "society" were raised even prior to the pretest. During the back-translation process, the translators had difficulty agreeing upon a precise set of symbols for that concept in Arabic. This suggests a degree of validity for these procedures.

The methodological problem of external validity arises in the question of the generalizability of this study. What degree of confidence is there in these procedures as a method to determine the accuracy of all translations? This study was done only as an example. There was only a single sample of text being translated to a single language (Arabic), using a small select sample of observers of that language. The majority of this group were Palestinian, a cultural group involved in social conflict and change. It is not surprising that their perception of this term was different than American students. It should be pointed out, however, that this difference was also found between the back-translation and the original, suggesting that the discrepancy may be the result of the translation process. Still, it is unclear how generalizable these results are to all Arabic speakers regardless of the translated document. Future research should be conducted with other texts using other languages to determine the applicability of these procedures to evaluate the quality of translation.

One theoretical issue concerns how much the differences resulting from these measurements reflect cultural differences and how much they involve linguistic differences. These procedures have been widely used both as a measure of culture and as a measure of semantics. In this study, the subjects varied both in language and culture. It was necessary to use the back-translation to control for cultural differences between the Arabic speakers and the American students. Thus any researcher using these procedures should be careful to control for cultural variation when evaluating translation.

Finally, there is the economic issue of marginal utility. These procedures are costly and time-consuming. To use them for every translation may inhibit intercultural communication rather than enhance cross-cultural understanding by creating a backlog and a reduction in the timeliness of the translated message. These procedures should be employed only when the precision of the translation is critical, such as for technical, scientific, or policy documents. Even in these situations, the problem arises as to how many iterations should be performed to ensure accuracy before the cost of analysis outweighs the benefits.

The problem suggests that future Galileo research should not concentrate on the translation of single documents, but should eventually lead to a kind of indexing of relative concepts as reference frames for limited translation situations. These references would include concepts that are found in particular kinds of technical documents. Unlike the static state of dictionary glossaries, these are easily updated and can be applied over time (Barnett, 1979, 1980).

Furthermore, the results of this study would also indicate that accurate premeasurements of the target population could sensitize and direct translators more quickly to the point of equivalence and convergence. Rather than relying on the highly variant skills and intuitive judgments of bilinguals, accurate measurements will give a more precise picture of the two worlds and indicate the best path toward a resolution of the differences. This could effectively cut the time and cost of the process.

SUMMARY

This chapter tested a method to measure translation accuracy using the Galileo method of metric multidimensional scaling, from a convergence theory perspective. It was argued that the equivalence of technical documents should not be determined solely by the judgments of bilingual "experts," but rather by comparison of the relevant semantic/conceptual domains of the text's users in both the original and target languages. The spatial manifolds generated by multidimensional scaling can be compared to determine problems in translation. These can be used to guide an iterative cybernetic process of testing and adjustment of the translation until convergence of congruence between the original document and its translation reaches an acceptable level of equivalence. A test of the proposed methods using English- and Arabic-speaking students was described that showed that the translated texts did not differentiate among the key concepts to the same degree as the original. The translation process produced greater uncertainty in the relations among the key concepts and the analysis identified the primary sources of error in the translation.

NOTES

1. The following section represents a brief summary of Palmer and Barnett (1984). An examination of that source is recommended for a complete discussion of the theoretical issues raised in this chapter.

2. This plot was produced from the coordinate values that resulted after the coordinates of the two translated groups were rotated to a least-squares best fit, which minimized the departure from congruence with the criterion space, the original English text.

3. Generally, the dimensionality of a space is equal to the number of scaled concepts minus one, although in some cases it may be less. In this case, all three texts were evaluated along nine dimensions (Barnett & Woelfel, 1979).

REFERENCES

Ball-Rokeach, S. J., & De Fleur, M. (1982). A dependency model of mass media effects. In G. Gumpert & R. Cathcart (Eds.), *Inter/media: Interpersonal communication in a media world*. New York: Oxford University Press.

Barnett, G. A. (1974, April). *Social system homophily as a function of communication*. Paper presented at the meeting of the International Communication Association, New Orleans.

Barnett, G. A. (1976). *Bilingual information processing: The effects of communication on semantic structure*. Unpublished doctoral dissertation, Michigan State University.

Barnett, G. A. (1977a). Linguistic relativity: The role of the bilingual. In B. Ruben (Ed.), *Communication yearbook 1* (pp. 397-414). New Brunswick, NJ: Transaction.

Barnett, G. A. (1977b). Bilingual semantic organization: A multidimensional analysis. *Journal of Cross-Cultural Psychology, 8*, 315-330.

Barnett, G. A. (1979, May). *On the nature of synonyms: And this little piggie*. Paper presented at the meeting of the Eastern Communication Association, Philadelphia.

Barnett, G. A. (1980, May). *Frequency of occurrence as an estimate for inertial mass: Pigs in space.* Paper presented at the meetings of the International Communication Association, Acapulco.

Barnett, G. A., & Kincaid, D. L. (1983). Cultural convergence: A mathematical theory. In W. B. Gudykunst (Ed.), *Intercultural communication theory: Current perspectives* (pp. 171-194). Beverly Hills, CA: Sage.

Barnett, G. A., & McPhail, T. L. (1980). An examination of the relationship of United States television and Canadian identity. *International Journal of Intercultural Relations, 4,* 219-232.

Barnett, G. A., Wigand, R. T., Harrison, R. B., Woelfel, J., & Cohen, A. A. (1981). Communication and cultural development. *Human Organization, 40,* 330-337.

Barnett, G. A. & Woelfel, J. (1979). On the dimensionality of psychological processes. *Quality and Quantity, 13,* 215-232.

Brislin, R. W. (1972). Translation issues: Multilanguage versions and writing translatable English. *American Psychologist, 7,* 299-300.

Brislin, R. W. (1974). Back translation for cross-cultural research. *Journal of Cross-Cultural Psychology, 24,* 21-35.

Brislin, R. W., & Sinaiko, W. H. (1973). Evaluating language translations: Experiments on three assessment methods. *Journal of Philosophy and Rhetoric, 57,* 328-334.

Cliff, N. (1959). Adverbs as multipliers. *Psychological Review, 66,* 27-44.

Danowski, J. A., Stoyanoff, N. J., & Barnett, G. A. (1977, June). *A simple-minded view of TV: A look at users' cognitive complexity.* Paper presented at the meetings of the International Communication Association, Berlin.

Ervin, S. M., & Bowers, R. F. (1952) Translation problems in international surveys. *Public Opinion Quarterly, 16,* 595-604.

Ervin, S. M., Osgood, C. E. (1954). Second language learning and bilingualism. *Journal of Abnormal Psychology, 49,* 139-146.

Kincaid, D. L. (1975). *The convergence model of communication.* Honolulu: East-West Communication Institute.

Kincaid, D. L., Yum, J. O., Woelfel, J., & Barnett, G. A. (1983). The cultural convergence of Korean immigrants in Hawaii: An empirical test of a mathematical theory. *Quality and Quantity, 18,* 59-78.

MacNamara, J. (1970). Bilingualism and thought. In J. E. Alatis (Ed.), *Georgetown roundtable of languages and linguistics* (pp. 25-40). Washington, DC: Georgetown University Press.

Nida, E. (1966). A review of *Syntactic Translation* by Wayne Tosh. *Language, 42,* 851-854.

Nida, E. (1975). *Language structure and translation.* Stanford, CA: Stanford University Press.

Osgood, C. E., May, W. H., & Miron, M. S. (1975). *Cross-cultural universals of affective meaning.* Urbana: University of Illinois Press.

Osgood, C. E., Suci, G. J., & Tannenbaum, P. H. (1957). *The measurement of meaning.* Urbana: University of Illinois Press.

Palmer, M. T. (1981) *Linguistics and translation.* Unpublished master's thesis, Rensselaer Polytechnic Institute.

Palmer, M. T., & Barnett, G. A. (1982, May). *A method to measure accuracy of language translation.* Paper presented at the meeting of the International Communication Association, Boston.

Palmer, M. T., & Barnett, G. A. (1984). Using a spatial model to verify language translation. In W. B. Gudykunst & Y. Y. Kim (Eds.), *Methods for intercultural communication research* (pp. 129-146). Beverly Hills, CA: Sage.

Rogers, E. M., & Kincaid, D. L. (1981). *Communication networks: Toward a new paradigm.* New York: Free Press.

Shannon, C., & Weaver, W. (1949). *The mathematical theory of communication.* Urbana: University of Illinois Press.

Stoyanoff, N. J., & Fink, E. L. (1981, May). *A metric multidimensional scaling of cognitive structure.* Paper presented at the meeting of the International Communication Association, Minneapolis.

Thurstone (1927). A law of comparative judgement. *Psychological Review, 34,* 273-286.

Wigand, R. T., & Barnett, G. A. (1976). Multidimensional scaling of cultural processes: The case of Mexico, South Africa and the United States. In F. Casmir (Ed.), *International-intercultural communication annual—III* (pp. 139-161). Falls Church, VA: Speech Communication Association.

Woelfel, J., Cody, M. J., Gillham, J. R., & Holmes, R. (1980). Basic premises of multidimensional attitude theory. *Human Communication Research, 6,* 153-167.

Woelfel, J., & Fink, E. L. (1980). *The measurement of communication process: Galileo theory and method.* New York: Academic.

Woelfel, J., Holmes, R., & Kincaid, D. L. (1979, May). *Rotation to congruence for general Riemann surfaces under theoretical constraints.* Paper presented at the meeting of the International Communication Association, Philadelphia.

VII ● POLITICAL COMMUNICATION

26 ● Media Agenda-Setting and Public Opinion: Is There a Link?

DAVID WEAVER

Indiana University

MOST of the media agenda-setting research in the past decade has been concerned with cognitions—public awareness of and concern over issues or problems emphasized by the mass media (Becker, 1982; McCombs, 1982; Shaw & McCombs, 1977; Weaver, Graber, McCombs, & Eyal, 1981). The key proposition tested in most agenda-setting studies is that concentration by the mass media over time on relatively few issues and subjects generally leads to the public regarding these issues and subjects as more salient, or more important, than other issues and subjects.

This emphasis on cognitions (what we think *about,* or the images in our minds) has led to a decrease in interest in attitudes and opinions (what we *think,* or how we feel) on the part of many researchers who study the effects of mass communication, even though the earlier studies of the effects of mass media concentrated heavily on media influence on public opinion (see Chaffee, 1980; Katz, 1980; Klapper, 1960; Weiss, 1969). Because of this shift in emphasis from opinions and attitudes to cognitions, the role of mass communication in shaping public opinion has not been of great interest to most media effects researchers in the past ten years or so.

AUTHOR'S NOTE: An earlier version of this chapter was presented at an international seminar on public opinion and communication in Tokyo, September 1983, and was published in the *Bulletin of the Institute for Communications Research of Keio University,* March 1984. I appreciate the support and encouragement of Professor Youichi Ito of Keio University, who planned the seminar, and the feedback from colleagues who attended the seminar.

Correspondence and requests for reprints: David Weaver, School of Journalism, Indiana University, Bloomington, IN 47405.

Becker and McLeod (1976), for example, propose a model of media effects that distinguishes between two types of media behaviors (content emphasis and content direction) and two types of media effects (cognitive, including saliences and general perceptions and beliefs, and evaluative, including positions on issues or attitudes toward candidates). They note that the relationship between cognitions and attitudes is important, but it is not specified in their model.

Becker and McLeod (1976, p. 11) write that it is important to analyze the relationship between cognitions and attitudes because the importance of agenda-setting studies depends on "the unique effect of saliences on the political variables." But very few researchers studying agenda-setting effects have shown much interest in trying to link cognitive effects of mass media to attitudinal effects. Instead, the tendency has been to focus on specifying contingent conditions under which agenda-setting is more or less likely to occur. This is a worthwhile endeavor, because we need to understand the agenda-setting process better, but studying contingent conditions does little to link agenda-setting research with the broader field of mass communication and public opinion.

Even though the perceived salience of issues and problems by the public is a highly important media effect, it is only one of a number of possible media effects on public opinion. Deciding which issues are most important is not the same thing as deciding which positions to take on those issues or which candidate or party to support in an election. Obviously, directional decisions are crucial to the outcome of any campaign or election, once the most important issues have been established. But recently there is evidence to suggest that there are links between the perceived importance of issues and images and voters' *preferences* for certain political parties and candidates.

Our year-long study of the 1976 U.S. presidential election (Weaver et al., 1981), for example, suggests that by concentrating on certain characteristics of candidates Jimmy Carter and Gerald Ford and deemphasizing others, the mass media contributed to voter *evaluations* of these candidates as well as to cognitive images of them. This finding supports Katz's (1980) conclusion that "as a latent consequence of telling us what to think *about*, the agenda-setting effect can sometimes influence what we think."

The primary purposes of this chapter are to review some recent studies that have begun to build a bridge between media agenda-setting effects and the opinions of the public and to suggest some questions that future studies should explore. The key assumption underlying this effort is that there is a link between what we know and are concerned about and what opinions we hold. Just as feelings, or opinions, are not constructed out of thin air, but rather on the basis of beliefs (cognitions), likewise cognitions may be formed in response to certain opinions through selective exposure, attention, and retention (Klapper, 1960; Sears & Freedman, 1967).

MEDIA AGENDA-SETTING
RESEARCH

Before reviewing studies linking agenda-setting with public opinion, it is necessary to discuss briefly the evidence regarding media agenda-setting effects. There are two major assumptions behind agenda-setting research: (1) The press does not reflect reality, but rather filters and shapes it; and (2) concentration by the media over time on relatively few issues leads to the public perceiving these issues as more salient or more important than other issues. Most of the research on agenda-setting in the United States during the past decade has focused on testing the second assumption, with little concern shown for the first—that the press shapes and filters reality, rather than simply mirroring society.

After a decade of empirical studies on agenda-setting, there is still some scholarly debate as to whether media content does tend to shape our perceptions of what is important and thus tell us what to think *about,* if not what to think. But this debate is centered not so much on whether media have influence as it is on the contingent conditions that make for more or less of this influence. The strength of support for an agenda-setting influence of the mass media does vary, however, according to what kinds of studies are consulted. As McCombs (1982) notes, agenda-setting can be studied through either aggregate (grouped) data from a population or individual (ungrouped) data. The research can focus on a single issue (or several issues considered separately) or on the principal set of issues before the public. The combination of these decisions yields a four-cell typology defined by aggregate versus individual data and single issues versus issue sets (see McCombs, 1982, p. 124).

Type I Studies

When one looks at McCombs's quadrant I (studies employing aggregate data and a set of issues), it is clear that the research of McCombs and his associates (McCombs and Shaw, 1972; Weaver, McCombs, & Spellman, 1975; Shaw & McCombs, 1977; Weaver et al., 1981) falls into this category. These studies range in design from the one-shot survey and content analysis employed in the original McCombs and Shaw (1972) study, to the five-month panel study of the 1972 election reported in Shaw and McCombs (1977), to the one-year panel study reported in Weaver et al. (1981).

The evidence mustered by these studies suggests that the influence of both newspapers and television on public concern over issues is greatest during the spring and summer and least during the final few months of a U.S. presidential election campaign. This media influence seems to be confined mainly to those issues least likely to have a direct impact on most voters' daily lives—"unobtrusive" issues, such as foreign affairs, government credibility, government spending and size, crime, the environment, and energy.

Weaver et al. (1981) also found that the distinctions between newspapers and television as issue agenda-setters became less pronounced as the campaign progressed. During the primary elections in the spring of 1976, we found evidence of the newspaper issue agenda remaining stable over time, the television issue agenda converging toward the newspaper agenda, and the voter issue agendas becoming more similar to the television issue agenda. But after the summer party conventions, the newspaper and television issue agendas became nearly identical and changed little.

In contrast to the declining importance of newspapers and television as issue agenda-setters later in the year, the orientations of voters seemed to become more important as the election campaign drew to a close. Although motivation to follow the campaign had fairly minor effects on voter issue agendas during the spring and summer seasons, this was not true during the fall period. Those voters with a high need for orientation (high interest and high uncertainty about whom to support) had issue agendas in the fall that were substantially more similar to the media agendas than were those of other voters.

Of course, it must be remembered that the evidence of agenda-setting supplied by our 1976 study (Weaver et al., 1981) and by other Type I studies is based on comparisons of media rankings of sets of issues with rankings of the same sets of issues by groups of respondents, not by individuals. Typically, in such studies, randomly selected individual voters or members of the public are asked about the issues of most concern to them, and typically they mention one or two issues. These responses from individuals are then aggregated into a ranking of issues that reflects no single person, but rather a group, or groups, of persons. Thus in Type I agenda-setting studies it is not accurate to speak of the media influencing individuals' agendas, but rather of the media influencing the *distribution* of the top one or two issues among representative groups of voters or the public. Even though this is not as dramatic an effect as some advocates of agenda-setting might hope for, it is still an important phenomenon, for it suggests that the relative amount of emphasis on various issues by the media determines the size of various groups of individuals in a given community or society who are most concerned about these same issues. And those Type I studies conducted over time (Weaver, McCombs, & Spellman, 1975; Shaw & McCombs, 1977; Weaver et al., 1981) suggest that the direction of influence is often from the media to the public, rather than the other way around.

Type II Studies

Those agenda-setting studies using sets of issues and individual-level data, such as McLeod, Becker, and Byrnes (1974), Siune and Borre (1975),

Weaver, Stehle, Auh, and Wilhoit (1975), and Auh (1977), find less support for media agenda setting than do Type I, III, or IV studies. This is not surprising, considering that Type II studies are testing the most radical version of the agenda-setting hypothesis—that the ranking of an entire set of issues by the media determines the ranking of the same set of issues for each individual member of the public. This is a considerably more stringent test than that employed by Type I studies, which compare the ranking of a set of issues between a group (or groups) of the public and the media. It is also a more stringent test than those employed by Type III and Type IV studies, which compare increases or decreases in public concern over single issues (measured by aggregate or individual data) with increases or decreases in emphasis on those issues by the mass media.

Of the Type II studies cited here, only the panel study of the 1971 Danish election by Siune and Borre (1975) offers much support for agenda setting, and part of this support is based on an issue-by-issue matching of the voters' agenda of nine issues with different media agendas, making this study both Type II and Type III because it employs both individual-level and aggregate-level data. Siune and Borre (1975, pp. 67-68) conclude that "the mass media played a major role in altering the priority of issues in the public's mind," but the public didn't "discard its pet issues altogether."

In contrast, the one-shot survey study by McLeod et al. (1974), which compared the agendas of two newspapers in Madison, Wisconsin, and the readers of those papers, found that using individual-level data produced much weaker correlations than using aggregated data from groups of voters. And Weaver, Stehle, Auh, and Wilhoit (1975), in a two-wave panel study of the 1974 off-year election in Bloomington, Indiana, found very weak evidence of individual-level agenda-setting with a set of issues emphasized in the leading newspapers, as did Auh (1977). But Auh found considerably more support for agenda-setting using aggregate measures of audience agendas.

In short, there is not much support for media agenda-setting from the few studies that compare the ranking of a set of issues (usually five to ten) emphasized by the media with the ranking of those same issues by individuals.

Type III Studies

The few studies that employ aggregate data to measure public concern over a single issue (or issues) find considerable support for media agenda-setting, especially MacKuen and Coombs's (1981) study of public concern over various issues from 1960 to 1977, using Gallup aggregate public opinion data and measures of media emphasis from three national news magazines (*Time, Newsweek,* and *U.S. News & World Report*) as well as "real-world" measures of unemployment, inflation, crime rates, heating-fuel prices, and troop levels in Vietnam. MacKuen and Coombs (1981, p. 141) conclude that "the shape of citizen agendas clearly reflects the editorial judgments defining news coverage, but is also sensitive to the real world . . . independent of the media's orientations." They also find that the *character* of events (how dramatic they are) is more important than the *amount* of news coverage in accounting for media impact on public agendas, but the relationship between amount of coverage and public concern "stands strong and there seems little doubt that such a correspondence exists" (p. 22).

Lang and Lang (1981), in an analysis of how the issue of Watergate became salient to the American public between June 1972 and the following summer, conclude that the news media were necessary, but not sufficient, in setting the public agenda. Using data from various studies and from Gallup, the Opinion Research Center, Harris, and the Michigan 1972 national election study, Lang and Lang argue that Watergate did not become a highly salient issue by virtue of heavy media coverage alone. Instead, they conclude that it took the participation of other institutions, such as the courts and Congress, and the involvement of other political elites to make the issue of high concern to the public. Lang and Lang call this an "agenda-building" process to distinguish it from the agenda-setting research that has concentrated on the media agenda-audience agenda relationship and has not been much concerned with how issues originate.

Thus the Type III studies, which employ aggregate audience data and analyze issues separately, provide substantial support for media agenda-setting.

Type IV Studies

The evidence with regard to media agenda-setting provided by the studies employing individual-level audience data and analyzing issues one by one varies considerably, depending on the design of the study. The weakest design, a one-shot survey by Erbring, Goldenberg, and Miller (1980), yields the weakest evidence for media agenda-setting, but even this evidence is no weaker than that provided by "real-world" measures or individual characteristics. On the other hand, the Type IV studies with the strongest designs—the field experiment by Cook et al. (1983) and the experiments by Iyengar, Peters, and Kinder (1983)—yield the strongest evidence in support of media agenda-setting. The panel studies by Schoenbach (1982) and Schoenbach and Weaver (1983) produce some support, although they do not directly compare media content with audience concerns.

Although the Erbring et al. (1980) study is one of the most sophisticated agenda-setting studies in terms of data analysis techniques, it is based on data from the 1974 Michigan Center for Political Studies national election study (a one-shot survey), and the measure of issue salience for each person is a simple dichotomy of mention/no mention. This study does allow for predictors of issue salience other than media coverage (real-world conditions as measured by local unemployment and crime rates, political attitudes, membership in unions, recent unemployment in one's family, demographics, and frequency of discussion with other persons about issues), and it finds that media coverage interacts with the audience's preexisting sensitivities to produce changes in issue concerns.

The studies by Schoenbach (1982) and Schoenbach and Weaver (1983) are based on a three-wave panel study of 459 West German voters during the 1979 European parliamentary elections. These are not true agenda-setting studies because no content analysis of media is included, but various measures of media exposure are used so that the individual change in the issue concerns of each respondent can be related to his or her individual media use. Schoenbach (1982) found that exposure to media coverage of the European election was more influential than routine media use in raising the salience of various domestic and foreign policy issues, and that print media were more powerful predictors of changes in issue salience than was television.

Schoenbach and Weaver (1983) found that exposure to media coverage of the European election was weakly correlated with the salience of European issues for all voters combined, and moderately correlated for those voters uncertain of which way to vote but not much interested in the campaign. But these correlations existed only during the campaign, and disappeared soon after the election.

Cook et al. (1983, p. 24) found a "clear agenda-setting effect" of an NBC televised investigative news report on fraud in federally funded home health care. Using a before-after experimental design with 300 members of the general public randomly selected from Chicago telephone numbers to watch either the NBC news program or another program airing at the same time, Cook and her associates found a substantial increase in concern over this issue among members of the experimental group who viewed the program, but not among members of the control group who viewed the other program. They also found an increase in concern over the problem among government decision makers who heard of or viewed the program, but not among those who were not exposed to the NBC program. And they found that government decision makers who were exposed to the news report on fraud and abuse in home health care were much more likely to advocate policy action to correct the problem than were those who were not exposed, suggesting that media agenda-setting is not confined to the general public, but applies to governmental elites as well.

In two other experiments employing individual-level data and analyzing single issues, Iyengar et al. (1983) found evidence that "strongly supports" the agenda-setting hypothesis. They altered television newscasts for six days for each study by substituting previously videotaped stories from the Vanderbilt Archive to change the amount of attention the evening TV news appeared to be paying to defense, energy problems, and inflation. Subjects were told they were simply watching evening newscasts in Yale University offices as part of a study of citizens' reactions to television newscasts.

Iyengar and his colleagues found increases in concern for two of the problems emphasized in the newscasts (defense inadequacies and pollution from energy generation), but not for the third (inflation), among those respondents exposed to the newscasts. They found no increases in concern among those respondents who viewed other versions of the newscasts. No agenda-setting effect was found for the issue of inflation, probably because concern over that issue was already very high.

In short, Type IV media agenda-setting studies offer support for the hypothesis in direct proportion to the strength of the study design. The two experiments (the strongest designs for assessing media effects) produced the strongest support for media agenda-setting. The two panel studies produced only moderate support, and the one-shot survey by Erbring et al. (1980) produced the weakest support.

In all, support from key studies of media agenda-setting in the last decade is mixed, depending on the kind of audience data used (aggregate or individual), the measurement of issues (singly or as a set), and the design of the study (one-shot survey, panel, or experiment). There is moderate to strong support for media agenda-setting from all the panel studies and experiments except for those employing a set of issues and individual data (Type II), but this is not terribly surprising, given the stringency of the test (media ranking of a set of issues transferred intact to each individual in the study).

On the basis of this review of key studies, it appears that media emphasis on an issue is likely to result in increased concern over that issue by individuals, but the precise ranking of a set of issues by the media is not likely to be reflected in the ranking of these issues by individual persons, although it is often reflected in group rankings of unobtrusive (not directly experienced) issues. Given these conclusions, what does the evidence indicate about the links between media agenda-setting and public opinion?

AGENDA-SETTING AND PUBLIC OPINION

The relationship between information gain and attitude (or opinion) change has been of interest to social psychologists for many years, but, as Carter (1965) pointed out some years ago, information gain is not always correlated with attitude change. Such a correlation is more likely to exist, according to Carter, if the information makes salient certain discriminating attributes that enable a person to assign a favorable or unfavorable value to an object (such as a political candidate or party). To the extent that certain issues stressed by the news media help a potential voter to discriminate between candidates or parties, we should expect increased salience of such issues to lead to a more favorable evaluation of one candidate or party over others.

There are a few empirical studies that give partial support to this expectation. Davidson and Parker (1972) found sheer media exposure to be the largest correlate of the public's support for Congress, as measured by favorable evaluations of representatives' performance. The use of media was a more powerful predictor of public support for Congress than political participation, party affiliation, political efficacy, and other variables. Davidson and Parker (1972, p. 610) speculate that "perhaps it is not the content of the media messages, but simply the fact of extensive coverage that elevates the standing of governmental institutions." This conjecture about the effects of the media in conferring status combines notions of agenda-setting (heightened salience) and public opinion (more favorable evaluations), and suggests a positive correlation between increased salience and increased public support for U.S. representatives.

On the other hand, Mazur (1981), in a study of magazine coverage of fluoridation and nuclear power and public opinion polls on these issues from 1950 to 1975, found a correlation between amount of media coverage of these controversial issues and public reaction against them, suggesting that media attention elicited negative public opinion. Mazur (1981, p. 109) suggests that "media coverage of scientific controversies may do more than define and amplify an event; it may have profound effects on public attitudes, the precise nature of which is difficult to specify." He also argues that the quantity of coverage of a technical controversy can have as much effect on public attitudes as the semantic content of the stories presented.

It seems clear from Mazur's study that one cannot always assume a positive correlation between increased salience of an issue and favorable public opinion toward that issue. Obviously, it depends on the issue and on the label given the issue in the study questionnaire. Both Davidson and Parker (1972) and Mazur (1981) found more than just increased salience as a result of heavy media coverage. They also found correlations (one positive and one negative) between media emphasis and public opinion, suggesting that increased salience of an issue or a person has attitudinal consequences, although the *direction* of these consequences depends largely on the nature of the issue or the person being covered and on the label given the issue when the question is asked.

Iyengar et al. (1983, p. 4), in their experiments on network television agenda-setting, speculate that "by lavishing attention on some problems and ignoring others, the press may not only be setting the public's priorities, it may also be altering the criteria by which the public evaluates government performance." And from their experimental data, they conclude that there is "considerable, if not overwhelming, evidence for the general proposition that the media's agenda alters the criteria the public relies on in evaluating its president" (p. 15).

Iyengar and his colleagues found that when participants in one of their experiments were asked to evaluate President Carter after a week's worth of stories emphasizing alleged weaknesses in American defense capability, defense performance was powerful in determining the ratings. They explain this as a result of a psychological process called "priming," whereby television emphasis on particular issues not only confers status (or increased salience), but also activates in viewers' memories previously acquired information about these issues. And that information is used in forming opinions about persons, groups, or institutions linked to these issues.

Iyengar et al. also found that the issues emphasized by the television networks influenced subjects' evaluations of President Carter's performance most of all, impressions of his competence secondarily, and judgments of his trustworthiness not at all. They interpret these findings as consistent with the Collins and Loftus (1975) "spreading-activation" model of memory, where the closer the concept to the one directly activated (defense performance in this case), the stronger the spreading effect. They reason that the president's performance is more closely associated with the defense capability of the country, that his competence is less so associated, and that his trustworthiness is not associated with it at all.

The findings from the experiments of Iyengar et al. (1983) support the conclusion of Lang and Lang (1981, p. 449), from their intensive study of the development of Watergate as a public issue, that "what people think may not be as easily separable from what they think about, as the various formulations of agenda-setting have implied. On the contrary, many differences of opinion originate from the different weights people attach to elements in a complex situation."

CONCLUSIONS

The few studies that have examined the relationship between media agenda-setting with regard to public issues and public opinion suggest that there is likely to be a relationship among media emphasis on an issue, the salience of that issue, and public opinion regarding actors (persons or institutions) associated with the issue. In view of this, it seems that Katz's (1966) description of the stages of public opinion formation needs revision. His four stages in public opinion formation are as follows:

(1) the salience of some problem (issue) for a number of people, even a small
    minority;
(2) the discussion of the problem, resulting in increased salience;
(3) the formation of alternative solutions and the narrowing of alternatives; and
(4) the final mobilization of opinion to affect the collective decision, either
    through a majority vote (as in an election or referendum) or through the
    assessment by leaders of the strength of mobilized opinion.

It is apparent from the studies of media agenda-setting reviewed here
that the media have an important role in making some issues or problems
more salient than others (stage 1 of Katz's model), but it also seems true that
the very salience of an issue often has immediate consequences for opinion
formation regarding persons or institutions linked to that issue. Another point
emerging from the experiments by Iyengar and his colleagues is that media
emphasis on certain issues often not only increases their salience, but also
activates in audience members' memories previously acquired information
about these issues. Thus no issue is made salient, discussed, and acted upon
in isolation from other issues and previous happenings, as Katz's (1966) description implies. It is not simply a matter of proceeding from increased salience to the formation of opinion about each issue in an orderly manner;
rather, the increased salience of an issue (resulting from increased media emphasis, personal experience, and/or discussion with others) is likely to invoke
a mixture of cognitions and feelings linked to that issue. And this mixture is
likely to have a direct impact on public opinion regarding not only that issue,
but also those persons and institutions associated with that issue.

From the point of view of a citizen of a certain political system, then, the
distinction between cognitions and opinions is likely to be irrelevant, as
Chaffee (1975) has argued. From the point of view of a mass communication effects researcher, the distinction seems more important, since we have
been able to demonstrate stronger and more consistent effects of mass communication on cognitions (knowledge) than on opinions and attitudes (feelings). But the studies reviewed here should caution us against assuming that
mass media have a very limited, or negligible, role in shaping public opinion. And they should encourage us to include measures of opinions and
behaviors in future studies of media agenda-setting.

REFERENCES

Auh, T. S. (1977). *Issue conflict and mass media agenda-setting during the 1974 Indiana senatorial campaign.* Unpublished doctoral dissertation, Indiana University.
Becker, L. B. (1982). The mass media and citizen assessment of issue importance: A reflection
on agenda-setting research. In D. C. Whitney & E. Wartella (Eds.), *Mass communication
review yearbook* (Vol. 3). Beverly Hills, CA: Sage.
Becker, L. B., & McLeod, J. M. (1976). Political consequences of agenda-setting. *Mass Communication Review, 3,* 8-15.
Carter, R. F. (1965). Communication and affective relations. *Journalism Quarterly, 42,*
203-212.

Chaffee, S. H. (1975). The diffusion of political information. In S. H. Chaffee (Ed.), *Political communication: Issues and strategies for research*. Beverly Hills, CA: Sage.

Chaffee, S. H. (1980). Mass media effects: New research perspectives. In G. C. Wilhoit & H. deBock (Eds.), *Mass communication review yearbook* (Vol. 1). Beverly Hills, CA: Sage.

Collins, A. M., & Loftus, E. F. (1975). A spreading-activation theory of semantic processing. *Psychological Review, 82*, 407-428.

Cook, F. L., Tyler, T. R., Goetz, S. G., Gordon, M. G., Protess, D., Leff, D. R., & Molotch, H. L. (1983). Media and agenda-setting: Effects on the public, interest group leaders, policy makers, and policy. *Public Opinion Quarterly, 47*, 16-35.

Davidson, R., & Parker, G. (1972). Positive support for political institutions: The case of Congress. *Western Politics Quarterly, 25*, 600-612.

Erbring, L., Goldenberg, E. N., & Miller, A. H. (1980). Front-page news and real-world cues: A new look at agenda-setting by the media. *American Journal of Political Science, 24*, 16-49.

Iyengar, S., Peters, M., & Kinder, D. (1983). Experimental demonstrations of the "not-so-minimal" consequences of television news programs. In E. Wartella & D. C. Whitney (Eds.), *Mass communication review yearbook* (Vol. 4). Beverly Hills, CA: Sage.

Katz, D. (1966). Attitude formation and public opinion. *Annals of the American Academy of Political and Social Science, 367*, 150-162.

Katz, E. (1980). On conceptualizing media effects. *Studies in Communications, 1*, 119-141.

Klapper, J. (1960). *The effects of mass communication*. New York: Free Press.

Lang, G., & Lang, K. (1981). Watergate: An exploration of the agenda-building process. In G. C. Wilhoit & H. deBock (Eds.), *Mass communication review yearbook* (Vol. 2). Beverly Hills, CA: Sage.

MacKuen, M. B., & Coombs, S. L. (1981). *More than news: Media power in public affairs*. Beverly Hills, CA: Sage.

Mazur, A. (1981). Media coverage and public opinion on scientific controversies. *Journal of Communication, 31*, 106-115.

McCombs, M. E. (1982). The agenda-setting approach. In D. Nimmo & K. Sanders (Eds.), *Handbook of political communication*. Beverly Hills, CA: Sage.

McCombs, M. E., & Shaw, D. L. (1972). The agenda-setting function of mass media. *Public Opinion Quarterly, 36*, 176-187.

McLeod, J. M., Becker, L. B., & Byrnes, J. E. (1974). Another look at the agenda-setting function of the press. *Communication Research, 1*, 131-166.

Schoenbach, K. (1982, May). *Agenda-setting effects of print and television in West Germany*. Paper presented at the 32nd Annual Meetings of the International Communication Association, Boston.

Schoenbach, K., & Weaver, D. H. (1983, May). *Cognitive bonding and need for orientation during political campaigns*. Paper presented at the 33nd Annual Meetings of the International Communication Association, Dallas.

Sears, D. O., & Freedman, J. L. (1967). Selective exposure to information: A critical review. *Public Opinion Quarterly, 31*, 194-213.

Shaw, D. L., & McCombs, M. E. (1977). *The emergence of American political issues: The agenda-setting function of the press*. St. Paul, MN: West.

Siune, K., & Borre, O. (1975). Setting the agenda for a Danish election. *Journal of Communication, 25*, 65-73.

Weaver, D. H., Graber, D. A., McCombs, M. E., & Eyal, C. (1981). *Media agenda-setting in a presidential election: Issues, images, and interest*. New York: Praeger.

Weaver, D. H., McCombs, M. E., & Spellman, C. (1975). Watergate and the media: A case study of agenda-setting. *American Politics Quarterly, 3*, 485-471.

Weaver, D. H., Stehle, T. E., Auh, T. S., & Wilhoit, G. C. (1975, August). *A path analysis of individual agenda-setting during the 1974 Indiana senatorial campaign*. Paper presented at the annual meetings of the Association for Education in Journalism, Ottawa.

Weiss, W. (1969). Effects of the mass media on communication. In G. Lindzey & E. Aronson (Eds.), *The handbook of social psychology*. Reading, MA: Addison-Wesley.

27 ● Reagan on Radio

JOE S. FOOTE

Cornell University

R ECENT presidents have supplemented their power and prestige through direct, almost automatic, access to the commercial television networks. Not only has the use of presidential television increased presidents' visibility and allowed them to present their message unfiltered to the American people, but it has tilted the executive-legislative balance further toward the presidency and away from Congress (Minow, Martin, & Mitchell, 1973). The most formidable tool of presidential television has been the presidential address, followed by news conferences and carefully engineered media appearances. Radio has been viewed by presidential publicists as a purely secondary medium, a mere accompaniment to its more glamorous offspring. Thus it was somewhat surprising that President Reagan turned to network radio in 1982 for what was to become the longest regular, sustained use of broadcasting by a president in American history.

On April 4, 1982, President Reagan delivered the first of a series of ten five-minute radio addresses to the nation. In late August, after an eleven-week hiatus, the president resumed his radio speeches. By mid-October 1983, he had delivered seventy Saturday radio addresses and planned to continue them until his formal announcement for reelection in 1984. This chapter examines the Reagan radio initiative, the congressional replies that have accompanied the president's speeches, and major media coverage of both.

AUTHOR'S NOTE: I wish to thank the Department of Communication Arts at Cornell University for funding assistance, Joan Payton and Nancy A. Hannula for research assistance, and Ellen Boyle in Speaker O'Neill's office for providing transcripts of congressional replies. This chapter is based on information available through October 15, 1983. Material covering October 16, 1983, to January 29, 1984, may be obtained from the author.

Correspondence and requests for reprints: Joe S. Foote, Department of Communication Arts, Cornell University, 640 Stewart Avenue, Ithaca, NY 14850

RESEARCH STRATEGY

The *Weekly Compilation of Presidential Documents* was used to analyze the president's remarks from April 4, 1982, to October 15, 1983. This publication contained the complete unedited transcript of each speech, the time it was broadcast, and the location from which it was broadcast. Information on congressional replies to presidential speeches, including transcripts, was obtained from the Office of the Speaker of the U.S. House of Representatives.

Major television and newspaper coverage of the Saturday speeches was also analyzed. The *Television News Index & Abstracts* to the Vanderbilt Television News Archive was used to examine coverage patterns for Saturday-evening broadcasts on CBS and NBC from April 1982 to June 1983. ABC did not have an early-evening Saturday broadcast. Frequently, sports broadcasts preempted the evening news on either NBC or CBS.

For newspaper coverage, two dailies with traditions of thorough coverage of the Congress and the president, the *Washington Post* and the *New York Times,* were chosen. The front news sections of the Sunday editions of both papers from April 4, 1982, to October 15, 1983, were examined for content and coverage patterns. These data were supplemented by personal interviews conducted with officials from the White House, Congress, and the news media who were involved with the production and coverage of the radio broadcasts.

HISTORICAL PERSPECTIVE

When radio dominated the airwaves, it was only natural that presidents gravitated toward it. President Harding delivered several live radio addresses and even had a transmitter installed in his railroad car. "Silent Cal" Coolidge spoke an average of 9000 words per month on radio and Herbert Hoover even had to turn down a network offer to make a live radio talk every week. While President Roosevelt seemed to dominate the airwaves, and, indeed, delivered at least twenty live radio addresses during his first ten months in office, he averaged only one "fireside chat" a year during his first term. Still, those few prime-time, informal addresses captivated a nation and left a romantic residue that subsequent presidents have tried to resurrect (Brown, Brown, & Rivers, 1978).

When television ascended to preeminence, radio was forgotten as a tool of presidential communication. It became so low key that President Nixon used radio in 1973 to downplay the strident debate over highly controversial budget initiatives, choosing to deliver his State of the Union address as a series of radio speeches rather than make a formal, more visible presentation before Congress and a nationwide television audience.

After more than thirty years, perhaps the time had come for a president to rediscover radio. No president has been better prepared to deal with that medium than Ronald Reagan. His career began in radio in the early 1930s, when he worked as a sports announcer in Iowa, becoming one of the leading play-by-play announcers in the Midwest. In 1975, after his term as governor of California, Reagan began a series of short radio commentaries, which were broadcast by about 300 radio stations across the country. He stopped the broadcasts in 1976 to seek the Republican presidential nomination, but resumed them after he lost the primary battle and continued on radio until 1979, when he announced his intention to run for president in 1980 (Denton, 1982). Thus President Reagan came to the microphone to begin his radio initiative better prepared than any of his predecessors to exploit the advantages that medium offered.

GETTING ON THE AIR

The initiative for the Reagan radio broadcasts came from the White House. The administration saw radio as an opportunity to take its case directly to the people on a sustained basis in a way that would allow the White House to control the broadcasts totally. At a time when the president's popularity was sagging, the radio addresses also presented an attractive complement to a broad multimedia offensive. Because the addresses would be broadcast on a traditionally "slow news day," the White House expected abundant residual media exposure on Saturday network radio and television newscasts and in Sunday newspapers. Finally, the White House staff realized how effective "the great communicator" could be using a medium with which he felt so confident.

Mark Goode, a White House consultant, initiated media contact in March 1982, surveying the radio networks' interest in carrying a series of ten five-minute radio addresses by the president. Mutual was the first to accept, but only on the condition that the speeches be live. Mutual News Vice President Tom O'Brian (personal communication, October 18, 1983) believed that recorded speeches would be appropriate only for excerpts in regularly scheduled newscasts, but that live speeches would be "hot news." After Mutual accepted, ABC, NBC, UPI, AP, Westinghouse, and RKO followed. Of the major commercial networks, only CBS declined to carry the speeches, citing "potential fairness doctrine implications." Surprisingly, National Public Radio, then in its high-flyer mode, also refused to carry the president live (Denton, 1982).

While the stakes were low by television standards, the White House assembled a sizable network at a time when many Americans were likely to be radio listeners. Furthermore, according to Goode, there was a public relations benefit with the radio industry, which "doesn't get anything that is strictly theirs" (Denton, 1982).

The White House had achieved radio access in an entirely controlled way. There would be no editing of material, no filtering through reporters' minds, no distracting or nagging questions by the press. It would be a perfect opportunity to "let Reagan be Reagan." Even in the residual coverage, when reporters could edit as they wished, White House aides believed the Reagan momentum would still be present. As veteran Washington correspondent Roscoe Drummond once said, "A reporter has a responsibility to expound what a president is trying to do before he gets to the question of analyzing it and criticizing it" (Grossman & Kumar, 1979).

THE LOYAL OPPOSITION

When word spread that President Reagan would begin a ten-week series of radio addresses, the Democratic leadership in Congress sought air time to reply. On March 31, 1982, Speaker of the House Thomas P. O'Neill, Jr., and Senate Minority Leader Robert Byrd sent a letter to the radio networks planning to carry President Reagan's radio addresses, asking them for reply time on the same day the president spoke. The leadership claimed that the presidential speeches were coming at a "critical time" in the resolution of important policy questions and implied that the president was using the speeches to shore up his domestic initiatives at a time when his popularity was slipping. In part, the letter said:

> The issues that the President will discuss will undoubtedly be among those most important to the vitality of our nation. We believe that the airing of these Presidential addresses without meaningful response by the opposition would seriously erode, if not destroy entirely, the carefully balanced presentation of conflicting views you strive to preserve. Such an imbalance would be intolerable in a nation that thrives upon open and robust debate at a time when so much hangs in the balance.

Initially, some of the networks were noncommittal on the Democratic leadership's request. ABC at first said it would make a decision on a "week-by-week" basis, an unusual stance since it had already made a commitment to the president for ten weeks without advance knowledge of the content of the speeches (UPI, 1982). Mutual believed from the beginning that if the president were aired, the Democratic opposition in Congress should receive comparable time on the same day (T. O'Brian, personal communication, October 18, 1983). In the end, this view prevailed. The Democratic leadership was notified two days before President Reagan's first speech that it would be given reply time one hour after the president gave his speech (A. Dunn, personal communication, March 29, 1983). It would be up to the networks' affiliates whether they carried the President's speech or the congressional reply. The networks said they would urge their affiliates to carry both if one were carried.

While the network decision was a minor one in terms of the value of air time, it was precedent setting in its recognition of the opposition party in Congress. Never before had the networks given such a sweeping allocation of air time to those opposing a president. The decisions on television, and even on radio in 1973 with President Nixon, had always been made on a case-by-case basis with both the president and Congress. The opposition parties in Congress had consistently asked for time over the past twenty years; the networks had consistently denied it. Only with the State of the Union messages broadcast once a year had the networks given the congressional opposition a regular opportunity to reply. Rarely did this access achieve parity with that given the president.

Thus, symbolically, the Democrats in Congress in 1982 achieved a significant victory. They were recognized for the first time on an institutional basis as being the legitimate counterbalance to the president of the United States. The networks, apparently mindful of the implications of such a decision, delivered that decision orally and never stated their policy publicly (E. Boyle, personal communication, March 25, 1983). There is no indication that the television networks are likely to recognize opposition parties. In fact, there have been some indications that the opposition is losing ground on television. At a symposium in Washington, D.C., in October 1983, sponsored by ABC and Harvard, ABC News President Roone Arledge strongly implied that his network was dissatisfied with the Democrats' pretaped, professionally produced response to the State of the Union speech in 1983 and that ABC might reconsider its traditional offer of time (Arledge, 1983).

In addition to the precedent set by networks in favor of the congressional opposition, the Democratic leadership received an opportunity to articulate its position in a magnified forum and solidify its position as the opposition force to the president in the American political system. While the exposure of individual members of Congress has increased significantly in recent years, the exposure of the opposition party position has not. Competition is keen on the network news and the congressional position is likely to be reported in fragmented form, reflecting the diversity and divisions within the institution. The party position, while much weaker than forty years ago, still provides an organized alternative to the president. A sustained response by the opposition party helps to increase its status as the countervailing force to the president and also promotes party cohesion. Because competition for broadcast exposure is intense among many members of Congress, the weekly replies give the party leadership a few opportunities to reward "back-bench" representatives. For some, making the reply may be a rare opportunity for national exposure.

THE TEN-WEEK TEST

On Saturday, April 3, 1983, President Reagan began his radio initiative in the oval office with the first of ten five-minute speeches. The president said that he was making the speeches to overcome "all the confusion and all the conflicting things that come out of Washington" by bringing "the facts to the people as simply as I can and as much as I can in five minutes" (Raines, 1982). Aides said it was an effort to prevent having his message "truncated" or "filtered" by the news media (Denton, 1982).

The White House staff said that Mr. Reagan wrote most of the first ten speeches himself, often rejecting drafts and writing the script in longhand shortly before air time. He set a folksy, conversational tone in the first address by beginning, "I'll be back every Saturday at this same time, same station, live. I hope you'll tune in." After the speech, Mr. Reagan said the experience reminded him of his sportscasting days: "I keep waiting for someone to steal second" (Raines, 1982). The president's personal input sometimes startled aides. The second speech, which was broadcast from Barbados, was to be relayed live to several islands in the Caribbean in an effort to gain support for the president's policies in that region. At the last minute, President Reagan dropped the Caribbean Basin initiative speech and decided to concentrate the bulk of his time on student financial aid, causing one of his surprised aides to quip, "Next Saturday we'll go to a school in the United States and discuss foreign aid" (Cannon, 1982).

When President Reagan settled into his radio routine, it was obvious his targets were the Democrats in Congress. The president used six of his first ten speeches to defend his economic programs and attack the Democratic House for not supporting him. Not surprisingly, these speeches gained the greatest press coverage; the *Washington Post* covered all six of them on the front page and the broadcasting networks gave them prominent placement on the evening news. While it is not difficult for the president to make news, it can be difficult for him to make news that he controls. Therefore, extensive regular coverage in Sunday newspapers and on Saturday network news about subjects that he initiated was a positive sign. Not surprisingly, when President Reagan signed off for the last of his ten speeches, he said, "I'll be back before too long."

By the end of the ten-week radio series, some ground rules for speech content and media coverage had emerged:

(1) The general tone of the speeches was partisan, with economic messages dominating. The rhetoric was more strident than the president used on television.
(2) The one-hour time difference between the president's speech and the opposition's response precluded an in-depth rebuttal from the Democratic opposition. Congressional spokespersons usually devoted a minute to a superficial response to the president before going to their prepared texts.
(3) The news organizations examined in this study assigned White House reporters to cover the speeches, almost guaranteeing that the congressional response would be an add-on at the end of the story. Also, congressional coverage usually increased in proportion to the coverage given the president.
(4) The *Washington Post* and the *New York Times* began an institutionalized type of coverage, which guaranteed the president some type of coverage for even nonpartisan, ceremonial speeches.

To understand the extent of network television news coverage of the president's radio speeches, one must compare it to the subsequent eleven weeks, when he was off radio. During the ten weeks the speeches were broadcast, CBS and NBC covered them every week, usually placing them within the first three minutes of the newscast. Even though there was no visual focus for the story, the networks, on 15 of 17 newscasts, used the president's voice over a still photograph. This heavy coverage contrasted with the following 11 weeks, when there were no radio broadcasts; during this period, the president did not appear once on tape and was mentioned in only 6 of 22 newscasts. Thus it appears that the radio initiative focused regular broadcast attention on the president that he might not have otherwise received.

THE ELECTION-YEAR OFFENSIVE

President Reagan picked an auspicious time to resume his weekly radio speeches—ten weeks before the November congressional elections. The president implied that his latest radio series would be a permanent one, opening his broadcast by saying, "I hope this is the first of many broadcasts to come. I've missed these weekly visits." The president set a confrontational tone that would dominate the ten-week presidential-congressional exchange in the first speech by announcing his veto of the supplemental appropriation bill. This was the first time that Reagan had used a radio address to release a major announcement, and he saved the surprise for the last sentence of the speech.

Six weeks later, the president made a second major pronouncement on radio: the withdrawal of most-favored-nation status from Poland. Although this announcement came less than a month before the election, the official Democratic reply, made by Representative Henry Reuss of Wisconsin, received no coverage on any of the media examined in this study. It appeared, therefore, that the Democrats' notion of piggybacking on Reagan's publicity-getting powers had curvilinear dimensions. The Democrats' coverage increased in proportion to the president's until that coverage became so prominent that the Democrats were dropped altogether. This phenomenon occurred six times during the seventy speeches examined. Thus there were only two types of occasions when the congressional opposition was not covered: when Reagan's speeches were of such low value that they weren't covered at all and when his speeches were of such high value that they totally eclipsed the opposition.

The preelection offensive climaxed during the last two weeks in October, when two prominent Democrats, Speaker Thomas P. O'Neill, Jr., and Senator Edward Kennedy, responded to the president. In the first speech, on October 23, the president tried to erase "six big myths" about his economic program, but O'Neill took the offensive. Rather than waiting to reply to the president, O'Neill taped his speech on Friday and released it to the news media in an effort to dominate the dialogue. Both speeches received extensive and prominent coverage in the media covered by this study. Interestingly, the *Washington Post* broke its coverage pattern by assigning a congressional correspondent to the story and having a White House reporter file an insert. Not surprisingly, O'Neill's position got top billing:

> Democrats took the offensive yesterday for the first time in their weekly radio battle with President Reagan, bringing in House Speaker Thomas P. O'Neill, Jr., to elevate and sharpen the dispute over who should be blamed for the condition of the economy.
>
> In a taped message released three hours before the President's live broadcast, O'Neill charged that the administration's program "is not working because the program is not fair—and just as important, because the people themselves know it is not fair."
>
> It was the first time a Democrat of O'Neill's stature had taken part in the Saturday broadcasts and the first time the party launched a political assault rather than responding to Reagan's remarks.
>
> Reagan, sticking with previous strategy in his five-minute live radio broadcast from Camp David, Md., ignored O'Neill's charges, even though they had been available in wire service news reports since Friday evening. A White House spokesman said Reagan had not seen the reports. (Omang, 1982)

It is difficult to assess why the focus of the coverage shifted from the White House to the Congress for this speech. Certainly, Speaker O'Neill's status, his early release of the tape, the approaching congressional election, and the *Post*'s decision to assign a congressional reporter to the story were all factors. Speaker O'Neill's and Senator Kennedy's preelection speeches clearly represented the apex of congressional opposition coverage. While Speaker O'Neill received good coverage the following year in a second-page *Post* story, replies by congressional leaders such as Senate Minority Leader Byrd and House Majority Leader Wright were often given no more than routine coverage.

THE TRANQUIL TRANSITION

After the November elections, in which his party suffered losses in the House of Representatives but retained control of the Senate, President Reagan abandoned his strident preelection rhetoric and concentrated more on wooing bipartisan support. Even his speeches on the budget during January and February were more explanatory than promotional. From November through mid-March, the president covered a variety of topics, from the MX missile to drunk driving. He also took two opportunities to break front-page news: new sanctions against the Soviet pipeline and the announcement that Vice President George Bush would be sent to Europe to discuss arms control. As mentioned earlier, congressional opposition replies in these situations were overshadowed by the breaking news. Senator Moynihan's reply on the pipeline sanctions, for example, received no coverage in any of the media surveyed.

THE BUDGET WARS

In mid-March 1983, President Reagan accelerated another confrontation over his budget, much like the one a year earlier that prompted his use of radio to confront his critics. The speech the president delivered on March 19, 1983, was but one of thirty he devoted to the economy during his first seventy radio speeches. In virtually all of them, the theme was the same: President Reagan inherited massive economic problems and it was through his initiatives that the economy was turning around. The only threats to the rebounding economy were the "tax and spend" policies of the liberal Democrats in Congress. Seldom has a president had the opportunity to deliver a message with such repetition. The following is an excerpt from President Reagan's October 19, 1983, radio address:

> Right now, House liberals are pushing a budget—the so-called liberal Democratic budget—that, if implemented, would reverse the progress we've made and wreck our program to rebuild the economy. . . . To cite just one example, Medicare would be driven into bankruptcy. . . . Now, how do they propose to

pay for their reckless binge? Two ways: by compromising America's defense security and by slapping massive new tax increases on every working family.

But this isn't just my struggle; it's yours, too. You're not spectators, and I need your help. Together we still have time to beat back the unfair tax increases, hold the line on spending, and keep America strong. If you can't make the big spenders see the light, you can make them feel the heat. Please tell your representatives not to turn back the clock and squander America's future.

Despite the direct conflict between the president and Congress posed in this speech, the *Washington Post* was able to summarize the rebuttal of the Democratic respondent in one sentence.

In a five-week period from the end of April through May 1983, President Reagan taped three of his speeches rather than broadcast them live. This trend concerned the Mutual Broadcasting System, which announced on May 21, 1983, that it would no longer carry the president's speeches. Three days later, however, Mutual rescinded its decision after receiving assurances from the Reagan administration that future talks would be live (T. O'Brian, personal communication, October 18, 1983).

Less than a month after the Mutual flap, President Reagan rewarded the networks carrying his speeches by using radio to make one of the biggest news announcements of his administration: the reappointment of Paul Volcker as chairman of the Federal Reserve Board. Reagan, who decided to include the announcement in his June 18 speech just a few hours before air time, obviously enjoyed relaying the message to his listeners:

As the saying goes, we interrupt this program for a news flash. Some years ago, a favorite movie theme was the crusading reporter. In every such picture, the reporter—hat on the back of his head, clutching the phone—would yell, "Give me the city desk. I've got a story that'll crack this town wide open!" I've read that line a few times myself. Well, I'm not wearing a hat or clutching a phone, but before getting into today's broadcast, I'd like to make an important announcement.

The announcement of such an important administration appointment in such a casual way was unprecedented. Yet, it demonstrated President Reagan's affinity for the radio medium and was his fourth opportunity to use the speeches to make surprise pronouncements.

THE FOREIGN AFFAIRS FIXATION

With the Congress headed toward its traditional summer recess and the major budget decisions made, President Reagan, by mid-July 1983, had cooled his partisan rhetoric and veered his radio speeches toward foreign affairs and less partisan causes, such as appeals for organ donations. During his first seventy radio speeches, President Reagan spoke about foreign affairs issues sixteen times. Nine of those came during a fourteen-week period from late summer to early fall.

With the tragic bombing incident in Lebanon and the U.S. invasion of Grenada in October 1983, it appeared that foreign affairs would continue to be the focus of President Reagan's radio speeches for the near future.

President Reagan's radio broadcasts drew renewed interest when the Soviet Union shot down a Korean airliner in early September. The president delivered four successive radio speeches on the airliner incident and relations with the Soviet Union. He delivered the last one live from the studios of the Voice of America, where it was relayed simultaneously in five languages, including Russian, to a prime-time audience in the Soviet Union. White House aides kept the international broadcast of the speech a secret to prevent the Soviets from jamming the president's remarks.

THE DEMOCRATS SPEAK

The automatic replies to President Reagan's first 70 radio speeches gave 24 senators, 32 representatives, and 3 noncongressional Democrats an opportunity to go head-to-head with the president. Speaker O'Neill chose the House spokesperson, and Minority Leader Byrd chose those from the Senate. Spokespersons wrote their own speeches, but guidance was available from the leadership if it was requested.

While a broad range of senators and members of Congress gained radio access, their geographic representation was tilted heavily toward the East at the expense of the South. For example, 21 percent of eastern House Democrats had an opportunity to reply to the president, compared with only 6 percent of southern House Democrats. Likewise, 73 percent of eastern senators spoke, compared with 36 percent of southern Senators. The regional bias could also be seen by examining state delegations. The three largest Democratic delegations in the House of Representatives were California (28); Texas (22); and New York (20). Of the New York delegation, 30 percent were chosen for replies compared with 18 percent of the California delegation and only 15 percent of the Texas delegation. However, while House Majority Leader Jim Wright was the lone Texan to be chosen, he delivered four replies, more than any other House member.

The opportunity to reply to one of President Reagan's radio speeches was sought by several rank-and-file members, especially younger, less visible representatives. It was considered an honor and a sign of approval to be asked by the Speaker to make the reply. Many members were more interested in the local audiences in their districts than they were in the nationwide audience. Some media-conscious members of Congress heavily promoted the speeches in advance, advising their constituents to listen on Saturday.

The lure of a radio replay was not as appealing to senators and senior House members. The Saturday afternoon time posed an obstacle to recruiting the best and brightest of the party. Many senior members had important weekend commitments that they were not willing to change. Some senators resented the double standard the networks imposed on the Congress. The broadcasters followed President Reagan anywhere in the world for his Saturday speeches, but made members of Congress and senators come to a studio in downtown Washington. This gave President Reagan great flexibility—he gave fewer than one-third of his speeches from the White House—but posed a logistical problem for the Democrats in Congress. Furthermore, listening to the president, drafting a relevant reply, rehearsing it, and presenting it all in one hour did not strike some legislators as the most relaxing way to spend a Saturday afternoon. Still, the opportunity for the "loyal opposition" to have automatic, direct access to the president of the United States was unprecedented, and the Democrats took full advantage of the opportunity.

MEDIA COVERAGE

The heavy media coverage of President Reagan's first ten radio speeches in 1982 set a standard for the first seventy speeches. Table 27.1 shows that the president was able to sustain newspaper interest throughout his radio initiative. Only in a few instances did the *Washington Post* and the *New York Times* fail to cover one of his speeches. Even in those rare cases,

Table 27.1
Newspaper Coverage of Reagan Radio
Addresses (N = 70)

| | Washington Post | | New York Times | |
| | Number of | | Number of | |
	Stories	Percentage	Stories	Percentage
Reagan speech coverage	65	93	62	89
Opposition speech coverage	44	63	39	56
Front page coverage (Reagan)	38	54	24	34

some of the speeches were not covered because the president overshadowed himself by making more important news that day. This happened often when the president was making a domestic or foreign trip.

While the *Post* and the *Times* both gave extensive coverage to the president's speeches, the *Post* featured them far more prominently. For example, 99 percent of the *Post* stories were printed on the first ten pages of the front section, compared to 37 percent in the *Times*. Furthermore, the *Post* used its own correspondent to report the stories 98 percent of the time, in contrast to the *Times*, whose reporters wrote only 60 percent of the stories. The two papers also displayed differences in news judgment. Their percentages of agreement in placement were as follows: both covering story on front page, 29 percent; both covering opposition in paper, 39 percent neither covering opposition, 20 percent; and neither covering president, 20 percent.

There was little independent analysis in either the *Post* or *Times* stories, but the *Post*, with its own reporters covering the speeches, provided more perspective. Most of the stories were straightforward news accounts of the president's speech, with mention of the congressional respondent. Occasionally, the writer would gather reaction from noncongressional sources or members of Congress and senators not designated as the official respondent. In big stories such as the Volcker reappointment, the pipeline embargo, and the Polish trade sanctions, extensive background and reaction would be given. In general, however, the president succeeded in setting the agenda for coverage of his speeches, especially when wire service stories were used.

In both the *Post* and the *Times*, the congressional opposition coverage lagged behind the president by roughly the same percentages. While the two newspapers carried the congressional opposition a majority of the time, coverage was often limited to one or two sentences at the end of the story. From the beginning, the *Times*, in about 20 percent of its stories, presented the congressional respondent in a separate wire service story. The *Post* tried to integrate the opposition for most of its 65 stories. In September 1983, however, it suddenly veered toward separate coverage in 4 of its last 6 stories, something it had done only twice in the previous 64 weeks. The *Post* had been left in the awkward position many times of inserting congressional quotes in presidential stories that dealt with entirely different topics. While the best stories seemed to be those of like content that could be woven together, the separate story idea made more sense when the content was dissimilar.

Network broadcast coverage was difficult to measure because ABC did not have an early evening newscast and either NBC or CBS did not have an evening newscast on 17 of the 54 weeks surveyed. In fact, the networks were in head-to-head competition only 65 percent of the time. On only half of those occasions did NBC and CBS both carry stories about President Reagan's speech during 47 of the 54 weeks in which coverage was examined.

Table 27.2
Network Television Coverage of Reagan
Radio Addresses

| | CBS (N = 42) | | NBC (N = 46) | |
	Number of Stories	Percentage	Number of Stories	Percentage
Reagan speech coverage	33	79	30	65
Opposition speech coverage	19	45	9	20
Reagan actuality (including voice over)	18	43	24	52
Opposition actuality	11	26	6	13

Table 27.2 shows that network coverage of the Reagan radio speeches, while not as extensive as that of the *Post* and the *Times,* was still substantial, especially considering the small news hole of television broadcasts. One can assume that the speeches being delivered on Saturdays, traditionally a slow broadcast news day, had an effect on the high level of network coverage. While the two networks covered the president in a comparable way, there was a disparity in coverage of the congressional opposition. NBC used the congressional opposition replies only 9 times in 46 weeks. Of the 9 opposition replies carried on NBC, 7 were broadcast during the first 20 weeks; none was broadcast during the final 20 weeks. CBS, on the other hand, covered the congressional replies steadily over the entire 54-week period.

It was interesting that the networks broadcast twice as many actualities (taped segments) of Reagan as the opposition, when the networks had access only to audiotapes of Reagan but had access to full videotapes of the opposition. This example shows that the appeal of the presidency is strong enough to offset the conventional wisdom that television will always choose an interesting picture over no picture.

CONCLUSION

While television continues to be the prime presidential media instrument, President Reagan has developed radio as a formidable alternative. Through a series of seventy Saturday radio addresses over a period of a year and a half, the president has generated substantial residual coverage on Saturday network television shows and Sunday newspapers in addition to the exposure he has received from the radio addresses themselves. The *Washington Post* and the *New York Times* have covered nearly every speech and have frequently given the speeches front-page coverage.

As important as the quality of the coverage for the White House has been the quality. By controlling the content of the broadcasts and having the advantage of repetition, President Reagan has been able to present an unfiltered message to the American people and also set the agenda for residual coverage. There have been few instances where the media have strayed from the themes established by the president. President Reagan has also been able to use the regularity of the radio addresses to reinforce his message continually.

The Democratic opposition, long frustrated by its inability to gain television time to reply to the president, has also benefited from the presidential radio initiative. The Democrats have been given an automatic right of reply for the first time, allowing them an unprecedented opportunity for national exposure. Still, the opposition speeches merit far less coverage than those of the president. On only a few occasions have the Democrats in Congress been given equal media exposure. While increasing attention on the president usually raises the visibility of the opposition, the biggest news stories tend to eclipse the congressional responses totally.

President Reagan's radio speeches, after only a year and a half, have become the longest-running regularly scheduled broadcast media initiative ever taken by an American president. Ronald Reagan could well be remembered as the president who resurrected radio as a persuasive tool of the presidency.

REFERENCES

Arledge, R. (1983). Remarks at *ABC*/Harvard Symposium on Electoral Participation, Washington, D.C.

Balutis, A. (1977). The presidency and the press: The expanding presidential image. *Presidential Studies Quarterly, 7,* 244-251.

Brown, C., Brown, T. R., & Rivers, W. L. (1978). *The media and the people.* New York: Holt, Rinehart & Winston.

Cannon, L. (1982, April 11). Reagan denies plan will cut student aid. *Washington Post.*

Denton, H. (1982, April 4). Before the mike. *Washington Post.*

Grossman, M. B., & Kumar, M. J. (1979). The White House and the news media: The phases of their relationship. *Political Science Quarterly, 94,* 37-53.

Grossman, M. B., & Kumar, M. J. (1981). *Portraying the president: The White House and the news media.* Baltimore: Johns Hopkins University Press.

Minow, N. N., Martin, J. B., & Mitchell, L. M. (1973). *Presidential television.* New York: Basic Books.

Omang, J. (1982, October 24). O'Neill sharpens Democrat's attack. *Washington Post.*

Paletz, D. L., & Entman, R. M. (1981) *Media power politics.* New York: Free Press.

Raines, H. (1982, April 4). President defends his economic plan. *New York Times.*

Rubin, R. L. (1981). The presidency in the age of television. *In Power to Govern, 34,* 138-152.

28 ● Persuading the Blue-Collar Voter: Issues, Images, and Homophily

KATHLEEN E. KENDALL ● JUNE OCK YUM

State University of New York — Albany

R HETORICIANS and communication researchers have long been interested in the political campaign as a persuasive phenomenon. Just as the communication process has the components of a source sending a message through a channel to a receiver and receiving feedback in a cycle of information exchange, so a campaign has the components of candidates (sources) sending messages (speeches, commercials, and so on) through television or radio or newspapers (channels) to the intended voters (receivers) and receiving their applause, their response to polls, and ultimately their voting decisions (feedback). In studying this process, researchers have speculated about what variable most influences a voter's decision. McCleneghan (1980) lists eleven independent variables that have acceptable reliability in predicting which candidate might win office: incumbency, newspaper coverage, newspaper editorial endorsement, newspaper advertising, television news coverage, television advertising, candidate image, political philosophy, amount of money spent in the election by a candidate, the economic climate, and voter turnout. And this list is not complete. The variables of party registration, issue positions, and homophily should certainly be added, based on the extensive research done on these topics.

No one study can consider all fourteen of these factors as persuasive or situational phenomena. This study of the 1980 presidential campaign fo-

Correspondence and requests for reprints: Kathleen E. Kendall, Department of Communication, HU 355, State University of New York, 1400 Washington Avenue, Albany, NY 12222.

cuses on three variables—issue, image, and homophily—in seeking further illumination of the question of what makes people vote as they do. These factors were chosen because, in contrast to situational factors, the candidate can exercise some direct control over image and homophily, and even over issues, in terms of the positions he or she takes and the emphasis given to them. The candidate's decisions about these variables will be the "stuff" of the campaign, particularly of the advertising.

The voters in this study are blue-collar workers and their families. The blue-collar subjects were selected in an effort to broaden the study of voter behavior to a population not often specifically studied. In this chapter we use the following definitions. "Issue" means an important topic in the campaign about which there is disagreement. "Image" means the mental picture people have about a candidate, the candidate's "publicly perceived attributes" (Bowes & Strentz, 1978, p. 398). "Homophily" means the degree to which the voters see themselves and the candidates as "similar in certain ways, such as attitudes, beliefs, background, education" (Andersen & Todd de Mancillas, 1978, p. 169). "Blue-collar worker" refers to people in the following job categories: craftsmen, foremen, and kindred workers; operatives, except transport; transport equipment operatives; laborers, except farm; service workers; and private household workers.[1]

Voter surveys in the 1940s found that party registration was the best predictor of voting decisions (for example, see Lazarsfeld, Berelson, & Gaudet, 1944; Berelson, Lazarsfeld, & McPhee, 1954). But this is no longer true in many cases. Since the 1960s, ticket splitting has been widespread (DeVries & Tarrance, 1972). Three of the explanations of voter behavior since the onset of widespread ticket splitting are those based on issue, image, and homophily.

THEORY

The Influence of Issues

Some analysts believe that issues have dominated election outcomes since 1964, in a major change in the "structure of citizen attitudes" (Nie, Verba, & Petrocik, 1979; compare Miller, Miller, Raine, & Brown, 1976, p. 31). In order for people to engage in issue voting, certain minimum conditions must exist, according to Nie et al. (1979, p. 158): (1) The voter must prefer one position over another and (2) "the candidates must offer a choice on the issues." In a summary of voting research between 1970 and 1976, Dennis, Chaffee, and Choe (1979, p. 314) report that "specific issue positions [have] replaced party ties as the strongest predictor in voting research."

But the assumption that specific issues are the main vote determinants is open to question. Converse (1964) argues that only about 10 to 15 percent of American adults can recognize policy issues and have clear positions of their own. Carmines and Stimson (1980, p. 78) agree, seeing issue voting as a "final result of a sophisticated decision calculus" that few voters are capable of making. While the masses are capable of "gut responses" to candidates and parties on the basis of "easy issues," Carmines and Stimson (1980, p. 84) say, only the "well-educated, well-informed, concerned and active segment of the electorate" can really discern the "hard issues" and vote accordingly. Rabinowitz, Prothro, and Jacoby (1982, p. 53), in a study of issue salience (the perceived importance of an issue to an individual), found that "salience plays a substantial but not overwhelming role in determining candidate evaluations." However, they failed to find the public making voting decisions "solely on the basis of the issue of particular concern to them" (p. 57).

Some researchers have focused more on the influence of clusters of issues in persuading voters, rather than on single issues. Gopian (1982), in a review of the CBS News-*New York Times* 1976 primary election exit surveys for twenty presidential primaries, categorized issues as "economic" and "noneconomic." He found that knowledge of a voter's issue positions improved predictions of the vote only 13 percent over random guessing, and that noneconomic issues were better predictors than economic issues. Barnett, Serota, and Taylor (1976), investigating political attitude formation in a longitudinal study prior to the 1974 congressional elections, found that when voters identified a candidate with the issues clustering closest to themselves, they moved the candidate closer to themselves on a metric multidimensional scale, and were more likely to vote for the candidate. The convergence of the candidate's position on several issues with the voter's own positions was a much better predictor of vote than the study of a single issue. The concept of homophily proved valuable in this research, as the authors examined the degree to which the voters perceived similarities between themselves and candidates in reference to issues.

The Influence of Image

Among political communication researchers generally, the candidate's image is thought to be the main determinant of voting behavior. The concept of image is very close to that of "ethos," or "source credibility," which has been measured and studied closely for more than three decades, and which originates with Aristotle's *Rhetoric*. Aristotle believed that ethos, or the audience's perception of the rhetor's character, was the most potent means of persuasion. He said that ethos had three main constituents: authoritativeness, trustworthiness, and good will. A recent summing up of research on ethos found that there are two clear dimensions of ethos, competence and character, and that the construct of goodwill or intention depends on the person's perceptions of the source's character (McCroskey & Young, 1981).

While image researchers often work without reference either to Aristotle's *Rhetoric* or ethos research, their findings are basically the same. Roberts (1981, p. 64), in a 1976 panel study of voters in Florida, found that one factor, the voter's perception of the candidate's trustworthiness, had fairly consistent loadings across time and candidates, and usually accounted "for half the variance and almost 90 percent of the common variance in the initial or unrotated factor solution." Issues, on the other hand, were of no value in predicting the vote early in the campaign (February), but became good predictors by the end of the campaign. Williams, Weber, Haaland, Mueller, and Craig (1976, p. 37), in an ambitious study of issues and images in the 1972 New Hampshire primary, found that "candidate personal attributes were identified by the majority of voters as more important dimensions in deciding for whom to vote than candidate issue positions." Given 11 personal attributes and 19 issues to evaluate, voters most frequently cited honesty and leadership capability as the most important factors in their vote. Dennis et al. (1979, p. 321), in a 1976 study of issues and images in presidential voting, found that at all stages of their survey image differences were "the most highly associated with intended vote." Of those image traits, honesty and integrity loomed especially large, with leadership, strength, and decisiveness also important. Not only do most image studies concur that honesty and competence are the most influential components of political image, but these traits also emerge as the most important attributes when people are asked to describe the qualities of an ideal public figure (Sigel, 1966; Hellweg, 1979).

The Influence of Homophily

Another way of looking at voter behavior is through a Burkean perspective, that is, by examining the extent to which voters identify with the candidate, or feel homophilous with the candidate. Burke (1972, p. 28) writes of the power of persuasion in which people "spontaneously, intuitively, and often unconsciously" persuade themselves by identifying with a particular group or idea (in contrast to the Aristotelean idea of persuasion by the "deliberate design" of another). He calls this kind of self-persuasion "identification" and describes three types. An audience is likely to identify with someone who makes them aware that he or she (1) shares the same background or ideas they do, (2) is against the same things they are against, or (3) subtly encourages identification by using the word "we" to show their communality, glossing over their differences.

The concept of homophily, or sender-receiver similarity, is very close to that of identification, especially when the emphasis is on subjective homophily, meaning the communicator's perception of similarity with another communicator (in contrast to objective homophily, which refers to the observable rather than perceived similarities of sender and receiver). Through homophily scales we can test the degree of voter identification with the candidate, by seeing whether the voter thinks the candidate shares the same background and the same ideas. The most subtle level of identification, through the use of the word "we," would require a close content analysis, however.

Andersen and Todd de Mancillas (1978, pp. 177-178) focused on the *perceived* or subjective similarity between two communicators rather than objective, observable similarities, on the grounds that "people's behavior is based on their subjective perceptions of reality regardless of the accuracy of those perceptions." They found that "homophily with public figures is a multidimensional construct consisting of at least two factors: attitude homophily and background homophily." They define attitude homophily as "the extent to which a person perceives that another person shares his or her attitudes, beliefs or values, " and background homophily as "the extent to which a person perceives that another person shares his or her educational and social background." Using their homophily scale in a U.S. Senate race in Florida, Andersen and Kibler (1976) found that "the attitude homophily scale predicted 58% of the variance in voter preference while the background homophily dimension accounted for 6% of the variance in voter preference." In short, people tended to vote for candidates they thought had views similar to their own.

The composition of those views or "attitudes" is vague in attitudinal homophily. And they do not necessarily meet a strict definition of political attitudes as "relatively enduring orientations toward objects . . . that provide individuals with mental frameworks for making economical sense of the world." Instead, the views measured are more like opinions, or "immediate orientations toward contemporary political objects" (Hennessy, 1972, pp. 27-28). We cannot be sure what the homophily scales measure; they ask the voter to compare the candidate's "attitudes" to his or her own, and the definition of those views are all in the voter's mind. Yet the scales do test the extent to which voters approach candidates from an abstract perspective, the extent to which they use global attributes to assess the candidate. It is possible that voters make decisions by judging that "the candidate is like me" and "the other candidate is less like me" on two or three broad attributes, and when we know what those attributes are and what the voter positions on them are, we will know how the vote will go.

Hypotheses

While there have been numerous studies of the role of issues, images, and homophily in influencing voter behavior, few studies have examined the three factors concurrently. Issues, images, and homophily are not totally independent of each other but are interrelated in such a way that a voter's image of a candidate may be influenced by his or her perception of homophily, and a voter's perception of issues may be influenced by his or her image of the candidate. Therefore, it is important to investigate the unique contribution of each factor in predicting the vote decision, controlling the other two factors.

Our reading of several major theories of behavior suggests that homophily may be more influential in voting decisions than either issues or images. Convergence theory emphasizes the relative position of those who communicate with one another (the difference between them) rather than the position of either one of them taken separately (Rogers & Kincaid, 1981; Kincaid, 1983). When this theory is applied to the current study, it suggests that homophily is the basic determinant of vote decisions. In Barnett et al.'s (1976) study, the voter's homophily with the candidate on several issues was a key factor in the vote decision. In other words, it is not issues as independent objects that are important, but the level of similarities between voters and candidates in reference to certain issues. The cognitive congruity theory predicts that if a receiver perceives a source positively, the receiver adjusts his or her positions on certain issues, making those issue positions congruent with the positions of the source (Osgood & Tannenbaum, 1955).

Also, when people make judgments about or create images of other people, those judgments or images are usually affected by the judge's own self-image. Therefore, it is hypothesized that homophily is a more important predictor of vote decision than images or issues.

> H_1: Among blue-collar voters, perceived homophily with the candidate is a more important predictor of voter decision than issue valence or perceptions of candidate images.

Previous research has demonstrated that attitudinal homophily is a more significant predictor of the variance in vote preference than background homophily. This finding is logical, considering the fact that there are generally only two candidates for each political office, and those two people cannot possibly have the same educational, cultural, and class backgrounds of all the voters or even of most of the voters. It is also logical that in selecting such an important leader as a president, voters would like to vote for someone who is better educated than they are, someone whose background provides better preparation for the presidency than the voters have had. On the other hand, it is understandable that people would like to elect a president who has a belief system similar to theirs. It is thus hypothesized that atttitudinal homophily is a more important predictor in voting decisions than background homophily.

H₂: Among blue-collar voters, perceived attitudinal homophily with the candidate is a more important predictor of voter decision than perceived background homophily.

METHODS AND PROCEDURES

Sampling

The subjects for this study were Albany, New York, residents who live in an area having a high density of blue-collar workers. We used the 1970 census tracts to identify this area of the city, and when the 1980 census tracts became available the blue-collar composition of the area was confirmed. Of the approximately 2,000 employed persons in the census tract, over 600 were service workers, about 300 "operators, fabricators, and laborers," over 250 in wholesale and retail trade, 250 in manufacturing, and 200 in precision production, craft, and repair occupations. The median family income was $10,993, the mean $12,195. Only 51.4 percent of the residents had completed high school; 16 percent had attended college (U.S. Department of Commerce, 1983).

The streets in the census tract were identified and a random sample of 1,000 names and telephone numbers drawn from the city directory. Of those, 202 were interviewed by telephone, a number sufficient to generalize to the blue-collar population of the city (47,354) at a confidence level of ±3 percent. Only 20 percent of the people called could be interviewed, as about half were not registered voters, some did not answer or were no longer at that number, and others refused to be interviewed. The interviewers were trained communication students from the State University of New York at Albany.[2]

The telephone calls were made in March 1981, four months after the 1980 presidential election. In spite of the time lag between the election and the interviews, the authors are relatively confident that the subjects answered accurately. When we checked the voting results in each of the wards in the census tract and compared them to the interview results, we found that the percentages compared almost perfectly, which gave us an independent confirmation of the interviewees' honesty. The actual vote (rounded off) in the wards was as follows: Carter, 63 percent; Reagan, 25 percent; Anderson, 10.5 percent; and other, 2 percent (*Official Canvass*, 1981). In our study, the vote was Carter, 64 percent; Reagan, 26 percent; Anderson, 10 percent; and other, .5 percent.

The composition of the sample interviewed was representative of the blue-collar district, but with two exceptions, gender and education. We in-

Table 28.1
Demographic Profile of Subjects
Interviewed (N = 202)

	Number	Percentage
Sex		
male	76	38
female	126	62
Education		
0-11 years	35	17
high school graduate	91	45
some college	43	21
college graduate	19	9
some graduate school	9	5
no answer	5	3
Annual family income		
under $10,000	43	21.3
$10,000-$15,000	57	28.2
$15,000-$20,000	37	18.3
$20,000-$29,000	19	9.4
$30,000-$39,000	6	3
$40,000-$49,000	—	—
$50,000 or over	1	.5
no answer	39	19.3
Age		
range	20 to 89	
mean	47	
median	45	
Party		
Democrats	150	74
Republicans	20	10
independents	9	4.5
other	7	3.5
no answer	16	8
Vote		
Carter	117	58
Reagan	48	24
Anderson	18	9
other	1	9
no answer	18	
Employment		
employed	115	57
unemployed, or temporarily laid off	11	5
other (retired, homemaker, student)	68	34
no answer	8	4

terviewed more women than men and people with more years of schooling than the census tract. But our assumption is that women vote much as men do in blue-collar families, so the overproportion of women should not change the results. Our requirement that only registered voters could be interviewed undoubtedly excluded many people of lower educational levels. Table 28.1 reports the demographic profile of our sample.

The first question asked in the telephone interview was, "Did you vote in the presidential election last fall?" Only those people who answered yes were interviewed, as the study focuses on voters, not nonvoters. The hypotheses were then tested by asking the voters to respond to three scales— one on issue salience, one on image, and one on homophily—as well as to answer several demographic questions. To determine the salience of issues, the interviewers asked respondents to answer on a 5-point scale how important each of six issues was in the voter's decision about how to vote, with 1 being "unimportant" and 5 being "very important." The issues were the state of the economy, the Iranian crisis, military preparedness, the Equal Rights Amendment, unemployment, and energy. These issue areas were selected by reviewing information on exit polls and other analyses at the time of the election. A summary of the subjects' responses shows that the state of the economy was the most important issue to them, with unemployment second and energy third. Table 28.2 summarizes the means of the issue valence answers. The answers to the six issue valence questions were combined to create a total issue valence index. The mean of the total issue valence is 23.17, with a standard deviation of 4.15.

The respondents were then asked to rate each of the presidential candidates on 5-point scales on a list of five image traits; for example, 1 would mean "very dishonest" and 5 would mean "very honest." The traits included honesty and competence, the most significant image traits in most studies, as well as experience (related to competence), strength, and sympathy. The word "sympathy" was selected to convey a meaning similar to "em-

Table 28.2
Means and Standard Deviations of Issue
Valence Answers

Issue	Mean	S.D.
State of the economy	4.52	.784
Unemployment	4.33	.97
Energy	4.07	1.09
Iranian crisis	3.78	1.3
Military preparedness	3.77	1.27
Equal Rights Amendment	3.49	1.48

Note: The higher the mean, the more important the issue.

Table 28.3

Means and Standard Deviations of Image Answers

	Experience		Competence		Honesty		Sympathy		Strength	
	Mean	S.D.	Mean	S.D.	Mean	S.D.	Mean	S.D.	Mean	S.D.
Carter	3.42	1.23	3.35	1.21	4.17	1.07	4.00	1.14	2.95	1.18
Reagan	2.84	1.18	3.15	1.24	3.45	1.29	2.86	1.21	3.85	1.14

Note: The higher the mean, the more positive the image in the voters' minds.

Table 28.4

Means and Standard Deviations for

Homophily Answers

	Carter		Reagan	
	Mean	S.D.	Mean	S.D.
His political attitudes were about the same as yours.[a]	2.73	1.07	3.28	1.07
His political beliefs were different from yours.[b]	3.24	1.01	2.77	1.08
His goals for the country were the same as yours.[a]	2.62	1.10	3.10	1.15
He didn't share your beliefs.[b]	3.26	1.03	2.79	1.05
He liked the same politicians that you liked.[a]	2.92	.97	3.32	.94
His political party was different from yours.[b]	3.54	.99	2.48	.99
His background is similar to yours.[a]	3.19	.96	3.64	.81
His educational background is similar to yours.[a]	3.40	.93	3.61	.85
He is from a different class than you are.[b]	2.81	.96	2.54	.96
His cultural background is similar to yours.[a]	3.33	.93	3.55	.90

a. The lower the mean, the closer the voter feels to the candidate.
b. The lower the mean, the farther the voter feels from the candidate.

pathy," as sympathy is a more widely understood word. The results showed that Jimmy Carter was rated highest on honesty and sympathy, and lowest on strength, while Ronald Reagan was rated highest on strength and lowest on experience. Except on the quality of "strength," Carter was rated far more positively than Reagan on image traits. Table 28.3 summarizes the means of the image answers. To create the Carter image index, we combined the five Carter image scores. This index has a mean of 17.76, with a standard deviation of 4.49. The Reagan image index was calculated in the same way; it has a mean of 13.15, with a standard deviation of 4.96.

For the homophily concept, we used the homophily scale developed by Andersen and Todd de Mancillas (1978), asking the respondents to compare themselves to the candidates on a list of attitudinal and background homophily traits, on a 5-point scale ranging from "strongly agree" to "strongly disagree." The attitudinal traits were political attitudes, political beliefs, goals for the country, and liking the same politicians. The background traits were political party, educational background, class, and cultural background. Based on the results, the voters placed themselves closest to Carter in goals for the country and political attitudes, and not close to Reagan on any trait. Table 28.4 summarizes the means of the homophily answers.

Two different indices were calculated for homophily: attitudinal homophily and background homophily. The attitudinal homophily index was calculated by combining the scores on political attitudes, political beliefs, goals for the country, and liking the same politicians. The mean for attitudinal homophily was 26.78, with a standard deviation of 7.55. The background homphily index was calculated by combining the scores on political party, educational background, class, and cultural background. The mean of this index was 26.61, with a standard deviation of 5.62. When statements in the scale stressed differences rather than similarities with the candidate, the scales were reversed in calculating the homophily indices.

The dependent variable, vote decisions, was measured by asking the respondent for whom he or she voted. Those who voted for Carter were coded as 1 and those who voted for Reagan were coded as 2. The rest of the answers were treated as missing. In the analysis, vote decision was entered as the dummy variable, and the final analysis was based on only the 165 respondents who voted for Carter or Reagan.

The interviews ended with a series of demographic questions, on age, years of schooling completed, family income range, employment status, party registration, and vote in the 1980 presidential race. The interviewer reported the gender of the respondent. These results are reported in Table 28.1.

RESULTS

Multiple regression techniques were employed in the analysis because they allow us to understand the unique contribution of an independent variable after controlling for the effects of the other variables in the system. The vote decision was regressed on the issue variable, two homophily variables (attitudinal homophily and background homophily), and two image variables (Carter image and Reagan image). Table 28.5 reports the final results.

Table 28.5
Results of the Multiple Regression of
the Vote Decision (N=165)

Independent Variable	Multiple R	R^2 Change	Zero-Order Correlation	Beta	F
Issues	.07	.01	−.07	−.00	.001
Attitudinal homophily	.67	.44	.67	.53	38.93**
Background homophily	.67	.00	.44	−.02	.07
Carter's image	.68	.02	−.43	−.13	3.72
Reagan's image	.70	.02	−.49	−.16	5.70*
	$R^2 = .49$	$F = 29.90$	($p < .001$)		

*The regression coefficient is statistically significant beyond the .05 level.
**The regression coefficient is statistically significant beyond the .001 level.

The multiple correlation of vote decision on all five independent variables combined is .70, which is statistically significant beyond the .001 level. These five variables explain 49 percent of the variance of vote decision. Of the five variables, attitudinal homophily alone explains 45 percent of the variance controlling the effect of the other variables, while the impact of issue valence is negligible. Of the two image variables, Reagan's image adds 2 percent of explanation of the variance of vote decision and is statistically significant beyond the .05 level. When compared to the homophily variable, however, the explanatory power of the image variables is much smaller. This result supports the first hypothesis, which states that perceived homophily is a more important predictor of vote decision than issue valence or images.

Background homophily demonstrates no explanatory power on vote decision, while attitudinal homophily is the best predictor of all the variables studied. Therefore, the second hypothesis is also supported by the results: Attitudinal homophily is a more important predictor of vote decision than background homophily. It is interesting to note, however, that the zero-order correlation between background homophily and vote decision is .44, which is statistically significant beyond the .001 level. But this correlation disappears when the effects of attitudinal homophily and image variables are controlled. It appears that the effect of background homophily is preempted by the effect of attitudinal homophily.

DISCUSSION

The present study has made three contributions to existing literature on political communication. First, by focusing the study on blue-collar workers rather than on the general public, we were able to broaden the study of voter behavior to a population not often specifically studied. Second, by investigating the three factors—homophily, issues, and images—at the same time, we were able to determine the unique contribution of each factor while controlling the effects of the other two. Third, our study was audience centered in that we looked at the voters' self-persuasion process through their perceived homophily, issue salience, and perceived images of the candidates, rather than from the perspective of the persuaders' overt efforts. This approach is consistent with Burke's emphasis on identification rather than persuasion by deliberate design. The underlying assumption of the study was that voters are not passive receivers of the campaign messages bombarding them, but active participants in the communication process. With that assumption we proposed that perceived homophily between voters and candidates would be the most important predictor of vote decision, and the research results supported our hypotheses.

As is true in other voter studies, we could not include all the relevant variables. We investigated only three factors we believed to be important, but even with those three we were able to explain almost half of the variance in the vote decisions, mainly through one variable, attitudinal homophily.

The present study confirmed the view that blue-collar voters use broad concepts and personal preferences to make their voting decisions, rather than the specific issues of the campaign. Some would lament this finding, arguing that only an educated electorate making careful choices based on well-developed issues can protect democracy against those who would "sell" candidates as though they were bars of soap. Certainly a well-educated electorate and careful choices are highly desirable. But there is a hidden elitism in the view that intelligent voting decisions must be based on specific issues, an assumption that any other way of doing it is inadequate and inappropriate. This view seems unjustified on the evidence and, certainly, snobbish. Issues are often time bound and transient, important only for a few months or a year. For instance, energy was an important issue four years ago, but due to the drop in oil prices and voluntary conservation by the public, it is not an issue at the moment. If the public chooses a president because of his or her stance on an issue, the public may be sorry once the specific issue fades and the president turns out to have views alien to theirs in many respects. The blue-collar voter apparently selects a president in much the same way one selects friends, noting their personal qualities and beliefs and attitudes, particularly as they relate to one's own though expecting a president to be better educated and trained. Who is to say that such a basis for judgment is any worse than a judgment based on campaign issues in the mysterious game of predicting future presidential behavior on a wide range of issues?

One unexpected finding of the study was that perceived images of Reagan had a significant relationship to voter decision, but the images of Carter did not. This means that the relatively negative images of Reagan influenced the blue-collar vote for Carter more than positive images of Carter. This finding has an important theoretical implication. So far, most research on image and perceived homophily has ignored the possibility that a homophily gap, or "heterophily," may work differently than homophily, and negative images of a certain candidate may have a different influence on vote decisions than positive images of the other candidate. Further research could help to illuminate the phenomenon of "negative voting."

The present study has two methodological limitations, one resulting from sampling procedure and the other from measurement procedure. Our respondents were mainly blue-collar workers or family members who were similar to each other in background, and therefore their perceived background homophily with the candidates was similar. The resultant reduced variance may have contributed to the negligible relationship that background homophily had with voter decision. Also, blue-collar workers historically favor Democratic candidates, and our respondents were no exception. Almost 60 percent of the respondents voted for Carter, and consequently the distribution of the dependent variable was skewed. This distribution was the result of random sampling procedures. While future research with a similar sampling frame might try to match the number of voters who vote for each candidate, such a procedure could distort the other variables, since Republican blue-collar workers may differ from the general population of blue-collar workers.

Issue valence was measured by asking the respondents how important each issue was in their decisions on how to vote. This procedure may have evoked the "socially desirable response" syndrome. Most respondents answered positively, that is, they perceived all the issues as important or very important. In effect, respondents used only half of the five-point scale. When a variable has a truncated range, it is difficult to observe its relationship with other variables. However, the explanatory power of issue valence was so negligible that it is unlikely that reduced variance alone contributed to such a result.

The present study has demonstrated a need for new directions in the study of voter decision processes. Issue valence and candidate images should not be studied as isolated objects separated from candidates and from voters. The relative positions of voters and candidates toward the issues and images and the changes in these relative positions over time should be the focal point of study. The process by which voters and candidates converge or diverge (increase or decrease their homophily) deserves more attention among political communication researchers, in terms of the voters' perception of issues, their judgments about the personality traits important for good leadership, and their general political beliefs.

NOTES

1. These are job categories used in the U.S. Census. The system of data analysis is that used by Duncan, Featherman, and Duncan (1972).

2. We would like to express our appreciation to the students who helped to develop the study and who did the interviewing: Amy Adelman, Robert Blasenstein, Thomas Clark, Rick Honen, Arlene Konsens, and Mildred Treis. We also want to thank Robert Kuchay and Rick Holmes for their great assistance with the computer analysis.

REFERENCES

Andersen, P. A., & Kibler, R. J. (1976). *The effect of source credibility, attraction and homophily on voter preference.* Paper presented at the annual meeting of the International Communication Association, Portalnd, OR.

Andersen, P. A., & Todd de Mancillas, W. (1978). Scales for the measurement of homophily with public figures. *Southern Speech Communication Journal, 43,* 169-179.

Barnett, G. A., Serota, K. B., & Taylor, J. A. (1976). Campaign communication and attitude change: A multidimensional analysis. *Human Communication Research, 2,* 227-244.

Berelson, B. R., Lazarsfeld, P. F., & McPhee, W. N. (1954). *Voting.* Chicago: University of Chicago Press.

Bowes, J. E., & Strentz, H. (1978). Candidate images: Stereotyping and the 1976 debates, in B. Ruben (Ed.), *Communication yearbook 2.* New Brunswick, NJ: Transaction.

Burke, K. (1972) *Dramatism and development.* Barre, MA: Clark University Press.

Carmines, E. G., & Stimson, J. A. (1980). The two faces of issue voting. *American Political Science Review, 74,* 78-91.

Converse, P. (1964). The nature of belief systems in mass publics. In D. Apter (Ed.), *Ideology and discontent.* New York: Free Press.

Dennis, J., Chaffee, S. H., & Choe, S. Y. (1979). Impact on partisan image and issue voting. In S. Kraus (Ed.), *The great debates: Carter vs. Ford, 1976.* Bloomington: Indiana University Press.

DeVries, W., & Tarrance, V. L. (1972). *The ticket-splitter: A new force in American politics.* Grand Rapids, MI: William B. Eerdmans.

Duncan, O. D, Featherman, D. L., & Duncan, D. (1972). *Socioeconomic background and achievement.* New York: Seminar.

Gopian, D. (1982). Issue preferences and candidate choice in presidential primaries. *American Journal of Political Science, 26,* 523-546.

Hellweg, S. (1979). An examination of voter conceptualizations of the ideal political candidate. *Southern Speech Communication Journal, 44,* 373-385.

Hennessy, B. (1972). A headnote on the existence and study of political attitudes. In D. D. Nimmo & C. M. Bonjean (Eds.), *Political attitudes and public opinion.* New York: David McKay.

Kincaid, D. L. (1983). *Recent Developments in the Network/convergence paradigm of communication.* Paper presented at the annual meeting of the International Communication Association, Dallas.

Lazarsfeld, P. F., Berelson, B. R., & Gaudet, H. (1944). *The people's choice.* New York: Columbia University Press.

McCleneghan, J. S. (1980). Media and non-media effects in Texas mayoral elections. *Journalism Quarterly, 57,* 129-134, 201.

McCroskey, J. C., & Young, T. J. (1981). Ethos and credibility: The construct and its measurement after three decades. *Central States Speech Journal, 32,* 24-34.

Miller, A. H., Miller, W. E., Raine, A. S., & Brown, T. A. (1976). A majority party in disarray: Policy polarization in the 1972 election. *American Political Science Review, 70,* 753-778.

Nie, N. H., Verba, S., & Petrocik, J. R. (1979). *The changing american voter.* Cambridge, MA: Harvard University Press.

Official canvass of the county of Albany for the election held Tuesday, November 4, 1980. (1981). Albany, NY.

Osgood, C. E., & Tannenbaum, P. H. (1955). The principle of congruity in the prediction of attitude change. *Psychological Review, 62,* 42.55.

Rabinowitz, G., Prothro, J. W., & Jacoby, W. (1982). Salience as a factor in the impact of issues on candidate evaluation. *Journal of Politics, 44,* 41-63.

Roberts, C. L. (1981). From primary to presidency: A panel study of images and issues in the 1976 election. *Western Journal of Speech Communication, 45,* 60-70.

Rogers, E. M., & Kincaid, D. L. (1981). *Communication networks.* New York: Free Press.

Sigel, R. S. (1966). Image of the American presidency: Part II of an exploration in popular views of presidential power. *Midwest Journal of Political Science, 10,* 123-137.

U.S. Department of Commerce, Bureau of the Census. (1983). *1980 Census of Population and Housing, Albany-Schenectady-Troy, New York.* Washington, DC: Government Printing Office.

Williams, D. C., Weber, S. J., Haaland, G. A., Mueller, R. H., & Craig, R. E. (1976). Voter decisionmaking in a primary election: An evaluation of three models of choice. *American Journal of Political Science, 20,* 37-49.

VIII ● INSTRUCTIONAL COMMUNICATION

29 ● Power in the Classroom IV: Alternatives to Discipline

PATRICIA KEARNEY ● TIMOTHY G. PLAX ●
VIRGINIA P. RICHMOND ●
JAMES C. McCROSKEY

West Virginia University

A S Wlodkowski (1982, p. 2) has noted, "If anything could ever had been made real by wishing for it or wanting it, we would have made disciplined students the norm long ago." Demands for disciplined and obedient students are a clearly defined part of our cultural orientation. The public continues to clamor for more classroom discipline, claiming that uncontrolled students are the number one problem facing our schools (Gallup, 1981). In this way, discipline is construed as the panacea for all learning-related problems. Educators are retained and tenured on their ability to *make* students learn. Surveys of elementary and secondary teachers indicate that good teaching in their schools is equated with student control (see Hoy, 1968). Experienced teachers and administrators most frequently advocate a rigidly disciplined classroom and are quick to reprimand beginning instructors for their permissiveness (Hoy, 1968). The pervasiveness of the disciplinarian mentality is staggering (see Willever & Jones, 1963; Check, 1979).

Ironically, discipline alone may actually work against learning (see Hoy, 1968; Glasser, 1978). Highly disciplined schools fail to stimulate greater learning and are generally associated with increased incidence of student misbehaviors (Wlodkowski, 1982; Lufler, 1978). No research evidence suggests that more or better discipline, in and of itself, leads to greater teacher effectiveness (see Wlodkowski, 1982). On the contrary, teachers who employ frequent discipline interventions tend to find their classrooms even

Correspondence and requests for reprints: Patricia Kearney, Department of Speech Communication, West Virginia University, Morgantown, WV 26506.

more disruptive and hard to manage (Rutter, Maughan, Mortimore, Ouston, & Smith, 1979). More rules, harsher penalties, and "get tough" policies fail to gain student compliance and conformity (Clegg & Megson, 1968; Heal, 1978; Lufler, 1978).

Historically, corporal punishment has been the most notable means of imposing discipline. Advocates claim that the educational system is handicapped without the implicit or explicit threat of punitive sanctions (Coy, 1980). Educators often assert that corporal controls are an expedient way of managing student misbehaviors. Parents also demand teacher authority through physical punishment, indicating that such measures are *good* for some students. Others, who argue against corporal actions, indicate that punishment leads to student rebellion and revenge. Moreover, it is argued that such controls set up inappropriate, punitive models that interfere with affective learning and discourage educators from employing other forms of control in managing their classrooms (Coy, 1980). In schools where corporal punishment has been restricted, however, teachers have been left wanting. What alternative control techniques are available to public school professionals? The present investigation attempts to expand upon and clarify what is known about teachers' use of management strategies in the classroom. Of primary concern in this study were the available alternative teacher communication techniques that can be employed to control student behaviors necessary for learning.

"Power in the classroom" refers to the teacher's capacity to influence students to do something they would not have done had they not been influenced (McCroskey & Richmond, 1983). Thus the ability of teachers to employ power influences the effectiveness of their classroom management. Power strategies are actually behavior alteration techniques that teachers communicate to control or modify student actions (Kearney, Plax, Richmond, & McCroskey, 1983). Since learning requires that teachers assume control in order to optimize classroom environments conducive to learning, teachers must "strategically communicate messages that compel students to engage in learning" (Kearney et al., 1983, p. 1). Consequently, power strategies are critical for managing the classroom.

This study was designed to explore the use of power in the classroom by expanding and refining the classification of behavior alteration techniques and messages that teachers report are representative of the classroom environment. The result of this investigation is a comprehensive, classroom-relevant taxonomy of alternative behavior alteration techniques that teachers can and do employ to modify or elicit student behaviors. As with earlier investigations, the research and thinking in the areas of power and classroom management provided directions for the present study.

CLASSROOM MANAGEMENT

Discipline traditionally has been linked to control—"student acceptance of or submission to teacher authority" (Wlodkowski, 1982, p. 2). There
is little doubt that this perspective was especially pertinent to historical interpretations, in which schools were conceived as despotic structures (Waller,
1932). In early discussions, teachers were defined as dominating rulers and
students as "subjects" to be "civilized" (see Waller, 1932; Durkheim, 1961;
Boocock, 1983). In this way, students were expected to submit to teacher
authority (Waller, 1932; Wlodkowski, 1982; Hoy, 1968). This long-standing
teacher-student characterization is still reflected in the contemporary custodial orientation toward education.

Administrators and teachers who communicate impersonality, mistrust, and pessimism to students reflect a custodial environment. Schools
with such an environment emphasize autocracy, teacher dominance, rigidly
defined teacher-student role hierarchies, and strict, unilateral teacher control (Hoy, 1968). Novice teachers quickly shed permissive pupil control ide-
ologies advocated in their training programs and adopt an increasingly custodial orientation after their student teaching experience and again after
their first year of teaching (Hoy, 1968). These noticeable teacher changes
are alarming when evidence indicates that custodial-type schools are no
longer effective in controlling student behavior (Glasser, 1978; Lufler,
1978; Wlodkowski, 1982).

While traditional schools may have defined discipline as the optimal
goal, contemporary educators can ill afford to demand student submission
as a function of teacher authority (Glasser, 1978; Rutter et al., 1979). In this
decade, "education for education's sake" holds little meaning for our youth.
While formal education may have been equated with political, social and
economic opportunities in the past, students question the relative efficacy of
education's meeting those obligations today. According to Boocock (1983),
the current crisis in education is a function of credential inflation and surplus
absorption. That is, students no longer believe that academic credentials
ensure them either professional opportunities or the training necessary for
on-the-job performance. Additionally, students may view schools as "holding places" where young people are kept so as to exclude them from a work
force already glutted. Consequently, formal education has lost much of its
value for our youth. This declining value of education has inevitably led to a
loss of teacher authority (Boocock, 1983). Discipline techniques designed to
make students learn, then, may have little or no effect.

In response to these concerns, instructional researchers have recently
focused on student control as it relates directly to learning (Hoy, 1968).
Given this contemporary perspective, effective teachers are competent in

both instructional (that is, instructional technologies, learning objectives, content, and evaluation) and classroom management skills. Within the context of classroom management, discipline loses its name, its meaning, and its pervasive emphasis (Rutter et al., 1979; Wlodkowski, 1982). Instead, "classroom management" refers to those teacher behaviors that "produce high levels of student involvement in classroom activities, minimal amounts of student behaviors that interfere with the teacher's or student's work, and efficient use of instructional time" (Emmer & Evertson, 1980, p. 342).

Consistent with this orientation, Richmond and Andriate (1982) define "classroom misbehavior" as any student behavior that interferes with learning. Effective managers, then, are able both to encourage behaviors appropriate for learning and to reduce student misbehavior. In this way, students assume a more positive stance relative to the overall learning environment. Rather than forcing students to learn in the antiquated discipline sense, the teacher creates and manages a classroom where techniques are employed to influence students to *want* to learn. Two separate research areas have converged on this problem. One area emphasizes the encouragement of on-task behaviors and the other the reduction of student misbehaviors. While these emphases address classroom management from different points of departure, both ultimately prescribe conditions that lead to management effectiveness.

From the first perspective, student involvement in initiating and maintaining on-task behavior is a necessary condition for effective classroom management. The use of prompts (Krantz & Scarth, 1979), positive questioning techniques (Borg & Ascione, 1979), motivational messages, structured transitions, teacher-led group activities (Good & Beckerman, 1978), and other teacher strategies all promote greater task persistence.

The second perspective is represented in the body of research on control techniques designed to minimize student disruptions or misbehaviors. Unlike discipline, these control strategies are inextricably tied to learning or on-task behavioral requirements. As such, while student misbehaviors are discouraged, these approaches provide concurrent rewards for appropriate behaviors conducive to learning. Such positive control techniques include token economy (Jenson, 1978), behavioral contracts (Harris, 1972), incentive systems (Emmer & Evertson, 1980), extinction, reinforcement, time-outs (Shrigley, 1979), and others.

Recently, a third perspective on classroom management has emerged from the instructional communication literature (McCroskey & Richmond, 1983; Richmond & McCroskey, in press; Kearny et al., 1983). The most recent research in this area (Kearney et al., 1983) examines the application of behavior alteration techniques. This approach examines classroom management from both relational and message-based orientations. In contrast to other perspectives on classroom management, this approach is based on the teacher's use of power in the classroom.

POWER IN THE CLASSROOM

For the purpose of classroom management, the term "power-based strategies" refers to the teacher's potential to affect student on-task behaviors and student disruptions to learning. The most suitable framework for defining power-based strategies within the classroom is provided by French and Raven (1968). McCroskey and Richmond (1983) interpreted this conceptualization for their research on power in the classroom. Within the classroom, *coercive* power emanates from student's perceptions that they will be punished by the teacher if they fail to comply with the teacher's influence attempts. *Reward* power is based on students' perceptions that they will be rewarded if they comply with teacher demands. *Legitimate,* or assigned, power stems from students' perceptions that the teacher has the right to prescribe behavior. *Referent* power is based on students' desire to comply in order to please or identify with the teacher. Finally, *expert* power arises from students' desire to comply because they perceive that the teacher is competent in specific areas.

McCroskey and Richmond (1983) examined teachers' and students' perceptions of teacher use of each of these five types of power in the classroom. Junior high, high school, and college teachers and their students were found to share somewhat similar perceptions. Both teachers and students perceived that reward, referent, and expert power were employed more frequently than either legitimate or coercive power. However, teachers perceived that they used expert power more than their students believed they did, while students perceived their teachers as using more coercive power than their teachers perceived themselves as using.

Richmond and McCroskey (in press) examined the effects of power type/usage on students' affective and cognitive learning. Their results indicated that teacher use of coercive and, to a lesser degree, legitimate power was negatively related to both affective and cognitive learning. However, both referent and, to a lesser degree, expert power were positively related to both learning outcomes. Reward power was not found to be meaningfully associated with learning.

Teacher authority and discipline in the traditional sense have little or no meaning in today's classroom. McCroskey and Richmond (1983) demonstrate that influence in the classroom is relational. Teachers do not automatically possess power; students must perceive its existence. According to teacher and student perceptions, then, power and subsequent influence evolve relationally within the classroom. Further, Richmond and Mc-Croskey (in press) found that legitimate (or assigned) power and coercive (or punishment) power were both negatively associated with learning. These types of emergent power most closely resemble authority and discipline. These power types, then, may be detrimental to classroom management. Such influence attempts may fail to either encourage on-task behaviors or discourage misbehaviors to create an atmosphere necessary to optimal learning.

Based upon these findings, Kearney et al. (1983) studied the bases of power available to teachers in order to broaden the range of alternatives available to teachers in their efforts at classroom management. This third investigation focused on the generation of an initial list of potential power strategies for classroom use. A college student sample was employed to generate an open-ended list of potential influence statements. This list was coded into a typology of eighteen behavior alteration techniques (BATs) that were best represented by a combination of statements or behavioral alteration messages (BAMs). Each unique set of BAMs provided an inductive basis for labeling each of the eighteen separate BATs. The grouping of BAMs were then given to elementary and secondary teachers for an assessment of their usage and effectiveness in changing behavior in the classroom. Teachers reported that seven of the BATs were used frequently and were perceived as effective. Results also indicated that teacher use of BATs was not meaningfully associated with instructor gender, grade level, or years taught.

Overall, the results demonstrated power need not be restricted to direct teacher appeals. That is, teacher power need not rely on externally based sanctions. Unlike the bases of power explicated in McCroskey and Richmond (1983) and Richmond and McCroskey (in press), BATs employed in the classroom can be indirect. In other words, additional BATs that teachers reported they used frequently were "student centered," referencing inherent student benefits through compliance. Most pertinent to the classroom environment specifically, teachers reported that they also relied on "student audience effect" techniques or those strategies that appeal to students' peers and reference groups for compliance.

RESEARCH QUESTIONS

Defining effective teaching from a classroom management perspective constructively diverges from traditional views of instruction. While numerous teachers are still forced to operate within a custodial orientation, the research evidence indicates that discipline *cannot be* the goal of instruction. In fact, the classroom management literature suggests that discipline "may actually be a force against learning" (Wlodkowski, 1982, p. 8). Effective managers are those who view student control only as it relates to the over-riding goal of learning. Instead of emphasizing discipline, then, classroom managers seek to gain student compliance by shaping an optimal learning environment that encourages learning. Behavior alteration techniques offer teachers a useful approach to achieving this objective through communicating student-centered messages that offer reasons for compliance.

Thus far, the generation of an initial pool of BATs has relied on college student reports (Kearney et al., 1983). Unlike previous research on compliance-gaining strategies (see, for example, Marwell & Schmitt, 1967; Miller, Boster, Roloff, & Seibold, 1977; Cody, McLaughlin, & Jordan, 1980; Schenck-Hamlin, Wiseman, & Georgacarakos, 1982), the format employed in generating BATs purposefully omitted hypothetical scenarios or reference to specific relationships in order to elicit a wide range of potential responses. While this approach was essential for an initial, comprehensive list of BATs, the results of the Kearney et al. (1983) study suggest that additional BATs may exist for the classroom. That is, the uniqueness of "student-centered" and "audience effect" techniques indicate that classroom strategies are qualitatively different from other compliance-gaining typologies. Thus the present study was designed to extend, validate, and refine the BAT typology through teacher input. Additionally, classroom-relevant BAMs that represent each technique are more appropriately derived from sources of those messages themselves—teachers. Therefore, the following research questions have been formulated:

RQ1: What types of behavior alteration techniques are available for teacher use in the classroom?

RQ2: What representative messages do teachers generate when they employ each BAT?

Based on the revisions of both BATs and BAMs specifically applicable to the classroom, the third question was asked in order to isolate those techniques teachers use most and least frequently with their students.

RQ3: What BATs do teachers perceive that they employ most frequently; which do they use least frequently?

Kearney et al. (1983) suggest that teachers employ primarily positive BATs in the classroom. However, earlier research indicates that teachers are more likely to use a more discipline-oriented model of student control (Hoy, 1968). Either teachers are unwilling to report or they are unaware that they frequently use such custodial forms of control. According to student perceptions, coercive power is frequently used more than teachers report (Mc-

Croskey & Richmond, 1983). By assessing what strategies teachers perceive that *other* teachers employ, teachers may be more willing to identify additional BATs being used in the classroom. Therefore, we asked the following question:

> RQ4: What BATs do teachers perceive that *other* teachers employ for the same grade level taught?

Since teachers may report that they use one set of BATs and that other teachers employ a different set, the fifth research question was asked to determine teachers' perceptions of the relative effectiveness of each BAT.

> RQ5: What BATs do teachers perceive to be effective in the classroom?

Finally, Kearney et al. (1983) failed to demonstrate any meaningful association between specific teacher variables and the selection and perceived effectiveness of BATs employed in the classroom. However, the revised BATs and BAMs, as well as the inclusion of *other* teachers' use of BATs, may produce quite different results. Therefore, we asked:

> RQ6: Are the BATs teachers perceive they use those they perceive that other teachers use and those BATs they find effective a function of: (a) instructor gender, (b) number of years teaching, or (c) grade level taught?

PROCEDURES

Data Collection

Data for this study were collected in three phases. The first two phases involved the same group of subjects. The third phase employed subjects not involved in the previous phases.

Phase 1. A total of 343 teachers in grades K-12 were provided a form with the following instructions:

> As a teacher you often try to get your students to do things that they may not want to do. The student usually thinks, and often asks, "Why should I do this?" Please give us the most common answers you would give to this question.

The form provided 25 numbered spaces for responses. Subjects were informed that if they had more responses they should provide those on the back of the form.

Subjects in this phase were enrolled in a basic graduate course in communication in instruction. The form was administered the first day of class, before any instruction in the content of the course. The teaching experience of the subjects ranged from 1 to 37 years.

Phase 2. The subjects from Phase 1 were divided into 55 groups of 5-7 members each, representing level of grade taught (K-3, N = 10; 4-6, N = 10; 7-9, N = 9; 10-12, N = 9; other, N = 17). While most of the subjects taught in clearly distinct categories within elementary or secondary schools, an "other" category was necessary to accommodate subjects who taught at multiple levels (speech pathologists, music teachers, special education teachers, and so on).

Each group was provided a copy of the behavior alteration technique categories and representative messages generated in the Kearney et al. (1983) study. They were also provided a form with each category label. Substantial space was provided between labels on the forms. Each group was asked to go over the messages they had generated in Phase 1 and place the ones they could in the categories provided. After they had completed this task, they were asked to review the messages they had been unable to classify and attempt to group them in new categories and to label the new categories.

Phase 3. On the basis of the results of the first two phases (discussed below), 22 categories of behavior alteration techniques with representative behavior alteration messages were generated (see Table 29.2). Subjects (N = 402) were provided a form that included the 22 BATs and corresponding message examples. The subjects were asked to indicate (on a 1-5 scale, 5 = high) how frequently they used each of the techniques, how frequently they believed other teachers at their same grade level used the technique, and how effective they perceived the technique to be in modifying student behaviors at that grade level. The subjects were also asked to indicate how many years they had taught, the level at which they taught, and their gender. The range of experience was 1-24 years, with a mean of 4.8 years. There were 66 males and 336 females in the sample. The sample size for each level taught was as follows: K-3, 115; 4-6, 81; 7-9, 56; 10-12, 66; other, 84.

Data Analyses

The data from Phase 1 and Phase 2 were analyzed to obtain answers to our first two research questions. The data obtained in Phase 2 (group responses) were examined to determine the number of groups at each teaching level that generated behavior alteration messages that the group could classify for each of the Kearney et al. (1983) BAT categories. In addition, these data were examined to determine whether the groups had generated categories beyond those provided them. Potential new categories were rejected only if all of the behavior alteration messages provided as examples could clearly be classified in one or a combination of the Kearney et al. (1983) categories by two of the investigators. All other new categories were accepted. Finally, all of the responses from Phase 1 were classified by the investigators into Kearney et al. (1983) categories plus the new categories generated by the analysis of the Phase 2 data. The unclassifiable messages (approximately 2 percent) were examined to determine whether additional categories could be formed.

In a supplementary analysis (for which no research question was posed in advance) a sample of 1217 behavior alteration messages was drawn from the total responses provided in Phase 1 (total was slightly in excess of 3650 responses). These messages were classified into three categories: prosocial (for example, reward-type), antisocial (for example, punishment and legitimate types), and other. This analysis was performed to determine whether there was either a pro- or antisocial bias in the data obtained. The analysis indicated that there were 542 prosocial messages, 535 antisocial messages, and 140 that were classified as other. Since there was no apparent pro- or antisocial bias, this issue was not considered subsequently.

The data from Phase 3 were analyzed to obtain answers to research questions 3-6. To determine frequency of self-use, other use, and perceived effectiveness of each of the techniques, means for each response across the entire sample were computed. In addition, frequency analysis was performed to determine the percentage of respondents reporting high (4 or 5) use or effectiveness and those reporting low (1 or 2) use or effectiveness.

To determine whether teacher gender, length of teaching experience, or level taught affects perceived use or effectiveness of the techniques, multivariate analyses of variance were computed for each of these predictors, with the use and effectiveness responses as criterion variables. Where significant multivariate results were obtained, univariate analyses of variance were computed to probe the results.

Finally, since the data on use and effectiveness were collected during the same sitting, correlations among responses were examined to determine the existence of any meaningful patterns. Separate factor analyses were computed for self-use, other use, and effectiveness. A liberal criterion of an eigen-value of 1.0 was set for termination of factor extraction. Both orthogonal and oblique rotational analyses were examined. In addition, the unrotated analyses were examined. A minimum loading of .60 was set for considering an item loaded on a factor. In addition to the factor analyses, the correlations were computed between responses for self-use and other use, self-use and effectiveness, and other use and effectiveness for each BAT.

RESULTS

Phases 1 and 2

Analysis of the data provided by the various teacher groupings indicated that instructors at each teaching level generated behavioral alteration

Table 29.1
Number of Groups Generating Behavior Alteration
Messages for Each Behavior
Alteration Technique

BAT	K-3	4-6	7-9	10-12	Other	Total
			Teaching Level			
Reward from Behavior	10	10	9	9	16	54
Reward from Others	8	7	5	6	7	33
Punishment from Source	8	9	9	7	11	44
Referent-Model	3	3	5	4	7	22
Legitimate-Higher Authority	10	8	6	7	14	45
Guilt	7	4	7	6	12	36
Reward from Source	7	10	5	7	13	42
Normative Rules	8	8	8	6	14	44
Personal Responsibility	6	6	7	6	13	38
Expert	5	5	3	5	7	25
Punishment from Behavior	7	7	8	8	9	39
Self-Esteem	8	6	7	8	12	41
Debt	2	5	4	3	6	20
Personal Relationship-Negative	4	2	1	2	5	14
Altruism	3	5	7	2	7	24
Personal Relationship-Positive	7	6	5	5	6	29
Duty	5	4	6	3	7	25
Legitimate-Personal Authority	10	10	9	8	15	52
Number of Groups	10	10	9	9	17	55

messages for each of the original eighteen BAT categories (Kearney et al., 1983). However, no particular BAT was represented by a spontaneously generated message from any single member in any of the groups sampled (see Table 29.1). The BATs for which the most groups reported messages were Reward from Behavior and Legitimate-Personal Authority. The fewest groups reported messages for Personal Relationship-Negative, Debt, and Referent-Model. Clearly, all of the BATs generated by the student sample employed in the Kearney et al. (1983) research are appropriate for teachers. However, some BATs seem to be more a part of what teachers indicate they use than others.

Four new BATs were generated in the data provided by the teacher groups: Deferred Reward from Behavior, Punishment from Others, Peer Modeling, and Teacher Feedback. The first of these represents a splitting of the original BAT of Reward from Behavior into two categories—Immediate

Table 29.2
Revised Behavior Alteration Techniques and Messages

Technique	Sample Messages
(1) Immediate Reward from Behavior	You will enjoy it. It will make you happy. Because it's fun. You'll find it rewarding/interesting. It's a good experience.
(2) Deferred Reward from Behavior	It will help you later on in life. It will prepare you for college (or high school, job, etc.). It will prepare you for your achievement tests. It will help you with upcoming assignments.
(3) Reward from Teacher	I will give you a reward if you do. I will make it beneficial to you. I will give you a good grade (or recess, extra credit) if you do. I will make you my special assistant.
(4) Reward from Others	Others will respect you if you do. Others will be proud of you. Your friends will like you if you do. Your parents will be pleased.
(5) Self-Esteem	You will feel good about yourself if you do. You are the best person to do it. You are good at it. You always do such a good job. Because you're capable!
(6) Punishment from Behavior	You will lose if you don't. You will be unhappy if you don't. You will be hurt if you don't. It's your loss. You'll feel bad if you don't.
(7) Punishment from Teacher	I will punish you if you don't. I will make it miserable for you. I'll give you an "F" if you don't. If you don't do it now, it will be homework tonight.
(8) Punishment from Others	No one will like you. Your friends will make fun of you. Your parents will punish you if you don't. Your classmates will reject you.
(9) Guilt	If you don't, others will be hurt. You'll make others unhappy if you don't. Your parents will feel bad if you don't. Others will be punished if you don't.
(10) Teacher-Student Relationship: Positive	I will like you better if you do. I will respect you. I will think more highly of you. I will appreciate you more if you do. I will be proud of you.
(11) Teacher-Student Relationship: Negative	I will dislike you if you don't. I will lose respect for you. I will think less of you if you don't. I won't be proud of you. I'll be disappointed in you.

(continued)

Table 29.2 (Continued)

(12) Legitimate-Higher Authority	Do it, I'm just telling you what I was told. It is a rule, I have to do it and so do you. It's a school rule. It's school policy. The principal said so.
(13) Legitimate-Teacher Authority	Because I told you to. You don't have a choice. You're here to work! I'm the teacher, you're the student. I'm in charge, not you. Don't ask, just do it.
(14) Personal (Student) Responsibility	It is your obligation. It is your turn. Everyone has to do his/her share. It's your job. Everyone has to pull his/her own weight.
(15) Responsibility to Class	Your group needs it done. The class depends on you. All your friends are counting on you. Don't let your group down. You'll ruin it for the rest of the class (team).
(16) Normative Rules	We voted, and the majority rules. All of your friends are doing it. Everyone else has to do it. The rest of the class is doing it. It's part of growing up.
(17) Debt	You owe me one. Pay your debt. You promised to do it. I did it the last time. You said you'd try this time.
(18) Altruism	If you do this, it will help others. Others will benefit if you do. It will make others happy if you do. I'm not asking you to do it for yourself; do it for the good of the class.
(19) Peer Modeling	Your friends do it. Classmates you respect do it. The friends you admire do it. Other students you like do it. All your friends are doing it.
(20) Teacher Modeling	This is the way I always do it. When I was your age, I did it. People who are like me do it. I had to do this when I was in school. Teachers you respect do it.
(21) Expert Teacher	From my experience, it is a good idea. From what I have learned, it is what you should do. This has always worked for me. Trust me — I know what I'm doing. I had to do this before I became a teacher.
(22) Teacher Feedback	Because I need to know how well you understand this. To see how well I've taught you. To see how well you can do it. It will help me know your problem areas.

and Deferred. Punishment from Others, similarly, represents an additional BAT stemming from the Punishment from Source and Punishment from Behavior categories in the original study. The Peer Modeling BAT represents the splitting of the Referent-Model category into Teacher Modeling and Peer Modeling. The final BAT, Teacher Feedback, represents a completely new category. Each of these new BATs was generated across several of the teacher groups, although the labels that were attached by the teachers were not all identical.

Less than 2 percent of the spontaneously generated messages from Phase 1 could not be classified into the original BAT categories or the four new categories. Almost all of these came from teachers who clearly did not understand the assignment or provided responses that the investigators could not interpret (for example, "It is 2:30"; "Tell a joke"; "Are you passing all your other classes?"). No new BAT could be generated from these responses.

On the basis of these results the 22 Bats appearing in Table 29.2 were included in Phase 3 of the present study. Additionally, the sample statements used by Kearney et al. (1983) were modified by including specific statements generated by the teachers in Phases 1 and 2. Also, some of the labels for the BAT categories were modified to relate specifically to the teacher-student relationship.

Phase 3

Table 29.3 reports the mean self-use, other use, and effectiveness scores for each of the BATs. The percentages of respondents indicating high or low use of effectiveness are also reported. Employing a majority percentage criterion, four of the BATs were found to be used frequently by the teachers sampled: Immediate Reward from Behavior, Deferred Reward from Behavior, Self-Esteem, and Teacher Feedback. Employing the same criterion, ten of the BATs were found to be used infrequently: Punishment from Behavior, Punishment from Teacher, Punishment from Others, Guilt, Teacher/Student Relationship-Negative, Legitimate-Teacher Authority, Debt, Altruism, Peer Modeling, and Teacher Modeling.

Results with regard to the teachers' perceptions of the use of the BATs by other teachers at their same grade level were substantially different. A majority reported that six techniques are frequently used by other teachers: Immediate Reward from Behavior, Deferred Reward from Behavior, Punishment from Teacher, Legitimate-Higher Authority, Legitimate-Teacher Authority, and Teacher Feedback. In contrast, a majority of the teachers reported only four techniques that are infrequently used by other teachers: Punishment from Others, Guilt, Teacher/Student Relationship-Negative, and Debt.

In terms of effectiveness, the majority of the teachers reported only

Table 29.3
Mean Self-Use, Other Use, and Effectiveness Ratings and
Frequency Percentages of High and Low Self-Use,
Other Use, and Effectiveness

	Self-Use %			Other Use %			Effectiveness %		
BAT[a]	$\overline{X}$	High Use	Low Use	$\overline{X}$	High Use	Low Use	$\overline{X}$	High Effect	Low Effect
1	3.9	69	8	3.6	53	11	3.9	66	10
2	3.5	54	20	3.6	60	14	3.0	34	33
3	3.0	39	37	3.4	48	20	3.5	55	20
4	2.8	27	39	3.1	34	25	3.1	33	35
5	3.9	72	9	3.4	46	14	4.0	73	6
6	2.2	16	63	3.0	33	32	2.3	14	59
7	2.3	22	61	3.4	56	23	2.4	21	56
8	1.4	3	89	2.3	13	60	2.0	12	69
9	1.8	6	77	2.4	16	52	2.0	10	68
10	3.1	44	30	3.1	40	25	3.3	44	24
11	1.7	4	80	2.4	17	56	2.0	9	67
12	3.0	31	32	3.6	59	14	2.7	24	44
13	2.4	24	54	3.5	56	18	2.4	14	55
14	3.2	39	25	3.4	43	15	2.9	25	32
15	2.7	28	43	3.1	34	27	2.9	30	37
16	2.7	26	43	3.0	31	30	2.7	24	37
17	1.6	5	84	2.2	12	62	1.9	5	76
18	2.3	15	61	2.4	15	49	2.5	18	48
19	2.4	17	55	2.9	29	36	3.1	39	31
20	2.4	19	57	2.9	33	35	2.4	19	51
21	2.9	33	37	3.2	41	24	2.8	26	41
22	4.0	73	7	3.6	55	13	3.7	60	12
Overall	2.7	30.3	46.0	3.1	37.5	29.8	2.8	29.8	41.4

a. See Table 29.2 for category labels.

four techniques that are highly effective: Immediate Reward from Behavior, Reward from Teacher, Self-Esteem, and Teacher Feedback. In contrast, a majority reported that eight techniques are ineffective: Punishment from Behavior, Punishment from Teacher, Punishment from Others, Guilt, Teacher/Student Relationship-Negative, Legitimate-Teacher Authority, Debt, and Teacher Modeling.

The multivariate analyses for the impact of teacher gender on perceived use and effectiveness were all significant ($< .0001$). Table 29.4 reports the results of the univariate analyses. Only four analyses yielded significant results for self-use. Females were found to use Immediate Reward from Behavior, Self-Esteem, and Teacher Feedback more than males.

Table 29.4
Mean Self-Use, Other Use, and Effectiveness Ratings
for Significant Sex Differences

BAT	Male	Female	F	R^2
Self-use				
Immediate Reward				
from Behavior	3.4	4.0	19.03	.05
Self-Esteem	3.6	4.0	8.99	.02
Expert Teacher	3.3	2.9	6.67	.02
Teacher Feedback	3.7	4.0	7.10	.02
Other use				
Immediate Reward				
from Behavior	3.3	3.6	4.69	.01
Self-Esteem	3.2	3.5	4.94	.01
Teacher Feedback	3.3	3.6	5.39	.01
Effectiveness				
Self-Esteem	3.7	4.1	12.48	.03
Teacher Feedback	3.4	3.7	6.50	.02

Males were found to use Expert Teacher more than females. Results were significant on three BATS for other use. Females reported that other teachers use Immediate Reward from Behavior, Self-Esteem, and Teacher Feedback more often than males reported they did. With regard to effectiveness, significance was obtained only for Self-Esteem and Teacher Feedback. Females reported that both BATs were more effective than did the males.

The multivariate analyses for the impact of teaching level on perceived use and effectiveness also were all significant ($< .0001$). In these analyses, the subjects in the "other" category were omitted due to the very diverse nature of the members of the group. Table 29.5 reports the results of the univariate analyses.

Results relating to self-use were significant for six BATs. Teachers in the upper grades reported more use of Deferred Reward from Behavior, Punishment from Teacher, Debt, and Expert Teacher. Teachers in lower grades reported more use of Reward from Teacher and Reward from Others.

Significant results were obtained for eight BATs pertaining to other use. Teachers in upper grades reported that their colleagues use more Deferred Reward from Behavior, Punishment from Teacher, Legitimate-Higher Authority, Debt, and Teacher Modeling. Teachers in lower grades saw their colleagues using more Immediate Reward from Behavior, Reward from Others, and Self-Esteem.

In terms of effectiveness, only two results were significant. Teachers in

Table 29.5
Mean Self-Use, Other Use, and Effectiveness Ratings
for Significant Teaching Level Differences

BAT	K-3	4-6	7-9	10-12	F	R^2
Self-use						
Deferred Reward from						
Behavior	2.9[b]	3.7[a]	4.0[a]	4.0[a]	15.31	.13
Reward from Teacher	3.3[a]	3.1[a,b]	3.0[a,b]	2.7[b]	3.42	.03
Reward from Others	3.0[a]	2.9[a]	2.6[b]	2.5[b]	2.86	.03
Punishment from Teacher	2.1[b]	2.6[a]	2.6[a]	2.4[a]	3.03	.03
Debt	1.4[b]	1.6[a,b]	1.8[a]	1.7[a]	2.83	.03
Expert Teacher	2.7[b]	3.0[a]	3.2[a]	3.1[a]	2.50	.02
Other use						
Immediate Reward from						
Behavior	3.8[a]	3.6[a,b]	3.3[b,c]	3.2[c]	5.03	.05
Deferred Reward from						
Behavior	3.1[b]	3.7[a]	3.9[a]	4.0[a]	14.32	.13
Reward from Others	3.2[a]	3.2[a,b]	2.9[b,c]	2.7[c]	4.99	.05
Self-Esteem	3.6[a]	3.5[a]	3.4[a,b]	3.2[b]	2.80	.03
Punishment from Teacher	3.2[a]	3.5[a,b]	3.5[a,b]	3.8[b]	3.15	.03
Legitimate-Higher Authority	3.5[a]	3.6[a]	3.7[a,b]	4.0[b]	2.52	.02
Debt	1.9[a]	2.1[a,b]	2.4[b,c]	2.6[c]	5.72	.05
Teacher Modeling	2.7[a]	3.0[a,b]	3.1[a,b]	3.3[b]	2.78	.03
Effectiveness						
Deferred Reward from						
Behavior	2.6[b]	3.1[a]	3.2[a]	3.4[a]	5.89	.06
Reward from Teacher	3.7[a]	3.7[a]	3.5[a,b]	3.2[b]	2.46	.02

Note: Means with same superscript are not significantly different.

upper grades saw Deferred Reward from Behavior as more effective, while teachers in lower grades saw Reward from Teacher as more effective.

The multivariate analyses for the impact of years of teaching experience were all nonsignificant. Thus, on the basis of the data obtained, teaching experience does not appear to alter teachers' use of BATs, their perceptions of their colleagues' use, or the effectiveness of the techniques.

An examination of the factor-analytic results indicated no meaningful factor structure for the BAT items for self-use, other use, or effectiveness. On the unrotated factor solutions, no item met the .60 eigenvalue criterion, strongly suggesting the presence of multiple factors. However, rotated solutions that produced five factors indicated that no factor included more than two items with high loadings. Thus, even though there were some meaningful correlations between BAT category scores, there did not appear to be an

Table 29.6
Correlations Among Ratings of Self-Use,
Other Use, and Effectiveness

BAT	Self-Use/ Other Use	Self-Use/ Effectiveness	Other Use/ Effectiveness
Immediate Reward from Behavior	.51	.60	.28
Deferred Reward from Behavior	.56	.57	.42
Reward from Teacher	.54	.67	.44
Reward from Others	.51	.51	.46
Self-Esteem	.42	.47	.29
Punishment from Behavior	.49	.56	.34
Punishment from Teacher	.50	.51	.37
Punishment from Others	.38	.32	.28
Guilt	.43	.48	.34
Teacher-Student Relationship: Positive	.61	.64	.47
Teacher-Student Relationship: Negative	.46	.50	.32
Legitimate-Higher Authority	.50	.55	.33
Legitmate-Teacher Authority	.49	.58	.41
Personal (Student) Responsibility	.64	.58	.47
Responsibility to Class	.63	.61	.58
Normative Rules	.50	.61	.44
Debt	.49	.59	.46
Altruism	.57	.62	.55
Peer Modeling	.55	.48	.42
Teacher Modeling	.53	.66	.45
Expert Teacher	.55	.72	.48
Teacher Feedback	.48	.63	.35

underlying structure that would permit reduction in the number of categories employed.

The obtained correlations among rating of self-use, other use, and effectiveness for the 22 BAT categories are reported in Table 29.6. All of the obtained correlations were significant and most were moderate to moderately high. Clearly, these perceptions are not independent. Generally, the higher correlations were between self-use and effectiveness. This would appear reasonable, since it should be expected that teachers would choose to use techniques that they believe will be effective. The very substantial correlations between self-use and other use are more difficult to interpret. These relationships may indicate the presence of patterns of BAT use that are relatively consistent across teachers in a given school. However, they may also be a function of teachers not really knowing what their colleagues do and, as

a result, responding to our instrument with their own behavior heavily influencing their perceptions.

DISCUSSION

Consistent with the primary objective of this study, a revised and extended typology of classroom-relevant behavior alteration techniques and
messages was generated. Research question 1 was asked in order to isolate
classroom strategies available for teacher use. Based on teacher input, the
original eighteen BATs (Kearney et al., 1983) were modified to enable more
precise discriminations among existing strategies and extended to include
new categories. These modifications suggest that strategies teachers employ in the classroom are in some cases similar to existing compliance-
gaining typologies, but are qualitatively different in several fundamental
ways.

The first difference is that teachers employ BATs that rely on direct as
well as mediated appeals. That is, teachers may provide either direct rewards and punishments (among others) to obtain compliance, or mediate
those appeals by referencing students' peer groups as sources of power.
Second, teachers employ BATs that exemplify the evaluative role of teachers in the classroom environment. Teacher Feedback obtains compliance by
calling attention to the teacher's task-oriented objective, to assess student
learning and teaching effectiveness. Third, while several of the BATs may
seem similar to existing compliance-gaining strategies in the abstract sense,
teachers appear to be constrained by the specific types of messages they
generate to employ each BAT. Accountability to students, parents, and administrators may require that teachers selectively employ BATs by communicating BAMs that are appropriate to teachers as student role models.

Further modifications of the available BATs for teacher use were addressed in research question 2. Whereas the BAMs derived in Kearney et al.
(1983) relied on college students' input, in this study teachers themselves
generated classroom-relevant messages. These teacher BAMs were an obvious extension and revision of those previously isolated. Blending the
former BAMs with teacher BAMs resulted in empirically refined configurations of classroom-representative BAMs. These configurations, then, can
now serve as sets of operational statements for each BAT that teachers use.

Based on the revised BATs, research question 3 was concerned with
those BATs teachers use most and least frequently. Similar to the results
obtained by Kearney et al. (1983), teachers reported that they used primarily reward-type or prosocial BATs. However, teachers in this sample did not
indicate that they most frequently employed "student audience effect-type

BATs or mediated appeals. Instead, teachers rated highly a new BAT, Teacher Feedback. Additionally, teachers claimed to use least frequently those BATs that were primarily punishment oriented or antisocial. These findings would seem to suggest that teachers in this study were better able to discriminate among BATs and BAMs since category labels and messages were refined to be more clearly representative of classroom-specific applications.

Research question 4 was asked to explore those BATs instructors perceived that other teachers used with students at the same grade level. While prosocial and Teacher Feedback BATs made up half of the list of strategies most frequently used by others, teachers also perceived others as frequently using a variety of antisocial BATs. Whereas teachers may be reluctant to report using antisocial BATs themselves, these results indicate that teachers can readily identify their use by other teachers. Perhaps teachers are guilty of projection ("A friend of mine has this problem . . ."). Given this interpretation, teachers may employ both pro- and antisocial BATs. Such use is supported by the initial classification of messages teachers generated in Phase I. Teachers consistently recalled almost equal frequencies of both pro- and antisocial messages. Furthermore, the results of Power 1 (McCroskey & Richmond, 1983) indicated that students perceived their teachers as using more coercive power than did their teachers.

Teachers also appear to be selective in their use of antisocial BATs. That is, teachers reported that other teachers *least* frequently used other types of antisocial BATs. An examination of antisocial BATs most and least frequently employed suggests that teachers perceive others as using antisocial BATs that reflect legitimate power or teacher authority and rarely rely on student or peer sources of punishment. This observation is consistent with the custodial model of classroom discipline. Following this model, new teachers are evaluated on their ability to adopt this authority-based discipline orientation (Hoy, 1968).

Interpreting the results pertinent to research question 5, teachers perceived that the BATs they most frequently used themselves were also most effective in controlling student behavior. Similarly, those they found least effective were also the BATs they employed least. Generally, effective BATs were primarily prosocial, whereas ineffective BATs were primarily antisocial. While reward-type strategies may be effective for optimizing student control, Richmond and McCroskey (in press) found that the use of reward power was not meaningfully associated with student learning. This result calls into question the relative efficacy of prosocial BATs for classroom management.

No single antisocial BAT was perceived as effective. However, teachers perceived that others frequently used antisocial BATs. Perhaps teachers recognize that such BATs are ineffective, but resort to their use regardless. Potentially, the custodial expectation of their school systems may mandate the use of more traditional sources of discipline. Teachers might also employ such strategies simply because they *prefer* the use of punishment to control student misbehaviors (Siggers, 1980), in spite of its ineffectiveness.

Finally, research question 6 asked whether teacher use, others' use, and effectiveness of BATs were a function of teacher gender, years taught, and grade level. Results indicated that primarily prosocial BATs were perceived as used and effective by female teachers significantly more than by males. In contrast, male teachers perceived Expert Teacher as used and effective significantly more than did females. These findings reflect the influence of traditional gender-based roles. That is, females may employ BATs that indicate responsiveness to and support of the student (for example, "You will enjoy it"; "You always do such a good job"; "To see how well you can do it"). Males, however, may rely on self-perceptions of their own credibility and may actively assert this stance ("This has always worked for me"; "Trust me—I know what I'm doing"; and so on).

Years taught was not shown to be a function of the use (self and other) or effectiveness of particular BATs employed in the classroom. Although disappointing, this result is consistent with the findings obtained by Kearney et al. (1983). Different results might be obtained by eliciting experienced teachers' perceptions of inexperienced teachers' use and effectiveness of BAT employment (see Hoy, 1968). In any case, this issue remains open.

Grade-level data proved to be particularly interesting. While teachers reported self- and other use of prosocial-type BATs for the lower grades, upper-grade-level teachers reported self- and other use of primarily antisocial and Expert Teacher BATs. These results are consistent with traditional elementary and junior/senior high teacher-student orientations. That is, elementary teachers may rely on a variety of reward-type strategies to control student behavior because younger students are more easily influenced by external sources of reward. Older students, however, may no longer perceive that teachers have the ability to provide relevant rewards for compliance (see Boocock, 1983). Instead, teachers in upper grades may resort to punishment or demonstration of teacher competence in the content area taught. Similarly, secondary and college teachers and students have reported the frequent use of teacher expert power (McCroskey & Richmond, 1983). These same students also perceived their teachers as using more coercive power than their teachers perceived themselves using.

One notable exception to upper-grade-level self- and other use of BATs in the present study was the frequent employment of Deferred Reward. In addition, upper-grade-level teachers perceived Deferred Reward to be significantly more effective than lower-grade teachers. While upper-grade-level students may not perceive teachers to have reward influence potential, these same students may rely on future sources of reward that can benefit them directly (for example, "It will prepare you for a job"; "It will help you later on in life"). In contrast, lower-grade-level teachers found Reward from Teacher to be significantly more effective. Elementary students may attribute to teachers the ability to provide meaningful rewards. Further, such students may require more immediate and tangible rewards, which teachers can readily provide.

The results reported here illustrate the need for a variety of additional investigations. Currently, investigations are under way that examine the types of BATs teachers employ with students of different academic abilities. In addition, the present study assessed only teacher perceptions of BAT usage in the classroom. Research is being conducted that examines student perceptions as well. Moreover, since years of teaching experience failed to predict types of BATs employed, studies should be designed either to tap experienced teachers' perceptions of inexperienced teachers or to observe and code BAT employment in the classroom directly. Finally, this continued research program on teacher power in the classroom will focus on the relative effectiveness of each BAT on both classroom management and student learning outcomes.

REFERENCES

Boocock, S. (1983). Public schools and education. In M. L. DeFleur (Ed.), *Social problems in American society.* Boston: Houghton Mifflin.

Borg, W. R., & Ascione, F. R. (1979). Changing on-task, off-task, and disruptive pupil behavior in elementary mainstreaming classrooms. Journal of Educational Research, 72, 243-252.

Check, J. F. (1979). Classroom discipline—Where are we now? *Education, 100,* 134-137.

Clegg, A., & Megson, B. (1968). *Children in distress.* Harmondsworth: Penguin.

Cody, M. J., McLaughlin, M. L., & Jordan, W. J. (1980). A multidimensional scaling of three sets of compliance-gaining strategies. *Communication Quarterly, 28,* 34-46.

Coy, S. C. (1980). *Discipline: There are alternatives! A handbook for elementary teachers and principals* (ERIC Document Reproduction Service No. ED 221 916).

Durkheim, E. (1961). *Moral education.* New York: Free Press.

Emmer, E. T., & Evertson, C. (1980). *Effective classroom management at the beginning of the year in junior high school classrooms.* Report No. 6107. Austin: University of Texas, Research and Development Center for Teacher Education.

French, J.R.P., Jr., & Raven, B. (1968). The bases of social power. In D. Cartwright (Ed.), *Studies in social power.* Ann Arbor: University of Michigan Press.

Gallup, G. F. (1981). The 13th annual Gallup Poll of the public's attitudes toward the public schools. *Phi Delta Kappan, 62,* 33-47.

Glasser, W. (1978). Disorders in our schools: Causes and remedies. *Phi Delta Kappan, 51,* 331-333.

Good, T. L., & Beckerman, T. M. (1978). Time-on-task: A naturalistic study in sixth-grade classrooms. *Elementary School Journal, 78,* 193-201.

Harris, M. B. (1972). *Classroom uses of behavior modification.* Columbus, OH: Charles E. Merrill.

Heal, K. H. (1978). Misbehavior among school children: The roles of the school in strategies for prevention. *Policy and Politics, 6,* 321-332.

Hoy, W. K. (1968). The influence of experience on the beginning teacher. *School Review, 76,* 312-323.

Jenson, W. R. (1978). Behavior modification in secondary schools: A review. *Journal of Research and Development in Education, 11*(4), 53-61.

Kearney, P., Plax, T. G., Richmond, V. P., & McCroskey, J. C. (1983). *Power in the classroom III: Teacher communication techniques and messages.* Paper presented at the annual meeting of the Speech Communication Association, Washington, DC.

Krantz, M., & Scarth, L. (1979). Task persistence and adult assistance in the preschool. *Child Development, 50,* 578-581.

Lufler, H. S., Jr. (1978). Discipline: A new look at an old problem. *Phi Delta Kappan, 59,* 424.

Marwell, G., & Schmitt, D. R. (1967). Dimensions of compliance-gaining behavior: An empirical analysis. *Sociometry, 30,* 350-364.

McCroskey, J. C., & Richmond, V. P. (1983). Power in the classroom I: Teacher and student perceptions. *Communication Education, 32,* 176-184.

Miller, G. R., Boster, F., Roloff, M., & Seibold, D. (1977). Compliance-gaining message strategies: A typology and some findings concerning effects of situational differences. *Communication Monographs, 44,* 37-51.

Richmond, V. P., & Andriate, G. (1982). *Advanced study: Instructional communication.* Morgantown, WV: West Virginia University, Department of Speech Communication.

Richmond, V. P., & McCroskey, J. C. (in press). Power in the classroom II: Power and learning. *Communication Education.*

Rutter, M., Maughan, B., Mortimore, P., Ouston, J., & Smith, A. (1979). *Fifteen thousand hours.* Cambridge, MA: Harvard University Press.

Schenck-Hamlin, W. J., Wiseman, R. L., & Georgacarakos, G. N. (1982). A model of properties of compliance-gaining strategies. *Communication Quarterly, 30,* 92-100.

Shrigley, R. L. (1979). Strategies in classroom management. *Educational Digest, 45,* 7-10.

Siggers, W. W. (1980). Changing teacher correcting behavior: Using aversive and positive contingencies. *Educational Research Quarterly, 5,* 25-32.

Waller, W. (1932). *The sociology of teaching.* New York: John Wiley.

Willever, D. J., & Jones, R. G. (1963). When pupil control becomes an institutional theme. *Phi Delta Kappan, 45,* 107-109.

Wlodkowski, R. J. (1982). *Discipline: The great false hope* (ERIC Document Reproduction Service No. ED 224 782).

30 ● Compliance-Resisting Behaviors: The Effects of Age, Agent, and Types of Request

JEFFREY S. McQUILLEN ●
DOROTHY C. HIGGINBOTHAM ●
M. CLAIRE CUMMINGS

Texas A&M University ● University of Oklahoma

I N its broadest sense, all behavior is directed at achieving some level of control over the environment. Persuasion may be viewed as one of our major means of achieving control over our *social* environment. The term "persuasion," however, is accompanied by a great deal of restrictive philosophical/epistemological baggage.

Historically, the field of communication has viewed the social influence process as a one-way activity, with the initiator or "sender" controlling the encounter. This limited paradigm discounts the interdependent, reciprocal nature of persuasion. In a scholarly crusade against the traditional approach to persuasion research, Miller and Burgoon (1978) have criticized the prevailing research paradigm, which has operationally defined persuasion as a "linear, unidirectional activity." Following this line of thought, an active persuader exerts influence over a passive target. This unidirectional view of persuasion discounts the notion of participant reciprocity or interdependence in communication.

Because the traditional approach to persuasion has posed such an impoverished conceptual foundation for related research, an expanded view of this concept is being considered. The alternative approach to the traditional view of persuasion, which has received considerable attention in recent literature, has been termed "compliance-gaining."

Correspondence and requests for reprints: Jeffrey S. McQuillen, Division of Speech Communication, Department of English, Texas A&M University, College Station, TX 77843.

In contrast to previous persuasion research, the compliance-gaining approach focuses on *message selection* rather than on *message impact*. The empirical efforts employing this approach have been concerned with the development of taxonomies of compliance-gaining strategies (Marwell & Schmitt, 1967; Clark, 1979; Fitzpatrick & Winke, 1979) and the effect of relevant situational and personality variables on the selection of specific strategies (Miller, Boster, Roloff, & Seibold, 1977; Roloff & Barnicott, 1978; Hunter & Boster, 1979).

Research exploring the *development* of compliance-gaining behaviors suggests a number of developmental trends that appear with some consistency in the acquiring of compliance-gaining behaviors. First, research consistently shows that the size of a child's repertoire of compliance-gaining strategies increases with age. These findings report two general age-related increases: the number of strategies a subject employs for a given task increases with age and the number of different types of strategies a subject employs also increases with age (Wood, Weinstein, & Parker, 1967; Alvy, 1973; Finley & Humphreys, 1974; Clark & Delia, 1976, 1977; Haslett, 1983).

An additional finding emphasizes an age-related increase in children's strategy differentiation across targets. Children as young as 6 years old display the ability to vary strategies across differing targets (Wood et al., 1967; Flavell, Botkin, Fry, Wright, & Jarvis, 1968; Alvy, 1973; Clark & Delia, 1976, 1977; Howie-Day, 1977).

Most of the research efforts focusing on the explication of the social influence process have been limited to experimental analysis of the actions and resources available to the compliance-gaining agent. This one-way approach confines our understanding of the process of interpersonal influence to a cause-effect relationship—the agent acts and the target responds. The reciprocal interdependence between the participants of this type of communicative interaction is not captured by this unidirectional approach. If a detailed analysis of the social influence process is to be achieved, research needs to focus on those tactics and resources available to both the agent and the target of a communication episode. Berlo (1977, p. 20) explains the benefit of adopting an interactional approach to the study of communication:

> If we look on the "source" as intentional and initiatory and the "receiver" as passive and a receptive container—e.g., if the message is stimulus and the effect is response—the relationship is directional. On the other hand, if the relationship is one in which both users approach the engagement with expectations, plans, and anticipation, the uncertainty reduction attributable to the contact may be better understood in terms of how one person uses the contact to direct the other.

McLaughlin, Cody, and Robey (1980), in an attempt to address this deficiency, proposed the concept of compliance-*resisting* strategies. According to McLaughlin et al., compliance-resisting strategies are verbal attempts by a target to gain the agent's acceptance of the target's unwillingness to comply. Complementary to McLaughlin et al.'s definition, compliance-resisting can be viewed as "reflexive persuasion." Resistance strategies are messages constructed by the persuadee or target as he or she assumes the role of the persuader in an attempt to secure the initial persuader's acceptance of the target's unwillingness to agree to the conditions of a compliance-gaining appeal. In this conceptualization, compliance-resisting can be considered a "special type" of interpersonal influence.

Compliance-resisting is not self-initiated; it results from incompatibility between the agent's request and the target's unwillingness to fulfill the conditions requisite to the request. To date only two empirical studies have focused directly on those strategic alternatives available to the target of a compliance-gaining appeal (McLaughlin et al., 1980; Cody, O'Hair, & Schneider, 1982). McLaughlin et al. (1980) propose a four-category typology of compliance-resisting strategies deductively derived by synthesizing the taxonomic work contained in three previous social influence studies (Fitzpatrick & Winke, 1979; Clark, 1979; Cody, McLaughlin, Jordan, & Schneider, 1979). The categories identified are as follows:

(1) *Nonnegotiation:* inflexible, unapologetic refusal to assent to the agent's request
(2) *Identity management:* the indirect manipulation of the image of the agent or the target or both, either positively or negatively
(3) *Justifying:* offering support, based on the projected outcomes of compliance or noncompliance, for one's unwillingness to comply
(4) *Negotiation:* proposal to engage in mutual talks that will result in maximized goals for both involved parties

McLaughlin et al.'s (1980) research differs from previous taxonomic work in that its categories focus explicitly on defining the tactics available to the resister and not on the agent of the compliance-gaining appeal. Situational effects associated with this taxonomy are highly complex and inhibit the positing of clear experimental trends. The major finding of compliance-resisting studies (McLaughlin et al., 1980; Cody et al., 1982) suggests that strategy selection is based on the relevant risk associated with the use of compliance-resisting (Tedeschi, 1972; McLaughlin et al., 1980).

The most serious deficiencies in these initial studies of compliance-resisting behaviors are related to methodological limitations. First, the employment of the likelihood-of-use technique has been criticized by several authors (Clark, 1979; Clark & Delia, 1976; Wiseman & Schenck-Hamlin, 1981; Schenck-Hamlin, Wiseman, & Georgacarakos, 1982; Cody et al., 1982). This method of examining communication behaviors unnecessarily restricts subjects' responses and may reflect a response bias in which higher preference ratings are awarded those strategies accommodating more closely to the target's perspective.

Second, the methodological approach should be expanded to include the examination of the interactive nature of compliance-gaining and compliance-resisting strategies. McLaughlin et al. (1980, p. 35) have suggested that "additional research should examine the resistance process by varying the kinds of compliance-gaining strategies the agent initially uses." This expanded approach would more adequately resemble the interactive nature of the social influence process. Targets do not resist situations; they resist specific compliance-gaining appeals generated within the context of specific situations. Therefore, examination of the influential effects of different types of initial compliance-gaining strategies on the selection of compliance-resisting strategies is warranted.

Finally, research should systematically examine the development of compliance-resisting strategies. In other words, how do children of different ages resist compliance-gaining attempts by an agent?

DEVELOPMENT OF
COMPLIANCE-RESISTING BEHAVIORS

Based on a sociolinguistic study of children's ability to use and react to requests for action, Garvey (1975) offers some insight into the development of compliance-resisting behaviors. To examine adequately the sequential behaviors involved in the compliance process, Garvey proposes a structural unit that she calls the "domain" of a request. The request domain is defined as the "scope of discourse within which the attention of the speaker and the addressee is directed to the accomplishment of the request" (Garvey, 1975, p. 49). This domain maps out the boundaries of the request and related behaviors (acknowledgments). Requests and their acknowledgments (that is, noncompliant responses) follow both optional and obligatory orders that suggest the basis for conversational sequencing. According to this structural analysis, speaker and addressee assume complementary roles that entail reciprocal responsibilities. This interdependence between interactants and structural elements asserts that previous communicative behavior within a given request domain will constrain the following behaviors within the same domain.

According to Garvey's (1975, p. 61) research, children as young as 4 years old are aware of the interpersonal meanings that underlie requests and request refusals and are able to employ this knowledge effectively. According to her findings, Garvey (1975, p. 63) suggests that the complementary role structure requires the speaker (S) and the addressee (A) to fulfill reciprocal responsibilities:

S is responsible for producing an intelligible, reasonable, appropriate and effective request, while A must offer an intelligible, reasonable, appropriate and effective acknowledgement, regardless of whether he wishes to comply or not.

Garvey offers no empirical evidence supporting the systematic development of compliance-resisting behaviors. Her analysis was limited to the explanation of the acquisition of discourse rules. No attempts were made to assess directly the relationship between development and the acquisition of specific strategies for resisting compliance.

In summary, little empirical research is available that focuses on compliance-resisting behavior. Our understanding of the development of this communicative skill is even more limited. Because of this paucity, research should focus on the investigation of the resistance process, specifically focusing on the relationship between compliance-resisting skills and the development of social competence.

The present investigation is an initial step in providing a systematic analysis of the development of verbal compliance-resisting strategies.

THE STUDY

The purpose of the present study was to determine how children of different ages (first, fourth, and ninth graders) use their language to resist persuasion. An inductive approach to message construction was employed (Clark, 1979). Subjects were required to generate compliance-resisting strategies in response to three communication situations. These situations were developed following criteria established by Wiseman and Schenck-Hamlin (1981). Each task situation is associated with a different age/status agent (mother, peer, younger sibling). These agents were chosen because they maintain a similar degree of familiarity to the subject, and they also represent the major situational participants typically manipulated in previous investigations of communication development. These task situations were concluded with a compliance-gaining appeal, which the subjects were required to resist.

The three strategies that served as stimuli for the resistance tasks (simple request, incentive request, and altruistic request) were selected because each clearly illustrated one of the structural properties posited by Wiseman and Schenck-Hamlin (1981). For example, a simple request stresses message directness associated with the structural property "explicitness of intent"; an incentive request is characteristic of "manipulation of sanction"; and an altruistic request emphasizes the power of the request as regulated by "others" (norms) and is illustrative of "locus of control."

Subjects were asked to generate a compliance-resisting strategy. These compliance-resisting strategies were triggered by a specific compliance-gaining strategy. This procedure allowed the communication task to approximate a naturalistic communication interaction more closely.

In an attempt to determine whether children's use of compliance-resisting behaviors display developmental trends, the study was designed to answer the following research questions:

(1) Do communicators vary their selection of compliance-resisting strategies as a function of age?
(2) Do communicators vary their selection of compliance-resisting strategies as a function of the agent of the compliance-gaining attempt?
(3) Do communicators vary their selection of compliance-resisting strategies as a function of the type of compliance-gaining strategy employed by the agent of the attempt?

METHODOLOGY

Subjects

The subjects for this study were 118 children attending schools in a metropolitan area. Children were drawn from each of three age groups. The sample was limited to 36 first-grade, 41 fourth-grade, and 41 tenth-grade subjects. These categories of subjects were selected because in previous research these age groups have demonstrated the greatest developmental progression in communicative performance (Alvy, 1973; Clark & Delia, 1976; Howie-Day, 1977; Delia, Kline, & Burleson, 1979). Since testing was done in the summer months, the grade levels reported represent those the subjects had just completed.

Materials

The stimulus materials consisted of line drawings of three common environments (kitchen, TV room, living room). These environments constituted the settings for the compliance-gaining attempts. In addition, each of the task settings included an artist's representation of one of three potential compliance-gaining agents. These agents differed in terms of their age and status (mother, peer, younger sibling). For convenience, the line drawings were identified by referencing the appropriate agent in each.

Each drawing was accompanied by a brief scenario that posed a hypothetical communicative interaction that might occur in that setting. All three scenarios concluded with one of three types of compliance-gaining strategies: (1) a simple request, "Will you let me watch my TV show?"; (2) an incentive request (promise), "If you help me clean up the kitchen, I'll let you stay up an hour later tonight"; or (3) an altruistic request (invocation of a normative behavior), "You should read a story for me because all the other people who watch me read me a story."

Procedures

Each subject was brought individually to a quiet room and was interviewed by one of three trained interviewers. The interviewer first introduced him- or herself and explained to the subject that the study was being conducted to see how people avoid doing those things they do not want to do.

The subject was seated at a small table and informed that the session would be tape-recorded. After the recorder was turned on, the subject was asked a number of demographic questions.

As a verbal pretest to alert the subjects as to the concept under consideration (compliance-resisting), subjects were asked if their best friends had ever requested them to do something they didn't want to do. If an affirmative answer was given, the subject was asked to give an example of such a disagreement and how he or she handled it. If an example was not readily available, the subject was aksed if his or her mother had ever asked him or her to do something he or she did not want to do. All subjects were able to provide an example of this second trial.

All subjects were presented with a series of three 8 × 11-inch line drawings, each depicting one of three agents (mother, best friend, or younger sibling) in a common communicative environment. Each drawing was presented separately. The subject was asked to imagine that the agent in the picture represented the appropriate "real-person" counterpart—for example, the subject was told, "Imagine the figure in the picture is your mother." The order of presentation of these drawings was randomized across all subjects.

Subjects within each age group were assigned randomly to one of three stimulus conditions: (1) simple request strategy, (2) incentive request strategy, (3) altruistic request strategy. These conditions represented the type of compliance-gaining strategy the subjects were asked to resist. The strategy assigned to each subgroup was held constant across all three task agents. For example, subjects assigned to Condition 1 were asked to resist a simple request strategy from mother, best friend, and younger sibling.

The interviewer read to the subjects a brief scenario designed to establish the specific communicative demands of the situation. This information was followed by the condition-matched compliance-gaining strategy. The subject was then asked what resistance strategy he or she would use to resist the actions requested by the agent.

After this initial presentation, the interviewer explained that in many instances the first attempt at refusing an agent's appeal for compliance is not effective. The scenario and appeal were read a second time, and the subject was asked to construct verbally the compliance-resisting strategy he or she would use in a second attempt.

These procedures were repeated for each of the three pictorial contexts. All responses were tape-recorded for future analysis. At the conclusion of the interview, the subject was thanked for his or her assistance. In the case of the elementary school groups, subjects were given a small reward for their participation.

Measurement Procedures

The study reported here employed one dependent measure: The category of compliance-resisting strategy employed by the subject. Transcriptions of the subjects' responses were prepared and scored according to the following procedures.

The compliance-resisting strategies constructed by the subjects were coded according McLaughlin et al.'s (1980) typology of compliance-resistance strategies. Each subject-constructed strategy was assigned to one of the four major categories. Subcategories were employed only to assist in coding the compliance-resisting message into one of these major categories.

Data Analysis

The data analysis employs a $3 \times 3 \times 3$ factorial design, with the third measure being repeated. The factors are age (first-, fourth-, and tenth-grade subjects), compliance-gaining strategies (simple request, incentive request, altruistic request), and agents (mother, peer, younger sibling).

To test the possible effects that the independent variables have on the use of the compliance-resisting strategies, a series of chi-square tests were used. The results of these tests were used to examine the effects of age, compliance agent, and compliance-gaining strategies on the use of specific categories of compliance-resisting strategies.

RESULTS

Subjects for this study produced 602 codable utterances. There were 262 responses coded as nonnegotiation strategies, 87 responses coded as justification strategies, 192 responses coded as negotiation strategies, and 61 responses coded as identity management strategies.

Effect of Age on
Compliance-Resisting

A 4×3 (categories of resistance strategies by subject's grade level) contingency table analysis was employed to examine the impact of age on

Table 30.1
Proportion of Compliance-Resisting Strategies
Used by Subjects at Each Grade Level

Strategies	First Grade	Fourth Grade	Tenth Grade
Nonnegotiation			
row %	36.3	34.7	29.0
column %	54.3	42.9	35.2
Justification			
row %	19.9	35.2	44.9
column %	8.6	16.0	18.5
Negotiation			
row %	27.1	35.4	37.5
column %	29.7	32.1	33.3
Identity management			
row %	21.7	31.7	46.7
column %	7.4	9.0	13.0

subjects' use of compliance-resisting strategies. Table 30.1 presents the results of this analysis. Based on a chi-square test of statistical independence ($\chi^2 = 18.68097$, df = 6, p < .004), it was concluded that children of different ages differ significantly in their use of compliance-resisting strategies.

There were marked differences between the age of the subject and the use of three of the four major categories of resistance strategies. Subjects' use of nonnegotiation strategies displayed a clear decrease with age. Approximately 54 percent of the resistance strategies constructed by first graders were categorized as instances of nonnegotiation. Only 43 percent and 35 percent of the strategies used by fourth- and tenth-grade subjects, respectively, were instances of this category.

A second developmental trend was suggested by the data. The frequency of justification and identity management strategies increased as a function of the age of the subject. Of the resistance strategies constructed by first-grade subjects, approximately 19 percent were instances of justification, in contrast to a 45 percent frequency of use of justification by the tenth-grade subjects. A similar increase in the frequency of use of identity management strategies was also apparent (first grade, 22 percent; fourth grade, 32 percent; and tenth grade, 47 percent).

As may be observed from the above summary, the age trend in category usage of the four categories of compliance-resisting strategies is quite consistent and provides support for a possible developmental progression in the use of compliance-resisting strategies. The use of the less socially sensi-

Table 30.2
Proportion of Compliance-Resisting Strategies Used by All Groups in
Response to Differing Compliance-Gaining Strategies Employed by the Agent

Strategies	Simple Request	Incentive Request	Altruistic Request
Nonnegotiation			
row %	37.5	33.7	28.7
column %	43.6	51.2	36.6
Justification			
row %	30.3	33.7	36.0
column %	12.0	17.4	15.6
Negotiation			
row %	44.3	22.9	32.8
column %	37.8	25.6	30.7
Identity management			
row %	25.0	16.7	58.3
column %	6.7	5.8	17.1

tive category of resistance, nonnegotiation, declines with age. The other
more socially sensitive strategies show an increase with age.

Effect of Compliance-Gaining Strategy on Compliance-Resisting Response

For the purposes of measuring the association between the type of
strategy used to gain compliance and the category of strategies subjects
used to resist those attempts, a chi-square test of independence was performed on a 4 × 3 contingency table (types of resistance strategy by types of
compliance-gaining strategies).

As is evident from Table 30.2, there is a significant difference in the
types of strategies subjects employed as a function of the type of strategy a
subject was asked to resist ($\chi^2 = 27.18352$, df = 6, p < .0001). In response
to the simple request condition, approximately 82 percent of all strategies
used were instances of nonnegotiation (44 percent) or negotiation (38 percent). Within the incentive request condition, nonnegotiation accounted for
approximately 51 percent of all strategies employed. Finally, identity management strategies were used more frequently in response to the altruistic
request condition (58 percent) than with the other two types of compliance-
gaining strategies (simple request, 25 percent; incentive request, 18 percent).

It should be noted that the frequency of all compliance-resisting strategies constructed by the subjects varied as a function of the compliance-gain-

Table 30.3
Proportion of Compliance-Resisting Strategies
Used in Response to Differing Agents

Strategies	Mother	Peer	Younger Sibling
Nonnegotiation			
row %	23.3	36.6	40.5
column %	31.3	46.3	52.2
Justification			
row %	69.7	8.9	21.3
column %	31.8	3.9	9.3
Negotiation			
row %	30.2	36.5	33.3
column %	29.7	34.1	31.5
Identity management			
row %	23.3	53.3	23.3
column %	7.2	15.6	6.9

ing strategy used by the agent. It is concluded, therefore, that the type of strategy used to gain compliance will affect the type of strategy a target selects in attempts to resist.

Effect of Compliance-Gaining Agent on Choice of Resistance Strategy

A chi-square test was used to examine the effect different compliance-gaining agents may have on the types of compliance-resisting strategies a target will employ. A positive association was found between these two factors ($\chi^2 = 79.977$, df = 6, p < .001) (see Table 30.3).

In the case of mother as agent, subjects employed more justification strategies (70 percent) and fewer nonnegotiation strategies (23 percent) than when responding to one of the other agents. In response to the peer condition, 9 percent of subjects' responses were in the justification category and 36 percent were nonnegotiation. When the younger sibling was the agent of the request, justification and nonnegotiation constituted 21 percent and 41 percent, respectively, of the compliance-resisting strategies. The greatest percentage of identity management strategies was used when the peer was the compliance-gaining agent (53 percent). Nonnegotiation was the predominant category employed when the younger sibling was the agent (52 percent).

To further clarify the association of agent and compliance-resistance, a

Table 30.4
Proportion of Compliance-Resisting Strategies
by First-Grade Subjects in Response
to Differing Agents

Strategies	Mother	Peer	Younger Sibling
Nonnegotiation			
row %	32.6	32.6	34.7
column %	54.3	49.2	60.0
Justification			
row %	46.6	26.7	26.7
column %	12.3	6.3	7.2
Negotiation			
row %	32.6	40.4	26.9
column %	29.8	33.3	25.5
Identity Management			
row %	15.4	53.8	30.8
column %	3.5	11.1	7.3

Table 30.5
Proportion of Compliance-Resisting Strategies
by Fourth-Grade Subjects in Response
to Differing Agents

Strategies	Mother	Peer	Younger Sibling
Nonnegotiation			
row %	20.9	35.2	43.9
column %	28.8	44.4	54.1
Justification			
row %	67.6	8.8	23.5
column %	34.8	4.1	10.8
Negotiation			
row %	26.5	41.2	32.4
column %	27.3	38.9	29.7
Identity Management			
row %	31.6	47.4	21.1
column %	9.0	12.5	5.4

Table 30.6
Proportion of Compliance-Resisting Strategies
by Tenth-Grade Subjects in Response
to Differing Agents

Strategies	Mother	Peer	Younger Sibling
Nonnegotiation			
row %	14.5	42.1	43.4
column %	15.3	45.7	44.6
Justification			
row %	80.0	2.5	17.5
column %	44.4	1.4	9.5
Negotiation			
row %	31.9	29.2	38.9
column %	31.9	30.0	37.8
Identity Management			
row %	21.4	57.1	21.4
column %	8.3	22.9	8.1

series of chi-square tests controlling for grade level of subject were performed. As presented in Tables 30.4, 30.5, and 30.6, the chi-squares for the fourth- and tenth-grade subjects reach statistical significance (fourth: $\chi^2 = 30.7433$, df = 6, p < .001). However, the chi-square for the first-grade group did not attain an acceptable level of significance ($\chi^2 = 4.91$, df = 6, p > .05).

DISCUSSION

The results of the chi-square analyses support a significant positive association between the three major independent variables (age of subject, type of request used to gain compliance, and the agent of the compliance attempt) and the dependent variable (category of compliance-resisting strategy). This study is an initial step in describing how children develop compliance-resisting competence. The general findings of this investigation suggest that the types of strategies subjects used to resist compliance-gaining attempts differ significantly with the age of the resister. The quality of this difference suggests a possible developmental trend. The frequency of use of nonnegotiation strategies for the first-grade subjects is extremely high, but the reliance on this type of strategy as the primary means of resisting decreases with age.

The nonnegotiation strategy, according to McLaughlin et al. (1980), is a high-risk strategy. The use of such a nonapologetic, inflexible method of declining compliance can negatively affect relational maintenance. Therefore, as the child becomes more aware of the feelings and needs of others and the effect one's communication has on these receiver characteristics, a tendency to use more prosocial strategies may appear. The findings of this study support the argument that first-grade children rely heavily on the use of nonnegotiation strategies to the exclusion of the other major strategies, while fourth- and tenth-grade subjects use a wider range of compliance-resisting strategies. This finding is consistent with the developmental literature on compliance-gaining which suggests that a child's persuasive repertoire increases with age (Wood et al., 1967).

The data reveal a second developmental trend. As the age of subject increased, the tendency to vary the type of resistance strategy as a function of the intended receiver also increased. This "target differentiation" is, theoretically, related to the child's growing awareness of the other's perspective (Flavell et al., 1968). Accordingly, the better able the child is at adapting his or her resistance strategy to differing targets, the more developed his or her compliance-resisting skills appear.

Finally, all age groups varied their categories of resistance as a function of the type of strategy they were asked to resist. This finding supports the argument that the selection of a specific resistance strategy is not only influenced by what is being asked, but also by *how* it is asked.

This study suggests the need to investigate further the relationship between a child's social cognitive development and his or her ability to construct competent compliance-resisting strategies. Findings from numerous studies (Alvy, 1973; Clark & Delia, 1976; Haslett, 1983) support a relationship between perspective-taking skills and compliance-gaining competence. The results reported here indicate that a parallel relationship exists between social perspective-taking and compliance-resisting competence.

REFERENCES

Alvy, K. T. (1973). The development of listener adapted communication in grade-school children from different social-class backgrounds. *Genetic Psychology Monographs, 87,* 33-104.

Berlo, D. K. (1977). Communication as process: Review and commentary. In B. D. Ruben (Ed.), *Communication Yearbook 1* (pp. 11-27). New Brunswick, NJ: Transaction.

Clark, R. A. (1979) The impact of selection of persuasive strategies on self-interest and desired liking. *Communication Monographs, 46,* 257-273.

Clark, R. A., & Delia, J. G. (1976). The development of functional persuasive skills in childhood and adolescence. *Child Development, 47,* 1008-1014.

Clark, R. A., & Delia, J. G. (1977). Cognitive complexity, social perspective-taking, and functional persuasive skills in second- to ninth-grade children. *Human Communication Research, 3,* 128-134.

Cody, M. J., McLaughlin, M. L., & Jordan, W. J. (1980). A multidimensional scaling of three sets of compliance-gaining strategies. *Communication Quarterly, 28,* 34-45.

Cody, M. J., McLaughlin, M. L., Jordan, W. J., & Schneider, M. J. (1979). *A proposed working typology of compliance-gaining message strategies.* Unpublished manuscript, Texas Tech University.

Cody, M. J., McLaughlin, M. L., & Schneider, M. J. (1981). The impact of relational consequences and intimacy on the selection of interpersonal persuasion strategies: A reanalysis. *Communication Quarterly, 29,* 91-106.

Cody, M. J., O'Hair, H. D., & Schneider, M. J. (1982, May). *The impact of intimacy, rights to resist, Machiavellianism and psychological gender on compliance-resisting strategies: How pervasive are response effects in communication surveys?* Paper presented at the meeting of the International Communication Association, Boston. 1982.

Delia, J. G., & Clark, R. A. (1977). Cognitive complexity, social perception, and the development of listener-adapted communication in six-, eight-, ten-, and twelve-year-old boys. *Communication Monographs, 44,* 326-345.

Delia, J. G., Kline, S. L., & Burleson, B. R. (1979). The development of persuasive communication strategies in kindergarteners through twelfth-graders. *Communication Monographs, 46,* 241-256.

Delia, J. G., & O'Keefe, B. J. (1979). Constructivism: The development of communication in children. In E. Wartella (Ed.), *Children communicating: Media and development of thought, speech, understanding.* Beverly Hills, CA: Sage.

Finley, G. E., & Humphreys, C. A. (1974). Naive psychology and the development of persuasive appeals in girls. *Canadian Journal of Behavioral Science, 6,* 75-80.

Fitzpatrick, M., & Winke, J. (1979). You always hurt the one you love: Strategies and tactics in interpersonal conflict. *Communication Quarterly, 27,* 3-11.

Flavell, J. H., Botkin, P. T., Fry, C. L., Jr., Wright, J. W., & Jarvis, P. E. (1968). *The development of role-taking and communication skills in children.* New York: John Wiley.

Garvey, C. (1975). Requests and response in children's speech. *Journal of Child Language, 2,* 41-63.

Haslett, B. (1983). *Preschoolers' communicative strategies in gaining compliance from peers: A developmental study. Quarterly Journal of Speech, 69,* 84-99.

Howie-Day, A. M. (1977). *Meta persuasion: The development of reasoning about persuasive strategies.* Unpublished doctoral dissertation, University of Minnesota.

Hunter, J. E., & Boster, F. J. (1981). *Situational differences in the selection of compliance-gaining messages.* Paper presented at the meeting of the Speech Communication Association, Anaheim, CA.

Marwell, G., & Schmitt, D. R. (1967). Dimensions of compliance-gaining behavior: An empirical analysis. *Sociometry, 30,* 350-364.

McLaughlin, M. L., Cody, M. J., & Robey, C. S. (1980). Situational influences on the selection of strategies to resist compliance-gaining attempts. *Human Communication Research, 1,* 14-36.

Menig-Peterson, C. L. (1975). The modification of communicative behaviors in preschoolaged children as a function of the listener's perspective. *Child Development, 46,* 1015-1018.

Miller, G. R., Boster, F., Roloff, M. E., & Seibold, D. (1977). Compliance-gaining message strategies: A typology and some findings concerning effects of situational differences. *Communication Monographs, 44,* 37-51.

Miller, G. R., & Burgoon, M. (1978). Persuasion research: Review and commentary. In B. D. Ruben (Ed.), *Communication yearbook 2.* New Brunswick, NJ: Transaction.

Piche, G. L., Rubin, D. L., & Michlin, M. L. (1978). Age and social class in children's use of persuasive communicative appeals. *Child Development, 49,* 773-780.

Ritter, E. M. (1979). Social perspective-taking ability, cognitive complexity and listener-adapted communication in early and late adolescence. *Communication Monographs, 46.*

Rodnick, R., & Wood, B. (1973). The communication of strategies of children. *Speech Teacher, 22,* 114-124.

Roloff, M. E., & Barnicott, E. F. (1978). The situational use of pro-and anti-social compliance-gaining strategies by high and low Machiavellian. In B. D. Ruben (Ed.), *Communication yearbook 2*. New Brunswick, NJ: Transaction.

Ruben, B. D. (Ed.). (1978). *Communication yearbook 2*. New Brunswick, NJ: Transaction.

Schenck-Hamlin, W. A., Wiseman, R. L., & Georgacarakos, G. N. (1982). A model of properties of compliance-gaining strategies. *Communication Quarterly*, 1982, *30*, 92-100.

Tedeschi, J. T. (1972). *Social influence process*. Chicago: Aldine.

Wiseman, R. L., & Schenck-Hamlin, W. A. (1981). *A multidimensional scaling validation of an inductively derived set of compliance-gaining strategies*. Paper presented at the meeting of the Speech Communication Association, Anaheim, CA.

Wood, B. S. (1976). *Children and communication: Verbal and nonverbal language development*. Englewood Cliffs, NJ: Prentice-Hall.

Wood, J. R., Weinstein, E. A., & Parker, R. (1967). Children's interpersonal tactics. *Sociological Inquiry, 37, 129-138*.

IX ● HEALTH COMMUNICATION

31 ● When an M.D. Gives an R.N. a Harmful Order: Modifying a Bind

MARY ANN CUNNINGHAM ●
JAMES R. WILCOX

North Central College ● Bowling Green State University

T HE focus of this research is nurses' communication in the "inappropriate-order" situation—an episode in which the nurse believes a physician's order is not in the patient's best interest. The situation itself seems to put the nurse in a "bind," a term described by Bavelas (1983) and Bavelas and Smith (1982):

> caught between two or more incompatible aspects of the situation, and furthermore, still required to communicate (Bavelas, 1983, p. 132)

> an avoidance-avoidance conflict, in which two unappealing choices repel the individual, who will leave the field if possible—in this case, communicationally, by evasive or indirect communication (Bavelas & Smith, 1982, pp. 138-139)

Bavelas's five experiments tested the effects of bind and nonbind situations on communication choices, supporting her hypothesis that indirect or disqualified responses are preferred to lies, directness—bold honesty—or a statement of both sides of an issue. Such indirect (evasive, avoidant, ambiguous) communication styles allow the person to leave the field of the bind and reduce risk. Indirect communicator style, as a response to risky situations, has been observed by other communication researchers (Goffman, 1959, 1967; Ervin-Tripp, 1976; Brown & Levinson, 1978; Pomerantz, 1980).

In the inappropriate-order situation, the nurse is legally and ethically (in harmful situations) required to confront the situation and to seek actively to

Correspondence and requests for reprints: Mary Ann Cunningham, Department of Speech Communication, North Central College, Naperville, IL 60566.

prevent harm (Murchison, Nichols, & Hanson, 1982). Two undesirable and seemingly contradictory alternatives are compliance or noncompliance with the order. If the former is done, the patient's welfare is risked. If the latter is done, the relationship with the physician, and perhaps future effective patient care, is risked. The nurse confronts a situation in which meeting both patient and physician demands is difficult.

Rushing (1962-1963) noted the two potentially conflicting demands. Most nurses in his study said they responded with indirect influence attempts, that is, by trying to secure a change either from the physician's superior or from the physician by stating patient observations that contraindicated the order, or by indicating that they did not understand the order. In other words, they reported using an indirect style of communication with the physician, avoiding a statement of the problem and potential solutions (based on knowledge the nurse may have) in the hope that the physician would take the hint and change the order. Rushing observes that these attempts satisfy both patient and physician concerns: They acknowledge the physician's authority while circumventing or even violating it by hinting that he or she may be wrong.

An indirect style of nurse communication with physicians has achieved notoriety as the "Doctor-Nurse Game" (Stein, 1967). The key rule of the game is avoidance—avoidance of disagreement, the appearance of being direct and of commitment to positions "before a subrosa agreement on that position has already been established" (Stein, 1967, p. 699). The more significant the recommendation the more subtly and delicately it must be expressed. The nurse's paradox is that he or she is expected to be knowledgeable and

> when her good sense tells her a recommendation would be helpful to him [the doctor] she is not allowed to communicate directly nor is she allowed not to communicate it. The way out of the bind is to use the doctor-nurse game and communicate . . . without appearing to do so. (p. 703).

Stein (1967, p. 703) contends that the game "supports and protects the rigid organizational structure with the physician in clear authority."

However, a contemporary conception of the nurse-physician relationship is that nurses and physicians are supposed to form a collaborative, interdependent team. Nurses are not expected to be passive servants, but active patient advocates. But have nurses' selected communication styles changed since the early Rushing (1962-1963) and Stein (1967) articles? Is the nature or quality of the bind constant or might it vary with specific relevant situational elements? This research attempted to explore these questions of selective style in coping with the inappropriate-order situation and the nature of the bind this situation puts the nurse in.

The inappropriate-order situation may elicit a nurse response that depends on the characteristics of the situation itself, particularly those associated with risk. Two key risks are patient health and physician-interpersonal risks. Communication and nursing research have identified three specific situational factors related to the two risks. First, there is *potential patient consequences* if the order is carried out (slight discomfort versus serious harm). Stanley (1979) found differences between life-threatening and non-life-threatening situations in terms of nurses' reported initial actions in handling these situations. The second factor is that of the *expected physician response* if the nurse approaches the physician about the problem. Both Goffman (1967) and Redland (1983) suggest that expected reaction (positive or negative) may cause communicator style to vary. Goffman implies that expected negative response will inspire caution (even with a familiar other); Redland speculates that anticipated success with the physician may make the nurse less accommodative. The third factor is *physician's status* (first-year resident versus experienced attending physician, for example). Coser (1962) indicates that nurses may relate to interns on a basis of greater equality than they relate to experienced physicians. Hinted (or indirect) communication, according to Goffman (1959), may be a safe way to make and refuse out of character requests that, if done openly, might require altering the relationship more than temporarily. With first-year residents, nurses may be more out of character when they communicate indirectly; with experienced physicians, directness may be more out of character.

When the physician risks are low (a positive expected response, a first-year resident), a more direct, forceful behavior may be expected. When the patient risk is high (serious harm), more directness should also result. But whether the directness comes initially or later is not known, and whether consulting with the physician would be done initially or later is not known. Most studies of the inappropriate-order situation draw conclusions based on nurses' choices of initial actions to handle the situation or initial comments to the physician, usually not both, and further actions are not explored. Furthermore, the studies do not explore these three risk factors together.

The present study distinguishes among an initial handling of the situation, initial comments to the physician to secure change, and follow-up actions or discourse if the initial attempt with the physician is not successful. The objective of the study was to explore the effects of the three risk factors on nurses' communication choices and ratings in these three potential phases of the inappropriate-order situation. Specifically, this study addressed the following questions:

(1) How will R.N.s rate and select given communicator choices within three potential phases of the inappropriate order situation?
    (a) an initial response
    (b) a confrontation with the physician to secure an order change
    (c) a follow-up to an unsuccessful verbal confrontation with the physician
(2) What will R.N.s expect they would do or say to follow up an unsuccessful initial confrontation with the physician?

(3) Will potential patient consequences (slight discomfort versus serious harm) significantly affect nurses' ratings and selections of communicator choices in the three potential phases?

(4) Will expected physician response (positive versus negative) significantly affect nurses' ratings and selections of communicator choices in the three potential phases?

(5) Will physician status (experienced attending physician versus first-year resident) significantly affect nurses' ratings and selections of communicator choices in the three potential phases?

METHODS

Subjects

Research participants were 298 nonmanagement female registered nurses drawn from two midwestern hospitals. Hospital A is a relatively small, 350-bed medical school hospital with a nursing school. It is a progressive hospital, and the majority of the units use a primary nursing model in which each patient has a primary nurse who manages and is accountable for the patient's total nursing care, in contrast to a team-nursing model, in which nursing care tasks are divided among members of the nursing team. Attending physicians at this hospital are medical school professors. Hospital B is a relatively large, 850-bed hospital with a nursing school and an affiliation with Hospital A's medical school. Units in the hospital are just beginning conversion to a primary nursing model. Some of the attending physicians at Hospital B are also on the faculty of Hospital A's medical school.

Subjects' ages ranged from 21 to 60, with medians of 28.5 and 31 for Samples 1 (N = 139) and 2 (N = 159), respectively.

Procedures

The instruments were distributed by head nurses, clinical managers, or mail, and were returned to a designated point in each hospital. Each nurse received one of eight versions of the instrument; the distribution was determined by randomizing procedures.

Instrument

Each instrument described one of eight hypothetical situations, constructed in such a way as to include all combinations of the three risk factor levels. The situation and the elements, which were varied in the different treatment conditions, are as follows:

[A first-year resident/an experienced attending physician] has left a written order which you are expected to carry out for one of your patients. You feel certain that the order will have [seriously harmful/slightly uncomfortable] consequences for the patient. You know of an alternate order which would eliminate this [serious harm/slight discomfort] and be beneficial to the patient. This [first-year resident/experienced attending physician] has been [negative/positive] about your making recommendations in the past, and you would tend to expect a [negative/positive] response if you made a recommendation.

Nurses were instructed to imagine themselves in the situation and to respond to questions regarding their probable communication behavior in (1) the initial handling of the situation, (2) their initial comments to the physician to secure an order change, and (3) further action if initial comments to the physician are unsuccessful in securing change.

Six initial action choices to handle the situation were presented (in a different random order on each sample's instrument), derived from alternatives described in nursing studies (Rushing, 1962-1963; Hofling, Brotzman, Dalrymple, Graves, & Pierce, 1966; Rank & Jacobson, 1977; Stanley, 1979). These alternative choices varied from submissive (DOM 1) to dominant (DOM 6), and the scale was validated by a small group of nurses prior to instrument administration:

DOM 1: Carry out the order.
DOM 2: Confer with the supervising or head nurse, and let him/her handle it.
DOM 3: Confer with another physician and let him/her handle it.
DOM 4: Confer with someone else (supervisor, other physician, peers, etc.) for advice and then the physician.
DOM 5: Confer with the physician to secure an order change.
DOM 6: Tell the physician you refuse to carry out the order.

For each choice presented, nurses were asked to indicate on a seven-point Likert-type scale their degree of agreement/disagreement with two statements: (1) "I would probably do this first," and (2) "I would probably avoid doing this first." Additionally, each nurse selected one most probable choice and gave written reasons for that choice. Ratings were used to provide more precise information about all alternative choices and to test for interactions. The top choice variable was used to complement the ratings information, to simulate more closely "real-world" demands to make a single choice, and to provide a basis for the requested rationale.

Four initial comment choices were constructed based on previous work (Rushing, 1962-1963; Stein, 1967) and on reports of "typical" nurses' comments, as reported by a group of consulting head nurses. These choices were also varied on a direct/indirect continuum based on relevant definitions of that concept (Rushing, 1962-1963; Stein, 1967; Bavelas & Smith, 1982; Bavelas, 1983; Goffman, 1959, 1967; Brown & Levinson, 1978; Ervin-Tripp, 1976; Falbo & Peplau, 1980; Johnson, 1978). Placement of comments on the continuum below was validated by a small group of nurses consulted for this research:

DIR 1: Doctor, I'm not sure I understand this order. Would you clarify it for me?
DIR 2: Doctor, I'm concerned about possible negative effects with this order. Could you explain the order to me?
DIR 3: Doctor, I'm concerned about X and Y effects with this order. Would some other order eliminate these effects?
DIR 4: Doctor, I recommend a change to order Z. In my experience it has eliminated the X and Y effects.

After nurses were asked to suppose they were to confer with the physician to secure a changed order, they rated their degree of agreement/disagreement with two statements: (1) "I would probably say something like this first," and (2) "I would probably avoid saying something like this first." As in the initial action section, each nurse also selected a most probable choice and wrote reasons for that choice.

Finally, nurses were asked to indicate ("yes" or "no") whether they would pursue the matter if their initial comment choices were unsuccessful and to specify what further action they would take.

Statistical Analyses

The top choice data were analyzed by chi-square tests of association. Due to several low to no frequency cells, DOM 1, 2, 3, and 6 were excluded from these analyses. Chi-square tests analyzed associations between each of the three risk factors and each of the three sets of remaining choices, resulting in nine tests for each sample.

The effects of the risk factors and their interactions on initial action and on initial comment ratings were analyzed by general linear model tests of univariate and multivariate analyses of variance, respectively (see Tables 31.1 and 31.2). After determining that the ratings for the conversely worded statements were significantly correlated ($p < .0001$), one rating score was reflected. The mean of the two resultant scores was used in subsequent analyses.

Content Analysis

Responses specifying how the matter would be pursued further if initial comments were unsuccessful were content analyzed. Mutually exclusive categories that emerged from an examination of the data were used to classify responses. Additional subcategories were formed for further data description. Frequencies and percentages for each category were computed.

RESULTS

The following is a presentation of both descriptive (including content analysis) and experimental results (see Tables 31.1 and 31.2). No interac-

Table 31.1
Summary of Main Effect MANOVAs

Risk Factor	Sample					
	1			2		
	F	df	p	F	df	p
Initial action ratings set (DOM)						
potential patient consequences	9.99	6,124	.0001	8.32	6,156	.0001
expected physician response	4.14	6,124	.0008	5.55	6,156	.0001
physician status	1.09	6,124	.3721	2.94	6,156	.0098
Initial comment ratings set (DIR)						
potential patient consequences	6.83	4,128	.0001	5.41	4,147	.0004
expected physician response	.70	4,128	.5910	2.39	4,147	.0536
physician status	1.32	4,128	.2647	.75	4,147	.5593

Note: Interaction effects were not significant (p range: .1572 to .9732).

tions were found. A more detailed reporting of results may be found in Cunningham (1983).

Descriptive Results

The most preferred initial action choices were those involving conferring with the physician, while the least preferred were carrying out or refusing the order. Moderate initial comment choices were generally selected over the most and least direct comments. However, the risk factors did significantly affect nurses' responses.

The content analyses of responses to the open-ended question about pursuing the matter further resulted in four mutually exclusive categories: (1) further interaction with the physician (more than 40 percent for both samples), which largely entailed giving specific information on reasons for change, alternate orders, and refusals; (2) involving others (approximately 25 percent of each sample); (3) further interaction with the physician followed by involving others (12 percent for Sample 1, 20 percent for Sample 2); (4) miscellaneous responses, which made up less than 4 percent of each sample. Thus, conferring with the physician further in a more direct, specific, and forceful manner was the preference of the majority of respondents.

Table 31.2
Summary of Overall Ranks and Risk Factor Associations

	Overall Rank	Potential Patient Consequence Discomfort	Harm	Expected Physician Response Negative	Positive	Physician Status Experienced	First Year
Initial action choices[a]							
DOM 1	6	1[cd],2[cd]					
DOM 2	3			1[cd]			
DOM 3	4			1[cd]			2[cd]
DOM 4	2		1[b],2[b]	1[bc],2[b]			
DOM 5	1	1[b],2[b]			1[bc],2[bc]		
DOM 6	5		1[cd],2[cd]				2[cd]
Initial comment choices[a]							
DIR 1	3		1[c],2[b]				
DIR 2	2		1[cb],2[cb]				
DIR 3	1	1[b],2[bc]					
DIR 4	4						
Pursuing the matter further							
yes	1		1[b],2[b]		2[b]		2[b]
no	2	1[bd],2[bd]		2[bd]	2[bd]		

Note: Entries 1 and 2 indicate a significant association with the particular risk factor level for Sample 1 and Sample 2.
a. Described in the text.
b. Chi-square test ($p<.05$) on top-choice data (cells <5 were omitted from analysis).
c. GLM ANOVA tests performed after GLM MANOVA on each set of continuous variables. (Critical levels were adjusted conservatively due to multiple, related variables in each set: DOM $p = .05/6, .0083$; DIR $p = .05/4, .0125$.)
d. Not a preferred choice overall, though more likely to occur than expected.

Potential Patient Consequences

Nurses' responses depended on whether the potential patient consequences were seriously harmful or slightly uncomfortable. This was the most potent risk factor, compared to expected physician response and physician status.

Slight patient discomfort was significantly associated with the following:

(a) DOM 5, a dominant action, conferring directly with the physician (Samples 1 and 2 chi-squares)
(b) DOM 1, a very submissive action, carrying out the order (Samples 1 and 2 ANOVAs, means in the disagree range)
(c) DIR 3, a direct comment, specifying effects and inquiring about another order (Samples 1 and 2 chi-squares, Sample 2 ANOVA)
(d) not pursuing the matter further (Samples 1 and 2 chi-squares, although a majority would pursue the matter further)

Serious patient harm was significantly associated with the following:

(a) a moderately dominant action, DOM 4, seeking advice and then conferring with the physician (Samples 1 and 2 chi-squares)
(b) a highly dominant action, DOM 6, refusing to carry out the order (Samples 1 and 2 ANOVAs, means in the disagree range)
(c) an indirect action, DIR 2, mentioning possible effects and asking for an explanation (Samples 1 and 2 chi-squares and ANOVAs)
(d) the most indirect action, DIR 1, asking for a clarification (Sample 2 chi-square, Sample 1 ANOVA)
(e) pursuing the matter further, which usually consisted of involving others and/ or giving the physician more information on reasons and/or alternate orders or refusing the order (Samples 1 and 2 chi-squares)

Nurses given the serious harm situations reported that they would use less dominant/more indirect initial actions (seeking advice and then conferring with the physician, DOM 4) and more indirect initial comments (DIR 1 and 2) than those nurses given the slight discomfort situations. While DOM 4 and DIR 1 and 2 appear to be less effective actions for the patient who may face serious harm, the nurses in this condition also reported a greater likelihood of pursuing the matter further, which often entailed more direct, specific information about reasons for a change and alternate orders, refusals of the order, and/or enlisting others' help in securing a changed order. Carrying out the order and not pursuing the matter were choices made more often than expected in the patient discomfort situation, but these choices were rejected by a majority of respondents.

Expected Physician Response

Expected physician response, the next most potent factor, also affected nurses' choices and ratings, but principally initial action variables. Some effects were not consistent across the two samples (see Table 31.1). A negative physician response was associated with the following:

(a) DOM 4, seeking advice before conferring with the physician (Samples 1 and 2 chi-squares, Sample 1 ANOVA)
(b) DOM 2 and 3, letting others handle the situation (Sample 1 ANOVA, means in the disagree range)
(c) not pursuing the matter further (Sample 2 chi-square, majority would pursue matter further)

A positive physician response was associated with the following:

(a) DOM 5, conferring with the physician directly to secure change (Samples 1 and 2 chi-squares, ANOVAs);
(b) pursuing the matter further (Sample 2 chi-square)

R.N.s given the negative physician response situations were more likely than expected to report a less dominant/more indirect initial action (DOM 4 again, as in serious patient harm) than those nurses in the positive physician response condition, who preferred DOM 5, conferring with the physician to secure change. A negative response was also more likely to elicit letting others handle the situation (DOM 2 and 3) and not pursuing the matter further, though these choices were not preferred in general and the effects were limited to one sample.

Physician Status

The physician status factor seemed to make a difference only with sample 2, and the affected choices were, in general, not preferred ones. Physician status was a sample-specific factor and similar to expected physician response; it did not significantly affect initial comment variables.

An experienced attending physician was associated with not pursuing the matter further (Sample 2 chi-square, the majority would pursue the matter further).

A first-year resident was associated with the following:

(a) DOM 3, letting another physician handle the situation (Sample 2 ANOVA, means in the disagree range)
(b) DOM 6, refusing to carry out the order (Sample 2 ANOVA, means in the disagree range)
(c) pursuing the matter further (Sample 2 chi-square)

A more dominant action, refusing the order, letting another physician handle the situation, and pursuing the matter further were associated with the first-year resident condition and not with the experienced attending physician condition. When an experienced attending physician was involved, R.N.s reported that they were more likely not to pursue the matter further, although this choice was not preferred by the majority.

Physician status effects should be interpreted cautiously, since pursuing the matter further was the choice of the majority in both independent variable levels, and both DOM 3 and DOM 6 means were in the disagree range.

In sum, when patient or physician risks were high (harm to the patient or a negative physician response), more avoidant, cautious initial communication was likely, but the matter was likely to be pursued further in a more direct, forceful way. When the patient or physician risks were low, more initial directness in handling the situation and in commenting to the physician was likely, but the matter was less likely than expected to be pursued further. However, the most direct comment (DIR 4) was the least preferred choice of the nurses in all conditions.

DISCUSSION

Is the Inappropriate-Order Situation a Bind?

Based on the results of this study, it appears that the situation is more a bind initially, but less a bind as interaction evolves. Nurses seem to reject the extreme initial choices of noncompliance (refusing the order) and compliance (carrying out the order), *two undesirable and contradictory choices*. They also reject extreme directness in initial comments to the physician (recommending a specific change even though they may have knowledge of an alternate order in the situation). Thus less direct choices are preferred initially, as in Bavelas's (1983) studies on binds. In addition, nurses' responses indicate *a requirement to communicate* to handle the situation; communicating with the physician was the most preferred choice of the subjects in this study. However, when the matter is pursued further, a choice of the majority of nurses, more direct comments and forceful actions are reported. The bind is altered, then, when nurses fail to secure an order change from the physician initially. Studies that make judgments about nurses' behavior based only on initial actions or initial comments to the physician, then, can be misleading if they do not take into account subsequent communication when success does not occur initially.

Although the situation in general is more binding than not binding *initially,* the bind can be loosened or tightened by the risk factors. In particular, serious patient harm and a negative physician response present risks that tighten the bind. Patient discomfort and positive physician response conditions loosen the bind and allow more initial directness either of action or of comment. The nature of the bind, then, is that it is not a constant—it varies according to the nurse's perception of risk, both to the patient and to his or her continued working relationship with the physician.

Implications for the Nurse-Physician Role Relationship and the "Doctor-Nurse Game"

Nurses in this study seem to take their role of patient advocate very seriously: They choose to confer with the physicians themselves, a more dominant action than one might expect given the antiquated dictum that nurses must obey physicians' orders unquestioningly. Though it may be harder for them to be more direct when the patient risks are high, since their own judgments could be in error, they report they would persist and use more direct comments and forceful actions later. That nurses say they would use influence attempts, as in Rushing's (1962-1963) study, that satisfy patient concerns and that conform with but also circumvent the physician's authority by suggesting a need for change, is perhaps a reflection of the transitional nature of the nurse-physician relationship.

A tendency toward a contemporary, interdependent, collaborative nurse-physician relationship is evidenced by nurses' preferences for using some of their knowledge in their influence attempts, as in DIR 2 and 3, the most preferred choices. DIR 2 is problem oriented in its reference to possible effects, and DIR 3 is problem and solution oriented in its mention of specific negative effects and its inquiry about some other order. However, DIR 1 involves some dependency seeking by its reliance on the physician to ferret out the problem initially and come up with a solution; some nurses called this "playing dumb." Some may view the nurses' rejection of DIR 4, which presents a more independent problem and solution, as a reflection of the handmaiden role. But making a direct recommendation statement was perceived by nurses as inhibiting lines of communication before all the issues could be explored. Many nurses noted in their written rationales that choices other than DIR 4 had the potential to open lines of communication so that mutual learning and joint problem solving were possible. And, as noted, initial indirectness does not preclude later directness.

It is not difficult to find condemnations of nurses' indirect communication styles, the "Doctor-Nurse Game" (Stein, 1967; Bullough, 1975). Johnson (1978) equates indirectness with manipulation and points out that if indirect but effective strategies are not detected by the other person, the influencer does not get credit and cannot build a basis for future influence. In other words, the physician gets the credit and the nurse gets nothing. One nurse in the present study reflects this concern:

> Responses 11 and 12 [DIR 1 and 2] are truly wimp responses, perpetuating the nurse-handmaiden image, decreasing the odds physicians will ever consider nurses as colleagues rather than servants.

If all the "game" entails is indirect language or hints throughout the episode, then these views are worth considering. But clearly the "game" can involve more than *initial* hints, as one nurse's written response indicates:

> I am willing to play the game for the pts. sake—would call, ask for advice, explanations, etc., try to suggest alternatives and reach compromise before I refused the order.

The rules of the Doctor-Nurse Game, then, may be only opening moves. While initial comments may be indirect, subsequent comments may be more direct and specific when the matter is pursued further, a choice of the majority of the nurses in this study. Furthermore, the initial indirectness can serve as an introduction to a collaborative approach, as lines of communication are opened and joint problem solving is encouraged.

The Applications of This Research

This study suggests directions for communication training for nurses and physicians. The results indicate that communication that is beneficial in one situation may not be in another: Patient and interpersonal risks need to be taken into account. Adaptation to the demands of the situation, a characteristic of communicative competence (Weimann, 1977; Knapp, 1978; Fisher, 1982; Spitzberg, 1983), then, is recommended. In her recommendations on how to handle the inappropriate-order situation, Stanley (1979, p. 29) concurs: "Tailor the nature of your response to the situation." One nurse's written comment is consistent with this view: "Again, I want to be fair with the Doctor, not come off like I'm being assertive for assertiveness' sake!" For example, while discussing the problem directly with the physician is generally recommended, Stanley (1979) advises enlisting others' assistance when dealing with a difficult physician. A particularly urgent crisis situation involving patient harm may require highly forceful, direct action, although Stanley (1979, p. 23) advises, in general, using a more cautious, questioning initial approach with the physician because "the deck is stacked against the nurse in this situation" and initial comments "can make a big difference in the outcome of the confrontation."

A prerequisite of adaptation, though, is knowledge of what one is adapting to, which can be gained from an analysis of the situation. Knowledge of the key factors of the situation, some of which were considered in this study, are helpful in the analysis. Other factors not considered here are the urgency of the situation (the serious harm situation in this study was not depicted as requiring immediate action), the nurses' own abilities, the hospitals' protocols for dealing with the inappropriate-order situation, the supportiveness of the hospital organizations, and, most important, the patients' rights. Training in considering these factors may allow a quick sizing-up of the situation in the actual episode.

Building a wide repertoire of communication behaviors that can be flexibly adapted and implemented when needed is recommended. A limitation of this present study is that nurses' responses were based on what they said they would do when given a set of choices upon which they had time to reflect. Whether nurses would think of or use these responses in the heat of the situation is not known. Having a wide repertoire of communicative approaches, however, may enable nurses to make quicker, more adaptive selections in the actual situation.

Physician communication training is also important. Two physicians we interviewed indicated that they desire direct communication styles from nurses. A study reported by Bullough (1975) supports this physician preference, although older physicians tended to prefer more indirectness. But whether physicians encourage direct communication in actual situations has not been verified. Real concerns voiced by nurses in this study were the fear of being in error, offending the physician, or putting the doctor on the defensive by being too direct. Physicians need to understand these fears, whether they are warranted or not. When physicians indicate their preferences for nurses' communicative approaches, support their preferences in interaction, and solicit nurses' communicative preferences, some of nurses' uncertainties about the physicians' responses in inappropriate-order situations may be reduced, and perhaps more energy can be invested in patients' welfare. One physician we interviewed indicated how she supports her preferences in interaction with nurses. She gives positive, explicit feedback to nurses for direct, specific, to-the-point communication, even when the nurses are in error, because she does not want to inhibit this type of communication from nurses in other situations where it may be vital to the patient's welfare.

SUMMARY AND IMPLICATIONS

Communication theorists and researchers, in conceptualizing and studying the notion of binds, have suggested that the logical response to a bind may be evasive, avoidant, or indirect behavior. This research, generating data in a specific and specialized environment in order to gain insight into a particular type of bind (the Doctor-Nurse Game), has supported the expectation of indirectness. Additionally, these findings enhance our understanding of binds and bind coping behaviors (including indirection) by showing that the nature and quality of a bind may be dependent on certain situational circumstances—in this case, perceived risks. In other words, it may be possible to conceptualize binds as "tighter" or "looser" at the outset of a process in which indirection may serve as a bind "loosener" by functioning to open and maintain collaboration with another. Further, given a range of alternatives on a continuum of directness-indirectness, the middle or moderate may be most productive in bind loosening and the extremes least likely to affect the bind. If a bind may be affected by situational factors and if a certain degree of indirectness may serve to loosen the bind as at least an opening move in an evolving interaction, then several questions become important for future research and thinking in both nurse-doctor interaction and other situations:

(1) What situational factors have the greatest and the least effects on the nature and quality of binds?
(2) What kinds and degrees of indirectness/directness serve as openers to bind-loosening interaction and what kinds and degrees serve to tighten binds and inhibit interaction (or at least increase the likelihood of avoidance or evasion)?
(3) How does a certain degree of indirectness actually function in interaction to elicit continuity, collaboration, relational change, mutual problem solving, and even greater degrees of directness?

The prevailing ideology of the last fifteen or twenty years has promoted directness as a preferred communicator style. There is, however, growing recognition, reflected in a small body of research, that some indirection may serve a variety of functions, some of which may be socially or pragmatically desirable. These findings, relevant in particular to the so-called Doctor-Nurse Game, may be relevant as well for similar relational situations.

REFERENCES

Bavelas, J. B. (1983). Situations that lead to disqualification. *Human Communication Research, 9,* 130-145.

Bavelas, J. B., & Smith, B. J. (1982). A method for scaling verbal disqualification. *Human Communication Research, 8,* 214-227.

Brown, P., & Levinson, S. (1978). Universals in language usage: Politeness phenomena. In E. N. Goody (Ed.), *Questions and politeness: Strategies in social interaction.* Cambridge: Cambridge University Press.

Bullough, B. (1975). Barriers to the nurse practitioner movement: Problems of women in a woman's field. *International Journal of Health Services, 5,* 225-233.

Coser, R. L. (1962). *Life in the ward.* East Lansing: Michigan State University Press.

Cunningham, M. A. (1983). *Coping with a bind: The effects of three risk factors on nurses' communication in the inappropriate-order situation.* Unpublished doctoral dissertation, Bowling Green State University.

Ervin-Tripp, S. (1976). Is Sybil there? The structure of some American English directives. *Language in Society, 5,* 25-66.

Fisher, B. A. (1982). Communication pragmatism: Another legacy of Gregory Bateson. *Journal of Applied Communication Research, 10,* 38-49.

Falbo, T., & Peplau, L. A. (1980). Power strategies in intimate relationships. *Journal of Personality and Social Psychology, 38,* 618-628.

Goffman, E. (1959). *The presentation of self in everyday life.* Garden City, NY: Doubleday.

Goffman, E. (1967). *Interaction ritual: Essays on face to face behavior.* Garden City, NY: Doubleday.

Hofling, C. K., Brotzman, E., Dalrymple, S., Graves, N., & Pierce, C. M. (1966). An experimental study in nurse-physician relationships. *Journal of Nervous and Mental Diseases, 143,* 171-180.

Johnson, P. B. (1978). Women and interpersonal power. In I. H. Frieze, J. C. Parsons, P. B. Johnson, D. N. Ruble, & G. L. Zellman (Eds.), *Women and sex roles.* New York: Norton.

Knapp, M. L. (1978). *Social intercourse: From greeting to goodbye.* Boston: Allyn & Bacon.

Murchison, I., Nichols, T. S., & Hanson, R. (1982). *Legal accountability in the nursing process* (2nd. ed.). St. Louis: C. V. Mosby.

Pomerantz, A. (1980). Telling my side: "Limited access" as a fishing device. *Sociological Inquiry, 50,* 186-198.

Rank, S. G., & Jacobson, C. K. (1977). Hospital nurses' compliance with medication overdose orders: A failure to replicate. *Journal of Health and Social Behavior, 18,* 188-193.

Redland, A. R. (1983). *An investigation of nurses' interaction styles with physicians and suggested patient care interventions.* Paper presented at the meetings of the International Communication Association, Dallas.

Rushing, W. A. (1962-1963). Social influence and the social-psychological function of deference: A study of psychiatric nursing. *Social Forces, 41,* 142-148.

Spitzberg, B. H. (1983). Communication competence as knowledge, skill, impression. *Communication Education, 32,* 323-329.

Stanley, L. (1979). Doctors: What to do when the MD is wrong. *RN, 42,* 23-30.

Stein, L. I. (1967). The doctor-nurse game. *Archives of General Psychiatry, 16,* 699-703.

Weimann, J. M. (1977). Explication and test of a model of communicative competence. *Human Communication Research, 3,* 195-213.

32 ● Communication and Job Stress in a Health Organization

BEVERLY DAVENPORT SYPHER ●
EILEEN BERLIN RAY

University of Kentucky

O VER the past several years, the relationship of communication to job stress has received much attention in both the popular and academic presses. Burnout, a reaction to chronic job-related stress, is often the focus in this literature. It is characterized by physical, attitudinal, and emotional exhaustion (Cherniss, 1980; Edelwich, 1980; Freudenberger, 1974; Kafry & Pines, 1980; Mattingly, 1977). Maslach (1976) describes it as a wearing out because of job demands.

While there is some discrepancy between what is found on burnout in the popular press and in empirical research (Ray, 1983a), there tends to be some agreement on the importance of communication relationships as a buffer to job burnout. The popular press tends to emphasize formal communication relationships with both superiors and peers (Cherniss, 1980; Edelwich, 1980; Freudenberger, 1974; Veninga & Bradley, 1981). Empirical research in different types of human service organizations reveals that communication variables such as work relationships (Maslach & Jackson, 1979; Maslach & Pines, 1977; Pines & Kafry, 1978; Pines & Maslach, 1978), support (Pines & Kafry, 1978), and social feedback (Pines & Kafry, 1978) are negatively related to burnout.

AUTHORS' NOTE: We wish to thank Nanci Williamson and other students at the University of Kentucky for their help in data collection.

Correspondence and requests for reprints: Beverly Davenport Sypher, College of Communications, University of Kentucky, Lexington, KY 40506.

Unfortunately, much of this research is fragmented and lacks a guiding theoretic framework (Albrecht, 1982; Kanner, Kafry, & Pines, 1978). In an attempt to provide this framework, recent studies have examined more explicitly the role of communication to burnout. Albrecht (1982), for example, found that several relational coping strategies mediated burnout for nurses. Another investigation revealed that child-care workers integrated in an organizational communication network reported less burnout than those less integrated (Albrecht, Irey, & Mundy, 1982). However, for nurses, network integration in their work unit was not significantly related to their burnout level (Ray, 1983a). These findings suggest that burnout may be mediated by integration in an organizational, as opposed to work unit, network.

Findings from these studies and others suggest that the burnout process is more complex than much of the literature asserts. Ray (1983a), for example, tested a causal model of burnout examining job stress, network integration in the work unit, and cognitive distance between nurses' perceptions of self and job. The only significant path in the model was job-related stress to burnout. In another study, Ray (1983b) found that high- and low-burnout respondents perceived different subsets of stressors as salient and that these stressors combined in different ways to predict burnout. Moreover, several of the stressor variables with the highest means were not significantly related to burnout.

What is becoming increasingly apparent in this area of research is the importance of examining individual organizations in the study of communication and organizational outcomes such as burnout. How organization members shape their perceptions and make sense of their work environment is largely due to their interaction with others in their organizations. Through this interaction, members develop and define their shared realities and, communicatively, change or maintain their perceptions of this enacted reality. As a result, what may be perceived as stressful in one organization may be ignored in another. Similar communication practices may be interpreted differently by members in different organizations. This context-dependent nature of communication affirms the necessity of studying individual organizations as unique collectivities and looking for the specific communication behaviors related to job burnout in each particular organization.

This study examined the perceptions of specific communication behaviors and burnout in a health-related organization. It was guided by the following research questions:

RQ 1: How do organization members perceive communication in the organization?

RQ 2: What is the relationship between communication and burnout?

RQ 3: Do high- and low-burnout respondents differ in their perceptions of communication in the organization?

METHOD

The Organization Studied

The organization studied is a nonprofit blood center located in a southern city. Organizational goals include recruiting donors and safely and economically supplying hospitals with needed blood. At the time of this study, ninety employees worked in one of six different areas: administration, administrative services, lab, mobile units, donor drawing, and recruitment. The results reported here are part of a larger, ongoing study of the organization.

Procedures

The choice of both qualitative (interview) and quantitative (survey) data-gathering strategies was based on the strengths of multiple methods procedures: (a) Weaknesses of one method may be balanced by another (Albrecht & Ropp, 1982); (b) confidence in the findings, whether they converge or diverge, is increased (Jick, 1979); and (c) convergent validation is possible (Denzin, 1978; Jick, 1979). Delia, O'Keefe, and O'Keefe (1982, p. 181) also maintain that methodological triangulation resulting from studying phenomena under diverse conditions is "the best practical means of assuring accommodations to the empirical world."

Interviews. A stratified random sample of approximately 30 percent (n = 32) of the organization was chosen from the six different work areas. Structured interviews with each of these persons focused on the strengths and weaknesses of the organization's communication practices. Most of these interviews lasted approximately 45 minutes, but they ranged in length from 20 minutes to 2 hours. Respondents were asked to describe communication within the organization, focusing on interpersonal relationships, conflicts, overall communication satisfaction, and their general feelings about their jobs and the organization.

Survey. Data gathered from the individual interviews provided input into the construction of a questionnaire designed specifically to investigate communication and burnout. Interview data suggested that intergroup relationships were poor, conflicts were not resolved, and communication in general was unsatisfactory. Based on these findings, we included scales specifically designed to measure burnout, conflict resolution, and communication satisfaction. Approximately 68 percent (n = 61) of all organization members completed the survey. Respondents completed the survey in a special assigned room at the site location.

Measures

Burnout. The Tedium Scale (Kafry & Pines, 1980) is a 21-item questionnaire that assesses physical, attitudinal, and emotional exhaustion.

Items are rated on a 7-point Likert-type scale bounded by "never" at 1 and "always" at 7, and mean scores are computed. The higher the mean score, the greater the burnout. This scale has been used in numerous burnout studies, with test-retest reliabilities of .79 (Albrecht et al., 1982) and .89 (Kanner et al., 1978) and internal reliabilities (Cronbach's alpha) of .84 (Albrecht et al., 1982) and .86 (Ray, 1983a) reported. In this study, the internal reliability (Cronbach's alpha) was .87.

Divergent validity of burnout was assessed by correlating the Tedium Scale with job satisfaction. Correlations of −.58 (Kanner et al., 1978) and −.54 (Albrecht et al., 1982) have been reported. In this study, job satisfaction was measured by a 3-item scale developed by Cammann, Fichman, Jenkins, and Klesh (1978) as part of the general attitudes module of the Michigan Organizational Assessment Questionnaire (MOAQ). This particular scale provides an indication of employees' overall affective responses to their jobs. Cammann et al. (1978) report a .77 internal consistency reliability coefficient for the scale. In this study, a correlation of −.54 (p ⩽ .001) was found between burnout and the MOAQ job satisfaction scale, indicating further validity of the burnout measure.

Conflict Resolution. A 14-item scale was used to measure respondents' perceptions of the ways in which conflict was resolved in their organization. This measure was developed as part of the intergroup relations module of the Michigan Organizational Assessment Package (MOAP, 1975). The internal reliability (Cronbach's alpha) for the measure in this study was .81. Respondents used 5-point Likert-type scales to indicate how frequently various methods of conflict resolution were used. The scale was bounded by "never" at 1 and "always" at 5. The scale was further broken into five subscales focusing on strategies used to deal with conflict, as suggested in the MOAP (1975): ignoring the problem, smoothing, third-party intervention, confrontation, and problem solving.

Communication Satisfaction. Respondents also completed the Faces Scale (Kunin, 1955; Dunham & Herman, 1975) measure of organizational communication satisfaction as modified by Roberts and O'Reilly (1974). This one-item scale is intended to measure subjects' degree of satisfaction with communication in general, including the amount of information they receive, contacts with their immediate supervisors and others, and the accuracy of the information available. Roberts and O'Reilly (1974) reported test-retest reliabilities of .60 and .73.

RESULTS

Research Question 1

Interview Data. From all indications, this organization is very much like what Deal and Kennedy (1982) called a "process culture." This type of organization has low financial stakes, depends heavily on written communication (memos, reports, procedures, forms, and so on) ignores problems until errors are made, provides little recognition and feedback, and focuses on how something is done rather than what is done.

An example of a process orientation was revealed when one respondent was asked to describe her work:

> For myself, I'm busy from the time I walk in the door until the time I walk out in the afternoon. It's a full eight hour day—just a busy, busy job. There are a lot of things to do.

Another interviewee elaborated:

> Most of the time we're taking orders, shipping blood, writing up transfer memos; we have a card for every unit of blood and every time that a unit of blood moves, we have to write on that card where it goes. Then whatever is transfused, we have to write the hospital name, the hospital number, the date it was transfused, and then it must be entered on a transfer report sheet.

A response from top management reaffirms the process nature of this organizational culture:

> We have a product [blood] to get out. If we have time for those other things [staff meetings, informal communication, participation in decision making, solving problems, and so on] after, it would be nice.

The norms set by top management seemed to be directly related to members' perceptions of communication. Organization members felt little attention was directed toward "people kinds of issues." Overall, the interview data revealed a general lack of communication. Interviewees especially complained about the inadequate amount of downward communication. They said there was too much written and "unimportant" communication and not enough informal communication. Over 65 percent of the interviewees listed an overreliance on written communication among the organization's communication weaknesses.

These respondents also referred to a "communication gap" between the various levels in the organization's hierarchy. Lack of information from top management was repeatedly cited in interviews as a source of dissatisfaction. When asked to consider all sources, interviewees felt that the least amount of information originated from the top. Interviewees felt that they were not included in decision making, not given any feedback, and not encouraged to offer input. As a result, they felt "personality clashes" were ignored, and problems were usually left to take care of themselves.

Some respondents said that they thought employees were "too busy"

Table 32.1
Descriptive Statistics[a] and Correlations for Conflict
Resolution and Communication Satisfaction
with Burnout

Variable	X	S.D.	r (Burnout)
Conflict resolution	3.21	.53	*−.36
ignoring the problem	3.24	.66	−.10
smoothing	3.31	.88	−.26
third-party intervention	2.97	.76	−.13
confrontation	3.22	.75	*−.42
Communication satisfaction	3.67	1.18	**−.33
Burnout	3.35	.52	—

a. The range for all variables except for burnout was 1—5. The range for the burnout variable was 1—7.
*$p \leqslant .05$; **$p \leqslant .01$.

with their work to deal with personal problems, while other respondents said the organization had just gotten too large to deal with its problems. One interviewee remarked:

> We started out with two employees and now there's so many people I don't even know. I don't see them because we're so busy, busy, busy.

And yet another respondent said top management did not encourage employees to discuss their problems:

> Everyone around here, especially top management, tends to ignore problems until someone makes a mistake. Then, everyone hears about it.

Taken together, the interview data revealed that this organization's members perceived a general lack of downward-directed communication, an overreliance of written communication, a focus only on work-related communication, and a tendency to ignore problems and avoid conflict.

Survey Data. More specific answers to the first research question were available from the survey data. Findings revealed that organization members were not especially satisfied with communication, but neither were they dissatisfied. The mean score for communication satisfaction was 3.67 (S.D. = 1.18; see Table 32.1).

This question was also answered by measuring organization members' perceptions of how frequently various types of conflict-resolution strategies were used. The results of the descriptive statistics for the overall scale and its subscale items are presented in Table 32.1. The survey respondents felt that their coworkers tried to avoid offending one another ($\bar{X}$ = 3.31, S.D. = .88) more often than they attempted to meet issues head on ($\bar{X}$ = 3.22, S.D. = .75) and solve problems ($\bar{X}$ = 3.01, S.D. = .91). They also felt problems were ignored ($\bar{X}$ = 3.24) more often than confronted and resolved.

Research Question 2

This question examined the relationship of communication in the organization to burnout. Data were analyzed using Pearson product-moment correlations (see Table 32.1). The relationship between overall conflict resolution and burnout was significant (r = −.36, p ⩽ .05), as were the specific strategies of confrontation (r = −.42, p ⩽ .05) and problem solving (r = −.42, p ⩽ .05). Organization members were moderately satisfied with communication in general ($\bar{X}$ = 3.67, S.D. = 1.18) and reported low to moderate burnout ($\bar{X}$ = 3.35, S.D. = .52). A significant relationship was also found for communication satisfaction and burnout (r = −.33, p ⩽ .05).

Research Question 3

In order to test whether high- and low-burnout respondents differed in their perceptions of the communication relationships in the organization, t-tests were computed. In this study, subjects were divided into high- or low-burnout groups. Those scoring above the median (median = 3.33) made up the high group, while those scoring below the median made up the low group. The results of the t-tests (see Table 32.2) revealed significant differences between the high- and low-burnout groups for overall conflict resolution (t = 2.64, p. ⩽ .05), and the specific strategies of smoothing (t = 2.45, p. ⩽ .05), confrontation (t = 2.67, p. ⩽ .05), and problem solving (t = 2.06, p. ⩽ .05). The groups also differed significantly on communication satisfaction (t = 2.24, p ⩽ .05).

Table 32.2
T-Tests for High- and Low-Burnout Respondents

Variable	$\bar{X}$ Low	$\bar{X}$ High	t
Conflict resolution	3.43	3.04	*2.64
ignoring the problem	3.44	3.18	n.s.
smoothing	3.58	3.04	*2.46
third-party intervention	3.07	2.81	n.s.
confrontation	3.51	3.00	*2.76
problem solving	3.28	2.79	*2.06
Communication satisfaction	4.07	3.42	*2.24

*⩽.05 (two-tailed test).

DISCUSSION

The purpose of this study was to examine perceptions of communication relationships and job burnout in a health-related organization. The
results reveal several interesting relationships. Specifically, the use of confrontation and problem-solving conflict-resolution strategies and organizational communication satisfaction appear to mediate job burnout.

The use of multiple methods provided a more complete understanding
of these relationships. Based on the interview data, respondents felt that
most conflicts were ignored and few face-to-face strategies were used.
These findings were consistent with the survey data, which revealed that the
strategy of smoothing was considered to be used most often, followed by
ignoring the problem, confrontation, problem solving, and, last, third-party
intervention. Only confrontation and problem-solving strategies had significant negative relationships to burnout.

These findings suggest that the two strategies found to mediate burnout were used less frequently than smoothing or ignoring the problem. Both
confrontation and problem solving require direct interaction between those
involved. Smoothing and ignoring the problem are lower-risk strategies, not
requiring an open, direct approach to dealing with the problem or the parties involved. However, these data suggest that by openly dealing with conflict, members may circumvent a potentially stressful situation as well as
strengthen their interpersonal relationships (Ivancevich & Matteson, 1980;
Maslach, 1982). Given the importance of interpersonal relationships as a
mediator to burnout, it makes sense that open interaction in dealing with
conflict would be an effective preventive strategy.

In addition, perceptions of conflict strategies differed depending on
burnout level. Low-burnout respondents felt that smoothing, confrontation,
and problem solving were used to resolve conflicts more often than the other
strategies. Even though other studies have reported differences in perceptions based on burnout level (Albrecht, 1982; Ray, 1983b), this is the first
study to examine burnout in terms of perceived conflict-resolution strategies.

In terms of communication satisfaction, the interview and survey data
tended to diverge. The interview data revealed a high level of dissatisfaction
with communication in general. Interviewees cited an overall lack of face-to-
face communication and reported an overreliance on written communication. Given this, we would have expected the survey mean score for communication satisfaction to have been relatively low. However, the mean was
more than moderate ($\bar{X} = 3.67$, S.D. $= .18$). Since we interviewed only one-
third of the population, it is possible that the more dissatisfied organization
members were chosen randomly. On the other hand, it is possible that an
aggregated communication satisfaction score across departments failed

to capture satisfaction levels within individual departments. Another possible problem is the use of a one-item measure of communication satisfaction. Since the overall mean was higher than expected, the global measure may have failed to reveal the specific dimensions of communication satisfaction in this organization. However, this measure appeared to capture a more general level of satisfaction and proved to be one indication that communication in fact mediates job burnout.

Despite this divergence, the results regarding communication satisfaction contribute to our understanding of burnout. The significant negative correlation ($r = -.33$, $p \leq .01$), although low, revealed that the more satisfied organization members reported less burnout. Previous research has reported significant, negative relationships between burnout and job satisfaction (Albrecht et al., 1982; Kanner et al., 1978; Maslach & Pines, 1977; Pines & Maslach, 1978) and between burnout and life satisfaction (Kanner et al., 1978), but no other studies have examined the relationship between burnout and communication satisfaction.

Finally, the communication practices discussed by interviewees reflected feelings of burnout, but the survey data revealed only a low to moderate level of burnout. It is possible that people experiencing burnout were unwilling to spend the necessary time and energy required to complete a questionnaire. On the other hand, subjects may indeed be less burned out than the interview data led us to believe. Regardless of the level of burnout or satisfaction, these data suggest that perceptions of these two variables were linked.

In addition to the findings previously discussed, several limitations of this study deserve consideration. First, this research focused on organizational, not individual, conflict-resolution strategies. Examination of individual strategies as well would provide a more complete operationalization of conflict resolution. Second, data were collected only at one point in time. As a result, the stability of organization members' perceptions is not known. Longitudinal studies in similar and different types of organizations would increase generalizability and reveal patterns of communication relationships and burnout over time (Albrecht, 1982; Ray, 1983b). Third, these data are perceptions and should be understood in those terms. We cannot be sure that perceptions actually parallel strategies used. Nevertheless, these perceptions, regardless of actual behavior, appear to mediate burnout.

Despite these limitations, the results of this study illustrate the importance of a multiple-methods approach for understanding the complexity of this organization's communication relationships and job burnout. The survey data provide a picture of the general aggregated perceptions of organization members and help to answer the question of what the organization members perceive. The interview data provide specific explanations for these perceptions and help answer the question of why these perceptions exist. Previous burnout research has typically used only survey methods. This study underscores the necessity of using multiple methods in order to appreciate fully the complexity of job burnout and its relationship to communication.

REFERENCES

Albrecht, T. L. (1982). Coping with occupational stress: Relational and individual strategies of nurses in acute health care settings. In M. Burgoon (Ed.), *Communication yearbook 6*. Beverly Hills, CA: Sage.

Albrecht, T. L., Irey, K. V., & Mundy, A. K. (1982). Integration in communication networks as a mediator of stress: The case of a protective services agency. *Social Work, 27*, 225-236.

Albrecht, T. L., & Ropp, V. A. (1982). The study of network structuring in organizations through the use of method triangulation. *Western Journal of Speech Communication, 46*, 162-179.

Cammann, C., Fichman, M., Jenkins, D., & Klesh, J. (1978). *The Michigan organizational assessment questionnaire.* Unpublished manuscript, University of Michigan, Institute for Social Research.

Cherniss, C. (1980). *Staff burnout: Job stress in the human services.* Beverly Hills, CA: Sage.

Deal, T., & Kennedy, A. (1982). *Corporate cultures: The rites and rituals of corporate life.* Reading, MA: Addison-Wesley.

Delia, J., O'Keefe, B., & O'Keefe, D. (1982). The constructivist approach to communication. In F. X. Dance (Ed.), *Human communication theory.* New York: Harper & Row.

Denzin, N. (1978). *Sociological methods: A sourcebook.* Chicago: Aldine.

Dunham, R., & Herman, J. (1975). Development of a female faces scale for measuring job satisfaction. *Journal of Applied Psychology, 60*, 629-631.

Edelwich, J. (1980). *Burn-out: Stages of disillusionment in the helping professions.* New York: Human Sciences.

Freudenberger, H. J. (1974). Staff burn-out. *Journal of Social Issues, 30*, 159-165.

Ivancevich, J. M., & Matteson, M. T. (1980). *Stress and work: A managerial perspective.* Glenview, IL: Scott, Foresman.

Jick, P. (1979). Mixing qualitative and quantitative methods: Triangulation in action. *Administrative Science Quarterly, 24*, 602-611.

Kafry, D., & Pines, A. (1980). The experience of tedium in life and work. *Human Relations, 33*, 477-503.

Kanner, A. D., Kafry, D., & Pines, A. (1978). Conspicuous in its absence: The lack of positive conditions as a source of stress. *Journal of Human Stress, 4*, 33-39.

Kunin, T. (1955). The construction of a new type of attitude measure. *Personnel Psychology, 8*, 65-78.

Maslach, C. (1976). Burned-out. *Human Behavior, 5*, 16-22.

Maslach, C. (1982). *Burnout: The cost of caring.* Englewood Cliffs, NJ: Prentice-Hall.

Maslach, C., & Jackson, S. E. (1979,May). Burned-out cops and their families. *Psychology Today*, pp. 59-62.

Maslach, C., & Pines, A. (1977). The burn-out syndrome in the day care setting. *Child Care Quarterly, 6*, 100-113.

Mattingly, M. A. (1977). Sources of stress and burn-out in professional child care work. *Child Care Quarterly, 6*, 127-137.

Michigan organizational assessment package [MOAP]. (1975). Progress Report II. Ann Arbor: University of Michigan, Institute for Social Research.

Pines, A., & Kafry, D. (1978, November). Occupational tedium in social services. *Social Work*, pp. 499-507.

Pines, A., & Maslach, C. (1978). Characteristics of staff burn-out in mental health settings. *Hospital and Community Psychiatry, 29*, 233-237.

Ray, E. B. (1983a). Job burnout from a communication perspective. In R. Bostrom (Ed.), *Communication yearbook 7*. Beverly Hills, CA: Sage.

Ray, E. B. (1983b). Identifying job stress in a human service organization. *Journal of Applied Communication Research 11, 109-119.*

Roberts, K., & O'Reilly, C. (1974). Measuring organizational communication. *Journal of Applied Psychology, 59,* 321-326.

Veninga, R. L., & Bradley, J. P. (1981). *The work stress connection: How to cope with job burnout.* New York: Ballantine.

AUTHOR INDEX

SUBJECT INDEX

ABOUT THE EDITOR

ROBERT N. BOSTROM is Professor of Communication in the College of Communications at the University of Kentucky. He received his Ph.D. from Iowa University in 1961. He has been a member of the International Communication Association since 1961, having originally been affiliated with the NSSC. His latest book, *Competence in Communication*, was published in 1984 by Sage Publications.

BRUCE H. WESTLEY is Professor Emeritus in the College of Communications at the University of Kentucky. Professor Westley, formerly Chairman of the Department of Journalism, has often been called the father of modern research in mass communication.

ABOUT THE AUTHORS

TERRANCE L. ALBRECHT (Ph.D., Michigan State University, 1978) is Assistant Professor in the Department of Speech Communication at the University of Washington. Her research interests are based primarily on the consequences of larger network linkage patterns on micro-level processes in organizational contexts.

HANA NOOR AL-DEEN (M.A., English; M.A., behavioral science in education, California State University, Sacramento) is currently a doctoral candidate in communication at the State University of New York at Buffalo. Her primary research interest is in the transfer of the benefits of the new telecommunication's technologies to Third World nations.

JAMES L. APPLEGATE (Ph.D., University of Illinois—Urbana-Champaign) is Associate Professor and Chair of the Department of Communication at the University of Kentucky. His major research interests include interpersonal communication and social cognition and communication. He is coeditor (with Howard E. Sypher) of Volume 5 in the Sage Series in Interpersonal Communication, *Communication by Children and Adults: Social Cognitive and Strategic Processes.*

LARRY L. BARKER (Ph.D., Ohio University) is Professor of Speech Communication at Auburn University. He has authored or coauthored over twenty textbooks in speech communication and listening as well as numerous articles in professional journals. He has served as an officer in several professional communication organizations. He is President of Spectra Communication Associates.

GEORGE A. BARNETT (Ph.D., Michigan State University, 1976) is Associate Professor in the Department of Communication at the State University of New York at Buffalo. His research interests include the mathematical modeling of social and cultural processes, including language and organizational communication.

CHARLES R. BERGER (Ph.D., Michigan State University) is Professor of Communication Studies and Director of the Communication Research Center at Northwestern University. He is the author of articles examining the study of communication in initial phases of interpersonal interaction, development and disintegration of relationships, and interpersonal epistemology. He is currently the editor of *Human Communication Research.*

FRANKLIN J. BOSTER (Ph.D., Michigan State University, 1978) is Associate Professor in the Department of Communication, Arizona State University. His research interests are in the areas of persuasion and communication and small group behavior.

JENNINGS BRYANT (Ph.D., Indiana University, 1974) is Professor of Communication and Head of the Department of Communication at the University of Evansville, Indiana.

MILTON CHEN is a Ph.D. candidate in the Institute for Communication Research, Stanford University. His research involves the educational potential of communication technologies. He was formerly director of research at Children's Television Workshop for *3-2-1 Contact,* a television series on science, and has been a guest lecturer at the Beijing Broadcasting Institute in the People's Republic of China.

MICHAEL J. CODY (Ph.D., Michigan State University, 1978) is Assistant Professor of Communication at the University of Southern California. His research interests include face-to-face social influence, nonverbal communication, and reciprocity effects in conversations.

M. CLAIRE CUMMINGS (M.A., University of Oklahoma, 1983) is a doctoral candidate at the University of Oklahoma. She is currently developing a training model to prepare employers for participation in a performance appraisal interview. Her other areas of interest include superior-subordinate communication, communication of organizational culture, and the impact of automation on human communication in the workplace.

MARY ANN CUNNINGHAM (Ph.D., Bowling Green State University, 1983) is an Assistant Professor of Speech Communication at North Central College, Illinois. She is involved in health care communication training and research in hospitals in addition to her interests in male-female communication, conflict management, and organizational communication.

MARY E. DIEZ (Ph.D., Michigan State University, 1983) is an Assistant Professor of Communication at Alverno College, Milwaukee, Wisconsin. Her interests focus on communication competence in group decision-making situations.

JAMES P. DILLARD (Ph.D., Michigan State University, 1983) is Assistant Professor of Communication at the University of Wisconsin—Madison. His research interests include interpersonal and organizational communication.

R. LEWIS DONOHEW (Ph.D., University of Iowa) is Professor in the Department of Communication, University of Kentucky. His master's degree is in political science. Over the past several years, he has been involved in a program of research on human information exposure. His most recent work has been on physiological and affective responses to message designs.

JO ELLEN FAIR (M.A., Indiana University, 1984) is a doctoral student in the Department of Journalism at Indiana University. Her research interests include the legal implications of satellite communications and national development.

GAIL T. FAIRHURST (Ph.D., University of Oregon, 1978) is an Associate Professor in the Department of Communication at the University of Cincinnati. Her research interests include superior-subordinate relationships and controlling ineffective performance in organizations. Her research has been published in the *Academy of Management Journal, Academy of Management Review, Western Journal of Speech Communication,* and *Human Communication Research.*

RAYMOND L. FALCIONE is Associate Professor in the Department of Communication and Director of the Speech Communication Division at the University of Maryland. He is Chairperson of the Organizational Communication Division of the ICA, and his publications have appeared in *Human Communication Research, Communication Yearbook 1, Personnel Journal, Journal of Business Communication, Journal of Applied Communication Research,* and *Nursing Research.* He is also coauthor (with Howard Greenbaum) of *Organizational Communication Abstracts,* Volumes 1-9. His most recent book is titled *A Guide to Effective Communication in Government Service.* He has conducted communication audits and organizational diagnoses in various settings and has consulted for numerous government agencies, private corporations, and service organizations.

EDWARD L. FINK (Ph.D., University of Wisconsin—Madison) is Associate Professor of Communication Arts and Theatre at the University of Maryland. His research interests involve the measurement and modeling of cognition and attitude change, interpersonal communication, and issues in theory construction and data analysis. His work has been published in *Human Communication Research*, *Sociological Methods and Research*, *Journal of Experimental Social Psychology*, *Behavioral Science*, *Communication Monographs*, and *Communication Yearbooks 6* and *7*. He is also coauthor (with J. Woelfel) of *The Measurement of Communication Processes* (Academic Press, 1980).

SETH FINN (Ph.D., Stanford University, 1982) is Assistant Professor in the Department of Radio, Television and Motion Pictures at the University of North Carolina. He was formerly a television news producer at KRON-TV, San Francisco.

JOE S. FOOTE (Ph.D., University of Texas, 1979) is a Visiting Professor in the Department of Communication Arts at Cornell University. He was formerly Administrative Assistant to Congressman Dave McCurdy and Press Secretary to former Speaker of the House Carl Albert. He has taught at the University of Texas and the University of Oklahoma and has worked as a broadcast journalist in Oklahoma and Washington, D.C.

MYRNA FOSTER (M.A., Texas Tech University, 1982) is currently a doctoral candidate at Pennsylvania State University. Her research interests include nonverbal communication, correlates of deception, and research on conversations.

STEPHEN G. GREEN (Ph.D., University of Washington, 1976) is an Associate Professor of Organizational Behavior in the Department of Management at the University of Cincinnati. His research interests focus on leader-member and control processes within organizational settings, and his work has been published in the *Academy of Management Journal*, *Organizational Behavior and Human Performance*, *Journal of Applied Psychology*, and *Human Communication Research*.

BRADLEY S. GREENBERG (Ph.D., University of Wisconsin) is Professor of Telecommunication and Communication at Michigan State

University. He has published widely on children and television, and his current research interests include the role of communications technology in people's lives. He is the author of *Life on Television* and *Mexican Americans and the Mass Media.*

BETH HASLETT (Ph.D., University of Minnesota, 1971) is Associate Professor in the Department of Communication, University of Delaware. She has published numerous articles on children's communication and communication theory. Her primary research interests are in the areas of discourse analysis, pragmatics, children's communication, and communication theory, especially the relationship between oral and written communication.

MARGARET FITCH HAUSER (Ph.D., University of Oklahoma) is Assistant Professor of Business Communication, College of Business Administration, University of Oklahoma. Her teaching experience has included teaching public speaking, business writing, interviewing, interpersonal communication, and listening. She has served as a consultant for workshops in these areas as well. She was named one of the Outstanding Young Women of America in 1982.

DOROTHY C. HIGGINBOTHAM (Ph.D., Northwestern University, 1961) is Professor of Communication at the University of Oklahoma. Her interests include style variables in communication, social cognition, language, and communication development.

FREDRIC M. JABLIN (Ph.D., Purdue University, 1977) is Associate Professor of Speech Communication at the University of Texas at Austin. His research has been published in communication, psychology, and management journals, and he has served as a consultant-researcher to a number of organizations. His current research interests include communication and organizational assimilation, influence processes in superior-subordinate interaction, and communication correlates of the selection interview.

J. DAVID JOHNSON (Ph.D., Michigan State University, 1978) is Assistant Professor of Communication at Arizona State University. He has prior experience at the University of Wisconsin—Milwaukee and with the Office of Research of the U.S. Information Agency. He is the author of numerous articles, convention papers, grant reports, and government documents. He has published in his three primary interest areas—social interaction, organizational communication, and international communication—in such journals as *Communication Monographs, Communication Research, Journalism Quarterly,* and *Academy of Management Review.*

ELYSE A. KAPLAN (M.A., University of Maryland) is Corporate Director, Training and Development, for Goldome, the second largest savings bank in the United States, headquartered in Buffalo, New York. She formerly served as Corporate Director, Human Resource Planning, for Marriott Corporation. She has coauthored several papers presented at the meetings of the SCA, the ICA, and the American Marketing Association, and her work has been published in *Human Communication Research.*

STAN A. KAPLOWITZ (Ph.D., University of Michigan) is Professor of Sociology at Michigan State University. Among his publications are articles on the interaction of moral and instrumental thinking (*Journal of Conflict Resolution*), on the social psychology of power attribution (*Social Psychology Quarterly*), and on the detection of falsified data (*Public Opinion Quarterly*). His current research interests are in the areas of attitude change, public opinion, and formal theory construction. He and E. L. Fink are collaborating on a theory of attitude change and cognition, and parts of their research have appeared in *Communication Yearbook 6, Communication Monographs,* and *Behavioral Science.*

PATRICIA KEARNEY (Ed.D., West Virginia University, 1979) is Assistant Professor of Speech Communication at West Virginia University. Her teaching and research activities center on communication in the classroom. Specifically, she has developed a research program on compliance-gaining or teacher power-based strategies and student resistance in classroom management.

KATHY KELLERMANN (M.A., Wake Forest University; M.S. and Ph.D., Northwestern University) is an Assistant Professor in the Department of Communication Arts at the University of Wisconsin—Madison. Her research interests concern the mathematical modeling of social information processing and interpersonal interaction.

KATHLEEN E. KENDALL (Ph.D., Indiana University, 1966) is Associate Professor and Chair of the Department of Communication, State University of New York at Albany. Her main area of interest is political communication. She has published in *Quarterly Journal of Speech, Communication Education,* and *Central States Speech Journal.*

SHIRLEY WILLIS MAASE is a doctoral student in the Program in Public Communication at the University of Maryland—College Park, and an instructor in the university's overseas program. Her dissertation is a test of some of the theoretical models discussed in her coauthored chapter included in this *Yearbook*. In addition to her work on humor and cognition, she has specialized in persuasion, small group communication, and sex roles in communication. She has authored or coauthored papers presented at the meetings of the International Communication Association, the Speech Communication Association, and other scholarly associations.

PETER J. MARSTON (B.A., Occidental College, 1980) is currently a doctoral candidate at the University of Southern California. His research in nonverbal communication demonstrates a strong concern for the effects of cognitive planning and processing, and for the role of temporality of interaction events, especially in acts of deception.

MICHAEL MAYER (Ph.D., University of Kansas, 1979) is Associate Professor in the Department of Communication, Arizona State University. His research interests include argumentation and communication and small group behavior.

KAREN B. McCOMB (M.A., University of Texas—Austin, 1983) is a Personnel Interviewer at InterFirst Bank—Austin, Texas. She has presented papers at several ICA conventions and is a coauthor of an article that will soon be appearing in *Critical Studies in Mass Communication*. Her recently completed master's thesis examined the verbal communication correlates of interviewer empathy in selection interviews.

JAMES C. McCROSKEY (Ed.D., Pennsylvania State University, 1966) is Professor and Chairperson, Department of Speech Communication, West Virginia University. He is a Fellow of ICA, former editor of *Human Communication Research*, and a former member of the ICA Board of Directors. He is past president of the Eastern Communication Association and present Vice-President of the World Communication Association.

STEVEN T. McDERMOTT (Ph.D., Michigan State University) is Assistant Professor of Speech Communication at the University of Georgia. His major research interests are in children's communication and persuasive effects. His research on children has appeared in assorted publications, including *Journalism Quarterly, Journal of Broadcasting,* and *Communication*.

JEFFREY S. McQUILLEN (Ph.D., University of Oklahoma, 1984) is
Assistant Professor of Speech Communication, Department of English,
at Texas A&M University. His interests include communication and
language development, social cognition, and the social influence
process. He is investigating the relationship between social perception
and the system of interpersonal accounts.

PAUL MONGEAU (M.A., Arizona State University, 1983) is engaged in
graduate study in the Department of Communication, Michigan State
University. His research interests are in the areas of persuasion and
interpersonal communication.

MURALI NAIR is a doctoral student in communication at the University
of Kentucky. His primary research interest is in the area of
communication and national development.

CHRISTINE L. OGAN (Ph.D., University of North Carolina—Chapel
Hill, 1976) is Assistant Professor of Journalism at Indiana University.
Her research interests include the impacts of new technologies, in
particular direct-broadcast satellites and videocassette recorders, on
communication policies and development. She is currently working
(with Ardyth Sohn and John Polich) on a book on newspaper
management to be published by Prentice-Hall.

GARRETT J. O'KEEFE is Professor and Chairperson at the Department
of Mass Communications, University of Denver. His research interests
include social and political uses and effects of mass media, including
political socialization and campaign effects. His recent work has focused
on public information campaigns and attitudes toward crime. His work
has appeared in a variety of scholarly books and journals.

WILLIAM PAISLEY (Ph.D., Stanford University, 1965) is Associate
Professor in the Institute for Communication Research, Stanford
University. His research focuses on the social and cognitive impacts
of new communication technologies and on knowledge utilization
among scientists, professionals, and the public. He is coeditor of
Public Communication Campaigns (with Ronald E. Rice;
Sage, 1981) and *Knowledge Utilization Systems in Education*
(with Matilda Butler; Sage, 1983).

MARK T. PALMER (M.S., Rensselaer Polytechnic Institute, 1981) is
currently a doctoral candidate at the University of Wisconsin—Madison.
The focus of his research is interpersonal communication and the
information processing of language.

PHILIP PALMGREEN (Ph.D., University of Michigan) is Associate Professor in the Department of Communication, University of Kentucky. His research is concerned with audience uses of the mass media, with recent research focusing on the relationships between gratifications sought and obtained, and on expectancy-value approaches to uses and gratifications. He is coeditor (with Karl Erik Rosengren and Lawrence Wenner) of *Media Gratifications Research: Current Perspectives* (Sage, forthcoming).

TIMOTHY G. PLAX (Ph.D., University of Southern California, 1974) is Associate Professor of Speech Communication at West Virginia University. A former internal consultant for Rockwell International, his teaching focuses primarily on organizational and applied communication. His current research emphasizes persuasive strategies and message comprehension and resistance.

EILEEN BERLIN RAY (Ph.D., University of Washington, 1981) is Assistant Professor of communication at the University of Kentucky. Her primary research interest is in organizational communication, focusing on quality of work life issues, social structure, and comparative organizational research.

VIRGINIA P. RICHMOND (Ph.D., University of Nebraska, 1977) is Associate Professor and Coordinator of Graduate Studies in Speech Communication at West Virginia University. She has published several articles in international, national, and regional journals, and has presented numerous papers at various international, national, and state conventions. She was awarded the Distinguished Research Award by the Association of Teacher Educators in 1982-1983. Her major research areas include instructional, interpersonal, and organizational communication.

HEMANT SHAH (M.A., Purdue University, 1982) is a doctoral student in the Department of Journalism at Indiana University. His research interests focus on communication and national development.

B. KAY SNAVELY (M.B.A., Miami University, 1979) is an Instructor in the Department of Management at Miami University, Oxford, Ohio, and a doctoral student in organizational behavior in the Department of Management at the University of Cincinnati. Her research interests include controlling ineffective performance in organizations, job design, turnover, and leadership. Her research has been published in the *Academy of Management Journal, Academy of Management Review,* and *Human Communication Research.*

BRIAN H. SPITZBERG (Ph.D., University of Southern California, 1981) is Assistant Professor of Communication at North Texas State University. His research interests include interpersonal competence and impression formation in dyadic interaction.

BEVERLY DAVENPORT SYPHER (Ph.D., University of Michigan, 1981) is Assistant Professor in the Department of Communication at the University of Kentucky. Her research focuses on individual differences and communicative abilities among organizational members.

HOWARD E. SYPHER (Ph.D., University of Michigan) is Associate Professor of Communication and Director of Graduate Studies for the College of Communications at the University of Kentucky. His research interests include communication theory, interpersonal communication, and social cognition and communication. He is coeditor (with James L. Applegate) of Volume 5 in the Sage Series in Interpersonal Communication, *Communication by Children and Adults: Social Cognitive and Strategic Processes.*

RON TAMBORINI (Ph.D., Indiana University, 1982) is Assistant Professor in the Department of Communication at Michigan State University.

KITTIE W. WATSON (Ph.D., Louisiana State University) is Assistant Professor, Department of Communication, Tulane University. She is the coauthor of three books, and has published numerous book chapters and journal articles. She is Chair of the Research Committee of the International Listening Association and Vice President of Spectra Communication Associates, a communication consulting firm.

DAVID WEAVER (Ph.D., University of North Carolina, 1974) is Professor of Journalism at Indiana University and Director of the Bureau of Media Research in the School of Journalism. He is the author of *Videotex Journalism* (Erlbaum, 1983), senior author of *Media Agenda-Setting in a Presidential Election* (Praeger, 1981), and coauthor of *Newsroom Guide to Polls and Surveys* (American Newspaper Publishers Association, 1980). He has also published numerous book chapters and articles on media agenda-setting, newspaper readership, and foreign news coverage. He has worked as an editor and reporter on four daily newspapers.

JAMES R. WILCOX (Ph.D., Purdue University, 1973) is Associate Professor in the School of Speech Communication at Bowling Green

State University. His interests and recent research efforts include sex roles and interpersonal communication, functions of metaphor in discourse, and communication in the hospital setting.

JUNE OCK YUM (Ph.D., University of Southern California, 1979) is Assistant Professor, Department of Communication, State University of New York at Albany. She has conducted research on communication patterns of immigrants, political campaigns and the mass media, and natural helping networks. She has published in *Human Communication Research*, *International Journal of Inter-Cultural Relations*, and *Quality and Quantity*.

DOLF ZILLMANN (Ph.D., University of Pennsylvania, 1969) is Professor of Communication, Psychology, and Semiotics, and Director of the Institute for Communication Research at Indiana University.